Live audio source problems   619
LMHOSTS file, overview   796
Locations-based call admission control   624, 636
Masks, overview   495
Methodology for troubleshooting   4
MGCP overview   218
Microsoft Performance (PerfMon)   68
Modem passthrough configuration   441
Modem passthrough, overview   437
Modem troubleshooting methodology   447
MOH—live audio source problems   619
MOH—multicast and unicast problems   615
MOH—no music when calls are on hold   611, 617
MOH—reading CCM traces   607
MOH—troubleshooting methodology   611
MWI problems (Personal Assistant)   659
MWI problems (SMDI)   682
MWI problems (Unity)   659
MWI problems (VG248)   690
"No conference bridge available" message   587
No-way audio   405, 410
Octel integration   693
One-way audio   405, 406, 410
Outside dial tone played at the wrong time   465
Park problems   531
Partitions, overview   469
Personal Assistant is not intercepting calls   785
Personal Assistant—MWI problems   659
Phone—busy signal not heard   310
Phone—failover and failback   154, 155, 158
Phone—inline power problems   114
Phone—network connectivity and Skinny registration   117
Phone stuck in SRST mode   730
Phone—switch port operation   161
Phone—TFTP configuration file   121
Phone—understanding the difference between restart and reset   156
Phone—understanding the Skinny protocol   139
Phone—VLAN configuration   118
Phone won't register   127
Pickup/group pickup problems   533
PRI backhaul channel status   256
PRI—CallManager sends the proper digits to the PSTN, but call won't route properly   269
PRI signaling troubleshooting   210, 262
Publisher-Subscriber model, overview   793, 796
Q.931 Translator   95
Registration problems on IP phone   127
Replication problems   796, 804, 807
Reset vs. restart   156
Ringback problems   307, 309
Route filters, overview   506
SDL traces—how to read   60

Search for a user fails   824
services button doesn't work   160
Silence suppression—effect on voice quality   402
SMDI—check configuration parameters   686
SMDI—integration   662
SMDI integration with VG248   686
SMDI—MWI problems   682
SoftPhone has no lines   788
SoftPhone—one-way audio over VPN   787
SoftPhone shows line but won't go off-hook   786
SQL database replication problems   796, 804, 807
SQL—re-establishing a broken subscription   807
SQL—reinitializing a subscription   809
SRST and phone registration   712
SRST—DHCP issues   731
SRST—features lost during operation   707
SRST—phones still registered after WAN connection is restored   730
SRST—transfer problems   729
SRST—voice mail and forwarding issues   731
T1 CAS signaling troubleshooting   214
T1 interface troubleshooting   208
"Temporary Failure" message   561
Time synchronization   38
Toll fraud prevention   544, 548
Tone on hold plays instead of music   615, 617
Transcoder—out of resources   578
Transcoder—understanding codec selection between devices   570
Transfer problems   529
Transformation troubleshooting   513
Transformations and masks, overview   486
Transformations, overview   496, 500
Translation pattern troubleshooting   501
Unity—MWI problems   659
Unity—TSP configuration   656
VAD—effect on voice quality   402
VG248—MWI problems   690
Voice mail—MWI problems (DPA 7610/7630)   702
Voice mail—MWI problems (SMDI)   682
Voice mail—MWI problems (Unity)   659
Voice mail—MWI problems (VG248)   690
Voice mail—Octel integration   693
Voice quality problems   384, 389, 396, 400, 402, 405, 410
WS-X6608/6624 gateway troubleshooting   313, 314, 320, 324
WS-X6608—D-channel is down   326, 337, 340, 343, 344
WS-X6608—dropped calls   326
WS-X6608—T1 CAS problems   359
WS-X6608 T1/E1 configuration troubleshooting   325, 326
WS-X6608—unexpected resets   326, 345
WS-X6624 FXS analog gateway configuration   367

P9-DTI-340

Troubleshooting Cisco IP Telephony

Paul Giralt, CCIE No. 4793
Addis Hallmark
Anne Smith

Cisco Press

800 East 96th Street
Indianapolis, IN 46240 USA

Troubleshooting Cisco IP Telephony

Paul Giralt, CCIE No. 4793

Addis Hallmark

Anne Smith

Copyright© 2003 Cisco Systems, Inc.

Published by:
Cisco Press
800 East 96th Street
Indianapolis, IN 46240 USA

Printed in the United States of America   9 0

Ninth Printing November 2006

Library of Congress Cataloging-in-Publication Number: 2001096407

ISBN: 1-58705-075-7

Trademark Acknowledgments

Warning and Disclaimer

This book is designed to provide information about troubleshooting the various components of a Cisco IP Telephony network. Every effort has been made to make this book as complete and accurate as possible, but no warranty or fitness is implied.

The information is provided on an "as is" basis. The authors, Cisco Press, and Cisco Systems, Inc., shall have neither liability nor responsibility to any person or entity with respect to any loss or damages arising from the information contained in this book or from the use of the discs or programs that may accompany it or be referenced by it.

The opinions expressed in this book belong to the authors and are not necessarily those of Cisco Systems, Inc.

Portions of Chapter 6 are extracted from RFC 2705 which defines MGCP. The following copyright statement applies to any information derived from RFC 2705:

Full Copyright Statement

Copyright © The Internet Society (1999). All Rights Reserved.

This document and translations of it may be copied and furnished to others, and derivative works that comment on or otherwise explain it or assist in its implementation may be prepared, copied, published and distributed, in whole or in part, without restriction of any kind, provided that the above copyright notice and this paragraph are included on all such copies and derivative works. However, this document itself may not be modified in any way, such as by removing the copyright notice or references to the Internet Society or other Internet organizations, except as needed for the purpose of developing Internet standards in which case the procedures for copyrights defined in the Internet Standards process must be followed, or as required to translate it into languages other than English.

The limited permissions granted above are perpetual and will not be revoked by the Internet Society or its successors or assigns.

This document and the information contained herein is provided on an "AS IS" basis and THE INTERNET SOCIETY AND THE INTERNET ENGINEERING TASK FORCE DISCLAIMS ALL WARRANTIES, EXPRESS OR IMPLIED, INCLUDING BUT NOT LIMITED TO ANY WARRANTY THAT THE USE OF THE INFORMATION HEREIN WILL NOT INFRINGE ANY RIGHTS OR ANY IMPLIED WARRANTIES OF MERCHANTABILITY OR FITNESS FOR A PARTICULAR PURPOSE.

Corporate and Government Sales

Cisco Press offers excellent discounts on this book when ordered in quantity for bulk purchases or special sales.

For more information please contact: **U.S. Corporate and Government Sales** 1-800-382-3419 corpsales@pearsontechgroup.com

For sales outside the U.S. please contact: **International Sales** international@pearsoned.com

Feedback Information

At Cisco Press, our goal is to create in-depth technical books of the highest quality and value. Each book is crafted with care and precision, undergoing rigorous development that involves the unique expertise of members of the professional technical community.

Reader feedback is a natural continuation of this process. If you have any comments regarding how we could improve the quality of this book, or otherwise alter it to better suit your needs, you can contact us through e-mail at feedback@ciscopress.com. Please be sure to include the book title and ISBN in your message.

We greatly appreciate your assistance.

iv

Publisher	John Wait
Editor-In-Chief	John Kane
Cisco Representative	Anthony Wolfenden
Cisco Press Program Manager	Sonia Torres Chavez
Cisco Marketing Communications Manager	Tom Geitner
Cisco Marketing Program Manager	Edie Quiroz
Acquisitions Editor	Amy Moss
Production Manager	Patrick Kanouse
Development Editor	Christopher Cleveland
Copy Editor	Gayle Johnson
Technical Editors	Shawn Armstrong, Dave Goodwin, Christina Hattingh, Phil Jensen, Ketil Johansen, Chris Pearce, Ana Rivas, Markus Schneider, Gert Vanderstraeten, Liang Wu
Team Coordinator	Tammi Barnett
Book Designer	Gina Rexrode
Cover Designer	Louisa Adair
Compositor	Mark Shirar
Indexer	Tim Wright

CISCO SYSTEMS

Corporate Headquarters
Cisco Systems, Inc.
170 West Tasman Drive
San Jose, CA 95134-1706
USA
www.cisco.com
Tel: 408 526-4000
    800 553-NETS (6387)
Fax: 408 526-4100

European Headquarters
Cisco Systems International BV
Haarlerbergpark
Haarlerbergweg 13-19
1101 CH Amsterdam
The Netherlands
www-europe.cisco.com
Tel: 31 0 20 357 1000
Fax: 31 0 20 357 1100

Americas Headquarters
Cisco Systems, Inc.
170 West Tasman Drive
San Jose, CA 95134-1706
USA
www.cisco.com
Tel: 408 526-7660
Fax: 408 527-0883

Asia Pacific Headquarters
Cisco Systems, Inc.
Capital Tower
168 Robinson Road
#22-01 to #29-01
Singapore 068912
www.cisco.com
Tel: +65 6317 7777
Fax: +65 6317 7799

Cisco Systems has more than 200 offices in the following countries and regions. Addresses, phone numbers, and fax numbers are listed on the
Cisco.com Web site at www.cisco.com/go/offices.

Argentina • Australia • Austria • Belgium • Brazil • Bulgaria • Canada • Chile • China PRC • Colombia • Costa Rica • Croatia • Czech Republic
Denmark • Dubai, UAE • Finland • France • Germany • Greece • Hong Kong SAR • Hungary • India • Indonesia • Ireland • Israel • Italy
Japan • Korea • Luxembourg • Malaysia • Mexico • The Netherlands • New Zealand • Norway • Peru • Philippines • Poland • Portugal
Puerto Rico • Romania • Russia • Saudi Arabia • Scotland • Singapore • Slovakia • Slovenia • South Africa • Spain • Sweden
Switzerland • Taiwan • Thailand • Turkey • Ukraine • United Kingdom • United States • Venezuela • Vietnam • Zimbabwe

About the Authors

Paul Giralt, CCIE No. 4793, is an escalation engineer at the Cisco Systems Technical Assistance Center in Research Triangle Park, N.C., where he has worked since 1998. He has been troubleshooting complex IP Telephony networks since the release of CallManager 3.0 as a TAC engineer, a technical lead for the Enterprise Voice team, and now as an escalation engineer supporting the complete Cisco line of IP Telephony products. Paul has troubleshot problems in some of Cisco's largest IP Telephony deployments and has provided training for TAC teams around the globe. Prior to working on IP Telephony, he was a TAC engineer on the LAN Switching team. He holds a B.S. in computer engineering from the University of Miami.

Addis Hallmark, CCNA, CIPT, is a senior technical marketing engineer with Cisco Systems. He has been installing, configuring, administering, and troubleshooting the Cisco IP Telephony solution since the 2.3 release of CallManager. He has contributed to numerous design guides, application notes, and white papers on a variety of IP Telephony subjects, including CallManager, IP Phones, and IP gateways.

Anne Smith is a technical writer in the CallManager engineering group at Cisco Systems. She has written technical documentation for the Cisco IP Telephony solution since CallManager release 2.0 and was part of the Selsius Systems acquisition in 1998. Anne writes internal and external documents for CallManager, IP phones, and other Cisco IP Telephony products. She is a co-author of *Cisco CallManager Fundamentals* (ISBN: 1-58705-008-0) and *Developing Cisco IP Phone Services* (ISBN: 1-58705-060-9), both from Cisco Press.

About the Technical Reviewers

Shawn Armstrong is an IT engineer working in Cisco's Core Hosting group. She has been with Cisco for four years and is responsible for managing NT and Windows 2000 servers within Cisco's Information Technology group.

Dave Goodwin, CCIE No. 4992, is a customer diagnostic engineer for Cisco's Advanced Engineering Services. He is responsible for discovering and resolving problems in new Cisco IP Telephony products while administering internal field trials for these systems. He also works closely with Cisco's development and TAC support teams to provide support for anything from troubleshooting to quality issues to tools. He has been at Cisco for almost five years and has worked as a network engineer for eight years.

Christina Hattingh is a member of the Technical Marketing organization at Cisco Systems. In this role she works closely with product management and engineering. Christina focuses on helping Cisco sales engineers, partners, and customers design and tune enterprise and service provider Voice over Packet network infrastructures with particular focus on QoS. Prior to this she was a software engineer and engineering manager of PBX Call Center products at Nortel Networks. Her earlier software development experience in X.25 and network management systems provide background for the issues involved today in migrating customers' traditional data and voice networks to packet-based technologies. Christina has a graduate degree in computer science and mathematical statistics.

Phil Jensen, CCIE No. 2065, is a consulting systems engineer for Cisco in the southeastern U.S. He has focused on helping Cisco's largest customers design and troubleshoot AVVID IP Telephony solutions for the past three years. He has worked as a network engineer for more than 14 years.

Ketil Johansen, CCIE No. 1145, is a business development manager with Cisco Systems, working with companies integrating their applications with Cisco CallManager. He has worked with networking technologies for more than 18 years and has been a CCIE since 1994. The last three years he has focused on IP Telephony technologies.

Chris Pearce is a technical leader in the Cisco CallManager software group at Cisco Systems, Inc. He has ten years of experience in telecommunications. His primary areas of expertise include call routing, call control, and telephone features. He was a member of the team that developed and implemented the Cisco CallManager software from its early stages, and he was directly involved in developing the system architecture and design.

Ana Rivas, CCIE No. 3877, is an escalation engineer in Cisco's EMEA region. She is one of the technical leaders for AVVID solutions in the Cisco TAC. She is responsible for technically leading the resolution of some of the most critical problems in voice and IP Telephony, spreading technical knowledge to other teams, and working with Cisco business units and the field to head IP Telephony solutions. She has been working as a network engineer for more than five years.

Markus Schneider, CCIE No. 2863, is a diagnostic engineer for Cisco's Advanced Engineering Services. He is responsible for helping Cisco customers design, implement, and troubleshoot IP Telephony solutions in their environment. He has been working for Cisco as a network engineer for more than six years.

Gert Vanderstraeten has been working as a telecom/datacom engineer for companies such as Alcatel, Bell, and Lucent Technologies since 1993. Since 1998 he has been an independent contractor for the Cisco Systems' IT department. During the course of his tenure, his main focus has been the design, implementation, and maintenance of VoIP, IP Telephony, voice and video applications, and the integration of AVVID technologies into solutions. He is currently operating within the Cisco Systems global Enterprise Architecture Solutions team.

Liang Wu is a software engineer in the CallManager software group at Cisco Systems, Inc. For the last seven years, he has been focusing on PBX/Enterprise communication systems. He spent more than eight years in the Class 4/5/AIN telephone switching industry.

Dedications

Paul Giralt

I dedicate this book to my parents, Vicia and Pedro, for being the best parents anyone could ask for and always providing the opportunity and encouragement to continue learning.

Addis Hallmark

I want to dedicate this book to my lovely wife, Stephanie. Her companionship is the most precious thing in the world to me. Her patience, understanding, and encouragement helped me write this book. I love and appreciate her dearly.

Anne Smith

For Herb for seeing me through the long nights and weekends without complaint. And, of course, for all those backrubs.

Acknowledgments

Paul Giralt

I want to first thank Anne Smith for all her hard work and guidance throughout this entire project. There is no way this book would exist without her constant dedication and attention to detail.

Thanks to Chris Cleveland for his excellent work as development editor on this book and for being so flexible when it comes to the unpredictable schedules of a TAC engineer.

Thank you to the worldwide Enterprise Voice and AVVID TAC teams, especially the RTP Enterprise Voice team for being such a world-class group of engineers to work with.

Thanks to the RTP Voice Network Team (VNT) for all the excellent VoX documentation. Special thanks to Gonzalo Salgueiro and Mike Whitley for the VoX boot camp material and to Steve Penna for knowing everything.

Thanks to Dave Hanes for his excellent fax troubleshooting presentations and Andy Pepperell for his explanation of fax and modem passthrough.

Thanks to all the technical reviewers—Ana Rivas, Chris Pearce, Dave Goodwin, Ketil Johansen, Markus Schneider, Phil Jensen, Gert Vanderstraeten, Liang Wu, Shawn Armstrong, and especially Christina Hattingh—for always being on top of everything in the world of Cisco IOS gateways.

Thanks to all the developers in Richardson and San Jose that I have worked with over the years. Your insight into the inner workings of CallManager has helped me understand how to better troubleshoot the product. Special thanks to Bill Benninghoff for always answering any question I throw his way and for always being so thorough in his explanations. Also thanks to Chris Pearce for his excellent grasp on the intricacies of call routing.

Thank you to all the contributors to the VNT Voice University website as well as the AVVID TAC tips website on Cisco.com. Also thanks to all the other unnamed authors for the documentation scattered throughout various web pages.

Thanks to all the customers I have worked with over the past several years on AVVID issues for being my teachers. Every customer I work with helps me understand a little more about IP Telephony.

Addis Hallmark

First, I'd like to thank Paul Hahn and Richard Platt for bringing me on at Cisco. Paul in particular spent a lot of time with me, bringing me up to speed on these technologies, and for that, I am indebted to him.

I'd also like to thank all the brilliant development engineers who patiently helped me understand CallManager so well over the past few years.

I'd like to thank Susan Sauter. She is a brilliant engineer, and so much of what I know about IP Phones came from her patient instruction.

Chris Pearce has also helped me so much over the last few years in understanding dial plans.

The chapter on applications is based on the hard work of Dave Bicknell. Without his efforts, that chapter would not be even close to what it should be.

Manish Gupta and his team were a tremendous source of help on the LDAP Directory chapter. Stefano Giorcelli's excellent directory documentation also was so very helpful!

The TAC is on the front lines of troubleshooting, and much of the help I received was from the experiences that only solid TAC engineers could provide.

Also, the technical reviewers of this book were so helpful. Thank you so much to everyone for their hard work!

I really believe this is a great book, and one of the biggest reasons for that is Paul Giralt's invaluable contribution and hard work on this project. I couldn't have done this without him!

My manager, Shaik Kaleem, was very supportive of this project that I undertook on my own time, and I greatly appreciate that support.

Finally, I'd like to thank Anne Smith. This project would never have happened without her tireless work and skillful help. I am so grateful for Anne's effort. She worked so very hard over this past year, and Paul Giralt and I would have been lost without her.

Anne Smith

My many thanks go to Paul Giralt and Addis Hallmark for making this book a reality with their knowledge, experience, hard work, and sacrifice. In particular, I thank Paul for a highly enjoyable working experience. Paul's dedication to the quality, accuracy, and comprehensiveness of this book was unsurpassed; he spent countless hours reviewing every page of technical information and his experience with the many components in the Cisco AVVID IP Telephony solution made his extensive contribution invaluable. At every turn, Paul's dedication, commitment to quality, tireless drive for accuracy, and constant positive attitude made working with him a rewarding experience.

As always, my thanks and great admiration go to Richard Platt and Scott Veibell. Without their continued support there would be no Cisco IP Telephony-related Cisco Press books.

I would like to thank Chris Pearce for his help on the Call Routing chapter, Travis Amsler for his assistance on the Cisco CRA and extension mobility sections, and Brian Sedgley and Ken Pruski for their help with CCM and SDL tracing. Appreciation and recognition also go to the engineers who created and developed Dick Tracy: Rick Baugh, Jim Brasher, Long Huang, and David Patton.

Contents at a Glance

Foreword   xxv

Introduction   xxvi

Chapter 1   Troubleshooting Methodology and Approach   3

Chapter 2   IP Telephony Architecture Overview   23

Chapter 3   Understanding the Troubleshooting Tools   37

Chapter 4   Skinny Client Registration   113

Chapter 5   IP Phones   139

Chapter 6   Voice Gateways   169

Chapter 7   Voice Quality   383

Chapter 8   Fax Machines and Modems   433

Chapter 9   Call Routing   459

Chapter 10   Call Preservation   551

Chapter 11   Conference Bridges, Transcoders, and Media Termination Points   565

Chapter 12   Music on Hold   601

Chapter 13   Call Admission Control   623

Chapter 14   Voice Mail   655

Chapter 15   Survivable Remote Site Telephony (SRST)   707

Chapter 16   Applications   735

Chapter 17   SQL Database Replication   793

Chapter 18   LDAP Integration and Replication   819

Appendix A   Cisco IP Telephony Protocol and Codec Information and References   849

Appendix B   NANP Call Routing Information   857

Appendix C   Decimal to Hexadecimal and Binary Conversion Table   881

Appendix D   Performance Objects and Counters   891

Glossary   927

Index   947

Contents

Foreword   xxv

Introduction   xxvi

Chapter 1   Troubleshooting Methodology and Approach 3

Developing a Troubleshooting Methodology or Approach 4
   Production Versus Nonproduction Outages 5
   Step 1: Gathering Data About the Problem 6
      Identifying and Isolating the Problem 6
      Using Topology Information to Isolate the Problem 7
      Gathering Information from the User 10
      Determining the Problem's Timeframe 10
   Step 2: Analyzing the Data Collected About the Problem 11
      Using Deductive Reasoning to Narrow the List of Possible Causes 11
      Verifying IP Network Integrity 12
      Determining the Proper Troubleshooting Tool 13

Case Study: Resolving a Problem Using Proper Troubleshooting Methodology 13
   Gathering the Data 14
   Analyzing the Data 18
   Conclusions 20

Summary 21

Chapter 2   IP Telephony Architecture Overview 23

Network Infrastructure 23

IP Telephony Infrastructure 23
   Call Processing 24
      Single-Site Deployment Model 24
      Multiple-Site Deployment Model 25
      Centralized Deployment Model 26
      Distributed Deployment Model 27
   Cisco AVVID IP Telephony Infrastructure 28
   Clients 29
      Cisco IP Phone Models 7960 and 7940 31
      Cisco IP Phone Expansion Module 7914 31
      Cisco IP Phone 7910 32
      Cisco IP Conference Station 7935 32
   Voice Gateways 32

Cisco AVVID IP Telephony Applications 33

Summary 34

Chapter 3   Understanding the Troubleshooting Tools 37

Time Synchronization 38
Configuring Automatic Time Synchronization on CallManager Servers 39
Synchronizing Time Manually on CallManager Servers 40
Synchronizing Time on Cisco IOS Devices 40
Synchronizing Time on CatOS Devices 41

Reading CCM (or SDI) Traces 42
Setting the Appropriate Trace Level and Flags 42
Reading CCM Traces 50
A Sample CCM Trace for a Call Between Two IP Phones 51
Tracing a Call Through an MGCP T1 PRI Gateway 58

Reading SDL Traces 60
SDL Overview 60
Enabling SDL Trace and Setting the Appropriate SDL Trace Level 63

Microsoft Performance (PerfMon) 68
Comparing PerfMon and the Real-time Monitoring Tool (RTMT) 68
PerfMon Advantages 68
RTMT Advantages 68
Using PerfMon to View Real-Time Statistics 69
Using Counter Logs 71
Using Alerts 75

CCEmail 76
Alerting Methods During Production and Non-production Hours 81
Acquiring CCEmail 82

CallManager Serviceability 82
Alarms 82
Tracing 83
Using XML-enabled Traces 83
Searching for Devices with XML Traces 84
Web-based Q.931 Translator 84
Service Activation 84
Control Center 85
Real-Time Monitoring Tool (RTMT) 85
Performance Tab 86
Devices Tab 86
CTI Apps Tab 88

Call Detail Records (CDR) and the CDR Analysis and Reporting (CAR) Tool 89

CDR Time Converter 90
Acquiring the CDR Time Converter 91

Event Viewer 91

Q.931 Translator and Enhanced Q.931 Translator 95
    Enhanced Q.931 Translator 98
    Acquiring Enhanced Q.931 Translator 100

Dick Tracy 101
    Using the Dick Tracy Tool 102
    Using the CLI Tracy/Embedded Tracy Tool 105
    Acquiring Dick Tracy 105

Sniffer Traces 106

Voice Codec Bandwidth Calculator 106

Bug Toolkit (Formerly Bug Navigator) 106

Remote Access Tools 107
    Terminal Services 107
    Virtual Network Computing (VNC) 108

Websites and Further Reading 108

Best Practices 109
    VNC Best Practices 109

Summary 110

Chapter 4 Skinny Client Registration 113

Troubleshooting Inline Power 114

Troubleshooting Network Connectivity and
  Skinny Registration 117
    Verifying VLAN configuration 118
    Verifying IP Addressing Information 118
    Verifying TFTP Configuration File Download 121
    Understanding Skinny Registration 127
    Troubleshooting Skinny Registration 130

Additional Tools for Troubleshooting Skinny Client Registration Problems 133
    Checking IP Phone Status Messages 133
    Checking Registration with the Real-Time Monitoring Tool 135

Best Practices 137

Summary 137

Chapter 5   IP Phones 139

    Understanding IP Phone Behavior 139
        Understanding the Skinny Protocol 139
            Call Processing Behavior 140
            Examining Skinny Protocol Messages in a CCM Trace 148
        Understanding Failover and Failback 154
            Failover Behavior 155
            Failback Behavior 156
        Understanding the Difference Between Restart and Reset 156

    Troubleshooting IP Phone Problems 157
        Dropped Calls 157
        "CM Down, Features Disabled" 158
        Reasons for Failover 158
        Directory and Service Problems 160

    79xx Series IP Phone 3-port Switch Operation 161

    Best Practices 165
        Check Your Firmware 165
        Press the Help (i or ?) Button Twice During Active Calls 165
        Use a Custom Phone Service That Tracks Voice Quality Statistics 166
        Check the IP Phone Configuration Via Web Browser 167

    Summary 167

Chapter 6   Voice Gateways 169

    Cisco IOS Voice Gateways 169
        Cisco VG200 170
        Cisco 2600 Series Routers 171
        Cisco 3600 Series Routers 172
        Cisco 3700 Series Routers 173
        Cisco Catalyst 4224 173
        Cisco Catalyst 4000 Access Gateway Module (AGM) 174
        Cisco WS-SVC-CMM Communications Media Module (CMM) 174
        Other Cisco IOS Gateways 174

    Understanding Dial Peer Matching in Cisco IOS Software 175

    Understanding Cisco IOS Debugs and show Commands 184
        Correctly Setting the Timestamps 185
        Enabling Cisco IOS Software Debugs 185

    Troubleshooting TDM Interfaces on Cisco IOS Gateways 187
        Useful show Commands for Troubleshooting TDM Interfaces 187
        Using debug Commands to Troubleshoot TDM Interfaces 192
            Understanding Cisco IOS CCAPI Debugs 196

Understanding the FXO Disconnect Problem 205

Troubleshooting Digital Interfaces 208
    Checking Physical Layer Connectivity on Digital Interfaces 208
    Troubleshooting ISDN PRI Signaling 210
    Troubleshooting T1 CAS 214

Understanding MGCP 218
    MGCP Endpoint Identifiers 219
    MGCP Commands 219
    MGCP Parameter Lines 221
    MGCP Packages 229
        Generic Media Package (G) 231
        DTMF Package (D) 231
        MF Package (M) 232
        Trunk Package (T) 233
        Line Package (L) 234
        Handset Emulation Package (H) 235
        RTP Package (R) 236
        DTMF Trunk Package (DT) 236
        MF Trunk Package (MS) 237
    MGCP Response Headers and Response Codes 238

Cisco IOS MGCP Gateways 240
    MGCP FXS/FXO 249
    Cisco IOS MGCP PRI 256
        Reading ISDN Messages 258
        Table of Q.850 Cause Codes 262
        Numbering Type and Plan Mismatches 269
        Troubleshooting Calling Name Display Problems 270
        Understanding ISDN Timers 271
    Cisco IOS MGCP T1 CAS 276

Cisco IOS Gateways Using the H.323 Protocol 281
    H.225 Signaling 283
        H.225 Messages 283
        H.225 Information Elements 284
        H.225 Call Flow 287
    H.245 Signaling 295
        Master/Slave Determination 296
        Terminal Capabilities Exchange 297
        Logical Channel Signaling 300
        DTMF Relay 303
    Additional H.323 Debugs in Cisco IOS Software 305

Troubleshooting Problems with Ringback and Other Progress Tones 307
    No Ringback on an IP Phone When Calling the PSTN 308
    No Ringback on a PSTN Phone When Calling an IP Phone 309

No Ringback When Transferring a Call 309
The IP Phone User Does Not Hear In-band Messages When a Call Is Disconnected 310

Intercluster Trunks 311

Troubleshooting the WS-X6608 and WS-X6624 Voice Gateways 313
Recognizing and Powering the Module 313
Troubleshooting DHCP, TFTP, and Registration Problems 314
Troubleshooting DHCP Problems 314
Troubleshooting TFTP Problems 320
Troubleshooting Registration Problems 324
Catalyst WS-X6608 T1/E1 Digital Gateway Configuration 325
Troubleshooting Configuration Issues 326
Getting the D-channel Established 337
Checking Physical Layer Statistics on the WS-X6608 340
Verifying D-channel Configuration 343
Advanced Troubleshooting for D-channel Problems 344
Unexpected Resets 345
Using Dick Tracy to Analyze a WS-X6608 Port 345
Troubleshooting T1 CAS Problems on the WS-X6608 359
Catalyst WS-X6624 FXS Analog Gateway Configuration 367

Best Practices 380

Summary 381

Chapter 7   Voice Quality 383

Fixed and Variable Delays 384
Fixed Delay Sources 385
Coder (Processing) Delay 386
Packetization Delay 386
Serialization Delay 387
Propagation Delay 389
Variable Delay Sources 389
Queuing/Buffering Delay 390
Low-speed Links 391
Dejitter Delay 393
The Effects of Delay on Signaling 395

Analyzing and Troubleshooting Choppy and Garbled Audio 396
Packet Drops 397
Queuing Problems 400
The Effect of VAD on Voice Quality 402

Troubleshooting Problems with One-way or No-way Audio 405
Verifying IP Connectivity 405
One-way Audio on Cisco IOS Software Gateways 406
NAT, PAT, and Firewalls 410

Troubleshooting Echo Problems 410
Sources of Echo 411
Electrical Echo 411
Acoustic Echo 412
Talker Versus Listener Echo 412
What Makes Echo a Problem 414
How an Echo Canceller Works 416
Eliminating Echo 418
Eliminating Echo on Cisco IOS Software Gateways 421
Eliminating Echo on the WS-X6608 and DT-24+/DE-30+ 424
Eliminating Echo Problems on Cisco IP SoftPhone 428

Best Practices 429

Summary 430

Chapter 8   Fax Machines and Modems 433

Understanding Fax Machine Operation 433
Basic Fax Machine Operation 434
T.30 Messages 435

Understanding Fax/Modem Passthrough Versus Fax Relay 437
Fax/Modem Passthrough 437
Named Service Events and Named Telephony Events 438
Basic Fax/Modem Passthrough Operation 439
Modem Passthrough Operation 439
Fax Passthrough Operation 440
Verifying Fax and Modem Passthrough Configuration 441
Fax Relay Basics 444

The Effect of Packet Loss and Jitter on Fax
Machines and Modems 446

First Steps in Troubleshooting Fax and Modem Problems 447
Checking for Physical Layer Problems on Digital Circuits 447

Isolating and Troubleshooting Fax Problems 449
Adjusting the Fax Relay Data Rate 451
Disabling Error Correction Mode 452
Changing the Nonstandard Facilities Field 453
Changing the Fax Protocol 454
Checking the fax interface-type Command 454
Enabling Fax Relay Debugs 455

Best Practices 457

Summary 457

Chapter 9   Call Routing 459

Understanding Closest-match Routing 461
Common Problems Associated with Closest-match Routing 465
Outside Dial Tone Played at the Wrong Time 465
Delayed Routing When Placing Seven-digit Local Calls 466

Understanding Calling Search Spaces and Partitions 469
Calling Search Space/Partition Rules 474
The First Partition Takes Precedence 474
The Line-level Calling Search Space Takes Precedence over the Device-level Calling Search Space 476
Event-specific Calling Search Spaces 478
Call Forwarding Calling Search Spaces 479
Call Forward No Answer (CFNA) 479
Call Forward Busy (CFB) 480
Call Forward All (CFA) 480
Call Forward on Failure (CTI Ports and CTI Route Points Only) 485

Understanding and Troubleshooting Transformations and Masks 486
Digit Discard Instructions (DDIs) 486
Understanding the Concept of Masks 495
Transformation Rules 496
Order of Applied Transformations 496
Cumulative Transformations 497
Cumulative Transformation on Calling Party Number Example 497
Cumulative Transformation on Called Party Number Example 498
Overwritten Transformations 499
Service Parameter-related Transformations 500

Understanding and Troubleshooting Translation Patterns 501

Understanding Route Filters 506

Digit Transformation Troubleshooting 513

Call Routing Troubleshooting 515
Reading CCM Traces for Call Routing Information 516

Troubleshooting Hold, Transfer, Park, and Call Pickup 521
Call Hold and Resume 522
Call Transfer 529
Call Park 531
Call Pickup 533

Getting the Dialing Forest Traces 538

Best Practices 544
Toll Fraud Prevention 544
Preventing Transfers to Extension 9011 or Your Equivalent International Access Code 545

Using PLAR to Control Rogue Auto-registered IP Phones 545
Restricting the Call Forward All Field on IP Phones 546
Restricting Voice Mail Systems by Using Calling Search Spaces 547
Blocking Certain Area Codes 548

Summary 549

Chapter 10 Call Preservation 551

Understanding Call Preservation 551
Survivable Endpoints 552
IP Phones 552
MGCP Gateways 553
Nonsurvivable Endpoints 557
Skinny Gateways 557
H.323 Gateways 558
CTI/TAPI Endpoints 559
Media Processing Resources 560

Troubleshooting Call Preservation Issues 561

Best Practices 562

Summary 562

Chapter 11 Conference Bridges, Transcoders, and Media Termination Points 565

Media Resource Groups (MRGs) and Media Resource Group Lists (MRGLs) 566
MRGL Selection 567

Understanding Codec Selection 568

Transcoder Resources 570
Regions and the Regions Codec Matrix 570
Out-of-resource Conditions 578
Use of Transcoders in Conjunction with Other Media Resources 580
Transcoders in Conjunction with Conference Bridge Resources 581
Transcoders in Conjunction with MOH Servers 585

Conference Bridge Devices 586
Types of Conference Bridges 586
Troubleshooting "No Conference Bridge Available" 587
Troubleshooting Conference Failures 591
Other Conferencing Error Messages 597
"Already In Conference" 597
"Exceeds maximum parties" 597

Best Practices 598

Summary 598

Chapter 12   Music on Hold 601

Understanding MOH 601

Troubleshooting Data Points 603
Performance Counters 604
CCM Trace Files 607

Troubleshooting MOH 611
Resolving Problems Related to Multicast and Unicast 615
Determining Why Tone on Hold Is Playing 617
Troubleshooting the Audio Translator 617
Troubleshooting the Live Audio Source 619
Configuring the Correct MOH Fixed Audio Source Device 619
Selecting the Proper Recording Input 620

Best Practices 620

Summary 621

Chapter 13   Call Admission Control 623

Locations-based CAC 624
Setting LocationsTraceDetailsFlag and CDCC Values 626
The Role of Regions in CAC 627
Locations-based CAC in Action 627
Locations Reservations for Media Resources 631
Locations-based CAC Reservations for Music on Hold Resources 631
Locations-based CAC Reservations for Ad Hoc or Meet-Me Conferences 633
Finding Bandwidth Leaks 635
Locations and Call Preservation Interaction 636
Troubleshooting Automated Alternate Routing 637

Gatekeeper Call Admission Control 638
Checking Gatekeeper Configuration 640
Verifying Gatekeeper Configuration on CallManager 641
CallManager Registration with Gatekeeper 645
Call Setup with Gatekeeper 647

Best Practices 652

Summary 652

Chapter 14   Voice Mail 655

Cisco Unity 655
CallManager Integration 655
Verifying Version Compatibility 656
Verifying TSP Configuration 656

Verifying Cisco Unity Switch Configuration 658
Message Waiting Indicator (MWI) 659
Dual-Tone Multifrequency (DTMF) Relay Problems 661
Additional Unity Troubleshooting 662
More Troubleshooting Resources for Unity 662

SMDI Integration 662
Understanding SMDI Messages 663
Call History Information for Calls to Voice Mail from CallManager 664
Message Waiting Indicator On/Off Messages 665
Error Messages 666
Cisco Messaging Interface 666
CMI Configuration Parameters 667
Reading CMI Traces 674
Using HyperTerminal to Diagnose SMDI Problems 679
Message Waiting Indicator Problems 682
Cisco VG248 SMDI Integration 686
Verifying Configuration Parameters 686
Message Waiting Indicator Problems 690

Octel Voice Mail Digital Integration Via a DPA Voice Mail Gateway 693
Verify Cabling 693
Check Port Status 697
Troubleshooting DPA MWI Problems 702
Using the DPA Event Log 703

Best Practices 703

Summary 704

Chapter 15   Survivable Remote Site Telephony (SRST) 707

SRST Operation 707
SRST Configuration 709
IP Phone Registration 712
SRST Dial Plan 718
Debugging Call Control in SRST Mode 719
Problems with Transferring Calls in SRST Mode 729
IP Phones Stuck in SRST Mode 730
Voice Mail and Forwarding Features in SRST Mode 731
DHCP Considerations When Using SRST 731

Best Practices 732

Summary 733

Chapter 16   Applications 735

    Customer Response Applications (CRA) 736
        Checking TSP or JTAPI Plugin Versions 736
        IP IVR and IP AA 737
          CRA Administration Problems 738
          Directory Configuration 741
          Verifying Configuration 744
          Engine Status 745
          Collecting Traces 748
        Extension Mobility for CallManager 3.1 and 3.2 756
          CallManager Extension Mobility Configuration 758
          CRA Extension Mobility Configuration 759
          Configuration Summary 762
          Understanding the Login and Logout process 763
          Troubleshooting Extension Mobility on CallManager 3.1 and 3.2 765
        Extension Mobility for CallManager 3.3 773
          Understanding the Login and Logout Process 775
        Troubleshooting Extension Mobility on CallManager 3.3 777

    Cisco CallManager Attendant Console 779
        Understanding the Server Components 780
        Understanding the Attendant Console Client 781
        Troubleshooting Attendant Console 782

    Cisco Personal Assistant 785
        Call Routing Problems and Personal Assistant 785
        Personal Assistant and Message Waiting Indicator Issues 786

    Cisco IP SoftPhone 786
        Line Number Displays, But No Dial Tone 786
        Echo Problems with Cisco IP SoftPhone 787
        One-way Audio and Using Cisco IP SoftPhone over VPN 787
        Cisco IP SoftPhone Has No Lines 788

    Cisco IP Phone Services 788

    Cisco IP Videoconferencing (IP/VC) 789

    Cisco Conference Connection 789
        Ensure the Necessary Services Are Started 790
        Using Event Viewer with Conference Connection 791

    Cisco Emergency Responder (ER) 791

    Summary 791

Chapter 17 SQL Database Replication 793

Understanding the Publisher-Subscriber Model 793
Troubleshooting the Publisher-Subscriber Relationship 796

The Role of Name Resolution and Passwords in Replication 796

Microsoft SQL Server Enterprise Manager 802

Correcting Replication Errors 804
Re-establishing a Broken SQL Replication Subscription 807
Deleting the Subscription from the Publisher 807
Adding the Subscription to the Subscriber SQL Server 808
Starting the Snapshot Agent 809
Reinitializing a Subscription 809

CDR Replication Issues 809
Subscriber Is Not Configured to Generate CDRs 810
Database Layer Monitor Is Not Running Properly 812
Additional Problems with Writing CDRs 813

Best Practices 815

Summary 816

Chapter 18 LDAP Integration and Replication 819

Directory Integration Versus Directory Access 820
Providing Endpoints with Corporate Directory Access 821
Troubleshooting Corporate Directory Access 823

Using the CallManager Embedded Directory 823
Troubleshooting the CallManager Embedded Directory 824
Reconfiguring DC Directory on the Publisher 827
CallManager 3.3 Reconfiguration Steps 828
CallManager 3.0–3.2 Reconfiguration Steps 830
Reconfiguring DC Directory on Subscribers 835

Understanding and Troubleshooting Active Directory Integration 837
Troubleshooting Common Problems with Installing the Customer Directory
Configuration Plugin 839
Preparing Active Directory to Allow Schema Modifications 840
Ensuring Domain Name Accuracy for Active Directory 841
Verifying Distinguished Name Administrative Rights After Cisco Customer
Directory Configuration Plugin Failure 842
Checking Log Files for Errors 842
Miscellaneous Troubleshooting Items 843

Understanding and Troubleshooting Netscape iPlanet Integration 844

Best Practices 845

Summary 846

Appendix A Cisco IP Telephony Protocol and Codec Information and References 849

      Protocols 849

      Codecs 855

Appendix B NANP Call Routing Information 857

Appendix C Decimal to Hexadecimal and Binary Conversion Table 881

Appendix D Performance Objects and Counters 891

      Cisco Performance Objects and Counters 891
        Cisco Analog Access Object 892
        Cisco CallManager Object 893
        Cisco CallManager Attendant Console Object—Release 3.3(2) 898
        Cisco CallManager System Performance Object 900
        Cisco CTI Manager Object 903
        Cisco Gatekeeper Object 904
        Cisco H.323 Object 904
        Cisco HW Conference Bridge Device—Release 3.3(2) 904
        Cisco Lines Object 905
        Cisco Locations Object 906
        Cisco Media Streaming App Object 906
        Cisco Media Termination Point Object—Through Release 3.3(2) 909
        Cisco Messaging Interface Object 910
        Cisco MGCP FXO Device Object 911
        Cisco MGCP FXS Device Object 912
        Cisco MGCP Gateways Object 912
        Cisco MGCP PRI Device Object 913
        Cisco MGCP T1 CAS Device Object 914
        Cisco MOH Device Object 915
        Cisco MTP Device Object 916
        Cisco Music on Hold Server Object—Through Release 3.3(2) 916
        Cisco Phones Object 918
        Cisco SW Conference Bridge Object—Through Release 3.3(2) 918
        Cisco SW Conference Bridge Device Object—Release 3.3(2) 919
        Cisco TFTP Object 920
        Cisco Transcode Device Object 923
        Cisco Unicast Hardware Conference Object 924
        Cisco Unicast Software Conference Bridge Device Object—Through Release 3.3(1) 924
        Cisco WebAttendant Object—Through Release 3.3(1) 924

      Windows 2000 Objects 924

Glossary   927

Index   947

Foreword

In November of 1998, Cisco Systems acquired a small startup called Selsius Systems. For over a year this small company had been shipping the world's first IP phones and Windows NT-based call management software consisting of close to a million lines of C++ code with a small development staff of about 40 engineers. Since the acquisition, the code base has evolved into many millions of lines of C++, XML, and Java code, and the development staff now has over 500 engineers. The level of sophistication and capability has increased dramatically and is a key component of the Cisco Architecture for Voice, Video, and Integrated Data (AVVID). Current deployments range from extremely distributed enterprises with hundreds of remote offices to small 50-person offices. Geographically, systems are deployed across the world, including exotic locations such as Antarctica and the International Space Station!

AVVID's IP Telephony components (including the IP phones, gateways, and Cisco CallManager) comprise a telephony system that is both richer than and different from traditional TDM-based phone systems. For example, manageability and serviceability are achieved through either a browseable interface or an XML SOAP-based protocol for integration with existing IT systems. Geography disappears as a problem because telephony functions, manageability, and serviceability all traverse the IP network. Proprietary databases disappear in favor of standard SQL databases and LDAP directories. Nevertheless, this unification and standardization of telephony on IP networks also presents unique challenges. Voice quality can be impacted by poor IP network design. Capacity planning requires consideration of IP address numbering. Music on Hold as a multicast stream requires proper switch and router configuration. These are only a few examples of the unique considerations that must be given to IP Telephony deployments.

This book incorporates the authors' real-life experiences in planning and troubleshooting IP Telephony within the AVVID solution. The wisdom contained herein has been gained over the course of thousands of real customer experiences. Paul Giralt and Addis Hallmark are two of the very best troubleshooters in the industry, and Anne Smith has written about and worked with the system since the earliest releases. Paul has been with Cisco's customer support organization for several years. His depth and breadth of knowledge across all Cisco products are legendary, including his most recent focus on IP Telephony. I have seen him in action at some very large and sensitive customer installations, where he resolved extremely difficult problems and provided excellent guidance during upgrades and installations. We were fortunate to get him back, inasmuch as our customers were loathe to let him leave! Addis has been involved in the development and testing of many AVVID products. He has been personally engaged with many key customers during deployment and operation and has received numerous rave reviews from customers. Addis also has been instrumental in the security design aspects of Cisco CallManager. Anne is an author and the technical editor for this and several other AVVID books. She has been engaged with the technology since its inception at Selsius Systems.

I highly recommend this book to any individual or organization involved in installing, operating, or troubleshooting one of the most exciting advances in the long history of telephony. Written by three of its pioneers, this book serves as a guide for the rest of the pioneers who aren't afraid to help their organization communicate in its own way, the better way, the IP way.

Richard B. Platt
Vice President for Enterprise Voice, Video Business Unit
Cisco Systems, Inc.

Introduction

This book teaches you the troubleshooting skills you need to isolate and resolve IP telephony problems. IP telephony is a relatively new technology with many different components. The Cisco IP Telephony (CIPT) solution revolves around Cisco CallManager, the core call processing engine. CIPT includes many different endpoints, such as IP phones, various gateways, and various applications such as Cisco IP IVR, Cisco CallManager Attendant Console, Cisco IP SoftPhone, Cisco Conference Connection, extension mobility, and more. Additionally, the network infrastructure plays an important role in prioritizing voice packets to ensure quality of service (QoS).

With all these components involved in transmitting voice across packet networks, it is essential that you be able to identify and resolve issues in the entire solution. This requires knowledge of the functionality of these components and how they interact with each other, as well as what tools are available to help you find the root cause when problems arise. This book educates you about the techniques, tools, and methodologies involved in troubleshooting an IP telephony system.

Target CallManager Release

This book is written to CallManager release 3.3. Updates to this book may be provided after publication. You should periodically check the ciscopress.com web site for updates (go to ciscopress.com and search for "Troubleshooting Cisco IP Telephony").

Goals and Methods

This book intends to deliver a methodology you can follow when troubleshooting problems in an IP telephony network, particularly a Cisco IP Telephony solution. This book provides detailed troubleshooting information that applies to a variety of problems that can occur in any IP telephony deployment.

"Best Practices" sections in each chapter provide tips and design considerations to help you avoid common configuration problems.

Who Should Read This Book?

This book is designed to teach you how to isolate and correct problems in an IP telephony network. If you are a networking professional responsible for administering a Cisco IP Telephony (CIPT) system, this book is for you. Although this book's main focus is on CIPT, some concepts apply to IP telephony in general as well.

You will best be able to assimilate the information in this book if you already have a working knowledge of a CIPT network.

How This Book Is Organized

Although you could read this book cover-to-cover, it is designed to help you find solutions to specific problems. The chapters are organized by the various components of a Cisco IP Telephony solution. Four appendixes provide reference information.

- **Chapter 1, "Troubleshooting Methodology and Approach"** — You can troubleshoot even the most complex problems if you have a good methodology in place for finding the root cause. This chapter focuses on teaching that methodology: learning how to find clues and track down your "suspect" by breaking the problem into smaller pieces and tackling each piece individually.

- **Chapter 2, "IP Telephony Architecture Overview"**—Cisco AVVID includes many different components that come together to form a comprehensive architecture for voice, video, and integrated data. This chapter covers the basic components of the IP Telephony architecture in order to provide a big-picture view of the system.

- **Chapter 3, "Understanding the Troubleshooting Tools"**—To effectively troubleshoot problems in a Cisco IP Telephony network, you must be familiar with the many tools at your disposal. In addition, you need to know how to best use those tools to achieve maximum results. This chapter describes the various tools and their different uses.

- **Chapter 4, "Skinny Client Registration"**— IP phone registration is a common source of problems. This chapter describes how Skinny protocol-based device registration works, including discussions of inline power, network connectivity, and potential TFTP and CallManager issues.

- **Chapter 5, "IP Phones"**—IP phones can encounter various problems, from unexpected resets to directory and service problems, and more. This chapter explains proper IP phone behavior and examines problems that can occur after an IP phone successfully registers.

- **Chapter 6, "Voice Gateways"**—Voice gateways are the interface that bridges the Voice over IP (VoIP) world with the Public Switched Telephone Network (PSTN). Voice gateways can be Cisco IOS Software gateways or modules within voice-enabled LAN switches. They can be analog or digital, and they can use a wide variety of signaling protocols. This chapter teaches you how to identify and resolve gateway problems by breaking these components into logical groups and following a methodical trouble-shooting approach.

- **Chapter 7, "Voice Quality"**—Voice quality is a broad term that covers the following conditions: delayed audio, choppy or garbled audio, static and noise, one-way or no-way audio, and echo. This chapter focuses on the information you need to investigate and resolve voice quality problems in an IP Telephony network.

- **Chapter 8, "Fax Machines and Modems"**—Fax machines and modems present unique challenges when carried over an IP Telephony network, primarily due to their unforgiving nature concerning any modification to the audio stream. This chapter discusses the effect of packet loss and jitter, fax passthrough, fax relay, and how to troubleshoot modems and faxes.

- **Chapter 9, "Call Routing"**—Possessing a strong understanding of call routing is arguably one of the most important aspects of a smooth-operating CIPT solution. This chapter discusses closest-match routing, calling search spaces and partitions, trans-formations, and translation patterns as well as troubleshooting hold, transfer, park, and call pickup.

- **Chapter 10, "Call Preservation"**—Call preservation is easier to predict when you understand the protocol interaction with CallManager. This chapter provides guidelines for determining call survivability based on endpoint type and protocol.

- **Chapter 11, "Conference Bridges, Transcoders, and Media Termination Points"**—Conference bridges, transcoders, and media termination points are media resources. This chapter discusses the role of media resource groups and media resource group lists, codec selection, and troubleshooting transcoder and conference bridge resources.

- **Chapter 12, "Music on Hold"**—The Music on Hold feature allows callers to hear streaming audio while on hold. This chapter describes this feature and provides steps to take if you encounter problems.

- **Chapter 13, "Call Admission Control"**—Call admission control is used in situations where a limited amount of bandwidth exists between telephony endpoints such as phones and gateways. This chapter discusses the two types of call admission control—locations-based and gatekeeper—and the mechanisms available to reroute calls through the PSTN in the event of WAN congestion.

- **Chapter 14, "Voice Mail"**—CallManager is compatible with a variety of voice mail systems that integrate with CallManager through various methods. This chapter focuses on troubleshooting the integration of CallManager and three types of voice mail systems: Cisco Unity, third-party voice mail systems integrated via Simple Message Desk Interface (SMDI), and Octel Voice Mail, integrated through Cisco DPA Voice Mail gateways.

- **Chapter 15, "Survivable Remote Site Telephony (SRST)"**—SRST allows a router at a remote branch to assume call processing responsibilities in the event that phones at a remote site are unable to contact the central CallManager. This chapter describes SRST and provides detailed information about the various problems that can occur.

- **Chapter 16, "Applications"**—Cisco AVVID allows for the creation of many different applications to interoperate within the converged network. This chapter discusses some of the primary applications in a Cisco AVVID IP Telephony solution, such as IP AA and IP IVR, extension mobility, Cisco IP SoftPhone, Personal Assistant, and Cisco CallManager Attendant Console.

- **Chapter 17, "SQL Database Replication"**—The SQL relational database stores the majority of CallManager configuration information. This chapter discusses the Publisher-Subscriber model for database replication, name resolution, Enterprise Manager, Replication Monitor, broken subscriptions, and CDR database replication.

- **Chapter 18, "LDAP Integration and Replication"**—User information is stored in a Lightweight Directory Access Protocol (LDAP) database. This chapter describes directory integration versus directory access, using the CallManager embedded directory, and integrating with Active Directory and Netscape iPlanet.

- **Appendix A, "Cisco IP Telephony Protocol and Codec Information and Reference"**—Cisco IP Telephony employs many different protocols and codecs. This appendix provides a list of applicable protocols and codecs with descriptions and the standards body corresponding to the protocol or the Request for Comments (RFC) number. Compression rates are given for each codec.

- **Appendix B, "NANP Call Routing Information"**—CallManager provides a built-in dial plan for the North American numbering plan (NANP). This appendix provides information from the NANP file located in the C:\Program Files\Cisco\Dial Plan directory. This file shows you how each part of an NANP number corresponds to a specific placeholder. It is particularly useful when you're learning how to apply route filters.

- **Appendix C, "Decimal to Hexadecimal and Binary Conversion Table"**—This appendix provides a cheat sheet that shows you how to quickly convert between decimal, hexadecimal, and binary values.

- **Appendix D, "Performance Objects and Counters"**—Microsoft Performance (PerfMon) and the Real-Time Monitoring Tool allow you to monitor your system through the use of performance counters. This appendix lists and describes the performance objects and counters in a Cisco IP Telephony network. Some pertinent Windows 2000 counters are also described.

- **Glossary**—The glossary defines terms and acronyms used in this book.

Best Practices

In a perfect world, there would be no need for this book, because systems would always run perfectly. Unfortunately, in the real world, problems do arise, and they usually don't go away on their own. However, an administrator/installer can proactively take steps to ensure reliability and high availability and minimize the number of problems that arise.

Best practices include not only design considerations but also monitoring and management. A properly monitored system can detect failures before they become service-affecting. Each chapter contains a section outlining best practices as they apply to the chapter topic.

In a properly designed network, you can achieve 99.999 percent reliability—a rating that is expected of a telephone system.

High Availability in an IP Telephony Environment

High availability for IP telephony is based on distribution and core layers in the network and servers (call processing, application servers, and so on). BellCore Specification GR-512 defines what criteria must be met to achieve "five 9s" (99.999 percent) reliability. A careful examination of this document is recommended if you are interested in understanding 99.999 percent reliability. Note that many "events" are not counted against five 9s reliability. Some of these events include the following:

- Outages of less than 64 devices
- Outages less than 30 seconds in duration
- Outages due to outside causes, such as power loss from utility or network circuit failures caused by the provider
- Outages due to planned maintenance

The Cisco AVVID IP Telephony solution can achieve 99.999 percent reliability per the BellCore FR-512 specification.

Command Syntax Conventions

The conventions used to present command syntax in this book are the same conventions used in the IOS Command Reference. The Command Reference describes these conventions as follows:

- Vertical bars | separate alternative, mutually exclusive elements.

- Square brackets [ ] indicate an optional element.

- Braces { } indicate a required choice.

- Braces within brackets [{ }] indicate a required choice within an optional element.

- **Boldface** indicates commands and keywords that are entered literally as shown. In actual configuration examples and output (not general command syntax), boldface indicates commands that the user inputs (such as a **show** command).

- *Italic* indicates arguments for which you supply actual values.

OSI Reference Model

Throughout the book, a few references are made to the OSI model. Table I-1 provides a brief primer on the OSI reference model layers and the functions of each. You can learn more about the OSI model in any of the Cisco Press books that target the CCNA certification.

Table I-1 *OSI Reference Model Overview*

OSI Layer Name	Functional Description	Examples
Physical (Layer 1)	Responsible for moving bits of data between devices. Also specifies characteristics such as voltage, cable types, and cable pinouts.	EIA/TIA-232, V.35
Data link (Layer 2)	Combines bytes of data into frames. Provides access to the physical media using a Media Access Control (MAC) address, which is typically hard-coded into a network adapter. Also performs error detection and recovery for the data contained in the frame.	802.3/802.2, HDLC
Network (Layer 3)	Uses logical addressing which routers use for path determination. Can fragment and reassemble data if the upper-layer protocol is sending data larger than the data link layer can accept.	IP, IPX
Transport (Layer 4)	Provides reliable or unreliable delivery of data packets. Allows for multiplexing of various conversations using a single network-layer address. Can also ensure data is presented to the upper layers in the same order it was transmitted. Can also provide flow control.	TCP, UDP
Session (Layer 5)	Sets up, coordinates, and terminates network connections between applications. Also deals with session and connection coordination between network endpoints.	Operating systems and application access scheduling

Table I-1 *OSI Reference Model Overview (Continued)*

OSI Layer Name	Functional Description	Examples
Presentation (Layer 6)	Defines how data is presented to the application layer. Can perform special processing, such as encryption, or can perform operations such as ensuring byte-ordering is correct.	JPEG, ASCII
Application (Layer 7)	Interface between network and application software.	Telnet, HTTP

Comments for the Authors

The authors are interested in your comments and suggestions about this book. Please send feedback to the following address:

troubleshootingcipt@external.cisco.com

Further Reading

The authors recommend the following sources for more information.

Cisco Documentation

This book provides comprehensive troubleshooting information and methodology. However, details about common procedures might not be provided. You should be familiar with and regularly use the documentation that is provided with the Cisco IP Telephony system to supplement the information in this book.

You can find Cisco IP Telephony documentation by searching for a specific product on Cisco.com or by starting at the following link:

www.cisco.com/univercd/cc/td/doc/product/voice/index.htm

You can examine the following books at a technical bookseller near you or online by entering the title in the search box at www.ciscopress.com.

Cisco CallManager Fundamentals: A Cisco AVVID Solution

You can find detailed information about CallManager's inner workings in the book *Cisco CallManager Fundamentals* (ISBN 1-58705-008-0).

Developing Cisco IP Phone Services: A Cisco AVVID Solution

You can find instructions and tools for creating custom phone services and directories for Cisco IP Phones in the book *Developing Cisco IP Phone Services* (ISBN 1-58705-060-9).

Cisco IP Telephony

You can find installation, configuration, and maintenance information for Cisco IP Telephony networks in the book *Cisco IP Telephony* (ISBN 1-58705-050-1).

Integrating Voice and Data Networks

You can find information on how to integrate and configure packetized voice networks in the book *Integrating Voice and Data Networks* (ISBN 1-57870-196-1).

Cisco Router Configuration, Second Edition

Cisco Router Configuration, Second Edition (ISBN 1-57870-241-0) provides example-oriented Cisco IOS Software configuration for the three most popular networking protocols used today—TCP/IP, AppleTalk, and Novell IPX.

Icons Used in This Book

Throughout this book, you will see a number of icons used to designate Cisco-specific and general networking devices, peripherals, and other items. The following icon legend explains what these icons represent.

Network Device Icons

CallManager

IP Phone

Stations

SRST Router

Used For:
Application Server
DHCP
DNS
MOH Server
MTP
SW Conference Bridge
Voice Mail Server

Router

Switch

Layer 3 Switch

PIX Firewall

Gateway or
3rd-party
H.323
Server

Modem

Access Server

ATM Switch

Used For:
Analog Gateway
Gatekeeper
Gateway
H.323 Gateway
Voice-enabled Router

PBX/PSTN Switch

PBX (Small)

Cisco
Directory
Server

Local Director

DAT Tape

PC

Laptop

Server

PC w/Software

Used For:
HW Conference Bridge
Transcoder
Voice-enabled Switch

POTS Phone

Relational
Database

Fax Machine

Media/Building Icons

Network Cloud

Ethernet Connection

Serial Connection

Telecommuter

Building

Branch
Office

## CHAPTER 1

Troubleshooting Methodology and Approach

It's 5:30 a.m. on a Monday and your pager goes off. You recognize the phone number— it's your CEO's administrative assistant. As the administrator of the company's 8000-phone IP Telephony network, you assume there's a big problem. You rush into work and find the CEO's administrative assistant, who states that several calls for the CEO have been disconnected in the middle of the call, including a call from a very important customer. Where do you start?

Troubleshooting a Cisco IP Telephony network can be a daunting task. Rather than describing step-by-step how to solve specific problems (subsequent chapters provide that information), this chapter focuses on teaching a good troubleshooting methodology: learning how to find clues and track down your "suspect" by breaking the problem into smaller pieces and tackling each piece individually.

A typical IP Telephony network consists of—at the very least—one or more of the following components:

- Cisco CallManager servers
- IP phones
- Voice gateways

These components are in addition to the data network infrastructure that supports voice over IP (VoIP) traffic. More-complex installations can have dozens of servers for different services and redundancy, each server running a variety of applications, as well as hundreds or thousands of IP phones and a large number of voice gateways.

Before exploring the myriad of tools, traces, and techniques available to you that aid in troubleshooting, you must develop a systematic method by which you can focus on the problem and narrow it down until you determine the root cause.

In addition to the information in this book, you should become familiar with the various standard protocols that are used in an IP Telephony network, such as the following:

- H.323
- Media Gateway Control Protocol (MGCP)
- Telephony Application Programming Interface/Java Telephony Application Programming Interface (TAPI/JTAPI)

You should also become familiar with the protocols used when interfacing with the traditional time-division multiplexing (TDM)-based Public Switched Telephone Network (PSTN), such as the following:

- Q.931 (an ISDN protocol)
- T1- or E1-Channel Associated Signaling (T1-CAS or E1-CAS)
- Foreign Exchange Office (FXO)
- Foreign Exchange Station (FXS)

Additionally, because an IP Telephony network runs over a data network, it is important to understand the protocols that transport VoIP data, such as the following:

- Internet Protocol (IP)
- Transmission Control Protocol (TCP)
- User Datagram Protocol (UDP)
- Real-Time Transport Protocol (RTP)

Later chapters cover some of these concepts. However, each of the mentioned protocols could take up an entire book on its own, so you should refer to the specifications and RFCs or to other materials that go into detail about these protocols. Appendix A, "Cisco IP Telephony Protocol and Codec Information and References," provides references to where you can find additional information for each protocol discussed in this book.

On the other hand, because the Skinny Client Control Protocol (SCCP or Skinny protocol, the Cisco-developed protocol that Cisco IP Phones use) is not the product of an industry-wide standards body, this book goes into additional detail about how this protocol works. Understanding the Skinny protocol is essential to understanding how the phone operates and how to troubleshoot problems with it. The Skinny protocol is covered in greater detail in Chapter 5, "IP Phones."

Developing a Troubleshooting Methodology or Approach

To track down a problem and resolve it quickly, you must assume the role of detective. First, you need to look for as many clues as you can find. Some clues lead you to additional clues, and others lead you to a dead end. As soon as you've got all the clues, you need to try to make sense of them and come up with a solution. This book shows you where to look for these clues and track down the problem while trying to avoid as many dead ends as possible.

Troubleshooting a problem can be broken down into two stages: data gathering and data analysis, although your analysis might lead you to collect additional data. The following list is a general guide for steps to take when troubleshooting an IP Telephony problem:

Step 1 Gather data about the problem:

(a) Identify and isolate the problem.

(b) Use topology information to isolate the problem.

(c) Gather information from the end users.

(d) Determine the problem's timeframe.

Step 2 Analyze the data you collected about the problem:

(a) Use deductive reasoning to narrow the list of possible causes.

(b) Verify IP network integrity.

(c) Determine the proper troubleshooting tool(s), and use them to find the root cause.

Production Versus Nonproduction Outages

Troubleshooting a problem can occur in one of two timeframes:

- During a scheduled outage window, such as when you're installing a new system, adding components, or upgrading for new features or functionality

- During production hours when the problem affects end users or service

Although the methodology to troubleshoot problems in either of these two situations is similar, the focus on how to resolve the problem should be different. In the case of a service-affecting problem during production hours, the focus should be to quickly restore service by either resolving the problem or finding a suitable workaround.

In contrast, when a problem is found during a new install or scheduled outage window, the focus should be on determining the root cause to ensure the problem is completely diagnosed and resolved so that it does not have the potential to become service-affecting.

For example, if users are encountering a delayed dial tone or sluggish behavior on their phones, you might discover that a high-level process on CallManager is consuming 100 percent of the CPU on one of the servers. During a new install or scheduled outage window, it's a good idea to investigate what is causing the CPU consumption to ensure that the problem does not return during production hours.

However, if this problem occurs during production hours, the best approach is to stop or restart the offending process and let the redundant systems take over to quickly restore service. After you restore service, perform a root-cause analysis to try to determine why that process was consuming the CPU. The downside of this approach is that you might not be able to further troubleshoot the problem when the process is restarted. Fortunately, CallManager provides many diagnostic traces (if they are enabled prior to the problem) that you can reference after a problem has occurred to see what was happening on CallManager at the time of the problem.

Note that although 100 percent CPU of a high-level process can cause sluggish behavior or delayed dial tone, do not infer from this that 100 percent CPU is necessarily always a bad thing. As of CallManager 3.3(1), low priority tasks (such as phone registrations) can consume 100 percent CPU without causing adverse effects to the ability to place or receive calls. Look at the 100 percent CPU as a possible symptom but not necessarily the root cause. In this case, you observe the symptoms of sluggish or delayed dial tone and 100 percent CPU utilization and make a correlation between the two.

If you encounter an event where you are unable to determine the root cause due to insufficient information, it is a good idea to turn on the appropriate traces to ensure that if the problem reoccurs, you will have enough data to identify the root cause.

Sometimes, several service-affecting problems occur simultaneously. In fact, this is not uncommon, because multiple problems often manifest themselves as symptoms of the same root cause. When multiple problems occur simultaneously, focus on the problem that has the greatest impact on users. For example, if some users are reporting dropped calls and others are reporting occasional echo, the two problems are probably unrelated. Troubleshoot the dropped-call problem first because keeping calls connected is more critical than removing the occasional echo on an active call.

Step 1: Gathering Data About the Problem

So you've just installed a new IP Telephony network, or you've been given the task of maintaining one—or maybe you've taken your first CallManager out of the box and are having problems getting it to run. You've encountered a problem. The first thing to do is gather as much information about the problem as possible.

Identifying and Isolating the Problem

Half the battle in troubleshooting a problem is determining which piece of the puzzle is the source of the problem. With so many different pieces composing an IP Telephony network, the first step is to isolate the problem and, if multiple problems are being reported, determine which of the problems might be related to each other and which should be identified as separate problems.

You must also determine which parts of the problem are symptoms and which are the root cause of the problem. For example, if a user complains of a phone resetting itself, it might seem logical to first assume that something is wrong with the phone. However, the problem might lie with CallManager or one of the many routers and switches that make up the underlying data network. So although the symptom is a phone reset, the root cause could be a WAN network outage or CallManager failure. You must always remember to look at the big picture when searching for the root cause and not let the symptoms of the problem lead you in the wrong direction. To help you visualize the big picture, detailed topology information is essential.

Using Topology Information to Isolate the Problem

You can take many proactive steps to help make the troubleshooting process easier. One of the first lines of defense is possessing current topology information. One of the most important pieces of topology information is a detailed network diagram (usually created using Microsoft Visio or a similar application). The network diagram should include network addressing information and the names of all the devices. It should also clearly show how the devices are interconnected and the port numbers being used for these interconnections. This information will prove invaluable when you try to isolate which components are involved in a particular problem.

For medium- to larger-sized networks, you should have a high-level overview topology that gives you a general idea of how things are connected and then several more-detailed diagrams for each piece of the network that drill down to the interface level on your network devices.

Figure 1-1 shows a typical high-level topology diagram for a large enterprise IP Telephony network. Notice that device names and IP addresses are listed in the diagram. This makes troubleshooting easier by allowing you to quickly look up devices to access them. Because Figure 1-1 is a high-level diagram, it does not get down to the interface level of each device.

Most networks are not as large as the one shown in Figure 1-1. However, no matter the size of your network, a similar topology diagram is very useful for quickly sharing information about your network with others who might be assisting you in troubleshooting.

In addition to the network diagram, you should use some method to store information such as IP address assignments, device names, password information, and so on. For a small network, you can use something as simple as a spreadsheet or even a plain text file. For larger deployments, some kind of database or network management application such as CiscoWorks is recommended. Many customers keep all this topology information on a web server as well, making it quickly and easily accessible to others when it is needed the most. Be sure to keep this information in a secure location.

You also need documentation of your dial plan. Some deployments, especially those heavily utilizing toll-bypass, have very complex dial plans. Knowing where a call is supposed to go just by knowing the phone number and from where it is dialed helps you quickly understand a problem.

Figure 1-1 *Sample High-Level Topology Diagram*

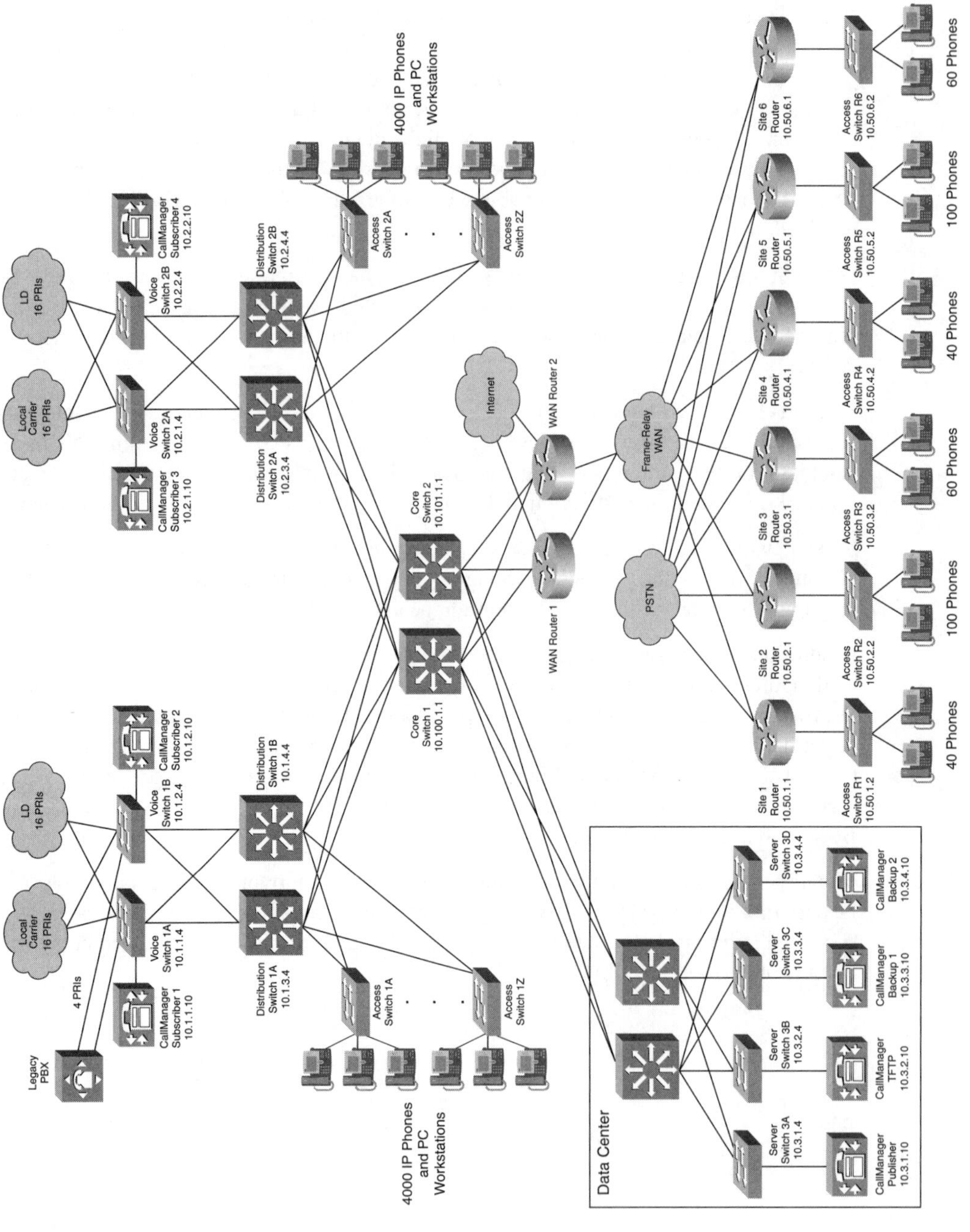

When your topology information is complete, it should include all the following information:

- Interconnection information for all devices, including device names and port numbers. If any patch panels exist between devices, the port numbers should be listed.
- IP addressing for all network devices (routers, switches, and so on)
- IP addressing for all telephony and application servers and voice gateways (including data application servers)
- IP addressing for endpoints (that is, scopes of a DHCP pool)
- WAN and PSTN service provider names and Circuit IDs for each circuit
- Spanning-tree topology, including root bridges for all VLANs and which ports should be forwarding and blocking
- Dial plan information
- Software version information for all devices

If you are troubleshooting a network you didn't design, topology is one of the first pieces of information you should obtain, if it's available. If a topology drawing is not available, it is a good idea to spend time obtaining this information from someone who is familiar with the network and then making a quick sketch. A general topological understanding of the network or at least the piece of the network in question helps when you're trying to differentiate the problem from its symptoms. It's necessary when you're trying to isolate the problem to a particular part of the network.

For example, if a user reports hearing choppy audio when making a conference call, it is essential to know exactly where in the network the conference bridge device is located in relation to the user's phone, including all the intermediate network devices. Without a network diagram, finding this information could waste precious time. Assume that the network you are troubleshooting looks like Figure 1-1. If the user's phone is connected to Access Switch 1A, the other conference participants are on Access Switch 1Z, and the conference bridge device is on Voice Switch 1A, you can see that the number of devices is greatly reduced from 100 or more switches and routers to four or five.

What is worse than not having topology information? Having *incorrect* topology information can lead to countless hours heading down the wrong path. If you're going to keep topology information (highly recommended), make sure you keep it current.

Use all the topology information you have to narrow down which pieces of the network might be involved in the problem you are trying to troubleshoot. To further isolate the problem, interview the end users who reported the problem to gather additional information.

Gathering Information from the User

Information the user provides can be vital to your ability to correct a problem. Try to gather as much detail as possible on exactly what the problem is. Often when troubleshooting a problem, you might realize that what you've been troubleshooting for hours is not really the problem the user encountered. The more detail about the problem you can gather before you begin troubleshooting, the easier it is to find a resolution—and that means less frustration for you. Here is some general information to collect from users:

- Details about exactly what the user experienced when the problem occurred.

- Phone numbers for all parties involved in the problematic call or calls. You can use this as search criteria if you need to look through traces.

- Actions performed by the user when the problem occurred. This includes what buttons were pressed and in what order.

- User observations. This includes text messages displayed on the phone or recorded announcements.

- Information about the user's device. For example, if the user experienced a problem while using a 7960 phone, get the phone's MAC address and IP address, along with registration information and any other statistics available from the phone.

Sometimes the information provided by an end user is not enough to even begin troubleshooting. For example, if a user has trouble transferring calls, you should ask what steps the user took when the problem happened and, if possible, when the problem occurred so that you can examine traces. Sometimes the proper diagnostic tools are not enabled when the problem occurs, forcing you to ask the user to inform you the next time the problem occurs. Be sure to turn on tracing or debugs before making the request so that when the problem occurs again, you will have captured the data. Users can get quite irritated if you have to ask them for the same piece of information two or three times. Also point out to the user the importance of letting you know immediately after a problem occurs, as many of the diagnostic trace files overwrite themselves within several hours or days (depending on the amount of traffic on your system).

Determining the Problem's Timeframe

In addition to *what* the problem is, you should try to determine *when* the problem occurred. Determining the problem's earliest occurrence can help correlate the problem with other changes that might have been made to the system or other events that occurred around the same time. For example, assume that a regular workday begins at 9 a.m. and ends around 6 p.m. Many users report that they get a busy signal when dialing into their voice mail. It is important to know whether they are attempting to do this at 9:10 a.m., a time when the voice mail system is likely under attack from many users all trying to access the system at once. This might change the problem from a troubleshooting issue to a load-balancing or equipment-expansion issue. You check the voice mail system and notice that at the time the problem was reported, all the voice mail ports were in use. Clearly in this example you need more voice mail ports or servers to handle call volume. However, if the problem occurs at 10:30 p.m., capacity is likely not the problem, so it's time to start troubleshooting your network and voice mail system. As another example, if a user reports that her phone was not working for 10 minutes and you know there was a network outage in her part of the building at that time, you can be relatively sure that the problem was due to the network outage.

When relying on end users to give "when" information about a problem, ask them to note the time on their phone when the problem occurred. The phone's time is synchronized with the clock on the CallManager to which the phone is registered. As long as you have the time on your CallManagers and network devices synchronized, having a phone-based time from the user makes finding the proper trace files very easy.

In some cases, the information about when a problem occurred might be the only piece of information you have other than a limited description of the problem at hand. If you have information about when, you might be able to look through trace files during that timeframe to search for anything abnormal.

TIP   Although it is important to use information about *when* the problem started happening, it is equally important to not assume that the problem was a direct result of an event. For example, if a user reports a problem the day after an upgrade was performed on CallManager, you might give some credence to the notion that the upgrade might have caused the problem, but don't automatically assume that this is the root cause.

Step 2: Analyzing the Data Collected About the Problem

Now that you have collected data from a variety of sources, you must analyze it to find the root cause and/or workaround for your problem.

Using Deductive Reasoning to Narrow the List of Possible Causes

The next part of your fact-finding mission is to identify the various components that might be involved and to eliminate as many components as possible. The more you can isolate the problem, the easier it is to find the root cause. For example, if a user complains about choppy voice quality, consider some of the following questions to help isolate the real problem, and think about how the answer will help narrow your focus:

- Does the problem happen on only one phone? If so, you can probably eliminate hundreds or thousands of other phones as suspects. However, keep in mind a single user's perspective. He might think the problem happens only on his phone, so you'll have to ask other users to see if the problem is more widespread than a single phone.

- What numbers are being called when the problem occurs? The answer to this question helps determine which parts of the system are being used when the problem occurs. For example, if the user never experiences poor audio quality when calling certain numbers but always experiences it when calling other numbers, this is a big clue.

- Does the problem happen only between IP phones, only through one or more voice gateways, or both? The user probably won't know the answer, but you'll be able to answer this question yourself after you answer the preceding question about which numbers are being called when the problem happens.

You will find more detailed questions similar to these throughout this book when troubleshooting particular problems.

Although not all of the following apply to every problem, where applicable, you must check all of the following pieces involved in the call. Use your topology information to help obtain this information.

- CallManager nodes involved in the signaling
- Network devices that signaling and/or voice traffic traverse
- Gateways or phones involved in the call
- Other devices involved, such as conference bridges or transcoders

Concentrate your energy on the smallest subset of devices possible. For example, if all the users on a particular floor are having the same problem, concentrate on the problem a particular user is having. If you fix the problem for that one user, in most cases you fix it for all the affected users.

Verifying IP Network Integrity

One thing that people often forget is that your IP Telephony network is only as good as your IP network. A degraded network or a network outage can cause a wide range of problems, ranging from slight voice quality problems to a total inability to make or receive calls on one or more phones. The network is always a consideration when you encounter certain problems, so network health issues are covered throughout this book. Network health is especially important during the discussion of voice quality problems in Chapter 7, "Voice Quality," because most voice quality problems stem from packet delay and/or loss.

Always remember to keep the IP network in mind and look at every layer in the OSI model, starting from Layer 1. Check your physical layer connectivity (cables, patch panels, fiber connectors, and so on). Then make sure you have Layer 2 connectivity by checking for errors on ports, ensuring that Layer 2 switches are functioning properly, and so forth. Continue working your way up the stack until you reach the application layer (Layer 7). As an example, two of the most common reasons for one-way audio (where one side of the conversation cannot hear the other) are the lack of an IP route from one phone to another and the lack of a default gateway being configured on a phone. Taking the layered approach, you would first check the cabling and switches to make sure that there are no errors on the ports. You would then check Layer 3, the network layer, by ensuring that IP routing is working correctly. When you reach this layer, you discover that for some reason the IP packets from one phone are unable to reach the other phone. Upon further investigation, you might discover that there was a missing IP route on one of the routers in the network or a missing default gateway on one of the end devices (such as an IP phone or voice gateway).

Determining the Proper Troubleshooting Tool

After you narrow down the appropriate component(s) causing a problem and have detailed information from the user(s) experiencing the problem, you must select the proper tool(s) to troubleshoot the problem. Most components have multiple troubleshooting tools available to help you. Chapter 3, "Understanding the Troubleshooting Tools," provides more details about some of the tools available for troubleshooting CallManager. You should use the tracing and debugging facilities available in CallManager and other devices to determine exactly what is happening. Additional tools and traces are covered in the chapter associated with diagnosing certain types of problems. For example, Chapter 6, "Voice Gateways," covers debugging Cisco IOS Software voice gateways. Because CallManager is central to almost all problems, information about various portions of the CCM trace facilities appears throughout this book.

This step is the most demanding on your troubleshooting skills because you analyze the detailed information provided in the various tools and use it to search for additional clues using other tools. Sometimes the problem description you have is not detailed enough to determine which tool to use. In this case, you should try various tools in search of anything that looks out of the ordinary.

The following case study shows how this troubleshooting methodology works in a real-world scenario.

Case Study: Resolving a Problem Using Proper Troubleshooting Methodology

It is 6 a.m., and you have arrived at work to resolve your CEO's problem. The only data you have is the page you received at 5:30 a.m. that says "CEO's calls keep dropping. Please help ASAP!" You need a bit more information than that to fix the problem.

This case study applies the methodology previously described. You must gather the data before you can begin the analysis.

Gathering the Data

As part of the data-gathering stage, you should do the following:

- Identify and isolate the problem
- Use topology information to isolate the problem
- Gather data from the end users
- Determine the problem's timeframe

You find the CEO's administrative assistant and begin your fact-finding mission. He states that at various times during the previous day and one time this morning, the CEO is on the phone when, all of the sudden, the call is disconnected. Eager to resolve the problem, you ask the administrative assistant for the following information:

- The exact date and times the problem occurred
- Whether the dropped calls were incoming or outgoing
- What number was dialed if it was an outbound call or what number the call came from if it was an inbound call

The assistant states that the call was dropped around 5:15 a.m. because the CEO was in early to prepare for the stockholders meeting. This is the extent of the information he remembers. Most users do not pay attention to specifics like this unless they have been instructed to, but all is not lost. The CEO has a 7960 phone that stores information locally about missed calls, received calls, and placed calls. You head into the CEO's office and look at the list of received calls and placed calls for the morning. You notice that a call was received at 5:05 a.m. and a call placed at 5:25 a.m. You notice that the second call was placed to the same area code and prefix as the call that was received.

You ask the CEO about the two calls. She remembers that she was on the phone with a customer for about 15 minutes when the call was disconnected. She immediately called the customer back. She also confirms that the first call that was received was the dropped call. Now you know that the problematic call was received at approximately 5:05 a.m. and was dropped just before 5:25 a.m.

While you are looking at the CEO's phone, you also go into the Settings menu (press the **settings** button > **Network Configuration > CallManager 1**) to see which CallManager the CEO's phone is registered to. This lets you isolate which CallManager in the cluster is involved in the signaling for this phone.

Armed with this information, you can begin the task of isolating the problem. You refer to your topology diagram to isolate the components that are involved. Figure 1-2 shows a high-level diagram of the network topology.

Figure 1-2   *High-Level Topology Diagram*

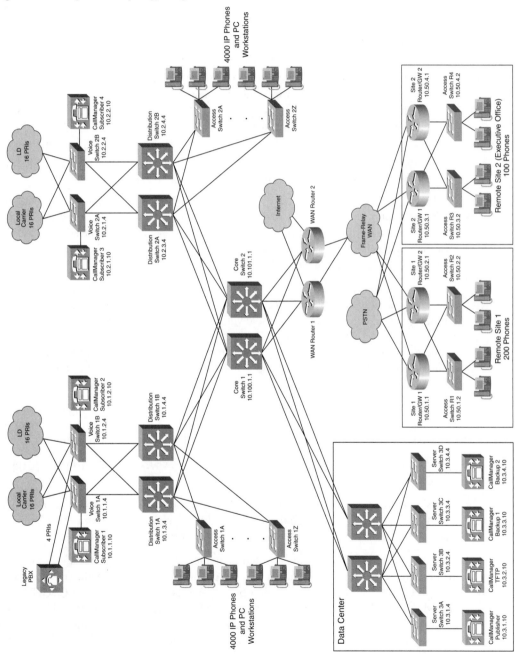

Reinforcing the topology in Figure 1-2, assume the following setup:

- A cluster with eight CallManager nodes

- 32 voice gateway connections to the PSTN for outgoing calls at your main site—16 for local calls and 16 for international and long distance

- 32 more voice gateways at your main campus where all your inbound calls come in. The telephone company has set up the inbound calls so that the 32 gateways are redundant whereby if one of the gateways is down, all your incoming calls can still use any of the other remaining gateways.

- Two gateways at each remote site used for both inbound and outbound calls. All outbound calls prefer the first gateway, and inbound calls prefer the second gateway, although each can handle both inbound and outbound calls should one fail.

As shown in Figure 1-2, the executive offices are at a remote site across the WAN. With just the information you have so far, you can eliminate a large portion of the network. So far you know that the problematic call was to the CEO. You also know that the problematic call was an inbound call. You ask the CEO and her admin if all the dropped calls were inbound calls. As far as they can remember, they were.

You know that the call this morning was during a time of day where there is little phone activity. Remember that all inbound calls to the remote site come in through Primary Rate Interfaces (PRIs) connected to the remote voice gateways and that inbound calls to the site prefer the second gateway. It is unlikely that all the channels on the first PRI were in use during a time of low call volume, so you assume that the call probably came in through the second gateway, although you still keep it in the back of your mind that the call might have come in through the first gateway at the remote site.

You then look at the configuration for the two gateways at Remote Site 2 and note that they are both configured to send incoming calls to CallManager Subscriber 3 as their preferred CallManager and CallManager Backup 1 in case CallManager Subscriber 3 fails.

With the information you have so far, you can narrow down the possible suspect devices to the network shown in Figure 1-3.

Armed with this knowledge, you can immediately isolate the problem to the user's phone and the two gateways being used for inbound calls. Keep in mind that you haven't elimi-nated the possibility that the problem is on CallManager or is network-related.

Now that you know the problem is related to inbound calls, it makes sense to try to understand the call flow for an inbound call to this user. Determine whether these calls all come directly to the user or if the call flow has any intermediate steps, such as Cisco IP Auto Attendant (Cisco IP AA) or an operator who transfers the call to the end user. For the sake of this example, assume that the user has a Direct Inward Dialing (DID) number, so the call comes straight from the PSTN through a gateway to the user, and a Cisco IP AA or operator is not involved. You have now eliminated Cisco IP AA from the picture, as well as the possibility that other phones or users are involved in this user's problems. This is not to say that other users are not experiencing similar problems, but the focus here is on solving this particular user's problem. If the problem is more widespread than this one user, you will probably find it as you continue to troubleshoot this user's problem.

Figure 1-3   *Network After You Narrow Down the Possible Suspects*

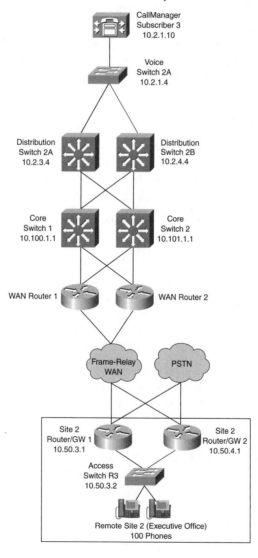

At this point, the problem has been isolated to the following culprits:

- The CEO's phone
- CallManager Subscriber 3
- Site 2 Router/GW 1 and Site 2 Router/GW 2
- The underlying network connecting these devices

It might seem like you haven't made much progress in this example, but in reality you have eliminated a large portion of the system as possible culprits. This concludes the data-gathering piece of your investigation. Now it is time to start analyzing the data. After you isolate the problem, you must break it into smaller pieces.

Analyzing the Data

As soon as you have a clear understanding of the problem you're trying to resolve, and you have isolated the piece or pieces of the network that are involved, the next step is to break the problem into pieces to find the root cause. As part of the data analysis stage, you should do the following:

- Use deductive reasoning to narrow the list of possible causes
- Verify IP network integrity
- Determine the proper troubleshooting tools, and use them to find the root cause

Continuing with the case study example, you now know the pieces involved in the puzzle, but you still don't know why the call is being dropped. For the sake of this example, this chapter keeps things general, but later chapters go into far greater detail on exactly what to look for. In this case, the problem is likely caused by the phone, CallManager, the gateway, the PSTN, or the IP network. So how do you determine which one is causing the problem?

One important distinction to make that will become evident as you read through this book is that many problems can be narrowed down to being either signaling-related or voice packet-related. In this case, you are dealing with a signaling-related problem, because the problematic call is being torn down—a problem that must occur in the signaling path between devices.

Because nearly all signaling for a call must go through one or more CallManager servers, the first tool you decide to use is a trace from CallManager Subscriber 3. You can then analyze the trace files to discover the device that disconnects the call from CallManager's perspective—in other words, "Who hung up first?" Using the information provided by the user, you must find the proper trace file and try to reconstruct the call from beginning to end.

A call between the CEO's phone and the voice gateway has two distinct signaling connections. One is the communication between CallManager and the voice gateway. The other is the communication between CallManager and the phone. The phone and voice gateway never directly exchange signaling data. All signaling goes through CallManager.

The trace includes all the messaging between CallManager and both the phone and the gateway. Chapter 3 provides more details on where to find these traces and how to read them.

You know that the call in question was set up around 5:05 a.m., so you look through the traces during that timeframe, searching for the phone number you retrieved from the CEO's phone. After combing through the trace file, you determine that the gateway is sending a message to CallManager, telling it to disconnect the call. The CCM traces (discussed in Chapter 3) indicate which gateway the calls are coming from. This eliminates the CEO's phone as a cause of the problem because the disconnect message is coming from the gateway. Because the user indicated that there were three drops, you can now go through the same process of looking through the CCM trace files for each instance of a dropped call and reconstructing those calls to see if the problem is isolated to one gateway. If you don't know the times that the other calls were dropped, you should just concentrate on the one call you do have data for.

Because CallManager received a message from the gateway telling it to disconnect the call, it is unlikely that a network problem is causing the calls to disconnect. If there were a network problem, you would likely see an indication that there was a problem communicating between CallManager and the gateway. In this case, the gateway had no problem sending the disconnect message to CallManager. It would not hurt to look through the network devices between CallManager and the voice gateway to ensure that there are no network errors, but with a problem like this, the network is an unlikely culprit.

At this point, you have narrowed down the problem to be originating from either the voice gateway or the PSTN. Figure 1-4 shows you've narrowed down the network to only a few devices.

The next step is to go to the suspected gateway and try to determine why one of the calls was dropped. This involves turning on additional debugs on the gateway to determine if the gateway is disconnecting the call or just passing along information from the PSTN about disconnecting the call. Unfortunately, it is unlikely that you had the debugs enabled at the time the problem occurred, so you need to enable the proper debugs and wait for the problem to happen again. This is why it is so important to narrow down the problem to a small subset of devices: You do not want to turn on debugs on dozens of gateways.

Which debugs to use depends on the gateway model and the type of interface to the PSTN. Chapter 6 discusses these considerations in detail. While waiting for the problem to reoccur, you discover that a message to disconnect the call is coming from the PSTN. If you are using an ISDN voice circuit for connectivity to the PSTN, the disconnect message is accompanied by a cause code that provides a general reason why the call was disconnected. Depending on what you discover on the gateway debugs, the next step might be to contact the local service provider or perhaps debug the gateway further to find the root cause.

Figure 1-4 *Network After You Continue Narrowing Down the Possible Suspects*

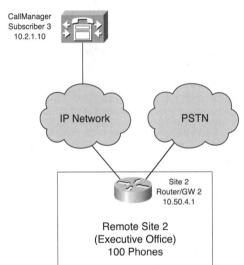

Conclusions

As this case study has demonstrated, the more information you can obtain about the problem, the easier it is to get to the root cause. For example, without the times the dropped calls occurred, it would have been almost impossible to find them in the trace files on a busy system. When deployed in a large enterprise, it is good to arm your help desk with a list of questions to ask depending on the problem being reported.

The point of this example is not to teach you how to troubleshoot a specific problem or to find out exactly why the user's calls are being dropped. It is to show you how to approach a problem in order to isolate it and break it into more manageable pieces. The same principles can be applied to almost any problem you are troubleshooting.

So remember, first put on your detective hat and gather enough information to isolate the problem to a few pieces of the system. Then dig deeper into each component by breaking the problem into more manageable pieces. Finally, apply your expertise to each of the smaller pieces until you find the resolution to your problem.

Summary

This chapter discussed the methodology you should employ to successfully troubleshoot problems in an IP Telephony network. You should become familiar with the methodologies discussed here. It is vital that you always follow a consistent approach to troubleshooting. Many basic problems can be avoided by using a consistent troubleshooting approach.

Also, be sure that you understand the big picture of IP Telephony architecture. What areas are you unsure about? Are you strong in IP but weak in call processing skills? Are you familiar with the basic protocols that are used? Consider where you are now, and as you move forward, pay particular attention to strengthening your weak areas.

As you begin this journey, hopefully this book can bring some illumination to the sometimes daunting task of troubleshooting an IP Telephony network.

## CHAPTER 2

IP Telephony Architecture Overview

Cisco AVVID (Architecture for Voice, Video and Integrated Data) includes many different components that come together to form a comprehensive architecture for voice, video, and integrated data.

This chapter covers the basic components of the IP Telephony architecture in order to get a big-picture viewpoint of the system. With this overview as the starting point, the ensuing chapters address each of these components.

Cisco AVVID IP Telephony can be characterized as having three primary layers:

- Network infrastructure
- IP Telephony infrastructure
- Applications

Network Infrastructure

The network infrastructure is a key piece of the IP Telephony architecture. The infrastructure includes switches and routers, and it connects local-area networks (LANs), metropolitan-area networks (MANs), and wide-area networks (WANs). Your network design must be built for high availability, and the Cisco series of switches and routers provides that capability. A voice-enabled network is a quality of service (QoS)-enabled network that gives precedence to voice, call signaling, and data to ensure good voice quality and rapid call signaling.

IP Telephony Infrastructure

The IP Telephony infrastructure includes the Cisco CallManager call processing engine and the various endpoints that carry voice. This includes client endpoints and various voice gateways that are interfaces to the Public Switched Telephone Network (PSTN).

Call Processing

The CallManager software is the heart of Cisco AVVID IP Telephony that provides call processing features and capabilities to network devices in the enterprise. IP phones, voice gateways, media processing devices, and multimedia applications are just some of the network devices for which CallManager provides call processing.

CallManager is installed on the Cisco Media Convergence server and other approved IBM and Compaq servers. CallManager is shipped with integrated voice applications and utilities such as Cisco CallManager Attendant Console (formerly Cisco WebAttendant), software conferencing, and the Bulk Administration Tool (BAT).

Multiple CallManager servers are clustered and managed as a single entity. CallManager clustering yields scalability of up to 36,000 users per cluster with version 3.3. By interlinking multiple clusters, system capacity can be increased up to one million users in a 100-site system. Triple call processing server redundancy improves overall system availability.

The benefit of this distributed architecture is improved system availability and scalability. *Call admission control* ensures that voice QoS is maintained across constricted WAN links and automatically diverts calls to alternative PSTN routes when WAN bandwidth is unavailable.

The four primary call processing models that are used to meet the needs of the enterprise are

- Single-site deployment model
- Multiple-site deployment model
- Centralized deployment model
- Distributed deployment model

Single-Site Deployment Model

In this deployment model, CallManager, applications, voice mail, and digital signal processor (DSP) resources are located at the same physical location. Figure 2-1 shows an example of these components located at a single site.

Figure 2-1   *Single-Site Deployment Model*

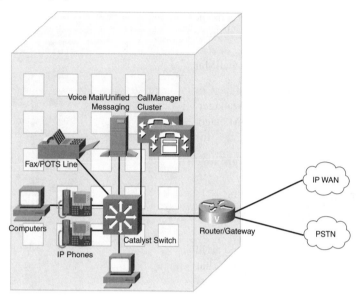

Multiple-Site Deployment Model

In this deployment model, CallManager, applications, voice mail, and DSP resources are located at one physical location. Multiple sites exist, and they connect to each other via the PSTN. Figure 2-2 shows an example of each separate site connecting via the PSTN.

Figure 2-2   *Multiple-Site Deployment Model*

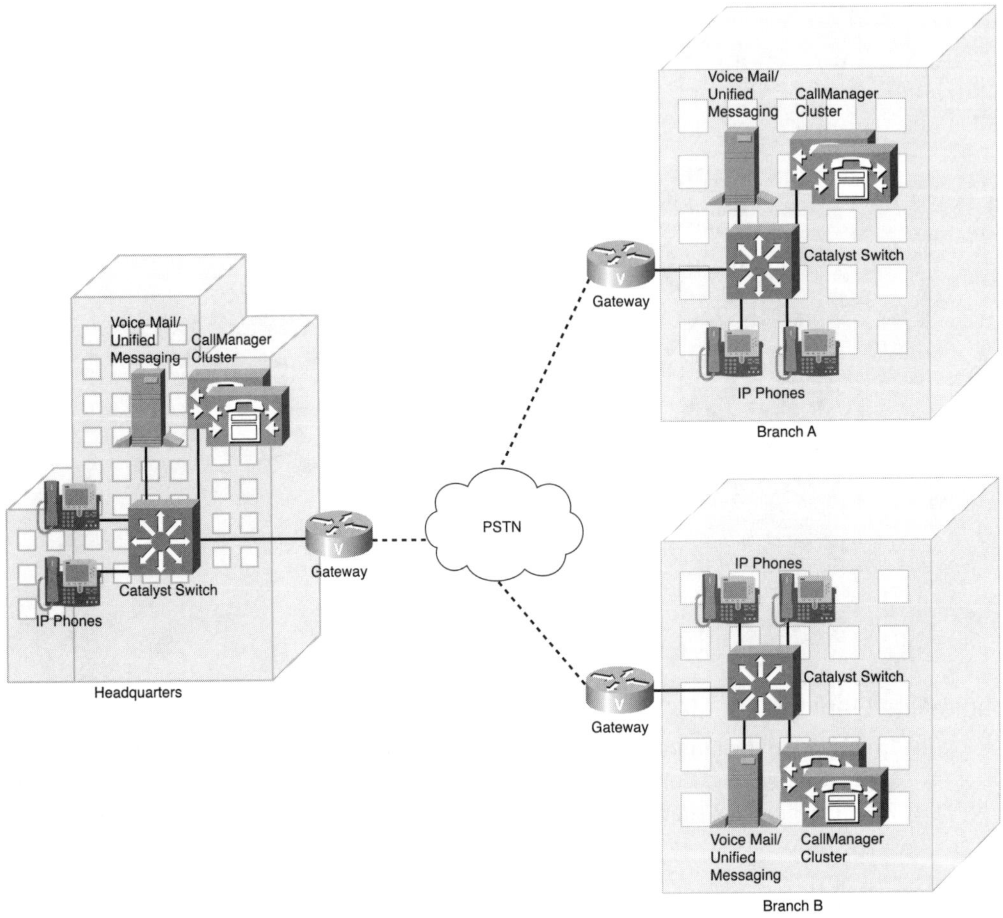

Centralized Deployment Model

A centralized call processing deployment model centrally locates CallManager, applications, voice mail, and DSP resources while many remote locations connect to the central site for all these services. Locations-based call admission control prevents oversubscription of the WAN. At each remote site, Survivable Remote Site Telephony (SRST) ensures that call processing continues in the event of a WAN outage. The centralized call processing model is really the same as the single-site deployment model with the addition of remote sites across the WAN. Figure 2-3 illustrates the centralized deployment model.

Figure 2-3   *Centralized Deployment Model*

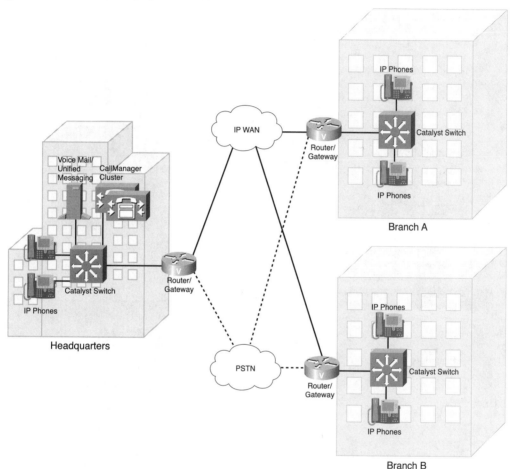

Distributed Deployment Model

In a distributed deployment model, CallManager and applications are located at each site with up to 36,000 IP phones per cluster. One hundred or more sites could be interconnected via H.323 using a gatekeeper for call admission control and dial plan resolution. Transparent use of the PSTN is available if the WAN is down. Figure 2-4 depicts a distributed deployment model.

Figure 2-4 *Distributed Deployment Model*

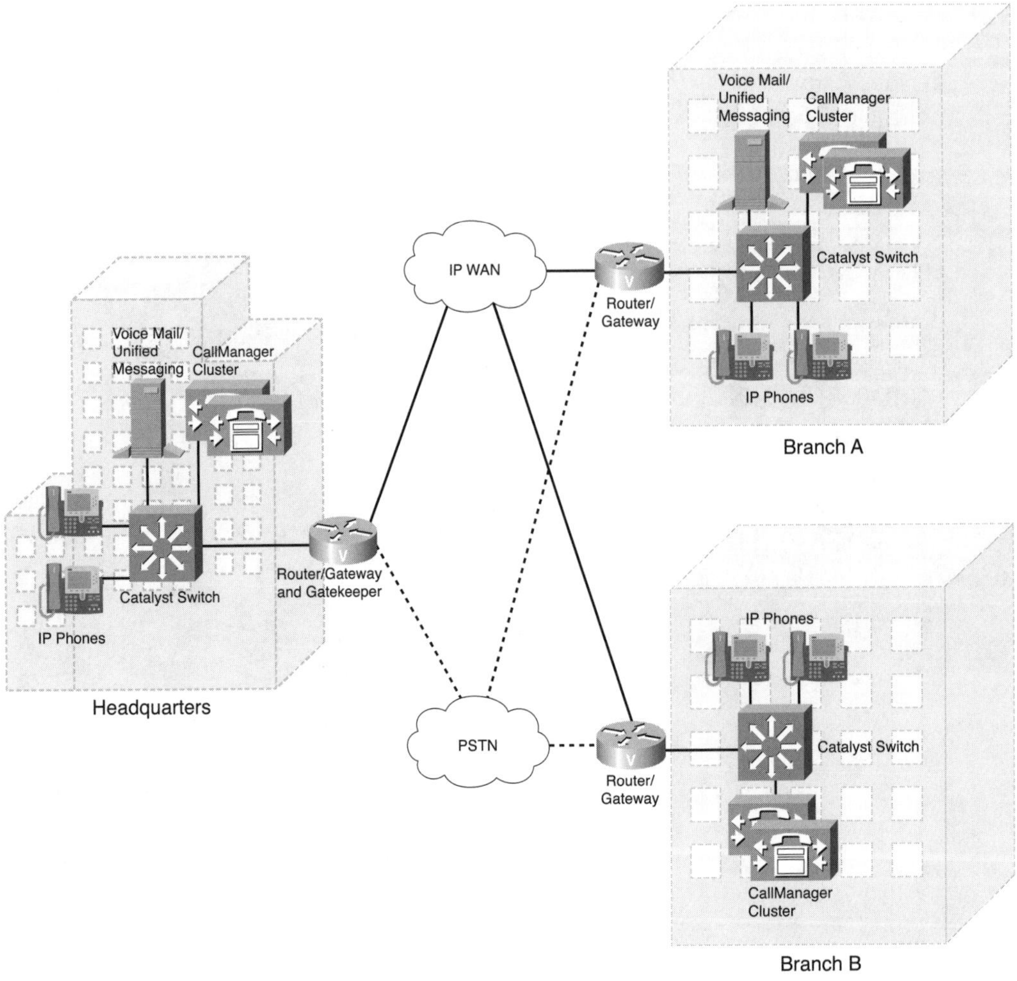

Cisco AVVID IP Telephony Infrastructure

The Cisco AVVID IP Telephony infrastructure includes Cisco Media Convergence Servers and other certified servers running CallManager, Cisco Unity, or other applications, such as IP Auto Attendant, IP Interactive Voice Response (IVR), and IP Integrated Contact Distribution (ICD). Switches, routers, and voice gateways are all part of this infrastructure as well. Although infrastructure is not the primary focus of this book, it is an important part of the IP Telephony architecture, and you will see discussion of some infrastructure aspects when dealing with a Cisco AVVID IP Telephony deployment.

Clients

Clients consist primarily of IP phones. Cisco offers several models with different functions, and these are deployed throughout the IP Telephony infrastructure. Additionally, several third-party companies throughout the world have developed IP phones for their markets. Figure 2-5 shows the Cisco family of IP Phones.

Figure 2-5   *Cisco Family of IP Phones*

7910

7940

7960

7960 with one 7914 expansion module

7935 Conference Station

Table 2-1 provides highlights of each phone and its features.

Table 2-1   *Descriptions of IP Phone Models*

Phone Model	Description
Cisco IP Phone 7960	A full-featured, six-line business set that supports the following features: • A help (**i** or **?**) button • Six programmable line or speed dial buttons • Four fixed buttons for accessing voice mail messages, adjusting phone settings, and working with services and directories • Four soft keys for displaying additional call functionality, such as hold, transfer, conference, and so on • A large liquid crystal display (LCD) that shows call detail and soft key functions • An internal two-way speakerphone and microphone mute
Cisco IP Phone 7940	A full-featured, two-line business set with all the same features as the Cisco IP Phone model 7960, except only two lines.
Cisco IP Phone 7914 Expansion Module	An expansion module for the Cisco IP Phone 7960 that provides 14 additional line or speed dial buttons. It has the following features: • An LCD to identify the function of the button and the line status • The capability to daisy-chain two Cisco IP Phone 7914 Expansion Modules to provide 28 additional line or speed dial buttons for a total of 34 line or speed dial buttons
Cisco IP Phone 7910/ 7910+SW	A single-line, basic feature phone designed primarily for common-use areas with medium telephone traffic, such as lobbies or break rooms. It includes the following features: • Four dedicated feature buttons for Line, Hold, Transfer, and Settings • Six programmable feature buttons that you can configure through phone button templates in Cisco CallManager Administration. Available features include call park, redial, speed dial, call pickup, conference, forward all, group call pickup, message waiting, and Meet-Me conference • A two-line LCD (24 characters per line) that indicates the directory number, call status, date, and time • An internal speaker designed to be used for hands-free dialing • A handset cord jack that can also be used for a headset • (7910+SW only) A Cisco two-port switch with 10/100BaseT interface

Table 2-1   *Descriptions of IP Phone Models (Continued)*

Phone Model	Description
Cisco IP Conference Station 7935	A full-featured, IP-based, full-duplex, hands-free conference station for use on desktops, in offices, and in small- to-medium-sized conference rooms. It includes the following features: • Three soft keys and menu navigation keys that guide a user through call features and functions. Available features include call park, call pickup, group call pickup, transfer, conference, and Meet-Me conference • An LCD that indicates the date and time, calling party name, calling party number, digits dialed, and feature and line status • A digitally-tuned speaker and three microphones allowing conference participants to move around while speaking • Microphone mute

Cisco IP Phone Models 7960 and 7940

The 7960/7940 phones are the most common clients in a Cisco IP Telephony network. These phones feature a large pixel-based display that allows for XML-based applications on the phone. Because these phones are largely soft key-based, new features can easily be added via software upgrades instead of requiring the purchase of new hardware.

The internal three-port Ethernet switch allows for a direct connection to a 10/100BaseT Ethernet network via an RJ-45 interface with single LAN connectivity for both the phone and a co-located PC. The system administrator can designate separate VLANs (802.1Q) for the PC and Cisco IP Phone. The 7960/7940 phones can also receive power down the line from any of the Cisco inline power-capable switches or the Cisco inline power patch panel.

A dedicated headset port eliminates the need for a separate, external amplifier when you use a headset, consequently reducing desk clutter. The 7960/7940 phones feature a high-quality, full-duplex speakerphone, as well as a speaker on/off button and microphone mute buttons.

Cisco IP Phone Expansion Module 7914

The Cisco IP Phone Expansion Module 7914 extends the capabilities of the Cisco IP Phone 7960 with additional buttons and an LCD. The Expansion Module lets you add 14 buttons to the existing six buttons on the 7960 phone, increasing the total number of buttons to 20 with one module or 34 when you add two 7914s. Up to two Cisco 7914s can be connected to a 7960.

The 14 buttons on each 7914 Expansion Module can be programmed as directory numbers or speed dial buttons, just like the 7960. Multicolor button illumination allows you to identify which lines are ringing, on hold, or in use.

Cisco IP Phone 7910

This low-end phone features on-hook dialing and call monitor mode but does not include speakerphone capability. The phone provides a mute button for the handset and headset microphones. You can attach a headset by removing the handset and using the port into which the handset cord was attached.

The 7910 plugs into a standard RJ-45 Ethernet connection. A second version of the 7910 phone, the 7910+SW, provides a Cisco two-port switch with a 10/100BaseT interface. The 7910+SW phone model provides a single RJ-45 connection at the desktop for the phone and an additional LAN device, such as a PC.

The 7910 phones can also receive power down the line from any of the Cisco inline power-capable switches or the Cisco inline power patch panel.

Cisco IP Conference Station 7935

The Cisco IP Conference Station 7935 is a conference room speakerphone utilizing speakerphone technologies from Polycom with the Cisco AVVID voice communication technologies. The 7935 is an IP-based, full-duplex, hands-free conference station for use on desktops and offices and in small- to-medium-sized conference rooms. Although the 7935 does not accept inline power from a Cisco inline power-capable switch, it does feature a power interface module (PIM) that provides power interface and network connectivity.

Voice Gateways

Many Cisco voice gateways are available for use in the IP Telephony network. These gateways interoperate with CallManager using various protocols. They interface with the PSTN using different TDM-based protocols such as T1/E1-PRI, T1-CAS, FXO, FXS, and so on.

One of the primary protocols used by Cisco voice gateways is MGCP. Gateways that support MGCP as of CallManager Release 3.1 include the following:

- Cisco VG200
- Cisco 3700, 3600 and 2600
- Cisco Catalyst 6000 E1/T1 Voice and Service modules
- Cisco Catalyst 4000 Access Gateway Module
- Cisco DE-30+
- Cisco DT-24+

When MGCP is used, CallManager controls routing and tones and provides supplementary services to the gateway. MGCP provides the following services:

- Call preservation (calls are maintained during switchover to a backup CallManager and switch back to the primary CallManager)

- Redundancy

- Dial plan simplification (no dial-peer configuration is required on the gateway)

- Hookflash transfer

- Tone/music on hold

MGCP-controlled gateways do not require a media termination point (MTP) to enable supplementary services such as hold, transfer, call pickup, and call park.

H.323 is another protocol used by Cisco voice gateways. Cisco IOS Software integrated router gateways can also use the H.323 protocol to communicate with CallManager. Intercluster trunks for connecting remote CallManagers across the IP WAN are also configured as H.323 gateways. Compared to MGCP, H.323 requires more configuration on the gateway because the gateway must maintain the dial plan and route patterns.

Two gateways, the VG248 and the ATA-186, use the Skinny Client Control Protocol (SCCP or Skinny protocol), the same protocol used by IP phones, to communicate with CallManager. Each port on these gateways registers individually as a phone device, so from the CallManager perspective, it does not treat the gateway as a single entity but rather treats each port the same way it treats an IP phone. Using Skinny on these gateways allows the gateway to provide features such as message waiting indicators (MWI), conferencing, and transfer to non-IP phones that would not be possible using any of the other supported protocols.

Finally, some older Cisco voice gateways use the Skinny Gateway Control Protocol (SGCP), such as the Cisco Analog Access AT-2, AT-4, AT-8, AS-2, AS-4, and AS-8.

Cisco AVVID IP Telephony Applications

The following list describes some voice and video applications in the application layer of Cisco AVVID IP Telephony:

- **Cisco Unity**—A messaging application that provides voice and/or unified messaging to enterprise communications.

- **Video IP/TV and IP videoconferencing products**—Applications that enable distance learning and workgroup collaboration.

- **Cisco IP IVR**—An IP-powered interactive voice response (IVR) solution, the IP IVR, combined with Cisco IP Auto Attendant, provides an open and feature-rich foundation for delivering IVR solutions over an IP network. Cisco IP IVR and IP AA are built on the Cisco Customer Response Applications (CRA) platform.

- **Cisco IP ICD**—An automatic call distributor (ACD) for enterprise organizations. Cisco IP ICD is built on the Cisco Customer Response Applications (CRA) platform.

- **Cisco CallManager Attendant Console**—A flexible and scalable application that replaces the traditional PBX manual attendant console.

- **Cisco IP SoftPhone**—A software computer-based phone for Windows 98, Windows NT, Windows 2000, and Windows XP that provides communication capabilities that increase efficiency and promote collaboration.

- **Personal Assistant**—A software application that selectively handles calls and helps you make outgoing calls. Personal Assistant provides rule-based call routing, speech-enabled directory dialing, voice mail browsing, and simple Ad Hoc conferencing.

- **Cisco Conference Connection**—A Meet-Me audio conference server that provides integrated operation with CallManager.

- **Cisco Emergency Responder**—An application that allows emergency agencies to identify the location of 911 callers and eliminates the need for any administration when phones or people move from one location to another. Cisco ER features a real-time location-tracking database and improved routing capabilities to direct emergency calls to the appropriate Public Safety Answering Point (PSAP) based on the caller's location.

Summary

This chapter provided an overview of the primary components that are involved in the Cisco IP Telephony architecture, including the deployment models, clients, voice gateways, and Cisco AVVID IP Telephony applications. When troubleshooting, it is important that you have the big picture of all the architecture components to implement the troubleshooting methodology covered in Chapter 1, "Troubleshooting Methodology and Approach."

## CHAPTER 3

Understanding the Troubleshooting Tools

To effectively troubleshoot problems in a Cisco IP Telephony (CIPT) network, you must be familiar with the many tools at your disposal. In addition, you need to know how best to use those tools to achieve maximum results. This chapter describes the various tools and their different uses.

Depending on the problem you encounter and your particular skill set, you might find certain tools more helpful than others. Nevertheless, knowing what tools are available and how they can help you solve the problem is essential to a successful resolution. Also, some tools might be more useful to you based on your past experience. If you are strong in IP, a sniffer trace might be your preferred tool when applicable. However, if you are stronger in call processing-related traces, the Cisco CallManager (CCM, also sometimes called SDI) traces might prove helpful once you understand how they work.

Later chapters demonstrate the use of these tools in different scenarios you might encounter.

This chapter covers the following topics:

- **Time synchronization**—Explains how to synchronize the clocks on all devices in an IP telephony network to ensure that timestamps on your trace files and debugs are synchronized with each other.

- **Reading CCM (or SDI) traces**—Describes one of the most important trace files you use to troubleshoot CallManager-related problems. CCM trace files provide information about call processing events and all messages exchanged between Skinny, MGCP, and H.323 endpoints.

- **Reading SDL traces**—Discusses the components of the less-used Signal Distribution Layer (SDL) trace files in CallManager. SDL traces describe the events occurring in the CallManager software at a code level. These traces are usually reserved for Cisco development engineering use; however, there are a few key pieces of information you can use to your advantage when troubleshooting CallManager problems.

- **Microsoft Performance (PerfMon)**—Details the capabilities of PerfMon, a built-in Windows 2000 utility that helps you troubleshoot CallManager.

- **CCEmail**—Details the third-party alerting tool that can be used in conjunction with PerfMon to configure alerts for the performance counters.

- **CallManager Serviceability**—Discusses various web-enabled tools provided with CallManager for reading alarms and XML-based tracing.

- **Real Time Monitoring Tool (RTMT)**—Describes the Cisco web-based monitoring application that allows you to view CallManager cluster details, monitor performance objects (much like PerfMon), and monitor devices and CTI applications.

- **Call detail records (CDR) and the CDR Analysis and Reporting (CAR) Tool**—Describes the CAR tool that helps you analyze the raw data that comprises the CDR database and create reports based on your search criteria.

- **CDR Time Converter**—Describes how to use this small utility that allows you to convert the UNIX Epoch-based date and time format stored in a CDR to standard date and time format.

- **Event Viewer**—Briefly explains the function of another built-in Windows 2000 tool that plays a key role in troubleshooting CallManager.

- **Q.931 Translator and Enhanced Q.931 Translator**—Describes two tools that read a CCM trace file and analyze all Q.931 and H.225 messages. The various information elements are decoded for ease of reading. The Enhanced Q.931 Translator also adds additional search and filtering options and decodes more information elements than the original Q.931 Translator.

- **Dick Tracy**—Describes an important tool used to troubleshoot the WS-X6608 and WS-X6624 voice gateways for the Catalyst 6000 series switches.

- **Sniffer traces**—Discusses when and why to use a network packet-capture tool.

- **Voice Codec Bandwidth Calculator**—Describes how to use the Voice Codec Bandwidth Calculator to determine the bandwidth used by different codecs with various voice protocols over different media.

- **Cisco Bug Toolkit (formerly Bug Navigator)**—Describes the web-based tool that allows you to find known bugs based on software version, feature set, and keywords. The resulting matrix shows when each bug was integrated or fixed if applicable.

- **Remote Access Tools**—Describes applications like Terminal Services and Virtual Network Computing, which allow you to access a server from a remote location.

- **Websites and Further Reading**—Provides URLs for websites that contain additional troubleshooting information. Also points you to a section in the "Introduction" with a recommended reading list.

Time Synchronization

Time synchronization is simply making sure that all the participating CallManager servers and network devices have the same exact time. Time synchronization is critical. A large CallManager cluster can have eight or more separate servers, not including any voice mail servers or application servers. This distributed architecture creates a highly available and scalable system. It also makes the troubleshooting process more involved because you have to collect traces from all participating servers to see the full picture of what happened.

As endpoints such as IP phones and voice gateways call each other, signaling occurs between CallManager and the endpoint device. Signaling also occurs between the respective CallManagers of each endpoint device. If a problem occurs, you need to consolidate trace files from all involved servers. CallManager Serviceability, discussed later in this chapter, can collect this information into one file. However, if the timestamps of each file are mismatched, it can be impossible to tell what the real series of call processing events is.

All the CallManager servers can be time-synched using the Network Time Protocol (NTP). When you synchronize the time on all involved servers, all the trace files are timestamped the same. When trace files are collected for analysis, you can follow the true series of call processing events with accuracy.

In addition to CallManager servers, you should ensure all network devices such as switches, routers, and voice gateways are synchronized to the same time source as the CallManager servers. This ensures consistent timestamps regardless of which device you are looking at.

Configuring Automatic Time Synchronization on CallManager Servers

Use the following steps to configure the CallManager server to automatically synchronize— and stay synchronized—with a Time Server.

Step 1 Verify that the NetworkTimeProtocol service is configured to launch automatically upon startup. Right-click **My Computer** and select **Manage**.

Step 2 Expand the **Services and Applications** section, and select **Services**.

Step 3 Double-click the **NetworkTimeProtocol** service, and ensure that Startup Type is set to **Automatic**.

Step 4 Configure the **C:\WINNT\ntp.conf** file. This file contains the list of time servers that CallManager will synchronize with. You can configure CallManager to point to specific time servers (see Example 3-1), or you can configure it to receive NTP broadcasts (see Example 3-2) on the local LAN segment from the router (as long as the router is configured to do so).

Example 3-1 *Sample ntp.conf File Using Static Time Servers*

```
server 10.0.0.10
server 10.1.0.10
driftfile %windir%\ntp.drift
```

Example 3-2 *Sample ntp.conf File Using an NTP Broadcast Router*

```
broadcastclient
driftfile %windir%\ntp.drift
```

Step 5 Go to the Services Control Panel and stop/start the NetworkTimeProtocol service. Allow several minutes for the update to take place.

Synchronizing Time Manually on CallManager Servers

Use the following steps to manually configure time synchronization.

Step 1 Stop the NetworkTimeProtocol service in the Services Control Panel.

Step 2 Synchronize the clock by using one of the following commands from a command prompt.

To synchronize with a remote Time Server, use the following command where *x.x.x.x* is the IP address of the Time Server:

```
ntpdate x.x.x.x
```

To synchronize with a Broadcast Router, use the command where *x.x.x.x* is the IP address of the Ethernet port of the router:

```
ntpdate x.x.x.x
```

Step 3 Restart the NetworkTimeProtocol service in the Services Control Panel.

Synchronizing Time on Cisco IOS Devices

In addition to your CallManager servers, you should also ensure the time is synchronized on all your network devices, including IOS voice gateways, switches, and routers.

For Cisco IOS devices, you can use the Network Time Protocol (NTP) to synchronize the time. To enable NTP, you must configure the time zone the IOS device is in along with the IP address of the NTP server. You should configure the IOS device to take daylight savings time into account as well if you live in a time zone that observes daylight savings time.

First you must configure the time zone. Use the command **clock timezone** *name_of_time_zone offset_from_GMT* to configure the time zone. For example, the following command configures the IOS device for Eastern Standard Time (EST):

```
clock timezone EST -5
```

If you are in a time zone that observes daylight savings time, use the command **clock summer-time** *name_of_time_zone* **recurring** to enable automatic daylight savings time. For example, the following configures Eastern Daylight Savings Time:

```
clock summer-time EDT recurring
```

You can determine time zones by performing a search at Google.com; search for a string such as "time zone GMT." Any one of the many hits should point you to a table showing the various time zones around the world, including daylight savings time.

Once your time zone is configured properly, you can enable NTP. If you do not have a device on the network running NTP, you can make an IOS device into an NTP master clock. You can do this by configuring the command **ntp master** on the IOS device. If you are not making the device an NTP master, you should configure the IP address of the NTP server using the command **ntp server** *NTP_server_IP_address*. For example, the following tells the IOS device to synchronize its clock with the NTP server at IP address 172.18.109.1:

```
ntp server 172.18.109.1
```

Once you have enabled NTP, all IOS devices should synchronize their clocks with the central NTP server. You should also synchronize the clocks on non-IOS network devices such as switches running CatOS software.

Synchronizing Time on CatOS Devices

You can use NTP to synchronize the clocks on switches running CatOS software. The configuration is similar to configuring NTP on a device running Cisco IOS Software.

First you must configure the time zone the switch is in using the command **set timezone** *name_of_time_zone offset_from_GMT*. For example, the following sets the clock to Eastern Standard Time:

```
set timezone EST -5
```

You can also configure daylight savings time using the command **set summertime enable** *name_of_time_zone*. For example, the following enables Eastern Daylight Savings Time:

```
set summertime enable EDT
```

You can determine time zones by performing a search at Google.com; search for a string such as "time zone GMT." Any one of the many hits should point you to a table showing the various time zones around the world, including daylight savings time.

Once you have the time zone configured properly, you can set the NTP server IP address and enable the NTP client on the switch. First set the NTP server IP address using the command **set ntp server** *NTP_server_IP_address*. Then enable the NTP client using the command **set ntp client enable**. The following shows the configuration to use the NTP server with IP address 172.18.109.1:

```
set ntp server 172.18.109.1
set ntp client enable
```

Once you have enabled proper time synchronization in your network, you can move on to reading the variety of trace files available to you for troubleshooting problems in an IP Telephony network.

Reading CCM (or SDI) Traces

CCM (also known as System Diagnostic Interface or SDI) traces are the user-friendliest call processing trace files you have available to you. After you learn a few tricks, it is easy to follow the call flows and find the potential problem. Although you might see "SDI" and "CCM" used interchangeably to refer to this type of trace, in this book we primarily refer to this type of trace as a CCM trace. Some pages in CallManager Serviceability refer to CCM traces as SDI traces.

Because CallManager is at the heart of a CIPT network, CCM traces are usually the first place to look when troubleshooting most problems. You can analyze problems related to device registration, call flow, digit analysis, and related devices such as IP phones, gateways, gatekeepers, and more. By the end of this section, you should be able to follow some basic call flows in the CCM trace. Future chapters continue to show CCM trace examples as you learn how to troubleshoot more problems. Later in this chapter you also learn about the Q.931 Translator, which is useful for quickly troubleshooting a variety of gateway problems. It is not a substitute for learning how to read the CCM trace, but it helps you quickly examine a trace in a graphical format without having to wade through irrelevant debugs. See the later "Q.931 Translator and Enhanced Q.931 Translator" section for more information.

Setting the Appropriate Trace Level and Flags

CallManager allows you to select from a variety of different options that adjust which events are logged to the CCM trace files. If you know exactly what you are looking for, you can configure CallManager to log only specific events in the CCM trace file. If you configure the trace to collect too much information, the trace becomes more difficult to analyze. However, if you do not configure the trace to collect enough information, you might miss the problem you are trying to find. When you are beginning to learn how to read CCM trace files, it is best to enable more debugs than less. As you learn which trace settings are required for specific problems, you can enable just the settings you need.

Unfortunately you can never predict what problems will come up, so if you do not have a high level of tracing enabled, you may have to wait for a problem to happen a second time after enabling the appropriate trace settings before you can troubleshoot. For this reason, it is usually best to leave a majority of the trace flags enabled during normal operating conditions so you have trace data available if a problem occurs.

You configure a CCM trace in Cisco CallManager Serviceability (**Trace > Configuration**). Figure 3-1 shows the top half of the Trace Configuration page, and this section discusses the relevant fields and settings on that page.

Figure 3-1   *Trace Configuration (Part 1) in CallManager Serviceability*

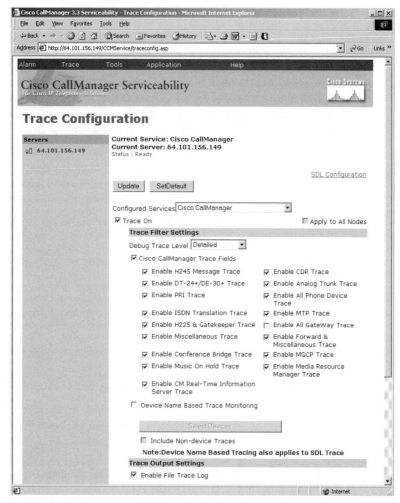

First thing to note is the **Trace On** checkbox. This must be selected for any of the trace settings to be available.

The **Apply to All Nodes** checkbox allows you to apply the specified trace settings to all CallManager servers in the cluster. This is useful when you are troubleshooting a problem that is occurring on more than one CallManager server. You generally want to keep the same level of tracing enabled on all the servers in the cluster unless you are absolutely certain the problem is isolated to a single server in the cluster. Because of the distributed nature of CallManager, you may think a process only involves a single server when in reality part of the processing for a particular call is occuring on another server in the cluster.

The Trace Filter Settings area allows you to specify the exact parameters of your trace. First, you set the level of tracing you want to perform in the **Debug Trace Level** field.

CallManager Serviceability provides six different levels, but for nearly every kind of problem that you'll want traces for, the recommended levels are either Detailed or Arbitrary:

- **Detailed**—Provides detailed debug information and highly repetitive messages that are primarily used for debugging, including KeepAlives and responses. For CallManager releases 3.1 and earlier, be cautious about using this level during normal production hours on a heavily loaded system. It can cause performance degradation on CallManager. In release 3.2 and later, CallManager uses asynchronous tracing to reduce the impact that trace file generation has on call processing.

- **Arbitrary**—Provides low-level debug traces. This level is best suited for debugging difficult problems. This level includes nearly everything that is included in Detailed with the exception of KeepAlives. If you are not troubleshooting problems related to missed KeepAlives, this level is good for day-to-day troubleshooting.

Other trace levels are provided, but generally, they don't offer as much information as the Detailed and Arbitrary levels. The other levels are

- **Error**—Provides traces generated in abnormal conditions, such as coding errors or other errors that normally should not occur.

- **Special**—Provides traces for all informational, non-repetitive messages such as process startup messages, registration messages, and so on. All system and device initialization traces are at this level.

- **State Transition**—Provides traces for call processing events or normal events traced for the subsystem (signaling layers).

- **Significant**—Provides traces for media layer events.

Second, make sure the **Enable CallManager Trace Fields** checkbox is selected, which gives you the opportunity to select which specific traces you want to run and to choose your traces. Table 3-1 describes the trace fields to choose from. Most are reasonably self-explanatory. For example, if you're having problems with an H.323 device, you would enable the **H245 Message Trace** and **Enable H225 & Gatekeeper Trace** options. Likewise, for music on hold (MOH) issues, the **Enable Music on Hold** option would display trace relating to all MOH activity.

Table 3-1 *Cisco CallManager Trace Fields*

Field Name	Description
Enable H245 Message Trace	Debugs H.245 signaling for H.323 calls, including the media processing messages.
Enable DT-24+/DE-30+ Trace	Activates the logging of events related to the legacy gateways, Cisco Digital Access DT-24+/DE-30+.
Enable PRI Trace	Activates a trace of Primary Rate Interface (PRI) devices.
Enable ISDN Translation Trace	Activates a Layer 3 trace of Q.931 (ISDN messages).

Table 3-1   *Cisco CallManager Trace Fields (Continued)*

Field Name	Description
Enable H225 & Gatekeeper Trace	Activates a trace showing H.225 signaling messaging for H.323 calls.
Enable Miscellaneous Trace	Activates a trace of miscellaneous devices.
Enable Conference Bridge Trace	Activates a trace of the conference bridges. Use this level to trace conference bridge statuses such as • Registered with CallManager • Unregistered with CallManager • Resource allocation processed successfully • Resource allocation failed
Enable Music on Hold Trace	Activates a trace of MOH devices. Use this level to trace MOH device statuses such as • Registered with CallManager • Unregistered with CallManager • Resource allocation processed successfully • Resource allocation failed
Enable CM Real-Time Information Server Trace	Activates CallManager real-time information traces used by the real-time information server.
Enable CDR Trace	Enables tracing of call detail record (CDR) processing. However, this trace flag does not provide much information about CDRs because CDR processing is mostly handled by the Database Layer Monitor and CDR Insert services discussed in Chapter 17, "SQL Database Replication."
Enable Analog Trunk Trace	Activates a trace of all MGCP-based devices using an analog interface.
Enable All Phone Device Trace	Activates a trace of phone devices, including Cisco IP SoftPhones, and shows events such as on-hook, off-hook, key presses, and so on.
Enable MTP Trace	Activates a trace of media termination point devices and transcoders. Use this level to trace MTP device statuses such as • Registered with CallManager • Unregistered with CallManager • Resource allocation processed successfully • Resource allocation failed
Enable All Gateway Trace	Activates a trace of all analog and digital gateways.

continues

Table 3-1 *Cisco CallManager Trace Fields (Continued)*

Field Name	Description
Enable Forward and Miscellaneous Trace	Activates a trace of call forwarding and all subsystems not covered by another checkbox.
Enable MGCP Trace	Activates a trace showing media gateway control protocol (MGCP) messages for MGCP-based devices.
Enable Media Resource Manager Trace	Activates a trace for media resource manager (MRM) activities.

Next, you can trace based on a specific device name by selecting the **Device Name Based Trace Monitoring** checkbox. When that checkbox is selected, you can click the **Select Devices** button to choose from a list of devices to trace. Tracing based on specific devices is very useful when you know which devices are involved in the problem, such as specific phones or gateways, and want to see trace output only for those devices.

The non-device option is a catch-all; if you're having issues that are not device-related, you can select the **Include Non-device Traces** checkbox to see traces not related to devices.

Figure 3-2 shows the bottom half of the Trace Configuration page.

Figure 3-2 *Trace Configuration (Part 2) in CallManager Serviceability*

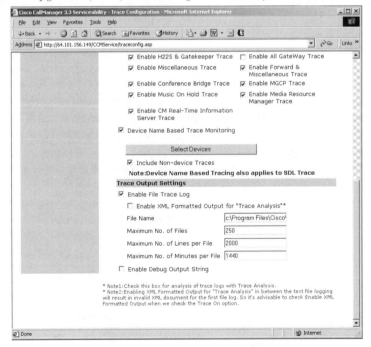

For traces to be logged to a file, the **Enable File Trace Log** checkbox must be selected. The trace output is then sent to the path specified in the **File Name** field, which is C:\Program Files\Cisco\Trace\CCM\ccm.txt by default.

We're going to skip discussion of the **Enable XML Formatted Output for "Trace Analysis"** checkbox for a moment to finish the fields related to file settings.

The Trace Configuration page in CallManager Serviceability validates the filename and ensures that it has a .txt extension. Do not use a filename that exists on another computer. Use a filename that exists on the computer running the trace. It is a good practice to have each server use a filename format that has the server name in it. This could be **servera-ccm.txt**, for example. That way, if trace files are collected from several servers, each file is easily distinguished from those collected on a different server. One downside to this, though, is that you can't use the **Apply to all nodes** option. If you did, you would have to go back and change the names of the files on all nodes.

The **Maximum No. of Files** field defaults to 250. Normally, a maximum of 250 is never enough files because the files write in round-robin fashion—when the maximum limit is met, the next file starts at the beginning and overwrites the first file. Frequently, this means that the trace information you need to troubleshoot a problem that began occurring yesterday or the day before has already been overwritten by new files. For each server on which you're running trace, determine how much free disk space you have, deduct a safety net of 500 MB, and then use the rest of your disk space for trace space. Assuming you don't go above 10,000 lines—which we don't recommend—you can calculate the size of your trace files by figuring the average CCM trace at 10,000 lines consumes about 2.5 MB; the average SDL trace at 10,000 lines consumes about 3.5 MB. We don't recommend going above 10,000 lines because you want to keep your trace files at a manageable size. At these average sizes, you can easily zip the file and e-mail it if needed.

The default of 1440 for the **Maximum No. of Minutes per File** is adequate; you'll probably never reach it.

The **Enable XML Formatted Output for "Trace Analysis"** checkbox takes the trace output and formats it in XML, which is required if you want use the Trace Analysis feature in CallManager Serviceability. With Trace Analysis, you can view the trace files in a web page, and the XML tagging lets you filter the trace results. The downside, however, is that the number of lines per file is limited to 2000 instead of 10,000. In most cases, you'll probably want to stick with standard text-based tracing because the 2000 line limit severely restricts the amount of information in the trace file. Also, reading XML-formatted traces manually can be far more time-consuming than non-XML-formatted traces because you need to weed out all the extra XML tags that get added to each trace line. If you do not enable XML-formatted output, the log file compiles in text format.

The **Enable Debug Output String** checkbox sends debugging information to a Microsoft development tool useful only to Cisco development engineers. You should never need to or be asked to enable this checkbox.

Click **Update** to save your settings. The new trace settings take effect immediately when you click **Update**.

Once you've specified the trace settings, you can go to the Trace Collection page (**Trace > Collection**) to collect traces from one or more servers after an event has occurred. Set the service you want to retrieve the trace files for (such as Cisco CallManager), along with the date and time period you want to trace and click the **Submit Form** button. Depending on the time period you specified, tracing can impact performance, so be sure to trace short intervals that won't impact CallManager or during non-production hours.

It is usually quicker and easier to manually collect the traces yourself using either Terminal Services or VNC (discussed later in this chapter) to access the CallManager server and copy the files to another machine for analysis.

Once the trace has been gathered, you are given the option to view it in a new window or use Save As to save the output to a file. If you choose to view the text-based output in a new window, it looks similar to Figure 3-3.

Figure 3-3 *Viewing Text-based Trace Output in Web Browser*

If you choose the Save As option, the text-based output displays in the CallManager Serviceability window in the same format as Figure 3-3, and you can click **File > Save As** to save the file.

We generally recommend that you do not use the trace collection utility for anything other than very small traces on a system that is not busy. Manually copy the traces off the server(s) in question and analyze them offline.

If you selected the **Collect XML Trace File(s)** checkbox and choose to view the output in a new window, the Trace Analysis dialog appears. In this dialog box, you can filter the trace results based on the options described in Table 3-2.

Table 3-2   *Trace Analysis Filtering*

Field Name	Description
CallManager Host	Choose ALL CallManagers or select just one CallManager.
Device Name	Choose ALL or specify the device's name. If you specify a device name, only trace information pertaining to that device name appears in the search results.
IP Address	Choose ALL or a specific server's IP address.
Trace Type	Choose ALL, Alarm, or Trace. Trace shows all events as specified in the trace settings. Alarm shows only specific messages that meet the criteria of being an information Alarm message.
Cluster	Select this checkbox if you want to include the cluster name in the trace output.
Date and Time	Select this checkbox if you want to include the date and time of each event listed in the trace output.
CM Node	Select this checkbox if you want to include the CallManager node (IP address or host name) in the trace output.
Trace Type	Select this checkbox if you want to include the trace type in the trace output.
IP Address	Select this checkbox if you want to include the device's source IP address in the trace output.
Correlation Tag	Select this checkbox if you want to include the number that correlates traces with each other in the trace output.
Application Name	Select this checkbox if you want to include the directory numbers (DNs) and other service-specific information in the trace output.
Information	Select this checkbox if you want to include a description of what the trace found in the trace output.
Device Name	Select this checkbox if you want to include the device name in the trace output.

Figure 3-4 shows a trace file formatted as XML output and filtered to display only one CallManager host, one IP address, and the fields Cluster, Date and Time, CM Node, Source IP, and Information.

Figure 3-4   *Filtered Trace Output in XML Format*

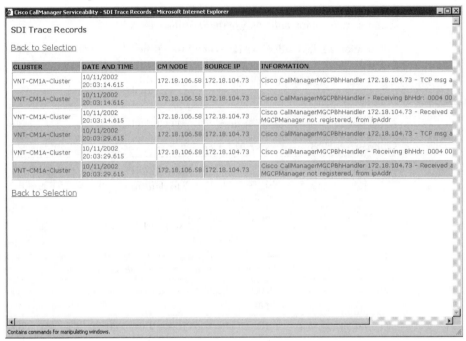

You can click the **Back to Selection** link to return to the Trace Analysis dialog and filter based on different criteria.

As you can see, reading through a large amount of trace files using the trace collection utility can be very cumbersome and time-consuming in relation to reading the trace files manually. You should learn how to read the CCM traces directly from the text files to help you troubleshoot problems more quickly and accurately. For that reason, all the examples of CCM traces that we show in this book are in plain text files. The following section describes how to read a text-based CCM trace.

Reading CCM Traces

This section shows you a few call flow examples and highlights key information in each example that helps you understand the CCM trace.

For brevity, the header and tail of the trace line have been omitted in many examples. For example, the complete trace would look like the following:

```
03/15/2001 05:34:41.956 CCM |StationInit: 1a3e8b54 OffHook.|
  <CLID::DLS2-CM152-SRV4-Cluster><NID::DLS2-CM152-SRV4><CT::1,100,96,1.69>
  <IP::172.28.238.62><DEV::SEP003094C2D11F>
```

But for many examples, the header and tail do not add value. So the same trace is shown in this book as

```
StationInit: 1a3e8b54 OffHook.
```

The header portion of the trace line just specifies the date and time when the trace event was generated and which trace file you are looking at. For a CCM trace file, every line starts with the date and time followed by the letters "CCM." Prior to CallManager 3.3 the trace files begin with the date and time followed by the words "Cisco CallManager."

You should understand a few things about CCM traces:

- Many places in the trace files use hexadecimal equivalents for the IP addresses—The IP address 172.28.232.164 is shown in trace files as a4e81cac, which is a hexadecimal representation of 172.28.232.164. You can determine the IP address by working backwards: take the last two digits, **ac**, which is hex for 172; then **1c**, which is hex for 28; then **e8**, which is hex for 232; and finally, **a4**, which is hex for 164. The IP address is 172.28.232.164. Appendix C, "Decimal to Hexadecimal and Binary Conversion Table," provides a quick cheat sheet to determine how to quickly convert between decimal, hexadecimal, and binary values.

- Trace files sometimes use ASCII for directory numbers—Consider the value 33 30 30 31, which is how the directory number 3001 is sometimes displayed in the trace file.

- Trace files may include messages for a variety of protocols—Details on each of these protocols is described in the appropriate chapters. For example, the Skinny protocol is discussed in Chapter 4, "Skinny Client Registration," and Chapter 5, "IP Phones." Other protocols such as H.323 and MGCP are discussed in Chapter 6, "Voice Gateways." Appendix A, "Cisco IP Telephony Protocol and Codec Information and References," lists the protocols in an IP Telephony environment and the standards body or specification governing the protocol.

When you first open a CCM trace file, you might feel intimidated by the large amount of information presented in the trace file. We recommend that you use the default trace settings for CCM traces except you set the trace level to either **Arbitrary** or **Detailed**. Click the **SetDefault** button on the Trace Configuration page for CCM traces in CallManager Serviceability (**Trace > Configuration**) and then change the **Debug Trace Level** setting to **Detailed**.

A Sample CCM Trace for a Call Between Two IP Phones

As a first example at looking at CCM traces, go through a simple call between two IP phones. IP phones use the Skinny protocol to communicate with CallManager. All messages to and from a Skinny device are preceded by either the words **StationInit** or **StationD**.

For example, assume you have two phones, Phone A and Phone B. Phone A calls Phone B. Phone A goes off-hook and you see the following line in the CCM trace:

```
StationInit: 1a3e8b54 OffHook.
```

StationInit means that an inbound Transmission Control Protocol (TCP) message from a Skinny station reached CallManager. A Skinny station is any endpoint that uses the Skinny protocol to communicate with CallManager. This includes the Cisco 79*xx* family of

IP phones. In other words, any message that starts with StationInit is a message *from* an IP phone.

1a3e8b54 is probably the most important piece of this trace example. It is called a *TCP handle* and it represents a unique value that identifies a specific IP phone registered to this CallManager server. With the TCP handle, you can follow every message to and from that IP phone and see the full series of messages exchanged between CallManager and the phone. When searching through a CCM trace file in Notepad, copy the TCP handle to the clipboard (**Ctrl+C**), then open the Find box in Notepad (**Ctrl+F**), and paste the TCP handle (**Ctrl+V**). Once you get into the habit of highlighting the TCP handle and then pressing Ctrl+C, Ctrl+F, and Ctrl+V to enter the TCP handle into the Find window, you will be able to search for Skinny messages related to a device very quickly.

If you want to find the TCP handle for a particular IP phone, obtain the MAC address of the phone from either CallManager Administration or from the phone itself and search for the MAC address in the CCM trace until you find a KeepAlive to that phone. For example,

```
StationInit - InboundStim - KeepAliveMessage -
  Send KeepAlive to Device Controller. DeviceName=SEP003094C2D11F,
  TCPHandle=1a3e8b54, IPAddr=10.80.1.147, Port=51763,
  Device Controller=[2,89,2992]
```

Notice the KeepAlive message contains both the TCP handle and the device name for the IP phone. Once you find the KeepAlive message, copy the TCPHandle field and use that to search through the CCM trace.

The **OffHook** message means that CallManager received a Skinny message indicating the phone went off-hook.

The next message is

```
StationD:    1a3e8b54 DisplayText text='                   3000                '
```

Notice that instead of **StationInit** you see **StationD**. This signifies that CallManager is sending a Skinny message to the phone. StationInit messages are sent from the IP phone to CallManager, while StationD messages are sent from CallManager to the IP phone. Skinny message transmission such as this between the IP phone and CallManager occurs for every action undertaken by the IP phone, including initialization, registration, on-hook, off-hook, dialing of digits, key presses on the phone, and so much more.

Again you see the same TCP handle, 1a3e8b54, listed for this message.

The number **3000** represents the directory number of the phone. If you know the phone number of the calling IP phone, you can often find the beginning of a call by simply searching for the calling phone's directory number. In CallManager 3.3 and later the DisplayText message actually shows

```
StationOutputDisplayText don't need to send, because mIsALegacyDevice = 0
```

The reason for this message is that the 79*xx* series Cisco IP Phones never paid attention to the DisplayText message in the first place, so in CallManager 3.3 and beyond, the message is no longer sent. This means that if you search for the directory number of the IP phone, you might not find exactly the beginning of the sequence of events. It is best to search for the device name you are looking for and find a KeepAlive to get the TCP handle as discussed earlier.

Other messages sent to the IP phone include the following:

```
StationD:      1a3e8b54 StartTone tone=33(InsideDialTone), direction=0
StationD:      1a3e8b54 SetLamp stimulus=9(Line) stimulusInstance=1
  lampMode=2(LampOn).
StationD:      1a3e8b54 CallState callState=1 lineInstance=1 callReference=16777217
StationD:      1a3e8b54 DisplayPromptStatus timeOutValue=0
  promptStatus='Enter number' lineInstance=1 callReference=16777217.
StationD:      1a3e8b54 SelectSoftKeys instance=1 reference=16777217
  softKeySetIndex=4 validKeyMask=-1.
StationD:      1a3e8b54 ActivateCallPlane lineInstance=1.
```

Again you see that all the trace lines begin with **StationD** indicating that these are messages from CallManager to the IP phone and you see each line has the same TCP handle.

Do not concern yourself at this point about exactly what each of the pieces in the trace mean. These are all Skinny messages sent to the IP phone. At this point, you should just familiarize yourself with the basic call flow to understand how to read the trace files, not necessarily what each piece of the trace file means. Chapters 4 and 5 provide additional detail relating to the Skinny messaging you see in the preceding output. In particular, see Table 5-1, "Skinny Message Definitions," and the section, "Examining Skinny Protocol Messages in a CCM Trace" in Chapter 5 for detailed explanations.

You will notice, however, that many of the trace messages are relatively self-explanatory. For example, the **StartTone** message with **tone=33(InsideDialTone)** tells the IP phone to start playing dial tone.

Note the **callReference** ID. A callReference ID is created for each participant in a call and you can use this ID to track a particular call through a CCM trace. A new callReference ID is created for each participant in a call and when some features are invoked, such as transfer and conference. Each leg of a call gets its own callReference ID assigned, so in a call between two IP phones, each phone gets assigned a separate callReferenceID.

So far you have only seen Skinny protocol messages; however, this callReference ID can help you correlate the Skinny messages with other messages to devices involved in the same call.

Next, the user on the IP phone begins dialing digits. This time, notice the difference between **StationD** and **StationInit** messages, indicating communication back and forth between CallManager and the IP phone.

```
StationInit: 1a3e8b54 KeypadButton kpButton=3
StationD:      1a3e8b54 StopTone
StationD:      1a3e8b54 SelectSoftKeys instance=1 reference=16777217
  softKeySetIndex=6 validKeyMask=-1
StationInit: 1a3e8b54 KeypadButton kpButton=0
StationInit: 1a3e8b54 KeypadButton kpButton=0
StationInit: 1a3e8b54 KeypadButton kpButton=1
Digit analysis: match(fqcn="3000", cn="3000", pss="IPMA:PA:Line1", dd="3001")
```

Notice that a 3 is dialed and a tone is then stopped. The Skinny protocol does not provide a mechanism to specify which tone to stop, so it sends a generic **StopTone** message. This stops any tones the IP phone happened to be playing at the time. In this case, remember you saw CallManager instruct the IP phone to play inside dial tone in the previous trace section.

The **kpButton=** message is always followed by the dialed digit. As soon as the first digit is dialed, the phone is told to stop playing dial tone. That makes sense because when you pick up the phone, you hear dial tone, but as soon as you dial a digit, the tone stops. Notice that after the phone is told to stop the tone, the soft keys are updated on the display. By looking at all the **kpButton=** messages, you can see that 3001 is the number dialed.

Note that the digit * is shown in a trace as the letter **e** and a # is shown as **f**. So for example, the message **kpButton=e** means the user entered the * key.

CallManager is constantly analyzing the digits the user dials, and once it finds an exact match, digit analysis returns the results for the match. Now it is time to ring Phone B, which is configured with DN 3001. Chapter 9, "Call Routing" provides additional detail about how digit analysis works in CallManager. There is, however, one important concept you should understand about digit analysis: Whenever digit analysis makes a match for a call, it displays the digit analysis results in the CCM trace. For example,

```
Digit analysis: analysis results
| PretransformCallingPartyNumber=3000
| CallingPartyNumber=3000
| DialingPartition=Line1
| DialingPattern=3001
| DialingRoutePatternRegularExpression=(3001)
| DialingWhere=
| PatternType=Enterprise
| PotentialMatches=NoPotentialMatchesExist
| DialingSdlProcessId=(2,34,3500)
| PretransformDigitString=3001
| PretransformTagsList=SUBSCRIBER
| PretransformPositionalMatchList=3001
| CollectedDigits=3001
| UnconsumedDigits=
| TagsList=SUBSCRIBER
| PositionalMatchList=3001
| VoiceMailbox=
| VoiceMailCallingSearchSpace=IPMA:PA:Line1
| VoiceMailPilotNumber=5678
| DisplayName=James
| RouteBlockFlag=RouteThisPattern
| InterceptPartition=
| InterceptPattern=
| InterceptWhere=
| InterceptSdlProcessId=(0,0,0)
| InterceptSsType=0
| InterceptSsKey=0
| WithTags=
| WithValues=
| CgpnPresentation=NotSelected
| CallManagerDeviceType=UserDevice
```

Do not be concerned about what each of the fields means at this point. Chapter 9 explains some of the concepts such as partitions and calling search spaces. The important concept to grasp here is that any time digit analysis makes a match, you see a digit analysis result similar to this one in the CCM trace. These digit analysis results are easy to spot in a CCM trace because of the white space to the right of the digit analysis results. If you look at a CCM trace, you will see that the majority of trace lines are over 100 characters in length; however, the digit analysis results are usually no more than 20 to 30 characters long, making the digit analysis results easy to find while scrolling quickly through a CCM trace file.

Because CallManager has collected all the required digits, it is ready to notify the destination IP phone there is an incoming call. The next example shows CallManager sending Skinny messages to Phone B.

```
StationD:      1a3e8af0 DisplayText text='                    3001          '
StationD:      1a3e8af0 CallState callState=4 lineInstance=1 callReference=16777218
StationD:      1a3e8af0 CallInfo callingPartyName='James' callingParty=3000
                        cgpnVoiceMailbox=
                        calledPartyName='Mary' calledParty=3001 cdpnVoiceMailbox=
                        originalCalledPartyName='Mary' originalCalledParty=3001
                        originalCdpnVoiceMailbox= originalCdpnRedirectReason=0
                        lastRedirectingPartyName='Mary' lastRedirectingParty=3001
                        lastRedirectingVoiceMailbox=
                        lastRedirectingReason=0
                        callType=1(InBound) lineInstance=1
                        callReference=16777218
StationD:      1a3e8af0 SetLamp stimulus=9(Line) stimulusInstance=1
   lampMode=5(LampBlink)
StationD:      1a3e8af0 SetRinger ringMode=2(InsideRing)
StationD:      1a3e8af0 DisplayNotify timeOutValue=10 notify='From 3000'
StationD:      1a3e8af0 DisplayPromptStatus timeOutValue=0 promptStatus='From 3000'
   lineInstance=1 callReference=16777218
StationD:      1a3e8af0 SelectSoftKeys instance=1 reference=16777218
   softKeySetIndex=3 validKeyMask=-1
```

Notice first that a **StationD** message is generated. This means that a message is sent from CallManager to the IP phone. Also notice that the TCP handle is different than in the preceding trace output. Each IP phone has a unique TCP handle assigned to it at registration. You can use the unique TCP handle to differentiate between the Skinny messages sent to and from Phone A (TCP handle 1a3e8b54) and those sent to and from Phone B (TCP handle 1a3e8af0). A new TCP handle is assigned any time an IP phone such as Phone A unregisters and reregisters to CallManager, resets, or fails over or back from one CallManager to another.

Notice also that the **callReference** value (16777218) is different from the previous output. As we mentioned earlier, this is because each leg of a call is assigned a different call reference. In this case, this is the call reference for Phone B. This call reference persists for the duration of the call on Phone B.

Phone B rings and the call information shows that James called Mary. You see several messages that seem to suggest the call is being redirected; it's not. These are just standard messages sent by CallManager.

Once again, do not be concerned about exactly what each message means at this point. Future chapters go into detail about each message; however, you can see from reading the trace that Phone B is being told to ring (**SetRinger ringMode=2(InsideRing)**) and display "From 3000" on the prompt line of the IP phone (**promptStatus='From 3000'**).

Now that a call is in progress, Phone A gets some updated information, including display information such as called and calling party names.

```
StationD:    1a3e8b54 SelectSoftKeys instance=1 reference=16777217
  softKeySetIndex=8 validKeyMask=-1.
StationD:    1a3e8b54 CallState callState=12 lineInstance=1 callReference=16777217
StationD:    1a3e8b54 CallInfo callingPartyName='James' callingParty=3000
             cgpnVoiceMailbox= calledPartyName='Mary' calledParty=3001
             cdpnVoiceMailbox= originalCalledPartyName='' originalCalledParty=
             originalCdpnVoiceMailbox= originalCdpnRedirectReason=0
             lastRedirectingPartyName='' lastRedirectingParty=
             lastRedirectingVoiceMailbox= lastRedirectingReason=0
StationD:    1a3e8b54 StartTone tone=36(AlertingTone).
StationD:    1a3e8b54 CallState callState=3 lineInstance=1 callReference=16777217
StationD:    1a3e8b54 SelectSoftKeys instance=1 reference=16777217
  softKeySetIndex=8 validKeyMask=-1.
StationD:    1a3e8b54 DisplayPromptStatus timeOutValue=0 promptStatus='Ring Out'
  lineInstance=1 callReference=16777217.
```

Basically, these messages perform two actions. First, the display on Phone A changes now that the call is in progress. Second, the phone is told to play an alerting tone. The alerting tone is the standard ringback tone you hear when placing a call. You also see the first **callReference** value, 16777217, indicating the original call placed by Phone A. Remember each call reference is only valid for one leg of the call.

```
StationInit: 1a3e8af0 OffHook
StationD:    1a3e8af0 ClearNotify
StationD:    1a3e8af0 SetRinger ringMode=1(RingOff)
StationD:    1a3e8af0 SetLamp stimulus=9(Line) stimulusInstance=1
  lampMode=2(LampOn)
StationD:    1a3e8af0 CallState callState=1 lineInstance=1 callReference=16777218
StationD:    1a3e8af0 ActivateCallPlane lineInstance=1
```

The **StationInit OffHook** message indicates that Phone B goes off-hook and answers the call. CallManager sends a **SetRinger ringMode=1(RingOff)** message, which tells Phone B to stop ringing, and the preparation is now complete for the actual media connection.

Next, we'll examine how the audio stream is set up. As with all VoIP protocols, Skinny uses Real-Time Transport Protocol (RTP) streams over User Datagram Protocol (UDP) packets to send and receive Voice over IP (VoIP) samples. Each RTP stream is called a logical channel. A logical channel is a unidirectional RTP stream, so to have a two-way conversation, you must have two logical channels opened—one from the calling device to the called device and one from the called device to the calling device.

In a call involving a Skinny device, CallManager asks the IP phone to open a connection to receive RTP streams. CallManager asks the IP phone for specific parameters for this connection, including the codec and packet size. You can see the following **OpenLogicalChannel** messages from CallManager to each IP phone requesting that they open a connection to receive RTP packets using G.711.

```
StationD:    1a3e8b54 OpenReceiveChannel conferenceID=0
  passThruPartyID=17 millisecondPacketSize=20
  compressionType=4(Media_Payload_G711Ulaw64k)
  qualifierIn=?.   myIP: 3eee1cac (172.28.238.62)
StationD:    1a3e8af0 OpenReceiveChannel conferenceID=0
  passThruPartyID=33 millisecondPacketSize=20
  compressionType=4(Media_Payload_G711Ulaw64k)
  qualifierIn=?.   myIP: 2fee1cac (172.28.238.47)
```

Upon receiving an **OpenReceiveChannel** message, the IP phone selects the UDP port number it wants to use to receive RTP packets and reports this information back to CallManager in an **OpenReceiveChannelAck** message. Phone A responds first:

```
StationInit: 1a3e8b54 OpenReceiveChannelAck
   Status=0, IpAddr=0x3eee1cac, Port=20096, PartyID=17
```

Once CallManager receives this information from Phone A, it can tell Phone B where to send its RTP stream. Until this point, CallManager could not tell Phone B which UDP port number to use because Phone A had not reported it to CallManager. Once CallManager receives the port number in the **OpenReceiveChannelAck** message from Phone A, it sends a **StartMediaTransmission** message to Phone B giving it the IP address and port number of Phone A along with information about which voice codec to use.

```
StationD:    1a3e8af0 StartMediaTransmission
   conferenceID=0 passThruPartyID=33
   remoteIpAddress=3eee1cac(172.28.238.62)
   remotePortNumber=20096 milliSecondPacketSize=20
   compressType=4(Media_Payload_G711Ulaw64k)
   qualifierOut=?. myIP: 2fee1cac (172.28.238.62)
```

Next, CallManager receives an **OpenReceiveChannelAck** from Phone B containing the UDP port number information and passes this on to Phone A in a **StartMediaTransmission** message.

```
StationInit: 1a3e8af0 OpenReceiveChannelAck Status=0,
   IpAddr=0x2fee1cac, Port=19648, PartyID=33
StationD:    1a3e8b54 StartMediaTransmission
   conferenceID=0 passThruPartyID=17
   remoteIpAddress=2fee1cac(172.28.238.47)
   remotePortNumber=19648 milliSecondPacketSize=20
   compressType=4(Media_Payload_G711Ulaw64k) qualifierOut=?.
   myIP: 3eee1cac (172.28.238.47)
```

So at this point, Phone A (TCP handle 1a3e8b54) is sending RTP packets to 172.28.238.47, which happens to be Phone B, and Phone B (TCP handle 1a3e8af0) is sending RTP packets to 172.28.238.62, which happens to be Phone A.

Notice that for the duration of this call, Phone A has never sent nor received any Skinny signaling to or from Phone B. This is because all the signaling goes through CallManager. The only time IP phones send packets to each other is for the actual voice stream. This is what allows CallManager to set up calls between devices that use different signaling protocols. For example, if Phone A called a phone number on the PSTN instead of another IP phone, the signaling between CallManager and Phone A remains the same. Phone A has no idea that it is sending RTP packets to a voice gateway and vice versa.

When reading CCM traces, you can usually separate each leg of the call and concentrate on one part at a time. For example, if you have a call that goes out through a voice gateway, once you have verified that the IP phone dialed the correct digits and CallManager is routing the call to a voice gateway, you can focus on the gateway debugs to determine how the call gets set up.

Also it is important to separate the signaling aspects of a call set up from the RTP media streams. All VoIP devices are blindly told to send RTP packets to an IP address and port number without knowing what type of device they are sending these packets to. As long as the terminating device provided the correct IP address and port number and CallManager relayed this information correctly, everything works properly. However, pay attention to the signaling aspects to ensure that the port number received from the terminating device is the same as the port number reported to the originating device.

Tracing a Call Through an MGCP T1 PRI Gateway

The next call to dissect is an IP phone (3000) making a call through a WS-X6608-T1 PRI MGCP gateway. MGCP is not described in detail in this example; however, you will see ISDN Q.931 messages because this is the protocol used over the PRI D-channel. A detailed discussion on troubleshooting ISDN PRI problems can be found in Chapter 6. Appendix A includes the standards body and specification for ISDN Q.931.

All Q.931 and H.323 (including intercluster trunk) calls look basically the same in a CCM trace. Also, some non-ISDN gateways such as the WS-X6624 and the WS-X6608 when using T1 CAS also use Q.931 messages to communicate with CallManager. This makes understanding the basic structure of this kind of trace message important.

The majority of information presented in the CCM trace file for a gateway call is in hexadecimal notation. The Q.931 specification states that phone numbers should be encoded in ASCII as well as character strings, such as display names. The CCM trace also uses hexadecimal equivalents for the IP addresses on some occasions. Do not be intimidated by the hexadecimal values. Once you understand how to decode them, they are actually easy to understand. Appendix C provides a cheat sheet for conversions.

Whenever an H.323 or Q.931 call is made, you will see a section of trace similar to the following outgoing ISDN setup message:

```
Out Message -- PriSetupMsg -- Protocol= PriNi2Protocol.
Ie - Ni2BearerCapabilityIe IEData= 04 03 80 90 A2
Ie - Q931ChannelIdIe IEData= 18 03 A9 83 97
Ie - Q931CallingPartyIe IEData= 6C 06 00 80 33 30 30 30
Ie - Q931CalledPartyIe IEData= 70 05 80 33 30 30 31
MMan_Id= 0. (iep=  0 dsl=  0 sapi=  0 ces=  0 IpAddr=a4e81cac IpPort=2427)
IsdnMsgData2= 08 02 00 09 05 04 03 80 90 A2 18 03 A9 83 97 6C 06 00 80 33 30 30
     30 70 05 80 33 30 30 31
```

The first line gives you information about the direction of the call (either **Out Message** or **In Message**) followed by the type of message (**PriSetupMsg**) and the protocol used for the message (**PriNi2Protocol**). The direction is from the perspective of CallManager, so this means a device registered to CallManager is placing a call out through a gateway.

As with the IP phone, a unique identifier is used to keep track of the call. Use the hexadecimal IP address **IpAddr=a4e81cac** in conjunction with call reference number **02 00 09** to track the call throughout the trace. When viewing an ISDN trace, look at the **IsdnMsgData2** line to find the call reference ID. In some cases you will see **IsdnMsgData** or **IsdnMsgData1** instead of **IsDNMsgData2**. They are equivalent. Ignore the first two numbers (usually **08**). The next two numbers are the call reference length (**02**), and the next four are the call reference value (**00 09**).

You might be wondering how **a4e81cac** is converted to an IP address in dotted decimal notation. This is a hexadecimal representation of the IP address. You can figure out the IP address by working backwards. In this example, first, take the last two digits, **ac**, which is hex for 172. Next, consider the **1c**, which is hex for 28. Third, take **e8**, which is hex for 232. Finally, take **a4**, which is hex for 164. The IP address is 172.28.232.164.

NOTE   Appendix C provides a quick cheat sheet to determine how to quickly convert between decimal, hexadecimal, and binary values.

So far you know you are looking at an outbound setup message on a PRI configured for the NI2 ISDN protocol, all of which you determined from the first line of the trace. You also know the call reference from decoding the first few bytes of the **IsdnMessageData2**. The lines in the middle that begin with **Ie** are ISDN Q.931 information elements. Information elements are covered in detail in Chapter 6; however, they are all formatted the same way in the CCM trace. For example, the following is the called party information element (IE):

```
Ie - Q931CalledPartyIe IEData= 70 05 80 33 30 30 31
```

Each information element line begins with the letters **Ie** followed by the name of the information element, in this case **Q931CalledPartyIe**. After the name follows the data contained in that information element. The format of the data that follows is dependent on the particular information element. The Q.931 and H.225 specifications describe the format of each information element. Having a copy of the ITU-T Q.931 specification can prove to be invaluable when troubleshooting ISDN problems because you can get down to the exact details of each bit in the IE data.

Fortunately for most day-to-day activities you do not need to reference the Q.931 specification because the information you need is easily identifiable. For example, in the called party number information element shown above, notice the IE data contains the sequence **33 30 30 31**, which is 3001 in ASCII. This represents the directory number that is being called. Now you can follow the call's events.

Just as you searched through the CCM trace for the TCP handle of the IP phone to find the next message associated with a particular phone, you can do the same for a Q.931 or H.323 call. The call reference for a call remains the same for the duration of a call. The first bit, however, of the call reference is flipped depending on the direction of the call. Chapter 6 goes into detail about how this works, so don't worry about it right now. All you need to know is to search for the call reference minus the first digit. In this case the call reference is **00 09**, so search for **0 09**.

If you search through the CCM trace, you come to the next message. Notice that the message that follows is an **In Message**. This means it is an inbound message sent to CallManager by the ISDN network:

```
In  Message -- PriCallProceedingMsg -- Protocol= PriNi2Protocol
Ie - Q931ChannelIdIe -- IEData= 18 03 A9 83 97
MMan_Id= 0. (iep=  0 dsl=  0 sapi=  0 ces= 0 IpAddr=a4e81cac IpPort=2427
IsdnMsgData1= 08 02 80 09 02 18 03 A9 83 97
```

Notice that the call reference is now **02 80 09**. The most-significant bit (MSB) is set on the call reference value. This bit determines if this message is the originating or terminating side; however, you do not need to know what this bit means because CallManager clearly tells you which direction the message is going when it says **In Message** or **Out Messsage**. When searching, you need to look for **02 00 09** or **02 80 09** to track all events relating to this call event, although searching for just **0 09** is usually good enough.

These are just some of the tricks that help you follow call flows through the CCM trace. Subsequent chapters provide additional trace examples as we investigate other trouble-shooting scenarios. Half the battle in reading a CCM trace is knowing which pieces of the trace file to ignore so that you can focus on the important messages in the trace. As you read through the following chapters, you will get a better understanding of the different messages you might find in a CCM trace.

Reading SDL Traces

An SDL trace is a very detailed trace mainly used by Cisco development engineers for code-level analysis of call processing events. To the average CallManager administrator, SDL trace files are far too detailed for normal practical use.

If you're working with the Cisco Technical Assistance Center (TAC) on problem resolution, TAC might ask you to collect SDL traces so that it can forward them to CallManager developers for analysis. You need to know how to configure the trace files to capture the right information for TAC.

Although the SDL trace files are generally not used for troubleshooting purposes, you will find a few occasions in this book where you must look in the SDL trace file to get a full understanding of a particular problem. In cases like this, we will provide details on exactly what to look for.

SDL Overview

SDL traces provide a C programming language interface to alarms and trace information in CallManager. Alarms are used to inform a TAC engineer or CallManager developer of unexpected events, such as being unable to access a file, database, Winsock, or other operating system resources.

SDL traces can span multiple servers, allowing a process on one server to communicate with a process on another server transparently. This mechanism is supported by the use of

SDL links. An SDL link spans from one server supporting SDL to another server supporting SDL.

SDL maintains a circular queue of files to log information. Over time, a file will be overwritten. The number of files (determined by the CallManager service parameter **SdlTraceTotalNumFiles**) and the number of lines per file (determined by the CallManager service parameter **SdlTraceMaxLines**) governs how long it takes to overwrite old log files.

SDL generates two types of files:

- **Log files**—Contain the actual tracing information.
- **Index files**—Indicate which log file in the circular queue is currently being used for writing. An index file allows SDL logging to start where it left off each time an application is restarted.

Log filenames are composed of the following:

SDL*nnn_qqq_xxxxxx*.txt

where

> *nnn* represents the node ID
> *qqq* represents the application ID (CallManager = 100)
> *xxxxxx* represents the unique file index

Index filenames are composed of the following:

SDL*nnn_qqq*.index

where

> *nnn* represents the node ID
> *qqq* represents the application ID (CallManager = 100)

The actual SDL log and index files are text-based. All columns in a log entry are delimited by a vertical bar (|) character (0x7c). A log entry is broken into two components, prefix and detail, which appear in the following format:

```
| Prefix Component | Detail Component |
```

Every log entry contains a prefix. The prefix always has the same format. The common prefix of a trace line is as follows:

```
uuuuuuuuu | yy/mm/dd-hh:mm:ss:vvv | nnn | xxxx |
```

where

> *uuuuuuuuu* represents a unique line sequence timestamp
> *yy* represents the year
> *mm* represents the month
> *dd* represents the day
> *hh* represents the hour
> *mm* represents the minutes
> *ss* represents the seconds

vvv represents the milliseconds

nnn represents the node ID

xxxx represents the log entry type (which defines the type of entry being logged)

The SDL process running on each CallManager allows each node in the cluster to communicate with other nodes in the cluster to exchange information. SDL is what allows CallManager clustering to work by allowing processing for tasks to run on any node in the cluster. Generally, processing for an event occurs on the node where the device performing the given action is registered. For example, if an IP phone is registered to a particular CallManager in a cluster, that CallManager usually handles all call processing operations for that phone. But what if an IP phone registered to one CallManager in the cluster places a call out a gateway registered to a different CallManager in the cluster? In this case, some of the processing might occur on one node while the rest of the processing occurs on another node.

CallManager functions by sending *signals* from one process to another. These signals are just messages from one piece of software to another internal to CallManager. These signals can be sent to a piece of code on an entirely different CallManager node in the cluster. The SDL trace lets you see this happening. The best way to see this is by looking at the log entry type field at the beginning of an SDL trace file. For example,

```
011381785 | 02/09/16 14:51:37.874 | 002 | SdlSig-O
```

The log entry type is SdlSig-O. This means this CallManager server sent an SDL signal to another node (O means outgoing). Conversely, if you see SdlSig-I, this tells you the CallManager node you are looking at received an SDL signal from another node or another process. The CallManager and CTI Manager process communicate with each other using SDL links as well, so you see communication to and from CTI Manager in the SDL trace as SdlSig-O and SdlSig-I.

So how do you know which node the signal was coming from or destined to? After the SdlSig-O or SdlSig-I message you should see several columns of text separated by the vertical bar (I) character. For example,

```
SdlSig-O | DbDeviceClose | initialized   | Db(1,100,20,1) | Db(2,100,20,1)   |
```

An actual SDL trace has many more columns and spaces between columns than what is shown here. We have condensed the trace to fit on the printed page. The two columns to examine are the third and fourth columns after SdlSig-O. These describe the process sending the signal and the process to which the signal is being sent. The third column shows the destination (**Db(1,100,20,1)**) and the fourth shows the source (**Db(2,100,20,1)**).

Now you need to understand what you are looking at when you see Db(2,100,20,1). Db is the process name. You do not need to understand what the various process names signify. The important part is the four comma-separated numbers that follow the process name. The four numbers represent (in this order)

- Node number
- Application number (100 = CallManager, 200 = CTI Manager)
- Process type
- Process instance

The only ones you should be concerned with are the node number and the application number. In this case, you can see the signal is from CallManager on node 2 to CallManager on node 1.

You might be wondering why you need to know all this. Because CallManager is a distributed architecture, you might find that when looking at a CCM trace the events occurring don't seem to make sense. For example, you might see an IP phone making a call but never see the call go out a gateway to its destination, or you might see an IP phone told to play reorder for no apparent reason. When you see an unexplained event in the CCM trace, look at the same timestamp in the SDL trace to see if there was a signal from another node at that time. If so, look in the CCM trace on the other node at the same time to see if there is any additional detail about the call on the other node. This is the reason why having the clocks synchronized on all servers is so vitally important. Without time synchronization, you would have a very difficult task trying to match the events shown in the CCM trace on one server with the events on another server.

Although you will never read through an SDL trace the way you read through a CCM trace, you might occasionally have to look at the SDL trace to see what triggered a particular event in the CCM trace. In some cases, you will take the timestamp for an event in the CCM trace and match up that same timestamp in the SDL trace.

Enabling SDL Trace and Setting the Appropriate SDL Trace Level

Now that you know what the SDL trace is for, you need to know how to turn on SDL tracing and set the appropriate bit mask for the data you need. A *bit mask* is a string of bits that each represent a particular trace setting. For example, 10010011 is a bit mask. Each 1 in the bit mask indicates that a particular trace should be enabled, while each 0 indicates that a particular trace should be disabled. Bit masks are usually represented as strings of hex digits. For example, 10010011 is 0x93.

Detailed SDL tracing consumes a lot of disk space and affects the processor on the CallManager server, which can result in performance degradation under very high call volumes. However, as of CallManager 3.3, SDL trace writing is performed asynchronously which means CallManager is allowed first access to the disk and CPU for call processing. If insufficient disk or CPU bandwidth exists to write the trace file, lines are skipped in the trace, but call processing is not affected.

SDL traces are enabled in the **Service > Service Parameter** area in CallManager Administration. Table 3-3 shows the parameters you can adjust.

Table 3-3 *SDL Service Parameters*

SDL Service Parameter	Description
SdlListeningPort	This is the TCP port with which SDL links can be established between nodes in a cluster. The port is 8002 by default. There is rarely any reason to change this value.
SdlMaxRouterLatencySecs	Indicates the maximum number of seconds of signal latency before forcing a restart of the CallManager service. The default is 20.
SdlMaxUnHandledExceptions	Specifies the maximum number of CallManager exceptions that can occur before CallManager stops running. The default is 5.
SdlTraceDataFlags	This is a bit mask used to enable the tracing of SDL non-application-specific components or to modify the behavior of SDL tracing. • The recommended value for normal system debugging is **0x110**. • The recommended value when tracking problems with SDL links is **0x13D**. See Table 3-4 for details.
SdlTraceFlushImmed	Determines whether SDL trace entries are to be flushed to disk immediately. If this parameter is set to False, SDL trace entries are flushed to disk when there is spare disk bandwidth not being used for call processing. Setting this parameter to True causes higher disk input/output but ensures that all entries are written to the disk in the unlikely event of a software error. You should set this to False during normal operating conditions. The default is True.
SdlXmlTraceFlag	Determines whether XML-formatted tracing is allowed for SDL traces. The default is False.
SdlTraceDataSize	For signal types, this constrains the number of bytes that can be dumped from the data portion of a signal. This information appears in the freeform information column at the end of each line in the SDL trace file. The default is 100 bytes.
SdlTraceFilePath	This is the directory path that SDL uses to generate the log files. If this path is not defined or is defined incorrectly, SDL uses the default root path: C:\ProgramFiles\Cisco\Trace\SDL\.
SdlTraceFlag	This is a Boolean flag that indicates if SDL tracing is enabled or disabled. Set this flag to True to turn tracing on or False to turn tracing off. The default is True.

Table 3-3   *SDL Service Parameters (Continued)*

SDL Service Parameter	Description
SdlTraceMaxLines	This value indicates the maximum number of lines written to a log file before a new log file is created. The default is 10,000 lines.
SdlTraceTotalNumFiles	This value indicates the maximum number of files that can be created for logging purposes. The default is 250 files. Normally, a maximum of 250 files is not enough because the files write in round-robin or circular fashion—when the maximum limit is met, the next file starts at the beginning and overwrites the first file.
	Determine how much free disk space you have, deduct a safety net of 500 MB, and then use the rest of your disk space for trace space. You can calculate the size of your trace files by figuring the average CCM trace at 10,000 lines consumes about 2.5 MB; the average SDL trace at 10,000 lines consumes about 3.5 MB. Be sure to monitor free disk space by using other tools mentioned in this chapter such as PerfMon or CCEmail.
SdlTraceTypeFlags	This field indicates the bit mask value for collecting the trace type flag of choice.
	• The recommended value for normal call debugging is **SdlTraceTypeFlags=0x00000B04**.
	• The recommended value for low-level debugging or the debugging of voice gateways is **0xA000EB15**.
	See Table 3-5 for more details.

The bit mask definitions shown in Table 3-4 correlate to the Trace Characteristics on the SDL Trace Configuration page in CallManager Serviceability (**Trace > Configuration >** *select a server* **> Cisco CallManager >** *click the link to* **SDL Configuration**).

Table 3-4   *Non-application-specific Bits*

Name	Trace Characteristic in CallManager Serviceability	Bit Mask	Description
traceSdlLinkState	Enable SDL Link States Trace	0x00000001	Enables the tracing of SDL link states.
traceSdlLowLevel	Enable Low-level SDL Trace	0x00000002	Enables low-level SDL tracing.
traceSdlLinkPoll	Enable SDL Link Poll Trace	0x00000004	Enables the tracing of SDL link poll.

continues

Table 3-4 *Non-application-specific Bits (Continued)*

Name	Trace Characteristic in CallManager Serviceability	Bit Mask	Description
traceSdlLinkMsg	Enable SDL Link Messages Trace	0x00000008	Enables the tracing of SDL Link messages.
traceRawData	Enable Signal Data Dump Trace	0x00000010	Enables signal data dump.
traceSdlTagMap	Enable Correlation Tag Mapping Trace	0x00000020	Enables the tracing of correlation tag mapping.
traceCreate	Enable SDL Process States Trace	0x00000100	Enables the tracing of SDL process states.
traceNoPretyPrint	Disable Pretty Print of SDL Trace	0x00000200	Enables no pretty print of the SDL trace. Pretty print adds tabs and spaces in a trace file without performing post processing.
traceSdlEvent	Enable SDL TCP Event Trace	0x80000000	Enables TCP event traces.

The bit mask definitions shown in Table 3-5 correlate to the Trace Filter Settings on the SDL Trace Configuration page in CallManager Serviceability (**Trace > Configuration >** *select a server* **> Cisco CallManager >** *click the link to* **SDL Configuration**).

Table 3-5 *Bit Mask Definitions*

Name	Trace Filter Setting in CallManager Serviceability	Bit Mask	Description
traceLayer1	Enable All Layer 1 Trace	0x00000001	Enables all Layer 1 traces.
traceDetailLayer1	Enable Detailed Layer 1 Trace	0x00000002	Enables detailed Layer 1 trace.
Not used	—	0x00000008	This bit is not used.
traceLayer2	Enable All Layer 2 Trace	0x00000010	Enables all Layer 2 traces.
traceLayer2Interface	Enable Layer 2 Interface Trace	0x00000020	Enables Layer 2 interface trace.
traceLayer2TCP	Enable All Layer 2 TCP Trace	0x00000040	Enables Layer 2 TCP trace.

Table 3-5   *Bit Mask Definitions (Continued)*

Name	Trace Filter Setting in CallManager Serviceability	Bit Mask	Description
traceDetailLayer2	Enable Detailed Dump Layer 2 Trace	0x00000080	Enables a detailed dump of Layer 2 frames.
traceLayer3	Enable All Layer 3 Trace	0x00000100	Enables all Layer 3 traces.
traceCc	Enable All Call Control Trace	0x00000200	Enables all Call Control traces.
traceMiscPolls	Enable Miscellaneous Polls Trace	0x00000400	Enables miscellaneous polls traces.
traceMisc	Enable Miscellaneous Trace (Database Signals)	0x00000800	Enables miscellaneous traces (database signals).
traceMsgtrans	Enable Message Translation Signals Trace	0x00001000	Enables message translation signals **TranslateIsdnToSdlReq**, **TranslateIsdnToSdlRes**, **TranslateSdlToIsdnReq**, **TranslateSdlToIsdnRes** traces.
traceUuie	Enable UUIE Output Trace	0x00002000	Enables UUIE output traces.
traceGateway	Enable Gateway Signals Trace	0x00004000	Enables gateway signals traces.
traceCti	Enable CTI Trace	0x00008000	Enables CTI signal traces.
traceNetworkSvc	Enable Network Service Data Trace	0x10000000	Enables network service data traces.
traceNetworkEvent	Enable Network Service Event Trace	0x20000000	Enables network service event traces.
traceIccpAdmin	Enable ICCP Admin Trace	0x40000000	Enables Intracluster Control Protocol (ICCP) administration traces.
traceDefault	Enable Default Trace	0x80000000	Enables default traces.

Microsoft Performance (PerfMon)

Microsoft Performance is an administrative tool provided by the Windows 2000 operating system. It is colloquially referred to as PerfMon. PerfMon can be used to monitor a variety of performance objects. A *performance object* is a set of counters reported by a process or application running on the system that can be monitored. An example of a standard performance object is the Processor object, which contains a variety of processor-related counters such as processor utilization. PerfMon allows you to look at real-time statistics. It contains logging facilities to take snapshots of any counter at user-defined intervals.

The StatisticsEnabled service parameter in CallManager Administration (**Service > Service Paramaters >** *select a server* **> Cisco CallManager**) must be set to True to generate data in the counters. If statistics are disabled, neither PerfMon nor the Real-Time Monitoring Tool (RTMT) can collect data. Statistics are enabled by default.

CallManager includes several performance objects that let you monitor various counters related to the operation of the CallManager services and associated devices. The RTMT, which is discussed later in this chapter as part of the "CallManager Serviceability" section, provides much the same functionality as PerfMon.

Comparing PerfMon and the Real-Time Monitoring Tool (RTMT)

Although PerfMon and the RTMT allow you to view the same performance objects, each tool has its strengths and weaknesses.

PerfMon Advantages

You can configure PerfMon to log specific counters to a comma-separated values (CSV) file. This CSV file can then be imported into a spreadsheet application for further analysis.

A third-party tool called CCEmail (discussed in the next section) allows you to configure alerts in PerfMon.

Another advantage PerfMon has over RTMT is that the RTMT web browser must always be running for the counters to be monitored and alerts to be sent. However, that will likely be fixed in releases of RTMT subsequent to release 3.3(3).

RTMT Advantages

You can run the RTMT from a web browser on any PC that has IP connectivity to CallManager. PerfMon can be run only from a Windows NT/2000/XP PC that has PerfMon installed.

You can configure specific counters and save the configurations in RTMT. Then, each time you run RTMT, the pre-defined configurations are available.

In addition to performance-monitoring capabilities, RTMT provides two tabs—Devices and CTI Apps. The tabs allow you to search for devices and check the state of TAPI and JTAPI applications that are connected to CallManager.

You'll read more about the additional capabilities of the RTMT later in this chapter.

Using PerfMon to View Real-time Statistics

PerfMon's most basic function is to view real-time statistics on a machine. For example, you might want to know how many calls are currently active on CallManager or the status of the channels on a PRI. This kind of information can easily be obtained through PerfMon.

An example of how to view some real-time statistics with PerfMon will better familiarize you with the tool. Launch PerfMon from a CallManager server by selecting **Start > Programs > Administrative Tools > Performance**. The application looks similar to Figure 3-5.

Figure 3-5   *PerfMon*

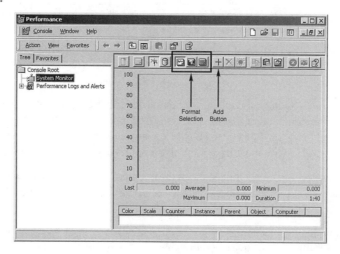

PerfMon has three formats to display data: chart, histogram, and report. Three buttons on the toolbar shown in Figure 3-5 are used to switch between the different formats. For viewing real-time statistics, you usually want to use the report format. Click the **View Report** button on the toolbar to gray out the area below.

Next, add the counters you want to monitor. Click the **Add** button on the toolbar, as shown in Figure 3-5. You see a dialog box similar to Figure 3-6.

Figure 3-6   *PerfMon Add Counters Dialog Box*

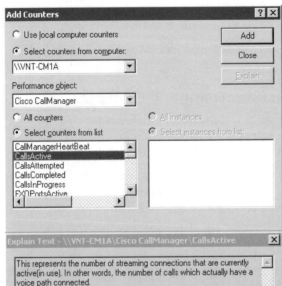

From this screen, you can add counters from either the machine on which you are running PerfMon or any other machine that has IP connectivity to the machine on which you are running PerfMon. For you to be able to view counters on remote machines, the account you are logged in with must have administrator privileges on the machine you want to monitor.

Next, select the object that contains the counter(s) you want to monitor. For example, if you want to monitor the number of active calls on a CallManager, select the Cisco CallManager object.

Below the object selection you can choose which counter to monitor. If you select the Cisco CallManager object, you see a counter labeled CallsActive. Select this counter and click **Add**. The dialog box remains open so that you can continue selecting and adding counters. To monitor all the counters for a particular object, click the **All counters** button. You can click the **Explain** button to get a short description of the counter, as shown in Figure 3-6. When you are done adding counters, click **Close**. Figure 3-7 shows all the counters in the Cisco CallManager object. You can see that the counters are updated every second or so.

Appendix D, "Performance Objects and Counters," describes the meanings of each of these counters, as well as the rest of the CallManager-related objects.

Objects and counters are only available for installed components. For example, if you do not have Cisco CallManager Attendant Console installed on the server you are trying to monitor, you will not see the Cisco CallManager Attendant Console object.

Figure 3-7   *PerfMon Displaying the CallManager Performance Object*

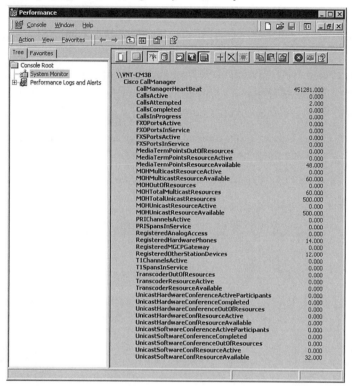

Some counters give you the option of selecting a specific instance of the counter to monitor. For example, the Cisco Lines object has only one counter, named **Active**. However, for this one counter, you can select one or more instances to monitor. In this case, each instance corresponds to a particular line on CallManager. You can select a range by holding down the Shift key and clicking the first and last instances in the range. Or you can select several individual instances by holding down the Ctrl key while clicking to select specific instances.

See Appendix D for detailed descriptions of all the Cisco CallManager-related performance objects and counters available in either PerfMon or the RTMT.

Using Counter Logs

One of PerfMon's most powerful features is the ability to periodically log performance information to a file. This can be useful for monitoring trends or determining exactly what time a problem occurred. Probably the most common use of counter logs is to monitor memory and CPU utilization for trends. If memory utilization continues to increase, you might be running into a memory leak. If the CPU spikes during specific times, you might be encountering one of many problems that cause high CPU utilization, such as a call routing loop.

Use the following steps to configure a counter log to monitor memory and CPU utilization on a per-process basis:

Step 1 On a CallManager server, open PerfMon by selecting **Start > Programs > Administrative Tools > Performance**.

Step 2 In the left column, in the **Performance Logs and Alerts** section, select **Counter Logs**.

Step 3 Select **Action > New Log Settings**.

Step 4 In the New Log Settings dialog box, type a name for the log, such as **CPU and Memory Logging**.

Step 5 A dialog box similar to the one shown in Figure 3-8 appears. Click **Add**.

Figure 3-8   *Counter Log Configuration Dialog Box*

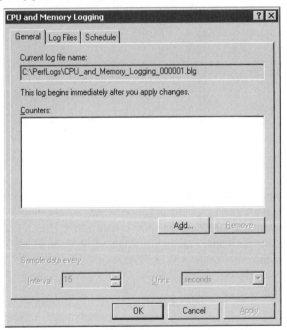

Step 6 The Select Counters dialog box appears (previously shown in Figure 3-6). The **Processor** object and **% Processor Time** counter are selected by default. Click **Add** to add this counter to the log.

Step 7 In the **Performance object** field, select the **Memory** object.

Step 8 In the list of counters, select the **Available MBytes** counter.

Step 9 Click **Add** and then **Close** to return to the counter log configuration dialog box.

Step 10 In the **Sample data every** area, adjust the interval depending on how often you want to monitor. For example, set it to 5 seconds to take a snapshot of the selected counters every 5 seconds. Microsoft recommends this counter not be set lower than 2 seconds when logging many different counters.

Step 11 Select the **Log Files** tab.

Step 12 In the **Location** field, type the path where you want to save the log files (the default is C:\PerfLogs).

Step 13 In the **File Name** field, type a filename for this log file, such as **CPU_and_Memory_Logging**.

Step 14 The **End file names with** checkbox and popup menu let you append a number to the end of the filename based on either the date and time the file is created or just an arbitrary number that increments each time a new log file is created. Select the **End file names with** checkbox, and choose a date format from the popup menu.

Step 15 Change the **Log file type** from **Binary File** to **Text File – CSV**. With the data in a CSV format. you can take the resulting data and import it into a variety of applications. Figure 3-9 shows the Log Files tab as described in the preceding steps.

Figure 3-9   *Log Files Tab for CPU and Memory Logging in PerfMon*

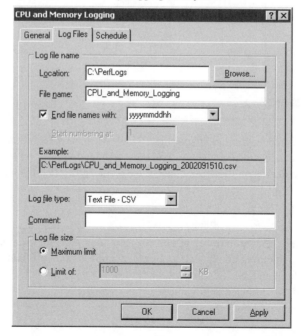

Step 16 Click the **Schedule** tab. If this is the first log on this system, you'll be asked if you want to create the directory, C:\PerfLogs. Click **Yes**.

Step 17 Instead of creating one huge log file, you can have PerfMon automatically create a new file periodically. To do this, in the **Stop log** area, click **After** and select how often you want to create a new file. For example, to create a new file every day, enter **1** and set the **Units** to days.

Step 18 Check the **Start a new log file** checkbox so that PerfMon starts a new file for the frequency you specified.

Step 19 Click **OK**.

If you followed the preceding instructions, you should now see a log with a green icon to the left of it on the Counter Logs screen, as shown in Figure 3-10.

Figure 3-10 *CPU and Memory Logging Counter Log in PerfMon*

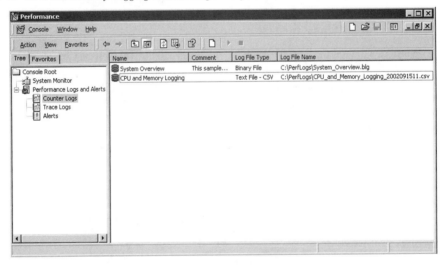

If the icon is red, right-click it and select **Start**. An error message should appear, telling you PerfMon is unable to start the log. The error will likely refer you to the Windows event log to get more details on the error. Correct the error, right-click the icon again, and select **Start**.

CAUTION When logging a small number of objects, as in the preceding example, setting the logging interval to something small such as 1 or 2 seconds is not a problem. However, if you are logging a large number of counters, be careful not to set the interval too low because this can lead to performance degradation.

CAUTION   Unlike CCM trace files, PerfMon log files do not have a way to do circular wrapping (also known as round-robin). This means that if left unattended, PerfMon log files can use up all the available hard drive space on the server, leading to a multitude of other potential problems. If you are using PerfMon logging, ensure you periodically delete old files to free up hard drive space.

Using Alerts

PerfMon allows you to configure alerts based on selected counters. For example, you can monitor the OutOfResources counter in the Cisco HW Conference Bridge Device object and be alerted when the value in that counter crosses a threshold you specify. Figure 3-11 shows some common alerts you may want to configure.

Figure 3-11 *Alerts in PerfMon*

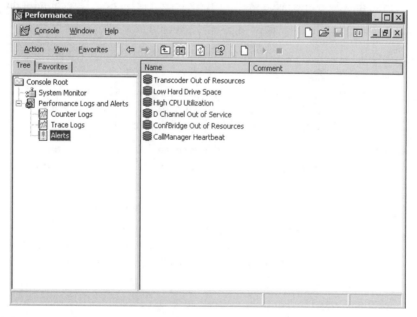

Other common things you might want to set an alert for are low disk space, low available memory, the D-channel going out of service on an MGCP gateway, and the number of registered phones falling below a certain value. You can place an alert on any counter in PerfMon, so the reasons and counters you may want to monitor vary based on your system.

The default action for an alert is to log an entry in Event Viewer. You can also configure the alert to send a network message to a computer you specify, run a counter log, or have a specified program run when the alert is triggered.

The Help in PerfMon (**Help > Help Topics**) provides detailed configuration steps for setting alerts.

The RTMT in CallManager Serviceability also allows you to configure alerts based on counters. However, in RTMT, you can have the alert sent as a network message to a computer you specify (just like in PerfMon) or to a pager or via e-mail to a specified recipient. You can also achieve this functionality using the CCEmail tool in combination with PerfMon.

CCEmail

You can use the Windows 2000-based tool CCEmail in conjunction with PerfMon to configure alerts for the performance counters. Alerts can be sent via pager or e-mail so long as the CallManager node for which the alert is configured has connectivity to an SMTP server. Also, the pager specified to receive alerts must be capable of receiving alphanumeric pages through an e-mail.

As part of the free tools provided with this book, you can download a copy of CCEmail from the Cisco Press web site. See the "Acquiring CCEmail" section for details.

Perform the following steps to install and configure CCEmail:

Step 1   Create a folder called **ccemail** on the C: drive of each CallManager server where monitoring is to take place.

Step 2   Download the CCEmail program from the Cisco Press website (as specified in the "Acquiring CCEmail" section) and save it to the C:\ccemail directory on each CallManager server.

Step 3   Open PerfMon (**Start > Programs > Administrative Tools > Performance**) and click on **Performance Logs and Alerts** and then **Alerts**.

Step 4   Right-click in the window and select **New Alert Settings**.

Step 5   In the **Name** field, type **minor**. Once you finish all the steps in this section, you are asked to repeat them again to create two alert settings, minor and major. The second time you perform this step, type **major** instead.

Step 6   Click **OK**.

Step 7   (Optional) Add a comment, such as **Alert settings for minor alarms** or **Alert settings for major alarms**.

Step 8   Click **Add**. The Select Counters dialog box appears.

Step 9   Make sure that **Select counters from computer** is selected and select the name of the CallManager server.

Step 10   In the **Performance object** list, choose **Cisco CallManager**.

Step 11 With the **Select counters from list** button selected, select counters you want to include in the alert and click **Add**. Add as many counters as you want to monitor with this alert. You can press and hold the Control key while clicking on counters from the list.

Some recommended counters to include for the minor alert are

— RegisteredAnalogAccess

— RegisteredDigitalAccess

— RegisteredPhones

Some recommended counters to include for the major alert are

— CallManagerHeartBeat

— RegisteredAnalogAccess

— RegisteredDigitalAccess

— RegisteredPhones

Step 12 In the **Performance object** list, choose **Process**. Select the **Private Bytes** counter and the instance _**Total**.

Step 13 In the **Performance object** list, choose **Processor**. Select the **% Processor Time** counter and the instance _**Total**.

Step 14 Click **Add** and then **Close**.

Step 15 Click on the first counter in the **Counters** list and set the threshold for when to be notified. Refer to Table 3-6 for suggestions for determining thresholds.

Table 3-6   *Threshold Recommendations*

Counter	Minor Alert	Major Alert
RegisteredAnalogAccess	Under 1 less than total	Under 50 percent less than total
RegisteredDigitalAccess	Under 1 less than total	Under 50 percent less than total
RegisteredPhones	Under 20 percent of total or 50, whichever is smaller	Under 40 percent of total or 150, whichever is smaller
Private Bytes (1 GB Total Memory)	900 MB	950 MB
Private Bytes (512 MB Total Memory)	450 MB	500 MB
% Processor Time	85 percent	95 percent

Step 16 Repeat the previous step until the thresholds have been set for all counters.

Step 17 Set the interval for how often the counters should be monitored. The recommended time is 15 minutes but you can choose any interval. Figure 3-12 shows the General tab for the minor alert.

Figure 3-12 *Minor Alert Settings, General Tab*

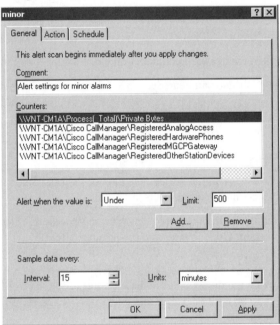

Step 18 Click the **Action** tab.

Step 19 Select the **Log an entry in the application event log** checkbox.

Step 20 Select the **Run this program** checkbox and click **Browse**.

Step 21 Navigate to the C:\ccemail directory and choose the proper .bat file.

If you only want to use e-mail alerts (no paging), choose email.bat. If you only want to use paging alerts (no e-mail), choose page.bat. You can also use one method for minor alarms and the other method for major alarms. For example, major alerts always page someone and minor alerts always e-mail someone. In that case, choose page.bat for the major alerts and email.bat for the minor alerts.

Figure 3-13 shows the Action tab for the minor alert.

Step 22 Click the **Schedule** tab.

Figure 3-13 *Minor Alert Settings, Action Tab*

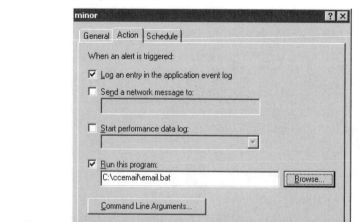

Step 23 In the **Start scan** area, make sure that **At** is selected.

Step 24 In the **Stop scan** area, make sure that **After** is selected and that the setting is **1 day**. Also, select the **Start a new scan** checkbox. Figure 3-14 shows the Schedule tab for the minor alert.

Step 25 Click **OK**.

Step 26 The alert settings for minor alarms are now complete. Repeat Steps 4 through 25 to create the alert settings for major alarms.

Figure 3-14 *Minor Alert Settings, Schedule Tab*

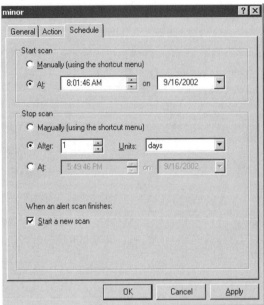

Perform the following steps to configure the .bat files for CCEmail:

Step 1 In the C:\ccemail directory, double-click **Setup.exe**.

Step 2 The CCEmail Setup Program displays. Click **Next**.

Step 3 In the Sender Information window, type the name of the SMTP server to be used and the sender's e-mail address.

Step 4 Click **Next**.

Step 5 Confirm the settings you just entered and click **Next** again.

Step 6 In the Email Addresses window, type the e-mail addresses, if any, to be e-mailed. For multiple addresses, separate entries with this string **-to:**.

For example: **sysadmin-alias@abc.com -to:john.smith@abc.com**

Step 7 Click **Next**.

Step 8 Confirm the settings you just entered and click **Next** again.

Step 9 In the Pager Addresses window, type the pager addresses, if any, to be paged. For multiple addresses, separate entries with this string, as described in Step 6 **-to:**.

Step 10 Click **Next**.

Step 11 Confirm the settings you just entered and click **Next** again.

Step 12 Click **Finish**.

Alerting Methods During Production and Non-production Hours

You can configure CCEmail to automatically switch between paging and e-mailing alerts depending on the time of day. Major alerts are typically important enough that a page should be received when the alert is triggered, regardless of the hour of day. Minor alerts are still important, but they're normally not considered critical enough to warrant a page during non-production hours, such as the middle of the night.

The following steps explain how to use .bat files and the Windows Task Scheduler so that minor alerts send pages during business hours and e-mails at night.

Step 1 Download the **ccemail_auto.exe** file from the Cisco Press website (as specified in the "Acquiring CCEmail" section) file and save it to the CallManager server where the changes are to be made.

Step 2 Double-click **ccemail_auto.exe** and make sure that the **Unzip to folder** field is set to **C:\ccemail**.

Step 3 Open the Windows Task Scheduler (**Start > Settings > Control Panel > Scheduled Tasks > Add Scheduled Task**).

Step 4 The Scheduled Task Wizard displays. Click **Next**.

Step 5 Click **Browse**, choose the **C:\ccemail\today.bat** file, and click **Open**.

Step 6 Type a name for the task (such as **today**), select **Daily** and click **Next**.

Step 7 For **Start time**, enter the beginning of business hours, such as 8:00 AM, select **Every Day**, and set the start date as today's date.

Step 8 Click **Next**.

Step 9 Enter the username and password of any user that has read/write permission for the C: drive and click **Next**.

Step 10 Click **Finish**.

Step 11 Repeat Steps 3 through 10 with the following changes:

- In Step 5, choose **tonight.bat** instead of today.bat.

- In Step 7, enter the end of business hours instead of the beginning, such as 6:00 PM.

Step 12 Open PerfMon (**Start > Programs > Administrative Tools > Performance**) and click on **Performance Logs and Alerts** and then click **Alerts**.

Step 13 Double-click on **minor** and click on the **Action** tab.

Step 14 In the **Run this program** field, click **Browse** and choose the **C:\ccemail\minor.bat** file.

Step 15 Click **OK** and close PerfMon.

Acquiring CCEmail

Check the Cisco Press website for a free downloadable file containing this tool (**www.ciscopress.com** > *type* **1587050757** *in the Search field* > *click the link to* **Troubleshooting Cisco IP Telephony**). Check the site regularly as there may also be updates to the tool or the book chapters.

CAUTION   This is not an officially supported tool. If you download, install, or use this tool, you do so at your own risk. Cisco Systems, Inc., is not responsible for correcting problems that may arise as a result of using this unsupported tool.

CallManager Serviceability

CallManager Serviceability is a collection of tools that help you troubleshoot various aspects of your CIPT system. CallManager Serviceability provides end user documentation online (make a selection from the **Help** menu) and on Cisco.com at the following location:

> **www.cisco.com/univercd/cc/td/doc/product/voice/c_callmg/index.htm** > *select your CallManager release* > **Serviceability**

CallManager Serviceability provides the following basic services:

- Alarms
- Tracing and the web-based Q.931 Translator
- Service Activation
- Control Center
- Real-Time Monitoring Tool

Alarms

Options under the Alarm menu let you configure the destination for the alarms (**Alarm > Configuration**) and search for alarm message definitions (**Alarm > Definitions**). *Alarms* are messages that notify you of basic errors. The messages can be inserted into CCM (SDI) and SDL traces and the Windows Event Viewer.

CallManager Serviceability provides pre-defined alarms, set at pre-defined levels. Use the Alarm Configuration page to set up which level of alarm you want to receive and where you want those alarms sent. Table 3-7 describes the alarm event levels.

Table 3-7   *Alarm Event Levels*

Level	Description
Emergency	This level designates the system as unusable.
Alert	This level indicates that immediate action is needed.
Critical	This level indicates that CallManager detects a critical condition.
Error	This level signifies that an error condition exists.
Warning	This level indicates that a warning condition is detected.
Notice	This level designates a normal but significant condition.
Informational	This level designates information messages only.
Debug	This level designates detailed event information used for debugging.

Tracing

Options under the Trace menu let you configure trace levels and parameters for CallManager, Database Layer, CTI Manager, and other core services. CallManager Serviceability then allows you to collect this information from one node or all nodes in the cluster when necessary. You can select trace information at the device level to target one or more specific devices in the trace output. The log files generated by the trace can be .txt format or XML-enabled for detailed analysis. We have already discussed text-based and XML-based tracing in the previous sections "Reading CCM Traces" and "Reading SDL Traces." In this section, we focus on XML-formatted tracing.

Using XML-enabled Traces

Using XML-enabled traces can make reading traces easier. Earlier in this chapter, you learned how to read trace files in their raw, text-based format and saw comparisons of standard text-based tracing and XML-formatted tracing. In some cases, you might find it easier to use XML-enabled traces and let the system do the searching for you. With XML-based tracing, you are given certain trace filters that you can apply to the trace output. Also, you can have the system search and compile trace information on just the devices you need (this feature is also available for standard text-based tracing). We don't normally recommend XML-based tracing because of a 2000-line limit in the trace files and the fact that searching through a large number of trace files is very slow. If you are searching a large amount of data, for instance, a problem that occurred over the course of several hours or several days, depending on the size of your system, you will probably need to use text-based tracing instead of XML-based tracing. If you select trace collection criteria that causes the trace output to be larger than XML-based tracing can handle, a message displays in CallManager Serviceability advising you that trace analysis cannot be performed on files greater than 2 MB in size. You are then given the option to save the result without filtering using **File > Save As** in your web browser.

The previous section, "Reading CCM Traces" detailed the steps used to configure XML-enabled tracing. Once trace files are collected, XML-based tracing allows you to filter the trace output using Trace Analysis.

Searching for Devices with XML Traces

Using the Trace Analysis feature, you can search for devices in the XML traces and narrow the scope of the trace search by choosing different search criteria and display fields. Instead of scanning thousands of lines of trace files looking for an event here and there, the XML-enabled trace can compile only the lines that relate to the devices or analysis criteria you have selected. In other words, all trace file lines you aren't looking for are filtered out so that you can concentrate on what is important to your search. Trace Analysis was discussed in detail in the previous section, "Reading CM Traces."

Web-based Q.931 Translator

The Trace menu in CallManager Serviceability provides a link to a web-based interface to the Q.931 Translator. Although convenient, the web-based interface may slow the performance of the Q.931 Translator. See the "Q.931 Translator and Enhanced Q.931 Translator" section for more information about this tool.

Service Activation

Service Activation in CallManager Serviceability (**Tools > Service Activation**) lets you activate and deactivate CallManager services. You can activate or deactivate CallManager-related services from Automatic mode by selecting or deselecting checkboxes next to specific services and then clicking the **Update** button. Then you can use the Control Center or the Windows Services Microsoft Management Console (*right-click* **My Computer** *and select* **Manage** > *double-click* **Services and Applications** > *click* **Services**) to start and stop services.

CAUTION   If you need to deactivate a service, you should do so from the Service Activation page. If you deactivate services from the Service Control Manager, you get an error message saying that some of the services are not configured properly. This is because deactivating services from the Service Control Manager does not remove the entries from the CallManager database; therefore, the services are out of sync with the configured services in the CallManager database.

Control Center

The Control Center in CallManager Serviceability (**Tools > Control Center**) lets you start and stop CallManager services and view their activation status. You can stop and start services in the Windows Services Microsoft Management Console as well if you have local access to the server. If not, you can use the Control Center web page in CallManager Serviceability to do the same thing.

Real-Time Monitoring Tool (RTMT)

The RTMT is a web-based application that provides up-to-the-second information about the state of a CallManager cluster, including run-time information about CallManager and CallManager-related components such as IP phones and gateways. This includes dozens of counters on items such as call activity, trunk usage, and even memory and processor utilization.

Appendix D describes the meanings of each of the CallManager-related performance objects and counters, as well as some commonly used Windows counters.

The RTMT provides much the same functionality as PerfMon in an easy-to-use web-based tool. See the section "Comparing PerfMon and the Real-Time Monitoring Tool (RTMT)," for more information about the differences the two tools provide. You may find yourself using PerfMon for some tasks and RTMT for others. The StatisticsEnabled service parameter in CallManager Administration (**Service > Service Paramaters** > *select a server* > **Cisco CallManager**) must be set to True to generate data in the counters. If statistics are disabled, neither the RTMT nor PerfMon can collect data. Statistics are enabled by default.

One very useful feature not provided by PerfMon (unless you use a third-party tool such as CCEmail described in this chapter) is the ability to configure alerts based on the objects. These alerts can be set to send a notification via pager, e-mail, or system message popups. These alerts can be configured for any performance object and can be set to trigger if a counter is greater or less than a specific threshold. The alerts can be configured to run only at specific times or all the time. Alerts are useful when you are troubleshooting problems because you can set the RTMT to alert you when a specific event you are trying to troubleshoot occurs. For example, if you are running out of channels on a gateway interface, you can set the RTMT to page or e-mail you when the counter for total calls to that gateway exceeds a certain value. Through release 3.3, the RTMT web browser must remain open and running for alerts to be sent. This requirement may change in future releases of CallManager Serviceability.

Objects and counters are only available for installed components. For example, if you do not have Cisco CallManager Attendant Console installed on the server you are trying to monitor, you will not see the Cisco CallManager Attendant Console object.

Performance Tab

The Performance tab in RTMT allows you to view CallManager cluster info as shown in Figure 3-15. To view this information, right-click on the cluster name and select **Properties**. The CallManager Cluster Info window displays basic statistic about the cluster, broken down by server.

Figure 3-15 *RTMT, Cluster Info*

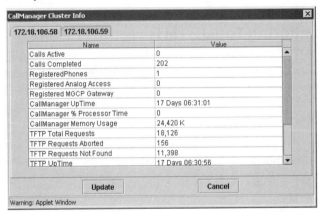

This is also the tab where performance monitoring occurs, much the same functionality as with PerfMon. However, in RTMT, you can configure tabs for specific counter configurations. Each time you use RTMT, the pre-defined configurations are displayed. Figure 3-16 shows several counters used to monitor general activities on a system.

To add a new category, right-click on one of the existing tabs and select **New Category**. Building the category is as easy as selecting a counter and then dragging and dropping it onto the tab's frame. Multiple counters can be piled in a single frame, and six frames per tab are provided.

Devices Tab

The Devices tab in RTMT allows you to view device information that you configure for various device types—phones, gateways, H.323 devices, CTI applications, voice mail, and Cisco IP Voice Media Streaming Application devices such as MOH servers, MTP resources, and conference bridges. The Devices tab is shown in Figure 3-17.

Figure 3-16 *RTMT, Performance Tab*

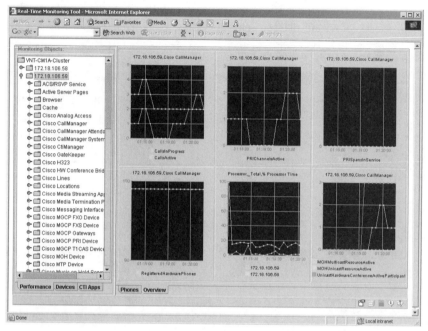

Figure 3-17 *RTMT, Devices Tab*

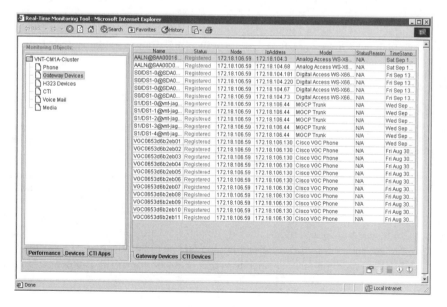

To add a new category, click on one of the existing tabs and select **New Category**. You build the category by first double-clicking on one of the device types and then making selections in a series of wizard-like screens that display, as shown in Figure 3-18 and 3-19.

Figure 3-18 *Device Search Criteria Screens, Part 1*

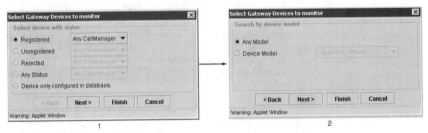

Figure 3-19 *Device Search Criteria Screens, Part 2*

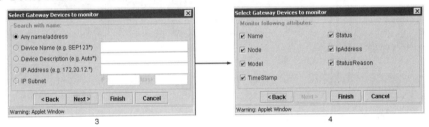

The screens shown in Figure 3-18 and 3-19 allow you to search for real-time information about devices in the cluster regardless of their registration status. You can search for devices based on device name, IP address, DN, IP subnet, and so on.

CTI Apps Tab

The CTI Apps tab in RTMT allows you to view application-, device-, and line-based information for CTI applications. You can check the registration status of TAPI and JTAPI applications such as Personal Assistant, Cisco IP Manager Assistant, Cisco IP SoftPhone, and so on. The CTI Apps tab shows whether the application has an open connection with CallManager and who's using it. The CTI Apps tab also shows you applications attempting to log in using an invalid username or password. Figure 3-20 shows the CTI Apps tab.

To add a new category, right-click on one of the existing tabs and select **New Category**. You build the category by first double-clicking on one of Applications, Devices, or Lines in the left frame and then making selections in a series of wizard-like screens that appear.

Figure 3-20 *RTMT, CTI Apps Tab*

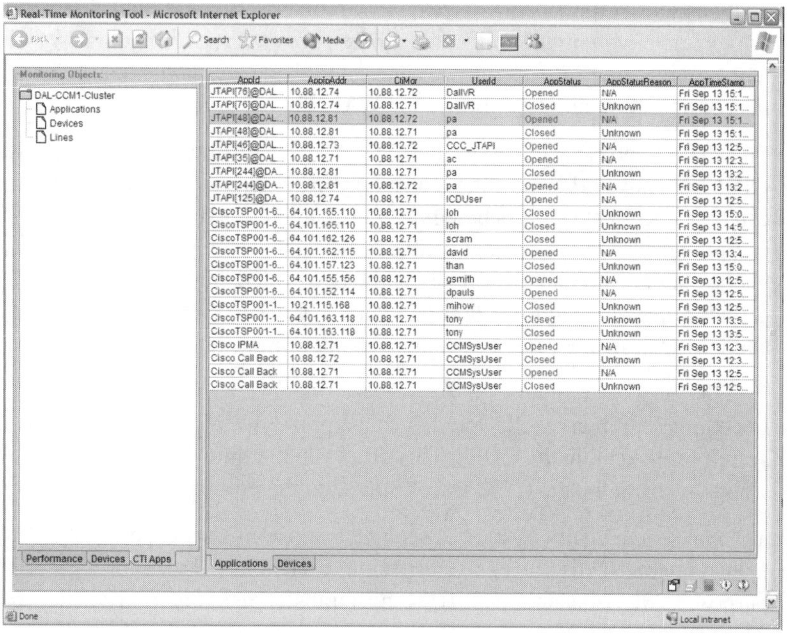

Call Detail Records (CDR) and the CDR Analysis and Reporting (CAR) Tool

CallManager can be configured to store CDRs for all calls generated throughout a CallManager cluster. Typically CDRs are used for billing and accounting purposes, but they can also be useful when troubleshooting certain types of problems. Usually CDRs do not provide enough information to diagnose a problem, but they can help you narrow down a problem and provide information about the specific time when a problem occurred, leading you to other trace files or debugging tools that might give you more details on the problem's root cause.

CDRs are stored in their own SQL database on the Publisher server in the CallManager cluster. For CallManager to generate CDRs, you must set the **CdrEnabled** service parameter on each CallManager to True (select **Service > Service Parameters**). This service parameter is set to False by default. For additional details, you should also enable the **Call Diagnostics Enabled** service parameter. If the **Call Diagnostics Enabled** service parameter is set to True, CallManager also generates Call Management Records (CMRs, also known as Diagnostic CDRs). CMRs contain data such as packets sent and received, packets lost, and jitter for the duration of the call. One CDR might have multiple CMRs associated with it because each media stream creates a CMR. This means that if a call is placed on hold and then resumed, two CMRs are created—one for the media stream before the call is on hold, and one for the media stream after the call is on hold. CMRs are especially useful for diagnosing voice quality problems because they allow you to see patterns. For example, you might notice that all the phones across a specific WAN link are experiencing high jitter or packet loss. This can indicate a possible quality of service (QoS) misconfiguration or line errors on the WAN link.

The CDR Analysis and Reporting (CAR) tool (**CallManager Serviceability > Tools > CDR Analysis and Reporting**) can help you analyze the raw data that comprises the CDR database and create reports based on your search criteria. For example, if you are receiving complaints of poor voice quality, one of the first things you should do is find out which phones or gateways are experiencing the poor voice quality. Although you can wait to collect data from additional user complaints, you can proactively use the data in the CDRs and CMRs to identify any trends in high jitter or packet loss to hone in on where the problem is.

For example, if a user tells you they had a problem calling someone, you can use CAR to search for the call in the CDRs. This gives you the time the call occurred, which helps you when you examine the CCM traces related to the problem.

You can search CDRs by user or specific extensions for the period that you specify. This helps you trace calls placed from specific extensions for diagnostic or informational purposes. All associated records, such as transfer and conference calls, appear together as a logical group.

CAR can also be used to send you alerts if the number of calls with poor QoS is exceeded or if the CDR database size exceeds a percentage of the maximum number of records.

For more information on the various features available in CAR, review the CAR section in the CallManager Serviceability documentation at

> **www.cisco.com/univercd/cc/td/doc/product/voice/c_callmg/index.htm** > *select your CallManager release* > **Serviceability > Serviceability System Guide > CDR Analysis and Reporting**

If you look at the raw timestamp information stored in the CallManager CDRs, you notice they are stored in a format that is not easily recognizable in standard date and time format. To quickly convert the date and time from the format in the CDRs to standard format, use the CDR Time Converter utility.

CDR Time Converter

Timestamps in the CallManager CDRs are stored in a format known as Epoch time. This is the number of milliseconds that have elapsed since midnight January 1, 1970 GMT. While this might be a convenient format for things like computers, humans usually prefer a more readable date and time format.

The CDR Time Converter utility allows you to enter the time as stored in a CDR—for example, 1030565084—and convert it to standard date and time format—such as 8/28/2002 3:04:44 PM. Figure 3-21 shows the output of the CDR Time Converter tool.

Figure 3-21 *CDR Time Converter Tool*

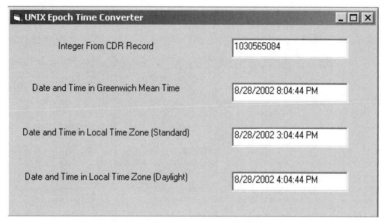

Notice the tool converts the number in Epoch time to Greenwich Mean Time (GMT) and the local time zone of the PC on which the tool is installed for both standard and daylight savings time.

Acquiring the CDR Time Converter

Check the Cisco Press website for a free downloadable file containing this tool (**www.ciscopress.com** > *type* **1587050757** *in the Search field* > *click the link to* **Troubleshooting Cisco IP Telephony**). Check the site regularly as there may also be updates to the tool or the book chapters.

CAUTION   This is not an officially supported tool. If you download, install, or use this tool, you do so at your own risk. Cisco Systems, Inc., is not responsible for correcting problems that may arise as a result of using this unsupported tool.

Event Viewer

Microsoft Event Viewer is a Windows 2000 Server application that displays system, security, and application events (including CallManager) for the Windows 2000 Server. These events are alarm messages generated by CallManager. CallManager Serviceability is used to configure alarm messages to be sent to the Event Viewer (**Alarm > Configuration**).

Open Event Viewer on the server running CallManager by clicking **Start > Settings > Control Panel > Administrative Tools > Event Viewer**. CallManager errors are logged in the Application log. You can double-click an event in the log to learn more about it.

Alarm definitions can be found in CallManager Serviceability (**Alarm > Definitions**).

Figure 3-22 shows an example of an alarm message in Event Viewer.

Figure 3-22 *Event Viewer*

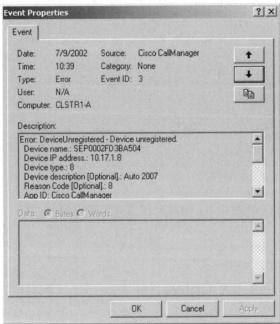

Notice the App ID and the Error message. This tells you that the IP phone specified in the Device Name details has unregistered from CallManager.

All alarms fall into seven catalogs, as shown in Table 3-8.

Table 3-8 *Alarm Definition Catalogs*

Catalog Name	Description
CallManager	All CallManager alarm definitions such as CallManagerFailure, DChannelOOS, DeviceUnregistered, and RouteListExhausted.
TFTPAlarmCatalog	All Cisco TFTP alarm definitions such as kServingFileWarning and kCTFTPConnectSendFileTimeoutOccurred.

Table 3-8   *Alarm Definition Catalogs (Continued)*

Catalog Name	Description
CMIAlarmCatalog	All Cisco Messaging Interface (CMI) alarm definitions such as kCCMConnectionError, kSMDIMessageError and kSerialPortOpenningError.
CtiManagerAlarmCatalog	All Cisco Computer Telephony Integration (CTI) alarm definitions such as kCtiProviderOpenRej, kCtiMaxConnectionReached, and kCtiProviderOpenFailure.
DBAlarmCatalog	All Cisco database alarm definitions such as kPrimaryDbIsLost, kUnableToConnectToDB, and kErrorBuildingCnfFile.
GenericAlarmCatalog	All generic alarm definitions shared by all applications such as OutOfMemory, ServiceStopped, and ServiceStartupFailed.
IpVmsAlarmCatalog	All Cisco IP Voice Media Streaming Application alarm definitions, including MOH, conference, media termination point, and transcoder alarms, such as kIPVMSDeviceDriverNotFound, CreateAudioSourcesFailed, and kDeviceDriverError.
JavaApplications	All Java applications that run on the CallManager server including extension mobility and Cisco IP Manager Assistant (IPMA), such as EMAppServiceError and IPMAApplicationError.

Based on the information given in the Event log entry in Figure 3-22 you can go to CallManager Serviceability to search for a better definition of the problem in question.

To search for alarm definitions, perform this procedure:

Step 1   In CallManager Administration, choose **Application > Cisco CallManager Serviceability**. The Cisco CallManager Serviceability window appears.

Step 2   Choose **Alarm > Definitions**.

Step 3   Choose the catalog of alarm definitions from the **Find alarms where** drop-down box, or click the **Enter Alarm Name** field to enter the alarm name. Figure 3-23 shows this interface.

Figure 3-23 *CallManager Alarm Message Definitions*

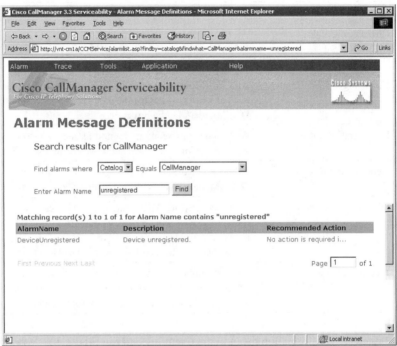

Step 4   Click the **Find** button. The definitions list appears for the alarm catalog or search string you entered.

Step 5   In the list, click the alarm definition for which you want alarm details. Based on the Event Viewer entry shown in Figure 3-22, choose the CallManager catalog and the DeviceUnregistered error. You see Figure 3-24, showing the severity, an explanation, and the recommended action. All alarm messages found in the Event Viewer can be researched in this fashion.

Figure 3-24 *CallManager Alarm Details*

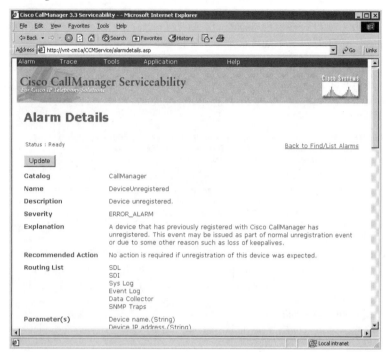

Q.931 Translator and Enhanced Q.931 Translator

Q.931 Translator is an application that takes a CCM trace and decodes the hex-formatted Q.931 messages into human-readable format. Depending on the version of CallManager you are using, there are two ways to access the application. Q.931 Translator is bundled with every CallManager installation. It can be found in the C:\Program Files\Cisco\bin directory. The file is called **Q931 translator.exe**. In CallManager version 3.2 and later, the application is also part of the CallManager Serviceability web page (select **Trace > Q931 Translator**).

Q.931 Translator is useful for quickly troubleshooting a variety of gateway problems. It is not a substitute for learning how to read the CCM trace, but it helps you resolve some gateway signaling problems without ever having to look in the CCM trace.

The name Q.931 Translator is a bit misleading because this application does more than just translate ISDN messages into a human-readable format. The Q.931 Translator also helps you troubleshoot problems with hardware that does not use the Q.931 protocol, including the WS-X6624 analog FXS card, T1 CAS on the WS-X6608 card, and calls to and from an

H.323 gateway. The Translator is helpful for troubleshooting problems with these hardware components because some of these gateways convert their native signaling to Q.931 messages. H.225 messages used in the H.323 protocol are based on the Q.931 specification; hence, the Q.931 Translator can decode H.225 messages.

The amount of information contained in a CCM trace can be intimidating. Q.931 Translator helps you quickly examine a trace in a graphical format without having to wade through irrelevant debugs. For example, the following sample is from a CCM trace of an outgoing call setup:

```
Out Message -- Pri250SetupMsg -- Protocol= Pri250Protocol
Ie - Ni2BearerCapabilityIe IEData= 04 03 80 90 A2
Ie - Q931ChannelIdIe IEData= 18 03 A9 83 94
Ie - Q931DisplayIe IEData= 28 0C B2 50 61 75 6C 20 47 69 72 61 6C 74
Ie - Q931CallingPartyIe IEData= 6C 0C 21 80 39 31 39 35 35 35 35 36 34 34
Ie - Q931CalledPartyIe IEData= 70 0D A1 39 31 32 31 30 35 35 35 32 35 30 30
MMan_Id= 0. (iep=  0 dsl=  0 sapi=  0 ces=  0 IpAddr=346812ac IpPort=2427)
IsdnMsgData2= 08 02 05 C8 05 04 03 80 90 A2 18 03 A9 83 94 28 0C B2 50 61 75
   6C 20 47 69 72 61 6C 74 6C 0C 21 80 39 31 39 35 35 35 35 36 34 34 70 0D A1
   39 31 32 31 30 35 35 35 32 35 30 30
```

Without a copy of the ITU Q.931 specification, which explains each bit in the trace information elements, this sample looks like a bunch of numbers and letters. However, the Q.931 Translator decodes the output into a readable format, as shown in Figure 3-25.

Figure 3-25 *Q.931 Translator Application*

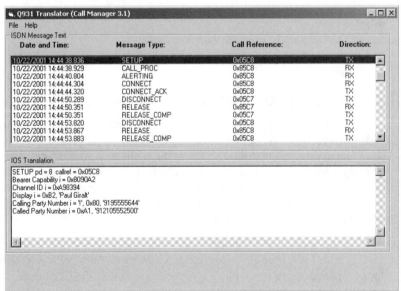

One thing you should know right away is not to trust the Direction column. Information in the Direction column can occasionally be inaccurate because of how the tool decodes hex messages. To be sure of the direction, look at the first line in the debug, which states **Out**

Message. This indicates that this is an outbound (TX) setup message. Similarly, an inbound (RX) message would show **In Message** in the CCM trace.

Calls in the trace can be distinguished by the call reference value. The most significant bit (MSB) of the call reference toggles between 0 and 1, depending on whether the message was inbound to CallManager or outbound from CallManager to the gateway. Table 3-9 shows the difference between the first bit being 1 versus being 0. This table also shows the binary representation of the hexadecimal digits to clearly show how the last three binary digits in the left and right columns are identical. The only difference between the left and right columns is that the MSB for all the digits in the left column is 0, and the MSB for all the digits in the right column is 1.

Table 3-9   *Binary Representation of Hexadecimal Digits*

MSB = 0	MSB = 1
0 (0000)	8 (1000)
1 (0001)	9 (1001)
2 (0010)	A (1010)
3 (0011)	B (1011)
4 (0100)	C (1100)
5 (0101)	D (1101)
6 (0110)	E (1110)
7 (0111)	F (1111)

The output in Figure 3-25 shows that the call reference is **0x05C8** in the transmit (TX) direction and **0x85C8** in the receive (RX) direction. Any row that has a 0x05C8 or 0x85C8 in the Call Reference column is a message for the same call. As Table 3-9 shows, 0 and 8 are equivalent, with the exception of the MSB, which is different. Call reference values are eventually reused, but it is impossible for the same call reference to appear in a single CCM trace file for one gateway because several hundred or thousand calls must occur before the value is reused.

Q.931 Translator shows the calling and called party numbers converted to easily readable text, along with the bearer channel identifier, bearer capability, and display information element. The channel identifier and bearer capability are not fully decoded. You need a copy of the Q.931 specification to understand what the various bits in those fields signify. Don't worry if you don't have this specification. Chapter 6 explains how to decode some of these. Some of these are decoded for you in the Enhanced Q.931 Translator explained in the next section.

Q.931 Translator is most useful for decoding cause codes that are sent as an information element (IE) in various Q.931 messages. These cause codes are always sent as part of a DISCONNECT message and may be included as part of other messages as well. Decoding the cause code IE gives you some insight into why the call was disconnected.

The following is a sample of a CCM trace showing a Q.931 DISCONNECT message:

```
Out Message -- PriDisconnectMsg -- Protocol= Pri250Protocol
Ie - Q931CauseIe IEData= 08 02 80 81
MMan_Id= 0. (iep=  0 dsl=  0 sapi=  0 ces=  0 IpAddr=a86a12ac IpPort=2427)
IsdnMsgData2= 08 01 AA 45 08 02 80 81
```

The first thing you should notice is that this is a DISCONNECT message being sent by CallManager to the PSTN. You can see that the hex representation of the data in the Q931CauseIe is **08 02 80 81**. These cause codes are defined in the ITU Q.850 specification; however, Q.931 Translator decodes these for you. Opening the trace file containing the DISCONNECT message in Q.931 Translator reveals the following:

```
DISCONNECT pd = 8  callref = 0xAA
Cause i = 0x8081 - Unallocated/unassigned number
```

You can see that 0x8081 is decoded to **Unallocated/unassigned number**, meaning that CallManager does not have a phone or route pattern that matches the digits that were sent to CallManager by the ISDN network.

NOTE   See Chapter 6 for additional information about what various cause codes mean and how to continue troubleshooting problems like these.

Enhanced Q.931 Translator

Although the Q.931 Translator allows you to quickly observe Q.931 and H.225 events, its functionality is somewhat limited. Two Cisco TAC engineers took the original source code for Q.931 Translator and enhanced it to provide additional functionality not available from the official Q.931 Translator product bundled with CallManager.

The Enhanced Q.931 Translator offers the following advantages over the standard Q.931 Translator:

- **Direction column is correct**—As mentioned earlier, the method by which the standard Q.931 Translator decodes the direction is flawed, and therefore, the direction column is sometimes incorrect. The Enhanced Q.931 Translator properly decodes the messages as **In** or **Out**.

- **Protocol column**—Tells you whether the message is a Q.931 message or an H.225 message.

- **Expanded IE decoding**—Decodes far more Q.931 information elements than the original Q.931 Translator, including bearer capability, channel ID, numbering plan and type in the calling and called party number IEs, call state, and many more.

- **Find in messages**—Allows you to search for any text that appears in the decoded message data. This means you can search for a calling or called party phone number, disconnect cause code, or any other value and quickly find the message you are looking for.

- **Filter messages**—Allows you to filter messages based on a specific call reference or protocol type. When filtering on call reference, Enhanced Q.931 Translator automatically includes all messages for that call reference regardless of the setting of the MSB of the call reference.

- **Raw ISDN message data**—After the decoded information, the raw hex bytes for the ISDN message are presented.

- **Resizable window**—Allows you to resize the window to view more messages.

- **File name display**—The currently-open filename is displayed in the title bar in case you forget where you left off when searching through several traces in a folder.

Figure 3-26 shows the same trace shown in Figure 3-25, this time as it looks in the Enhanced Q.931 Translator.

Figure 3-26 *Enhanced Q.931 Translator Application*

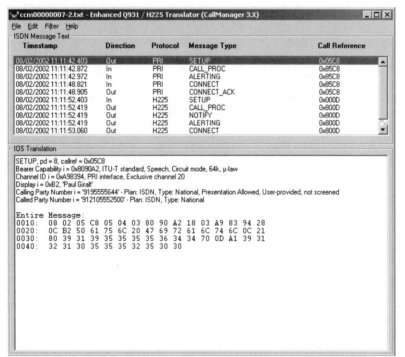

Notice the amount of additional data presented in the bottom pane of the tool. The bearer capability (ITU-T standard, Speech, Circuit mode, 64k, μ-law), channel ID (PRI interface, Exclusive channel 20), calling party numbering plan and type (Plan: ISDN, Type: National, Presentation Allowed, User-provided, not screened), and called party numbering plan and type (Plan: ISDN, Type: National) are all decoded for you automatically.

Future versions of CallManager may include the Enhanced Q.931 Translator, but until then, you must download the tool from the Cisco Press website (see "Acquiring Enhanced Q.931 Translator" later in this chapter).

One thing to remember is that the Q.931 Translator and Enhanced Q.931 Translator tools are not a replacement for the CCM trace. They are just another tool you can use to make decoding the CCM trace easier and finding the location of your problem quicker. Often you will have to refer back to the CCM trace after finding the call in Q.931 Translator to get additional detail regarding the events that surround a message. For example, if you find a message in Q.931 Translator indicating CallManager disconnected a call with a cause code of 0xAF, "Resources Unavailable," Q.931 Translator tells you the cause code and the timestamp in the CCM trace. You must then go to the CCM trace at that timestamp and determine what resource was unavailable that caused CallManager to disconnect the call.

As mentioned before, Q.931 Translator decodes more than just Q.931 messages. The H.225 protocol used to communicate between H.323 gateways and other CallManager clusters uses messages similar to ISDN Q.931. Q.931 Translator translates H.225 messages that appear in CCM traces.

Some gateways use Q.931 to communicate with CallManager even though the gateway's interface to the PSTN is not actually using Q.931. For example, the WS-X6624 24-port FXS gateway uses analog FXS signaling to communicate with analog phones, fax machines, and modems; however, this analog signaling is converted to Q.931 messages between the gateway and CallManager. These Q.931 messages appear in the CCM trace and are translated by the Q.931 Translator. The same is true of the WS-X6608-T1 gateway when communicating with the PSTN using channel associated signaling (CAS). The gateway converts CAS to Q.931 messages.

So if the gateways are converting these various protocols to Q.931, you might wonder how you can troubleshoot the signaling before it is converted to Q.931. This is one of the various uses of the Dick Tracy tool discussed in the section "Dick Tracy."

Acquiring Enhanced Q.931 Translator

Check the Cisco Press website for a free downloadable file containing this tool (**www.ciscopress.com** > *type* **1587050757** *in the Search field* > *click the link to* **Troubleshooting Cisco IP Telephony**). Check the site regularly as there may also be updates to the tool or the book chapters.

CAUTION   This is not an officially supported tool. If you download, install, or use this tool, you do so at your own risk. Cisco Systems, Inc., is not responsible for correcting problems that may arise as a result of using this unsupported tool.

Dick Tracy

The Dick Tracy tool is a complex and powerful tool used to troubleshoot problems on various gateways based on the Skinny or MGCP protocols. Specifically, the Dick Tracy tool is used on the following voice gateways:

- DT-24+
- DE-30+
- WS-X6608-T1
- WS-X6608-E1
- WS-X6624

There is little to no documentation on the Dick Tracy tool because it was created as an internal development tool. However, it has been released under the condition that the tool itself is unsupported. This means that no formal documentation or release mechanism exists for the tool. This also means that the tool's behavior might change from one release to another without warning, but as long as you understand the basics of how the tool works, you should be able to pick up any changes without too much difficulty. The "Acquiring Dick Tracy" section explains how you can download a copy of the Dick Tracy tool.

There are two versions of Dick Tracy:

- A standalone Windows 95/98/NT/2000/XP application that connects to the gateway you want to monitor over TCP/IP. This version is commonly called Dick Tracy.

- A version is embedded in the Catalyst 6000 operating system (CatOS). It can be invoked from the Catalyst 6000 command-line interface (CLI) to diagnose problems on WS-X6608 and WS-X6624 gateways in the chassis. This version is commonly called CLI Tracy or embedded Tracy.

The CLI Tracy tool can be used to connect only to gateways that are in the same Catalyst 6000 chassis to which you are connected. Using the Windows-based Dick Tracy tool is recommended here because it is more flexible and easier to use than CLI Tracy.

Why do you need the Dick Tracy tool? In case you've never seen a Cisco DT-24+ gateway, it is a PCI card that plugs into a PCI slot in any PC chassis. The gateway only uses the PCI slot to draw power. The PCI bus is not used for any kind of data transfer to or from the DT-24+. The DT-24+ also provides an Ethernet port and a T1 port. There is no console port or other method of out-of-band communication to the gateway; therefore, you need a tool to access the gateway so that you can determine what is going on inside the gateway. The WS-X6608 and WS-X6624 are similar to the DT-24+ because they use the Catalyst 6000 chassis they reside in for power and IP connectivity. Other than that, the Catalyst 6000 Supervisor (the management interface on the Catalyst 6000) has no out-of-band management interface to the gateways.

CAUTION   Before we discuss the tool itself, you should know that the Dick Tracy tool is not the most
                user-friendly piece of software. It also can damage your gateway if it's not used properly.
                A good working rule is that if you don't know what something does, you probably shouldn't
                mess with it—particularly most of the **set** commands that are available. This book covers a
                few useful **set** commands, but other than those, you should not need to use Dick Tracy to
                set commands on the gateways.

Using the Dick Tracy Tool

Figure 3-27 shows the Windows version of the Dick Tracy tool. The tool itself is a very
simple program. Clicking the **Connect** button on the toolbar reveals a box indicating
Connect to remote target device. Enter the IP address of the gateway you want to
troubleshoot in the **Target IP Address** box. The port number should always be 2005.

Figure 3-27 *Dick Tracy Tool for Windows*

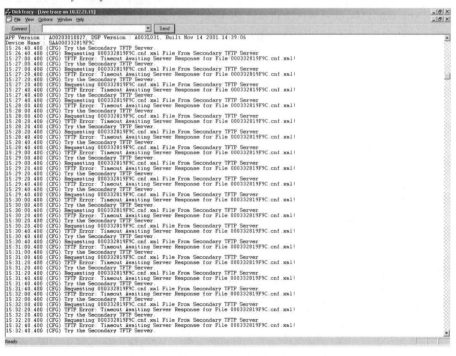

After you connect to a gateway, you see a text box labeled **Live trace on** *ip address,* where
ip address is your gateway's IP address. You can open additional connections to other
gateways using the same procedure. You will likely see several lines of tracing when you
connect. This is because the gateway buffers the last few lines of tracing and shows them
to you when you connect.

After you connect to a gateway, it is a good idea to enable logging of the live trace. Click **Options > Start Logging**. A dialog box appears, asking where you want to save the logged traces. Choose a convenient location on your hard drive that has enough space available. The traces are just a text log of everything you see on your screen while connected to the gateway. They usually do not get very big unless you are running a debug for an extended period of time. Logging does not affect the performance of Dick Tracy or the gateway. Enabling logging keeps a record of all the traces you capture until you close the trace window or stop logging using the menu.

At this point, you've started a trace, and the tool is up and running. On the menu bar you see a one-line text box and a **Send** button. Think of this field as the *command box* to communicate with the gateway. To communicate with the gateway, you must understand the concept of task IDs. Each gateway has various tasks that are responsible for various components of the software. For example, one of the tasks is responsible for sending and receiving messages to and from the digital signal processors (DSPs) on the gateway.

To view the list of available tasks on a gateway, enter the command **0 show tl** (this command uses the number 0, not the letter O, and the letter L, not the number 1) in the command box and click **Send** or press **Enter**. You should see something similar to the following sample:

```
03:15:15.450 (GEN) Lennon Tasks
        0 : GEN
        1 : AUD
        2 : TRC
        3 : SNMP
        4 : SPAN
        5 : NMP
        6 : DSP
        7 : LINE
        8 : CFG
        9 : GMSG
       10 : SOCK
       11 : TMR
       12 : Q921
       13 : XA
```

The 0 (zero) is the number of the task ID you want to issue a command to. In this case, you are issuing a command to the GEN task (ID 0). Each task has various commands that can be issued to it. Some tasks do not respond to commands at all. The **show tl** portion is the command being issued to task ID 0.

Dick Tracy offers context-sensitive help for the tasks that accept commands. For example, to see which commands are available for task 0, enter **0 ?** in the command box and press **Enter**. You see something similar to the following sample:

```
03:22:21.320 GEN  --> Help -> Available Commands:
03:22:21.320 reset <hard/soft>
03:22:21.320 read func[index] <count>
03:22:21.320 write func[index] <value>
03:22:21.320 show func
03:22:21.320 clear func
03:22:21.320 set func
```

You can see that **show** is one of the available commands for task ID 0. You can get additional context-sensitive help by entering **0 show ?**. You see the following:

```
03:24:31.500 GEN   Help: show modifiers ->
03:24:31.500 Show Task List : show tl
03:24:31.500 Show Ethernet Stat's : show ether
03:24:31.500 Show Version's : show ver
03:24:31.500 Show Time : show time
03:24:31.500 Show Reset : show reset
```

You can see that the command **show tl** performs the command **Show Task List** according to the context-sensitive help. It is difficult to provide a list of the available task IDs and Tracy commands because they vary from gateway to gateway and can change from one version of CallManager to the next. Chapter 6 covers some specific task IDs when discussing troubleshooting gateways.

You should always precede each command with a task ID. If you do not precede a command with a task ID, the gateway applies the command to the last task ID you sent a command to.

In addition to the various **show** commands, a few other commands are useful. One in particular is **set mask**. You use the **set mask** command to turn on various debugs. To view what debugs you can turn on for a particular task, issue the **show mask** command for the task in question. For example, issuing the command **6 show mask** details the various trace bits for the DSP task:

```
(DSP) Mask<0x0>
   Where Bit0 = Debug Msg's
         Bit1 = Call Progression Msg's
         Bit2 = Boot Msg's
         Bit3 = Stat Msg's
         Bit4 = Cmd Msg's
         Bit5 = RTP Msg's
         Bit6 = SID Frames
         Bit7 = Status Msg's
```

As you can see from this output, the mask is currently set to **0x0**, and eight different trace bits can be enabled. The mask is set as a hexadecimal digit. In this case because you have eight bits, 256 possible combinations of tracing can be turned on, depending on which bits are enabled. For example, to enable Debug Msg's (Bit0) and Call Progression Msg's (Bit1), the mask must be set to 00000011 in binary. This translates to 0x03 in hex. Therefore, the command is **6 set mask 0x03**.

CAUTION   Be sure to set the masks back to **0x0** after enabling any trace masks. The traces continue to run until the gateway is reset, even if you close your Dick Tracy session. Failure to turn off the debug masks could create a performance impact on the gateway.

For the time being, don't worry about what each of these trace masks or task IDs does. Chapter 6 covers the masks and IDs in detail.

Using the CLI Tracy/Embedded Tracy Tool

The less-used version of Dick Tracy is the CLI Tracy or embedded Tracy tool, available on the Catalyst 6000 CLI. To enable tracing for a particular port, enter the command **tracy_start** *module port,* where *module* and *port* are the module and port numbers of the port you want to debug. For example, for the gateway on port 6/3, you would enter

```
tracy_start 6 3
```

Notice that the syntax differs from the traditional Catalyst Operating System (CatOS) notation, in which ports are specified using *module/port*.

After you start CLI Tracy for a port, all the debug information for that port appears on your console or Telnet session. You can send Tracy commands to the port using the command **tracy_send_cmd** *module port taskid command*. When you need to send commands to a port, you should really use the Windows-based tool because sending commands via CLI Tracy can lead to switch instability. When you are done using the CLI Tracy tool, enter the command **tracy_close** *module port* to end the session. You can have only one CLI Tracy session open at any given time on the whole chassis. So if someone has a Tracy session open on the console port, you cannot start one from a Telnet session. Be sure to close the CLI Tracy session when you are done.

CLI Tracy does have one advantage over the Windows-based Dick Tracy tool: It can monitor a port before it obtains an IP address. For that reason, you can use CLI Tracy to troubleshoot problems where the port cannot obtain an IP address. The regular Dick Tracy tool cannot accomplish this because you need IP connectivity to the port in question before you can gather information from the port.

Acquiring Dick Tracy

Check the Cisco Press website for a free downloadable file containing this tool (**www.ciscopress.com** > *type* **1587050757** *in the Search field* > *click the link to* **Troubleshooting Cisco IP Telephony**). Check the site regularly as there may also be updates to the tool or the book chapters.

CAUTION   This is not an officially supported tool. If you download, install, or use this tool, you do so at your own risk. Cisco Systems, Inc., is not responsible for correcting problems that may arise as a result of using this unsupported tool.

Sniffer Traces

One of the most powerful tools for troubleshooting a large number of CallManager problems is a packet capture/analyzer tool such as Network Associates' Sniffer Pro (www.nai.com), Finisar Surveyor (www.finisar.com/product/product.php?product_id=104), or Ethereal (www.ethereal.com). Because of Sniffer Pro's widespread appeal, a trace file generated by any packet-capture tool is commonly called a *sniffer trace*. This term is used here to refer to any packet-capture software, not just Sniffer Pro.

A sniffer trace lets you see exactly what is happening on the network at any given time. Examining a sniffer trace requires a good understanding of the various layers of the OSI model, which were briefly described in the "Introduction" to this book.

To get the most benefit from a packet-capture tool, you should use a tool that can decode the various protocols you might encounter in an IP telephony network. This includes, but is not limited to, H.323 (H.225 and H.245), MGCP, RTP, SQL, and LDAP. Also extremely important is the capability to decode Skinny packets. Most newer versions of commercially available network capture application can decode Skinny. Finisar Surveyor can decode Skinny as part of the standard package while Network Associates Sniffer Pro requires you purchase the Sniffer Voice add-on to get Skinny decodes. Also, the free protocol analyzer Ethereal supports decoding Skinny as of version 0.8.20.

This book does not teach you how to use the network analysis software, but instead focuses on the kind of information you can obtain using network analysis software. Sniffer traces are most important when you're troubleshooting problems that can't be examined using standard trace files or debugs because the problem is either network-related or the appropriate diagnostic tool is not built into the product. For example, device registration problems are much easier to troubleshoot with a sniffer trace, as are most voice quality problems.

Voice Codec Bandwidth Calculator

Use the Voice Codec Bandwidth Calculator to determine the bandwidth used by different codecs with various voice protocols over different media.

To get a detailed analysis of all the headers for your particular medium, use the automated Voice Codec Bandwidth Calculator available on Cisco.com. You must be a registered user on Cisco.com to access the tool.

http://tools.cisco.com/Support/VBC/jsp/Codec_Calc1.jsp

Bug Toolkit (Formerly Bug Navigator)

Cisco provides a bug search feature that allows you to find known bugs based on software version, feature set, and keywords. The resulting matrix shows when each bug was integrated or fixed, if applicable. It also allows you to save the results of a search in Bug Groups and also create persistent Alert Agents that can feed those Groups with new defect alerts.

Bug Toolkit is only available to registered users on Cisco.com. Access the bug toolkit by searching for "bug toolkit" on Cisco.com or at the following link:

www.cisco.com/cgi-bin/Support/Bugtool/launch_bugtool.pl

Remote Access Tools

There are several tools you can use to remotely access your system. In this chapter, we briefly discuss Terminal Services and Virtual Network Computing (VNC).

Terminal Services

Windows Terminal Services is a feature that comes standard on all servers running Windows 2000 Server software. Terminal Services allows you to remotely access the Windows interface on a CallManager server.

Terminal Services is extremely useful for remotely troubleshooting problems on CallManager when you do not have immediate access to the console. To use Terminal Services, you must install the Terminal Services Client on any PC running most Microsoft Windows operating systems.

The installer for the Terminal Services Client is included on all CallManager servers in the C:\WINNT\system32\clients\tsclient folder. There are several folders for the 32-bit and 16-bit versions. Use the 32-bit client on any PC running Windows 95 or later.

Once installed, launch the Terminal Services Client and enter the IP address of CallManager and the screen resolution you want to connect with. You receive a login prompt for the server. Enter the administrator username and password to authenticate. Once authenticated, you have access to the CallManager desktop almost as if you were on the console.

If you need to open a hole through your firewall to access CallManager via Terminal Services, open TCP port 3389. This is the only port needed to access a Windows 2000 Server via Terminal Services.

CAUTION   Cisco does not support installing any CallManager applications, CallManager software patches, or operating system patches via Terminal Services. Terminal Services is designed for remote access to the CallManager server for troubleshooting purposes; however, some portions of the CallManager installer are not compatible with Terminal Services. You can use VNC to access the console of the server for performing upgrades and patches.

Virtual Network Computing (VNC)

VNC is basically a remote display system that allows you to view a remote desktop environment. VNC allows you to use one computer to drive actions on a target computer but differs from Terminal Services because, with VNC, any actions performed by you that occur on the target computer can be seen equally by the local user. All computers must have a local copy of VNC installed. You can use VNC to install, upgrade, or apply patches to CallManager.

You can access the VNC application and documentation files on the OS version 2000 2.2 and later CD or download. If you're running an older version of the OS, run the OS upgrade for version 2000 2.2 or later to gain access to the VNC files. OS upgrades are available on CCO at the following link:

www.cisco.com/cgi-bin/tablebuild.pl/cmva-3des

CAUTION   Using VNC can expose you to a security risk. Please review the "Security Best Practices" section in the Cisco-produced document for installing VNC, which is available on the OS 2000 version 2.2 and later CD or at the download link previously shown.

Websites and Further Reading

There's a wealth of information available on the Internet. When you're looking for more information, use the following resources:

- **Cisco Technical Assistance website**—Provides the latest information and technical documentation from Cisco's Technical Assistance Center (TAC). Use the TAC website to search for tech tips and documentation, download software updates, or open a TAC case to obtain additional information. Access the TAC website by searching for "TAC" on Cisco.com or at

  www.cisco.com/tac

- **Technical tips for IP Telephony applications, servers and associated technologies**—This site contains a variety of technical documents written by TAC engineers that are useful for solving commonly encountered problems. Access the IP Telephony Applications website by searching for "IP Telephony Applications" on Cisco.com or at

  www.cisco.com/pcgi-bin/Support/browse/index.pl?i=Technologies&f=1533

- **Networking Professionals Connection**—This site is the gathering place for net-working professionals to share questions, suggestions, and information about networking solutions, products, and technologies. Access the forum by searching for "networking professionals" on Cisco.com or at

  www.cisco.com/go/netpro

- **AnswerMonkey**—You'll find detailed information about Cisco Unity at the home page of one Unity's creators, Jeff Lindborg. Access the site by searching for "answermonkey" on Google.com or at

  www.answermonkey.net

- **Updates to this book**—Check the Cisco Press website regularly for updated information pertaining to the chapters in this book (**www.ciscopress.com >** *type* **1587050757** *in the Search field* **>** *click the link to* **Troubleshooting Cisco IP Telephony**).

Check out the section "Further Reading" in the "Introduction" to this book for additional books about IP Telephony and VoIP.

Best Practices

- Become familiar with the various troubleshooting tools at your disposal. Be sure to try each of them before you encounter a problem to understand how they work so you do not have to waste time learning the tool when under pressure to resolve a network outage.

- Keep a copy of all the tools in a centralized location and check frequently for updates that may add additional functionality.

- The only way to become efficient at reading CCM traces is by practicing. The more you look through CCM traces to troubleshoot problems, the better you will understand the intricacies of the CCM trace.

- Ensure remote access to your CallManager cluster is available before a problem occurs. If you need to be able to access the CallManager cluster from outside the office, make provisions for VPN or dialup access and use Terminal Services or VNC to access your CallManagers. Terminal Services works amazingly well even over slow dialup connections.

VNC Best Practices

- If you're using VNC and no longer plan to use Terminal Services for remote management, disable Terminal Services.

- Set the VNC service to Manual startup and start it only during remote management. This adds another layer of protection by requiring that users access the environment via Windows username/password authentication to start the VNC service.

- Use a complex alphanumeric password for VNC. VNC does not have a username/ password structure; it only uses a single password, so make sure the password you choose is difficult to crack. VNC limits the password to eight characters. A good password includes numbers, upper- and lowercase letters, and special characters and does not use any known word. For example, 123eye67 is not as good a password choice as 4hW9Lv#g.

Summary

This chapter covered the various troubleshooting tools and resources you have at your disposal to troubleshoot a CIPT network. Which tool you use depends largely on the problem at hand. However, some problems can be resolved using more than one tool. As you become more familiar with each of the tools in your tool belt, you will begin to favor some tools over others for specific tasks. No matter how much you read about these tools, you will not learn about them until you use them to troubleshoot a real problem on your own. As you advance through the rest of this book, you will see frequent references to the tools presented in this chapter because they play an integral part in CIPT troubleshooting.

## CHAPTER 4

Skinny Client Registration

"My phone won't register." If I had a dollar for every time I have heard that, I'd be pretty well off! The majority of Skinny client registration problems are caused by a misconfiguration on CallManager, the DHCP server, one or more network devices, or the IP phone itself.

In addition to IP phones, other Skinny clients exist such as the Cisco VG248, the ATA 186, and even Unity voice mail ports. Because all these devices utilize the Skinny Client Control Protocol (SCCP or Skinny protocol) for registration, they all can be approached with a very similar troubleshooting methodology.

To address a Skinny client registration problem, you need two primary things:

- Adherence to a solid troubleshooting methodology
- A basic understanding of how the Cisco IP Phone boots up

In most cases where an IP phone won't register, the cause proves to be a fundamental network-related problem. When troubleshooting an IP phone that will not register, it is important to work your way up the OSI layer. This is important. Most people skip ahead to investigate the application layer, only to find out that the IP phone doesn't even have an IP address. For more information about the OSI model, see the "Introduction" section in the front of the book.

The question, then, is what do you do when you encounter an IP phone that doesn't register properly with CallManager?

Step 1 Check for inline power issues.

Step 2 Check IP addressing and DHCP.

Step 3 Check for IP network connectivity.

Step 4 Check for Trivial File Transfer Protocol (TFTP) problems.

Step 5 Check for CallManager issues.

The following sections address the procedures involved with these troubleshooting steps.

Troubleshooting Inline Power

If an IP Phone doesn't have power, you obviously can't do anything else until you fix this problem. An IP Phone can be powered by a power brick or via inline power. Inline power is typically one of those things that either works or it doesn't. That doesn't mean, however, that you can't take steps to try to correct the loss of inline power.

It is important to treat inline power problems as Layer 1 issues first. If you plug in an IP Phone, and it doesn't receive power, maybe that cable doesn't go back to the inline power-capable port. Before assuming that the IP Phone has a problem receiving inline power, plug the IP Phone into a known good port. If you are using a known good port, and every IP Phone you plug in works except one, you have narrowed the problem to the IP Phone itself.

If you have a known good IP Phone, and it still doesn't work, you have to investigate for other potential physical layer issues. Also, make sure that you have plugged the cable into the right port on the back of the IP Phone. One port is for the IP Phone, and the other port is for a PC.

If there are any intermediate patch panels check those to ensure the cables are properly connected and, if possible, try a different cable run to narrow down the problem to either a particular cable or a particular switch port. Also try connecting another non-inline power network device to the same patch where inline power is not working to see if you can get a good Ethernet connection to the port. If you can get an Ethernet connection this is a sign that the physical path is good, although that doesn't make any guarantees on the quality of the connection.

If you have verified that there are no Layer 1 problems, you can investigate the switch settings for that port. An inline power port can basically be in an Auto or Off mode. There is no such thing as an On mode for an inline power port.

Catalyst 6000 series, 4006, 4224, 4500 series, and 3524XL-PWR switches all have an Auto mode that indicates that the phone discovery mechanism is in operation. The Catalyst 6000 series, 4500 series and 4006 have an Off mode. The Catalyst 3524XL-PWR and 4224 have a Never mode that is equivalent to the Off mode.

It might help to understand a bit about how inline power works. The following is a basic explanation of the method used to detect that an IP Phone is connected to a 10/100 Ethernet port used by a Catalyst inline power capable switch.

Step 1   Just like any 100 Mbps Fast Ethernet switch capable of autonegotiation, the port on the switch sends a signal called Fast Link Pulse (FLP) to any device that might be connected to it. However, when inline power is enabled (set to Auto), the switch modifies the FLP so that it is different than a standard FLP. This pulse is sent continuously unless the port is explicitly set to Off.

Step 2   If the port sees this "special" FLP returned to it by a connected device, it knows that it must supply inline power. A Cisco IP Phone 79xx is designed to forward this FLP signal back to the 10/100 Ethernet port on the switch. It does this because it has a relay that connects its Ethernet receive pairs with its Ethernet transmit pair. When no power is being supplied to the IP Phone, this relay is closed, allowing the FLP signal to return to the switch port. As soon as the switch receives this FLP signal, power is supplied, and the relay then remains in an open state. The Catalyst 6000 series switches check their power budget to determine if there is available power in the system to power the IP Phone. If there is enough power available, the IP Phone is powered up. If the switch detects a "standard" FLP, the switch knows the connected device is not inline power capable. In this case, the port immediately stops sending the modified FLP and switches to sending standard FLPs to negotiate the speed and duplex with the connected device.

Step 3   The port provides power to the IP Phone over pairs 1 and 2 as a common mode current; the same two pairs of Ethernet frames are carried over. The switch port is then taken out of phone-discover mode and is changed to normal 10/100 Ethernet autonegotiation mode.

Step 4   When this occurs, a "wait for link" timer in the switch starts. The IP Phone has five seconds to establish a link on the Ethernet port. If the switch doesn't detect a link on the port within five seconds, it shuts off power to the port and starts the phone-discovery process again.

After the IP Phone has booted up, it sends a Cisco Discovery Protocol (CDP) message to the switch. This message has Type, Length, and Value object (TLV) information that tells the switch how much power the IP Phone really needs. The switch receives this information and adjusts the power budget accordingly.

If you are using a Catalyst switch capable of per-port power management such as the Catalyst 6000 series, one important thing to check is whether or not the switch actually has enough power available to provide power to an IP Phone. Use the command **show environment power** to view the current power status for the switch. Example 4-1 shows the output of the **show environment power** command on a Catalyst 6509 switch.

Example 4-1   *Using* **show environment power** *to Show Current Power Status on a Catalyst 6509*

```
Console (enable) show environment power
PS1 Capacity: 1153.32 Watts (27.46 Amps @42V)
PS2 Capacity: 1153.32 Watts (27.46 Amps @42V)
PS Configuration : PS1 and PS2 in Redundant Configuration.
Total Power Available: 1153.32 Watts (27.46 Amps @42V)
Total Power Available for Line Card Usage: 1153.32 Watts (27.46 Amps @42V)
Total Power Drawn From the System: 997.92 Watts (23.76 Amps @42V)
Remaining Power in the System: 155.40 Watts ( 3.70 Amps @42V)
Default Inline Power allocation per port: 7.00 Watts (0.16 Amps @42V)
```

continues

Example 4-1 *Using* **show environment power** *to Show Current Power Status on a Catalyst 6509 (Continued)*

```
Slot power Requirement/Usage :

Slot Card Type          PowerRequested PowerAllocated CardStatus
                        Watts  A @42V  Watts  A @42V
---- ------------------ ------ ------  ------ ------  ----------
1    WS-X6K-SUP1A-2GE    138.60  3.30  138.60  3.30  ok
2    WS-SVC-CMM          252.00  6.00  252.00  6.00  ok
3    WS-X6408-GBIC        84.00  2.00   84.00  2.00  ok
4    WS-X6624-FXS         64.68  1.54   64.68  1.54  ok
5    WS-X6348-RJ-45      100.38  2.39  100.38  2.39  ok
6    WS-X6608-T1          84.00  2.00   84.00  2.00  ok
7    WS-X6408-GBIC        84.00  2.00   84.00  2.00  ok
8    WS-X6248-RJ-45      112.98  2.69  112.98  2.69  ok
9    WS-X6624-FXS         64.68  1.54   64.68  1.54  ok
```

Notice that in Example 4-1, the switch has 155.40 Watts of power available on the switch for additional line cards or IP Phones. If the card status shows **partial-deny** or **deny** this indicates there is not enough power to either power up the module or to provide power to one or more ports on the module.

To see exactly how much power a particular IP Phone is using, issue the command **show port inlinepower** or **show port inlinepower** *mod/port* for a specific port. Example 4-2 shows the output from **show port inlinepower**.

Example 4-2 *Using* **show port inlinepower** *to View Power Usage on an Individual Port*

```
Console (enable) show port inlinepower 5/37
Default Inline Power allocation per port: 7.00 Watts (0.16 Amps @42V)
Total inline power drawn by module 5:  12.60 Watts ( 0.30 Amps @42V)
Port     InlinePowered      PowerAllocated
      Admin Oper   Detected mWatt mA @42V
----- ----- ------ -------- ----- --------
 5/37 auto  on     yes      6300  150
```

Notice that 6.3 Watts of power is allocated to this particular port.

If you run out of power on the switch, you should see a message logged to the console, as well as your Syslog server if you have one configured, that states

```
%SYS-3-PORT_NOPOWERAVAIL:Device on port 5/12 will remain unpowered
```

If the switch provides power to a port but does not detect the link within five seconds, you will see this message:

```
%SYS-3-PORT_DEVICENOLINK:Device on port 5/26 powered but no link up
```

If you see this message once it might indicate that someone connected their IP Phone to a port and immediately unplugged it before the link came up. However, if you see this message multiple times for the same port, this indicates there is a problem. A bad IP Phone that does not power up to the point of establishing the link but is still detected as an inline power-capable device can cause the switch to continue toggling power to the port. Generally, a defective IP Phone causes this type of behavior, although cabling problems can cause problems like this as well—especially cable runs that exceed the Ethernet maximum distance of 100 meters.

In review, it is important to follow this basic procedure when troubleshooting inline power issues:

Step 1   If you suspect that the IP Phone doesn't work, plug it into a known good port.

Step 2   If you suspect that the port or cable might be bad, plug in a known good IP Phone.

Step 3   With this information, investigate any physical layer possibilities, such as cables not being plugged in, damaged cables, or cables not patched through correctly to the switch port.

Step 4   Check configuration and power issues on the switch itself. Make sure that the switch is in Auto mode and that the port in question hasn't been set to Off. Also check that sufficient power is available for the IP Phone.

Once the IP Phone is powered up, ensure the IP addressing information on the IP Phone is correct.

Troubleshooting Network Connectivity and Skinny Registration

If the IP Phone has power but won't register, the network configuration on the phone is the first thing to look at. IP Phones are very similar to any other network device that communicates using IP.

The approach to solving these types of problems involves starting with Layer 1 of the OSI reference model and working your way up.

First, a brief overview of the IP Phone boot-up service is in order. Upon receiving power, the IP Phone does the following:

Step 1   Obtains voice VLAN information from the switch to which the IP Phone is connected or uses statically defined voice VLAN information.

Step 2   Requests DHCP information or uses statically configured IP address information if DHCP is disabled on the IP Phone. The DHCP information or static configuration also provides the IP Phone with the IP address of the TFTP server.

Step 3   Contacts the TFTP server to download a configuration file. Among other things, this configuration file specifies the list of CallManagers to which the IP Phone should attempt to register.

Step 4   Attempts registration to its primary CallManager. If the primary CallManager is unavailable, the IP Phone tries subsequent servers from the list provided via the TFTP server.

If you troubleshoot each component one at a time, you can determine which piece of the registration process is not working and correct the problem. First check to see if the IP Phone is configured in the correct VLAN.

Verifying VLAN configuration

The first action an IP Phone attempts after powering up is to obtain voice VLAN information from the switch it is connected to. The IP Phone sends three CDP messages requesting the voice VLAN ID. If the IP Phone receives a VLAN ID, it tags all subsequent packets using the VLAN ID received via CDP. If the IP Phone does not receive a response, all packets are untagged by the phone.

It is possible to also statically configure a VLAN ID for the IP Phone to use. This is necessary in IP telephony deployments using non-Cisco switches or older Cisco switches that do not support auxiliary (voice) VLANs. To check the currently active voice VLAN, check the **Operational VLAN ID** setting on the IP Phone (**settings > 3-Network Configuration > 19-Operational VLAN Id**). If this VLAN ID does not match what you expect, check the VLAN configuration on the switch to which the IP Phone is attached and also check the static VLAN ID on the IP Phone to ensure it is not unintentionally statically configured (**settings > 3-Network Configuration > 20-Admin VLAN Id**).

Verifying IP Addressing Information

Once the IP Phone has determined the proper VLAN ID for voice packets, it must obtain the IP addressing information it will use to communicate with CallManager and other network devices. This can be accomplished by either statically configuring all the IP addressing parameters or via DHCP. Most deployments use DHCP for ease of administration. Check your IP Phone to determine which method is selected by checking the status of the **DHCP Enabled** parameter on the phone (**settings > 3-Network Configuration > 30-DHCP Enabled**). A setting of **YES** uses DHCP for IP addressing while a setting of **NO** allows you to configure a static IP address. If this parameter is not set as you expect, unlock the phone by entering ****#** on the IP Phone keypad and then use the soft keys to toggle between **YES** and **NO**.

If you are using DHCP, you can see if the IP Phone succeeds in its DHCP request. When looking at DHCP issues, there are two possible problems:

- The IP Phone is not getting an IP address from the DHCP server.
- The IP Phone is getting an IP address, but some part of the information is incorrect or incomplete.

DHCP works with four basic messages exchanged between the client and the DHCP server:

1 Discover—The client sends a Discover packet that has several requested fields.

2 Offer—The DHCP server answers with an Offer packet, filling in those fields with the information it has.

3 Request—The client then sends a Request packet, confirming its receipt of the information.

4 Acknowledge—The DHCP server then sends an Acknowledgment packet to the client.

When the IP Phone sends its Discover packet, it requests the following information:

- IP address
- Subnet mask
- Default gateway
- DNS server
- Domain name
- Option 66
- Option 150

You should recognize most of these fields as standard DHCP options that most IP endpoints, such as PCs, request from a DHCP server to be able to communicate on the IP network. The two that are unique to CallManager are Option 66 and Option 150.

For an IP phone to register with a CallManager node, the IP phone needs to know the IP address of the CallManager it is supposed to register with. CallManager places this information on the TFTP server in an XML configuration file. Option 66 and Option 150 are two of the six possible ways for an IP phone to determine the IP address of the TFTP server. The other four methods are discussed later. Although the IP phone requests both Option 66 and Option 150, you should use only one of the two.

The recommended practice is to use Option 150 because it allows you to specify an array of two IP addresses, allowing you to have redundant TFTP servers. Redundant TFTP servers are supported in CallManager release 3.2(1) and later. If your DHCP software does not support adding Option 150 it probably does allow you to configure Option 66. Option 66 is defined as a host name of the TFTP server; however, you can enter either a host name or IP address and IP phone interprets it properly. Note that a host name requires IP phone to perform a DNS lookup for CallManager's IP address, adding an additional level of complexity and another point of possible failure.

If your IP phone is not able to obtain an IP address via DHCP, check for any network connectivity problems between the IP phone and the DHCP server. If the DHCP server is not on the same subnet as the IP phone voice VLAN, ensure that you have properly configured an IP helper address on the local router (using the command **ip helper-address** *x.x.x.x* on the LAN interface).

If your IP Phone is still unable to obtain an IP address via DHCP, the next thing to try is to reset the phone to its factory default configuration and then hard-code (manually enter) all the necessary IP parameters. This eliminates possible DHCP and DNS issues from the IP Phone's perspective.

NOTE   If possible, connect the IP Phone to an IP subnet that has other working IP Phones on it. Use the same TFTP server IP address.

First erase the configuration in the IP Phone and reset to the factory defaults. This is a quick and easy way to purge any incorrect data, but you do lose all your settings.

If you want to reset a Cisco IP Phone to the factory defaults, follow these steps:

Step 1   Press ****#** to unlock Network Configuration on the IP Phone.

Step 2   Press **settings** and then **3** for **Network Configuration**.

Step 3   The Network Configuration padlock symbol in the upper-right corner of the IP Phone's display should appear unlocked. If it doesn't, press ****#** again. Press **33** or scroll down to **Erase Configuration**. Press the **Yes** soft key and then the **Save** soft key.

After being reset, the IP Phone reboots using the factory default settings.

Give the IP Phone about two minutes to try to obtain its IP addressing information via DHCP. After two minutes check the network configuration on the IP Phone (**settings > 3-Network Configuration**) to see if the phone has the expected IP addressing information.

If the IP Phone still is not able to obtain an IP address via DHCP, you might want to statically configure the information into the phone to determine whether the problem is an IP connectivity problem between the phone and the DHCP server or a problem with the DHCP server. To manually configure the IP parameters on a 79*xx* series Cisco IP Phone, do the following:

Step 1   Unlock the IP Phone by using the ****#** key sequence.

Step 2   Press **settings** and then **3** for **Network Configuration**.

Step 3   Press **30** or scroll down to **DHCP Enabled**. Set it to **No** by pressing the **No** soft key and then the **Save** soft key.

Step 4   Press **8** or scroll up to the **TFTP Server** field.

Step 5   Press the **Edit** soft key and enter a static IP address, then press the **Validat.** soft key.

NOTE   Use the numbers on the keypad to enter the IP addresses. The * key is used for the . between the sections of the IP addresses.

Step 6   Configure the **IP Address**, **Subnet Mask**, **Default Router 1**, and any other IP parameters you require.

Step 7   Press the **Save** soft key when you are finished.

After statically configuring the IP addressing information on the IP Phone, go to your DHCP server and try to ping the phone. This verifies end-to-end IP connectivity between the two. If the pings fail, next try a ping from the IP Phone's default gateway. If this also fails, you have isolated the problem to the local subnet. Verify the switch configuration to ensure it has IP connectivity to the default gateway.

If you can ping the IP Phone from the DHCP server and the phone still does not get an IP address, re-check your helper address configuration and ensure the DHCP server has addresses available in the scope where the phone is trying to get an IP address.

If all else fails, connect a sniffer to the network and observe where the problem is. Does the IP Phone send a DHCP Discover on the correct VLAN? Does the Discover get to the DHCP server? Does the DHCP server respond with an Offer? Does the IP Phone send a DHCP request in response to the Offer? Does the DHCP acknowledge the request? You will likely find either a problem on your DHCP server or on one of the intermediate network devices.

Also be sure to double-check the IP addressing information received from the DHCP server, particularly parameters like the default gateway that are essential for proper IP connectivity. You may end up in a situation where you are receiving IP address information from the DHCP server, but it is incorrect because of a configuration problem on the DHCP server.

After the IP Phone has the correct IP addressing information, it must contact the TFTP server to download its configuration information.

Verifying TFTP Configuration File Download

To find the IP address of a CallManager server to register with, an IP Phone must download a configuration file from the TFTP server that contains an ordered list of CallManager servers. An IP Phone can obtain the IP address of the TFTP server in a variety of ways.

The following list describes the order of precedence that the IP Phone uses to select the TFTP server address.

1 Statically configured TFTP server (Alternate TFTP).

2 DNS resolution for CiscoCM1.domain.name.

3 DHCP Option 150 or DHCP Option 66 with a dotted decimal address specified, whichever appears last in the options list.

4 DHCP si address (siaddr) field.

5 DHCP sname field.

6 DHCP Option 66 with a DNS name specified.

You can verify which IP address the IP Phone has chosen for its TFTP server from the Network Configuration menu (**settings > 3-Network Configuration > 8-TFTP Server 1**). If the address is not the one you expect, go through the preceding list and determine which method the IP Phone used to get the TFTD IP address. You might have to use a sniffer to look at the exact information being returned from the DHCP server.

Once you have verified that the TFTP server address is correct, you should verify that the IP Phone has IP connectivity to the TFTP server.

Because there is no way to initiate a ping from the IP Phone itself, a great way to verify two-way communication between the phone and the TFTP server is to ping the phone from the TFTP server. You can do this from the console of the TFTP server or via a Terminal Services window. A TFTP Timeout status message on the IP Phone tells you that the phone could not reach the TFTP server. Although a successful ping is a good sign that network connectivity is working, you cannot rule out the possibility of a firewall or access list blocking TFTP packets.

NOTE   Remember that if you plug a PC into the back of the IP Phone to perform a ping test, your results might be invalid. Because auxiliary VLANs can be used, the PC might be on a different subnet.

As soon as you know that no network-related issues exist between the IP Phone and the TFTP server, the next step is to verify that the IP Phone is able to properly download its configuration file from the TFTP server.

Take a look at what happens between the IP Phone and the TFTP server. The whole process can be summarized as follows (assuming that all DHCP-/IP-related information is correct):

1 The IP Phone requests OS79XX.txt from the TFTP server.

2 The IP Phone requests *DeviceName*.cnf.xml from the TFTP server.

NOTE	If the IP Phone is not configured in CallManager, this file request fails and the phone requests the file SEPDefault.cnf.xml.

3 Using the CallManager information in the configuration file, the IP Phone attempts to register to CallManager.

The first thing the IP Phone does after it has its IP addressing information is request a file from the TFTP server called OS79XX.txt. This file is used to determine whether to boot up as a Session Initiation Protocol (SIP), Media Gateway Control Protocol (MGCP), or Skinny protocol phone. If the file cannot be downloaded, or if the first four letters in the file match the current image, the universal boot sequence is bypassed and the IP Phone continues with its native initialization.

Next, the IP Phone connects to the TFTP server and attempts to get the configuration file that corresponds to the device type. The name of the file requested is *DeviceName*.cnf.xml, where *DeviceName* is "SEP" followed by the IP Phone's MAC address. Other Skinny clients use different device names. For example, the Cisco ATA gateways use "ATA" followed by the MAC address and the VG248 uses "VGC" followed by the MAC address.

If the IP Phone is not configured in the CallManager database, the file request fails because that file does not exist. This is because the TFTP service automatically generates these XML files when devices are configured in CallManager Administration. In this case, the IP Phone then asks for the XMLDefault.cnf.xml file. As soon as this file is retrieved, the IP Phone has enough information to register to CallManager.

The configuration file contains important information, including the following:

- The CallManager group, which lists up to three CallManagers plus an optional SRST router for the IP Phone to connect to
- Load information, which specifies the firmware version the IP Phone should be using
- The URLs for Directories, Services, Information, and Idle

After the XML configuration file is retrieved, the IP Phone parses the file and reads the load ID and the version stamp. It compares the load ID with its current load. If there is a mismatch, the IP Phone retrieves the new load from the TFTP server. As soon as it is downloaded, the IP Phone resets and repeats the entire boot up process.

Look at the complete configuration settings on the IP Phone by pressing the **settings** button and then **3** for Network Configuration. Table 4-1 lists all the settings on the 79*xx* IP Phone. The TFTP File Parameter? column tells you whether the specified network setting came from the TFTP configuration file.

Table 4-1 *79xx IP Phone Settings*

Network Setting	Description	TFTP File Parameter ?
DHCP Server	Displays the IP address of the DHCP server that the IP Phone used to obtain an IP address.	—
BootP Server	Indicates whether the IP Phone obtained its IP configuration from a Bootstrap Protocol (BootP) server rather than a DHCP server.	—
MAC Address	Identifies the IP Phone's unique MAC address.	—
Host Name	Identifies the unique host name assigned to the IP Phone.	—
Domain Name	Identifies the name of the DNS domain in which the IP Phone resides.	—
IP Address	Indicates the phone's IP address.	—
Subnet Mask	Indicates the subnet mask used by the IP Phone.	—
TFTP Server 1	Indicates the primary TFTP server used by the IP Phone to obtain configuration files.	—
Default Routers 1 to 5	Identifies the default gateway(s) used by the IP Phone.	—
DNS Servers 1 to 5	Indicates the DNS server(s) used by the IP Phone to resolve the TFTP server, CallManager system, and web server host names.	—
Operational VLAN Id	Indicates the VLAN of which the IP Phone is currently a member. The operational VLAN is obtained from the switch to which the IP Phone is attached through CDP or through the Admin. VLAN setting if you are using a non-Cisco switched network.	—
Admin VLAN Id	Allows you to configure the VLAN that the IP Phone will use to tag its packets. This overrides the VLAN configuration received via CDP from a Cisco switch or allows you to statically configure a VLAN ID when using a non-Cisco switch.	—
CallManager 1 to 5	Identifies the CallManager servers that this IP Phone can attempt to register with.	Yes
Information URL	Specifies the location (URL) of the help text for the help (**i** or **?**) button.	Yes
Directories URL	Specifies the server address (URL) from which the IP Phone obtains the directory menu displayed when the **directories** button is pressed.	Yes

Table 4-1   *79xx IP Phone Settings (Continued)*

Network Setting	Description	TFTP File Parameter?
Messages URL	Through CallManager release 3.3(1), this URL does not do anything. Future versions of software may utilize this field.	Yes
Services URL	Specifies the URL for Cisco IP Phone services.	Yes
DHCP Enabled	Indicates whether the IP Phone is using DHCP.	—
DHCP Address Released	Allows the IP address assigned by DHCP to be released.	—
Alternate TFTP	Indicates whether the IP Phone is using an alternate TFTP server. You must set this option to YES before you can configure the TFTP server option.	—
Erase configuration	Allows you to erase all locally-assigned settings on the IP Phone and reset values to the factory default settings.	—
Forwarding Delay	Indicates whether the IP Phone's internal switch begins forwarding packets between the PC port and switch (SW) port on your phone when your phone becomes active. If set to YES the IP Phone waits 10 seconds after link establishment before forwarding packets on the PC port.	Yes
Idle URL	Specifies a URL that the IP Phone displays when the phone has not been used for the time specified in the Idle URL Time setting. For example, your administrator can specify a logo to display on the LCD when the IP Phone has not been used for five minutes.	Yes
Idle URL Time	Displays the amount of time (in seconds) that elapses before the URL specified in the Idle URL setting appears. A setting of zero disables the Idle URL.	Yes
Authentication URL	Displays the URL that the IP Phone uses to validate requests made to the phone's web server.	Yes
Proxy Server URL	Specifies the host and port used to proxy HTTP requests for access to non-local host addresses from the IP Phone's HTTP client.	Yes
PC Port Disabled	Indicates whether the PC port on the IP Phone is enabled or disabled. The port is labeled **10/100 PC** on the back of the IP Phone. It is used to connect a PC or workstation to the IP Phone so that both phone and workstation can share a single network connection.	Yes

continues

Table 4-1   *79xx IP Phone Settings (Continued)*

Network Setting	Description	TFTP File Parameter?
SW Port Configuration	Indicates the switch port's speed and duplex. Valid values are • AUTO—autonegotiate • 10H—10BASE-T/half duplex • 10F—10BASE-T/full duplex • 100H—100BASE-T/half duplex • 100F—100BASE-T/full duplex	—
PC Port Configuration	Indicates the PC port's speed and duplex. Valid values are • AUTO—autonegotiate • 10H—10BASE-T/half duplex • 10F—10BASE-T/full duplex • 100H—100BASE-T/half duplex • 100F—100BASE-T/full duplex	—
TFTP Server 2	Indicates a secondary TFTP server used by the IP Phone to obtain configuration files if it is unable to contact the primary TFTP server.	—
User Locale	Indicates the localized language used on the IP Phone display screen and soft keys.	Yes
Network Locale	Indicates the localized sounds heard by the user, such as dial tone and ringback.	Yes
Handset Only Mode	Indicates whether the speakerphone and/or headset feature has been disabled for this IP Phone.	Yes
User Locale Version	Indicates the version of the user locale associated with the IP Phone. The user locale identifies a set of detailed information to support users, including language and font.	Yes
Network Locale Version	Indicates the version of the network locale associated with the IP Phone. The network locale contains a definition of the tones and cadences used by the phone in a specific geographic area.	Yes

Note that this is the information that the IP Phone uses to register to CallManager. If any of the TFTP values in Table 4-1 are incorrect or missing, the IP Phone might not be able to reach CallManager.

If one of the values does not match what is configured on CallManager, the IP Phone might not have successfully downloaded a new configuration file. If an IP Phone fails to download a new configuration file, it keeps its existing settings and uses them. Check the status messages on the IP Phone (**settings > 5-Status > 1-Status Messages**). Status messages can tell you whether the configuration file download failed. The message is simply "TFTP file download failed."

To troubleshoot a TFTP download problem, set the TFTP service traces to Detailed level. If there is a problem with the IP Phone downloading its file, it shows up in the TFTP trace and the Event Viewer.

The CCM trace file would have the following information:

```
Cisco TftpkServingFileWarning - Warning about error inside serving part of TFTP.
   ErrorNumber:1 FileName:SEP0003E348DDAE.cnf.xml IPAddress_Port:10.16.20.6:49787
   Mode:octet OpCode:1 Reason:File not found inside tftp() of CTFTPConnect
   class App ID:Cisco Tftp Cluster ID:CLSTR1-A-Cluster Node ID:10.89.242.12
```

Notice that this file warning indicates that there was a problem with the IP Phone that has a MAC address of **0003E348DDAE**. This message also tells you the IP address of the requesting phone and the IP address of the TFTP server. The IP Phone failed to get its configuration file. If the IP Phone is not configured in the CallManager database, this is normal, and the IP Phone would then request the XMLDefault.cnf.xml file.

Understanding Skinny Registration

The IP Phone attempts to register to CallManager based on the information in its TFTP configuration file. Table 4-1 specified the information that comes from the TFTP file. It is important to note that the TFTP configuration file information must be correct for the IP Phone to successfully register with CallManager.

Figure 4-1 illustrates the exchange of all registration messages between CallManager and the IP Phone during registration.

Figure 4-1   *Exchange of Registration Messages Between CallManager and an IP Phone*

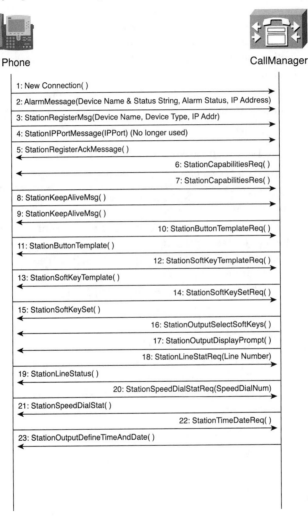

For device registration purposes, it is not necessary to know what every single message means. It *is* important to get a picture of this Skinny message exchange so that you know what has to happen for an IP Phone to register. Table 4-2 defines some of the more important messages.

Table 4-2   *Skinny Registration Messages Between the IP Phone and Cisco CallManager*

Message	Parameters
StationAlarmMessage Phone → CCM	**Message**—The message has the device name, the load of the IP Phone, the parms string, and the parameters parm1 and parm2. The **parms string** can be any one of the following, based on when the alarm message is sent: **Last=Phone-Loading**—This is sent if the IP Phone registers again due to version mismatch. **Last=CM-closed-TCP**—The IP Phone fails over to its backup. **Last=KeepaliveTO**—The IP Phone closed the TCP connection because of a KeepAlive timeout. **Last=Reset-Reset**—The IP Phone closed the TCP connection because it received a Reset/Reset from CallManager Administration. **Last=Reset-Restart**—The IP Phone closed the TCP connection because it received a Reset/Restart from CallManager Administration. **Last=Phone-Reg-Rej**—The IP Phone closed the TCP connection because it received a Registration Reject message. **Empty string**—Appears during normal operation. **parm1**—Contains the alarm status code. **parm2**—The IP Phone's IP address.
StationRegisterMessage Phone → CCM	This message has the following information: **DeviceName**—The device name that identifies the IP Phone. **StationIPAddress**—The IP Phone's IP address. **DeviceType**—The IP Phone's model type (7960, 7940, 7914, and so on).
StationRegisterAck Phone ← CCM	Sent when the IP Phone's registration request succeeds and CallManager successfully registers the phone. **KeepAliveInterval**—Indicates the time interval at which the IP Phone sends a KeepAlive message to CallManager. **SecondaryKeepAliveInterval**—Indicates the time interval at which the IP Phone sends a KeepAlive message to the backup CallManager.
StationRegisterReject Phone ← CCM	Sent by CallManager when the registration fails. **text**—Has a description of the reason for the message's rejection.
StationKeepAliveMsg Phone → CCM	Sent to CallManager to ensure that the communication between CallManager and the IP Phone is active.
StationKeepAliveAck Phone ← CCM	Sent by CallManager to ensure that the connection between the IP Phone and CallManager is active.

Troubleshooting Skinny Registration

Now that you've had a glimpse of the registration process, you can move on to troubleshooting registration problems.

If the IP Phone has the correct information but it still doesn't register, you need to do some additional investigating. Here are some common reasons why registration fails at this point:

- The CallManager service isn't started. Nothing can register if CallManager is down.

- The IP Phone can't reach CallManager. Maybe it could reach the TFTP server, but not CallManager. Try to ping the IP Phone from the CallManager server it is trying to register with. This will confirm bi-directional IP connectivity.

- If NAT, firewalls, or access lists are in use, be sure to check there as well to make sure that traffic is not being blocked, thus preventing proper communication. Skinny devices use TCP port 2000 to register with CallManager.

- If the IP Phone must resolve the CallManager name to register, a failure could occur if the DNS server is inaccessible or the DNS entry is incorrect. Generally it is a good idea not to rely on DNS at all. To use IP addresses instead of DNS names, configure the servers in the cluster by IP address in CallManager Administration (**System > Server**).

- The IP Phone firmware load specified by CallManager is not in the TFTP path. If the IP Phone load currently running on the phone is not compatible with the CallManager the phone is trying to register to, the registration might fail. Ensure that the IP Phone is running the firmware version specified in CallManager Administration (**System > Device Defaults**).

- If the IP Phone has never been entered into the CallManager database via CallManager Administration, CallManager does not allow that phone to register unless auto-registration is enabled. Auto-registration does not work unless it has available directory numbers to provide the registering IP Phone a DN. If the IP Phone is not configured in CallManager Administration and auto-registration is not enabled or CallManager has run out of DNs, the phone displays "Registration Rejected."

If two-way communication is verified and CallManager is running, you might need to look at the trace files. You can do this with XML-enabled CCM traces and CallManager Serviceability. Follow the directions in Chapter 3, "Understanding the Troubleshooting Tools," for searching for individual devices with XML-enabled traces. You can also just look at non-XML traces directly. This is also discussed in Chapter 3.

Table 4-3 dissects an excerpt from the CCM trace that shows the exact messages that appear when an IP Phone fails registration because of a database error.

Table 4-3   *Failed Device Registration Trace File Example*

Date and Time	Device Name	Source IP Address	Trace Type	Information
11/29/01 6:44 AM	SEP0003E348DDAE	10.16.20.6	Trace	Cisco CallManagerStationInit - Processing StationReg. regCount: 1 DeviceName=SEP0003 E348DDAE, TCPHandle=0x5626b6c , Socket=0x1e0, IPAddr=10.16.20.6, Port=49928
11/29/01 6:44 AM	SEP0003E348DDAE	10.16.20.6	Trace	Cisco CallManagerStationD: 5626b6c RegisterReject text='Error: DB Config'.
11/29/01 6:44 AM	SEP0003E348DDAE		Alarm	Cisco CallManagerDeviceTra nsientConnection - Transient connection attempt. Connecting Port:2000 Device name [Optional].:SEP0003E3 48DDAE Device IP address.:10.16.20.6 Device type. [Optional]:7 Reason Code [Optional].:1 App ID:Cisco CallManager Cluster ID:CLSTR1-A- Cluster Node ID:10.89.242.12
11/29/01 6:44 AM	SEP0003E348DDAE	10.16.20.6	Trace	Cisco CallManagerStationInit - StationCloseReq received: 0x5626b6c

Take a look at some of the messages in this trace file. The first trace message has the following information:

```
Cisco CallManagerStationInit - Processing StationReg. regCount: 1
  DeviceName=SEP0003E348DDAE, TCPHandle=0x5626b6c, Socket=0x1e0,
  IPAddr=10.16.20.6, Port=49928
```

This is a **StationInit** message. It indicates that a station—in this case, an IP Phone—initiated a connection with CallManager. **StationReg** tells you that this is a registration message. **DeviceName** tells you the IP Phone's MAC address. **IPAddr** is the IP Phone's IP address. **Port=49928** is the TCP port on which the IP Phone is listening.

CallManager responds by first rejecting the message:

```
Cisco CallManagerStationD: 5626b6c RegisterReject text='Error: DB Config'.
```

This is a **StationD** message, which always is a CallManager-initiated message. The **RegisterReject** message tells you that this is a registration reject. The **text=** field gives you the reason. In this case, the reason is a **DB Config** error, which means that something in the database is incorrect. Either the MAC address was entered incorrectly, or the MAC address is not in the database and auto-registration is not enabled or has no available directory numbers.

Next, CallManager generates an alarm message. As you learned in Chapter 3, these alarms can be configured to be sent to the Event Viewer. This same information is being shown as an event in the Event Viewer:

```
Cisco CallManagerDeviceTransientConnection - Transient connection attempt.
    Connecting Port:2000 Device name [Optional].:SEP0003E348DDAE
    Device IP address.:10.16.20.6 Device type. [Optional]:7
    Reason Code [Optional].:1 App ID:Cisco CallManager Cluster ID:
    CLSTR1-A-Cluster Node ID:20.10.242.12
```

This alarm has details about the problem:

- It designates this as a **CallManagerDeviceTransientConnection**. This can happen for a variety of other reasons, such as an IP Phone that fails back to another CallManager before completing its registration to the backup CallManager or because a device that is not in the database tried to register. This message is just a symptom of a failed registration but don't assume that this message always indicates a failed registration.

- It lists the device name and device IP address.

- It tells you the name and IP address of the CallManager node that the IP Phone attempted to register to.

Finally, the IP Phone sends a message closing its connection to CallManager:

```
Cisco CallManagerStationInit - StationCloseReq received: 0x5626b6c
```

This trace tells you that an IP Phone tried to register and was rejected for database-related reasons. The IP Phone is in the database, or its MAC address might have been entered incorrectly.

Additional Tools for Troubleshooting Skinny Client Registration Problems

In addition to the various trace files available for troubleshooting registration problems, there are additional tools available to help you understand why a Skinny client is not registering properly. These include

- Status messages on an IP Phone
- Real-Time Monitoring Tool (RTMT)

Status messages on the IP Phone give you specific information about why a particular phone does not register, while RTMT allows you to get a system-wide view on registration issues.

Checking IP Phone Status Messages

The 79*xx* IP Phone is an intelligent device. Most of the time, it knows what the problem is, and it can tell you.

The first clue to the condition of the IP Phone is the display. If the IP Phone display shows the copyright screen and nothing else, the phone doesn't even have an Ethernet link. You now know that the IP Phone has a Layer 1 issue, such as a bad or disconnected cable or a disabled port on the switch.

If the IP Phone display indicates that it is attempting to connect to the network, you can look at the status messages. To view the status messages, do the following:

Step 1   Press the **settings** button on the IP Phone, and then press **5** for **Status**.

Step 2   Press **1** for **Status Messages**.

The applicable status messages appear. Table 4-4 lists all the possible status messages and possible courses of action.

Table 4-4   *79xx IP Phone Status Messages*

Message	Explanation	Possible Course of Action
DHCP timeout	The DHCP server did not respond.	Restore/verify network connectivity between the DHCP server and the IP Phone.
		Ensure that the DHCP server is up and running.
		Check on the status of the DHCP server, and make sure that all necessary fields are correctly populated.
		Make sure that the router local to the IP Phone has an IP helper address if the DHCP server is not on the same IP subnet as the phone.

continues

Table 4-4 *79xx IP Phone Status Messages (Continued)*

Message	Explanation	Possible Course of Action
TFTP timeout	The TFTP server did not respond.	Restore/verify network connectivity between the IP Phone and the TFTP server.
		Verify that the network settings on the IP Phone are correct.
		Ensure that the TFTP server is up and running.
TFTP file not found	The requested file was not found in the TFTPPath directory.	Check the load ID assigned to the IP Phone, and make sure that the file is in the TFTPPath. This directory location is usually C:\Program Files\Cisco\TFTPPath.
TFTP access error	The TFTP server is not responding.	If you are using static IP addresses, make sure that you have added the correct TFTP server.
		If you are using DHCP, make sure that the correct TFTP IP address is specified in the Option 66 or Option 150 field.
		If the TFTP address is correct, check the other network settings on the IP Phone to be sure they are correct.
TFTP general error	All other TFTP failures.	Check the status of the TFTP server if this error is received.
DNS unknown host	The IP Phone could not resolve the Domain Name System (DNS) name of the TFTP server or CallManager.	Ensure that CallManager or the TFTP server name is properly configured in the DNS server, or switch to using IP addresses instead of DNS names.
		The best solution is to not rely on DNS at all. Switch to using IP addresses in CallManager Administration (**System > Server**).
DNS timeout	The DNS server did not respond.	Restore/verify network connectivity between the IP Phone and the DNS server.
		Ensure that the DNS server is up and running.
		The best solution is to not rely on DNS at all. Switch to using IP addresses in CallManager Administration (**System > Server**).
No DNS server IP	A name was specified, but DHCP or static IP configuration did not specify a DNS server address.	If the IP Phone has a static IP address, make sure the DNS server has been added.
		If the IP Phone uses DHCP, check the DHCP server configuration.
		The best solution is to not rely on DNS at all. Switch to using IP addresses in CallManager Administration (**System > Server**).

Table 4-4   *79xx IP Phone Status Messages (Continued)*

Message	Explanation	Possible Course of Action
Load ID incorrect	The software file's load ID is of the wrong type.	Check the load ID assigned to the IP Phone on the Phone Configuration page in Cisco CallManager Administration (**Device > Phone >** *find and select a phone*). Make sure that the load ID is entered correctly.
Checksum Error	The downloaded software file is corrupted.	Obtain a new copy of the IP Phone firmware and place it in the TFTPPath directory. This directory location is usually C:\Program Files\Cisco\TFTPPath. You should copy files into this directory only when the TFTP server is shut down. Otherwise, the files might be corrupted.
SEPDefault.cnf. xml or SEP*MAC Address*.cnf. xml	This is the name of the configuration file.	This is simply an informational message that indicates the IP Phone's configuration file name.
No default router	DHCP or static configuration did not specify a default router.	If the IP Phone has a static IP address, verify that the default router has been assigned. If the IP Phone uses DHCP, check the DHCP server configuration.
Duplicate IP	Another device is using the IP address assigned to the IP Phone.	If the IP Phone has a static IP address, verify that it is not a duplicate. If you are using DHCP, check the DHCP server configuration.

In addition to the status messages available on the IP Phone, you can use RTMT to check registration status.

Checking Registration with the Real-Time Monitoring Tool

The CallManager Serviceability RTMT is an invaluable source of information for registration problems. It gives you real-time information about the CallManager cluster. When you select real-time monitoring for IP Phones, you have the option of selecting IP Phones based on certain criteria.

For instance, you can choose to show all Registered, Unregistered, or Rejected IP Phones. You can even make this a cluster-wide search or a CallManager-specific search. If you need to get more specific, you can select devices based on directory number, device name, device description, IP address, or subnet. Figures 4-2 and 4-3 demonstrate this feature.

Figure 4-2 *Real-Time Monitoring Tool Setup Page*

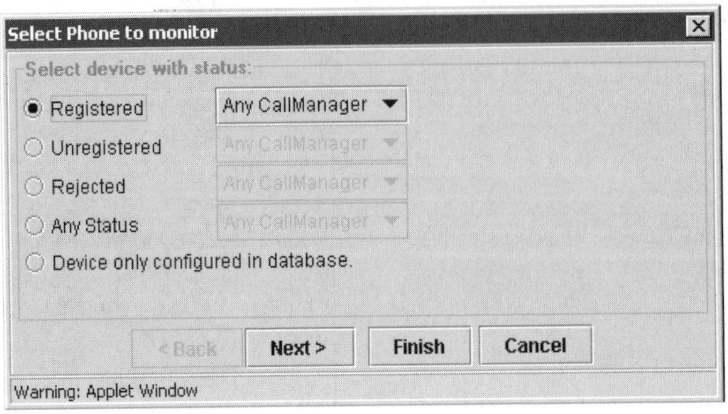

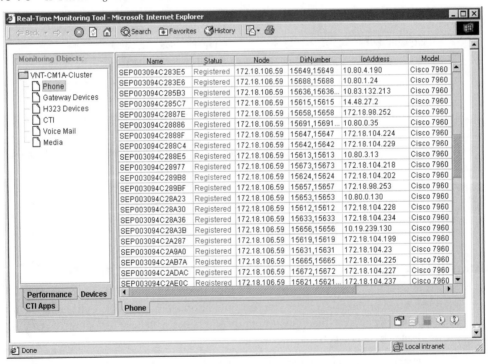

Figure 4-3 *IP Phone Registration Results in the RTMT*

This might seem strange, but a great question to ask is "What IP Phones are *not* registered?" If you have registration problems, it might be useful to see every IP Phone that currently isn't registered. By doing this, you might immediately see that they are all on the same subnet or on the same CallManager.

Best Practices

The following list documents some best practices and tips that might help you avoid some common device registration-related problems:

- Use IP addresses for CallManager nodes instead of host names because DNS can be a single point of failure, depending on the resiliency of the DNS infrastructure.

- Use IP addresses and Option 150 for the TFTP server address(es). Although Option 66 allows you to use an IP address just like Option 150, TFTP server redundancy is only available when using Option 150.

- Make sure your DHCP scopes are consistent, complete, and accurate across your enterprise before you start rolling out IP Phones.

- Remember to check the status messages on the IP Phone. That is the quickest way to see what the issue might be.

- Make sure you have two-way connectivity. It is possible that the IP Phone can successfully send CallManager a message but that CallManager cannot successfully respond to it. The same applies to two-way connectivity with the TFTP server.

Summary

This chapter should have given you a good understanding of how Skinny client registration works. The most important thing to remember is the methodology of troubleshooting these types of problems. Start with the physical layer. Proceed to investigate network-related issues. Finally, search the application layer by looking into CallManager and TFTP issues.

Other Skinny clients such as the Cisco VG248, the ATA 186, and Unity voice mail ports go through the same registration process described in this chapter, so keep in mind that the same approach can be used to figure out registration problems for those devices as well.

With experience, you will begin to quickly rule out certain common problems and get right to the root cause. Apply this approach and use the tools the system provides (as discussed in Chapter 3). You will find that you can quickly resolve registration issues with the right tools, the right knowledge, and the right approach.

## CHAPTER 5

IP Phones

The preceding chapter discussed problems related to Skinny client registration. Getting an IP phone registered is the first step. This chapter looks at problems that can occur after an IP phone is successfully registered.

Here are some possible sources of these problems:

- Unexpected resets
- IP phone failover and failback
- Directory and service problems

Before you dive into the pool of potential problems, it's important to have a good understanding of how the IP phone works.

Understanding IP Phone Behavior

As you saw in the preceding chapter, the IP phone must be registered to Cisco CallManager to be of any use. The IP phone depends on CallManager for almost everything. The 79*xx* series of Cisco IP Phones uses the Skinny Client Control Protocol (SCCP or Skinny protocol). The Skinny protocol provides a lightweight yet feature-rich way of facilitating a master/slave relationship between CallManager and the IP phone.

The following section looks at the nature of the interaction between the IP phone and CallManager.

Understanding the Skinny Protocol

Cisco Systems created a generalized messaging set to allow *Skinny clients*—such as IP phones—to communicate with CallManager. The Skinny protocol is a lightweight master/slave protocol. This means that CallManager controls nearly every function of the IP phone. CallManager, in turn, facilitates call signaling to other entities using MGCP, H.323, TAPI/JTAPI, and so on.

The phone cannot do very much on its own. For example, when a phone goes off-hook, it notifies CallManager that the user has gone off-hook. CallManager then sends a message to the phone telling it to play dial tone. The phone does not know when to play dial tone by itself.

The advantage of using the Skinny protocol over other protocols, such as H.323 or TAPI, is that the lightweight nature allows features to be added with little resource overhead on the phone. Generally adding more capacity to the CallManager server is easier than replacing hundreds or thousands of phones.

It is important to understand the roles that IP phones and CallManager each play in troubleshooting problems with the IP phone. Understanding which component is responsible for which action helps you quickly identify the likely culprit when a problem occurs. For instance, if a user goes off-hook but does not hear a dial tone for several seconds, you might be initially inclined to suspect the IP phone as the cause. However, because IP phones rely on CallManager to provide call signaling, the delay of a dial tone might actually be due to CallManager because CallManager did not send the message to start the dial tone, CallManager was too congested to send the message right away, or a network problem stopped the message from arriving at the phone.

CallManager and endpoints such as IP phones have a client/server relationship. The next section discusses this interaction in detail.

Call Processing Behavior

Take a look at a basic call from one IP phone to another. Take special note of the signaling between the calling phone and CallManager and between CallManager and the called phone (Table 5-1 defines many of the signals). Figure 5-1 shows the first part of this phone call.

Figure 5-2 shows the media setup portion of the signaling. Notice in particular the **StartMediaTransmission** and **OpenLogicalChannel** messages. At the bottom of Figure 5-2, the receiving IP phone hangs up, which causes the on-hook message to be sent to CallManager.

Figure 5-1   *Call Processing Behavior*

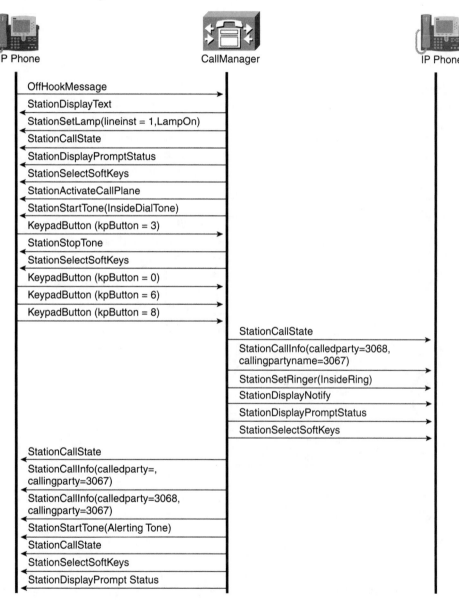

Figure 5-2   *Call Processing Behavior*

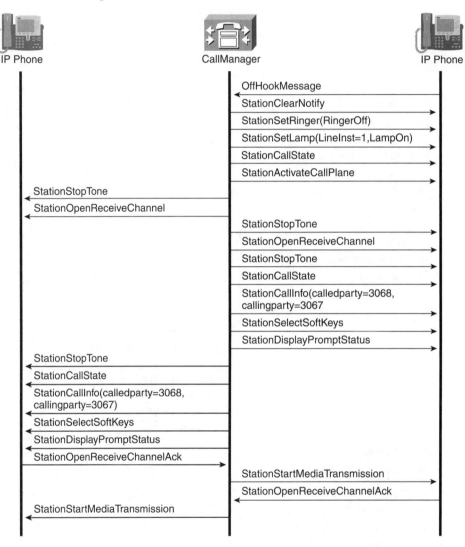

These messages are very significant. Before the **StartMediaTransmission** and **OpenLogicalChannel** messages, no audio stream is set up between these two IP phones. Until these messages are sent, the call setup is still in progress. As soon as both IP phones receive these messages, a voice stream is established.

Figure 5-3 shows the call being torn down. The IP phones are commanded to return to a normal state.

Figure 5-3   *Call Processing Behavior*

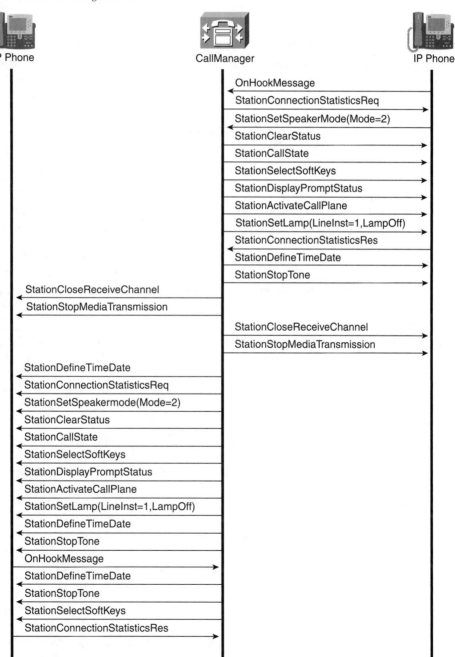

What do some of these messages mean? Table 5-1 defines them. It also shows which device sends the message. Phone → CCM means that the IP phone generates the message and sends it to CallManager while Phone ← CCM means CallManager generates a message and sends it to the IP phone.

Table 5-1 *Skinny Message Definitions*

To or From CCM	Message	Parameters
Phone → CCM	**OffHookMessage**	This message is sent when the user goes off-hook (such as by lifting the handset or pressing the **NewCall** soft key).
Phone ← CCM	**StationOutputDisplayText**	This message is not processed by the 79*xx* IP Phone. The legacy phone models 30VIP, 30SP+, and 12SP+ used this field to display the extension.
Phone ← CCM	**StationSetLamp**	This message is not processed by the 79*xx* IP Phone. The legacy phone models 30VIP, 30SP+, and 12SP+ used this field to light a lamp indicator on the IP Phone.
Phone ← CCM	**StationDisplayPromptStatus**	This message causes the phone to update the display for the line and a call on the line.
Phone ← CCM	**StationSelectSoftKeys**	This message loads the appropriate soft key set, depending on the call state.
Phone ← CCM	**StationActivateCallPlane**	This message contains the specified line appearance of the DN being called.
Phone ← CCM	**StationStartTone**	This message commands the IP phone to play a tone and specifies the tone type and duration. For example, tone types include dial tone, busy tone, reorder tone, and so on.
Phone → CCM	**StationKeypadButtonMessage**	This message indicates the keypad button that was pressed (number keys from 0 to 9, A to D, and the * and # keys). Note that * is represented at 0xe and # is represented as 0xf in some trace files.

Table 5-1   *Skinny Message Definitions (Continued)*

To or From CCM	Message	Parameters
Phone ← CCM	**StationCallState**	This message contains the state of the call. The call states are as follows: • **OffHook=1** • **OnHook=2** • **RingOut=3** • **RingIn=4** • **Connected=5** • **Busy=6** • **Congestion=7** • **Hold=8** • **CallWaiting=9** • **CallTransfer=10** • **CallPark=11** • **Proceed=12** • **CallRemoteMultiline=13** • **InvalidNumber=14**
Phone ← CCM	**StationCallInfo**	This message has the called party directory number and name and the calling party directory number and name.
Phone ← CCM	**StationSetRinger**	The IP phone sets the ringer to the specified ringing mode: **StationRingOff**—This message stops the ringer from ringing **StationInsideRing**—This ring indicates an OnNet call **StationOutsideRing**—This ring indicates an OffNet call **StationFeatureRing**—This ring is used by third-party applications to invoke special features, etc.
Phone ← CCM	**StationDisplayNotify**	This message causes the IP phone to discard the message text from **StationOutputDisplayText** and instead display the text contained in the **StationDisplayNotify** message.

continues

Table 5-1   *Skinny Message Definitions (Continued)*

To or From CCM	Message	Parameters
Phone ← CCM	**StationStopTone**	This message is sent by CallManager when a tone (such as a dial tone) needs to be stopped.
Phone ← CCM	**StationClearNotify**	This message is sent to the IP phone to clear the information sent in the **StationDisplayNotify** message.
Phone ← CCM	**StationOpenReceiveChannel**	This message contains the media payload information and the bit rate. This message asks the IP phone if it is ready to receive a Real-Time Transport Protocol (RTP) stream. This message is sent to both the calling and called parties.
Phone → CCM	**StationOpenReceiveChannelAck**	The IP phone selects a UDP port number on which it is listening for RTP packets and informs CallManager of its IP address and port number. This message provides information about the following: • The open receive channel status • The IP address the phone is listening on for RTP packets • The UDP port number the phone is listening on for RTP packets
Phone ← CCM	**StationStartMediaTransmission**	This message commands the IP phone to start streaming RTP. It includes the following information: • UDP port of the remote endpoint • IP address of the remote endpoint • Packet size • Compression type (Codec)
Phone ← CCM	**StationCloseReceiveChannel**	This message commands the IP phone to stop processing RTP messages sent to it.
Phone ← CCM	**StationStopMediaTransmission**	This message tells the IP phone to stop streaming RTP packets.
Phone ← CCM	**StationSetSpeakerMode**	This message turns the speakerphone off or on.
Phone ← CCM	**StationClearPromptStatus**	This message clears the IP phone's display prompt.
Phone ← CCM	**StationConnectionStatisticsRequest**	This message requests connection statistics from the IP phone.

Table 5-1   *Skinny Message Definitions (Continued)*

To or From CCM	Message	Parameters
Phone → CCM	**StationConnectionStatisticsResponse**	This message contains connection statistics from the last RTP stream that was active. Connection statistics include the number of discarded packets, jitter, delay, and so on.
Phone → CCM	**StationSoftKeyEventMessage**	This message indicates which soft key was pressed. Upon receipt of this message, CallManager invokes the action associated with the pressed soft key. For example, if **Hold** was the pressed soft key, CallManager places the active call on user hold.

In some trace files you might see a soft key number without the corresponding description. The following list defines each soft key number:

- **Redial = 1**
- **New Call = 2**
- **Hold = 3**
- **Transfer = 4**
- **Call Forward All = 5**
- **(not used) = 6**
- **(not used) = 7**
- **Backspace = 8**
- **End Call = 9**
- **Resume = 10**
- **Answer = 11**
- **Information = 12**
- **Conference = 13**
- **Park = 14**
- **(not used) = 15**
- **Meet Me Conference = 16**
- **Call Pick Up = 17**
- **Group Call Pick Up = 18**
- **Drop Last Conference Participant = 19**
- **None = 20**
- **Barge = 21**

Examining Skinny Protocol Messages in a CCM Trace

Unfortunately CallManager does not draw nice figures like those shown in Figures 5-1 through 5-3; however, CCM traces provide the same information in greater detail, provided that you understand how to read the trace files.

When searching through a CCM trace to determine what is happening with a particular phone, you should first determine the TCP handle of the phone. There are several ways to find this information. If you know the CCM trace you are looking at contains a call to or from a particular phone, search for the extension number of the phone. You should see a line in the trace that looks like this:

```
StationD:    56ac778 DisplayText text='                2001           '.
```

In this case 2001 is the extension number and 56ac778 is the TCP handle.

If you cannot find the extension number in the trace file, search for the MAC address of the phone. If you have Detailed tracing enabled, you should see a line in the trace every 30 seconds for KeepAlives. This line contains the MAC address and TCP handle of the phone.

Also remember that **StationD** and **StationInit** messages are not displayed in the CCM trace unless the trace level is set to **Arbitrary** or **Detailed**. KeepAlives are not displayed unless the trace level is set to **Detailed**.

Example 5-1 shows the beginning of a call from one IP phone to another. The calling IP phone's TCP handle is 56ac778. See Chapter 3, "Understanding the Troubleshooting Tools," to learn how to enable and view trace files. Remember StationInit shows messages from the IP phone to CallManager and StationD shows messages from CallManager to the IP phone.

Example 5-1 *Calling the IP Phone's Initial CallManager Interaction*

```
StationInit: 56ac778 OffHook.
StationD:    56ac778 DisplayText text='                2001           '.
StationD:    56ac778 SetLamp stimulus=9(Line) stimulusInstance=1
  lampMode=2(LampOn).
StationD:    56ac778 CallState callState=1(OffHook) lineInstance=1
  callReference=16777217
StationD:    56ac778 DisplayPromptStatus timeOutValue=0 promptStatus=
  'Enter number' lineInstance=1 callReference=16777217.
StationD:    56ac778 SelectSoftKeys instance=1 reference=16777217
  softKeySetIndex=4 validKeyMask=-1.
StationD:    56ac778 ActivateCallPlane lineInstance=1.
StationD:    56ac778 StartTone tone=33(InsideDialTone).
StationInit: 56ac778 KeypadButton kpButton=2.
StationD:    56ac778 StopTone.
StationD:    56ac778 SelectSoftKeys instance=1 reference=16777217
  softKeySetIndex=6 validKeyMask=-1.
StationInit: 56ac778 KeypadButton kpButton=0.
StationInit: 56ac778 KeypadButton kpButton=0.
StationInit: 56ac778 KeypadButton kpButton=2.
```

Notice in Example 5-1 that CallManager receives an **OffHook** message from the IP phone and responds by telling the phone to play inside dial tone. Next you can then see the phone presses the keypad button **2**. In response to receiving a digit, CallManager instructs the phone to stop playing dial tone.

Once again notice how the phone must be instructed by CallManager to do everything. If for some reason the **StopTone** Skinny message does not arrive at the phone, the phone will continue to play dial tone. However, remember that Skinny messages are carried over a TCP connection, so TCP takes care of retransmissions in the case of packet loss.

You can see the calling phone continues to dial more digits until the calling party has dialed **2002**. At this point CallManager determines that the dialed digits are a match and shows the digit analysis results. For every successful call (and some unsuccessful calls as well) you will see digit analysis results in the CCM trace.

Example 5-2 shows the digit analysis results. Chapter 9, "Call Routing," explains digit analysis in greater detail.

Example 5-2 *Digit Analysis of Dialed Digits*

```
|Digit analysis: match(fqcn="2001", cn="2001", pss="", dd="2002")
|Digit analysis: analysis results
|PretransformCallingPartyNumber=2001
|CallingPartyNumber=2001
|DialingPartition=
|DialingPattern=2002
|DialingRoutePatternRegularExpression=(2002)
|DialingWhere=
|PatternType=Enterprise
|PotentialMatches=NoPotentialMatchesExist
|DialingSdlProcessId=(1,34,13)
|PretransformDigitString=2002
|PretransformTagsList=SUBSCRIBER
|PretransformPositionalMatchList=2002
|CollectedDigits=2002
|UnconsumedDigits=
|TagsList=SUBSCRIBER
|PositionalMatchList=2002
|VoiceMailbox=2002
|DisplayName=
|RouteBlockFlag=RouteThisPattern
|InterceptPartition=
|InterceptPattern=
|InterceptWhere=
|InterceptSdlProcessId=(0,0,0)
|InterceptSsType=0
|InterceptSsKey=0
```

After the match completion and digit analysis, CallManager immediately sends a message to the calling IP phone, changing its display and preparing it for connectivity, as demonstrated in Example 5-3. Notice the phone is first put into the **Proceed** call state.

CallManager then tells the calling phone to play ringback (**AlertingTone**) and puts the phone into the **RingOut** state. Also notice that CallManager sends a **DisplayPromptStatus** instructing the phone to display the words "Ring Out" on the prompt line.

Example 5-3 *CallManager and Calling IP Phone Interaction*

```
StationD:    56ac778 SelectSoftKeys instance=1 reference=16777217
  softKeySetIndex=8 validKeyMask=-1.
StationD:    56ac778 CallState callState=12(Proceed) lineInstance=1
  callReference=16777217
StationD:    56ac778 CallInfo callingPartyName='' callingParty=2001
  cgpnVoiceMailbox=2001          calledPartyName='' calledParty=2002
  cdpnVoiceMailbox=2002          originalCalledPartyName=''
  originalCalledParty=2002 originalCdpnVoiceMailbox=2002
  originalCdpnRedirectReason=0          lastRedirectingPartyName=''
  lastRedirectingParty= lastRedirectingVoiceMailbox= lastRedirectingReason=0
  callType=2(OutBound) lineInstance=1 callReference=16777217."
StationD:    56ac778 DialedNumber dialedNumber=2002 lineInstance=1
  callReference=16777217.
StationD:    56ac778 CallInfo callingPartyName='' callingParty=2001
  cgpnVoiceMailbox=2001          calledPartyName='' calledParty=2002
  cdpnVoiceMailbox=2002          originalCalledPartyName=''
  originalCalledParty= originalCdpnVoiceMailbox= originalCdpnRedirectReason=0
  lastRedirectingPartyName='' lastRedirectingParty=2002
  lastRedirectingVoiceMailbox=2002 lastRedirectingReason=0
  callType=2(OutBound) lineInstance=1 callReference=16777217."
StationD:    56ac778 StartTone tone=36(AlertingTone).
StationD:    56ac778 CallState callState=3(RingOut) lineInstance=1
  callReference=16777217
StationD:    56ac778 SelectSoftKeys instance=1 reference=16777217
  softKeySetIndex=8 validKeyMask=-1.
StationD:    56ac778 DisplayPromptStatus timeOutValue=0
  promptStatus='Ring Out' lineInstance=1 callReference=16777217.
```

Example 5-4 shows the first message sent to the called IP phone. The called IP phone's TCP Handle is 56ac714. Notice that it is immediately instructed to change its display and start ringing.

Example 5-4 *First Messages Sent to the Called IP Phone*

```
StationD:    56ac714 DisplayText text='                    2002        '.
StationD:    56ac714 CallState callState=4(RingIn) lineInstance=1
  callReference=16777218
StationD:    56ac714 CallInfo callingPartyName='' callingParty=2001
  cgpnVoiceMailbox=2001          calledPartyName='' calledParty=2002
  cdpnVoiceMailbox=2002 originalCalledPartyName=''
  originalCalledParty=2002
  originalCdpnVoiceMailbox=2002 originalCdpnRedirectReason=0
  lastRedirectingPartyName='' lastRedirectingParty=2002
  lastRedirectingVoiceMailbox=2002 lastRedirectingReason=0
  callType=1(InBound) lineInstance=1 callReference=16777218."
StationD:    56ac714 SetLamp stimulus=9(Line)
```

Example 5-4 *First Messages Sent to the Called IP Phone (Continued)*

```
          stimulusInstance=1 LampMode=5(LampBlink).
    StationD:    56ac714 SetRinger ringMode=2(InsideRing).
    StationD:    56ac714 DisplayNotify timeOutValue=10 notify='From 2001'.
    StationD:    56ac714 DisplayPromptStatus timeOutValue=0 promptStatus=
      'From 2001' lineInstance=1 callReference=16777218.
    StationD:    56ac714 SelectSoftKeys instance=1 reference=16777218
      softKeySetIndex=3 validKeyMask=-1.
```

The next line, shown in Example 5-5, shows that the called IP phone goes off-hook to answer the call.

Example 5-5 *The Called IP Phone Answers*

```
    StationInit: 56ac714 OffHook.
    StationD:    56ac714 ClearNotify.
    StationD:    56ac714 SetRinger ringMode=1(RingOff).
    StationD:    56ac714 SetLamp stimulus=9(Line) stimulusInstance=1
      lampMode=2(LampOn).
    StationD:    56ac714 CallState callState=1(OffHook) lineInstance=1
      callReference=16777218
    StationD:    56ac714 ActivateCallPlane lineInstance=1.
    StationD:    56ac778 StopTone.
```

Notice that CallManager tells the called phone to stop ringing by sending a **SetRinger** message and also tells the calling IP phone to stop providing a ringback tone by sending a **StopTone** message.

In Example 5-6, CallManager tells the calling IP phone to prepare to listen to an RTP stream (**OpenReceiveChannel**) and then to start streaming RTP (**StartMediaTransmission**). Notice that the **StartMediaTransmission** message specifies the codec. This call is a G.711 μ-law call.

Please note that Example 5-6 is only showing the communication between CallManager and the calling IP phone, thus only showing one part of the signaling. At the same time some of these messages are exchanged with the calling phone, other messages are exchanged with the called phone.

In fact, the **StartMediaTransmission** message in Example 5-6 is specifying the IP address and port of the remote IP phone because it received that information in the **OpenReceiveChannel** as shown in the beginning of Example 5-7.

The full sequence of events is depicted in Figures 5-1 through 5-3. In Examples 5-6 through 5-9, each communication segment is separated out. If all of these examples were combined, they would follow the sequence shown in Figures 5-1 through 5-3. To see the messages exchanged between the calling IP phone and CallManager, review Example 5-6.

Example 5-6 *The Calling IP Phone Receives Media Stream Setup Instructions*

```
StationD:    56ac778 OpenReceiveChannel conferenceID=0
  passThruPartyID=17 millisecondPacketSize=20
  compressionType=4(Media_Payload_G711Ulaw64k) qualifierIn=?.
  myIP: 714100a (10.16.20.7)
StationD:    56ac778 StopTone.
StationD:    56ac778 CallState callState=5(Connected) lineInstance=1
  callReference=16777217
StationD:    56ac778 CallInfo callingPartyName='' callingParty=2001
  cgpnVoiceMailbox=2001calledPartyName='' calledParty=2002 cdpnVoiceMailbox=2002
  originalCalledPartyName='' originalCalledParty= originalCdpnVoiceMailbox=
  originalCdpnRedirectReason=0                    lastRedirectingPartyName=''
  lastRedirectingParty=2002 lastRedirectingVoiceMailbox=2002
  lastRedirectingReason=0
  callType=2(OutBound) lineInstance=1 callReference=16777217."
StationD:    56ac778 SelectSoftKeys instance=1 reference=16777217
  softKeySetIndex=1 validKeyMask=-1.
StationD:    56ac778 DisplayPromptStatus timeOutValue=0
  promptStatus='Connected' lineInstance=1 callReference=16777217.
StationD:    56ac778 StartMediaTransmission
  conferenceID=0 passThruPartyID=17
  remoteIpAddress=514100a(10.16.20.5) remotePortNumber=25138
  milliSecondPacketSize=20 compressType=4(Media_Payload_G711Ulaw64k)
  qualifierOut=?.  myIP: 714100a (10.16.20.7)
StationInit: 56ac778 OpenReceiveChannelAck Status=0, IpAddr=0x714100a,
  Port=17580, PartyID=17
```

In Example 5-7, the called IP phone is told to stop ringing, to **OpenReceiveChannel**, and to **StartMediaTransmission**. The display shown in Example 5-7 also changes as the media stream is established. Remember that Example 5-7 only shows messages sent to and from the called IP phone.

Example 5-7 *The Called IP Phone Receives Media Stream Setup Instructions*

```
StationD:    56ac714 StopTone.
StationD:    56ac714 OpenReceiveChannel conferenceID=0
  passThruPartyID=33 millisecondPacketSize=20
  compressionType=4(Media_Payload_G711Ulaw64k)
  qualifierIn=?.  myIP: 514100a (10.16.20.5)
StationD:    56ac714 StopTone.
StationD:    56ac714 CallState callState=5(Connected) lineInstance=1
  callReference=16777218
StationD:    56ac714 CallInfo callingPartyName='' callingParty=2001
  cgpnVoiceMailbox=2001              calledPartyName='' calledParty=2002
  cdpnVoiceMailbox=2002              originalCalledPartyName=''
  originalCalledParty=2002 originalCdpnVoiceMailbox=2002
  originalCdpnRedirectReason=0              lastRedirectingPartyName=''
  lastRedirectingParty=2002
  lastRedirectingVoiceMailbox=2002
```

Example 5-7   *The Called IP Phone Receives Media Stream Setup Instructions (Continued)*

```
      lastRedirectingReason=0
      callType=1(InBound) lineInstance=1 callReference=16777218."
    StationD:    56ac714 SelectSoftKeys instance=1 reference=16777218
      softKeySetIndex=1 validKeyMask=-1.
    StationD:    56ac714 DisplayPromptStatus timeOutValue=0
      promptStatus='Connected' lineInstance=1 callReference=16777218.
    StationInit: 56ac714 OpenReceiveChannelAck Status=0,
      IpAddr=0x514100a, Port=25138, PartyID=33
    StationD:    56ac714 StartMediaTransmission
      conferenceID=0 passThruPartyID=33
      remoteIpAddress=714100a(10.16.20.7) remotePortNumber=17580
      milliSecondPacketSize=20
      compressType=4(Media_Payload_G711Ulaw64k) qualifierOut=?.
      myIP: 514100a
      (10.16.20.5)]
```

The next message, shown in Example 5-8, displays the **OnHook** message. The called IP phone hangs up the call. The call is now torn down.

Example 5-8   *The Called IP Phone Hangs up the Call*

```
    StationInit: 56ac714 OnHook.
    StationD:    56ac714 SetSpeakerMode speakermode=2(Off).
    StationD:    56ac714 ClearPromptStatus lineInstance=1
      callReference=16777218.
    StationD:    56ac714 CallState callState=2(OnHook) lineInstance=1
      callReference=16777218
    StationD:    56ac714 SelectSoftKeys instance=0 reference=0
      softKeySetIndex=0 validKeyMask=7.
    StationD:    56ac714 DisplayPromptStatus timeOutValue=0
      promptStatus='Your current options' lineInstance=0 callReference=0.
    StationD:    56ac714 ActivateCallPlane lineInstance=0.
    StationD:    56ac714 SetLamp stimulus=9(Line) stimulusInstance=1
      lampMode=1(LampOff).
    StationD:    56ac714 DefineTimeDate timeDateInfo=?
      systemTime=1008173476.
    StationD:    56ac714 StopTone.
```

As demonstrated in Examples 5-9 and 5-10, the calling and called IP phones are told to **CloseReceiveChannel** (stop listening) and to **StopMediaTransmission** (stop streaming).

Example 5-9   *The Calling IP Phone Is Told to **CloseReceiveChannel** and **StopMediaTransmission***

```
    StationD:    56ac778 CloseReceiveChannel conferenceID=0
      passThruPartyID=17.  myIP: 714100a (10.16.20.7)
    StationD:    56ac778 StopMediaTransmission conferenceID=0
      passThruPartyID=17.  myIP: 714100a (10.16.20.7)
```

Example 5-10 *The Called IP Phone Is Told to* **CloseReceiveChannel** *and* **StopMediaTransmission**

```
StationD:    56ac714 CloseReceiveChannel conferenceID=0
  passThruPartyID=33.  myIP: 514100a (10.16.20.5)
StationD:    56ac714 StopMediaTransmission conferenceID=0
  passThruPartyID=33.  myIP: 514100a (10.16.20.5)
StationD:    56ac778 DefineTimeDate timeDateInfo=?
  systemTime=1008173476.
StationD:    56ac778 SetSpeakerMode speakermode=2(Off).
StationD:    56ac778 ClearPromptStatus lineInstance=1
  callReference=16777217.
StationD:    56ac778 CallState callState=2(OnHook) lineInstance=1
  callReference=16777217
StationD:    56ac778 SelectSoftKeys instance=0 reference=0
  softKeySetIndex=0 validKeyMask=7.
StationD:    56ac778 DisplayPromptStatus timeOutValue=0
  promptStatus='Your current options' lineInstance=0 callReference=0.
StationD:    56ac778 ActivateCallPlane lineInstance=0.
StationD:    56ac778 SetLamp stimulus=9(Line) stimulusInstance=1
  lampMode=1(LampOff).
StationD:    56ac778 DefineTimeDate timeDateInfo=?
  systemTime=1008173476.
StationD:    56ac778 StopTone.
```

As you can see from these examples, Skinny clients such as IP phones do not do anything without CallManager instructing them to do so. Fortunately the messages in the Skinny protocol are mostly in plain English and easy to understand. Hopefully you now have a feel for the interaction that occurs between the IP phone and CallManager.

Being able to read a CCM trace and reconstruct a call is very important because often users do not remember exactly what they did when they ran into a problem. If you can find the problem call in the CCM trace, you can go step-by-step searching through the trace for the phone's TCP handle to understand exactly what buttons were pressed and how CallManager responded to each action. You can then attempt to reproduce the problem by following the same sequence of events.

Understanding Failover and Failback

To understand IP phone failover and failback behavior, you must understand the operation of the TFTP configuration file and CallManager lists.

The TFTP configuration file received by the IP phone has a list of up to three CallManagers for registration purposes. The order of CallManagers indicates their priority. The first is the highest-priority CallManager for the IP phone. It is the first place the IP phone attempts to register. The highest-priority CallManager is also called the *primary CallManager*.

When the IP phone registers with its primary CallManager, it also establishes a standby TCP connection to the next-highest–priority available CallManager, sometimes called the *standby CallManager*, *secondary CallManager*, or *backup CallManager*. The IP phone knows that there is an alternative CallManager for quick failover if it loses connectivity with its primary CallManager.

At any given point in time, the CallManager to which the phone is registered is its *active* connection. The CallManager node that has a standby TCP connection for the IP phone is the *standby* connection.

Failover Behavior

Failover occurs under two conditions:

- If the TCP connection between the IP phone and the primary CallManager goes down. Incidentally, stopping the CallManager service on a server causes all the TCP connections to be closed and all the IP phones on that server to register to their standby.

- If CallManager has not responded to three consecutive KeepAlive messages sent from the IP phone.

Any number of network-related issues could cause the TCP connection to go down. When the IP phone registers with its standby CallManager, it registers with an alarm indicating why it failed over.

Under the second condition, CallManager fails to respond to three consecutive KeepAlives. The IP phone sends a KeepAlive message every 30 seconds by default. CallManager should answer each KeepAlive the IP phone sends with an acknowledgment message. If CallManager fails to respond to three consecutive KeepAlive messages, the IP phone marks the connection as "bad." The IP phone does not tear down the TCP connection, but it does not attempt to re-register with the "bad" CallManager either. It continues sending KeepAlive messages to the "bad" CallManager until CallManager tears down the TCP connection. This delay gives CallManager time to respond if it recovers quickly. After 10 minutes, the IP phone removes the "bad" tag and again tries to establish communication with CallManager using KeepAlive messages in the process just described. During this time, the IP phone attempts to establish a connection with its secondary CallManager (or its tertiary if the secondary is not available) and registers if possible.

If a call is in progress when an IP phone detects the loss of a TCP connection, the IP phone does not fail over until the call is finished. If CallManager fails to respond to three consecutive KeepAlive messages while an IP phone has an active call, the IP phone again waits until the call is finished before registering to its standby CallManager.

If no CallManagers are available, the IP phone may register to an SRST router. Chapter 15, "Survivable Remote Site Telephony (SRST)," discusses this topic in detail.

Failback Behavior

Before the IP phone attempts to reregister with its primary CallManager, it goes through a process to determine if it should begin to fail back. If the IP phone has a higher-priority CallManager that is not currently the active connection, it attempts to make a TCP connection to the higher-priority CallManager. If this connection attempt succeeds, the failback process begins.

With a successful TCP connection to the higher-priority CallManager, the IP phone sends a token request. This is essentially a test registration message. If CallManager can handle the failback, it sends an acknowledgment message back to the IP phone. As soon as the IP phone receives this message, it unregisters with its current CallManager and sends a registration message to the higher-priority CallManager. The failback to CallManager is randomized on the IP phones. The random time that failback occurs is between 0 and 300 seconds.

If CallManager cannot handle the failback, it sends a token reject message with a retry value. The retry value specifies when the IP phone should resend its request. This process repeats until the IP phone gets an acknowledgment to its request.

Upcoming sections discuss how to find out what is causing failover to occur.

Understanding the Difference Between Restart and Reset

You can reset or restart a phone in Cisco CallManager Administration. What is the difference between resetting and restarting? Basically, the **reset** command causes the IP phone to completely power-cycle and begin again as if it had just been plugged in. The **restart** command tells the IP phone to unregister and then reregister with CallManager. Making some changes to the Phone Configuration page in CallManager Administration (**Device > Phone >** *find and select a phone*) requires the IP phone to get a new configuration file. Because a **restart** does not cause the phone to re-download its configuration file via TFTP, a **reset** command is required to get the new information.

The actual Skinny message sent by CallManager is **StationReset**. It has two message types: DEVICE_RESET and DEVICE_RESTART. Table 5-2 describes the behavior of these message types in more detail.

Table 5-2 *IP Phone Behavior Based on Reset Type*

Reset Type	Phone Behavior
DEVICE_RESET	This message commands the IP phone to act as if it is being plugged in for the first time. This means that the following steps occur: • Get all IP information from the DHCP server. • Contact the TFTP server and download the phone's configuration file. • Register with the highest-priority CallManager. For details on the boot-up and registration behavior, see Chapter 4, "Skinny Client Registration." If a call is in progress, the IP phone waits until the call has ended before responding to this command.
DEVICE_RESTART	When this command is received, the IP phone immediately unregisters with CallManager. It tears down any TCP connection with CallManager and attempts to establish a new connection. If a call is in progress, the IP phone waits until the call has ended before responding to this command.

Troubleshooting IP Phone Problems

The preceding section examined the behavior of IP phones. This information should help you understand what to expect from the IP phone as it interacts with CallManager.

The following sections examine some of the more common issues you may experience:

• Dropped calls
• "CM Down, Features Disabled"
• Reasons for failover
• Directory and service problems

Dropped Calls

Chapter 10, "Call Preservation," is devoted to the subject of call preservation. Chapter 10 covers the details of call preservation, but this section addresses some key ideas as well.

IP phone-to-IP phone calls should never drop. Calls involving H.323 gateways and media resources such as conference bridges might, but pure IP phone-to-IP phone calls for two phones registered to the same CallManager cluster never will.

If you suspect that an IP phone-to-IP phone call has dropped, check the trace files. It is likely that one party bumped a button and hung up the call. Remember that CallManager is not involved with the media stream of a call after it is established. At this point, it is simply two point-to-point RTP media streams.

"CM Down, Features Disabled"

This message appears on the IP phone only if a call is established and the IP phone loses connectivity to its CallManager.

As you might remember, the IP phone sends a KeepAlive message to its active CallManager every 30 seconds. If an IP phone is in the middle of a call and it sends a KeepAlive that cannot reach CallManager or that is ignored by CallManager after three consecutive KeepAlive messages, the IP phone displays the "CM Down, Features Disabled" message.

The phone displays this message because the currently active CallManager is unavailable to process any request from the IP phone. If the user wanted to transfer, conference, park a call, or place a call on hold, he or she could not do so because CallManager is unavailable to process the request. Displaying the "CM Down, Features Disabled" message communicates to the user that he or she cannot invoke these features at this time.

The IP phone does not register to its standby CallManager until the phone call is finished. You should not encounter this message during normal operations, so an investigation into what caused the outage is in order. The most likely suspects are a network outage or a CallManager server failure.

Reasons for Failover

When you see that IP phones are failing over to their standby CallManager, it is time to investigate the reason. Fortunately, the IP phone supplies its reason for failover in its registration message with its standby CallManager. This is an alarm, and as such, it can be configured to display in the Event Viewer, the SDL trace files, and the CCM trace files.

When the IP phone registers to CallManager, it sends a **StationAlarmMessage** before it sends a **StationRegisterMessage**. During normal operation, the **StationAlarmMessage** message field is blank, indicating that this registration attempt is normal. When the IP phone is registering because of a potential problem or incident, it sends the **StationAlarmMessage** with an error message. Table 5-3 lists the different alarm messages sent in the **StationAlarmMessage** field.

Table 5-3   **StationAlarmMessage** *Alarm Definitions*

Alarm	Description
Last=CM-Closed-TCP	This alarm appears when an IP phone fails over to its backup CallManager because it can't reach the primary CallManager over the network. It also uses this message when the primary CallManager closes the TCP socket to the IP phone. For instance, if the primary CallManager is stopped manually, all the TCP sockets are closed.
Last=KeepaliveTO	This alarm indicates that the IP phone failed over because of a KeepAlive timeout. If the IP phone sends three consecutive KeepAlive messages to its primary CallManager without an acknowledgment, it registers to the backup CallManager. Note that this indicates a successful TCP transmission to CallManager, but not an acknowledgment. If there were a TCP failure, the message used would be **Last=CM-Closed-TCP**.
Last=Reset-Reset	This alarm indicates that the IP phone failed over because it received a reset command from CallManager Aministration or the phone keypad (the reset command on the keypad is ****#****). If the administrator pressed the **Reset** button in the Phone Configuration page in CallManager Administration (**Device > Phone >** *find and select a phone*), this alarm message indicates that the IP phone is registering because it was told to reset. A reset causes a full power cycle of the IP phone, as if it is being powered up for the first time.
Last=Reset-Restart	This alarm indicates that the IP phone failed over because it received a restart command from the Phone Configuration page in CallManager Administration (**Device > Phone >** *find and select a phone*). If the administrator pressed the **Restart** button in CallManager Administration, this alarm message indicates that the IP phone is registering because it was told to restart. A restart essentially commands the IP phone to unregister and then reregister with CallManager.
Last=Phone-Reg-Rej	This alarm indicates that the IP phone failed over due to receiving a Registration Reject message from CallManager. This means that the IP phone is registering to this CallManager because it was rejected from the last CallManager it attempted to register to.

By looking in the Event Viewer, CCM traces, or SDL traces for these alarms, you can narrow down the scope of the problem. Depending on the **StationAlarmMessage**, you can begin investigating your network infrastructure or perhaps begin a diagnosis of CallManager itself. Find out what event(s) caused the IP phone to failover, and then try to discover the series of events that transpired to cause the failover.

Most failover problems are the result of a network connectivity problem between CallManager and the phone. If more than one phone is failing over within a short period of time, list all the phones encountering this problem and see if they are all isolated to one part of the network. If they are, look for any sign of a network outage to that part of the network.

On the other hand, if a large number of phones are failing over but there is no geographic pattern as to their location, perhaps all the problem phones are registered to a particular CallManager in the cluster—indicating either a problem on CallManager itself or a problem with the network connectivity from that CallManager to the rest of the network. Layer 1 and Layer 2 issues such as a bad cable or a duplex mismatch are common causes for this kind of problem.

Directory and Service Problems

Any time you press the **services** or **directories** buttons on the IP phone, an HTTP request is sent to a web server. If this request fails, no services or directories can be displayed. Think about this in terms of your web browser. If you click a link in your web browser that leads to a server that is down or inaccessible, your browser gives you an error. The same thing happens on an IP phone.

Several activities can cause an HTTP request to originate from the IP phone. You can see the following URL fields in CallManager Administration (**System > Enterprise Parameters**):

- URL Authentication
- URL Directories
- URL Help
- URL Idle
- URL Idle Time
- URL Information
- URL Messages
- URL Proxy
- URL Services

The services URL looks like this:

http://*callmanager_name_or_IP_address*/CCMCIP/getservicesmenu.asp

The directory URL looks like this:

http://*callmanager_name_or_IP_address*/CCMCIP/xmldirectory.asp

With this information, what can you do to fix a problem with services or directory? There are a few usual suspects for this issue.

One common problem is with DNS resolution. This could occur because the IP phone doesn't have a DNS server to resolve the name for it. Or it could occur because the DNS server doesn't have the right CNAME (canonical name) or a record entry that resolves the name to the correct IP address. Or perhaps the phone does not know the DNS domain name that is necessary to ask for the web server's correct fully-qualified domain name. The IP phone displays a "Host Not Found" error on the screen in this case.

Another problem could simply be one of network connectivity. If there is no network connectivity to the DNS server or the web server, the request fails. Verify bidirectional connectivity if you suspect this is the cause. Chapter 4 discusses this procedure.

Finally, the web server itself could be the problem. Make sure that the web server is running and that the specified web pages exist. You should be able to access the services and directories URL from a standard web browser if you are running Microsoft Internet Explorer 5.5 or later, as it supports displaying XML content.

Now you have to consider one more critical piece of information. If you press the **services** button, you download an XML page listing the subscribed services for that IP phone. Each service is a URL of its own that can query any web server it is configured to point to. If you successfully download the initial services page and then have a problem reaching one of the subscribed services, use the tips just discussed to try to determine where the problem lies. Be aware that some services target a web server outside your control (such as Yahoo! or a weather web site). As such, the problem could come down to poor XML development by a web developer or a broken server outside your control.

For problems with XML services, the most useful troubleshooting tool is a sniffer. Capture a sniffer trace of the communication between the IP phone and the web server to determine where the problem lies.

79xx Series IP Phone 3-port Switch Operation

The Cisco 79xx series IP Phones (7960, 7940, and 7910+SW) all contain a 3-port Ethernet switch that allows for voice quality of service (QoS) guarantees, data and voice VLAN support, the ability to re-tag class of service (CoS) bits (802.1p priority bits) based on extended trust configuration from an attached Catalyst switch, broadcast suppression, and multicast group awareness.

Network administrators who have a strong switching background often ask the same question: "I plugged a packet analyzer (Network Associates Sniffer Pro, Finisar Surveyor, Ethereal, and so on) into the PC port on my phone and am seeing all the packets being sent to and from the phone. Doesn't the phone have a switch in it? If so, why am I seeing traffic that is not destined to my PC?"

Although at first glance this may appear to be improper behavior for a device being sold as a switch, the phone is actually behaving as intended.

Before discussing the architecture of the 79xx switch, we must first analyze why we would want to have a switch in the phone in the first place. Traditionally switches have been used in enterprise LANs to reduce the size of collision domains and to isolate traffic to only the network nodes that need to receive the traffic. This is especially important when you have several multi-Mbps streams between different hosts or several 100 Mbps hosts being aggregated to a 1 Gb (or more) port. Also, with the introduction of VLAN technology, network managers have been able to use switches to have separate broadcast domains on the same switch as well.

If the preceding information were to describe the function of a switch in the 79*xx* IP Phone, what would you be gaining? You would not be gaining much at all. The phone would be able to keep the small amount of traffic the phone generates from reaching the PC port and you would be able to keep broadcasts in the voice VLAN from reaching the PC connected to the phone. When we consider that even with wideband audio introduced in CallManager 3.1, which uses 16 kbps sampling and 16-bit samples and consumes 256 kbps, this is still only 0.25 percent utilization of a 100 Mbps Fast Ethernet connection. Even if you take into ac-count the worst-case scenario of 10 Mbps and wideband audio, the utilization still peaks at 2.5 percent.

So you ask, "Why do I need a switch in my IP Phone if the functions a switch normally performs gives me no perceivable advantage over having a hub in the phone?" Well, that is certainly a good question, and the answer is that there are many other functions a switch can perform that would make it ideal for residing in an IP Phone.

The important concept to understand is that the purpose of the switch in a 79*xx* phone is not to keep traffic away from the PC attached to the phone; the primary purpose of the switch is to guarantee voice quality regardless of what other traffic is present on the LAN. To do this, the switch must be able to prioritize voice traffic over data traffic no matter how much data traffic is trying to share the same bandwidth. This is accomplished by implementing various input and output queues in the switch fabric that prioritizes frames based on the 802.1p priority bits (CoS bits) or other criteria.

In the case of real-time data like voice and video, the switch must be able to give strict priority to voice/video traffic, meaning that if there are any voice/video frames in the queue, they are sent first regardless of how many other data packets are waiting to be sent. The 3-port switch in the 79*xx* series phones implements four separate queues per port. The most important of these is the strict priority queue in which traffic with a CoS of 5 is put. All voice traffic from the 79*xx* phone is marked with a CoS of 5 to ensure it gets into the priority queue.

Prioritizing the traffic is not the only thing the switch is used for. Once the voice traffic enters the rest of your LAN, it must be prioritized there as well. There are many ways to do this; however, managing your voice traffic can often be easier if you have your voice traffic on a different VLAN than your data traffic. More importantly, you typically do not want to waste valuable public IP address space for your IP phones.

To assist in these goals, the 79*xx* is capable of putting voice traffic on a separate VLAN than the data traffic. This allows you to have DHCP scopes with a private address space for the phones and keep existing data subnet scopes. This is also especially useful when using dual permanent virtual circuit (PVC) designs over the WAN to remote sites where traffic must be policy routed to the correct PVC. Having the traffic separated onto two different VLANs greatly simplifies this type of configuration.

One important point to note is that marking and prioritizing traffic is only useful if only the traffic you truly want to get priority gets marked. When a user plugs their PC into the back of a phone, you don't want them to be able to mark their data traffic with the same priority as the voice traffic—if not there will be no way to differentiate between high priority voice traffic and lower priority data traffic.

To ensure that the attached PC does not send its packets with precedence values that allow the packets into the strict priority queue, the 79xx IP Phone's switch can re-write the Layer 2 precedence bits (802.1p) being sent by the device attached to the PC port on the phone. Note that any Layer 3 precedence set by the PC (IP Precedence or Differentiated Services Code Point [DSCP]) is preserved through the phone. This is all configured from the access switch to which the phone is attached. The switch informs the phone whether the PC port is to be trusted or untrusted. If trusted, the priority bits are left alone and the traffic is prioritized according to the priority bits. If untrusted, the priority bits are reset to a user-configured value—generally configured to 0. This ensures that the data entering your LAN is marked correctly. For more information regarding the proper configuration of trust and extended trust, please refer to the Cisco IP Telephony QoS Design Guide available on Cisco.com at the following link:

www.cisco.com/univercd/cc/td/doc/product/voice/ip_tele/index.htm

Another advantage the switch in the phone offers is the ability to ensure that the connection between the phone's switch and the LAN switch is full-duplex. A high number of collisions can impact voice quality by generating variable delay (jitter). By having a switch in the phone, the connection from the phone to the LAN switch can be full-duplex and the connection to the attached PC can be either half- or full-duplex without impacting voice quality between the phone and the LAN switch. If the phone were to have a hub, the connection would have to be half-duplex since hubs are half-duplex by nature.

Enterprise LAN switches typically contain MAC address tables (CAM Tables) of 32,000 to 128,000 entries to be able to keep track of which port a particular device is connected to. To be able to decide which port to forward traffic to, the switch in the 79xx IP Phone also needs to have a Content Addressable Memory (CAM) table.

In reality, the 79xx switch has a CAM table that has space for 32 entries. Unlike what you might expect from a transparent bridge, the switch in the 79xx does not do any kind of dynamic MAC address learning. If it were to do this, it would require enough CAM entries for at least the number of hosts that are on the voice and data VLAN. This could easily be 500 to 1000 entries. While this is certainly possible, it is not practical because it would needlessly add complexity and cost to the phone. The only thing this would accomplish is to shield the PC from the traffic destined to the phone port. Because the switch knows what is connected to the internal phone Application Specific Integrated Circuit (ASIC) port, it can make sure that none of the data VLAN traffic affects the internal ASIC port—even if you pump a full 100 Mbps of bandwidth out the PC port.

In addition to unicast traffic, the switch in the phone must be able to protect the phone ASIC from broadcast and multicast traffic as well. The phone's switch has broadcast suppression automatically enabled to ensure a broadcast storm does not take down the phone. Additionally, the switch is able to talk to the phone's application software to add and remove multicast MAC addresses from the CAM table whenever the phone needs to join and leave a multicast group. This ensures the phone does not have to process unnecessary multicast traffic either.

One other point to note is that the switch in the phone does not have any color block logic (CBL), which means that it is not able to blindly block packets destined to a particular VLAN from exiting out a particular port. If the switch had CBL it would be able to stop broadcasts coming in to the voice VLAN from being sent out the PC port on the switch, but again this would be additional complexity that would buy you no real-world advantage.

One of the reasons for the behavior previously described is the ability to dual-home a phone to two LAN switches where extreme high availability is needed. In this configuration, in addition to being connected to an inline-power capable switch on the network port, the phone is also connected to another switch via a crossover Ethernet cable connected to the PC port. The phone itself does not run the Spanning Tree Protocol (STP); however, it passes bridge protocol data units (BPDUs) through the switch so that the attached switches can take care of blocking one of the ports connecting to the phone. The PC port does not accept inline power, so to function with the switch connected via the PC port, the phone must also be locally powered. This gives you no single point of failure other than the phone itself. Both power and network connectivity are redundant.

One added advantage of not having a CAM table on the phone is that this makes taking network capture traces extremely easy when trying to troubleshoot a problem on the phone. Just plug your network analyzer into the PC port on the phone and begin capturing. You will see the packets to and from the switch. This is much easier for troubleshooting than having to determine which access switch port the phone is connected to, go to the access switch to connect the network analyzer, and configure the switch to span the phone's port to the analyzer port. Additionally, because the access LAN switch does have a CAM table and only sends traffic to the ports that need the traffic, the only thing you can capture from the back of the phone is traffic to and from the phone you are connected to.

In summary, the 3-port switch subsystem of the Cisco 79xx series IP Phones provides the following advantages over a hub, which allow for ease of use and voice quality guarantees.

- Voice QoS priority queuing (802.1p)
- Data traffic 802.1p QoS reclassification and trust boundary enforcement
- 802.1q VLAN tagging
- Full-duplex Ethernet operation
- Multicast traffic management
- Broadcast suppression
- Inline power

Use this behavior to your advantage by connecting your network analyzer directly to the back of any phone you need to get a trace from.

Best Practices

Now that you understand how the IP phone and CallManager work together, this section offers some best practices and tips to increase your success when troubleshooting IP phone issues.

Check Your Firmware

If you recently upgraded CallManager, you also have upgraded the firmware on the IP Phones because a new firmware release is almost always included in a CallManager release. If a new IP Phone problem has popped up, it could be related to the new firmware it is running.

An easy way to check your firmware version is to go to the Phone Configuration page in CallManager Administration for the IP Phone that is experiencing problems and specify a different firmware version (**Device > Phone >** *find and select the phone > enter the phone load in the* **Phone Load Name** *field*). You could specify the old firmware version and run your test again. If the problem is fixed, you know that the new IP Phone firmware might be to blame.

Also, you might upgrade your CallManager or IP Phones to fix a problem only to find that some IP Phones are still experiencing the same problem. In this case, make sure that no IP Phones are running the old firmware version. This is easy to verify. In CallManager Administration, go to **Device > Firmware Load Information**. This page lists any devices that are not using the default firmware load as specified in the Device Defaults page (**System > Device Defaults**). On the IP Phone, two firmware loads can be found. One is the boot load, and the other is the application load. The application load is the one that matters.

You can find the application load on the IP Phone by pressing **settings > 5 > 3** or by pressing the **settings** button, selecting the **status** menu item, and then selecting the **firmware version** menu item.

Press the Help (i or ?) Button Twice During Active Calls

Another good practice is to press the help (**i** or **?**) button on the IP Phone during an active call. If a voice quality-related problem arises, place a call and press the help (**i** or **?**) button twice in rapid succession. Doing so displays a Call Statistics window that lists IP statistics such as the amount of jitter and lost packets. This can give you immediate insight into the call's quality. You can also teach users to do this when they experience poor audio quality during a phone call.

<table>
<tr><td>**TIP**</td><td>You can deploy a custom phone service that logs call statistics whenever a user presses the help (**i** or **?**) button twice in rapid succession during an active call. See the next section for more information.</td></tr>
</table>

The call statistics menu provides the following information:

- **rxtype/txtype**—These values indicate the codecs used in the call.
- **rxsize/txsize**—These values indicate the codec payload size.
- **rxcount/txcount**—These values indicate the number of packets sent and received during the call.
- **avgjtr**—This value indicates the estimated average jitter observed in the last 16 RTP packets.
- **maxjtr**—This value indicates the maximum jitter during the life of the RTP receive stream. Remember that this is not for the life of the call; it is for the life of the stream. If you put someone on hold, the stream terminates. When the call with the held party resumes, the **maxjtr** count restarts.
- **rxdisc**—This value indicates the number of inbound (received) packets that have been discarded for this IP Phone.

The **rxtype/txtype** values give you instant knowledge of what codec(s) are being used for the conversation between this phone and the other device. Make sure that the codecs match on both sides. Also, pay careful attention to the size of the sound samples—they should match. If they do not match, verify that either the other device can transcode the disparate codec or that a transcoder is in place to handle the service.

Chapter 7, "Voice Quality," covers voice quality in greater detail.

Use a Custom Phone Service That Tracks Voice Quality Statistics

Even easier than teaching users to press the help (**i** or **?**) button and then write down relevant information is developing a phone service that users can invoke when they experience voice quality problems. You can write the service yourself, or you can use the free one, Voice Anomaly Tracking (VAT), provided on the CD that accompanies the Cisco Press book *Developing Cisco IP Phone Services* (ISBN 1-58705-060-9). The VAT service polls the IP statistics when the user presses a specific soft key. The IP statistics are saved to a file for you to view anytime.

Check the IP Phone Configuration Via Web Browser

Finally, remember that the IP phone listens to HTTP requests. This means that you can browse to the IP phone using its IP address. You can also do this from CallManager Administration, where a link takes you to the IP phone (**Device > Phone >** *find a phone > click the link provided for IP Address*). You can then view all the configuration information on the IP phone from your browser. You can review the configuration information to determine if any items are misconfigured. Figure 5-4 demonstrates viewing the IP phone through a web browser.

Figure 5-4   *Obtaining IP Phone Information Via Web Browser*

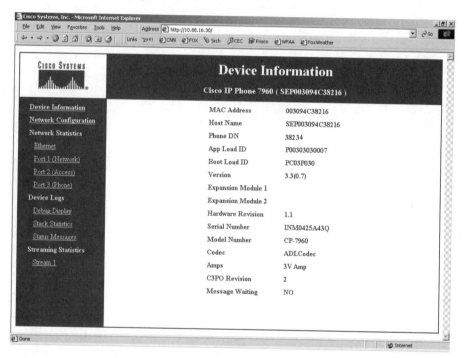

Summary

Knowing how the IP phone and CallManager interact provides great insight into determining where problems can reside. Although the IP phone depends on CallManager for everything it does, it is still smart enough to know why it is having trouble in many cases. If you check the IP phone's trace files and status messages, you can identify most basic problems immediately.

## CHAPTER 6

Voice Gateways

Voice gateways are the interfaces that bridge the voice over IP (VoIP) world with the Public Switched Telephone Network (PSTN) and legacy private branch exchange (PBX) networks. These gateways can be Cisco IOS gateways, voice modules within voice-enabled LAN switches, or one of many standalone gateway platforms.

The actual type of interface to the time-division multiplexing (TDM) world can be analog or digital. Voice gateways communicate using various signaling protocols, depending on their interface. If the interface is analog, the signaling protocols can be Foreign Exchange Station (FXS), Foreign Exchange Office (FXO), or Ear and Mouth (E&M). If the interface is digital, the signaling protocols can be ISDN Basic Rate Interface (BRI), T1/E1 Primary Rate Interface (PRI), or T1/E1 channel associated signaling (CAS).

By breaking these components into logical groups and following a methodical troubleshooting approach, you can identify and resolve gateway problems.

The following sections discuss the different types of voice gateways and interfaces and how to troubleshoot and resolve issues with them. This chapter covers troubleshooting the following gateways:

- TDM interfaces on Cisco IOS gateways
- Media Gateway Control Protocol (MGCP) signaling on Cisco IOS gateways
- H.323 signaling on Cisco IOS gateways
- WS-X6608 T1/E1 gateway (6608)
- WS-X6624 FXS gateway (6624)

Cisco IOS Voice Gateways

Cisco offers a large variety of voice gateways that run Cisco IOS Software. These gateways vary from the low-end Cisco 1750 all the way up to the Cisco 7500. The majority of these gateways are fully functional multiprotocol routers with added voice functionality. The decision of which gateway to use largely depends on the interface types needed, the number of calls that need to be processed, the density of interfaces needed, the features required, and any other functions you intend to perform with the same gateway.

The good news is that all these gateways run the same Cisco IOS Software, making them nearly identical from a troubleshooting standpoint. There are subtle platform-specific differences, but for the most part, if you learn how to troubleshoot one Cisco IOS voice gateway, you can master them all. The following sections examine some of the most commonly used Cisco IOS voice gateways.

Cisco VG200

The VG200 is a one-rack unit (1RU) standalone gateway. It has only static routing functionality and is designed to function only as a Cisco CallManager voice gateway, not as a router. The VG200 has one network module slot that can be populated with an NM-1V, NM-2V, NM-HDV, or NM-DSP-FARM.

The NM-1V and NM-2V are similar. The NM-1V has enough digital signal processors (DSP) for two voice calls and one voice interface card (VIC) slot, and the NM-2V has enough DSPs for four voice calls and two VIC slots. These VIC slots can be populated with any of the following modules:

- Two-port FXS (VIC-2FXS)
- Two-port FXO (VIC-2FXO)
- Two-port FXO for Europe (VIC-2FXO-EU)
- Two-port FXO with battery reversal detection and caller ID support (VIC-FXO-M1)
- Two-port FXO with battery reversal detection and caller ID support for Europe (VIC-FXO-M2)
- Two-port FXO for Australia (VIC-FXO-M3)
- Two-port analog E&M (VIC-VIC-2E/M)
- Two-port ISDN BRI (VIC-2BRI-S/T-TE)
- Two-port ISDN BRI with integrated NT1 (VIC-2BRI-NT/TE)
- Two-port analog DID (VIC-2DID)

The majority of the preceding VICs support one call per port, so each card can carry up to two calls. The NM-1V and NM-2V each support up to two calls per port, so that works out well. However, note that if you are using BRI, each BRI port is capable of two calls, for a total of four calls on a single VIC. To be able to place four calls from a single VIC-2BRI, you must insert it into an NM-2V and leave the second slot empty. The NM-2V allocates all four DSP resources to the one slot. If you exceed the number of DSP resources on the NM-1V or NM-2V, you see the following message:

```
%C542-1-INSUFFICIENT_DSPS: VNM(1), cannot support all voice channels on VICs
```

Also note that each VIC has the minimum level of Cisco IOS Software needed to recognize the card. You can find the latest information using the Software Advisor on Cisco.com. You can access the Software Advisor at the following link (requires registered user login):

www.cisco.com/cgi-bin/Support/CompNav/Index.pl

The VG200 can also accept a high-density voice module (NM-HDV). The NM-HDV has one slot that accepts a variety of digital T1 and E1 interfaces and has five internal slots for adding DSP modules. The interface slot can accept any of the following modules:

- One-port T1 (VWIC-1MFT-T1)
- Two-port T1 (VWIC-2MFT-T1)
- One-port E1 (VWIC-1MFT-E1)
- Two-port E1 (VWIC-2MFT-E1)
- Two-port T1 with Drop and Insert (VWIC-2MFT-T1-DI)
- Two-port E1 with Drop and Insert (VWIC-2MFT-E1-DI)

DSPs on most Cisco IOS gateways have a concept called codec complexity. You can select between medium and high complexity. Medium complexity allows you to place twice the number of calls per DSP as a high complexity call; however, there are certain limitations when using medium complexity. For example, when placing a call using the G.729 codec, high complexity uses the G.729 codec while medium complexity uses the G.729a codec. G.729a offers nearly the same voice quality while saving a good amount of processing power on the DSP.

The internal DSP slots are populated with packet voice/data module (PVDM)-12 modules that provide 12 medium-complexity channels or 6 high-complexity channels of DSP resources. This means that if you want to use two E1 ports to full capacity (a total of 60 channels), you need five PVDM-12 modules.

Finally, the NM-HDV-FARM is used as a pool of DSP resources for conferencing and transcoding. The hardware is identical to an NM-HDV with one or more PVDM-12 modules and nothing in the voice WAN interface card (VWIC) slot.

The VG200 also has two WAN interface card (WIC) slots. These slots are disabled on the VG200 and cannot be used for anything because the VG200 is not a router; it is only a voice gateway.

Cisco 2600 Series Routers

The Cisco 2600 series routers are nearly identical to the VG200, except that they are fully functional routers in addition to being voice gateways. The 2600 series routers have the same hardware support as described for the VG200. At times, Cisco might choose to release features on the VG200 prior to releasing them on the 26/3600 series. So although the hardware is compatible, be sure that the feature you need is also available on the 2600 series.

The 2600 has one network module slot just like the VG200. The biggest difference is that the two WIC slots are functional and a variety of WAN interfaces can be inserted into these slots. This functionality is not discussed here because it is outside the scope of this book. The 2600 series comes in a variety of models. The differences between these models are the built-in LAN interfaces, memory capacity, and CPU performance. The following outlines the various 2600 series routers:

- **Cisco 2650XM and Cisco 2651XM**—Up to 40,000 packets per second (pps), one and two autosensing 10/100 Mbps Ethernet ports, respectively

- **Cisco 2650 and Cisco 2651**—Up to 37,000 pps, one and two autosensing 10/100 Mbps Ethernet ports, respectively

- **Cisco 2620XM and Cisco 2621XM**—Up to 30,000 pps, one and two autosensing 10/100 Mbps Ethernet ports, respectively

- **Cisco 2620 and Cisco 2621**—Up to 25,000 pps, one and two autosensing 10/100 Mbps Ethernet ports, respectively

- **Cisco 2610XM and Cisco 2611XM**—Up to 20,000 pps, one and two autosensing 10/100 Mbps Ethernet ports, respectively

- **Cisco 2610 through Cisco 2613**—Up to 15,000 pps

  - Cisco 2613—One Token Ring port
  - Cisco 2612—One 10 Mbps Ethernet port, one Token Ring port
  - Cisco 2611—Two 10 Mbps Ethernet ports
  - Cisco 2610—One 10 Mbps Ethernet port

All listed XM models can expand to up to 32 MB of Flash and 128 MB of DRAM. The non-XM models can accommodate only 16 MB of Flash and 64 MB of DRAM.

In addition to these models is the 2691, which is a 2RU chassis with three WIC slots instead of the two that are offered on the other 2600 series routers.

None of the router differences matter much when you're troubleshooting IP Telephony problems on these platforms. Most of the troubleshooting occurs on the telephony interfaces (FXS, FXO, PRI, and so on). The type of LAN interface does not matter. The only factor that might come into play is CPU performance if you are trying to do several other things on the same router you are using as your voice gateway. If you do not have enough CPU power, the performance of the voice functionality is degraded. Also, due to Flash and memory restrictions, some platforms might not be able to load the newest software.

In addition to the modules supported on the VG200, the 2600 series routers also support the AIM-VOICE module, which allows a T1/E1 VWIC to use the DSP resources from the AIM-VOICE module instead of having to use the NM-HDV.

Cisco 3600 Series Routers

As a voice gateway, the Cisco 3600 series routers are nearly identical to the Cisco 2600 series routers. The Cisco 3600 series routers accept the same network modules and VICs as the Cisco 2600 series and VG200. The biggest difference is that the Cisco 3600 series router can achieve much higher port densities because of the additional network module slots. From a configuration and troubleshooting perspective, the 3600 series routers are no different from a VG200 or 2600. Four base models are available in the 3600 series product family:

- **Cisco 3620**—Two network module slots (although one needs to be used for LAN/WAN connectivity)

- **Cisco 3640**—Four network module slots (although one needs to be used for LAN/WAN connectivity)

- **Cisco 3661**—Six network module slots and a built-in Fast Ethernet port

- **Cisco 3662**—Six network module slots and two built-in Fast Ethernet ports

Cisco 3700 Series Routers

The Cisco 3700 series routers are very similar to the 3600 series routers. They use the same network modules and WIC/VIC cards. The biggest difference is that the 3700 series has two built-in autosensing 10/100 Fast Ethernet ports. The two available models are as follows:

- **Cisco 3725**—Two network module slots, one of which can accept a High-Density Service Module (HDSM), three WIC slots, two Advanced Integration Module (AIM) slots, 100,000 pps performance

- **Cisco 3745**—Four network module slots, two of which can accept an HDSM, three WIC slots, two AIM slots, 225,000 pps performance

Cisco Catalyst 4224

The Cisco Catalyst 4224 is an ideal platform for a small branch office. It offers 24 inline-power-capable ports, 3 VIC/WIC slots, and an 8-port FXS module that is field-upgradeable.

NOTE   As of October 2002, Cisco no longer offers the Catalyst 4224 for sale. Similar functionality to the 4224 can be found in Cisco 2600/3600/3700 IOS gateways with 16 or 36 port EtherSwitch modules in addition to WAN and Voice ports.

The Catalyst 4224 can accept the same VIC cards as the VG200, but the DSPs come on the motherboard of the 4224. Note that the 4224 has enough DSPs for 24 medium-complexity calls. A G.711 or G.729a call is considered a medium-complexity call, whereas a G.729 call is considered a high-complexity call. This means that you can do a full T1 or fractional E1 as long as you use one of the medium-complexity codecs. To be able to use all 24 channels for the VIC slots, you must disable the onboard 8-port FXS module, or you can use the 8-port FXS module and use the remaining 16 DSP channels for your VIC cards.

The nice thing about the Catalyst 4224 is that you can have everything you need to run a small office in one box because it can act as your WAN router, an inline-power-capable switch for your phones, a voice gateway for PSTN access, and an SRST router in the event of a WAN outage. (For more information about SRST, see Chapter 15, "Survivable Remote Site Telephony (SRST).")

Cisco Catalyst 4000 Access Gateway Module (AGM)

The Catalyst 4000 Access Gateway Module (AGM) is a module available for the Catalyst 4000 series switches. This module connects to the switch with a 1-gigabit (Gb) connection to the switch fabric. The module has three VIC/WIC slots and an expansion module for a high-density FXS module.

Cisco WS-SVC-CMM Communications Media Module (CMM)

The Catalyst 6000 CMM is a perfect fit for IP Telephony deployments requiring high-density T1, E1, and FXS interfaces. The CMM has interface slots that can accept one of the following modules:

- Six-port T1 card
- Six-port E1 card
- 24-port FXS card

In its first release, the CMM is only able to act as an MGCP gateway for CallManager. Future versions, however, might support other protocols such as H.323 or Session Intitiation Protocol (SIP).

The CMM runs Cisco IOS software and is designed to be a standalone voice gateway. It is not designed to provide routing functionality to the Catalyst switch. Configuration and troubleshooting of this module is identical to any other Cisco IOS voice gateway using MGCP to communicate with CallManager.

Other Cisco IOS Gateways

A variety of other Cisco IOS gateways can be used in an IP Telephony environment—namely, the 1751, 1760, 7200, and 7500. Although the hardware for these platforms is different from what is listed for the other specific gateway platforms, the troubleshooting methodology explained in this chapter applies to these platforms as well. However, note that not all the features, especially MGCP PRI backhaul, are supported on these platforms (although these platforms might close the feature gap with the 26/36/3700 series in the future).

Additionally, the AS5300, AS5400, and AS5800 series of gateways can also be used in an IP Telephony network. However, these gateways are targeted toward the service provider market. As such, they lack many features that are useful in an IP Telephony environment, such as CallManager MGCP support (these gateways do support MGCP, but they lack some features to allow them to be controlled by CallManager), multicast Music on Hold (MOH), XML autoconfiguration, and so on. As long as you do not need any of the additional features available on other platforms, the AS53/54/5800 series routers can all be used as an H.323 gateway in an IP Telephony network. Because all these platforms run Cisco IOS Software, troubleshooting is nearly identical between all platforms.

Understanding Dial Peer Matching in Cisco IOS Software

Call routing in Cisco IOS Software is controlled by a list of configuration structures called dial peers. A dial peer can be defined as either a Plain Old Telephone System (POTS) dial peer or one of several voice over packet dial peers. The discussion in this section focuses on VoIP peers, although Cisco IOS Software also supports voice over Frame Relay (VoFR) and voice over ATM (VoATM). CallManager does not support VoFR or VoATM, so they are not discussed in this book.

A *POTS dial peer* defines the characteristics of a traditional telephony network connection. The POTS dial peer maps a dial string to a specific voice port on the local gateway. Normally, the voice port connects the gateway to the local PSTN, a PBX, or an analog telephone.

A *VoIP dial peer* defines the attributes of a packet voice network connection. A VoIP dial peer maps a dial string to a remote network device and also sets the attributes of the network connection, such as the codec to use, the capability to do voice activity detection (VAD), and DTMF relay configuration. A VoIP dial peer can point to any H.323-compatible device, such as another gateway, a CallManager server, or an H.323 gatekeeper. VoIP peers can also use protocols other than H.323, such as Session Initiation Protocol (SIP). These are not discussed in the context of CallManager-gateway interaction because CallManager supports only H.323 and MGCP to communicate with a Cisco IOS gateway. MGCP configuration on a Cisco IOS gateway does not use VoIP dial peers.

The first thing to understand about dial peers is the concept of inbound and outbound call legs. Every call that traverses a Cisco IOS gateway must match both an inbound and an outbound peer, one for each call leg. Figure 6-1 shows how a call between an IP Phone and the PSTN has both a VoIP call leg and a POTS call leg.

Figure 6-1 *VoIP and POTS Call Legs on a Cisco IOS Gateway*

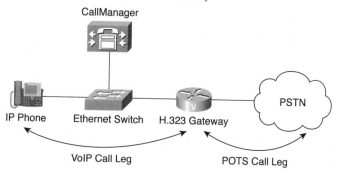

Each call leg can be either an inbound or an outbound call leg, depending on the call's direction. For a call from an IP Phone to the PSTN, the VoIP call leg is the inbound call leg, and the POTS leg is the outbound call leg. The opposite is true for a call from the PSTN to the IP Phone.

All this talk of inbound and outbound call legs is important because every call has an inbound and outbound call leg associated with it. Various rules govern which dial peers get selected for both the inbound and outbound call legs.

Example 6-1 looks at the configuration of some sample dial peers.

Example 6-1   *POTS and VoIP Dial Peer Configuration*

```
dial-peer voice 111 pots
 destination-pattern 9T
 port 1/1/1
!
dial-peer voice 110 pots
 application mgcpapp
 port 1/1/0
!
dial-peer voice 99 voip
 incoming called-number 9
 destination-pattern 156..
 session target ipv4:172.18.106.59
 dtmf-relay h245-alphanumeric
 codec g711ulaw
 no vad
!
```

Each dial peer starts with the keywords **dial-peer voice** followed by a dial peer number. This number is locally significant to the gateway and plays no part in the call routing logic. In fact, dial peers appear in the configuration in the order they are entered, not in the order of the dial peer numbers. After the dial peer number is a keyword that identifies what kind of peer it is. For this discussion, the keyword is either **voip** or **pots**, although **vofr** and **voatm** are valid for voice over Frame Relay and voice over ATM networks.

Each dial peer can contain a variety of parameters. Some parameters are valid only for VoIP dial peers, others are valid only for POTS dial peers, and a few are valid for all dial peers.

One function of dial peers is to select where to route a call. The dial peer configuration parameter **destination-pattern** is used to configure call routing. A text string follows the **destination-pattern** parameter and can contain any of the following:

- Any digit from 0 to 9, *, #, or A to D.
- **T** indicates zero or more digits.
- . matches exactly one digit.
- [*digit(s)*] matches one or more digits exactly once. For example, [**24-6**] matches the digit 2, 4, 5, or 6.
- , pauses for 1 second (this is available only on a POTS dial peer).

For example, **destination-pattern 156..** matches a range of numbers between 15600 and 15699. The command **destination-pattern 9T** matches the digit **9** followed by zero or more digits. The command **destination-pattern [2-5]....** matches the digits 20000 through 59999.

It is possible for multiple dial peers to match a given digit string. Cisco IOS Software attempts to perform longest-match routing in most cases. That means that if you have two patterns, **555....** and **55512..**, and the called party number is 5551234, Cisco IOS Software matches the peer with **55512..**; however, if the call to that peer fails, the gateway attempts to use the other peer that matches.

Also note that a dial peer with a **T** introduces an interdigit timeout because it can accept a variable number of digits on interfaces that can accept digits one at a time. This includes all POTS interfaces except PRI and BRI, unless overlap sending is being used. In the case of overlap sending, PRI and BRI also send digits one at a time.

You might also have more than one peer with the same destination pattern configured. In that case, the **preference** command on the dial peer is the tiebreaker. The peer with the lowest preference gets the highest priority, which might seem counterintuitive. The default preference is 0.

Table 6-1 shows five sample dial peers.

Table 6-1   *Sample Dial Peers to Illustrate Dial Peer Matching*

Dial Peer	Destination Pattern	Preference	Session Target
1	4085551048	1	voip 1
2	408555....	0	voip 2
3	408555....	1	pots 1
4	....	1	pots 2
5	....	0	voip 3

Assume that a call arrives with a Digital Number Identification Service (DNIS, also known as the called party number) of 4085551048. Try to determine the order in which the dial peers are matched.

The correct order is 1, 2, 3, 5, 4. Dial peer 1 has the longest match, so it comes first even though its preference is higher. Dial peers 2 and 3 both have the next-closest match, but dial peer 2 has a lower preference, so it is chosen first. Finally, dial peers 4 and 5 are the last match based on destination pattern, but dial peer 5 has a lower preference than dial peer 4, so dial peer 5 comes first.

Dial peer matching gets more complicated when variable-length destination patterns are involved. Table 6-2 shows an example of three dial peers with variable lengths.

Table 6-2   *Sample Dial Peers to Illustrate Variable-Length Matching*

Dial Peer	Destination Pattern	Preference	Session Target
1	4085551048	0	voip 1
2	408...	1	voip 2
3	408...	0	voip 3

In the case where matching occurs one digit at a time (as opposed to a PRI using enbloc sending, where all the DNIS digits are delivered at once in the setup message), dial peer matching for variable lengths is more complex. The longest match on the destination pattern applies immediately whenever the first match is hit. This means that in Table 6-2, dial peer 3 is matched first, followed by dial peer 2. Dial peer 1 is never matched because as soon as dial peer 2 and 3 are matched, the call is routed and no more digits are accepted by the voice gateway. This is not the case when digits arrive at the same time. For example, a PRI or BRI usually sends the digits at one time, especially in North America. Also, when a voice gateway receives an H.323 call setup from CallManager, all the digits arrive at the same time, so it is possible to match dial peer 1 in that scenario.

Assuming a call in which the DNIS is 4085551048 and all the digits are presented to the voice gateway at the same time (that is, ISDN or H.323 call setup), the dial peer matching order is 1, 3, 2.

Dial peer matching is further complicated when dial peers have a **T** in the destination pattern. As mentioned earlier, **T** matches on zero or more digits. Because it can match on a variable length of digits, a **T** in a destination pattern causes the voice gateway to wait for more digits up until the interdigit timeout expires. If all the dial peers that match a given string of digits have a T, the voice gateway continues collecting digits until the interdigit timeout before making a match. Table 6-3 shows two dial peers to illustrate this.

Table 6-3   *Sample Dial Peers to Illustrate Variable-Length Matching and Interdigit Timeout*

Dial Peer	Destination Pattern	Preference	Session Target
1	408555104.T	1	voip 1
2	408...T	0	voip 2

If a call with DNIS 4085551048 is dialed on a voice gateway configured as shown in Table 6-3, after the 8 is dialed, the calling party must wait for the interdigit timeout to expire (10 seconds by default) before the voice gateway makes a routing decision. Dial peer 1 is selected because it is the longest match, followed by dial peer 2, which is a less-specific match.

After a dial peer has been matched, you must tell the gateway where to route the call. On a POTS dial peer, the destination corresponds with a physical port on the gateway. For example, to route any call that starts with 9 and zero or more additional digits to port 1/1/1 on a gateway, use the configuration shown in Example 6-2.

Example 6-2   *Example of a POTS Dial Peer*

```
dial-peer voice 111 pots
  destination-pattern 9T
  port 1/1/1
```

When a call is routed to a POTS dial peer, *the default behavior is to strip any digits that were explicitly matched and pass the rest.* For example, if you were using the dial peer shown in Example 6-2, the **9** would be stripped, and any remaining digits would be passed to the PSTN. This is a common cause of calls not completing correctly when being routed out an H.323 gateway. To override the default behavior, use the dial peer configuration command **no digit-strip** or use the command **forward-digits all**. You can also use the **prefix** command to put back the digits that were stripped or prefix different digits than those that were stripped.

In the case of a VoIP dial peer, you must tell the gateway what IP address to send the call to. You do this using the **session-target ipv4:***ip address* command. For example, to route any call from 15600 through 15699 to a CallManager with IP address 172.18.106.59, you would use the configuration shown in Example 6-3.

Example 6-3   *Example of a VoIP Dial Peer*

```
dial-peer voice 99 voip
  destination-pattern 156..
  session target ipv4:172.18.106.59
```

You can configure a variety of commands on the VoIP and POTS dial peers to set various characteristics of a call that is routed via that dial peer. On a VoIP dial peer, some of these parameters include codec, DTMF relay, and VAD. These parameters are very important because a mismatch can cause calls to fail or can result in suboptimal voice quality. Table 6-4 lists the most commonly used parameters for VoIP dial peers.

Table 6-4   **dial-peer voice voip** *Optional Parameters*

Parameter	Description
codec	Specifies the codec to be attempted when using this dial peer.
dtmf-relay	Transports DTMF digits across the IP link. Valid options are **h245-alphanumeric**, **h245-signal**, and **cisco-rtp**. This should always be set to **h245-alphanumeric** when the dial peer is pointing to CallManager.
fax rate	Configures fax relay. The default is **fax rate voice**, which tries to use the highest speed possible depending on the codec being used. **fax rate disable** can be used to disable fax relay.

continues

Table 6-4   **dial-peer voice voip** *Optional Parameters (Continued)*

Parameter	Description
fax-relay	Disables error correction mode (ECM) when you're using fax relay.
huntstop	Stops hunting on dial peers.
ip qos **ip precedence**	Sets Layer 3 Differentiated Services Code Point (DSCP) or IP Precedence bits for voice traffic on calls matching the peer. The **ip precedence** command has been replaced with **ip qos** in Cisco IOS Software Release 12.2(2)T and later.
max-conn	Sets the maximum number of simultaneous calls using this dial peer.
playout-delay	Configures the voice playout delay (jitter) buffer.
preference	Configures this dial peer's preference order. If two dial peers have the same destination pattern configured, the **preference** command is the tiebreaker. Lower numbers get higher preference. The default preference is 0.
translate-outgoing	Matches a translation rule before the call is routed using this peer.
vad	Enables/disables voice activity detection.
voice-class codec	Sets an ordered list of codecs in preference order instead of using the **codec** command to select a single codec.
voice-class h323	Sets an H.225 TCP timeout value. Can also be used to enable or disable H.323 Fast Connect.

POTS dial peers also have various parameters that can be used to change the characteristics of calls that match the dial peer. You've already read about the **digit-strip** and **forward-digits** parameters. Table 6-5 lists the most commonly used parameters on a POTS dial peer.

Table 6-5   **dial-peer voice pots** *Optional Parameters*

Parameter	Description
application	Invokes a variety of applications when a call is received on a port. In the case of CallManager, you use **application MGCPAPP** to enable MGCP on a port. The default is the **session** application.
digit-strip	Strips all explicitly matched digits on a POTS dial peer. The default is **enabled**. You can disable this using the command **no digit-strip**.
direct-inward-dial	Uses the called party number to route the call immediately instead of providing dial tone and waiting for digits. Used on ISDN PRI and BRI interfaces when called party number information is provided by the service provider/PBX. Do not use this for analog or T1 CAS interfaces. Doing so results in calls being dropped immediately because the gateway needs to wait for digits from these interfaces prior to routing the call.

Table 6-5   **dial-peer voice pots** *Optional Parameters (Continued)*

Parameter	Description
forward-digits	Lets you forward a specific number of digits. Valid values are as follows: • **0 to 32**—Indicates the number of right-justified dialed digits to forward. • **all**—Forwards all digits without stripping any. • **extra**—Sends all the digits that are not explicitly matched (this is the default behavior).
huntstop	Stops hunting on dial peers.
max-conn	Sets the maximum number of simultaneous calls using this dial peer.
numbering-type	Sets the calling/called party numbering type for interfaces that support sending this information (ISDN).
preference	Configures this dial peer's preference order. If two dial peers have the same destination pattern configured, the **preference** command is the tiebreaker. Lower numbers get higher preference. The default preference is 0.
prefix	Indicates the pattern to be dialed before the dialed number.
progress_ind	Allows the progress indicator information element to be overwritten for specific messages. Possible values are **alert**, **connect**, **progress**, and **setup**. The use of this command is discussed in detail in the later section "Troubleshooting Problems with Ringback and Other Progress Tones."
translate-outgoing	Used to match a translation rule before the call is routed using this peer.

Remember that every H.323 call that is processed by a Cisco IOS gateway must match both an inbound and outbound dial peer. Matching the called party number with the **destination-pattern** command is *always* used to match an outbound dial peer. So how does the inbound peer get selected, and why is this important?

When a call goes from CallManager to a gateway, the call's outbound leg is the POTS side of the call. Matching the proper dial peer uses the **destination-pattern** command, as mentioned earlier. However, how do you determine what parameters to use for VoIP-specific parameters such as codec, DTMF relay, and VAD? Without inbound peer matching, there would be no way to accomplish this. In this case, the inbound peer dictates how the VoIP parameters get set. The inbound peer does not affect where the call is routed, but it does determine all the call properties for the VoIP side of the call, regardless of what outbound peer it terminates on.

A couple of dial peer configuration commands that have not yet been covered let you choose which inbound dial peer gets selected for a given call. These commands are **incoming called-number** and **answer-address**.

The **incoming called-number** and **answer-address** commands are used only to match inbound peers. They are never used for call routing or choosing an outbound peer. Similar to the **destination-pattern** command, the **incoming called-number** command matches based on the called party number; however, this command does not play a role in where the call is routed. It is used only to select the inbound peer. For example, assume that the dial peers shown in Example 6-4 are configured on an H.323 gateway.

Example 6-4   *Dial Peer Examples Showing the Use of* **incoming called-number**

```
dial-peer voice 111 pots
 destination-pattern 9T
 port 1/1/1
!
dial-peer voice 99 voip
 incoming called-number 9
 destination-pattern 156..
 session target ipv4:172.18.106.59
 dtmf-relay h245-alphanumeric
 codec g711ulaw
 no vad
```

When a call arrives from CallManager, the gateway must select an inbound dial peer. Assume that the called number is 95551212 and that the calling party number is 5155515600. In this case, the gateway matches dial peer **99** because 95551212 matches the statement **incoming called-number 9**. This means that the VoIP parameters are set in accordance with the configuration of dial peer **99**. Next the gateway must select the outbound peer. In this case it must use **destination-pattern** as the criteria for matching, so you match dial peer 111 for the outbound peer.

If you do not have any peer with **incoming called-number** configured that matches the called party number, the next possibility for matching an inbound peer involves the command **answer-address**. The **answer-address** command tries for a match using the calling party number information instead of the called party number. The **answer-address** command is followed by a pattern just like the **destination-pattern** and **incoming called-number** commands. The important thing to remember is that the match is on the calling party information. For example, if you configured a VoIP dial peer with the configuration command **answer-address 515551....**, a call with the calling party number 5155515600 would use that peer for the VoIP parameters. This assumes that no peer matched based on **incoming called-number** first.

If no peer matches based on **incoming called-number** or **answer-address**, there is one final check. The calling party information is matched against the **destination-pattern** commands configured on your dial peers. Remember that the focus here is on matching for the inbound peer characteristics, not for any routing information. Also note that it is the calling party number information that is matched. For example, assume that the dial peers are configured as shown in Example 6-5.

Example 6-5   *Sample Dial Peers Showing Inbound Peer Matching Based on Destination Pattern*

```
dial-peer voice 111 pots
 destination-pattern 9T
 port 1/1/1
!
dial-peer voice 99 voip
 destination-pattern 156..
 session target ipv4:172.18.106.59
 dtmf-relay h245-alphanumeric
 codec g711ulaw
 no vad
```

Assume that a call comes in with a called party number of 95551212 and a calling party number of 15600. No peer matches **incoming-called number** for 95551212, and there is no peer with an **answer-address** that matches 15600, so the last resort is to look for a destination-pattern that matches 15600. You see that **dial peer 99** has a **destination-pattern** of **156..**, which matches 15600, so **dial peer 99** is selected as the inbound peer. The gateway still needs to select the outbound peer; that match is **111** based on the **destination-pattern** match on the called party number of 95551212.

For calls that are originating on a POTS port, the same rules for selecting an inbound peer apply, with one additional possibility. If a match cannot be made using any of the three methods previously detailed, the inbound dial peer is matched based on port configuration. The dial peer that is used is the first dial peer in the configuration that specifies the port the call came in on.

If no inbound peer can be matched using any of the criteria already listed, the inbound peer is set to **peer ID 0**. The characteristics of **peer ID 0** cannot be changed. For an inbound VoIP call, **peer ID 0** has the following characteristics:

- Any supported codec
- No DTMF relay
- IP precedence 0
- VAD-enabled
- No RSVP support
- Fax-rate voice

For an incoming call on a POTS port, peer ID 0 has the following characteristics:

- No application
- No direct inward dial

You should always try to avoid using **peer ID 0** when possible. You should always have a peer with **incoming called-number** configured correctly to ensure that you always match a VoIP peer with the parameters you want when placing outbound calls through a Cisco IOS gateway. A large number of problems with calling out through a Cisco IOS gateway are due to codec/VAD/DTMF-relay misconfiguration because peer ID 0 is being matched. To see which dial peers are being matched for an active call, use the command **show call active voice brief**. Refer to Example 6-11 to see sample output for this command.

NOTE   When a call comes in via VoIP, the voice gateway searches for an inbound peer by looking through all the configured VoIP dial peers. Using regular digit-matching rules, it tries to match in this order:

1. Match the called number with the incoming called number.

2. Match the calling number with the answer-address.

3. Match the calling number with the destination pattern.

4. Otherwise, use peer ID 0.

When a call comes in via POTS, the voice gateway searches for an inbound peer by looking through all the configured POTS dial peers. Using regular digit-matching rules, it tries to match a peer in the following order.

If the inbound interface is PRI or BRI the following rules are used:

1. Match the called number with the incoming called number.

2. Match the calling number with the answer-address.

3. Match the calling number with the destination pattern.

If the inbound interface is not PRI or BRI, or if a PRI or BRI interface does not match a dial peer using the preceding three rules, the voice gateway matches a POTS dial peer that has the inbound port configured as long as any of the following are configured: **destination-pattern**, **answer-address**, or **incoming called-number**. Note that **answer-address** in this case overwrites the call's calling-party number (ANI).

Understanding Cisco IOS Debugs and show Commands

Now that you understand how dial peer matching works, you need to examine the various troubleshooting facilities that are available in Cisco IOS Software to help you find the solution to your problem.

As you can see, Cisco IOS gateways support a wide variety of TDM-based telephony interfaces. The following sections cover each of these protocols and the associated debugs to troubleshoot problems related to these protocols. In addition to these protocols, you must also examine the signaling protocols being used on the packet telephony side. CallManager can use either H.323 or MGCP to communicate with a Cisco IOS gateway. Some TDM-based interfaces are supported on either H.323 or MGCP but not both; however, the majority of interfaces are supported on both. For example, analog E&M interfaces are supported only on H.323.

Correctly Setting the Timestamps

Before you start troubleshooting a gateway running Cisco IOS Software, the first thing you should do is make sure your timestamps are set correctly. By default, the timestamps show the amount of time since the gateway was booted. The units are granular down to the minute. This is usually unacceptable for telephony debugging. What you want is to get the timestamps down to the millisecond level, and you want them to show you the exact date and time using the local time zone. Add the following commands to your configuration:

```
service timestamps debug datetime localtime msec
service timestamps log datetime localtime msec
```

Also, just like the recommendation to keep your CallManager server time synchronized with a Network Time Protocol (NTP) server, you should do the same on all your Cisco IOS gateways. Doing so lets you correlate debugging information from the gateway to that in the CCM traces.

The timestamp setting is also important for troubleshooting problems involving timeouts. If you see a call being rejected as a result of a timeout, the debugs show you exactly how much time elapsed before the timeout occurred. This can help you determine which timeout you are running into. We discuss various timeouts later in this chapter.

Enabling Cisco IOS Software Debugs

Enabling debugs in Cisco IOS Software is fairly easy; however, you should be aware of a few things when working with debugging facilities in Cisco IOS Software.

The first thing to be aware of is the various places where debugging information can be displayed. Depending on your configuration, debugs can be displayed on the console port, via a vty session (for example, Telnet, ssh, rsh, and so on), to a remote syslog server, or to the logging buffer in Cisco IOS Software.

The one to be most careful with is the console port. Most Cisco IOS gateways default to a console baud rate of 9600 baud. Most voice debugs are quite verbose and therefore generate a large amount of debug output in a short period of time. The console port almost never can keep up with the more verbose debugs. Additionally, the console port is interrupt-driven and consumes a high amount of CPU power when it is overloaded with debug messages. For this reason, you should disable logging to the console port while debugging most voice problems. This is usually not a problem if you are generating only one call at a time, but in a production environment, be especially careful with the number of debugs you enable and where they are being logged. To disable logging to the console, enter the configuration mode command **no logging console**.

Most of the time you should do your debugging from a vty session such as a Telnet or secure shell (ssh) session. You must do two things to be able to get debug output from a vty session:

- Make sure that **logging monitor** is configured on the gateway. This is the default setting, so it does not show up in the Cisco IOS configuration. If you see **no logging monitor** in the configuration, remove it by configuring **logging monitor**.

- Enable logging each time you establish a vty session. You issue the command to do this from the enable prompt on the gateway, not in configuration mode. The command to issue is **terminal monitor**. After you enter **terminal monitor**, all debugging information is displayed in your vty session. Note that you must issue this command every time you access the gateway via a vty session. You can issue the command **terminal no monitor** to disable logging messages to the vty session; however, debugs remain enabled and are output to any of the other previously mentioned locations (console, syslog server, and so on).

The last place to send debugging information is to the Cisco IOS Software logging buffer. This buffer uses up dynamic RAM (DRAM), so be careful how large you set this. First, take a look at how your logging settings are currently configured by issuing the command **show log**, as demonstrated in Example 6-6.

Example 6-6   **show log** *Command Showing the Current Logging Level*

```
Router#show log
Syslog logging: enabled (0 messages dropped, 0 messages rate-limited, 0 flushes,
   0 overruns)
    Console logging: level debugging, 358 messages logged
    Monitor logging: level debugging, 37 messages logged
        Logging to: vty66(0)
    Buffer logging: disabled
    Logging Exception size (4096 bytes)
    Trap logging: level informational, 16 message lines logged
```

As you can see, console logging is enabled, monitor logging is enabled, and buffer logging is disabled. You also can see that the user connected via vty66 has issued the **terminal monitor** command because the output says **Logging to: vty66(0)**.

To determine a safe level to set your buffer logging to, issue the command **show memory summary**. Example 6-7 shows the output.

Example 6-7   **show memory summary** *Command Showing the Largest Free Memory Block*

```
Router#show memory summary
                 Head     Total(b)    Used(b)    Free(b)    Lowest(b)   Largest(b)
Processor    80EFC7F0    13645840    4372260    9273580     9248948     9243044
      I/O     1C00000     4194304    1813624    2380680     2378192     2380636
```

You want to look at the **Processor** line and the column labeled **Largest(b)**. This indicates the largest free contiguous piece of memory. As you can see, this gateway has more than 9 MB of memory available, so setting the logging buffer to 512 KB should not be a problem.

To set the logging buffer to 512 KB, configure the following:

```
logging buffered 512000 debugging
```

You enable Cisco IOS Software debugs from the command line in enable mode. As soon as your logging is configured correctly, as just explained, you can enable a variety of debugs by entering **debug** followed by the debug you want to enable. For example, the **debug isdn q931** command enables Q.931 protocol debugging. Debugs are cumulative, so enabling one debug does not disable previously enabled debugs. You can view which debugs are enabled at any given time by entering **show debug**. You can stop a particular debug by entering **no** before the command you used to enable the debug. For example, to disable the Q.931 protocol debugging, enter **no debug isdn q931**. If you want to turn off all debugging, issue the command **no debug all** or **undebug all**. You can shorten **undebug all** to **un al** if you need to turn off debugs quickly. This is especially helpful if you notice you've turned on a debug that might be generating too much output.

Troubleshooting TDM Interfaces on Cisco IOS Gateways

This section looks at some of the Cisco IOS Software debugs and **show** commands available for the myriad of analog and digital TDM-based interfaces.

The good news is that much of the information that applies to one TDM interface applies to both H.323 and MGCP. For this reason, covering the debugs and **show** commands specific to each TDM-based interface is the first topic of discussion, followed by discussing the debugs and **show** commands associated with H.323 and MGCP.

The majority of Cisco AVVID installations use one or more of the following TDM interfaces for PSTN and traditional analog device connectivity:

- FXS
- FXO (loop start or ground start)
- Analog E&M
- Analog Direct Inward Dial (DID)
- ISDN PRI
- ISDN BRI
- T1/E1 Channel Associated Signaling (E&M wink start or immediate start)

Depending on the interface you are using, you need to enable one or more debugs on the Cisco IOS gateway to examine what is happening.

Useful show Commands for Troubleshooting TDM Interfaces

You can use a variety of **show** commands to diagnose the state of ports on a Cisco IOS gateway.

The first is **show voice port summary**. Example 6-8 shows typical output from this command.

Example 6-8   **show voice port summary** *Command Displays POTS Port Status*

```
Router#show voice port summary
                IN    OUT
PORT   CH  SIG-TYPE     ADMIN OPER STATUS   STATUS   EC
====== == ============ ===== ==== ======== ======== ==
1/0/0  -- fxs-ls       up    up   on-hook  ringing  y
1/0/1  -- fxs-ls       up    up   off-hook idle     y
1/1/0  -- fxo-ls       up    dorm idle     on-hook  y
1/1/1  -- fxo-ls       up    dorm idle     on-hook  y
```

As you can see, this gateway has a total of four analog ports—two FXS ports and two FXO ports. Port 1/0/0 is currently on-hook and ringing because of an incoming call, and port 1/0/1 is off-hook, so either it is on a call or the phone was left off the hook. The two FXO ports are idle.

You can get more details if you issue the same command without the **summary** option at the end. You can specify a port to look at as well. For example, you can issue the command **show voice port 1/0/0**, as demonstrated in Example 6-9.

Example 6-9   **show voice port 1/0/0** *Command Shows a Detailed Port Status*

```
Router#show voice port 1/0/0
Foreign Exchange Station 1/0/0 Slot is 1, Sub-unit is 0, Port is 0
 Type of VoicePort is FXS
 Operation State is DORMANT
 Administrative State is UP
 No Interface Down Failure
 Description is not set
 Noise Regeneration is enabled
 Non Linear Processing is enabled
 Non Linear Mute is disabled
 Non Linear Threshold is -21 dB
 Music On Hold Threshold is Set to -38 dBm
 In Gain is Set to 0 dB
 Out Attenuation is Set to 3 dB
 Echo Cancellation is enabled
 Echo Cancellation NLP mute is disabled
 Echo Cancellation NLP threshold is -21 dB
 Echo Cancel Coverage is set to 8 ms
 Playout-delay Mode is set to default
 Playout-delay Nominal is set to 60 ms
 Playout-delay Maximum is set to 200 ms
 Playout-delay Minimum mode is set to default, value 40 ms
 Playout-delay Fax is set to 300 ms
 Connection Mode is normal
 Connection Number is not set
 Initial Time Out is set to 10 s
 Interdigit Time Out is set to 10 s
 Call Disconnect Time Out is set to 60 s
 Ringing Time Out is set to 180 s
```

Example 6-9   **show voice port 1/0/0** *Command Shows a Detailed Port Status (Continued)*

```
Wait Release Time Out is set to 30 s
Companding Type is u-law
Region Tone is set for US

Analog Info Follows:
Currently processing none
Maintenance Mode Set to None (not in mtc mode)
Number of signaling protocol errors are 0
Impedance is set to 600r Ohm
Station name None, Station number None

Voice card specific Info Follows:
Signal Type is loopStart
Ring Frequency is 25 Hz
Hook Status is On Hook
Ring Active Status is inactive
Ring Ground Status is inactive
Tip Ground Status is inactive
Digit Duration Timing is set to 100 ms
InterDigit Duration Timing is set to 100 ms
No disconnect acknowledge
Ring Cadence is defined by CPTone Selection
Ring Cadence are [20 40] * 100 msec
```

This command gives you more information than you probably care to know about the voice port, but sometimes it is very useful in catching problems that otherwise might be difficult to track down.

Another useful command for checking the state of your voice ports is **show voice call summary**, as demonstrated in Example 6-10.

Example 6-10   **show voice call summary** *Shows Call State Information*

```
Router#show voice call summary
PORT          CODEC     VAD VTSP STATE            VPM STATE
============  ========  === ====================  ======================
1/0/0         -         -   -                     FXSLS_ONHOOK
1/0/1         None      y   S_ALERTING            FXSLS_OFFHOOK
1/1/0         -         -   -                     FXOLS_ONHOOK
1/1/1         -         -   -                     FXOLS_ONHOOK
```

This gives you a snapshot of the various ports on the gateway and their states. You can see that port 1/0/1 is in the alerting state and is currently off-hook.

Some of the states listed are relatively self-explanatory; however, others are not. Table 6-6 lists the valid values for the VTSP STATE column.

Table 6-6   *Voice Telephony Service Provider (VTSP) States and Descriptions*

VTSP State	Description
S_NULL	Uninitialized state machine.
S_SETUP_FAIL	The setup was processed, but it failed to get a DSP channel.
S_SETUP_IND_PEND	A setup is indicated. Wait for a DSP channel to open.
S_SETUP_INDICATED	Indicated setup to application.
S_DIGIT_COLLECT	DTMF/pulse digit collection mode.
S_PROCEEDING	The call is proceeding (still unconnected).
S_ALERTING	Performing local alerting (still unconnected).
S_WAIT_RELEASE_NC	The application terminated an unconnected call waiting for telephony disconnect (generate error tone).
S_WAIT_RELEASE_RESP	An unconnected application terminated the call. The user disconnect is waiting on a telephony service provider (TSP) release response.
S_WAIT_HOST_DISC	The caller hung up before the connection. Wait for the application disconnect.
S_WAIT_ERROR_STAT	Wait for DSP error statistics.
S_CONNECT	The call is connected.
S_SETUP_REQ_PROC	An outbound setup request was sent to the telephony service provider.
S_SETUP_REQ_FAIL	DSP request for outbound call failed. Wait for a CCAPI termination request.
S_SETUP_REQ_PEND	Setup requested. Wait for DSP channel.
S_SETUP_REQ_DISC	CCAPI disconnected while waiting for DSP channel.
S_CLOSE_DSPRM	Call processing is complete. Waiting for close_complete from DSP Resource Manager (DSPRM).
S_WAIT_STATS	Gather final call statistics.
S_WAIT_RELEASE	The application terminated the connected call.
S_LFAX_WAIT_ACK	Waiting for a remote fax switchover acknowledgment.
S_LFAX_DOWNLOAD	Downloading a fax due to local tone detect.
S_LFAX_WAIT_FAX	Wait for codec_fax before starting fax_mode.
S_FAX	Operating in fax relay mode.
S_RFAX_DOWNLOAD	Downloading a fax due to a remote fax detection.
S_RFAX_WAIT_ACK	Wait for fax acknowledgment before starting fax mode.
S_DOWNLOAD_TERM	Received a disconnect while downloading a fax. Terminate on download completion.

Table 6-6   *Voice Telephony Service Provider (VTSP) States and Descriptions (Continued)*

VTSP State	Description
S_FAX_TERM	Wait for voice download completion after disconnecting.
S_SETUP_IND_NO_DSP	No DSP is available on setup from the telephony service provider.
S_SETUP_REQUEST	Setup requested. Waiting for call proceeding.
S_SETUP_REQ_NO_DSP	No DSP is available on setup from CCAPI.
S_WAIT_STATS_RETRY	Retry one more time.
S_PCM_SWITCHOVER	Fax/modem PCM switchover in progress.
S_RFAX_SERVICE	Waiting for DSP fax service (remote side).
S_LFAX_SERVICE	Waiting for DSP fax service (local side).
S_LFAX_WAIT_CAPS_ACK	Waiting for T.38 fax relay capabilities.
S_ALLOC_DSP_PEND	Pending DSP open for allocate_dsp.
S_ALLOC_DSP	DSP allocated.
S_SETUP_PROGRESS	SETUP sent to telephony service provider and received PROGRESS.
UNKNOWN STATE	Unknown finite state machine (FSM) state.

By looking at the VTSP state, you can see the state of a call on a voice port at any given time.

One command that is very useful when you're troubleshooting any problem on a Cisco IOS gateway is **show call active voice** and the short version, **show call active voice brief**. Example 6-11 shows the output of **show call active voice brief**.

Example 6-11   *Output of* **show call active voice brief**

```
Router#show call active voice brief
<ID>: <start>hs.<index> +<connect> pid:<peer_id> <dir> <addr> <state>
  dur hh:mm:ss tx:<packets>/<bytes> rx:<packets>/<bytes>
 IP <ip>:<udp> rtt:<time>ms pl:<play>/<gap>ms lost:<lost>/<early>/<late>
  delay:<last>/<min>/<max>ms <codec>
  MODEMPASS <method> buf:<fills>/<drains> loss <overall%> <multipkt>/<corrected>
   last <buf event time>s dur:<Min>/<Max>s
 FR <protocol> [int dlci cid] vad:<y/n> dtmf:<y/n> seq:<y/n>
  sig:<on/off> <codec> (payload size)
 ATM <protocol> [int vpi/vci cid] vad:<y/n> dtmf:<y/n> seq:<y/n>
  sig:<on/off> <codec> (payload size)
 Tele <int>: tx:<tot>/<v>/<fax>ms <codec> noise:<l> acom:<l> i/o:<l>/<l> dBm
 Proxy <ip>:<audio udp>,<video udp>,<tcp0>,<tcp1>,<tcp2>,<tcp3> endpt: <type>/
<manf>
 bw: <req>/<act> codec: <audio>/<video>
  tx: <audio pkts>/<audio bytes>,<video pkts>/<video bytes>,<t120 pkts>/<t120 bytes>
  rx: <audio pkts>/<audio bytes>,<video pkts>/<video bytes>,<t120 pkts>/<t120 bytes>
```

continues

Example 6-11   *Output of* **show call active voice brief** *(Continued)*

```
Total call-legs: 4
1216 : 2134033hs.1 +413 pid:101 Answer 15801 active
 dur 00:00:22 tx:1127/180320 rx:1140/182400
 Tele 1/0/1:39: tx:22800/22800/0ms g711ulaw noise:0 acom:0  i/0:-48/-51 dBm

1216 : 2134335hs.1 +111 pid:99 Originate 15644 active
 dur 00:00:22 tx:1129/180640 rx:1127/180320
 IP 0.0.0.0:0 rtt:0ms pl:7370/40ms lost:0/0/0 delay:54/54/65ms g711ulaw

121A : 2134583hs.1 +1 pid:100 Answer  active
 dur 00:00:21 tx:747/119520 rx:878/140480
 Tele 1/0/0:41: tx:17560/17560/0ms g711ulaw noise:0 acom:0  i/0:-46/-42 dBm

121A : 2134970hs.1 +-1 pid:0 Originate  connecting
 dur 00:00:00 tx:749/119840 rx:747/119520
 IP 172.18.104.74:19496 rtt:0ms pl:14745/0ms lost:0/2/0 delay:54/54/65ms g711ulaw
```

The first part of the output explains the output shown for each call. There are two active calls on this gateway. Each active call has two call legs. Notice that the first field for each call leg is the ID parameter and that each pair of call legs has the same ID. You can use that to correlate the two call legs as one call.

The **pid:** parameter indicates which dial peer is matched for this particular call leg. Notice that for each call, an inbound and outbound peer are matched. In the case of the call with call ID 121A, you can see that peer ID 0 was matched, indicating that no specific configured dial peer matched this call.

You might be wondering why the first call lists the IP address as **0.0.0.0.** This is because the call is currently on hold. When using MOH, there is only an audio stream from the MOH server to the gateway, not in the reverse direction. Therefore, the gateway shows **0.0.0.0** because it does not transmit packets to any IP address during that time.

Using debug Commands to Troubleshoot TDM Interfaces

The states listed in Table 6-6 are also used in several debugs available in Cisco IOS Software. The most commonly used debugs for troubleshooting the TDM side of a call are

```
debug vtsp [session | dsp | tone | all]
debug vpm [signal | all]
```

The following is the output of **debug vtsp all** and **debug vtsp tone** for an FXS port. For some reason, **debug vtsp tone** is not included as part of **debug vtsp all**, so it must be enabled separately. Throughout the debug you see lines that look like this:

```
Jan 16 15:36:42.481: vtsp:[1/0/1:31, S_DIGIT_COLLECT, E_CC_GEN_TONE]
```

Whenever you see a line like this, it indicates a state machine event. You can see that this is port 1/0/1 and that the state is S_DIGIT_COLLECT. The event that has occurred is E_CC_GEN_TONE, which indicates that a tone is being played by the DSP. If you have

debug vtsp tone enabled, you see a line such as this, indicating what the tone is, for example:

```
Jan 16 15:36:42.481: act_gen_tone: Tone Dial generated in direction Network
```

Take a look at the whole debug. Don't be concerned with what every line means; learn to weed out the unimportant information. Most of these debugs are not the most user-friendly to read, so it takes a little practice to sort out the unimportant from the important.

First, the phone connected to the FXS port goes off-hook, and the gateway generates dial tone, as shown in Example 6-12.

Example 6-12   *VTSP Debug Information*

```
Router#debug vtsp all
Router#debug vtsp tone
Jan 16 15:36:42.465: vtsp_tsp_call_setup_ind (sdb=0x811AF7E4, tdm_info=0x0,
  tsp_info=0x811AF3B0, calling_number= calling_oct3 = 0x0, called_number=
  called_oct3 = 0x81, oct3a=0x0): peer_tag=101
Jan 16 15:36:42.465: : ev.clg.clir is 0
 ev.clg.clid_transparent is 0
 ev.clg.null_orig_clg is 1
 ev.clg.calling_translated is false

Jan 16 15:36:42.469: vtsp_do_call_setup_ind
Jan 16 15:36:42.469: vtsp_allocate_cdb,cdb 0x80F0A494
Jan 16 15:36:42.469: vtsp_do_call_setup_ind: Call ID=98350, guid=80F0A9F4
Jan 16 15:36:42.469: vtsp_do_call_setup_ind: type=2, under_spec=0, name=xQ$8,
  id0=0, id1=0, id2=1, calling=, called= subscriber=RegularLine
Jan 16 15:36:42.469: vtsp_do_normal_call_setup_ind
Jan 16 15:36:42.469: vtsp_insert_cdb,cdb 0x80F0A494
Jan 16 15:36:42.473: vtsp_open_voice_and_set_params
Jan 16 15:36:42.473: vtsp_modem_proto_from_cdb: cap_modem_proto 1073741824
Jan 16 15:36:42.473: vtsp_modem_proto_from_cdb:
  cap_modem_proto 1073741824playout default

Jan 16 15:36:42.473: set_gains:  gain->output=65506
Jan 16 15:36:42.477: vtsp_report_digit_control: enable=1: digit reporting enabled
Jan 16 15:36:42.477: : vtsp_get_digit_timeouts
Jan 16 15:36:42.477: vtsp:[1/0/1:31, S_SETUP_INDICATED, E_CC_SETUP_ACK]
Jan 16 15:36:42.477: act_setup_ind_ack act_setup_ind_ack(): vtsp_dsp_dtmf_mode()

Jan 16 15:36:42.477: vtsp_modem_proto_from_cdb: cap_modem_proto 0
Jan 16 15:36:42.477: vtsp_modem_proto_from_cdb: cap_modem_proto 0act_setup_ind_ack:
  modem_mode = 0, fax_relay_on = 1
Jan 16 15:36:42.481: act_setup_ind_ack(): dsp_dtmf_mode()

Jan 16 15:36:42.481: vtsp_timer: 1964036
Jan 16 15:36:42.481: vtsp:[1/0/1:31, S_DIGIT_COLLECT, E_CC_GEN_TONE]
Jan 16 15:36:42.481: act_gen_tone
Jan 16 15:36:42.481: act_gen_tone: Tone Dial generated in direction Network

Jan 16 15:36:42.481: vtsp:[1/0/1:31, S_DIGIT_COLLECT, E_CC_GEN_TONE]
Jan 16 15:36:42.481: act_gen_tone
Jan 16 15:36:42.481: act_gen_tone: Tone Dial generated in direction Network
```

Example 6-13 shows where the gateway begins collecting digits. Unfortunately, this debug does not show you the actual digits being collected. When you look at the **debug voip ccapi inout** output beginning in Example 6-18, you can see the digits there.

Example 6-13 *VTSP Debugs Showing Digits Being Collected*

```
Jan 16 15:36:44.605: vtsp:[1/0/1:31, S_DIGIT_COLLECT, E_DSP_DTMF_DIGIT_BEGIN]
Jan 16 15:36:44.605: act_report_digit_begin
Jan 16 15:36:44.745: vtsp:[1/0/1:31, S_DIGIT_COLLECT, E_DSP_DTMF_DIGIT]
Jan 16 15:36:44.745: act_report_digit_end
Jan 16 15:36:44.745: vtsp_timer_stop: 1964262
Jan 16 15:36:44.749: vtsp_timer: 1964262
Jan 16 15:36:44.877: vtsp:[1/0/1:31, S_DIGIT_COLLECT, E_DSP_DTMF_DIGIT_BEGIN]
Jan 16 15:36:44.877: act_report_digit_begin
Jan 16 15:36:44.977: vtsp:[1/0/1:31, S_DIGIT_COLLECT, E_DSP_DTMF_DIGIT]
Jan 16 15:36:44.977: act_report_digit_end
Jan 16 15:36:44.977: vtsp_timer_stop: 1964285
Jan 16 15:36:44.977: vtsp_timer: 1964285
Jan 16 15:36:45.105: vtsp:[1/0/1:31, S_DIGIT_COLLECT, E_DSP_DTMF_DIGIT_BEGIN]
Jan 16 15:36:45.105: act_report_digit_begin
Jan 16 15:36:45.205: vtsp:[1/0/1:31, S_DIGIT_COLLECT, E_DSP_DTMF_DIGIT]
Jan 16 15:36:45.205: act_report_digit_end
Jan 16 15:36:45.205: vtsp_timer_stop: 1964308
Jan 16 15:36:45.209: vtsp_timer: 1964308
Jan 16 15:36:45.345: vtsp:[1/0/1:31, S_DIGIT_COLLECT, E_DSP_DTMF_DIGIT_BEGIN]
Jan 16 15:36:45.345: act_report_digit_begin
Jan 16 15:36:45.465: vtsp:[1/0/1:31, S_DIGIT_COLLECT, E_DSP_DTMF_DIGIT]
Jan 16 15:36:45.465: act_report_digit_end
Jan 16 15:36:45.465: vtsp_timer_stop: 1964334
Jan 16 15:36:45.469: vtsp_timer: 1964334
Jan 16 15:36:45.585: vtsp:[1/0/1:31, S_DIGIT_COLLECT, E_DSP_DTMF_DIGIT_BEGIN]
Jan 16 15:36:45.585: act_report_digit_begin
Jan 16 15:36:45.685: vtsp:[1/0/1:31, S_DIGIT_COLLECT, E_DSP_DTMF_DIGIT]
Jan 16 15:36:45.685: act_report_digit_end
Jan 16 15:36:45.685: vtsp_timer_stop: 1964356
Jan 16 15:36:45.689: vtsp_timer: 1964356
Jan 16 15:36:45.689: vtsp_report_digit_control: enable=0: digit reporting disabled
Jan 16 15:36:45.689: : vtsp_get_digit_timeouts
Jan 16 15:36:45.689: vtsp_save_dialpeer_tag: tag = 99
Jan 16 15:36:45.689: vtsp:[1/0/1:31, S_DIGIT_COLLECT, E_CC_PROCEEDING]
Jan 16 15:36:45.693: act_dcollect_proc
Jan 16 15:36:45.745: vtsp_get_dialpeer_tag: tag = 99
Jan 16 15:36:45.945: vtsp_get_dialpeer_tag: tag = 99
```

Next the call transitions into the call proceeding state, and the gateway generates ringback, as shown in Example 6-14.

Example 6-14 *VTSP Debug Showing the Call Proceeding State and Ringback Generation*

```
Jan 16 15:36:45.945: vtsp:[1/0/1:31, S_PROCEEDING, E_CC_ALERT]
Jan 16 15:36:45.945: act_alert
Jan 16 15:36:45.945: vtsp_timer_stop: 1964382
Jan 16 15:36:45.945: act_alert: Tone Ring Back generated in direction Network
```

Notice the gap in the timestamps between Examples 6-14 and 6-15. During this time, the calling party is hearing ringback, and the called party is ringing. After 5 seconds, the remote phone answers, and the gateway begins setting up the audio stream prior to ending up in the **S_CONNECT** state, as shown in Example 6-15.

Example 6-15 *VTSP Debug Showing the Transition from Alerting State to Connect State*

```
Jan 16 15:36:50.281: vtsp_get_dialpeer_tag: tag = 99
Jan 16 15:36:50.281: vtsp:[1/0/1:31, S_ALERTING, E_CC_BRIDGE]
Jan 16 15:36:50.281: act_bridge
Jan 16 15:36:50.281: vtsp:[1/0/1:31, S_ALERTING, E_CC_CAPS_IND]
Jan 16 15:36:50.285: act_caps_ind
Jan 16 15:36:50.285: act_caps_ind: passthrough: cap_modem_proto 0,
  cap_modem_codec 0, cap_modem_redundancy 0, payload 100
Jan 16 15:36:50.285: act_caps_ind:CC_CAP_ENCAP_RTP Encap 1, Vad 1, Codec 0x1,
  CodecBytes 160,
            FaxRate 2, FaxBytes 20, FaxNsf 0xAD0051
            SignalType 1
            DtmfRelay 32, Modem 0, SeqNumStart 0xE21
Jan 16 15:36:50.285: act_caps_ind: [ mode:0,init:60, min:40, max:200]
Jan 16 15:36:50.285: vtsp:[1/0/1:31, S_ALERTING, E_CC_CAPS_ACK]
Jan 16 15:36:50.285: act_caps_ack
Jan 16 15:36:50.285: act_caps_ack: passthrough: cap_modem_proto 0,
  cap_modem_codec 0, cap_modem_redundancy 0, payload 100
Jan 16 15:36:50.289: act_switch_codec: codec = 5

Jan 16 15:36:50.289: vtsp_modem_proto_from_cdb: cap_modem_proto 0
Jan 16 15:36:50.289: vtsp_rtp_nse_payload_from_cdb: payload 100
Jan 16 15:36:50.289: vtsp_modem_proto_from_cdb: cap_modem_proto 0
Jan 16 15:36:50.289: vtsp:[1/0/1:31, S_ALERTING, E_CC_CONNECT]
Jan 16 15:36:50.289: act_alert_connect
Jan 16 15:36:50.293: vtsp_ring_noan_timer_stop: 1964817
Jan 16 15:36:53.906: vtsp:[1/0/1:31, S_CONNECT, E_DSP_GET_TX]
```

Finally, the gateway begins the process of tearing down the call, as indicated in Example 6-16.

Example 6-16 *VTSP Debugs Showing a Call Being Torn Down*

```
Jan 16 15:36:55.022: vtsp:[1/0/1:31, S_CONNECT, E_CC_BRIDGE_DROP]
Jan 16 15:36:55.022: act_bdrop
Jan 16 15:36:55.022: vtsp:[1/0/1:31, S_CONNECT, E_CC_DISCONNECT]
Jan 16 15:36:55.022: act_disconnect
Jan 16 15:36:55.026: vtsp_ring_noan_timer_stop: 1965290
Jan 16 15:36:55.026: vtsp_pcm_tone_detect_timer_stop: 1965290
Jan 16 15:36:55.026: vtsp_pcm_switchover_timer_stop: 1965290
Jan 16 15:36:55.026: vtsp_timer_stop: 1965290
Jan 16 15:36:55.026: vtsp_timer: 1965290
Jan 16 15:36:55.034: vtsp:[1/0/1:31, S_WAIT_STATS, E_DSP_GET_ERROR]
Jan 16 15:36:55.034: act_get_error
Jan 16 15:36:55.034: vtsp_print_error_stats: rx_dropped=0 tx_dropped=0
  rx_control=8071 tx_control=28202 tx_control_dropped=64249
  dsp_mode_channel_1=64504 dsp_mode_channel_2=64507 c[0]=65398 c[1]=30460
  c[2]=64632 c[3]=64375 c[4]=29559 c[5]=31995 c[6]=63995 c[7]=64511 c[8]=30072
  c[9]=64252 c[10]=31742 c[11]=63484 c[12]=32508 c[13]=64504 c[14]=63862
  c[15]=31610
```

continues

Example 6-16   *VTSP Debugs Showing a Call Being Torn Down (Continued)*

```
Jan 16 15:36:55.038: vtsp_timer_stop: 1965291
Jan 16 15:36:55.038: vtsp_timer: 1965291
Jan 16 15:36:55.038: vtsp:[1/0/1:31, S_WAIT_STATS, E_DSP_GET_LEVELS]
Jan 16 15:36:55.038: act_get_levels
Jan 16 15:36:55.038: vtsp:[1/0/1:31, S_WAIT_STATS, E_DSP_GET_TX]
Jan 16 15:36:55.042: act_stats_complete
Jan 16 15:36:55.042: vtsp_timer_stop: 1965292
Jan 16 15:36:55.042: vtsp_ring_noan_timer_stop: 1965292
Jan 16 15:36:55.042: vtsp_timer: 1965292
Jan 16 15:36:55.998: vtsp:[1/0/1:31, S_WAIT_RELEASE, E_TSP_CALL_FEATURE_IND]
Jan 16 15:36:55.998: act_call_feature_ind
Jan 16 15:36:55.998: vtsp:[1/0/1:31, S_WAIT_RELEASE, E_TSP_DISCONNECT_CONF]
Jan 16 15:36:55.998: act_wrelease_release
Jan 16 15:36:55.998: vtsp_timer_stop: 1965387vtsp_do_call_historyvtsp_do_call_
    history CoderRate 5
Jan 16 15:36:56.002: vtsp:[1/0/1:31, S_CLOSE_DSPRM, E_DSPRM_CLOSE_COMPLETE]
Jan 16 15:36:56.002: act_terminate
Jan 16 15:36:56.002: vtsp_free_cdb,cdb 0x80F0A494
```

Examining each line of these traces would take a whole book by itself. It also would require a detailed understanding of the underlying source code. Instead of trying to understand every line, half the battle is knowing which **show** commands and debugs to enable when you're having problems. The commands detailed here should give you plenty of ammunition to isolate where a problem exists.

When working with analog FXS or FXO interfaces, never underestimate the troubleshooting power of a $7 analog phone. One of the first things to check when you're having problems with an FXO port is to unplug the FXO port from the line, plug an analog phone into the line, and simply make sure the line works the way you expect it to. If you're having problems dialing some numbers, try calling them directly from an analog phone. If you have FXS ports connected to a nonphone device such as an analog voice mail system or IVR system, plug the phone into the analog port on the FXS port to ensure that you can perform the actions that the device connected to the port is attempting to perform. The more you can simplify the problem, the better off you will be.

Understanding Cisco IOS CCAPI Debugs

In the Cisco IOS Software voice architecture, the call control application programming interface (CCAPI) is the heart of call processing within the voice gateway. The command **debug voip ccapi inout** shows you the inner workings of the CCAPI in Cisco IOS Software. This is the best way to look at what call routing decisions the gateway is making and what dial peers are being matched. The call flow won't be discussed in advance so that you can figure it out as you look through the debug.

The gateway this debug was taken from has the dial peers shown in Example 6-17 configured.

Example 6-17 *Dial Peer Configuration for the CCAPI Debug Example*

```
dial-peer voice 101 pots
 destination-pattern 15801
 port 1/0/1
!
dial-peer voice 111 pots
 destination-pattern 5T
 port 1/1/1
!
dial-peer voice 99 voip
 incoming called-number 5
 destination-pattern 156..
 session target ipv4:172.18.106.59
 dtmf-relay h245-alphanumeric
 codec g711ulaw
 ip qos dscp cs5 media
 no vad
!
dial-peer voice 999 voip
 destination-pattern 9T
 session target ipv4:172.18.106.59
 dtmf-relay h245-alphanumeric
 codec g711ulaw
 no vad
```

After you have verified your configuration, enable the debug by entering the command **debug voip ccapi inout**, and then place a call through the voice gateway. You see debug output similar to that shown in Example 6-18.

Example 6-18 *New Call Setup as Seen Using* **debug voip ccapi inout**

```
Router#debug voip ccapi inout
Jan 16 22:46:21.259: cc_api_supported_data data_mode=0x10002
Jan 16 22:46:21.263: cc_api_call_setup_ind (vdbPtr=0x810EF588,
  callInfo={called=15801,called_oct3=0x80,calling=15644,calling_oct3=0x0,
  calling_oct3a=0x81,calling_xlated=false,subscriber_type_str=Unknown,fdest=1,
  peer_tag=99, prog_ind=0},callID=0x81330C9C)
```

First, you see the **callInfo** structure as part of the **cc_api_callsetup_ind** message. In this message you can see the called party number, calling party number, progress indicator, and the incoming peer that is being matched.

From this information you now know that the calling party number is **15644** and the called party number is **15801**. Also, dial peer 99 is a VoIP dial peer, so you know the call is coming in from the VoIP side.

In Example 6-19, notice the dial peer that is matched is being matched because the calling party number of 15644 matches the **destination-pattern** configured on **dial peer 99**. At this point, ignore the **callID** parameter because this value has not been filled in yet.

Example 6-19 debug voip ccapi inout *Output Showing Dial Peer 99 Being Matched*

```
Jan 16 22:46:21.263: cc_api_call_setup_ind type 0 , prot 1
Jan 16 22:46:21.263: cc_api_call_setup_ind (vdbPtr=0x810EF588,
  callInfo={called=15801, calling=15644, fdest=1 peer_tag=99}, callID=0x81330C9C)
Jan 16 22:46:21.267: cc_process_call_setup_ind (event=0x81185528)
```

Next, in Example 6-20, you see the call get assigned a callID (**cid**) of **18** in decimal. Later in this debug, the callID is shown in hex (18 = 0x12).

Example 6-20 debug voip ccapi inout *Output Showing callID 18 Being Assigned*

```
Jan 16 22:46:21.267: >>>>CCAPI handed cid 18 with tag 99 to app "DEFAULT"
Jan 16 22:46:21.267: sess_appl: ev(24=CC_EV_CALL_SETUP_IND), cid(18), disp(0)
Jan 16 22:46:21.271: sess_appl: ev(SSA_EV_CALL_SETUP_IND), cid(18), disp(0)
Jan 16 22:46:21.271: ssaCallSetupInd
Jan 16 22:46:21.271: ccCallSetContext (callID=0x12, context=0x81335E18)
Jan 16 22:46:21.271: ssaCallSetupInd cid(18), st(SSA_CS_MAPPING),oldst(0),
  ev(24)ev->e.evCallSetupInd.nCallInfo.finalDestFlag = 1
Jan 16 22:46:21.271: ssaCallSetupInd finalDest cllng(15644), clled(15801)
Jan 16 22:46:21.271: ssaCallSetupInd cid(18), st(SSA_CS_CALL_SETTING),
  oldst(0), ev(24)dpMatchPeersMoreArg result= 0
```

Next, in Example 6-21, you see the match for the outbound dial peer. In this case, it is **peer 101**, which makes sense because **dial peer 101** has **destination-pattern 15801** configured on it. Notice that five digits are matched and that no prefix is configured.

Example 6-21 debug voip ccapi inout *Output Showing Dial Peer 101 Being Matched*

```
Jan 16 22:46:21.271: ssaSetupPeer cid(18) peer list: tag(101) called number (15801)
Jan 16 22:46:21.275: ssaSetupPeer cid(18), destPat(15801), matched(5), prefix(),
  peer(812DE308), peer->encapType (1)
```

Next, in Example 6-22, the call enters the call proceeding state. Notice that the callID is listed in hex now instead of decimal. Also notice that the progress indicator is 0.

Example 6-22 debug voip ccapi inout *Output Showing the Call Proceeding State*

```
Jan 16 22:46:21.275: ccCallProceeding (callID=0x12, prog_ind=0x0)
Jan 16 22:46:21.275: ccCallSetupRequest (Inbound call = 0x12, outbound peer =101,
dest=,
        params=0x8118EEA8 mode=0, *callID=0x8118F210, prog_ind = 0)
Jan 16 22:46:21.275: ccCallSetupRequest numbering_type 0x80
Jan 16 22:46:21.275: dest pattern 15801, called 15801, digit_strip 1
Jan 16 22:46:21.275: callingNumber=15644, calledNumber=15801,
  redirectNumber= display_info=Paul Giralt calling_oct3a=81
Jan 16 22:46:21.275: accountNumber=, finalDestFlag=1,
guid=006a.f3c3.ff28.711d.0100.b0cb.0a53.8102
Jan 16 22:46:21.275: peer_tag=101
Jan 16 22:46:21.279: ccIFCallSetupRequestPrivate: (vdbPtr=0x811AFC78,
```

Example 6-22   **debug voip ccapi inout** *Output Showing the Call Proceeding State (Continued)*

```
dest=, callParams={called=15801,called_oct3=0x80, calling=15644,
calling_oct3=0x0, calling_xlated=false,  subscriber_type_str=Unknown,
fdest=1, voice_peer_tag=101},mode=0x0) vdbPtr type = 6
```

Next, in Example 6-23, the gateway sets up the outbound leg of this call using the outbound peer that was matched. Notice that this leg gets its own callID assigned. This new callID is **0x13** or **19** in decimal.

Example 6-23   **debug voip ccapi inout** *Output Showing callID 19 Being Assigned*

```
Jan 16 22:46:21.279: ccIFCallSetupRequestPrivate: (vdbPtr=0x811AFC78,
  dest=, callParams={called=15801, called_oct3 0x80,  calling=15644,
  calling_oct3 0x0, calling_xlated=false,  fdest=1, voice_peer_tag=101},
  mode=0x0, xltrc=-5)
Jan 16 22:46:21.279: ccSaveDialpeerTag (callID=0x12, dialpeer_tag=
Jan 16 22:46:21.279: ccCallSetContext (callID=0x13, context=0x813349DC)
Jan 16 22:46:21.279: ccCallReportDigits (callID=0x12, enable=0x0)
Jan 16 22:46:21.279: cc_api_call_report_digits_done (vdbPtr=0x810EF588,
  callID=0x12, disp=0)
Jan 16 22:46:21.283: sess_appl: ev(53=CC_EV_CALL_REPORT_DIGITS_DONE), cid(18),
  disp(0)
Jan 16 22:46:21.283: cid(18)st(SSA_CS_CALL_SETTING)ev(SSA_EV_CALL_REPORT_DIGITS
_DONE)
oldst(SSA_CS_MAPPING)cfid(-1)csize(0)in(1)fDest(1)
Jan 16 22:46:21.283: -cid2(19)st2(SSA_CS_CALL_SETTING)oldst2(SSA_CS_MAPPING)
Jan 16 22:46:21.283: ssaReportDigitsDone cid(18) peer list: (empty)
Jan 16 22:46:21.283: ssaReportDigitsDone callid=18 Reporting disabled.
Jan 16 22:46:21.287: cc_api_call_proceeding(vdbPtr=0x811AFC78, callID=0x13,
    prog_ind=0x0)
Jan 16 22:46:21.287: cc_api_call_cut_progress(vdbPtr=0x811AFC78, callID=0x13,
  prog_ind=0x8, sig_ind=0x2)
Jan 16 22:46:21.291: sess_appl: ev(21=CC_EV_CALL_PROCEEDING), cid(19), disp(0)
Jan 16 22:46:21.291: cid(19)st(SSA_CS_CALL_SETTING)ev(SSA_EV_CALL_PROCEEDING)
oldst(SSA_CS_MAPPING)cfid(-1)csize(0)in(0)fDest(0)
Jan 16 22:46:21.291: -cid2(18)st2(SSA_CS_CALL_SETTING)oldst2(SSA_CS_CALL_SETTING)
Jan 16 22:46:21.291: ssaCallProc
Jan 16 22:46:21.291: ccGetDialpeerTag (callID=0x12)
Jan 16 22:46:21.291: ssaIgnore cid(19), st(SSA_CS_CALL_SETTING),oldst(1), ev(21)
Jan 16 22:46:21.291: sess_appl: ev(22=CC_EV_CALL_PROGRESS), cid(19), disp(0)
Jan 16 22:46:21.291: cid(19)st(SSA_CS_CALL_SETTING)ev(SSA_EV_CALL_PROGRESS)
oldst(SSA_CS_CALL_SETTING)cfid(-1)csize(0)in(0)fDest(0)
Jan 16 22:46:21.291: -cid2(18)st2(SSA_CS_CALL_SETTING)oldst2(SSA_CS_CALL_SETTING)
Jan 16 22:46:21.295: ssaCutProgress
Jan 16 22:46:21.295: ccGetDialpeerTag (callID=0x12)
Jan 16 22:46:21.295: ccCallCutProgress (callID=0x12, prog_ind=0x8, sig_ind=0x2)
```

Next, in Example 6-24, the gateway attempts to join the two call legs. Don't be confused by the word **CONFERENCE**. This is just a point-to-point call, not a multipoint conference of any kind. Notice that **callID 0x12** and **callID 0x13** get joined into **confID 0x6**.

Example 6-24   **debug voip ccapi inout** *Output Showing the Two Call Legs Being Joined*

```
Jan 16 22:46:21.295: ccConferenceCreate (confID=0x8118F29C, callID1=0x12,
  callID2=0x13, tag=0x0)
Jan 16 22:46:21.295: cc_api_bridge_done (confID=0x6, srcIF=0x810EF588,
  srcCallID=0x12, dstCallID=0x13, disposition=0, tag=0x0)
Jan 16 22:46:21.295: cc_api_bridge_done (confID=0x6, srcIF=0x811AFC78,
  srcCallID=0x13, dstCallID=0x12, disposition=0, tag=0x0)
Jan 16 22:46:21.295: cc_api_caps_ind (dstVdbPtr=0x810EF588, dstCallId=0x12,
  srcCallId=0x13,
        caps={codec=0x2EBFB, fax_rate=0xBF, vad=0x3, modem=0x2
            codec_bytes=0, signal_type=3})
Jan 16 22:46:21.299: cc_api_caps_ind (Playout: mode 0, initial 60,min 40, max 300)
Jan 16 22:46:21.307: sess_appl: ev(29=CC_EV_CONF_CREATE_DONE), cid(18), disp(0)
Jan 16 22:46:21.307: cid(18)st(SSA_CS_CONFERENCING_PROGRESS)ev(SSA_EV_CONF_CREATE
  _DONE)
oldst(SSA_CS_CALL_SETTING)cfid(6)csize(0)in(1)fDest(1)
Jan 16 22:46:21.307: -cid2(19)st2(SSA_CS_CONFERENCING_PROGRESS)oldst2(SSA_CS_CALL
  _SETTING)
Jan 16 22:46:21.307: ssaConfCreateDoneAlert
Jan 16 22:46:21.307: cc_process_notify_bridge_done (event=0x811868E8)
```

Next, the two call legs agree on capabilities. Capabilities are represented by a series of bits, each of which represents a particular capability.

For example, the codec value represents a series of bits that correspond to the supported codecs. For the sake of this example, assume that the following bits are defined for codec capabilities:

- **G.711 μ-law**—0x1 or 0001 in binary
- **G.711 A-law**—0x2 or 0010 in binary
- **G.729**—0x4 or 0100 in binary

To advertise that an endpoint is capable of G.711 μ-law, G.711 A-law, and G.729, you must do a binary addition of the capabilities. In this case, the result is 0111 in binary, which is 0x7 in hex. The actual capabilities tables are much larger than this, but the same concepts apply.

Reference Tables 6-7 through 6-10 to decode the various capabilities bits.

Table 6-7   *Codec Capabilities Bits*

Codec	Capability Bit
G.711 μ-law	0x1
G.711 A-law	0x2
G.729	0x4

Table 6-7   *Codec Capabilities Bits (Continued)*

Codec	Capability Bit
G.729a	0x8
G.726r16	0x10
G.726r24	0x20
G.726r32	0x40
G.728	0x80
G.723r63	0x100
G.723r53	0x200
GSM	0x400
G.729b	0x800
G.729ab	0x1000
G.723ar63	0x2000
G.723ar53	0x4000
G.729	0x8000
T.38 Fax	0x10000
Clear channel codec	0x20000
GSM EFR	0x40000

Table 6-8   *Fax Capabilities Bits*

Fax Speed Capability	Capability Bit
None	0x01
Voice	0x02
2400	0x04
4800	0x08
7200	0x10
9600	0x20
12000	0x40
14400	0x80

Table 6-9 *VAD Capabilities Bits*

VAD Capability	Capability Bit
VAD off	0x1
VAD on	0x2

Table 6-10 *DTMF Relay Capabilities Bits*

DTMF Relay Capability	Capability Bit
Disabled	0x0
In-band voice	0x1
RTP	0x2
NSE	0x4
Out of band	0x8
H.245 signal	0x10
H.245 alphanumeric	0x20
Hookflash	0x40

As you can see in Example 6-25, both call legs report G.711 μ-law (0x1), fax rate voice (0x2), and no VAD (0x1).

Example 6-25   **debug voip ccapi inout** *Output Showing Capabilities for Each Call Leg*

```
Jan 16 22:46:22.015: cc_api_caps_ind (dstVdbPtr=0x811AFC78, dstCallId=0x13,
  srcCallId=0x12,     caps={codec=0x1, fax_rate=0x2, vad=0x1, modem=0x0
           codec_bytes=160, signal_type=1})
Jan 16 22:46:22.019: cc_api_caps_ind (Playout: mode 0, initial 60,min 40, max 300)
Jan 16 22:46:22.019: cc_api_caps_ack (dstVdbPtr=0x811AFC78, dstCallId=0x13,
  srcCallId=0x12,     caps={codec=0x1, fax_rate=0x2, vad=0x1, modem=0x0
           codec_bytes=160, signal_type=1, seq_num_start=6594})
Jan 16 22:46:22.019: cc_api_caps_ack (dstVdbPtr=0x810EF588, dstCallId=0x12,
  srcCallId=0x13,     caps={codec=0x1, fax_rate=0x2, vad=0x1, modem=0x0
           codec_bytes=160, signal_type=1, seq_num_start=6594})
Jan 16 22:46:22.023: cc_api_voice_mode_event , callID=0x13
Jan 16 22:46:22.023: Call Pointer =813349DC
Jan 16 22:46:22.023: sess_appl: ev(51=CC_EV_VOICE_MODE_DONE), cid(19), disp(0)
Jan 16 22:46:22.023: cid(19)st(SSA_CS_CONFERENCED_ALERT)ev(SSA_EV_VOICE_MODE_DONE)
oldst(SSA_CS_CALL_SETTING)cfid(6)csize(0)in(0)fDest(0)
Jan 16 22:46:22.023: -cid2(18)st2(SSA_CS_CONFERENCED_ALERT)
  oldst2(SSA_CS_CONFERENCING_PROGRESS)
Jan 16 22:46:22.027: ssaIgnore cid(19), st(SSA_CS_CONFERENCED_ALERT),
  oldst(4), ev(51)
Jan 16 22:46:22.163: cc_api_caps_ind (dstVdbPtr=0x811AFC78, dstCallId=0x13,
  srcCallId=0x12,     caps={codec=0x1, fax_rate=0x2, vad=0x1, modem=0x0
           codec_bytes=160, signal_type=1})
```

Example 6-25   **debug voip ccapi inout** *Output Showing Capabilities for Each Call Leg (Continued)*

```
Jan 16 22:46:22.163: cc_api_caps_ind (Playout: mode 0, initial 60,min 40, max 300)
Jan 16 22:46:22.163: cc_api_caps_ack (dstVdbPtr=0x811AFC78, dstCallId=0x13,
  srcCallId=0x12,
     caps={codec=0x1, fax_rate=0x2, vad=0x1, modem=0x0
            codec_bytes=160, signal_type=1, seq_num_start=6594})
Jan 16 22:46:22.167: cc_api_caps_ack (dstVdbPtr=0x810EF588, dstCallId=0x12,
  srcCallId=0x13,
     caps={codec=0x1, fax_rate=0x2, vad=0x1, modem=0x0
            codec_bytes=160, signal_type=1, seq_num_start=6594})
Jan 16 22:46:22.167: cc_api_voice_mode_event , callID=0x13
Jan 16 22:46:22.167: Call Pointer =813349DC
Jan 16 22:46:22.171: sess_appl: ev(51=CC_EV_VOICE_MODE_DONE), cid(19), disp(0)
Jan 16 22:46:22.171: cid(19)st(SSA_CS_CONFERENCED_ALERT)ev(SSA_EV_VOICE_MODE_DONE)
oldst(SSA_CS_CONFERENCED_ALERT)cfid(6)csize(0)in(0)fDest(0)
Jan 16 22:46:22.171: -cid2(18)st2(SSA_CS_CONFERENCED_ALERT)
  oldst2(SSA_CS_CONFERENCING_PROGRESS)
Jan 16 22:46:22.171: ssaIgnore cid(19), st(SSA_CS_CONFERENCED_ALERT),oldst(4),
  ev(51)
Jan 16 22:46:22.367: cc_api_caps_ind (dstVdbPtr=0x811AFC78, dstCallId=0x13,
  srcCallId=0x12,
     caps={codec=0x1, fax_rate=0x2, vad=0x1, modem=0x0
            codec_bytes=160, signal_type=1})
Jan 16 22:46:22.371: cc_api_caps_ind (Playout: mode 0, initial 60,min 40, max 300)
Jan 16 22:46:22.371: cc_api_caps_ack (dstVdbPtr=0x811AFC78, dstCallId=0x13,
  srcCallId=0x12,
     caps={codec=0x1, fax_rate=0x2, vad=0x1, modem=0x0
            codec_bytes=160, signal_type=1, seq_num_start=6594})
Jan 16 22:46:22.371: cc_api_caps_ack (dstVdbPtr=0x810EF588, dstCallId=0x12,
  srcCallId=0x13,
     caps={codec=0x1, fax_rate=0x2, vad=0x1, modem=0x0
            codec_bytes=160, signal_type=1, seq_num_start=6594})
Jan 16 22:46:22.375: cc_api_voice_mode_event , callID=0x13
Jan 16 22:46:22.375: Call Pointer =813349DC
Jan 16 22:46:22.375: sess_appl: ev(51=CC_EV_VOICE_MODE_DONE), cid(19), disp(0)
Jan 16 22:46:22.375: cid(19)st(SSA_CS_CONFERENCED_ALERT)ev(SSA_EV_VOICE_MODE_DONE)
oldst(SSA_CS_CONFERENCED_ALERT)cfid(6)csize(0)in(0)fDest(0)
Jan 16 22:46:22.375: -cid2(18)st2(SSA_CS_CONFERENCED_ALERT)
  oldst2(SSA_CS_CONFERENCING_PROGRESS)
Jan 16 22:46:22.375: ssaIgnore cid(19), st(SSA_CS_CONFERENCED_ALERT),
  oldst(4), ev(51)
```

Finally, as Example 6-26 confirms, the phone connected to port 1/0/1 goes off-hook, so the call is connected. Notice that the connect comes from **callID=0x13**, which is the outbound leg of the call going out the POTS port.

Example 6-26   **debug voip ccapi inout** *Output Showing the Call Connect*

```
Jan 16 22:46:29.668: cc_api_call_connected(vdbPtr=0x811AFC78, callID=0x13),
  prog_ind = 2cc_api_call_connected: setting callEntry->connected to TRUE

Jan 16 22:46:29.672: sess_appl: ev(8=CC_EV_CALL_CONNECTED), cid(19), disp(0)
Jan 16 22:46:29.672: cid(19)st(SSA_CS_CONFERENCED_ALERT)ev(SSA_EV_CALL_CONNECTED)
```

continues

Example 6-26 **debug voip ccapi inout** *Output Showing the Call Connect (Continued)*

```
oldst(SSA_CS_CONFERENCED_ALERT)cfid(6)csize(0)in(0)fDest(0)
Jan 16 22:46:29.672: -cid2(18)st2(SSA_CS_CONFERENCED_ALERT)
  oldst2(SSA_CS_CONFERENCING_PROGRESS)
Jan 16 22:46:29.672: ssaConnectAlert
Jan 16 22:46:29.672: ccGetDialpeerTag (callID=0x12)
Jan 16 22:46:29.672: ccCallConnect (callID=0x12), prog_ind = 2ccCallConnect:
  setting callEntry->connected to TRUE

Jan 16 22:46:29.676: ssaFlushPeerTagQueue cid(18) peer list: (empty)
Jan 16 22:46:42.292: ccAuditEndptsValidate()
```

Now the call will be disconnected. This is one of the most important lines in this debug
because it lets you know which side of the call disconnected the call. This is important when
you troubleshoot issues with dropped calls out a gateway because this line gives you the
callID for the call leg that disconnected the call, as well as the cause code for the disconnect.
In this case, you see that the disconnect came from **callID=0x12**, which is the inbound call
leg (VoIP leg). Also, the cause code is **0x10**. Table 6-27 later in this chapter lists all the
Q.850 cause codes. This cause code is derived from the cause codes in that table. Convert
the cause code you receive from the debug to decimal (0x10 = 16), and then look it up in
Table 6-27. You can see that 0x10 means normal call clearing. This means that the IP phone
user disconnected the call. Example 6-27 shows this portion of the debug.

Example 6-27 **debug voip ccapi inout** *Output Showing the Call Disconnecting*

```
Jan 16 22:46:44.744: cc_api_call_disconnected(vdbPtr=0x0, callID=0x12, cause=0x10)
Jan 16 22:46:44.748: sess_appl: ev(11=CC_EV_CALL_DISCONNECTED), cid(18), disp(0)
Jan 16 22:46:44.748: cid(18)st(SSA_CS_ACTIVE)ev(SSA_EV_CALL_DISCONNECTED)
oldst(SSA_CS_CONFERENCING_PROGRESS)cfid(6)csize(0)in(1)fDest(1)
Jan 16 22:46:44.748: -cid2(19)st2(SSA_CS_ACTIVE)oldst2(SSA_CS_CONFERENCED_ALERT)
Jan 16 22:46:44.748: ssa: Disconnected cid(18) state(5) cause(0x10)
```

Finally, the conference and the two call legs are torn down, as shown in Example 6-28.

Example 6-28 **debug voip ccapi inout** *Output Showing the Call Legs Being Torn Down*

```
Jan 16 22:46:44.748: ccConferenceDestroy (confID=0x6, tag=0x0)
Jan 16 22:46:44.748: cc_api_bridge_drop_done (confID=0x6, srcIF=0x810EF588,
  srcCallID=0x12, dstCallID=0x13, disposition=0 tag=0x0)
Jan 16 22:46:44.748: cc_api_bridge_drop_done (confID=0x6, srcIF=0x811AFC78,
  srcCallID=0x13, dstCallID=0x12, disposition=0 tag=0x0)
Jan 16 22:46:44.752: sess_appl: ev(30=CC_EV_CONF_DESTROY_DONE), cid(18), disp(0)
Jan 16 22:46:44.752: cid(18)st(SSA_CS_CONF_DESTROYING)ev(SSA_EV_CONF_DESTROY_DONE)
oldst(SSA_CS_ACTIVE)cfid(-1)csize(0)in(1)fDest(1)
Jan 16 22:46:44.752: -cid2(19)st2(SSA_CS_CONF_DESTROYING)
  oldst2(SSA_CS_CONFERENCED_ALERT)
Jan 16 22:46:44.752: ssaConfDestroyDone
Jan 16 22:46:44.756: ccCallDisconnect (callID=0x12, cause=0x10 tag=0x0)
Jan 16 22:46:44.756: ccCallDisconnect (callID=0x13, cause=0x10 tag=0x0)
Jan 16 22:46:44.760: cc_api_icpif: expect factor = 0
```

Example 6-28 **debug voip ccapi inout** *Output Showing the Call Legs Being Torn Down (Continued)*

```
Jan 16 22:46:44.760: g113_calculate_impairment (delay=78,
    loss=0), Io=0 Iq=0 Idte=0 Idd=0 Ie=0 Itot=0
Jan 16 22:46:44.764: cc_api_call_disconnect_done(vdbPtr=0x0, callID=0x12, disp=0,
  tag=0x0)
Jan 16 22:46:44.768: sess_appl: ev(12=CC_EV_CALL_DISCONNECT_DONE), cid(18), disp(0)
Jan 16 22:46:44.768:
cid(18)st(SSA_CS_DISCONNECTING)ev(SSA_EV_CALL_DISCONNECT_DONE)
oldst(SSA_CS_CONF_DESTROYING)cfid(-1)csize(0)in(1)fDest(1)
Jan 16 22:46:44.768: -cid2(19)st2(SSA_CS_DISCONNECTING)
  oldst2(SSA_CS_CONFERENCED_ALERT)
Jan 16 22:46:44.768: ssaDisconnectDone
Jan 16 22:46:44.948: ccAuditEndptsValidate()
Jan 16 22:46:47.320: ccAuditEndptsValidate()
Jan 16 22:46:47.644: cc_api_call_feature: (vdbPtr=0x811AFC78, callID=0x13,
  feature_ind.type=5

Jan 16 22:46:47.648: cc_api_call_disconnect_done(vdbPtr=0x811AFC78, callID=0x13,
  disp=0, tag=0x0)
Jan 16 22:46:47.648: sess_appl: ev(28=CC_EV_CALL_FEATURE), cid(19), disp(0)
Jan 16 22:46:47.648: cid(19)st(SSA_CS_DISCONNECTING)ev(SSA_EV_CALL_FEATURE)
oldst(SSA_CS_CONFERENCED_ALERT)cfid(-1)csize(1)in(0)fDest(0)
Jan 16 22:46:47.652: ssaIgnore cid(19), st(SSA_CS_DISCONNECTING),oldst(7), ev(28)
Jan 16 22:46:47.652: sess_appl: ev(12=CC_EV_CALL_DISCONNECT_DONE), cid(19), disp(0)
Jan 16 22:46:47.652:
cid(19)st(SSA_CS_DISCONNECTING)ev(SSA_EV_CALL_DISCONNECT_DONE)
oldst(SSA_CS_DISCONNECTING)cfid(-1)csize(1)in(0)fDest(0)
Jan 16 22:46:47.652: ssaDisconnectDone
```

As mentioned previously, **debug voip ccapi inout** is a fairly complex debug, but if you know what to look for, you can determine what is happening in the routing decisions made by the Cisco IOS call routing code.

Understanding the FXO Disconnect Problem

When loop start signaling is used, a gateway's FXO interface looks like a phone to the switch (PBX, PSTN, Key-System) it is connecting to. The FXO interface closes the loop to indicate off-hook, just as an analog phone does when it is physically lifted off-hook. The switch always provides battery, so there is no disconnect supervision from the switch side. Because a switch expects a phone user (which an FXO interface behaves like) to hang up the phone when the call is terminated (on either side), it also expects the FXO port on the router to hang up. This "human intervention" is not built into the router. The FXO port expects the switch to tell it when to hang up (or remove battery to indicate on-hook). Because of this, it cannot be guaranteed that a near-end or far-end FXO port will disconnect the call after either end of the call has hung up.

This problem usually manifests itself when a call from the PSTN is forwarded to voice mail. Because the voice mail system continues recording while the call is still active, it might not disconnect the call until several minutes later, when the message length timeout is reached. This could result in users getting long, silent messages or messages of announcements from the PSTN like "If you would like to make a call, please hang up and try again."

This problem also manifests itself when a PSTN user calling into the IP network hangs up before the IP phone user answers. Without disconnect supervision, the IP phone continues to ring. If it is answered, the user might get either some kind of recording from the PSTN or even dial tone in some cases.

The problem is even worse if a call arrives from the PSTN on an FXO port and is forwarded back out the PSTN via a different FXO port. If neither port gets proper disconnect supervision, both ports remain off-hook indefinitely, resulting in ports that appear to be in a "hung" state. Not only does this interrupt service, but it could cost extra money on your phone bill if the number called is a toll call or if the inbound call is a toll-free call that you pay for.

There are several ways to resolve this problem. The first is to not use FXO loop start signaling. This might seem like a ridiculous idea, but loop start circuits are notorious for having problems with disconnect supervision. Solving these kinds of problems usually involves a good amount of time calling your service provider to get them to either enable disconnect supervision or make adjustments to how they perform disconnect supervision. Even if you get everything working, there is a chance you can still run into problems because of the nature of an analog loop start circuit.

If you must use FXO, try to use ground start signaling. If the PBX or PSTN switch can be configured to provide a ground start connection, switch over to ground start operation. This option is available on the Cisco 1750, 2600, 3600, and 3810 routers and VG200 gateways. Unfortunately, it might not be available on all PBX/switches. If it is available, the switch removes ground from the connection when the call finishes (disconnects) and the FXO port goes on-hook. Use the command **show voice port** to see if the FXO port is configured to ground start or loop start signaling. This is configured on the voice port in the Cisco IOS gateway configuration. The command to enable ground start is **signal groundStart**, and to enable loop start it is **signal loopStart**.

If none of these options are viable for you, the next best alternative is to have the gateway's FXO port respond to power denial. Power denial, illustrated in Figure 6-2, is an interruption of line power that can be generated by some PBXs and service providers for approximately 600 ms. Cisco IOS gateways require a minimum interruption of 350 ms. The FXO voice interface card detects that power is no longer present and interprets this as a supervisory disconnect. Cisco IOS gateways have this functionality enabled by default. You can disable it by configuring **no supervisory disconnect** under the voice port, although keeping this enabled is a recommended practice. Disconnect supervision is available on the Cisco 1750, 2600, 3600, 3810, and VG200 analog FXO ports in all versions of Cisco IOS Software. You can use the command **show voice port** to see if **supervisory disconnect** is active.

Figure 6-2   *Power Denial Supervisory Disconnect*

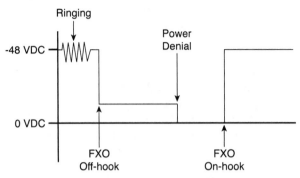

If you do not have any of the options discussed for resolving FXO disconnect problems, you might be able to get away with using supervisory disconnect tone, illustrated in Figure 6-3. If the FXO supervisory disconnect tone feature is configured and the DSP detects a tone from the PSTN or PBX, the analog FXO port goes on-hook. You can configure the router's FXO voice port to detect supervisory disconnect tones before or after the call is answered.

Figure 6-3   *Supervisory Disconnect Tone*

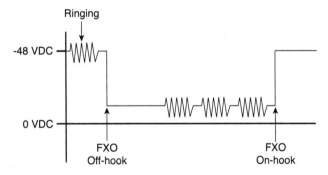

Suppose that the router receives a call on an FXO voice port and the calling party goes on-hook before the called party answers the call. If the switch is configured to provide a supervisory tone, the router's FXO port interprets this as supervisory disconnect and disconnects the call to the far end. This is the signal the router is looking for when the command **no supervisory disconnect** is configured on the voice port. The FXO supervisory disconnect tone feature applies only to analog FXO ports with loop start signaling.

Getting the supervisory disconnect tone to work can be a challenge because you need to know the frequency and cadence of the disconnect tone to be able to detect it.

For more information on the FXO supervisory disconnect tone feature, search Cisco.com for the document "FXO Supervisory Disconnect Tone" or use the following link:

www.cisco.com/en/US/products/sw/iosswrel/ps1834/
products_feature_guide09186a00800801d1.html

In some cases you can use a feature called *battery reversal*. When battery reversal is enabled, the battery polarity is reversed by the PBX's FXS port to indicate that a call is connected (far-end answer). The polarity is reversed throughout the entire conversation. When the far end disconnects, the FXS port returns the battery polarity to normal to indicate that the call has disconnected. This feature is offered on some PBXs and is typically not offered by service providers.

Battery reversal is supported on the VIC-2FXO-M1, VIC-2FXO-M2, and NM-HDA for the Cisco 2600/3600 routers and VG200 gateway. It is not supported on the standard VIC-2FXO.

Troubleshooting Digital Interfaces

You can use a variety of digital interfaces available for Cisco IOS gateways to interface with the TDM world. At the physical layer, these interfaces can be either T1 or E1 circuits. On either interface you can do either PRI signaling or CAS. From a signaling perspective, each of these requires its own troubleshooting methodology; however, you should check a few things at the physical layer before troubleshooting the higher-layer problems.

Checking Physical Layer Connectivity on Digital Interfaces

The first thing to examine when troubleshooting a T1 or E1 connection is the physical layer statistics. Use the command **show controllers [t1 | e1]** to show all the T1 or E1 interfaces on the gateway. You can also specify a particular port at the end of the command to view the statistics for a single port. If you issue the command without a port number, the output looks like Example 6-29.

Example 6-29 *Displaying Physical Layer Statistics for a T1 or E1 Port*

```
Router#show controllers t1
T1 1/0 is down.
  Applique type is Channelized T1
  Cablelength is long gain36 0db
  Transmitter is sending remote alarm.
  Receiver has loss of signal.
  alarm-trigger is not set
  Version info Firmware: 20010315, FPGA: 15
  Framing is ESF, Line Code is B8ZS, Clock Source is Line.
  Data in current interval (246 seconds elapsed):
     0 Line Code Violations, 0 Path Code Violations
     0 Slip Secs, 246 Fr Loss Secs, 0 Line Err Secs, 0 Degraded Mins
     0 Errored Secs, 0 Bursty Err Secs, 0 Severely Err Secs, 246 Unavail Secs
  Total Data (last 24 hours)
     0 Line Code Violations, 0 Path Code Violations,
     0 Slip Secs, 86400 Fr Loss Secs, 0 Line Err Secs, 0 Degraded Mins,
```

Example 6-29 *Displaying Physical Layer Statistics for a T1 or E1 Port (Continued)*

```
      0 Errored Secs, 0 Bursty Err Secs, 0 Severely Err Secs, 86400 Unavail Secs
T1 1/1 is up.
  Applique type is Channelized T1
  Cablelength is long gain36 0db
  No alarms detected.
  alarm-trigger is not set
  Version info Firmware: 20010315, FPGA: 15
  Framing is ESF, Line Code is B8ZS, Clock Source is Line.
  Data in current interval (247 seconds elapsed):
     0 Line Code Violations, 0 Path Code Violations
     0 Slip Secs, 0 Fr Loss Secs, 0 Line Err Secs, 0 Degraded Mins
     0 Errored Secs, 0 Bursty Err Secs, 0 Severely Err Secs, 0 Unavail Secs
  Total Data (last 24 hours)
     0 Line Code Violations, 0 Path Code Violations,
     0 Slip Secs, 0 Fr Loss Secs, 0 Line Err Secs, 0 Degraded Mins,
     0 Errored Secs, 0 Bursty Err Secs, 0 Severely Err Secs, 0 Unavail Secs
```

You can see that T1 1/0 is down and T1 1/1 is up. Note that T1 1/0 indicates that **Receiver has loss of signal**, so it is sending a remote alarm. This is called a *red alarm*. A red alarm informs the remote side that the local interface is not receiving any framing.

In addition to red alarm, there is also a condition called *yellow alarm*. Yellow alarm means that the side in yellow alarm is receiving frames that indicate that the far end is in red alarm.

For example, if the voice gateway is connected to a PBX and the PBX is not receiving framing, the PBX sends a red alarm indication. If the path from the PBX to the voice gateway is good, the gateway sends a yellow alarm toward the PBX indicating that it is receiving a red alarm. If you see a yellow alarm, there is very likely a problem with one of the pairs in the T1/E1 cable. In this example, the fault is on the cable that goes from the transmitter of the voice gateway to the receiver on the PBX. If you are seeing red or yellow alarms, check the cabling and, if possible, replace it.

In the **show controllers** output you can also see the framing, line code, and clock source settings. Ensure that the framing and line code settings match with the switch the gateway is attached to. Ensure that one side of the connection is providing clock while the other is deriving clock from the line.

T1 1/1 is up and running correctly. Notice that no alarms are detected and that no errors are listed in the current interval or the total data section. If you are seeing errors in the total data section but not in the current interval, you can issue the **show controllers** command including the port number, such as **show controllers t1 1/1**. This lists up to 96 of the last 15-minute intervals (24 hours). You can determine whether the errors that have accumulated have been accumulating slowly or if they are perhaps the result of a one-time event such as a cable being disconnected or tampered with.

If you are seeing errors in the **show controllers** output, double- and triple-check the clocking, framing, and line coding configuration. The error type is usually indicative of the problem. For example, clock slips are usually the result of improperly configured clocking, and line code and path code violations usually indicate a problem with line coding or framing. Check or replace your cables and, if necessary, ask your service provider to test the line. If the problem persists, there's always the possibility of bad hardware. If you have a second port to test with, try a different port to see if the problem resolves itself.

Note that the Catalyst 4000 AGM has an important difference in the way it handles clocking. The TDM clock reference on the AGM can be derived from one of seven sources. These are the free running onboard clock and two recovered clock sources from each VIC slot that contains an E1/T1 card.

The default reference is the onboard clock. You can use the **frame-clock-select** command to select one of the E1/T1 ports as the primary reference. You can also use this command to select up to three prioritized backups that can be used if the primary clock fails. Switching to a backup source is nonrevertive—the system does not switch back to a higher-priority clock if it recovers after a failure.

This command has the following syntax:

```
[no] frame-clock-select priority [t1 | e1] slot/port
```

For the most part, the ports on an NM-HDV module are clocked independently from the ports on another NM-HDV in the same chassis. In contrast, platforms with a TDM backplane (2600 series, 3660, and 3700 series) using the AIM-VOICE module can use the clock from a single source to provide clock synchronization to other T1/E1 ports in the chassis.

Future Cisco IOS voice gateways might also use the **frame-clock-select** configuration command, so always check for the existence of this command if you are having clocking problems.

As soon as you have verified physical layer connectivity, you can proceed to troubleshoot higher-layer problems.

Troubleshooting ISDN PRI Signaling

ISDN PRI signaling is probably the easiest of the TDM protocols to troubleshoot. This is mainly because ISDN is a message-based protocol and therefore provides a great deal of information regarding error conditions.

The first thing you must check when having problems on an ISDN PRI is whether the D-channel has been established. ISDN uses the D-channel to pass all the signaling information. The ITU-T ISDN Q.921 and Q.931 specifications provide documentation about ISDN. Q.921 documents the Layer 2 protocol, and Q.931 documents the Layer 3 signaling. Q.921 is basically used to ensure reliable delivery of the ISDN messages and is also used to establish the D-channel.

One of the most useful commands for troubleshooting an ISDN PRI is **show isdn status**. This command shows you the status of each layer, as demonstrated in Example 6-30.

Example 6-30   *Checking ISDN Port Status Using the* **show isdn status** *Command*

```
Router#show isdn status
ISDN Serial1/1:23 interface
        dsl 1, interface ISDN Switchtype = primary-dms100
        L2 Protocol = Q.921  L3 Protocol(s) = CCM-MANAGER
    Layer 1 Status:
        ACTIVE
    Layer 2 Status:
        TEI = 0, Ces = 1, SAPI = 0, State = MULTIPLE_FRAME_ESTABLISHED
    Layer 3 Status:
        0 Active Layer 3 Call(s)
    Active dsl 1 CCBs = 0
    The Free Channel Mask:  0x807FFFFF
    Number of L2 Discards = 0, L2 Session ID = 26
    Total Allocated ISDN CCBs = 0
```

You can see that Layer 1 is ACTIVE on this PRI. If Layer 1 is not ACTIVE, go back and check the **show controllers** output because there is a problem at the physical layer. The Layer 2 status is listed as **MULTIPLE_FRAME_ESTABLISHED**. This indicates that the D-channel is up. If the D-channel is not coming up, verify your switch type and network/user-side configuration. Every PRI should have one side as network side and the other as user side. When you connect to a public carrier, the carrier is nearly always the network side. When integrating with another PBX, you must select one side to be network and the other to be user. Cisco IOS Software does not support network side on all interfaces. Network-side PRI currently is supported only on primary-ni, primary-qsig, and primary-net5 in Cisco IOS Software version 12.2(11)T; however, future software versions might allow the configuration of network-side on other switch types.

After checking the switch type and network/user side configuration, if you are still not getting MULTIPLE_FRAME_ESTABLISHED, you can enable Q.921 debugs to see what the problem is using the command **debug isdn q921**.

When they are working correctly, the gateway and switch should start synchronizing with each other automatically. The negotiation begins with a Set Asynchronous Balanced Mode Extended (SABME) message being sent by one of the two endpoints. Either side can send the message and try to initialize with the other side. If the gateway receives the SABME message, it should send back an Unnumbered Acknowledge frame (UAf). The gateway then changes the Layer 2 status to MULTIPLE_FRAME_ESTABLISHED. If the gateway sends a SABME, the switch should respond with a UAf.

Turn on Q.921 debugs with the command **debug isdn q921**. After you have enabled the debug, go into configuration mode and do a **shut/no shut** on the controller, as shown in Example 6-31.

Example 6-31   *Displaying Q.921 D-channel Messages Using* **debug isdn q921**

```
vnt-vg200-gw1#config t
Enter configuration commands, one per line.  End with CNTL/Z.
vnt-vg200-gw1(config)#contr t1 1/1
vnt-vg200-(config-controller)#shut
```

continues

Example 6-31 *Displaying Q.921 D-channel Messages Using* **debug isdn q921** *(Continued)*

```
vnt-vg200-(config-controller)#
Jan 15 22:45:35.044: %CONTROLLER-5-UPDOWN: Controller T1 1/1, changed state to
  administratively down
vnt-vg200-(config-controller)#no shut
vnt-vg200-(config-controller)#
Jan 15 22:45:53.705: %CONTROLLER-5-UPDOWN: Controller T1 1/1, changed state to up
Jan 15 22:45:54.061: ISDN Se1/1:23: TX -> SABMEp c/r = 0 sapi = 0  tei = 0
Jan 15 22:45:54.065: ISDN Se1/1:23: RX <- UAf c/r = 0  sapi = 0  tei = 0
Jan 15 22:45:54.069: %ISDN-6-LAYER2UP: Layer 2 for Interface Se1/1:23,
  TEI 0 changed to up
Jan 15 22:46:04.069: ISDN Se1/1:23: RX <- RRp sapi = 0  tei = 0 nr = 0
Jan 15 22:46:04.069: ISDN Se1/1:23: TX -> RRp sapi = 0  tei = 0 nr = 0
Jan 15 22:46:04.073: ISDN Se1/1:23: TX -> RRf sapi = 0  tei = 0  nr = 0
Jan 15 22:46:04.077: ISDN Se1/1:23: RX <- RRf sapi = 0  tei = 0  nr = 0
```

If you are seeing SABME messages being sent but not acknowledged with a UAf, check the equipment attached to the gateway to ensure that the D-channel is enabled. This might involve calling your service provider.

If the voice gateway is acting as the network side instead of the user side, you should see the opposite direction for the messages seen in Example 6-31. The far end would transmit a SABME and the IOS gateway would then respond with a UAf to establish the D-channel.

After the D-channel is established, you should see Receiver Ready (**RRf** and **RRp**) messages every 10 seconds. These function as KeepAlives. If you have a problem with your D-channel bouncing, turn on **debug isdn q921** to ensure that you are not missing any Receiver Ready messages. As soon as four KeepAlives are missed, the D-channel is brought down, and the link establishment procedure must begin again.

If you see the gateway sending SABME messages and not getting a reply, you can verify that they are indeed being transmitted out the port by plugging a loopback plug into the T1/E1 port on the gateway. Be sure to change the clock to use the internal clock source and ensure that the controller comes up. Enable the **debug isdn q921** and **shut/no shut** the controller again. After the gateway transmits the SABME message, it should get looped back toward the gateway, and the following message should appear:

```
RX <- BAD FRAME(0x00017F)Line may be looped!
```

If you see this message, everything is working correctly from the gateway's point of view. The gateway sees its own packet and marks it as a bad frame. This means the frame was sent out to the port, got looped by the loopback plug, and was received by the gateway. You can continue performing loopback tests further down the line to the point where the SABME is no longer returned. If you are connected to the PSTN, you likely need to get your service provider involved.

Some service providers, especially those in Europe, require that the carrier's switch initiate the Terminal Endpoint Identifier (TEI) negotiation. If you are having problems establishing the D-channel on a BRI in Europe, try configuring the command **isdn tei first-call** under the BRI interface.

In Germany (and possibly in other countries), local telephone companies offer an ISDN line called *Anlagenanschluss*. This line is intended for connecting only one ISDN device, such as a PBX.

To use these ISDN lines on a Cisco IOS voice gateway, configure the **isdn static-tei 0** interface configuration command on the BRI interface(s), as shown in Example 6-32.

Example 6-32 *Assigning a Static TEI to Interface with "Anlagenanschluss" Service*

```
Router#configure terminal
Router(config)# interface bri 0
Router(config-if)# isdn static-tei 0
Warning: Interface must be cleared after reconfiguring the TEI.
Router(config-if)#
!--- do a shutdown and no shutdown to activate new TEI configuration
Router (config-if)# shutdown
Router (config-if)# no shutdown
```

Without the **isdn static-tei 0** command, the ISDN Layer 2 status gets stuck in the TEI_ASSIGNED state, and **debug isdn q921** output repeats the following two lines:

```
RX SABMEp c/r = 1 sapi = 0 tei = 0
RX IDCKRQ ri = 0 ai = 0
```

As soon as you are sure your D-channel is active, debugging Q.931 messages is easy. Just enable **debug isdn q931**, and you will experience one of the best debugs available in Cisco IOS Software, as demonstrated in Example 6-33.

Example 6-33 *Debugging Q.931 Messages*

```
Router#debug isdn q931
Jan 16 00:19:11.299: ISDN Se1/1:23: RX <-  SETUP pd = 8  callref = 0x00DD
Jan 16 00:19:11.303:           Bearer Capability i = 0x8090A2
Jan 16 00:19:11.303:           Channel ID i = 0xA98302
Jan 16 00:19:11.303:           Calling Party Number i = 0x0080, '9195555644',
  Plan:Unknown, Type:Unknown
Jan 16 00:19:11.311:           Called Party Number i = 0x80, '50781',
  Plan:Unknown, Type:Unknown
Jan 16 00:19:11.355: ISDN Se1/1:23: TX ->  CALL_PROC pd = 8  callref = 0x80DD
Jan 16 00:19:11.355:           Channel ID i = 0xA98302
Jan 16 00:19:11.359: ISDN Se1/1:23: TX ->  ALERTING pd = 8  callref = 0x80DD
Jan 16 00:19:11.359:           Progress Ind i = 0x8088 - In-band info or appropriate
  now available
Jan 16 00:19:27.371: ISDN Se1/1:23: TX ->  NOTIFY pd = 8  callref = 0x80DD
Jan 16 00:19:27.371:           Notification Ind i = 0xF1
Jan 16 00:19:27.375:           Display i = 'Voicemail'
Jan 16 00:19:27.379: ISDN Se1/1:23: TX ->  NOTIFY pd = 8  callref = 0x80DD
Jan 16 00:19:27.379:           Notification Ind i = 0xF1
Jan 16 00:19:27.383:           Display i = 'Paul', 0x20, 'Giralt'
Jan 16 00:19:27.687: ISDN Se1/1:23: TX ->  CONNECT pd = 8  callref = 0x80DD
Jan 16 00:19:27.687:           Display i = 'Voicemail'
Jan 16 00:19:27.715: ISDN Se1/1:23: RX <-  CONNECT_ACK pd = 8  callref = 0x00DD
Jan 16 00:19:38.092: ISDN Se1/1:23: RX <-  DISCONNECT pd = 8  callref = 0x00DD
Jan 16 00:19:38.092:           Cause i = 0x8290 - Normal call clearing
Jan 16 00:19:38.116: ISDN Se1/1:23: TX ->  RELEASE pd = 8  callref = 0x80DD
Jan 16 00:19:38.132: ISDN Se1/1:23: RX <-  RELEASE_COMP pd = 8  callref = 0x00DD
```

As you can see, **debug isdn q931** shows you each Q.931 message, along with all the information elements. Most of the information elements are also decoded for you. As you can see, the calling and called numbering plan and type are decoded, along with the progress indicator information element. You can also see that the display information element is decoded in plain text.

Because of the similarities between H.225 and Q.931, the messages and call flow for ISDN Q.931 are discussed in greater detail in the section "H.225 Signaling."

Troubleshooting T1 CAS

Troubleshooting T1 CAS on Cisco IOS gateways is relatively straightforward. Before you look at debugs, it helps to understand how CAS signaling works. The majority of T1 CAS circuits use E&M wink start signaling. CallManager does not support immediate start for MGCP-controlled ports, so the focus here is on wink start signaling. The same concepts apply to immediate start in H.323 mode, except that you don't have to worry about the complexity of waiting for a wink. What is a wink? Let's take a look.

CAS is also called *robbed-bit signaling* because some bits from each T1 speech bearer channel are "robbed" and used for signaling. On a T1 with Superframe (SF) framing, these are called the A and B bits, whereas a T1 with Extended Superframe (ESF) framing has A, B, C, and D bits. A gateway uses these bits to indicate on-hook, off-hook, and ringing.

For E&M signaling, an off-hook indication is transmitted as all 1s for the A, B, C, and D bits. On-hook is transmitted as all 0s.

Figure 6-4 shows how an E&M wink start call works.

Figure 6-4   *E&M Wink Start Signaling*

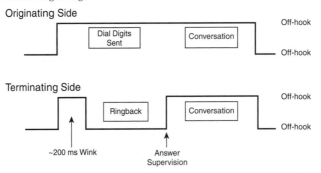

Either side can go off-hook to indicate it wants to set up a call. When the terminating side is ready to receive the digits, it goes off-hook for approximately 200 ms and then goes back on-hook. This is called a wink. The originating side then sends the digits as either DTMF or MF tones, depending on how each side is configured. If you are having problems where calls are not going through and the terminating side does not appear to be receiving any digits, be sure to check that both sides are using the same tones for sending digits.

As soon as the terminating side has accepted the digits, it plays ringback toward the originating side. When the final recipient of the call answers, the terminating side sends answer supervision by going off-hook. Either side can send disconnect supervision by going on-hook.

Unfortunately, there is no way to view the states of the ABCD bits directly on the majority of Cisco IOS gateways; however, several debugs and **show** commands show you the state transitions.

You can take a look at the current state of all the channels by issuing the command **show voice call summary**, just as you did for FXS/FXO ports. Example 6-34 demonstrates the output from this command.

Example 6-34   *Checking Channel State*

```
vnt-vg200-gw1#show voice call summary
PORT            CODEC    VAD VTSP STATE            VPM STATE
============    ======== === ==================    =======================
1/0:1.1         g711ulaw  n  S_CONNECT            EM_CONNECT
1/0:1.2         g711ulaw  n  S_SETUP_REQ_PROC     EM_WAIT_FOR_ANSWER
1/0:1.3         g711ulaw  n  S_DIGIT_COLLECT      EM_OFFHOOK
1/0:1.4         -         -  -                    EM_ONHOOK
1/0:1.5         -         -  -                    EM_ONHOOK
1/0:1.6         -         -  -                    EM_ONHOOK
1/0:1.7         -         -  -                    EM_ONHOOK
1/0:1.8         -         -  -                    EM_ONHOOK
1/0:1.9         -         -  -                    EM_ONHOOK
1/0:1.10        -         -  -                    EM_ONHOOK
1/0:1.11        -         -  -                    EM_ONHOOK
1/0:1.12        -         -  -                    EM_ONHOOK
1/0:1.13        -         -  -                    EM_ONHOOK
1/0:1.14        -         -  -                    EM_ONHOOK
1/0:1.15        -         -  -                    EM_ONHOOK
1/0:1.16        -         -  -                    EM_ONHOOK
1/0:1.17        -         -  -                    EM_ONHOOK
1/0:1.18        -         -  -                    EM_ONHOOK
1/0:1.19        -         -  -                    EM_ONHOOK
1/0:1.20        -         -  -                    EM_ONHOOK
1/0:1.21        -         -  -                    EM_ONHOOK
1/0:1.22        -         -  -                    EM_ONHOOK
1/0:1.23        -         -  -                    EM_ONHOOK
1/0:1.24        -         -  -                    EM_ONHOOK
```

As you can see, the first channel on this T1 is in an active call. The second has an outbound call, and the gateway is waiting for an answer from the far end. The third call is an inbound call on the T1, and the gateway is off-hook collecting digits.

One of the most common problems with CAS is a mismatch between the configurations on each side of the CAS trunk. If one side is configured for wink start, and the other is configured for immediate start, calls will fail because the side doing immediate start won't send a wink to indicate it is ready to begin receiving digits. This will be evident in the debugs because you will get a timeout waiting on the wink.

To debug CAS in Cisco IOS Software, enable **debug vpm signal** on the gateway. This debug is not very user-friendly. However, if you can understand the basics of the trace you should be able to troubleshoot most T1 CAS problems.

Example 6-35 shows an inbound call on a T1 CAS trunk.

Example 6-35 *Output of* **debug vpm signal** *Showing T1 CAS Signaling*

```
Router#debug vpm signal
Jan 17 12:58:35.448: htsp_process_event: [1/0:1(1), EM_ONHOOK, E_DSP_SIG_1100]
  em_onhook_offhook htsp_setup_ind
Jan 17 12:58:35.448: [1/0:1(1)] get_local_station_id calling num=
  calling name= calling time=01/17 12:58
Jan 17 12:58:35.448: htsp_timer - 3000 msec
Jan 17 12:58:35.460: htsp_process_event: [1/0:1(1), EM_WAIT_SETUP_ACK,
  E_HTSP_SETUP_ACK]em_wait_setup_ack_get_ack
Jan 17 12:58:35.460: htsp_timer_stop
Jan 17 12:58:35.460: htsp_timer2 - 168 msec
Jan 17 12:58:35.476: htsp_process_event: [1/0:1(1), EM_WAIT_SETUP_ACK,
  E_HTSP_VOICE_CUT_THROUGH]
Jan 17 12:58:35.628: htsp_process_event: [1/0:1(1), EM_WAIT_SETUP_ACK,
  E_HTSP_EVENT_TIMER2]em_wait_prewink_timer
Jan 17 12:58:35.628: em_offhook (0)[recEive and transMit1/0:1(1)]
  set signal state = 0x8
  em_onhook (200)[recEive and transMit1/0:1(1)]
  set signal state = 0x0
Jan 17 12:58:36.316: htsp_digit_ready: digit = 32
Jan 17 12:58:36.316: htsp_process_event: [1/0:1(1), EM_OFFHOOK,
  E_VTSP_DIGIT]em_offhook_digit_collect
Jan 17 12:58:36.516: htsp_digit_ready: digit = 32
Jan 17 12:58:36.516: htsp_process_event: [1/0:1(1), EM_OFFHOOK,
  E_VTSP_DIGIT]em_offhook_digit_collect
Jan 17 12:58:36.716: htsp_digit_ready: digit = 38
Jan 17 12:58:36.716: htsp_process_event: [1/0:1(1), EM_OFFHOOK,
  E_VTSP_DIGIT]em_offhook_digit_collect
Jan 17 12:58:36.916: htsp_digit_ready: digit = 33
Jan 17 12:58:36.916: htsp_process_event: [1/0:1(1), EM_OFFHOOK,
  E_VTSP_DIGIT]em_offhook_digit_collect
Jan 17 12:58:37.116: htsp_digit_ready: digit = 31
Jan 17 12:58:37.116: htsp_process_event: [1/0:1(1), EM_OFFHOOK,
  E_VTSP_DIGIT]em_offhook_digit_collect
Jan 17 12:58:37.144: htsp_process_event: [1/0:1(1), EM_OFFHOOK,
  E_HTSP_VOICE_CUT_THROUGH]em_offhook_voice_cut
Notice the first line in the trace:
htsp_process_event: [1/0:1(1), EM_ONHOOK, E_DSP_SIG_1100]
  em_onhook_offhook htsp_setup_ind
```

The message **htsp_process_event** indicates a change in the T1 CAS state machine. The message is followed by three items in square brackets. The first is the port number where this event was observed. The second is the current state of the port and the third is the event. The current state of **EM_ONHOOK** is easy enough to understand that the port is currently on-hook; however, **E_DSP_SIG_1100** is not obvious. To help clarify what that event means, look at the text that follows the square brackets, **em_onhook_offhook**

htsp_setup_ind. This indicates that a transition from on-hook to off-hook was detected and tells you that the port is receiving an incoming seizure.

Any message that says **set signal state** indicates a change in what the gateway is transmitting out the T1 CAS port towards the attached device. You can see the messages **em_offhook** and **set signal state = 0x8**. These indicate that the gateway is transmitting an off-hook indication by setting the ABCD bits to 1.

Immediately after that, you see **em_onhook (200)** and **set signal state = 0x0**. These messages indicate that the port went on-hook after 200 ms. This sequence of events means the gateway is transmitting a wink on the port that indicates to the calling device that the gateway is ready to receive digits.

After the wink you can see the port receives DTMF digits 22831 from the calling device. Finally you see the line

```
htsp_process_event: [1/0:1(1), EM_OFFHOOK,
  E_HTSP_VOICE_CUT_THROUGH]em_offhook_voice_cut
```

This message indicates the current receive state is off-hook and the port is now transitioning to the voice cut-through state. At this point the call has been accepted by the voice gateway and depending on what signaling protocol is being used on the VoIP side of the call, the call is extended to CallManager using either H.323 or MGCP. The protocol is irrelevant because at this point you are only looking at the T1 CAS debugs. The VoIP signaling protocol does not matter.

At this point the calling party should be hearing ringback generated by the voice gateway. Eventually the IP phone answers the call, so the gateway needs to send an off-hook indication to the connected device. You can see this in Example 6-36.

Example 6-36   *Output of* **debug vpm signal** *Showing T1 CAS Signaling*

```
Jan 17 12:58:45.656: htsp_process_event: [1/0:1(1), EM_OFFHOOK, E_HTSP_CONNECT]
  em_offhook_connect
Jan 17 12:58:45.656: htsp_timer2 - 40 msec
Jan 17 12:58:45.656: em_offhook (250)[recEive and transMit1/0:1(1)]
  set signal state = 0x8
Jan 17 12:58:45.700: htsp_process_event:
  [1/0:1(1), EM_CONNECT_MIN, E_HTSP_EVENT_TIMER2]
```

The important message to pay attention to in Example 6-36 is **set signal state = 0x8**. This indicates that the gateway port is transitioning to an off-hook state.

Finally the call is released. How the call is released is important because often when troubleshooting dropped calls, you need to be able to determine which leg of the call caused the call to drop. For T1 CAS, look for the message **E_DSP_SIG_0000**. If the release request event (**RELEASE_REQ**) occurs before the **E_DSP_SIG_0000** event, then the call was disconnected from the VoIP side. If the **E_DSP_SIG_0000** comes first, then the call was disconnected from the POTS side. You can see the **set signal state=0** message also comes before the **E_DSP_SIG_0000**. The message **set signal state=0** means the T1 CAS port is transmitting an on-hook indication. Example 6-37 shows the call disconnecting from the VoIP side.

Example 6-37   *Output of* **debug vpm signal** *Showing T1 CAS Signaling of a Call Disconnect*

```
Jan 17 12:58:53.397: htsp_process_event: [1/0:1(1), EM_CONNECT,
  E_HTSP_RELEASE_REQ]em_conn_release
Jan 17 12:58:53.397: htsp_timer_stop
Jan 17 12:58:53.397: htsp_timer_stop2 em_onhook (0)[recEive and transMit1/0:1(1)]
  set signal state = 0x0
Jan 17 12:58:53.401: em_start_timer: 400 ms
Jan 17 12:58:53.401: htsp_timer - 400 msec
Jan 17 12:58:53.801: htsp_process_event: [1/0:1(1), EM_WAIT_ONHOOK,
  E_HTSP_EVENT_TIMER]em_wait_timeout
Jan 17 12:58:53.801: em_stop_timers
Jan 17 12:58:53.801: htsp_timer_stop
Jan 17 12:58:53.801: em_start_timer: 400 ms
Jan 17 12:58:53.801: htsp_timer - 400 msec
Jan 17 12:58:53.833: htsp_process_event: [1/0:1(1), EM_CLR_PENDING,
  E_DSP_SIG_0000]htsp_report_onhook_sig
Jan 17 12:58:54.217: htsp_process_event: [1/0:1(1), EM_CLR_PENDING,
  E_HTSP_EVENT_TIMER]em_clr_timeout
Jan 17 12:58:54.221: em_stop_timers
Jan 17 12:58:54.221: htsp_timer_stop
Jan 17 12:58:54.221: em_start_timer: 10000 ms
Jan 17 12:58:54.221: htsp_timer - 10000 msec
Jan 17 12:58:54.221: htsp_process_event: [1/0:1(1), EM_PARK,
  E_DSP_SIG_0000]em_park_onhook
Jan 17 12:58:54.221: htsp_timer_stop
Jan 17 12:58:54.225: htsp_timer_stop2 htsp_report_onhook_sig
```

Now that you understand how to troubleshoot the various TDM interfaces available on Cisco IOS voice gateways, you must understand the protocols used for signaling between CallManager and the voice gateways. CallManager uses either MGCP or H.323 to communicate with a voice gateway. The more common of the two is MGCP.

Understanding MGCP

MGCP plays an important role in CallManager's communication with various voice gateways, including the WS-X6624 and WS-X6608, as well as the majority of Cisco IOS gateways when configured to use MGCP. To understand many of the debugs and traces available to you for troubleshooting voice gateways, you must understand how MGCP works. If you are very comfortable with MGCP, you can skip this section. Otherwise, read through this section to gain a better understanding of the protocol. Either way, use it as a reference when decoding the output of the various traces and debugs covered throughout this chapter.

MGCP is a plain-text protocol, meaning that the messages are sent as ASCII-encoded text. This makes reading MGCP debugs very consistent whether you're looking at a CCM trace, a Cisco IOS Software debug, or a sniffer trace. To understand MGCP debugs, you need to understand the protocol's syntax.

RFC 2705 defines MGCP. It is a master/slave protocol whereby a call agent—in this case, CallManager—controls the function of a particular port. This is very different from H.323, which is a peer-to-peer protocol. In H.323, each gateway controls its own interfaces and communicates with other gateways using ISDN-like signaling. Most MGCP gateways are "dumb" devices in that they don't make any call routing decisions. They are just a slave to whatever the call agent (CallManager) tells them to do. This master/slave relationship has several advantages, the most important being that the gateways do not need to know anything about the dial plan. The call agent has all the call routing intelligence. The other major advantage is that because most of the intelligence is in the call agent, new features can be implemented at the call agent with little or no modification of the software running on the gateways. However, to support a new interface type, a software change is typically required on both the call agent and the voice gateway.

MGCP Endpoint Identifiers

MGCP uses the concept of *endpoints* to identify a particular trunk to the PSTN. In a Cisco IP Telephony network, these endpoints can be either an analog port (such as an FXS or FXO port) or a channel (DS0) on a digital trunk such as a T1 or E1.

Each endpoint has a unique endpoint identifier. The endpoint identifier consists of a domain name for the gateway, along with local names for each endpoint within that particular gateway. For example, an analog port on a Cisco IOS gateway might be identified as follows:

```
AALN/S1/SU0/0@pgiralt-test
```

In the case of this endpoint identifier, **pgiralt-test** is the domain name. This can also be configured to be a fully qualified domain name (**pgiralt-test.cisco.com**) as long as both the call agent and the gateway are configured to use the same fully qualified domain name. **AALN/S1/SU0/0** is the local name for a particular analog port on the gateway. It breaks down as follows:

- AALN indicates that this is an analog port.
- S1 means slot 1.
- SU0/0 is subunit 0/0—in other words, port 0/0 on the module in slot 1.

MGCP Commands

For any MGCP call, CallManager must create a connection between an endpoint and the packet network or, in some cases, between two endpoints directly, such as when hairpinning a call. As soon as the connection is created, CallManager can make changes to that connection by sending a message to modify the connection. When a call needs to be torn down, CallManager sends a command to delete the connection. When a connection is made to an endpoint, the gateway assigns a connection identifier for each connection. In the case of CallManager, there is never more than one connection to an endpoint at any given time.

Each MGCP call is also assigned a call identifier. This call identifier is unique for the entire CallManager cluster.

MGCP uses a series of commands to communicate between CallManager and the gateway. Table 6-11 lists the four-letter codes for each of the possible MGCP commands, along with their definitions.

Table 6-11   *MGCP Commands*

Code	Message Name	Description
AUEP	AuditEndpoint	Used by CallManager to determine the status of a given endpoint.
AUCX	AuditConnection	Used by CallManager to retrieve the parameters attached to a connection.
CRCX	CreateConnection	Used to create a connection between two endpoints.
DLCX	DeleteConnection	From CallManager: Used to terminate a connection. As a side effect, it collects statistics on the connection's execution.
		From the VoIP gateway: In some circumstances, a gateway might need to clear a connection. For example, maybe it has lost the resource associated with the connection, or maybe it has detected that the endpoint is no longer able or willing to send or receive voice.
EPCF	EndpointConfiguration	Used to specify the encoding of the signals that the endpoint receives. For example, in certain international telephony configurations, some calls carry μ-law encoded audio signals, and others use A-law. The call agent uses the **EndpointConfiguration** command to pass this information to the gateway.
MDCX	ModifyConnection	Used to modify the characteristics of a gateway's "view" of a connection. This "view" of the call includes both the local connection descriptors and the remote connection descriptor.
RQNT	NotificationRequest	Used to ask the gateway to send notifications upon the occurrence of specified events in an endpoint. For example, a notification might be requested for when a gateway detects a DTMF digit.
NTFY	Notify	Used by the gateway to inform CallManager when an observed event occurs.
RSIP	RestartInProgress	Used by the gateway to signal that an endpoint or a group of endpoints is put into or taken out of service.

The easiest way to understand MGCP is to look at an example of a command. Example 6-38 shows an MGCP command.

Example 6-38   **MDCX** *MGCP Command*

```
MDCX 229 S1/DS1-1/1@vnt-vg200-gw1.cisco.com MGCP 0.1
C: D00000000200000900000000080000003
I: E
X: 1
L: p:20, a:PCMU, s:off
M: recvonly
R: D/[0-9ABCD*#]
Q: process,loop
```

Look at the lines one at a time to understand what everything means. The first part of the message is **MDCX**. As noted in Table 6-11, this is a **ModifyConnection** message.

The next number, **229**, is the transaction ID. The transaction ID is like a sequence number that increments each time CallManager sends a new MGCP message. The transaction ID is used to detect lost messages. Because each MGCP message must be acknowledged, the same transaction ID is used in the acknowledgment to indicate which message is being acknowledged. Keep this in mind when looking through debugs and traces because if you see the same transaction ID repeated, it means that the device sending the duplicate transaction ID is probably retransmitting because it did not see an acknowledgment. This could signify some kind of network degradation, leading to packet loss.

Following the transaction ID is the endpoint identifier discussed previously (**S1/DS1-1/1@vnt-vg200-gw1.cisco.com**). As you can see, this message is for the endpoint that corresponds to slot 1, **DS1 1/1** on the gateway named **vnt-vg200-gw1.cisco.com**. This particular port happens to be a T1 PRI, which is why it is labeled as a DS1.

Following the endpoint identifier is the version of MGCP being used—in this case, **MGCP 0.1**.

MGCP Parameter Lines

The next set of lines in Example 6-38 look rather cryptic, but with your secret decoder ring, you will quickly understand what each character in the message means. These lines are called parameter lines. Each parameter line consists of one or two characters that comprise the parameter name, a colon, a space, and the parameter value. The values vary depending on what the parameter is. Table 6-12 lists each of the MGCP parameter names and their values. Tables 6-12 through 6-14 are a useful reference when you troubleshoot MGCP problems. The more you read MGCP debugs, the more of these parameters you will begin to memorize. This information is available in greater detail in RFC 2705; however, the information presented here should give you all you need to troubleshoot the interaction between CallManager and a gateway.

Table 6-12 *MGCP Parameter Lines*

Code	Parameter Name	Parameter Value
A	Capabilities	Used to inform CallManager of an endpoint's capabilities. The encoding of capabilities is based on the local connection options encoding for the parameters that are common to both. In addition, capabilities can also contain a list of supported packages and a list of supported modes. Refer to Table 6-14 for the list of local connection options. In addition, two other options might be present: • **Event packages**—The event packages supported by this endpoint are encoded as the keyword **v**, followed by a colon and a character string. If a list of values is specified, these values are separated by a semicolon. The first value specified is the default package for that endpoint. • **Modes**—The modes supported by this endpoint are encoded as the keyword **m**, followed by a colon and a semicolon-delimited list of supported connection modes for this endpoint.
B	BearerInformation	Defines the coding on the TDM side of the connection. Can be either **A** for A-law or **mu** for μ-law.
C	CallId	A globally unique hexadecimal string of up to 32 characters that identifies the call that is active on an endpoint. If multiple endpoints are involved in a single call, they have the same CallId.
D	DigitMap	A text encoding of a digit map. This parameter is not used with CallManager.
E	ReasonCode	Used by the gateway when deleting a connection to inform CallManager of the reason for deleting the connection. Can also be used in a **RestartInProgress** command to indicate the restart reason. The following are valid ReasonCode parameters: • **000**—Endpoint state is nominal. (This code is used only in response to audit requests.) • **900**—Endpoint malfunctioning. • **901**—Endpoint taken out of service. • **902**—Loss of lower-layer connectivity.
ES	EventStates	For events that have auditable states associated with them, this parameter indicates the event corresponding to the state the endpoint is in. For example, this is **off-hook** if the endpoint is off-hook. The definition of the individual events indicates whether the event in question has an auditable state associated with it.

Table 6-12 *MGCP Parameter Lines (Continued)*

Code	Parameter Name	Parameter Value
F	RequestedInfo	Contains a comma-delimited list of parameter codes being requested, as defined in this table. For example, if you wanted to audit the value of the following parameters: NotifiedEntity, RequestIdentifier, RequestedEvents, SignalRequests, QuarantineHandling, and DetectEvents, you would enter this RequestedInfo parameter: **F:N,X,R,S,Q,T**
I	ConnectionId	A locally-significant hexadecimal string of up to 32 characters that identifies a connection within an endpoint. This parameter is locally significant only to each endpoint.
I2	SecondConnectionId	Used to identify the ConnectionId in response to a **CreateConnection** that has a Second Endpoint ID. This parameter is not used in CallManager.
K	ResponseAck	Used to acknowledge one or more previously received MGCP commands. The acknowledgment identifiers are sent as a comma-delimited list and may include ranges by using a hyphen. For example, **K: 100,200-202** acknowledges previously received commands 100, 200, 201, and 202.
L	LocalConnectionOptions	Specifies the operational parameters that CallManager suggests to the gateway. Table 6-14 describes these parameters.
LC	LocalConnection Descriptor	A list of fields that describe the local media session according to the Session Description Protocol (SDP) standard defined in RFC 2327.
M	ConnectionMode	Refer to Table 6-13 for the various parameters.
N	NotifiedEntity	Contains the endpoint identifier that should be notified of the events being requested. This is an optional parameter. If it is absent, the **Notify** and **DeleteConnection** commands are sent to the endpoint that originated the **CreateConnection** command.
O	ObservedEvents	Denotes a list of events that the gateway detected. A single notification may report a list of events. They are reported in the order in which they were detected. The list may contain only the identification of events that were requested in the RequestedEvents parameter of the triggering **NotificationRequest**. Event names are composed of an optional package name separated from the name of the actual event by a slash (*/*). The event name can optionally be followed by an at sign (@) and the identifier of a connection on which the event should be observed.

continues

Table 6-12 *MGCP Parameter Lines (Continued)*

Code	Parameter Name	Parameter Value
P	ConnectionParameters	A string of type and value pairs separated by an equals sign. Each parameter is separated by a comma. The valid types are as follows: • **PS**—Packets sent • **OS**—Octets sent • **PR**—Packets received • **OR**—Octets received • **PL**—Packets lost • **JI**—Jitter • **LA**—Latency Here's an example of connection parameter encoding: **P: PS=1245, OS=62345, PR=0, OR=0, PL=0, JI=0, LA=48**
Q	QuarantineHandling	Specifies the handling of events that were detected by the gateway before the arrival of a **NotificationRequest** command but that have not been communicated to CallManager. Valid keywords are **process** and **discard** to indicate the handling of quarantined events. The default is **process**. The keywords **step** and **loop** indicate whether at most one notification is expected or whether multiple notifications are allowed. The default is **step**. For example, to process the quarantined events and indicate multiple notifications are allowed, the parameter is **Q: process,loop**

Table 6-12   *MGCP Parameter Lines (Continued)*

Code	Parameter Name	Parameter Value
R	RequestedEvents	Denotes a list of events that the gateway should notify CallManager of, such as off-hook or on-hook transitions. Event names are composed of an optional package name, separated from the name of the event by a slash (/). The event name can optionally be followed by an at sign (@) and the identifier of a connection on which the event should be observed.
		Each event can be qualified by a requested action or list of actions. The actions, when specified, are encoded as a list of keywords, enclosed in parentheses and separated by commas. The codes for the various actions are as follows:
		• **N**—Notify immediately
		• **A**—Accumulate
		• **D**—Treat according to digit map
		• **S**—Swap
		• **I**—Ignore
		• **K**—Keep signal(s) active
		• **E**—Embedded notification request
		When no action is specified, the default action is to notify CallManager of the event immediately. This means that, for example, **ft** and **ft(N)** are equivalent. Events that are not listed are ignored.
		The requested list is encoded on a single line, with event/action groups separated by commas. For example: **R: hu(N), hf(S,N)**
RC	RemoteConnectionDescriptor	A list of fields that describe the remote media session according to the SDP standard defined in RFC 2327.
RD	RestartDelay	A number of seconds in decimal. This parameter specifies the delay if the RestartMethod requires one. If not specified, the default is null.
		For example, the following indicates a 2-second restart delay: **RD:2**

continues

Table 6-12 *MGCP Parameter Lines (Continued)*

Code	Parameter Name	Parameter Value
RM	RestartMethod	Specifies the type of restart. The value can be one of the following: • **graceful**—Indicates that the specified endpoints will be taken out of service after the delay specified in the RestartDelay parameter. The established connections are not yet affected, but the call agent should not try to establish any new connections to this endpoint. • **forced**—The specified endpoints are abruptly taken out of service. The established connections, if any, are lost. • **restart**—Service will be restored on the endpoints after the specified RestartDelay. No connections are currently established on the endpoints. • **disconnected**—The endpoint has become disconnected and is now trying to establish connectivity. The RestartDelay parameter specifies how long in seconds the endpoint has been disconnected. Established connections are not affected. • **cancel-graceful**—A gateway is canceling a previously issued **graceful** RestartMethod command.
S	SignalRequests	A set of signals that the gateway is asked to apply to the endpoint, such as dial tone or ringback. Event names are composed of an optional package name, separated from the name of the event by a slash (/). The event name can optionally be followed by an at sign (@) and the identifier of a connection on which the event should be observed.
T	DetectEvents	A comma-delimited list of events that should be detected by the gateway.
X	RequestIdentifier	A hexadecimal string of up to 32 characters that is used to correlate this request with the notifications it triggers.
Z	SpecificEndpointID	Used to return a specific endpoint to the call agent if the call agent sent a request to create a connection on the gateway but used a wildcard to match more than one endpoint. This parameter is not used in CallManager.
Z2	Second Endpoint ID	Identifies a second endpoint to which a connection should be created. This connection is treated as a separate connection that can be modified and deleted on its own. This parameter is not used in CallManager.

Table 6-13 describes the possible parameters for the ConnectionMode parameter line.

Table 6-13   *ConnectionMode Parameters*

Mode	Meaning
M: sendonly	The gateway should only send packets.
M: recvonly	The gateway should only receive packets.
M: sendrecv	The gateway should send and receive packets.
M: confrnce	The gateway should place the connection in conference mode.
M: inactive	The gateway should neither send nor receive packets.
M: loopback	The gateway should place the circuit in loopback mode.
M: cottest	The gateway should place the circuit in test mode.
M: netwloop	The gateway should place the connection in network loopback mode.
M: netwtest	The gateway should place the connection in network continuity test mode.
M: data	The gateway should use the circuit for data network access (Point-to-Point Protocol [PPP], Serial Line Internet Protocol [SLIP], and so on).

Table 6-14 lists the various options that can be included in the LocalConnectionOptions parameter line.

Table 6-14   *LocalConnectionOptions Parameters*

Keyword	Connection Option	Description
p	Packetization period	A decimal number in milliseconds. Ranges can be designated with a hyphen.
a	Preferred compression algorithm	A character string with a list of codecs. Create a list by separating each codec value with a semicolon.
b	Bandwidth	A decimal number representing the bandwidth in kilobits per second. A range can be specified using a hyphen.
e	Echo cancellation	Determines whether echo cancellation should be enabled or disabled. Valid values are **on** and **off**.
gc	Gain control	Sets the call's gain control. This can be either the keyword **auto** or a decimal number (positive or negative) representing the number of decibels of gain.
s	Silence suppression	Enables or disables silence suppression (VAD). Valid values are **on** and **off**.
t	Type of service	The value is encoded as two hexadecimal digits.

continues

Table 6-14 *LocalConnectionOptions Parameters (Continued)*

Keyword	Connection Option	Description
r	Resource reservation	Valid values are as follows: • **g**—Guaranteed service • **cl**—Controlled load • **be**—Best effort
k	Encryption key	Specified as defined for the **K** parameter of SDP (RFC 2327).
nt	Type of network	The type of network. Network types are encoded as one of the following keywords: **IN**, **ATM**, or **LOCAL**.

Keep Tables 6-12 through 6-14 close by because you will refer to them often when trying to decode MGCP messages. Let's get back to the message in Example 6-39, which repeats the message shown in Example 6-36.

Example 6-39 **MDCX** *MGCP Command*

```
MDCX 229 S1/DS1-1/1@vnt-vg200-gw1.cisco.com MGCP 0.1
C: D000000002000009000000080000003
I: E
X: 1
L: p:20, a:PCMU, s:off
M: recvonly
R: D/[0-9ABCD*#]
Q: process,loop
```

If you match Tables 6-12 through 6-14 with the sample message, you can see that you have CallId (C) , ConnectionId (I), RequestIdentifier (X), LocalConnectionOptions (L), ConnectionMode (M), RequestedEvents (R), and QuarantineHandling (Q) parameters being delivered as part of the **ModifyConnection** command. To digest this better, look at each line one at a time.

First you see the CallId parameter (D000000002000009000000080000003). This is sent from CallManager and uniquely identifies this call. This parameter is useful in troubleshooting because you can use it to match up messages between the gateway debugs and the CCM traces.

```
C: D000000002000009000000080000003
```

Next is the ConnectionID, which is set to **0xE** (14 decimal):

```
I: E
```

The request identifier is set to **1**. This means that any notify commands sent back to CallManager use **1** as the request identifier so that CallManager knows which request the notification corresponds to.

```
X: 1
```

Table 6-14 defines the LocalConnectionOptions. This message means that the packetization period is 20 ms, the codec is G.711 μ-law, and silence suppression (VAD) is disabled:

```
L: p:20, a:PCMU, s:off
```

The ConnectionMode parameter indicates that the connection is being put in a one-way audio state of receive only, meaning that the gateway should only receive packets and not send packets.

```
M: recvonly
```

Next, CallManager asks to be notified of any DTMF digit. You still don't know why **D/[0-9ABCD*#]** means any DTMF digit. The **D/** signifies the DTMF package, and the information enclosed in square brackets is the parameters for that package.

```
R: D/[0-9ABCD*#]
```

The next section explains each of the packages in detail and lists all their possible parameters.

Finally, CallManager tells the gateway it wants to process any quarantined events, and the **loop** value indicates that CallManager wants to know about all instances of the events:

```
Q: process,loop
```

Because CallManager asked to be notified of all DTMF digits, the gateway should then report any DTMF digit events that were quarantined before this message was sent to the gateway.

That might seem like an awful lot of work just to decode a single message, but it will get easier over time. Keep this chapter nearby when debugging MGCP messages so that you can decode each message. As previously mentioned, the last piece of information you need for your secret decoder ring is the list of MGCP packages and definitions of the symbols in the packages.

MGCP Packages

To understand some of the parameters sent in MGCP commands, you must understand what an MGCP package is and how to decode the messages. An *MGCP package* is a grouping of the events and signals supported by a particular type of MGCP endpoint. Each package is assigned one or more letters. These letters should not be confused with the letters used for the MGCP parameter lines listed in Table 6-12. Table 6-15 shows the relevant packages used between CallManager and MGCP gateways. For information about various other packages that are part of the MGCP specification, refer to RFC 2705.

Table 6-15 *MGCP Package Names*

Package Symbol	Package Name
G	Generic media package
D	DTMF package
M	MF package
T	Trunk package
L	Line package
H	Handset emulation package
R	RTP package
DT	DTMF trunk package
MS	MF trunk package

The following sections each contain a table that defines the symbols available for the nine different packages listed in Table 6-15. Each event table has five columns, as shown in Table 6-16.

Table 6-16 *Event Column Definitions*

Column	Description
Symbol	The unique symbol used for the event. This is typically one or two lowercase letters or numbers.
Definition	A short description of the event.
R	An x appears in this column if the event can be requested by CallManager for notification. Alternatively, one or more of the following symbols may appear: • **P**—Indicates that the event is persistent • **S**—Indicates that the event is an event state that may be audited • **C**—Indicates that the event/signal may be detected/applied on a connection. If C is associated with an event, this refers to an event that can occur on the media stream.
S	If nothing appears in this column for an event, CallManager cannot signal the event on command. Otherwise, the following symbols identify the type of event: • **On/off signal (OO)**—The signal is turned on until commanded by the call agent to turn it off, and vice versa. On/off signals can be parameterized with a + to turn the signal on or a – to turn the signal off. • **Timeout signal (TO)**—The signal lasts for a given duration unless it is superseded by a new signal. • **Brief signal (BR)**—The event has a short, known duration.
Duration	Specifies the duration of Timeout (TO) signals.

Generic Media Package (G)

The generic media package groups the events and signals that can be observed on several types of endpoints. Table 6-17 describes the meaning of each symbol in the package. Table 6-16 defined the meaning of each of the column headings.

Table 6-17   *Generic Media Package Symbol*

Symbol	Definition	R	S	Duration
mt	Modem detected	x	—	—
ft	Fax tone detected	x	—	—
ld	Long-duration connection	x	—	—
pat(###)	Pattern ### detected	x	OO	—
rt	Ringback tone	—	TO	—
rbk(###)	Ringback on connection	—	TO	180 seconds
cf	Confirm tone	—	BR	—
cg	Network congestion tone	—	TO	—
it	Intercept tone	—	OO	—
pt	Preemption tone	—	OO	—
of	report failure	x	—	—

DTMF Package (D)

The DTMF package is used to send and detect DTMF digits. Table 6-18 describes the meaning of each symbol in the package. Table 6-16 defined the meaning of each of the column headings.

Table 6-18   *DTMF Package Symbols*

Symbol	Definition	R	S	Duration
0	DTMF 0	x	BR	—
1	DTMF 1	x	BR	—
2	DTMF 2	x	BR	—
3	DTMF 3	x	BR	—
4	DTMF 4	x	BR	—
5	DTMF 5	x	BR	—
6	DTMF 6	x	BR	—
7	DTMF 7	x	BR	—
8	DTMF 8	x	BR	—

continues

Table 6-18 *DTMF Package Symbols (Continued)*

Symbol	Definition	R	S	Duration
9	DTMF 9	x	BR	—
#	DTMF #	x	BR	—
*	DTMF *	x	BR	—
A	DTMF A	x	BR	—
B	DTMF B	x	BR	—
C	DTMF C	x	BR	—
D	DTMF D	x	BR	—
L	Long-duration indicator	x	—	2 seconds
X	Wildcard; matches any digit from 0 to 9	x	—	—
T	Interdigit timer	x	—	4 seconds
of	Report failure	x	—	—

MF Package (M)

The MF package is used to send and detect multifrequency (MF) digits as well as signal seizure and wink conditions on an MF trunk. Table 6-19 describes the meaning of each symbol in the package. Table 6-16 defined the meaning of each of the column headings.

Table 6-19 *MF Package Symbols*

Symbol	Definition	R	S	Duration
0	MF 0	x	BR	—
1	MF 1	x	BR	—
2	MF 2	x	BR	—
3	MF 3	x	BR	—
4	MF 4	x	BR	—
5	MF 5	x	BR	—
6	MF 6	x	BR	—
7	MF 7	x	BR	—
8	MF 8	x	BR	—
9	MF 9	x	BR	—
X	Wildcard; matches any digit from 0 to 9	x	—	—
T	Interdigit timer	x	—	4 seconds
K0	MF K0 or KP	x	BR	—

Table 6-19 *MF Package Symbols (Continued)*

Symbol	Definition	R	S	Duration
K1	MF K1	x	BR	—
K2	MF K2	x	BR	—
S0	MF S0 or ST	x	BR	—
S1	MF S1	x	BR	—
S2	MF S2	x	BR	—
S3	MF S3	x	BR	—
wk	Wink	x	BR	—
wko	Wink off	x	BR	—
is	Incoming seizure	x	OO	—
rs	Return seizure	x	OO	—
us	Unseize circuit	x	OO	—
of	Report failure	x	—	—

Trunk Package (T)

The trunk package is used to generate test tones and other trunk maintenance procedures. This package is not used by CallManager.

Table 6-20 describes the meaning of each symbol in the package. Table 6-16 defined the meaning of each of the column headings.

Table 6-20 *Trunk Package Symbols*

Symbol	Definition	R	S	Duration
c01	Continuity tone (single tone or return tone)	x	OO	—
c02	Continuity test (go tone in dual-tone procedures)	x	OO	—
lb	Loopback	—	OO	—
om	Old milliwatt tone (1000 Hz)	x	OO	—
nm	New milliwatt tone (1004 Hz)	x	OO	—
tl	Test line	x	OO	—
zz	No circuit	x	OO	—
as	Answer supervision	x	OO	—
ro	Reorder tone	x	TO	30 seconds
of	Report failure	x	—	—
bl	Blocking	—	OO	—

Line Package (L)

The line package is used for a variety of purposes, including detecting on-hook and off-hook transitions as well as Flash hook. It is also used to generate tones such as ringback, busy, and reorder. Table 6-21 lists the symbols available in the line package. Table 6-16 defined the meaning of each of the column headings.

Table 6-21 *Line Package Symbols*

Symbol	Definition	R	S	Duration
adsi(string)	ADSI display	—	BR	—
vmwi	Visual message waiting indicator	—	OO	—
hd	Off-hook transition	x	—	—
hu	On-hook transition	x	—	—
hf	Flash hook	x	—	—
ht	Tone on Hold	—	BR	—
aw	Answer tone	x	OO	—
bz	Busy tone	—	TO	30 seconds
ci(ti,nu,na)	Caller-id	—	BR	—
wt	Call waiting tone	—	TO	30 seconds
wt1, wt2, wt3, wt4	Alternative call waiting tones	—	—	—
dl	Dial tone	—	TO	16 seconds
mwi	Message waiting indicator	—	TO	16 seconds
nbz	Network busy	x	OO	—
ro	Reorder tone	—	TO	30 seconds
rg	Ringing	—	TO	180 seconds
r0, r1, r2, r3, r4, r5, r6, or r7	Distinctive ringing	—	TO	180 seconds
rs	Ringsplash	—	BR	—
p	Prompt tone	x	BR	—
e	Error tone	x	BR	—
sl	Stutter dial tone	—	TO	16 seconds
v	Alerting tone	—	OO	—
y	Recorder warning tone	—	OO	—
sit	SIT tone	—	—	—

Table 6-21   *Line Package Symbols (Continued)*

Symbol	Definition	R	S	Duration
z	Calling card service tone	—	OO	—
oc	Report on completion	x	—	—
ot	Off-hook warning tone	—	TO	Infinite
s(###)	Distinctive tone pattern	x	BR	—
of	Report failure	x	—	—

Handset Emulation Package (H)

The handset emulation package is an extension of the line package, to be used when the gateway can emulate a handset. The difference with the line package is that events such as off-hook can be signaled as well as detected. Table 6-22 describes the meaning of each symbol in the package. Table 6-16 defined the meaning of each of the column headings.

Table 6-22   *Handset Emulation Package Symbols*

Symbol	Definition	R	S	Duration
adsi(string)	ADSI display	x	BR	—
hd	Off-hook transition	x	OO	—
hu	On-hook transition	x	OO	—
hf	Flash hook	x	BR	—
aw	Answer tone	x	OO	—
bz	Busy tone	x	OO	—
wt	Call waiting tone	x	TO	30 seconds
dl	Dial tone (350 + 440 Hz)	x	TO	120 seconds
nbz	Network busy (fast cycle busy)	x	OO	—
rg	Ringing	x	TO	30 seconds
r0, r1, r2, r3, r4, r5, r6, or r7	Distinctive ringing	x	TO	30 seconds
p	Prompt tone	x	BR	—
e	Error tone	x	BR	—
sdl	Stutter dial tone	x	TO	16 seconds
v	Altering tone	x	OO	—
y	Recorder warning tone	x	OO	—
t	SIT tone	x	—	—

continues

Table 6-22 *Handset Emulation Package Symbols (Continued)*

Symbol	Definition	R	S	Duration
z	Calling card service tone	x	OO	—
oc	Report on completion	x	—	—
ot	Off-hook warning tone	x	OO	—
s(###)	Distinctive tone pattern	x	BR	—
of	Report failure	x	—	—

RTP Package (R)

The RTP package allows an endpoint to report to a call agent when certain parameters regarding the media stream change, such as the codec, sampling rate, or jitter buffer size. It also provides a mechanism to generate test tones to check for continuity between two devices.

Table 6-23 describes the meaning of each symbol in the package. Table 6-16 defined the meaning of each of the column headings.

Table 6-23 *RTP Package Symbols*

Symbol	Definition	R	S	Duration
UC	Used codec changed	x	—	—
SR(###)	Sampling rate changed	x	—	—
JI(###)	Jitter buffer size changed	x	—	—
PL(###)	Packet loss exceeded	x	—	—
qa	Quality alert	x	—	—
co1	Continuity tone (single tone or return tone)	x	OO	—
co2	Continuity test (go tone in dual-tone procedures)	x	OO	—
of	Report failure	x	—	—

DTMF Trunk Package (DT)

The DTMF trunk package is not defined in RFC 2705 where all the other packages discussed so far are defined. Rather, it is defined in RFC 3064 which defines the MGCP CAS packages. This package lets CallManager control T1 CAS wink start and immediate start trunks on a Cisco IOS gateway. It uses DTMF tones to send digits to the PSTN. This package allows CallManager to control a T1 CAS port by using signaling similar to ISDN

Q.931. Table 6-24 describes the meaning of each symbol in the package. Table 6-16 defined the meaning of each of the column headings.

Table 6-24   *DTMF Trunk Package Symbols*

Symbol	Definition	R	S	Duration
ans	Call answer	P	BR	—
bl	Call block	S	BR	—
bz	Busy tone	—	TO	30 seconds
dl	Dial tone	—	TO	16 seconds
ft	Fax tone	x	—	—
ma	Media start	—	—	—
mt	Modem tone	x	—	—
oc	Operation complete	x	—	—
of	Operation failure	x	—	—
rel	Release call	P	BR	—
res	Resume call	P	BR	—
rlc	Release complete	P, S	BR	—
ro	Reorder tone	—	TO	30 seconds
rt	Ringback tone	—	TO	180 seconds
sup	Call setup	P, S	TO	When signal completes out-pulsing
sus	Suspend call	P	BR	—

MF Trunk Package (MS)

Similar to the DTMF trunk package, the MF trunk package is also defined in RFC 3074. This package lets CallManager control T1 CAS wink start and immediate start trunks on a Cisco IOS gateway using multifrequency tones to send digits to the PSTN. This package allows CallManager to control a T1 CAS port by using signaling similar to ISDN Q.931. Table 6-25 describes the meaning of each symbol in the package. Table 6-16 defined the meaning of each of the column headings.

Table 6-25   *MF Trunk Package Symbols*

Symbol	Definition	R	S	Duration
ans	Call answer	P	BR	—
bl	Call block	S	BR	—
bz	Busy tone	—	TO	30 seconds

continues

Table 6-25   *MF Trunk Package Symbols (Continued)*

Symbol	Definition	R	S	Duration
ft	Fax tone	x	—	—
inf(digits)	Information digits	x	—	—
ma	Media start	—	—	—
mt	Modem tone	x	—	—
oc	Operation complete	x	—	—
of	Operation failure	x	—	—
rel	Release call	P	BR	—
res	Resume call	P	BR	—
rlc	Release complete	P, S	BR	—
ro	Reorder tone	—	TO	30 seconds
rt	Ringback tone	—	TO	180 seconds
sup	Call setup	P, S	TO	When signal completes out-pulsing
sus	Suspend call	P	BR	—

MGCP Response Headers and Response Codes

Each MGCP command, regardless of its direction, must be acknowledged. MGCP is a UDP-based protocol; therefore, retransmissions must be handled at the application layer (Layer 7). If a device that sent a message does not receive an acknowledgment within a specified timeframe, it retransmits the message.

The acknowledgments are called *response headers*. A response header is composed of a response line, optionally followed by headers that contain additional parameters.

An example of response header could be

```
200 1203 OK
```

The response line starts with a three-digit response code—200 in this case. The code is followed by the transaction identifier, 1203, and an optional comment, **OK**.

The response codes are divided into four ranges:

- 100 to 199 indicates a provisional response
- 200 to 299 indicates a successful completion
- 400 to 499 indicates a transient error
- 500 to 599 indicates a permanent error

Transient errors typically indicate a problem with a single call or a short-lived problem. A permanent error indicates a problem that likely requires operator intervention to resolve, such as a circuit going out of service or a hardware failure.

Table 6-26 lists the possible response codes. Keep this table handy when you're troubleshooting MGCP gateways so that you can understand why a gateway is returning an error.

Table 6-26   *MGCP Response Codes*

Response Code	Definition
100	The transaction is currently being executed. An actual completion message follows later.
200	The requested transaction was executed normally.
250	The connection was deleted.
400	The transaction could not be executed due to a transient error.
401	The phone is already off-hook.
402	The phone is already on-hook.
403	The transaction could not be executed because the endpoint does not have sufficient resources at this time.
404	Insufficient bandwidth at this time.
500	The transaction could not be executed because the endpoint is unknown.
501	The transaction could not be executed because the endpoint is not ready.
502	The transaction could not be executed because the endpoint does not have sufficient resources.
510	The transaction could not be executed because a protocol error was detected.
511	The transaction could not be executed because the command contained an unrecognized extension.
512	The transaction could not be executed because the gateway is not equipped to detect one of the requested events.
513	The transaction could not be executed because the gateway is not equipped to generate one of the requested signals.
514	The transaction could not be executed because the gateway cannot send the specified announcement.
515	The transaction refers to an incorrect connection-id (it might already have been deleted).
516	The transaction refers to an unknown call-id.
517	Unsupported or invalid mode.

continues

Table 6-26 *MGCP Response Codes (Continued)*

Response Code	Definition
518	Unsupported or unknown package.
519	The endpoint does not have a DigitMap.
520	The transaction could not be executed because the endpoint is "restarting."
521	The endpoint was redirected to another call agent.
522	No such event or signal.
523	Unknown action or illegal combination of actions.
524	Internal inconsistency in LocalConnectionOptions.
525	Unknown extension in LocalConnectionOptions.
526	Insufficient bandwidth.
527	Missing RemoteConnectionDescriptor.
528	Incompatible protocol version.
529	Internal hardware failure.
530	CAS protocol error.
531	Failure of a grouping of trunks (for example, facility failure).

Some response headers contain information in addition to the response codes listed in Table 6-22. In the case of a response to a **CreateConnection** message, the response line is followed by a ConnectionId parameter. It also might be followed by a SpecificEndpointId parameter if the creation request was sent to a wildcard endpoint identifier. When a positive response code is sent in response to a **CreateConnection**, the messages should also contain a LocalConnectionDescriptor parameter.

In the case of a response to a **DeleteConnection** message, the response line is followed by a ConnectionParameters parameter.

Cisco IOS MGCP Gateways

Up to two signaling channels are involved in a Cisco IOS MGCP gateway that interfaces with CallManager, depending on the POTS interface in use:

- The UDP-based MGCP signaling discussed thus far
- A signaling channel for PRI gateways

All protocols use the UDP-based MGCP signaling. Only gateways that terminate an ISDN PRI connection use the second signaling channel.

The signaling channel for PRI gateways is used to backhaul the ISDN Q.931 messages received from the PSTN to CallManager for processing. Unlike H.323, which terminates the D-channel on the gateway for processing, CallManager's implementation of MGCP backhauls the Q.931 messages received on the PRI to CallManager via a TCP connection. This lets the Q.931 signaling terminate on CallManager for processing, whereas Q.921 terminates in the gateway. CallManager then uses MGCP to control the gateway.

When troubleshooting a Cisco IOS gateway configured to use MGCP, the first thing to check is the status of the gateway's registration with CallManager. Issue the command **show ccm-manager**, as demonstrated in Example 6-40.

Example 6-40 *Checking Gateway Registration Status*

```
vnt-vg200-gw1#show ccm-manager
MGCP Domain Name: vnt-vg200-gw1.cisco.com
Priority          Status                   Host
==============================================================
Primary           Registered               172.18.106.59
First Backup      Backup Ready             172.18.106.58
Second Backup     None

Current active Call Manager:     172.18.106.59
Backhaul/Redundant link port:    2428
Failover Interval:               30 seconds
Keepalive Interval:              15 seconds
Last keepalive sent:             3d23h (elapsed time: 00:00:23)
Last MGCP traffic time:          3d23h (elapsed time: 00:00:23)
Last failover time:              3d21h from (172.18.106.58)
Switchback mode:                 Graceful
MGCP Fallback mode:              Not Selected
Last MGCP Fallback start time:   00:00:00
Last MGCP Fallback end time:     00:00:00

PRI Backhaul Link info:
    Link Protocol:     TCP
    Remote Port Number: 2428
    Remote IP Address:  172.18.106.59
    Current Link State: OPEN
    Statistics:
        Packets recvd:   19
        Recv failures:   0
        Packets xmitted: 12
        Xmit failures:   0
    PRI Ports being backhauled:
      Slot 1, port 1
      Slot 1, port 0
Configuration Auto-Download Information
========================================
Current version-id: {20565D8B-596C-4CCB-A5CE-4F98368F170F}
Last config-downloaded:3d18h
Current state: Waiting for commands
Configuration Download statistics:
        Download Attempted        : 27
```

continues

Example 6-40 *Checking Gateway Registration Status (Continued)*

```
              Download Successful        : 27
              Download Failed            : 0
          Configuration Attempted        : 3
            Configuration Successful      : 3
            Configuration Failed(Parsing): 0
            Configuration Failed(config) : 0
Last config download command: New Registration
Configuration Error History:
FAX mode: cisco
```

As you can see, the output in Example 6-40 is from a PRI because there is a section for **PRI Backhaul Link info**. On a Cisco IOS gateway that does not have PRI interfaces, this does not appear.

In the first line of the output, you can see the MGCP domain name for this gateway. The MGCP domain name is always the gateway's host name. If the command **ip domain-name** is configured on the gateway, it is concatenated with the host name to form a fully qualified domain name.

CAUTION   If you change your gateway's host name, the MGCP domain name changes as well, making your gateway unable to register with CallManager. Make sure that if you change your gateway's host name, you also change the MGCP domain name that is configured in CallManager.

The next few lines show you up to three CallManagers that the gateway is configured to connect to in order of priority and the status of each. For the gateway to function, at least one CallManager should show **Registered**. If you do not see the gateway registered, this could be due to a misconfiguration or a connectivity issue.

First, issue the command **show running-config** to check the gateway's running configuration. Ensure that the following lines are configured:

```
mgcp
mgcp call-agent CallManager IP Address
ccm-manager mgcp
```

This is the minimum configuration required to get the gateway to register with CallManager. If the gateway is configured as shown and it still does not register, make sure you have IP connectivity to CallManager. The easiest way to do this is by issuing the **ping** command from the gateway with CallManager's IP address, as demonstrated in Example 6-41

Example 6-41   *Confirming IP Connectivity to CallManager*

```
pgiralt-test#ping 172.18.106.58

Type escape sequence to abort.
Sending 5, 100-byte ICMP Echos to 172.18.106.58, timeout is 2 seconds:
!!!!!
Success rate is 100 percent (5/5), round-trip min/avg/max = 60/61/64 ms
```

Just because the **show ccm-manager** command shows the gateway registered does not mean that everything is actually configured correctly. In versions of Cisco IOS Software prior to Release 12.2(11)T, all it really means is that the gateway could connect to TCP port 2428 on the CallManager server. So you might be wondering what TCP has to do with this, considering the earlier mention of MGCP using UDP port 2427. The TCP connection on 2428 is used for the gateway to exchange KeepAlives with CallManager and for sending PRI backhaul information. If a PRI is not being used, the TCP connection is just used to determine whether the primary and backup CallManagers are up and running.

In Cisco IOS Software Release 12.2(11)T and later, the output looks like Example 6-42.

Example 6-42   **show ccm-manager** *Command Output in Cisco IOS Software Release 12.2(11)T*

```
pgiralt-test#show ccm-manager
MGCP Domain Name: pgiralt-test
Priority          Status                      Host
================================================================
Primary           Registering with CM        172.18.106.58
First Backup      Backup Ready                172.18.106.59
Second Backup     None

Current active Call Manager:      None
Backhaul/Redundant link port:     2428
Failover Interval:                30 seconds
Keepalive Interval:               15 seconds
Last keepalive sent:              00:03:36 (elapsed time: 00:03:43)
Last MGCP traffic time:           00:07:16 (elapsed time: 00:00:02)
Last failover time:               00:07:16 from (172.18.106.59)
Switchback mode:                  Graceful
MGCP Fallback mode:               Not Selected
Last MGCP Fallback start time:    00:00:00
Last MGCP Fallback end time:      00:00:00

Configuration Auto-Download Information
========================================
 No configurations downloaded
Current state: Automatic Configuration Download feature is disabled
Configuration Error History:
FAX mode: Cisco
```

Notice that instead of saying **Registered**, it says **Registering with CM**. If it stays this way, there is a problem.

To see if the endpoints are registering correctly, the easiest thing to do is to force them to try to reregister by turning on **debug mgcp packet** and then restarting the MGCP process, as shown in Example 6-43.

Example 6-43 *Forcing Endpoint Reregistration*

```
pgiralt-test#terminal monitor
pgiralt-test#debug mgcp packet
Media Gateway Control Protocol packets debugging is on
pgiralt-test#configure terminal
Enter configuration commands, one per line.  End with CNTL/Z.
pgiralt-test(config)#no mgcp
pgiralt-test(config)#mgcp
```

Shortly after entering the commands shown in Example 6-43, you should see the MGCP debugs showing the gateway trying to register, as shown in Example 6-44.

Example 6-44 **debug mgcp packet** *Output Showing a Gateway Registration*

```
pgiralt-test#debug mgcp packet
Jan 11 12:23:30.913: send_mgcp_msg, MGCP Packet sent --->

Jan 11 12:23:30.913: RSIP 1 *@pgiralt-test MGCP 0.1
RM: restart
<---
Jan 11 12:23:31.005: MGCP Packet received -
500 1
```

As you can see, the gateway sent an MGCP restart in progress (**RSIP**) message. This message is for all endpoints in the MGCP domain pgiralt-test because of the wildcard character (*) before the domain. If you reference Table 6-12, you can see that the RestartMethod (RM) is **restart**.

The next message, shown in Example 6-45, is the response from CallManager. As you can see, the response code is 500. As shown in Table 6-26, 500 means "The transaction could not be executed because the endpoint is unknown." This is a clear sign that there is probably a misconfiguration on either the gateway or CallManager.

You can also look at the CCM traces from the same time period to see what this looks like from CallManager's perspective.

Example 6-45 *MGCP Gateway* **RestartInProgress**

```
MGCPHandler received msg from: 10.83.129.8
RSIP 1 *@pgiralt-test MGCP 0.1
RM: restart

MGCPInit - //// RSIP <restart> from *@pgiralt-test
DeviceTransientConnection - Transient connection attempt. Connecting Port:2427
  Device name [Optional].:*@pgiralt-test Device IP address.:10.83.129.8
  Device type. [Optional]:254 Reason Code [Optional].:2 App ID:Cisco CallManager
  Cluster ID:VNT-CM1A-Cluster Node ID:172.18.106.58
Device Transient deviceName : *@pgiralt-test, IPAddress : 10.83.129.8
```

Example 6-45   *MGCP Gateway* **RestartInProgress** *(Continued)*

```
DebugMsg deviceName : *@pgiralt-test, DeviceType : 254, risClass: 2
MGCPHandler send msg SUCCESSFULLY to: 10.83.129.8
500 1
MGCPBhHandler 10.83.129.8 - Unregistered but TCP remains open
```

As you can see, the MGCP portion of the debug is nearly identical to what you see on the gateway MGCP debug. The next step in troubleshooting this problem is to check CallManager Administration to see if there really is a configured gateway named pgiralt-test:

Step 1   **Select Device > Gateway**.

Step 2   Search for the name of your gateway (in this case, pgiralt-test).

If you don't get any matches, the problem is obviously that the gateway is not configured. If you do get a match, however, compare carefully. Figure 6-5 shows the results when you search the test system for pgiralt-test.

Figure 6-5   *CallManager Administration Gateway Search Page*

As you can see in Figure 6-5, the device name of the gateway that matched the search is pgiralt-test.cisco.com. This is not the same thing as pgiralt-test, so that's why CallManager is responding to the **RSIP** with a 500. In this case, there are two ways to resolve the problem. You can either change the configuration in CallManager from **pgiralt-test.cisco.com** to **pgiralt-test**, or you can add **ip domain-name cisco.com** to the gateway configuration so that it registers with the name **pgiralt-test.cisco.com**. The following examples demonstrate how the registration looks after this problem is corrected.

First, the gateway sends an **RSIP** to register with CallManager, as shown in Example 6-46.

Example 6-46 *MGCP* **RestartInProgress**

```
Jan 11 17:02:28.014: send_mgcp_msg, MGCP Packet sent to 172.18.106.58 --->

Jan 11 17:02:28.018: RSIP 1 *@pgiralt-test MGCP 0.1
RM: restart
<---
```

Next, CallManager responds with a 200, meaning that the transaction was completed successfully, as shown in Example 6-47.

Example 6-47 *MGCP Acknowledgment from CallManager*

```
Jan 11 17:02:28.142: MGCP Packet received from 172.18.106.58-
200 1
```

Then the gateway sends a **Notify** message indicating that it is not observing any events on any port, as shown in Example 6-48.

Example 6-48 *MGCP Acknowledgment from CallManager*

```
Jan 11 17:02:28.146: send_mgcp_msg, MGCP Packet sent to 172.18.106.58 --->

Jan 11 17:02:28.146: NTFY 2 *@pgiralt-test MGCP 0.1
X: 0
O:
<---
```

CallManager then sends a notification request for port 1/0/0, as shown in Example 6-49. CallManager is asking to be informed of any off-hook transition. The QuarantineHandling parameter tells the gateway it can inform CallManager of the off-hook event several times as opposed to just once, and if an off-hook event has already occurred, the gateway should inform CallManager.

Example 6-49 *MGCP* **NotificationRequest** *of Off-Hook Transitions*

```
Jan 11 17:02:28.150: MGCP Packet received from 172.18.106.58-
RQNT 29 AALN/S1/SU0/0@pgiralt-test MGCP 0.1
X: 2
R: L/hd
Q: process,loop
```

The gateway replies with a 200, acknowledging the notification request on port 1/0/0, as shown in Example 6-50.

Example 6-50 *MGCP Acknowledgment from a Gateway*

```
Jan 11 17:02:28.154: send_mgcp_msg, MGCP Packet sent to 172.18.106.58 --->

Jan 11 17:02:28.154: 200 29 OK
<---
```

CallManager sends a similar notification request for port 1/0/0, also asking to be informed of any off-hook transitions, as shown in Example 6-51.

Example 6-51   *MGCP* **NotificationRequest** *of Off-Hook Transitions*

```
Jan 11 17:02:28.222: MGCP Packet received from 172.18.106.58-
RQNT 30 AALN/S1/SU1/0@pgiralt-test MGCP 0.1
X: 0
R: L/hd
Q: process,loop
```

In Example 6-52, the gateway acknowledges the notification request on port 1/1/0.

Example 6-52   *MGCP Acknowledgment from a Gateway*

```
Jan 11 17:02:28.226: send_mgcp_msg, MGCP Packet sent to 172.18.106.58 --->

Jan 11 17:02:28.226: 200 30 OK
<---
```

CallManager now acknowledges the **Notify** command that the gateway sent previously, as shown in Example 6-53.

Example 6-53   *MGCP Acknowledgment from CallManager*

```
Jan 11 17:02:28.290: MGCP Packet received from 172.18.106.58-
200 2
```

In Example 6-54, CallManager sends an **AuditEndpoint** (AUEP) message for port 1/0/0, requesting the port capabilities (A), the value of the RequestIdentifier (X), and the ConnectionId (I).

Example 6-54   *MGCP* **AuditEndpoint** *Message for Port 1/0/0*

```
Jan 11 17:02:28.290: MGCP Packet received from 172.18.106.58-
AUEP 31 AALN/S1/SU0/0@pgiralt-test MGCP 0.1
F: X, A, I
```

The gateway responds with the requested information, as shown in Example 6-55. Notice that the ConnectionId (I) field is blank because there is no active call on the port. If there were an active call (for example, if a call was being preserved), the gateway would report the preserved call's connection identifier. The rest of the information reports the port's capabilities. You can see that the message is actually broken into two packets.

Example 6-55   *MGCP Acknowledgment from a Gateway Including Audit Information*

```
Jan 11 17:02:28.298: send_mgcp_msg, MGCP Packet sent to 172.18.106.58 --->

Jan 11 17:02:28.298: 200 31
I:
X: 2
L: p:10-20, a:PCMU;PCMA, b:64, e:on, gc:-6-14, s:on, t:00-FF, r:g, nt:IN,
  v:L;G;D;T;H
```

continues

Example 6-55 *MGCP Acknowledgment from a Gateway Including Audit Information (Continued)*

```
L: p:10-220, a:G.729a;G.729b;G.729, b:8, e:on, gc:-6-14, s:on, t:00-FF, r:g, nt:IN,
   v:L;G;D;T;H
L: p:10-110, a:G.726-16;G.728, b:16, e:on, gc:-6-14, s:on, t:00-FF, r:g, nt:IN,
   v:L;G;D;T;H
L: p:10-70, a:G.726-24, b:24, e:on, gc:-6-14, s:on, t:00-FF, r:g, nt:IN,
   v:L;G;D;T;H
L: p:10-50, a:G.726-32, b:32, e:on, gc:-6-14, s:on, t:00-FF, r:g, nt:IN,
   v:L;G;D;T;H
L: p:30-270, a:G.723.1-H;G.723.1a-H, b:6, e:on, gc:-6-14, s:on, t:00-FF, r:g,
   nt:IN, v:L;G;D;T;H
L: p:30-330, a:G.723.1-L;G.723.1a-L, b:5, e
Jan 11 17:02:28.302: :on, gc:-6-14, s:on, t:00-FF, r:g, nt:IN, v:L;G;D;T;H
M: sendonly, recvonly, sendrecv, inactive, loopback, conttest, netwloop, netwtest
<---
```

Finally, CallManager does a similar **AuditEndpoint** for port 1/1/0 and receives a similar response from the gateway, as shown in Example 6-56.

Example 6-56 *MGCP **AuditEndpoint** Message for Port 1/1/0*

```
Jan 11 17:02:28.314: send_mgcp_msg, MGCP Packet sent to 172.18.106.58 --->

Jan 11 17:02:28.342: MGCP Packet received from 172.18.106.58-
AUEP 32 AALN/S1/SU1/0@pgiralt-test MGCP 0.1
F: X, A, I


Jan 11 17:02:28.350: send_mgcp_msg, MGCP Packet sent to 172.18.106.58 --->

Jan 11 17:02:28.350: 200 32
I:
X: 0
L: p:10-20, a:PCMU;PCMA, b:64, e:on, gc:-6-14, s:on, t:00-FF, r:g, nt:IN,
   v:L;G;D;T;H
L: p:10-220, a:G.729a;G.729b;G.729, b:8, e:on, gc:-6-14, s:on, t:00-FF, r:g, nt:IN,
   v:L;G;D;T;H
L: p:10-110, a:G.726-16;G.728, b:16, e:on, gc:-6-14, s:on, t:00-FF, r:g, nt:IN,
   v:L;G;D;T;H
L: p:10-70, a:G.726-24, b:24, e:on, gc:-6-14, s:on, t:00-FF, r:g, nt:IN,
   v:L;G;D;T;H
L: p:10-50, a:G.726-32, b:32, e:on, gc:-6-14, s:on, t:00-FF, r:g, nt:IN,
   v:L;G;D;T;H
L: p:30-270, a:G.723.1-H;G.723.1a-H, b:6, e:on, gc:-6-14, s:on, t:00-FF, r:g,
   nt:IN, v:L;G;D;T;H
L: p:30-330, a:G.723.1-L;G.723.1a-L, b:5, e
Jan 11 17:02:28.350: :on, gc:-6-14, s:on, t:00-FF, r:g, nt:IN, v:L;G;D;T;H
M: sendonly, recvonly, sendrecv, inactive, loopback, conttest, netwloop, netwtest
<---
```

You might have noticed that CallManager only attempted to audit the endpoints for ports 1/0/0 and 1/1/0, not for 1/0/1 and 1/1/1. The reason for this is that the only ports configured on CallManager are ports 1/0/0 and 1/1/0; the other ports are not configured. If one or more ports are not functioning properly, you should check to ensure that the port has actually been configured in CallManager Administration.

Now that your gateway and all its endpoints are registered, it's time to start making some calls.

MGCP FXS/FXO

Analog FXO and FXS signaling are nearly identical from an MGCP signaling perspective. Now that you have read about how MGCP works, understanding the call flow will be easy. Take a look at a call from an FXS port. **debug mgcp packet** has been enabled on the gateway. Figure 6-6 shows the call flow for the call you are about to examine in detail. The acknowledgments have been omitted for the sake of brevity.

Figure 6-6 *FXS Port MGCP Call Flow*

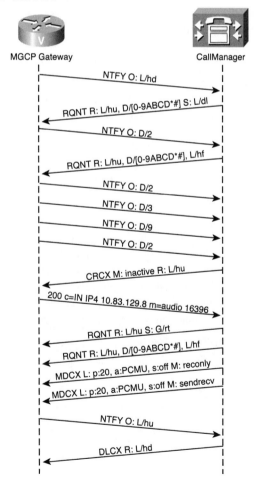

First, the analog phone connected to the FXS port goes off-hook. When the gateway first registered, CallManager requested that it be informed whenever an off-hook transition occurs. Because of this, you see the message in Example 6-57 sent from the gateway to CallManager.

Example 6-57   *MGCP* **Notify** *of an Off-hook Translation*

```
Jan 12 16:44:16.038: send_mgcp_msg, MGCP Packet sent to 172.18.106.58 --->

Jan 12 16:44:16.042: NTFY 3811 AALN/S1/SU0/0@pgiralt-test MGCP 0.1
X: 1e
O: L/hd
<---
Jan 12 16:44:16.106: MGCP Packet received from 172.18.106.58-
200 3811
```

You can see that the gateway sent a notify (**NTFY**) command. The **O: L/hd** indicates that the observed event comes from the line package and that the event is an off-hook. You can also see that CallManager responded with a **200**, indicating that it processed the command successfully. CallManager then sends the command shown in Example 6-58 to the gateway.

Example 6-58   *MGCP* **NotificationRequest**

```
Jan 12 16:44:16.126: MGCP Packet received from 172.18.106.58-
RQNT 37 AALN/S1/SU0/0@pgiralt-test MGCP 0.1
X: 1f
R: L/hu, D/[0-9ABCD*#]
S: L/dl
Q: process,loop
```

Example 6-58 shows the **NotificationRequest** command. The gateway uses the RequestIdentifier of **1f** to send any responses to this **NotificationRequest**. CallManager is asking to be informed of an on-hook transition (**L/hu**) and any DTMF digit (**D/[0-9ABCD*#]**). CallManager also tells the gateway to play dial tone with the command **L/dl**. Finally, CallManager also wants to know about any quarantined events. This is important because it is possible that the person using the analog phone might have gone on-hook before the gateway receives this message. The gateway acknowledges the message with a **200**, indicating successful completion of the command, as shown in Example 6-59.

Example 6-59   *MGCP Acknowledgment from a Gateway*

```
Jan 12 16:44:16.134: send_mgcp_msg, MGCP Packet sent to 172.18.106.58 --->

Jan 12 16:44:16.134: 200 37 OK
<---
```

Now the analog phone begins dialing the phone number it wants to call. Example 6-60 shows an MGCP message for each of the digits that have been detected. Notice that the

RequestIdentifier is **1f** because this notify message is in response to the
NotificationRequest that CallManager previously sent.

Example 6-60   *MGCP* **Notify** *Message Indicating a Digit of 2*

```
Jan 12 16:44:18.162: send_mgcp_msg, MGCP Packet sent to 172.18.106.58 --->

Jan 12 16:44:18.162: NTFY 3812 AALN/S1/SU0/0@pgiralt-test MGCP 0.1
X: 1f
O: D/2
<---
Jan 12 16:44:18.226: MGCP Packet received from 172.18.106.58-
200 3812
```

After receiving the preceding message with the digit **2**, CallManager responds with the
message shown in Example 6-61.

Example 6-61   *MGCP* **NotificationRequest** *Message*

```
Jan 12 16:44:18.230: MGCP Packet received from 172.18.106.58-
RQNT 38 AALN/S1/SU0/0@pgiralt-test MGCP 0.1
X: 20
R: L/hu, D/[0-9ABCD*#], L/hf
S:
Q: process,loop
```

This message tells the gateway to stop playing dial tone because the SignalRequests
parameter line is blank. This message also contains a request to be notified of a hookflash
event (**L/hf**) in addition to an on-hook transition or DTMF digit.

The user continues to dial digits, as shown in the debugs in Example 6-62. Notice that the
following digits all have a RequestIdentifier of **20** because they are all in response to the
latest **NotificationRequest** command from CallManager.

Example 6-62   *MGCP* **Notify** *Messages Showing Digits Being Dialed*

```
Jan 12 16:44:18.234: send_mgcp_msg, MGCP Packet sent to 172.18.106.58 --->

Jan 12 16:44:18.234: 200 38 OK
<---
Jan 12 16:44:18.530: send_mgcp_msg, MGCP Packet sent to 172.18.106.58 --->

Jan 12 16:44:18.530: NTFY 3813 AALN/S1/SU0/0@pgiralt-test MGCP 0.1
X: 20
O: D/2
<---
Jan 12 16:44:18.594: MGCP Packet received from 172.18.106.58-
200 3813


Jan 12 16:44:19.922: send_mgcp_msg, MGCP Packet sent to 172.18.106.58 --->

Jan 12 16:44:19.922: NTFY 3814 AALN/S1/SU0/0@pgiralt-test MGCP 0.1
X: 20
```

continues

Example 6-62 *MGCP **Notify** Messages Showing Digits Being Dialed (Continued)*

```
O: D/3
<---
Jan 12 16:44:19.986: MGCP Packet received from 172.18.106.58-
200 3814


Jan 12 16:44:20.530: send_mgcp_msg, MGCP Packet sent to 172.18.106.58 --->

Jan 12 16:44:20.530: NTFY 3815 AALN/S1/SU0/0@pgiralt-test MGCP 0.1
X: 20
O: D/9
<---
Jan 12 16:44:20.598: MGCP Packet received from 172.18.106.58-
200 3815


Jan 12 16:44:21.050: send_mgcp_msg, MGCP Packet sent to 172.18.106.58 --->

Jan 12 16:44:21.050: NTFY 3816 AALN/S1/SU0/0@pgiralt-test MGCP 0.1
X: 20
O: D/2
<---
Jan 12 16:44:21.114: MGCP Packet received from 172.18.106.58-
200 3816
```

At this point the user has dialed the digits 22392, which happens to be a valid extension on this CallManager. As a result, CallManager sends the **CreateConnection** command, as shown in Example 6-63.

Example 6-63 *MGCP **CreateConnection** Message*

```
Jan 12 16:44:21.134: MGCP Packet received from 172.18.106.58-
CRCX 39 AALN/S1/SU0/0@pgiralt-test MGCP 0.1
C: A0000000020000d0
X: 21
M: inactive
R: L/hu
Q: process,loop
```

The **CreateConnection** has a CallId of **A0000000020000d0** and a RequestIdentifier of **21**, and the ConnectionMode is **inactive**, indicating that there are no media streams at this point. CallManager also wants to know about any on-hook events.

The gateway then responds to the **CreateConnection** with the results shown in Example 6-64.

Example 6-64 *MGCP Acknowledgment Including SDP-Encoded Parameters*

```
Jan 12 16:44:21.150: send_mgcp_msg, MGCP Packet sent to 172.18.106.58 --->

Jan 12 16:44:21.150: 200 39
I: A
```

Example 6-64 *MGCP Acknowledgment Including SDP-Encoded Parameters (Continued)*

```
v=0
o=- 10 0 IN IP4 10.83.129.8
s=Cisco SDP 0
c=IN IP4 10.83.129.8
t=0 0
m=audio 16396 RTP/AVP 0 8 96 97 98 2 99 100 101 102 103 104 18
a=rtpmap:96 G.729a/8000/1
a=rtpmap:97 G.726-16/8000/1
a=rtpmap:98 G.726-24/8000/1
a=rtpmap:99 G.728/8000/1
a=rtpmap:100 G.723.1-H/8000/1
a=rtpmap:101 G.723.1-L/8000/1
a=rtpmap:102 G.729b/8000/1
a=rtpmap:103 G.723.1a-H/8000/1
a=rtpmap:104 G.723.1a-L/8000/1
<---
```

The response in Example 6-64 is a Session Description Protocol (SDP) encoded message sent from the gateway informing CallManager that it wants to use IP address **10.83.129.8** and UDP port number **16396** to receive the RTP stream. The message also lists several codecs that it can support for this connection.

Next, CallManager sends another **NotificationRequest** to the gateway, as shown in Example 6-65.

Example 6-65 *MGCP **NotificationRequest** Message*

```
Jan 12 16:44:21.598: MGCP Packet received from 172.18.106.58-
RQNT 40 AALN/S1/SU0/0@pgiralt-test MGCP 0.1
X: 22
R: L/hu
S: G/rt
Q: process,loop


Jan 12 16:44:21.602: send_mgcp_msg, MGCP Packet sent to 172.18.106.58 --->

Jan 12 16:44:21.602: 200 40 OK
<---
```

The message in Example 6-65 tells the gateway that CallManager wants to know about an on-hook transition. It also tells the gateway to play ringback tone toward the analog phone.

About 6 seconds later, CallManager sends the message shown in Example 6-66. If you do not have the timestamps set correctly, you will not know how many seconds elapsed between messages. This message corresponds with the called party answering his or her phone.

Example 6-66   *MGCP* **NotificationRequest** *Message*

```
Jan 12 16:44:27.415: MGCP Packet received from 172.18.106.58-
RQNT 41 AALN/S1/SU0/0@pgiralt-test MGCP 0.1
X: 23
R: L/hu, D/[0-9ABCD*#], L/hf
S:
Q: process,loop


Jan 12 16:44:27.419: send_mgcp_msg, MGCP Packet sent to 172.18.106.58 --->

Jan 12 16:44:27.419: 200 41 OK
<---
```

As you can see, the SignalRequests parameter line is now blank, indicating that ringback should stop. Again, CallManager wants to be informed of an on-hook event, any DTMF digit, or a hookflash. Next, CallManager sends a **ModifyConnection** to begin setting up the RTP stream, as shown in Example 6-67.

Example 6-67   *MGCP* **ModifyConnection** *Message*

```
Jan 12 16:44:27.483: MGCP Packet received from 172.18.106.58-
MDCX 42 AALN/S1/SU0/0@pgiralt-test MGCP 0.1
C: A0000000020000d0
I: A
X: 24
L: p:20, a:PCMU, s:off
M: recvonly
R: L/hu
Q: process,loop


Jan 12 16:44:27.491: send_mgcp_msg, MGCP Packet sent to 172.18.106.58 --->

Jan 12 16:44:27.491: 200 42 OK
<---
```

The **ModifyConnection** command has a ConnectionId of **0xA** and a TransactionId of **0x24**. CallManager is requesting that the call be a G.711 μ-law call with VAD disabled. Also, CallManager is telling the gateway to only receive packets, not send them. This is because CallManager still needs to determine the IP address and port number that the destination device wants to use before CallManager can tell the gateway where to send its RTP stream.

After CallManager has determined the IP address of the destination device, CallManager sends a message, as shown in Example 6-68.

Example 6-68 *MGCP Modify Connection Message*

```
Jan 12 16:44:27.603: MGCP Packet received from 172.18.106.58-
MDCX 43 AALN/S1/SU0/0@pgiralt-test MGCP 0.1
C: A0000000020000d0
I: A
X: 25
L: p:20, a:PCMU, s:off
M: sendrecv
R: L/hu, L/hf, D/[0-9ABCD*#]
S:
Q: process,loop

v=0
o=- 10 0 IN EPN AALN/S1/SU0/0@pgiralt-test
s=Cisco SDP 0
t=0 0
c=IN IP4 10.83.129.3
m=audio 27252 RTP/AVP 96
a=rtpmap:96 PCMU


Jan 12 16:44:27.615: send_mgcp_msg, MGCP Packet sent to 172.18.106.58 --->

Jan 12 16:44:27.615: 200 43 OK
<---
```

With this **ModifyConnection** command, CallManager provides the IP address and port
number of the destination device to the gateway for it to send its RTP stream. Also,
CallManager is telling the gateway to change mode to send and receive packets, thereby
opening a full-duplex audio stream.

After a few seconds, the phone on port 1/0/0 goes back on-hook, so the gateway sends
CallManager a **Notify** message, indicating the on-hook event for this endpoint. This results
in CallManager sending a **DeleteConnection** message to the gateway to tear down the call,
as shown in Example 6-69.

Example 6-69 *MGCP* **Notify** *and* **DeleteConnection** *Messages*

```
Jan 12 16:44:35.403: send_mgcp_msg, MGCP Packet sent to 172.18.106.58 --->

Jan 12 16:44:35.403: NTFY 3817 AALN/S1/SU0/0@pgiralt-test MGCP 0.1
X: 25
O: L/hu
<---
Jan 12 16:44:35.467: MGCP Packet received from 172.18.106.58-
200 3817


Jan 12 16:44:35.471: MGCP Packet received from 172.18.106.58-
DLCX 44 AALN/S1/SU0/0@pgiralt-test MGCP 0.1
C: A0000000020000d0
I: A
X: 26
```

continues

Example 6-69   *MGCP* **Notify** *and* **DeleteConnection** *Messages (Continued)*

```
R: L/hd
S:
Q: process,loop
```

Finally, the gateway sends a response with code **250**, indicating that the connection was deleted. It also includes the ConnectionParameters, indicating the call's statistics, as shown in Example 6-70.

Example 6-70   *MGCP Acknowledgment Including Call Statistics*

```
Jan 12 16:44:35.483: send_mgcp_msg, MGCP Packet sent to 172.18.106.58 --->

Jan 12 16:44:35.483: 250 44
 P: PS=393, OS=62880, PR=392, OR=62720, PL=0, JI=432, LA=0
 <---
```

And that's all there is to it. If you can understand the call flow examined in this section, you should be able to understand the MGCP messaging for almost any MGCP call. There are a few other things to consider for digital trunks such as PRIs and T1 CAS trunks. The following sections explain these points in greater detail.

Cisco IOS MGCP PRI

The one thing that distinguishes a PRI from other interfaces is the fact that the data that is received from the PSTN on the D-channel needs to be carried in its raw form back to CallManager for processing. The gateway does not process or modify this information. To do this, Cisco IOS MGCP gateways use a protocol called PRI backhaul.

The way PRI backhaul works is that everything up to the Layer 2 information, including all the Q.921 signaling, terminates on the gateway. This means that the gateway takes care of D-channel establishment, but only under CallManager's direction. The gateway does not bring up the D-channel unless it can communicate with CallManager to backhaul the Q.931 messages contained in the D-channel.

To check the current status of the backhaul channel, use the command **show ccm-manager backhaul**, as demonstrated in Example 6-71. This output is also included as part of the generic **show ccm-manager** command.

Example 6-71   *Current Status of the Backhaul Channel Using* **show ccm-manager backhaul**

```
Router#show ccm-manager backhaul
PRI Backhaul Link info:
    Link Protocol:     TCP
    Remote Port Number: 2428
    Remote IP Address:  172.18.106.59
    Current Link State: OPEN
    Statistics:
        Packets recvd:    2068
        Recv failures:    0
```

Example 6-71   *Current Status of the Backhaul Channel Using* **show ccm-manager backhaul** *(Continued)*

```
        Packets xmitted: 1521
        Xmit failures:   0
    PRI Ports being backhauled:
        Slot 1, port 1
```

You can see the active CallManager and that the link state is open. If the backhaul is not coming up, you can enable **debug ccm-manager backhaul packet**, as shown in Example 6-72.

Example 6-72   *Using* **debug ccm-manager backhaul packet** *to Troubleshoot PRI Backhaul Connectivity Problems*

```
Router #debug ccm-manager backhaul packet
Jan 17 18:11:49.699:
cmbrl_send_pak: --> Sending backhauled msg for Se1/1:23 :
        ¦ bk_msg_type = RELEASE_IND
        ¦ bk_chan_id (slot:port) = 1:1
        ¦ Q.931 length = 0

Jan 17 18:11:50.371: %CONTROLLER-5-UPDOWN: Controller T1 1/1, changed state to up
Jan 17 18:11:50.783:
cmbh_rcv_callback: <-- Receiving backhaul msg for Se1/1:23 :
        ¦ bk_msg_type = ESTABLISH_REQ
        ¦ bk_chan_id (slot:port) = 1:1
        ¦ Q.931 length = 0

Jan 17 18:11:50.791: %ISDN-6-LAYER2UP: Layer 2 for Interface Se1/1:23, TEI 0
    changed to up
Jan 17 18:11:50.791:
cmbrl_send_pak: --> Sending backhauled msg for Se1/1:23 :
        ¦ bk_msg_type = ESTABLISH_CFM
        ¦ bk_chan_id (slot:port) = 1:1
        ¦ Q.931 length = 0
```

You can see that when the controller comes up, the gateway sends a **RELEASE_IND** message to CallManager. CallManager then sends an **ESTABLISH_REQ**, asking the gateway to establish the D-channel. When the D-channel is up, the gateway sends an **ESTABLISH_CFM** back to CallManager to confirm that the D-channel is now up.

The same Q.921 debugging information discussed previously in the section "Troubleshooting ISDN PRI Signaling" applies to MGCP backhauled calls as well, so always check physical layer connectivity with **show controllers [t1 | e1]**, and check the Layer 2 status with **show isdn status**.

With **debug ccm-manager backhaul packet** enabled, you also see all the Q.931 messages sent to CallManager in their raw form. If you want to see them decoded, it's still best to enable **debug isdn q931**. However, Example 6-73 shows what a setup message looks like with **debug ccm-manager backhaul packet** enabled.

Example 6-73   *Q.931 Setup Message from the Output of* **debug ccm-manager backhaul packet**

```
Router#debug ccm-manager backhaul packet
Jan 17 18:14:57.317:
cmbrl_send_pak: --> Sending backhauled msg for Se1/1:23 :
         ¦ bk_msg_type = DATA_IND
         ¦ bk_chan_id (slot:port) = 1:1
         ¦ Q.931 length = 45
         ¦ Q.931 message type: SETUP
         ¦ Q.931 message =
080201DF0504038090A21803A98301280B5061756C20476972616C746C070080323238333170
06803230373831
```

Even though the D-channel is being backhauled, **debug isdn q931** still works for backhauled calls. This lets you quickly look at ISDN debug information on the gateway instead of having to search through the CCM trace files.

Other than getting the backhaul channel established, troubleshooting PRI calls on a Cisco IOS gateway is no different from troubleshooting a call on a WS-X6608. The CCM traces and MGCP messages look identical. You can enable the same MGCP debugs on the gateway (that is, **debug mgcp packet**) as you would for an FXS/FXO card and troubleshoot it the same way. The following section describes how to read the ISDN messages in a CCM trace.

Reading ISDN Messages

Reading ISDN traces is critical in troubleshooting many problems on a PRI connection. By reading these traces, you can determine what calling numbers and called numbers are involved in a call. Also, you can determine the reason for a call's termination by looking at the cause code (see Table 6-27) in the disconnect message.

ISDN messages are defined in the ITU-T Q.931 specification.

The easiest way to read ISDN traces is with the Q.931 Translator. Still, it is nice to know how to read the raw trace from the CCM trace file. In this section, you'll look at both.

First, Example 6-74 examines the ISDN trace message from the CCM trace file. This is an incoming call to extension 2001 from extension 2000. These numbers could be 7-digit, 10-digit, or even international-length numbers. (Now might be a good time to review the section "Q.931 Translator" in Chapter 3, "Understanding the Troubleshooting Tools.")

Example 6-74   *ISDN Trace Message from a CCM Trace File*

```
Out Message -- PriSetupMsg -- Protocol= PriNi2Protocol
Ie - Ni2BearerCapabilityIe IEData= 04 03 80 90 A2
Ie - Q931ChannelIdIe IEData= 18 03 A9 83 97
Ie - Q931CallingPartyIe IEData= 6C 06 00 80 32 30 30 30
Ie - Q931CalledPartyIe IEData= 70 05 80 32 30 30 31
```

Example 6-74 *ISDN Trace Message from a CCM Trace File (Continued)*

```
MMan_Id= 0. (iep=  0 dsl=  0 sapi=  0 ces=  0 IpAddr=61e100a IpPort=2427)
IsdnMsgData2= 08 02 00 02 05 04 03 80 90 A2 18 03 A9 83 97 6C
   06 00 80 32 30 30 30 70 05 80 32 30 30 31
```

This setup message reveals a lot of information. The critical data is highlighted. Notice that this is an outbound setup message toward the PSTN. The digits for calling and called party numbers are encoded in ASCII. Fortunately, the digits 0 through 9 are represented by ASCII characters 30 through 39, so you can just remove the leading 3 from each byte to obtain the digit. For example, the trace shows **32 30 30 30** in the **Q931CallingPartyIe** field. If you ignore the 3s, you can see that the calling party is 2000. Similarly, you can see that the called party is 2001 by looking at the **Q931CalledPartyIe**, which shows **32 30 30 31**.

The IP address of this gateway is important too. Notice that it is **61e100a**. As discussed in Chapter 3, this is read in hex as follows:

```
0x0a = 10
0x10 = 16
0x1e = 30
0x6 = 6
```

The IP address of this gateway is 10.16.30.6.

Also, this call is being sent out on channel 23 of the PRI. You can determine this by decoding the channel ID information element using the Q.931 specification. In this case, look at the last octet of the channel ID information element—in this case, **0x97**. You need to get rid of the most-significant bit. 0x9 is 1001 in binary. Removing the most-significant bit, you are left with 0001, which is 0x1. Similarly, if the value begins with 0x8, which is 1000 in binary, this becomes 0000 in binary or 0x0 in hex. In this example, you are left with 0x17. If you convert 0x17 to decimal, you get 23. Because a PRI has only 23 B-channels, the value of the channel IE is between 0x80 (channel 0) and 0x97 (channel 23).

Finally, the **IsdnMsgData2** line contains a hex dump of the entire Q.931 packet. If you look at the **IsdnMsgData2** line, it always begins with **08** for most signaling messages. The exception is link-management messages, such as service messages that use **03**. The following byte represents the length of the call reference and is either **01** or **02**. You usually see a 2-byte call reference. Depending on the length, the next 1 or 2 bytes are what you are interested in. These bytes are set to **00 02** in Example 6-75. This is the call reference value. If you recall from Chapter 3 in the discussion of call reference values, the most-significant bit toggles depending on the message's direction. A recommended practice is that you copy the last three digits and search through the file for that. So in this case you would search for **0 0F**. You see that all the following messages have **0 0F** in the third and fourth bytes of **IsdnMsgData**.

Example 6-75 *ISDN Trace Proceeding Message from a CCM Trace File*

```
In  Message -- PriCallProceedingMsg -- Protocol= PriNi2Protocol
Ie - Q931ChannelIdIe -- IEData= 18 03 A9 83 97
MMan_Id= 0. (iep=  0 dsl=  0 sapi=  0 ces= 0 IpAddr=61e100a IpPort=2427)
IsdnMsgData1= 08 02 80 02 02 18 03 A9 83 97
```

Example 6-75 shows an outbound Call Proceeding message. Also notice the **0 02** call reference value.

Example 6-76 shows an inbound Alerting message. Notice that the progress indicator is set to 8. This means that CallManager must cut through the audio because in-band information is available. Progress indicators are discussed in more detail in the section "Cisco IOS Gateways Using the H.323 Protocol." You also see the **0 02** call reference value again.

Example 6-76 *ISDN Trace Alerting Message from a CCM Trace File*

```
In  Message -- PriAlertingMsg -- Protocol= PriNi2Protocol
Ie - Q931ProgressIndIe -- IEData= 1E 02 80 88
MMan_Id= 0. (iep=  0 dsl=  0 sapi=  0 ces= 0 IpAddr=61e100a IpPort=2427)
IsdnMsgData1= 08 02 80 02 01 1E 02 80 88
```

Example 6-77 shows an inbound Connect message with a 0 02 call reference value.

Example 6-77 *ISDN Trace Connect Message from a CCM Trace File*

```
In  Message -- PriConnectMsg -- Protocol= PriNi2Protocol
MMan_Id= 0. (iep=  0 dsl=  0 sapi=  0 ces= 0 IpAddr=61e100a IpPort=2427)
IsdnMsgData1= 08 02 80 02 07
```

Example 6-78 shows an outbound Connect Ack message with a call reference value of 0 02.

Example 6-78 *ISDN Trace Connect Acknowledge Message from a CCM Trace File*

```
Out Message -- PriConnectAcknowledgeMsg -- Protocol= PriNi2Protocol
MMan_Id= 0. (iep=  0 dsl=  0 sapi=  0 ces=  0 IpAddr=61e100a IpPort=2427)
IsdnMsgData2= 08 02 00 02 0F
```

Example 6-79 shows an important message. There is an inbound Disconnect message. It tells you that the PSTN leg of the call initiated the disconnect. Notice in the **Q931CauseIe** message that the cause of this disconnect is 90. Table 6-27 in the next section lists and describes all the valid cause codes based on the ITU-T Q.850 specification.

Example 6-79 *ISDN Trace Disconnect Message from a CCM Trace File*

```
In  Message -- PriDisconnectMsg -- Protocol= PriNi2Protocol
Ie - Q931CauseIe -- IEData= 08 02 80 90
MMan_Id= 0. (iep=  0 dsl=  0 sapi=  0 ces= 0 IpAddr=61e100a IpPort=2427)
IsdnMsgData1= 08 02 80 02 45 08 02 80 90
```

Example 6-80 shows the outbound Release message with the same call reference.

Example 6-80 *ISDN Trace Release Message from a CCM Trace File*

```
Out Message -- PriReleaseMsg -- Protocol= PriNi2Protocol
MMan_Id= 0. (iep=  0 dsl=  0 sapi=  0 ces=  0 IpAddr=61e100a IpPort=2427)
IsdnMsgData2= 08 02 00 02 4D
```

Example 6-81 shows an inbound Release Complete message with the same call reference value.

Example 6-81 *ISDN Trace Release Complete Message from a CCM Trace File*

```
In  Message -- PriReleaseCompleteMsg -- Protocol= PriNi2Protocol
MMan_Id= 0. (iep=  0 dsl=  0 sapi=  0 ces= 0 IpAddr=61e100a IpPort=2427)
IsdnMsgData1= 08 02 80 02 5A
```

If reading hex isn't exactly your idea of fun, there is an easier way. The Q.931 Translator tool can take the hex output from a CCM trace and decode it for you.

If you run the Q.931 Translator on the file from which this trace derives, you get the information shown in Example 6-82.

Example 6-82 *Q.931 Translator Data Output from a CCM Trace File*

```
==============================
11:14:03.863              Out
0x0002 -> SETUP, pd = 8, callref = 0x0002
Bearer Capability i = 0x8090A2, ITU-T standard, Speech, Circuit mode, 64k, μ-law
Channel ID i = 0xA98397, PRI interface, Exclusive channel 23
Calling Party Number i = '2000' - Plan: Unknown, Type: Unknown,
  Presentation Allowed, User-provided, not screened
Called Party Number i = '2001' - Plan: Unknown, Type: Unknown
==============================
11:14:04.035              In
0x8002 -> CALL_PROC, pd = 8, callref = 0x8002
Channel ID i = 0xA98397, PRI interface, Exclusive channel 23
==============================
11:14:04.035              In
0x8002 -> ALERTING, pd = 8, callref = 0x8002
Progress Ind i = 0x8088 - In-band info or appropriate now available
==============================
11:14:05.535              In
0x8002 -> CONNECT, pd = 8, callref = 0x8002
==============================
11:14:05.535              Out
0x0002 -> CONNECT_ACK, pd = 8, callref = 0x0002
==============================
11:14:16.723              In
0x8002 -> DISCONNECT, pd = 8, callref = 0x8002
Cause i = 0x8090 - Normal call clearing
==============================
11:14:16.723              Out
0x0002 -> RELEASE, pd = 8, callref = 0x0002
==============================
11:14:16.754              In
0x8002 -> RELEASE_COMP, pd = 8, callref = 0x8002
```

The Q.931 Translator spells out all the data contained in the Q.931 messages. It breaks out the calling and called numbers. It shows the call reference value and type of message sent. Best of all, it shows the cause code for the disconnect message and offers an explanation. The Q.931 Translator is part of CallManager Serviceability. A standalone client can also be found in the C:\Program Files\Cisco\bin directory. For best results, download the Enhanced Q.931 Translator from the Cisco Press web site (www.ciscopress.com) by searching the Cisco Press website for "Troubleshooting Cisco IP Telephony". For more information on using the Q.931 Translator tool, refer to Chapter 3.

Table of Q.850 Cause Codes

The CCM trace shows ISDN messages that often include cause codes. A cause code is a standard Q.931 information element that indicates the reason for a disconnection or failure to connect a call. These codes are useful for troubleshooting ISDN PRI connections.

Table 6-27 lists the codes used for the Q.931 cause information element. Wherever possible, suggestions for troubleshooting your PRI connection when certain cause codes appear have been included. The columns include the code's hex representation as it appears in most debug output and the actual cause code number in decimal.

Table 6-27 *Q.850 Cause Codes for Q.931 Signaling*

Hexadecimal Code with High-Order Bit Set	Hexadecimal Code Without High-Order Bit Set	Decimal Code	Description
0x81	0x01	1	Unallocated (unassigned) number. This cause indicates that the destination requested by the calling user cannot be reached because the number is unassigned. This number is not in the routing table, or it has no path across the ISDN network.
0x82	0x02	2	No route to specified transit network (National use). This number was dialed with a transit network code such as 108880 to go from AT&T and MCI, and there is no route across. The wrong transit network code was dialed.
0x83	0x03	3	No route to the destination. The dialed number is in the routing plan, but there is no physical route to the destination. The most likely cause of this is that the PRI D-channel is down, or the span or WAN is not connected correctly.

Table 6-27 *Q.850 Cause Codes for Q.931 Signaling (Continued)*

Hexadecimal Code with High-Order Bit Set	Hexadecimal Code Without High-Order Bit Set	Decimal Code	Description
0x84	0x04	4	Send special information tone.
0x85	0x05	5	Misdialed trunk prefix (National use).
0x86	0x06	6	Channel unacceptable.
0x87	0x07	7	Call awarded and being delivered in an established channel.
0x88	0x08	8	Preemption.
0x89	0x09	9	Preemption. Circuit reserved for reuse.
0x90	0x10	16	Normal call clearing. This is one of the most common codes and is received for many reasons. It usually occurs because someone hung up the call.
0x91	0x11	17	User busy. The number dialed is busy and cannot receive any more calls.
0x92	0x12	18	No user responding. The number that is being dialed has an active D-channel, but the far end chooses not to answer.
0x93	0x13	19	No answer from the user (user alerted). The number that is being dialed has an active D-channel, but the far end chooses not to answer.
0x94	0x14	20	Subscriber absent.
0x95	0x15	21	Call rejected.
0x96	0x16	22	Number changed. This cause code is generated when a subscriber on the PSTN has changed his or her phone number. Usually this message is accompanied by a progress indicator stating that in-band information is available. The PSTN provides an announcement in-band indicating the new phone number, if available.

continues

Table 6-27 *Q.850 Cause Codes for Q.931 Signaling (Continued)*

Hexadecimal Code with High-Order Bit Set	Hexadecimal Code Without High-Order Bit Set	Decimal Code	Description
0x9A	0x1A	26	Nonselected user clearing.
0x9B	0x1B	27	Destination is out of order. The number dialed is a working number, but the span is not active.
0x9C	0x1C	28	Invalid number format (address incomplete). This can happen when you are calling out using a network type number (enterprise) when you should be calling out Unknown or National.
0x9D	0x1D	29	Facility rejected.
0x9E	0x1E	30	Response to STATUS ENQUIRY.
0x9F	0x1F	31	Normal, unspecified. This is a very common code. It happens when the network cannot determine what to do with the call being made.
0xA2	0x22	34	No circuit/channel is available. No B-channels are available to make the selected call.
0xA6	0x26	38	Network is out of order.
0xA7	0x27	39	Permanent frame mode connection is out of service.
0xA8	0x28	40	Permanent frame mode connection is operational.
0xA9	0x29	41	Temporary failure. The call was disconnected due to a network failure. This code might show up if you are using MCI and the hunt sequence is incorrect. PRI lines must be set up for a flex hunt sequence (not a float hunt sequence).
0xAA	0x2A	42	Switching equipment congestion.

Table 6-27   *Q.850 Cause Codes for Q.931 Signaling (Continued)*

Hexadecimal Code with High-Order Bit Set	Hexadecimal Code Without High-Order Bit Set	Decimal Code	Description
0xAB	0x2B	43	Access information discarded. Usually reported when the far-end ISDN switch removes some piece of information before tandem-switching a call. For example, some PBXs strip the display IE before sending a call out toward the PSTN and send back a message with this cause code.
0xAC	0x2C	44	Requested circuit/channel is unavailable. This happens when you get in a glare condition: Both sides are selected top-down or bottom-up. Change the Allocation Direction (so that one end is top-down and the other is bottom-up).
0xAE	0x2E	46	Precedence call blocked.
0xAF	0x2F	47	Resource unavailable, unspecified. Whenever you see CallManager initiate a disconnect with cause code 0xAF, 99% of the time the problem is related to a media setup failure. Check for codec capabilities mismatches, especially your regions configuration.
0xB1	0x31	49	Quality of service unavailable.
0xB2	0x32	50	Requested facility not subscribed. This code typically indicates you are trying to use a service you are not permitted to use. For example, you might be trying to make a voice call on an ISDN circuit provisioned for data only.
0xB5	0x35	53	Outgoing calls barred within Closed User Group (CUG).
0xB7	0x37	55	Incoming calls barred within CUG.
0xB9	0x39	57	Bearer capability not authorized. This code indicates that you are placing a call with a bearer capability you are not allowed to use.

continues

Table 6-27   *Q.850 Cause Codes for Q.931 Signaling (Continued)*

Hexadecimal Code with High-Order Bit Set	Hexadecimal Code Without High-Order Bit Set	Decimal Code	Description
0xBA	0x3A	58	Bearer capability not presently available. This code indicates that you are placing a call with a bearer capability for which the service provider does not currently have capacity to supply.
0xBE	0x3E	62	Inconsistency in designated outgoing access information and subscriber class.
0xBF	0x3F	63	Service or option unavailable, unspecified.
0xC1	0x41	65	Bearer capability not implemented. The cause could be one of the following occurrences: • You need to change the PCM Type value to the setting appropriate for your country. This is the most common cause, especially in countries where G.711 A-law companding is the standard. If your gateway is configured for μ-law and the service provider or PBX is expecting A-law, you will see calls disconnected with this cause code. • The Central Office (CO) does not understand an information element in the setup message. • You are connected to a PBX and you are sending out a network type number when the switch accepts only Unknown or National. • You are selecting European PRI and you have the progress indicators turned on when they should be off.
0xC2	0x42	66	Channel type not implemented.
0xC5	0x45	69	Requested facility not implemented.
0xC6	0x46	70	Only restricted digital information bearer capability is available (National use).
0xCF	0x47	79	Service or option not implemented, unspecified.

Table 6-27   *Q.850 Cause Codes for Q.931 Signaling (Continued)*

Hexadecimal Code with High-Order Bit Set	Hexadecimal Code Without High-Order Bit Set	Decimal Code	Description
0xD1	0x51	81	Invalid call reference value. This code indicates that the far-end switch did not recognize the call reference for a message sent by the gateway.
0xD2	0x52	82	Identified channel does not exist. This code indicates a call attempt on a channel that is not configured on the far end. This could happen if you are using a fractional PRI. As of CallManager version 3.3, CallManager does not support fractional PRIs.
0xD3	0x53	83	A suspended call exists, but this call identity does not.
0xD4	0x54	84	Call identity in use.
0xD5	0x55	85	No call suspended.
0xD6	0x56	86	Call having the requested call identity has been cleared.
0xD7	0x57	87	User is not a member of CUG.
0xD8	0x58	88	Incompatible destination. The cause could be one of the following occurrences: • The number being dialed is not capable of the type of call. • You are calling a restricted line in unrestricted mode. • You are calling a POTS phone using unrestricted mode.
0xDA	0x5A	90	Nonexistent CUG.
0xDB	0x5B	91	Invalid transit network selection (National use).
0xDF	0x5F	95	Invalid message, unspecified.

continues

Table 6-27 *Q.850 Cause Codes for Q.931 Signaling (Continued)*

Hexadecimal Code with High-Order Bit Set	Hexadecimal Code Without High-Order Bit Set	Decimal Code	Description
0xE0	0x60	96	Mandatory information element is missing. The far-end switch states that a message was received missing an information element it considers to be mandatory per the Q.931 specification.
0xE1	0x61	97	Message type nonexistent or not implemented.
0xE2	0x62	98	Message is incompatible with the call state, or the message type is nonexistent or not implemented. This code is usually indicative of an ISDN protocol mismatch. Each ISDN protocol variant has a slightly different state machine based on the state machines defined in the Q.931 specification. If the two sides of an ISDN connection are not configured for the same protocol, one side might violate the other's call state machine. If an ISDN message is sent that is not expected in the current call state, this cause is generated.
0xE3	0x63	99	An information element or parameter does not exist or is not implemented.
0xE4	0x64	100	Invalid information element contents. The cause could be one of the following occurrences: • The call has an information element that is not understood by the switch being called. The E4 is usually followed by the information element that is causing the problem. • The most common problem is that you are trying to place a call using a network number when the switch being called accepts only National, International, or Unknown dialing. • This code is also generated when you are using Network-Specific Facilities as an element when they are not needed.

Table 6-27   *Q.850 Cause Codes for Q.931 Signaling (Continued)*

Hexadecimal Code with High-Order Bit Set	Hexadecimal Code Without High-Order Bit Set	Decimal Code	Description
0xE5	0x65	101	The message is incompatible with the call state. This code is usually indicative of an ISDN protocol mismatch. Each ISDN protocol variant has a slightly different state machine based on the state machines defined in the Q.931 specification. If the two sides of an ISDN connection are not configured for the same protocol, one side might violate the other's call state machine. If an ISDN message is sent that is not expected in the current call state, this cause is generated.
0xE6	0x66	102	Recovery on timer expiry. This occurs when ISDN messages don't arrive in specified time according to the Q.931 specification. The E6 is sometimes followed by the timer that has expired (for example, 03 01 00—the 310 timer). The section "Understanding ISDN Timers" defines the various ISDN timers.
0xE7	0x67	103	Parameter nonexistent or not implemented—passed on (National use).
0xEE	0x6E	110	Message with unrecognized parameter discarded.
0xEF	0x6F	111	Protocol error, unspecified.
0xFF	0x7F	127	Interworking, unspecified.

Numbering Type and Plan Mismatches

The calling and called party number information elements contain fields called numbering plan and numbering type. In the majority of cases, these fields are ignored by most ISDN switches. However there are times when ISDN switches base their call routing decision partially on the numbering plan or type and some PBXs use the calling party numbering plan information for number presentation purposes.

The easiest way to look at the numbering plan and type information is to open the CCM trace file with the Enhanced Q.931 Translator. You will see the calling and called party number information, including the ISDN numbering plan and type information. For example, the following line shows a numbering plan and type of Unknown:

```
Called Party Number i = '2001' - Plan: Unknown, Type: Unknown
```

If you see CallManager sending the proper digits to the PSTN, but the call is not being routed properly, check to make sure that the numbering plan and type are set in accordance with the way the device connected to the gateway is configured.

By default, for calls to route patterns containing the @ NANP wildcard, the called party numbering type is classified as National (International if 011 is dialed), and the called numbering plan is ISDN. For calls to route patterns not containing the @ NANP wildcard, the called party numbering plan and type are classified as Unknown. The calling party numbering plan and type can be classified differently, depending on the digits to be sent.

Note that this automatic selection occurs only if the outbound PRI gateway has the numbering plan and type configured to "Cisco CallManager." Any other settings override the automatic assignment from the NANP.

If you suspect a problem with the numbering plan or type, try changing the calling and called party numbering plan to National and the numbering type to ISDN. If the country you are in has a different numbering type, experiment with the different values to see if they help.

Whatever the case, make sure that the called and calling party are being classified correctly so that the CO can process that call. If you are unsure what the plan and type should be set to, contact your service provider and ask what they expect to see.

Troubleshooting Calling Name Display Problems

A common problem encountered when interfacing between an IP Telephony network and a traditional PBX environment is the ability to pass calling name information. CallManager uses the display information element to pass and receive calling name information on all PRI variants with the exception of Q.Sig. The display information element is defined as part of the Q.931 specification and is the standard way to pass calling name information.

Many legacy PBXs do not support calling name display via the display information element and require Q.Sig for calling name display to work. Q.Sig uses the Facility information element to pass calling name information. CallManager supports calling name display via the facility IE only on Q.Sig trunks as of CallManager version 3.3.

Some service providers provide calling name display service from the PSTN on ISDN PRIs configured for the NI3 switch type. NI3 also uses a facility information element to send calling name information. As of CallManager 3.3, CallManager supports only the NI2 switch type. Therefore, CallManager cannot accept calling party name information from a service provider that sends the name in a facility information element, but it supports any device sending the name in a display information element.

The only requirement in CallManager for calling name display to work is that the **Display IE Delivery** checkbox be enabled on the gateway (either H.323 or MGCP) on which you want name delivery. Q.931 traces (either CCM traces or **debug isdn q931** on a Cisco IOS gateway) show you the calling name information being sent or received. If you see the name being presented to the far end and it is not showing up, you need to work with the administrators of that equipment to determine why they are not accepting the name information.

As a general rule, Lucent/Avaya PBX equipment can send and receive calling name information using most switch types as long as it is configured to send the display information in codeset 0 (this is a trunk group configuration parameter on the PBX).

Nortel PBXs, on the other hand, generally provide calling name information via the display information element only when using the DMS100 switch type. Most Nortel PBXs, however, do not support network-side DMS100, so you need to use a gateway on the CallManager side that supports network-side DMS100 to get this to work or configure the Nortel PBX for network-side SL100 switch type and use user-side DMS100 on the CallManager side.

Understanding ISDN Timers

The ISDN Q.931 specification lists a variety of timers that dictate how long an ISDN device should wait for a certain event to occur before taking corrective action. The Q.921 specification also lists a variety of timers related to D-channel establishment procedures, however adjusting these timers is seldom required.

Understanding how these timers work and when they are used is important, especially if you are troubleshooting calls that are being disconnected with a cause code of 0xE6, "Recovery on timer expiry." This cause code indicates the call was disconnected because a timer expired and there was no further corrective action that could be taken other than disconnecting the call.

The cause code in the cause information element is sometimes followed by the name of the timer that has expired (for example, 03 01 00—the 310 timer).

For example, if CallManager sends a call out to the PSTN by sending a SETUP message and receives a CALL PROCEEDING from the PSTN as expected, the T310 timer starts. This timer specifies that CallManager must receive either ALERTING, CONNECT, or DISCONNECT from the PSTN before the timer expires. By default, this timer is 10 seconds. After 10 seconds, CallManager sends a DISCONNECT with a cause of "Recovery on Timer Expiry."

Tables 6-28 and 6-29 list the timers defined in the Q.931 specification for both the network side and the user side of a call.

Table 6-28 *ISDN Q.931 Timers on the Network Side*

Timer Name	Call State	Cause for Start	Normal Stop	Action Upon First Expiry	Action Upon Second Expiry
T301	Call received	ALERTING received.	CONNECT received.	Clear the call.	—
T302	Overlap sending	SETUP ACK sent. Receipt of INFO restarts T302.	Sending Complete indication, ALERTING, or CONNECT received.	Clear call if call information is incomplete; otherwise, send CALL PROCEEDING.	—
T303	Call present	SETUP sent.	ALERTING, CONNECT, CALL PROCEEDING, RELEASE COMPLETE, or SETUP ACK received.	Retransmit SETUP; Restart T303. If RELEASE COMPLETE has been received, clear the call.	Clear network connection. Enter call abort state.
T304	Overlap receiving	SETUP ACK received. Sending of INFO restarts T304.	Send INFO; Receive CALL PROCEEDING, ALERTING, or CONNECT.	Clear the call.	—
T305	Disconnect indication	DISCONNECT without progress indicator of 8 sent.	RELEASE or DISCONNECT received.	Network sends RELEASE.	—
T306	Disconnect indication	DISCONNECT with progress indicator of 8 sent.	RELEASE or DISCONNECT received.	Stop the tone/ announcement. Send RELEASE.	—

Table 6-28   *ISDN Q.931 Timers on the Network Side (Continued)*

Timer Name	Call State	Cause for Start	Normal Stop	Action Upon First Expiry	Action Upon Second Expiry
T307	—	SUSPEND ACK sent.	RESUME ACK sent.	Clear the network connection. Release call identity.	—
T308	Release request	RELEASE sent.	RELEASE COMPLETE or RELEASE received.	Retransmit RELEASE and restart T308.	Place B-channel in maintenance condition. Release call reference.
T309	Any stable state	Data link disconnection. Calls in stable states are not lost.	Data link reconnected.	Clear network connection. Release B-channel and call reference.	—
T310	Incoming call proceeding	CALL PROCEEDING received.	ALERTING, CONNECT, or DISCONNECT received.	Clear the call.	—
T312	Call present, call abort	SETUP sent.	Timeout.	In call abort state, the call reference is released. Otherwise, no action is taken.	—
T314	Receiving segmented message	Message segment received.	Last message segment received.	Discard message.	—
T316	Restart request	RESTART sent.	RESTART ACK received.	RESTART may be retransmitted several times.	RESTART may be retransmitted several times.
T317	Restart	RESTART received.	Internal clearing of call references.	Maintenance notification.	—

continues

Table 6-28   *ISDN Q.931 Timers on the Network Side (Continued)*

Timer Name	Call State	Cause for Start	Normal Stop	Action Upon First Expiry	Action Upon Second Expiry
T321	Any call state	D-channel failure.	Response to Layer 3 message received.	Send DL-ESTABLISH request on both D-channels.	—
T322	Any call state	STATUS ENQUIRY sent.	STATUS, DISCONNECT, RELEASE, or RELEASE COMPLETE received.	STATUS ENQUIRY may be retransmitted several times.	STATUS ENQUIRY may be retransmitted several times.

Table 6-29   *ISDN Q.931 Timers on the User Side*

Timer Name	Call State	Cause for Start	Normal Stop	Action Upon First Expiry	Action Upon Second Expiry
T301	Call delivered	ALERTING received.	CONNECT received.	Clear the call.	—
T302	Overlap receiving	SETUP ACK sent. Receipt of INFO restarts T302.	Sending Complete indication; or internal alerting; or internal connection; or a determination that sufficient information has been received.	Clear the call if call information incomplete; otherwise, send CALL PROCEEDING.	—
T303	Call initiated	SETUP sent.	ALERTING, CONNECT, CALL PROCEEDING, RELEASE COMPLETE, or SETUP ACK received.	Retransmit SETUP; Restart T303. If RELEASE COMPLETE has been received, clear the call.	Clear internal connection. Send RELEASE COMPLETE; Enter null state.

Table 6-29 *ISDN Q.931 Timers on the User Side (Continued)*

Timer Name	Call State	Cause for Start	Normal Stop	Action Upon First Expiry	Action Upon Second Expiry
T304	Overlap sending	INFO sent; Sending of INFO restarts T304 again.	CALL PROCEEDING, ALERTING, CONNECT, DISCONNECT or progress indicator of 1 or 2 received.	DISCONNECT sent.	—
T305	Disconnect request	DISCONNECT sent.	RELEASE or DISCONNECT received.	RELEASE sent.	—
T308	Release request	RELEASE sent.	RELEASE COMPLETE or RELEASE received.	Retransmit RELEASE and restart T308.	Place B-channel in maintenance condition. Release call reference.
T309	Any stable state	Data link disconnection. Calls in stable states are not lost.	Data link reconnected.	Clear network connection. Release B-channel and call reference.	—
T310	Outgoing call proceeding	CALL PROCEEDING received.	ALERTING, CONNECT, or DISCONNECT received.	Send DISCONNECT.	—
T313	Connect request	CONNECT sent.	CONNECT ACK received.	Send DISCONNECT.	—
T314	Receiving segmented message	Message segment received.	Last message segment received.	Discard message.	—
T316	Restart request	RESTART sent.	RESTART ACK received.	RESTART may be retransmitted several times.	RESTART may be retransmitted several times.

continues

Table 6-29   *ISDN Q.931 Timers on the User Side (Continued)*

Timer Name	Call State	Cause for Start	Normal Stop	Action Upon First Expiry	Action Upon Second Expiry
T317	Restart	RESTART received.	Internal clearing of call references.	Maintenance notification.	—
T318	Resume request	RESUME sent.	RESUME ACK or RESUME REJECT received.	Send RELEASE message with cause No. 102.	—
T319	Suspend request	SUSPEND sent.	SUSPEND ACK or SUSPEND REJECT received.	Enter active state; Notify user application.	—
T321	Any call state	D-channel failure.	Response to Layer 3 message received.	Send DL-ESTABLISH request on both D-channels.	—
T322	Any call state	STATUS ENQUIRY sent.	STATUS, DISCONNECT, RELEASE, or RELEASE COMPLETE received.	STATUS ENQUIRY may be retransmitted several times.	STATUS ENQUIRY may be retransmitted several times.

The various ISDN timers defined in the preceding tables can be adjusted on a cluster-wide basis in CallManager Administration on the Service Parameters Configuration page (**Service > Service Parameters >** *select a server >* **Cisco CallManager**). The timers are named **TimerT301_msec** through **TimerT322_msec**. In CallManager 3.3 and later, similar timers exist for H.225 messages named **TimerH225T301_msec** through **TimerH225T322_msec**. Prior to CallManager 3.3, H.225 messages used the same Q.931 timers used for PRIs. Note that these values are all defined in milliseconds, so to set the T310 timer to 20 seconds, you must set the **TimerT310_msec** service parameter to 20000.

Cisco IOS MGCP T1 CAS

T1 CAS on MGCP-enabled ports works like a cross between an FXS/FXO port and a PRI. Cisco IOS MGCP T1 CAS uses only MGCP messages to communicate signaling between CallManager and the gateway. Even though the messaging is all MGCP, T1 CAS MGCP uses two packages that are defined in RFC 3064. These were discussed briefly earlier, but now you will see how these are used for MGCP T1 CAS. The two packages in question are the DT (DTMF trunk) package and the MS (MF trunk) package.

The DT and MS packages use ISDN-like messages over MGCP to communicate call signaling. This means that CallManager does not need to be aware of the states of the ABCD bits. Instead, CallManager just sends a generic message like the one shown in Example 6-83.

Example 6-83 *MGCP* **CreateConnection** *Message for a T1 CAS Call Setup*

```
CRCX 14413 S1/DS1-0/1@vnt-vg200-gw1.cisco.com MGCP 0.1
C: A00000000020019d8
X: 0
M: inactive
R: DT/oc
S: DT/sup(addr(1,2,8,3,1))
Q: process,loop
```

Refer to Table 6-24. CallManager is signaling to the gateway to perform a call setup on endpoint **S1/DS1-0/1**, which corresponds to port 1/0 channel 1, with the digits **12831**. Because the gateway is already configured to do T1 CAS E&M wink start signaling, it can take this message and convert it to an off-hook indication on channel 1, wait for a wink, and then send the digits. CallManager also sends a RequestedEvents parameter line, asking to be notified when the operation is complete.

Example 6-84 shows the gateway responding with its capabilities in an attempt to establish the media channel. Detailed coverage of these messages is unnecessary because this is identical to what you saw with FXS/FXO ports in the section "MGCP FXS/FXO."

Example 6-84 *MGCP Response Indicating the Endpoint Capabilities*

```
Jan 17 18:31:55.330: send_mgcp_msg, MGCP Packet sent to 172.18.106.59 --->

Jan 17 18:31:55.330: 200 14413
I: 19B

v=0
c=IN IP4 172.18.106.202
m=audio 16444 RTP/AVP 0 8 96 97 98 2 99 18
a=rtpmap:96 G.729a/8000/1
a=rtpmap:97 G.726-16/8000/1
a=rtpmap:98 G.726-24/8000/1
a=rtpmap:99 G.729b/8000/1
<---
Jan 17 18:31:56.962: send_mgcp_msg, MGCP Packet sent to 172.18.106.59 --->
```

When the gateway finishes setting up the call on the T1 CAS port, it responds to CallManager with a **Notify** message containing an Operation Complete message indicating that it completed the setup successfully, as shown in Example 6-85.

Example 6-85 *MGCP T1 CAS Call and Media Setup*

```
Jan 17 18:31:56.962: NTFY 41133 S1/DS1-0/1@vnt-vg200-gw1.cisco.com MGCP 0.1
X: 0
O: DT/oc(dt/sup)
<---
Jan 17 18:31:57.222: MGCP Packet received from 172.18.106.59-
200 41133


Jan 17 18:31:57.402: MGCP Packet received from 172.18.106.59-
MDCX 14415 S1/DS1-0/1@vnt-vg200-gw1.cisco.com MGCP 0.1
C: A0000000020019d8
I: 19B
X: 0
L: p:20, a:PCMU, s:off
M: recvonly
S:


Jan 17 18:31:57.410: send_mgcp_msg, MGCP Packet sent to 172.18.106.59 --->

Jan 17 18:31:57.414: 200 14415 OK
<---
Jan 17 18:31:57.494: MGCP Packet received from 172.18.106.59-
MDCX 14416 S1/DS1-0/1@vnt-vg200-gw1.cisco.com MGCP 0.1
C: A0000000020019d8
I: 19B
X: 0
L: p:20, a:PCMU, s:off
M: sendrecv
S:

v=0
o=- 411 0 IN EPN S1/DS1-0/1@vnt-vg200-gw1.cisco.com
s=Cisco SDP 0
t=0 0
c=IN IP4 172.18.104.74
m=audio 19780 RTP/AVP 96
a=rtpmap:96 PCMU


Jan 17 18:31:57.506: send_mgcp_msg, MGCP Packet sent to 172.18.106.59 --->

Jan 17 18:31:57.506: 200 14416 OK
<---
```

When the end party answers, the gateway notifies CallManager that the call was answered, as shown in Example 6-86. CallManager then sends a **NotificationRequest** for any DTMF digit or a release from the POTS side.

Example 6-86 *MGCP T1 CAS Call Clearing*

```
Jan 17 18:32:14.315: send_mgcp_msg, MGCP Packet sent to 172.18.106.59 --->

Jan 17 18:32:14.315: NTFY 41134 S1/DS1-0/1@vnt-vg200-gw1.cisco.com MGCP 0.1
X: 0
O: DT/ans
<---
Jan 17 18:32:14.323: MGCP Packet received from 172.18.106.59-
200 41134


Jan 17 18:32:14.327: MGCP Packet received from 172.18.106.59-
RQNT 14419 S1/DS1-0/1@vnt-vg200-gw1.cisco.com MGCP 0.1
X: 0
R: D/[0-9ABCD*#], DT/rel
S:
Q: process,loop


Jan 17 18:32:14.335: send_mgcp_msg, MGCP Packet sent to 172.18.106.59 --->

Jan 17 18:32:14.339: 200 14419 OK
<---
```

Example 6-87 shows the MGCP messages required to clear a call after the IP phone hangs up. In this case, the call is dropped from the CallManager side. This is evident because CallManager initiates the call clearing by first sending a **ModifyConnection** to the gateway to make the call **recvonly**. CallManager then sends a **DeleteConnection** with a release call message, asking the gateway to let it know when a release complete occurs. In other words, CallManager asks the gateway to tear down the call and notify it when the gateway is finished tearing down the call. When translated to the T1 CAS world, this means that the gateway should go on-hook and inform CallManager when it sees the far end go on-hook. Example 6-87 shows CallManager clearing the call by sending a **ModifyConnection** followed by a **DeleteConnection**.

Example 6-87 *CallManager Clearing a T1 CAS Call*

```
Jan 17 18:32:20.655: MGCP Packet received from 172.18.106.59-
MDCX 14422 S1/DS1-0/1@vnt-vg200-gw1.cisco.com MGCP 0.1
C: A0000000020019d8
I: 19B
X: 0
M: recvonly
R: D/[0-9ABCD*#], DT/rel
S:
Q: process,loop
```

continues

Example 6-87 *CallManager Clearing a T1 CAS Call (Continued)*

```
Jan 17 18:32:20.663: send_mgcp_msg, MGCP Packet sent to 172.18.106.59 --->

Jan 17 18:32:20.667: 200 14422 OK
<---
Jan 17 18:32:20.671: MGCP Packet received from 172.18.106.59-
DLCX 14423 S1/DS1-0/1@vnt-vg200-gw1.cisco.com MGCP 0.1
C: A0000000020019d8
I: 19B
X: 0
R: DT/rlc
S: DT/rel
Q: process,loop


Jan 17 18:32:20.683: send_mgcp_msg, MGCP Packet sent to 172.18.106.59 --->

Jan 17 18:32:20.683: 250 14423
P: PS=1158, OS=185280, PR=1159, OR=185440, PL=0, JI=512, LA=0
<---
```

Finally, in Example 6-88, the gateway notifies CallManager that the call has been released successfully. CallManager responds with a **NotificationRequest** asking for any incoming call setups.

Example 6-88 *MGCP T1 CAS Call Completion*

```
Jan 17 18:32:21.511: send_mgcp_msg, MGCP Packet sent to 172.18.106.59 --->

Jan 17 18:32:21.511: NTFY 41135 S1/DS1-0/1@vnt-vg200-gw1.cisco.com MGCP 0.1
X: 0
O: DT/rlc
<---
Jan 17 18:32:21.515: MGCP Packet received from 172.18.106.59-
200 41135


Jan 17 18:32:21.519: MGCP Packet received from 172.18.106.59-
RQNT 14426 S1/DS1-0/1@vnt-vg200-gw1.cisco.com MGCP 0.1
X: 0
R: DT/sup
Q: process,loop


Jan 17 18:32:21.527: send_mgcp_msg, MGCP Packet sent to 172.18.106.59 --->

Jan 17 18:32:21.527: 200 14426 OK
<---
```

You should be able to troubleshoot any part of a T1 CAS connection by combining this knowledge with what you learned in the sections on troubleshooting the TDM side of a T1 CAS connection. Each piece was explained separately on purpose because it is important to break your problem into components. Troubleshoot each leg of the call one at a time. For example, if you see an Operation Failed (**DT/of**) message sent by the gateway in response to a call setup request (**DT/sup**), you should enable the T1 CAS debugs and see why the call is not going through on the TDM side. As a general rule, start with the CCM trace to see how far the call is getting, and proceed toward the endpoint that is causing the problem.

Now that the topic of MGCP troubleshooting has been exhausted, it's time to look at the other form of signaling that is supported for CallManager on Cisco IOS gateways—H.323.

Cisco IOS Gateways Using the H.323 Protocol

H.323 is an umbrella recommendation from the ITU that sets standards for multimedia communications over packet-based networks. The reason it is considered an umbrella recommendation is that most of the signaling protocols used by H.323 devices are actually defined in various other ITU specifications. H.323 uses other specifications to control call setup (H.225) and to exchange endpoint capabilities (H.245).

NOTE   Cisco supports H.323v2 as of Cisco IOS Software Release 12.0(5)T in all H.323-enabled devices; however, you do not want to use Cisco IOS Software Release 12.0(5)T code. Significant changes went into Cisco IOS Software Release 12.1(3)XI, which was eventually rolled into Cisco IOS Software Release 12.1(5)T. This eventually became the Cisco IOS Software Release 12.2 mainline train. We suggest that you use a 12.2-based or later Cisco IOS Software release if you will use that device as a voice gateway.

Because H.323 is a standard, CallManager can, in theory, use any H.323 device as a gateway. The focus here is on Cisco IOS gateways; however, the same concepts apply to any other H.323 gateway.

H.323 is very different from MGCP. As mentioned previously, MGCP is a master/slave protocol in which CallManager has direct control over every endpoint on a gateway. H.323 is a peer-to-peer protocol. H.323 uses messages similar to ISDN Q.931 to communicate between endpoints. This means that if you are familiar with ISDN Q.931 signaling, H.323 should be very easy to learn. When dealing with H.323 gateways, CallManager has no control over the individual endpoints. In fact, CallManager does not even know what kind of interface is being used on an H.323 gateway. To CallManager, an FXO port and a PRI look the same. The advantage of this is that troubleshooting is easier because the H.323 piece of the connection is the same regardless of the physical interface. The disadvantage is that it makes troubleshooting more difficult because there is more complexity on the gateway side because it has to have some degree of call routing intelligence. Make your own decision as to whether the advantages outweigh the disadvantages. In general, MGCP might be more preferable when it's an option because the dial plan administration is far easier because it is all done from CallManager. Also, H.323 does not support some features like call preservation.

Because several protocols are involved in setting up a call through an H.323 device, it is important to understand the role each protocol plays to be able to effectively troubleshoot such a call. Figure 6-7 shows a basic call flow for an H.323 call.

Figure 6-7 *H.323 Call Flow*

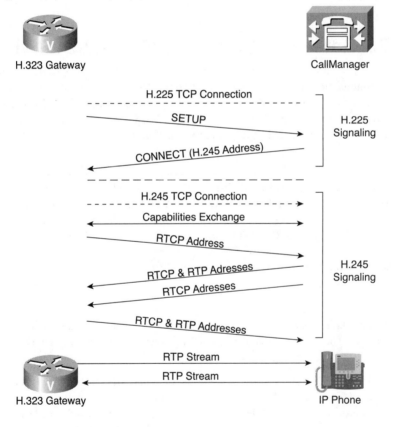

Although this might seem rather complex, if you take a look at each piece one at a time and understand how things are supposed to work, it is not bad at all. The following section begins with the H.225 signaling portion.

H.225 Signaling

H.225 is used for call control functions. H.225 is very similar to ISDN Q.931. In fact, many parts of the H.225 specification make references to the Q.931 specification. H.225 uses messages such as setup, call proceeding, connect, and release complete to establish and tear down a call.

H.225 signaling is carried over a TCP connection. H.323 devices, including CallManager and gateways, listen on TCP port 1720 for incoming connections. Note that by default CallManager does not accept a connection from a device that is not configured in the CallManager database as an H.323 gateway. This provides some level of security by not allowing rogue devices to place calls through CallManager. In CallManager 3.3 and later, all nodes in a CallManager cluster do not accept inbound H.323 connections. Only servers that are part of the device pool configured on a gateway in CallManager Administration (**Device > Gateway**) will accept an inbound H.323 call setup.

H.225 Messages

Table 6-30 lists and describes the messages that may be used in an H.225 call setup.

Table 6-30 *H.225 Call Setup Messages*

Message	Description
Setup	This message is sent by a calling H.323 device to indicate its desire to set up a connection to the called device.
Setup Acknowledge	This message typically indicates that the called device wants to do overlap sending and can accept more digits before proceeding with the call.
Call Proceeding	This message is sent by the called device to indicate that it has received all the information it needs to route the call to its destination.
Progress	This message can be sent by an H.323 gateway to indicate a call's progress. You typically see progress messages when internetworking with a non-ISDN network because audio cut-through must be treated differently in this case.
Alerting	This message might be sent by the called phone to indicate that the called phone is being alerted of the incoming call. In other words, the destination phone is ringing.
Connect	This message is sent by the called device to the calling device to indicate that the call has been accepted or answered.
User Information	This message can be sent to provide additional information. It can be used to provide information for call establishment in the case of overlap sending or miscellaneous call-related information. It can also be used to deliver proprietary features. CallManager and Cisco IOS gateways use this message to get around the fact that H.323 gateways do not normally provide ringback when a call is transferred and also to generate tone on hold.
Release Complete	This message is sent by a device to indicate the call's release.

continues

Table 6-30   *H.225 Call Setup Messages (Continued)*

Message	Description
Status Inquiry	This message can be used to request call status. Normally the device receiving this message responds with a Status message indicating the current call state for the given call reference.
Status	This message is used to respond to an unknown call signaling message or to a Status Inquiry message.
Information	This message is used to send additional information for a call. For example, when using overlap sending, each digit is sent one at a time in an Information message.
Notify	This message is used to notify a device of a change that has occurred in the call. CallManager uses this message to carry a display information element with the called party name when a call is connected.

If you are familiar with ISDN Q.931, you can see that the messages used in H.225 are nearly identical to those used in ISDN Q.931. One notable exception is the lack of Disconnect or Release messages in H.225. In an ISDN Q.931 call, disconnecting a call is a three-step procedure:

Step 1   The party disconnecting the call sends a Disconnect message.

Step 2   The other party replies to this messages with a Release message.

Step 3   The disconnecting party replies to the Release with a Release Complete.

In H.225, the party disconnecting the call sends a Release Complete, which is replied to with a Release Complete.

H.225 Information Elements

Each of the messages listed in Table 6-30 can contain one or more information elements. An *information element* (IE) carries a specific piece of information within an H.225 message. For example, the Called Party Number information element contains the digits and numbering plan information for the endpoint that is being called. This information element is usually sent as part of a Setup message to indicate the destination number that is being called.

The following list describes some of the most commonly used information elements. This is by no means a complete list of information elements. For the complete list along with the coding for each, refer to the ITU-T Q.931 specification.

- **Call Reference**—Allows an H.323 device to associate a particular message with a specific call. Using this information, you can search for messages associated with a specific call.

- **Bearer Capability**—Describes the capabilities requested of the PSTN bearer path. This is not very important in an H.323 call because the codec negotiations determine the audio path characteristics. However, the H.225 specification states that the bearer capability should be set to G.711 (A-law or μ-law) to indicate a voice call or to H.221 and H.242 to indicate a video call. Because CallManager currently supports only voice calls, this value should always end in either 0xA2 (μ-law) or 0xA3 (A-law).

- **Call State**—Indicates the ISDN call state. Table 6-31 lists the valid call states.

Table 6-31   *H.225 Call States*

Call State ID	Call State
0x00	Null
0x01	Call Initiated
0x02	Overlap Sending
0x03	Outgoing Call Proceeding
0x04	Call Delivered
0x06	Call Present
0x07	Call Received
0x08	Connect Request
0x09	Incoming Call Proceeding
0x0A	Active
0x0B	Disconnect Request
0x0C	Disconnect Indication
0x0F	Suspend Request
0x11	Resume Request
0x13	Release Request
0x19	Overlap Receiving

- **Called Party Number**—Contains the digits for the phone number being dialed. This is also called the Digital Number Identification Service (DNIS). Along with the phone number is the called party number numbering plan and numbering type. As explained later, if these are set incorrectly, the call might fail. Table 6-32 lists the valid values for the numbering types, and Table 6-33 lists the valid numbering plans.

Table 6-32   *Q.931 Numbering Type Identifiers*

Identifier	Name
0x0	Unknown
0x1	International Number

continues

Table 6-32   *Q.931 Numbering Type Identifiers (Continued)*

Identifier	Name
0x2	National Number
0x3	Network-Specific Number
0x4	Subscriber Number
0x6	Abbreviated Number
0x7	Reserved

Table 6-33   *Q.931 Numbering Plan Identifiers*

Identifier	Name
0x0	Unknown
0x1	ISDN (E.164)
0x3	Data (X.121)
0x4	Telex (F.69)
0x8	National standard
0x9	Private
0xF	Reserved

- **Calling Party Number**—This IE is similar to the Called Party Number IE, except that it contains the digits for the calling party's phone. This IE also contains numbering type and plan information, as shown in Tables 6-32 and 6-33.

- **Cause**—This IE is one of the most important when it comes to troubleshooting calls to H.323 gateways. The Cause IE tells you why a particular message was sent. In particular, you should be most interested in the Cause IE when it arrives in a Release Complete message. These cause codes give you insight into why a call might have been disconnected unexpectedly or why a particular call will not go through. These cause codes are the same cause codes used for troubleshooting PRIs and are all defined in the ITU-T Q.850 specification. Table 6-27 lists the most commonly used cause codes.

- **Display**—Carries text information that can be associated with a call. Typically this is used to send information about the calling or called party name. Devices that support the Display information element should display the contents of the information on the user's device. For example, if a CallManager is connected to a PBX via an H.323 gateway, when CallManager sends a setup to the PBX, it sends the calling party's name information in the Display information element so that the PBX phone can see not only the number of the calling party, but the name as well.

- **Progress Indicator**—This IE provides information about the call's progress. It is usually sent as part of a Progress message, although in some cases it might appear in other messages such as a Setup message. This IE is used to indicate whether the origination or destination addresses are non-ISDN. It also is used to signal an audio cut-through because in-band information is available. Table 6-34 lists the possible progress indicators.

Table 6-34   *Q.931 Progress Indicator Identifiers*

Progress Indicator	Description
0x1	The call is not end-to-end ISDN. Further progress information might be available in-band.
0x2	The destination address is non-ISDN.
0x3	The origination address is non-ISDN.
0x4	The call has returned to the ISDN.
0x5	Interworking has occurred and has resulted in a telecommunications service change.
0x8	In-band information or an appropriate pattern is now available.

- **Sending Complete**—Indicates the end of the called party number when using overlap sending. In some countries, if this IE is not sent, you must wait for the interdigit timeout before your call is routed, resulting in a period of dead air after you dial the number until the call is routed.

- **User-User**—This is perhaps one of the most important IEs in H.323. It carries H.323-specific information such as signaling IP addresses. The User-User IE is coded in a format called Abstract Syntax Notation (ASN.1). This chapter covers some ASN.1 output later.

- **Redirecting Number**—This IE is sometimes called the original called party number or the Redirected Dialed Number Identification Service (RDNIS). This element is typically used to convey information about the original called party to a voice mail system. When a call is forwarded to a voice mail system across H.323, the called party number is the number of the voice mail system, so there needs to be a place to put the phone number that was originally called so that the correct mailbox greeting can be played.

H.225 Call Flow

Now that you understand the building blocks of an H.225 call, take a look at an actual call from a phone attached to an H.323 gateway and an IP phone registered to a CallManager. Remember that because H.323 is a peer-to-peer protocol, it doesn't matter that this call is from an FXS port. If it were from an FXO or PRI, the call flow would be identical. Figure 6-8 gives you a quick look at the call flow.

Figure 6-8 *FXS Port H.225 Call Flow*

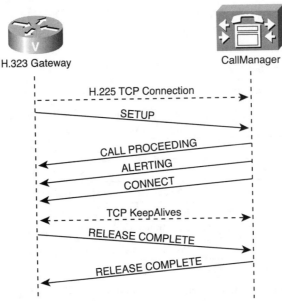

To review the details of this call, there are a variety of places you can look. The most readable of all the debugs are actually the CCM trace files. The CCM traces do a good job of decoding the H.225 signaling for you. In fact, you can even take the quick route and use the Q.931 Translator (discussed in Chapter 3), but doing it the hard way might be more helpful in the grand scheme of things. After looking at these trace files a few times, you won't even bother using the Q.931 Translator.

Sometimes finding the right place in the trace file is the hardest part of troubleshooting these types of calls. In the case where a large number of calls are occurring, it might be a good idea to use Q.931 Translator to quickly search through the trace for ISDN and H.323 calls to find the timestamp of the message you are looking for, and then you can go to that timestamp in the CCM trace. Even with a relatively high call volume, you should be able to search through the trace file manually if you know the approximate time of the incident you are looking for. Always remember that the time on Cisco IP Phones is synchronized with CallManager's clock, so if you are trying to troubleshoot occurrences of user-affecting problems, ask the users to give you the time on their phone when the problem occurred. When searching through CCM traces, you will notice blocks in the trace that look like Example 6-89.

Example 6-89   *Digit Analysis Match from a CCM Trace*

```
PretransformCallingPartyNumber=15801
CallingPartyNumber=15801
DialingPartition=Line1
DialingPattern=15644
DialingRoutePatternRegularExpression=(15644)
DialingWhere=
PatternType=Enterprise
PotentialMatches=NoPotentialMatchesExist
DialingSdlProcessId=(2,37,205)
PretransformDigitString=15644
PretransformTagsList=SUBSCRIBER
PretransformPositionalMatchList=15644
CollectedDigits=15644
UnconsumedDigits=
TagsList=SUBSCRIBER
PositionalMatchList=15644
VoiceMailbox=15644
VoiceMailCallingSearchSpace=
VoiceMailPilotNumber=15678
DisplayName=Paul Giralt
RouteBlockFlag=RouteThisPattern
InterceptPartition=Line1
InterceptPattern=15644
InterceptWhere=
InterceptSdlProcessId=(2,27,1)
InterceptSsType=33554436
InterceptSsKey=410
```

These blocks are usually very easy to find because of the amount of white space on the right. If you scroll through the trace file, you see a block like this every time a call is placed, assuming it can match a pattern that is configured in CallManager. Sometimes the problem you're troubleshooting is that CallManager is not matching a pattern, so don't always rely on the abundant white space rule.

Whenever you are looking for a call to an H.323 gateway, you can search through the CCM trace for the keywords **In Message** (notice there are two spaces between the words **In** and **Message**) or **Out Message** (just one space here). In searching through the trace, you would come upon the message shown in Example 6-90.

Example 6-90   *Inbound H.225 **Setup** Message as Seen in a CCM Trace*

```
In  Message -- H225SetupMsg -- Protocol= H225Protocol
Ie - H225BearerCapabilityIe -- IEData= 04 03 90 90 A3
Ie - H225CallingPartyIe -- IEData= 6C 06 80 31 35 38 30 31
Ie - Q931CalledPartyIe -- IEData= 70 06 81 31 35 36 34 34
Ie - H225UserUserIe -- IEData= 7E 00 8E 05 20 80 06 00 08 91 4A 00 02 08 80 01 3C
   05 01 00 00 CA F2 7A 78 07 E4 11 D6 81 34 A7 45 3B B2 6A 16 00 45 1C 07 00 0A 53
   81 08 2B 87 11 00 CA F2 7A 78 07 E4 11 D6 81 35 A7 45 3B B2 6A 16 32 02 12 00 00
   00 0C 60 13 80 0A 04 00 01 00 0A 53 81 08 48 CB 1D 40 00 00 06 04 01 00 4C 60 13
```

continues

Example 6-90 *Inbound H.225* **Setup** *Message as Seen in a CCM Trace (Continued)*

```
80 11 14 00 01 00 0A 53 81 08 48 CA 00 0A 53 81 08 48 CB 01 00 01 00 06 A0 01 80
13 01 40 B5 00 00 12 0C C0 01 00 02 80 06 00 04 00 00 00 03
MMan_Id= 0. (iep=  0 dsl=  0 sapi=  0 ces= 0 IpAddr=881530a IpPort=1720)
IsdnMsgData1= 08 02 00 0F 05 04 03 90 90 A3 6C 06 80 31 35 38 30 31 70 06 81 31 35
36 34 34 7E 00 8E 05 20 80 06 00 08 91 4A 00 02 08 80 01 3C 05 01 00 00 CA F2 7A
78 07 E4 11 D6 81 34 A7 45 3B B2 6A 16 00 45 1C 07 00 0A 53 81 08 2B 87 11 00 CA
F2 7A 78 07 E4 11 D6 81 35 A7 45 3B B2 6A 16 32 02 12 00 00 00 0C 60 13 80 0A 04
00 01 00 0A 53 81 08 48 CB 1D 40 00 00 06 04 01 00 4C 60 13 80 11 14 00 01 00 0A
53 81 08 48 CA 00 0A 53 81 08 48 CB 01 00 01 00 06 A0 01 80 13 01 40 B5 00 00 12
0C C0 01 00 02 80 06 00 04 00 00 00 03
```

Don't worry about all that mess of hex. Most of it is ignored here anyway. On the first line, you can see that this is an incoming H.225 Setup message. The direction is relative to CallManager, so this means that the message was sent by the gateway and received by CallManager.

Next you see all the information elements listed. The first is the Bearer Capability information element. Notice that the last hex digit is **0xA3**. This indicates G.711 A-law. Even though this call will eventually be a G.711 μ-law call, the important thing is that this is set to G.711 to indicate a voice call. The codec used for the media stream will be negotiated later in the H.245 negotiations. In fact, it doesn't even have to be G.711 at all. As long as it is either **0xA2** or **0xA3**, it is valid.

The next information elements are the Calling and Called Party Number information elements. Both have the same format. You can ignore the first 2 bytes. The third byte is the numbering type and plan information, as discussed in Tables 6-32 and 6-33. In this case, **0x80** is the numbering plan and type for the calling party number and **0x81** is the numbering plan and type for the called party number. So how do you decode that? First, you need to ignore the high-order bit. To do this, take the first hex number (8 in this case) and convert it to binary. That leaves 1000. The high-order bit is the first digit that can be changed to a 0. You are now left with 0000, which is 0x0 in hex. This means that the calling party numbering type and plan are **0x00**. The first digit is the type, and the second is the plan. Looking at Tables 6-32 and 6-33 you can see that the type is unknown and the plan is unknown. If you do the same thing for the called party information, you convert from **0x81** to **0x01** by ignoring the high-order bit. Decoding that, you can see that the called party numbering type is unknown and the numbering plan is ISDN. Q.931 Translator performs this decode automatically as you saw when decoding traces for an ISDN PRI. It does the same decode for H.225 messages as well.

After the numbering type and plan information, you see the actual digits that represent calling and called party numbers. The digits are encoded in ASCII. Fortunately, you can determine the decimal digit by just ignoring the first half of each byte. The first half is always a 3. So **31 35 38 30 31** means the calling party number is 15801 and **31 35 36 34 34** means the called party number is 15644.

Most of the rest of the data can be safely ignored for now, with one notable exception. The User-User information element is shown, but there is an easy way to decode it, as we'll explain in a moment. The last line that begins with **IsdnMsgData** is the raw hex representation of the message. This is the data that the Q.931 Translator uses to decode the packet. There is one important piece of information buried in this string of hex that you should take note of.

In case you didn't notice, none of the information so far has given you the call reference value for this call. Without a call reference value, how can you find any subsequent H.225 messages for this same call? If you look at the **IsdnMsgData**, it always begins with **08**. The following byte represents the length of the call reference and is either **01** or **02**. You usually see a 2-byte call reference. Depending on the length, the next 1 or 2 bytes are what you are interested in. These bytes are set to **00 0F** in Example 6-90. This is the call reference value. If you recall from Chapter 3 in the discussion of call reference values, the most-significant bit toggles depending on the direction of the message. A recommended practice is that you copy the last three digits and search through the file for that. In this case, you would search for **0 0F**. You will see that all the following messages have **0 0F** in the third and fourth bytes of the IsdnMsgData.

In response to the **Setup** message, CallManager sends a **Call Proceeding** message, as shown in Example 6-91.

Example 6-91 *Outbound H.225* **CallProceeding** *Message as Seen in a CCM Trace*

```
Out Message -- H225CallProceedingMsg -- Protocol= H225Protocol
Ie - H225UserUserIe IEData= 7E 00 32 05 21 80 06 00 08 91 4A 00 02 02 01 60 11 00
   CA F2 7A 78 07 E4 11 D6 81 35 A7 45 3B B2 6A 16 06 A0 01 00 0E 01 40 B5 00 00
   12 07 80 44 04 00 01 01 00
   MMan_Id= 0. (iep=  0 dsl=  0 sapi=  0 ces=  0 IpAddr=881530a IpPort=1720)
   IsdnMsgData2= 08 02 80 0F 02 7E 00 32 05 21 80 06 00 08 91 4A 00 02 02 01 60 11
   00 CA F2 7A 78 07 E4 11 D6 81 35 A7 45 3B B2 6A 16 06 A0 01 00 0E 01 40 B5 00
   00 12 07 80 44 04 00 01 01 00
```

As you can see, the only IE in the **Call Proceeding** message is the User-User IE. Also note that the call reference value for this message is **80 0F**, which you should expect; the most-significant bit is flipped because this message is in the opposite direction.

Immediately after sending the **Call Proceeding** message, CallManager sends an **Alerting** message, as shown in Example 6-92.

Example 6-92 *Outbound H.225* **Alerting** *Message as Seen in a CCM Trace*

```
Out Message -- H225AlertMsg -- Protocol= H225Protocol
Ie - H225UserUserIe IEData= 7E 00 32 05 23 80 06 00 08 91 4A 00 02 02 01 60 11 00
   CA F2 7A 78 07 E4 11 D6 81 35 A7 45 3B B2 6A 16 06 A0 01 00 0E 01 40 B5 00 00
   12 07 80 44 04 00 01 01 00
   MMan_Id= 0. (iep=  0 dsl=  0 sapi=  0 ces=  0 IpAddr=881530a IpPort=1720)
   IsdnMsgData2= 08 02 80 0F 01 7E 00 32 05 23 80 06 00 08 91 4A 00 02 02 01 60 11 00
   CA F2 7A 78 07 E4 11 D6 81 35 A7 45 3B B2 6A 16 06 A0 01 00 0E 01 40 B5 00 00 12
   07 80 44 04 00 01 01 00
```

The **Alerting** message also contains only a User-User IE. Note again that the call reference value is **80 0F**.

When the destination IP phone answers the call, CallManager sends a **Connect** message to the gateway, as shown in Example 6-93.

Example 6-93 *Outbound H.225* **Connect** *Message as Seen in a CCM Trace*

```
Out Message -- H225ConnectMsg -- Protocol= H225Protocol
Ie - Q931DisplayIe IEData= 28 0B 50 61 75 6C 20 47 69 72 61 6C 74
Ie - H225UserUserIe IEData= 7E 00 4A 05 22 C0 06 00 08 91 4A 00 02 00 AC 12 6A 3B
   04 92 02 00 CA F2 7A 78 07 E4 11 D6 81 34 A7 45 3B B2 6A 16 0B 00 11 00 CA F2
   7A 78 07 E4 11 D6 81 35 A7 45 3B B2 6A 16 06 A0 01 00 0E 01 40 B5 00 00 12 07
   80 44 04 00 01 01 00
   MMan_Id= 0. (iep=  0 dsl=  0 sapi=  0 ces=  0 IpAddr=881530a IpPort=1720)
   IsdnMsgData2= 08 02 80 0F 07 28 0B 50 61 75 6C 20 47 69 72 61 6C 74 7E 00 4A 05 22
   C0 06 00 08 91 4A 00 02 00 AC 12 6A 3B 04 92 02 00 CA F2 7A 78 07 E4 11 D6 81 34
   A7 45 3B B2 6A 16 0B 00 11 00 CA F2 7A 78 07 E4 11 D6 81 35 A7 45 3B B2 6A 16 06
   A0 01 00 0E 01 40 B5 00 00 12 07 80 44 04 00 01 01 00
```

The **Connect** message contains a Display information element. The data contained in the Display information element is also ASCII-coded data. The easiest way to look at this information is to use the Q.931 Translator, although it is possible to decode it manually. The first 2 bytes you can ignore. Starting from the third byte, you get the following:

```
0x50 = 'P'
0x61 = 'a'
0x75 = 'u'
0x6C = 'l'
0x20 = ' '
0x47 = 'G'
0x69 = 'i'
0x72 = 'r'
0x61 = 'a'
0x6C = 'l'
0x74 = 't'
```

So if you put it together, you get "Paul Giralt" as the display information being delivered. CallManager sends this as part of the **Connect** message to deliver the called party name to the person who placed the call.

When the conversation is over, the IP phone user hangs up the phone, and CallManager sends a **Release Complete** message to the gateway, indicating the end of the call, as shown in Example 6-94.

Example 6-94 *Outbound H.225* **Release Complete** *Message as Seen in a CCM Trace*

```
Out Message -- H225ReleaseCompleteMsg -- Protocol= H225Protocol
Ie - Q931CauseIe IEData= 08 02 80 90
Ie - H225UserUserIe IEData= 7E 00 21 05 25 80 06 00 08 91 4A 00 02 01 11 00 CA F2
   7A 78 07 E4 11 D6 81 35 A7 45 3B B2 6A 16 06 80 01 00
   MMan_Id= 0. (iep=  0 dsl=  0 sapi=  0 ces=  0 IpAddr=881530a IpPort=1720)
   IsdnMsgData2= 08 02 80 0F 5A 08 02 80 90 7E 00 21 05 25 80 06 00 08 91 4A 00 02 01
   11 00 CA F2 7A 78 07 E4 11 D6 81 35 A7 45 3B B2 6A 16 06 80 01 00
```

The most important information element in this message is the Cause information element. It tells you why the call is being disconnected. If you refer to Table 6-27, you can see that 0x90 means normal call clearing.

The gateway responds to the **Release Complete** with another **Release Complete** message, as shown in Example 6-95.

Example 6-95   *Inbound H.225 **Release Complete** Message as Seen in a CCM Trace*

```
In  Message -- H225ReleaseCompleteMsg -- Protocol= H225Protocol
Ie - Q931CauseIe -- IEData= 08 02 80 90
Ie - H225UserUserIe -- IEData= 7E 00 21 05 25 80 06 00 08 91 4A 00 02 01 11 00 CA
   F2 7A 78 07 E4 11 D6 81 35 A7 45 3B B2 6A 16 06 80 01 00
   MMan_Id= 0. (iep=  0 dsl=  0 sapi=  0 ces= 0 IpAddr=881530a IpPort=1720)
   IsdnMsgData1= 08 02 00 0F 5A 08 02 80 90 7E 00 21 05 25 80 06 00 08 91 4A 00 02 01
   11 00 CA F2 7A 78 07 E4 11 D6 81 35 A7 45 3B B2 6A 16 06 80 01 00
```

If you need to dig deeper into the User-User information element and you want to see the decoded ASN.1 output, you can enable an additional trace flag on CallManager.

To enable this flag in CallManager version 3.1, do the following:

Step 1   In CallManager Administration, select **Service > Service Parameters**.

Step 2   Select the server on which you want to enable the trace.

Step 3   Select **Cisco CallManager** from the list of services.

Step 4   Change the **SdlTraceTypeFlags** parameter to **0x8000EB15**.

Step 5   Repeat Steps 1 through 4 for each server you want to enable the trace for.

To enable this flag in CallManager version 3.2 and later, do the following:

Step 1   In CallManager Administration, select **Application > Cisco CallManager Serviceability**.

Step 2   Select **Trace > Configuration**.

Step 3   Select the server on which you want to enable the trace.

Step 4   Select **Cisco CallManager** from the Configured Services list.

Step 5   Select **SDL Configuration** in the upper-right corner.

Step 6   Check the **Enable UUIE Output Trace** checkbox.

Step 7   If you want this to apply to all nodes, check the **Apply to All Nodes** checkbox.

Step 8   Click **Update**.

NOTE   Although you are configuring the trace parameters for the SDL trace, the UUIE decode actually shows up in the CCM trace along with the rest of the H.225 messages, not the SDL trace file.

As soon as the **Enable UUIE Output** flag is enabled, the CCM trace files contain the decoded ASN.1 output. For example, the User-User information element for the **Connect** message you looked at in Example 6-93 is decoded in the trace shown in Example 6-96.

Example 6-96   *ASN.1 Decode of a User-User Information Element*

```
value H323-UserInformation ::=
{
  h323-uu-pdu
  {
    h323-message-body connect :
      {
        protocolIdentifier { 0 0 8 2250 0 2 },
        h245Address ipAddress :
          {
            ip 'AC126A3B'H,
            port 1170
          },
        destinationInfo
        {
          terminal
          {
          },
          mc FALSE,
          undefinedNode FALSE
        },
        conferenceID 'CAF27A7807E411D68134A7453BB26A16'H,
        callIdentifier
        {
          guid 'CAF27A7807E411D68135A7453BB26A16'H
        }
      },
    h245Tunneling FALSE,
    nonStandardControl
    {
      {
        nonStandardIdentifier h221NonStandard :
          {
            t35CountryCode 181,
            t35Extension 0,
            manufacturerCode 18
          },
        data '80440400010100'H
      }
    }
  }
}
```

The one useful piece of information you can obtain from the ASN.1 output is the H.245 signaling address that is being sent in the **Connect** message. The IP address is coded in hex, so **AC.12.6A.3B** decodes to 172.18.106.59. You can also see that the port number is set to **1170**.

The **Enable UUIE Output** flag is far more useful for troubleshooting H.245 signaling problems than it is for H.225 messages.

The H.225 messages in the CCM trace files help you solve the majority of H.323-related problems; however, some problems require you to look at the H.245 negotiations as well.

H.245 Signaling

H.225 is responsible only for setting up the call and routing it to the proper destination. H.225 does not have any mechanism for exchanging capabilities or setting up and tearing down media streams. The called H.323 device is responsible for sending the IP address and port number that are used to establish the TCP connection for H.245 signaling. This information can be sent by the called device in either the **Alerting** or **Connect** message.

CallManager must always send this information in the **Connect** message because in the majority of scenarios, CallManager does not know which device will answer the call until the call has been answered. For example, consider two phones that have a shared line appearance. In this case, CallManager does not know the IP address of the device that will answer the call until it is answered, so CallManager cannot tell the gateway which IP address to send the media stream to. The same thing applies to a phone that is being forwarded to voice mail. The call's IP address could be that of the phone being called, or it could be the IP address of the voice mail system. Until the call is answered, it is impossible to know. The same applies to the devices' capabilities. The phone being called might support one codec, and the voice mail system might support another.

As soon as the originating H.323 device receives the IP address and port number for H.245 negotiations, it initiates a second TCP connection to carry out the necessary capabilities exchange and logical channel negotiations. This TCP session is primarily used to do four things:

- Master/slave determination
- Terminal capabilities exchange
- Logical channel signaling
- DTMF relay

Figure 6-9 shows a typical H.245 message exchange between CallManager and an H.323 gateway.

Figure 6-9 *H.245 Message Exchange*

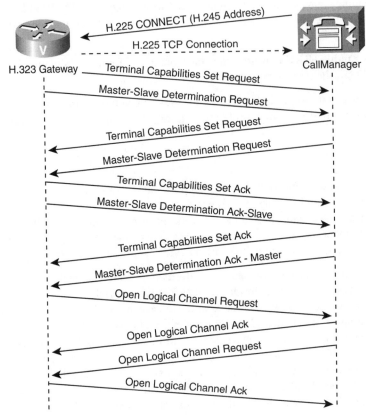

Master/Slave Determination

Master/slave determination is used to resolve conflicts that might exist when two endpoints in a call request the same thing, but only one of the two can gain access to the resource at a time. This is typically used for H.323 devices that handle multiparty conferences. Because CallManager does not operate as an H.323 conference device, master/slave determination is unimportant.

You see master/slave determination in the CCM traces if you have the **Enable UUIE Output** flag turned on. The messages look like Example 6-97.

Example 6-97   *H.245 Master/Slave Determination Message*

```
H245ASN - Incoming -value MultimediaSystemControlMessage ::= request :
  masterSlaveDetermination :
    {
      terminalType 60,
      statusDeterminationNumber 921
    }
H245ASN - Outgoing -value MultimediaSystemControlMessage ::=
  response : masterSlaveDeterminationAck :
    {
      decision master : NULL
    }
```

Rarely is this a problem when interfacing between CallManager and an H.323 gateway.

Terminal Capabilities Exchange

Terminal capabilities exchange is one of the most important functions of the H.245 protocol. It is how CallManager and the gateway let each other know what capabilities they support for a particular call. The two capabilities of concern are the supported audio codecs and the capability to use DTMF relay. Because the H.323 protocol is designed for far more than just basic audio calls, you can safely ignore a huge number of capabilities listed in the H.245 capabilities exchange when dealing with CallManager and associated gateways. The terminal capabilities set request sent from the gateway to CallManager looks like Example 6-98.

Example 6-98   *H.245 Terminal Capability Set Request*

```
H245ASN - Incoming -value MultimediaSystemControlMessage ::= request :
  terminalCapabilitySet :
    {
      sequenceNumber 1,
      protocolIdentifier { 0 0 8 245 0 3 },
      multiplexCapability h2250Capability :
        {
          maximumAudioDelayJitter 20,
          receiveMultipointCapability
          {
            multicastCapability FALSE,
            multiUniCastConference FALSE,
            mediaDistributionCapability
            {
              {
                centralizedControl FALSE,
                distributedControl FALSE,
                centralizedAudio FALSE,
                distributedAudio FALSE,
                centralizedVideo FALSE,
                distributedVideo FALSE
              }
            }
          },
```

continues

Example 6-98 *H.245 Terminal Capability Set Request (Continued)*

```
                  transmitMultipointCapability
                  {
                    multicastCapability FALSE,
                    multiUniCastConference FALSE,
                    mediaDistributionCapability
                    {
                      {
                        centralizedControl FALSE,
                        distributedControl FALSE,
                        centralizedAudio FALSE,
                        distributedAudio FALSE,
                        centralizedVideo FALSE,
                        distributedVideo FALSE
                      }
                    }
                  },
                  receiveAndTransmitMultipointCapability
                  {
                    multicastCapability FALSE,
                    multiUniCastConference FALSE,
                    mediaDistributionCapability
                    {
                      {
                        centralizedControl FALSE,
                        distributedControl FALSE,
                        centralizedAudio FALSE,
                        distributedAudio FALSE,
                        centralizedVideo FALSE,
                        distributedVideo FALSE
                      }
                    }
                  },
                  mcCapability
                  {
                    centralizedConferenceMC FALSE,
                    decentralizedConferenceMC FALSE
                  },
                  rtcpVideoControlCapability FALSE,
                  mediaPacketizationCapability
                  {
                    h261aVideoPacketization FALSE
                  },
                  logicalChannelSwitchingCapability FALSE,
                  t120DynamicPortCapability FALSE
                },
              capabilityTable
              {
                {
                  capabilityTableEntryNumber 17,
                  capability receiveAndTransmitDataApplicationCapability :
                    {
                      application nonStandard :
```

Example 6-98 *H.245 Terminal Capability Set Request (Continued)*

```
                                {
                                   nonStandardIdentifier h221NonStandard :
                                     {
                                        t35CountryCode 181,
                                        t35Extension 0,
                                        manufacturerCode 18
                                     },
                                   data '52747044746D6652656C6179'H
                                },
                              maxBitRate 0
                            }
                        },
                        {
                          capabilityTableEntryNumber 23,
                          capability receiveUserInputCapability : hookflash : NULL
                        },
                        {
                          capabilityTableEntryNumber 22,
                          capability receiveUserInputCapability : dtmf : NULL
                        },
                        {
                          capabilityTableEntryNumber 19,
                          capability receiveUserInputCapability : basicString : NULL
                        },
                        {
                          capabilityTableEntryNumber 1,
                          capability receiveAudioCapability : g711Ulaw64k : 20
                        }
                    },
                    capabilityDescriptors
                    {
                      {
                        capabilityDescriptorNumber 1,
                        simultaneousCapabilities
                        {
                          {
                            23
                          },
                          {
                            22,
                            19,
                            17
                          },
                          {
                            1
                          }
                        }
                      }
                    }
                }
            }
```

The first line of the message indicates that this is an incoming message; therefore, CallManager received it from the gateway. Next, take a look at the four highlighted lines in the **capabilityTable** section of the message. These are the capabilities you are interested in. The first capability listed is **hookflash**. The next two, **dtmf** and **basicString**, are two methods of performing DTMF relay. The **basicString** capability corresponds with the Cisco IOS configuration **dtmf-relay h245-alphanumeric**, and **dtmf** corresponds with the Cisco IOS configuration **dtmf-relay h245-signal**. The last capability indicates that this gateway supports only the G.711 μ-law codec with up to a 20-ms sample size. If the gateway is configured to use multiple codecs, instead of listing a single codec, the gateway lists all the supported codecs in the order it wants to use them.

CallManager sends a similar terminal capabilities set request to the gateway. Both the gateway and CallManager acknowledge each other's capabilities requests by sending an acknowledgment like the one shown in Example 6-99.

Example 6-99 *H.245 Terminal Capability Set Acknowledgment*

```
H245ASN - Incoming -value MultimediaSystemControlMessage ::=
  response : terminalCapabilitySetAck :
    {
      sequenceNumber 1
    }
```

You can see the identical output from the Cisco IOS gateway side by enabling **debug h225 asn1** for H.225 ASN.1 messages and **debug h245 asn1** for H.245 ASN.1 messages. Everyone has their preference as to how they want to look at this information, but in theory, the ASN.1 output should be identical regardless of which side you look at it from.

Although the H.323 specification allows for asymmetrical capabilities, such as G.711 for transmit and G.729 for receive for the same call, Cisco IOS Software does not currently support this. The codec on a gateway must be the same for transmit as well as receive for a call to complete successfully. Also important to note is that the H.323 protocol states that all H.323 devices must support the G.711 codec as a minimum.

Logical Channel Signaling

In the context of a Cisco IP Telephony network, a *logical channel* is nothing more than a one-way audio stream. The H.323 protocol allows for a logical channel to be far more complex when multiparty conferences and video are involved, but these concepts do not apply in the case of a CallManager communicating with an H.323 gateway. This means that to form a two-way audio conversation, a logical channel must be opened in each direction.

As of H.323 version 2, it is possible to open and close logical channels in the middle of a call. Opening and closing logical channels is how CallManager accomplishes supplementary services such as hold, transfer, and conference on an H.323 device. For example, to put a call on hold, all CallManager has to do is close the logical channels while keeping the call up. Remember that H.245 messages are independent of H.225 signaling, so although no logical channels are open, the call is still in the connected state as far as H.225 is concerned. If MOH is being used, a new logical channel is opened to the MOH server while the call is on hold. When the call is retrieved from hold, the logical channel to the MOH server is closed, and a new pair of logical channels is opened between the IP phone and gateway to continue the call.

The procedure for opening and closing logical channels is relatively straightforward. Each H.323 device involved in the call sends an **OpenLogicalChannel** message with a parameter called **mediaControlChannel**. This parameter corresponds to the IP address and port number to be used for the reverse real time control protocol (RTCP) channel. Example 6-100 shows an **OpenLogicalChannel** message.

Example 6-100 *H.245* **OpenLogicalChannel** *Message*

```
H245ASN - Outgoing -value MultimediaSystemControlMessage ::=
   request : openLogicalChannel :
      {
         forwardLogicalChannelNumber 45,
         forwardLogicalChannelParameters
         {
            dataType audioData : g711Ulaw64k : 20,
            multiplexParameters h2250LogicalChannelParameters :
               {
                  sessionID 1,
                  mediaControlChannel unicastAddress : iPAddress :
                     {
                        network 'AC126A3B'H,
                        tsapIdentifier 4001
                     },
                  silenceSuppression TRUE
               }
         }
      }
H245ASN - Incoming -value MultimediaSystemControlMessage ::=
   request : openLogicalChannel :
      {
         forwardLogicalChannelNumber 2,
         forwardLogicalChannelParameters
         {
            dataType audioData : g711Ulaw64k : 20,
            multiplexParameters h2250LogicalChannelParameters :
               {
                  sessionID 1,
                  mediaControlChannel unicastAddress : iPAddress :
                     {
                        network '0A538108'H,
                        tsapIdentifier 18635
                     }
               }
         }
      }
```

You can see that both logical channels are using G.711 μ-law, as you would expect from the previous capabilities exchange. You can see that CallManager is sending IP address **172.18.106.59** port **4001** as the **mediaControlChannel** parameter, and the gateway is sending **10.83.129.8** port **18635**. Note that the port numbers should always be odd-numbered. Also notice that the IP address and port number CallManager sends for RTCP is its own IP address. This is because the IP phones do not listen for RTCP, but then again, neither does CallManager. RTCP packets are ignored. In place of RTCP, IP phones store call statistics locally and send these statistics to CallManager when a call is completed.

Example 6-101 shows how CallManager and the gateway each reply to each other's open logical channel message with an open logical channel acknowledgment.

Example 6-101 *H.245 ASN.1 Output of an Open Logical Channel Acknowledgment*

```
H245ASN - Outgoing -value MultimediaSystemControlMessage ::=
  response : openLogicalChannelAck :
    {
      forwardLogicalChannelNumber 2,
      forwardMultiplexAckParameters h2250LogicalChannelAckParameters :
        {
          sessionID 1,
          mediaChannel unicastAddress : iPAddress :
            {
              network '0A538102'H,
              tsapIdentifier 19580
            },
          mediaControlChannel unicastAddress : iPAddress :
            {
              network '0A538102'H,
              tsapIdentifier 19581
            }
        }
    }
H245ASN - Incoming -value MultimediaSystemControlMessage ::=
  response : openLogicalChannelAck :
    {
      forwardLogicalChannelNumber 45,
      forwardMultiplexAckParameters h2250LogicalChannelAckParameters :
        {
          sessionID 1,
          mediaChannel unicastAddress : iPAddress :
            {
              network '0A538108'H,
              tsapIdentifier 18634
            },
          mediaControlChannel unicastAddress : iPAddress :
            {
              network '0A538108'H,
              tsapIdentifier 18635
            },
          flowControlToZero FALSE
        }
    }
```

The open logical channel acknowledgment has two IP address/port number pairs. The important one is the **mediaChannel parameter**. It indicates the IP address and port number to which the RTP stream should be sent. Notice that CallManager sends this to the phone's IP address, not to its own IP address. In this case you can see that the IP address is **10.83.129.2** with port number **19580**. The gateway sends its own IP address because it is terminating the RTP stream. It sends IP address **10.83.129.8** port **18634**.

At this point you have an active call between a CallManager and an H.323 gateway. Once the call is over, you see a **closeLogicalChannel** message that looks like Example 6-102.

Example 6-102 *H.245 ASN.1 Output of a Close Logical Channel Message*

```
H245ASN - Outgoing -value MultimediaSystemControlMessage ::=
  request : closeLogicalChannel :
    {
      forwardLogicalChannelNumber 45,
      source user : NULL
    }
H245ASN - Incoming -value MultimediaSystemControlMessage ::=
  response : closeLogicalChannelAck :
    {
      forwardLogicalChannelNumber 45
    }
```

That's all there is to an H.323 call. Understanding how things are supposed to function helps you understand why something is not working when it breaks.

DTMF Relay

The last activity that H.245 is used for is DTMF relay. VoIP networks typically do not carry DTMF tones in-band because tones can be distorted when transported over compressed codecs such as G.729. This is because compressed codecs such as G.729 are designed to carry human voice, not tones. To get around this problem, DTMF tones are carried via the signaling channel instead of the voice channel. Cisco IOS gateways support three methods of passing DTMF relay:

- **h245-signal** — Uses an H.245 message and specifies how long the tone was pressed so that it can be reproduced exactly at the receiving end. The duration is initially set to 4000 ms in the signal UserInput Indication, but it is extended if the tone has not ended when 50 ms remains. An initial length of 4 seconds is used because it is unlikely that someone will press a DTMF digit for longer than 4 seconds; however, the duration can be extended in increments of 1000 ms by sending additional signalUpdates every second until the end of the tone is detected, at which time a final signalUpdate is sent the actual duration. To indicate a tone shorter than 4000 ms, such as a 250 ms tone, the gateway would send an initial message indicating 4000 ms and then after 250 ms send a new message indicating the tone duration is only 250 ms, triggering the terminating gateway to stop playing the tone.

- **h245-alphanumeric**—Uses an H.245 message and specifies that a tone was pressed. It doesn't give the tone's length. It only pulses fixed-length digits at the receiving end for a period of 100 ms.

- **cisco-rtp**—A proprietary method that uses Payload Type 121 in the rtp header. It has the same packet format as FRF.11 Annex A. Currently no method exists to debug inbound VoIP packets that are DTMF except **debug ip rtp packet** (but it shows only payload type, not digit(s) contained within the packet). This was created before a standardized way of doing DTMF relay was created. It is never used in conjunction with CallManager.

As discussed in the earlier section "Understanding Dial Peer Matching in Cisco IOS Software," to properly interoperate with CallManager, Cisco IOS gateways should be configured to use h245-alphanumeric. What is confusing is that CallManager sends DTMF relay using h245-signal but accepts DTMF relay using h245-alphanumeric. Cisco IOS gateways always accept any form of DTMF relay, but CallManager accepts only h245-alphanumeric.

Because of that, you see different messages depending on whether CallManager or the gateway is sending DTMF relay.

For example, for a DTMF relay digit from a Cisco IOS gateway to CallManager, you see the message shown in Example 6-103.

Example 6-103 *H.245 ASN.1 Output of an H.245 Alphanumeric DTMF Relay Message*

```
Router#debug h245 asn1
H245 MSC OUTGOING PDU ::=

value MultimediaSystemControlMessage ::= indication : userInput : alphanumeric : "4"
```

However, on a DTMF relay digit from CallManager to a Cisco IOS gateway, you see the message shown in Example 6-104.

Example 6-104 *H.245 ASN.1 Output of an H.245 Signal DTMF Relay Message*

```
Router#debug h245 asn1
H245 MSC INCOMING PDU ::=

value MultimediaSystemControlMessage ::= indication : userInput : signal :
    {
      signalType "4"
      duration 300
    }
```

As you can see, CallManager is sending the digit as an h245-signal message; however, instead of setting the duration to 4000 ms and then modifying it later, CallManager always sets this to 300 ms. You can change this length by modifying the CallManager service parameter **H225DTMFDuration**. The default is 300 and is represented in milliseconds. You might find that voice mail or IVR systems on the PSTN require that this be changed, particularly if you are using Octel voice mail systems, which are networked via analog integration. These systems typically require that the DTMF tone duration be shorter.

Additional H.323 Debugs in Cisco IOS Software

So far, all the debugging information examined has been from CallManager's perspective. All the ASN.1 debugs you have looked at are available in identical form in Cisco IOS Software by using the following commands:

```
debug h225 asn1
debug h245 asn1
```

The output of these debugs is not included here because they provide the same information, just from the gateway side. Unfortunately, there is no easy way to look at the non-ASN.1 information, as you saw with the H.225 messages. However, a few debugs provide some useful H.225 information. What follows is a list of useful debugs in Cisco IOS Software:

```
debug cch323 h225
debug cch323 h245
debug h225 events
debug h245 events
debug voip ccapi inout
```

For instance, Example 6-105 shows the output from **debug h225** events. You can see the basic H.225 messages, but you cannot easily identify the information within the packets.

Example 6-105 *Troubleshooting an H.323 Call Using* **debug h225 events**

```
Router#debug h225 events
Hex representation of the SETUP TPKT to send.
030000AF0802001A0504039090A36C06803135383303170068131353634347E008E052080060008914A
  00020880013C050100005F74239D093011D68198A7453BB26A1600451C07000A538108303311005F
  74239D093011D68199A7453BB26A16320120000000C6013800A040001000A53810843BD1D400000
  060401004C60138011140001000A53810843BC000A53810843BD0100010006A00180130140B50000
  120CC00100028006000400000003
Jan 15 15:50:45.117: h225SetupRequest: Q.931 SETUP sent from socket [1]
  h323chan_chn_process_read_socket: fd (1) of type CONNECTED has data

Hex representation of the received
TPKT0300003E0802801A027E003205218006008914A000202016011005F74239D093011D68199A745
  3BB26A1606A001000E0140B50000120780440400010100
Jan 15 15:50:45.229: h225ParseData: Q.931 CALL PROCEEDING received on socket [1]
  h323chan_chn_process_read_socket: fd (1) of type CONNECTED has data

Hex representation of the received
TPKT0300003E0802801A017E003205238006008914A000202016011005F74239D093011D68199A745
  3BB26A1606A001000E0140B50000120780440400010100
Jan 15 15:50:45.497: h225ParseData: Q.931 ALERTING received on socket [1]
  h323chan_chn_process_read_socket: fd (1) of type CONNECTED has data

Hex representation of the received
TPKT030000630802801A07280B5061756C20476972616C747747E004A0522C0060008914A000200AC126A
  3B045D02005F74239D093011D68198A7453BB26A160B0011005F74239D093011D68199A7453BB26A
  1606A001000E0140B50000120780440400010100
Jan 15 15:50:49.565: h225ParseData: Q.931 CONNECT received on socket [1]
  Changing to new event: CONNECT
```

continues

Example 6-105 *Troubleshooting an H.323 Call Using* **debug h225 events** *(Continued)*

```
h323chan_chn_connect: connecting to 172.18.106.59:1117

changing from CONNECTING state to CONNECTED state

Hex representation of the received
TPKT030000310802801A5A080280907E0021052580060008914A00020111005F74239D093011D68199
  A7453BB26A1606800100
Jan 15 15:50:52.806: h225ParseData: Q.931 RELEASE COMPLETE received on socket [1]
Hex representation of the RELEASE COMPLETE TPKT to send.
030000310802001A5A080280907E0021052580060008914A00020111005F74239D093011D68199A745
  3BB26A1606800100
Jan 15 15:50:52.814: h225TerminateRequest: Q.931 RELEASE COMPLETE sent from
  socket [1]. Call state changed to [Null].
Jan 15 15:50:52.818:        h323chan_close: TCP connection from socket [1] closed
Jan 15 15:50:52.822:        h323chan_close: TCP connection from socket [2] closed
```

As you can see, **debug h225** events shows you which messages are being sent but does not decode any of the information elements. The hex information before each message could technically be decoded if you have a lot of time on your hands, but in most cases, the best course of action is to look at the CCM trace files or use the Q.931 Translator.

If you have a problem where calls are not getting to CallManager from an H.323 gateway, you might want to enable **debug h225 events** to see if the gateway is even sending the H.225 setup message (or receiving it if the problem is for calls being routed to the gateway).

If you see that the gateway cannot send an H.225 message, there might be a problem at a lower layer. Remember that for a gateway to send an H.225 setup, it must first establish a TCP connection to CallManager. Use the command **debug ip tcp transactions** to troubleshoot TCP-level problems. Example 6-106 shows the output of **debug ip tcp transactions**.

Example 6-106 *Using* **debug ip tcp transactions** *to Troubleshoot TCP or IP Layer Issues*

```
Router#debug ip tcp transactions
Jul 25 13:16:19.184: TCB62FFC300 created
Jul 25 13:16:19.184: TCB62FFC300 setting property TCP_PID (8) 62A74DFC
Jul 25 13:16:19.184: TCB62FFC300 setting property TCP_NO_DELAY (1) 62A74E00
Jul 25 13:16:19.184: TCB62FFC300 setting property TCP_NONBLOCKING_WRITE (10)
  62A74E88
Jul 25 13:16:19.184: TCB62FFC300 setting property TCP_NONBLOCKING_READ (14)
  62A74E88
Jul 25 13:16:19.184: TCB62FFC300 setting property unknown (15) 62A74E88
Jul 25 13:16:19.184: TCB62FFC300 setting property TCP_ALWAYSPUSH (17) 62A74E44
Jul 25 13:16:19.188: TCP: sending SYN, seq 3011021527, ack 0
Jul 25 13:16:19.188: TCP0: Connection to 10.4.3.2:1720, advertising MSS 536
Jul 25 13:16:19.188: TCP0: state was CLOSED -> SYNSENT [11005 -> 10.4.3.2(1720)]
Jul 25 13:16:19.188: TCP0: ICMP destination unreachable received
Jul 25 13:16:19.188: TCP0: state was SYNSENT -> CLOSED [11005 -> 10.4.3.2(1720)]
Jul 25 13:16:19.192: TCB 0x62FFC300 destroyed
```

As you can see in Example 6-106, the Cisco IOS gateway is attempting to establish a TCP connection to IP address 10.4.3.2 on port 1720. You can see that the gateway is receiving an ICMP destination unreachable message, which causes the TCP connection to be destroyed. This indicates that either there is an IP connectivity problem between CallManager and the gateway, or the CallManager service is not running.

Example 6-107 shows another example of the **debug ip tcp transactions** command.

Example 6-107 *Using* **debug ip tcp transactions** *to Troubleshoot TCP or IP Layer Issues*

```
Jul 25 13:25:14.308: TCB63043FD0 created
Jul 25 13:25:14.308: TCB63043FD0 setting property TCP_PID (8) 62A74DFC
Jul 25 13:25:14.308: TCB63043FD0 setting property TCP_NO_DELAY (1) 62A74E00
Jul 25 13:25:14.308: TCB63043FD0 setting property TCP_NONBLOCKING_WRITE (10)
  62A74E88
Jul 25 13:25:14.308: TCB63043FD0 setting property TCP_NONBLOCKING_READ (14)
  62A74E88
Jul 25 13:25:14.308: TCB63043FD0 setting property unknown (15) 62A74E88
Jul 25 13:25:14.308: TCB63043FD0 setting property TCP_ALWAYSPUSH (17) 62A74E44
Jul 25 13:25:14.308: TCP: sending SYN, seq 3715094991, ack 0
Jul 25 13:25:14.308: TCP0: Connection to 14.84.41.229:1720, advertising MSS 536
Jul 25 13:25:14.308: TCP0: state was CLOSED -> SYNSENT [11006 -> 14.84.41.229(1720)]
Jul 25 13:25:28.309: TCP0: timeout #3 - timeout is 16000 ms, seq 3715094991
Jul 25 13:25:28.309: TCP: (11006) -> 14.84.41.229(1720)
Jul 25 13:25:29.309: TCP0: state was SYNSENT -> CLOSED [11006 -> 14.84.41.229(1720)]
Jul 25 13:25:29.309: TCB 0x63043FD0 destroyed
```

In Example 6-107, you can see that the Cisco IOS gateway sends a TCP SYN packet to establish the TCP connection but does not receive a response. If you look at the timestamps, you can see that 16 seconds elapses before the connection times out and is destroyed. This indicates that either there is no IP connectivity or CallManager is not on the network.

Troubleshooting Problems with Ringback and Other Progress Tones

Lack of ringback is a problem that affects many IP Telephony installations. Fortunately, in the majority of cases, one or more configuration changes can resolve the problem. Ringback issues are most prevalent when an H.323 gateway is being used to interface with the PSTN. The most common ringback and progress tone problems are as follows:

- No ringback on an IP phone when calling the PSTN
- No ringback on a PSTN phone when calling an IP phone
- No ringback when transferring a call
- The IP phone user does not hear busy tone or other in-band messages when a call is disconnected

No Ringback on an IP Phone When Calling the PSTN

One common problem is lack of ringback when dialing out to the PSTN from an IP phone. Figure 6-10 shows an example of this scenario.

Figure 6-10 *No Ringback on an IP Phone When Dialing the PSTN*

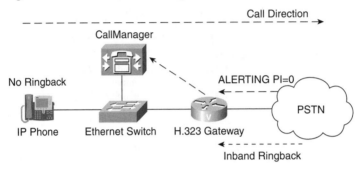

The problem in this scenario is that CallManager automatically cuts through audio to the H.323 gateway as soon as the logical channel signaling is complete. The problem arises because the alerting message sent by the PSTN does not contain a progress indicator indicating that in-band information is available. Typically in an end-to-end ISDN environment, the end device is responsible for locally generating ringback upon receiving an alerting message. Unfortunately, CallManager does not operate this way. It relies on in-band ringback when calling out an H.323 gateway. To fix this problem, configure **progress_ind alert enable 8** under the POTS dial peer that gets matched for this call's outbound call leg. For some reason, this command is hidden in some versions of Cisco IOS software, but if you enter it, the gateway accepts it, and it shows up in your configuration. Consider Example 6-108.

Example 6-108 *POTS Dial Peer to Fix Outbound Ringback Problems*

```
dial-peer voice 9 pots
  destination-pattern 9T
  progress_ind alert enable 8
  direct-inward-dial
  port 1/0:23
```

As soon as this is configured, Cisco IOS Software treats an alerting message as if it came in with a progress indicator of 8. A progress indicator of 8 means that in-band information is available, so the gateway cuts through audio upon receiving an alerting message. Table 6-34 listed the various progress indicator values.

No Ringback on a PSTN Phone When Calling an IP Phone

A similar ringback problem can occur for calls coming into the IP Telephony network from the PSTN. When a Cisco IOS gateway receives a setup message without a progress indicator, it does not play ringback toward the PSTN. This is because the gateway assumes that the PSTN is end-to-end ISDN and therefore handles playing ringback to the originating device upon receiving the alerting message. If the network is not end-to-end ISDN, the setup message should arrive with a progress indicator of 3, indicating that the origination address is non-ISDN. In the case of a failure, the device on the PSTN does not send a progress indicator. Figure 6-11 shows an example of this problem.

Figure 6-11 *No Ringback on a PSTN Phone When Dialing an IP Phone*

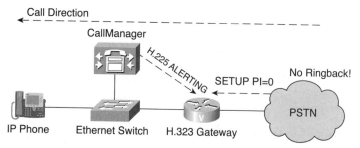

To resolve this problem, you need to configure the gateway to play ringback toward the PSTN regardless of the progress indicator in the setup message. To accomplish this, configure **progress_ind setup enable 3** on the VoIP dial peer that is being matched for this inbound call. Note that even though you are trying to fix a problem with ringback on the POTS side, this parameter must be configured on the VoIP dial peer. If you have multiple VoIP dial peers that might be matched, be sure to put the command under all of them. This command forces the Cisco IOS gateway to treat every setup message as if it has a progress indicator of 3. This forces the gateway to play in-band ringback toward the PSTN.

No Ringback When Transferring a Call

A third common ringback problem is the lack of ringback toward the PSTN user when an IP phone user transfers a call to another phone. The reason for this is a limitation of the H.323 protocol as it is implemented on the gateways and in Cisco IOS. When a call is transferred, the logical channels for that call are torn down between the gateway and the transferring device. During this time, the PSTN user hears no audio because no logical channels are open.

To get around this limitation, a solution is in place as of Cisco IOS Software Release 12.2(3) and later. This solution also requires CallManager 3.0(8) or later. To get it to work, make sure you are running the correct version of Cisco IOS Software, and make sure the **ToSendH225UserInfoMsg** service parameter is set to **True**. In CallManager 3.2(3) and later, this service parameter accepts a numeric value of 0, 1, or 2 instead of True or False. These values mean the following:

- **0**—Do not send any progress tone information.
- **1**—Use the H225UserInfo message to send progress tone information.
- **2**—Use the H225Info message to send progress tone information.

CallManager versions prior to 3.2(3) do not understand receiving these messages in the H225Info message, so for backward compatibility with CallManager clusters prior to 3.2(3), use a value of 1 (True). Otherwise, choose a value of 2.

As long as you have met these conditions, you should get ringback on transfer. See Figure 6-12.

Figure 6-12 *H225UserInfo Message Initiates Ringback on Transfer*

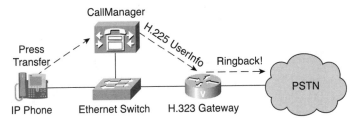

If you enable **debug h225 asn1** on the gateway, you should see a message similar to the following when you initiate the transfer:

```
H225.0 INCOMING PDU ::=
value H323_UserInformation ::=
```

Also, if you enable **debug vtsp tone**, you should get the following output:

```
act_gen_tone: Tone Ring Back generated in direction Network
```

The IP Phone User Does Not Hear In-band Messages When a Call Is Disconnected

In some cases, you might end up with IP phone users not hearing a busy signal when they call a busy number on the PSTN. This is a problem when the PSTN disconnects the call with a normal call clearing cause code instead of setting the cause to user busy. In this case, the PSTN might send a disconnect similar to the one shown in Example 6-109.

Example 6-109 *ISDN Disconnect Message with a Progress Indicator Indicating In-Band Information*

```
00:09:40.627: ISDN Se3/0:15: RX <- DISCONNECT pd = 8  callref = 0x8004
00:09:40.627:          Cause i = 0x8590 · Normal call clearing
00:09:40.627:          Progress Ind i = 0x8588 · In-band info or appropriate now
    available
00:09:40.631: cc_api_call_disc_prog_ind (callID=0x8),prog_ind 8 cause 10
```

As you can see, the disconnect message has a progress indicator information element set to **8**, indicating that in-band information is available. The disconnect message, however, causes the gateway and CallManager to release the call.

As of Cisco IOS Software Release 12.2(1), you can remedy this problem by configuring the **voice call convert-discpi-to-prog** command in global configuration mode. Doing so converts a disconnect with a progress indicator to a progress message with a progress indicator so that audio is cut through and the IP phone can hear the disconnect tones and/or announcement from the PSTN.

Intercluster Trunks

An intercluster trunk is used to connect different CallManager clusters. An intercluster trunk is really just a special case of an H.323 gateway. Although the H.323 protocol is used for intercluster trunks, an intercluster trunk must be configured slightly differently than a normal H.323 gateway, such as a Cisco IOS gateway. The H.323 signaling used between CallManager servers configured for intercluster trunk contains some additional messages that are not found when CallManager communicates with an H.323 gateway.

Because the protocol being used is H.323, troubleshooting intercluster trunks is identical to troubleshooting any other H.323 gateway.

First, the obvious fact must be stated about the network: If there is no connectivity between these two clusters, intercluster trunking won't work. If you are referring to these gateways by DNS name and you cannot resolve the name for some reason, intercluster trunking won't work.

What are the things you need to pay special attention to with intercluster trunks? One important distinction is that both sides of the cluster must be configured for the trunk to work. If you build one intercluster trunk on one cluster but don't build it on another, the connection will not work. This is especially important when you have a cluster of CallManagers talking to another cluster via an intercluster trunk. Figure 6-13 shows two clusters connected over a WAN. Cluster 1 has three CallManagers, and Cluster 2 has two.

As shown in Figure 6-13, a call can originate from any CallManager in a cluster and can terminate on any of the CallManager servers on the opposite cluster. You must ensure that you have properly configured each cluster so that all these combinations will work correctly.

For this to work correctly, Cluster 1 must have CallManager 2A and CallManager 2B configured in its database so that it will accept calls from either of those CallManager nodes. Cluster 1 should also have a route list that includes both CallManager 2A and CallManager 2B so that it can fail over if one CallManager is unavailable.

Figure 6-13 *Intercluster Trunk Topology*

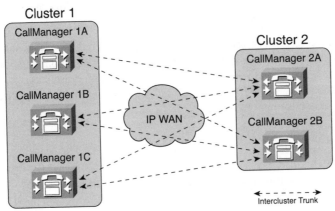

The same holds true for the configuration on Cluster 2. Cluster 2 must have CallManager 1A, CallManager 1B, and CallManager 1C configured in its database so that the CallManager servers in the cluster will accept calls from any of the CallManager nodes in Cluster 1. You must also have a route list with all three CallManager nodes in Cluster 1 so that failover can occur.

If you are missing one of the servers from either side, the symptoms you experience are typically either dead air when calling out through an intercluster trunk or a long delay before hearing ringback. This is usually indicative of one CallManager not being configured on the opposite side.

The exception to this rule is if you are using a gatekeeper-controlled trunk (called AnonymousDevice prior to CallManager version 3.3). In this case, CallManager accepts a call that originates from a gatekeeper even if the final endpoint is not explicitly configured in CallManager.

In CallManager version 3.3 and later, intercluster trunk devices can contain up to three IP addresses, greatly simplifying the configuration, especially for a large cluster. In Figure 6-13, Cluster 1 would contain a single intercluster trunk device with the IP addresses of CallManager 2A and CallManager 2B. Cluster 2 would contain a single intercluster trunk device with the IP addresses of CallManager 1A, CallManager 1B, and CallManager 1C.

Codec mismatches can also be a problem. If regions have been imposed on one side, restricting the codec to one type, and the other cluster has specified another codec, the call could fail. Make sure a codec mismatch isn't the problem.

Other than that, treat an intercluster trunk as you would any other H.323 gateway.

Troubleshooting the WS-X6608 and WS-X6624 Voice Gateways

The WS-X6608 and WS-X6624 voice gateways both use MGCP to communicate with CallManager. Therefore, understanding MGCP helps you understand the operation of these gateways.

Both the WS-X6608 and WS-X6624 voice gateways are modules that must reside in a Catalyst 6000 series chassis. Troubleshooting power, Dynamic Host Configuration Protocol (DHCP), Trivial File Transfer Protocol (TFTP), and registration issues are all basically the same for both modules.

The WS-X6624 provides 24 analog loop start FXS ports, and the WS-X6608 provides eight ports that can be used as a PRI (T1 and E1) or CAS (T1 only) interface.

One difference to note is that each of the eight individual ports on the WS-X6608 registers with CallManager with its own IP address and operates independent of the other ports. Conversely, the entire WS-X6624 module registers with one IP address. Although the WS-X6624 has 24 individual FXS ports, it uses a single IP address and signaling channel to communicate with CallManager. From CallManager's perspective, the WS-X6624 is treated as a single gateway, whereas each port on the WS-X6608 is treated as a single gateway.

When looking at the different issues in the following sections, remember that you need to look at individual ports on the WS-X6608 and the whole module for the WS-X6624.

Recognizing and Powering the Module

Before addressing registration or configuration issues, you must get the module powered up and recognized by the switch. This is an easy process and can be quickly resolved when you encounter any problems.

The module should power up immediately upon being inserted into the chassis. There are two reasons that the module will not receive power:

- Insufficient power is being supplied to the switch
- The module has explicitly been powered down

The **set module power up** *mod* command turns the power on to that module.

If the module is not being recognized, it is most likely that the software on the switch is not up to date. Verify your current version of switch software to make sure it is compatible with the WS-X6608 and WS-X6624 voice module. The WS-X6608 and WS-X6624 modules are supported in Catalyst OS Software version 5.5(3) and later. Neither module is supported in Native IOS on the Catalyst 6000. You must run CatOS on the supervisor for these modules to be recognized.

To verify that the module is recognized and powered up, use the command **show environment power**, which returns information similar to the output shown in Example 6-110.

Example 6-110 **show environment power** *Command Output Verifies Module Recognition and Power Status*

```
evoice-cat6k-6a (enable) show environment power 7
Module 7:
Slot power Requirement/Usage :

Slot Card Type          PowerRequested PowerAllocated CardStatus
Watts   A @42V Watts   A @42V
----  -----------------  -------  ------  -------  ------  ----------
3     WS-XWS-X6608-T1          83.16   1.98    83.16   1.98  ok
```

If the card type shows up correctly, the module was recognized. The **CardStatus** field displays **other** during the power-up process but changes to **ok** after successful bootup. If the **CardStatus** field displays **deny**, there is not enough power to power up the module. Consult your Catalyst 6000 documentation for information on power requirements.

Troubleshooting DHCP, TFTP, and Registration Problems

After a module has been supplied with power and correctly recognized, the registration process should begin immediately. Each port on the WS-X6608 module and the WS-X6624 module as a whole needs to have the following steps completed successfully in order to boot up and register with CallManager:

Step 1 Successfully contact the DHCP server or read static IP addressing information from the switch configuration file.

Step 2 Receive complete and accurate IP information.

Step 3 Successfully download a configuration file from the TFTP server.

Step 4 Successfully register.

The following section examines troubleshooting DHCP-specific issues.

Troubleshooting DHCP Problems

When looking at DHCP issues, there are generally two reasons you might run into problems:

- The port/module isn't getting an IP address from DHCP
- The port/module receives an IP address but some part of the information is incorrect or incomplete

DHCP works with four basic messages exchanged between the client and the DHCP server—Discover, Offer, Request, and Acknowledge. The DHCP message exchange works as follows:

Step 1   The client sends a Discover packet that has several requested fields.

Step 2   The DHCP server answers with an Offer packet, filling in those fields with the information it has.

Step 3   The client sends a Request packet confirming its receipt of the information.

Step 4   The DHCP server sends an Acknowledge packet to the client.

When the port/module sends its Discover packet, it requests the following information:

- IP address
- Subnet mask
- Default gateway
- DNS server
- Domain name
- Option 66
- Option 150
- ARP cache timeout

NOTE   Although the gateway requests both Option 66 and Option 150, only one of the two should be used. Option 66 provides the host name of the TFTP server, and Option 150 provides one or more IP addresses. You should use Option 150 unless you have a good reason not to because in CallManager version 3.2 and later, you can specify an array of two IP addresses for TFTP server redundancy.

Also, although Option 66 is designed to take a host name, the WS-X6624 and the WS-X6608 also attempt to interpret the name passed via Option 66 as an IP address. For example, if you configure Option 66 to be **callmanager.cisco.com**, the gateway attempts to resolve that name to an IP address using DNS. However, if Option 66 is set to an IP address, such as **10.1.1.1**, the gateway sees that this "name" is really an IP address, so it uses the IP address 10.1.1.1 without doing a DNS query.

Using a host name in Option 66 forces your voice gateways to rely on DNS for name resolution. Using Option 150 does not.

To determine that the WS-X6608 port has received its IP-related information, all you have to do is enter the **show port** *mod/port* command. Example 6-111 shows the port as not being registered.

Example 6-111 show port *Command Output Indicates an Unregistered Port*

```
Console (enable) show port 3/4
Port  Name                     Status      Vlan        Duplex Speed Type
----- --------------------     ----------  ----------  ------ ----- ------------
 3/4                           enabled     17          full   -     unknown

Port  DHCP    MAC-Address        IP-Address       Subnet-Mask
----- ------- ----------------   --------------   ---------------
 3/4  enable  00-01-c9-d8-55-77  10.192.17.109    255.255.255.0

Port  Call-Manager(s)   DHCP-Server     TFTP-Server     Gateway
----- ---------------   -------------   ------------    ---------------
 3/4  -                 172.18.112.11   172.18.112.17   10.192.17.254

Port  DNS-Server(s)    Domain
----- -------------    -------------------------------------------------
 3/4  161.44.15.250*   cisco.com
      161.44.21.250
(*): Primary

Port  CallManagerState DSP-Type
----- ---------------- --------
 3/4  notregistered    C549

Port  NoiseRegen NonLinearProcessing
----- ---------- -------------------
 3/4  -          -

Port  Trap     IfIndex
----- -------- -------
 3/4  disabled 1265
```

With this one command, you learn not only the basic IP information, such as IP address and subnet mask, but also the TFTP server and even registration status. If there is no IP information here, the port most likely failed to receive anything from DHCP. Also, you can see if DHCP is even enabled.

The same command can be used with the WS-X6624. Although the returned information is in a different format, the IP and registration information is the same. The **show port** command on the WS-X6624 returns the output shown in Example 6-112 (this example is of a registered module).

Example 6-112 **show port** *Command Output Indicates a Registered Port*

```
evoice-cat6k-6a (enable) show port 7
Port  Name                  Status    Vlan       Duplex Speed Type
----- --------------------- --------- ---------- ------ ----- ------------
 7/1                        onhook    400          full  64k FXS
 7/2                        onhook    400          full  64k FXS
 7/3                        onhook    400          full  64k FXS
 7/4                        onhook    400          full  64k FXS
 7/5                        onhook    400          full  64k FXS
 7/6                        onhook    400          full  64k FXS
 7/7                        onhook    400          full  64k FXS
 7/8                        onhook    400          full  64k FXS
 7/9                        onhook    400          full  64k FXS
 7/10                       onhook    400          full  64k FXS
 7/11                       onhook    400          full  64k FXS
 7/12                       onhook    400          full  64k FXS
 7/13                       onhook    400          full  64k FXS
 7/14                       onhook    400          full  64k FXS
 7/15                       onhook    400          full  64k FXS
 7/16                       onhook    400          full  64k FXS
 7/17                       onhook    400          full  64k FXS
 7/18                       onhook    400          full  64k FXS
 7/19                       onhook    400          full  64k FXS
 7/20                       onhook    400          full  64k FXS
 7/21                       onhook    400          full  64k FXS
 7/22                       onhook    400          full  64k FXS
 7/23                       onhook    400          full  64k FXS
 7/24                       onhook    400          full  64k FXS

Port    DHCP    MAC-Address        IP-Address       Subnet-Mask
------- ------- ------------------ ---------------- ----------------
7/1-24  enable  00-10-7b-00-13-de  10.123.9.15      255.255.255.0

Port    Call-Manager(s)    DHCP-Server       TFTP-Server       Gateway
------- ------------------ ----------------- ----------------- ----------------
7/1-24  10.123.9.2         10.123.9.2        10.123.9.2        10.123.9.1

Port    DNS-Server(s)      Domain
------- ------------------ -------------------------------------------------
7/1-24  10.123.9.2         evoice.com

Port    CallManagerState DSP-Type
------- ---------------- --------
7/1-24  registered       C549

Port    ToneLocal     Impedance InputGain(dB) OutputAtten(dB)
------- ------------- --------- ------------- ---------------
7/1-24  northamerica  600       0             0

Port    RingFreq Timing     Timing           Timing     Timing
        (Hz)     Digit(ms)  InterDigit(ms)   Pulse(ms)  PulseDigit(ms)
------- -------- ---------- ---------------- ---------- --------------
7/1-24  20       100        100              0          0
```

If the port does not seem to be receiving IP information, it is time to use the CLI Tracy troubleshooting tool. Refer to Chapter 3 for more information about how to use this utility. To begin, type the command **tracy_start** *mod port* from the command-line interface (CLI) in the Catalyst 6000.

NOTE	You should use the Windows Dick Tracy client utility whenever possible, but the port must have an IP address to use it. Therefore, CLI Tracy is the only version that works for troubleshooting this kind of problem. Limit the use of CLI Tracy to situations where the port/module does not have an IP address and therefore the Dick Tracy utility cannot be used.

From the command line in enable mode, enter **tracy_start** *mod port*. If the port is not contacting the DHCP server successfully, you see the information shown in Example 6-113 returned on the Catalyst CLI.

Example 6-113 *Output When the Catalyst WS-X6608 Port Is Not Successfully Contacting the DHCP Server*

```
dtl7-1-cat6000-a (enable) tracy_start 4 1



         | |             | |
         | |             | |
       | | |           | | |
       | | |           | | |
      | | | | |        | | | | |
      | | | | |        | | | | |
   . .| | | | | | | . . . . .| | | | | | | . . .
   . .: | | | | | | |: . . . .: | | | | | | |: . .
C i s c o    S y s t e m s
CAT6K Digital Gateway
APP Version : D004G300, DSP Version : D005B300, Built Sep 13 2000 15:06:02
Device Name : SDA0001C9D85577
02:38:26.620 (CFG) DHCP Timeout Waiting on Server, DHCPState = INIT
02:38:58.620 (CFG) DHCP Timeout Waiting on Server, DHCPState = INIT
02:39:02.620 (CFG) DHCP Timeout Waiting on Server, DHCPState = INIT
```

Example 6-114 shows the results for the WS-X6624.

Example 6-114 *Output When the Catalyst WS-X6624 Port Is Not Successfully Contacting DHCP Server*

```
   |                 |
   |                 |
       | |             | |
       | |             | |
      | | |           | | |
      | | |           | | |
     | | | | |        | | | | |
     | | | | |        | | | | |
   . .| | | | | | | . . . . .| | | | | | | . . .
   . .: | | | | | | |: . . . .: | | | | | | |: . .
C i s c o    S y s t e m s
CAT6K Analog Gateway
APP Version : A0020300, DSP Version : A0030300, Built Jun  1 2000 16:33:01

ELVIS>> 00:00:00.020 (XA) MAC Addr : 00-10-7B-00-13-DE
00:00:00.050 NMPTask:got message from XA Task
```

Example 6-114 *Output When the Catalyst WS-X6624 Port Is Not Successfully Contacting DHCP Server (Continued)*

```
00:00:00.050 (NMP) Open TCP Connection ip:7f010101
00:00:00.050 NMPTask:Send Module Slot Info
00:00:00.060 NMPTask:get DIAGCMD
00:00:00.160 (DSP) Test Begin -> Mask<0x00FFFFFF>
00:00:01.260 (DSP) Test Complete -> Results<0x00FFFFFF/0x00FFFFFF>
00:00:01.260 NMPTask:get VLANCONFIG
00:00:02.870 (CFG) Starting DHCP
00:00:02.870 (CFG) Booting DHCP for dynamic configuration.
00:00:06.570 (CFG) DHCP Request or Discovery Sent, DHCPState = INIT_REBOOT
00:00:06.570 (CFG) DHCP Server Response Processed, DHCPState = INIT_REBOOT
00:00:06.780 (CFG) IP Configuration Change!  Restarting now...
00:00:10.480 (CFG) DHCP Request or Discovery Sent, DHCPState = INIT
00:00:14.480 (CFG) DHCP Timeout Waiting on Server, DHCPState = INIT
00:00:22.480 (CFG) DHCP Timeout Waiting on Server, DHCPState = INIT
00:00:38.480 (CFG) DHCP Timeout Waiting on Server, DHCPState = INIT
```

These messages confirm your suspicion that the port is not getting a response from the DHCP server. Some of the possible reasons for this problem are as follows:

- The DHCP server could be down.

- The port could be in a VLAN that cannot reach the DHCP server.

- The DHCP Discover message is not being forwarded to the DHCP server.

To resolve these problems, start by making sure the DHCP server is up and running. If the VLAN is wrong, change it by entering **set vlan** *vlan_num mod/port*, where *vlan_num* is the correct VLAN number. After changing the VLAN for a port, it is usually best to reset the module to ensure that the change takes effect immediately. If you do not reset the module, the VLAN change might take several minutes to take effect.

If the DHCP server is not on the same VLAN as the WS-X6608 port or the WS-X6624 module, make sure the appropriate IP Helper addresses have been configured to forward the DHCP requests to the DHCP server. If you suspect that the router might not be forwarding the DHCP request, check it and add an IP Helper address if necessary. You do this by adding the command **ip helper-address** *x.x.x.x* to the appropriate interface on your router.

As soon as you have established connectivity between the requesting port and the DHCP server, the port should get its IP information. The **show port** *mod/port* command should display the IP information for the port now. Check the **CallManagerState** field to see if the port is registered or unregistered. If it shows unregistered, carefully examine the IP-related fields to make sure the port has been given complete and accurate information.

The Dick Tracy information should now show a successful DHCP attempt by the port, as shown in Example 6-115.

Example 6-115 *Output When the Catalyst WS-X6608 Port Successfully Contacts the DHCP Server*

```
Console (enable) tracy_start 4 1
00:09:05.620 (CFG) DHCP Server Response Processed, DHCPState = REQUESTING
00:09:05.620 (CFG) DHCP Server Response Processed, DHCPState = BOUND
00:09:05.620 (CFG) Requesting DNS Resolution of CiscoCM1
00:09:05.620 (CFG) DNS Error on Resolving TFTP Server Name.
00:09:05.620 (CFG) TFTP Server IP Set by DHCP Option 150 = 10.123.9.2
```

In this example, the debug information shows that the TFTP server address was set using Option 150. It also shows the IP address that was specified. The WS-X6624 returns identical information, as shown in Example 6-116.

Example 6-116 *Output When the Catalyst WS-X6624 Port Successfully Contacts the DHCP Server*

```
Console (enable) tracy_start 4 1
00:09:05.620 (CFG) DHCP Server Response Processed, DHCPState = REQUESTING
00:09:05.620 (CFG) DHCP Server Response Processed, DHCPState = BOUND
00:09:05.620 (CFG) Requesting DNS Resolution of CiscoCM1
00:09:05.620 (CFG) DNS Error on Resolving TFTP Server Name.
00:09:05.620 (CFG) TFTP Server IP Set by DHCP Option 150 = 10.123.9.2
```

Incorrect or missing information is still a potential problem. Any network device must have an IP address and a correct subnet mask. If the device must communicate with devices on another network, it must have a default gateway. If the device will communicate with other devices by host name, it needs a DNS server specified to resolve those names. Make sure everything is correct and complete, or TFTP and CallManager connectivity might not succeed.

Troubleshooting TFTP Problems

For the WS-X6608 port and the WS-X6624 module to register to a CallManager, the port or module must first download a configuration file from the TFTP server. The module determines the TFTP server's IP address from the IP address information provided by the DHCP server in Option 66 or Option 150 just as an IP phone does.

So if the information appears to be complete and correct, what could be preventing the port or module from getting its TFTP file? The most common causes are as follows:

- No bidirectional network connectivity exists between the port and the TFTP server.
- No bidirectional network connectivity exists between the port and the DNS server.
- The TFTP server is not running.
- No DNS server exists for the device to resolve a host name when one is used for the TFTP server.
- The DNS server does not have an entry to resolve the name of the TFTP server if host names are being used for TFTP.

The quickest way to determine what the device has identified as the problem is with CLI Tracy. Start CLI Tracy by entering the **tracy_start** *mod port* command. If the WS-X6608 port or WS-X6624 module cannot reach the TFTP server, or if it does not get a response from the TFTP server, the error message in Example 6-117 appears.

Example 6-117 *Output When the Catalyst WS-X6608 Port Cannot Communicate with the TFTP Server*

```
Console (enable) tracy_start 4 1
00:09:05.620 (CFG) Requesting 0001C9D85577.cnf.xml File From TFTP Server
00:09:18.620 (CFG) TFTP Error: Timeout Awaiting Server Response for .cnf.xml File!
```

Another problem could be that the requested file is not found on the TFTP server. If that is the problem, the error message in Example 6-118 appears.

Example 6-118 *Output When the File Requested by the Catalyst WS-X6608 Cannot Be Located on the TFTP Server*

```
Console (enable) tracy_start 4 1
00:00:06.560 (CFG) TFTP Server IP Set by DHCP Option 150 = 172.18.106.58
00:00:06.560 (CFG) TFTP Server Backup IP Set by DHCP Option 150 = 172.18.106.59
00:00:06.560 (CFG) Requesting 0030F2709105.cnf.xml File From TFTP Server
00:00:26.560 (CFG) TFTP Error: Timeout Awaiting Server Response for File
0030F2709105.cnf.xml!
00:00:26.560 (CFG) Try the Secondary TFTP Server.
00:00:26.560 (CFG) Requesting 0030F2709105.cnf.xml File From Secondary TFTP Server
00:00:46.560 (CFG) TFTP Error: Timeout Awaiting Server Response for File
0030F2709105.cnf.xml!
```

Example 6-119 shows the same error message generated by the WS-X6624.

Example 6-119 *Output When the File Requested by the Catalyst WS-X6624 Cannot Be Located on the TFTP Server*

```
Console (enable) tracy_start 4 1
00:00:02.240 (CFG) TFTP Server IP Set by DHCP Option 150 = 172.18.106.58
00:00:02.240 (CFG) TFTP Server Backup IP Set by DHCP Option 150 = 172.18.106.59
00:00:02.250 (CFG) Requesting 00D097385F65.cnf.xml File From TFTP Server
00:00:22.250 (CFG) TFTP Error: Timeout Awaiting Server Response for File
00D097385F65.cnf.xml!
00:00:22.250 (CFG) Try the Secondary TFTP Server.
00:00:22.250 (CFG) Requesting 00D097385F65.cnf.xml File From Secondary TFTP Server
00:00:42.250 (CFG) TFTP Error: Timeout Awaiting Server Response for File
00D097385F65.cnf.xml!
```

You see trace information in the Tracy ouput in addition to what is shown in the preceding examples. If you do not understand what some of the debug information means, don't worry; most of this debug information is designed for development engineers.

To give you a feel for what the full debug looks like, Example 6-120 provides the full debug information for the WS-X6608 and the WS-X6624 to help you understand how these messages would be extracted from the plethora of data.

Example 6-120 *Catalyst WS-X6608 Debug Output*

```
Console (enable) tracy_start 4 1
             |             |
             |             |
             |             |
           | | |         | | |
           | | |         | | |
          | | | | |     | | | | |
          | | | | |     | | | | |
    ..:|||||||||:....:|||||||||:..
    C i s c o   S y s t e m s
    CAT6K Digital Gateway
    APP Version : D00403010035, DSP Version : D005L031, Built Dec  8 2001 12:38:20
    Device Name :
    00:00:00.060 (XA) MAC Addr : 00-30-F2-70-91-05
    00:00:00.060 (NMP) Received message from XA Task
    00:00:00.060 (NMP) Opening TCP Connection to IP 127.1.1.1 (0x7F010101)
    00:00:00.070 (NMP) Sending Module Slot Info
    00:00:00.070 (NMP) Received DIAGCMD
    00:00:00.070 (NMP) Sending DIAGCMD TCP ACK
    00:00:00.070 SPAN: Transmit clock slaved to span 7
    00:00:00.070 SPAN: Transmit clock set to internal osc.
    00:00:00.620 (DSP) Test Begin -> Mask<0x00FFFFFF> Framer<T1>
    00:00:01.610 SPAN: Transmit clock slaved to span 7
    00:00:01.610 SPAN: Transmit clock set to internal osc.
    00:00:01.620 (DSP) Test Complete -> Results<0x00FFFFFF/0x00FFFFFF>
    00:00:03.260 (NMP) Received VLANCONFIG
    00:00:06.300 (CFG) Starting DHCP
    00:00:06.300 (CFG) Booting DHCP for dynamic configuration.
    00:00:06.560 (CFG) DHCP Request Sent, DHCPState = INIT_REBOOT
    00:00:06.560 (CFG) DHCP  dtmf_on = 0, dtmf_off = 0
    00:00:06.560 (CFG) DHCP Server ACK Processed, DHCPState = BOUND
    00:00:06.560 (CFG) DHCP  dtmf_on = 0, dtmf_off = 0
    00:00:06.560 (CFG) Requesting DNS Resolution of CiscoCM1
    00:00:06.560 (CFG) DNS Unable to resolve TFTP Server Name CiscoCM1.
    00:00:06.560 (CFG) TFTP Server IP Set by DHCP Option 150 = 172.18.106.58
    00:00:06.560 (CFG) TFTP Server Backup IP Set by DHCP Option 150 = 172.18.106.59
    00:00:06.560 (CFG) Requesting 0030F2709105.cnf.xml File From TFTP Server
    00:00:26.560 (CFG) TFTP Error: Timeout Awaiting Server Response for File
      0030F2709105.cnf.xml!
    00:00:26.560 (CFG) Try the Secondary TFTP Server.
    00:00:26.560 (CFG) Requesting 0030F2709105.cnf.xml File From Secondary TFTP Server
    00:00:46.560 (CFG) TFTP Error: Timeout Awaiting Server Response for File
      0030F2709105.cnf.xml!
```

Example 6-121 shows the full WS-X6624 debug.

Example 6-121 *Catalyst WS-X6624 Debug Output*

```
Console (enable) tracy_start 4 1
             |             |
             |             |
             |             |
           | | |         | | |
           | | |         | | |
          | | | | |     | | | | |
          | | | | |     | | | | |
    ..:|||||||||:....:|||||||||:..
    C i s c o   S y s t e m s
```

Example 6-121 *Catalyst WS-X6624 Debug Output (Continued)*

```
CAT6K Analog Gateway
APP Version : A00203010028, DSP Version : A003L031, Built Dec  8 2001 12:41:35
Device Name :
00:00:00.020 (XA) MAC Addr : 00-D0-97-38-5F-65
00:00:00.050 (NMP) Received message from XA Task
00:00:00.050 (NMP) Opening TCP Connection to IP 127.1.1.1 (0x7F010101)
00:00:00.060 (NMP) Sending Module Slot Info
00:00:00.060 (NMP) Received DIAGCMD
00:00:00.170 (DSP) Test Begin -> Mask<0x00FFFFFF>
00:00:01.270 (DSP) Test Complete -> Results<0x00FFFFFF/0x00FFFFFF>
00:00:01.270 (NMP) Received VLANCONFIG
00:00:02.020 (CFG) Starting DHCP
00:00:02.020 (CFG) Booting DHCP for dynamic configuration.
00:00:02.240 (CFG) DHCP Request Sent, DHCPState = INIT_REBOOT
00:00:02.240 (CFG) DHCP   dtmf_on = 0, dtmf_off = 0
00:00:02.240 (CFG) DHCP Server ACK Processed, DHCPState = BOUND
00:00:02.240 (CFG) DHCP   dtmf_on = 0, dtmf_off = 0
00:00:02.240 (CFG) Requesting DNS Resolution of CiscoCM1
00:00:02.240 (CFG) DNS Unable to resolve TFTP Server Name CiscoCM1.
00:00:02.240 (CFG) TFTP Server IP Set by DHCP Option 150 = 172.18.106.58
00:00:02.240 (CFG) TFTP Server Backup IP Set by DHCP Option 150 = 172.18.106.59
00:00:02.250 (CFG) Requesting 00D097385F65.cnf.xml File From TFTP Server
00:00:22.250 (CFG) TFTP Error: Timeout Awaiting Server Response for File
   00D097385F65.cnf.xml!
00:00:22.250 (CFG) Try the Secondary TFTP Server.
00:00:22.250 (CFG) Requesting 00D097385F65.cnf.xml File From Secondary TFTP Server
00:00:42.250 (CFG) TFTP Error: Timeout Awaiting Server Response for File
   00D097385F65.cnf.xml!
00:00:42.250 (CFG) Try the Secondary TFTP Server.
00:00:42.250 (DelBugTrap) Resetting in 30 second(s), Code<0x0807>
00:00:42.250 (CFG) Requesting 00D097385F65.cnf.xml File From Secondary TFTP Server
00:01:02.250 (CFG) TFTP Error: Timeout Awaiting Server Response for File
   00D097385F65.cnf.xml!
```

You can also observe the error from the point of view of the TFTP service on CallManager. Some errors are reported in the Event Log while other require you to look in the TFTP trace file. By default, the **Alarm Event Level** on the Alarm Configuration page in CallManager Serviceability (**Alarm > Configuration >** *select the TFTP server* **> Cisco TFTP**) for the TFTP service is set to **Error**. This is sufficient to see errors like when a file is not found.

Example 6-122 shows an Application Event Log (from the Windows Event Viewer) error message indicating that a TFTP request for the file SDA0001C9D85577.cnf.xml was not serviced because the file was not found.

Example 6-122 *Event Log Message Indicating a File Is Not Found*

```
Error: UNKNOWN_ALARM:kServingFileWarning
  ErrorNumber: 1
  FileName: SDA0001C9D85577.cnf.xml
  IPAddress_Port: 10.26.22.26:49787
  Mode: octet
  OpCode: 1
  Reason: File not found inside tftp() of CTFTPConnect class
```

This message also provides the IP address of the requesting port and the IP address of the TFTP server. The port failed to get its configuration file because the file was not found on the TFTP server. This can occur if that port's MAC address is not correctly entered into the CallManager database.

Another indication that the port is not getting its TFTP file is the reset information appearing in the console. This is not the Tracy debug information. This is a normal error indication that appears in the console, indicating a problem. Example 6-123 shows what appears every 2 minutes if the port cannot contact the TFTP server.

Example 6-123 *Catalyst 6000 CLI Output for WS-X6608 or WS-X6624 Port Resets*

```
2000 Apr 14 19:24:08 %SYS-4-MODHPRESET:Host process (860) 7/1 got reset
  asynchronously
2000 Apr 14 19:26:05 %SYS-4-MODHPRESET:Host process (860) 7/1 got reset
  asynchronously
2000 Apr 14 19:28:02 %SYS-4-MODHPRESET:Host process (860) 7/1 got reset
  asynchronously
```

Review the areas of potential problems, and resolve them so that the port can get its TFTP configuration file. Remember to check for network issues and confirm that the TFTP server is up and running. Using the CLI Tracy utility, you can find out exactly why the port cannot successfully reach the TFTP server.

Troubleshooting Registration Problems

If the port successfully received its configuration file, it should be ready to register to CallManager. As shown in earlier examples, the **show port** *mod/port* command provides many details about the port, including its registration state. If the **show port** command shows an unregistered state, some additional investigation must take place.

You are troubleshooting only registration now because registration cannot take place unless a TFTP configuration file is received. You must know that the TFTP configuration file has been received before proceeding.

As soon as the WS-X6608 port or WS-X6624 module has successfully received an IP address and downloaded its configuration file, you should use the Dick Tracy utility on a separate PC instead of using CLI Tracy to minimize the possibility of causing problems on the Catalyst 6000 switch.

A possible registration problem could be that the application load specified in the configuration file is not found on the TFTP server. You see all this registration information from the Dick Tracy utility by just connecting to the module. In this case, Dick Tracy clearly shows that the TFTP server reported that the file is not found, as demonstrated in Example 6-124.

Example 6-124 *Dick Tracy Report Indicating That the TFTP Server Cannot Find the Requested File*

```
00:00:07.390 GMSG: CCM#0 CPEvent = REGISTER_REQ --> CPState = SentRegister
00:00:08.010 GMSG: TFTP Request for application load D00403011300
00:00:08.010 GMSG: CCM#0 CPEvent = LOADID --> CPState = AppLoadRequest
00:00:08.010 GMSG: *** TFTP Error: File Not Found ***
00:00:08.010 GMSG: CCM#0 CPEvent = LOAD_UPDATE --> CPState = LoadResponse
```

You can see that the port is requesting application load **D00403011300**. This file is not found by the port. Further investigation usually reveals that the specified file does not exist on the TFTP server or that the filename is incorrectly specified in CallManager. The same problem can occur when a new application load needs to get its corresponding DSP load. If the new DSP load is not found, a similar message appears.

What are some other reasons that registration might be failing? The most common causes are as follows:

- No bidirectional network connectivity exists between the port and the CallManager server.

- The CallManager server is not running.

- If a host name is used for the CallManager server, the WS-X6608 port must have a DNS server to resolve the name for it.

- There might not be bidirectional network connectivity between the port and the DNS server.

- The DNS server might not have an entry to resolve the name of the CallManager server if host names are being used for CallManager servers.

After you have a registered port or module, you can begin looking into other potential problems. Now that you have looked at the common areas that the WS-X6624 and WS-X6608 share, the next section focuses on the WS-X6608.

Catalyst WS-X6608 T1/E1 Digital Gateway Configuration

The Catalyst WS-X6608 T1/E1 module is essentially a big digital signal processor (DSP) farm with a T1 or E1 framer. Because of its architecture, each of the eight ports of the WS-X6608 can be provisioned as a T1/E1 interface, conference bridge, or transcoder. For example, you can have three ports as T1 gateway ports, three conference bridge ports, and two transcoder ports.

Most of the configuration for this module is performed in CallManager Administration. CallManager tells each port if it is a T1/E1 interface, a conference bridge, or a transcoder. If it is a T1/E1 interface, CallManager controls which protocols are used, as well as several other key parameters. For any of these configuration parameters to have meaning, the module must be registered to CallManager.

NOTE	The T1 and E1 versions are different hardware modules altogether. The basic functionality, however, is the same in terms of how they register and the services they provide. You can determine which model you have by looking at the module's front panel or by issuing the command **show module** from the Catalyst 6000 CLI. You see WS-X6608-T1 for the T1 module and WS-X6608-E1 for the E1 module.

Now that you are familiar with power, DHCP, TFTP, and registration issues, you can investigate some configuration problems that can occur.

Troubleshooting Configuration Issues

After your gateway is registered, many other problems can arise. After a gateway like the WS-X6608 registers, it does its job of bridging the packet-switched world and the circuit-switched world. It must speak the language of the circuit-switched world to work properly, and this is where configuration problems often occur.

Some typical problems that you might fix with configuration changes are as follows:

- The D-channel is down
- Number presentation (calling ID, calling name, and so on)
- Unexpected resets
- Numbering type mismatches
- Dropped calls

There are other issues as well. The following issues are deserving of in-depth discussion, so they are covered in other chapters:

- **Echo**—Covered in Chapter 7, "Voice Quality"
- **Bad audio**—Covered in Chapter 7
- **Call routing**—Covered in Chapter 9, "Call Routing"

First, take a look at the many fields that can be configured on a T1/E1 PRI gateway. These fields are configured in CallManager Administration (select **Device > Gateway >** *find and select a gateway*). Table 6-35 shows the different fields and gives information about their function and use.

Table 6-35 *T1/E1 WS-X6608 Port Configuration*

Field	Description and Usage Information
MAC Address	Specify the MAC address. The MAC address identifies the WS-X6608 port's hardware-based device name.
Description	Provide a simple description that can be used to better identify the port. Make this as descriptive as possible to help you identify this gateway among the potentially dozens of gateways you might have in your system.

Table 6-35   *T1/E1 WS-X6608 Port Configuration (Continued)*

Field	Description and Usage Information
Device Pool	Choose a device pool. The device pool specifies a collection of properties for this device, including CallManager group, date/time group, and region.
Network Locale	Choose the locale associated with the gateway. The network locale contains a definition of the tones and cadences used by the device in a specific geographic area.
Media Resource Group List	Choose a media resource group list. This list provides a prioritized grouping of media resource groups. An application chooses the required media resource, such as an MOH server, from among the available media resources according to the priority order defined in a media resource group list.
Location	Choose the appropriate location for this device. The location specifies the total bandwidth available for calls to and from this location. For more information about locations-based call admission control, refer to Chapter 13, "Call Admission Control."
AAR Group	Choose the automated alternate routing (AAR) group for this device. The AAR group provides the prefix digits used to route calls that are otherwise blocked due to insufficient bandwidth. An AAR group setting of **None** specifies that no rerouting of blocked calls will be attempted. Refer to Chapter 13 for additional information about AAR.
Load Information	The value you enter here overrides the default firmware load for this type of gateway.
PRI Protocol Type	Choose the ISDN switch type to which the gateway is connected. The switch type on both sides of a PRI connection must match for ISDN signaling to work properly. For E1 PRI spans, three options exist: • **PRI AUSTRALIAN**—Australian TS014 switch • **PRI EURO**—European NET5 switch • **ISO QSIG**—ISO Q.Sig switch type. Used to connect to other PBXs that support the ISO Q.Sig standard. T1 PRI spans have several options, depending on the carrier or switch: • **4ESS**—AT&T 4ESS Class 4 switch. Generally only used to connect to Interexchange carriers (IXC). • **5E8**—AT&T 5ESS Class 5 switch software version 8. Note that some 5ESS switches might use software that complies with the National ISDN (NI2) standard. Ask your service provider what switch type they are using on their 5ESS before assuming the switch type is 5ESS. • **5E8 CUSTOM**—A variant of the 5ESS switch type used on some PBXs.

continues

Table 6-35 *T1/E1 WS-X6608 Port Configuration (Continued)*

Field	Description and Usage Information
PRI Protocol Type *(continued)*	• **5E8 INTECOME**—A variant of the 5ESS switch type used on Intecom PBXs
	• **5E8 TELEOS**—A variant of the 5ESS switch type used on Teleos (Madge) ISDN switches.
	• **5E9**—AT&T 5ESS Class 5 switch software version 9.
	• **DMS-100**—Nortel DMS-100 Class 5 Switch. Many PBXs including Nortel PBXs emulate the DMS-100 switch.
	• **DMS-250**—Nortel DMS-250 Class 4 Switch.
	• **ETSI SC**—Uses the same protocol as the European NET5 switch, but on a T1 instead of an E1. This switch type is common in Asia.
	• **ISO QSIG**—ISO Q.Sig switch type. Used to connect to other PBXs that support the ISO Q.Sig standard.
	• **NI2**—Also known as National ISDN switch type. One of the most commonly used switch types in North America and on many PBXs.
	• **NTT**—Japanese NTT switch type.
Protocol Side	Choose the appropriate ISDN protocol side. This setting specifies whether the gateway connects to a Central Office/ Network device or to a User device.
	Make sure the two ends of the PRI connection use opposite settings. For example, if you connect to a PBX and the PBX uses **User** as its protocol side, choose **Network** for this device. Typically, you use **User** for central office connections.
	Note that on some devices, the protocol side configuration is different than on CallManager. In CallManager you define which protocol side the gateway is going to use. On some PBXs you configure which protocol side the connected device is using. If you are unsure of the terminology being used on the connected device, consult the documentation for that device or just try both **Network** and **User** to see if one of the two come up.
Channel Selection Order	Choose the order in which channels or ports are enabled, from first (lowest-number port) to last (highest-number port) or from last to first.
	Valid entries include **Top Down** (first to last) and **Bottom Up** (last to first). You should set this to be the opposite of the device connected to the port. For example, if your service provider is sending calls **Top Down**, then configure the port for **Bottom Up**, and vice versa.

Table 6-35 *T1/E1 WS-X6608 Port Configuration (Continued)*

Field	Description and Usage Information
Channel IE Type	Choose one of the following values to specify whether channel selection is presented as a B-channel or a slot map: **Timeslot Number**—Specifies the B-channel to use for a call as a number. For example, for a call on B-channel 5, the Channel IE contains the number 5. **Continuous Number**—Specifies the B-channel to use for a call as a number, but does not take the D-channel timeslot into account. This option only applies to an E1 PRI where the D-channel is on timeslot 16. When this option is selected, the timeslot numbers are sent as 1-30 instead of 1-15 and 17-31. **Slotmap**—Specifies the B-channel to use for a call as a slot map. A *slot map* is a field that can exist in an ISDN Q.931 Channel IE which uses a bit mask to represent all the channels. Using a slot map, an endpoint can use more than one B-channel for a call. CallManager never uses more than one B-channel for a call. **Use Number When 1B**—Specifies the B-channel to use for a call as a timeslot number for one B-channel but is a slot map if more than one B-channel is required for the call.
PCM Type	Specify the digital encoding format. Choose one of the following formats: • **μ-law**—Use for North America and Japan • **A-law**—Use for Europe and the rest of the world.
Delay for first restart (1/8 sec ticks)	Enter the rate at which the spans are brought into service. The delay occurs when many PRI spans are enabled on a system and the **Inhibit Restarts at PRI Initialization** checkbox is deselected. For example, set the first five cards to 0, and set the next five cards to 16 (wait 2 seconds before bringing them into service). This spaces out the initialization of the PRI line.
Delay between restarts (1/8 sec ticks)	Enter the time between restarts. The delay occurs when a PRI RESTART is sent if the **Inhibit Restarts** checkbox is unselected.
Inhibit restarts at PRI initialization	A RESTART message confirms the status of the ports on a PRI span. If RESTARTs are not sent, CallManager assumes that the ports are in service. When the D-channel successfully connects with another PRI D-channel, it sends RESTARTs when this checkbox is not selected. If you see problems where B-channels are being placed out of service for an unexplained reason, try selecting this checkbox. Some switches do not properly support RESTART messages and selecting this checkbox inhibits CallManager from sending them.

continues

Table 6-35 *T1/E1 WS-X6608 Port Configuration (Continued)*

Field	Description and Usage Information
Enable status poll	Select the checkbox to view the status of the B-channels in the CCM trace files.
Significant Digits (release 3.3 and later)	Choose the number of significant digits to collect, from 0 to 32. CallManager counts significant digits starting from the right (the last digit) of the number called.
	If **All** is selected, no digits are discarded for inbound calls.
	This parameter applies to CallManager release 3.3 and later.
Num Digits (pre-release 3.3)	Choose the number of significant digits to collect, from 0 to 32. CallManager counts significant digits starting from the right (the last digit) of the number called.
	Use this field if you select the **Sig Digits** checkbox. Use it to process incoming calls and to indicate the number of digits starting from the last digit of the called number used to route calls coming into the gateway. See **Sig Digits** and **Prefix DN**.
	Use the Significant Digits parameter in place of the Num Digits parameter in CallManager release 3.3 and later.
Sig Digits (pre-release 3.3)	Select or deselect this box depending on whether you want to limit digit collection to only a specific number of significant digits.
	Significant digits represents the number of final digits a PRI span should retain on inbound calls. A trunk with significant digits enabled truncates all but the final few digits of the address provided by an inbound call.
	If the checkbox is deselected, CallManager does not truncate the inbound number. If the checkbox is selected, you also need to choose the number of significant digits to collect by using the **Num Digits** field.
	This parameter is no longer present in CallManager release 3.3 and later.
Calling Search Space	Choose the appropriate calling search space for incoming calls through the gateway. A calling search space designates a collection of partitions that are searched to determine how a called number should be routed.
	If you are having problems receiving calls from the PSTN, ensure that the calling search space for the gateway can reach the partition for the end devices. For more information about partitions and calling search spaces, refer to Chapter 9.

Table 6-35   *T1/E1 WS-X6608 Port Configuration (Continued)*

Field	Description and Usage Information
AAR Calling Search Space	Chose the appropriate calling search space for inbound calls when being redirected through the user of the AAR feature when there is insufficient locations bandwith available.
	Refer to Chapter 13 for more information about locations-based CAC and AAR.
Prefix DN	Enter the prefix digits that are appended to the digits that this trunk receives on incoming calls. CallManager adds prefix digits after first truncating the number in accordance with the Num Digits setting.
	Note that this is parameter only applies to inbound calls. It does not apply to outbound calls.
	This parameter, in conjunction with **Sig Digits** and **Num Digits**, can be used to transform the called party number from the PSTN to a format that matches your internal dial plan.
	For example, if your service provider is sending the called party number with digits 972555XXXX, but your internal extension range is 6XXXX, select the **Sig Digits** checkbox, set **Num Digits** to 4 so that only the last four digits are used, and then set **Prefix DN** to 6 to prepend the 6 to the last four digits.
Calling Party Presentation	Controls the behavior of the presentation bit in the calling party number IE in a Q.931 SETUP message. When the presentation bit is set to **Restricted**, the calling party number is still delivered to the PSTN; however, the presentation bit causes the far-end switch to not present the number to the called party. The caller ID display of the called party typically displays a message such as "Private."
	In CallManager 3.3 and later, there is an option for **Default**. If set to **Default**, the presentation bit is set on a per-route pattern basis.

continues

Table 6-35 *T1/E1 WS-X6608 Port Configuration (Continued)*

Field	Description and Usage Information
Calling Party Selection	Any outbound call on a gateway can send calling party number number information. Choose which directory number is sent:
	Originator—Sends the directory number of the calling device.
	First Redirect Number—Sends the directory number of the first redirecting device.
	Last Redirect Number—Sends the directory number of the last redirecting device.
	First Redirect Party (External)—Sends the directory number of the first redirecting device with the external phone mask applied.
	Last Redirect Party (External)—Sends the directory number of the last redirecting device with the external phone mask applied.
	If only one device has redirected a call, the first redirecting device and the last redirecting device are the same. If no device redirected the call, the calling number of the originator is used.
Called party IE number type unknown	Choose the value for the numbering type field in Q.931 Called Party Number information element.
	You might need to change the default in Europe because CallManager does not recognize European national dialing patterns. You can also change this setting when connecting to PBXs using routing as a non-national type number.
	Choose one of the following options:
	• **Cisco CallManager**—CallManager automatically sets the numbering type. If the called party number matches a pattern with the @ wildcard, the numbering type is set appropriately based on the dialed number. If the called party number does not match a route pattern with the @ wildcard, the numbering type is set to **Unknown**.
	• **International**—Use when you are dialing outside the dialing plan for your country.
	• **National**—Use when you are dialing within the dialing plan for your country.
	• **Subscriber**—Use when you are dialing within a private network or as required by a PBX.
	• **Unknown**—If the dialing plan is unknown, try the Unknown setting.

Table 6-35 *T1/E1 WS-X6608 Port Configuration (Continued)*

Field	Description and Usage Information
Calling party IE number type unknown	Choose the value for the numbering type field in Q.931 Calling Party Number information element. You might need to change the default in Europe because CallManager does not recognize European national dialing patterns. You can also change this setting when connecting to PBXs using routing as a nonnational type number. Choose one of the following options: • **Cisco CallManager**—CallManager automatically sets the numbering type. • **International**—Use when you are dialing outside the dialing plan for your country. • **National**—Use when you are dialing within the dialing plan for your country. • **Subscriber**—Use when you are dialing within a private network or as required by a PBX. • **Unknown**—If the dialing plan is unknown, use the Unknown setting.
Called Numbering Plan	Choose the value for the numbering plan field in Q.931 Called Party Number information element. You might need to change the default in Europe because CallManager does not recognize European national dialing patterns. You can also change this setting when connecting to PBXs using routing as a nonnational type number. Choose one of the following options: • **Cisco CallManager**—CallManager automatically sets the numbering plan. If the called party number matched a pattern with the @ wildcard, the numbering plan is set appropriately based on the dialed number. If the called party number does not match a route pattern with the @ wildcard, the numbering plan is set to Unknown. • **ISDN**—Use when you are dialing outside the dialing plan for your country. • **National Standard**—Use when you are dialing within the dialing plan for your country. • **Private**—Use when you are dialing within a private network. • **Unknown**—If the dialing plan is unknown, use the Unknown setting.

continues

Table 6-35 *T1/E1 WS-X6608 Port Configuration (Continued)*

Field	Description and Usage Information
Calling Numbering Plan	Choose the value for the numbering plan field in Q.931 Calling Party Number information element.
	You might need to change the default in Europe because CallManager does not recognize European national dialing patterns. You can also change this setting when connecting to PBXs using routing as a nonnational type number.Choose the value for the numbering plan field in Q.931 Calling Party Number information element.
	You might need to change the default in Europe because CallManager does not recognize European national dialing patterns. You can also change this setting when connecting to PBXs using routing as a nonnational type number.
	Choose one of the following options:
	• **Cisco CallManager**—CallManager automatically sets the numbering plan.
	• **ISDN**—Use when you are dialing outside the dialing plan for your country.
	• **National Standard**—Use when you are dialing within the dialing plan for your country.
	• **Private**—Use when you are dialing within a private network.
	• **Unknown**—If the dialing plan is unknown, use the Unknown setting.
Number of digits to strip	Choose the number of digits to strip on outbound calls, from 0 to 32. For example, suppose 99725551234 is dialed and the number of digits to strip is 1. In this example, CallManager strips 9 from the outbound number and sends 9725551234.
Caller ID DN	Enter the pattern you want to use for caller ID, from 0 to 24 digits.
	For example, in North America:
	972555XXXX = variable caller ID, where X equals an extension number. The CO usually appends the number with the area code if you do not specify it.
	9725555000 = fixed caller ID, where you want the corporate number to be sent instead of the exact extension from which the call is placed.
	For more information about the **Caller ID DN** parameter and how transformation masks work, refer to Chapter 9

Table 6-35 *T1/E1 WS-X6608 Port Configuration (Continued)*

Field	Description and Usage Information
Display IE Delivery	Select the checkbox to enable delivery of the Display information element in SETUP, NOTIFY, and CONNECT messages for the calling and called party name delivery service. The default leaves the checkbox unselected.
Redirecting Number IE Delivery - Outbound	Select the checkbox to include the Redirecting Number IE in the SETUP message to indicate the first redirecting number and the redirecting reason of the call when call forwarding occurs.
	This setting applies to the SETUP message only on all protocols for digital access gateways.
	This is often used with voice mail systems where the original called number must be retained for presentation to the voice mail system.
Redirecting Number IE Delivery - Inbound	Select the checkbox to accept a Redirecting Number IE in a SETUP message. When present, the redirecting number becomes the original called party number for a call. This means that if a call forwards to voice mail, the information in the Redirecting Number IE is presented to the voice mail system as the original called party number.
	This setting applies to the SETUP message only on all protocols for digital access gateways.
Send Extra Leading Character In Display IE	This setting is used only when connecting to a Nortel PBX. Nortel PBXs using the DMS100 switch type expect the first byte of the display IE to be a character that indicates additional information about the display name, such as whether the name is the calling party name or the called party name.
	Select the checkbox to send a special leading character in the outbound Display IE. Deselect the checkbox to send the Display IE without modifying it.
	If the first character of the display name is missing when sending a call to a Nortel PBX, select this checkbox.
Setup non-ISDN Progress Indicator IE Enable	Enable this setting only if users are not receiving ringback tones on outbound calls. The default leaves this setting disabled (unselected).
	When this setting is enabled, CallManager sends Q.931 Setup messages with the Progress Indicator information element set to **origination address is non-ISDN**.
	This message notifies the destination device that the CallManager gateway is non-ISDN and that the destination device should play in-band ringback.
	This setting is usually enabled for CallManagers that connect to PBXs through digital gateways.

continues

Table 6-35 *T1/E1 WS-X6608 Port Configuration (Continued)*

Field	Description and Usage Information
Interface Identifier Present	Select the checkbox to indicate that an interface identifier is present. By default, CallManager leaves this checkbox unselected. This setting applies only to the DMS100 protocol for digital access gateways in the Channel Identification information element of the SETUP, CALL PROCEEDING, ALERTING, and CONNECT messages.
Interface Identifier Value	Enter the value obtained from the PBX provider. This field applies to the DMS100 protocol only and is only used if the **Interface Identifier Present** checkbox is selected. Valid values range from 0 to 255.
Country Code	Choose the country in which the gateway is located to determine the frequency and cadence of call progress tones such as ringback and busy tones. This parameter is only available in CallManager 3.0 and 3.1. In CallManager 3.2 and later, use the **Network Locale** parameter to select the progress tones to use.

Table 6-36 shows the product-specific settings for this gateway.

Table 6-36 *T1/E1 Product-specific Settings*

Field	Description and Usage Information
Clock Reference	Specifies from where the master clock is derived. Normally this is the network because the CO is typically the master clock.
TX-Level CSU	This parameter only applies to T1 PRIs. Specifies the transmit level based on the distance between the gateway and the nearest repeater. The default is full power (0 dB). Other choices are 7.5dB, –15dB, and –22.5dB.
FDL Channel	This parameter only applies to T1 PRIs. Determines what, if any, facility data link (FDL) the span supports. The FDL is a maintenance channel that allows remote troubleshooting of link layer problems and remote monitoring of the link's performance statistics.
Framing	Determines the span's multiframe format. This is typically Extended Super Frame (ESF) for a T1 PRI and cyclical redundancy check #4 (CRC4) for an E1 PRI.
Audio Signal Adjustment into IP Network	Specifies the gain or loss applied to the received audio signal from the PSTN or PBX to which the gateway is connected. Use this parameter to increase or decrease the volume level heard by the IP phone user from the PSTN.

Table 6-36   *T1/E1 Product-specific Settings (Continued)*

Field	Description and Usage Information
Zero Suppression	Determines how the T1 or E1 span electrically codes binary 1s and 0s on the wire. This is also referred to as the line coding selection. This should be B8ZS on a T1 and HDB3 on an E1.
Digit On Duration	The length of time a DTMF digit is played out towards the PSTN.
Interdigit Duration	The amount of time the gateway waits between digits when playing out a string of DTMF digits.
Adaptive Gain Control Enable	Causes the gateway to automatically boost or attenuate the signal level from the PSTN to keep the signal level constant. Note that this option may introduce echo and should not be used unless the gateway is connected to an IVR or voice mail system.
SNMP Community String	Sets the SNMP community string for the gateway to allow polling of SNMP statistics directory from the gateway.
Debug Port Enable	Used by Cisco development engineering and should not be changed.
Hold Tone Silence Duration	Specifies the amount of time between tones when using tone on hold.

The Gateway Configuration page also has a section for Fax and Modem Parameters and Playout Delay Parameters. These are discussed in Chapter 8, "Fax Machines and Modems."

Hopefully the descriptions have shed some light on the multitude of fields you can configure. Once you have the gateway configured, you ensure the D-channel is established.

Getting the D-channel Established

When using a PRI interface, it is important to understand that nothing is going to work without the D-channel being established. The D-channel carries the signaling that allows calls to be set up and torn down over the Bearer channels. How do you know the D-channel is up, and what can you do if it isn't?

Imagine everything is working properly until one day you pick up your IP phone and try to place a call to the PSTN and you get immediate reorder. One likely cause is that the D-channel is down. It could also be because something in your dial plan changed and is no longer configured correctly, but it is worth checking PerfMon or CallManager Serviceability for verification.

The counter to examine is the DataLinkInService counter in the Cisco MGCP PRI Device performance object for the gateway you are trying to troubleshoot. It is set to **1** when the D-channel is up and to **0** when the D-channel is down. If the D-channel is up and the calls aren't going through, this could be the result of a dial plan configuration problem. Chapter 9 discusses dial plan problems in greater detail.

There are other ways to check the status of the D-channel. Telnet to the switch where the WS-X6608 module is installed and issue the command **show port** *module/port* to see the status of an individual port or **show port** *module* to see the status of all the ports on the module. You should see something similar to the output in Example 6-125.

Example 6-125 *Checking the D-channel Status from the Catalyst 6000 CLI*

```
vnt-c6k-main (enable) show port 6
Port  Name                    Status      Vlan       Duplex Speed Type
----- --------------------    ----------  ---------- ------ ----- -----------

 6/1  PRI Corp->VNT           connected   51          full 1.544 T1
 6/2  PRI VNT->Corp           connected   104         full 1.544 T1
 6/3  VNT-CMDEV-1             connected   104         full 1.544 T1
 6/4  VNT-CMDEV-1             notconnect  104         full 1.544 T1
 6/5  VNT-CM1 XCoder          enabled     104         full    -  MTP
 6/6  VNT-CM1 CFB             enabled     104         full    -  Conf Bridge
 6/7  VNT-CM1 PRI             notconnect  104         full 1.544 T1
 6/8  VNT-CM1 PRI             notconnect  104         full 1.544 T1
```

Notice the status of ports 6/4, 6/7, and 6/8 shows **notconnected**. This means the D-channel is down.

A final way to check the D-channel status is by using a web browser to view statistics on the WS-X6608 port. Remember each port has its own IP address. You can find this IP address from the output of **show port** on the Catalyst switch or from the gateway's configuration page in CallManager Administration (**Device > Gateway**). Once you browse to the web page, select D-Channel Statistics. Figure 6-14 shows the **D-Channel Statistics** web page on a WS-X6608 port.

Figure 6-14 *D-channel Statistics Web Page on a WS-X6608 Port*

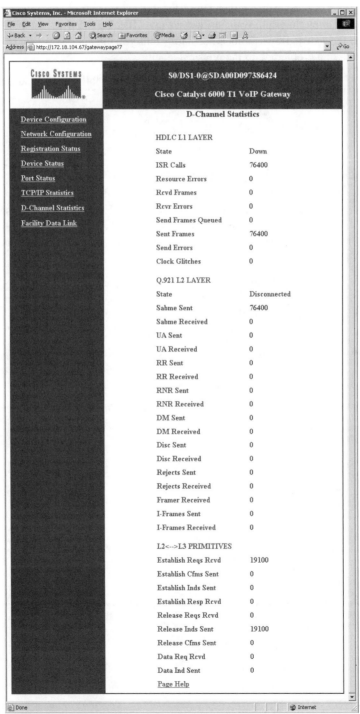

Notice in Figure 6-14 that there is a section for **Q.921 L2 LAYER**. This corresponds to the D-channel. Notice the state says **Disconnected**. This means the D-channel is down. If you look higher on the page, you can also see that **HDLC L1 Layer**, the physical layer, also shows the state is **Down**. This immediately tells you that the reason the D-channel is down: because of a problem with the physical layer.

If the D-channel is down, the possible reasons usually fall into two categories:

- Physical layer problems
- Configuration problems

Checking Physical Layer Statistics on the WS-X6608

Physical layer problems could be something like a bad cable or one that is simply too long. A reversal of transmit or receive pairs or an open receive pair can also cause errors. The pins on a RJ-45/48 jack are numbered from 1 to 8. With the metal pins facing toward you, pin 1 is the leftmost pin. The receive pair should be on lines 1 and 2, and the transmit pair should be on lines 4 and 5.

There are a variety of ways to check the physical layer statistics on a WS-X6608 port. You already saw in Figure 6-14 that you can see the physical layer status from the D-channel Statistics web page on the WS-X6608 port. Unfortunately, this page does not offer you the detail needed to accurately diagnose what physical layer statistics exist.

The best way to get physical layer statistics for a WS-X6608 port is to use the Dick Tracy client utility. Connect to the IP address of the WS-X6608 port and issue the command **4 show status**. The output of the command is shown in Example 6-126.

Example 6-126 *Checking the D-channel Status on T1/E1 Interfaces with the* **show status** *Command*

```
00:00:36.160 SPAN: CLI Request --> Show Span Summary Status
    E1 6/1 is up
        No alarms detected.
    Alarm MIB Statistics
        Yellow Alarms ------> 1
        Blue Alarms ---------> 0
        Frame Sync Losses ---> 0
        Carrier Loss Count --> 0
        Frame Slip Count ----> 0
        D-chan Tx Frame Count ----> 5
        D-chan Tx Frames Queued --> 0
        D-chan Tx Errors ---------> 0
        D-chan Rx Frame Count ----> 5
        D-chan Rx Errors ---------> 0
00:00:51.310 SPAN: CLI Request --> Show Span Summary Status
    T1 6/1 is down
        Transmitter is sending Remote Alarm
        Receiver has AIS Indication
    Alarm MIB Statistics
```

Example 6-126 *Checking the D-channel Status on T1/E1 Interfaces with the* **show status** *Command (Continued)*

```
        Yellow Alarms  ------->  1
        Blue Alarms    --------->  2
        Frame Sync Losses  --->  2
        Carrier Loss Count  -->  0
        Frame Slip Count  ---->  0
        D-chan Tx Frame Count  ---->  43
        D-chan Tx Frames Queued  -->  0
        D-chan Tx Errors  --------->  0
        D-chan Rx Frame Count  ---->  0
        D-chan Rx Errors  --------->  0
```

Notice the first port shown in Example 6-126 is an E1 port and the E1 physical layer is up and there are no alarms. This is the normal operating condition. Notice there has been one yellow alarm since the port booted up. As long as the number of alarms is not incrementing, this is okay.

The second port shown in Example 6-126 is a T1, and the T1 physical layer is down. The output indicates the transmitter is sending a remote alarm, which means the port is not receiving any framing on its receive pair. If the port is down or you are seeing a large number of alarms in the output of **4 show status**, you need to get additional details using the Dick Tracy client utility.

To get detailed physical layer information on a WS-X6608 port, issue the Dick Tracy command **4 show fdlintervals** *number of intervals*. Example 6-127 shows the output of the command **4 show fdlintervals 3**.

Example 6-127 *Checking Detailed Physical Layer Information on a WS-X6608 Port*

```
16:56:09.590 SPAN: CLI Request --> Dump local FDL 15-min interval history
  96 Complete intervals stored.
  Data in current interval (356 seconds elapsed):
    0 Line Code Violations, 0 Path Code Violations
    0 Slip Secs, 255 Fr Loss Secs, 0 Line Err Secs
    0 Errored Secs, 0 Bursty Err Secs, 0 Severely Err Secs, 356 Unavail Secs
  Data in interval 1:
    0 Line Code Violations, 0 Path Code Violations
    0 Slip Secs, 255 Fr Loss Secs, 0 Line Err Secs
    0 Errored Secs, 0 Bursty Err Secs, 0 Severely Err Secs, 900 Unavail Secs
  Data in interval 2:
    0 Line Code Violations, 0 Path Code Violations
    0 Slip Secs, 255 Fr Loss Secs, 0 Line Err Secs
    0 Errored Secs, 0 Bursty Err Secs, 0 Severely Err Secs, 900 Unavail Secs
  Data in interval 3:
    0 Line Code Violations, 0 Path Code Violations
    0 Slip Secs, 255 Fr Loss Secs, 0 Line Err Secs
    0 Errored Secs, 0 Bursty Err Secs, 0 Severely Err Secs, 900 Unavail Secs
  24-Hr Totals:
    0 Line Code Violations, 0 Path Code Violations
    0 Slip Secs, 255 Fr Loss Secs, 0 Line Err Secs
    0 Errored Secs, 0 Bursty Err Secs, 0 Severely Err Secs, 65535 Unavail Secs
```

The output of this command should look familiar because the format is identical to the **show controllers [t1 | e1]** command discussed in the section "Checking Physical Layer Connectivity on Digital Interfaces" earlier in this chapter. Follow the same methodology discussed in that section here as well.

Issue the command **4 show fdlintervals 3** several times to see if any of the counters are incrementing. Each interval spans a period of 15 minutes. If you see any errors in the current interval, you very likely have some kind of physical layer problem. If you see errors in the **24-Hr Totals** section, but not in the current interval, they are probably due to some physical layer condition that existed but is now resolved. For example, if you unplug the cable and then plug it back in, errors are logged. They show up in the 24-Hr Totals section but not the current interval if it has been more than 15 minutes since the event occurred.

If you do not have access to the Dick Tracy client utility, you can issue the command **show port voice fdl** *mod/port* from the Catalyst 6000 CLI to display the facilities data link (FDL) statistics for the specified ports. FDL is a link management protocol used to help diagnose problems and gather statistics. As shown in Example 6-128, the **show port voice fdl 3/1-3** command displays information for the ports on the WS-X6608 T1 module. Note that FDL is supported only on T1 interfaces, so you see the message "Feature not supported on Module 3" if you issue the command on an E1 module.

Example 6-128 show port voice fdl *Command Output Displays Facilities Data Link Statistics for the Specified Ports*

```
Console> (enable) show port voice fdl 3/1-3

Port  ErrorEvents          ErroredSecond        SeverlyErroredSecond
      Last 15' Last 24h Last 15' Last 24h Last 15' Last 24h
----- -------- -------- -------- -------- -------- ----------
 7/1  17       18       19       20       21       22
 7/2  17       18       19       20       21       22
 7/3  17       18       19       20       21       22


Port  FailedSignalState FailedSignalSecond
      Last 15' Last 24h Last 15' Last 24h
----- -------- -------- -------- ---------
 7/1  37       38       39       40
 7/2  37       38       39       40
 7/3  37       38       39       40

Port       LES              BES              LCV
      Last 15' Last 24h Last 15' Last 24h Last 15' Last 24h
----- -------- -------- -------- -------- -------- --------
 7/1  41       48       49       50       53       54
 7/2  41       48       49       50       53       54
 7/3  41       48       49       50       53       54
```

Table 6-37 describes the FDL fields.

Table 5-4   *FDL Field Descriptions*

Field	Description
ErrorEvents	Count of errored events
ErroredSecond	Count of errored seconds
SeverelyErroredSecond	Count of severely errored seconds
FailedSignalState	Count of failed signal state errors
FailedSignalSecond	Number of seconds the signal has failed
LES	Line errored seconds detected
BES	Bursty errored seconds detected
LCV	Line code violation seconds detected

If any of the previously-mentioned commands show you any indication of physical layer problems, there are four configuration parameters to check:

- Clock Reference
- Framing
- Line Coding (Zero Suppression)
- CSU Level

Ensure one side of the connection is providing clock and the other side is deriving clock. Ensure both sides are configured with the same framing and line coding. Failure to properly match these statistics results in physical layer errors.

CAUTION   It is possible that each end of the PRI span can have its clock reference set the same, and a D-channel could still be established. Sometimes their respective internal clocks are close enough to keep in sync. As a result, a D-channel might stay up for a while and then go down suddenly. Make sure your clock reference is right. Don't assume that it is right just because you previously established a D-channel. Any clocking mismatches appear as physical layer errors.

Verifying D-channel configuration

Once you have eliminated any physical layer problems, if your D-channel still does not come up, there are several configuration parameters to verify.

- **Protocol or Switch Type**—Specifies the ISDN Q.931 variant being used to communicate between devices. Although Q.931 is a standard, there are several variants on the standard that have been implemented by different switch makers such as Lucent and Nortel that depart from the Q.931 standard. As a result, you must ensure the switch type setting matches between the two devices connected to each other. Because all switch types are based on the Q.931 standard, they are all roughly the same. This means that you might be able to get the D-channel up and place basic calls even with a switch type mismatch and then run into problems later under specific circumstances. If you start seeing calls disconnected with errors like "Unknown IE Contents" or "Mandatory IE Missing," check to make sure the switch type is configured the same on both sides of the T1 or E1 PRI.

- **Protocol Side**—Choose the appropriate protocol side. This setting specifies whether the gateway emulates a Central Office/Network device or a User device. Choose **User** or **Network** and make sure it is the opposite of what has been configured on the far end. Protocol side is extremely important for D-channel establishment. A mismatch between protocol sides almost guarantees that the D-channel will not come up.

Advanced Troubleshooting for D-channel Problems

If you have verified physical layer connectivity and have ensured that the configuration between the two PRI devices matches, but the D-channel still does not come up, there are several other tasks you can perform to determine the root cause.

The most useful tool is the D-Channel Statistics web page you saw in Figure 6-14. This page not only shows you the status of the D-channel but also shows you statistics about the packets sent on the D-channel.

As mentioned in the section "Troubleshooting ISDN PRI Signaling," to establish a D-channel the user side must send a SABME message on the D-channel and the network side must respond with a UAf message. Check the D-Channel Statistics web page to see whether the WS-X6608 port is sending or receiving packets on the D-channel. If you see the **Sabme Sent** counter incrementing but the **Sabme Received** and **UA Received** counters are not incrementing, this indicates the far end is not responding to attempts to bring up the D-channel.

The next thing to do is verify that the WS-X6608 is indeed sending out the SABMEs. Disconnect the cable that is connected to the WS-X6608 port and connect a T1 loopback plug. A T1 loopback plug has pin 1 connected to pin 4 and pin 2 connected to pin 5. Once you have a loopback up, look at the D-Channel Statistics web page again. You should see the **Sabme Sent** and **Sabme Received** counters incrementing. This means the WS-X6608 is receiving the SABMEs it is sending because of the loopback plug. If you are not seeing the SABMEs returned back, this could indicate either a hardware failure or your loopback plug is faulty.

If you have two free ports on your WS-X6608 module, you can test the ports to ensure they are working by connecting a T1 crossover cable between two ports and registering both ports to CallManager. Set one port to network clock and network protocol side and set the other port to internal clock and user protocol side. If both ports are registered and you have a good T1 crossover cable between the two ports, the D-channel should come up.

During normal operation, you should see the **RR Sent** and **RR Received** counters increment every few seconds on the D-Channel Statistics page.

Unexpected Resets

Sometimes a gateway port seems to reset unexpectedly. The following is a partial list of potential reasons that might cause this type of activity:

- Other ports on the module are not configured, causing them to continually reset. This can cause a fully registered and functional gateway to reset because the ports share the same Philips Semiconductor 16-bit 80C51XA micro-controller (XA) processor. Be sure to configure all ports on the WS-X6608 module, even if they will not be used. You can also use the **set port disable** command on the unused ports.

- A network problem could be causing the reset. If the port loses connectivity with CallManager for a long-enough period of time, it might end up resetting.

- A DHCP lease expiration could cause the port to reset if the DHCP server becomes unavailable when the port tries to renew its lease. The port is smart enough to not reset during a call, but it resets as soon as there are no calls on the span.

Use the Dick Tracy tool to monitor the module. The debug information indicates any one of these reasons as possible causes.

Using Dick Tracy to Analyze a WS-X6608 Port

In the majority of situations, you should never have to enable debugs on on the Dick Tracy utility. However, using the Dick Tracy application is the best way to get detailed information on the port itself. This section examines some trace information obtained from the Dick Tracy client utility.

What tasks are available in the trace? Example 6-129 shows the general WS-X6608 port tasks. This is the same list you saw in Chapter 3, "Understanding the Troubleshooting Tools." Refer to Chapter 3 for details on how to use the Dick Tracy utility.

As firmware loads change, the number associated with each type of trace could change. The DSP and GMSG traces remain the most helpful. Enter **0 show tl** to generate the list shown in Example 6-129.

Example 6-129 *Available Trace Tasks for WS-X6608 Port*

```
07:16:02.240 (GEN) Lennon Tasks
        0 : GEN
        1 : AUD
        2 : TRC
        3 : SNMP
        4 : SPAN
        5 : NMP
        6 : DSP
        7 : LINE
        8 : CFG
        9 : GMSG
       10 : SOCK
```

continues

Example 6-129 *Available Trace Tasks for WS-X6608 Port (Continued)*

```
11 : TMR
12 : Q921
13 : XA
```

The next few examples examine tasks 6 and 9 (some of these tasks don't do anything).

Use the command **show mask** to find out which debugs are available for a particular task. Example 6-130 shows the list of debugs available for task ID 6 by issuing the command **6 show mask**.

Example 6-130 *Output of the 6 show mask Command in Dick Tracy*

```
Where Bit0 = Debug Msg's
      Bit1 = Call Progression Msg's
      Bit2 = Boot Msg's
      Bit3 = Stat Msg's
      Bit4 = Cmd Msg's
      Bit5 = RTP Msg's
      Bit6 = SID Frames
      Bit7 = Status Msg's
```

Example 6-131 shows the list of debugs available for task ID 9 by issuing the command **9 show mask**.

Example 6-131 *Output of the 9 show mask Command in Dick Tracy*

```
Where Bit0 = GW Status Msg's
      Bit1 = CP States
      Bit2 = GW States
      Bit3 = Detail Msg's
      Bit4 = TCP Msg's
      Bit5 = MGCP Msg's
      Bit6 = MGCP List Msg's
      Bit7 = MGCP KA Msg's
```

To understand the type of information available through the Dick Tracy utility, it is best to see the output of these debugs for a real call. The call investigated here is a call from extension 2000 through a T1 PRI to extension 2001 on a legacy PBX connected to the WS-X6608 port. The calling party (extension 2000) dials **52001**. The **5** represents the routing pattern causing the call to go out the T1 PRI.

First, look at task 6 with all the masks set. Task 6 is the DSP task; you will see events associated with setting up and tearing down media streams. In the Dick Tracy command window, enter **6 set mask ff**.

The calling phone dials 2001, and CallManager begins allocating a port on the T1, as demonstrated in Example 6-132. The port number corresponds to the B-channel being used for the call.

Example 6-132 *Task 6 Trace with All Masks Set (***6 set mask ff***)*

```
07:16:15.350 (DSP) Status Check
07:16:17.140 (DSP) CRCX -> Port<22>
07:16:17.140 (DSP7) get_stat<83> PktLen<10> Chan<3> Reset<1>
07:16:17.140 (DSP7) get_stat<84> PktLen<10> Chan<3> Reset<1>
07:16:17.140 (DSP7) get_stat<6> PktLen<10> Chan<3> Reset<1>
07:16:17.140 (DSP7) get_stat<86> PktLen<10> Chan<3> Reset<1>
07:16:17.140 (DSP7) get_stat<87> PktLen<10> Chan<3> Reset<1>
07:16:17.140 (DSP7) get_stat<89> PktLen<10> Chan<3> Reset<1>
07:16:17.140 (DSP7) get_stat<88> PktLen<10> Chan<3> Reset<1>
```

Example 6-133 shows where the voice stream is set up. Notice the output indicates which UDP port number is being used for the media stream and also shows that G.711 is being used as the codec for this call. Near the end you see the DSP begins transmitting packets to 10.16.20.6.

Example 6-133 *Voice Stream Setup of Call*

```
07:16:17.140 (DSP) RTP RxOpen -> Port<22> UDP Port<0x5C64 (23652)>
07:16:17.140 (DSP) RTCP RxOpen -> Port<22> UDP Port<0x5C65 (23653)>
07:16:17.220 (DSP) MDCX -> Port<22>
07:16:17.220 (DSP7) open_voice_channel<74> PktLen<16> Chan<3>
                    Comp<0> Sig<0> TS<2> SP<0>
07:16:17.220 (DSP7) set_gains <91> PktLen<12> Chan<3> In<0> Out<0>
07:16:17.220 (DSP7) idle_mode<68> PktLen<8> Chan<3>
                    Mode : RECVONLY
Just go to voice mode
07:16:17.230 (DSP) Voice Mode -> Port<22> Comp<G711_ULAW_PCM>
07:16:17.230 (DSP7) set_playout_delay<76> PktLen<18> Chan<3>
                    Mode<1> Initial<60> Min<4> Max<200> Fax<300>
07:16:17.230 (DSP7) encap_config<92> PktLen<28> Chan<3> Prot<2>
                    txSSRC<0x1E070116> rxSSRC<0x00000000>
                    txVPXCC<0x0080> rxVPXCC<0x0000> SID<0> NSE<101> SEQ<0>
07:16:17.230 (DSP7) voice_mode<73> PktLen<24> Chan<3> Codec<1> PktSize<160>
                    VAD<0> Echo<256> Noise<1> Detect<0x0421> Mode<3> AGC<0>
07:16:17.230 (DSP7) rx_echo_delay_control<109> PktLen<10> Chan<3> Delay<16>
07:16:17.230 (DSP7) echo_canceller_control<66> PktLen<10> Chan<3> Mode<0x0000>
                    Enabling Digit Detection
07:16:17.260 (DSP) MDCX -> Port<22>
                    Mode : SENDRECV
07:16:17.260 (DSP) RTP TxOpen -> Port<22> Remote IP<10.16.20.6> UDP Port<0x4912
    (18706)>
07:16:17.260 (DSP) RTCP TxOpen -> Port<22> Remote IP<10.16.20.6> UDP Port<0x4913
    (18707)>
                    Enabling Digit Detection
07:16:17.350 (DSP7) get_stat<86> PktLen<10> Chan<3> Reset<0>
07:16:17.360 (DSP) Status Check
07:16:17.360 (DSP) Port 22 Tx Stats
```

continues

Example 6-133 *Voice Stream Setup of Call (Continued)*

```
07:16:18.360 (DSP7) get_stat<87> PktLen<10> Chan<3> Reset<0>
07:16:18.370 (DSP) Port 22 Rx Stats
07:16:19.360 (DSP7) get_stat<89> PktLen<10> Chan<3> Reset<0>
07:16:19.360 (DSP) Status Check
07:16:19.370 (DSP) Port 22 Level Stats
07:16:20.360 (DSP7) get_stat<83> PktLen<10> Chan<3> Reset<0>
07:16:20.370 (DSP) Port 22 VPOD Stats
```

After the call is established, the calling party hangs up the call. Example 6-134 shows where the call is torn down. Notice the output indicates the number of packets that were received and lost for the call. This is useful for determining the root cause of voice quality problems. If you see packet loss you are probably going to experience voice quality problems. Refer to Chapter 7, "Voice Quality," for more information on troubleshooting voice quality problems.

Example 6-134 *Voice Stream Teardown of Call*

```
07:16:21.030 (DSP) MDCX -> Port<22>
                    Mode : RECVONLY
07:16:21.030 (DSP) RTP TxClose -> Port<22>
                    Enabling Digit Detection
07:16:21.070 (DSP) DLCX -> Port<22> From<GMSG >
07:16:21.070 (DSP) RTP RxClose -> Port<22>
07:16:21.070             Pkts Rcvd<187> Pkts Lost<0> Total Pkts Lost<0>
07:16:21.070             Underrun<0> Overrun<0>
07:16:21.070 (DSP7) idle_mode<68> PktLen<8> Chan<3>
07:16:21.070 (DSP7) get_stat<83> PktLen<10> Chan<3> Reset<1>
07:16:21.070 (DSP7) get_stat<84> PktLen<10> Chan<3> Reset<1>
07:16:21.070 (DSP7) get_stat<6> PktLen<10> Chan<3> Reset<1>
07:16:21.070 (DSP7) get_stat<86> PktLen<10> Chan<3> Reset<1>
07:16:21.070 (DSP7) get_stat<87> PktLen<10> Chan<3> Reset<1>
07:16:21.070 (DSP7) get_stat<89> PktLen<10> Chan<3> Reset<1>
07:16:21.070 (DSP7) get_stat<88> PktLen<10> Chan<3> Reset<1>
07:16:21.070 (DSP7) close_voice_channel<75> PktLen<8> Chan<3>
07:16:21.360 (DSP) Status Check
07:16:23.360 (DSP) Status Check
```

Now, look at the same call with each individual mask bit set. Example 6-135 shows the call using the **6 set mask 1** command. The number 1 is 00000001 in binary, so this enables bit 0, which shows debug messages according to Example 6-130.

Example 6-135 *Task 6 Trace with Mask 1 Set (**6 set mask 1***)*

```
07:16:27.580 (DSP) Voice Mode -> Port<22> Comp<G711_ULAW_PCM>
```

This tells you the B-channel used for the call and the codec type.

Example 6-136 shows the call using the **6 set mask 2** command. The number 2 is 00000010 in binary, so this enables bit 1, which shows call progression messages according to Example 6-130.

Example 6-136 *Task 6 Trace with Mask 2 Set (***6 set mask 2***)*

```
07:16:39.270 (DSP) CRCX -> Port<22>
07:16:39.340 (DSP) MDCX -> Port<22>
                    Mode : RECVONLY
Just go to voice mode
                    Enabling Digit Detection
07:16:39.370 (DSP) MDCX -> Port<22>
                    Mode : SENDRECV
                    Enabling Digit Detection
07:16:42.760 (DSP) MDCX -> Port<22>
                    Mode : RECVONLY
                    Enabling Digit Detection
07:16:42.800 (DSP) DLCX -> Port<22> From<GMSG >
```

You see the B-channel used for the call and the transmit modes being set (RECVONLY and SENDRECV). Notice each of these corresponds to the MGCP commands to create and modify the connection.

No data shows up with the mask set to 4 during a call because that enables bit 2, which shows boot messages. You should not have to use this bit to troubleshoot calls.

Example 6-137 shows the call using the **6 set mask 8** command. The number 8 is 00001000 in binary, so this enables bit 3, which shows DSP status messages according to Example 6-130. The output of this bit is relatively meaningless because it does not show any of the statistics being collected. However, the fact that statistics are being collected lets you know that at least the DSP is still functioning and there is an active call on that DSP.

Example 6-137 *Task 6 Trace with Mask 8 Set (***6 set mask 8***)*

```
07:16:55.370 (DSP) Port 22 Level Stats
07:16:56.370 (DSP) Port 22 VPOD Stats
07:16:57.370 (DSP) Port 22 VPOE Stats
07:16:58.370 (DSP) Port 22 Error Stats
07:16:59.370 (DSP) Port 22 Tx Stats
07:17:00.370 (DSP) Port 22 Rx Stats
07:17:01.370 (DSP) Port 22 Level Stats
07:17:02.370 (DSP) Port 22 VPOD Stats
```

Example 6-138 shows the call using the **6 set mask 10** command. Remember the values presented to the Dick Tracy utility are in hex, so the hex number 0x10 is 00010000 in binary. This enables bit 4, which is the command messages trace according to Example 6-130. This trace shows you the messages being sent to the DSP to open and close logical channels and is one of the more useful bit masks to set on a WS-X6608. This is a verbose command and should be used carefully because too much traffic can have adverse effects on the gateway and could—in the worst-case scenario—reset the gateway port.

Example 6-138 *Task 6 Trace with Mask 8 Set* (**6 set mask 10**)

```
07:54:16.890 (DSP7) get_stat<83> PktLen<10> Chan<3> Reset<1>
07:54:16.890 (DSP7) get_stat<84> PktLen<10> Chan<3> Reset<1>
07:54:16.890 (DSP7) get_stat<6> PktLen<10> Chan<3> Reset<1>
07:54:16.890 (DSP7) get_stat<86> PktLen<10> Chan<3> Reset<1>
07:54:16.890 (DSP7) get_stat<87> PktLen<10> Chan<3> Reset<1>
07:54:16.890 (DSP7) get_stat<89> PktLen<10> Chan<3> Reset<1>
07:54:16.890 (DSP7) get_stat<88> PktLen<10> Chan<3> Reset<1>
07:54:16.990 (DSP7) open_voice_channel<74> PktLen<16> Chan<3>
                        Comp<0> Sig<0> TS<2> SP<0>
07:54:16.990 (DSP7) set_gains <91> PktLen<12> Chan<3> In<0> Out<0>
07:54:16.990 (DSP7) idle_mode<68> PktLen<8> Chan<3>
07:54:16.990 (DSP7) set_playout_delay<76> PktLen<18> Chan<3>
                        Mode<1> Initial<60> Min<4> Max<200> Fax<300>
07:54:16.990 (DSP7) encap_config<92> PktLen<28> Chan<3> Prot<2>
                        txSSRC<0x1E070116> rxSSRC<0x00000000>
                        txVPXCC<0x0080> rxVPXCC<0x0000> SID<0> NSE<101> SEQ<0>
07:54:16.990 (DSP7) voice_mode<73> PktLen<24> Chan<3> Codec<1> PktSize<160>
                        VAD<0> Echo<256> Noise<1> Detect<0x0421> Mode<3> AGC<0>
07:54:16.990 (DSP7) rx_echo_delay_control<109> PktLen<10> Chan<3> Delay<16>
07:54:16.990 (DSP7) echo_canceller_control<66> PktLen<10> Chan<3> Mode<0x0000>
07:54:17.470 (DSP7) get_stat<86> PktLen<10> Chan<3> Reset<0>
07:54:18.470 (DSP7) get_stat<87> PktLen<10> Chan<3> Reset<0>
07:54:19.470 (DSP7) get_stat<89> PktLen<10> Chan<3> Reset<0>
07:54:20.470 (DSP7) get_stat<83> PktLen<10> Chan<3> Reset<0>
07:54:21.470 (DSP7) get_stat<84> PktLen<10> Chan<3> Reset<0>
07:54:22.470 (DSP7) get_stat<6> PktLen<10> Chan<3> Reset<0>
07:54:23.290 (DSP7) idle_mode<68> PktLen<8> Chan<3>
07:54:23.290 (DSP7) get_stat<83> PktLen<10> Chan<3> Reset<1>
07:54:23.290 (DSP7) get_stat<84> PktLen<10> Chan<3> Reset<1>
07:54:23.290 (DSP7) get_stat<6> PktLen<10> Chan<3> Reset<1>
07:54:23.290 (DSP7) get_stat<86> PktLen<10> Chan<3> Reset<1>
07:54:23.290 (DSP7) get_stat<87> PktLen<10> Chan<3> Reset<1>
07:54:23.290 (DSP7) get_stat<89> PktLen<10> Chan<3> Reset<1>
07:54:23.300 (DSP7) get_stat<88> PktLen<10> Chan<3> Reset<1>
07:54:23.300 (DSP7) close_voice_channel<75> PktLen<8> Chan<3>
```

Example 6-139 shows the call using the **6 set mask 20** command. The hex number 0x20 is 00100000 in binary, so this mask enables the RTP messages debug according to Example 6-130. This mask allows you to see opening and closing of RTP streams and the IP address information related to RTP streams.

Example 6-139 *Task 6 Trace with Mask 20 Set* (**6 set mask 20**)

```
07:54:31.020 (DSP) RTP RxOpen -> Port<22> UDP Port<0x5C8C (23692)>
07:54:31.030 (DSP) RTCP RxOpen -> Port<22> UDP Port<0x5C8D (23693)>
07:54:31.120 (DSP) RTP TxOpen -> Port<22> Remote IP<10.16.20.6> UDP Port<0x4934
   (18740)>
07:54:31.120 (DSP) RTCP TxOpen -> Port<22> Remote IP<10.16.20.6> UDP Port<0x4935
```

Example 6-139 *Task 6 Trace with Mask 20 Set (**6 set mask 20**) (Continued)*

```
(18741)>
07:54:35.960 (DSP) RTP TxClose -> Port<22>
07:54:36.000 (DSP) RTP RxClose -> Port<22>
07:54:36.000               Pkts Rcvd<241> Pkts Lost<0> Total Pkts Lost<0>
07:54:36.000               Underrun<0> Overrun<0>
```

This command provides RTP/UDP setup information. It indicates the port you are using, that port's IP address, and the UDP ports used for this call. The tail end of the output summarizes the packets received and lost.

In this particular call, no debugs appeared with the mask set to 40. This is because the hex number 0x40 is 01000000 in binary, corresponding to the Silence Information Description (SID) frames debug according to Example 6-130. SID frames are only generated when using VAD for a call. In this case, VAD was disabled, so no SID frames were generated or accepted. If you want to see when VAD is being enabled and disabled, use bit mask 40.

Finally, Example 6-140 shows the call using the **6 set mask 80** command. The hex number 0x80 is 10000000 in binary, which corresponds to the status messages debug according to Example 6-130. Like **6 set mask 8**, this mask does not provide much useful information during normal operating conditions, however if there are problems with the DSP, you might see error messages indicated here.

Example 6-140 *Task 6 Trace with Mask 80 Set (**6 set mask 80**)*

```
07:54:57.480 (DSP) Status Check
07:54:59.480 (DSP) Status Check
07:55:01.480 (DSP) Status Check
07:55:03.480 (DSP) Status Check
07:55:05.480 (DSP) Status Check
07:55:07.480 (DSP) Status Check
```

This simply indicates that the DSP is functioning properly.

You have just gone through all the task 6 (DSP task) debugs created during a call. Now let's look at task 9.

Task 9 (GMSG task) provides different information, such as the MGCP messages used during the call. Refer to the "Understanding MGCP" section for details on decoding these messages. Also, keep in mind that the CCM trace in CallManager logs the MGCP messages as well.

Remember that MGCP is a UDP-based protocol. UDP has no provisions for retransmissions, so it relies on the MGCP protocol layer to handle retransmissions. If you suspect you are having packet loss problems, enable these masks on the gateway using the Dick Tracy utility and log the output to a file. Then compare the messages seen in the Dick Tracy utlity with those found in the CCM trace on CallManager. If there is a discrepancy or you see retransmissions, comparing the output will show you whether the message was lost in the network. If you are seeing inconsistencies between the Dick Tracy output and the CCM trace, check for errors on the network devices between CallManager and the WS-X6608 port. Simple misconfigurations like Ethernet duplex mismatches can lead to packet loss.

Example 6-141 shows the whole trace using the **9 set mask ff** command. This example shows the same call as before from extension 2000 to a phone on an external PBX with extension 2001. The calling phone dials 52001 and CallManager routes the call to this gateway.

Example 6-141 *Task 9 Trace with Mask 1ff Set (***9 set mask ff***)*

```
07:18:55.040 (MGCP)Incoming Msg:
        CRCX 876 S0/DS1-0/23@SDA0001C9B102B0 MGCP 0.1
        C: D000000001000090000000000000000000c
        M: inactive
07:18:55.040 (MGCP) Incoming CMD: Adding transID<876> CMD to incoming list
07:18:55.040 (MGCP) Outgoing RSP: Matching transID<876> found on incoming list,
  removing CMD
07:18:55.040 (MGCP) Outgoing RSP: Adding transID<876> RSP to outgoing list
07:18:55.040 (MGCP) Outgoing RSP: Re-starting list timer
07:18:55.050 (MGCP)Outgoing Msg:
        200 876
        I: 23

        v=0
        o=- D000000001000090000000000000000000c 0 IN IP4 10.16.30.6
        s=Cisco SDP 0
        c=IN IP4 10.16.30.6
        t=0 0
        m=audio 23670 RTP/AVP 0
07:18:55.080 (GMSG) Rcv TCP Msg, Post to Q921
07:18:55.080 GMSG TX BUFFER : len=2a Ptr=1d1aa0
  ->0004000000100000001001e0802000c0504038090a21803a983976c060080
07:18:55.170 (GMSG) Rcv Q921 Msg, Post to TCP
07:18:55.170 GMSG RX BUFFER : len=16 Ptr=18b8f8 ->
  0004000000110000000001000a0802800c021803a98397
07:18:55.180 (GMSG) Rcv Q921 Msg, Post to TCP
07:18:55.180 GMSG RX BUFFER : len=15 Ptr=18c0f8 ->
  00040000001100000001000090802800c011e028088
07:18:55.280 (MGCP)Incoming Msg:
        MDCX 877 S0/DS1-0/23@SDA0001C9B102B0 MGCP 0.1
        C: D000000001000090000000000000000000c
        I: 23
        X: 17
        L: p:20, a:PCMU, s:off
        M: recvonly
        R: D/[0-9ABCD*#]
        Q: process,loop
07:18:55.280 (MGCP) Incoming CMD: Adding transID<877> CMD to incoming list
07:18:55.280 (MGCP) Incoming CMD: Matching port<22> found on outgoing list,
  removing RSP
07:18:55.290 (MGCP) Outgoing RSP: Matching transID<877> found on incoming list,
  removing CMD
```

Example 6-141 *Task 9 Trace with Mask 1ff Set (***9 set mask 1ff***) (Continued)*

```
07:18:55.290 (MGCP) Outgoing RSP: Adding transID<877> RSP to outgoing list
07:18:55.290 (MGCP)Outgoing Msg:
          200 877
07:18:55.320 (MGCP)Incoming Msg:
          MDCX 878 S0/DS1-0/23@SDA0001C9B102B0 MGCP 0.1
          C: D000000001000090000000000000000c
          I: 23
          X: 17
          L: p:20, a:PCMU, s:off
          M: sendrecv
          R: D/[0-9ABCD*#]
          S:
          Q: process,loop

          v=0
          o=- 35 0 IN EPN S0/DS1-0/23@SDA0001C9B102B0
          s=Cisco SDP 0
          t=0 0
          c=IN IP4 10.16.20.6
          m=audio 18102 RTP/AVP 96
          a=rtpmap:96 PCMU
07:18:55.330 (MGCP) Incoming CMD: Adding transID<878> CMD to incoming list
07:18:55.330 (MGCP) Incoming CMD: Matching port<22> found on outgoing list,
   removing RSP
07:18:55.330 (MGCP) Outgoing RSP: Matching transID<878> found on incoming list,
   removing CMD
07:18:55.330 (MGCP) Outgoing RSP: Adding transID<878> RSP to outgoing list
07:18:55.330 (MGCP)Outgoing Msg:
          200 878
07:18:55.740 (MGCP) Timer: Outgoing transID<878> RSP timed out, removing RSP
07:18:56.670 (GMSG) Rcv Q921 Msg, Post to TCP
07:18:56.670 GMSG RX BUFFER : len=11 Ptr=18c8f8 ->
   00040000001100000001000050802800c07
07:18:56.680 (GMSG) Rcv TCP Msg, Post to Q921
07:18:56.680 GMSG TX BUFFER : len=11 Ptr=1d12a0 ->
   0004000000100000000100050802000c0f
07:18:59.010 (GMSG) Rcv Q921 Msg, Post to TCP
07:18:59.010 GMSG RX BUFFER : len=15 Ptr=18d8f8 ->
   0004000000110000000100090802800c4508028090
07:18:59.030 (MGCP)Incoming Msg:
          MDCX 879 S0/DS1-0/23@SDA0001C9B102B0 MGCP 0.1
          C: D000000001000090000000000000000c
          I: 23
          X: 17
          M: recvonly
          R: D/[0-9ABCD*#]
          Q: process,loop
07:18:59.030 (MGCP) Incoming CMD: Adding transID<879> CMD to incoming list
07:18:59.030 (MGCP) Outgoing RSP: Matching transID<879> found on incoming list,
   removing CMD
07:18:59.030 (MGCP) Outgoing RSP: Adding transID<879> RSP to outgoing list
```

continues

Example 6-141 *Task 9 Trace with Mask 1ff Set* (**9 set mask 1ff**) *(Continued)*

```
07:18:59.030 (MGCP) Outgoing RSP: Re-starting list timer
07:18:59.030 (MGCP)Outgoing Msg:
        200 879
07:18:59.050 (GMSG) Rcv TCP Msg, Post to Q921
07:18:59.060 GMSG TX BUFFER : len=11 Ptr=1bd2a0 ->
  00040000001000000001000050802000c4d
07:18:59.070 (GMSG) Rcv Q921 Msg, Post to TCP
07:18:59.070 GMSG RX BUFFER : len=11 Ptr=18e8f8 ->
  00040000001100000001000050802800c5a
07:18:59.080 (MGCP)Incoming Msg:
        DLCX 880 S0/DS1-0/23@SDA0001C9B102B0 MGCP 0.1
        C: D00000000100009000000000000000000c
        I: 23
        X: 17
        S:
07:18:59.090 (MGCP) Incoming CMD: Adding transID<880> CMD to incoming list
07:18:59.090 (MGCP) Incoming CMD: Matching port<22> found on outgoing list,
  removing RSP
07:18:59.090 (MGCP) Outgoing RSP: Matching transID<880> found on incoming list,
  removing CMD
07:18:59.090 (MGCP) Outgoing RSP: Adding transID<880> RSP to outgoing list
07:18:59.090 (MGCP)Outgoing Msg:
        250 880
        P: PS=185, OS=29600, PR=184, OR=29440, PL=0, JI=0, LA=0
07:18:59.530 (MGCP) Timer: Outgoing transID<880> RSP timed out, removing RSP
```

Example 6-141 contains a lot of information. To better understand the information presented in Example 6-141, take a look at each of the debug mask bits enabled individually.

Example 6-142 shows the call using the **9 set mask 1** command. The number 1 is 00000001 in binary, so this mask enables the gateway status messages debug according to Example 6-131. This debug shows that the gateway is maintaining its TCP connection to two CallManagers which correspond to CP#0 and CP#1.

Example 6-142 *Task 9 Trace with Mask 1 Set* (**9 set mask 1**)

```
07:19:05.900 (GMSG) Statusing TCP Socket for CP#1
07:19:19.900 (GMSG) Statusing TCP Socket for CP#0
07:19:20.900 (GMSG) Statusing TCP Socket for CP#1
```

To determine which CallManager addresses correspond with CP#0 and CP#1, issue the command **9 show gatewayinfo**. Example 6-143 shows the output of the command **9 show gatewayinfo**.

Example 6-143 *Output of* **9 show gatewayinfo**

```
19:17:39.330 (GMSG) CLI Request --> Show Gateway Info
        Cat6K slot --> 6
        Blade CPU no. --> 3
        VLAN ID --> 104
        Gateway State --> Run
        Timer --> 47 secs
        CCM KeepAlive Timeout --> 30 secs
        Country Code --> 7
        Active CCM --> #1
        Backup CCM --> #2
        Next CCM --> #3
        CCM Rollover Count --> 0
        LinkEst --> True.
```

Notice Example 6-143 lists the Active and Backup CallManagers in the fields marked
Active CCM and **Backup CCM. CP#0** corresponds with the **Active CCM** and **CP#1**
corresponds with the **Backup CCM**. To determine what #1 and #2 corresponds to, issue the
command **9 show callmgrinfo**.

Example 6-144 shows the output of **9 show callmgrinfo**.

Example 6-144 *Output of* **9 show callmgrinfo**

```
19:22:38.860 (GMSG) CLI Request --> Show CallManager Info
    Priority    IP_Address       State       Timer
       1      172.18.106.59    ActiveCCM     17200
       2      172.18.106.58    BackupCCM      3200
```

In this case, 172.18.106.59 is #1 and 172.18.106.58 is #2, so 172.18.106.58 is CP#0 and
172.18.106.59 is CP#1. If there are any connectivity issues between the WS-X6608 port
and CallManager, you will see errors in the output of **9 set mask 1**.

Bits 1 through 4 (**9 set mask 2, 4, 8,** and **10**) do not generate any debug output during a call
setup or teardown.

When you use the 9 set mask 20 command, however, you get detailed information on the
MGCP messages, as shown in Example 6-145. The number 20 in hex is 00100000 in binary,
which corresponds to the MGCP messages debug according to Example 6-131. This is the
most useful of the debug masks for task 9 because it shows you the MGCP messages being
received from and transmitted to CallManager.

Example 6-145 *Task 9 Trace with Mask 20 Set (***9 set mask 20***)*

```
07:55:33.090 (MGCP)Incoming Msg:
        CRCX 1047 S0/DS1-0/23@SDA0001C9B102B0 MGCP 0.1
        C: D0000000010000c0000000000000001b
        M: inactive
07:55:33.090 (MGCP)Outgoing Msg:
        200 1047
        I: 23
```

continues

Example 6-145 *Task 9 Trace with Mask 20 Set (**9 set mask 20**) (Continued)*

```
                  v=0
                  o=- D0000000010000c00000000000000001b 0 IN IP4 10.16.30.6
                  s=Cisco SDP 0
                  c=IN IP4 10.16.30.6
                  t=0 0
                  m=audio 23700 RTP/AVP 0
07:55:33.180 (MGCP)Incoming Msg:
                  MDCX 1048 S0/DS1-0/23@SDA0001C9B102B0 MGCP 0.1
                  C: D0000000010000c00000000000000001b
                  I: 23
                  X: 17
                  L: p:20, a:PCMU, s:off
                  M: recvonly
                  R: D/[0-9ABCD*#]
                  Q: process,loop
07:55:33.180 (MGCP)Outgoing Msg:
                  200 1048
07:55:33.210 (MGCP)Incoming Msg:
                  MDCX 1049 S0/DS1-0/23@SDA0001C9B102B0 MGCP 0.1
                  C: D0000000010000c00000000000000001b
                  I: 23
                  X: 17
                  L: p:20, a:PCMU, s:off
                  M: sendrecv
                  R: D/[0-9ABCD*#]
                  S:
                  Q: process,loop

                  v=0
                  o=- 35 0 IN EPN S0/DS1-0/23@SDA0001C9B102B0
                  s=Cisco SDP 0
                  t=0 0
                  c=IN IP4 10.16.20.6
                  m=audio 24940 RTP/AVP 96
                  a=rtpmap:96 PCMU
07:55:33.220 (MGCP)Outgoing Msg:
                  200 1049
07:55:36.180 (MGCP)Incoming Msg:
                  MDCX 1050 S0/DS1-0/23@SDA0001C9B102B0 MGCP 0.1
                  C: D0000000010000c00000000000000001b
                  I: 23
                  X: 17
                  M: recvonly
                  R: D/[0-9ABCD*#]
                  Q: process,loop
07:55:36.180 (MGCP)Outgoing Msg:
                  200 1050
07:55:36.220 (MGCP)Incoming Msg:
                  DLCX 1051 S0/DS1-0/23@SDA0001C9B102B0 MGCP 0.1
                  C: D0000000010000c00000000000000001b
                  I: 23
                  X: 17
                  S:
```

Example 6-145 *Task 9 Trace with Mask 20 Set (***9 set mask 20***) (Continued)*

```
07:55:36.230 (MGCP)Outgoing Msg:
        250 1051
        P: PS=149, OS=23840, PR=147, OR=23520, PL=0, JI=0, LA=0
```

Example 6-146 shows the call using the **9 set mask 40** command. The number 40 in hex is 01000000 in binary, which corresponds to the MGCP list messages debug according to Example 6-131. This trace shows the gateway's processing of MGCP messages. As mentioned earlier, MGCP must handle retransmissions itself because the lower-layer protocols do not take care of retransmissions. This debug shows the gateway adding transactions to the list of outstanding transactions (**Adding transID=**) and removing them when a resonse to the transaction is received (**found on incoming list, removing CMD**). If there is a packet lost on the network, you see the transaction get added to the list, but it is not removed. In this case, there is no packet loss so you can see each transaction get added and removed successfully.

Example 6-146 *Task 9 Trace with Mask 40 Set (***9 set mask 40***)*

```
07:55:41.890 (MGCP) Incoming CMD: Adding transID<1052> CMD to incoming list
07:55:41.890 (MGCP) Outgoing RSP: Matching transID<1052> found on incoming list,
    removing CMD
07:55:41.890 (MGCP) Outgoing RSP: Adding transID<1052> RSP to outgoing list
07:55:41.890 (MGCP) Outgoing RSP: Re-starting list timer
07:55:41.980 (MGCP) Incoming CMD: Adding transID<1053> CMD to incoming list
07:55:41.980 (MGCP) Incoming CMD: Matching port<22> found on outgoing list,
    removing RSP
07:55:41.980 (MGCP) Outgoing RSP: Matching transID<1053> found on incoming list,
    removing CMD
07:55:41.980 (MGCP) Outgoing RSP: Adding transID<1053> RSP to outgoing list
07:55:42.010 (MGCP) Incoming CMD: Adding transID<1054> CMD to incoming list
07:55:42.010 (MGCP) Incoming CMD: Matching port<22> found on outgoing list,
    removing RSP
07:55:42.020 (MGCP) Outgoing RSP: Matching transID<1054> found on incoming list,
    removing CMD
07:55:42.020 (MGCP) Outgoing RSP: Adding transID<1054> RSP to outgoing list
07:55:42.490 (MGCP) Timer: Outgoing transID<1054> RSP timed out, removing RSP
07:55:46.020 (MGCP) Incoming CMD: Adding transID<1055> CMD to incoming list
07:55:46.020 (MGCP) Outgoing RSP: Matching transID<1055> found on incoming list,
    removing CMD
07:55:46.030 (MGCP) Outgoing RSP: Adding transID<1055> RSP to outgoing list
07:55:46.030 (MGCP) Outgoing RSP: Re-starting list timer
07:55:46.060 (MGCP) Incoming CMD: Adding transID<1056> CMD to incoming list
07:55:46.060 (MGCP) Incoming CMD: Matching port<22> found on outgoing list,
    removing RSP
07:55:46.060 (MGCP) Outgoing RSP: Matching transID<1056> found on incoming list,
    removing CMD
07:55:46.060 (MGCP) Outgoing RSP: Adding transID<1056> RSP to outgoing list
07:55:46.530 (MGCP) Timer: Outgoing transID<1056> RSP timed out, removing RSP
07:55:49.990 (MGCP) Outgoing CMD: Adding transID<1904> CMD to outgoing list
07:55:49.990 (MGCP) Outgoing CMD: Re-starting list timer
07:55:50.000 (MGCP) Incoming RSP: Matching transID<1904> found on outgoing list,
    removing CMD
```

Finally, Example 6-147 shows the call using the **9 set mask 80** command. The hex number 80 is 10000000 in binary, which corresponds to the MGCP KeepAlive messages debug according to Example 6-131. The WS-X6608 uses MGCP notify messages as KeepAlives to CallManager. You can enable this debug if your WS-X6608 is unregistering with CallManager because of missed KeepAlives.

Example 6-147 *Task 9 Trace with Mask 80 Set (***9 set mask 80***)*

```
07:56:04.990 (MGCP)Outgoing Msg:
        NTFY 1905 *@SDA0001C9B102B0 MGCP 0.1
        X: 0
        O:
07:56:05.000 (MGCP)Incoming Msg:
        200 1905
```

In addition to the debug commands available by using the **set mask** command, there are some **show** commands that provide useful information as well. You already saw the output of **9 show callmgrinfo** and **9 show gatewayinfo**. You can use the **show port** *B-channel* command to get information on a call's status. The channel numbers are zero-based, so for B-channel 1 use the command **6 show port 0**. To execute this command for this example, enter **6 show port 24**. This returns summary data for the whole span, as demonstrated in Example 6-148.

Example 6-148 *Trace of the* **6 show port 24** *Command*

```
(DSP) Show Port ->
        Port< 0> <-->
        Port< 1> <-->
        Port< 2> <-->
        Port< 3> <-->
        Port< 4> <-->
        Port< 5> <-->
        Port< 6> <-->
        Port< 7> <-->
        Port< 8> <-->
        Port< 9> <-->
        Port<10> <-->
        Port<11> <-->
        Port<12> <-->
        Port<13> <-->
        Port<14> <-->
        Port<15> <-->
        Port<16> <-->
        Port<17> <-->
        Port<18> <-->
        Port<19> <-->
        Port<20> <-->
        Port<21> <-->
        Port<22> <--> 10.16.20.6 (0x0A101406)
        Port<23> <-->
```

You can see there is only one call up on port 22, which corresponds to B-channel 23. For greater detail, enter **6 show port** *B-channel*. In Example 6-149, the command is **6 show port 22**.

Example 6-149 *Trace of the* **6 show port 22** *Command*

```
(DSP) Show Port -> Port<22> :
       DSP/Channel = 7/3
       CxMode = SENDRECV
       State = Voice
       Local RTP Port = 0x5C9C (23708)
       Remote RTP Port = 0x6B06 (27398)
       Remote IP Address = 10.16.20.6 (0x0A101406)
       Connection ID = 23
       Call ID = D0000000010000cc000000000000001f
       Request ID = 17
       Packet Period/Size = 20/160
       Compression = G711_ULAW_PCM
       VAD = Disabled
       Preserved = False
```

This information provides the packet size, codec selection, VAD status, and RTP ports, which can help you identify the network components involved in this call, as well as the codec used for the RTP stream between them.

You can use the **Call ID** field to look through a CCM trace and find how the call got set up in the first place. If there is a call up and you know which channel it is on, but don't know how it got set up, copy the **Call ID** field (D0000000010000cc000000000000001f in this case) and search through the CCM traces for it. You should be able to find the **CRCX** MGCP message that set up the call. It will have the same call ID in the message.

Also note the last entry in Example 6-149. The **Preserved = False** line indicates that this is not a preserved call. If the call was a preserved call, the output would show **Preserved = True**.

When you are done using the Dick Tracy utility, don't forget to set any masks you enabled back to 0. Failure to do so leaves the debugs running even when you disconnect from the port. If the debugs are verbose, they may cause the port to reset from the load.

Now that you have seen how to use the Dick Tracy utility for a PRI call, you should understand the value of this utility when troubleshooting T1 CAS problems on the WS-X6608.

Troubleshooting T1 CAS Problems on the WS-X6608

T1 CAS on the WS-X6608 works differently from other MGCP-controlled gateways. The WS-X6608 converts the CAS signaling to ISDN Q.931 messages that are backhauled to CallManager just as if the signals had come in from a PRI. From CallManager's perspective, the call looks just like a PRI call setup, but behind the scenes, the WS-X6608 gateway translates between T1 CAS and ISDN Q.931. The only way to observe the CAS signaling states is by using the Dick Tracy utility.

When troubleshooting a T1 CAS call through a WS-X6608, troubleshoot the call using CCM traces as you would for a PRI call. If the WS-X6608 is not behaving as you would expect for a PRI call, you must use the Dick Tracy utility to debug the CAS signaling. For example, if CallManager sends a SETUP message to the WS-X6608 and the WS-X6608 responds with a DISCONNECT that has a cause code of resources unavailable, you need to enable debugs on the WS-X6608 to determine why the WS-X6608 is not able to process the call.

The section "Troubleshooting T1 CAS" earlier in this chapter explains how T1 CAS signaling works. If you are unfamiliar with T1 CAS signaling, please refer to that section.

The call investigated in the following example is a call from extension 2000 through a T1 CAS trunk configured for E&M Wink Start to extension 2001. The calling party (extension 2000) dials **52001**. The **5** is the route pattern causing the call to go out the T1 PRI.

On a WS-X6608 port configured for T1 CAS, task 7, the line task, provides information about T1 CAS signaling states. Issue the command **7 show mask** to get a list of the various debug flag bits that can be enabled for the line task. Example 6-150 shows the output of **7 show mask**.

Example 6-150 *Debug Mask Bits for the Line Task (Task 7)*

```
04:02:47.150 (LINE) --> TraceMask value = 00000000
            Where Bit0 = Call Control Statess
                  Bit1 = Q931
                  Bit2 = Q931 Msg's
                  Bit3 = Line Restarts
                  Bit4 = E&M Trunk States/Events
                  Bit5 = Ground Start Trunk States/Events
                  Bit6 = Loop Start Trunk States/Events
                  Bit7 = Robbed Bit Signaling Changes
```

First, look at the output for a call with all the bits set for task 7. In the Dick Tracy command window, enter **7 set mask ff** and place a call to get the results shown in Example 6-151.

Example 6-151 *Debug Trace with the Task 7 Mask Set to ff*

```
04:02:48.310 Q931: callref=8016  CCM Setup --> State = CALL_PRESENT -->
  CCM Release_Complete
04:02:48.310 E&M Q931 --> LINE: 00  EVENT: SetupInd        STATE: CSIdle
04:02:48.310 SIGNAL channel 0:signal F
04:02:48.310 LINE 0: Q931 SetupInd        --> State To CSEmWaitFarEndWink
04:02:48.980 EM RX WINK -- channel=0, In Wink Valid=100ms, Wink Dur=200ms
04:02:48.980 E&M Line --> LINE: 00  EVENT: E&M Rx Wink/Delay  STATE:
  CSEmWaitFarEndWink
04:02:48.980 Q931: callref=8016  LINE ProceedReq --> State = IN_CALL_PROCEED -->
  CCM Call_Proceeding
04:02:48.980 LINE 0: Event E&M Rx Wink/Dela --> State To CSEmWaitTOtoSendDigit -->
  Q931 ProceedReq
04:02:49.250 E&M Line --> LINE: 00  EVENT: LINE Timeout
  STATE: CSEmWaitTOtoSendDigit
```

Example 6-151 *Debug Trace with the Task 7 Mask Set to ff (Continued)*

```
04:02:49.260 LINE 0: Event LINE Timeout
04:02:50.060 E&M Line --> LINE: 00  EVENT: DTMF Sent
  STATE: CSEmDoneDialAddress
04:02:50.060 Q931: callref=8016  LINE AlertReq --> State = CALL_RECVD -->
  CCM Alerting
04:02:50.060 LINE 0: Event DTMF Sent --> State To CSEmWaitFeOffHookOr2ndWink -->
  Q931 AlertReq
04:02:51.660 CAS RX A=1 -- channel=0
04:02:51.660 E&M Line --> LINE: 00  EVENT: E&M Off Hook
  STATE: CSEmWaitFeOffHookOr2ndWink
04:02:51.660 Q931: callref=8016  LINE SetupResp --> State = CONNECT_REQ -->
  CCM Connect
04:02:51.660 LINE 0: Event E&M Off Hook --> State To CSEmWaitSetupCmpInd -->
  Q931 SetupResp
04:02:51.680 Q931: callref=8016  CCM Connect_Acknowledge --> State = ACTIVE
04:02:51.680 E&M Q931 --> LINE: 00  EVENT: SetCmpInd
  STATE: CSEmWaitSetupCmpInd
04:02:51.680 LINE 0: Q931 SetCmpInd      --> State To CSEmConnected
04:02:53.140 E&M RX Disconnect -- channel=0
04:02:53.140 E&M Line --> LINE: 00  EVENT: E&M On Hook
  STATE: CSEmConnected
04:02:53.140 SIGNAL channel 0:signal 0
04:02:53.140 Q931: callref=8016  LINE DiscReq --> State = DISCONNECT_REQ -->
  CCM Disconnect
04:02:53.140 E&M Line --> LINE: 00  EVENT: E&M On Hook
  STATE: CSCallAbandon
04:02:53.170 Q931: callref=8016  CCM Release --> State = NULL -->
  CCM Release_Complete
04:02:53.170 E&M Q931 --> LINE: 00  EVENT: ReleaseInd        STATE: CSCallAbandon
04:02:53.170 LINE 0: Q931 ReleaseInd --> State To CSIdle --> Q931 DiscReq
04:02:53.190 E&M Line --> LINE: 00  EVENT: Close Channel      STATE: CSIdle
04:02:53.190 LINE 0: Event Close Channel
```

With all the mask bits enabled, the output can be intimidating and difficult to read. However, if you look at the output for each individual bit mask, you can selectively enable the debugs you need to troubleshoot a specific problem.

As mentioned earlier, the WS-X6608 uses Q.931 to communicate with CallManager and must convert these Q.931 messages to T1 CAS. To do this, the WS-X6608 maintains a state machine that correlates Q.931 states to T1 CAS states. According to Example 6-151, bit 0 for the line task provides information about the call control states. Example 6-152 shows the trace using the command **7 set mask 1**.

Example 6-152 *Debug Trace with the Task 7 Mask Set to 1*

```
04:03:08.430 LINE 0: Q931 SetupInd            --> State To CSEmWaitFarEndWink
04:03:09.120 LINE 0: Event E&M Rx Wink/Dela --> State To CSEmWaitTOtoSendDigit -->
      Q931 ProceedReq
04:03:09.400 LINE 0: Event LINE Timeout
04:03:10.210 LINE 0: Event DTMF Sent          --> State To CSEmWaitFeOffHookOr2ndWink
      --> Q931 AlertReq
04:03:12.280 LINE 0: Event E&M Off Hook       --> State To CSEmWaitSetupCmpInd
      --> Q931 SetupResp
04:03:12.290 LINE 0: Q931 SetCmpInd           --> State To CSEmConnected
04:03:13.760 LINE 0: Q931 ReleaseInd          --> State To CSIdle
      --> Q931 DiscReq
04:03:13.780 LINE 0: Event Close Channel
```

Example 6-152 helps correlate the Q.931 states with signaling states on the T1 CAS side. For example, the second line in Example 6-152 reads

```
Event E&M Rx Wink/Dela --> State To CSEmWaitTOtoSendDigit --> Q931 ProceedReq
```

Lines that begin with the word **Event** such as this one indicate that there was a state change on the T1 CAS side. Lines that begin with **Q931** indicate a Q.931 message from CallManager. In this case, the event indicates that the WS-X6608 received an E&M Wink from the line. The next section indicates that this event caused a state change to the state named **CSEmWaitTOtoSendDigit**. This state change also triggered a state change on the ISDN state machine causing the WS-X6608 to send a Call Proceeding message to CallManager indicating that the WS-X6608 has begun the process of setting up the call. Notice that the Call Proceeding message is sent after the WS-X6608 successfully receives a wink from the far-end device.

According to Example 6-150, bit 1 for the line task provides information about Q.931 messages. Example 6-153 shows the trace using the command **7 set mask 2**. Notice the familiar Q.931 messages including Setup, Call Proceeding, Alerting, Connect, Disconnect, and Release Complete. What you do not get from this output are details about the information elements contained in each of these messages. Notice each line contains the Q.931 call reference for the call. This allows you to correlate the Dick Tracy output with a CCM trace by matching up the call reference values.

Although not intuitive, this debug indicates whether the message was sent to CallManager or received from CallManager. Immediately after the call reference field (**callref=**), you see either the letters **CCM** or the word **LINE**. If the line begins with the letters CCM, this is a message that came *from* CallManager. If the line begins with the word **LINE**, the message was sent *to* CallManager.

Example 6-153 *Debug Trace with the Task 7 Mask Set to 2*

```
04:03:20.600 Q931: callref=8018  CCM Setup --> State = CALL_PRESENT -->
  CCM Release_Complete
04:03:21.280 Q931: callref=8018  LINE ProceedReq --> State = IN_CALL_PROCEED -->
  CCM Call_Proceeding
04:03:22.350 Q931: callref=8018  LINE AlertReq --> State = CALL_RECVD -->
  CCM Alerting
04:03:24.640 Q931: callref=8018  LINE SetupResp --> State = CONNECT_REQ -->
  CCM Connect
04:03:24.650 Q931: callref=8018  CCM Connect_Acknowledge --> State = ACTIVE
04:03:27.500 Q931: callref=8018  LINE DiscReq --> State = DISCONNECT_REQ -->
  CCM Disconnect
04:03:27.520 Q931: callref=8018  CCM Release --> State = NULL -->
  CCM Release_Complete
```

The trace output in Example 6-153 does not provide you with any more detail than what you would see in the CCM trace when looking at Q.931 messages. However, when this mask bit is combined with others that show you the T1 CAS signaling, it lets you see the sequence of events. For example, if you see an on-hook indication from the T1 CAS side followed by a Q.931 Disconnect message sent from the WS-X6608 to CallManager, you can understand that the Disconnect message was due to the device connected to the WS-X6608 port sending an on-hook indication.

Example 6-153 also shows you how T1 CAS states are mapped to Q.931 states. For example, the second line, **LINE ProceedReq --> State = IN_CALL_PROCEED --> CCM Call_Proceeding**, indicates that a call proceeding request came from the T1, which corresponds to a wink as you saw in Example 6-152. The call proceeding request from the line causes a state change to the IN_CALL_PROCEED state and also triggers the port to send a Q.931 Call Proceeding to CallManager as indicated by the message **CCM_Call_Proceeding**.

Bits 2 and 3, which correspond to the commands **7 set mask 4** and **7 set mask 8**, do not provide any useful debug information when troubleshooting a T1 CAS call. Example 6-154 shows the trace output with the mask set to **10**. This is probably the most useful bit for viewing the states of the T1 CAS signaling.

Example 6-154 *Debug Trace with the Task 7 Mask Set to 10*

```
04:03:57.930 E&M Q931 --> LINE: 00  EVENT: SetupInd
  STATE: CSIdle
04:03:57.930 SIGNAL channel 0:signal F
04:03:58.620 E&M Line --> LINE: 00  EVENT: E&M Rx Wink/Delay
  STATE: CSEmWaitFarEndWink
04:03:58.900 E&M Line --> LINE: 00  EVENT: LINE Timeout
  STATE: CSEmWaitTOtoSendDigit
04:03:59.710 E&M Line --> LINE: 00  EVENT: DTMF Sent
  STATE: CSEmDoneDialAddress
04:04:01.260 E&M Line --> LINE: 00  EVENT: E&M Off Hook
  STATE: CSEmWaitFeOffHookOr2ndWink
04:04:01.280 E&M Q931 --> LINE: 00  EVENT: SetCmpInd
  STATE: CSEmWaitSetupCmpInd
```

continues

Example 6-154 *Debug Trace with the Task 7 Mask Set to 10 (Continued)*

```
04:04:04.220 E&M Line --> LINE: 00  EVENT: E&M On Hook
  STATE: CSEmConnected
04:04:04.220 SIGNAL channel 0:signal 0
04:04:04.220 E&M Line --> LINE: 00  EVENT: E&M On Hook
  STATE: CSCallAbandon
04:04:04.260 E&M Q931 --> LINE: 00  EVENT: ReleaseInd
  STATE: CSCallAbandon
04:04:04.280 E&M Line --> LINE: 00  EVENT: Close Channel
  STATE: CSIdle
```

This trace is only useful if you understand what the various states and events in the trace signify. To better understand this debug, take a look at the components of a single trace line. For example,

```
E&M Line --> LINE: 00  EVENT: E&M Rx Wink/Delay
  STATE: CSEmWaitFarEndWink
```

The first part, **E&M Line --> LINE**, indicates the event is coming from the line. **E&M Q931 --> LINE** indicates an event from CallManager. This is followed by the line number, 00 in this case. This indicates the B-channel where this event is occurring.

Next you see an event (**EVENT:**) followed by the current state in the state machine (**STATE:**). The state machine is in the **CSEmWaitFarEndWink** call state, which means the port is waiting for a wink from the far end. The event **E&M Rx Wink/Delay** means the port received a wink.

Table 6-38 lists the various call states available for T1 CAS E&M. Table 6-39 lists the various events that can come from CallManager and Table 6-40 lists the various events that can come from the line.

Table 6-38 *T1 CAS E&M Call States on the WS-X6608*

State Name	Description
CSIdle	Line is in an Idle state.
CSEmWaitFeCmReady	Sent setup request to CallManager and waiting for a response.
CSEmWaitWinkTO	Sending a wink to the far end.
CSEmWaitFeDialAddress	Waiting for the far end to dial digits and CallManager to process them.
CSEmWaitFarEndWink	Waiting for a wink or delay from the far end (depending on whether the port is configured for wink start or delay start).
CSEmWaitTOtoSendDigit	Waiting for a delay to start dialing after receiving a wink or delay (depending on whether the port is configured for wink start or delay start).

Table 6-38 *T1 CAS E&M Call States on the WS-X6608 (Continued)*

State Name	Description
CSEmDoneDialAddress	Sending digits out on the line.
CSEmWaitSetupCmpInd	Waiting for a setup complete message from CallManager, such as a call proceeding or alerting message.
CSEmWaitFeOffHookOr2ndWink	Waiting for an off-hook from the far end.
CSEmConnected	Call is connected.
CSXferActive	Received a hookflash from the far end and informed CallManager with a feature activation information element.
CSSeizeCall2	Received a response from CallManager for a feature activation information element and sent a setup request to CallManager for the second call.
CSDialCall2	Passing the digits from the far end to CallManager.
CSDisconnect	The line is in a disconnect state after receiving a disconnect request from CallManager.
CSCallAbandon	For an outgoing call, indicates a disconnect from the far end.
CSCallClearing	During disconnection, sent an on-hook over the line and waiting for an on-hook from the far end.
CSCallGlare	Received an off-hook before the gateway was finished transmitting digits or while the gateway is waiting for a wink from far end.
CSCallAborted	Call disconnected during call setup.
CSCallReject	Call rejected on a line that is busy.

Table 6-39 *T1 CAS E&M Events from CallManager on the WS-X6608*

Event Name	Description
CCSetupInd	Setup indication from CallManager indicating an outgoing call.
CCDiscInd	Disconnect indication from CallManager.
CCMoreInfoInd	Indication from CallManger asking the gateway to receive digits on the line and pass them to CallManager.
CCReleaseInd	CallManager is requesting that the gateway release the line.
CCProceedInd	CallManager has received all the digits sent by the gateway.
CCAlertInd	CallManager has begun alerting the terminating IP phone.
CCSetupCfm	Call setup confirmation from CallManager.
CCSetCmpInd	Call setup from CallManager is complete.

Table 6-40 *T1 CAS E&M Events from the Line on the WS-X6608*

Event Name	Description
E&M On Hook	Received an on-hook from the far end.
E&M Off Hook	Received an off-hook from the far end.
E&M Rx Wink/Delay	Received a wink or delay from the far end (depending on whether the port is configured for wink start or delay start).
E&M Rx Flash	Received a hookflash from the far end. Note that as of CallManager release 3.3, hookflash is not supported on T1 CAS trunks.
LINE Timeout	A timer expired that was started during the previous state transition. For example, if a wink or delay timer is started, you see this as an event when the timer expires.
DTMF Sent	The gateway has finished sending digits on the line.
Close Channel	Close the channel in response to an MGCP **DLCX** message from CallManager.
Abort Channel	The gateway lost communication with CallManager and the channel is not in sendrecv mode, so the call cannot be preserved.

Other than the event and state descriptions, you should also note the lines that begin with **SIGNAL channel**. For example, in Example 6-154 you can see the following **SIGNAL channel** messages:

```
04:03:57.930 SIGNAL channel 0:signal F
04:04:04.220 SIGNAL channel 0:signal 0
```

0 indicates the B-channel number (zero-indexed so this is B-channel 1) and **signal** indicates the transmit state of the ABCD bits. In this case, **F** means 1111 (because 0xF = 1111 in binary) and **0** means 0000 (because 0x0 = 0000 in binary).

You can see how the gateway receives a **SetupInd** event from CallManager, indicating CallManager wants to set up a new call, which causes the gateway to send **signal F** indicating an off-hook.

Later in the trace you see the event **E&M On Hook** indicating the gateway received an on-hook indication from the far end. This causes the gateway to also go on-hook by sending **signal 0**. By observing which side goes on-hook first, you can determine which side disconnected the call. In this case the far end device disconnected because the gateway received an on-hook prior to going on-hook itself.

There is no trace output with the mask set to **20** or **40** because these are used for troubleshooting FXO loop start and ground start calls. This call is an E&M call and, therefore, provides the state and event information using mask **10**.

Example 6-155 shows the trace output with the mask set to **80**.

Example 6-155 *Debug Trace with the Task 7 Mask Set to 80*

```
04:04:30.620 EM RX WINK -- channel=0, In Wink Valid=100ms, Wink Dur=200ms
04:04:33.360 CAS RX A=1 -- channel=0
04:04:39.680 E&M RX Disconnect -- channel=0
```

This debug provides some additional detail regarding the status of the A bit received on the channel and the wink duration. Normally the information presented in Example 6-154 for mask **10** is enough to troubleshoot most T1 CAS problems; however, you might want to add this bit for additional detail.

You should have to resort to using the preceding debugs only if you identify a problem with the signaling that is sent as Q.931 to CallManager. If there is a problem setting up the call from the T1 CAS point of view, the WS-X6608 port returns a cause code from Table 6-27 that indicates an error. If you are getting an error such as Resources Unavailable, it is a good idea to use the Dick Tracy utility to look at the T1 CAS signaling.

Catalyst WS-X6624 FXS Analog Gateway Configuration

The WS-X6624 Port FXS Analog Interface Module provides 24 FXS ports for connecting to analog phones, fax machines, modems, and legacy voice mail systems. This module also supports fax relay, which enables compressed fax transmission over the IP WAN.

The WS-X6624 Port FXS Analog Interface Module provides the following features:

- 24-port RJ-21 FXS module
- Modem passthrough
- Fax passthrough
- Cisco fax relay
- MGCP interface to CallManager

Like T1 CAS on the WS-X6608, the WS-X6624 module uses Q.931 backhauled messages to communicate with CallManager. This means that in a CCM trace, all you see is Q.931 messages to and from the WS-X6624 just as if the WS-X6624 were a PRI gateway. This again makes troubleshooting easy if you understand the Q.931 protocol. However, if you need to see the FXS loop start signaling on the analog ports, you must access the gateway via the Dick Tracy utility to analyze the signaling on the port.

For example, if CallManager sends a setup message to the WS-X6624, this should cause the analog phone connected to the WS-X6624 port to ring, but if the phone does not ring, no amount of traces from CallManager can tell you why. At that point, you need to look at the loop start signaling on the WS-X6624 using the Dick Tracy utility.

Just like the WS-X6608, the WS-X6624 has several different tasks that run on it. Each of these tasks is assigned a number that must be entered at the beginning of all Dick Tracy commands.

Example 6-156 lists the WS-X6624 tasks. The command **0 show tl** lists the available tasks for the WS-X6624.

Example 6-156 *WS-X6624 Debugging Tasks*

```
01:56:42.220 (GEN) Elvis Tasks
         0 : GEN
         1 : AUD
         2 : TRC
         3 : SNMP
         4 : NULL
         5 : NMP
         6 : DSP
         7 : LINE
         8 : CFG
         9 : GMSG
        10 : SOCK
        11 : TMR
        12 : CDC
        13 : XA
```

To troubleshoot the WS-X6624 gateway, you should understand how to troubleshoot the WS-X6608 using Dick Tracy. Architecturally, the two modules are very similar. For example, the output of task 9 (GMSG) is identical on the WS-X6608 and the WS-X6624, so if you understand how to read the traces for task 9 on the WS-X6608, you can do the same on the WS-X6624.

Unfortunately there is no easy way to observe events like off-hook and on-hook except by inferring the events occurred based on other events. For example, if you see the WS-X6624 send a **CreateConnection** MGCP message to CallManager, you can infer that the analog port on the WS-X6624 went off-hook.

The WS-X6624 has a few traces that differ from the WS-X6608. The DSP task **6** option is the most helpful for the majority of problems you might encounter. As with the WS-X6608, you can enable several debug masks on the DSP using the command **6 set mask**. To get a list of the available debug masks for the WS-X6624 DSP task, issue the command **6 show mask**. Example 6-157 shows the output of **6 show mask** on a WS-X6624.

Example 6-157 *Output of* **6 show mask** *on a WS-X6624 Module*

```
(DSP) Mask<0x0>
    Where Bit0 = Debug Msg's
          Bit1 = Call Progression Msg's
          Bit2 = Boot Msg's
          Bit3 = Stat Msg's
          Bit4 = Cmd Msg's
          Bit5 = RTP Msg's
          Bit6 = SID Frames
          Bit7 = Status Msg's
          Bit8 = DSP Low Level Debug Msg's
          Bit9 = Fax Relay Debug Msg's
          Bit10 = Restart Debug Msg's
          Bit11 = Statistics Query Msg's
          Bit12 = Latency Debug Msg's
```

To collect traces with the Dick Tracy client utility, you must first start the Dick Tracy utility and connect to the port you want to troubleshoot and then set the trace mask to enable the desired debugs.

To enable all the debug flags, set the mask on a WS-X6624 module to 1fff by connecting to the IP address of the WS-X6624 and issuing the command **6 set mask 1fff**.

CAUTION	When you are done debugging with the masks, make sure you set the mask back to **0**. Otherwise, even if you've closed the Dick Tracy utility, the debug information continues to be displayed on the 860 console port, thereby degrading system performance and possibly leading to an 860 reset. You can double-check the mask's status before closing the Dick Tracy utility with the command *task ID* **show mask**, so for task ID 6, you would enter the command **6 show mask**.

Example 6-158 shows a call between two phones connected to a WS-X6624 module. The calling phone is on port 4/1 with extension 58908, and the called party is on port 4/2 with extension 58909.

Example 6-158 *Dick Tracy Trace Output on a WS-X6624 with a Mask of 0x1fff Set*

```
14:46:30.480 (DSP) CRCX -> Port<0>
14:46:30.480 (DSP) RTP RxOpen -> Port<0> UDP Port<0x698A (27018)> Handle<3>
14:46:30.480 (DSP) RTCP RxOpen -> Port<0> UDP Port<0x698B (27019) Handle<4>>
14:46:30.490 (DSP) RQNT -> Port<0> From<LINE>
14:46:30.490 (DSP0) proc<0x4d72> open_voice_channel<74> PktLen<16> Chan<1>
                    Comp<0> Sig<0> TS<0> SP<0>
14:46:30.490 (DSP0) proc<0x4d73> set_gains <91> PktLen<12> Chan<1> In<0> Out<0>
14:46:30.490 (DSP0) proc<0x4d74> idle_mode<68> PktLen<8> Chan<1>
                    Enabling Digit Detection
14:46:30.490 (DSP0) proc<0x4d75> dial_mode<65> PktLen<10> Chan<1> Detect<0>
14:46:30.490 (DSP0) proc<0x4d76> echo_canceller_control<66> PktLen<12> Chan<1>
  Mode<0x0000>
                    Generating CP Tone<CPTONE_BUSY>
14:46:30.490 (DSP0) proc<0x4d77> cp_tone_on<72> PktLen<54> Chan<1>
                    NumFreq<2> Level1<9806> Level2<9806> Dir<0x0001>
                    Freq1<350/440> Cad1<65535/0> Cad2<0/0>
                    Cad3<0/0> Cad4<0/0>
14:46:32.180 (DSP) Status Check
14:46:34.180 (DSP) Status Check
14:46:34.400 (DSP) Digit Rcvd -> Port<0> Digit<5>
14:46:34.400 (DSP) RQNT -> Port<0> From<LINE>
                    Stopping Tones
14:46:34.400 (DSP0) proc<0x4d78> cp_tone_off<71> PktLen<8> Chan<1>
14:46:34.560 (DSP) Dial Digit End -> Port<0> Digit<5> Duration<195>
14:46:35.350 (DSP) Digit Rcvd -> Port<0> Digit<8>
14:46:35.530 (DSP) Dial Digit End -> Port<0> Digit<8> Duration<215>
14:46:36.180 (DSP) Status Check
```

continues

Example 6-158 *Dick Tracy Trace Output on a WS-X6624 with a Mask of 0x1fff Set (Continued)*

```
14:46:36.700 (DSP) Digit Rcvd -> Port<0> Digit<9>
14:46:36.880 (DSP) Dial Digit End -> Port<0> Digit<9> Duration<215>
14:46:37.610 (DSP) Digit Rcvd -> Port<0> Digit<0>
14:46:37.770 (DSP) Dial Digit End -> Port<0> Digit<0> Duration<195>
14:46:38.180 (DSP) Status Check
14:46:38.580 (DSP) Digit Rcvd -> Port<0> Digit<9>
14:46:38.580 (DSP) CRCX -> Port<1>
14:46:38.590 (DSP) RTP RxOpen -> Port<1> UDP Port<0x698C (27020)> Handle<5>
14:46:38.590 (DSP) RTCP RxOpen -> Port<1> UDP Port<0x698D (27021)> Handle<6>>
14:46:38.590 (DSP) RQNT -> Port<1> From<LINE>
14:46:38.590 (DSP0) proc<0x4d79> open_voice_channel<74> PktLen<16> Chan<2>
                    Comp<0> Sig<0> TS<1> SP<0>
14:46:38.590 (DSP0) proc<0x4d7a> set_gains <91> PktLen<12> Chan<2> In<0> Out<0>
14:46:38.590 (DSP0) proc<0x4d7b> idle_mode<68> PktLen<8> Chan<2>
                    Generating CP Tone<CPTONE_STUTT_DIALTONE>
14:46:38.590 (DSP0) proc<0x4d7c> dial_mode<65> PktLen<10> Chan<2> Detect<0>
14:46:38.590 (DSP0) proc<0x4d7d> echo_canceller_control<66> PktLen<12> Chan<2>
  Mode<0x0000>
14:46:38.590 (DSP0) proc<0x4d7e> cp_tone_on<72> PktLen<54> Chan<2>
                    NumFreq<1> Level1<65535> Level2<0> Dir<0x0001>
                    Freq1<20/0> Cad1<100/0> Cad2<0/0>
                    Cad3<0/0> Cad4<0/0>
14:46:38.600 (DSP) RQNT -> Port<0> From<GMSG>
                    Enabling Digit Detection
                    Generating CP Tone<CPTONE_CONGESTION>
14:46:38.600 (DSP0) proc<0x4d7f> cp_tone_on<72> PktLen<54> Chan<1>
                    NumFreq<2> Level1<10386> Level2<10386> Dir<0x0001>
                    Freq1<440/480> Cad1<2000/4000> Cad2<0/0>
                    Cad3<0/0> Cad4<0/0>
14:46:38.760 (DSP) Dial Digit End -> Port<0> Digit<9> Duration<215>
14:46:40.180 (DSP) Status Check
14:46:42.180 (DSP) Status Check
14:46:44.180 (DSP) Status Check
14:46:46.180 (DSP) Status Check
14:46:46.890 (DSP) RQNT -> Port<1> From<LINE>
                    Stopping Tones
14:46:46.890 (DSP0) proc<0x4d80> cp_tone_off<71> PktLen<8> Chan<2>
14:46:46.900 (DSP) MDCX -> Port<0>
                    Mode : RECVONLY
Just go to voice mode
14:46:46.900 (DSP) Voice Mode -> Port<0> Comp<G711_ULAW_PCM> agcEnable<0>
14:46:46.900 (DSP0) proc<0x4d81> set_playout_delay<76> PktLen<18> Chan<1>
                    Mode<1> Initial<60> Min<20> Max<150> Fax<0>
14:46:46.900 (DSP0) proc<0x4d82> encap_config<92> PktLen<30> Chan<1> Prot<2>
                    txSSRC<0x68ED0100> rxSSRC<0x00000000>
                    txVPXCC<0x0080> rxVPXCC<0x0000> SID<0> NSE<101> SEQ<0>
(DSP0) proc<0x4d83> voice_mode<73> PktLen<26> Chan<1> Codec<1> PktSize<160>
  VAD<0> Echo<256> Noise<1> Detect<0x0421> Mode<3> AGC<0> V21<65535>
14:46:46.900 (DSP0) Current PID: S<0x4d83> E<0x4d82> Last PID: S<0x4d82>
  E<0x4d82>
14:46:46.900 (DSP0) proc<0x4d84> echo_canceller_control<66> PktLen<12> Chan<1>
  Mode<0x8197>
```

Example 6-158 *Dick Tracy Trace Output on a WS-X6624 with a Mask of 0x1fff Set (Continued)*

```
14:46:46.900 (DSP0) proc<0x4d85> agc_control<98> PktLen<10> Chan<1> Mode<0x0000>
                    Enabling Digit Detection
14:46:46.900 (DSP) MDCX -> Port<1>
                    Mode : RECVONLY
Just go to voice mode
14:46:46.910 (DSP) Voice Mode -> Port<1> Comp<G711_ULAW_PCM> agcEnable<0>
14:46:46.910 (DSP0) proc<0x4d86> set_playout_delay<76> PktLen<18> Chan<2>
                    Mode<1> Initial<60> Min<20> Max<150> Fax<0>
14:46:46.910 (DSP0) proc<0x4d87> encap_config<92> PktLen<30> Chan<2> Prot<2>
                    txSSRC<0x68ED0101> rxSSRC<0x00000000>
                    txVPXCC<0x0080> rxVPXCC<0x0000> SID<0> NSE<101> SEQ<0>
(DSP0) proc<0x4d88> voice_mode<73> PktLen<26> Chan<2> Codec<1> PktSize<160>
  VAD<0> Echo<256> Noise<1> Detect<0x0421> Mode<3> AGC<0> V21<65535>
14:46:46.910 (DSP0) Current PID: S<0x4d88> E<0x4d87> Last PID: S<0x4d87>
  E<0x4d87>
14:46:46.910 (DSP0) proc<0x4d89> echo_canceller_control<66> PktLen<12> Chan<2>
  Mode<0x8197>
14:46:46.910 (DSP0) proc<0x4d8a> agc_control<98> PktLen<10> Chan<2> Mode<0x0000>
                    Enabling Digit Detection
14:46:46.910 (DSP) RQNT -> Port<0> From<GMSG>
                    Stopping Tones
14:46:46.910 (DSP0) proc<0x4d8b> cp_tone_off<71> PktLen<8> Chan<1>
14:46:46.910 (DSP) RQNT -> Port<0> From<LINE>
14:46:46.920 (DSP) MDCX -> Port<1>
                    Mode : SENDRECV
14:46:46.920 (DSP) RTP TxOpen -> Port<1> Remote IP<172.18.104.236>
  UDP Port<0x698A (27018)> Handle<0>
14:46:46.920 (DSP) RTCP TxOpen -> Port<1> Remote IP<172.18.104.236>
  UDP Port<0x698B (27019)> Handle<0>
                    Enabling Digit Detection
14:46:46.920 (DSP) MDCX -> Port<0>
                    Mode : SENDRECV
14:46:46.920 (DSP) RTP TxOpen -> Port<0> Remote IP<172.18.104.236>
  UDP Port<0x698C (27020)> Handle<0>
14:46:46.920 (DSP) RTCP TxOpen -> Port<0> Remote IP<172.18.104.236>
  UDP Port<0x698D (27021)> Handle<0>
                    Enabling Digit Detection
14:46:47.180 (DSP0) proc<0x4da6> get_stat<84> PktLen<10> Chan<1> Reset<0>
14:46:47.180 (DSP0) proc<0x4da7> get_stat<84> PktLen<10> Chan<2> Reset<0>
14:46:47.190 (DSP) DSP<0> Chan<1> VPOESt PR<0> Int<0> Sil<0>Ret<0> Ov<0>
  TSE<1536076>
14:46:47.190 (DSP) DSP<0> Chan<2> VPOESt PR<0> Int<0> Sil<0>Ret<0> Ov<0>
  TSE<1536076>
14:46:48.180 (DSP0) proc<0x4e0c> get_stat<6> PktLen<10> Chan<1> Reset<0>
14:46:48.180 (DSP0) proc<0x4e0d> get_stat<6> PktLen<10> Chan<2> Reset<0>
14:46:48.180 (DSP) Status Check
14:46:48.190 (DSP) DSP<0> Chan<1> ErrSt drRxH<0> drTxO<0> Rx<496>Tx<157>
  drTx<0> drRx<0>
14:46:48.190 (DSP) DSP<0> Chan<2> ErrSt drRxH<0> drTxO<0> Rx<83>Tx<4>
  drTx<0> drRx<0>
14:46:49.180 (DSP0) proc<0x4e72> get_stat<86> PktLen<10> Chan<1> Reset<0>
14:46:49.180 (DSP0) proc<0x4e73> get_stat<86> PktLen<10> Chan<2> Reset<0>
```

continues

Example 6-158 *Dick Tracy Trace Output on a WS-X6624 with a Mask of 0x1fff Set (Continued)*

```
14:46:49.190 (DSP) DSP<0> Chan<1> voicePkts<113> CN<0> Dur<2270>,
  vTxDur<227> faxTxDur<0>
14:46:49.190 (DSP) DSP<0> Chan<2> voicePkts<113> CN<0> Dur<2270>,
  vTxDur<227> faxTxDur<0>
14:46:50.180 (DSP0) proc<0x4ed8> get_stat<87> PktLen<10> Chan<1> Reset<0>
14:46:50.180 (DSP0) proc<0x4ed9> get_stat<87> PktLen<10> Chan<2> Reset<0>
14:46:50.180 (DSP) Status Check
14:46:50.190 (DSP) DSP<0> Chan<1> sigPkts<162> CN<0> rxDur<3250> OOS<0> Bad<0>
  Late<0> Early<0>
14:46:50.190 (DSP) DSP<0> Chan<2> sigPkts<162> CN<0> rxDur<3250> OOS<0> Bad<0>
  Late<0> Early<0>
14:46:51.180 (DSP0) proc<0x4f3e> get_stat<89> PktLen<10> Chan<1> Reset<0>
14:46:51.180 (DSP0) proc<0x4f3f> get_stat<89> PktLen<10> Chan<2> Reset<0>
14:46:51.190 (DSP) Port 0 Level Stats
14:46:51.190 (DSP) Port 1 Level Stats
14:46:52.180 (DSP0) proc<0x4fa4> get_stat<108> PktLen<10> Chan<1> Reset<0>
14:46:52.180 (DSP0) proc<0x4fa5> get_stat<108> PktLen<10> Chan<2> Reset<0>
14:46:52.180 (DSP) Status Check
14:46:52.190 (DSP) DSP<0> Chan<1> fill<0> drain<0> overall loss<0>consecutive
  loss<0> RFC 2198 loss<0> time<0> max duration<0> min duration<0>
14:46:52.190 (DSP) DSP<0> Chan<2> fill<0> drain<0> overall loss<0>consecutive
  loss<0> RFC 2198 loss<0> time<0> max duration<0> min duration<0>
14:46:53.180 (DSP0) proc<0x500a> get_stat<88> PktLen<10> Chan<1> Reset<0>
14:46:53.180 (DSP0) proc<0x500b> get_stat<88> PktLen<10> Chan<2> Reset<0>
14:46:54.120 (DSP) MDCX -> Port<0>
                       Mode : RECVONLY
14:46:54.120 (DSP) RTP TxClose -> Port<0>
14:46:54.120 (DSP) Set DSP Idle<HOLD>, hold_state<1> previous state<0>
                       Enabling Digit Detection
14:46:54.120 (DSP) MDCX -> Port<1>
                       Mode : RECVONLY
14:46:54.120 (DSP) RTP TxClose -> Port<1>
14:46:54.120 (DSP) Set DSP Idle<HOLD>, hold_state<1> previous state<0>
                       Enabling Digit Detection
14:46:54.130 (DSP) DLCX -> Port<1> From<LINE >
14:46:54.130 (DSP) RTP RxClose -> Port<1>
14:46:54.130              Pkts Rcvd<360> Pkts Lost<0> Total Pkts Lost<0>
14:46:54.130              Underrun<0> Overrun<0>
14:46:54.130 (DSP0) proc<0x506a> idle_mode<68> PktLen<8> Chan<2>
14:46:54.130 (DSP0) proc<0x506b> close_voice_channel<75> PktLen<8> Chan<2>
14:46:54.130 (DSP) DLCX -> Port<1> From<GMSG >
14:46:54.180 (DSP0) proc<0x506c> get_stat<1468> PktLen<10> Chan<1> Reset<0>
14:46:54.180 (DSP) Status Check
14:46:55.180 (DSP0) proc<0x506d> get_stat<83> PktLen<10> Chan<1> Reset<0>
14:46:55.190 (DSP) DSP<0> Chan<1> VPODSt Clk<0> Del<44> Lo<44>Hi<65>
14:46:56.180 (DSP0) proc<0x506e> get_stat<84> PktLen<10> Chan<1> Reset<0>
14:46:56.180 (DSP) Status Check
14:46:56.190 (DSP) DSP<0> Chan<1> VPOESt PR<30> Int<10> Sil<0>Ret<20> Ov<1>
  TSE<1536076>
14:46:57.180 (DSP0) proc<0x506f> get_stat<6> PktLen<10> Chan<1> Reset<0>
14:46:57.190 (DSP) DSP<0> Chan<1> ErrSt drRxH<0> drTxO<0> Rx<505>Tx<164>
  drTx<0> drRx<0>
14:46:58.180 (DSP0) proc<0x5070> get_stat<86> PktLen<10> Chan<1> Reset<0>
14:46:58.180 (DSP) Status Check
```

Example 6-158 *Dick Tracy Trace Output on a WS-X6624 with a Mask of 0x1fff Set (Continued)*

```
14:46:58.190 (DSP) DSP<0> Chan<1> voicePkts<564> CN<0> Dur<11280>,
  vTxDur<1128> faxTxDur<0>
14:46:59.130 (DSP) RQNT -> Port<0> From<LINE>
                        Generating CP Tone<CPTONE_RING>
14:46:59.130 (DSP) Set DSP voice Mode Hold_state<2> previous state<1>
14:46:59.130 (DSP0) proc<0x5071> cp_tone_on<72> PktLen<54> Chan<1>
                        NumFreq<2> Level1<9256> Level2<9256> Dir<0x0001>
                        Freq1<480/620> Cad1<250/250> Cad2<0/0>
                        Cad3<0/0> Cad4<0/0>
14:46:59.180 (DSP0) proc<0x5072> get_stat<87> PktLen<10> Chan<1> Reset<0>
14:46:59.190 (DSP) DSP<0> Chan<1> sigPkts<359> CN<0> rxDur<12260> OOS<0> Bad<0>
  Late<0> Early<0>
14:47:00.180 (DSP0) proc<0x5073> get_stat<89> PktLen<10> Chan<1> Reset<0>
14:47:00.180 (DSP) Status Check
14:47:00.190 (DSP) Port 0 Level Stats
14:47:01.180 (DSP0) proc<0x5074> get_stat<108> PktLen<10> Chan<1> Reset<0>
14:47:01.190 (DSP) DSP<0> Chan<1> fill<0> drain<0> overall loss<0>consecutive
  loss<0> RFC 2198 loss<0> time<0> max duration<0> min duration<0>
14:47:01.440 (DSP) DLCX -> Port<0> From<LINE >
14:47:01.440 (DSP) RTP RxClose -> Port<0>
14:47:01.440                 Pkts Rcvd<360> Pkts Lost<0> Total Pkts Lost<0>
14:47:01.440                 Underrun<0> Overrun<0>
14:47:01.440 (DSP0) proc<0x5075> dial_mode<65> PktLen<10> Chan<1> Detect<0>
14:47:01.440 (DSP0) proc<0x5076> cp_tone_off<71> PktLen<8> Chan<1>
14:47:01.440 (DSP0) proc<0x5077> close_voice_channel<75> PktLen<8> Chan<1>
14:47:01.440 (DSP) DLCX -> Port<0> From<GMSG >
```

To better understand each of the pieces of the trace, enable each trace bit one at a time to understand what each of them do.

First enable Bit0 which corresponds to the debug messages trace according to Example 6-157 by entering the Dick Tracy command **6 set mask 1**. The output for the same call from 58908 to 58909 is shown in Example 6-159.

Example 6-159 *Debug with the Dick Tracy Task 6 Mask Set to 1*

```
   (DSP) Set Mask -> Mask<0x1>
14:47:37.900 (DSP) Dial Digit End -> Port<0> Digit<5> Duration<155>
14:47:38.180 (DSP) Dial Digit End -> Port<0> Digit<8> Duration<185>
14:47:38.510 (DSP) Dial Digit End -> Port<0> Digit<9> Duration<215>
14:47:39.340 (DSP) Dial Digit End -> Port<0> Digit<0> Duration<165>
14:47:39.580 (DSP) Dial Digit End -> Port<0> Digit<9> Duration<135>
14:47:44.350 (DSP) Voice Mode -> Port<0> Comp<G711_ULAW_PCM> agcEnable<0>
14:47:44.350 (DSP) Voice Mode -> Port<1> Comp<G711_ULAW_PCM> agcEnable<0>
```

Example 6-159 shows you any DTMF digits detected by the WS-X6624 gateway. You can also see which port on the WS-X6624 the DTMF digits correspond to. In this case the port number is **Port<0>**, which is actually port 1 on the gateway. The gateway port numbers go from 1 through 24, however Dick Tracy displays them as 0 through 23.

You can also see both port 0 and port 1 are put into voice mode using the G.711 codec. Other trace masks shown in the following examples give you better information about codec selection during a call. Next, enable Bit1, which corresponds to the call progression messages trace according to Example 6-157, by entering the Dick Tracy command **6 set mask 2**. The output for the same call from 58908 to 58909 is shown in Example 6-160.

Example 6-160 *Debug with the Dick Tracy Task 6 Mask Set to 2*

```
           (DSP) Set Mask -> Mask<0x2>
14:48:03.390 (DSP) CRCX -> Port<0>
14:48:03.400 (DSP) RQNT -> Port<0> From<LINE>
                   Enabling Digit Detection
                   Generating CP Tone<DIAL>
14:48:03.400 (DSP) Set DSP voice Mode Hold_state<2> previous state<1>
14:48:05.440 (DSP) Digit Rcvd -> Port<0> Digit<5>
14:48:05.440 (DSP) RQNT -> Port<0> From<LINE>
                   Stopping Tones
14:48:05.700 (DSP) Digit Rcvd -> Port<0> Digit<8>
14:48:05.940 (DSP) Digit Rcvd -> Port<0> Digit<9>
14:48:06.180 (DSP) Digit Rcvd -> Port<0> Digit<0>
14:48:06.430 (DSP) Digit Rcvd -> Port<0> Digit<9>
14:48:06.440 (DSP) CRCX -> Port<1>
14:48:06.440 (DSP) RQNT -> Port<1> From<LINE>
                   Generating CP Tone<RING>
14:48:06.450 (DSP) Set DSP voice Mode Hold_state<2> previous state<1>
14:48:06.450 (DSP) RQNT -> Port<0> From<GMSG>
                   Enabling Digit Detection
                   Generating CP Tone<RINGBACK>
14:48:09.900 (DSP) RQNT -> Port<1> From<LINE>
                   Stopping Tones
14:48:09.910 (DSP) MDCX -> Port<0>
                   Mode : RECVONLY
14:48:09.910 (DSP) Set DSP Idle<HOLD>, hold_state<1> previous state<2>
Just go to voice mode
                   Enabling Digit Detection
14:48:09.910 (DSP) MDCX -> Port<1>
                   Mode : RECVONLY
14:48:09.910 (DSP) Set DSP Idle<HOLD>, hold_state<1> previous state<2>
Just go to voice mode
                   Enabling Digit Detection
14:48:09.910 (DSP) RQNT -> Port<0> From<GMSG>
                   Stopping Tones
14:48:09.920 (DSP) MDCX -> Port<1>
                   Mode : SENDRECV
14:48:09.920 (DSP) set Dsp voice Mode hold_stae<0> previous state<1>
                   Enabling Digit Detection
14:48:09.920 (DSP) MDCX -> Port<0>
                   Mode : SENDRECV
14:48:09.920 (DSP) set Dsp voice Mode hold_stae<0> previous state<1>
                   Enabling Digit Detection
14:48:09.920 (DSP) RQNT -> Port<0> From<LINE>
14:48:14.790 (DSP) MDCX -> Port<0>
                   Mode : RECVONLY
14:48:14.790 (DSP) Set DSP Idle<HOLD>, hold_state<1> previous state<0>
                   Enabling Digit Detection
```

Example 6-160 *Debug with the Dick Tracy Task 6 Mask Set to 2 (Continued)*

```
14:48:14.790 (DSP) MDCX -> Port<1>
                        Mode : RECVONLY
14:48:14.790 (DSP) Set DSP Idle<HOLD>, hold_state<1> previous state<0>
                        Enabling Digit Detection
14:48:14.800 (DSP) DLCX -> Port<1> From<LINE >
14:48:14.800 (DSP) DLCX -> Port<1> From<GMSG >
14:48:16.710 (DSP) DLCX -> Port<0> From<LINE >
14:48:16.710 (DSP) DLCX -> Port<0> From<GMSG >
```

The call progression debug trace provides you with some good information. First, when you see the message **CRCX -> Port<0>** it indicates that a new connection was created for port 1 on the module, which corresponds with port 0 in the debugs. This is usually an indication that the port went off-hook.

This trace also shows you all the call progress tones for the call. The message **Generating CP Tone** is followed by a description of the tone being generated, such as RING for ring tone, RINGBACK for ringback tone, and DIAL for dial tone. Notice the message always indicates which port the message corresponds with. To stop a tone, you see **Stopping Tones** in the trace.

Finally, the call progression debug trace shows you when the ports go on-hook with the message **DLCX -> Port<0>**.

Setting the mask to **0x4** (Boot Messages) does not produce any debug output during the course of a normal call because the flag is only useful while the port is booting up.

Next, enable Bit3, which corresponds to statistics messages trace according to Example 6-157, by entering the Dick Tracy command **6 set mask 8**. The output for the same call from 58908 to 58909 is shown in Example 6-161.

Example 6-161 *Debug with the Dick Tracy Task 6 Mask Set to 8*

```
14:49:01.190 (DSP) DSP<0> Chan<1> VPODSt Clk<0> Del<64> Lo<64>Hi<65>
14:49:01.190 (DSP) DSP<0> Chan<2> VPODSt Clk<0> Del<64> Lo<64>Hi<65>
14:49:02.190 (DSP) DSP<0> Chan<1> VPOESt PR<0> Int<0> Sil<0>Ret<0> Ov<0>
  TSE<1536076>
14:49:02.190 (DSP) DSP<0> Chan<2> VPOESt PR<0> Int<0> Sil<0>Ret<0> Ov<0>
  TSE<1536076>
14:49:03.190 (DSP) DSP<0> Chan<1> ErrSt drRxH<0> drTx0<0> Rx<605>Tx<230>
  drTx<0> drRx<0>
14:49:03.190 (DSP) DSP<0> Chan<2> ErrSt drRxH<0> drTx0<0> Rx<160>Tx<22>
  drTx<0> drRx<0>
14:49:04.190 (DSP) DSP<0> Chan<1> voicePkts<183> CN<0> Dur<3670>, vTxDur<367>
  faxTxDur<0>
14:49:04.190 (DSP) DSP<0> Chan<2> voicePkts<183> CN<0> Dur<3660>, vTxDur<366>
  faxTxDur<0>
14:49:05.190 (DSP) DSP<0> Chan<1> sigPkts<231> CN<0> rxDur<4640> OOS<0> Bad<0>
  Late<0> Early<0>
14:49:05.190 (DSP) DSP<0> Chan<2> sigPkts<232> CN<0> rxDur<4650> OOS<0> Bad<0>
  Late<0> Early<0>
```

continues

Example 6-161 *Debug with the Dick Tracy Task 6 Mask Set to 8 (Continued)*

```
14:49:06.190 (DSP) Port 0 Level Stats
14:49:06.190 (DSP) Port 1 Level Stats
14:49:07.190 (DSP) DSP<0> Chan<1> fill<0> drain<0> overall loss<0>
  consecutive loss<0> RFC 2198 loss<0> time<0> max duration<0> min duration<0>
14:49:07.190 (DSP) DSP<0> Chan<2> fill<0> drain<0> overall loss<0>
  consecutive loss<0> RFC 2198 loss<0> time<0> max duration<0> min duration<0>
14:49:10.190 (DSP) DSP<0> Chan<1> VPODSt Clk<0> Del<44> Lo<44>Hi<65>
14:49:10.190 (DSP) DSP<0> Chan<2> VPODSt Clk<0> Del<44> Lo<44>Hi<65>
14:49:11.190 (DSP) DSP<0> Chan<1> VPOESt PR<0> Int<0> Sil<0>Ret<20> Ov<0>
  TSE<1536076>
14:49:11.190 (DSP) DSP<0> Chan<2> VPOESt PR<0> Int<0> Sil<0>Ret<20> Ov<0>
  TSE<1536076>
14:49:12.190 (DSP) DSP<0> Chan<1> ErrSt drRxH<0> drTxO<0> Rx<614>Tx<237>
  drTx<0> drRx<0>
14:49:12.190 (DSP) DSP<0> Chan<2> ErrSt drRxH<0> drTxO<0> Rx<169>Tx<29>
  drTx<0> drRx<0>
14:49:13.190 (DSP) DSP<0> Chan<2> voicePkts<633> CN<0> Dur<12670>, vTxDur<1267>
  faxTxDur<0>
14:49:14.190 (DSP) DSP<0> Chan<2> sigPkts<597> CN<0> rxDur<13660> OOS<0> Bad<0>
  Late<0> Early<0>
14:49:15.190 (DSP) Port 1 Level Stats
14:49:16.190 (DSP) DSP<0> Chan<2> fill<0> drain<0> overall loss<0>
  consecutive loss<0> RFC 2198 loss<0> time<0> max duration<0> min duration<0>
14:49:19.190 (DSP) DSP<0> Chan<2> VPODSt Clk<0> Del<44> Lo<44>Hi<65>
14:49:20.190 (DSP) DSP<0> Chan<2> VPOESt PR<30> Int<10> Sil<0>Ret<20> Ov<1>
  TSE<1536076>
14:49:21.190 (DSP) DSP<0> Chan<2> ErrSt drRxH<0> drTxO<0> Rx<179>Tx<36>
  drTx<0> drRx<0>
14:49:22.190 (DSP) DSP<0> Chan<2> voicePkts<1083> CN<0> Dur<21670>, vTxDur<2167>
  faxTxDur<0>
```

The DSP statistics are sent to the 860 CPU every second, as shown in Example 6-161. It takes six seconds to retrieve all the statistics for a port because only one statistic is updated every second, and there are six different statistics.

The numbers displayed are DSP statistics for a particular DSP channel, so you must correlate the DSP channel number with the port number. To do this, use the command **6 show port**[*port_number*]. For example, **show port[0]** shows:

```
(DSP) Show Port -> Port< 0> :
        DSP/Channel = 0/1
        No Connection
```

This means that port 0 corresponds with DSP 0 channel 1. You also need to know which DSP corresponds to a particular port to use the next debug, which is the command messages trace.

Bit4 corresponds to the command messages trace according to Example 6-157. Enable this trace by entering the Dick Tracy command **6 set mask 10**. The output for the same call from 58908 to 58909 is shown in Example 6-162.

Example 6-162 *Debug with the Dick Tracy Task 6 Mask Set to 0x10*

```
14:49:34.660 (DSP0) proc<0x5b11> open_voice_channel<74> PktLen<16> Chan<1>
                    Comp<0> Sig<0> TS<0> SP<0>
14:49:34.660 (DSP0) proc<0x5b12> set_gains <91> PktLen<12> Chan<1> In<0> Out<0>
14:49:34.660 (DSP0) proc<0x5b13> idle_mode<68> PktLen<8> Chan<1>
14:49:34.660 (DSP0) proc<0x5b14> dial_mode<65> PktLen<10> Chan<1> Detect<0>
14:49:34.660 (DSP0) proc<0x5b15> echo_canceller_control<66> PktLen<12> Chan<1>
  Mode<0x0000>
14:49:34.660 (DSP0) proc<0x5b16> cp_tone_on<72> PktLen<54> Chan<1>
                    NumFreq<2> Level1<9806> Level2<9806> Dir<0x0001>
                    Freq1<350/440> Cad1<65535/0> Cad2<0/0>
                    Cad3<0/0> Cad4<0/0>
14:49:35.820 (DSP0) proc<0x5b17> cp_tone_off<71> PktLen<8> Chan<1>
14:49:36.870 (DSP0) proc<0x5b18> open_voice_channel<74> PktLen<16> Chan<2>
                    Comp<0> Sig<0> TS<1> SP<0>
14:49:36.870 (DSP0) proc<0x5b19> set_gains <91> PktLen<12> Chan<2> In<0> Out<0>
14:49:36.870 (DSP0) proc<0x5b1a> idle_mode<68> PktLen<8> Chan<2>
14:49:36.870 (DSP0) proc<0x5b1b> dial_mode<65> PktLen<10> Chan<2> Detect<0>
14:49:36.870 (DSP0) proc<0x5b1c> echo_canceller_control<66> PktLen<12> Chan<2>
  Mode<0x0000>
14:49:36.870 (DSP0) proc<0x5b1d> cp_tone_on<72> PktLen<54> Chan<2>
                    NumFreq<1> Level1<65535> Level2<0> Dir<0x0001>
                    Freq1<20/0> Cad1<100/0> Cad2<0/0>
                    Cad3<0/0> Cad4<0/0>
14:49:36.870 (DSP0) proc<0x5b1e> cp_tone_on<72> PktLen<54> Chan<1>
                    NumFreq<2> Level1<10386> Level2<10386> Dir<0x0001>
                    Freq1<440/480> Cad1<2000/4000> Cad2<0/0>
                    Cad3<0/0> Cad4<0/0>
14:49:41.370 (DSP0) proc<0x5b1f> cp_tone_off<71> PktLen<8> Chan<2>
14:49:41.380 (DSP0) proc<0x5b20> set_playout_delay<76> PktLen<18> Chan<1>
                    Mode<1> Initial<60> Min<20> Max<150> Fax<0>
14:49:41.380 (DSP0) proc<0x5b21> encap_config<92> PktLen<30> Chan<1> Prot<2>
                    txSSRC<0x68ED0100> rxSSRC<0x00000000>
                    txVPXCC<0x0080> rxVPXCC<0x0000> SID<0> NSE<101> SEQ<0>
(DSP0) proc<0x5b22> voice_mode<73> PktLen<26> Chan<1> Codec<1> PktSize<160>
  VAD<0> Echo<256> Noise<1> Detect<0x0421> Mode<3> AGC<0> V21<65535>
14:49:41.380 (DSP0) proc<0x5b23> echo_canceller_control<66> PktLen<12> Chan<1>
  Mode<0x8197>
14:49:41.380 (DSP0) proc<0x5b24> agc_control<98> PktLen<10> Chan<1> Mode<0x0000>
14:49:41.380 (DSP0) proc<0x5b25> set_playout_delay<76> PktLen<18> Chan<2>
                    Mode<1> Initial<60> Min<20> Max<150> Fax<0>
14:49:41.380 (DSP0) proc<0x5b26> encap_config<92> PktLen<30> Chan<2> Prot<2>
                    txSSRC<0x68ED0101> rxSSRC<0x00000000>
                    txVPXCC<0x0080> rxVPXCC<0x0000> SID<0> NSE<101> SEQ<0>
(DSP0) proc<0x5b27> voice_mode<73> PktLen<26> Chan<2> Codec<1> PktSize<160>
  VAD<0> Echo<256> Noise<1> Detect<0x0421> Mode<3> AGC<0> V21<65535>
14:49:41.380 (DSP0) proc<0x5b28> echo_canceller_control<66> PktLen<12> Chan<2>
  Mode<0x8197>
14:49:41.380 (DSP0) proc<0x5b29> agc_control<98> PktLen<10> Chan<2> Mode<0x0000>
```

continues

Example 6-162 *Debug with the Dick Tracy Task 6 Mask Set to 0x10 (Continued)*

```
14:49:41.390 (DSP0) proc<0x5b2a> cp_tone_off<71> PktLen<8> Chan<1>
14:49:46.510 (DSP0) proc<0x5d34> idle_mode<68> PktLen<8> Chan<2>
14:49:46.510 (DSP0) proc<0x5d35> close_voice_channel<75> PktLen<8> Chan<2>
14:49:48.750 (DSP0) proc<0x5d38> idle_mode<68> PktLen<8> Chan<1>
14:49:48.750 (DSP0) proc<0x5d39> close_voice_channel<75> PktLen<8> Chan<1>
```

As you can see, this is one of the more verbose debugs available. Be careful using this mask bit, especially if several calls are going simultaneously.

The command messages trace shows you messages to the DSP to generate call progress tones and adjust DSP parameters such as playout delay (jitter buffer size) and dB levels. The call progression messages trace in Example 6-160 showed the names of the call progress tones; however, the command messages trace indicates the exact frequency and cadence of the tone being played. For example, the following is an extract from Example 6-162 of the first call progress tone generated:

```
14:49:34.660 (DSP0) proc<0x5b16> cp_tone_on<72> PktLen<54> Chan<1>
                    NumFreq<2> Level1<9806> Level2<9806> Dir<0x0001>
                    Freq1<350/440> Cad1<65535/0> Cad2<0/0>
                    Cad3<0/0> Cad4<0/0>
```

Notice that the trace indicates there are two frequencies as part of this tone: 350 Hz and 440 Hz. The cadence is 65535 which indicates a continuous tone. This is the frequency and cadence for dial tone in North America. If you are using a different network locale you should see a different frequency and cadence that matches the configured network locale.

You can also use this trace mask to ensure any audio gain or attenuation parameters configured on the Gateway Configuration page in CallManager Administration (**Device > Gateway**) are being applied. In the trace above, you can see that the gains are being set to zero for both input and output by looking at the line that says **set_gains <91> PktLen<12> Chan<1> In<0> Out<0>**.

Bit5 corresponds to the RTP messages trace according to Example 6-157. Enable this trace by entering the Dick Tracy command **6 set mask 20**. The output for the same call from 58908 to 58909 is shown in Example 6-163.

Example 6-163 *Debug with the Dick Tracy Task 6 Mask Set to 0x20*

```
14:50:00.540 (DSP) RTP RxOpen -> Port<0> UDP Port<0x69A4 (27044)> Handle<3>
14:50:00.540 (DSP) RTCP RxOpen -> Port<0> UDP Port<0x69A5 (27045) Handle<4>>
14:50:03.340 (DSP) RTP RxOpen -> Port<1> UDP Port<0x69A6 (27046)> Handle<5>
14:50:03.350 (DSP) RTCP RxOpen -> Port<1> UDP Port<0x69A7 (27047) Handle<6>>
14:50:09.160 (DSP) RTP TxOpen -> Port<1> Remote IP<172.18.104.236>
   UDP Port<0x69A4 (27044)> Handle<0>
14:50:09.170 (DSP) RTCP TxOpen -> Port<1> Remote IP<172.18.104.236>
   UDP Port<0x69A5 (27045)> Handle<0>
14:50:09.170 (DSP) RTP TxOpen -> Port<0> Remote IP<172.18.104.236>
   UDP Port<0x69A6 (27046)> Handle<0>
14:50:09.170 (DSP) RTCP TxOpen -> Port<0> Remote IP<172.18.104.236>
   UDP Port<0x69A7 (27047)> Handle<0>
```

Example 6-163 *Debug with the Dick Tracy Task 6 Mask Set to 0x20 (Continued)*

```
14:50:17.100 (DSP) RTP TxClose -> Port<0>
14:50:17.100 (DSP) RTP TxClose -> Port<1>
14:50:17.110 (DSP) RTP RxClose -> Port<1>
14:50:17.110              Pkts Rcvd<397> Pkts Lost<0> Total Pkts Lost<0>
14:50:17.110              Underrun<0> Overrun<0>
14:50:20.220 (DSP) RTP RxClose -> Port<0>
14:50:20.220              Pkts Rcvd<397> Pkts Lost<0> Total Pkts Lost<0>
14:50:20.220              Underrun<0> Overrun<0>
```

The RTP messages trace is useful for determining when RTP streams are opened and closed and to which IP address and port number the RTP streams are being created. Notice in this example the **Remote IP** field is set the same for both ports. This is because the call is between two analog phones on the same module, so the module basically sends RTP packets to itself to communicate from one port to the other.

At the end of the trace when the RTP stream is closed (indicated by the **RTP RxClose** message), you see packet statistics for the call. You can use this if you are having voice quality problems and you suspect packet loss. The RTP messages trace confirms or denies whether you are having problems with packet loss. For more information on troubleshooting voice quality problems, refer to Chapter 7, "Voice Quality."

For this particular call, Bit5, which corresponds with the SID frames trace, did not produce any output because SID frames are only generated when VAD is enabled. VAD was disabled for this call.

Finally, Bit6 corresponds to the status messages trace according to Example 6-157. Enable this trace by entering the Dick Tracy command **6 set mask 80**. The output for the same call from 58908 to 58909 is shown in Example 6-164.

Example 6-164 *Debug with the Dick Tracy Task 6 Mask Set to 80*

```
14:50:56.190 (DSP) Status Check
14:50:58.190 (DSP) Status Check
14:51:00.190 (DSP) Status Check
14:51:02.190 (DSP) Status Check
14:51:04.190 (DSP) Status Check
```

As you can see, this trace is not very exciting. It just shows you the same message every two seconds. If you are having DSP-related problems such as a DSP that has crashed, this debug might provide some additional insight. If, however, you have a DSP crashing, you might have to reset the module to recover from the failure.

Best Practices

You can apply several best practices to gateways to help make troubleshooting that much easier:

- Use IP addresses for your H.323 gateways instead of host names. Put the host name in the description. The last thing you need to do is rely on your DNS servers unnecessarily.

- Put your service provider's circuit ID and phone number in the description field of your gateways. This helps you quickly get the information you need to contact your service provider.

- Use Syslog to log messages from all your Cisco IOS gateways to be able to catch any errors that occur before they become a problem.

- Ensure the clocks on all your CallManager nodes and voice gateways are synchronized with a centralized NTP clock source as described in Chapter 3. Synchronized clocks makes correlating events between gateway debugs and CCM traces easier.

- Hard-code the IP addresses on your gateways, or give them DHCP reservations to ensure that they always have the same IP address.

- Make sure that IP routing is enabled on all voice gateways, even if they are not performing routing functionality. The voice code uses the IP routing code to send the voice packets to their final destination.

- Make sure you have two-way IP connectivity. It is possible for the gateway to successfully send a message to CallManager but for CallManager's response to get lost in the network. The same applies to two-way connectivity with the TFTP server.

- Hard-code speed and duplex only on static devices such as gateways and servers. Use autonegotiation for all client devices, such as phones and PCs.

- When possible, use MGCP instead of H.323. MGCP offers call preservation and easier dial plan configuration. H.323 calls are not preserved in the event of a CallManager or network failure. Also note that when you use MGCP, you must take into account WAN failover scenarios because an MGCP interface does not work when connectivity is lost to the call agent (CallManager). As of Cisco IOS Software Release 12.2(11)T, MGCP endpoints can revert to H.323 in a failure scenario to work in conjunction with Survivable Remote Site Telephony (SRST).

- Always use an **incoming called number** configuration parameter to match an inbound dial peer for H.323 calls. It has been mentioned several times, but the importance of making sure you always match an inbound dial peer as opposed to matching peer ID 0 can't be stressed enough.

Summary

Gateways are one of the most important elements of an IP Telephony network. They provide connectivity to the outside world through a variety of TDM-based interfaces.

If you have you finished reading the whole chapter, you probably are overwhelmed by the amount of information presented. With the right tools and approach, the complexity can be significantly reduced. Consider the following:

- Every gateway mentioned can suffer from network misconfiguration or network outages. Therefore, never forget to take each problem one piece at a time and one layer of the OSI model at a time.

- Don't forget that connectivity to your gateway is only as good as your IP network. Regardless of which gateway it is, it must have bidirectional network connectivity to the other devices it communicates with.

- If the gateway is Cisco IOS-based, the debugging tools are virtually the same for all the platforms. If you learn how to use them, it doesn't matter if it is a 2600, 3600, or 5300.

- If the gateway is a WS-X6608 or WS-X6624 module, the debugging tools are the same. Dick Tracy can be used with either module, and many tasks are very similar in their output during tracing. Both modules have the same types of power needs and follow identical procedures to register with CallManager.

- Two primary VoIP signaling protocols are used, H.323 and MGCP. H.323 is used between CallManager and other CallManager clusters, as well as Cisco IOS gateways. MGCP is used between CallManager and Cisco IOS gateways, as well as between CallManager and the WS-X6608 and WS-X6624 modules. As soon as you know the basic signaling for MGCP and H.323, you can apply that knowledge to any of the gateways mentioned.

- T1 PRI and T1 CAS signaling are the same regardless of the platform. As soon as you understand the basic messages, you can apply that knowledge to any of the gateways using those protocols.

At this point, you might be thinking that this is still a lot of information. Understanding the protocols used in the packet-switched and circuit-switched realms can apply to all the gateways referenced in this chapter. For example, if you learn ISDN Q.931 signaling, you will be able to troubleshoot Q.931 on any of the gateways described here. As a bonus, you will understand a good piece of H.323 signaling in the process. In essence, it is these basic skills that transcend individual platforms and allow you to troubleshoot gateway problems effectively.

## CHAPTER 7

Voice Quality

"I got echo during a call this morning." "I was on the phone with a client this afternoon, and the call didn't sound good." "I was on a conference call, and the sound was choppy." These kinds of problem reports are typical voice quality problems you might encounter in a telephony environment. Phrases such as "this morning" and "didn't sound good" don't provide the details you need to diagnose a problem's root cause. This chapter focuses on what information you need and how to investigate and resolve voice quality problems in an IP telephony network.

The best way to troubleshoot a voice quality problem is to understand what elements contribute to good or bad quality and the various sources of problems that could affect each of these elements. Voice quality is a broad term that covers the following elements:

- Delayed audio
- Choppy or garbled audio
- Static and noise
- One-way or no-way audio
- Echo

Voice quality problems are some of the most difficult to troubleshoot because most voice quality problems are caused by problems in the IP network transporting the voice packets. Therefore, a good understanding of your network is absolutely essential to troubleshooting voice quality issues. This chapter focuses on explaining the various elements that contribute to voice quality and the possible factors that can cause a problem in one or more of these elements.

When presented with a voice quality problem, examine the symptoms to determine which element of voice quality is a problem and investigate the potential causes for the problem methodically. Most voice quality problems involve multiple network devices, so identify the two endpoints involved in the call and search for the root cause in the network devices between the two endpoints, one device at a time.

Fixed and Variable Delays

Delay is an important factor to consider when designing an IP telephony network, particularly if WAN connectivity is involved. *Delay* is the amount of time it takes the sound from a talker's mouth to reach the far-end listener's ear. Because of the nature of a packet voice network, several factors can cause delay. Some of these factors you can control, and others you cannot. Delays in a packet voice network can be subdivided into fixed delays and variable delays.

The International Telecommunication Union (ITU) considers network delay for voice applications in Recommendation G.114. This recommendation defines three bands of one-way delay, as shown in Table 7-1. The recommended ranges for private networks, such as Cisco IP telephony solutions, differ, as explained later in this section.

Table 7-1 *Recommendation G.114 Delay Specifications*

ITU Recommendation— Range in Milliseconds	Private Network Recommendation— Range in Milliseconds	Description
0 to 150	0 to 200	Acceptable for most user applications.
150 to 400	200 to 250	Acceptable provided that administrators are aware of the transmission time and its impact on the transmission quality of user applications.
Above 400	Above 250	Unacceptable for general network planning purposes. However, it is recognized that in some exceptional cases, this limit will be exceeded (for example, satellite connections).

These recommendations are for connections in which echo is adequately controlled, which implies that echo cancellers are used. Echo cancellers are required when one-way delay exceeds 25 ms, as described in the section "What Makes Echo a Problem?"

The ITU recommendations are written with telephone companies and service providers in mind. The level of delay acceptable for most user applications is more stringent than what might be required in a private voice network because in a private voice network, you control the total end-to-end delay. A telephone company likely has additional equipment connected at the customer premises that might introduce additional delay that it must account for. For a private network, 200 ms is a reasonable goal, and 250 ms should be an absolute maximum. The important thing is to know what your delay budget is so that if there is a problem, you have a known-good value to compare to. Remember that these numbers are total end-to-end delay, not just the delays introduced on the WAN side of a connection. These recommendations are also geared toward planning for end-to-end delay for the voice path, but they do not take into account delays associated with signaling. The section "The Effects of Delay on Signaling" discusses this problem in more depth.

To troubleshoot a problem with delayed audio, you must

- Understand where the delay is coming from
- Take measures to minimize the amount of delay at each hop in the path between two endpoints

First, let's determine the potential sources of delay in a packet voice network.

Fixed Delay Sources

Fixed delay refers to delays that are constant for every call regardless of varying network conditions. For example, the propagation delay between two points over the same medium is always the same because the speed of light does not change. Sources of fixed delay include the following:

- Coder (processing) delay
- Packetization delay
- Serialization delay
- Propagation delay

Figure 7-1 shows where the various forms of fixed delays are introduced in a network.

Figure 7-1   *Fixed Delays*

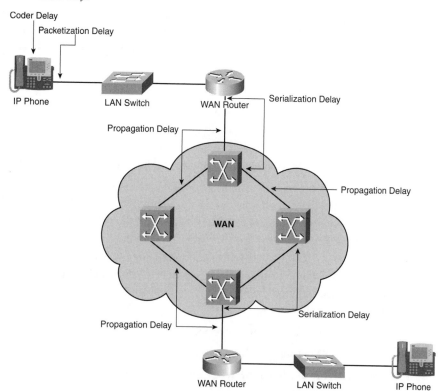

Coder (Processing) Delay

Coder delay, also known as processing delay, is the time taken by the digital signal processor (DSP) to compress a block of pulse code modulation (PCM) samples. Because different coders work in different ways, this delay varies with the voice codec used and processor speed. For example, Algebraic Code Excited Linear Prediction (ACELP) algorithms (for example, G.723) work by analyzing a 10-ms block of PCM samples and then compressing them.

The compression time for a Conjugate Structure Algebraic Code Excited Linear Prediction (CS-ACELP) process (for example, G.729) ranges from 2.5 ms to 10 ms, depending on the loading of the DSP. If the DSP is fully loaded with four voice channels, the coder delay is 10 ms. If the DSP is loaded with only one voice channel, the coder delay is 2.5 ms. This occurs after the sample has been taken and before the packetization begins. For example, G.729 has a 10-ms sample size, so the codec gathers 10 ms of data and then compresses it. The codec can compress while it gathers future samples, so the codec delay applies only once per packet, not once per sample.

Uncompressed codecs such as G.711 don't have any coder delay because they do not have to compress the sampled waveforms; however, as you will see in the next section, packetization delay is the limiting factor.

Most compressed codecs use information about the next sample to generate the current sample. For example, when a G.729 coder tries to compress a 10-ms block of audio, it looks at the subsequent 5 ms of audio to make the calculation for the current 10-ms sample. This means that the current 10-ms sample must be delayed an additional 5 ms before being compressed. This additional look-ahead delay is called *algorithmic delay.* G.729 has an algorithmic delay of 5 ms, and G.723.1 has an algorithmic delay of 7.5 ms.

Packetization Delay

Packetization delay is the time taken to fill a packet payload with encoded/compressed speech and add the various IP/UDP/RTP headers. This delay is a function of the sample block size required by the coder and the number of blocks placed in a single frame.

The packetization delay must be a multiple of the sample size that a given codec uses. For example, G.729 uses 10-ms samples, so the information must be packetized in 10-ms blocks. For G.711 and G.729, the default packet (payload) size is a 20-ms sample. G.723 uses 30-ms samples, so the packet size must be a multiple of 30.

The packet size for the various codecs is user-configurable on a system-wide basis in Cisco CallManager Administration (**Service > Service Parameters >** *select a server >* **Cisco CallManager**). Three CallManager service parameters control the packet size, one for each supported codec:

- **PreferredG711MillisecondPacketSize**
- **PreferredG723MillisecondPacketSize**
- **PreferredG729MillisecondPacketSize**

You want to try to minimize packetization delay because it can contribute a fair amount of delay to your delay budget. You must keep in mind, however, that the smaller the packet size, the more packets per second you need to generate for the same Real-Time Protocol (RTP) stream. Also, the size of the IP, User Datagram Protocol (UDP), and RTP headers remains constant regardless of the sample size being used, so the smaller the packet size, the greater the header overhead will be in proportion to the total packet size.

For example, in the worst-case scenario of using 10-ms samples for a G.729 packet, the G.729 sample is 10 bytes and the IP, UDP, and RTP headers are 40 bytes. This means that you have 400 percent overhead! By changing to 20-ms samples, you now have 20 bytes of audio and 40 bytes of headers, so the overhead is 200 percent. This is still a huge number; however, you can see what a significant difference increasing the packet size makes. Also, by going from 10 ms to 20 ms, you change the number of packets per second from 100 to 50. Depending on your network infrastructure, you might not be able to handle 100 packets per second when you multiply that by the number of active RTP streams in your network. Also, some gateways might not be able to handle such a high packet rate associated with the lower sample sizes. If you are seeing high CPU utilization or dropped packets in output queues on WAN routers carrying voice traffic or gateways terminating voice traffic, check the number of packets per second that router/gateway is processing by using the **show interface** command. This will tell you if you are going over the stated capacity of the particular router/gateway that is experiencing the high CPU utilization. This is especially important on routers performing compressed RTP (cRTP) on WAN links because cRTP is a CPU-intensive operation.

Also be aware that the larger your packet size, the greater the impact that losing a single packet has on voice quality. For example, if you lose a 10-ms sample, most codecs can compensate for this very easily by guessing what the missing waveform is. However, if you are missing 50 ms, there might be a noticeable audio glitch.

In general, the only portion of the coder delay that is important is the algorithmic delay because you need to wait for the packetization delay before sending the packet anyway. As a rough estimate, the algorithmic delay plus the packetization delay gives you a value that is good enough for making calculations. If you want to be conservative, add a few milliseconds to the calculation to compensate for any additional processing delays that the packet might undergo before being sent onto the network.

Serialization Delay

Serialization delay is the fixed delay required to clock an IP packet out a network interface. It is directly related to the clock rate on the interface.

Table 7-2 shows the serialization delay required for different frame sizes at different line speeds.

Table 7-2 *Serialization Delay for Different Frame Sizes*

	1 Byte	64 Bytes	128 Bytes	256 Bytes	512 Bytes	1024 Bytes	1500 Bytes
56 kbps	143 μs	9 ms	18 ms	36 ms	72 ms	144 ms	214 ms
64 kbps	125 μs	8 ms	16 ms	32 ms	64 ms	128 ms	187 ms
128 kbps	62.5 μs	4 ms	8 ms	16 ms	32 ms	64 ms	93 ms
256 kbps	31 μs	2 ms	4 ms	8 ms	16 ms	32 ms	46 ms
512 kbps	15.5 μs	1 ms	2 ms	4 ms	8 ms	16 ms	23 ms
768 kbps	10 μs	640 μs	1.28 ms	2.56 ms	5.12 ms	10.24 ms	15 ms
1536 kbps	5 μs	320 μs	640 μs	1.28 ms	2.56 ms	5.12 ms	7.5 ms

* μs=microseconds

For a 20-ms G.729 packet with IP, UDP, and RTP headers, the packet size is 60 bytes plus any Layer 2 overhead, equaling roughly 64 bytes. This means that on a 64-kbps WAN connection, it takes approximately 8 ms to put the entire packet on the wire. If there are multiple hops, you must take the serialization delay for each packet into account because each router needs to receive the entire packet before it can begin sending it out the destination interface.

Table 7-3 shows the header length for various protocols you might encounter. Every voice packet has at least an IP, UDP, and RTP header in addition to the voice sample payload and Layer 2 headers.

Table 7-3 *Header Lengths for Various Protocols*

Protocol Header	Header Length in Bytes
IP	20
UDP	8
RTP	12
Ethernet	18
Frame Relay	6
PPP	6
HDLC	6

To get a detailed analysis of all the headers for your particular medium, use the automated Voice Codec Bandwidth Calculator available on Cisco.com:

http://tools.cisco.com/Support/VBC/jsp/Codec_Calc1.jsp

So far, the discussion has been focused on the serialization delay of a single voice packet without taking into account any buffering that might be required to serialize other packets in the buffer. The section "Variable Delay Sources" discusses this in greater detail.

Propagation Delay

Propagation delay is the amount of time it takes for a single bit of data to get from one side of a digital connection to the other. Propagation delay is usually close to the speed of light, depending on the medium over which the packet is being carried (copper, fiber, and so on). The propagation delay over a digital copper or fiber-optic connection is approximately 1 ms per 100 miles. For example, the distance between New York and London is approximately 3500 miles. This means that the propagation delay between New York and London is approximately 35 ms.

Other devices can contribute to propagation delay. Physical layer devices such as multiplexers and repeaters can introduce a small amount of delay that is usually negligible; however, if several such devices are in use, the delay can add up.

Propagation delay is usually a concern only when you're dealing with long distances. Within a metropolitan area, propagation delay is negligible.

Variable Delay Sources

Fixed delay is relatively easy to calculate because all the fixed delay sources have a way to determine exactly how much delay is caused by each delay source. *Variable delay,* as the name implies, can change depending on network conditions. Packet voice depends on a steady stream of voice packets. Typically, you'll use a 20-ms packet size, so the receiving device expects to see a packet every 20 ms. The fixed delay sources dictate how long it takes the first packet to get from the sender to the receiver; however, after the first packet has reached the receiver, regardless of how long it took to get there, subsequent packets are expected to arrive every 20 ms. If any sources of variable delay exist in the network, some packets might arrive later than 20 ms. If appropriate actions are not taken, the receiving device has no audio samples to play during the time the packet is variably delayed. Variable delay is called *jitter*. You should do everything possible to minimize the amount of jitter in your network. To understand how to minimize jitter, you must first understand what causes it.

Figure 7-2 shows what can happen if your network has variable delay.

Figure 7-2 *Jitter (or Variable Delay) in a Network*

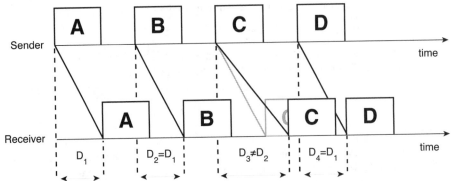

Notice that packets A, B, C, and D are all sent at regular intervals, such as every 20 ms. Packet A arrives at the receiving device after a specific amount of time, D_1. This value represents the total delay between the sender and the receiver. If there are no variable delay sources in the network, all packets take exactly D_1 time to get from the sender to the receiver. However, in Figure 7-2, you can see that Packet C takes longer to arrive than expected. *Jitter* is the difference in time between the expected arrival time and the time the packet actually arrives.

Most jitter is caused by the fact that somewhere in the network a packet needs to wait for other packets that are in front of it to be sent. Most jitter is introduced as a result of queuing or buffering on the network, especially when low-speed links are involved.

Queuing/Buffering Delay

After the compressed voice payload is built, a header is added and the frame is queued for transmission on the network connection. Assuming that you have configured your quality of service (QoS) correctly, voice should have absolute priority on all routers and switches in your network. Therefore, a voice frame should only have to wait either for a data frame already in the process of being transmitted or for other voice frames that arrived at the router or switch ahead of it. Essentially, the voice frame is waiting for the serialization delay of any preceding frames in the output queue. Queuing delay is a variable delay and is dependent on the line speed and the queue's state. As you can see, random elements are associated with the queuing delay.

For example, on a 64-kbps line, assume that a packet is queued behind one data frame (128 bytes) and one voice frame (60 bytes). Because there is a random aspect as to how much of the 128-byte frame has played out, you can safely assume, on average, that half the data frame has been played out. Using the data from Table 7-2, the data frame component is as follows:

$$16 \text{ ms} \times 0.5 = 8 \text{ ms}$$

Adding the time for another voice frame ahead in the queue (8 ms) gives you a total time of 16 ms of queuing delay at this particular moment in time. If the other voice sample hadn't been there, the total would have been just 8 ms. If nothing had been in the queue, there would have been no delay.

Low-speed Links

Jitter is more likely to occur on low-speed links because even a single packet in the queue on a low-speed link can dramatically affect the amount of time a voice packet needs to wait in the queue before being transmitted. Jitter can be an even bigger problem if you do not have priority queuing (that is, Low Latency Queuing [LLQ]) enabled on your WAN connections or if you have it misconfigured. It is essential that voice traffic get absolute priority over any data traffic. For more information on using LLQ to prioritize voice samples over data, refer to the *Cisco IP Telephony QoS Design Guide*, available on Cisco.com (search for "Cisco IP Telephony QoS Design Guide") or at the following link:

www.cisco.com/univercd/cc/td/doc/product/voice/ip_tele/avvidqos/

Low-speed links also require special consideration when data traffic is also present to ensure that a large data packet does not cause excessive jitter. Generally on WAN links that are 768 kbps or slower, you should use some form of fragmentation and interleaving to ensure that large data packets do not starve smaller voice packets. Remember that even with LLQ enabled, if a data packet is in the process of being transmitted when a voice packet arrives, the voice packet must wait for that data packet to be completely sent before the voice packet can be sent.

Taking the worst-case scenario, suppose you have a 64-kbps Frame Relay connection, and a 1500-byte data packet arrives. A voice packet arrives at the router and is transmitted to the WAN. At this point, no more voice packets need to be sent, so the 1500-byte data packet is allowed to go to the WAN. After the first byte of the 1500-byte packet is transmitted, a second voice packet arrives. From Table 7-2, you can see that the 1500-byte packet takes 187 ms to transmit before the voice packet can begin being transmitted. That single 1500-byte data packet just introduced 187 ms of jitter. You are trying to target a one-way delay of 150 ms, and this single data packet just caused the variable delay to exceed the total delay budget. Clearly, this is unacceptable.

To correct this, you can introduce one of several methods for performing link fragmentation and interleaving (LFI). LFI tools are used to fragment large data frames into regular-sized pieces and to interleave voice frames into the flow so that the end-to-end delay can be predicted accurately. This places bounds on jitter by preventing voice traffic from being delayed behind large data frames, as illustrated in Figure 7-3. The two techniques used for this process are FRF.12 for Frame Relay and Multilink Point-to-Point Protocol (MLP) for point-to-point serial links.

Figure 7-3 *Link Fragmentation and Interleaving*

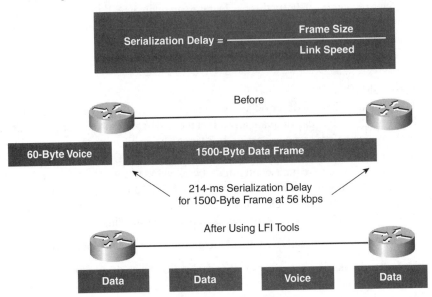

If you are seeing high amounts of jitter over a low-speed link, it's quite likely that improperly configured LFI is the problem. This is assuming that you are not oversubscribing the WAN link with more voice traffic than what you are prioritizing with your QoS policy.

For more information on how to configure LFI, refer to the *Cisco IP Telephony QoS Design Guide*.

In a properly designed network, all voice traffic should take strict priority over all other data traffic. Although this ensures that no more than one data packet is allowed to exit the router before a voice packet (because it was already being transmitted prior to the voice packet's arrival), voice packets still need to wait behind other voice packets that are in the queue because all voice packets get priority treatment. This means that the maximum queuing delay is determined by the amount of voice traffic on the link, which is controlled by one of the various call admission control mechanisms discussed in Chapter 13, "Call Admission Control," and the maximum frame size on the link.

For example, if you allow four G.729 voice calls over a 128-kbps WAN, it takes approximately 4 ms to transmit one voice sample. The worst-case scenario is that there are four simultaneous voice calls, and all four voice samples arrive at the same time. This means that the fourth sample needs to wait behind the other three that arrived immediately before it. So although the serialization delay for one voice packet is 4 ms, there is an additional queuing delay of 12 ms for the other three voice packets that arrived shortly before the fourth packet. Additionally, assuming that the link's fragmentation size is 128 bytes, it is likely that a data fragment was in the process of being transmitted when the first of the four voice samples arrived. 128 bytes of data takes 8 ms to transmit on a 128-kbps link, so in the worst case, the fourth voice sample might have to wait for the one data fragment plus the three other voice samples that arrived in front of it. This equals a 20-ms total queuing delay for the one packet.

Dejitter Delay

Every network has a certain amount of jitter due to its various queues. Because speech is a constant bit rate (CBR) service, the jitter from all the variable delays must be removed before the audio is played back to the recipient. In Cisco voice gateways and IP Phones, this is accomplished with a dejitter buffer at the receiving voice gateway or IP Phone. The *dejitter buffer* transforms the variable delay into a fixed delay by holding the first sample received for a period of time before playing it. This holding period is called the *initial playout delay*. Figure 7-4 shows the buffering that normally occurs in a dejitter buffer.

Figure 7-4   *Dejitter Buffer Operation*

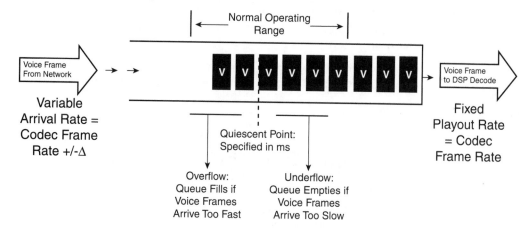

Proper handling of the dejitter buffer is critical. If samples are held for too short a time, variations in delay can cause the buffer to underrun and cause gaps in the speech. If the sample is held for too long a time, the buffer can overrun, and the dropped packets again cause gaps in the speech. Also, packets that are held for too long a time affect the connection's overall delay, causing it to rise to unacceptable levels.

The optimum initial playout delay for the dejitter buffer is equal to the total variable delay along the connection. Because this is not something that is typically known as an absolute, some best guesses are necessary. Some platforms allow you to configure the initial playout delay, but the majority of non-IOS voice gateways and IP phones do not.

Assume that the playout delay is initially set to 40 ms. The first voice sample received when the dejitter buffer is empty is held for 40 ms before it is played. This implies that a subsequent packet received from the network can be delayed as much as 40 ms (with respect to the first packet) without any loss of voice continuity. If it is delayed more than 40 ms, the dejitter buffer empties, and the next packet received is held for 40 ms before playout to reset the buffer. This results in a gap in the voice played for about 40 ms. As long as voice packets are arriving at the correct packet rate, the dejitter buffer has enough packets to play 40 ms of audio before running out of packets. This means that the variable delay in the network can be up to 40 ms without noticeable voice quality degradation on the receiving end.

The dejitter buffer's actual contribution to delay is the dejitter buffer's initial playout delay plus the actual amount the first packet was buffered in the network.

Most Cisco voice gateways and Cisco IP Phones have variable dejitter buffers that can adapt to network conditions. If an IP Phone detects that the maximum jitter on a network connection exceeds the initial playout delay, it increases the size of the dejitter buffer to accommodate for larger variable delay. This has the positive effect of making the voice sound good instead of sounding choppy or broken; however, it has the side effect of introducing additional one-way delay. The dejitter buffer in the 79xx series of IP Phones can actually grow up to 1 second; however, there must be extremely bad network conditions to cause this to occur. At that point, the conversation would be extremely annoying because of the additional delay.

To look at the jitter statistics on a 79xx IP Phone, press the help (**i** or **?**) button twice in quick succession during an active call. The call statistics appear on the screen, as shown in Figure 7-5.

Figure 7-5   *Call Statistics from a 7960 Phone*

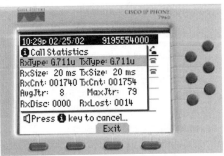

Notice that in Figure 7-5 the average jitter (AvgJtr) is only 8 ms, but the maximum jitter (MaxJtr) for this call is 79 ms. This means that the dejitter buffer is likely slightly more than 79 ms to compensate for the jitter that is being encountered on the line. The average jitter value is the amount of jitter experienced for the last 16 packets processed by the IP Phone. In this case, the buffering delays that caused the 79 ms of jitter are no longer present because the jitter is only 8 ms. The dejitter buffer adds 80 ms to whatever other fixed delays exist between the two endpoints. Depending on how you have designed your network, 80 ms might or might not be acceptable. If several low-speed links along the way between two endpoints are heavily loaded with voice traffic, the queuing delay from the network can contribute to significant variable delay. If you are in a LAN environment and are seeing 79 ms of jitter, you probably have a problem somewhere. A very common reason for jitter like this in a LAN environment is a duplex mismatch between two network devices connecting the two endpoints. Such a condition would likely cause choppy or garbled audio as well. The section "Analyzing and Troubleshooting Choppy and Garbled Audio" goes into details on how to troubleshoot choppy or garbled audio.

The Effects of Delay on Signaling

So far you have seen the effects of fixed and variable delay on voice packets, but signaling traffic is also affected by delay.

When a call is set up between two endpoints, the servers in the CallManager cluster are responsible for setting up the media streams between each of the endpoints involved in the call. Because most messages require some kind of response before the message exchange can continue, any delay slows down the message exchange. The user does not hear any audio until all the messages required to open the media streams are completed. If the delay is long enough, the caller might not hear the first few words of the conversation when the user answers the phone. This is mostly a problem when using H.323 gateways.

As you saw in Chapter 6, "Voice Gateways," CallManager and an H.323 gateway exchange several messages to complete H.245 negotiations. If you refer to Figure 6-7, you can see that H.245 negotiations involve opening the H.245 TCP connection, capabilities exchange, and logical channel negotiation. Table 7-4 shows the number of messages required to accomplish each step of the H.245 negotiation.

Table 7-4   *Messages Required to Complete H.245 Negotiations*

H.245 Negotiation Step	Messages
Connect message	1
Three-way handshake to open H.245 TCP connection	3
Capabilities exchange/master-slave determination	2
Open logical channel	1
Open logical channel acknowledgment	1

If you add up the number of messages shown in Table 7-4, you see that it takes a minimum of eight messages to open a media stream on an H.323 gateway. If a WAN with 100-ms one-way delay separates CallManager and the H.323 gateway, audio cut-through takes at least 800 ms without taking into account the processing delays on the H.323 gateway and CallManager.

The worst-case scenario is when both an H.323 gateway and an IP phone are at one location and CallManager is across the WAN at another location. In this case, you also need to take into account the number of messages to open the media stream to the IP phone. Having an IP phone at the other end introduces at least three more messages because CallManager needs to complete the negotiation with the IP phone before it can complete the negotiations with the gateway. This means that at least 11 one-way trips are required to open the media stream. In the case of 100 ms of WAN delay, this means 1.1 seconds before the calling party hears the called party.

There are several things you can do to minimize the impact of WAN delays on signaling. One change that significantly reduces the messaging is switching from H.323 to MGCP. MGCP requires significantly fewer messages to open the media streams. In the case of an MGCP gateway and an IP phone at one location and CallManager across the WAN, the total number of messages required to open the logical channels is only six. This number might be reduced to four in future versions of CallManager and Cisco IOS Software.

An alternative is to enable H.323 Fast Connect (also called FastStart). To enable Fast Connect, set the CallManager service parameter **H323FastStartInbound** to True on all nodes in the cluster (**Service > Service Parameters >** *select a server >* **Cisco CallManager**). This causes CallManager to use Fast Connect when an inbound H.323 setup message contains the FastStart element. When you use Fast Connect, all H.245 negotiations are bypassed, and audio is cut through with far less messaging than without Fast Connect.

Note that even though Fast Connect greatly improves media stream establishment times when a call is first answered, the H.245 negotiations still occur when the media stream is redirected, such as in the case of putting a call on hold or transferring a call, so you might still see delays in these situations. The best alternative is to use MGCP.

Analyzing and Troubleshooting Choppy and Garbled Audio

One of the most common voice quality problems is choppy or garbled audio. Nearly all voice quality problems can be attributed to some kind of degradation on the IP network that the voice traffic traverses. Network problems that might not be noticeable for normal data traffic are very apparent in a voice conversation due to the necessity of minimizing packet loss and variable delay in an IP telephony network.

A variety of issues can result in choppy or garbled audio:

- Packet drops
- Queuing problems
- Voice activity detection (VAD)

Packet Drops

Packet loss is probably the most common reason for voice quality problems in an IP telephony network. IP telephony demands that voice packets reach their destination within a predicable amount of time and without being dropped somewhere along the path from the source to the destination.

In a properly designed network with appropriate QoS provisioning in place, packet loss should be near zero. All voice codecs can tolerate some degree of packet loss without dramatically affecting voice quality. Upon detecting a missing packet, the codec decoder on the receiving device makes a best guess as to what the waveform during the missing period of time should have been. Most codecs can tolerate up to five percent random packet loss without noticeable voice quality degradation. This assumes that the five percent of packets being lost are not being lost at the same time, but rather are randomly dropped in groups of one or two packets. Losing multiple simultaneous packets, even as a low percentage of total packets, can cause noticeable voice quality problems. You should design your network for zero packet loss for packets that are tagged as voice packets. A converged voice/data network should be engineered to ensure that only a specific number of calls are allowed over a limited-bandwidth link. You should guarantee the bandwidth for those calls by giving priority treatment to voice traffic over all other traffic.

For more information on prioritizing voice over data, refer to the *Cisco IP Telephony QoS Design Guide*, available on Cisco.com (search for "Cisco IP Telephony QoS Design Guide") or at the following link:

> www.cisco.com/en/us/netsol/ns110/ns165/ns268/
> networking_solutions_design_guidances_list.html

There are various tools you can use to determine whether you are experiencing packet loss in your network and where in the network the packets are getting dropped.

The first place to look for lost packets is the call statistics screen on the Cisco 7940 and 7960 IP Phones, as you saw when looking for jitter measurements earlier. You access these statistics by pressing the help (**i** or **?**) button on the IP Phone twice in quick succession during an active call. You should see a statistics screen similar to the one shown in Figure 7-6.

Figure 7-6   *Call Statistics from a 7960 Phone*

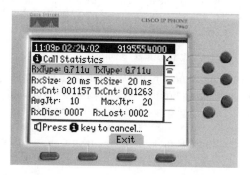

Notice the last two lines of the display. The counters RxDisc and RxLost are the counters you are interested in. RxLost measures the number of packets that were never received because they were dropped in the network somewhere. By detecting a missing RTP sequence number, the IP Phone can determine that a packet has been lost. RxDisc corresponds to packets that were received but were discarded because they could not be used at the time they arrived. RxDisc can come from an out-of-order packet or a packet that arrived too late. If either of these two counters increments, you should investigate to learn why packets are being lost or discarded. The call shown in Figure 7-6 has no noticeable degradation in voice quality because only nine packets out of 1263 have been lost. This is only 0.07 percent packet loss.

Regardless of how low your packet loss is, if is not zero, you should investigate the root cause because it might be a sign of a bigger problem that will get worse with higher call volume. Also, although small packet loss might not be perceptible in a conversation between two people, it can be detrimental to fax and modem transmissions as discussed in Chapter 8, "Fax Machines and Modems." The packet loss can be occurring at any layer of the OSI model, so be sure to check for all possibilities for each hop. For example, if there is a Frame Relay connection over a T1 between two sites, you should check to make sure there are no errors at the physical layer on the T1, check to see if you are exceeding your committed information rate (CIR) on the Frame Relay connection, and make sure you are not dropping the packets at the IP layer because you are exceeding your buffer sizes or have your QoS improperly configured. Also be aware of service providers that tell you they do not provide a CIR but guarantee that they will not drop any packets. In a voice environment, delay is as important as packet loss. Many service providers' switches can buffer a large amount of data, thereby causing a large amount of jitter. Ensure that your service provider not only guarantees packet delivery but also guarantees a low-jitter link.

One common cause of drops in an Ethernet environment is a duplex mismatch. Check all the switch ports through which a given call must travel, and ensure that there are no alignment or frame check sequence (FCS) errors. Alignment and FCS errors are usually a sign of a duplex mismatch—that is, when one side of a connection is set to full duplex and the other is at half duplex. Poor cabling or connectors can also contribute to such errors; however, duplex mismatches are a far more common cause of this kind of problem. To check for duplex mismatches, look at each link between the two endpoints experiencing packet loss, and check to make sure the speed and duplex settings match on either side. For more information about troubleshooting duplex mismatches, refer to the Cisco document "Configuring and Troubleshooting Ethernet 10/100/1000Mb Half/Full Duplex Auto-Negotiation" at the following URL:

www.cisco.com/warp/public/473/3.html

Although duplex mismatches are responsible for a large number of packet loss problems, there are many other opportunities for packet loss in other places in the network as well. When voice traffic must traverse a WAN, there are several places to look. First, check each interface between the two endpoints, and look for packet loss. On all Cisco IOS Software platforms, you can find this information using the **show interface** command. If you are seeing dropped packets on any interface, there is a good chance you are oversubscribing the link. This could also be indicative of some other traffic you are not expecting on your network. The best solution in this case is to take a sniffer trace to examine which traffic is congesting the link.

Sniffers are invaluable in troubleshooting voice quality problems. Chapter 3, "Understanding the Troubleshooting Tools," provides more information about collecting sniffer traces. With a sniffer, you can examine each packet in an RTP stream to see if packets are really being lost and where in the network they are being lost. To troubleshoot using a sniffer, start at the endpoint that is experiencing the poor-quality audio where you suspect packet loss. Take a sniffer trace of a poor-quality call and filter it so that it shows you only packets from the far end to the endpoint hearing the problem. The packets should be equally spaced, and the sequence numbers should be consecutive with no gaps. If you are seeing all the packets in the sniffer trace, continue taking traces after each hop until you get a trace where packets are missing. As soon as you have isolated the point in the network where the packet loss is occurring, look for any counters on that device that might indicate where the packets are being lost. Figure 7-7 shows part of a sniffer trace that has been filtered to show a single RTP stream. Notice that the sequence numbers increment consecutively from 15252 to 15275 with no missing packets.

Figure 7-7   *Single RTP Stream in SnifferPro*

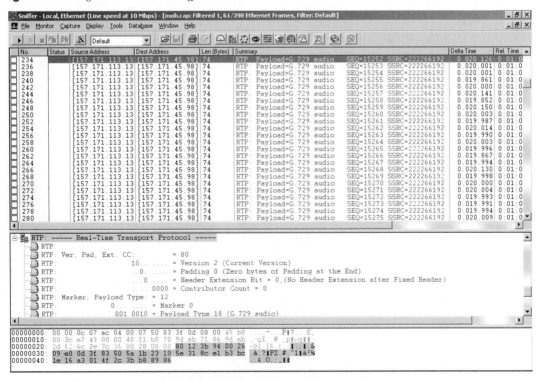

Also in Figure 7-7, notice that the Delta Time column is very close to 20 ms between each packet. This is expected because the packet size being used is 20 ms. An easy way to look for missing or delayed packets is to check the Delta Time column, looking for packets that have a delay much greater than 20 ms. Figure 7-8 shows an example of a call with more jitter than the trace in Figure 7-7.

Figure 7-8 *Single RTP Stream in SnifferPro with Jitter*

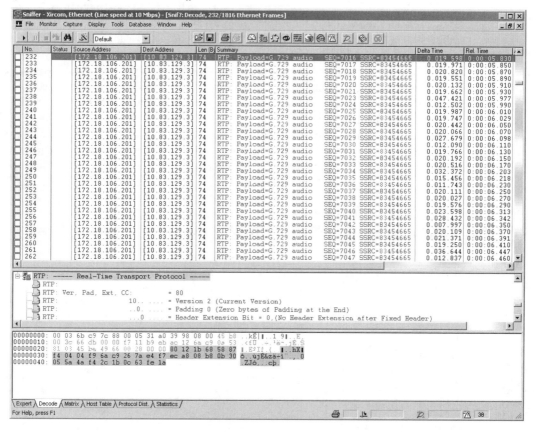

Notice the values in the Delta Time column are no longer very close to 20 ms. Also notice that between the sixth and seventh lines in the trace there is a packet that was lost. You can see this because the sixth line has a sequence number of 7021 (SEQ=7021) and the seventh line has a sequence number of 7023 (SEQ=7023). This means that the packet with sequence number 7022 was lost in the network somewhere.

Queuing Problems

As discussed in the section "Queuing/Buffering Delay," queuing delay can be a significant contributor to variable delay (jitter). When you have too much jitter end-to-end, you encounter voice quality problems.

A voice sample that is delayed over the size of the receiving device's jitter buffer is no better than a packet that is dropped in the network because the delay still causes a noticeable break in the audio stream. In fact, high jitter is actually worse than a small amount of packet loss because most codecs can compensate for small amounts of packet loss. The only way to compensate for high jitter is to make the jitter buffer larger, but as the jitter buffer gets larger, the voice stream is delayed longer in the jitter buffer. If the jitter buffer gets large enough such that the end-to-end delay is more than 200 ms, the two parties on the conference feel like the conversation is not interactive and start talking over each other.

Queuing problems over the WAN can be caused by the following:

- **Improperly configured LLQ**—If LLQ is not properly configured, data traffic is queued before voice traffic, causing the voice traffic to be delayed.

- **Improperly configured LFI**—If LFI is not properly configured to fragment large data packets, a single data packet could cause some voice packets to be severely delayed, even if LLQ is configured to properly offer priority to voice packets over data packets.

- **Improperly configured Frame Relay traffic shaping**—If your service provider guarantees a certain CIR and you exceed it, your packets might be dropped or delayed within the service provider. Always use Frame Relay traffic shaping to ensure that you do not exceed your CIR. Frame Relay traffic shaping ensures that bursts of data traffic are rate-limited and buffered so that the traffic does not exceed the CIR as it is transmitted towards the WAN. You can learn more by searching for "Frame Relay traffic shaping" on Cisco.com or at the following link:

  www.cisco.com/warp/public/125/traffic_shaping_6151.html

Remember that every network device between the two endpoints involved in a call (switches, routers, firewalls, and so on) is a potential source of queuing or buffering delays. The ideal way to troubleshoot a problem in which the symptoms point to delayed or jittered packets is to use a sniffer trace at each hop to see where the delay or jitter is being introduced.

Although less common, it is possible to have queuing problems on a LAN. This can occur if you do not prioritize your voice traffic over data traffic on the LAN or if you do not properly enforce QoS trust boundaries. A *QoS trust boundary* allows administrators to select which devices can be trusted to properly mark only critical traffic with a higher QoS precedence while leaving lower-priority traffic at a lower precedence. Cisco IP Phones mark their voice traffic with a Layer 2 priority (CoS) of 5 and a Layer 3 priority (ToS) of 5. As long as you enforce trust boundaries to ensure that you do not trust things such as PCs or other network devices, you can ensure that the traffic you are prioritizing is voice traffic.

For more information on LAN QoS and trust boundaries, refer to the *Cisco IP Telephony QoS Design Guide*, available on Cisco.com (search for "Cisco IP Telephony QoS Design Guide") or at the following link:

  www.cisco.com/univercd/cc/td/doc/product/voice/ip_tele/avvidqos/

The Effect of VAD on Voice Quality

Most customers who run voice over their WAN to remote sites want to use as little bandwidth as possible without sacrificing voice quality. This usually means using a compressed codec such as G.729; however, some customers choose to gain additional bandwidth savings by using voice activity detection (VAD), also known as silence suppression.

VAD (or *silence suppression*) detects when there is silence in a conversation. Instead of sending voice packets filled with silence, the device stops sending voice packets and indicates to the far end that there is a silent period. Because most conversations involve only one party talking at any given time, the opposite direction is usually quiet. This means that you can achieve substantial bandwidth savings by enabling VAD.

Unfortunately, VAD might affect voice quality. Most phone users never expect to hear complete silence when they are talking on the phone. There is a certain amount of noise, commonly referred to as *comfort noise*. This comfort noise is usually just a slight hiss on the line that makes users feel like there is still someone on the other end of the line. When VAD is enabled, this noise is suppressed because voice packets are no longer sent. To get around this limitation, most phones and voice gateways generate comfort noise when VAD is enabled and no one is speaking. This comfort noise might sound slightly different than the background noise that would be heard if VAD were disabled. Some users can detect the difference between normal background noise and artificially generated comfort noise.

As just mentioned, with VAD enabled, no voice packets are sent in periods of silence. Because there is usually never an absolute silence, a threshold is set that determines what levels are considered silence. After a period of silence, the IP phone or voice gateway must detect the beginning of normal speech and restart the transmission of voice packets. If the IP phone or gateway does not detect the beginning of a talk spurt in time, the beginning of the talk spurt can be truncated, causing the first syllable of speech to be lost.

For some customers, this minor hit on voice quality is acceptable because of the cost savings associated with the reduced bandwidth requirements of enabled VAD; however, most customers prefer to disable VAD. If you are encountering symptoms that are similar to the side effects caused when VAD is enabled, verify that you have VAD disabled in CallManager by checking service parameters for CallManager in Cisco CallManager Administration (**Service > Service Parameters >** *select a server* **> Cisco CallManager**). Ensure that **SilenceSuppressionSystemWide** and **SilenceSuppressionWithGateways** are both set to False. Setting these service parameters disables VAD for any device directly controlled by CallManager, including IP phones and MGCP gateways. The **SilenceSuppressionSystemWide** parameter selects the VAD setting for all Skinny endpoints (for example, IP phones and Skinny gateways) while **SilenceSuppressionWithGateways** selects the VAD setting for all MGCP gateways. It does not have an effect on H.323 gateways. VAD on H.323 gateways must be disabled on the gateway itself. Note that these two service parameters are only locally significant to a CallManager. So if you have multiple CallManager nodes in a single cluster where you always want to disable VAD, be sure to set these parameters for each CallManager node in the cluster.

If you are using a Cisco IOS Software gateway, VAD is enabled by default for H.323 calls. To disable VAD, you must match a VoIP dial peer that has the command **no vad** configured. In Example 7-1, the dial peer disables VAD for all outbound calls that start with 9 and inbound calls destined for extensions 15600 through 15699.

Example 7-1 *Disabling VAD on a Cisco IOS Software Gateway Using H.323*

```
dial-peer voice 15600 voip
  incoming called-number 9
  destination-pattern 156..
  ip precedence 5
  dtmf-relay h245-alphanumeric
  session-target ipv4:172.18.106.58
  no vad
```

Some codecs, such as G.729b and G.729ab, have VAD built into them, and it cannot be disabled. If you do not want to use VAD, use the standard G.729 or G.729a codecs instead.

Most platforms provide a way to look at whether VAD is enabled for a particular call. On the WS-X6608 or WS-X6624 voice gateway module, use the **show port voice active** *module/port* command. Look for the line that shows the status of VAD. Example 7-2 shows sample output from this command.

Example 7-2 **show port voice active** *Command Output Displays VAD Activity*

```
vnt-c6k-main (enable) show port voice active 6
Port  6/1 :
  Channel #1:
    Remote IP address                 : 10.1.2.3
    Remote UDP Port                   : 17550
    ACOM Level Current                : 0
    Call State                        : voice
    Codec Type                        : G711 ULAW PCM
    Coder Type Rate                   : 20
    ERL Level                         : 169
    Voice Activity Detection          : disabled
    Echo Cancellation                 : enabled
    Fax Transmit Duration (ms)        : 0
    Hi Water Playout Delay            : 65
    Low Water Playout Delay           : 64
    Receive Bytes                     : 58080
    Receive Delay                     : 64
    Receive Packets                   : 363
    Transmit Bytes                    : 58080
    Transmit Packets                  : 363
    Tx Duration (ms)                  : 4610
    Voice Tx Duration (ms)            : 461
```

On a call through a Cisco IOS Software gateway, use the **show call active voice** command. Look in the section labeled **VOIP:** for a line that says **VAD = enabled** or **VAD = disabled**, as shown in Example 7-3.

Example 7-3 **show call active voice** *Command Output Indicates That VAD Is Disabled*

```
Router#show call active voice
VOIP:
ConnectionId[0xA242B2 0x6F48711D 0x600CCCF 0xA538102]
IncomingConnectionId[0xA242B2 0x6F48711D 0x600CCCF 0xA538102]
RemoteIPAddress=10.83.129.2
RemoteUDPPort=29280
RoundTripDelay=0 ms
SelectedQoS=best-effort
tx_DtmfRelay=inband-voice
FastConnect=FALSE

AnnexE=FALSE

Separate H245 Connection=FALSE

H245 Tunneling=FALSE

SessionProtocol=cisco
SessionTarget=
OnTimeRvPlayout=23350
GapFillWithSilence=0 ms
GapFillWithPrediction=0 ms
GapFillWithInterpolation=0 ms
GapFillWithRedundancy=0 ms
HiWaterPlayoutDelay=65 ms
LoWaterPlayoutDelay=64 ms
ReceiveDelay=64 ms
LostPackets=0
EarlyPackets=0
LatePackets=0
VAD = disabled
CoderTypeRate=g711ulaw
CodecBytes=160
SignalingType=cas
CallerName=Paul Giralt
CallerIDBlocked=False
```

To see if VAD is enabled on an IP Phone, place a call to another phone, and then bring up the call statistics by pressing the help (**i** or **?**) button on the phone twice in quick succession. Pay attention to the receive count (RxCnt) and transmit count (TxCnt) counters. Be quiet on both sides of the conversation, and see if both counters continue to increment at the same rate. If they do, you know VAD is disabled. Note that the receive count depends on whether the opposite endpoint has VAD enabled. Also note that you should not use the mute button on the phone for this test because the phone stops sending RTP packets when mute is engaged, regardless of the VAD setting.

Troubleshooting Problems with One-way or No-way Audio

One-way audio and no audio at all (no-way audio) are problems that are fairly common during a new IP telephony network installation. The majority of these problems are caused by misconfigurations. For one-way audio problems, always pay attention to which direction the one-way audio is occurring. For no audio in either direction, the troubleshooting methodology is the same. You might need to repeat the procedure for each direction of audio, but more likely you will find the source of the problem when trying to troubleshoot one direction. There are various steps you can take to troubleshoot a one-way/no-way audio problem:

- Verify bidirectional IP connectivity

- Verify configuration parameters on H.323 gateways

- Check for NAT or firewall restrictions

Verifying IP Connectivity

You should verify IP connectivity as the first step in troubleshooting a one-way or no-way audio problem because IP connectivity must be present for voice packets to transmit between two devices. A large number of one-way or no-way audio problems are caused by lack of IP connectivity. If the two endpoints are on different IP subnets, check the default gateway and subnet mask settings on the two endpoints involved in the call to ensure they are correct. If one of the endpoints is an IP phone, the DHCP scope might have an incorrectly configured default gateway parameter. On a Cisco IOS Software gateway, the default route might be incorrect. Remember that signaling traffic is always between CallManager and the endpoint, whereas the RTP voice traffic is directly between the endpoints. So just because the endpoints are registered to CallManager and can set up a call through CallManager does not mean that the endpoints have proper IP connectivity between them.

If one of the endpoints is a Cisco IOS Software gateway, ping the other endpoint from the gateway. If the ping is successful, you know you have IP connectivity. If the ping is unsuccessful, perform a traceroute to determine where the problem is. Example 7-4 shows the output of the **traceroute** command on a Cisco IOS router.

As you can see in Example 7-4, the last successful hop in the network is the router with IP address 10.18.254.158. Because you do not see the final destination (192.168.1.1) in the output, you have now determined that the problem is either on 10.18.254.158 or the following hop after that router.

Example 7-4   **traceroute** *Command Output on a Cisco IOS Router*

```
Router#traceroute 192.168.1.1

Type escape sequence to abort.
Tracing the route to 192.168.1.1

  1 10.84.100.2 0 msec 0 msec 0 msec
  2 10.0.0.13 0 msec 0 msec 4 msec
  3 10.18.127.145 0 msec 4 msec 0 msec
  4 10.18.0.41 0 msec 4 msec 0 msec
  5 10.18.254.57 4 msec 0 msec 0 msec
  6 10.18.254.169 4 msec 0 msec 4 msec
  7 10.18.254.158 0 msec 4 msec 0 msec
  8  *   *   *
  9  *   *   *
```

Note that other platforms use different commands to invoke the traceroute tool. For example, the Microsoft Windows operating system uses the command **tracert**; however, the information presented is the same. If one of the endpoints is not a Cisco IOS Software gateway, such as if the problem is between two IP phones, the best you can do is to try to ping one endpoint from a PC that is on the same subnet as the opposite IP phone. Remember that if auxiliary VLANS are in use, a PC plugged into the back of the IP phone is in a different VLAN than the phone. For the ping test to be valid, you must ensure that the PC is on the same VLAN as the IP phone by either connecting to a switch port on the same VLAN as the phone or temporarily changing the data VLAN to match the voice VLAN.

Another useful tool for troubleshooting such a problem is the help (**i** or **?**) button on the Cisco 7940/7960 phones. Press the help (**i** or **?**) button twice in quick succession during an active call. The display shows you receive and transmit statistics for the call. If you do not see the receive counter (RxCnt) incrementing, it is likely that the packets are not arriving on that IP Phone. If you go to the originating IP Phone and the transmit count (TxCnt) is incrementing, the packets are probably being lost somewhere in the network. If a ping or traceroute does not provide enough information about where the packets are being lost, you might have to connect a sniffer to the network. First, connect the sniffer to the back of the originating IP Phone, and make sure the phone is really transmitting the packets. Make sure the IP address and MAC address information is correct. If they are, go to the terminating IP Phone to make sure that the packets are really not arriving at the terminating phone. If they are not, move the sniffer from hop to hop to try to determine where the packets are being dropped. A common reason for a problem such as this is a missing or improperly configured IP route.

After you have verified IP connectivity, there are several things you can check when a Cisco IOS Software gateway is involved, as the following sections cover in detail.

One-way Audio on Cisco IOS Software Gateways

There are various reasons why you might encounter one-way audio on calls to a Cisco IOS Software gateway. Most of these problems can be solved using simple configuration commands.

The first thing to check is that IP routing is enabled on the gateway you are using, even a standalone gateway such as a Cisco VG200. You do not need to be running a routing protocol such as RIP, EIGRP, or OSPF, but IP routing *must not* be disabled. Make sure the **no ip routing** command does not show up in your configuration. If it does, be sure to eliminate it by configuring **ip routing**. You can also issue the **show ip route** command to see if IP routing is enabled. If IP routing is disabled, the output looks like Example 7-5. Notice there are no routes listed, and the list of routing protocols is not present.

Example 7-5 *Confirming IP Routing Status: Disabled*

```
Router#show ip route
Default gateway is not set

Host            Gateway           Last Use    Total Uses  Interface
ICMP redirect cache is empty
```

If IP routing is enabled, however, you should see something like the output shown in Example 7-6. Notice there are several IP routes listed, and the output begins with a list of routing protocols.

Example 7-6 *Confirming IP Routing Status: Enabled*

```
Router#show ip route
Codes: C - connected, S - static, I - IGRP, R - RIP, M - mobile, B - BGP
       D - EIGRP, EX - EIGRP external, O - OSPF, IA - OSPF inter area
       N1 - OSPF NSSA external type 1, N2 - OSPF NSSA external type 2
       E1 - OSPF external type 1, E2 - OSPF external type 2, E - EGP
       i - IS-IS, L1 - IS-IS level-1, L2 - IS-IS level-2, ia - IS-IS inter area
       * - candidate default, U - per-user static route, o - ODR
       P - periodic downloaded static route

Gateway of last resort is 172.18.106.1 to network 0.0.0.0

     172.18.0.0/24 is subnetted, 1 subnets
C       172.18.106.0 is directly connected, FastEthernet0/0
S*   0.0.0.0/0 [1/0] via 172.18.106.1
```

The VoIP subsystem in Cisco IOS Software uses the IP routing code to aid in encapsulating and transmitting the VoIP packets, so it must be enabled to transmit and receive VoIP packets. It does not need the IP routing code to perform signaling such as H.323 or MGCP, so the signaling still works with IP routing disabled.

Another common cause of one-way audio occurs on Cisco IOS Software H.323 voice gateways that have more than one data interface, such as a gateway that has both an Ethernet connection to the LAN and a serial connection to the WAN. When an H.323 gateway is configured in CallManager Administration, you configure a specific IP address. CallManager always uses this IP address for all its signaling to the gateway; however, Cisco IOS Software voice gateways by default use the IP address of the interface closest to the destination. This could be a problem if CallManager is connected via one interface and the device the RTP audio stream is destined for is connected to a different interface. To force the voice gateway to always use the same IP address, configure **h323-gateway voip bind srcaddr** *ip address* on the interface you are using for signaling on the Cisco IOS Software voice gateway. Make sure this is the same IP address configured in CallManager Administration. Failure to do so could result in one-way audio when the gateway tries to use a different source interface than the one configured in CallManager.

Sometimes you have one-way audio problems only when calling specific numbers, such as 411 or 911 in the North American numbering plan (NANP) or after you transfer a call or put it on hold. If you are having these problems when going through a Cisco IOS Software voice gateway, be sure the **voice rtp send-recv** command is configured on the gateway. This is a global command that is supported as of Cisco IOS Software Release 12.1(5)T. Numbers such as 411 and 911 sometimes do not send back answer supervision (that is, an ISDN connect message) when the remote end answers. As a result, the Cisco IOS Software voice gateway does not cut through audio in both directions to prevent toll fraud. Configuring **voice rtp send-recv** forces the voice gateway to cut through audio in both directions immediately.

If you are using a Cisco AS5350 or AS5400 as a gateway, make sure you configure **no voice-fastpath enable** in global configuration mode. When enabled (**voice-fastpath enable**), this command causes the voice gateway to cache the IP address and UDP port number information for the logical channel opened for a specific call and forwards the packets using the cached information. This helps reduce CPU utilization marginally in high-call-volume scenarios. Because of how CallManager opens and closes logical channels to redirect RTP audio streams, such as in the case of a transfer or music on hold (MOH) server, the AS5350 and AS5400 cache the IP address information of the old IP address. Therefore, you end up with one-way audio when the call gets redirected to a new IP address because the voice gateway still uses the cached information instead of the newly negotiated information.

All the scenarios discussed so far are cases in which you have one-way audio or no-way audio from the beginning of the call or after a hold/transfer. Occasionally, however, you might encounter scenarios in which a call is up and suddenly becomes one-way, or audio disappears entirely. Network problems are largely to blame for failures of this sort. Ensure that network connectivity between the two endpoints still exists and that nothing on the network might be causing intermittent network connectivity. An example would be a flapping network connection—a network connection that is transitioning between up and down states over and over again—or a routing protocol that cannot converge correctly. Again, a sniffer trace is the best tool for diagnosing this kind of problem. The best place to start is on the device that originates the RTP stream to ensure that the stream is still being generated when the loss of audio occurs. If you discover that the originating device stops sending packets for no reason, you might be dealing with a software or hardware problem on the originating device.

A common cause of such a failure is a DSP crash. If the end device is a Cisco IOS Software voice gateway, you see an error displayed on the console that looks similar to the following:

```
%VTSP-3-DSP_TIMEOUT: DSP timeout on event 6: DSP ID=0x2312: DSP error stats
```

This message is also sent to a Syslog server if the Cisco IOS Software voice gateway is configured to send Syslog information to a Syslog server. On a Cisco VG200, 2600, or 3600, you can issue the following command to check the status of the DSPs:

test dsprm *slot #*

For instance, Example 7-7 is a test of the DSPs in an NM-HDV in slot 1 of a VG200. Note that for this command's output to appear on screen, you must either be on the console with console logging enabled or be in a Telnet session with terminal monitor enabled.

Example 7-7 *Testing the DSP on a Cisco IOS Software Voice Gateway*

```
vnt-vg200-gw2#test dsprm 1

Section:
1 - Query dsp resource and status
2 - Display voice port's dsp channel status
3 - Print dsp data structure info
4 - Change dsprm test Flags
5 - Modify dsp-tdm connection
6 - Disable DSP Background Status Query and Recovery
7 - Enable  DSP Background Status Query and Recovery
8 - Enable DSP control message history
9 - Disable DSP control message history
q - Quit
Select option : 1

Dsp firmware version: 3.4.49
Maximum dsp count: 15
On board dsp count: 12
Jukebox available
Total dsp channels available 48
Total dsp channels allocated 47
Total dsp free channels 1
Quering dsp status......
vnt-vg200-gw2#
9w2d: dsp 3 is ALIVE
9w2d: dsp 4 is ALIVE
9w2d: dsp 5 is ALIVE
9w2d: dsp 6 is ALIVE
9w2d: dsp 7 is ALIVE
9w2d: dsp 8 is ALIVE
9w2d: dsp 9 is ALIVE
9w2d: dsp 10 is ALIVE
9w2d: dsp 11 is ALIVE
9w2d: dsp 12 is ALIVE
9w2d: dsp 13 is ALIVE
9w2d: dsp 14 is ALIVE
```

Notice that all the DSPs show they are alive. The number displayed varies, depending on how many DSPs you have installed in your voice gateway. The **show voice dsp** command shows you which port and timeslot are allocated to each DSP. If **test dsprm** detects a DSP that has crashed, you can match this with the information obtained from a **show call active voice** (or **show call history voice** if the call has been disconnected) to see if the timeslot of the failed call is the same as the DSP that is no longer available. Unfortunately, the only way to recover from this condition is to reload the gateway.

The majority of DSP problems are the result of software defects in the DSP firmware. If you encounter issues that appear to be DSP crash-related, be sure to search Bug Navigator on Cisco.com for potential defects in the version of code you are running. (You can learn more about Bug Navigator in Chapter 3.)

NAT, PAT, and Firewalls

One common cause of one-way or no-way audio is when Network Address Translation (NAT), Port Address Translation (PAT), or firewalls exist between two endpoints.

The Skinny protocol embeds IP addresses in the IP packet's payload to signal which IP address to send RTP packets to. If the device performing NAT or PAT is unaware of this fact, the embedded IP addresses are not translated. Therefore, one-way or no-way audio results.

Firewalls can also be a problem if they are unaware of the voice traffic passing through them. Firewalls often are configured to block all UDP traffic going through them. Because voice traffic is carried over UDP, it might be blocked while the signaling carried over TCP is passed. A sniffer is the best tool for debugging such a scenario. If both devices appear to be transmitting audio but the audio is not reaching the opposite side, take a sniffer trace at each hop along the way until you find the hop where the audio is not passing through. You might need to open a hole in the firewall if it is blocking UDP packets to allow the voice traffic to traverse the firewall.

Troubleshooting Echo Problems

Echo is one of the more difficult voice quality problems to troubleshoot, but it's also one of the most commonly encountered problems. Echo is present in almost any telephony network; however, IP telephony in particular makes echo problems more apparent than they might be in a non-packet network. To understand how to troubleshoot echo problems, you must first understand the following:

- Sources of echo
- Types of echo (listener versus talker echo)
- What makes echo a problem
- How an echo canceller works
- Eliminating echo

Sources of Echo

To understand how to troubleshoot echo problems, you first must understand how echo is generated. The majority of echo is created in one of two forms:

- Electrical echo
- Acoustic echo

The more you understand about the nature of the echo you are encountering, the easier it is to troubleshoot.

Electrical Echo

The majority of echo you have to deal with comes in the form of electrical echo. Most electrical echo is caused by a device called a hybrid. What is a hybrid? Most analog circuits in the Public Switched Telephone Network (PSTN) are two-wire connections. For example, a standard residential phone line uses a two-wire connection between the home and the phone company. This means that both receive signals and transmit signals are carried on the same two wires. When going from analog to digital, the receive and transmit signals must be separated so that they can be transmitted separately in digital form. This is also true when converting from two-wire to four-wire analog circuits. The device that does this two-wire-to-four-wire conversion is called a *hybrid*.

A hybrid relies on a delicate balance between its internal impedance and the impedance of the two-wire circuit connected to it. If this impedance is out of balance, echo can be generated in either direction of the hybrid. Unfortunately, most hybrids are not perfectly balanced—some unbalanced worse than others. It is safe to assume that any call that goes through a hybrid has some amount of echo.

Because hybrids exist only on analog circuits, an all-digital network is not subject to hybrid echo. Perhaps someday we will get to the point where we have no analog telephony devices, but unfortunately a large number of analog lines are still in use today. As a result, hybrid echo is the biggest contributor to echo problems when an IP telephony network connects to the PSTN.

Several devices exist that contribute to hybrid echo. Anything that modifies the impedance of a two-wire loop causes the hybrid to become unbalanced. One such device is a *loading coil*. A loading coil is used when the local loop is longer than 18,000 feet to compensate for the capacitance of such a long cable run. These loading coils modify the loop's impedance and, therefore, can create an imbalance at the hybrid. Other such devices that can contribute to problems are bad patches or splices in the cable that can cause electrical reflections in the signal.

Electrical echo can also be caused by other inherent problems in an analog circuit. One such problem is crosstalk. *Crosstalk* is when the electrical energy in an analog circuit where the receive and transmit pairs are separate "leaks" from one side to the other because of inductance between the two pairs of wires. Perhaps at some point you have been on a call through the PSTN and you have heard parts of someone else's conversation faintly in the background. This is an example of crosstalk. However, in that case, the two pairs on which the crosstalk occurred are from different circuits, so instead of echo, you hear an entirely different conversation. Devices such as isolation transformers can contribute to crosstalk if they are not properly designed to minimize crosstalk. Other physical layer issues can also contribute to crosstalk, such as improperly shielded cables in close proximity to each other.

As you can see, all forms of electrical echo occur when the audio signal is in analog form. The fewer analog circuits you have to deal with, the fewer echo problems you will encounter.

Acoustic Echo

The second form of echo is acoustic echo. *Acoustic echo* occurs when the acoustic energy from a device such as a handset, headset, or speakerphone enters the microphone of the same device. This is of particular concern on speakerphones because the microphone can certainly pick up the audio signals being transmitted out the speaker. Fortunately, most speakerphones have circuitry built in to eliminate echo.

Acoustic echo can be generated only by endpoints such as phones and speakerphones because they are the only point where the signal takes the form of a sound wave that can be heard by a microphone device. Acoustic echo can also occur as a result of vibrations through a device. For example, the plastic of a telephone handset vibrates if the signal from the earpiece is loud enough. If this vibration is strong enough, it can be picked up by the microphone in the handset and heard as echo at the originating phone.

Acoustic echo is usually easier to diagnose because you can do things such as lower the device's volume or mute it. On the other hand, electrical echo generally requires that you either modify equipment you usually don't have access to or replace hardware. This means that instead of eliminating echo at the source, you are usually left trying to cancel it elsewhere in the network.

Talker Versus Listener Echo

All echo can be categorized as being either talker echo or listener echo. The difference between the two has to do with which party's voice is being echoed and which party heard the echo.

Talker echo means one party in the call hears himself echoed. Talker echo is by far the most common form of echo. Figure 7-9 shows an example.

Figure 7-9 *Talker Echo Example*

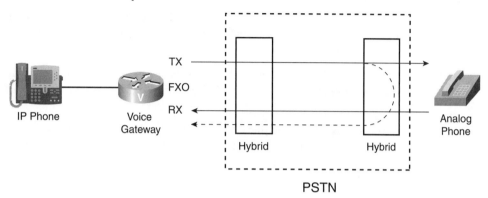

Listener echo means one party in the call hears the other person's words repeated. Listener echo is rare in comparison to talker echo. It results from the same audio being echoed twice, as shown in Figure 7-10.

Figure 7-10 *Listener Echo Example*

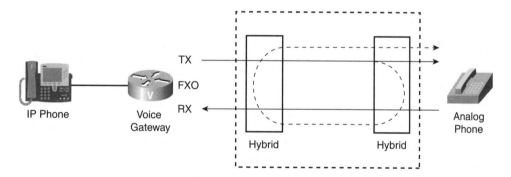

When troubleshooting an echo problem, one of the most basic pieces of information you need to collect is which side of the conversation hears the echo and whose voice the user heard being echoed—his own or the other party's. This lets you classify the call as either talker echo or listener echo and focus on the possible pieces of the network that could be the cause of the echo. Before you can begin troubleshooting echo, you must understand what makes echo a problem.

What Makes Echo a Problem

Although echo is usually present in any call over the PSTN that involves an analog circuit, it is not necessarily a problem. In fact, most of the time echo goes largely unnoticed. Three conditions must be met for echo to be a problem.

First, there must be some form of analog leakage between the transmit and receive signals. This can be in the form of either electrical (hybrid) or acoustic echo, as described previously.

Second, the echo must be of a significant-enough amplitude to be perceived as being a problem. If the echo's amplitude level is low, it goes unnoticed. Although most hybrids are not perfectly balanced and therefore generate some amount of echo, a lot of this echo is not loud enough to be noticed.

Finally, there must be enough delay between the time when the originating signal is transmitted and the time when the echo returns to make the echo perceptible. A minimum delay is needed for an echo to become perceptible. In almost every telephone device, some of the transmit signal is fed back into the earpiece so that the user can hear herself speaking. This is known as *sidetone*. The delay between the actual mouth signal and the sidetone signal is negligible, and sidetone is not perceived as an echo. Most people feel uncomfortable using a phone that does not generate sidetone. Also, a person's skull resonates during speech (an acoustic sidetone source), and the human auditory system has a certain *integration period* that determines the minimum time difference between events so that they can be perceived as separate events rather than a single event. Together, these phenomena set a lower boundary on the mouth-to-ear delay required for an echo signal to be perceived at all. Echoes must be delayed by at least 20 ms to be audible. Unfortunately, in a packet-based system, delays routinely exceed 20 ms. The G.131 specification states that echo cancellers should be used when the delay exceeds 25 ms.

The amplitude and delay determine whether the echo is perceived. If the delay is lower, the amplitude must be higher for the echo to be perceived. The opposite is also true. The longer the delay is, the lower the amplitudes at which echo is perceived. Figure 7-11 shows the relationship between amplitude and delay. Any values above the curve will likely be perceived as echo. Therefore, to eliminate echo, you need to lower the delay, lower the echo's amplitude, or both. The vertical axis in Figure 7-11 represents the Talker Echo Loudness Rating (TELR). TELR refers to the difference in amplitude between the talker's voice and the level of the echo. A low TELR value means that the echo is almost as loud as the orginial signal, whereas a high TELR means the echo is much softer than the orignial signal.

Figure 7-11 *Amplitude/Delay Relationship*

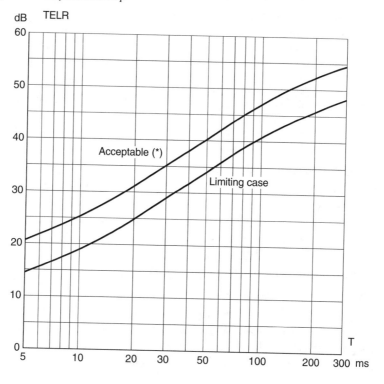

TELR	Talker Echo Loudness Rating
T	Mean one-way transmission time
(*)	The "Acceptable" curve is equivalent to the curve with "1%" probability of encountering objectionable echo.

In a time-division multiplexing (TDM)-based telephony environment, echo is of little concern when calls are being placed within a small geographic area. The transmission delay for a circuit-switched call is very short, and the delay increases as a function of distance. Therefore, long distances require echo cancellers. For this reason, many long distance carriers have echo cancellers in their network, especially for international circuits. In a TDM-based environment, as long as the distances are not very great, any echo is dismissed as sidetone.

In a packet-based telephony environment, things are very different. As mentioned earlier, latency in a packet-based network can easily be in the 50 to 150 ms range. This means that echo amplitude must be very low for echo to be imperceptible. An echo that might be interpreted as a sidetone on a TDM-based private branch exchange (PBX) is heard as echo on a packet-based IP telephony system because of the additional delay.

Fortunately, Cisco voice gateways and IP Phones include DSP code that can detect and suppress or cancel echo. Each platform behaves differently, but the concepts of how they work are the same.

How an Echo Canceller Works

Before we discuss how an echo canceller works, you need to be familiar with some terminology:

- Tail circuit
- Echo return loss (ERL)
- Echo return loss enhancement (ERLE)
- Combined loss (ACOM)

A *tail circuit* is the part of the telephony network facing out from an echo canceller. In an IP telephony environment, this encompasses everything from the voice gateway's connection to the PSTN all the way to the terminating phone. Figure 7-12 shows an example of all the components that might make up a tail circuit.

Figure 7-12   *Components of a Tail Circuit*

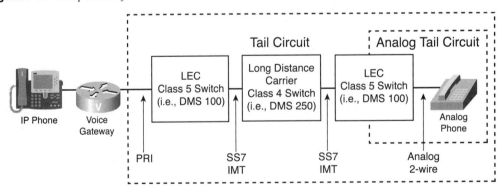

Figure 7-12 highlights the analog tail circuit as a subset of the tail circuit. Because echo is generated in the analog portion of the network, the analog tail circuit is the most likely candidate to be a source of echo. The other two switches between the voice gateway and the terminating Class 5 switch very likely do not contribute to the echo; however, they can add delay if the distances are long enough.

Figure 7-13 helps define the terms ERL, ERLE, and ACOM.

Figure 7-13 *Relationship Between ERL, ERLE, and ACOM*

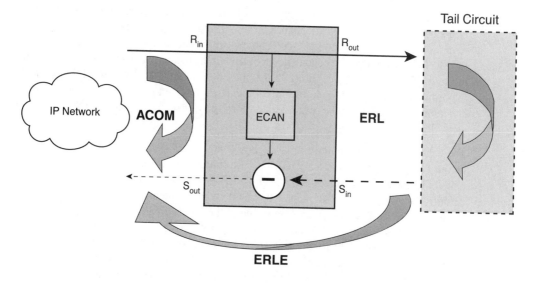

ERL is the level of echo returned from tail circuit. For example, if a speech signal enters the tail circuit from the network at a level of x dB, the level of the echo coming back from the tail circuit into the S_{in} terminal of the echo canceller is $x - ERL$ dB.

ERL is extremely important because the echo canceller needs the echo's volume level to be lower than the output signal by a certain amount for it to interpret the input signal as echo. Most Cisco echo canceller implementations require that the ERL be a minimum of 6 dB for the echo canceller to work correctly. If the ERL is lower (meaning that the echo is louder), the echo canceller does not cancel the echo. An ERL of 15 dB or greater is usually considered good; however, as mentioned, the echo cancellers can deal with echo that has an ERL as low as 6 dB.

ERLE refers to the additional echo loss obtained through the operation of the echo canceller. An echo canceller is not a perfect device, and the best it can do is attenuate the level of the returning echo. ERLE is a measure of this echo attenuation through the echo canceller. It is the difference in the level (in dB) between the signal arriving from the tail circuit at the S_{in} terminal of the echo canceller and the level of the signal leaving the echo canceller (and entering the network) at the S_{out} terminal.

ACOM is simply the total echo return loss seen across the echo canceller's R_{in} and S_{out} terminals. It is the sum of ERL and ERLE. This is the difference between the originating party's voice and the echo the originating party hears. The goal is to make the ACOM as large as possible because the larger the ACOM, the lower the level of echo the caller hears. For example, an ACOM of 60 dB means that the echo heard by the caller is 60 dB lower than the original sound he made.

One other factor that is important for echo canceller operation is the *tail circuit delay*. This is the time between the point where the original audio signal exits the echo canceller and the time it returns as echo. The echo canceller must keep a record of the audio it has sent for a certain amount of time, waiting to see if that same audio comes back as echo. The DSPs performing the echo cancellation have a limited amount of memory, so they can remember only so much; most Cisco echo cancellers support up to 32 ms of tail circuit length. This means that the echo canceller remembers the last 32 ms of audio that has gone through it. If the echo returns after 32 ms, the echo canceller cannot cancel the echo. The maximum length of the tail circuit the echo canceller converges on is called the *echo canceller coverage*. It can be configured on some platforms. The default setting for the echo canceller coverage varies by platform.

The echo canceller does not eliminate echo. What it does is attenuate the echo by a large amount (approximately 25 to 30 dB). The resulting signal is then fed into an algorithm called the nonlinear processor (NLP). The NLP looks at the total signal. If it is below a certain threshold, the NLP attenuates the whole signal. The idea is that if no one is talking on the far end, and the only signal returning to the talker is echo, the NLP completely removes it. It is important that the NLP disengage quickly when the far end starts talking. If it doesn't, the listener hears clipping at the beginning of the talk spurt. *Doubletalk* is when both parties on the call are talking at the same time. During times of doubletalk, the NLP must disengage so that both sides can hear each other. If the echo canceller does not attenuate the echoed signal enough, however, echo might be perceptible during doubletalk conditions.

Eliminating Echo

Now that you understand where echo comes from and how an echo canceller works, how do you troubleshoot echo problems in your network?

The first thing you need to do is try to find out where the echo is coming from. Try to characterize the echo as being either talker echo or listener echo by determining who heard the echo and what she heard. Does the echo occur only OnNet (IP phone to IP phone) or only on calls to the PSTN (OffNet)? Is a Cisco IP SoftPhone involved? If it happens only when calling out the PSTN, does it happen only to specific phone numbers? Is the destination a local, long distance, or international number? If you have call detail records (CDRs) enabled, look up the CDR for the call that experienced echo, and determine which devices were involved in the call (phones or gateways). It's also important to find out if the echo persisted for the duration of the call or if it occurred only during parts of the call.

The majority of echo problems involve some kind of PSTN connection, so it is important to find out as much as possible about where the call occurred and which gateway was involved. If possible, also learn which port on the gateway was used. For a call out an MGCP gateway, just look through the CCM traces until you find the particular call, and then look to see which gateway it went out. It is very important to get the approximate time the call occurred so that you can look back through the trace files.

For example, assume an IP phone user reports having echo on a call to the PSTN at 11:21 a.m. and indicates she called a local number, 555-2900. The user heard herself echoed, meaning she had talker echo. This means the source of the echo is somewhere on the PSTN. First, find out which CallManager the user's phone is registered to, and look in the CCM trace for that user. Search for 5552900, and you should find the call. Example 7-8 shows the contents of the trace file.

Example 7-8   *Trace File for a Call to 5552900*

```
02/18/2002 11:20:40.089 Cisco CallManager || PretransformCallingPartyNumber=15644
|CallingPartyNumber=9195555644
|DialingPartition=Local
|DialingPattern=9.[2-9]XXXXXX
|DialingRoutePatternRegularExpression=(9)([2-9]XXXXXX)
|DialingWhere=
|PatternType=Enterprise
|PotentialMatches=NoPotentialMatchesExist
|DialingSdlProcessId=(2,87,6)
|PretransformDigitString=95552900
|PretransformTagsList=ACCESS-CODE:SUBSCRIBER
|PretransformPositionalMatchList=9:5552900
|CollectedDigits=95552900
|UnconsumedDigits=
|TagsList=ACCESS-CODE:SUBSCRIBER
|PositionalMatchList=9:5552900
|VoiceMailbox=
|VoiceMailCallingSearchSpace=
|VoiceMailPilotNumber=
|DisplayName=
|RouteBlockFlag=RouteThisPattern
|InterceptPartition=
|InterceptPattern=
|InterceptWhere=
|InterceptSdlProcessId=(0,0,0)
|InterceptSsType=0
|InterceptSsKey=0
```

After you have found the call, continue through the trace, as shown in Example 7-9, to find out which gateway the call went out.

Example 7-9   *Trace File: Determining the Gateway of Origin*

```
RouteListCdrc - RouteListName = PSTN; Processing route number 1;
   Trying to locate DeviceName = S0/DS1-0@SDA00D097386425.
RouteListCdrc; Device S0/DS1-0@SDA00D097386425 located.
RouteListCdrc (2,86,165) extending call to Device (2,61,6)
MGCPpn9d:restart0_CcSetupReq - S0/DS1-0@SDA00D097386425 My Region=Default,
   Other Side Region=Default
RouteListCdrc - RouteListName = PSTN; Processing route number 2;
   Trying to locate DeviceName = S0/DS1-0@SDA00D097386424.
RouteListCdrc; Device S0/DS1-0@SDA00D097386424 located.
RouteListCdrc (2,86,165) extending call to Device (2,61,9)
MGCPpn9d:restart0_CcSetupReq - S0/DS1-0@SDA00D097386424 My Region=Default,
   Other Side Region=Default
```

Then, after a few lines, you see the following:

```
CRCX 1840 S0/DS1-0/23@SDA00D097386424 MGCP 0.1
```

So you see that CallManager has created a connection using the gateway named S0/DS1-0/23@SDA00D097386424, which happens to be a port on a WS-X6608-T1. You can also see that it first attempted to use the gateway named S0/DS1-0@SDA00D097386425 and then continued to S0/DS1-0/23@SDA00D097386424. This happened because the gateway was not registered, the D-channel was not up, or all the channels on that gateway were in use. Next you see the outgoing setup message, as shown in Example 7-10.

Example 7-10 *Outgoing Setup Message*

```
Out Message -- Pri250SetupMsg -- Protocol= Pri250Protocol
Ie - Ni2BearerCapabilityIe IEData= 04 03 80 90 A2
Ie - Q931ChannelIdIe IEData= 18 03 A9 83 97
Ie - Q931DisplayIe IEData= 28 0B 50 61 75 6C 20 47 69 72 61 6C 74
Ie - Q931CallingPartyIe IEData= 6C 0C 21 80 39 31 39 35 35 35 35 36 34 34
Ie - Q931CalledPartyIe IEData= 70 08 80 35 35 35 32 39 30 30
MMan_Id= 0. (iep=  0 dsl=  0 sapi=  0 ces=  0 IpAddr=a46812ac IpPort=2427)
```

You can see that the IP address is **a46812ac**, which translates to 172.18.104.164 (as discussed in Chapter 6). So now you know which port on the WS-X6608 was involved for this call. If the call was sent out an H.323 gateway, determining the port number is a bit more complicated, but similar. Example 7-11 shows another similar call that was routed out an H.323 gateway instead.

Example 7-11 *Outgoing Setup Message from an H.323 Gateway*

```
Out Message -- H225SetupMsg -- Protocol= H225Protocol
Ie - H225BearerCapabilityIe IEData= 04 03 80 90 A2
Ie - Q931DisplayIe IEData= 28 0B 50 61 75 6C 20 47 69 72 61 6C 74
Ie - H225CallingPartyIe IEData= 6C 0C 00 81 39 31 39 35 35 35 35 36 34 34
Ie - Q931CalledPartyIe IEData= 70 09 A1 39 35 35 35 32 39 30 30
Ie - H225UserUserIe IEData= 7E 00 69 05 20 B0 06 00 08 91 4A 00 02 01 40 0A 00 50
   00 61 00 75 00 6C 00 20 00 47 00 69 00 72 00 61 00 6C 00 74 02 00 01 03 80 C6 C5
   5C 33 00 80 AD 11 BA 95 42 71 1D 04 00 0A 52 0A 52 F1 BA 00 49 0C 11 00 80 AD 11
   BA 95 42 71 1D 04 00 0A 52 0A 52 F1 BA 01 00 01 00 06 A0 01 00 0E 01 40 B5 00 00
   12 07 80 44 04 00 01 01 00
MMan_Id= 0. (iep=  0 dsl=  0 sapi=  0 ces=  0 IpAddr=c96a12ac IpPort=1720)
```

Now that you have the gateway's IP address, 172.18.106.201, Telnet or SSH into the gateway and issue the **show call history voice brief** command, as demonstrated in Example 7-12.

Example 7-12 show call history voice brief *Command Output Displays the Port for an Active Call*

```
Router#show call history voice brief
351D : 847453131hs.282 +370 +617 pid:1 Answer 9195555644
 dur 00:00:02 tx:264/42240 rx:131/20960 10  (normal call clearing.)
 IP 10.82.241.186:21002 rtt:0ms pl:1610/0ms lost:0/10/0 delay:64/64/65ms g711ulaw

351D : 847453141hs.283 +360 +608 pid:9 Originate 95552900
 dur 00:00:02 tx:130/20800 rx:264/42240 10  (normal call clearing.)
 Telephony 1/1:23 (283): tx:5310/5310/0ms g711ulaw noise:0dBm acom:34dBm
```

You can identify the call by the calling and called party numbers. You can also see that the call was delivered to the PSTN on port **1/1:23**, which happens to be a Primary Rate Interface (PRI). By default, the call history information is retained for only the last 15 minutes. This is probably too short in most cases because by the time the problem is reported to you, the call has been removed from the history list. You can increase the time before entries are deleted with the **call-history-mib retain-timer** *minutes* command. You can also increase the number of entries that are retained to up to 500 entries with the **call-history-mib max-size** *minutes* command. Both commands are global configuration parameters in Cisco IOS Software.

Now that you know which gateway and port are involved, how do you eliminate the echo? If the echo persists for the duration of the call, there are really only two reasons this would occur:

- The call's ERL was less than 6 dB.

- The tail circuit was greater than the configured echo canceller coverage.

Ideally, the best way to troubleshoot such a problem is by trying to reproduce the echo. If you can't, it will be hard to get quantitative data to help you troubleshoot, not to mention that you won't know if the changes you make are helping you eliminate the problem.

If you know the number from which the echo came, try making multiple calls to that number in an attempt to reproduce the echo. If you can reproduce it, the best thing to do is try to determine the circuit's ERL. How you do this depends on the platform. Troubleshooting Cisco IOS Software gateways is different from troubleshooting the WS-X6608. The following section examines how to do this on a Cisco IOS Software gateway.

Eliminating Echo on Cisco IOS Software Gateways

The first thing you want to do is get a measurement of the ERL for a particular tail circuit. The best way to do this is with a tone generator that can generate a 1004 Hz test tone at −15 dB. Don't have a tone generator? No problem. You can use any 7960 IP Phone on your network to perform this function. One important limitation to note is that this function works only for G.711 calls, so if you are using G.729 to a particular gateway, temporarily switch to G.711 for the purposes of echo testing.

To enable the tone generator on your 7960, you must first unlock the phone by entering the keypad sequence **#. Next, place a call to another phone and hang up. You must do this because the sequence **#** is the phone's reset sequence, and the next command you will enter also starts with **. With the IP Phone unlocked and on-hook, enter **3 on the keypad. You have now enabled the IP Phone's tone generator. As soon as this mode is enabled, it remains enabled until the IP Phone is reset.

Before making your test call, be sure no adjustments for **output attenuation** or **input gain** are configured on the voice port on the Cisco IOS Software gateway. If either is configured, remove it from the configuration, and then restart the voice port by shutting it down and re-enabling it (**shutdown** followed by **no shutdown**). When you shut down the voice port, all active calls are dropped, so be sure to do this during a scheduled outage window in which you won't affect production traffic.

Now place a call to the number that is the suspected source of echo. As soon as the called party answers the phone, speak to him for a few seconds and then ask him to remove the handset from his ear because you're going to send a test tone. It is important to have some speech before generating the test tone. It is not easy for the echo canceller to converge on a tone, so you want the echo canceller to try to converge before generating the test tone. Also make sure that you have absolute silence on the remote end so that nothing is transmitted to you other than the echoed tone. Press the phone's help (**i** or **?**) button twice in quick succession. You should see the call statistics screen appear on your IP Phone. In the lower-left corner of the screen you should see a soft key labeled **Tone**. When you press the **Tone** soft key, a –15 dB tone at 1004 Hz is generated for the duration of the call.

With the call still up, issue the command **show call active voice** on the gateway, and find your call. You should see three lines that look like the following:

```
OutSignalLevel=-15
InSignalLevel=-18
ERLLevel=25
```

Notice that the output signal level is –15 dB and the input signal level is –18 dB. Assuming that the terminating side of the call is being silent, the –18 dB of input signal is all echo. If you subtract the **InSignalLevel** from the **OutSignalLevel**, you get the ERL, which is 3 dB in this case. Notice that the gateway actually reports an ERL of 25 dB. This is because the ERL is not high enough for the echo canceller to converge on the echo, so at this point the echo canceller is confused and does not interpret the echo as echo because the echo is too loud. To get the ERL within the acceptable range, there are several things you can do.

Ideally, the best thing you can do is eliminate the echo at the source. However, most of the time this is impossible because you have no control over the devices generating the echo. When echo comes from the PSTN, the best you can do is try to get the ERL within the range where the echo canceller can operate. You can do this in one of two ways:

- Attenuate the output signal after the echo canceller has examined it.
- Attenuate the input signal coming from the PSTN before the echo canceller looks at it.

When attenuating levels, you are not just attenuating the echo; you are attenuating the entire signal. So always keep in mind that you are affecting the volume level that is heard by the two parties in the conversation. The opposite also holds true: Use extreme caution when using the **input gain** and **output attenuation** commands to boost the levels coming into and out of the gateway. You might end up fixing a low-volume problem and introducing echo.

In this example, you need to get the ERL up to at least 6 dB for the echo canceller to converge, so you must attenuate the signal by an additional 3 dB. On a Cisco IOS Software gateway, you can do this with the **output attenuation** and **input gain** commands. The **output attenuation** command takes effect after the echo canceller has analyzed the signal. For example, if you add the **output attenuation 2** command to the voice port configuration, the audio signal level out toward the PSTN is actually –17 dB even though the echo canceller sees –15 dB. Because the ERL on the tail circuit is still 3 dB, when the echo returns to the gateway, the signal level is –20 dB. From the echo canceller's point of view, the ERL in this case is 5 dB. If you also add the **input gain -1** command, the gateway attenuates the input signal (including the echo) by an additional decibel. This attenuation is performed before the echo canceller looks at the input signal.

NOTE	Changes to the **output attenuation** and **input gain** commands might not take effect until the voice port on which they are configured is shut down and re-enabled. Failure to issue the **shutdown** command followed by the **no shutdown** command on the voice port can result in inaccuracies.

Now assume you have the following configured on the Cisco IOS Software gateway:

```
voice-port 1/1:23
  input gain -1
  output attenuation 2
```

Place the same call and generate the –15 dB test tone again. Issue the command **show call active voice** again. The output should look like the following:

```
OutSignalLevel=-17
InSignalLevel=-21
ERLLevel=6
```

Notice that the **ERLLevel** now shows 6 dB, which is correct. Note that the difference between the **OutSignalLevel** and **InSignalLevel** is only 4 dB, but that is because the **OutSignalLevel** already has 2 dB attenuated due to the **output attenuation** command. At this point, you should not hear echo anymore.

What if your dB levels appear correct, but the echo is still there? The other possibility is that your echo canceller coverage is set too low. On Cisco IOS Software gateways, this value can be adjusted from 8 ms to 32 ms. The default value is 8 ms. You can change this on the voice port with the **echo-cancel coverage** *value* command. Without sophisticated test equipment, it is difficult to determine the actual delay on the tail circuit, so you'll need to try various values until you arrive at a point where you no longer have echo. This command also requires that you perform the **shutdown** command followed by the **no shutdown** command on the voice port for the configuration change to take effect.

You might be wondering why you wouldn't just set the echo canceller coverage to the maximum of 32 ms and forget about it. All echo cancellers have a certain convergence time needed to determine the echo's characteristics before they can begin canceling the echo. The longer you make the echo canceller coverage, the longer this convergence time is. At the maximum of 32 ms, the echo cancellers can take up to five seconds to converge at the beginning of the call. Although this is certainly better than having echo for the duration of a call, you should try to keep the echo canceller coverage as low as possible without going below the tail circuit length.

If you are experiencing convergence echo at the beginning of a call, there is a new feature available in Cisco IOS Software release 12.2(8)T5, 12.2(11)T and later that adds an echo suppressor for the beginning of the call that virtually eliminates convergence echo. This feature is disabled by default and can be enabled with the voice-port command **echo-cancel suppressor**. You can adjust the amount of time the echo suppressor is active at the beginning of a call. The default is seven seconds. For example, to enable the echo suppressor for the first five seconds of a call, configure the voice-port as follows:

```
voice-port 1/1:23
  echo-cancel coverage 32
  echo-cancel suppressor 5
  input gain -1
  output attenuation 2
```

Most service providers put echo cancellers on long distance circuits, so you might encounter echo only on local phone calls and not long distance calls. This is especially true when you're dealing with calls that are still considered local calls yet are geographically dispersed. 32 ms should be a worst case in most scenarios because service providers typically insert echo cancellers when delays exceed 25 ms. Although 32 ms should be the worst case, there are some exceptions in which the tail circuit exceeds 32 ms.

Several projects are currently under way to improve the performance of the Cisco IOS Software echo cancellers to increase the echo canceller coverage from 32 ms to 64 ms and even 128 ms on some platforms. These projects are scheduled to be available on some platforms in Cisco IOS Software Releases 12.2(13)T and 12.3.

Eliminating Echo on the WS-X6608 and DT-24+/DE-30+

The Cisco WS-X6608 and DT-24+/DE-30+ gateways are configured differently than Cisco IOS Software gateways. Therefore, troubleshooting echo on these platforms is different than on a Cisco IOS Software gateway. Although the configuration and troubleshooting tools are different, the concept is the same. The same concepts discussed in the previous sections about ERL and echo cancellation coverage apply.

If you get a report of echo and you discover that the call went out a WS-X6608 gateway, try to reproduce the echo the same way as described for a Cisco IOS Software gateway. Place a call to the number in question, and generate a test tone. Telnet into the Catalyst 6500 switch where the WS-X6608 is installed, and issue the **show port voice active** *module/port* command, as demonstrated in Example 7-13.

Example 7-13 **show port voice active** *Command Output Displays Echo Canceller Information*

```
Switch (enable)show port voice active 4/8
Port  4/8 :
  Channel #23:
    Remote IP address                : 172.18.104.74
    Remote UDP Port                  : 24526
    ACOM Level Current               : 45
    Call State                       : voice
    Codec Type                       : G711 ULAW PCM
    Coder Type Rate                  : 20
    ERL Level                        : 61
    Voice Activity Detection         : disabled
    Echo Cancellation                : enabled
    Fax Transmit Duration (ms)       : 0
    Hi Water Playout Delay           : 65
    Low Water Playout Delay          : 64
    Receive Bytes                    : 503840
    Receive Delay                    : 64
    Receive Packets                  : 3149
    Transmit Bytes                   : 504160
    Transmit Packets                 : 3151
    Tx Duration (ms)                 : 62440
    Voice Tx Duration (ms)           : 62440
```

Notice that there is no indication of what the input and output levels are, as you see on Cisco IOS Software gateways. Because of this, troubleshooting is a bit more difficult. The two useful pieces of information from this command are **ACOM Level Current** and **ERL Level**. These values are listed in 1/10 decibels. This means that the ERL level listed in Example 7-13 is really 6.1 dB. The ACOM level is listed as 4.5 dB. If the echo canceller was really canceling the test tone, the ACOM level would be much higher than just 4.5 dB. Again you see that the ERL level is a bogus number because the echo canceller has not converged. This is not immediately obvious until you look at the ACOM level.

The problem here is that you don't know how much to adjust the input and output levels to get over the 6 dB ERL. One way you can do this is by purposely lowering the dB levels by 6 dB and looking at the reported value of ERL. For example, if the PSTN returns an ERL of 3 dB, but you don't know this because the WS-X6608 doesn't provide enough information, change the input and output attenuation levels (as explained shortly) by 3 dB each. Now the ERL is 9 dB. When you issue the **show port voice active** command, you see the ERL Level listed as 90, which means 9.0 dB. Now you know that the PSTN ERL is 3 dB because 9 dB – 6 dB = 3 dB. This gives you 3 dB to play with if you really need to increase the level because users are complaining about low volume. Adjusting the level any higher results in being under the required 6 dB ERL, and the echo is not cancelled.

Figure 7-14 shows the Product Specific Configuration section of the Gateway Configuration page in CallManager Administration (**Device > Gateway >** *find and select a gateway*) for a WS-X6608 gateway.

Figure 7-14 *Product Specific Configuration for a WS-X6608 Gateway*

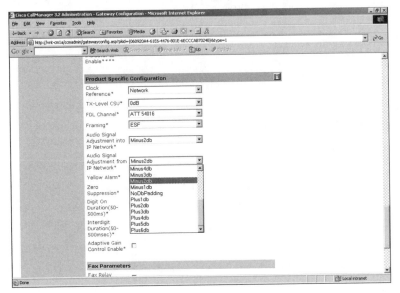

Notice the configuration parameters for Audio Signal Adjustment into IP Network and Audio Signal Adjustment from IP Network. Audio Signal Adjustment into IP Network is synonymous with the **input gain** command in Cisco IOS Software, and Audio Signal Adjustment from IP Network is synonymous with output attenuation. However, the **output attenuation** command in Cisco IOS Software decreases the level for positive values, and Audio Signal Adjustment from IP Network requires a negative value to decrease the level. After you change either of these configuration options, you must click the **Update** button on the Gateway Configuration page and then reset the gateway from CallManager Administration for the change to take effect.

| NOTE | Changes to the audio signal adjustment settings do not take effect until the gateway is reset. You can do this by simply clicking the **Reset Gateway** button on the Gateway Configuration page in CallManager Administration. |

Assume that you set both options to Minus3db and place the same call as before while generating a test tone. Example 7-14 shows the resulting output from **show port voice active**.

Example 7-14 **show port voice active** *Command Output Displays Echo Canceller Information*

```
Switch (enable)show port voice active 4/8
Port  4/8 :
  Channel #23:
    Remote IP address                 : 172.18.104.74
    Remote UDP Port                   : 24526
    ACOM Level Current                : 339
    Call State                        : voice
    Codec Type                        : G711 ULAW PCM
    Coder Type Rate                   : 20
    ERL Level                         : 89
    Voice Activity Detection          : disabled
    Echo Cancellation                 : enabled
    Fax Transmit Duration (ms)        : 0
    Hi Water Playout Delay            : 65
    Low Water Playout Delay           : 64
    Receive Bytes                     : 503840
    Receive Delay                     : 64
    Receive Packets                   : 3149
    Transmit Bytes                    : 504160
    Transmit Packets                  : 3151
    Tx Duration (ms)                  : 62440
    Voice Tx Duration (ms)            : 62440
```

Notice that the ERL level is now 8.9 dB and the ACOM level is 33.9 dB. This means that the echo canceller is attenuating the echo by 33.9 dB, making it inaudible. Because the ERL is 8.9 dB and you are attenuating by 6 dB, the ERL from the PSTN is 2.9 dB.

Unfortunately, the Cisco DT-24+ and DE-30+ are not as easy to troubleshoot. There is no way to look at the dB levels, ERL levels, or ACOM levels because there is no command-line interface (CLI) on these gateways. As a result, the best you can do is lower the dB levels gradually until the echo goes away. You can use this approach on any other gateway as well if you do not want to go through the trouble of making test calls and generating test tones; however, by doing proper testing, you can better understand what limitations you are running into and adjust for them accordingly.

Neither the WS-X6608 nor the DT-24+/DE-30+ offers a way to adjust the echo cancellation coverage. They are both designed to cancel a tail circuit up to 32 ms long. The WS-X6608 has some additional echo suppression logic that helps remove the possibility of having echo for the first three to five seconds of a call while the echo canceller converges.

Eliminating Echo Problems on Cisco IP SoftPhone

Cisco IP SoftPhone presents a unique set of challenges when it comes to echo. If configured improperly, SoftPhone can easily be a major source of acoustic echo. SoftPhone uses the sound card of the PC it is installed on for audio input and output. It uses the currently selected recording source as the input device and uses the wave-out device as the output. On a normal PC, the PC speakers are the output device, and an external or built-in microphone is the input. Left this way, echo is a huge problem because the sound coming out of the PC speakers is picked up by the microphone and is heard as echo on the other side. The SoftPhone user is not the one who experiences the echo. Rather, the party speaking to the SoftPhone user hears severe echo.

To ensure good voice quality when using SoftPhone, you should purchase a good handset or headset that connects to the PC's sound card. This isolates the output signal from being picked up by the microphone. Some headsets connect to the USB port on the PC and have a built-in sound card that gives even better audio performance than the built-in sound card on the PC.

Some sound cards can feed the output signal (speaker output) directly into the record source. When you're using SoftPhone, this is particularly bad because the sound card basically generates echo by feeding the output signal back into the input. To check what the recording source is set to on a Windows PC, follow these instructions:

Step 1 Open **Sounds and Multimedia** in the Control Panel.

Step 2 Click the **Audio** tab.

Step 3 Under **Sound Recording**, click the **Volume** button.

Step 4 On the **Options** menu, make sure **Advanced Controls** is selected.

Step 5 Select **Options > Properties**.

Step 6 Under **Adjust volume for**, select **Recording**.

Step 7 Check all the boxes in the **Show the following volume controls** box. Be sure to scroll down because the list is probably longer than just four entries.

Step 8 Click **OK**.

You should now see the Recording Control, as shown in Figure 7-15.

Figure 7-15 *Confirming the Recording Source Settings*

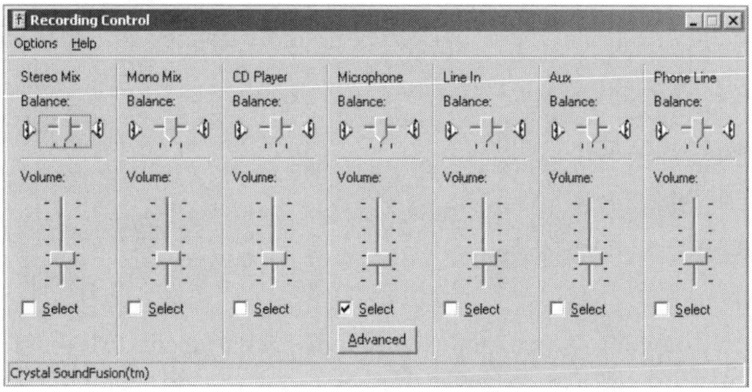

Notice that the Microphone Balance column has a checkbox to select it as the recording source. Some sound cards allow multiple sources to be used as the recording source. The two that are particularly dangerous in Figure 7-15 are Stereo Mix Balance and Mono Mix Balance because they echo anything that comes out the speakers directly to the recording source. Be sure you have only the source you want to use as your input (usually Microphone Balance) selected.

Best Practices

You can take several steps to ensure you do not run into voice quality problems:

- Your voice quality will be only as good as the reliability of your data network. Spend considerable time and effort up front to make sure your data network is ready to handle the voice traffic and prioritize it over data traffic.

- Check for duplex mismatches throughout your network. This is one of the primary causes of packet loss, resulting in choppy voice or jitter.

- Make sure you have enough bandwidth available on your WAN to handle the voice traffic, and use call admission control to ensure that the bandwidth allocated for voice traffic is not exceeded.

- For WAN links slower than 768 kbps, use LFI to ensure that large data packets don't cause excessive jitter for the smaller voice packets.

- Before going into production, test your voice quality by making a variety of OnNet, local, long distance, and international phone calls. Ensure that the call has no echo and that the volume is adequate. Echo usually exhibits itself only when you call specific numbers, so the more areas you can test, the more likely you are to find any potential echo problems.

- Make every effort not to exceed a total one-way delay budget of 150 ms.

- Use network management tools such as the CDR Analysis and Reporting (CAR) tool to proactively monitor for packet loss and network congestion. This helps you correct issues that could potentially cause voice quality problems before users report them.

Summary

Voice quality is a broad topic that can be roughly divided into the following:

- Delayed audio
- Choppy or garbled audio
- Static and noise
- One-way or no-way audio
- Echo

To properly diagnose voice quality problems, get as accurate a description of the problem as possible from the user experiencing the problem, and search through the pieces of the network one at a time for the root cause.

Many voice quality problems are actually a result of problems with the underlying data network. A good understanding of your data network infrastructure allows you to better troubleshoot voice quality problems in a timely manner.

## CHAPTER 8

Fax Machines and Modems

The move to an e-mail and high-speed Internet access-driven society reduces the need for fax machines and modems; however, fax machines and modems are still a big part of most businesses today. As a result, being able to properly transport fax and modem tones over a voice over IP (VoIP) network is essential for any customer who implements IP telephony.

Fax machines and modems present unique challenges when carried over an IP telephony network, primarily due to their unforgiving nature for any modification to the audio stream. Human voice can be modified slightly before reaching the listener without any noticeable difference in the quality of the audio. However, minor changes to the audio stream can lead fax machines and modems to fail or perform poorly. As a result, special features have been added to a variety of Cisco voice gateways to give calls through fax machines and modems different treatment than a normal voice call.

To better troubleshoot fax and modem problems, you should have a good understanding of how fax machines and modems operate and the various features available that help provide reliable fax and modem transmission over an IP telephony network. This chapter discusses:

- Overview of fax machine operation
- Fax/modem passthrough
- Fax relay
- The effect of packet loss and jitter on fax machines and modems
- Checking for clocking problems
- Isolating and troubleshooting fax problems
- Adjusting fax relay parameters

Understanding Fax Machine Operation

To better understand how to troubleshoot fax problems, it is best to understand how fax transmissions work. Most modern fax devices are Group 3-compliant. *Fax Group 3* is a standards-based technology that is made up primarily of the T.4 and T.30 ITU recommendations. T.4 pertains to how the fax image is encoded by a fax device, and T.30 details the fax negotiations and communication protocol.

Group 3 fax devices are designed for use over the PSTN. Because the PSTN is designed for human speech, Group 3 uses analog encoding or modulated signals to transmit the fax data. This modulated signal can be heard as varying audio tones. Group 3 fax machines take 6 to 30 seconds to transmit a page, plus about 15 seconds for the first page initial handshake.

Basic Fax Machine Operation

For ease of understanding, a fax call can be divided into two parts:

*   Fax negotiation
*   Page transmission

The fax negotiation occurs at the beginning of a fax call. V.21 modulated high-level data link control (HDLC) data frames are passed at a speed of 300 bps. These data frames are sent in a standard sequence between the originating and terminating fax devices. During this period, each fax device exchanges its capabilities, and both fax devices agree on the fax session characteristics before the page transmission takes place.

Some capabilities that are exchanged and negotiated include the following:

*   Page transmission speed
*   Error Correction Mode (ECM)
*   Resolution
*   Page coding
*   Scan time

Page transmission speed (*training*) is an important negotiation that determines the speed at which the fax will send its information. Faxes always try to train at the highest modulation speed possible based on the parameters exchanged initially. Fax devices retrain to a lower speed if the training at a higher speed fails.

Page transmission occurs when the training part of the fax negotiation phase is complete. The page information is coded into scan lines with a standard resolution of 203H × 98V dots per inch. Fax images are typically compressed and encoded using either Modified Huffman (MH) or Modified Read (MR) encoding. MH usually compresses at a 20:1 ratio. MR encoding typically provides a 20 percent compression improvement over MH but is slightly less resilient to errors.

When page transmission occurs, a bit rate is used that is higher than the initial 300 bps used in the call setup negotiation. Following are some of the common rates used in fax page transmission:

*   **V.27ter**—2400/4800 bps
*   **V.29**—7200/9600 bps
*   **V.17**—14.4 kbps

Although you do not need to completely understand the intricacies of how fax negotiation works, it is good to have a general understanding of the various T.30 messages used in a fax call.

T.30 Messages

To help you understand how a fax call works, Figure 8-1 illustrates the basic T.30 transactions that occur for a single-page fax transmission. Each message used in a T.30 fax transmission is represented by a three-letter code, as shown in Table 8-1.

Figure 8-1   *T.30 Single-page Fax Transmission*

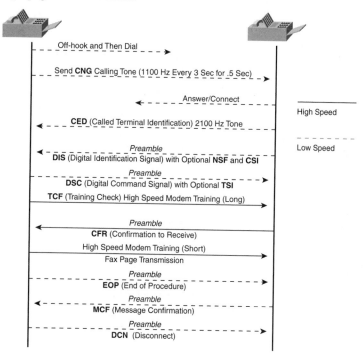

Describing the details of the protocol is beyond the scope of this book; however, Table 8-1 describes the basic transactions that are seen during a fax call. This table does not include all the messages in T.30, but it does represent the ones you are most likely to see. Not all these messages are mandatory for a successful fax transmission. Table 8-1 notes which parameters are optional. For additional information about fax messaging, refer to the ITU T.30 specification.

Table 8-1 *T.30 Fax Message Descriptions*

T.30 Message	Description
CED (Called Terminal Identification)	A 2100-Hz signal that is transmitted by the terminating fax device when a fax call is answered.
CFR (Confirmation to Receive)	A response confirming that the previous messaging and training have been completed and that fax page transmission can begin.
CNG (Calling Tone)	An 1100-Hz tone that is on for half a second and then off for 3 seconds. This signal identifies the fax terminal as a non-speech device. The signal also indicates that the initiating fax terminal is awaiting the Digital Identification Signal (DIS) from the terminating fax terminal.
CRP (Command Repeat)	(Optional) A response that indicates that the previous command was received in error and needs to be repeated.
CSI (Called Subscriber Identification)	(Optional) Provides the specific identity of the called fax terminal through its international telephone number.
DCN (Disconnect)	Ends the fax call and requires no response.
DCS (Digital Command Signal)	Provides the response to the capabilities identified by the DIS signal. This message is where the calling fax terminal matches its capabilities with the ones provided in the called fax terminal's DIS message.
DIS (Digital Identification Signal)	Identifies the capabilities of the called fax terminal.
EOM (End of Message)	Indicates the end of a complete page of fax information.
EOP (End of Procedure)	Indicates the end of a complete page of fax information. No further pages are to be sent. Proceed to the disconnect phase of the fax call.
FTT (Failure to Train)	Used to reject a training signal and to request a retrain. (Retrains usually occur at lower modulation speeds.)
MCF (Message Confirmation)	Indicates that a message has been satisfactorily received.
MPS (Multipage Signal)	Indicates the end of a complete page of fax information and that the receiver is ready for additional pages.
NSF (Nonstandard Facilities)	(Optional) Identifies specific capabilities or requirements that are not covered by the T-series specifications.
RTN (Retrain Negative)	Indicates that a previous message has not been satisfactorily received. Retraining is needed to proceed (usually at a lower modulation speed).
RTP (Retrain Positive)	Indicates that a complete message has been received and that additional messages might follow after retraining.

Table 8-1 *T.30 Fax Message Descriptions (Continued)*

T.30 Message	Description
TCF (Training Check)	Sent through the higher-speed T.4 modulation system (versus the 300 kbps V.21 modulation used for the previous T.30 signaling) to verify training and indicate the acceptability of sending fax pages at this transmission rate.
TSI (Transmitting Subscriber Identification)	(Optional) Identifies the transmitting (calling) fax terminal.

Understanding Fax/Modem Passthrough Versus Fax Relay

Because fax machines and modems are extremely intolerant of any modification of the tones used to transport fax and modem data, various features have been implemented in most Cisco voice gateways to help ensure fax and modem traffic traverses the IP network with as little distortion as possible.

The two primary features available in Cisco voice gateways designed to help transport fax and modem data over an IP network are fax/modem passthrough and fax relay. Fax/modem passthrough ensure the path being used to carry the audio samples containing fax or modem data are as distortion-free as possible, while fax relay actually demodulates the fax tones and passes the fax information as data packets over the IP network. Both fax/modem passthrough and fax relay are discussed in detail in the following sections.

Fax/Modem Passthrough

Gateways in an IP telephony network initially treat voice, fax, and modem calls the same. All calls cause the gateway to load the configured voice compression codec in the digital signal processor (DSP). For calls over the WAN, the codecs are usually high-compression codecs so that less bandwidth is used for each voice call. High-compression codecs such as G.729 and G.723 are optimized for voice. They do a good job of compressing the voice to a low bandwidth while maintaining good voice quality. However, G.729 and other high-compression codecs are not optimized for fax or modem. In fact, the modulated signals of fax and modem transmissions usually do not correctly pass through when these codecs are used, and fax and modem calls fail as a result.

In most cases, faxes can be transmitted successfully when using codecs with lower compression ratios or no compression at all (such as G.726 and G.711 with no VAD and sometimes without echo cancellation). Modems generally require that the echo canceller be disabled while fax machines usually do not. This method of sending faxes and modem transmissions through the voice codec is usually called *fax passthrough* or *modem passthrough*. In a Cisco IP Telephony network, G.711 is currently the only codec that can support fax/modem passthrough; however, you should make proper provisions to ensure that VAD is disabled for the call and for increased performance. Other codecs, such as clear-channel codec and even G.726, can do fax passthrough as well, but neither of these codecs is supported in an IP Telephony environment at this time.

With fax/modem passthrough, the codec encodes the modulated signal from the fax machine on the source gateway and passes it across the VoIP network just as if it were a voice sample. The terminating gateway then decompresses and decodes the sample and plays it to the terminating fax machine. This is no different from what the gateway does for a voice call.

Any gateway configured to use G.711 supports fax passthrough in theory, although most gateways are more intelligent in that they can automatically detect fax and modem tones and automatically disable both VAD and the echo canceller as necessary. A number of gateways have this capability; however, not all of them can currently interoperate with each other because different gateways use different methods to communicate fax and modem passthrough information. Although both methods of passing this information are very similar, they use different packet formats to accomplish the same task, making them incompatible.

Named Service Events and Named Telephony Events

To better understand how fax and modem passthrough work on Cisco voice gateways, you must understand what a Named Service Event (NSE) and Named Telephony Event (NTE) are. Although the two are very similar, their differences are enough to cause incompatibilities between various gateway platforms.

NTEs are defined in the IETF standards document RFC 2833. The actual purpose of this document is to define a system of transporting tones and other telephony events over RTP, similar to DTMF relay discussed in Chapter 6, "Voice Gateways."

On the wire, an NTE consists of an RTP packet with the same source and destination IP addresses and UDP ports as the rest of the media stream. However, to allow the receiver to be able to distinguish this from the audio packets that make up the stream, a different RTP payload type is used.

The NTE packet structure is fully defined within RFC 2833. There are three significant values encoded within a 4-byte payload. These are

- **Event type**—The type of tone being conveyed (8 bits)
- **Volume**—The amplitude of the tone detected (6 bits)
- **Duration**—The length of the tone (16 bits)

As per RFC 2833, the payload type for NTEs is a dynamic, negotiable value. However, not all Cisco voice gateways use protocols capable of performing such negotiation. For example, the Skinny Client Control Protocol (SCCP or Skinny protocol) has no such capability. Because of this, Cisco devices standardize this value and always use payload type 101 to send NTEs. If you see an RTP packet with payload type 101, you know the gateways are exchanging NTE packets.

NSEs have a very similar packet structure in that they are also RTP packets; however, on Cisco voice gateways NSEs are normally sent with RTP payload type 100 rather than 101. Also, the event type values have different meanings, so although the data might appear similar to an NTE, that meaning of that data is completely different. In addition, there are some values defined for Cisco NSEs for which there is no corresponding NTE event type. If you see an RTP packet with payload type 100, you know the gateways are exchanging NSE packets.

Basic Fax/Modem Passthrough Operation

Whether NSEs or NTEs are used, fax and modem passthrough works the same way on all Cisco gateway devices that support fax and modem passthrough. Although there are a few differences between dealing with a fax call versus a modem call in passthrough, they are virtually the same.

Modem Passthrough Operation

When a modem calls out, it should be calling another modem. When the far-end modem answers the call, it first plays an "answer tone" often termed ANS. The answer tone is a 2100 Hz tone. When this tone reaches a voice gateway to enter the IP telephony network, the gateway to which the remote modem is connected is responsible for recognizing this tone and acting accordingly. In the case of a call from a user connected to an FXS port on a local gateway going out to the PSTN via a PRI, the PRI gateway is considered the far-end gateway even though the modem is technically not directly connected to the PRI (same thing applies if the connection to the PSTN is BRI, FXO, or CAS). The important thing to know is that this is the point where it enters the IP telephony world. The two actions the terminating gateway must perform at this point are

- Change the characteristics of its audio path to the originating gateway to eliminate anything that might obstruct the modem audio signals. This involves switching to G.711 transmission if a different audio codec was in use, turning off any auxiliary processing such as high pass filters (which remove all frequencies that occur below a certain frequency, such as 300 Hz), disabling silence suppression (VAD), and changing the jitter buffer properties to make the receive path as resilient to network jitter as possible.

- Translate the answer tone to an NSE or NTE and send as an "event" packet to the originating gateway.

When the originating gateway receives the NSE or NTE that signifies that a modem answered the call at the terminating gateway, this causes the originating gateway to perform the same changes to the audio path (G.711, no VAD, and so on) as the terminating gateway did.

After playing a 2100 Hz answer tone, the called modem plays a slightly modified version of this tone. The modification is to reverse the phase of the sine wave every 450 ms. This tone instructs any devices through which the tone passes to turn off any echo cancellers that are currently in use.

When the terminating gateway detects this tone (along with the phase reversal) it performs the following two actions:

- Disables any echo cancellers that it currently has activated for the call's media stream
- Translates this new audio tone (2100 Hz + 450 ms phase reversal) to an NSE or NTE and send as an IP packet to the originating gateway

On receipt of the NSE or NTE that corresponds to the 2100 Hz tone with phase reversal being detected, the originating gateway should disable its own echo cancellers for the call.

At this stage both the originating and terminating gateways should be running as clear a channel as possible because the gateways have detected two tones—one pure 2100 Hz signal and one 2100 Hz tone with phase reversal every 450 ms. The clear channel will use G.711 encoding, no silence suppression, no high pass filters, and no echo cancellation with the jitter buffers' depths set for maximum resilience to network jitter.

Fax Passthrough Operation

A fax call starts off in a very similar manner to a modem call. The called fax machine first plays a 2100 Hz tone to the calling fax machine that is detected by the terminating gateway. This causes the terminating gateway to change the codec to G.711, turn off silence suppression, disable any audio filters in place, and use larger jitter buffers in order to make the receive path as resilient to network jitter as possible, the same way it did with the modem call.

However, unlike a modem, the fax machine typically does not play a 2100 Hz tone with 450 ms phase reversal. This means that echo cancellers in the network should typically remain enabled during a fax call, even though some fax machines are designed to transmit a 2100 Hz signal with phase reversal, which causes the echo cancellers to be disabled.

At some point after the 2100 Hz signal is sent out and the voice path is set up as a clear channel, the sending and receiving fax machine start to converse using the V.21 protocol as mentioned in the section "Basic Fax Machine Operation." This conversation (known as the fax preamble) can be detected by the originating and terminating gateways because it uses specific known tone frequencies.

Before receiving the V.21 tones, it is not possible for the gateway to distinguish between a fax machine and a modem. When the voice gateway detects the V.21 tones it knows the call is a fax call and if the gateway is configured to do so, it may try to negotiate fax relay with the peer gateway.

Verifying Fax and Modem Passthrough Configuration

After reading the previous sections, you should have a good understanding of how fax and modem passthrough works. With that knowledge, now you can check to ensure fax and modem passthrough are configured correctly.

To ensure that fax and modem passthrough are enabled, first check the Fax and Modem Parameters area on the Gateway Configuration page in Cisco CallManager Administration (**Device > Gateway**) to ensure that fax relay is disabled (see Figure 8-2). On the WS-X6608, this is done on a per-T1/E1 basis, and on the WS-6624, fax relay can be disabled on a per-port basis. To use fax and modem passthrough, uncheck the **Fax Relay Enable** checkbox.

Figure 8-2   *Fax Configuration Parameters for a WS-X6608 Port*

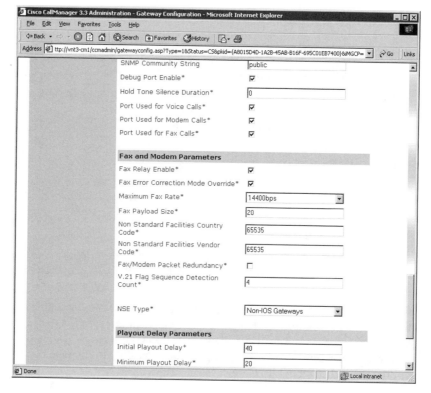

To enable fax passthrough on the WS-X6624, select the port you want to configure in CallManager Administration and uncheck the **Fax Relay Enable** checkbox in the Fax Parameters section of the Port Configuration page, as shown in Figure 8-3.

Figure 8-3 *Fax Configuration Parameters for a WS-X6624 Port*

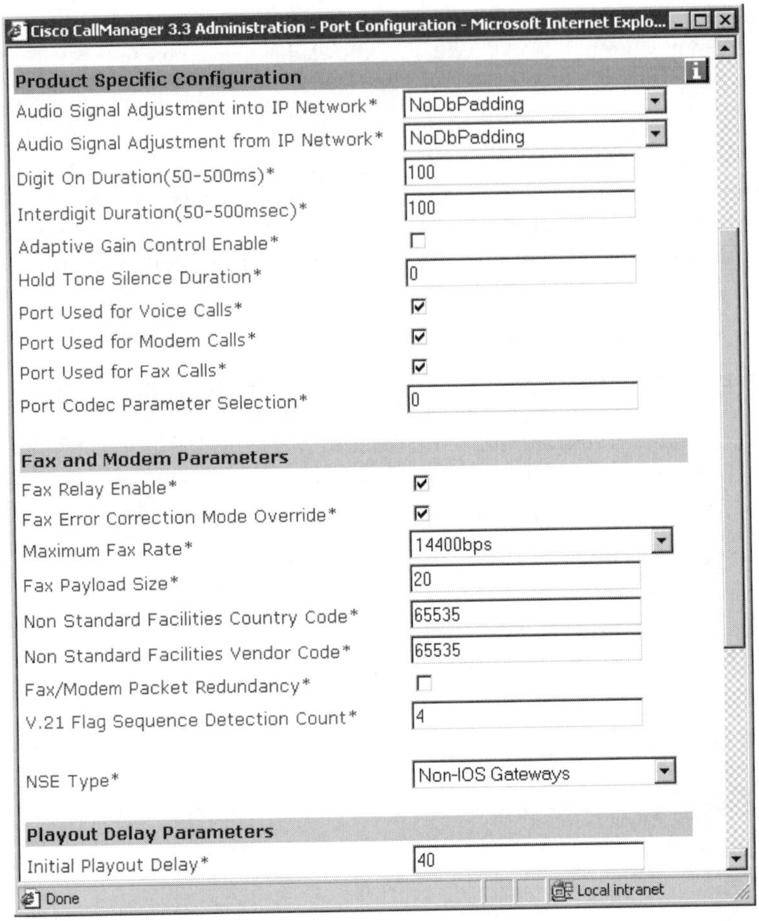

In addition to the **Fax Relay Enable** checkbox, there are a few other settings that apply to fax and modem passthrough. One of the most important is the **NSE Type** parameter. This parameter can be set to **Non-IOS Gateways** or **IOS Gateways**. When set to **Non-IOS Gateways**, the gateway uses NTEs (RTP payload type 101) to communicate fax relay information. When set to **IOS Gateways** the gateway uses NSEs (RTP payload type 100) to communicate fax relay information. If you only have WS-X6608 and WS-X6624 gateways in your network, all you have to do is make sure the settings match throughout. However, if you are using any IOS gateways (which must be running Cisco IOS Software version 12.2(11)T or later) you must set the **NSE Type** parameter to **IOS Gateways**. Other gateways such as the VG248 use NTEs or NSEs depending on the version of software. VG248 software version 1.2(1) and later uses NSEs while earlier versions use NTEs. To be absolutely sure of which method is being used by a particular gateway, take a sniffer trace of a fax transmission between the two gateways and observe the value of the RTP payload type.

Another set of checkboxes that can be configured when using fax and modem passthrough are labeled **Port Used for Voice Calls**, **Port Used for Modem Calls**, and **Port Used for Fax Calls**. If all three checkboxes are selected, the gateway port switches among voice, fax passthrough, and modem passthrough as needed. If you know a particular port is going to be used solely for a fax or modem, disable the checkboxes that do not apply. This forces the port into fax or modem passthrough mode for all calls, reducing the chance of the gateway not properly detecting fax or modem tones and switching to passthrough.

The remaining parameters mostly apply to fax relay and are discussed in the following section.

After you have verified that the gateways are properly configured for fax and modem passthrough, you can confirm that passthrough is working for a particular call by using the **show port voice active** *mod/port* command while the fax or modem call is active on the Catalyst 6000 switch in which the WS-X6608 or WS-X6624 gateway resides (see Example 8-1).

Example 8-1 *Confirming Fax Passthrough with the* **show port voice active** *mod/port Command*

```
Console> (enable) show port voice active 5/2
Port  5/2 :
  Channel #1:
    Remote IP address                  : 14.84.211.104
    Remote UDP Port                    : 26636
    ACOM Level Current                 : 200
    Call State                         : fax
    Codec Type                         : G711 ULAW PCM
    Coder Type Rate                    : 20
    ERL Level                          : 200
    Voice Activity Detection           : disabled
    Echo Cancellation                  : enabled
    Fax Transmit Duration (ms)         : 0
    Hi Water Playout Delay             : 64
    Low Water Playout Delay            : 64
    Receive Bytes                      : 202720
    Receive Delay                      : 64
    Receive Packets                    : 1267
    Transmit Bytes                     : 203840
    Transmit Packets                   : 1274
    Tx Duration (ms)                   : 14070
    Voice Tx Duration (ms)             : 14070
```

Notice that the Call State is listed as **fax**, and VAD is disabled automatically. The echo canceller remains enabled because the fax machine did not send a 2100 Hz tone with phase reversal every 450 ms. The output would indicate **modem** if the call was a modem passthrough call. If the output of **show port voice active** displays **fax relay** or **voice**, go back and double-check your configuration to ensure that fax relay is disabled on *both* the gateways involved in the call.

On most Cisco IOS Software voice gateways, Cisco fax relay is enabled by default (fax relay is discussed in the next section). To use fax passthrough, you must disable fax relay.

You disable fax relay by using the dial peer configuration command **fax rate disable**. The AS5*xxx* series of Cisco IOS Software voice gateways use T.38 fax relay by default as opposed to Cisco fax relay. Example 8-2 demonstrates the dial peer configuration after enabling fax passthrough.

Example 8-2 *Dial Peer Configuration for Disabling Fax Relay on an H.323 Cisco IOS Software Gateway*

```
dial-peer voice 3 voip
  destination-pattern 555....
  dtmf-relay h245-alphanumeric
  codec g711ulaw
  fax rate disable
  ip qos dscp cs5 media
  no vad
```

Notice that VAD is disabled with the command **no vad**, and fax relay is disabled with the command **fax rate disable**. If you remember the dial peer matching rules from Chapter 6, this dial peer is matched for an inbound call from the PSTN or for an outbound call only if the calling party number matches the destination pattern. Use the **incoming called-number** command to ensure that a dial peer with **fax rate disable** configured is matched if you want to disable fax relay for outbound calls.

Fax Relay Basics

Fax relay functions are very different from fax passthrough. *Fax relay* is a protocol that terminates the modulated signal, extracts the digital information, and then relays the digital information through the data network using data packets. At the terminating side, the digital information is extracted from the packet, modulated, and played out. This means that the fax tones are not carried over the data network. Instead, the fax data itself is carried across the network.

Fax relay is a technique used to overcome the deficiency in high-compression voice codecs (G.729, G.723, and so on) when these codecs try to pass fax traffic. Generally, fax relay is required only when fax information is carried over a WAN where high-compression codecs are being used. Fax relay is also used across the WAN to preserve bandwidth. WAN links do not often have the capacity to deal with fax passthrough. Also, fax relay decouples the clocking dependencies on each side of the network so that synched clocking is not required in the network to make it work properly.

Because a fax call is treated as a regular voice call, the DSP in each gateway is put into voice mode, after which human speech is expected to be received and processed. During the life of the call, if a fax answer (CED) or calling (CNG) tone is heard, the DSP does not interfere with the speech processing. It allows the tone to continue across the VoIP call leg.

A normal fax machine, after generating a CED or hearing a CNG, transmits a T.30 DIS message as part of fax handshaking. This process usually occurs at the terminating fax machine. The terminating gateway's DSP then detects the HDLC flag sequence at the start of the DIS message and initiates fax relay switchover. This means it unloads the voice codec and loads a fax relay codec to handle the fax call that is taking place.

Notification is also sent to the DSP on the other side of the network so that the DSPs on each side of the fax call use the fax relay codec. The notification mechanism differs depending on the fax relay protocol used. With the fax codec loaded, the DSPs demodulate the T.30 HDLC frames, extract the fax information, and pass it between the routers using one of the following fax relay protocols:

- **Proprietary Cisco fax relay for VoIP**—Fax relay is the default mode for passing faxes through a VoIP network. Cisco fax relay is the default fax relay type. This capability is supported in Cisco IOS Software Releases 11.3 and later, and is widely available. It uses RTP to transport the fax data. Cisco fax relay is also available on the WS-X6608, WS-X6624, and VG248 voice gateways.

- **Standards-based T.38 fax for VoIP**—T.38 has been available in Cisco IOS Software Releases 12.1(3)T and later on some platforms. It can be enabled with the **fax relay protocol t38** command configured under the VoIP dial peer. It uses UDP to transport fax data. Unfortunately, Cisco CallManager does not support T.38 fax, so in an IP Telephony environment (as opposed to a non-CallManager VoIP environment), T.38 should not be used. Ensure that T.38 fax is disabled on any Cisco IOS Software voice gateway. T.38 fax support is planned for future releases of CallManager.

It is important to understand that, unlike fax passthrough, fax relay converts the T.30 fax tones into the actual HDLC data frames, transmits the information across the VoIP network using the fax relay protocol, and then converts the data back into tones at the far side by creating a new modulated signal. The fax machines on either end send and receive tones and are unaware that a demodulation/modulation fax relay process is occurring.

Figure 8-4 shows how fax tones are demodulated and carried as data over the IP network and modulated at the far end.

Figure 8-4   *Fax Relay Over an IP Network*

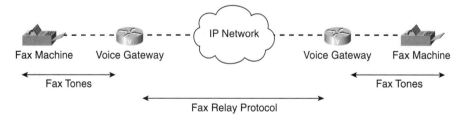

When using Cisco fax relay, first ensure that fax relay is enabled on both of the gateways involved in the call. Refer to Figures 8-2 and 8-3 for the CallManager Administration pages for configuring fax relay. Ensure that the **Fax Relay Enable** checkbox is enabled for the gateways on which you want to enable fax relay. You must reset the gateway from CallManager Administration for the change to take effect.

For a Cisco IOS Software voice gateway, Cisco fax relay is enabled by default. Look at the VoIP dial peer that applies to the call in question, and make sure it does *not* have the command **fax rate disable**.

The Effect of Packet Loss and Jitter on Fax Machines and Modems

Now that you understand how fax/modem passthrough and fax relay work, you can understand how to troubleshoot a fax or modem problem. There are several conditions that can adversely affect a fax or modem transmission. The worst of these is any problem that causes packet loss or jitter.

Chapter 7, "Voice Quality," discusses the effect of packet loss and variable delay (jitter) on voice quality. Chapter 7 states that some degree of packet loss can be concealed by the various codecs and jitter buffers that adapt to accommodate variable delay conditions. However, when you start transporting fax and modem tones over an IP network, these techniques are not nearly as effective at preserving fax and modem tone quality, which is critical to the success of those devices.

Fax machines and modems typically have to retrain or possibly even drop the call when a small number of packets are lost in the network—especially when more compressed codecs that are optimized for human speech, such as G.729, are used. Additionally, digital signal processors (DSPs) are optimized to predict a wave pattern of human speech, so even if a packet is lost, the waveform can be reconstructed fairly well. This is not the case with modem/fax tones. Some fax machines and modems are more resilient when handling varying line conditions. For this reason, for successful fax and modem transmissions, the first step is to ensure perfect or near-perfect network conditions. Refer to the troubleshooting methodology in Chapter 7 for various places to look for voice quality problems. If you are having any voice quality issues in your network, tackle those first because whatever is causing your voice quality problem is likely causing fax and modem problems as well.

Fax and modem tones have very different requirements than human voice. First, fax machines and modems are typically full-duplex, meaning that both sides constantly transmit and receive data at the same time. This is different from a phone conversation, in which typically only one person is speaking at any given time.

For this reason, voice activity detection (VAD) is of no use on a fax or modem call. In fact, serious problems can occur if VAD is enabled at any point in a fax or modem call. For this reason, ensure that VAD is disabled for any call involving a fax or modem. As discussed in the section "Basic Fax/Modem Passthrough Operation," most gateways disable VAD dynamically upon detecting a fax or modem tone when configured properly.

First Steps in Troubleshooting Fax and Modem Problems

You should check a few basic things before getting too involved in troubleshooting a fax or modem problem. Often a problem report comes in, indicating that a user is unable to send faxes, receive faxes, or both. The first thing to check is to make sure that a regular voice call can be completed to the port where the fax or modem resides. Take a plain analog phone and connect it to the gateway in place of the fax or modem. If possible, use the same cable that is currently connected to the fax or modem to ensure that none of the physical layer components are at fault.

If you can make a voice call successfully without any voice quality problems, there are a few other things to check. First, determine whether the problem occurs only on inbound calls, outbound calls, or both. Many IP telephony deployments use different gateways for inbound and outbound calls. If the fax/modem problems occur in only one direction, this points you in the direction of the gateway for inbound or outbound, depending on the problem you are encountering.

One common reason for fax and modem problems, especially problems transmitting multipage faxes and long modem calls, is physical layer errors on digital interfaces.

Checking for Physical Layer Problems on Digital Circuits

If the fax call traverses any T1 or E1 digital connections, ensure that the connection is error-free. Fax machines and modems are extremely sensitive to errors on the line, and they fail even when voice quality is good.

On a Cisco IOS Software gateway, use the command **show controllers** (demonstrated in Example 8-3) to look for physical layer problems.

Example 8-3 *Search for Physical Layer Problems with the* **show controllers** *Command*

```
Router#show controllers t1 1/1 brief
T1 1/1 is up.
  Applique type is Channelized T1
  Cablelength is long gain36 0db
  No alarms detected.
  alarm-trigger is not set
  Version info Firmware: 20020306, FPGA: 11
  Framing is ESF, Line Code is B8ZS, Clock Source is Line.
  Data in current interval (237 seconds elapsed):
     0 Line Code Violations, 0 Path Code Violations
     0 Slip Secs, 0 Fr Loss Secs, 0 Line Err Secs, 0 Degraded Mins
     0 Errored Secs, 0 Bursty Err Secs, 0 Severely Err Secs, 0 Unavail Secs
  Total Data (last 24 hours)
     0 Line Code Violations, 0 Path Code Violations,
     0 Slip Secs, 0 Fr Loss Secs, 0 Line Err Secs, 0 Degraded Mins,
     0 Errored Secs, 0 Bursty Err Secs, 0 Severely Err Secs, 0 Unavail Secs
```

Notice in Example 8-3 that all the counters are 0 for the past 24-hour period. If you see any errors, use the command **clear counters** to reset all the counters to 0, and then monitor to see if the errors return while you are having fax or modem problems. If you are seeing any physical layer problems, they are very likely contributing to your fax and modem problems.

The same statistics can be obtained for the WS-X6608 gateway using the Dick Tracy utility as described in the section "Getting the D-Channel Established" in Chapter 6.

The most common error is clock slips, which are typically caused by improperly configured clocking. Any two endpoints communicating with each other using a synchronous TDM interface such as a T1 or E1 must agree upon a single clock to keep both endpoints synchronized. This is referred to as *clocking*. If the clock configuration is incorrect on either side of the connection, clock slips occur.

One side of the T1/E1 should be configured as the clock source, and the other side should be configured to derive clocking from the line. Ideally, all your TDM-connected devices (that is, T1/E1 CAS/PRI connections) should derive clocking from the same source. This can sometimes be difficult if you have various trunks to different service providers. In such a case, you should at least ensure that two different service providers are not connected to the same voice gateway.

On some Cisco platforms, including the Cisco MC3810 and the AIM-VOICE card in a 2600, 3600, or 3700 series voice gateway, you need to configure the **network-clock-select** command and then issue the **show network-clocks** command to make sure the configuration has taken effect. For a good general overview of hierarchical clocking, refer to the following URL or search "Configuring Synchronized Clocking" on Cisco.com:

> www.cisco.com/en/US/products/hw/routers/ps1904/products_configuration_guide_
> chapter09186a008007dc3f.html

Similarly, on the Catalyst 4224, Cisco 7200VXR, and WS-X4604 Access Gateway Module platforms, the **frame-clock-select** command is required for the voice cards to properly synchronize the voice gateway's clock with the device to which the gateway is attached. Failure to configure this command will likely result in clock slips.

Example 8-4 shows the output of the **show network-clocks** command.

Example 8-4 *Output of the **show network-clocks** Command*

```
Router#show network-clocks
Router#  Network Clock Configuration
- - - - - - - - - - - - - - - - - - - - - - - - - -
  Priority      Clock Source    Clock State    Clock Type

     5            Backplane         Good            PLL

  Current Primary Clock Source
- - - - - - - - - - - - - - - - - - - - - - - - - -
  Priority      Clock Source    Clock State    Clock Type

     5            Backplane         Good            PLL
```

Notice the backplane is currently being used as the clock source, which means this gateway is providing clocking to all the ports.

If you have checked for packet loss and clocking problems and are still encountering fax or modem transmission failures, you should attempt to further isolate the problem and troubleshoot the fax/modem passthrough or fax relay settings.

Isolating and Troubleshooting Fax Problems

As with any other problem you are trying to troubleshoot, the first step is to isolate the problem to two fax machines or modems that are experiencing problems. Although you cannot reproduce all problems 100 percent of the time, most fax and modem failures are usually easily reproduced within a few attempts.

As soon as you have found a pair of fax machines or modems where you can reproduce the failure, determine which gateways are involved, and double-check the configuration to ensure the gateways are configured for either fax passthrough or fax relay. Ensure that the configuration is consistent on both gateways and that you don't have one gateway configured for pass-through and the other configured for relay.

If a Cisco IOS Software voice gateway is involved, use the command **show call active voice brief** to ensure that the dial peer is being matched that contains the fax configuration you want. Example 8-5 shows some sample output from this command.

Example 8-5   *Ensuring That the Correct Dial Peer Is Matched with the* **show call active voice brief** *Command*

```
Router#show call active voice brief
321D : 98177135hs.1 +388 pid:9 Answer 9195551000 active
 dur 00:00:03 tx:178/3531 rx:186/3720
 IP 172.18.106.59:19554 rtt:0ms pl:1990/0ms lost:0/0/0 delay:69/69/70ms g729r8

321D : 98177146hs.1 +377 pid:1 Originate 95552000 active
 dur 00:00:03 tx:186/3720 rx:178/3531
 Tele 1/1:23 (45): tx:3700/3550/0ms g729r8 noise:-78 acom:-20  i/0:-44/-44 dBm
```

The output in Example 8-5 indicates that the VoIP leg of the call matches dial peer 9. You should check dial peer 9 to ensure that it has the fax configuration you intend to use.

If a dial peer other than the one you expect is being selected, refer to the dial peer selection rules covered in Chapter 6. If you are matching peer ID 0, follow the instructions in Chapter 6 and create a dial peer that contains the fax configuration you want. Check the configuration on both sides to ensure that they match. A common cause of problems is a mismatch, such as fax relay configured on one side and not the other, or the fax relay protocol set to Cisco on one side and T.38 on the other. Another common problem is when the gateways are configured to use a high-compression codec such as G.729 with fax passthrough. When using any kind of compressed codec, use fax relay.

Now that you know which dial peers are being used and the gateways involved, you can start trying various things to resolve the fax problems. First, it cannot be stressed enough that you should ensure that there are no network problems that are causing high jitter or packet loss. Also, check for clock slips on your digital TDM circuits (as discussed in the section "Checking for Physical Layer Problems on Digital Circuits"). Finally, make sure a voice call is working properly between the two endpoints. Connect analog phones in place of the fax machines or modems and make sure you can make a voice call between them.

If you are having problems with fax relay, the first thing to try is switching to fax passthrough. Although fax relay helps in situations where low bandwidth is required because it needs to understand the T.30 signaling, some fax machines that do not completely adhere to the T.30 specification can cause fax calls to fail when traversing a Cisco fax relay network. If the fax call is still unsuccessful with fax passthrough and you are sure there are no clock slips or packet loss, try bypassing the VoIP network entirely and ensure that there is not a problem with the two fax machines independent of the VoIP network.

CAUTION   Be careful when switching from fax relay to fax passthrough if the call must traverse a WAN link because it is likely you are using a compressed codec over the WAN. Switching to fax passthrough requires that you use G.711, which takes up considerably more bandwidth. If your call admission control and QoS policy are not set up to allow a G.711 call to work properly over the WAN, fax passthrough calls fail as well. You also might cause oversubscription of your WAN if a call that is supposed to be 24 kbps actually consumes 80 kbps, causing voice quality problems for the other calls using that WAN link.

If you are still having problems with fax passthrough, there are several other parameters you can try to use to resolve the issue. If this is a WS-X6608 or WS-X6624 gateway, force the two ports to use either fax or modem by selecting the **Port Used for Fax Call** or **Fax Used for Modem Call** checkbox and disabling the other checkboxes. This forces the port into fax or modem passthrough. Also, ensure the **NSE Type** parameter is consistent throughout. If you are having problems between different types of gateways, ensure the **NSE Type** matches the gateway to which you are connecting. The recommended setting is **IOS Gateways** as long as you are using a gateway that supports fax passthrough negotiation using NSE packets.

One last thing you can try is to increase the size of the jitter buffer by adjusting the Playout Delay Parameters as shown in Figures 8-2 and 8-3. Set the **Initial Playout Delay** and **Minimum Playout Delay** parameters to a large value, such as 100 ms. This ensures the jitter buffer is always at least 100 ms in size to compensate for up to 100 ms of jitter on the network. You should not have this much jitter in any network, so if this resolves the problem, go back again and troubleshoot the network for any sources of jitter.

If switching from fax relay to fax passthrough resolves the problem there are several settings you can change on the various voice gateways to tune the performance of fax relay.

The various settings you can change on a Cisco IOS voice gateways and the WS-X6608 and WS-X6624 to tune the performance of fax relay are

- Fax relay data rate
- Error correction mode
- Nonstandard facilities
- Fax protocol (Cisco IOS only)
- Fax interface type (Cisco IOS only)

Adjusting the Fax Relay Data Rate

Fax relay allows you to use much less bandwidth than fax passthrough. When traversing a WAN, you should ensure you do not use more bandwidth for a fax call than what you allow for a voice call.

On a Cisco IOS gateway, the **fax rate** command is configured under the VoIP dial peer that is matched for your fax call. The default setting is **fax rate voice.** This *does not* appear in the configuration under each dial peer. The **fax rate voice** setting restricts the fax rate to the codec bandwidth. This means that if the dial peer is configured to use the default G.729 voice codec that compresses voice to 8 kbps, the **fax rate voice** setting does not allow fax calls to exceed this codec bandwidth. The fax is limited to a bandwidth of 7200 bps, even if it tries to initially negotiate at a higher bandwidth of 14.4 kbps or 9600 bps.

A common complaint is that faxes that used to complete within a certain time when connected via the PSTN now take twice as long over a VoIP network. If a low-bandwidth codec such as G.729 has been configured with the default fax rate voice setting, this behavior is expected because the highest rate that can be negotiated is 7200 bps. Negotiation can be as high as 14.4 kbps over a standard POTS line. Using the **fax rate** command, you can configure fax transmissions to use a bandwidth greater than the codec compression. For example, the command **fax rate 14400** allows fax calls to negotiate to a maximum of 14.4 kbps regardless of the voice codec configured. This configuration resolves the problem of longer completion times.

Be extremely careful if you decide to change the fax rate for calls that should use no more than 8 kbps. Failure to take the additional bandwidth into account can result in an oversubscription of your WAN unless you specifically engineer your Low Latency Queuing (LLQ) and other Quality of Service (QoS) mechanisms to take fax calls into account. Oversubscribing the WAN causes fax failures and voice quality problems for other calls because oversubscription results in packet loss. The **fax rate voice** setting is the default because it ensures that both voice and fax calls use the same amount of bandwidth within the VoIP network.

Some fax machines do not operate well at lower fax rates, so you might want to set the fax rate to **fax rate 14400** temporarily to see if a particular fax machine has problems operating at a lower fax rate. If this is the case, you should provision your WAN to ensure that fax calls that exceed the codec bandwidth do not oversubscribe the WAN.

On the WS-X6608 and WS-X6624 voice gateways, the fax relay data rate is configured under the **Maximum Fax Rate** parameter in the Fax and Modem Parameters section of the Gateway Configuration page in CallManager Administration, as shown in Figures 8-2 and 8-3. Note that these gateways do not have an equivalent command to **fax rate voice** on a Cisco IOS gateway, so you must ensure the fax rate is set lower than the bandwidth allocated for a voice call. For example, if you are using G.729 over the WAN, you need to make sure the **Maximum Fax Rate** is set to less then 8000 bps. The data rates for each codec are defined in Appendix A, "Cisco IP Telephony Protocol and Codec Information and References."

Disabling Error Correction Mode

Another useful parameter for troubleshooting fax relay problems is the Error Correction Mode (ECM) configuration.

The **fax-relay ecm disable** command is issued to disable ECM negotiation between a pair of fax machines. ECM ensures that the faxed pages are transmitted error-free. This feature is usually found on higher-end fax machines. Unfortunately, ECM has a low tolerance for jitter and packet loss (approximately two percent). Therefore, when this negotiated feature is enabled, it might result in a higher fax failure rate in networks where there is some packet loss. Incomplete output on the terminating fax is a symptom of failures due to packet loss.

If both fax machines agree during the fax negotiation phase, ECM is enabled. When using fax relay, the gateways demodulate the fax tones into their true HDLC frame format. Because they have the actual fax data instead of modulated tones, the gateways can intercept and overwrite the field in the frame that indicates ECM status. If a fax machine transmits that it is capable of ECM, the gateway can change this parameter so that the other fax machine believes that ECM is not supported. Both fax machines are then forced to disable ECM, which means transmitting the fax data using standard T.4 data.

Fax reliability is increased greatly with ECM disabled, even with much higher packet loss (about 10 percent) and delay. In addition, this command automatically enables a Cisco IOS Software feature called *packet loss concealment,* in which lost scan lines are repeated to spoof the receiving fax machine into believing that it is receiving all the data.

Note that although ECM might improve the success rate of fax transmissions in an IP network with packet loss, the underlying network problems should be addressed because they indicate a more serious problem that could lead to voice quality degradation.

To disable ECM, use the VoIP dial peer configuration command **fax-relay ecm disable**. To enable ECM, use the command **no fax-relay ecm disable**. The dial peer shown in Example 8-6 has fax relay enabled, but ECM is disabled.

Example 8-6 *Configuring a Dial Peer to Disable ECM*

```
dial-peer voice 3 voip
 destination-pattern 555....
 dtmf-relay h245-alphanumeric
 ip qos dscp cs5 media
 fax-relay ecm disable
```

ECM can also be disabled on the WS-X6608 and WS-X6624 voice gateways. ECM is disabled by default; however, you can check to ensure it is disabled in CallManager Administration. Refer to Figures 8-2 and 8-3. Beneath the **Fax Relay Enable** checkbox is a **Fax Error Correction Mode Override** checkbox. When this box is checked, ECM is disabled.

Changing the Nonstandard Facilities Field

The Nonstandard Facilities (NSF) field is used to exchange proprietary fax capabilities between two fax machines. Some fax machines use proprietary techniques to provide additional features that are not available as part of the standard T.30 specification. Usually these features work only when you send faxes between like fax machines. Because the router's fax relay implementation demodulates and decodes the fax tones based on the T.30 specification, transactions or encodings that are proprietary break fax relay and cause the fax transmissions to fail. This capability notification takes place using the optional Nonstandard Facilities field during fax negotiation.

This field can be overridden in Cisco IOS voice gateways and the WS-X6608 and WS-X6624 voice gateways. Use the **fax nsf** command to prevent the transfer of proprietary fax capabilities on Cisco IOS gateways.

If you use the **fax nsf** command, the voice gateway overwrites the NSF so that only standard fax transactions occur. Vendor-specific facilities that are beyond the standard Group 3 requirements are prevented from being used. Usually the NSF is set to all zeros (0) when this command is issued. This should fix problems caused by proprietary fax features.

You can also reset the NSF field when using a WS-X6608 or WS-X6624 gateway. The Gateway Configuration page in CallManager Administration provides two fields to modify NSF parameters: **Non Standard Facilities Country Code** and **Non Standard Facilities Vendor Code**. When these parameters are set to 65535, the NSF field is passed transparently without modification. To erase the NSF field completely, set these fields to zero.

Changing the Fax Protocol

The **fax protocol** command is used to specify which fax relay protocol (T.38 or Cisco fax relay) is used. This command is only available on Cisco IOS gateways. There are three options:

- The **cisco** option configures Cisco fax relay.

- The **t38** option disables Cisco fax relay and enables T.38.

- The **system** option allows the dial peer to inherit the fax relay protocol that is configured globally with the **voice service voip** command. If nothing is configured under the **voice service voip** command, the default is Cisco fax relay.

Currently, CallManager and all gateways under its direct control do not support T.38 fax relay, so you must ensure that the fax protocol is always configured for Cisco fax relay.

This presents a problem on certain voice platforms, such as the Cisco 5350 and 5400, which support only T.38. If you have one of these platforms, you must resort to using fax passthrough.

The default setting for the **fax protocol** command is the **system** option. Because the **system** option defaults to Cisco fax relay, VoIP dial peers always default to Cisco fax relay when nothing is explicitly configured globally.

Checking the fax interface-type Command

On some Cisco IOS Software platforms, including the Cisco 3660, 5300, 5350, 5400, and 5800, the gateway defaults to **fax interface-type modem**. The **fax interface-type modem** global configuration command forces fax calls to a modem (usually for T.37 Store and Forward fax), not a DSP. For Cisco fax relay to work, the fax call must be sent to a DSP, which means you must configure it by issuing the **fax interface-type vfc** command. This is an issue only when you're using fax relay. It does not apply to fax passthrough. You must reload the router for a change to the **fax interface-type** configuration to take effect.

Example 8-7 shows a Cisco IOS gateway using H.323 with the NSF set to all zeros and ECM disabled.

Example 8-7 *Dial Peer Configuration to Disable ECM and Set the NSF to 0*

```
dial-peer voice 3 voip
  destination-pattern 555....
  dtmf-relay h245-alphanumeric
  ip qos dscp cs5 media
  fax nsf 000000
  fax-relay ecm disable
```

Enabling Fax Relay Debugs

If you have exhausted all configurations, or if you have determined that fax passthrough works but fax relay does not, you can enable fax relay debugs on Cisco IOS Software gateways to find the source of the problem. Enable fax relay debugging with the command **debug fax relay t30 all**.

Example 8-8 shows output from **debug fax relay t30 all** from a failed fax call.

Example 8-8   **debug fax relay t30 all** *Output from a Failed Fax Call*

```
Dec 5 07:49:13.073: 1/2:62 1281347052 fr-entered (10ms)
Dec 5 07:49:17.985: 1/2:62 1281351950 fr-msg-det CRP
Dec 5 07:49:20.105: 1/2:62 1281354070 fr-msg-tx NSF
Dec 5 07:49:20.655: 1/2:62 1281354620 fr-msg-tx good crc, 19 bytes
Dec 5 07:49:20.720: 1/2:62 1281354680 fr-msg-tx DIS
Dec 5 07:49:22.350: 1/2:62 1281356310 fr-msg-det TSI
Dec 5 07:49:23.045: 1/2:62 1281357000 fr-msg-det DCS
Dec 5 07:49:27.346: 1/2:62 1281361290 fr-msg-tx FTT
Dec 5 07:49:28.836: 1/2:62 1281362780 fr-msg-det TSI
Dec 5 07:49:29.531: 1/2:62 1281363470 fr-msg-det DCS
Dec 5 07:49:29.740: 1/2:62 1281363680 fr-msg-det bad crc, 0 bytes
Dec 5 07:49:30.362: 1/2:62 1281364300 fr-msg-det bad crc, 0 bytes
Dec 5 07:49:30.804: 1/2:62 1281364740 fr-msg-det bad crc, 0 bytes
Dec 5 07:49:30.852: 1/2:62 1281364790 fr-msg-det bad crc, 0 bytes
Dec 5 07:49:33.868: 1/2:62 1281367800 fr-msg-tx FTT
Dec 5 07:49:35.414: 1/2:62 1281369340 fr-msg-det TSI
Dec 5 07:49:36.113: 1/2:62 1281370040 fr-msg-det DCS
Dec 5 07:49:36.515: 1/2:62 1281370440 fr-msg-det bad crc, 0 bytes
Dec 5 07:49:36.908: 1/2:62 1281370830 fr-msg-det bad crc, 0 bytes
Dec 5 07:49:37.559: 1/2:62 1281371480 fr-msg-det bad crc, 0 bytes
Dec 5 07:49:37.784: 1/2:62 1281371700 fr-msg-det bad crc, 0 bytes
Dec 5 07:49:37.900: 1/2:62 1281371820 fr-msg-det bad crc, 0 bytes
Dec 5 07:49:40.133: 1/2:62 1281374050 fr-msg-tx FTT
Dec 5 07:49:41.888: 1/2:62 1281375800 fr-msg-det TSI
Dec 5 07:49:42.583: 1/2:62 1281376490 fr-msg-det DCS
Dec 5 07:49:43.173: 1/2:62 1281377080 fr-msg-det bad crc, 0 bytes
Dec 5 07:49:44.937: 1/2:62 1281378840 fr-msg-det bad crc, 0 bytes
Dec 5 07:49:45.386: 1/2:62 1281379290 fr-msg-det bad crc, 0 bytes
Dec 5 07:49:46.941: 1/2:62 1281380840 fr-msg-tx FTT
Dec 5 07:49:48.503: 1/2:62 1281382400 fr-msg-det DCN
Dec 5 07:49:50.631: 1/2:62 1281384520 fr-end-dcn
```

The debug output in Example 8-8 shows the T.30 events that take place in the DSP during fax relay. The debugs indicate what is taking place from the perspective of the DSP interacting with the fax device. Therefore, any **fr-msg-tx** (transmit message) is transmitted from the DSP to the connected fax device. Any message that the DSP says it detects (a **fr-msg-det** message) is a message it received from the connected fax device. Figure 8-5 shows the direction of the messages when you view the output from **debug fax relay t30 all**.

Figure 8-5 *Messages to and from the DSP as Shown in* **debug fax relay t30 all**

In the failed fax transaction shown in Example 8-8, you can see several **bad crc** messages, followed by a Failure to Train (FTT) message from the far side. From the debugs, it looks like the problem involves the training signal. The **bad crc** errors and the FTT message returned from the other side indicate that the signal is corrupted or is incompatible with the Cisco fax relay protocol. This debug is taken from a fax relay problem that occurs with a V.34-capable fax machine that attempts to connect at V.34 rates. V.34 is a data modem standard used by computer modems to transmit information at up to 28.8 kbps. It is not supported in Cisco fax relay. Some fax manufacturers have devised proprietary methods to use modem technology to send faxes at higher data rates, but they are not standards-compliant and, therefore, cause the training errors shown in Example 8-8. This is one example of how fax machines performing out of specification can cause fax relay to fail.

Example 8-9 shows an example of a working fax relay debug taken from both ends of the call. Notice that the debugs are identical, except that the directions are opposite.

Example 8-9 *Fax Relay Debug from the Transmitting and Receiving Ends of the Call*

```
! Originating fax machine:
Oct 25 14:33:02.001: 6/0:1:8 3698358 fr-entered (10ms)
Oct 25 14:33:03.193: 6/0:1:8 3699550 fr-msg-tx NSF
Oct 25 14:33:03.433: 6/0:1:8 3699790 fr-msg-tx CSI
Oct 25 14:33:04.125: 6/0:1:8 3700480 fr-msg-tx DIS
Oct 25 14:33:05.905: 6/0:1:8 3702260 fr-msg-det TSI
Oct 25 14:33:06.701: 6/0:1:8 3703060 fr-msg-det DCS
Oct 25 14:33:11.201: 6/0:1:8 3707560 fr-msg-tx CFR
Oct 25 14:35:47.261: 6/0:1:8 3863620 fr-msg-det EOP
Oct 25 14:35:49.601: 6/0:1:8 3865960 fr-msg-tx MCF
Oct 25 14:35:51.157: 6/0:1:8 3867510 fr-msg-det DCN
Oct 25 14:35:53.304: 6/0:1:8 3869660 fr-end-dcn

! Terminating fax machine:
Oct 25 10:33:01.801: 6/0:1 (8) 3183322 fr-entered (10ms)
Oct 25 10:33:02.885: 6/0:1 (8) 3184410 fr-msg-det NSF
Oct 25 10:33:03.125: 6/0:1 (8) 3184650 fr-msg-det CSI
Oct 25 10:33:03.817: 6/0:1 (8) 3185340 fr-msg-det DIS
Oct 25 10:33:06.205: 6/0:1 (8) 3187730 fr-msg-tx TSI
Oct 25 10:33:07.009: 6/0:1 (8) 3188530 fr-msg-tx DCS
Oct 25 10:33:10.897: 6/0:1 (8) 3192420 fr-msg-det CFR
Oct 25 10:35:47.565: 6/0:1 (8) 3349090 fr-msg-tx EOP
Oct 25 10:35:49.293: 6/0:1 (8) 3350820 fr-msg-det MCF
Oct 25 10:35:51.469: 6/0:1 (8) 3352990 fr-msg-tx DCN
Oct 25 10:35:53.457: 6/0:1 (8) 3354980 fr-end cause unknown 0x1
```

Best Practices

Use fax relay when using a variety of gateways in your network or make sure both gateways are configured to use NSEs or NTEs when using fax passthrough.

Always use fax relay when transmitting faxes over the WAN unless you can afford to use the extra bandwidth required for fax passthrough and you have provisioned your WAN QoS policy to allow for the extra bandwidth requirements.

If you encounter compatibility problems between certain fax machines, fax passthrough is more tolerant of proprietary fax protocols and fax machines that vary from the T.30 specification. However, fax passthrough requires 80 kbps of bandwidth because you must use the G.711 codec. Also, some gateways such as the ATA 186 force you to use fax passthrough because they do not support fax relay.

Summary

Fax machine and modem problems can be some of the more difficult problems to diagnose due to the limited number of troubleshooting tools available. However, the majority of fax and modem problems are actually voice quality problems that might not be severe enough to be noticed in a normal voice conversation. Because fax machines and modems are less tolerant of errors, fax calls might fail and modem calls might drop often. Because voice quality is so important to the successful operation of fax machines and modems, be sure to review the information in Chapter 7.

## CHAPTER 9

Call Routing

Troubleshooting call routing problems can seem difficult at times. Because an IP telephony network can be such a complex system, much of the difficulty revolves around your level of understanding of the elements involved in routing a call. Sometimes you understand certain aspects of the dial plan well, and others you don't. The result is that you might not have the full story and therefore do not have the information necessary to determine what the problem might be.

Hopefully this chapter can clear things up. First, there is no better explanation of CallManager call routing than the one found in Chapter 2 of *Cisco CallManager Fundamentals* (ISBN 1-58705-008-0). Because the authors of this book are the architects of the system, it makes sense that their explanation would be comprehensive in nature. With this in mind, understand that although this chapter discusses call routing elements, its focus is troubleshooting and fixing call routing problems. In most cases, basic explanations of the call routing components are not given. For an exhaustive treatment of dial plans and call routing concepts, you should consult *Cisco CallManager Fundamentals*.

This chapter discusses the following topics:

- Closest-match routing
- Calling search spaces and partitions
- Understanding and troubleshooting transformations and masks
- Translation patterns
- Route filters
- Troubleshooting digit transformation
- Troubleshooting call routing

CallManager Wildcard Summary

A note about wildcards from the Cisco Press book *Cisco CallManager Fundamentals*:

Route patterns use *wildcards*, digit placeholders that permit you to quickly specify a range of matching digits. For example, instead of configuring every individual number from 7000 to 7999 in order to route a call across a gateway to another network, by configuring 7XXX, you can tell the gateway to receive all calls that begin with the digit 7 and are followed by three digits within the range 0 to 9.

Table 9-1 describes the basic wildcards you'll be seeing in the examples in this chapter.

Table 9-1   *Wildcard Summary (Courtesy Chapter 2 of* Cisco CallManager Fundamentals*)*

Wildcard	Description
0, 1, 2, 3, 4, 5, 6, 7, 8, 9, *, #	These look like digits, but they are actually simple wildcards. Each matches exactly one occurrence of the corresponding digit in a dialed digit string.
[xyz...]	This notation allows you to specify a set of matching digits—for example, [357] matches one occurrence of either the digit 3, 5, or 7.
[...x-y...]	Placing a hyphen between any two digits within square brackets causes one occurrence of any digits within the range to match, including the digits themselves. You can use range notation along with set notation—for example, [3-69] matches one occurrence of a digit 3, 4, 5, 6, or 9.
[^x-y]	If the first character after the open square bracket is a caret, the expression matches one occurrence of any digit (including * and #) *except* those specified—for example, [^1-8] matches one occurrence of a digit 9, 0, *, or #.
wildcard?	A question mark following any wildcard or bracket expression matches zero or more occurrences of any digit that matches the previous wildcard—for example, 9[12]? matches the empty string, 9, 91, 92, 912, 9122, 92121, and many others.
wildcard+	A plus sign following any wildcard or bracket expression matches one or more occurrences of any digit that matches the previous wildcard—for example, 3[1-4]+ matches 31, 3141, 3333, and many others.
X	The X wildcard is a convenience wildcard that matches one occurrence of any digit in the range 0 to 9. This wildcard is functionally equivalent to the range expression [0-9].
!	The ! wildcard is a convenience wildcard that matches one or more occurrences of any digit in the range 0 to 9. This wildcard is functionally equivalent to the range expression [0-9]+.

Table 9-1   *Wildcard Summary (Courtesy Chapter 2 of* Cisco CallManager Fundamentals*) (Continued)*

Wildcard	Description
@	The @ wildcard does not represent any particular set of matching characters. The @ wildcard causes CallManager to add the set of national route patterns for the numbering plan you specify in the Numbering Plan field on the Route Pattern or Translation Pattern Configuration pages in CallManager Administration. One way to think of the @ pattern is that it matches any number that you can dial from your North American home phone—for example, specifying the @ pattern along with the North American Numbering Plan (NANP) allows users to dial 911 and 555 1212 and 1 800 555 1212 and 011 33 12 34 56 78 90.
.	The . wildcard is unlike other wildcards in that it does not match digits at all. The . wildcard functions solely as a delimiter. When it appears in a route pattern, it divides the dial string into PreDot and PostDot sections. This has no effect on what digit strings the route pattern matches. Rather, you use the . wildcard in conjunction with digit discarding instructions.

Understanding Closest-match Routing

Before we talk about the different components involved in call routing, you must understand the concept of closest-match routing. This is also a good place to discuss digit analysis behavior, which can best be described as digit-by-digit analysis.

CallManager matches the dialed number with the most explicit match. For example, if someone dials extension 2001, several patterns might match the dialed digits. Consider the following matches:

- XXXX
- 2XXX
- 20XX
- 200X
- 2001
- 2!

All of these are matches, but only one is the most explicit. The most explicit match is selected based on the number of possible matches that could occur for a given pattern. For example, 200X can match up to 10 different patterns (2000 through 2009). 20XX can match up to 100 different patterns (2000 through 2099), and so on.

The 2! pattern is a bit more complex. Theoretically the ! wildcard matches an infinite number of digits; however, for the purposes of shortest match routing, the determination is made by examining the number of digit strings *of the same length as the provided digits* that could match the specified pattern. In the case of a user dialing 2001, 2! matches 1000 patterns of 4 digits in length (2000 through 2999).

Because 2001 only matches one pattern, it is the closet match.

The next example is a little more challenging. What is the closest match for the dialed digits 99725551212 given the following matches?

- 9.@
- 9.972XXXXXXX
- 9.@ where LOCAL-AREA-CODE==972
- 9.XXXXXXXXXX

You might be inclined to think the answer is 9.972XXXXXXX; however, the answer is actually 9.@ where LOCAL-AREA-CODE==972, although all four patterns are matches. You must look through each of the matches for the most specific match.

The first pattern, 9.@, is a macro that includes approximately 300 individual route patterns that encompass everything in the NANP. For closest-match routing purposes, it is important to understand that each individual pattern is matched within the NANP. In this case, the dialed pattern, 99725551212, matches the pattern 9.[2-9][02-9]X[2-9]XXXXXX.

The third pattern, 9.@ where LOCAL-AREA-CODE==972, also uses the @ symbol that encompasses any number in the NANP that has 972 as the local area code—not a long distance area code. The distinction between the two is that in the NANP, a long distance area code is preceded by a 1 or 0 while a local area code is not (in the case of 10-digit local dialing). (See the section "Understanding Route Filters" later in this chapter to understand exactly why this pattern is matched.) Remember CallManager matches specific route patterns that encompass the @ pattern, not the sum of the patterns. In this case, the particular pattern that is matched is 9.972[2-9][02-9]XXXXX.

If you look at the specific patterns for the route patterns that have an @, you end up with these patterns:

- 9.[2-9][02-9]X[2-9]XXXXXX
- 9.972XXXXXXX
- 9.972[2-9][02-9]XXXXX
- 9.XXXXXXXXXX

To determine which of these four is the closest match, you need to calculate how many possible matches there are for each route pattern.

- $9.[2-9][02-9]X[2-9]XXXXXX = 8 \times 9 \times 10 \times 9 \times 10^6 = 6,480,000,000$ possible matches
- $9.972XXXXXXX = 10^7 = 10,000,000$ possible matches
- $9.972[2-9][02-9]XXXXX = 8 \times 9 \times 10^5 = 7,200,000$ possible matches
- $9.XXXXXXXXXX = 10^{10} = 10,000,000,000$ possible matches

$9.972[2-9][02-9]XXXXX$ is the smallest with 7,200,000 possible matches. Remember this pattern was one of the patterns that makes up the @ pattern. Therefore, 9.@ where LOCAL-AREA-CODE==972 is the best match.

So why is CallManager's digit analysis behavior considered "digit-by-digit"? An example will help illustrate the concept. For this example, assume that the following patterns have been configured in CallManager Administration:

- 100X
- 110X
- 122X
- 123X
- 44XX
- 56XX

As soon as an IP phone goes off-hook, CallManager enters digit analysis mode. The first digit dialed in this example is 1. CallManager analyzes this digit and already can rule out two of the six configured patterns:

- 44XX
- 56XX

CallManager knows these patterns don't match the first dialed digit, which narrows down the scope of possible matches. The second digit dialed in this example is 2. This means that CallManager has received the digits, 12, so far. Now CallManager can rule out the following patterns:

- 100X
- 110X

This means that only two of the six configured patterns are left as possible matches:

- 122X
- 123X

In this example, the next dialed digit determines which pattern CallManager uses to route the call. If the user dials a 2, the pattern 122X is the only remaining pattern choice for CallManager. If the user dials a 3, the pattern 123X is the only remaining pattern choice for CallManager. For this example, the third dialed digit is 3. This means that CallManager has already determined which pattern is the match (123X). Whatever digit the user dials next results in the call being routed by CallManager. The remaining pattern is considered a *potential match* until the user actually dials the last digit.

If the user dialed any other number than 2 or 3, CallManager would have instructed the IP phone to play reorder tone because in that case there were no patterns configured in CallManager that would have matched. Likewise, if the user does not dial any other number before the interdigit timer expires, CallManager instructs the phone to play reorder tone. You'll learn more about interdigit timeout in the "Seven-Digit Dialing and Delayed Routing" section later in this chapter.

One other common source of confusion is the # character. In many cases the # character is used as an end-of-dialing character to signify that the user has finished entering the called party number. This is especially important in places where variable-length dial plans exist. The end-of-dialing character allows a user to avoid having to wait for the interdigit timeout.

For example, assume the following pattern is configured in CallManager:

9.!

This allows the user to enter the digit 9 followed by any number of digits. This means that any of the following are matches:

- 91
- 912
- 9123
- 91234567
- 9123456789012345

Remember from Table 9-1 that the ! pattern matches any digit between 0 and 9 but does not include * or #. If a user dials 912, CallManager waits for more digits because the ! pattern has more potential matches if the user dials more digits. So what happens if a user dials 9123#? The user expects the call to be immediately routed to the number 9123. However, because the # is not considered part of the ! pattern, the call fails. You must explicitly configure another pattern with 9!# if you want to allow users to be able to terminate the dial string with a # character.

In some versions of CallManager, you are able to terminate dialed strings with a # without having it explicitly configured. This, however, is a result of a change made to accommodate overlap sending, and this functionality is likely to be modified in the future. Just remember that in CallManager there is no special meaning associated with the # character, so if you want to use it as an end of dialing character, you must explicitly configure it as such.

Common Problems Associated with Closest-match Routing

Some common problems that occur because of the closest-match routing behavior in CallManager are

- Outside dial tone played at the wrong time
- Delayed routing when placing seven-digit local calls

The following sections examine these problems in greater detail.

Outside Dial Tone Played at the Wrong Time

When a user goes off-hook on an IP phone, CallManager tells their IP phone to play dial tone. This initial dial tone is referred to as *inside dial tone*. For OffNet calls, most administrators want to configure CallManager to provide outside dial tone (sometimes called secondary dial tone) after a one-digit access code is pressed. In some rare situations, some administrators want outside dial tone after two or more digits are entered, but in most cases a single digit is desired.

When you create a route pattern, you can choose to have outside dial tone played. This does not, however, guarantee that CallManager always plays outside dial tone after the first digit. If multiple patterns exist with the same first digit and at least one of the patterns is not configured to provide outside dial tone, outside dial tone is not played unless all the remaining potential matches are configured to provide it. Many administrators run into a problem when they configure the patterns 9.@ and 911. If both patterns exist, and 9.@ is configured to play outside dial tone, why would outside dial tone not occur until the second digit is pressed?

Think through this problem in a digit-by-digit pattern-match process. CallManager receives a 9 from an endpoint dialing a number. CallManager can rule out many patterns, but in this example, two potential matches exist:

- 9.@ with Provide Outside Dial Tone selected
- 911 without Provide Outside Dial Tone selected

NOTE   Be careful when using the emergency number pattern (such as 911 in NANP or the local emergency number in your country) for testing. You may occupy emergency phone lines that are needed for real emergencies. Most local emergency response offices allow you to schedule a time for testing your 911 access. Check with your local emergency response office for more detail.

CallManager does not command the IP phone to play outside dial tone because CallManager still has two potential matches and one of the two is not configured to provide outside dial tone. Therefore, CallManager must wait until it has received enough information to determine whether to play outside dial tone.

You can fix this problem in a couple of ways:

- Check the box on the 911 route pattern that tells it to play outside dial tone.
- Change the 911 pattern to 9.911 instead and check the box that tells it to play outside dial tone (although 9.911 is already included as part of 9.@).

In either case, CallManager tells the phone to play outside dial tone after a user dials a 9 because both potential matches have the same need for outside dial tone, even though the final pattern hasn't been determined.

NOTE   If you encounter a problem such as outside dial tone played at the wrong time, check to make sure you don't have a conflict with lines configured on phones, voice mail ports, MWI on/off numbers, Meet-Me conference numbers or call park patterns. For example, a phone with extension 9234 conflicts with the route pattern 9.@ and CallManager does not instruct the phone to play outside dial tone until 9234 is no longer a potential match because a phone directory number (DN) never has Provide Outside Dial Tone.

Any pattern that is similar to the digits dialed can cause outside dial tone to play at the wrong time because CallManager must wait for the next digit before determining which pattern to use. A good way to isolate the problem is to view the Route Plan Report in Cisco CallManager Administration (**Route Plan > Route Plan Report**).

Any time outside dial tone is not played at the expected time, it is almost certain that multiple potential matches exist. This knowledge should lead you to check all patterns of any kind that could be causing this conflict.

Delayed Routing When Placing Seven-digit Local Calls

Another problem commonly encountered is delayed routing. Delayed routing is when a user dials the number they want to call but CallManager does not route the call immediately. For example, a user goes off-hook and dials an access code and then a 7-digit local number. He waits 10 seconds before CallManager routes the call. This waiting period is called the *interdigit timeout*. In this case, CallManager must wait some amount of time before routing the call because there are other route patterns configured that could potentially be matched if the user enters more digits.

For the sake of this example, assume that someone has configured 9.@ as the only pattern in CallManager. As mentioned earlier, the @ pattern represents everything in the NANP. This, of course, includes local, long distance, and international numbers. Local numbers can be 7 or 10 digits long depending on the dial plan in your local area. If someone dials seven digits, how can CallManager know that three more aren't coming to make a 10-digit local call? In this example, CallManager cannot know more digits aren't coming, so it waits for the interdigit timeout to expire (which is 10 seconds by default). If no additional digits are dialed within the interdigit timeout, CallManager routes the call based on the digits it has received so far.

NOTE You can adjust interdigit timeout using the service parameter **TimerT302_msec**. However, in most cases this is not the best way to address the problem of delayed routing.

As mentioned previously, when configured to use the NANP, the @ wildcard is a shortcut for about 300 individual route patterns that match local, long distance, international, and other types of numbers in the NANP. The @ wildcard represents many items, including the patterns shown in Table 9-2, which lists only six of the nearly 300 patterns included as part of the @ wildcard.

Table 9-2   *Excerpt of @ Patterns when Using the NANP*

Route Pattern Type	Format	Description
7-digit local calls	([2-9][02-9]X)(XXXX)	OFFICE-CODE:SUBSCRIBER
	([2-9]X[02-9])(XXXX)	
10-digit local calls	([2-9]X[02-9]) ([2-9]XX)(XXXX)	LOCAL-AREA-CODE:OFFICE-CODE:SUBSCRIBER
	([2-9][02-9]X) ([2-9]XX)(XXXX)	
11-digit direct-dialed long distance calls	(1)([2-9][02-9]X) ([2-9]XX)(XXXX)	LONG-DISTANCE-DIRECT-DIAL:AREA-CODE:OFFICE-CODE:SUBSCRIBER
	(1)([2-9]X[02-9]) ([2-9]XX)(XXXX)	

For the sake of simplicity, look at these patterns:

```
[2-9]XXXXXX
[2-9]XXXXXXXXX
1[2-9]XXXXXXXXX
```

When a user goes off-hook and dials 1, the only pattern that matches is 1[2-9]XXXXXXXXX and the call completes if the remaining ten digits are dialed. There is no problem here.

However, if the user goes off-hook and dials a digit in the range of 2 to 9, there are now two possible matches for this example. One is [2-9]XXXXXX, and the other is [2-9]XXXXXXXXX. If six more digits are dialed, [2-9]XXXXXX is a match; however, [2-9]XXXXXXXXX is still considered a potential match because it could be a match if the user dials three more digits. If 10 seconds elapse without another digit being dialed, CallManager assumes that the match is for the [2-9]XXXXXX pattern because there are no other matches and routes it accordingly.

You can easily address this issue by being a little more specific with the patterns. For instance, if the two local area codes are 972 and 214, you can add two patterns and take one away. Instead of the three previously mentioned patterns, you would have four:

```
[2-9]XXXXXX
972[2-9]XXXXXX
214[2-9]XXXXXX
1[2-9]XXXXXXXXX
```

Now the problem with interdigit timeout is fixed, assuming there are no 7-digit numbers that begin with 972 or 214. Typically when a service provider has overlapping 7- and 10-digit dialing in a local area, they ensure the local area codes do not overlap with the 3-digit office code in the 7-digit number.

When a user goes off-hook and begins dialing, CallManager can distinguish quickly if the pattern will match a local 10-digit pattern, an 11-digit long distance pattern, or a 7-digit local pattern. Because the pattern is known to be only seven digits long (as soon as 1, 972, and 214 are ruled out), the call immediately routes to the Public Switched Telephone Network (PSTN).

Incidentally, this can also be accomplished with route filters. This is discussed in the section "Understanding Route Filters," but for reference, the route filter patterns are as follows:

9.@ where INTERNATIONAL-ACCESS DOES-NOT EXIST AND SERVICE DOES-NOT-EXIST AND LOCAL-AREA-CODE DOES-NOT-EXIST and AREA-CODE DOES-NOT-EXIST.
9.@ where LOCAL-AREA-CODE == 972 OR LOCAL-AREA-CODE == 214
9.@ where AREA-CODE EXISTS

Using Call Routing to Your Advantage

Remember that to take full advantage of the cost savings IP telephony provides across company sites on the LAN and WAN, you need to configure route patterns, route filters, route groups, route lists, dialing transformations, partitions, and calling search spaces that allow you to place calls between remote sites using the IP network, rather than the PSTN. A well-designed network uses the PSTN only when you have exceeded the network capacity or in the case of a network outage. Troubleshooting a complex dial plan that involves multiple sites designed to take advantage of these features all comes down to the fundamental basic components that allow you to create the dial plan. As long as you understand how each of the pieces work, you can troubleshoot any call routing problem.

See the "Cisco IP Telephony Network Design Guide" for more information on designing your network to take advantage of routing calls over the WAN whenever possible:

www.cisco.com/univercd/cc/td/doc/product/voice/ip_tele/network/index.htm

Understanding Calling Search Spaces and Partitions

Understanding calling search spaces and partitions is essential to successfully troubleshooting call routing problems. Calling search spaces and partitions are the foundation to build your call routing knowledge on. We can't overemphasize the importance of fully understanding the concepts of calling search spaces and partitions.

When you think about calling search spaces, you might find it useful to associate them with calling devices. As for partitions, you might think of them as dialed numbers. So when you are using or troubleshooting calling search space or partitions, you are really asking a simple question:

> What dialed numbers (inside a partition) can this calling device reach (with an assigned calling search space)?

To answer this question, you must understand how calling search spaces and partitions relate to each other. Route patterns and directory numbers (DNs) on IP phones are essentially the same. In either case, a pattern is associated with a device or list of devices or even MWI numbers, translation patterns, call park numbers, and so on. Normally, you group patterns that have similarities.

Some basic groupings for called destinations could be internal numbers, local numbers, long distance numbers, and international numbers. You might, therefore, create these four partitions in CallManager. For this example, call them P_Internal, P_Local_Calls, P_LD_Calls, and P_INTL_Calls. If you have a multiple site deployment using a centralized CallManager or a multiple tenant environment, you might create four such partitions for each site or tenant.

Remember that partitions are just logical groupings of route patterns (including phone DNs) and have nothing to do with where you can call *from* these devices.

So far all you have are categorical groupings of numbers that have similar characteristics. Next you would assign different patterns to those partitions:

- Configure the DN of every IP phone to be in the P_Internal partition.

- Configure all route patterns that allow for local calling to be in the P_Local_Calls partition.

- Configure all route patterns that allow for long distance calling to be in the P_LD_Calls partition.

- Configure all route patterns that allow for international calling to be in the P_INTL_Calls partition.

Table 9-3 shows examples of these partitions, with the corresponding patterns with which they are associated.

Table 9-3 *Four Basic Partitions with Associated Patterns*

Partition	Associated Patterns
P_Internal	2000
	2001
	2002
	2003
	2004
	2005
P_Local_Calls	9.411
	9.911
	9.[2-9][02-9]XXXXX
	9.[2-9]X[02-9]XXXX
P_LD_Calls	9.1[2-9]XXXXXXXXX
P_INTL_Calls	9.011!
	9.011!#
	The # on the end of this international pattern allows the user to dial her number and then press the # key so that she does not have to wait for the interdigit timeout.

You just logically grouped types of numbers into the types of destinations you want to reach by putting the route patterns into separate partitions. Now you need to decide which devices can call those destinations. If you have an IP phone in the lobby, you might want it to be able to call only internal phone numbers. To do that, you need a calling search space that defines the partitions that device can call. Call it CSS_Internal_Only.

You add the P_Internal partition to the CSS_Internal_Only calling search space. Figure 9-1 demonstrates how to do this in CallManager Administration.

Figure 9-1   *Adding P_Internal Partitions to the CSS_Internal_Only Calling Search Space*

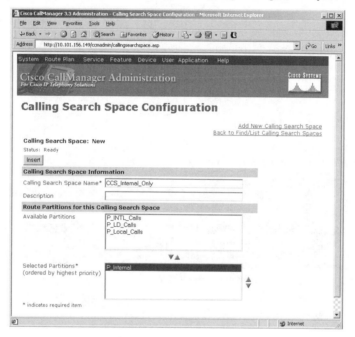

Devices in the CSS_Internal_Only calling search space can call any pattern in the P_Internal partition, which has the patterns 2000, 2001, 2002, 2003, 2004, and 2005. Figure 9-2 depicts this relationship.

Finally, the calling device is assigned a calling search space. This could be a gateway, an IP phone, a CTI port, or even a voice mail port.

Dial plans are usually not that simple, so a more complex example using the same calling search space/partitions is in order. A reasonable assumption is that a device might need to reach internal, local, long distance, and international numbers. To accomplish this, you need a new calling search space. This calling search space has access to all four sample partitions. Figure 9-3 shows this in CallManager Administration.

Figure 9-2 *P_Internal Partition Added to the CSS_Internal_Only Calling Search Space*

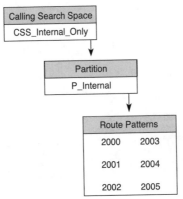

Figure 9-3 *CSS_All_Access Calling Search Space Configuration*

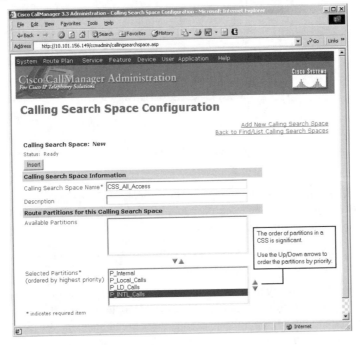

Figure 9-4 depicts this relationship, where a device configured with the calling search space CSS_All_Access can call patterns in the P_Internal, P_Local_Calls, P_LD_Calls, and P_INTL_Calls partitions. As such, any device with the calling search space set to CSS_All_Access can call the dialed patterns that reside in the partitions included in that calling search space.

The general logic behind this is that if a calling device cannot reach a particular dialed number, there is a break in the relationship between devices, calling search spaces, and partitions. This break could be due to a number of factors:

- The DN of the destination has been assigned the wrong partition

- The calling search space that is intended to provide access to the destination does not contain the destination's partition

- The caller has not been assigned the appropriate calling search space

Figure 9-4   *CSS_All_Access/Partitions Depiction*

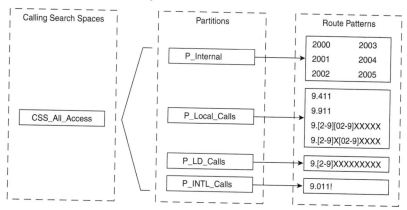

You may encounter some scenarios where the above three conditions are met and the call is still not arriving at the intended destination. The following are possible reasons why this could occur:

- The **Block This Pattern** checkbox may be checked on the route pattern. If a pattern with **Block This Pattern** is a closer match than all other patterns, the call is blocked.

- The partition associated with the target DN is correct, the calling search space contains the partition, and the caller is assigned the correct calling search space, but another partition within the calling search space contains an overlapping pattern that is a better match and that destination is selected as a result of the dialed digits.

- The partition associated with the target DN is correct, the calling search space contains the partition, and the caller is assigned the correct calling search space, but the *effective* calling search space of the caller contains an overlapping pattern that is a better match. Calls from an IP phone use a calling search space that is a combination of the device and the line calling search spaces.

Although it might appear that the routing selection is complex, it all comes down to one rule: CallManager searches through *all* partitions in the caller's effective calling search space, determines which pattern best matches the provided digits, and extends the call to the endpoint associated with that pattern. If there is more than one equal match, the calling search space order is used as a tie-breaker.

Here are the questions (from a calling search space/partition perspective) you need to ask to determine why a call isn't completing:

- Which partition is the dialed pattern in?
- What calling search space includes the partition that includes the dialed number you want to reach?
- Which calling search space is assigned to the calling device?

The "Call Routing Troubleshooting" section focuses on the methodology you should employ when fixing a routing problem. You will revisit these topics when you read that section.

Calling Search Space/Partition Rules

There are two rules to be aware of when using calling search spaces and partitions:

- The order of partitions listed in a calling search space can affect the way a call is routed. If two or more *equal* matches are found in all of the listed partitions, the match in the first partition from the top of the list is chosen to route the call.
- The line-level calling search space takes precedence over the device-level calling search space on a phone.

The following sections examine the conditions for these rules.

The First Partition Takes Precedence

If two or more equal patterns match in different partitions that are in the calling search space of a calling device, the first partition in the calling search space that contains the most explicit match is the one chosen. If two or more equal patterns exist in the *same* partition (for example, 200X and 20X0 both match exactly 10 patterns and are equal matches for the dialed number 2000) then the behavior is non-deterministic.

In other words, the order of partitions in a calling search space is significant *only* when multiple patterns are matched that have the same number of possible matches. For example, assume you have three partitions:

- PartitionA
- PartitionB
- PartitionC

You also have two calling search spaces defined as follows:

- CSS1 which contains
  - PartitionA
  - PartitionB
  - PartitionC

- CSS2 which contains
  - PartitionC
  - PartitionB
  - PartitionA

Finally, you have three route patterns configured as follows:

- RP1 = PartitionA/1XXX
- RP2 = PartitionB/1XXX
- RP3 = PartitionC/100X

If a phone with CSS1 dials 1000, which route pattern gets matched? Remember digit analysis performs closest-match routing *first* so RP3 is matched, even though PartitionA/1XXX appears first in the list of partitions for CSS1.

What if another IP phone configured with CSS2 dials 1010? In this case both RP1 and RP2 are equal matches, so the list of partitions in CSS2 is used as the tie-breaker. CSS2 has PartitionB before PartitionA, so RP2 is matched.

If the same call to 1010 is placed from an IP phone with CSS1, the call is routed to RP1 because PartitionA appears before PartitionB in CSS1.

The order of partitions being searched is clearly shown in a CCM trace when digit analysis is collecting digits and makes a match. Example 9-1 shows a call from extension 2000 to 1010. Note the line **pss="PartitionC:PartitionB:PartitionA"** indicates the order of partitions in the calling search space.

Example 9-1   *Digit Analysis Results for a Call from 2000 to 1010*

```
Digit analysis: match(fqcn="2000", cn="2000", pss="PartitionC:PartitionB:PartitionA",
    dd="1010")
Digit analysis: analysis results
|PretransformCallingPartyNumber=2000
|CallingPartyNumber=2000
|DialingPartition=PartitionB
|DialingPattern=1XXX
|DialingRoutePatternRegularExpression=(1XXX)
|DialingWhere=
|PatternType=Enterprise
|PotentialMatches=NoPotentialMatchesExist
|DialingSdlProcessId=(2,84,21)
|PretransformDigitString=1010
|PretransformTagsList=SUBSCRIBER
|PretransformPositionalMatchList=1010
|CollectedDigits=1010
|UnconsumedDigits=
|TagsList=SUBSCRIBER
|PositionalMatchList=1010
|VoiceMailbox=
|VoiceMailCallSearchSpace=
```

continues

Example 9-1 *Digit Analysis Results for a Call from 2000 to 1010 (Continued)*

```
| VoiceMailPilotNumber=
| DisplayName=
| RouteBlockFlag=RouteThisPattern
| InterceptPartition=
| InterceptPattern=
| InterceptWhere=
| InterceptSdlProcessId=(0,0,0)
| InterceptSsType=0
| InterceptSsKey=0
| WithTags=
| WithValues=
| CgpnPresentation=NotSelected
| CallManagerDeviceType=AccessDevice
```

The Line-level Calling Search Space Takes Precedence over the Device-level Calling Search Space

Calling search spaces can be assigned at the device level and at the line level on an IP phone device. The effective calling search space for a call placed from a line on an IP phone that has both a line calling search space and a device calling search space is a combination of both the line calling search space and the device calling search space. Remember that a calling search space is nothing more than a list of partitions. CallManager takes the two lists of partitions that make up the line calling search space and device calling search space and combines them to form a single effective calling search space. For example:

- CSS1 which contains
  - PartitionA
  - PartitionB
  - PartitionC
- CSS2 which contains
  - PartitionB
  - PartitionD

If an IP phone is configured with CSS1 on the line and CSS2 on the device, the effective calling search space becomes

- PartitionA (from CSS1)
- PartitionB (from CSS1)
- PartitionC (from CSS1)
- PartitionB (from CSS2)
- PartitionD (from CSS2)

Notice that PartitionB appears twice in the list. When calling search spaces are combined, any duplicates are removed and the first appearance of the partition is kept. For this example, the effective calling search space is actually

- PartitionA (from CSS1)
- PartitionB (from CSS1)
- PartitionC (from CSS1)
- PartitionD (from CSS2)

If CSS1 is configured on the device and CSS2 is configured on the line, the effective calling search space is

- PartitionB (from CSS2)
- PartitionD (from CSS2)
- PartitionA (from CSS1)
- PartitionC (from CSS1)

There is seldom a reason why you need to configure a calling search space at both the device level and the line level. Usually the only time this might be useful is when you have a shared line appearance that appears on two or more IP phones that are in different physical sites, which in turn necessitates different dial plan requirements depending on the location. Remember that a shared line can only have one calling search space no matter how many different phones it appears on, so the device level calling search space can be used to make any location-specific changes to the calling search space.

For example, the director of engineering in a business unit has two IP phones. One IP phone is in Dallas, and the other is in San Jose. While in San Jose, he makes all his calls as if he were in Dallas. He dials exactly the same in both instances. The calling search space assigned to the shared line is the same. The calling search space assigned to each device is different.

In this example, the calling search space assigned to the line is named CSS_Internal_Local_LD_Intl. As you might guess, this calling search space can call only internal, local, long distance, and international numbers. The San Jose (SJ) phone has a calling search space called SJ_911. This can call a 911 pattern that goes out a San Jose gateway. The Dallas phone has a calling search space called Dallas_911. This goes to a 911 pattern that goes out a Dallas gateway.

As you can see, both of these phones have the same dialing needs, with the exception of the emergency number. To properly dispatch emergency services when needed, the phone in Dallas must call out a Dallas gateway if 911 is dialed, notifying the local authorities. Likewise, the phone located in San Jose must call out a San Jose gateway if 911 is dialed. Apart from that exception, all other calls go to the same place (Dallas voice gateways in this example).

Note that it is extremely important to understand that the line calling search space takes priority over the device calling search space. If the line calling search space has a 911 route pattern, what will happen? The 911 pattern in the line calling search space takes priority over both of the device calling search space patterns, and the 911 call will be routed out a single gateway regardless of which phone with the shared line is in use. This would be a very bad situation to be in if the phone in San Jose is being used and the call is going to a 911 emergency center in Dallas. In this example, you must ensure that the line calling search space does not contain any patterns that have the 911 phone number in them so that the device calling search space can add the appropriate 911 pattern depending on the location.

TIP   Cisco Emergency Responder (ER) renders this example moot. With Cisco ER, the location of IP Phones is tracked dynamically. This application intercepts 911 calls and redirects them out the appropriate gateway automatically while presenting the correct calling party information. With the requirements of Enhanced 911, Cisco ER is the preferred means of dealing with 911 routing when multiple locations exist.

Event-specific Calling Search Spaces

Specific events can cause a calling search space to be used that is different than the calling search space configured on the calling party's phone. One example is a call forward busy calling search space on a DN. When a call is forwarded because of a busy line, the numbers that can be reached depend on the calling search space assigned to the call forward busy field on the busy line of the called party's phone.

Automatic alternate routing (AAR) is another example. AAR allows for PSTN fallback for remote locations using locations-based call admission control. Devices that use this feature have a calling search space for AAR. When an AAR event occurs, the AAR-specific calling search space is used.

The idea of event-specific calling search spaces will continue to expand in future CallManager releases. This capability provides a finer level of granularity for call routing because a specific calling search space is used depending on the type of event that is occurring. For example, future versions of CallManager might allow for a different calling search space when a call is being transferred.

The concept of calling search spaces remains the same. The only difference is that different events use different calling search spaces.

Call Forwarding Calling Search Spaces

When a call is extended to an IP phone, it can be forwarded to an alternate destination depending on how the line is configured. An IP phone's line configuration has three call forward fields:

- Call Forward No Answer (CFNA)
- Call Forward Busy (CFB)
- Call Forward All (CFA)

For CTI ports and CTI route points, an additional field is available: Call Forward on Failure (CFF).

In these call forward fields, you can set a DN to forward to and a calling search space that is used for each event. Each event can specify a different calling search space. This means that the numbers that can be reached depend on the calling search space and the type of forwarding used for the call.

NOTE   It is best to always assign a calling search space to every device and to put all DNs and patterns in route partitions. This way, you have explicitly specified which endpoint can reach these numbers. Patterns placed in the null partition can be reached by everyone and this can cause problems if there are conflicts with other patterns in valid partitions.

Call Forward No Answer (CFNA)

CFNA is used when a call is extended to the IP phone but the call goes unanswered. Typically the IP phone rings four times, and then the call is forwarded. Normally, CFNA is used to forward to a voice mail pilot number, but it can be any number assigned by the administrator. Only system administrators can configure CFNA.

The amount of time that passes before a call is considered not answered is specified by the CallManager service parameter **Forward No Answer Timeout**. The value for this parameter specifies the number of seconds before the forward no answer timer expires.

CallManager release 3.2 and later lets you create a voice mail profile and apply it to the DN. This essentially accomplishes the same result as configuring the voice mail pilot number and a calling search space that can reach the partition of the voice mail pilot number. However, the profile makes it easier for administrators by allowing you to just select the **Voice Mail** checkbox, and the forward destination and calling search space are selected based on the voice mail profile configuration.

Note that the voice mail profile that gets used is always that of the original called party. To better understand this, assume Phone A and Phone B are both configured to CFNA to voice mail; however, their voice mailboxes are on different voice mail systems, which means their voice mail profiles are different. Normally a call to Phone A forwards to voice mail system 1 if Phone A does not answer and Phone B forwards to voice mail system 2 if Phone B does not answer.

What if Phone A is set to forward all calls to Phone B? If someone calls Phone A, the call is immediately forwarded to Phone B and Phone B rings. If Phone B does not answer, the call forwards to voice mail because the **Voice Mail** checkbox is selected as the CFNA destination. CallManager always provides the original called party number to the voice mail system. In this case, that is Phone A because the caller originally dialed Phone A, which happened to be forwarded to Phone B. If the call were to forward following the voice mail profile of Phone B, the call would end up on voice mail system 2 which does not have a mailbox for Phone A. When using the **Voice Mail** checkbox and voice mail profiles, not only does the original called party number get used, but the destination DN and calling search space of the original called party's voice mail profile gets used as well. This means that the call is extended to voice mail system 1 with the original called party number of Phone A, so the call rolls to Phone A's voice mail even though the configuration of Phone B performed the forward operation to voice mail.

Call Forward Busy (CFB)

The CFB field works in the same way as CFNA. CFB has its own number for forwarding and its own calling search space. As such, it can be directed to a specific number based on the calling search space applied to the DN. In the event that a call is forwarded because the line is busy, the Call Forward Busy calling search space is used. You can also select the **Voice Mail** checkbox as the CFB destination. Only system administrators can configure CFB.

Call Forward All (CFA)

The CFA field also has its own calling search space and number for forwarding. There is a difference, however, because the end user as well the system administrator can configure a number to which all calls will be forwarded. Because the user has this ability, there is potential for fraudulent use and routing loops.

The calling search space for CFA behavior does not always work as you might expect. If you explicitly configure a calling search space, everything behaves as you expect where calls to the forwarded line use the calling search space configured for CFA to route the call immediately to the forward all destination.

However, if you leave the CFA field without an assigned calling search space (CFA calling search space configured as <none>), the CFA calling search space behaves differently than you might expect. If no calling search space is assigned to the CFA field, the rules are as follows:

- If the IP phone has a forward all designation configured from the IP phone itself or from the Cisco CallManager User Options web page, the calling search space of the device and the line on which the forwarding was configured is used as the CFA calling search space so that the IP phone can be forwarded in a location-sensitive manner. This means that on a shared line appearance, the CFA calling search space changes based on the device on which the CFA is performed, even though the CFA calling search space applies to a line.

- If the IP phone is forwarded in the Directory Number Configuration page in CallManager Administration, the configured CFA calling search space is applied. In other words, the CFA calling search space is effectively <none>, so calls can only be forwarded to DNs or route patterns in the null (<none>) partition.

Remember this behavior only applies when the CFA calling search space is configured to <none> in CallManager Administration. It is always best to explicitly apply a calling search space to the CFA field to restrict where users are allowed to forward their phones to.

NOTE   The behavior of the <none> calling search space on CFA is current as of CallManager release 3.3(2) but may change in the future to behave the same way all other calling search spaces behave where <none> always means the null partition. Consult the CallManager documentation and release notes if you are going to use the <none> calling search space for CFA. This is one more reason why you should always explicitly configure the CFA calling search space to prevent toll fraud.

One critical problem you want to avoid is routing loops. An important question to consider is: Can IP phone A forward to IP phone B, which could be configured to forward back to IP phone A?

Although this is a problem within one cluster, it is not a big deal because the maximum number of forwards is throttled through the use of a CallManager service parameter; by default, the **Forward Maximum Hop Count** parameter terminates the forwarding loop after 12 attempts. After the **Forward Maximum Hop Count** limit is reached, the calling party hears reorder tone. A forwarding loop is fairly easy to observe in a CCM trace because you see the same call go back and forth between two or more destinations repeatedly within a very short time span and then you see reorder tone played to the calling party. If the calling party is an IP phone, you see something like the following:

```
StationD:    000000753 StartTone tone=37(ReorderTone), direction=0.
```

Note that just because you see CallManager tell the phone to play reorder tone does not mean that there is a routing loop. Reorder tone is a symptom of many different problems. To find out whether this problem is a result of a routing loop, search backwards through the CCM trace looking for the TCP handle of the phone that received reorder (in our example, the TCP handle is 000000753) until you find where the call began. Then look at everything in the trace between the origination of the call to the point where the user receives reorder tone. If you see digit analysis continuously match the same numbers over and over again, you probably have a call routing loop.

For example, if you search back through the CCM trace that contained the StartTone message shown above for the TCP handle of this IP phone, the previous message in the trace shows the last digit the user dialed when placing the call:

```
StationInit: 000000753 KeypadButton kpButton=4.
Digit analysis: match(fqcn="9195555644", cn="15644", pss="PA:Line1:Cisco:Local:
    Long Distance:International", dd="15644")
```

The KeypadButton message in the trace has a timestamp of 00:18:00.854. The StartTone message telling the phone to play reorder tone has a timestamp of 00:18:00.917. This means that only 63 ms elapsed between these two messages; however, the trace file has 1355 lines of trace messages between these two timestamps. Even on a busy system, that is unusual. If you look through the file further, you see digit analysis repeatedly matching the same two numbers. For example, the following shows a call forwarded from extension 15644 to extension 15709. Notice that in between the two digit analysis blocks the calling search space changes to include just the Line1 partition because the CFA calling search space is configured to only allow calls to the Line1 partition:

```
09/02/2002 00:18:00.854 CCM || PretransformCallingPartyNumber=15644
|CallingPartyNumber=15644
|DialingPartition=Line1
|DialingPattern=15644
|DialingRoutePatternRegularExpression=(15644)
|DialingWhere=
|PatternType=Enterprise
|PotentialMatches=NoPotentialMatchesExist
|DialingSdlProcessId=(2,34,233)
|PretransformDigitString=15644
|PretransformTagsList=SUBSCRIBER
|PretransformPositionalMatchList=15644
|CollectedDigits=15644
|UnconsumedDigits=
|TagsList=SUBSCRIBER
|PositionalMatchList=15644
|VoiceMailbox=15644
|VoiceMailCallingSearchSpace=IPMA:PA:Line1
|VoiceMailPilotNumber=15678
|DisplayName=Paul Giralt
|RouteBlockFlag=RouteThisPattern
|InterceptPartition=Line1
|InterceptPattern=15644
|InterceptWhere=
|InterceptSdlProcessId=(2,25,1)
|InterceptSsType=33554436
|InterceptSsKey=452
```

```
|WithTags=
|WithValues=
|CgpnPresentation=NotSelected
|CallManagerDeviceType=UserDevice
Digit analysis: Changed  VoiceMailBox = 15644
Digit analysis: match(fqcn="9195555644", cn="15644", pss="Line1", dd="15709")
Digit analysis: analysis results
09/02/2002 00:18:00.854 CCM ||PretransformCallingPartyNumber=15644
|CallingPartyNumber=15644
|DialingPartition=Line1
|DialingPattern=15709
|DialingRoutePatternRegularExpression=(15709)
|DialingWhere=
|PatternType=Enterprise
|PotentialMatches=NoPotentialMatchesExist
|DialingSdlProcessId=(2,34,596)
|PretransformDigitString=15709
|PretransformTagsList=SUBSCRIBER
|PretransformPositionalMatchList=15709
|CollectedDigits=15709
|UnconsumedDigits=
|TagsList=SUBSCRIBER
|PositionalMatchList=15709
|VoiceMailbox=15709
|VoiceMailCallingSearchSpace=IPMA:PA:Line1
|VoiceMailPilotNumber=15678
|DisplayName=
|RouteBlockFlag=RouteThisPattern
|InterceptPartition=Line1
|InterceptPattern=15709
|InterceptWhere=
|InterceptSdlProcessId=(2,25,1)
|InterceptSsType=33554436
|InterceptSsKey=451
|WithTags=
|WithValues=
|CgpnPresentation=NotSelected
|CallManagerDeviceType=UserDevice
```

After a few lines of trace, you see the call forward again, this time from 15709 to 15644. Notice the timestamp has not changed.

```
09/02/2002 00:18:00.854 CCM || PretransformCallingPartyNumber=15644
|CallingPartyNumber=15644
|DialingPartition=Line1
|DialingPattern=15709
|DialingRoutePatternRegularExpression=(15709)
|DialingWhere=
|PatternType=Enterprise
|PotentialMatches=NoPotentialMatchesExist
|DialingSdlProcessId=(2,34,596)
|PretransformDigitString=15709
|PretransformTagsList=SUBSCRIBER
|PretransformPositionalMatchList=15709
|CollectedDigits=15709
|UnconsumedDigits=
|TagsList=SUBSCRIBER
|PositionalMatchList=15709
|VoiceMailbox=15709
|VoiceMailCallingSearchSpace=IPMA:PA:Line1
|VoiceMailPilotNumber=15678
|DisplayName=
|RouteBlockFlag=RouteThisPattern
|InterceptPartition=Line1
```

```
| InterceptPattern=15709
| InterceptWhere=
| InterceptSdlProcessId=(2,25,1)
| InterceptSsType=33554436
| InterceptSsKey=451
| WithTags=
| WithValues=
| CgpnPresentation=NotSelected
| CallManagerDeviceType=UserDevice
Digit analysis: Changed  VoiceMailBox = 15709
ForwardManager::wait_SsRegisterRejectionInterceptRes
Forwarding::awaitingCallResponse_SsRegisterRejectionInterceptRes
Digit analysis: match(fqcn="9195555644", cn="15644", pss="Line1", dd="15644")
Digit analysis: analysis results
09/02/2002 00:18:00.854 CCM||PretransformCallingPartyNumber=15644
| CallingPartyNumber=15644
| DialingPartition=Line1
| DialingPattern=15644
| DialingRoutePatternRegularExpression=(15644)
| DialingWhere=
| PatternType=Enterprise
| PotentialMatches=NoPotentialMatchesExist
| DialingSdlProcessId=(2,34,233)
| PretransformDigitString=15644
| PretransformTagsList=SUBSCRIBER
| PretransformPositionalMatchList=15644
| CollectedDigits=15644
| UnconsumedDigits=
| TagsList=SUBSCRIBER
| PositionalMatchList=15644
| VoiceMailbox=15644
| VoiceMailCallingSearchSpace=IPMA:PA:Line1
| VoiceMailPilotNumber=15678
| DisplayName=Paul Giralt
| RouteBlockFlag=RouteThisPattern
| InterceptPartition=Line1
| InterceptPattern=15644
| InterceptWhere=
| InterceptSdlProcessId=(2,25,1)
| InterceptSsType=33554436
| InterceptSsKey=452
| WithTags=
| WithValues=
| CgpnPresentation=NotSelected
| CallManagerDeviceType=UserDevice
```

The above sequence continues over and over again until the **Forward Maximum Hop Count** limit is reached. This is a clear indication that there is a routing loop.

If the calling party is not an IP phone, you do not see the StartTone Skinny message, but the digit analysis loop is still in the CCM trace. For example, if the call is coming in on a PRI, you see CallManager reject the call with a cause of 0xA9, which stands for temporary failure as shown in the following:

```
Out Message -- PriReleaseCompleteMsg -- Protocol= Pri250Protocol
Ie - Q931CauseIe IEData= 08 02 80 A9
MMan_Id= 0. (iep= 0 dsl= 101 sapi= 0 ces= 0 IpAddr=2c6a12ac IpPort=2427)
IsdnMsgData2= 08 01 9E 5A 08 02 80 A9
MGCPBhHandler - Sending BhHdr: 0004 0000 0010 0101 0001 0008
```

If you decode the CCM trace using Q.931 Translator you see

```
RELEASE_COMP, pd = 8, callref = 0x9E
Cause i = 0x80A9 - Temporary failure
```

Once again you must remember that this is just a symptom of a call routing loop, but this can be a symptom of other call routing related problems, so you must look at the rest of the trace to determine why the call is being disconnected.

When dealing with multiple clusters connected via intercluster trunks or routing loops between CallManager and the PSTN or another PBX, the situation is more complex. What if a user forwards their IP phone out the PSTN to their cell phone, which is in turn forwarded back to their IP phone? In this case CallManager sees each call leg as a separate call.

In these scenarios, the **MaxForwardsToDn** service parameter is used to stop routing loops. This forward feature counts how many pending forwards are targeted on a particular DN and rejects the call with a "User Busy" reason after the threshold is exceeded. Note that because the "User Busy" reason is returned, you must also ensure that the CallManager service parameter **StopRoutingOnUserBusyFlag** is set to True. If this parameter is set to False, CallManager attempts to reroute through any remaining gateways in a route list, which could cause further loops.

When **MaxForwardsToDn** stops a call forwarding loop, you see the following message in the CCM trace:

```
ForwardManager - wait_SsInterceptInd - Clearing call, too many forwards
    for Dn= 15709, InterceptKey= 0x1C3, Party= 0x2000B89, count= 12
```

TIP   How to read a CCM trace and use the Q.931 Translator are discussed in Chapter 3, "Understanding the Troubleshooting Tools."

Plan carefully when you decide where you want an IP phone to be able to CFA to. For calls within a cluster, use the **Forward Maximum Hop Count** service parameter (**Service > Service Parameters** > *select a server* > **Cisco CallManager**) to end a forwarding chain after a specified number of hops and use **MaxForwardsToDn** and **StopRoutingOnUserBusyFlag** to prevent routing loops that traverse other clusters or legacy TDM equipment.

Call Forward on Failure (CTI Ports and CTI Route Points Only)

When a CTI route point or CTI port is not registered with CallManager, the call is forwarded to the CFNA destination configured for that device. Many administrators are under the impression that the forward on failure destination is used in this case, but it is not. The forward on failure configuration is only used when a call is extended to a CTI route point or CTI port and the application does not respond or there is a failure with a request made by the application. This is useful for redirecting the call to a redundant system or attendant. Only system administrators can configure forward on failure.

For example, if you have redundant IP IVR servers, you should configure the CFNA destination on the route point for the first server to the route point for the second server. You may also want to put the CFF destination as the second server as well, in case some failure occurs on the first server while processing the call. Alternatively, you might want to send calls in the event of a failure to an operator or group of operators because a user who was in the IP IVR probably entered some data into the IVR and might get frustrated or confused when they are redirected back to the beginning of the menu on the redundant system. Forwarding the caller to a live person might help alleviate the confusion.

Understanding and Troubleshooting Transformations and Masks

Dialing transformations allow you to manipulate the called party numbers for routing and the calling party number for presentation purposes. Some transformations such as transform masks can apply to the calling and called number. Other transformations such as digit discard instructions (DDI) only apply to the called number.

NOTE   The acronym DDI in this chapter refers to "digit discard instruction" and not "direct dial in" which is commonly used to refer to direct inward dial (DID) numbers in some countries.

In this section, you learn how transformations work and how to troubleshoot them when a problem is encountered.

Dialing transformations generically apply to a variety of CallManager settings that allow you to change the called number for call routing purposes and the calling number for number presentation purposes.

Digit Discard Instructions (DDIs)

A DDI is really just a form of called number transformation. While there are many different DDIs to choose from, all DDIs apply only to a called number. Also, with one exception, a DDI works only when used with the @ wildcard (the exception is the PreDot DDI). Table 9-4 breaks down each DDI and provides examples of how a dialed number is transformed when you apply a DDI.

NOTE	It should be re-emphasized that DDI only works with the @ wildcard. Many people try to use a DDI with a route pattern that does not have the @ wildcard and are puzzled as to why it doesn't work. The only exception to this rule is the PreDot DDI that discards all digits before a dot in a route pattern. The PreDot DDI works with any route pattern that has a dot.

Table 9-4   *Digit Discard Instructions for the NANP*

DDI	Effect	Example
10-10-Dialing	This DDI removes the Interexchange Carrier (IXC) access code, such as 1010288.	Route pattern: 9.@ Dialed digit string: 910102889725555000 After applying DDI: 99725555000
10-10-Dialing Trailing-#	This DDI removes • IXC access code • End-of-dialing character for international calls	Route pattern: 9.@ Dialed digit string: 91010288011815555555# After applying DDI: 901181555555
11/10D->7D	This DDI removes • Long distance direct-dialing code • Long distance operator-assisted dialing code • IXC access code • Area code • Local area code This DDI creates a 7-digit local number from an 11- or 10-digit dialed number.	Route pattern: 9.@ Dialed digit string: 919725555000 or 99725555000 After applying DDI: 95555000
11/10D->7D Trailing-#	This DDI removes • Long distance direct-dialing code • Long distance operator-assisted dialing code • IXC access code • Area code • Local area code • End-of-dialing character for international calls This DDI creates a 7-digit local number from an 11- or 10-digit dialed number.	Route pattern: 9.@ Dialed digit string: 919725555000# or 99725555000# After applying DDI: 95555000

continues

Table 9-4 *Digit Discard Instructions for the NANP (Continued)*

DDI	Effect	Example
11D->10D	This DDI removes • Long distance direct-dialing code • Long distance operator-assisted dialing code • IXC access code	Route pattern: 9.@ Dialed digit string: 919725555000 After applying DDI: 99725555000
11D->10D Trailing-#	This DDI removes • Long distance direct-dialing code • Long distance operator-assisted dialing code • End-of-dialing character for international calls • IXC access code	Route pattern: 9.@ Dialed digit string: 919725555000# After applying DDI: 99725555000
Intl TollBypass	This DDI removes • International access code • International direct-dialing code • Country code • IXC access code • International operator-assisted dialing code	Route pattern: 9.@ Dialed digit string: 901181555555 After applying DDI: 9555555
Intl TollBypass Trailing-#	This DDI removes: • International access code • International direct-dialing code • Country code • IXC access code • International operator-assisted dialing code • End-of-dialing character	Route pattern: 9.@ Dialed digit string: 901181555555# After applying DDI: 9555555
NoDigits	This DDI removes no digits.	Route pattern: 9.@ Dialed digit string: 919725555000 After applying DDI: 919725555000

Table 9-4 *Digit Discard Instructions for the NANP (Continued)*

DDI	Effect	Example
PreAt	This DDI removes all digits prior to the NANP portion of the route pattern, including • CallManager external access code • Private branch exchange (PBX) external access code	Route pattern: 8.9@ Dialed digit string: 899725555000 After applying DDI: 9725555000
PreAt Trailing-#	This DDI removes all digits prior to the NANP portion of the route pattern, including • CallManager external access code • PBX external access code In addition, this DDI also removes the following: • End-of-dialing character for international calls	Route pattern: 8.9@ Dialed digit string: 8901181555555# After applying DDI: 01181555555
PreAt 10-10-Dialing	This DDI removes all digits prior to the NANP portion of the route pattern, including • CallManager external access code • PBX external access code In addition, this DDI also removes the following: • IXC access code	Route pattern: 8.9@ Dialed digit string: 89101028897255555000 After applying DDI: 9725555000
PreAt 10-10-Dialing Trailing-#	This DDI removes all digits prior to the NANP portion of the route pattern, including • CallManager external access code • PBX external access code In addition, this DDI also removes the following: • IXC access code • End-of-dialing character for international calls	Route pattern: 8.9@ Dialed digit string: 8910102880181555555# After applying DDI: 01181555555

continues

Table 9-4   *Digit Discard Instructions for the NANP (Continued)*

DDI	Effect	Example
PreAt 11/10D->7D	This DDI removes all digits prior to the NANP portion of the route pattern, including • CallManager external access code • PBX external access code In addition, this DDI also removes the following to create a 7-digit local number from an 11- or 10-digit dialed number: • Long distance direct-dialing code • Long distance operator-assisted dialing code • IXC access code • Area code • Local area code	Route pattern: 8.9@ Dialed digit string: 8919725555000 or 899725555000 After applying DDI: 5555000
PreAt 11/10D->7D Trailing-#	This DDI removes all digits prior to the NANP portion of the route pattern, including • CallManager external access code • PBX external access code In addition, this DDI also removes the following to create a 7-digit local number from an 11- or 10-digit dialed number: • Long distance direct-dialing code • Long distance operator-assisted dialing code • IXC access code • Area code • Local area code • End-of-dialing character for international calls	Route pattern: 8.9@ Dialed digit string: 8919725555000# or 899725555000# After applying DDI: 5555000

Table 9-4   *Digit Discard Instructions for the NANP (Continued)*

DDI	Effect	Example
PreAt 11D->10D	This DDI removes all digits prior to the NANP portion of the route pattern, including • CallManager external access code • PBX external access code In addition, this DDI also removes the following to create a 10-digit number from an 11-digit dialed number: • Long distance direct-dialing code • Long distance operator-assisted dialing code • IXC access code	Route pattern: 8.9@ Dialed digit string: 8919725555000 After applying DDI: 9725555000
PreAt 11D->10D Trailing-#	This DDI removes all digits prior to the NANP portion of the route pattern, including • CallManager external access code • PBX external access code In addition, this DDI also removes the following to create a 10-digit number from an 11-digit dialed number: • Long distance direct-dialing code • Long distance operator-assisted dialing code • IXC access code • End-of-dialing character for international calls	Route pattern: 8.9@ Dialed digit string: 8919725555000# After applying DDI: 9725555000

continues

Table 9-4 *Digit Discard Instructions for the NANP (Continued)*

DDI	Effect	Example
PreAt Intl TollBypass	This DDI removes all digits prior to the NANP portion of the route pattern, including • CallManager external access code • PBX external access code In addition, this DDI also removes the following: • International access code • International direct-dialing code • Country code • IXC access code • International operator-assisted dialing code	Route pattern: 8.9@ Dialed digit string: 8901181555555 After applying DDI: 555555
PreAt Intl TollBypass Trailing-#	This DDI removes all digits prior to the NANP portion of the route pattern, including • CallManager external access code • PBX external access code In addition, this DDI also removes the following: • International access code • International direct-dialing code • Country code • IXC access code • International operator-assisted dialing code • End-of-dialing character	Route pattern: 8.9@ Dialed digit string: 8901181555555# After applying DDI: 555555
PreDot	This DDI removes the CallManager external access code. Anything before the dot (.) is stripped. This DDI is an exception to the rule and can be used with patterns that do not have an @ wildcard.	Route pattern: 8.9@ Dialed digit string: 899725555000 After applying DDI: 99725555000

Table 9-4   *Digit Discard Instructions for the NANP (Continued)*

DDI	Effect	Example
PreDot Trailing-#	This DDI removes • CallManager external access code • End-of-dialing character for international calls	Route pattern: 8.9@ Dialed digit string: 8901181555555# After applying DDI: 901181555555
PreDot 10-10-Dialing	This DDI removes • CallManager external access code • IXC access code	Route pattern: 8.9@ Dialed digit string: 8910102889725555000 After applying DDI: 99725555000
PreDot 10-10-Dialing Trailing-#	This DDI removes • CallManager external access code • IXC access code • End-of-dialing character for international calls	Route pattern: 8.9@ Dialed digit string: 89101028801181555555# After applying DDI: 901181555555
PreDot 11/10D->7D	This DDI removes • CallManager external access code • Long distance direct-dialing code • Long distance operator-assisted dialing code • IXC access code • Area code • Local area code This DDI creates a 7-digit local number from an 11- or 10-digit dialed number.	Route pattern: 8.9@ Dialed digit string: 8919725555000 or 899725555000 After applying DDI: 95555000
PreDot 11/10D->7D Trailing-#	This DDI removes • CallManager external access code • Long distance direct-dialing code • Long distance operator-assisted dialing code • IXC access code • Area code • Local area code • End-of-dialing character for international calls This DDI creates a 7-digit local number from an 11- or 10-digit dialed number.	Route pattern: 8.9@ Dialed digit string: 8919725555000# or 899728135000# After applying DDI: 95555000

continues

Table 9-4 *Digit Discard Instructions for the NANP (Continued)*

DDI	Effect	Example
PreDot 11D->10D	This DDI removes • CallManager external access code • Long distance direct-dialing code • Long distance operator-assisted dialing code • IXC access code	Route pattern: 8.9@ Dialed digit string: 8919725555000 After applying DDI: 99725555000
PreDot 11D->10D Trailing-#	This DDI removes • CallManager external access code • Long distance direct-dialing code • Long distance operator-assisted dialing code • IXC access code • End-of-dialing character for international calls	Route pattern: 8.9@ Dialed digit string: 8919725555000# After applying DDI: 99725555000
PreDot IntlAccess IntlDirectDial	This DDI is typically used when connecting to an AT&T 4ESS Primary Rate Interface (PRI) ISDN connection. This DDI removes • CallManager external access code • International access code • International direct-dialing code • IXC access code • International operator-assisted dialing code • End-of-dialing character for international calls	Route pattern: 9.@ Dialed digit string: 9011442055551122# After applying DDI: 442055551122
PreDot Intl TollBypass	This DDI removes • CallManager external access code • International access code • International direct-dialing code • Country code • IXC access code • International operator-assisted dialing code	Route pattern: 8.9@ Dialed digit string: 8901181555555 After applying DDI: 9555555

Table 9-4   *Digit Discard Instructions for the NANP (Continued)*

DDI	Effect	Example
PreDot Intl TollBypass Trailing-#	This DDI removes • CallManager external access code • International access code • International direct-dialing code • Country code • IXC access code • International operator-assisted dialing code • End-of-dialing character	Route pattern: 8.9@ Dialed digit string: 8901181555555# After applying DDI: 9555555
Trailing-#	This DDI removes the end-of-dialing character for international calls. Remember, this DDI *only* applies to a pattern with the @ wildcard.	Route pattern: 9.@ Dialed digit string: 901181555555# After applying DDI: 901181555555

Understanding the Concept of Masks

A *mask* provides specific number presentation and digit manipulation. Use a mask to format a calling or called party number in a specific way.

To understand how a mask works, think of it as a math problem. The X allows the original number to fall through to the final transformed number. Masks can be used in conjunction with dialing transformations to transform the calling party number from a four or five digit extension to a 10-digit phone number in North America, allowing users on the PSTN to receive the proper caller ID information. For example, if your extension is 2000, you can set a mask for outbound calls. The mask could be 972555XXXX. For instance,

Original extension	2000
Mask	972555XXXX
Final result	9725552000

Or perhaps you want to apply a mask that completely changes the original number. This is useful when you want to hide the original number and display a general office number instead. That might look like the following:

Original extension	2000
Mask	9725551234
Final result	9725551234

Perhaps you might want some part of the original number to come through while keeping the rest of the original number the same. For example, if your internal extension range is

2000 through 2999, but the public phone number for these extensions is really (972) 555-1000 through (972) 555-1999, you could do the following:

Original extension	2000
Mask	9725551XXX
Final result	9725551000

What if you want a long number to be transformed to only the last four digits? The mask is applied from right to left, so you use only four Xs, allowing only the first four digits counting from the right to be applied. This is useful if the PSTN is providing the called party number as a 10-digit number but your internal extensions are only five digits. Notice the last five digits of 51234 are transformed to extension 21234:

Original extension	2145551234
Mask	2XXXX
Final result	21234

Finally, you could also prefix a digit to the original number:

Original extension	2145551234
Mask	1XXXXXXXXX
Final result	12145551234

This transformation activity works the same for calling and called party transformations.

Transformation Rules

Now that you have an understanding of the various components of calling and called party transformations, it is time to understand how these different components work together.

Order of Applied Transformations

Order is important when applying transformations. Calling and called party transformations are applied in this specific order:

Step 1   The External Phone Number Mask on the original calling device (when specified on a route pattern or translation pattern by the **Use Calling Party's External Phone Number Mask** checkbox.)

Step 2   A translation pattern

Step 3   A route pattern

Step 4   A route list using route group details

Step 5   Transformation on the terminating device

The steps in the list are performed by CallManager every time a call is routed. This list does not mean that every transformation step is always taken. For example, the External Phone Number Mask transformation only occurs if the route pattern or translation pattern has the **Use Calling Party's External Phone Number Mask** box checked. Also, Step 2 does not have an effect if the routed number is not matched to a translation pattern. The dialed number might immediately match a route pattern so it would not be processed through a translation pattern.

Steps 1, 2, 3 and 5 are are cumulative transformations. This means that the information from the previous step is used as the input into the next step. However, Step 4 can override any transformation done in Step 3.

Cumulative Transformations

The transformations described in this section (the same as Steps 1, 2, 3 and 5 in the list of transformations from the preceding section) represent the four areas of transformation that are cumulative:

- The original calling device (when specified on a route pattern or translation pattern by the **Use Calling Party's External Phone Number Mask** checkbox.)
- A translation pattern
- A route pattern
- Transformation on the terminating device

In other words, transformations done to any of these four areas are added together.

Cumulative Transformation on Calling Party Number Example

First, let's look at how a cumulative transformation can affect the calling party number. Changing the calling party number changes how the calling party number is presented to the called party.

For example, the original calling device has an extension of 2200. Assume the External Phone Number Mask for the line is configured as 1XXXX. If the **Use Calling Party's External Phone Number Mask** box is checked on a translation pattern, the External Phone Number Mask is applied to the extension number resulting in a new calling number of 12200 as shown in the following:

```
External Phone Number Mask transformation:
Original extension                    2200
External Phone Number Mask            1XXXX
_____
Result                                12200
```

The translation pattern itself can also have a calling party transformation mask. Assume the translation pattern has a calling party transformation mask of 5XXXX. The translation pattern can also have digit prefix instructions. Assume the translation pattern is configured to prefix the digits 55. The results are shown in the following:

Translation pattern transformations:	
Result from previous step	12200
Calling Party Transform Mask	5XXXX
Prefix digits 55	
Result	5552200

After going through the translation pattern, this call is directed toward a route pattern and the calling party transformation mask associated with that route pattern applies the mask 972XXXXXXX to the calling party number, resulting in a new calling number of 97255512200. The route pattern can also prefix digits to the calling party number. In this case assume no digits are prefixed. The results are shown in the following:

Route pattern transformations:	
Result from previous step	5552200
Calling Party Transform Mask	972XXXXXXX
Result	9725552200

Finally, the call is extended to a gateway where the gateway configuration parameter **Caller ID DN** can apply one last transformation to the calling party number before the call is routed out the gateway. In this case, assume the **Caller ID DN** field is left blank. After going through all these transformations, 9725552200 is the number that is presented as the calling party number to the called party.

Cumulative Transformation on Called Party Number Example

Now, let's look at how a cumulative transformation can affect the called party number. Changing the called party number changes how the number is routed.

For example, the dialed number is 5000. This matches a translation pattern of 5XXX. On this translation pattern, 9214555 is prepended to the 5000 making the new number 92145555000.

Translation pattern transformations:	
Dialed digits	5000
Called Party Transform Mask	9214555XXXX
Result	92145555000

This called party number is returned to digit analysis to be routed. This matches a route pattern of 9.@ that has a DDI to discard PreDot.

Route pattern transformations:

Dialed digits	92145555000
DDI of PreDot	
Result	2145555000

You can see how each transformation results in a new match that changes how the call is routed. It is important to note that calling and called party transformations can be occurring to the same call each step of the way. As a called number is changed, thus affecting the routing of the call, the calling party number can be changed, thus affecting the presentation of the calling party number.

All the examples so far have not involved transformations on the route group details of a route list. This is because transformations on the route group details of a route list overwrite transformations performed on a route pattern.

Overwritten Transformations

The route group details configuration on a route list overrides any calling or called party number transformations made on a route pattern. Note that although it overrides the transformations on the route pattern, any previous transformations (for example, if the call went through a translation pattern) are preserved. The best example of this is a DDI transformation. If the route pattern has a DDI of PreDot, and the route list has a DDI of NoDigits, the route list discards no digits because the route lists overrides the route pattern. By default, the DDI instruction is set to <None>. This simply means that nothing is done to the dialed number, so the transformations applied on the route pattern still apply. This is different from the DDI instruction of NoDigits, which literally discards no digits and ignores the transformations on the route pattern.

If we continue the last example where the user dialed 5000 and the final called party number was 2145555000 after going through a translation pattern and a route pattern, now assume the route pattern points to a route list. In that route list the route group details for a particular route group is configured to discard NoDigits. In this case, CallManager ignores the transformation on the route pattern (which had removed the 9 from the beginning of the dialed digit string) and removes no digits, so the final called party number ends up being 92145555000.

It is important to understand all the various places where a transformation can occur because CallManager is not very good at showing you the transformations as they occur in a CCM trace. In the trace, you suddenly see a number change but no indication is given as to what transformation caused this change to occur. If you see a calling or called party number change between two stages in a trace and don't understand why, check the various call routing configuration pages in CallManager Administration for any transformations that might be applied to the relevant patterns involved in the call. One final location where such transformations can occur is through various CallManager service parameters, as discussed in the next section.

Service Parameter-related Transformations

It is important to note that several service parameter-related dialing transformations exist. A common error made by administrators is looking at route patterns and translation patterns for transformations while ignoring service parameter-related settings. Table 9-5 describes CallManager service parameters that affect transformation for all gateways associated with this specific CallManager.

Table 9-5   *Service Parameter Transformations*

Service Parameter	Description
CallerID	Specifies a mask used to format the caller ID number for outbound calls. For example, if you set **CallerID** to 555XXXX and the DN of the calling party is 1234, CallManager sends the string 5551234 as the caller ID field for outbound calls from that DN.
CgpnScreeningIndicator	Specifies the value of the calling party number screening indicator that CallManager sends with outbound calls to the ISDN. Do not change this value unless the ISDN has rejected outbound calls because of an unacceptable screening indicator value. Allowed values for this field are as follows: • **0**—Calling number not screened • **1**—Calling number screened and passed • **2**—Calling number screened and failed • **3**—CallManager provides the calling number • **4**—CallManager sets the screening indicator value (this is the default setting) Regardless of this value, CallManager does not screen the calling number. If you change this setting, you change only the screening indicator value that CallManager sends to the ISDN switch.
MatchingCgpnWithAttendantFlag	Specifies whether CallManager uses the same analog trunk for both inbound and outbound calls for a particular DN. Valid values are True and False. This feature emulates a small PBX or key system. To use the same trunk for both inbound and outbound calls, set this flag to True, specify the target DN in the Attendant DN field of the gateway port that connects to the desired trunk, and create the appropriate route pattern and route list to route calls to the gateway. If you set this flag to False, CallManager may route outbound calls over a different trunk than inbound calls.

Table 9-5   *Service Parameter Transformations (Continued)*

Service Parameter	Description
OverlapReceivingForPriFlag	Indicates whether all Primary Rate Interface (PRI) trunks that use the PRI Backhaul mechanism should support Overlap Receiving procedures. Valid values are True (enable) and False. Overlap receiving allows the PSTN to send a setup message with only part of the called party number. CallManager responds with a setup ack message instead of a call proceeding message and waits for additional digits delivered in an information message. If this flag is set to False, CallManager rejects any inbound call that does not match a pattern.
	This parameter is typically set to True for non-North American markets to enable Overlap Receiving.
StripPoundCalledPartyFlag	Enables the stripping of # digits from the called party information element of the inbound and outbound Q.931 and H.225 SETUP message.
UnknownCallerId	Designates the DN to be displayed when the calling party number is unknown. The value can be any numeric value representing a general number for your system (if you want to provide caller ID functionality to called parties). A valid value is any valid telephone number.
UnknownCallerIdFlag	Relates to the **UnknownCallerIdText** service parameter. This is set to True by default. Cisco recommends that you keep this parameter set to True because it makes sure that the **UnknownCallerIdText** displays if no calling party caller ID information is available.
UnknownCallerIdText	Specifies a text string to be displayed to called parties who have caller ID capability. This text string appears on the IP Phone for an incoming call that does not have caller ID information. For example, "Unknown Caller."
	The first line is 20 characters long, and the second line is 14 characters long. Use a character setup that can be broken into two lines, each of which has the specified number of characters per line.
DialPlanPath	Specifies the location of the dial plan files used for digit analysis. The default path is C:\Program Files\Cisco\DialPlan. There is a file called NANP in this directory that describes the North American Numbering Plan.

Understanding and Troubleshooting Translation Patterns

A *translation pattern* allows you to take an originally dialed number and change all or part of the calling and called number into another number. A translation pattern transforms the calling and called party numbers through the use of calling and called party transformations that are configured as part of the translation pattern.

There is the added benefit of allowing the calling party to dial the translation pattern without being able to directly dial the translated number (if calling search spaces and partitions are set up correctly). The following steps help clarify:

Step 1   A number is dialed.

Step 2   The call routing engine in CallManager determines that a translation pattern is the closest match.

Step 3   The calling/called number is transformed, and potentially a new calling search space is applied.

Step 4   The call is sent to the call routing engine again to find the closest match based on the output of the translation pattern. This could mean that a different calling search space is used to find the closest match or the called party number has been transformed. Note that this basically takes you back Step 1. The closest match might be another translation pattern which is perfectly acceptable.

One important thing to note is that translation patterns are always treated as an *urgent priority* route pattern. An urgent priority route pattern is one where one of the rules of digit analysis is ignored—namely, when the dialed digits match an urgent priority pattern, the call is routed immediately even if there are other potential matches that might match if more digits are entered. CallManager does not wait for additional digits and routes the call immediately.

For example, if you have 1XXX configured on a translation pattern and you have an IP phone with DN 12345, when a calling party dials 1234, the call is routed to the 1XXX translation pattern immediately, even though 12345 is still a potential match if the user presses a 5. In this case there is no way for a user to directly dial 12345 because the translation pattern always routes the call immediately after four digits.

Remember that the calling and called number can be changed by a translation pattern. The transformation behavior is the same as the transformation on route patterns or route lists. Figure 9-5 shows the Translation Pattern Configuration page in CallManager Administration (**Route Plan > Translation Pattern**).

To better understand the significance of the contents of the Translation Pattern Configuration page, look at the Pattern Definition section. The first field is the translation pattern itself. Like any pattern, it can be placed in a partition (in this case, the **Internal** partition). Also, as with any route pattern, a numbering plan and route filter can be applied to the pattern, but these only apply if the translation pattern has the @ wildcard as part of the pattern.

Figure 9-5   *Translation Pattern Configuration Page*

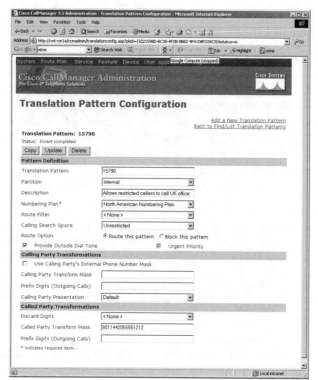

The translation pattern also includes a calling search space. After the translation pattern has done its work of transforming the called or calling party numbers, the information is presented back to CallManager's digit analysis engine as if it were a new call. As with any calling device, the digits need an associated calling search space to determine where the call can be routed.

For a moment, forget about translation patterns. Instead, think of a receptionist answering an IP phone. For the purpose of this example, assume that the receptionist can call internal phone numbers and local phone numbers. User A's IP phone can call only internal numbers, not local numbers. But if User A calls the receptionist and asks to be transferred to a local phone number, the receptionist can complete the call, enabling User A to reach a local number from his phone. In a sense, the receptionist "translates" the original number dialed by User A (the receptionist's phone number) into a different number, which is a local number.

Using translation patterns, you can "hop" from one calling search space to another in a controlled fashion—for example, you don't want to allow users to make international calls, yet there is a remote office that can only be reached via an international number. While there are many ways to solve this problem, one easy way is to create a translation pattern in a partition accessible for internal calls and translate the number to the international number while changing the calling search space to one that allows for international calls.

If you refer back to Figure 9-5, you can see that the translation pattern is 15790 and is in the **Internal** partition. This partition can be called by anyone with a calling search space that has the ability to call OnNet extensions. However, the calling search space for the translation pattern is configured as the **Unrestricted** calling search space. This calling search space is allowed to call any partition, including those that reach long distance and international destinations. You can see that the called party transform mask is 9011442055551212, which is an international phone number. Now anyone with access to the **Internal** partition can dial 15790 and reach this one particular international office without having to allow all the users access to the **International** partition.

When a dialed pattern matches a translation pattern, a few steps occur. Understand that the calling number and the called number can be modified. The calling party's external phone number mask can be used if the **Use Calling Party's External Phone Number Mask** checkbox is selected, and a transformation can be applied to the calling number.

When the called party transformation is applied, the original number can be modified or completely changed. The called number is changed and the calling search space is used to call that new pattern.

There is a box to check if you want to provide outside dial tone. As mentioned earlier, there is also an **Urgent Priority** checkbox. The **Urgent Priority** checkbox means that CallManager immediately routes any number that matches this pattern without waiting for any more digits if there are other potential matches. Remember that all translation patterns are urgent priority patterns and you cannot deselect the **Urgent Priority** checkbox.

An example of this is the pattern 9.911. If a 9.[2-9]XXXXXX pattern exists along with 9.911, both are seen as potential matches if a user dials the digits 9911. If the **Urgent Priority** box is selected on the 9.911 pattern, CallManager routes the call based on the 9.911 pattern and does not look for other matches.

It's important to note that because translation patterns have a calling search space, you can easily cause an internal routing loop if the called digits are not modified in the pattern and the calling search space includes the partition that the pattern itself exists in. To avoid an internal routing loop, make certain that the translation pattern does not end up pointing back to itself.

When you look at a CCM trace of a call where a translation pattern is involved, you will not see anything special indicating that the translation pattern is at work. You will just see the translated output mysteriously appear in the trace. Continuing the previous example where dialing 15790 routes the call to an international phone number, assume extension

15644 has a calling search space that only allows it to call the **Internal** partition. Example 9-2 shows extension 15644 dialing 15790. Notice the calling search space (**pss=**) field shows the only partition this phone is able to call is the **Internal** partition. "pss" stands for partition search space and indicates the calling search space for the device. However, the calling search space information is presented as an ordered list of partitions, not the name of the calling search space.

Example 9-2 *CCM Trace Showing Extension 15644 Dial 15790*

```
StationD:     000000889 StartTone tone=33(InsideDialTone), direction=0.
StationInit: 000000889 KeypadButton kpButton=1.
StationD:     000000889 StopTone.
StationD:     000000889 SelectSoftKeys instance=1 reference=33558243
  softKeySetIndex=6 validKeyMask=-1.
Digit analysis: match(fqcn="15644", cn="15644", pss="Internal", dd="1")
Digit analysis: potentialMatches=PotentialMatchesExist
StationInit: 000000889 KeypadButton kpButton=5.
Digit analysis: match(fqcn="15644", cn="15644", pss="Internal", dd="15")
Digit analysis: potentialMatches=PotentialMatchesExist
StationInit: 000000889 KeypadButton kpButton=7.
Digit analysis: match(fqcn="15644", cn="15644", pss="Internal", dd="157")
Digit analysis: potentialMatches=PotentialMatchesExist
StationInit: 000000889 KeypadButton kpButton=9.
Digit analysis: match(fqcn="15644", cn="15644", pss="Internal", dd="1579")
Digit analysis: potentialMatches=PotentialMatchesExist
StationInit: 000000889 KeypadButton kpButton=0.
Digit analysis: match(fqcn="15644", cn="15644", pss="Internal", dd="15790")
```

Immediately following the user dialing 15790 you see the digit analysis results; however, the results immediately show the output of the translation pattern with no indication that a translation pattern was matched. Example 9-3 shows the digit analysis results.

Example 9-3 *CCM Trace Showing Digit Analysis Results After a Translation Pattern Match*

```
Digit analysis: analysis results
|PretransformCallingPartyNumber=9195555644
|CallingPartyNumber=15644
|DialingPartition=International
|DialingPattern=9.@
|DialingRoutePatternRegularExpression=(9)(01)(1)(4[013-9])(X+)(#)
|DialingWhere=(INTERNATIONAL-ACCESS EXISTS)
|PatternType=International
|PotentialMatches=NoPotentialMatchesExist
|DialingSdlProcessId=(2,84,13)
|PretransformDigitString=9011442055551212#
|PretransformTagsList=ACCESS-CODE:INTERNATIONAL-ACCESS:INTERNATIONAL-DIRECT-DIAL:
  COUNTRY-CODE:NATIONAL-NUMBER:END-OF-DIALING
```

continues

Example 9-3 *CCM Trace Showing Digit Analysis Results After a Translation Pattern Match (Continued)*

```
|PretransformPositionalMatchList=9:01:1:44:2055551212:#
|CollectedDigits=9011442055551212#
|UnconsumedDigits=
|TagsList=ACCESS-CODE:INTERNATIONAL-ACCESS:INTERNATIONAL-DIRECT-DIAL:COUNTRY-CODE:
  NATIONAL-NUMBER:END-OF-DIALING
|PositionalMatchList=9:01:1:44:2055551212:#
|VoiceMailbox=
|VoiceMailCallingSearchSpace=
|VoiceMailPilotNumber=
|DisplayName=
|RouteBlockFlag=RouteThisPattern
|InterceptPartition=
|InterceptPattern=
|InterceptWhere=
|InterceptSdlProcessId=(0,0,0)
|InterceptSsType=0
|InterceptSsKey=0
|WithTags=
|WithValues=
|CgpnPresentation=NotSelected
|CallManagerDeviceType=AccessDevice
```

You can see the that the translation pattern transformed the calling party number from 15644 to 9195555644, changed the called party number to 9011442055551212# and changed the calling search space to one that contains the **International** partition because the 9.@ pattern that is matched in Example 9-3 is in the **International** partition. This behavior can be very confusing when reading through CCM traces because you may see a number change for what appears to be no reason. If you see behavior like this, check your translation pattern configuration in CallManager Administration to see if a translation pattern is being matched.

Understanding Route Filters

Route filters raise many questions: What does a filter do? Does it filter out the calls you don't want? Or does it allow through only the calls you want? This section explores how route filters work.

Route filters are used with numbering plans when using the @ wildcard. Every country has a numbering plan of some sort. As of CallManager Release 3.3, the only numbering plan supported by the @ wildcard is the NANP; therefore, route filters only apply to the NANP. Although this section only deals with the NANP, the concepts apply to any numbering plan when they are implemented in CallManager.

As mentioned several times, the @ wildcard corresponds to all the patterns in a given numbering plan. In this case it corresponds to every pattern in the NANP because that is the only numbering plan for which the @ pattern is currently supported. The NANP consists of almost 300 individual route patterns. Route filters allow you to selectively remove or restrict which of those 300 patterns are used.

Certain parts of a dialed number correspond to a substring. For example, in the NANP, a 10-digit number is composed of three substrings. The first three digits represent the local area code substring. The next three digits are the office code substring. The final four are the subscriber code substring. Figure 9-6 depicts this example.

Figure 9-6   *Numbering Plan Example*

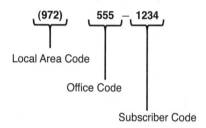

In the numbering plan file that defines the NANP, each substring within a route pattern is mapped to a tag. A *tag* indicates the placeholder in the NANP for a substring in a given route pattern. For example, one of the route patterns in the NANP numbering plan is ([2-9]11). Parentheses are used to designate substrings. This pattern only has one substring and the tag assigned to that substring is called SERVICE.

A more complex example is (1)([2-9][02-9]X)([2-9]XX)(XXXX). This pattern has four substrings. Tags are assigned to the substrings as follows:

- (1) = LONG-DISTANCE-DIRECT-DIAL
- ([2-9][02-9]X) = AREA-CODE
- ([2-9]XX) = OFFICE-CODE
- (XXXX) = SUBSCRIBER

You can find this information by looking at the numbering plan file. Appendix B, "NANP Call Routing Information," contains the output of the NANP dial plan. You can also find this on a CallManager system in C:\Program Files\Cisco\DialPlan\NANP. The following is the definition of the 1[2-9][02-9]X[2-9]XXXXXX pattern in the NANP file.

```
# 1+[2-9][02-9]X[2-9]XXXXXX
P:  1                LONG-DISTANCE-DIRECT-DIAL
P:  [2-9][02-9]X     AREA-CODE
P:  [2-9]XX          OFFICE-CODE
P:  XXXX             SUBSCRIBER
T:  N
```

Tags are just arbitrary names given by the CallManager developers to signify what a particular substring means in a given route pattern. Table 9-6 is a list of the tags available in CallManager as part of the NANP. If some other numbering plan is supported in the future, the names and significance of these tags will change depending on which numbering plan is chosen.

Table 9-6 *List of Tags in the NANP Available for Use in a Route Filter*

Tag	Description
AREA-CODE	This tag identifies the area code for long distance calls. In the NANP it is defined in the form [2-9]XX.
COUNTRY CODE	This tag identifies the one-, two-, or three-digit number that specifies the destination country for international calls.
END-OF-DIALING	This tag identifies the end of the dialed-digit string. The # character serves as the end-of-dialing signal for international numbers dialed within the NANP.
INTERNATIONAL-ACCESS	This access code specifies international dialing. The NANP uses 01 for this tag.
INTERNATIONAL-DIRECT-DIAL	This tag identifies a direct-dialed international call. The NANP uses 1 for this tag.
INTERNATIONAL-OPERATOR	This tag identifies an operator-assisted international call. The NANP uses 0 for this tag.
LOCAL-AREA-CODE	This tag identifies the area code for local calls. In the NANP it is defined in the form [2-9]XX.
LOCAL-DIRECT-DIAL	This tag identifies a direct-dialed local call. NANP calls use 1 for this tag.
LOCAL-OPERATOR	This tag identifies an operator-assisted local call. NANP calls use 0 for this tag.
LONG-DISTANCE-DIRECT-DIAL	This tag identifies a direct-dialed long distance call. NANP calls use 1 for this tag.
LONG-DISTANCE-OPERATOR	This tag identifies an operator-assisted, long distance call within the NANP. Operator-assisted calls use 0 for this tag, and operator access uses 00.
NATIONAL-NUMBER	This tag specifies the nation-specific part of the digit string for an international call.
OFFICE-CODE	This tag designates the first three digits of a seven-digit DN in the form [2-9]XX.

Table 9-6   *List of Tags in the NANP Available for Use in a Route Filter (Continued)*

Tag	Description
SATELLITE-SERVICE	This tag provides access to satellite connections for international calls.
SERVICE	This tag designates services such as 911 for emergency, 611 for repair, and 411 for information.
SUBSCRIBER	This tag specifies the last four digits of a seven-digit DN in the NANP.
TRANSIT-NETWORK	This tag identifies a long distance carrier using a four-digit carrier identification code. Do not include the leading 101 carrier access code prefix in the TRANSIT-NETWORK value. Refer to TRANSIT-NETWORK-ESCAPE for more information.
TRANSIT-NETWORK-ESCAPE	This tag precedes the long distance carrier identifier. The value for this field is 101 in the NANP. Do not include the four-digit carrier identification code in the TRANSIT-NETWORK-ESCAPE value. Refer to TRANSIT-NETWORK for more information.

Route filters allow you to filter out parts of the numbering plan by selecting patterns that have a particular tag, do not have a particular tag, or when the substring that matches a particular tag is set to a specific value.

This first example shows how to use a route filter to add only the patterns that contain a specific tag. To do this, select the value **EXISTS** for the tag you want to add. For example, assume you have a route pattern configured with a route filter as follows:

> 9.@ where AREA-CODE EXISTS

This means that this route pattern matches any route pattern in the numbering plan file that has the AREA-CODE tag in it. If you look in the NANP file, you can see there are eight route patterns that have the AREA-CODE tag:

- 0[2-9][02-9]X[2-9]XXXXXX
- 0[2-9]X[02-9][2-9]XXXXXX
- 101XXXX0[2-9][02-9]X[2-9]XXXXXX
- 101XXXX0[2-9]X[02-9][2-9]XXXXXX
- 101XXXX1[2-9][02-9]X[2-9]XXXXXX
- 101XXXX1[2-9]X[02-9][2-9]XXXXXX
- 1[2-9][02-9]X[2-9]XXXXXX
- 1[2-9]X[02-9][2-9]XXXXXX

These eight patterns allow you to dial 0 plus a 10-digit long distance number, 1 plus a 10-digit long distance number, or 101XXXX followed by 0 or 1 and the 10-digit number. This basically encompasses all the ways you can make a long distance call in North America. These eight patterns only correspond to the @ part of the route pattern, so a 9 is added in front of each pattern with a tag called ACCESS-CODE that corresponds to the 9. Next, take the case where you want to include all patterns that do not have a particular tag in them. To configure this, select the value **DOES-NOT-EXIST** for the tag you want to exclude. For example,

> 9.@ where AREA-CODE DOES-NOT-EXIST

This means that this route pattern will match any pattern in the numbering plan file that does not have the AREA-CODE tag in it. You already saw which patterns include the AREA-CODE tag in the previous example. In this case, this route pattern matches all the patterns in the numbering plan file except for the eight that are listed in the previous example because those eight have the AREA-CODE tag.

NOTE   You might be wondering how to distinguish an area code from a local area code. These two designations are just arbitrary names used to signify the area code when dialing a local number versus the area code when dialing a long distance number. In the NANP, the substring that matches the AREA-CODE tag (corresponding to a long distance area code) always has either a 1 or 0 in front of it. The 1 is referred to as the LONG-DISTANCE-DIRECT-DIAL tag and the 0 is referred to as the LONG-DISTANCE-OPERATOR tag. Without a 1 or 0 in front of the area code, it is considered a local area code. Consider the following examples:

> 972-555-5000: In this case, the 972 is a local area code
> 1-972-555-5000: In this case, the 972 is an area code

Remember, the AREA-CODE and LOCAL-AREA-CODE tags are just arbitrary tags for substrings of route patterns in the numbering plan file, so to completely understand which patterns you are adding or removing when using these tags in a route filter, you must refer to the numbering plan file.

Finally, you can use route filters to include only patterns where a substring that matches a particular tag is equal to a specific value. For example, if you want to include all the patterns that have the AREA-CODE tag and you want to limit the substring that matches the AREA-CODE tag to a specific area code, such as 972, you can configure:

> 9.@ where AREA-CODE == 972

The == operator is very similar to the **EXISTS** operator, except it takes the operation a step further. First you start by looking at all the route patterns where the AREA-CODE tag is present. You end up with the same list you saw before. Now, however, you must restrict the substring that matches AREA-CODE to the configured pattern. If you look at the North

American numbering plan file, you will see that the highlighted substrings of the route patterns shown below correspond with the AREA-CODE tag:

- 0[2-9][02-9]X[2-9]XXXXXX
- 0[2-9]X[02-9][2-9]XXXXXX
- 101XXXX0[2-9][02-9]X[2-9]XXXXXX
- 101XXXX0[2-9]X[02-9][2-9]XXXXXX
- 101XXXX1[2-9][02-9]X[2-9]XXXXXX
- 101XXXX1[2-9]X[02-9][2-9]XXXXXX
- 1[2-9][02-9]X[2-9]XXXXXX
- 1[2-9]X[02-9][2-9]XXXXXX

CallManager takes the intersection of the configured route filter value and the substring pattern in the dial plan file. In this case, two substrings appear for the AREA-CODE field:

- [2-9][02-9]X
- [2-9]X[02-9]

You must then take the intersection of 972 with each of these substrings. In both cases, the result is just 972. If you replace the substrings that correspond with the AREA-CODE tag with the intersection, 972, you are left with the following route patterns:

- 0972[2-9]XXXXXX
- 0972[2-9]XXXXXX
- 101XXXX0972[2-9]XXXXXX
- 101XXXX0972[2-9]XXXXXX
- 101XXXX1972[2-9]XXXXXX
- 101XXXX1972[2-9]XXXXXX
- 1972[2-9]XXXXXX
- 1972[2-9]XXXXXX

These eight patterns are added to digit analysis (with a 9 in front of each of them) when you configure **9.@ where AREA-CODE == 972** and these are the patterns that are used for closest-match routing purposes. Notice there are duplicate patterns after applying the route filter. In this case only the four unique patterns are added and the duplicates are ignored.

A route filter can also have multiple clauses. You can configure a route pattern such as **9.@ where AREA-CODE == 972 OR AREA-CODE == 214**. Using the same logic above, you take all the patterns that have the substring corresponding to the AREA-CODE tag equal to either 972 or 214. You basically end up adding all eight patterns twice—once with the 972 area code and once with the 214 area code. The resulting route patterns are

- 0972[2-9]XXXXXX
- 0972[2-9]XXXXXX
- 101XXXX0972[2-9]XXXXXX
- 101XXXX0972[2-9]XXXXXX
- 101XXXX1972[2-9]XXXXXX
- 101XXXX1972[2-9]XXXXXX
- 1972[2-9]XXXXXX
- 1972[2-9]XXXXXX
- 0214[2-9]XXXXXX
- 0214[2-9]XXXXXX
- 101XXXX0214[2-9]XXXXXX
- 101XXXX0214[2-9]XXXXXX
- 101XXXX1214[2-9]XXXXXX
- 101XXXX1214[2-9]XXXXXX
- 1214[2-9]XXXXXX
- 1214[2-9]XXXXXX

The ability to have multiple clauses allows you to get quite specific on a pattern. You could do something like the following:

Clause: (OFFICE-CODE == 555 AND LOCAL-AREA-CODE == 214) OR (LOCAL-AREA-CODE == 972 AND OFFICE-CODE == 444)

To determine the patterns that are added for this example, first find the route patterns that have the LOCAL-AREA-CODE tag in them:

- 101XXXX[2-9][02-9]X[2-9]XXXXXX
- 101XXXX[2-9]X[02-9][2-9]XXXXXX
- [2-9][02-9]X[2-9]XXXXXX
- [2-9]X[02-9][2-9]XXXXXX

Once you have this list, look through these four patterns for patterns that also include the OFFICE-CODE tag. In this case, all four of the patterns have the OFFICE-CODE tag.

To obtain the resulting route patterns from the first part of the clause, **OFFICE-CODE == 555 AND LOCAL-AREA-CODE == 214**, replace the substring that corresponds with the OFFICE-CODE tag with the intersection of [2-9]XX and 555, which is 555, and the substring that corresponds with the LOCAL-AREA-CODE tag with the intersection of

[2-9][02-9]X and [2-9]X[02-9] with 214, both of which are equal to 214. Then do the same for **LOCAL-AREA-CODE == 972 AND OFFICE-CODE == 444.** You end up with the following patterns:

- 101XXXX214555XXXX
- 101XXXX214555XXXX
- 214555XXXX
- 214555XXXX
- 101XXXX972444XXXX
- 101XXXX972444XXXX
- 972444XXXX
- 972444XXXX

Notice you end up with some duplicate route patterns. CallManager automatically eliminates duplicates and you are left with four route patterns:

- 101XXXX214555XXXX
- 214555XXXX
- 101XXXX972444XXXX
- 972444XXXX

Examining a few examples should dispel the mystery of route filters. It helps to analyze each piece of the route filter and write it out until you have a list of all the patterns that match the route filter.

Digit Transformation Troubleshooting

Digit transformation and call routing troubleshooting are linked. However, calling and called party transformations result in different types of problems. Calling party transformation problems primarily revolve around proper number and name presentation. As a result, call routing isn't affected by calling party transformations. A called party transformation does have call routing implications.

If the problem is only one of calling party number presentation, you don't have to be concerned with call routing—only presentation. Example 9-4 shows a calling party transformation taking place.

Example 9-4   *CCM Trace of Calling Party Information*

```
| Digit analysis: match(fqcn="2000", cn="2000",
  pss="P_Local:P_Internal", dd="95551212"
| Digit analysis: analysis results
| PretransformCallingPartyNumber=2000
| CallingPartyNumber=9725550000
```

continues

Example 9-4 *CCM Trace of Calling Party Information (Continued)*

```
|DialingPartition=P_Local
|DialingPattern=9.XXXXXXX
|DialingRoutePatternRegularExpression=(9)(XXXXXXX)
|DialingWhere=
|PatternType=Enterprise
|PotentialMatches=NoPotentialMatchesExist
|DialingSdlProcessId=(1,58,5)
|PretransformDigitString=95551212
|PretransformTagsList=ACCESS-CODE:SUBSCRIBER
|PretransformPositionalMatchList=9:5551212
|CollectedDigits=95551212
|UnconsumedDigits=
|TagsList=ACCESS-CODE:SUBSCRIBER
|PositionalMatchList=9:5551212
|VoiceMailbox=
|DisplayName=
|RouteBlockFlag=RouteThisPattern
|InterceptPartition=
|InterceptPattern=
|InterceptWhere=
|InterceptSdlProcessId=(0,0,0)
|InterceptSsType=0
|InterceptSsKey=0 |
```

The calling number is 2000, but the external calling party mask is 9725550000. The actual dialed number is 95551212. Notice that as soon as the dialed number is matched, the calling party number is transformed.

When you troubleshoot calling party transformations, the CCM trace file shows the transformation occurring. You should view this information while keeping in mind the order of transformation:

1 Original calling device (when specified on a route pattern or translation pattern by the **Use Calling Party's External Phone Number Mask** checkbox.)

2 Translation pattern

3 Route pattern

4 Route list

5 Terminating device

The original calling device when specified on a route pattern or translation pattern by the **Use Calling Party's External Phone Number Mask** checkbox, the translation pattern (if it exists), and the route pattern all perform a cumulative transformation. Don't forget any route list transformations override any route pattern transformations.

Call Routing Troubleshooting

Simplistically speaking, a call routing problem is when the call is not getting to where you expect it to be. The symptoms of this problem manifest themselves in different ways. It could be that the user picks up the phone, starts dialing, and gets reorder tone even before the dialing is completed, or the user might finish dialing and then get reorder. It is even possible that the user dials successfully but the call gets routed to the wrong place.

Remember that general call routing problems can occur on gateways and other devices too. Inbound calls might not be routed properly to users or voice mail systems or other applications such as auto attendants or interactive voice response servers.

As a first step to solving general call routing problems, follow the steps listed in Table 9-7.

Table 9-7   *Methodology for Resolving Call Routing Problems*

Step	Action
Step 1	Determine which calling device had the problem. This includes phones, gateways, CTI ports, voice mail ports, and so on. You can use CallManager Serviceability to search for the device in the CCM traces or just manually search through the CCM traces yourself. It helps to get the calling number and the time the call was placed and to find out if the problem can be reproduced.
Step 2	Identify the dialed number as dialed by the user or sent by the gateway. If the user received reorder prior to being able to completely dial the called number, identify the digits dialed prior to receiving reorder tone.
Step 3	Check the calling search space of the calling device to see which partitions were searched. Remember that the device and the line could have a calling search space if it is an IP phone. As such, check both keeping in mind that the line calling search space takes precedence over the device calling search space when two equal matches are found in two different partitions.
Step 4	If a match was made, check to see which pattern was matched and which partition the matched pattern is in. This is important because you know that a transformation might be taking place on the pattern or route list.
	If a match wasn't made, the calling party did not have access to the partition that had the pattern the calling party needed access to, or alternatively, the pattern might not even exist.
	See Example 9-4 for an example of this step.
Step 5	If the pattern is a translation pattern, check the called party transformation and the calling search space. The calling search space on the translation pattern must be able to access the transformed number in one of its partitions.
	If no translation pattern is used, skip this step.

continues

Table 9-7 *Methodology for Resolving Call Routing Problems (Continued)*

Step	Action
Step 6	If the matched pattern is a route pattern, check the DDIs as well as the calling and called party transformation. What DDI is being used? An incorrect DDI choice means that the wrong numbers might be presented to the PSTN. Consult Chapter 6, "Voice Gateways," for information on how to read the traces for outbound calling.
	If you know what numbers were presented to the PSTN, you know where you need to check for errors. The DDI might not be removing the digits it needs to. Or it might be removing part of the number that shouldn't be removed.
	A called party transformation might also be changing the dialed number in a way that the PSTN or PBX does not recognize.
Step 7	If the route pattern goes to a route list, check the DDIs, calling party transformations, and called party transformations on the route group details of the route list. Remember that this overrides any instruction or transformation specified on the route pattern.

Reading CCM Traces for Call Routing Information

At this point, it might be beneficial to walk through the CCM trace following the troubleshooting approach outlined in Table 9-7. The first thing you have to do is find the calling device in the trace file. This could be a gateway, IP phone, or CTI port.

Usually the best way to find a device in the CCM trace is by searching for the DN configured on the device. If the calling device is a gateway (the call is coming in on a gateway) and the gateway is not receiving calling party number information, you can search for the device name of the gateway in the trace.

Using CallManager Serviceability, you can search for the device, and all related traces can be displayed. See Chapter 3 for information about CallManager Serviceabilty. You can also just open the CCM trace file using Notepad and search through the file manually. Example 9-5 shows the beginning of the call.

Example 9-5 *CCM Trace File at the Beginning of an IP Phone Call*

```
StationInit: 766a71c OffHook
StationD:    766a71c DisplayText text='2000'
StationD:    766a71c SetLamp stimulus=9(Line) stimulusInstance=1
  lampMode=2(LampOn)
StationD:    766a71c CallState callState=1(OffHook)
  lineInstance=1 callReference=16777225
StationD:    766a71c DisplayPromptStatus timeOutValue=0
  promptStatus='Enter number' lineInstance=1 callReference=16777225
StationD:    766a71c SelectSoftKeys instance=1 reference=16777225
  softKeySetIndex=4 validKeyMask=-1
StationD:    766a71c ActivateCallPlane lineInstance=1
Digit analysis: match(fqcn="2000", cn="2000", pss="P_Local:P_Internal", dd="")
Digit analysis: potentialMatches=PotentialMatchesExist
```

On the **Digit analysis** line, look at the contents of the **match** section. What do they mean?

- **fqcn="2000"**—This is the fully qualified calling number, including any mask applied by the external phone number mask.

- **cn="2000"**—This is the calling party number.

- **pss="P_Local:P_Internal"**—"pss" stands for partition search space. This indicates the calling search space for the device, however the calling search space information is presented as an ordered list of partitions, not the name of the calling search space. These are the partitions that are being searched for a match in the order they are being searched. The calling search space on this device has only two partitions, so a match is being sought in only these two partitions (in addition to the null partition).

- **dd=""**—These are the digits dialed so far.

You can use this information to determine the dialed number as dialed by the user or sent by the gateway. For a call from an IP phone or other device that presents the digits to CallManager one at a time, the dialed digits are null, but more follow. If the call comes in from a gateway, the first digit analysis line will contain the complete called party number.

The third step is to see which partitions are being searched. This is also available in the digit analysis output by looking at the pss information.

Next, the first digit is dialed. In the CCM trace shown in Example 9-6, you can see that potential matches do exist within the two partitions being searched.

Example 9-6 *CCM Trace File of the First Dialed Digit, 2*

```
StationD:      766a71c StartTone tone=33(InsideDialTone)
StationInit: 766a71c KeypadButton kpButton=2.
StationD:      766a71c StopTone.
StationD:      766a71c SelectSoftKeys instance=1 reference=16777225
  softKeySetIndex=6 validKeyMask=-1.
Digit analysis: match(fqcn="2000", cn="2000",
  pss="P_Local:P_Internal", dd="2")
Digit analysis: potentialMatches=PotentialMatchesExist
```

In Example 9-7, a 0 is dialed.

Example 9-7 *CCM Trace File of the Second Dialed Digit, 0*

```
StationInit: 766a71c KeypadButton kpButton=0.
Digit analysis: match(fqcn="2000", cn="2000",
  pss="P_Local:P_Internal", dd="20")
Digit analysis: potentialMatches=PotentialMatchesExist
```

Digit analysis shows that potential matches still exist. Notice that the **dd=** field now shows **20**, because these are the digits dialed up to this point.

Example 9-8 shows that another 0 is dialed.

Example 9-8 *CCM Trace File of the Third Dialed Digit, 0*

```
StationInit: 766a71c KeypadButton kpButton=0.
Digit analysis: match(fqcn="2000", cn="2000",
  pss="P_Local:P_Internal", dd="200")
Digit analysis: potentialMatches=PotentialMatchesExist
```

More potential matches exist.

Now that you have the final match, check to see which pattern was used and which partition it was found in, as shown in Example 9-9.

This next digit finalizes the match in this case. Notice that as soon as a match occurs, digit analysis presents the results of the match.

Example 9-9 *CCM Trace File of the Fourth Dialed Digit, 1*

```
StationInit: 766a71c KeypadButton kpButton=1.
Digit analysis: match(fqcn="2000", cn="2000",
  pss="P_Local:P_Internal", dd="2001")
Digit analysis: analysis results
CallingPartyNumber=2000
DialingPartition=P_Internal
DialingPattern=2001
DialingRoutePatternRegularExpression=(2001)
DialingWhere=
PatternType=Enterprise
PotentialMatches=NoPotentialMatchesExist
DialingSdlProcessId=(1,34,16)
PretransformDigitString=2001
PretransformTagsList=SUBSCRIBER
PretransformPositionalMatchList=2001
CollectedDigits=2001
UnconsumedDigits=
TagsList=SUBSCRIBER
PositionalMatchList=2001
VoiceMailbox=2001
DisplayName=
RouteBlockFlag=RouteThisPattern
InterceptPartition=
InterceptPattern=
InterceptWhere=
InterceptSdlProcessId=(0,0,0)
InterceptSsType=0
InterceptSsKey=0
```

The digit analysis match shown in Example 9-9 tells you that the calling party is 2000. You also know that the partition the match is found in is called P_Internal. The dialing pattern (the called party number) is 2001.

Now look at another example, in which a local 7-digit call is placed. The dialed number is 95551212.

First, you find the calling device, as shown in Example 9-10.

Example 9-10 *CCM Trace File of a Call to 95551212*

```
StationInit: 766a71c OffHook.
StationD:    766a71c DisplayText text= 2000
StationD:    766a71c SetLamp stimulus=9(Line) stimulusInstance=1
  lampMode=2(LampOn)
StationD:    766a71c CallState callState=1(OffHook)
  lineInstance=1 callReference=16777227
StationD:    766a71c DisplayPromptStatus timeOutValue=0
  promptStatus='Enter number' lineInstance=1 callReference=16777227
StationD:    766a71c SelectSoftKeys instance=1 reference=16777227
  softKeySetIndex=4 validKeyMask=-1.
StationD:    766a71c ActivateCallPlane lineInstance=1.
Digit analysis: match(fqcn="2000", cn="2000",
  pss="P_Local:P_Internal", dd="")
Digit analysis: potentialMatches=PotentialMatchesExist
```

As before, a potential match is recognized within the two partitions shown. You are now on Steps 2 and 3 in the call routing methodology defined in Table 9-7. You know what partitions are being searched, and you are in the process of determining the final dialed number and the partition it is found in. Example 9-11 shows the first dialed digit, 9.

Example 9-11 *CCM Trace File of the First Dialed Digit, 9*

```
StationD:    766a71c StartTone tone=33(InsideDialTone)
StationInit: 766a71c KeypadButton kpButton=9.
StationD:    766a71c StopTone
StationD:    766a71c SelectSoftKeys instance=1 reference=16777227
  softKeySetIndex=6 validKeyMask=-1.
Digit analysis: match(fqcn="2000", cn="2000",
  pss="P_Local:P_Internal", dd="9")
Digit analysis: potentialMatches=PotentialMatchesExist
```

The second digit, 5, is dialed. Potential matches still exist, as confirmed by Example 9-12.

Example 9-12 *CCM Trace File of the Second Dialed Digit, 5*

```
StationInit: 766a71c KeypadButton kpButton=5.
Digit analysis: match(fqcn="2000", cn="2000",
  pss="P_Local:P_Internal", dd="95")
Digit analysis: potentialMatches=ExclusivelyOffnetPotentialMatchesExist
```

Here you see a difference. CallManager has enough information to know that this pattern is exclusively OffNet. An OffNet pattern is just a pattern that has **Provide Outside Dial Tone** configured. This trace line means that CallManager knows that outside dial tone must be played because all remaining potential matches have the **Provide Outside Dial Tone** checkbox selected. CallManager knows it needs to play outside dial tone for this call even though the final digits have not been dialed. Example 9-13 continues to show dialed digits.

Example 9-13 *CCM Trace File of the Remaining Dialed Digits*

```
StationD:       766a71c StartTone tone=34(OutsideDialTone).
StationInit:    766a71c KeypadButton kpButton=5.
StationD:       766a71c StopTone.
StationD:       766a71c SelectSoftKeys instance=1 reference=16777227
  softKeySetIndex=6 validKeyMask=-1.
Digit analysis: match(fqcn="2000", cn="2000",
  pss="P_Local:P_Internal", dd="955")
Digit analysis: potentialMatches=ExclusivelyOffnetPotentialMatchesExist
StationInit:    766a71c KeypadButton kpButton=5
Digit analysis: match(fqcn="2000", cn="2000",
  pss="P_Local:P_Internal", dd="9555")
Digit analysis: potentialMatches=ExclusivelyOffnetPotentialMatchesExist
StationInit:    766a71c KeypadButton kpButton=1.
Digit analysis: match(fqcn="2000", cn="2000",
  pss="P_Local:P_Internal", dd="95551")
Digit analysis: potentialMatches=ExclusivelyOffnetPotentialMatchesExist
StationInit:    766a71c KeypadButton kpButton=2.
Digit analysis: match(fqcn="2000", cn="2000",
  pss="P_Local:P_Internal", dd="955512")
Digit analysis: potentialMatches=ExclusivelyOffnetPotentialMatchesExist
StationInit:    766a71c KeypadButton kpButton=1.
Digit analysis: match(fqcn="2000", cn="2000",
  pss="P_Local:P_Internal", dd="9555121")
Digit analysis: potentialMatches=ExclusivelyOffnetPotentialMatchesExist
StationInit:    766a71c KeypadButton kpButton=2.
Digit analysis: match(fqcn="2000", cn="2000",
  pss="P_Local:P_Internal", dd="95551212")
Digit analysis: analysis results
```

The final match is found. After the pattern is matched, the analysis results are shown, as in Example 9-14.

Example 9-14 *CCM Trace File of Digit Analysis for the Dialed Number*

```
CallingPartyNumber=2000
DialingPartition=P_Local
DialingPattern=9.XXXXXXX
DialingRoutePatternRegularExpression=(9)(XXXXXXX)
DialingWhere=
PatternType=Enterprise
PotentialMatches=NoPotentialMatchesExist
DialingSdlProcessId=(1,58,8)
PretransformDigitString=95551212
PretransformTagsList=ACCESS-CODE:SUBSCRIBER
PretransformPositionalMatchList=9:5551212
CollectedDigits=95551212
```

Example 9-14 *CCM Trace File of Digit Analysis for the Dialed Number (Continued)*

```
UnconsumedDigits=
TagsList=ACCESS-CODE:SUBSCRIBER
PositionalMatchList=9:5551212
VoiceMailbox=
DisplayName=
RouteBlockFlag=RouteThisPattern
InterceptPartition=
InterceptPattern=
InterceptWhere=
InterceptSdlProcessId=(0,0,0)
InterceptSsType=0
InterceptSsKey=0
```

The calling number, dialing partition, dialing pattern, and actual dialed number are shown in this piece of the trace.

This gives you enough information to check the translation patterns or route patterns that match this pattern. Digit transformations can be analyzed to see how they affect the original dialed number.

Troubleshooting Hold, Transfer, Park, and Call Pickup

CallManager offers a variety of features, including but not limited to

- Hold/resume
- Transfer
- Call park
- Call pickup and group call pickup
- Conference

These features are usually invoked by pressing a soft key on an IP Phone corresponding to the feature. The VG248 voice gateway allows you to invoke some of these features through the use of the hook flash on an analog phone and feature codes entered as DTMF digits. However, the VG248 converts these analog messages to soft key messages that are sent to CallManager, so troubleshooting both scenarios is the same when you look at the CCM trace.

Hold/resume, transfer, call park, and call pickup/group call pickup are discussed in this chapter. Conferencing is discussed in Chapter 11, "Conference Bridges, Transcoders, and Media Termination Points."

Call Hold and Resume

Call hold is a very basic and often-used feature. It is important to understand because hold is invoked for a variety of other features to work, for example, a call transfer begins by putting the first call on hold while the user places a call to the desired transfer destination.

When a call is placed on hold, the RTP streams connecting the two parties on the call are torn down and either the held party gets music on hold (MOH) or tone on hold, depending on the CallManager configuration. Chapter 12, "Music on Hold," goes into detail about how to troubleshoot MOH problems.

When an IP phone user places a call on hold, you will see the following sequence of events in the CCM trace. First, you see the IP phone send a **SoftKeyEvent** message with a softKeyEvent of **3**. Also notice that the TCP handle of the phone that pressed this soft key is **000001140**, the line for which this soft key applies is line **1** on the phone, and the call reference for this call is **33560019**.

```
StationInit: 000001140 SoftKeyEvent softKeyEvent=3 lineInstance=1
   callReference=33560019
```

You may be wondering what softKeyEvent=3 means. In some versions of CallManager this event is decoded for you in the trace file; however, as you see in this example, it is not. Table 9-8 shows the list of valid soft key events:

Table 9-8   *List of Soft Key Events and Descriptions*

softKeyEvent Value	Description
1	Redial
2	New Call
3	Hold
4	Transfer
5	Call Forward All
6	Not used
7	Not used
8	Backspace
9	End Call
10	Resume
11	Answer
12	Information
13	Conference
14	Park

Table 9-8   *List of Soft Key Events and Descriptions (Continued)*

softKeyEvent Value	Description
15	Not used
16	Meet-Me Conference
17	Call PickUp
18	Group Call PickUp
19	Drop Last Conference Participant
20	Call Back
21	Barge

As you can see from Table 9-8, the message softKeyEvent=3 means that the user pressed the **Hold** soft key. When a call is put on hold, the first thing that happens is the media streams are torn down. Notice both the party that pressed hold that has TCP handle 000001140 and the held party with TCP handle 000001429 are told to stop streaming as shown in Example 9-15.

Example 9-15 *CCM Trace Showing a Call Being Placed on Hold*

```
ConnectionManager - wait_AuDisconnectRequest(33560019,33560020): STOP STREAMING
ConnectionManager - storeMediaInfo(33560019): EXISTING ENTRY DISCOVERED, tail == 2
ConnectionManager - storeMediaInfo(33560020): EXISTING ENTRY DISCOVERED, tail == 2
MediaCoordinator - wait_AuDisconnectRequest
MediaCoordinator - wait_AuDisconnectRequest - sending disconnect to
MediaManager(1437)
MediaManager - wait_AuDisconnectRequest
MediaManager - wait_AuDisconnectRequest - no proxy and StopStreaming send disconnect
to (70,1464)
StationD:     000001140 CloseReceiveChannel conferenceID=33560019
  passThruPartyID=4821.  myIP: 7e6812ac (172.18.104.126)
StationD:     000001140 StopMediaTransmission conferenceID=33560019
  passThruPartyID=4821.  myIP: 7e6812ac (172.18.104.126)
StationD:     000001429 CloseReceiveChannel conferenceID=33560020
  passThruPartyID=4831.  myIP: 5b6a12ac (172.18.106.91)
StationD:     000001429 StopMediaTransmission conferenceID=33560020
  passThruPartyID=4831.  myIP: 5b6a12ac (172.18.106.91)
MediaManager - wait_AuDisconnectReply
MediaManager - wait_AuDisconnectReply - received all disconnect replies,
  forwarding a reply for party1(33560019) and party2(33560020)
MediaCoordinator - wait_AuDisconnectReply
MediaCoordinator - wait_AuDisconnectReply - removing MediaManager(1437) from
connection list
ConnectionManager - wait_AuDisconnectReply(33560019,33560020): STOP STREAMING
```

Next, a new media stream is established between the IP phone and the MOH server. This part of the trace is covered in detail in Chapter 12, so it is omitted here.

In this example, the IP phone that placed the call on hold has a shared line appearance with three other phones. When the call is placed on hold, the displays of the other three IP phones are updated to indicate the call is on hold. Remember when a call is on hold on a shared line appearance, any of the appearances can resume that call. Example 9-16 shows phones with TCP handles 000000957, 000000125, and 000000969 updated with information that there is a call on hold. Notice the call reference stays consistent.

Example 9-16 *CCM Trace Showing Phones Placed into the Hold Call State*

```
StationD:     000000957 SetLamp stimulus=9(Line) stimulusInstance=1
  lampMode=3(LampWink).
StationD:     000000957 CallState callState=8 lineInstance=1 callReference=33560019
StationD:     000000957 SelectSoftKeys instance=1 reference=33560019
  softKeySetIndex=2 validKeyMask=-1.
StationD:     000000957 DisplayPromptStatus timeOutValue=0 promptStatus='__'
  content='Hold' lineInstance=1 callReference=33560019 ver=0x80000004.
StationD:     000000125 SetLamp stimulus=9(Line) stimulusInstance=1
  lampMode=3(LampWink).
StationD:     000000125 CallState callState=8 lineInstance=1 callReference=33560019
StationD:     000000125 SelectSoftKeys instance=1 reference=33560019
  softKeySetIndex=2 validKeyMask=-1.
StationD:     000000125 DisplayPromptStatus timeOutValue=0 promptStatus='Hold'
  content='Hold' lineInstance=1 callReference=33560019 ver=0x0.
StationD:     000000969 SetLamp stimulus=9(Line) stimulusInstance=1
  lampMode=3(LampWink).
StationD:     000000969 CallState callState=8 lineInstance=1 callReference=33560019
StationD:     000000969 SelectSoftKeys instance=1 reference=33560019
  softKeySetIndex=2 validKeyMask=-1.
StationD:     000000969 DisplayPromptStatus timeOutValue=0 promptStatus='__'
  content='Hold' lineInstance=1 callReference=33560019 ver=0x80000004.
```

After updating all the shared lines, Example 9-17 shows the IP phone that placed the call on hold (TCP handle 000001140) being updated with the same information as well.

Example 9-17 *CCM Trace Showing the IP Phone Placed into the Hold Call State*

```
StationD:     000001140 DefineTimeDate timeDateInfo=? systemTime=1031096027.
StationD:     000001140 CallState callState=8 lineInstance=1 callReference=33560019
StationD:     000001140 SelectSoftKeys instance=1 reference=33560019
  softKeySetIndex=2 validKeyMask=-1.
StationD:     000001140 DisplayPromptStatus timeOutValue=0 promptStatus='__'
  content='Hold' lineInstance=1 callReference=33560019 ver=0x80000004.
```

As you might have guessed, the callState field indicates the state for the call on the indicated line. In this case you see all the IP phones are notified that the call state has a value of 8. Table 9-9 lists the various call states that you might see in a CCM trace:

Table 9-9   *Definition of the Various callState Messages*

callState value	Description
0	Idle
1	Off-hook
2	On-hook
3	Ring Out
4	Ring In
5	Connected
6	Busy
7	Congestion
8	Hold
9	Call Waiting
10	Call Transfer
11	Call Park
12	Proceed
13	Call Remote Multiline
14	Invalid Number

As you can see from Table 9-9, all the IP phones are being told that the call is currently in the Hold call state. At this point the call is on hold. The held party is hearing either tone on hold or music on hold and the holding IP phones all show the call is on hold.

You keep looking through the CCM trace and you see the the information shown in Example 9-18. First, CallManager tells the held party's IP phone to open a logical channel and the four IP phones that were on hold (including the phone that put the call on hold in the first place) are told that the call state is now **callState=13**. Second, you see CallManager tell the held party (TCP handle 000001429) to start media transmission to IP address 172.18.104.52.

Example 9-18   *CCM Trace Showing a Call Being Resumed*

```
StationD:    000001429 OpenReceiveChannel conferenceID=33560020
  passThruPartyID=4833 millisecondPacketSize=20
  compressionType=4(Media_Payload_G711Ulaw64k) qualifierIn=?.
  myIP: 5b6a12ac (172.18.106.91)
StationD - Call Phase == CALL_REMOTE_MULTILINE
```

continues

Example 9-18 *CCM Trace Showing a Call Being Resumed (Continued)*

```
StationD - Call Phase == CALL_REMOTE_MULTILINE
StationD - Call Phase == CALL_REMOTE_MULTILINE
StationD - Call Phase == CALL_REMOTE_MULTILINE
StationD:    000000957 SetLamp stimulus=9(Line) stimulusInstance=1
  lampMode=2(LampOn).
StationD:    000000957 ClearNotify.
StationD:    000000957 CallState callState=13 lineInstance=1
  callReference=33560019
StationD:    000000957 SelectSoftKeys instance=1 reference=33560019
  softKeySetIndex=10 validKeyMask=-1.
StationD:    000000957 DisplayPromptStatus timeOutValue=0 promptStatus='_'
  content='In Use Remotely' lineInstance=1 callReference=33560019 ver=0x80000004.
StationD:    000000125 SetLamp stimulus=9(Line) stimulusInstance=1
  lampMode=2(LampOn).
StationD:    000000125 ClearNotify.
StationD:    000000125 CallState callState=13 lineInstance=1
  callReference=33560019
StationD:    000000125 SelectSoftKeys instance=1 reference=33560019
  softKeySetIndex=10 validKeyMask=-1.
StationD:    000000125 DisplayPromptStatus timeOutValue=0
  promptStatus='In Use Remotely' content='In Use Remotely' lineInstance=1
  callReference=33560019 ver=0x0.
StationD:    000000969 SetLamp stimulus=9(Line) stimulusInstance=1
  lampMode=2(LampOn).
StationD:    000000969 ClearNotify.
StationD:    000000969 CallState callState=13 lineInstance=1
  callReference=33560019
StationD:    000000969 SelectSoftKeys instance=1 reference=33560019
  softKeySetIndex=10 validKeyMask=-1.
StationD:    000000969 DisplayPromptStatus timeOutValue=0 promptStatus='_'
  content='In Use Remotely' lineInstance=1 callReference=33560019 ver=0x80000004.
StationD:    000001140 SetLamp stimulus=9(Line) stimulusInstance=1
  lampMode=2(LampOn).
StationD:    000001140 ClearNotify.
StationD:    000001140 CallState callState=13 lineInstance=1
  callReference=33560019
StationD:    000001140 SelectSoftKeys instance=1 reference=33560019
  softKeySetIndex=10 validKeyMask=-1.
StationD:    000001140 DisplayPromptStatus timeOutValue=0 promptStatus='_'
  content='In Use Remotely' lineInstance=1 callReference=33560019 ver=0x80000004.
StationInit: 000001429 OpenReceiveChannelAck Status=0, IpAddr=0x5b6a12ac,
  Port=22902, PartyID=18483
MediaManager - wait_AuConnectInfo
MediaManager - wait_AuConnectInfo - recieved response, forwarding
MediaCoordinator - wait_AuConnectInfoInd
StationD:    000001429 StartMediaTransmission conferenceID=33560020
  passThruPartyID=4833 remoteIpAddress=346812ac(172.18.104.52)
  remotePortNumber=16384 milliSecondPacketSize=20
  compressType=4(Media_Payload_G711Ulaw64k) qualifierOut=?.
  myIP: 5b6a12ac (172.18.106.91)
```

At this point you might be wondering "What just happened?" CallManager told the held party's phone to come off of hold and also informed the other four IP phones that were previously in call state 8 that the new call state is 13. According to Table 9-9, call state 13 means "Call Remote Multiline." This call state means that another phone with the same shared line is currently active on that line, but you do not see any indication in the trace that any of the IP phones retrieved the call from hold.

You might be thinking that something does not make sense here because there is a missing piece of the puzzle you have not looked at yet. Remember CallManager is a distributed system with multiple nodes in a cluster. CCM traces only show the activity of devices and processes running on the CallManager server where you are looking at the traces. It is possible that there is another IP phone registered to a different CallManager in the cluster that also has the same shared line. You will not see any indication of this IP phone in the traces of any server except for the one it is registered to.

If you have a large cluster with multiple call processing servers, you do not want to have to look through the trace files on each server searching for the one that might have caused this to happen. There is an easier way. To get to the bottom of this, you need to look at the SDL trace files. First, find the timestamp from the point where you saw the unexpected event occur. In this case the first unexpected event is the message telling the held party to resume the call from hold and the messages to the IP phones telling them that the call state has changed.

Although we have removed the timestamps from the preceding examples for the purposes of this book, the first message in Example 9-18 occurred at timestamp 19:33:48.438. If you search through the SDL trace on the same server for the same timestamp, you see the following message:

```
19:33:48.438 |002 | SdlSig-I  | CcUpdateRegistration
  | hold_idle              | LineControl(2,100,34,233)
  | StationCdpc(1,100,88,431)   | (1,100,90,1)
```

The exact messages in the line of SDL trace are not important. The significant part is the third section of the trace that says **SdlSig-I**. This means that this CallManager server received an inbound message on an SDL link from another server in the cluster. The **002** tells you that this server has a node ID of 002. If you remember from Chapter 3, the first of the four numbers shown in parenthesis after each process name is the node ID as well. In this case this piece of trace is showing you that a StationCdpc process on node 1 sent a message to a LineControl process on node 2. Do not be particularly concerned about what that means. All you need to know is that something on node 1 sent a message to something on node 2.

You know that the node you are looking at is node 2 because of the 002 in the trace, so now you need to identify which node in the cluster is node 1 so you can look at the trace on that server. It is times like this that you want to be sure that you have proper time synchronization between servers in the cluster. Although the messages do not have identical timestamps down to the millisecond because there is some delay in sending the message across the network, the timestamps will be very close if you are using NTP as explained in Chapter 3.

To determine which server in the cluster has a node ID of 1, you can look in CallManager Administration. Open the Cisco CallManager Configuration page in CallManager Administration (**System > Cisco CallManager**) and select each server in the cluster one at a time. Near the top of the page you will see a line that indicates the node ID. For node ID 1, the page shows **CTI ID: 1**. Figure 9-7 shows an example.

Figure 9-7 *Node ID on the Cisco CallManager Configuration Page*

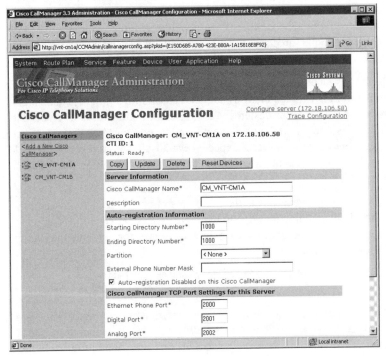

Now you know that the server with IP address 172.18.106.58 sent the message to the server you were originally looking at. If you go to that server, you should be able to find a nearly identical SDL trace message at a very similar timestamp. You go to that server and find this message:

```
19:33:48.424 |001 | SdlSig-O | CcUpdateRegistration
   | NotApplicable_RemoteSignal | LineControl(2,100,34,233)
   | StationCdpc(1,100,88,431)    | (1,100,90,1)
```

Notice the message is nearly identical except in this case the message is an outbound signal as shown by the **SdlSig-O** message. Now all you have to do is look at timestamp 19:33:48.424 in the CCM trace file on node 1 to find what caused this message to be sent in the first place.

You search the CCM trace that matches the same time frame for timestamp 19:33:48.424 and find:

```
StationInit: 000012618 SoftKeyEvent softKeyEvent=10 lineInstance=1 callReference
  =33560019.
```

If you refer back to Table 9-8, softKeyEvent=10 is the Resume soft key. The mystery is solved. It turns out that all along there has been another phone with a shared line appearance of the original holding party registered to a different CallManager in the cluster. After a phone registered to node 2 put the call on hold, the phone registered to node 1 retrieved it. You saw the phones registered to node 2 mysteriously show the line was in use again without any indication as to why it was occurring. That was because the call was resumed from a IP phone registered to a different CallManager server in the cluster.

This kind of behavior can occur for any event between two devices registered to different servers in the cluster. For this reason, it is important to always collect trace files from all nodes in the cluster when you experience a problem. You might later analyze the files and determine that additional information is needed from another server in the cluster, only to find out that the additional trace files have been overwritten by newer trace files.

Once you understand how to troubleshoot a call hold and resume, you can look at other features such as call transfer, call pickup, and park.

Call Transfer

A call transfer is a multiple step process. First a call is established. This can be an inbound or outbound call. For a transfer to occur, the call must be in the connected state.

Once you have an active call, a call transfer is initiated by pressing the transfer soft key on an IP phone or invoking the transfer feature code on a Skinny gateway such as the VG248. You see the following message in the CCM trace indicating the transfer soft key was pressed:

```
StationInit: 000001140 SoftKeyEvent softKeyEvent=4 lineInstance=1 callReference
  =33560831.
```

If you refer back to Table 9-8, softKeyEvent=4 means the transfer soft key. When transfer is invoked, the party being transferred is put on hold the same way you saw in the previous section. At this point the call is very similar to a call placed on hold, followed by a new call instance on the same line. Now the transferring IP phone has a call on hold and is receiving dial tone to call a new number, so the transferring phone makes a call to the transfer destination. This call can be to another phone, out through a gateway, to an IVR application, to voice mail, and so on. Troubleshoot this piece of the call as you would troubleshoot any other outbound call. Follow the methodology outlined in Table 9-7. Once a call is in the call proceeding state (in other words, the call has been routed to the destination and if the call is going out the PSTN, the PSTN has indicated that it is routing the call), the transfer soft key reappears on the IP phone that is transferring the call. If the transfer soft key is pressed before the second call is connected, a blind transfer is performed. This means that the transferring party never talks with the party to which the call is being transferred.

Remember that up to this point, the caller being transferred is still waiting on hold and hearing either music on hold or tone on hold. If a blind transfer is performed, CallManager takes the call off hold and plays ringback tone to the party being transferred. If the party being transferred that was on hold is connected through an H.323 gateway or an intercluster trunk, the user may not hear ringback. If this is the case, you must ensure two conditions are met to resolve it. If the call is through a Cisco IOS gateway using the H.323 protocol, you must be running an IOS version later than 12.2(5). For best performance you should be running 12.2(8)T5 or later. You must also enable the **ToSendH225UserInfoMsg** CallManager service parameter in CallManager Administration (**Service > Service Parameter**). In some versions of CallManager, this parameter must be set to **True**. In other versions this parameter is a numeric value. You should set it to **2** if you are using 12.2(8)T5 or later because this also gives you the ability to generate tone on hold using a Cisco IOS gateway. If you are using an IOS version prior to 12.2(8)T5, set the value to **1**.

For example, here you see the IP phone user press the transfer soft key for a second time to perform the blind transfer:

```
StationInit: 000001140 SoftKeyEvent softKeyEvent=4 lineInstance=1
    callReference=33560833
```

Notice the call reference for this call is different than the first time. This is because this is the call reference for the second call made to the transfer destination. After the transfer soft key is pressed the second time, you should see a message indicating the transfer is being performed:

```
TransferManager: SsInfoInd : complete transfer,
    TransferringSecondarSsParty=33560833,
    TransferringPartyDslAddr (0,0,2120749740,0),
    TransferringPartyPID (2,34,233),
    TransferDestinationSsParty=33560834,
    TransferDestinationDslAddr (0,0,1952977580,0),
    TransferDesinatonPID (2,34,236)
```

Notice the field that says **TransferDestinationSsParty**. This refers to the call reference for the transfer destination. A call reference in CallManager is used to describe one party in a call, so every call has two call references. When the initial call between two IP phones was set up, the phone that pressed transfer had a call reference of **33560831** for the first call and **33560833** for the second call to the transfer destination. The transfer destination had a call reference of **33560834**. When the transfer is completed, the two call references for the IP phone performing the transfer (**33560831** and **33560833**) operation are eliminated and the original call reference for the party being transferred is now associated to the new call reference for the transfer destination.

You may encounter a scenario where a user states he tried to transfer a call and the IP phone displayed a message stating "That key is not active here" when he pressed the transfer soft key. When a user transfers a phone call, CallManager places the current call on hold and allows the user to dial a number to call the transfer destination. All releases of CallManager up to Release 3.3 support up to two calls on any given line appearance. If a user has a call on a line appearance and call waiting is enabled on that line, a second call can arrive on the same line. Once two calls are active on a single line, you cannot transfer either of the two calls because there is no way to create a third call on that line appearance to call the transfer destination.

If you have users who need to be able to transfer inbound calls that arrive while they are on the phone with another caller, disable call waiting on the user's lines and create multiple line appearances that have call forward busy configured to hunt from one line to the next. This way, if a call is active on the first line on the phone and a second call arrives, it arrives on the second line appearance. When the call on the second line appearance is answered, there is still availability for a second call on that line appearance if the call needs to be transferred.

Call Park

Parking a call is really nothing more than a special case of putting a call on hold. The biggest difference between park and a call on hold is that a parked call gets assigned a call park number for the time the call is parked. The assignment of this number and the partition and calling search space implications can sometimes cause confusion, leading to the inability to park a call or retrieve a call that has been parked.

First, in order for call park to function, you must have one or more call park numbers defined in CallManager Administration. Call park numbers are added on the Call Park Configuration page in CallManager Administration (**Feature > Call Park**). A call park number can accept a range by using wildcards. For example, 1688X assigns the range of numbers 16880 through 16889 as call park numbers.

Note that when you create a call park number range you must assign a Cisco CallManager to that number range. This is a common source of configuration problems. When you select a particular CallManager server for a call park range, only calls that are under the control of that server can be parked using that range of numbers. This means that if you have six CallManager nodes in your cluster performing call processing, you must have at least six call park ranges defined—one for each CallManager server in the cluster. If you fail to assign a call park range to a particular server in the cluster, some phones might not be able park a call. Remember to add call park number ranges to all servers in the cluster, including servers that only handle calls when another server in the cluster fails. The majority of call park problems are caused by not having park numbers defined for all the servers in the cluster.

The second biggest cause for call park problems is a misconfiguration of the partition for the call park numbers. CallManager follows a few basic rules when dealing with partitions and call park.

When a user presses the **Park** soft key on their IP phone, CallManager searches for the first available park number assigned to the server on which the call is being processed. Once a park number is found, CallManager compares the calling search space on the device or line of the device that pressed the **Park** soft key to make sure the calling search space includes the partition of the park number that was selected. If the park number is not in the phone's calling search space, CallManager attempts to locate another available park number and repeats this process until it either finds a park number that is in a partition that is also part of the parking party's calling search space or until it runs out of park numbers and fails to park the call.

Many administrators are under the impression that the partition associated with the line that is used to park the call is somehow related to which partition is chosen to park the call. This is not the case. As long as the calling search space on the phone can access the partition the call park number is in, the phone can park the call at that number.

Once a call has been parked, any device that wants to be able to retrieve the parked call must have a calling search space that has access to the partition at which the call was parked.

A call park begins with the following Skinny message:

```
StationInit: 000001140 SoftKeyEvent softKeyEvent=14 lineInstance=1
   callReference=33560029.
```

You can see the IP phone with TCP handle **000001140** pressed soft key 14, which according to Table 9-8 is the **Park** soft key. Example 9-19 shows the call park manager allocate a call park number for the call. Notice that the call is parked on CallManager node 2. Various messages have been omitted from the trace to make reading easier.

Example 9-19 *CCM Trace Showing the Call Park Manager Allocating a Park Number*

```
CallParkManager - wait_SsInfoInd - Park Request. Party= 20015DD, Node= 2
CallPark Instance= 1 - Started
CallPark  - await_call_park_initiation_SsInfoInd - Initiating Call Park.
  ParkingParty= 20015DD, on Node= 2, Party to be Parked= 20015DC on Node= 2
CallPark - get_primary_call_info_SsCallInfoRes - Call Parked. ParkedParty= 20015DC
  NodeId= 2, State= 5
CallParkDcl - allocateParkCode - ParkCode= Line1 16890
CallPark  - get_primary_call_info_SsCallInfoRes - Parking call for Party= 20015DC
  on ParkCode= Line1 16890
CallPark - splitting_primary_call_SsSplitRes - Call parked - Reversion Timer set.
  Party= 20015DC Parked on Line1 16890
```

In Example 9-19 you can see the call gets parked at park number **16890** in the **Line1** partition. Example 9-20 shows how CallManager sends a message to the IP phone to show the park number on the IP phone display and sets the call state back to 2, which means on-hook.

Example 9-20 *CCM Trace Showing the Call Park Information Displayed on an IP Phone*

```
StationD:    000001140 DisplayNotify timeOutValue=10 notify='_! 16890'
  content='Parked At 16890' ver=0x80000004.
StationD:    000001140 CallState callState=2 lineInstance=1 callReference=33560029
```

Once a call is parked, the process of retrieving the call is identical to troubleshooting any other call because a call park retrieval is just a call to the park number. You must ensure that all call routing rules are adhered to, such as closest-match routing, partitions, and calling search spaces.

Call Pickup

Call pickup allows an IP phone to remotely redirect a call that is ringing on one IP phone to another IP phone so another party can answer it. For example, if a call comes in for extension 1000, extension 2000 can invoke the pickup feature to redirect the call to extension 2000 and answer the call for extension 1000.

There are two types of call pickup; however, both are really the same from a troubleshooting perspective. The first is called group call pickup or just group pickup. With group pickup, you place a group of phones into a pickup group. This pickup group is assigned a DN that is in a partition, just like any other DN in CallManager. When a call is ringing on any of the IP phones in that pickup group, another IP phone configured for call pickup can go off-hook and press the **GPickUp** soft key followed by the group pickup number, provided that the phone's calling search space allows access to the partition of the ringing phone's pickup number. The ringing call is redirected to the call that invoked the group pickup feature.

Call pickup works the same way as group pickup with one small exception. When a call is ringing on an IP phone in the pickup group, the phone that wants to retrieve the ringing call goes off-hook and presses the **PickUp** soft key. The pickup soft key is a shortcut for a group pickup using the pickup group number configured on the phone performing the pickup operation.

To help explain this better, take, for example, three IP phones with extension numbers 1000, 1001, and 1002. Extensions 1000 and 1001 are in pickup group 2000. Extension 1002 is in pickup group 3000. Assume a call comes in from the PSTN to ring extension 1000 (which is in pickup group 2000). If extension 1001 (also in pickup group 2000) goes off-hook and presses the **PickUp** soft key, the call is redirected from extension 1000 to extension 1001 because they are both in the same pickup group. If you take the same example where a call is coming into extension 1000 (which is in pickup group 2000), but you want to retrieve it from extension 1002 (which is in pickup group 3000), you must press the **GPickUp** soft key and enter the pickup group you want to retrieve the call from, in this case 2000.

Remember pickup group numbers are assigned a partition, so you can use partitions and calling search spaces to restrict access to specific pickup groups. If you have several groups of phones with pickup groups configured, you should configure each group in a different partition and use calling search spaces to allow or deny access to the pickup group as needed. You don't want anyone who knows a pickup group number to be able to answer another group's phone calls unless they have a reason to do so.

One important point to note is that any phone you want to be able to pick up a call from another phone must have a pickup group configured on the line you want to use to invoke the pickup feature. This is a very common reason for pickup not working. The CCM traces are very clear when this is the problem. Example 9-21 shows an IP phone attempting to invoke the group pickup feature without having a pickup group assigned. Refer to Table 9-8 to determine that softKeyEvent=18 is the group pickup soft key.

Example 9-21 *CCM Trace Showing a Phone Attempting to Invoke the Group Pickup Feature*

```
StationInit: 000002211 SoftKeyEvent softKeyEvent=18 lineInstance=1
  callReference=33561511.
Digit analysis: match(fqcn="9199915644", cn="15644",
  pss="PA:Line1:Cisco:Local:Long Distance:International", dd="")
Digit analysis: potentialMatches=PotentialMatchesExist
ForwardManager - wait_SsInfoInd - New Call Pickup attempt started.
  SsInfoInd sent to Forwarding. FID= 128, Party= 0x2001BA7, CallKey= 0x2C1
ForwardManager - addActiveCallTableEntry - Added entry for InterceptKey= 0x0,
  Party= 0x2001BA7 CallKey= 0x2C1
ForwardManager - sendCallInfoReq   - Sent to OrigParty= 0x2001BA7, CallKey= 0x2C1
Forwarding::awaitForwardInitiation_SsInfoInd
Forwarding - awaitForwardInitiation_SsInfoInd - Call Pickup Activated.
  CallKey= 0x2C1
ForwardManager - findInterceptTableEntry - Found Intercept table entry for
  dn= 15644:Line1, InterceptKey= 0x211
ForwardManager - wait_SsCallInfoRes - Call Terminated - Pickup requestor
  not in pickup group. Play re-order. OrigParty= 0x2001BA7, CallKey= 0x2C1
StationD:     000002211 StartTone tone=37(ReorderTone), direction=0.
```

Remember, pickup group numbers are in a partition, so if IP phone A attempts to invoke the pickup feature but does not have a calling search space that can access the pickup number configured on IP phone B, then IP phone A cannot pickup a call coming into the pickup group on IP phone B. Example 9-22 shows a successful group call pickup attempt. First the phone that wants to pick up a call goes off-hook and presses the **GPickUp** soft key and dials the pickup group number, **16702**.

Example 9-22 *CCM Trace Showing a Successful Group Call Pickup*

```
StationInit: 000002211 SoftKeyEvent softKeyEvent=18 lineInstance=1
  callReference=33561527.
Digit analysis: match(fqcn="9199915644", cn="15644",
  pss="PA:Line1:Cisco:Local:Long Distance:International", dd="")
Digit analysis: potentialMatches=PotentialMatchesExist
ForwardManager - wait_SsInfoInd - New Call Pickup attempt started.
  SsInfoInd sent to Forwarding. FID= 128, Party= 0x2001BB7, CallKey= 0x2C3
Forwarding - awaitForwardInitiation_SsInfoInd - Call Pickup Activated.
  CallKey= 0x2C3
ForwardManager - findInterceptTableEntry - Found Intercept table entry
  for dn= 15644:Line1, InterceptKey= 0x215
Forwarding - awaitingCallResponse_SsCallInfoRes  - Requesting Group Number.
  Party= 0x2001BB7 CallKey= 0x2C3
```

Example 9-22 *CCM Trace Showing a Successful Group Call Pickup (Continued)*

```
StationD:     000002211 StartTone tone=49(ZipZip), direction=0.
StationD:     000002211 SetLamp stimulus=128(undefined) stimulusInstance=1
  lampMode=4(LampFlash).
StationD:     000002211 DisplayPromptStatus timeOutValue=10 promptStatus='_ '
  content='Enter Number' lineInstance=1 callReference=33561527 ver=0x80000004.
StationInit: 000002211 KeypadButton kpButton=1.
StationD:     000002211 StopTone.
Digit analysis: match(fqcn="9199915644", cn="15644",
  pss="PA:Line1:Cisco:Local:Long Distance:International", dd="1")
Digit analysis: potentialMatches=PotentialMatchesExist
StationInit: 000002211 KeypadButton kpButton=6.
Digit analysis: match(fqcn="9199915644", cn="15644",
  pss="PA:Line1:Cisco:Local:Long Distance:International", dd="16")
Digit analysis: potentialMatches=PotentialMatchesExist
StationInit: 000002211 KeypadButton kpButton=7.
Digit analysis: match(fqcn="9199915644", cn="15644",
  pss="PA:Line1:Cisco:Local:Long Distance:International", dd="167")
Digit analysis: potentialMatches=PotentialMatchesExist
StationInit: 000002211 KeypadButton kpButton=0.
Digit analysis: match(fqcn="9199915644", cn="15644",
  pss="PA:Line1:Cisco:Local:Long Distance:International", dd="1670")
Digit analysis: potentialMatches=PotentialMatchesExist
StationInit: 000002211 KeypadButton kpButton=2.
Digit analysis: match(fqcn="9199915644", cn="15644",
  pss="PA:Line1:Cisco:Local:Long Distance:International", dd="16702")
```

Example 9-23 shows a digit analysis match for DN 16702. Notice the **DialingPattern** field is blank because this is not a normal DN; it is a DN corresponding to a feature.

Example 9-23 *Digit Analysis Results Showing a Match for the Pickup Group*

```
Digit analysis: analysis results
|PretransformCallingPartyNumber=15644
|CallingPartyNumber=15644
|DialingPartition=
|DialingPattern=
|DialingRoutePatternRegularExpression=
|DialingWhere=
|PatternType=Unknown
|PotentialMatches=NoPotentialMatchesExist
|DialingSdlProcessId=(0,0,0)
|PretransformDigitString=16702
|PretransformTagsList=
|PretransformPositionalMatchList=
|CollectedDigits=
|UnconsumedDigits=
|TagsList=
|PositionalMatchList=
|VoiceMailbox=
|VoiceMailCallingSearchSpace=
|VoiceMailPilotNumber=
```

continues

Example 9-23 *Digit Analysis Results Showing a Match for the Pickup Group (Continued)*

```
 |DisplayName=
 |RouteBlockFlag=BlockThisPattern
 |InterceptPartition=Line1
 |InterceptPattern=16702
 |InterceptWhere=
 |InterceptSdlProcessId=(2,25,1)
 |InterceptSsType=33554436
 |InterceptSsKey=65528
 |WithTags=
 |WithValues=
 |CgpnPresentation=NotSelected
 |CallManagerDeviceType=NoDeviceType
```

After digit analysis is complete, CallManager attempts the call pickup as shown in Example 9-24.

Example 9-24 *CallManager Attempts to Perform the Call Pickup Operation*

```
 Forwarding - awaitingCallResponse_SsOverlapRes  - Attempting call pickup.
   CallKey= 0x2C3 Forwarding::beginCallPickup
 Forwarding - beginCallPickup - Clearing requestors call. Party= 0x2001BB7,
   CallKey= 707
```

At this point the IP phone attempting to pick up the call momentarily goes back on-hook to wait for CallManager to redirect the call. Notice the call state is set to on-hook. Example 9-25 shows the IP phone going back into an idle state.

Example 9-25 *Phone Returns to an Idle State to Wait for the Call to Be Redirected*

```
 StationD:     000002211 CallState callState=2 lineInstance=1 callReference=33561527
 StationD:     000002211 SelectSoftKeys instance=0 reference=0 softKeySetIndex=0
   validKeyMask=-1.
 StationD:     000002211 DisplayPromptStatus timeOutValue=0 promptStatus='_$'
   content='You have a voice mail' lineInstance=0 callReference=0 ver=0x80000004.
 StationD:     000002211 ActivateCallPlane lineInstance=0.
 StationD:     000002211 SetLamp stimulus=9(Line) stimulusInstance=1
 lampMode=1(LampOff).
 StationD:     000002211 DefineTimeDate timeDateInfo=? systemTime=1031194413.
 StationD:     000002211 StopTone.
```

Finally, Example 9-26 shows CallManager redirecting the call to the IP phone that performed the pickup operation. Notice a digit analysis match is performed just as if the call had been forwarded to extension 15644, the IP phone that performed the pickup operation.

Example 9-26 *CallManager Completes the Pickup Operation by Redirecting the Original Call*

```
ForwardManager - removeCallPickupEntry - Group= 16702:Line1
ForwardManager - wait_SsDataInd - BASIC_CALL_RELEASE - mCallPickupTable -
  Removed Entry for Group= 16702:Line1, Key= 0x2C3, Party= 0x2001BB7
Forwarding::completeCallPickup
Forwarding::getCallPickupEntry
Forwarding - getCallPickupEntry - Returned Call Pickup entry for group= 16702:Line1
Forwarding::sendRedirectCallReq
Forwarding - sendRedirectCallReq Call Pickup -Redirected Party= 0x2001BB5,
  to Dn= 15644 CSS= Line1, CallKey= 0x2C2
Forwarding - completeCallPickup - Call entry found, Redirecting call with
  Party= 0x2001BB5, to requestor. CallKey= 706
Digit analysis: match(fqcn="", cn="9195552392", pss="IPMA:PA:Line1", dd="")
Digit analysis: potentialMatches=PotentialMatchesExist
Digit analysis: match(fqcn="", cn="9195552392", pss="Line1", dd="15644")
Digit analysis: analysis results
|PretransformCallingPartyNumber=9195552392
|CallingPartyNumber=9195552392
|DialingPartition=Line1
|DialingPattern=15644
|DialingRoutePatternRegularExpression=(15644)
|DialingWhere=
|PatternType=Enterprise
|PotentialMatches=NoPotentialMatchesExist
|DialingSdlProcessId=(2,34,233)
|PretransformDigitString=15644
|PretransformTagsList=SUBSCRIBER
|PretransformPositionalMatchList=15644
|CollectedDigits=15644
|UnconsumedDigits=
|TagsList=SUBSCRIBER
|PositionalMatchList=15644
|VoiceMailbox=15644
|VoiceMailCallingSearchSpace=IPMA:PA:Line1
|VoiceMailPilotNumber=15678
|DisplayName=Paul Giralt
|RouteBlockFlag=RouteThisPattern
|InterceptPartition=Line1
|InterceptPattern=15644
|InterceptWhere=
|InterceptSdlProcessId=(2,25,1)
|InterceptSsType=33554436
|InterceptSsKey=533
|WithTags=
|WithValues=
|CgpnPresentation=NotSelected
|CallManagerDeviceType=UserDevice
Forwarding - awaitingCallResponse_SsInterceptInd - Forwarded call Extended,
  or Call Pickup Call Extended. Party= 0x2001BB5, CallKey= 0x2C2
StationD:    000002211 CallState callState=4 lineInstance=1 callReference=33561529
StationD:    000002211 SetLamp stimulus=9(Line) stimulusInstance=1
  lampMode=5(LampBlink).
StationD:    000002211 SetRinger ringMode=3(OutsideRing).
```

continues

Example 9-26 *CallManager Completes the Pickup Operation by Redirecting the Original Call (Continued)*

```
StationD:     000002211 DisplayNotify timeOutValue=10 notify='__9195552392'
  content='From 9195552392' ver=0x80000004.
StationD:     000002211 DisplayPromptStatus timeOutValue=0
  promptStatus='__9195552392' content='From 9195552392' lineInstance=1
  callReference=33561529 ver=0x80000004.
```

At this point extension 15644 is ringing just as if the original caller from the PSTN had called 15644 directly. Now extension 15644 can answer the call normally or let the call forward to the call forward no answer destination.

Getting the Dialing Forest Traces

The entire dial plan can be dumped into the CCM traces for analysis. You can use a dialing forest trace to help troubleshoot many call routing problems.

For example, suppose you have a problem with delayed outside dial tone. Using a dialing forest trace, you can search through the trace files for all patterns that start with 9. Because the entire dial plan is in text format, this is easy to do. Table 9-10 shows the two dialing forest options.

Table 9-10 *Dialing Forest Options*

Sequence on IP Phone	Description
**##*2	Toggles terse and verbose made on and off
**##*4	Dumps the dial plan into the CCM trace

The dialing forest trace dump occurs when you go off-hook on an IP phone and dial one of the keypad sequences shown in Table 9-10 on an IP phone.

Example 9-27 demonstrates the results of dumping the dial plan into the CCM trace files in terse mode. Terse mode shows only the route pattern while verbose mode, shown later, includes additional details such as the route filter clause, tag list, network location, and so on. Notice that all the patterns are listed within each partition. The P_Access partition contains the 9.@ pattern. Notice you do not see the 9.@ pattern in the dialing forest, but rather you see each individual pattern that has been added to digit analysis after applying any route filters.

Also notice there are several patterns that have the word (Intercept) after the DN. This corresponds to patterns that have some kind of forwarding configured on them (CFA, CFNA, CFB, or CFF) or patterns that correspond to a feature like a call park number.

Example 9-27 *Sample Trace File When Dial Plans Are Dumped in Terse Mode*

```
02/26/2002 13:17:11.036 Cisco CallManager | | DialingForest=
{
|DigitForest=Dialing
 {
  |Partition=
  |Patterns=
  {
  |(**##*1)
  |(**##*2)
  |(**##*3)
  |(**##*4)
  |(2004) (Intercept)
  |(2000)
  |(2003)
  |(2002)
  |(2001)
  |(201X)
  |(2101)
  |(2102)
  |(5001) (Intercept)
  |(5002) (Intercept)
  |(5000) (Intercept)
  |(556677)
  |(5)(XXXX)
  |(99999) (Intercept)
  |(6667) (Intercept)
  |(6666) (Intercept)
  |(667788)
  |(b00110502009)
  |(b00110502010)
  |(b00110502011)
  |(b00110502012)
  |(b00110502013)
  |(b00110502014)
  |(b00110502015)
  |(b00110502016)
  |(3005)
  |(3004)
  |(3003)
  |(3002)
  |(3001)
  |(3009)
  |(3008)
  |(3000)
  |(3007)
  |(3006)
  |(3010)
  |(3666)
  }
 }
```

continues

Example 9-27 *Sample Trace File When Dial Plans Are Dumped in Terse Mode (Continued)*

```
{
|Partition=P_Access
|Patterns=
{
 |(9)(00)
 |(9)(0)([2-9][02-9]X)(XXXX)
 |(9)(0)([2-9][02-9]X)([2-9]XX)(XXXX)
 |(9)(0)([2-9]X[02-9])(XXXX)
 |(9)(0)([2-9]X[02-9])([2-9]XX)(XXXX)
 |(9)(01)(0)
 |(9)(01)(881)(X)(X+)(#)
 |(9)(01)(881)(X)(X+)
 |(9)(01)(88[02-9])(X+)(#)
 |(9)(01)(88[02-9])(X+)
 |(9)(01)(8[1246])(X+)(#)
 |(9)(01)(8[1246])(X+)
 |(9)(01)(8[03579]X)(X+)(#)
 |(9)(01)(8[03579]X)(X+)
 |(9)(01)(1)(881)(X)(X+)(#)
 |(9)(01)(1)(881)(X)(X+)
 |(9)(01)(1)(88[02-9])(X+)(#)
 |(9)(01)(1)(88[02-9])(X+)
 |(9)(01)(1)(8[1246])(X+)(#)
 |(9)(01)(1)(8[1246])(X+)
 |(9)(01)(1)(8[03579]X)(X+)(#)
 |(9)(01)(1)(8[03579]X)(X+)
 |(9)(01)(1)(2[07])(X+)(#)
 |(9)(01)(1)(2[07])(X+)
 |(9)(01)(1)(2[1-689]X)(X+)(#)
 |(9)(01)(1)(2[1-689]X)(X+)
 |(9)(01)(1)(3[0-469])(X+)(#)
 |(9)(01)(1)(3[0-469])(X+)
 |(9)(01)(1)(3[578]X)(X+)(#)
 |(9)(01)(1)(3[578]X)(X+)
 |(9)(01)(1)(4[013-9])(X+)(#)
 |(9)(01)(1)(4[013-9])(X+)
 |(9)(01)(1)(42X)(X+)(#)
 |(9)(01)(1)(42X)(X+)
 |(9)(01)(1)(5[1-8])(X+)(#)
 |(9)(01)(1)(5[1-8])(X+)
 |(9)(01)(1)(5[09]X)(X+)(#)
 |(9)(01)(1)(5[09]X)(X+)
 |(9)(01)(1)(6[0-6])(X+)(#)
 |(9)(01)(1)(6[0-6])(X+)
 |(9)(01)(1)(6[7-9]X)(X+)(#)
 |(9)(01)(1)(6[7-9]X)(X+)
 |(9)(01)(1)(7)(X+)(#)
 |(9)(01)(1)(7)(X+)
 |(9)(01)(1)(9[0-58])(X+)(#)
 |(9)(01)(1)(9[0-58])(X+)
 |(9)(01)(1)(9[679]X)(X+)(#)
 |(9)(01)(1)(9[679]X)(X+)
```

Example 9-27 *Sample Trace File When Dial Plans Are Dumped in Terse Mode (Continued)*

```
|(9)(01)(2[07])(X+)(#)
|(9)(01)(2[07])(X+)
|(9)(01)(2[1-689]X)(X+)(#)
|(9)(01)(2[1-689]X)(X+)
|(9)(01)(3[0-469])(X+)(#)
|(9)(01)(3[0-469])(X+)
|(9)(01)(3[578]X)(X+)(#)
|(9)(01)(3[578]X)(X+)
|(9)(01)(4[013-9])(X+)(#)
|(9)(01)(4[013-9])(X+)
|(9)(01)(42X)(X+)(#)
|(9)(01)(42X)(X+)
|(9)(01)(5[1-8])(X+)(#)
|(9)(01)(5[1-8])(X+)
|(9)(01)(5[09]X)(X+)(#)
|(9)(01)(5[09]X)(X+)
|(9)(01)(6[0-6])(X+)(#)
|(9)(01)(6[0-6])(X+)
|(9)(01)(6[7-9]X)(X+)(#)
|(9)(01)(6[7-9]X)(X+)
|(9)(01)(7)(X+)(#)
|(9)(01)(7)(X+)
|(9)(01)(9[0-58])(X+)(#)
|(9)(01)(9[0-58])(X+)
|(9)(01)(9[679]X)(X+)(#)
|(9)(01)(9[679]X)(X+)
|(9)(0)
|(9)(101)(XXXX)(0)([2-9][02-9]X)(XXXX)
|(9)(101)(XXXX)(0)([2-9][02-9]X)([2-9]XX)(XXXX)
|(9)(101)(XXXX)(0)([2-9]X[02-9])(XXXX)
|(9)(101)(XXXX)(0)([2-9]X[02-9])([2-9]XX)(XXXX)
|(9)(101)(XXXX)(01)(881)(X)(X+)(#)
|(9)(101)(XXXX)(01)(881)(X)(X+)
|(9)(101)(XXXX)(01)(88[02-9])(X+)(#)
|(9)(101)(XXXX)(01)(88[02-9])(X+)
|(9)(101)(XXXX)(01)(8[1246])(X+)(#)
|(9)(101)(XXXX)(01)(8[1246])(X+)
|(9)(101)(XXXX)(01)(8[03579]X)(X+)(#)
|(9)(101)(XXXX)(01)(8[03579]X)(X+)
|(9)(101)(XXXX)(01)(1)(881)(X)(X+)(#)
|(9)(101)(XXXX)(01)(1)(881)(X)(X+)
|(9)(101)(XXXX)(01)(1)(88[02-9])(X+)(#)
|(9)(101)(XXXX)(01)(1)(88[02-9])(X+)
|(9)(101)(XXXX)(01)(1)(8[1246])(X+)(#)
|(9)(101)(XXXX)(01)(1)(8[1246])(X+)
|(9)(101)(XXXX)(01)(1)(8[03579]X)(X+)(#)
|(9)(101)(XXXX)(01)(1)(8[03579]X)(X+)
|(9)(101)(XXXX)(01)(1)(2[07])(X+)(#)
|(9)(101)(XXXX)(01)(1)(2[07])(X+)
|(9)(101)(XXXX)(01)(1)(2[1-689]X)(X+)(#)
|(9)(101)(XXXX)(01)(1)(2[1-689]X)(X+)
```

continues

Example 9-27 *Sample Trace File When Dial Plans Are Dumped in Terse Mode (Continued)*

```
| (9)(101)(XXXX)(01)(1)(3[0-469])(X+)(#)
| (9)(101)(XXXX)(01)(1)(3[0-469])(X+)
| (9)(101)(XXXX)(01)(1)(3[578]X)(X+)(#)
| (9)(101)(XXXX)(01)(1)(3[578]X)(X+)
| (9)(101)(XXXX)(01)(1)(4[013-9])(X+)(#)
| (9)(101)(XXXX)(01)(1)(4[013-9])(X+)
| (9)(101)(XXXX)(01)(1)(42X)(X+)(#)
| (9)(101)(XXXX)(01)(1)(42X)(X+)
| (9)(101)(XXXX)(01)(1)(5[1-8])(X+)(#)
| (9)(101)(XXXX)(01)(1)(5[1-8])(X+)
| (9)(101)(XXXX)(01)(1)(5[09]X)(X+)(#)
| (9)(101)(XXXX)(01)(1)(5[09]X)(X+)
| (9)(101)(XXXX)(01)(1)(6[0-6])(X+)(#)
| (9)(101)(XXXX)(01)(1)(6[0-6])(X+)
| (9)(101)(XXXX)(01)(1)(6[7-9]X)(X+)(#)
| (9)(101)(XXXX)(01)(1)(6[7-9]X)(X+)
| (9)(101)(XXXX)(01)(1)(7)(X+)(#)
| (9)(101)(XXXX)(01)(1)(7)(X+)
| (9)(101)(XXXX)(01)(1)(9[0-58])(X+)(#)
| (9)(101)(XXXX)(01)(1)(9[0-58])(X+)
| (9)(101)(XXXX)(01)(1)(9[679]X)(X+)(#)
| (9)(101)(XXXX)(01)(1)(9[679]X)(X+)
| (9)(101)(XXXX)(01)(2[07])(X+)(#)
| (9)(101)(XXXX)(01)(2[07])(X+)
| (9)(101)(XXXX)(01)(2[1-689]X)(X+)(#)
| (9)(101)(XXXX)(01)(2[1-689]X)(X+)
| (9)(101)(XXXX)(01)(3[0-469])(X+)(#)
| (9)(101)(XXXX)(01)(3[0-469])(X+)
| (9)(101)(XXXX)(01)(3[578]X)(X+)(#)
| (9)(101)(XXXX)(01)(3[578]X)(X+)
| (9)(101)(XXXX)(01)(4[013-9])(X+)(#)
| (9)(101)(XXXX)(01)(4[013-9])(X+)
| (9)(101)(XXXX)(01)(42X)(X+)(#)
| (9)(101)(XXXX)(01)(42X)(X+)
| (9)(101)(XXXX)(01)(5[1-8])(X+)(#)
| (9)(101)(XXXX)(01)(5[1-8])(X+)
| (9)(101)(XXXX)(01)(5[09]X)(X+)(#)
| (9)(101)(XXXX)(01)(5[09]X)(X+)
| (9)(101)(XXXX)(01)(6[0-6])(X+)(#)
| (9)(101)(XXXX)(01)(6[0-6])(X+)
| (9)(101)(XXXX)(01)(6[7-9]X)(X+)(#)
| (9)(101)(XXXX)(01)(6[7-9]X)(X+)
| (9)(101)(XXXX)(01)(7)(X+)(#)
| (9)(101)(XXXX)(01)(7)(X+)
| (9)(101)(XXXX)(01)(9[0-58])(X+)(#)
| (9)(101)(XXXX)(01)(9[0-58])(X+)
| (9)(101)(XXXX)(01)(9[679]X)(X+)(#)
| (9)(101)(XXXX)(01)(9[679]X)(X+)
| (9)(101)(XXXX)(1)([2-9][02-9]X)(XXXX)
| (9)(101)(XXXX)(1)([2-9][02-9]X)([2-9]XX)(XXXX)
| (9)(101)(XXXX)(1)([2-9]X[02-9])(XXXX)
| (9)(101)(XXXX)(1)([2-9]X[02-9])([2-9]XX)(XXXX)
```

Example 9-27 *Sample Trace File When Dial Plans Are Dumped in Terse Mode (Continued)*

```
 |(9)(101)(XXXX)([2-9]11)
 |(9)(101)(XXXX)([2-9][02-9]X)(XXXX)
 |(9)(101)(XXXX)([2-9]X[02-9])(XXXX)
 |(9)(1)([2-9]11)
 |(9)(1)([2-9][02-9]X)(XXXX)
 |(9)(1)([2-9][02-9]X)([2-9]XX)(XXXX)
 |(9)(1)([2-9]X[02-9])(XXXX)
 |(9)(1)([2-9]X[02-9])([2-9]XX)(XXXX)
 |(9)([2-9]11)
 |(9)([2-9][02-9]X)(XXXX)
 |(9)([2-9]X[02-9])(XXXX)
}
```

When set to verbose mode, you get considerably more information for each entry. Example 9-28 shows a small piece of a verbose dialing forest. You can see there are two of the many patterns added as part of the route pattern **9.@ WHERE (AREA-CODE == 800) OR (AREA-CODE == 888) OR (AREA-CODE == 877) OR (AREA-CODE == 866) OR (AREA-CODE == 855) OR (SERVICE EXISTS)**. You can see not only the patterns, but also the substrings and the tags that are associated with each substring.

Example 9-28 *Sample Trace File When Dial Plans Are Dumped in Verbose Mode*

```
{
<
|RoutePattern=9.@
|WhereClause=(AREA-CODE == 800) OR (AREA-CODE == 888) OR
            (AREA-CODE == 877) OR (AREA-CODE == 866) OR
            (AREA-CODE == 855) OR (SERVICE EXISTS)
|Pattern=(9)(1)(855)([2-9]XX)(XXXX)
|SdlProcessId=(2,84,13)
|TagsList=ACCESS-CODE:LONG-DISTANCE-OPERATOR:AREA-CODE:OFFICE-CODE:SUBSCRIBER
|PatternType=National
|NetworkLocation=OffNet
|UseFullyQualifiedCallingPartyNumberYes
|CgpnPresentation=NotSelected
|CallManagerDeviceType=AccessDevice
>
<
|RoutePattern=9.@
|WhereClause=(AREA-CODE == 800) OR (AREA-CODE == 888) OR
            (AREA-CODE == 877) OR (AREA-CODE == 866) OR
            (AREA-CODE == 855) OR (SERVICE EXISTS)
|Pattern=(9)(1)(855)([2-9]XX)(XXXX)
|SdlProcessId=(2,84,13)
|TagsList=ACCESS-CODE:LONG-DISTANCE-OPERATOR:AREA-CODE:OFFICE-CODE:SUBSCRIBER
|PatternType=National
|NetworkLocation=OffNet
```

continues

Example 9-28 *Sample Trace File When Dial Plans Are Dumped in Verbose Mode (Continued)*

```
 | UseFullyQualifiedCallingPartyNumberYes
 | CgpnPresentation=NotSelected
 | CallManagerDeviceType=AccessDevice
 >
}
```

Best Practices

Call routing is a complex subject. As such, it is difficult to spell out additional best practices that have not already been covered in detail in this chapter. However, one area needs to be discussed.

One call routing problem you do not want to troubleshoot is toll fraud. You do not want to find out after the fact that someone has exploited your system and made fraudulent calls, or toll calls when they should not have been allowed to do so. Therefore, it is a best practice to lock down potential holes that some users might try to exploit.

Toll Fraud Prevention

Toll fraud is a serious issue. The fraudulent use of telecommunications technology can be very expensive for a company, and it is essential that administrators take the necessary precautions to prevent it. This section discusses some basic steps you should take to help prevent toll fraud.

This section is by no means complete and exhaustive. The intent here is to provide some core steps to get you on the way toward securing your system. It is up to you to stay up to date on new fraudulent practices in the telecommunications world so that you can take steps to prevent abuse.

The basic preventive measures covered here are as follows:

- Preventing transfers to an extension that provides out-of-country dialing (such as 9011)
- Using PLAR to control rogue auto-registered IP Phones
- Restricting the Forward All field on IP Phones
- Restricting voice mail systems by using calling search spaces
- Blocking certain area codes

Previous sections have discussed the behavior of calling search spaces. It is always a good idea to assign a calling search space to all your devices and put all dialed patterns in a partition. This way, you ensure that only devices with sufficient access can dial numbers in partitions that can be a potential source of toll fraud.

Preventing Transfers to Extension 9011 or Your Equivalent International Access Code

One common fraudulent abuse is having a caller call someone at a company and ask to be transferred to an extension that is equal to the digits dialed for out-of-country calls, such as 9011 in the U.S. or 900 in Great Britain. By doing this, the original caller is often given access to a line that will allow the caller to complete a call to an international number, all the while causing the international billing to go to the local company rather than the original caller. This scenario is only possible when overlap sending is used on gateways that connect to the PSTN, which is seldom the case in North America. Many European countries, however, use overlap sending for PSTN access.

Make sure that only authorized phones have a calling search space that can see a partition with an international pattern such as **9.011!**. By restricting access to international calling to only authorized phones, you can block this abuse to the general user community.

Any phone that can call international numbers is a phone that someone can call and ask to be "transferred" to 9011. Think carefully about which phones truly need international access. Again, remember that this would only be a problem if overlap sending is being used, but it is important to know about a potential problem such as this.

Using PLAR to Control Rogue Auto-registered IP Phones

Auto-registration allows IP phones not previously entered into the database to automatically register to CallManager. Auto-registration is a convenient feature for system administrators, but the concern is that these phones could be unauthorized for use, and fraudulent calls could be made from them.

You can deal with this situation easily using calling search spaces and partitions. Prevent fraud on auto-registered phones by causing an auto-registered phone to automatically dial a predetermined extension (this is known as PLAR, private line automatic ringdown) such as your telecom help desk or an IVR script that plays a prompt indicating what to do if they need legitimate access using that phone. Using the following steps, an auto-registered IP phone will use PLAR to be automatically routed to the help desk when the receiver is lifted.

Step 1   Create two new partitions called P_AutoPhones and P_PlarAutoPhones by opening the Partition Configuration page in CallManager Administration (**Route Plan > Partition >** *click the link in the upper right to* **Add a New Partition**).

Step 2   Create a calling search space called CSS_AutoPhones by opening the Calling Search Space Configuration page in CallManager Administration (**Route Plan > Calling Search Space >** *click the link in the upper right to* **Add a New Calling Search Space**). Add the P_PlarAutoPhones partition to this calling search space.

Step 3 On the Device Pool Configuration screen, create a new device pool called DP_AutoPhones and set the **Calling Search Space for Auto-Registration** field to CSS_AutoPhones (**System > Device Pool**).

Step 4 This device pool should now be set on the Device Defaults page (**System > Device Defaults**). Set this device pool on all IP phone types listed.

Step 5 On the Cisco CallManager Configuration page (**System > Cisco CallManager**), enter the Starting Directory Number and Ending Directory Number for auto-registration, and then select the **P_AutoPhones** partition.

Step 6 On the Translation Pattern Configuration page (**Route Plan > Translation Pattern >** *click the link in the upper right to* **Add a New Calling Translation Pattern**), leave the **Translation Pattern** field blank, set the partition to **P_PlarAutoPhones**, and set the calling search space to one that has access to the help desk number—for example, CSS_Internal. Also enter your help desk number as the called party transform mask.

What you have done is first tell CallManager that any IP phone that auto-registers is to be given a DN in the P_AutoPhones partition and a calling search space of CSS_PlarAutoPhones. Because there are no calling search spaces configured that have access to the P_AutoPhones partition, no one can call any of the rogue phones. The CSS_PlarAutoPhones calling search space has access to only one partition—the P_PlarAutoPhones partition. The only pattern in that partition is a translation pattern that matches no digits.

This means that when you go off-hook on an unconfigured auto-registered phone, the call immediately matches the translation pattern and dials the help desk number via the calling search space you have configured. Auto-registered phones are not able to call anywhere else and cannot be called by anyone.

This is the most restrictive approach because it prevents auto-registered phones from being able to call anyone except the help desk number. Alternatively, you can remove the translation pattern and give the IP phones a calling search space that allows them to call only internal extensions or your local emergency phone number. Choose the approach that provides the desired restriction.

Restricting the Call Forward All Field on IP Phones

Like most phones, IP phones can forward all calls to another number. This is convenient and helpful, but it can be a serious breach of toll security. Employees could forward their phone to their house and then have their family in another country call the company's toll-free number, dial the employee's extension, and then get a "free" call to them at home. Or, employees could forward their own phone to an international number, go home, and then call their own phone for a "free" call to the number they previously set.

You can deal with these toll fraud issues using calling search spaces and partitions. On the Directory Number Configuration page in CallManager Administration (**Device > Phone >** *search for and select a phone > click a line*), you can apply a calling search space to the **Forward All** field. In general, you might want to restrict most phones to be able to forward all calls to only another internal extension. For manager and executive phones, you might want to have a calling search space that allows for local and long distance forwarding.

Recognize that the Forward All feature is an area that can be abused, and use calling search spaces and partitions to restrict the Forward All field on a line-by-line level for each phone.

TIP   The Bulk Administration Tool (BAT) can accomplish many of these tasks for you. It depends on which version of BAT you are using, but investigate your version to see if you can modify these values. Using BAT will save you some time.

Restricting Voice Mail Systems by Using Calling Search Spaces

With some voice mail systems and automated attendant applications, it is possible to dial into the voice mail system, select an option to be transferred out, and then dial a long distance or international number. There is obvious potential for abuse, but appropriate use of calling search spaces and partitions can prevent this fraud. You can probably turn this capability off within the voice mail system, but it is prudent to restrict the calling rights as well.

There are two basic situations to deal with. The first involves using a voice mail system such as Cisco Unity that has voice mail ports configured in the database. The second involves interfacing to a third-party voice mail system such as Octel using Foreign Exchange Station (FXS) gateways. In either case, the approach is the same.

For Unity, each configured voice mail port is assigned a calling search space. This calling search space has the desired calling rights associated with it. The most restrictive approach is to assign a calling search space that can reach a partition that has only internal phone extensions. Cisco recommends this configuration for maximum security.

For FXS gateways that interface to a third-party voice mail system, the same type of calling search space is applied. Select the gateway that has the FXS ports going to the voice mail system, and assign a calling search space that can reach a partition that has only internal phone number extensions.

For CTI applications such as auto attendant or IP IVR, the configuration is slightly different. When a CTI application performs a redirect, the redirect uses the calling search space of the originating party. You want to restrict callers from the outside being able to transfer to another outside number, so configure the calling search space on all your gateways to only have access to internal numbers. This allows these CTI applications to transfer only internally.

Blocking Certain Area Codes

Some area codes are often used to host 900-type services that companies typically want to block. Calls to these area codes are often costly and might not always be business-related. As such, it is important to block as many of these as possible. However, if you do business with anyone located in one of these countries, you need to make sure that you can reach the necessary area codes. You can do this by allowing all calls to a specific area code, or preferably by creating a more specific route pattern that allows calls to reach that one company. Table 9-11 lists some area codes that you might want to consider blocking.

Table 9-11 *Blocked Area Codes List*

Country	Area Code	Blocked Pattern
Anguilla	264	9.1264XXXXXXX
Antigua and Barbuda	268	9.1268XXXXXXX
Bahamas	242	9.1242XXXXXXX
Barbados	246	9.1246XXXXXXX
Bermuda	441	9.1441XXXXXXX
British Virgin Islands	284	9.1284XXXXXXX
Cayman Islands	345	9.1345XXXXXXX
Dominica	767	9.1767XXXXXXX
Dominican Republic	809	9.1809XXXXXXX
Grenada	473	9.1473XXXXXXX
Jamaica	876	9.1876XXXXXXX
Montserrat	664	9.1664XXXXXXX
Puerto Rico	787	9.1787XXXXXXX
St. Kitts and Nevis	869	9.1869XXXXXXX
St. Lucia	758	9.1758XXXXXXX
St. Vincent and the Grenadines	784	9.1784XXXXXXX
Toll charge area code	900	9.1900XXXXXXX
Trinidad and Tobago	868	9.1868XXXXXXX
Turks and Caicos Islands	649	9.1649XXXXXXX
U.S. Virgin Islands	340	9.1242XXXXXXX

You have a couple of choices when implementing the blocked area codes list in CallManager, and you can choose whichever one you are most comfortable with.

First, you can simply create a separate route pattern for each area code, as shown in Table 9-11. To create separate route patterns, add the individual patterns to the Route Pattern Configuration page in CallManager Administration and select the **Block this pattern** option (**Route Plan > Route Pattern >** *click the link in the upper right to* **Add a New Route Pattern**). Repeat this step for each area code shown in Table 9-11.

Second, you can create a route filter specifying each area code in each clause (**Route Plan > Route Filter >** *click the link in the upper right to* **Add a New Route Filter**). The route filter has a character length limitation of 1024 characters, so you might not be able to put all the area codes in one route filter. You could, however, put about ten area codes in each filter.

These steps are only the beginning. Be diligent in making sure that you route calls to only the places you want them to go. Stay informed of new area codes that are sometimes used for fraudulent purposes.

Summary

The key to troubleshooting call routing problems is to understand the behavior of the involved components and to follow a methodical troubleshooting approach. This seems obvious, but dial plans can grow to be so huge and complex that even the best system administrators can lose sight of the basics.

When the complexity seems mind-boggling, apply the information presented in this chapter one step at a time. Taking everything in order and using the trace files lets you get to the root cause of your routing problems.

## CHAPTER 10

Call Preservation

Call preservation in Cisco CallManager 3.*x* might appear to be a complex issue. CallManager interacts with many different types of endpoints. These endpoints include Cisco IOS Software gateways, IP Phones, voice gateway modules, and computer telephony integration (CTI) applications. CallManager communicates with these endpoints using different protocols, including Skinny, Media Gateway Control Protocol (MGCP), H.323, and Telephony Application Programming Interface (TAPI). In addition, these various endpoints might be communicating via conference bridges, media termination points (MTPs), or transcoders. With so many endpoints and so many protocols, how do you know what calls survive and what calls don't when a failure occurs?

Fortunately, you can simplify these complexities by applying some straightforward rules. When you understand the protocol interaction with CallManager, you can categorize the various endpoints to simplify your understanding of how call preservation works.

The following sections look at these and other issues.

Understanding Call Preservation

Certain events can result in a Real-Time Transport Protocol/User Datagram Protocol (RTP/UDP) voice stream being lost between two endpoints. There are two places where a break in communication can potentially result in a dropped stream:

- Any Layer 2 or Layer 3 outage between the two endpoints results in a dropped call. This can include routing issues and spanning-tree loops. If the supporting infrastructure carrying the RTP/UDP stream between these endpoints suffers a failure, the call terminates.

- Any network outage between the endpoints and CallManager might result in a dropped call. A failure on the server itself can also result in a dropped call. In either case, the key idea to understand is that anything that prevents the endpoints from sending and receiving messages with CallManager might cause a problem.

The first case always results in a failure. The second case results in a failure only to nonsurvivable endpoints. Survivable endpoints continue streaming even if they cannot signal to CallManager.

For the purpose of this discussion, assume that endpoints fall into two categories:

- **Survivable endpoints**—These include IP Phones and MGCP gateways (this has nothing to do with the survivability features in Cisco IOS Software).
- **Nonsurvivable endpoints**—These include H.323 gateways, Skinny gateways, Unity ports, and CTI endpoints.

Even though Unity ports are Skinny client ports, the call still drops. This is a design decision made on the Unity TAPI Service Provider (TSP). Because the only thing preserved is the media stream, if you can't signal to Unity from CallManager, you can't enter any digits to enter options into Unity, so it doesn't help you to preserve the voice stream.

Before exploring each of these endpoints in more detail, you must apply two rules to your knowledge of call preservation:

- For a call to survive an outage, *both* endpoints must be *survivable* endpoints.
- Any involvement of media processing entities such as transcoders, conference bridges, and MTPs might result in an immediate or delayed termination of the stream.

Survivable Endpoints

The two types of survivable endpoints are IP Phones and MGCP gateways. If any of these devices are streaming to each other, the stream is preserved even if they cannot signal with CallManager.

The discussion at this point assumes that no intermediary media entities, such as transcoders, conference bridges, and MTPs, are involved in the call. Those are discussed in the "Media Processing Resources" section.

IP Phones

The nature of the relationship between IP Phones and CallManager allows for call preservation even if communication between them is lost. The Skinny protocol facilitates this capability. Figure 10-1 depicts the IP Phone signaling to CallManager.

The following list describes the series of transactions during signaling shown in Figure 10-1.

Step 1   Call setup

Step 2   Ringback

Step 3   Call setup

Step 4   Ring

Step 5   Off-hook

Step 6   Connect RTP stream

Figure 10-1 *IP Phone-to-CallManager Signaling*

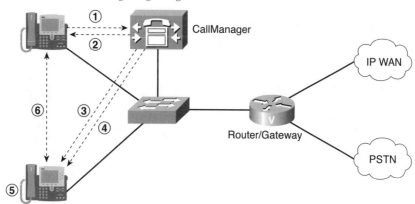

In the event that the IP Phone cannot signal with CallManager, the IP Phone sends KeepAlives every 30 seconds, even during a phone conversation. If three consecutive KeepAlives are sent without a response, or a TCP failure with CallManager is detected, the IP Phone continues streaming. As soon as the IP Phone goes on-hook, a registration message is sent to the standby CallManager.

Even though the conversation is preserved, the IP Phone can no longer invoke a feature such as transfer or a media resource such as a conference. The reason is simple: No connection exists to a CallManager that can carry out the signaling operations requested by the IP Phone.

MGCP Gateways

Many voice gateways can use H.323 or MGCP for protocol interaction with CallManager. MGCP has the advantage of call survivability. For this reason, many customers choose to use this protocol to ensure that the call is preserved even if communication with CallManager is lost.

In MGCP mode, the gateway translates T1 channel associated signaling (CAS), Foreign Exchange Station (FXS), and Foreign Exchange Office (FXO) signaling types into MGCP messages that are sent to CallManager for call control. If T1 Primary Rate Interface (PRI) is used, ISDN Layer 3 signaling is "backhauled" through the voice gateway directly to CallManager for processing. This means that the Layer 3 signaling is passed through the gateway back to CallManager.

Prior to CallManager version 3.1, Layer 2 signaling (Q.921) between the Public Switched Telephone Network (PSTN) and CallManager was transparently passed by the gateway back to CallManager. CallManager facilitated Layer 2 (Q.921) and Layer 3 (Q.931) signaling, so the loss of communication with that CallManager caused the loss of Layer 2 and Layer 3 signaling to the PSTN. If you lose Layer 2, you've lost your D-channel.

On a T1 PRI connection, the loss of the D-channel means the loss of all 23 bearer channels on the span.

Figure 10-2 shows the CallManager pre-version 3.1 Layer 2 backhaul behavior.

Figure 10-2 *CallManager Pre-3.1 Backhaul Behavior*

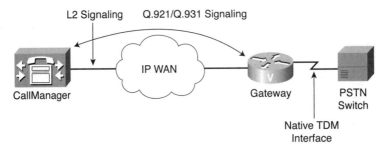

The three basic backhaul mechanisms used in MGCP are

- Reliable User Data Protocol (RUDP) (PRI backhaul to BTS10200)
- Simple Control Transmission Protocol (SCTP)
- TCP-based

CallManager 3.1 and later use the TCP backhaul mechanism. This PRI backhaul method uses two separate channels for communication between CallManager and the voice gateway. MGCP messages are sent over UDP streams between CallManager and the voice gateway. The Q.931 PRI messages are sent to CallManager by a generic backhaul channel on top of a TCP connection.

In other words, ISDN Layer 2 is handled by the voice gateway itself. ISDN Layer 3 is backhauled over a TCP connection to CallManager. If communication with CallManager is lost, the Layer 3 connection is established with the next available CallManager. Figure 10-3 shows the two separate channels established by the voice gateway. One is for the Q.931 TCP backhaul; the other is for UDP MGCP messages.

Figure 10-3 *UDP MGCP Channel and TCP Q.931 Backhaul*

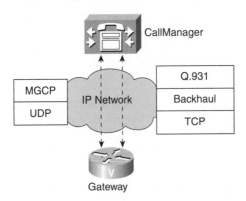

Because Layer 2 (Q.921) terminates on the voice gateway, when communication is lost between the gateway and CallManager, the gateway is able to keep the D-channel up. When the communications link to CallManager goes down, the gateway immediately attempts to reregister with the next available CallManager.

After the gateway registers with a new CallManager, the gateway preserves all the calls; however, the new CallManager has no state information about the calls that are up on the gateway. CallManager has a clever mechanism by which it re-learns the call state information.

Call preservation on a MGCP PRI gateway is a three-step process:

1 Send AuditEndpoint (AUEP) messages to the gateway to determine the state of each B-channel.

2 Send AuditConnection (AUCX) messages for any endpoints for which the gateway reports a preserved call.

3 Send Q.931 Status Enquiry Messages to the PRI device attached to the gateway to confirm the status of any calls CallManager believes are preserved.

After CallManager accepts the new connection from a gateway with preserved calls, the first thing CallManager does is determine which B-channels have preserved calls. CallManager does this by sending AuditEndpoint messages to the gateway for each B-channel.

The best way to understand this process is to look at an example. Example 10-1 shows the gateway initiating a new connection with a Restart In Progress (RSIP) message followed by the backhaul link opening.

Example 10-1 *MGCP Gateway Reregistering After a Failure*

```
MGCPInit - //// RSIP <restart> from S0/DS1-0/*@SDA0001C9B102B0
MGCPpn9d - Backhaul link OPEN for Devicename S0/DS1-0@SDA0001C9B102B0
```

Next, CallManager sends an AuditEndpoint MGCP message to the gateway for each B-channel. Example 10-2 shows two of these messages, although a PRI generates 23 or 30 of these messages depending on whether it is a T1 or E1 respectively. The two messages in Example 10-2 correspond to channels 1 and 23 on a T1.

Example 10-2 *CallManager Audits the Endpoints on a Gateway*

```
MGCPHandler send msg SUCCESSFULLY to: 10.16.30.7
AUEP 249 S0/DS1-0/1@SDA0001C9B102B0 MGCP 0.1
F: X, A, I
MGCPHandler send msg SUCCESSFULLY to: 10.16.30.7
AUEP 271 S0/DS1-0/23@SDA0001C9B102B0 MGCP 0.1
F: X, A, I
```

The gateway responds to each AuditEndpoint with information about the status of the endpoint. Among other things, the gateway returns a connection identifier for each endpoint (B-channel). If the connection identifier is blank, then there is no active call. If it contains a value, the connection identifier is the one that was assigned to the preserved call when it was first set up. Example 10-3 shows responses to the AuditEndpoint messages shown in Example 10-2. Notice channel 1 has no call active (**I:**); however, channel 23 has a call active with a connection identifier of 23 (**I: 23**).

Example 10-3 *Gateway Responds to AuditEndpoint Messages*

```
MGCPHandler received msg from: 10.16.30.7
200 249
X: 0
L: p:20, a:G.711u;G.711a, e:on, gc:-6-14, s:on, nt:IN, v:L;G;D;T
L: p:20, a:G.729a;G.729b-L;G.729;G.729b, e:on, gc:-6-14, s:on, nt:IN, v:L;G;D;T
M: sendonly, recvonly, sendrecv, inactive
I:
MGCPHandler received msg from: 10.16.30.7
200 271
X: 17
L: p:20, a:G.711u;G.711a, e:on, gc:-6-14, s:on, nt:IN, v:L;G;D;T
L: p:20, a:G.729a;G.729b-L;G.729;G.729b, e:on, gc:-6-14, s:on, nt:IN, v:L;G;D;T
M: sendonly, recvonly, sendrecv, inactive
I: 23
```

Now that CallManager knows there is an active call on channel 23 of the PRI with a connection identifier of 23 (**I: 23**), it sends an AuditConnection message to the gateway to get additional data about the preserved call. Example 10-4 shows the AuditConnection message and the gateway's response.

Example 10-4 *CallManager Sends AuditConnection Message and Gateway Responds*

```
GCPHandler send msg SUCCESSFULLY to: 10.16.30.7
AUCX 272 S0/DS1-0/23@SDA0001C9B102B0 MGCP 0.1
I: 23
F: C

MGCPHandler received msg from: 10.16.30.7
200 272
C: D00000000200000200000000000000001
```

The gateway responded to CallManager with the call identifier (**C: D00000000200000200000000000000001**) for the preserved call. Next CallManager requests that the gateway notify CallManager if it receives an Internet Control Message Protocol (ICMP) unreachable for the RTP stream. This allows CallManager to detect if the far-end IP endpoint preserving the call has hung up. Example 10-5 shows the notification request for an ICMP unreachable.

Example 10-5 *CallManager Requests an ICMP Unreachable Notification for Channel 23*

```
MGCPHandler send msg SUCCESSFULLY to: 10.16.30.7
RQNT 273 S0/DS1-0/23@SDA0001C9B102B0 MGCP 0.1
X: 17
R: R/iu
Q: process,loop
```

Finally, CallManager attempts to verify the status of the call with the far-end ISDN PRI switch. Remember that the device connected to the voice gateway has no idea that there was a failure on the CallManager side; however, it is possible that during the brief period of time that the failover was occurring, the ISDN PRI switch disconnected the call. To ensure both CallManager and the far-end switch agree on the status of each channel, CallManager sends a status enquiry ISDN message for each call it believes is still active to see if the far-end agrees. Example 10-6 shows the Q.931 status enquiry message sent to the far-end switch.

Example 10-6 *Status Enquiry ISDN Message*

```
Out Message -- PriStatusEnquiryMsg -- Protocol= PriNi2Protocol
MMan_Id= 0. (iep=  0 dsl=  0 sapi=  0 ces=  0 IpAddr=71e100a IpPort=2427)
IsdnMsgData2= 08 02 00 01 75
```

Upon receiving this message, the far-end switch might send back a status message indicating the state of the channel. If CallManager does not receive a status message in response, it will continue sending a status enquiry for that channel every four seconds. Now CallManager can use the PRI normally and maintain the status of the preserved calls.

Chapter 6, "Voice Gateways," provides detailed information on the MGCP messages exchanged between CallManager and voice gateways.

Nonsurvivable Endpoints

This section discusses nonsurvivable endpoints. As you will soon learn, some of these endpoints don't always fail. The following sections describe the circumstances under which they do.

Skinny Gateways

In the current Cisco AVVID IP Telephony architecture, Skinny gateways have been phased out and converted to MGCP. In CallManager 3.0, the Cisco Catalyst WS-X6608 module, WS-X6624 and Cisco Digital Access DT-24+/DE-30+ were Skinny protocol-based, but as of CallManager 3.1, MGCP is used. If you have any legacy gateways, such as the Cisco Access Analog Trunk or Analog Station gateways, they use the Skinny gateway protocol.

If you are using any of the legacy Skinny-based gateways on CallManager 3.0, be aware that there is no call preservation for calls through these gateways when communication with CallManager is lost.

In a Skinny gateway, the Layer 2 and Layer 3 D-channel is sent back to CallManager. All D-channel signaling is from CallManager where the gateway is registered to the PSTN. In any T1/E1 PRI, the loss of a D-channel drops all calls across that link.

H.323 Gateways

Calls made through H.323 gateways can fail if the H.225 session between CallManager and the H.323 gateway is terminated. It doesn't matter what type of PSTN interface is on the gateway, whether FXO, FXS, T1 PRI, or T1 CAS, because the signaling back to CallManager is still H.323.

The condition for a dropped H.323 call is as follows: An H.323 call drops if the H.225 session is broken.

This means that every time a call is made through an H.323 gateway, an H.225 session is established with CallManager. Figure 10-4 shows the H.225 session that is established for the duration of the call.

Figure 10-4 *H.225 Session Between CallManager and an H.323 Gateway*

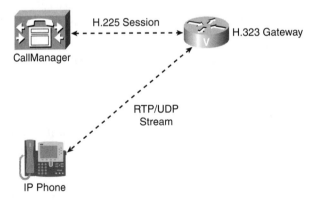

When the H.225 session between the voice gateway and CallManager is lost, the voice gateway terminates the RTP/UDP stream with the endpoint. The voice gateway might do this because CallManager stops responding or because the network between these devices goes down. In either case, the loss of the H.225 session causes the call to drop.

It is important to note that not all calls in a cluster will necessarily fail. Remember, the call fails only if the H.225 session is interrupted. Figure 10-5 illustrates an example of this scenario. If CallManager A fails, it has no effect on the call because the H.225 session is connected through CallManager B.

Figure 10-5 *H.225 Session Between CallManager in a CallManager Cluster and an H.323 Gateway*

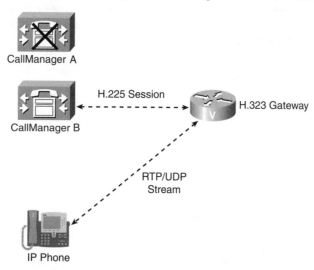

With CallManager 3.0(9) and earlier, the H.225 session was established on different CallManagers according to very complex criteria. In CallManager 3.0(10) and later, the H.225 session is established with the primary CallManager specified in the device pool. To better explain, the device pool assigned to that H.323 gateway has a CallManager failover list. The primary CallManager in that group is the one to which the H.225 session is established.

An H.323 call fails because this type of gateway does not register to CallManager. As such, CallManager has no knowledge of the interfaces being used on that gateway. Additionally, there are no provisions within the protocol itself to handle this kind of failover. In fact, the H.323 protocol states that if the H.225 TCP connection is lost for any reason, the call must be torn down. In contrast, MGCP gateways do register with CallManager. CallManager knows about the interfaces being used on that gateway, and MGCP has provisions in place for a failover of this type.

CTI/TAPI Endpoints

TAPI endpoints that connect to CTI ports on CallManager can preserve calls. These CTI/TAPI endpoints include the following:

- Cisco Customer Response applications, including the Cisco IP IVR, Cisco IP ICD, and Cisco IP AA

- Cisco Personal Assistant

Any calls in progress on any of these applications terminate immediately if connectivity with CallManager is lost.

Cisco IP SoftPhone preserves calls just like an IP phone. When communication with CallManager is lost, the media stream is preserved, but all features are disabled until the call ends and SoftPhone can re-register with a CallManager.

Media Processing Resources

Up to this point, everything discussed in this chapter assumes that no media processing resources were involved in the dropped call. The media resources that need to be considered are

- MTPs

- Transcoders

- Hardware conference bridges

- Software conference bridges

All of these media resources behave the same way in the event of a preserved call.

If a media resource is involved in a call and the CallManager controlling the media resource fails, all calls from the nonsurvivable endpoints fail. All calls from survivable endpoints continue in the call for up to 24 hours from the time the CallManager controlling the media resource failed. The 24-hour period is not configurable.

If the media resource re-registers with an available CallManager, there is no limit to the amount of time the media resource stream can stay connected. The 24-hour disconnect timer doesn't indicate the maximum duration of a media resource stream; it only indicates the maximum duration a media resource stream will stay up after losing connection with CallManager. If connected to CallManager, a media resource stream can actually be connected indefinitely.

This behavior allows the media resource to utilize a feature called ICMP unreachable detection, which allows continued streaming to the preserved endpoints in the call. However, if upon sending an RTP stream to a preserved endpoint the media resource receives an ICMP port unreachable, this is an indication that the endpoint is no longer listening on that port for the RTP stream. This is the queue to consider that participant disconnected. Once all the participants disconnect, the port is available for new media resource tasks.

Also, any media stream where no RTP packets are being received is actively monitored as well. Inactive channels are monitored every 10 minutes at which time the media resource sends a ping to that endpoint. If the endpoint does not respond, the media resource assumes that the endpoint is no longer on the network and de-allocates the media resource stream.

Remember that a call in the process of being set up fails if it is not yet in a connected state when communication with its CallManager fails.

Troubleshooting Call Preservation Issues

Troubleshooting is mainly a matter of knowing what is supposed to survive and what isn't. If a call goes down and it is determined that nonsurvivable endpoints were involved, there is no problem to investigate. However, if survivable endpoints encounter a dropped call, an investigation should take place.

When survivable endpoints have a dropped call, most of the time it is really a false alarm. As an administrator, I often received complaints about a dropped call that should not have been dropped. In almost every case, I found that the PSTN had sent a release complete ISDN message, causing the call to drop. Or the other IP Phone sent an on-hook message to CallManager, indicating that the other party terminated the call.

On a couple of other occasions, an infrastructure component such as a router or switch was misconfigured or was experiencing a hardware-related failure. Sometimes the problem might even be related to routing loops in the network itself. You should investigate these areas if a dropped call occurs between two survivable endpoints.

There are some clues that will tell you that the call preservation feature was activated. The first is obvious—when an IP phone preserves a call, the screen changes to say "CM Down, Features Disabled." This is an obvious clue of a problem; however, if an IP phone is communicating through an MGCP gateway and the gateway registers, the IP phones on active calls through that gateway displays the message "Temporary Failure."

The Temporary Failure message is used to indicate to the user on the IP phone that supplementary services for the active call are no longer available because CallManager no longer has the ability to manipulate the preserved call.

This message is also seen in the CCM trace when a failure occurs. This allows you to search for the words "Temporary Failure" and then look backwards through the trace to determine why the failure occurred. You will see a line in the trace that looks like this:

```
StationD:    5643f70 DisplayPromptStatus timeOutValue=0
  promptStatus='Temporary failure' lineInstance=1 callReference=33554436.
```

If you search back through the trace, you will find an indication as to why the failure may have occurred. In this case, the CallManager to which the gateway was registered to went down, but the CallManager to which the phone was registered stayed up. The CallManager where the phone was registered, which is the same place where you saw the Temporary Failure message, shows the following in the CCM trace:

```
SDLLinkOOS - SDL link to remote application out of service. Local node ID:1
  Local Application ID.:100 Remote IP address of remote application:10.89.242.13
  RemoteNodeID:2 Remote application ID.:100 Unique Link ID.:1:100:2:100
  App ID:Cisco CallManager Cluster ID:CLSTR1-A-Cluster Node ID:10.89.242.12
```

This message indicates that the SDL TCP connection went down to the node where the gateway was registered. At this point you would go investigate why the other node went down.

One final concept to understand about call preservation is its interaction with Survivable Remote Site Telephony (SRST). In Cisco IOS Software version 12.2(11)T and later, MGCP endpoints on a Cisco IOS Software voice gateway can be configured to convert themselves to H.323 endpoints in the event of a complete loss of connectivity to the CallManager cluster. When this occurs, calls are *not* preserved. This means that a CallManager failure where the IOS gateway can contact another CallManager results in call preservation. However, a WAN outage where the gateway loses all communication with the CallManager cluster results in calls being dropped as the gateway switches to H.323 mode.

Best Practices

From a best-practices perspective, knowing what survives and what doesn't makes the troubleshooting process easier. It is best to correlate the rules in this chapter with the detailed call flow information presented in Chapter 5, "IP Phones," and Chapter 6.

Chapters 5 and 6 present information on reading the trace files. With the information in this chapter, you know when you need to investigate the trace files because you know which calls survive and which don't.

Summary

The rules for call survivability can be summarized as follows:

- If the call involves nonsurvivable endpoints, and a CallManager involved in the call fails, the call fails. This is true regardless of whether a conference bridge, an MTP, or a transcoder is involved in the call and regardless of which CallManager (when there is more than one) fails. If the call involves one nonsurvivable endpoint and one survivable endpoint, the call fails only if the CallManager that the nonsurvivable endpoint is registered to fails.

- If the call involves only survivable endpoints, and one or more CallManagers involved in the call fails, the streaming connection between the endpoints is maintained. Note, however, that the endpoints do not have supplementary services available to them after the failure.

- If a hardware-based conference bridge is involved in a call, and the CallManager controlling the conference bridge fails, all calls from nonsurvivable endpoints fail. All calls from survivable endpoints continue in the conference.

- If a software-based conference bridge is involved in a call and the CallManager controlling the conference bridge fails, all calls from the nonsurvivable endpoints fail. All calls from survivable endpoints continue in the conference until the party terminates the call voluntarily. The conference bridge reregisters with an available CallManager.

- If a hardware- or software-based conference bridge is involved in a call and the CallManager controlling the conference bridge does not fail, all calls into the conference from CallManagers that did fail are terminated. All calls from CallManagers that did not fail continue in the conference.
- If the call involves an MTP or a transcoder, the call fails.
- If the call is in the process of being set up but is not yet in a connected state and a CallManager involved in the call fails, the call fails.

Conference Bridges, Transcoders, and Media Termination Points

An important part of any IP telephony network is a variety of media resources. A *media resource* is a network device that terminates a media stream to provide some service to IP telephony endpoints, such as IP phones and voice gateways. Three such media resources, conference bridges, transcoders, and media termination points (MTP), are discussed in this chapter. The fourth type of media resource, Music on Hold (MOH) servers, are discussed in Chapter 12, "Music on Hold."

The majority of IP Telephony networks require some form of conferencing resource to accommodate Ad Hoc or Meet-Me conferences of three or more parties. In a CallManager system, *Ad Hoc conferences* require a user (referred to as the conference controller) to include attendees to the conference by calling them individually; *Meet-Me conferences* allow attendees to dial into the conference after a conference controller has created the conference. Conference resources can reside on either a Cisco CallManager server or dedicated hardware when higher performance, functionality, or capacity are required.

Some topologies also require the use of one or more transcoders. *Transcoders* allow devices with incompatible codecs to communicate with each other. A transcoder connects a full-duplex RTP stream using one codec (such as G.711) to another full-duplex RTP stream using a different codec (such as G.729) in real time. Transcoding between two compressed codecs such as G.729 and G.723 can also be done as of CallManager release 3.1. However, this is typically not recommended because the voice quality degrades every time a compression/decompression cycle is added. Transcoding resources must reside on dedicated hardware because of the DSP resources required to convert from one codec to another.

A transcoder can also function as a *media termination point* (MTP), which allows for supplementary services such as hold and transfer to H.323 devices that otherwise would not support this functionality due to a lack of support for the null capabilities set H.323 feature.

MTP resources can also be provided in software. The distinction between a transcoder and a software MTP resource is that a software MTP resource only supports the G.711 codec. This allows a software MTP to provide supplementary services to H.323 endpoints that do not support the null capabilities set as long as the endpoint is configured to use the G.711 codec. All Cisco IOS voice gateways support the null capabilities set; MTP is generally only used when interoperating with third-party gateways.

Both software conferencing and software MTP are provided on any CallManager server or dedicated server that has the Cisco IP Voice Media Streaming Application installed.

NOTE   Note that although a transcoder can also function as an MTP, the opposite is not true. A software MTP cannot function as a transcoder because it only supports the G.711 codec.

This chapter covers the following topics:

- The role of media resource groups and media resource group lists
- Understanding how codec selection occurs
- Troubleshooting transcoder resources
- Troubleshooting conference bridge resources

Media Resource Groups (MRGs) and Media Resource Group Lists (MRGLs)

As of release 3.1, CallManager supports media resource groups (MRGs) and media resource group lists (MRGLs) to allow an administrator to allocate media resources to particular devices. The most common use of MRGs and MRGLs is to restrict media resource usage on a geographic basis. For example, if you have conference bridge resources at a remote site, you can create an MRGL for the IP phones at the remote site that only allows them to access the local conference bridge resource. This ensures that conferences created by IP phones at the remote site do not have to use WAN bandwidth for conferences within the same site. You can even configure the MRGL so that if the conference bridge at the remote site is out of resources or unavailable, resources from another site can be used as a backup. Figure 11-1 shows an example of a central site and a remote site controlled by a CallManager node at the central site.

Notice the IP phones at the remote site are using Conference Bridge 1 while the IP phones at the head site are using Conference Bridge 2. This is accomplished by configuring the MRGL on the IP phones at the remote site to have an MRG with Conference Bridge 1 first in the list. IP phones at the remote site will use all the resources available on Conference Bridge 1 before attempting to use Conference Bridge 2.

Figure 11-1 *Using MRGLs to Allocate a Specific Conference Bridge Resource*

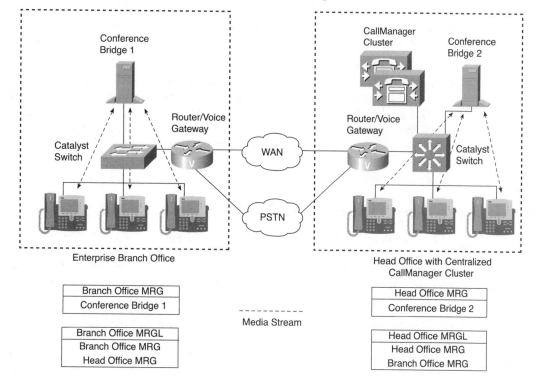

MRGL Selection

Understanding MRGLs is essential to troubleshooting conference bridge, transcoder, and MTP problems. MRGLs determine which resources a particular device has access to when it needs a media resource.

MRGs are logical groupings of media resources. A single MRG can contain hardware conference resources, software conference resources, transcoder resources, MOH servers, and software MTPs. An MRG has no user-defined order. All resources within an MRG are considered equal, so CallManager load-shares between resources of each type in one MRG.

MRGLs are just ordered lists of MRGs. MRGLs allow for a user-configurable order. All resources of a particular type must be exhausted in one MRG before CallManager will attempt to use a media resource from another MRG in the same MRGL.

A device can have access to more than one MRGL, depending on how you have configured CallManager. An MRGL can be configured on a per-device basis, which means that you can give specific devices access to media resources on an individual basis. A second MRGL can be configured on a per-device pool basis. The MRGL assigned to a device pool applies to all devices using that device pool. If a device has an MRGL configured at the device level as well as an MRGL at the device pool level, the MRGL on the device is searched first, followed by the MRGL on the device pool. Most administrators choose to configure MRGLs only at the device pool level.

The last place where a device can gain access to media resources is through the default MRGL. Any media resource that is not assigned to an MRG is automatically assigned to the default MRGL. As soon as a media resource is in an MRG, it is no longer available to devices via the default list. As you will see later in this chapter, the default list is always searched when looking for media resources. It is the last resort if no resources are available in the device-based MRGL and the device pool-based MRGL or if no MRGL is configured for the device at any level.

Understanding Codec Selection

Codec selection is an important concept to understand when dealing with conference bridges and transcoders. For any media stream between two devices, CallManager must decide which codec to use for that leg of the call. The majority of transcoding problems are due to a region misconfiguration in which a codec being selected is incompatible with the endpoint.

Codec selection in CallManager is performed via the configuration of a regions matrix in CallManager Administration (**System > Region**). Every device in CallManager is in a region. Regions are not explicitly configured on the device. Instead, they are configured as part of a device pool, and a device pool is then assigned to a device. This means that the device pool in which a device is assigned dictates which region the device is in and thereby dictates which codec to use when communicating with other devices.

For each region, you must configure which codec to use when communicating with any other region (or within the region). You must configure a codec between each pair of regions. This means that the number of regions configured increases exponentially. For example, if you have two regions, you need to configure only three different codec selections. Table 11-1 shows the codec configuration between two regions.

Table 11-1 *Sample Regions Matrix for Two Regions*

	Region A (Campus)	Region B (Remote Site)
Region A (Campus)	Wideband	G.729
Region B (Remote Site)	G.729	G.711

In this case, any call between two devices in Region A uses the wideband codec. Any call between two devices in Region B uses G.711. Any call between a device in Region A and a device in Region B uses G.729. Note that the selection is symmetrical, meaning that a call from Region A to Region B is the same as a call from Region B to Region A. So although the matrix shows four codecs, when you configure G.729 for Region A to Region B, you automatically configure the opposite as well. If you increase the number of regions to three, you now have a 3×3 matrix, for a total of nine codec selections. Again, some are repetitive due to the symmetrical nature of regions. However, with three regions, you have six distinct region pairs for which to configure a codec. Table 11-2 shows the regions matrix for three regions.

Table 11-2 *Sample Regions Matrix for Three Regions*

	Region A (Campus)	Region B (Transcoders)	Region C (Remote Site)
Region A (Campus)	Wideband	G.711	G.729
Region B (Transcoders)	G.711	G.711	G.729
Region C (Remote Site)	G.729	G.729	G.711

As you might have noticed, the number of region pairs you must configure a codec for increases exponentially for each region you add. The more regions you have, the more of a chance there is that one of them has been misconfigured, especially when transcoders are introduced.

Another important concept to understand is that when you configure a codec between two regions, CallManager doesn't exactly enforce the codec you configure. When you select a codec between two regions, you are actually telling CallManager that you do not want to use a codec that requires more bandwidth than the configured codec.

For example, if you configure G.729 between two regions, you are actually telling CallManager to use a codec that is 8 kbps or less. Table 11-3 shows the bandwidth requirements for each codec configurable in CallManager. Note that these values do not include the bandwidth required for IP/UDP/RTP headers and Layer 2 headers. Additional information about these codecs is available in Appendix A, "Cisco IP Telephony Protocol and Codec Information and References."

Table 11-3 *Codec Bandwidth Requirements*

Codec	Compression Rate Without Headers
Wideband	256 kbps
G.711 (A-law and μ-law)	64 kbps
GSM	13 kbps
G.729 (all variants)	8 kbps
G.723	5.3 kbps/6.3 kbps

Configuring G.729 between two regions automatically excludes G.711 and wideband. However, if two devices do not support G.729 but do support G.723, the call is connected successfully using G.723 even though you have configured G.729. This is because G.723 uses less bandwidth than G.729. Another example is if you configure wideband as the codec. Wideband is supported only between Cisco IP Phones; however, you can still place a call successfully between a phone and a gateway while configured for wideband codec. This is because G.711 uses less bandwidth than wideband and is therefore an acceptable alternative. Keep this in mind when looking through traces, because it might explain why you don't see the codec you expect to see. Traces later in this chapter show the codec negotiations.

Transcoder Resources

CallManager attempts to invoke a transcoder resource when it needs to connect a media stream between two devices that do not have a compatible codec without exceeding the configured codec bandwidth between regions. Transcoding resources are available only in hardware because they require high-speed digital signal processors (DSPs) to convert the media stream from one codec to another in real time.

Regions and the Regions Codec Matrix

The most important concept that is often overlooked when using transcoders is that the region selection between the two incompatible devices actually has nothing to do with the codec selection when the transcoder is in place. To further clarify this point, refer to Figure 11-2.

Figure 11-2 *Codec Selection with a Transcoder*

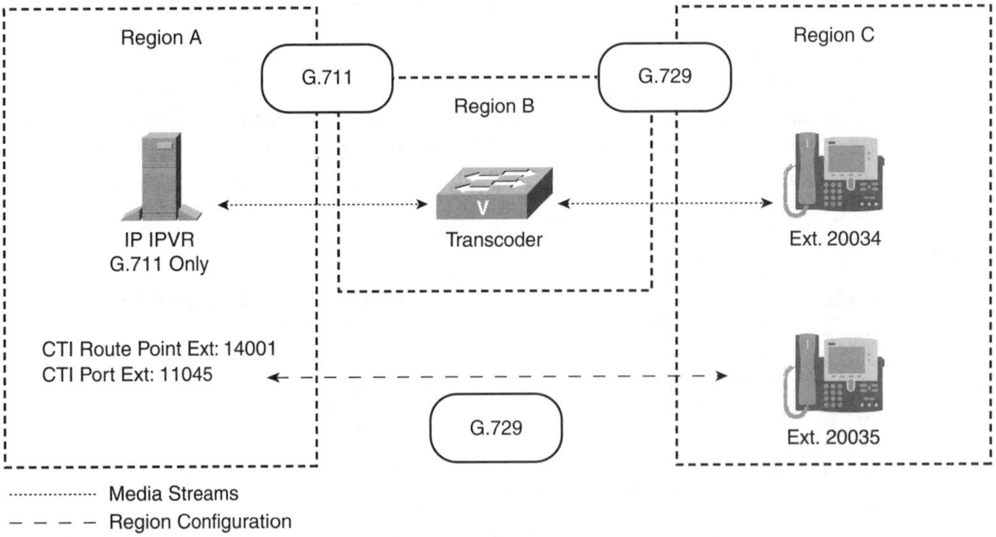

Figure 11-2 shows a device in Region A that supports only G.711; however, a remote site has IP phones that are using G.729 to conserve WAN bandwidth. Refer to Table 11-2 for the regions matrix for this example. The regions matrix states that a call from an IP phone in Region C to the IP IVR server in Region A must use a codec that consumes no more than 8 kbps because G.729 is the codec that is configured.

CallManager is always aware of the capabilities of the endpoints registered to it. When a call is placed from an IP phone in Region C to the IP IVR server in Region A, CallManager knows the two endpoints do not have a compatible codec that is 8 kbps or less, so it invokes a transcoder to attempt to connect the call. From the point where the transcoder is invoked, it is important to remember that the codec selected between Region A and Region C is irrelevant. This is because a media steam is no longer directly connected between Region A and Region C. When the transcoder is invoked, there are two individual media streams— one from Region A to Region B and one from Region B to Region C. CallManager uses the configuration for these two region pairs to select the codec for each leg of the transcoding session.

In this example, the regions matrix in Table 11-2 states that between Region A and Region B you want to use G.711, and between Region B and Region C you want to use G.729. As long as the transcoder is physically located on the same side of the WAN as Region A, this is okay. If the transcoder were at the remote site, the call would still complete. However, the media stream between the transcoder and the IP IVR server would be G.711 over the WAN, which defeats the whole purpose of using G.729. The transcoder should be physically located on the same LAN as the devices that require transcoding resources (and "on the same LAN" does *not* mean that they have to be on the same subnet). The majority of transcoder problems involve a misconfiguration in the regions between the transcoder and the endpoints. Many administrators do not pay attention to the region where the transcoder is located; however, it plays the most important role in determining which codecs get used when a transcoder is invoked.

Also remember that regions are not configured on a per-device basis but rather are configured at the device pool level. Because regions are configured at the device pool level, the device pool for which a transcoder is configured is a transcoder's most important configuration parameter.

The good news is that the traces for this kind of misconfiguration always look very similar, so you should be able to easily spot this as a problem when you see these symptoms in a CCM trace. To further your understanding, we'll examine traces of a call that failed because the regions were misconfigured. Example 11-1 shows a call from 20034, an IP phone at the remote site, calling IP IVR, 14001, located at the main site. The call is to CTI route point 14001. The IP IVR immediately redirects the call to CTI port 11045 for media termination.

Example 11-1 *CCM Trace of a Call from an IP Phone to an IP IVR*

```
| PretransformCallingPartyNumber=20034
| CallingPartyNumber=20034
| DialingPartition=
| DialingPattern=14001
| DialingRoutePatternRegularExpression=(14001)
| DialingWhere=
| PatternType=Enterprise
| PotentialMatches=NoPotentialMatchesExist
| DialingSdlProcessId=(1,73,2)
| PretransformDigitString=14001
| PretransformTagsList=SUBSCRIBER
```

continues

Example 11-1 *CCM Trace of a Call from an IP Phone to an IP IVR (Continued)*

```
|PretransformPositionalMatchList=14001
|CollectedDigits=14001
|UnconsumedDigits=
|TagsList=SUBSCRIBER
|PositionalMatchList=14001
|VoiceMailbox=14001
|DisplayName=
|RouteBlockFlag=RouteThisPattern
|InterceptPartition=
|InterceptPattern=
|InterceptWhere=
|InterceptSdlProcessId=(0,0,0)
|InterceptSsType=0
|InterceptSsKey=0
StationD:    67d2040 SelectSoftKeys instance=1 reference=16777383
  softKeySetIndex=8 validKeyMask=-1.
ConnectionManager - wait_AuDisconnectRequest(16777384,0): NO ENTRY FOUND IN TABLE
Locations: release: cdccPID=(1.13.93) no entry.
Digit analysis: match(fqcn="20034", cn="20034", pss="RTPLine1PT:RTPctiPortsPT:
  RTPVoicemail_2_PT:RTPVoicemail_1_PT:RTPTollFreePT:RTPTieLinesPT:
  RTPPAManagedPhones:RTPLongDistancePT:RTPLocalPT:RTPInternationalPT:
  RTPInternalCLT_PBX_PT:RTPInternalATL_PBX_PT:RTPCallParkPT:RTP911EmergencyPT:
  CLTVoicemail_1_PT:CHIVoicemail_1_PT", dd="11045")
Digit analysis: analysis results
|PretransformCallingPartyNumber=20034
|CallingPartyNumber=20034
|DialingPartition=RTPctiPortsPT
|DialingPattern=11045
|DialingRoutePatternRegularExpression=(11045)
|DialingWhere=
|PatternType=Enterprise
|PotentialMatches=NoPotentialMatchesExist
|DialingSdlProcessId=(2,34,44)
|PretransformDigitString=11045
|PretransformTagsList=SUBSCRIBER
|PretransformPositionalMatchList=11045
|CollectedDigits=11045
|UnconsumedDigits=
|TagsList=SUBSCRIBER
|PositionalMatchList=11045
|VoiceMailbox=
|DisplayName=VNT1Apps1Port45
|RouteBlockFlag=RouteThisPattern
|InterceptPartition=
|InterceptPattern=
|InterceptWhere=
|InterceptSdlProcessId=(0,0,0)
|InterceptSsType=0
|InterceptSsKey=0
StationD:    67d2040 SelectSoftKeys instance=1 reference=16777383
  softKeySetIndex=8 validKeyMask=-1.
ConnectionManager - wait_AuDisconnectRequest(16777385,0): NO ENTRY FOUND IN TABLE
Locations: release: cdccPID=(1.13.94) no entry.
```

Example 11-1   *CCM Trace of a Call from an IP Phone to an IP IVR (Continued)*

```
StationD:     67d2040 CallState callState=12(Proceed) lineInstance=1
  callReference=16777383
StationD:     67d2040 CallInfo callingPartyName='' callingParty=20034
  cgpnVoiceMailbox=10034  calledPartyName='VNT1Apps1Port45' calledParty=11045
  cdpnVoiceMailbox=  originalCalledPartyName=''  originalCalledParty=33000
  originalCdpnVoiceMailbox=33000 originalCdpnRedirectReason=0
  lastRedirectingPartyName=''  lastRedirectingParty=
  lastRedirectingVoiceMailbox= lastRedirectingReason=0
  callType=2(OutBound) lineInstance=1 callReference=16777383.
StationD::star_StationOutputCallInfo(): callInfo: CI=16777383,
  CallingPartyName=,  CallingParty=20034, CalledPartyName=VNT1Apps1Port45,
  CalledParty=11045, OriginalCalledPartyName=, OriginalCalledParty=33000,
  lastRedirectingPartyName=, lastRedirectingParty=
StationD:     67d2040 DialedNumber dialedNumber=33000 lineInstance=1
  callReference=16777383.
StationD:     67d2040 CallInfo callingPartyName='' callingParty=20034
  cgpnVoiceMailbox='10034  calledPartyName='VNT1Apps1Port45'
  calledParty=11045 cdpnVoiceMailbox=  originalCalledPartyName=''
  originalCalledParty= originalCdpnVoiceMailbox=
  originalCdpnRedirectReason=0 lastRedirectingPartyName=''
  lastRedirectingParty=14001 lastRedirectingVoiceMailbox=14001
  lastRedirectingReason=0 callType=2(OutBound) lineInstance=1
  callReference=16777383.
StationD::star_StationOutputCallInfo(): callInfo: CI=16777383, CallingPartyName=,
  CallingParty=20034, CalledPartyName=VNT1Apps1Port45, CalledParty=11045,
  OriginalCalledPartyName=, OriginalCalledParty=, lastRedirectingPartyName=,
  lastRedirectingParty=14001
StationD:     67d2040 StartTone tone=36(AlertingTone).
StationD:     67d2040 CallState callState=3(RingOut) lineInstance=1
  callReference=16777383
StationD:     67d2040 SelectSoftKeys instance=1 reference=16777383 softKeySetIndex=8
  validKeyMask=-1.
StationD:     67d2040 DisplayPromptStatus timeOutValue=0 promptStatus='Ring Out'
  lineInstance=1 callReference=16777383.
ConnectionManager - wait_AuConnectRequest(16777383,16777386): INFORM MEDIA LAYER
ConnectionManager - storeMediaInfo(16777383): ADD NEW ENTRY, tail == 54
ConnectionManager - storeMediaInfo(16777386): ADD NEW ENTRY, tail == 55
```

Up to this point, the call has proceeded normally. The IP phone placing the call should be hearing ringback, as indicated in the trace. Notice that the two parties involved in the call are identified by the endpoint IDs **16777383** and **16777386**. In Example 11-2, the media manager, which is the internal CallManager entity responsible for setting up and tearing down media streams, starts up to create the media stream.

Example 11-2   *CCM Trace Showing Media Manager Creating a Media Stream*

```
MediaCoordinator - wait_AuConnectRequest()
MediaCoordinator - wait_AuConnectRequest - starting MediaManager
  w/ existing (0) connections
MediaCoordinator - wait_AuConnectRequest - new MediaManager(40,84) started
MediaManager(84) started
MediaManager - wait_AuConnectRequest
```

In Example 11-3, the media manager realizes that no capabilities match and invokes a transcoder. Notice the line that says **ci=16777387**. This identifies the transcoder later when media streams are connected.

Example 11-3   *CCM Trace Showing Media Manager Introducing a Transcoder*

```
MediaManager - wait_AuConnectRequest - no caps match, introducing transcoder
MediaManager - wait_AuConnectRequest - allocating transcoder(ci=16777387)
MediaResourceManager::waiting_MrmAllocateXcoderResourceReq
```

In Example 11-4, the media manager searches through the MRGL to find an available transcoder. The MRGL contains a single MRG called **Single HW CFB**. As the name implies, it contains only a single hardware conference bridge device. Any time CallManager searches for a media resource, it also looks to see if any resources are available in the default list. In this case, you can see that CallManager finds a transcoder resource (MTP device) in the default list.

Example 11-4   *CCM Trace Showing Transcoder Allocation*

```
MediaResourceManager::waiting_MrmAllocateXcoderResourceReq -
  MRGL SEARCH,TRY CREATING CHILD USING MRGL LIST
MRM::convertScmStringToRWCString Single HW CFB
MRM::getXcodeDeviceGivenMrgl
MRM::getXcodeDeviceGivenMrgl GETTING XCODE FROM DEFAULT LIST
MRM::getXcodeDeviceGivenMrgl MTP0001C96AD659 Group=1 Counter=0
MediaResourceManager::waiting_MrmAllocateXcoderResourceReq -
  CREATED CHILD USING MRGL AND DEFAULT LIST
MediaResourceCdpc::sortDeviceGivenList
MediaResourceCdpc::sortDeviceGivenList Name=MTP0001C96AD659 Group=1 Counter=0
MediaResourceCdpc - Started
MediaResourceCdpc::waiting_MrmAllocateMtpResourceReq
MediaResourceCdpc::findDeviceGivenList
MediaResourceCdpc::waiting_MrmAllocateMtpResourceReq MtpDevice=MTP0001C96AD659
MediaResourceCdpc::device_lookup_DevicePidRes
MediaResourceCdpc::device_lookup_DevicePidRes MtpResource=MTP0001C96AD659
MediaResourceCdpc::resource_rsvp_AllocateMtpResourceRes
MediaResourceManager::waiting_MrmAllocateMtpResourceRes
MRM::updateMtpCounter MTP0001C96AD659
MRM::updateXcodeCounter MTP0001C96AD659
MRM::updateXcodeCounter allocateCounter=1
MediaResourceManager::waiting_MrmChildStopInd
MediaManager - wait_AllocateMtpResourceRes
```

As Example 11-5 demonstrates, now that the transcoder has been allocated, two new media streams are set up. Notice that the original endpoint IDs, 16777383 and 16777386, are now individually connected to endpoint ID 16777387, which is the transcoder.

Example 11-5   *CCM Trace Showing Connection Creation Between Endpoints and the Transcoder*

```
MediaManager - wait_AllocateMtpResourceRes - start 2 connections
MediaManager - wait_AuConnectRequest - assign null party A info with
  previous party B info
MediaManager - wait_AllocateMtpResourceRes - creating connection between
```

Example 11-5 *CCM Trace Showing Connection Creation Between Endpoints and the Transcoder (Continued)*

```
party1(16777383) and party2(16777387)
MediaManager - wait_AllocateMtpResourceRes - creating connection between
  party1(16777386) and party2(16777387)
MediaResourceCdpc::shutting_down_MrmChildStopConf
```

Next, CallManager allocates two streams for the call, as shown in Example 11-6.

Example 11-6 *CCM Trace Showing Resource Allocation Counters Incremented*

```
MediaCoordinator - wait_MediaCoordinatorAddResource - CI=16777387 count=1
MediaCoordinator - wait_MediaCoordinatorAddResource - CI=16777387 count=2
MediaManager - wait_AuConnectReply
MediaManager - wait_AuConnectReply
```

Up to this point, everything is working correctly. CallManager noticed that the capabilities between the two original endpoints (the remote IP phone and the IP IVR server) did not match and invoked a transcoder. Now CallManager needs to determine if it can match the capabilities between the transcoder and each of the endpoints. In Example 11-7, the trace shows that there was an error matching the capabilities.

Example 11-7 *CCM Trace Showing Media Capabilities Match Error*

```
MediaManager - wait_AuConnectReply - received 2 responses, fowarding reply
  for party1(16777383) and party2(16777386)
AgenaInterface - ERROR  waitForMXCapabilitiesExchanged_
  MediaExchangeCapabilitiesIncoming - match capabilities error
AgenaInterface - ERROR  waitForMXCapabilitiesExchanged_
  MediaExchangeCapabilitiesIncoming - match capabilities error
MediaCoordinator - wait_AuConnectReply
ConnectionManager - wait_AuConnectReply(16777383,16777386)
```

Example 11-8 shows the next error, **ERROR wait_AuConnectErrorInd**. This error is typical for any kind of media setup problem. Any time you have a codec mismatch or capabilities exchange timeout, you see something similar to the following five lines in the CCM trace. If you ever see something like this in a trace, pay special attention to things such as codec misconfigurations.

Example 11-8 *CCM Trace Showing Media Connect Errors*

```
MediaManager - ERROR  wait_AuConnectErrorInd
MediaManager - ERROR  wait_AuConnectErrorInd - sending disconnect to 2
  MediaExchanges
MediaManager - ERROR  wait_AuConnectErrorInd - sending AuConnectErrorInd to parent
MediaManager - ERROR  wait_AuConnectErrorInd - sending disconnect to (71,88)
MediaManager - ERROR  wait_AuConnectErrorInd - found sender(71,89), don't send
  disconnect
```

In Example 11-9, CallManager cleans up after the failure.

Example 11-9 *CCM Trace Showing CallManager Cleanup of the Failed Call*

```
MediaCoordinator - wait_MediaCoordinatorDelResource - CI=16777387 count=1
MediaCoordinator - wait_AuConnectErrorInd
MediaCoordinator - wait_AuConnectErrorInd - removing MediaManager(84)
  from connection list
StationD:    67d2040 StopTone.
StationD:    67d2040 OpenReceiveChannel conferenceID=0 passThruPartyID=1777
  millisecondPacketSize=20 compressionType=15(Media_Payload_G729AnnexB)
  qualifierIn=?.   myIP: c29540e (14.84.41.12)
MediaTerminationPointControl - stationOutputOpenReceiveChannel tcpHandle=65f4204
  myIP: 78d6540e (14.84.214.120)
MediaTerminationPointControl - ConferenceID: 16777229, MediaPartyId: 701,
  msecPacketSize: 20 compressionType: 15
ConnectionManager - wait_AuConnectErrorInd(16777383,16777386)
ConnectionManager - deleteMediaInfoEntry(16777383): ENTRY DELETED, tail == 54
ConnectionManager - deleteMediaInfoEntry(16777386): ENTRY DELETED, tail == 53
StationInit: 65f4204 OpenReceiveChannelAck Status=0, IpAddr=0x78d6540e,
  Port=16390, PartyID=1793
StationD:    67d2040 CloseReceiveChannel conferenceID=0 passThruPartyID=1777.
  myIP: c29540e (14.84.41.12)
StationD:    67d2040 StopMediaTransmission conferenceID=0 passThruPartyID=1777.
  myIP: c29540e (14.84.41.12)
MediaTerminationPointControl - stationOutputCloseReceiveChannel
  tcpHandle=65f4204 myIP: 78d6540e (14.84.214.120)
MediaTerminationPointControl - star_StationOutputCloseReceiveChannel -
  ConferenceID: 100000d, MediaPartyId: 701
MediaTerminationPointControl - stationOutputStopMediaTransmission
  tcpHandle=65f4204 myIP: 78d6540e (14.84.214.120)
MediaTerminationPointControl - star_StationOutputStopMediaTransmission -
  ConferenceID: 100000d MediaPartyId: 701
CTI: RoutePatternToCtiCommandData::findValue() : RP=20034:, bRc=0, T=, #entries=0
EnvProcessCdr::wait_DbCdrReq
MediaManager - ERROR  waitError_AuDisconnectReply
MediaManager - ERROR  waitError_AuDisconnectReply - received all
  disconnect replies, stopProcess()
StationD:    67d2040 StopTone.
StationD:    67d2040 CallState callState=5(Connected) lineInstance=1
  callReference=16777383
StationD:    67d2040 CallInfo callingPartyName='' callingParty=20034
  cgpnVoiceMailbox=10034 calledPartyName='VNT1Apps1Port45' calledParty=11045
  cdpnVoiceMailbox=   originalCalledPartyName='' originalCalledParty=
  originalCdpnVoiceMailbox= originalCdpnRedirectReason=0
  lastRedirectingPartyName='' lastRedirectingParty=14001
  lastRedirectingVoiceMailbox=14001 lastRedirectingReason=0
  callType=2(OutBound) lineInstance=1 callReference=16777383.
StationD::star_StationOutputCallInfo(): callInfo: CI=16777383,
  CallingPartyName=, CallingParty=20034, CalledPartyName=VNT1Apps1Port45,
  CalledParty=11045, OriginalCalledPartyName=, OriginalCalledParty=,
  lastRedirectingPartyName=, lastRedirectingParty=14001
StationD:    67d2040 SelectSoftKeys instance=1 reference=16777383
  softKeySetIndex=1 validKeyMask=-1.
```

Example 11-9 *CCM Trace Showing CallManager Cleanup of the Failed Call (Continued)*

```
StationD:    67d2040 DisplayPromptStatus timeOutValue=0 promptStatus='Connected'
  lineInstance=1 callReference=16777383.
MediaCoordinator - wait_MediaCoordinatorDelResource - CI=16777387 count=0
StationCdpc - INFO: clearType=0, mHoldFlag=0, mMediaConnFlag=1.
StationCdpc - INFO: NormalClear.
MRM::waiting_MrmDeallocateMtpResourceReq- Deallocate received for
  MRM TransactionId= 16777387
MRM::updateMtpCounter MTP0001C96AD659
MRM::updateXcodeCounter MTP0001C96AD659
MRM::updateXcodeCounter allocateCounter=0
StationD:    67d2040 DefineTimeDate timeDateInfo=? systemTime=1022218847.
```

Finally, in Example 11-10, CallManager tells the IP phone to play a reorder tone as a result of the error.

Example 11-10 *CCM Trace Showing Reorder Tone After a Call Failure*

```
StationD:    67d2040 StartTone tone=37(ReorderTone).
waiting_DeallocateMtpResourceReq - DeAllocateMtp = 1 CI=16777387
StationInit: 67d2040 OpenReceiveChannelAck Status=0, IpAddr=0xc29540e, Port=25104,
  PartyID=1777
EnvProcessCdr::insertCdrRecord Insert-Successful  CallingPartyDn: 20034
  CalledPartyDn: 11045  DateTimeDisconnect: 1022218847 DestNodeID: 2
  GlobalCallManagerId: 1    GlobalCallId: 42
```

CallManager then displays the regions matrix for debugging purposes, as Example 11-11 demonstrates.

Example 11-11 *CCM Trace Showing the Regions Matrix*

```
RegionsServer - displaying Regions Server Matrix
RegionA = Campus, RegionB =Campus, bandwith = 64
RegionA = Remote Site 729, RegionB =Remote Site 729, bandwith = 64
RegionA = Remote Site 729, RegionB =Campus, bandwith = 10
RegionA = Campus Transcoders, RegionB =Remote Site 729, bandwith = 10
RegionA = Campus Transcoders, RegionB =Campus Transcoders, bandwith = 64
RegionA = Campus Transcoders, RegionB =Campus, bandwith = 10
```

In this example, the IP IVR server is in the **Campus** region, the transcoder is in the **Campus Transcoders** region, and the IP phone is in the **Remote Site 729** region. Notice the last line of the trace, which says that between Campus Transcoders and Campus, the bandwidth is 10. This means that this region pair is configured for G.729. The call failed because the IP IVR server supports only G.711. Reconfiguring that region pair for G.711 results in a successful call.

Out-of-resource Conditions

One common reason for both conferencing and transcoding problems is a lack of DSP resources to perform the required function. This could occur either because you have run out of conference bridge or transcoder resources or because the device that requires the resource does not have any available in the MRGL it has been configured with.

For example, the call shown in Example 11-12 is similar to the call in the preceding section. A remote IP phone is attempting to call an IP IVR from a remote site.

Example 11-12 *CCM Trace Showing a Call from an IP Phone to an IP IVR Server*

```
StationD:    67d2040 StartTone tone=36(AlertingTone).
StationD:    67d2040 CallState callState=3(RingOut) lineInstance=1
  callReference=16777342
StationD:    67d2040 SelectSoftKeys instance=1 reference=16777342
  softKeySetIndex=8 validKeyMask=-1.
StationD:    67d2040 DisplayPromptStatus timeOutValue=0
  promptStatus='Ring Out' lineInstance=1 callReference=16777342.
ConnectionManager - wait_AuConnectRequest(16777342,16777345): INFORM MEDIA LAYER
ConnectionManager - storeMediaInfo(16777342): ADD NEW ENTRY, tail == 56
ConnectionManager - storeMediaInfo(16777345): ADD NEW ENTRY, tail == 57
MediaCoordinator - wait_AuConnectRequest()
MediaCoordinator - wait_AuConnectRequest - starting MediaManager
  w/ existing (0) connections
MediaCoordinator - wait_AuConnectRequest - new MediaManager(40,74) started
MediaManager(74) started
MediaManager - wait_AuConnectRequest
```

As the output in Example 11-13 shows, CallManager determines that no capabilities match exists and invokes a transcoder. CallManager gets a list of available resources from the MRGL and the default list; however, as you can see, no resources are listed.

Example 11-13 *CCM Trace Showing CallManager Introducing a Transcoder*

```
MediaManager - wait_AuConnectRequest - no caps match, introducing transcoder
MediaManager - wait_AuConnectRequest - allocating transcoder(ci=16777346)
MediaResourceManager::waiting_MrmAllocateXcoderResourceReq
MediaResourceManager::waiting_MrmAllocateXcoderResourceReq - MRGL SEARCH,
  TRY CREATING CHILD USING MRGL LIST
MRM::convertScmStringToRWCString Single HW CFB
MRM::getXcodeDeviceGivenMrgl
MRM::getXcodeDeviceGivenMrgl GETTING XCODE FROM DEFAULT LIST
MediaResourceManager::waiting_MrmAllocateXcoderResourceReq -
  CREATED CHILD USING MRGL AND DEFAULT LIST
MediaResourceCdpc::sortDeviceGivenList
MediaResourceCdpc - Started
MediaResourceCdpc::waiting_MrmAllocateMtpResourceReq
MediaResourceCdpc::findDeviceGivenList
```

Because no resources are available, an error occurs, as shown in the trace output of Example 11-14.

Example 11-14 *CCM Trace Showing Transcoder Allocation Failure*

```
MediaResourceCdpc::mtpErrorResponseToManager
MediaResourceManager::waiting_MrmAllocateMtpResourceErr
MRM::waiting_AllocateMtpResourceErr - ERROR - no resources are available
   -- ci = 16777346
MtpNoMoreResourcesAvailable - No more MTP resources available.
MediaResourceManager::waiting_MrmChildStopInd
MediaManager - errorWaitLastResponse - deallocating media resource(ci=16777346)
MediaManager - wait_AllocateMtpResourceErr
```

As Example 11-15 demonstrates, when CallManager fails to allocate an MTP resource (remember that a transcoder can also function as an MTP), it attempts to connect the two parties directly. However, you already know this attempt will fail because the reason CallManager allocated a transcoder in the first place was that it did not have a capabilities match.

Example 11-15 *CCM Trace Showing Endpoint Direct Connection and a Match Capabilities Error*

```
MediaManager - wait_AllocateMtpResourceErr - directly connecting
   party(16777342) and party(16777345)
MediaResourceCdpc::shutting_down_MrmChildStopConf
MediaCoordinator - wait_AuUpdateDisConnectStatus
MRM::waiting_MrmDeallocateMtpResourceReq- Deallocate received for
   MRM TransactionId= 16777346
MRM::waiting_DeallocateMtpResourceReq- ERROR  Deallocate received for
   an unknown Call Identifier  Ci = 16777346
MediaManager - wait_AuConnectReply
MediaManager - wait_AuConnectReply - received 1 responses, fowarding reply for
   party1(16777342) and party2(16777345)
AgenaInterface - ERROR  waitForMXCapabilitiesExchanged_
   MediaExchangeCapabilitiesIncoming - match capabilities error
AgenaInterface - ERROR  waitForMXCapabilitiesExchanged_
   MediaExchangeCapabilitiesIncoming - match capabilities error
MediaCoordinator - wait_AuConnectReply
ConnectionManager - wait_AuConnectReply(16777342,16777345)
```

Notice in Example 11-16 that you once again see the **ERROR wait_AuConnectErrorInd** error, indicating a failure to set up the media streams.

Example 11-16 *CCM Trace Indicating a Failure to Set Up Media Streams*

```
MediaManager - ERROR  wait_AuConnectErrorInd
MediaManager - ERROR  wait_AuConnectErrorInd - sending disconnect to
   1 MediaExchanges
MediaManager - ERROR  wait_AuConnectErrorInd - sending AuConnectErrorInd to
   parent
MediaManager - ERROR wait_AuConnectErrorInd - only (1) MediaExchange that
   reported error...going away.
MediaCoordinator - wait_AuConnectErrorInd
```

continues

Example 11-16 *CCM Trace Indicating a Failure to Set Up Media Streams (Continued)*

```
MediaCoordinator - wait_AuConnectErrorInd - removing MediaManager(74) from
   connection list
ConnectionManager - wait_AuConnectErrorInd(16777342,16777345)
ConnectionManager - deleteMediaInfoEntry(16777342): ENTRY DELETED, tail == 56
ConnectionManager - deleteMediaInfoEntry(16777345): ENTRY DELETED, tail == 55
```

Skipping a few lines of trace, eventually you see the IP phone receive reorder tone because of the error:

```
StationD:    67d2040 StartTone tone=37(ReorderTone).
```

Failures to allocate a media resource are also logged in PerfMon and RTMT by the counter **TranscoderOutOfResources** in the Cisco CallManager performance object.

If you have a successful call using a WS-X6608 as a transcoder and you want to determine which codecs are in use for each leg of the call, issue the command **show port voice active** *module/port*. Notice in Example 11-17 that the transcoding ID listed in the output corresponds to the ID shown in the CCM traces, so you can easily correlate the output of the **show** command with the trace data.

Example 11-17 *Determining Which Codecs Are in Use for Portions of a Call*

```
Switch (enable) show port voice active 6/6
Port  6/6 :
  Transcoding ID: 16777227
    Party ID: 1633
      Remote IP address               : 14.84.201.20
      UDP Port                        : 16420
      Codec Type                      : G711 ULAW PCM
      Packet Size (ms)                : 20
    Party ID: 1601
      Remote IP address               : 14.84.41.12
      UDP Port                        : 26116
      Codec Type                      : G729 A CS ACELP CISCO
      Packet Size (ms)                : 20
```

On the Catalyst 4604-GWY, you can obtain the same information by using the command **show voicecard transcode**. Also, when you use a VG200 as a DSP farm, you can obtain similar information by using the command **show sccp connections**.

Use of Transcoders in Conjunction with Other Media Resources

One often-overlooked problem along the same lines as the out-of-resource conditions just discussed is the failure to remember that other media resources such as conference bridges or MOH servers might need to invoke a transcoder if they do not have a common codec with the endpoint using the conference bridge or MOH server.

Transcoders in Conjunction with Conference Bridge Resources

Software conferencing supports only G.711. To support a G.729 or G.723 stream, for example, a transcoder must be invoked for each participant that is configured for a low-bandwidth codec. Another example is the Access Gateway Module (AGM) for the Catalyst 4000. Although the AGM is a hardware conference bridge, it supports only G.711. This is in contrast to the WS-X6608 module for the Catalyst 6000, which supports G.711, G.729, and G.723 endpoints natively in a conference. When you mix multiple media resources like this, the regions matrix can get very confusing because now you must consider the codec configured between the regions for the media resources without taking the endpoint into consideration.

For example, Figure 11-3 shows the devices you need to create a three-party conference between two IP phones and a NetMeeting client. Assume that the transcoders, conference bridge, and Endpoint A are all at the same physical location, with LAN connectivity between all devices. A WAN separates Endpoint B and Endpoint C from the rest of the devices.

Figure 11-3 *Devices for a Three-party Conference Involving Transcoders*

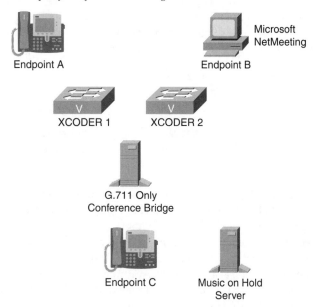

Table 11-4 shows the configured regions matrix for this example. Each device is in its own region for the sake of this example, but this configuration could be greatly simplified and achieve the same results. Notice that the regions named Endpoint C, XCODER 1, XCODER 2, and CFB all have identical regions configurations and all use G.711 within the region as well as between the regions listed above. This means that the devices in the

XCODER 1, XCODER 2, and CFB regions could just be put into the Endpoint C region allowing you to eliminate the XCODER 1, XCODER 2, and CFB regions.

Table 11-4 *Sample Regions Matrix for Six Regions*

	Endpoint A	Endpoint B	Endpoint C	XCODER 1	XCODER 2	CFB
Endpoint A	G.711	G.723	G.729	G.729	G.729	G.729
Endpoint B	G.723	G.711	G.723	G.723	G.723	G.723
Endpoint C	G.729	G.723	G.711	G.711	G.711	G.711
XCODER 1	G.729	G.723	G.711	G.711	G.711	G.711
XCODER 2	G.729	G.723	G.711	G.711	G.711	G.711
CFB	G.729	G.723	G.711	G.711	G.711	G.711

It is beneficial to go through the entire procedure of setting up a conference call to discover just how important the regions configuration is.

First, Endpoint A calls Endpoint C. Both of these devices are Cisco IP Phone models 7960. In Table 11-4 you can see that from Endpoint A to Endpoint C, G.729 has been configured as the codec. Because 7960 IP Phones support G.729 natively, a transcoder is not required. Figure 11-4 illustrates the call up to this point.

Figure 11-4 *Initial Call Setup Between Two Phones*

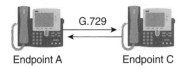

Endpoint A   Endpoint C

Next, Endpoint A presses the **Confrn** soft key to conference in Endpoint B. This causes Endpoint C to be put on hold. If MOH is enabled, the MRGL configured for Endpoint C determines which MOH server Endpoint C should be connected to. As soon as the server has been determined, the regions matrix is checked to determine which codec to use between the MOH server and the IP Phone. Assume for this example that the MOH server is in the same region as Endpoint C. According to the regions matrix shown in Table 11-4, you should use G.711 for calls within Endpoint C's region, so a media stream between the IP Phone and the MOH server is set up using G.711.

While this is happening, Endpoint A calls Endpoint B to add Endpoint B to the conference. Assume that Endpoint A waits for Endpoint B to answer before completing the conference. The regions matrix states that CallManager needs to use G.723 to set up this call. Because Endpoint A is a 7960, it does not support G.723. This means that CallManager must invoke a transcoder to find compatible codecs. The transcoder is chosen based on the MRGL for Endpoint B, so XCODER 2 is chosen. Now you must look at the regions matrix to determine what codec will be used between Endpoint A and XCODER 2, as well as between Endpoint B and XCODER 2. According to the regions matrix, G.729 has been configured between Endpoint A and XCODER 2 and G.723 between Endpoint B and XCODER 2. Figure 11-5 shows what the call looks like at this point.

Figure 11-5 *Calls Between Three Phones Before an Ad Hoc Conference Is Completed*

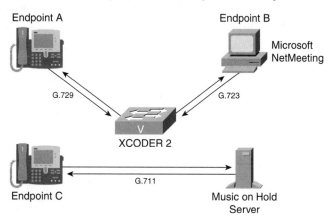

To complete the conference, Endpoint A presses the **Confrn** soft key again. At this point, all the media streams are torn down and redirected to the conference bridge device. The conference bridge device is chosen based on the conference controller's MRGL—in this case, Endpoint A.

Each media stream to the conference bridge is set up individually, and transcoders are allocated as needed. First, CallManager attempts to set up the media stream between Endpoint A and the conference bridge. According to the regions matrix in Table 11-4, the configured codec is G.729. Because the conference bridge supports only G.711, a transcoder is invoked. One very important point to note is that the MRGL used to select a transcoder is based on the conference bridge device's MRGL. You should note that there is no place to explicitly configure an MRGL for a conference bridge device, so you must have one of the two following conditions:

• Have a transcoder available in the default group.

• Ensure that the device pool configured for the conference bridge port has an MRGL assigned to it with one or more transcoder resources.

Now the codec decision must be made between Endpoint A and XCODER 1, as well as between the conference bridge and XCODER 1. According to the regions matrix in Table 11-4, Endpoint A to XCODER 1 is configured to use G.729, and XCODER 1 to the conference bridge is configured to use G.711.

Similarly, Endpoint B to the conference bridge is configured to use G.723. The conference bridge does not support G.723, so a transcoder is invoked from the MRGL of the terminating device (the conference bridge). Following the regions matrix defined in Table 11-4, G.711 is selected between the conference bridge and the transcoder, and G.723 is selected between the transcoder and Endpoint B.

Finally, Endpoint C is added to the conference bridge. The regions matrix indicates that between Endpoint C and the conference bridge, G.711 is used. Because both devices support G.711, a transcoder is not required. Figure 11-6 shows all the media streams and the various codecs after the conference is set up.

Figure 11-6 *Three-party Conference Using Transcoders*

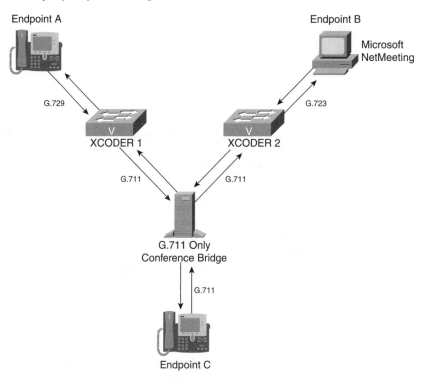

The most important thing to remember here is that if you are having problems setting up media streams, check your regions matrix to ensure that the codec configured between each device is configured such that any two endpoints always have a compatible codec. If a transcoder is involved, ensure that the regions configuration between the transcoder and all endpoints have compatible codecs.

Transcoders in Conjunction with MOH Servers

The example in the preceding section briefly mentioned an MOH server; however, many administrators fail to take into account the region in which the MOH server is located. This is especially important when low-bandwidth codecs are being used because, by default, the Cisco IP Voice Media Streaming Application is enabled only for G.711. The MOH feature of the IP Voice Media Streaming Application can support G.711 μ-law, G.711 A-law, G.729, and wideband codecs. It does not support G.723. As discussed in detail in Chapter 12, when a party is put on hold, the MRGL for the held device determines which MOH server is selected. After the device is selected, the regions configuration determines which codec to use for the MOH stream. If that codec is not enabled on the MOH server, a transcoder might be invoked. As with conference bridge ports, however, there is no way to configure an MRGL for an MOH server. So either a transcoder needs to be available in the default list, or an MRGL should be assigned to the device pool in which the MOH server is configured. Instead of wasting transcoding resources, the best action to take is to enable the codecs you want to use. You do this by going to the Service Parameters Configuration page in CallManager Administration for the Cisco IP Voice Media Streaming Application service (**Service > Service Parameters >** *select a server* **> Cisco IP Voice Media Streaming App**). This parameter is cluster-wide, so it applies to all MOH servers in the cluster. Figure 11-7 shows the **Supported MOH Codecs** parameter.

NOTE   The Supported MOH Codecs parameter was called Default MOH Codec in earlier versions of CallManager. It subsequently was renamed to reflect the true purpose of this parameter.

Figure 11-7 *Supported Codec Configuration for MOH*

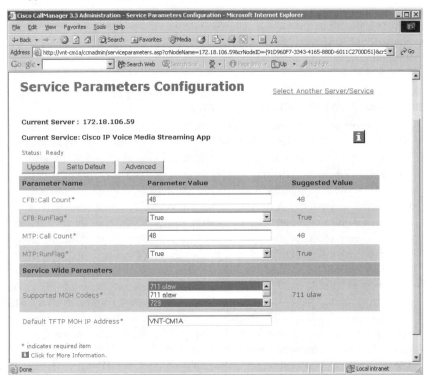

Conference Bridge Devices

CallManager invokes conference bridge resources when three or more audio streams need to be mixed together to form a multiparty conference. CallManager supports two general types of conference resources: software and hardware conference bridges.

Types of Conference Bridges

The most basic form of a conference resource in an IP telephony environment is software conferencing. When installed as a service on a CallManager server, the IP Voice Media Streaming Application provides software conference resources. The IP Voice Media Streaming Application is also responsible for MOH and software MTPs. The IP Voice Media Streaming Application can be installed on one or more CallManager nodes in a cluster. Be aware that because software conferencing consumes system resources, for larger deployments, you should use either a dedicated node in the cluster running the IP Voice Media Streaming Application or hardware conferencing.The IP Voice Media Streaming Application supports only G.711 μ-law and G.711 A-law codecs. It can provide up to 128 streams of conferencing on a standalone server or 24 streams when it coresides with CallManager on the same server.

Various hardware platforms are available that provide conference bridge resources for CallManager. The first of these is the WS-X6608 module. Each port on the WS-X6608 can be configured to be a gateway, a conference bridge, or a transcoder. When configured as a conference bridge, the module supports up to 32 simultaneous streams. These streams can be combined into any number of conferences of three parties or more. The WS-X6608 in conference bridge mode natively supports G.711, G.723, and G.729 for conference participants. The WS-X6608 can also perform conferencing for up to 24 participants using the Global System for Mobile Communications (GSM) codec. In other words, if some participants are using a codec other than G.711, the WS-X6608 conference bridge device converts all the streams to G.711, mixes this audio, and then converts the mixed stream back to the correct codec for each participant instead of having to use an external transcoder.

In contrast, the Catalyst 4000 AGM supports conferencing in hardware; however, it supports only G.711. This means that CallManager needs to use a transcoder if a call to the conference bridge on the AGM requires a low-bandwidth codec. The AGM provides up to 24 streams of conferencing.

The VG200 can be used as a DSP farm for conferencing and transcoding; however, it supports only G.711 and G.729 participants in a conference. Any other codec, such as G.723, requires a transcoder. The VG200 can support up to 90 streams of G.711 μ-law, G.711 A-law, G.729a, or G.729ab conference participants.

Although subtle differences in codec support of the various conference resources exist, from a CallManager perspective troubleshooting them is the same, keeping in mind that additional work needs to happen when a transcoder is required.

Troubleshooting "No Conference Bridge Available"

A common problem with either hardware or software conferencing occurs when a user states that he attempted to place a conference call and received a message on his IP Phone that indicated "No conference bridge available."

The first place to look is in PerfMon or CallManager Serviceability's Real-Time Monitoring Tool (RTMT). Expand the Cisco CallManager object and select all the conferencing counters. Through CallManager release 3.3(2), the counters start with **UnicastSoftware** and **UnicastHardware**. As of release 3.3(3), the counters start with **SWConference** and **HWConference**. Figure 11-8 shows a sample ouput from RTMT.

Figure 11-8 *Release 3.3(2) Conference Bridge Counters in RTMT*

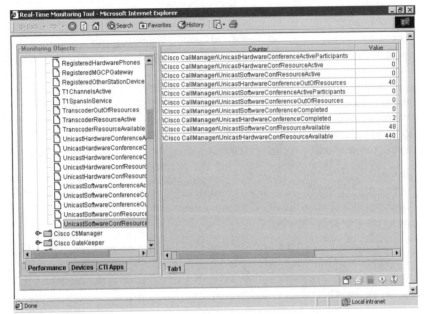

Notice that **UnicastHardwareConferenceOutOfResources**
[**HWConferenceOutOfResources** in release 3.3(3)] is a nonzero value. This indicates that
at some point there were not enough resources to create a software conference bridge.
Notice that in this case 440 hardware conference resources are available, along with 48
software conference resources. At this point the failures don't seem to make sense, because
ample resources appear to be available for conferencing. To troubleshoot, go to the IP
Phone in question and attempt to create a conference. When you do this, if the
UnicastHardwareConferenceOutOfResources [**HWConferenceOutOfResources** in
release 3.3(3)] counter continues to increment with plenty of resources available, there is a
good chance your MRG or MRGL is not configured properly. Looking at a CCM trace from
such an event gives you a better idea of what might be occurring.

The easiest way to quickly find the location in the trace where the error occurred is to search
for the exact text the user saw on his phone. Users often paraphrase the message they saw,
so if you are going to search for a message, make sure you get the exact message first;
otherwise, your search will fail. A less-exact but still-effective method is to obtain the
timestamp from the IP Phone in question at the time the error occurred, in order to have a
starting place in the trace file. In this case, searching for "No conference bridge available"
reveals the following line in the trace file:

```
StationD:      676376c DisplayNotify timeOutValue=10 notify='No conference bridge
      available'
```

You should then write down the TCP handle, **676376c**, and search up in the trace for 676376c until you find the place where the **Confrn** soft key was pressed. Eventually you find the output shown in Example 11-18, which shows the user pressing the **Confrn** soft key.

Example 11-18 *CCM Trace Showing the User Pressing the **Confrn** Soft Key*

```
StationInit: 676376c SoftKeyEvent softKeyEvent=13(Confrn) lineInstance=1
  callReference=16777269
Insert an entry into TransTable, now this table has 1 entries
Delete entries from TransTable, now this table has 0 entries
ConfereeInfo Table has 1 entries
ConfereeInfo Table has 2 entries
```

To create a conference, CallManager must search for an available conference bridge port from the MRGL assigned to the IP Phone. The following trace output shows the attempt to allocate a unicast conference bridge resource. **Ucb** stands for unicast conference bridge:

```
MediaResourceManager::waiting_MrmAllocateUcbResourceReq
```

The next line, shown in Example 11-19, shows that the MRGL for this device equals **0**, meaning that no MRGL is configured for this device. Note that the trace indicates that the default list is being used.

Example 11-19 *CCM Trace Showing MRGL=0*

```
MediaResourceManager::waiting_MrmAllocateUcbResourceReq -
  MRGL=0,CREATED CHILD USING DEFAULT LIST
MediaResourceCdpc::sortDeviceGivenList
MediaResourceCdpc - Started
MediaResourceCdpc::waiting_MrmAllocateUcbResourceReq
```

Notice that there is no list of devices after the **sortDeviceGivenList** line in the trace. This means that the list of media resources in the default list is empty. This then causes the failure to occur, as shown in Example 11-20.

Example 11-20 *CCM Trace Showing the Inability to Allocate a Conference Bridge*

```
MediaResourceCdpc::findDeviceGivenList
MediaResourceCdpc::ucbErrorResponseToManager
MediaResourceManager::waiting_MrmAllocateUcbResourceErr
MRM::waiting_MrmAllocateUcbResourceErr - ERROR - unable to identify requestor -
  ci = 16777272
MediaResourceManager::waiting_MrmChildStopInd
MediaResourceCdpc::shutting_down_MrmChildStopConf
```

As a result of the inability to allocate a conference bridge resource, CallManager displays the message "No conference bridge available" on the IP Phone:

```
StationD:     676376c DisplayNotify timeOutValue=10 notify=
  'No conference bridge available'
StationD:     676376c DisplayText text='No conference bridge available  '
```

Going through a working scenario will better familiarize you with what a successful call should look like. As Example 11-21 shows, again you see that the **Confrn** soft key is pressed.

Example 11-21 *CCM Trace Showing the User Pressing the **Confrn** Soft Key*

```
StationInit: 10d5d444 SoftKeyEvent softKeyEvent=13(Confrn) lineInstance=1
  callReference=16777974.
Insert an entry into MonitorPartyTable, now this table has 1 entries
Insert an entry into MonitorPartyTable, now this table has 2 entries
Insert an entry into TransTable, now this table has 1 entries
Delete entries from TransTable, now this table has 0 entries
ConfereeInfo Table has 1 entries
ConfereeInfo Table has 2 entries
```

In Example 11-22, the media resource manager is queried for an available conference bridge resource. This time, a list of resources is returned. The second line is a list of all the MRGs in the MRGL.

Example 11-22 *CCM Trace Showing the List of Configured MRGs*

```
MediaResourceManager::waiting_MrmAllocateUcbResourceReq
MRM::convertScmStringToRWCString BldgB HW CFB:BldgB XCODE:BldgC HW CFB:BldgC
XCODE:BldgD HW CFB:BldgD XCODE:Unicast MOH:Software CFB:Software MTP
```

Next, in Example 11-23, all the devices in the MRGL are listed, along with a counter indicating how many sessions are active on the port. The **Group** number indicates which MRG the device is in.

Example 11-23 *CCM Trace Showing Devices in an MRGL*

```
MRM::getUcbDeviceGivenMrgl
MRM::getUcbDeviceGivenMrgl CFB0001C96AD65A Group=0 Counter=0
MRM::getUcbDeviceGivenMrgl CFB0001C96AD65B Group=0 Counter=0
MRM::getUcbDeviceGivenMrgl CFB0002FCE16D7C Group=2 Counter=0
MRM::getUcbDeviceGivenMrgl CFB0002FCE16D7D Group=2 Counter=0
MRM::getUcbDeviceGivenMrgl CFB0002FCE17601 Group=4 Counter=0
MRM::getUcbDeviceGivenMrgl CFB00027E38DFB8 Group=4 Counter=0
MRM::getUcbDeviceGivenMrgl CFB_VNT1-MOH1 Group=7 Counter=0
MRM::getUcbDeviceGivenMrgl CFB_VNT1-MOH2 Group=7 Counter=0
```

In Example 11-24, all the devices in the default MRGL are added to the list as well. In this case there are no devices in the default list.

Example 11-24 *CCM Trace Showing a Device Request from the Default Media Resource Group List*

```
MRM::getUcbDeviceGivenMrgl GETTING UCB FROM DEFAULT LIST
MediaResourceManager::waiting_MrmAllocateUcbResourceReq -
  CREATED CHILD USING MRGL AND DEFAULT LIST
```

In Example 11-25, the list appears a second time, but this time sorted in order of preference.

Example 11-25 *CCM Trace Showing the Device List Ordered by Preference*

```
MediaResourceCdpc::sortDeviceGivenList
MediaResourceCdpc::sortDeviceGivenList Name=CFB0001C96AD65A Group=0 Counter=0
MediaResourceCdpc::sortDeviceGivenList Name=CFB0001C96AD65B Group=0 Counter=0
MediaResourceCdpc::sortDeviceGivenList Name=CFB0002FCE16D7C Group=2 Counter=0
MediaResourceCdpc::sortDeviceGivenList Name=CFB0002FCE16D7D Group=2 Counter=0
MediaResourceCdpc::sortDeviceGivenList Name=CFB0002FCE17601 Group=4 Counter=0
MediaResourceCdpc::sortDeviceGivenList Name=CFB00027E38DFB8 Group=4 Counter=0
MediaResourceCdpc::sortDeviceGivenList Name=CFB_VNT1-MOH1 Group=7 Counter=0
MediaResourceCdpc::sortDeviceGivenList Name=CFB_VNT1-MOH2 Group=7 Counter=0
MediaResourceCdpc - Started
MediaResourceCdpc::waiting_MrmAllocateUcbResourceReq
```

In Example 11-26, the media resource manager returns the device name for a conference bridge device.

Example 11-26 *CCM Trace Showing Conference Bridge Device Selection*

```
MediaResourceCdpc::findDeviceGivenList
MediaResourceCdpc::waiting_MrmAllocateUcbResourceReq UcbDevice=CFB0001C96AD65A
MediaResourceCdpc::device_lookup_DevicePidRes
MediaResourceCdpc::device_lookup_DevicePidRes UcbResource=CFB0001C96AD65A
MediaResourceCdpc::resource_rsvp_AllocateUcbResourceRes
MediaResourceManager::waiting_MrmAllocateUcbResourceRes
```

Finally, in Example 11-27, the counters are updated to indicate an allocation to this resource. A conference bridge ID also is allocated. In this example, **b00110526001** is the number assigned to this conference.

Example 11-27 *CCM Trace Showing Conference Bridge ID Assignment*

```
MRM::updateUcbCounter CFB0001C96AD65A
MRM::updateUcbCounter MRL allocateCounter=1
MRM::waiting_MrmAllocateUcbResourceRes - return to CC bridge =
   b00110526001 CFB0001C96AD65A
MediaResourceManager::waiting_MrmChildStopInd
MediaResourceCdpc::shutting_down_MrmChildStopConf
Insert an entry into TransTable, now this table has 1 entries
```

Troubleshooting Conference Failures

You might discover situations in which the resource selection is successful but the conference still fails. Before looking at the next set of traces, you must understand how a conference call is created in CallManager.

As shown in the trace in Example 11-27, after a conference resource has been allocated, CallManager assigns a conference bridge ID for the Ad Hoc conference. All participants who are added to the conference use this conference bridge identifier, which uniquely identifies the conference. An Ad Hoc conference is created when two parties are speaking and one of them uses the **Confrn** soft key to add a third participant. The user who wants to create the conference presses the **Confrn** soft key, dials the party she wants to add to the conference, and then presses the **Confrn** soft key again. The parties are not added to the conference bridge until the **Confrn** soft key is pressed a second time. The following trace excerpt shows how parties are added to a conference after the **Confrn** soft key is pressed:

```
StationInit: 64f1f8c SoftKeyEvent softKeyEvent=13(Confrn) lineInstance=1
  callReference=16778130
```

The first thing that happens after this event is that all the media streams are torn down. This is because CallManager needs to redirect all the media streams to the conference bridge device. The trace output shown in Example 11-28 demonstrates this.

Example 11-28 *CCM Trace Showing Conference Participants Being Redirected to the Conference Bridge*

```
ConnectionManager - wait_AuDisconnectRequest(16778130,16778131): STOP STREAMING
ConnectionManager - storeMediaInfo(16778130): EXISTING ENTRY DISCOVERED,
  tail == 64
ConnectionManager - storeMediaInfo(16778131): EXISTING ENTRY DISCOVERED,
  tail == 64
MediaCoordinator - wait_AuDisconnectRequest
MediaCoordinator - wait_AuDisconnectRequest - sending disconnect to
  MediaManager(265)
MediaManager - wait_AuDisconnectRequest
MediaManager - wait_AuDisconnectRequest - no proxy and StopStreaming send
  disconnect to (71,265)
StationD:    64f1f8c CloseReceiveChannel conferenceID=0 passThruPartyID=5937.
  myIP: 67dd540e (14.84.221.103)
StationD:    64f1f8c StopMediaTransmission conferenceID=0 passThruPartyID=5937.
  myIP: 67dd540e (14.84.221.103)
StationD:    669da80 CloseReceiveChannel conferenceID=0 passThruPartyID=5953.
  myIP: 64e7540e (14.84.231.100)
StationD:    669da80 StopMediaTransmission conferenceID=0 passThruPartyID=5953.
  myIP: 64e7540e (14.84.231.100)
```

This action goes on for several lines as the media streams for all three devices involved in the call are torn down. For brevity, the remainder of the media teardown has been excluded. Eventually you see what appears to be a call from one of the conference participants, but the phone number being dialed looks unusual. Take a look at the digit analysis results in Example 11-29.

Example 11-29 *CCM Trace Showing Conference Participants Being Added to the Conference Bridge*

```
Digit analysis: match(fqcn="20021", cn="20021",
  pss="RTPLine1PT:RTPctiPortsPT:RTPVoicemail_2_PT:RTPVoicemail_1_PT:RTPTollFreePT:
  RTPTieLinesPT:RTPPAManagedPhones:RTPLongDistancePT:RTPLocalPT:
  RTPInternationalPT:RTPInternalCLT_PBX_PT:RTPInternalATL_PBX_PT:RTPCallParkPT:
  RTP911EmergencyPT:CLTVoicemail_1_PT:CHIVoicemail_1_PT", dd="b00110548009")
Digit analysis: analysis results
|PretransformCallingPartyNumber=20021
```

Example 11-29 *CCM Trace Showing Conference Participants Being Added to the Conference Bridge (Continued)*

```
|CallingPartyNumber=20021
|DialingPartition=
|DialingPattern=b00110548009
|DialingRoutePatternRegularExpression=(b00110548009)
|DialingWhere=
|PatternType=Enterprise
|PotentialMatches=NoPotentialMatchesExist
|DialingSdlProcessId=(1,105,48)
|PretransformDigitString=b00110548009
|PretransformTagsList=SUBSCRIBER
|PretransformPositionalMatchList=b00110548009
|CollectedDigits=b00110548009
|UnconsumedDigits=
|TagsList=SUBSCRIBER
|PositionalMatchList=b00110548009
|VoiceMailbox=
|DisplayName=Call Manager
|RouteBlockFlag=RouteThisPattern
|InterceptPartition=
|InterceptPattern=
|InterceptWhere=
|InterceptSdlProcessId=(0,0,0)
|InterceptSsType=0
|InterceptSsKey=0
```

What this means is that extension 20021 is being added to the conference. You see a digit analysis match like the one in Example 11-29 for each of the three conference participants, as well as any additional participants added after the initial three. You can think of this as three IP Phones placing a call to one number that represents the conference.

In this case, the conference fails, as Example 11-30 confirms.

Example 11-30 *CCM Trace Showing a Failure to Add a Party to a Conference*

```
UnicastBridgeControl - ERROR CcSetup / Conference failed-
   no resources are available -- Ci = 1000394, Cdpn=b00110548009
Delete entries from TransTable, now this table has 30 entries
Insert an entry into CiCcp table, now this table has 63 entries
Insert an entry into TransTable, now this table has 31 entries
StationCdpc - INFO: clearType=0, mHoldFlag=0, mMediaConnFlag=1
StationCdpc - INFO: NormalClear
EnvProcessCdr::insertCdrRecord Insert-Successful  CallingPartyDn: 20019
   CalledPartyDn: 20021  DateTimeDisconnect: 1022208863 DestNodeID: 1
   GlobalCallManagerId: 1    GlobalCallId: 311
EnvProcessCdr::wait_DbCdrReq
StationD:    64f1f8c DefineTimeDate timeDateInfo=? systemTime=1022208863
StationD:    64f1f8c StartTone tone=37(ReorderTone)
```

Instead of being added to the conference, the participant is dropped immediately and hears a reorder tone. The same thing happens to the other two participants. Example 11-31 shows the digit analysis results for the second participant.

Example 11-31 *CCM Trace Showing an Attempt to Add a Party to a Conference*

```
Digit analysis: match(fqcn="20019", cn="20019",
  pss="RTPLine1PT:RTPctiPortsPT:RTPVoicemail_2_PT:RTPVoicemail_1_PT:RTPTollFreePT:
  RTPTieLinesPT:RTPPAManagedPhones:RTPLongDistancePT:RTPLocalPT:
  RTPInternationalPT:RTPInternalCLT_PBX_PT:RTPInternalATL_PBX_PT:RTPCallParkPT:
  RTP911EmergencyPT:CLTVoicemail_1_PT:CHIVoicemail_1_PT", dd="b00110548009")
Digit analysis: analysis results
|PretransformCallingPartyNumber=20019
|CallingPartyNumber=20019
|DialingPartition=
|DialingPattern=b00110548009
|DialingRoutePatternRegularExpression=(b00110548009)
|DialingWhere=
|PatternType=Enterprise
|PotentialMatches=NoPotentialMatchesExist
|DialingSdlProcessId=(1,105,48)
|PretransformDigitString=b00110548009
|PretransformTagsList=SUBSCRIBER
|PretransformPositionalMatchList=b00110548009
|CollectedDigits=b00110548009
|UnconsumedDigits=
|TagsList=SUBSCRIBER
|PositionalMatchList=b00110548009
|VoiceMailbox=
|DisplayName=Call Manager
|RouteBlockFlag=RouteThisPattern
|InterceptPartition=
|InterceptPattern=
|InterceptWhere=
|InterceptSdlProcessId=(0,0,0)
|InterceptSsType=0
|InterceptSsKey=0
```

Again the attempt to add a participant to the conference fails, and the user hears a reorder tone, as Example 11-32 confirms.

Example 11-32 *CCM Trace Showing a Failure to Add a Party to a Conference*

```
UnicastBridgeControl - ERROR  CcSetup / Conference failed- no resources
  are available -- Ci = 1000395, Cdpn=b00110548009
StationD:    64f1f8c SetLamp stimulus=125(Conference) stimulusInstance=1
  lampMode=1(LampOff)
Delete entries from TransTable, now this table has 30 entries
CTI: RoutePatternToCtiCommandData::findValue() : RP=20019:, bRc=0, T=, #entries=0
EnvProcessCdr::insertCdrRecord Insert-Successful  CallingPartyDn: 20021
  CalledPartyDn: b00110548009  DateTimeDisconnect: 1022208863 DestNodeID: 0
  GlobalCallManagerId: 1   GlobalCallId: 311
CTI: RoutePatternToCtiCommandData::findValue() : RP=20019:, bRc=0, T=, #entries=0
```

Example 11-32 *CCM Trace Showing a Failure to Add a Party to a Conference (Continued)*

```
Insert an entry into CiCcp table, now this table has 64 entries
Insert an entry into TransTable, now this table has 31 entries
StationCdpc - INFO: clearType=0, mHoldFlag=2, mMediaConnFlag=1
StationCdpc - INFO: NormalClear
EnvProcessCdr::wait_DbCdrReq
StationD:    669d2b0 DefineTimeDate timeDateInfo=? systemTime=1022208863
StationD:    669d2b0 StartTone tone=37(ReorderTone)
```

The same thing happens for the third participant. The traces for the third participant have been omitted for brevity because they are identical to the first two. After the third participant is dropped, the media resource is deallocated, as shown in Example 11-33.

Example 11-33 *CCM Trace Showing the Deallocation of Media Resources*

```
MediaResourceManager::waiting_MrmDeallocateUcbResourceReq
MRM::updateUcbCounter CFB0001C96AD65A
MRM::updateUcbCounter MRL allocateCounter=8
MRM::updateUcbCounter MRL allocateCounter=7
MRM::waiting_MrmDeallocateUcbResourceReq UcbDeviceDn=b00110548009
```

If you see an error such as this, you can look at the conference resource to see if it is out of resources. In this case, the conference resource in use is a port on a WS-X6608 card providing hardware conferencing. From the Catalyst 6000 command-line interface (CLI), issue the command **show port voice active**, which results in the output shown in Example 11-34.

Example 11-34 *Determining if a Conference Resource Is Out of Resources*

```
Console (enable) show port voice active
Port   Type          Total Conference-ID/ Party-ID IP-Address
                            Transcoding-ID
-----  ------------  ----- --------------- -------- ---------------
6/7   conferencing  8     16777217        49       14.84.231.101
                                          65       14.84.221.100
                                          97       14.84.221.103
                          16777218        145      14.84.213.121
                                          161      14.84.213.100
                                          193      14.84.221.104
                          16777219        241      14.84.231.100
                                          257      14.84.233.119
                                          289      14.84.223.100
                          16777220        385      14.84.231.104
                                          401      14.84.211.100
                                          372      14.84.211.102
                                          577      14.84.211.105
                                          609      14.84.223.103
                          16777221        481      14.84.223.106
                                          497      14.84.233.117
                                          513      14.84.233.121
                          16777222        705      14.84.41.13
```

continues

Example 11-34 *Determining if a Conference Resource Is Out of Resources (Continued)*

```
                             721        14.84.41.12
                             690        14.84.41.15
                             1233       14.84.233.123
                16777223     817        14.84.211.103
                             849        14.84.211.104
                             881        14.84.221.101
                             1121       14.84.223.102
                             804        14.84.211.101
                             1169       14.84.231.102
                16777224     945        14.84.213.118
                             1025       14.84.213.119
                             1057       14.84.221.102
                             1201       14.84.223.101
                             933        14.84.213.120
```

Notice that port 6/7 has 32 media streams allocated in a total of eight conferences. The WS-X6608 has a maximum limit of 32 streams per port, so this port is clearly full. If this occurs frequently, you might want to consider purchasing additional DSP resources to handle the Ad Hoc conferencing load.

From the Catalyst 6000 CLI you can obtain additional information about the currently active conferences. If you issue the command **show port voice active** *module/port*, you see detailed information about each conference participant, as Example 11-35 demonstrates.

Example 11-35 *Displaying Currently Active Conference Information*

```
Console (enable) show port voice active 6/7
  Conference ID: 16777217
    Party ID: 49
      Remote IP address            : 14.84.231.101
      UDP Port                     : 24966
      Codec Type                   : G711 ULAW PCM
      Packet Size (ms)             : 20
    Party ID: 65
      Remote IP address            : 14.84.221.100
      UDP Port                     : 22976
      Codec Type                   : G711 ULAW PCM
      Packet Size (ms)             : 20
    Party ID: 97
      Remote IP address            : 14.84.221.103
      UDP Port                     : 23196
      Codec Type                   : G711 ULAW PCM
      Packet Size (ms)             : 20
  Conference ID: 16777218
    Party ID: 145
      Remote IP address            : 14.84.213.121
      UDP Port                     : 20366
      Codec Type                   : G711 ULAW PCM
      Packet Size (ms)             : 20
    Party ID: 161
      Remote IP address            : 14.84.213.100
```

Example 11-35 *Displaying Currently Active Conference Information (Continued)*

```
            UDP Port                        : 20924
            Codec Type                      : G711 ULAW PCM
            Packet Size (ms)                : 20
       Party ID: 193
            Remote IP address               : 14.84.221.104
            UDP Port                        : 24032
            Codec Type                      : G711 ULAW PCM
            Packet Size (ms)                : 20
```

You can obtain similar information for the WS-X4604-GWY using the command **show voicecard conference**. If you are using a VG200 for conferencing resources, use the command **show sccp connections** to view this data.

Other Conferencing Error Messages

You might encounter a few other error messages when dealing with Ad Hoc conferences in CallManager. The following sections describe them.

"Already In Conference"

One common issue occurs when a user reports that he received a message that indicated "Already In Conference" when he pressed the **Confrn** soft key (or the **Conference** button on legacy IP Phones). This is not a problem you need to troubleshoot, other than explaining to the user how the **Confrn** soft key is designed to work.

The reason for the "Already In Conference" message is that the user does not have the right to add conference participants to an active conference. The party who originates an Ad Hoc conference is called the *conference controller*. The conference controller is the only member of the Ad Hoc conference who can add or drop participants from the conference. This might change in a future version of CallManager. If a party other than the conference controller presses the **Confrn** soft key while in a conference, the "Already In Conference" message appears. This feature operates as expected.

"Exceeds maximum parties"

Another common message displayed on IP Phones is "Exceeds maximum parties." This occurs when a user attempts to add a party to a conference after reaching the configured maximum. The maximum number of parties per Ad Hoc conference is user-configurable. Officially, Cisco supports up to six participants in a single Ad Hoc conference. Some hardware conference resources such as the AGM for the Catalyst 4000 and the VG200 DSP farm have a hardware limitation of six participants in a single conference. For this reason, you should not set the **MaxAdHocConference** service parameter to a value any greater than 6. To increase this number above the default value of 4, go to the CallManager service parameters and adjust the **MaxAdHocConference** service parameter (**Service > Service Parameters >** *select a server* **> Cisco CallManager >** *scroll down to* **Conference Bridge Parameters** *area*). Note that you need to configure this service parameter for each server. Failure to do so can result in some users being able to create larger conferences than others.

Best Practices

The following are some helpful tips to ensure best practices when dealing with conference bridges and transcoders:

- Keep your MRG/MRGL configuration as simple as possible. The more MRGLs you have, the better the chance of a misconfiguration.

- Always remember that when a media resource is assigned to *any* MRG, it is no longer available as part of the default MRGL. This means that endpoints that require the use of a media resource in an MRG must have an MRGL configured that contains that MRG. The opposite is also true—if a media resource is not in any MRG, it is in the default MRGL and therefore available to any endpoint, even endpoints with no MRGL configured.

- Monitor the PerfMon/RTMT counters mentioned earlier that report out-of-resource conditions. This proactively notifies you when users are having problems conferencing or invoking a transcoder or MTP.

- Be extremely careful when configuring your codec selections between regions. This is by far the most common cause of transcoder problems.

- As of CallManager 3.3, locations-based CAC (discussed in Chapter 13, "Call Admission Control") does not take transcoders into consideration, so you might end up allocating bandwidth that is not being used or vice versa because the wrong codec is used for the location's bandwidth reservation. For more information about locations, refer to Chapter 13.

Summary

Most IP telephony installations require the use of one or more conference bridge resources to provide multiparty conferencing, as well as transcoders to enable devices with incompatible codecs to interoperate. The configuration of the regions matrix for the various regions configured in CallManager is absolutely essential to ensuring that the correct codec is selected for a call terminating on a transcoder or conference bridge resource. Additionally, understanding MRG and MRGL configuration is essential to ensuring that devices requiring a media resource have one available.

## CHAPTER 12

Music on Hold

The Music on Hold (MOH) feature was introduced in Cisco CallManager version 3.1 and is a widely used feature. It is important to understand how it works so that any problems can be quickly resolved. This chapter begins with a discussion of how MOH works and then discusses how to troubleshoot it.

Understanding MOH

The MOH server allows users to place OnNet and OffNet callers on hold with music streamed from an MOH server. The actual service that facilitates MOH is the Cisco IP Voice Media Streaming Application. For MOH to work, this service must be running. If MOH isn't working, the first thing to check is that the service is running.

Here are some important facts about the MOH server:

- By default, the MOH server only streams using G.711 μ-law, but it can be configured to stream in G.711 A-law, G.729, and wideband as well.

- The MOH server can create unicast or multicast streams.

- You can configure two types of audio sources per device:

  - **User hold MOH audio source**—*User hold* means that the user pressed the **Hold** soft key.

  - **Network hold MOH audio source**—*Network hold* means that the user attempted to transfer, conference, or park a call, which requires CallManager to place the call on hold while performing the feature operation.

- You can configure a user hold MOH audio source and network hold MOH audio source at the cluster-wide level, device pool level, device level, and directory number (DN) level. The most explicit option is used. In other words, you can set MOH options on a device pool. This could affect hundreds of IP Phones. You could take some of those IP Phones and specify a different MOH source in the individual device settings for the phones. Because setting the MOH on the IP Phone is more explicit than the device pool, the setting at the IP Phone level (the device level), takes precedence.

- The MOH server communicates with CallManager using the Skinny protocol.

- IP Phones and gateways can have a user hold MOH audio source defined. Gateways don't have a network hold MOH audio source because they cannot invoke transfers, conferences, or call park.

- A sound card is needed only if a fixed audio source is used, such as a CD-ROM or external input device.

- You can select only one fixed audio source (live audio from a sound card) for an entire CallManager cluster, but you can specify up to 50 additional audio sources (one wave audio file for each source).

- The IP Phone invoking the hold determines which audio file should be played to the party on hold, but the party on hold must have access to an MOH server for the specified file to be played. If not, tone on hold is heard instead.

This list by no means spells out all the MOH server's capabilities. It should be enough, however, to provide a framework to work with as you troubleshoot potential problems.

One more critical function you must understand before looking into troubleshooting MOH is the operation of media resource groups (MRGs) and media resource group lists (MRGLs).

MRGs and MRGLs are important constructs in CallManager. Media resources include MOH servers, hardware and software conference bridges, transcoders, and media termination points (MTPs). Media resources are added to MRGs, and the priority of MRGs is defined in MRGLs. Endpoints are then configured with MRGs and MRGLs so that the endpoints can access the media resources defined in the MRGs. An endpoint must have an MRGL defined in its configuration to have access to media resources.

Before you can assume that there is a problem with the MOH server, you must know if the endpoints in question have access to an MOH resource on the MOH server via the MRG/MRGL construct.

Before proceeding, you should understand the following terms:

- **Holding party**—In an active, two-party call, the *holding party* initiates a hold action (either user hold or network hold). For example, if Party A is talking to Party B, and Party A presses the **Hold** soft key to initiate a hold action, Party A is considered the holding party.

- **Held party**—In an active, two-party call, the *held party* is the party who is placed on hold. For example, if Party A is talking to Party B, and Party A presses the **Hold** soft key to initiate a hold action, Party B is considered the held party.

With these terms in mind, consider the following scenario. Party A works in the marketing department and has a specific marketing MOH audio source specified. Party B works in engineering and has a specific engineering MOH audio source specified. There are two MOH servers in the cluster. Both have the same audio source files.

If Party A and Party B are having a conversation, and Party A presses the **Hold** button, what music does Party B hear, and where does it come from? Look at Figure 12-1 to determine the answer.

Figure 12-1 *MOH Example*

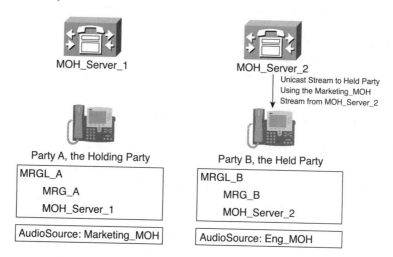

First, notice that the holding party controls what audio source is heard. Callers to Party A hear the same marketing audio file played when they are placed on hold, assuming that their IP Phones have access to an MOH server. Second, Party B hears this file from an MOH source in its own MRG/MRGL. What would happen if Party B did not have access to an MOH resource? The answer is that Party B would simply hear tone on hold.

These facts are critical. A gateway or IP Phone can hear an MOH audio stream only if it has an MRG/MRGL configured that includes an MOH server. If it has access to an MOH server, the IP Phone or gateway hears what the holding party wants it to hear (as specified in the holding party's user and network hold audio source configuration).

This same example applies to Party A attempting to transfer, conference, or call park. The only difference is that the *network* audio source is used for these actions. Normally the user and network audio sources are the same, but they could be different if a company chose so.

Troubleshooting Data Points

Before looking at the approach, take a look at what data points you can reference to help in troubleshooting MOH.

Performance Counters

Using Microsoft Performance (PerfMon) or the Real-Time Monitoring Tool in Cisco CallManager Serviceability, you can monitor the MOH server's current status. Several counters are available. For the server's overall status, use the Cisco Music on Hold Server object for CallManager releases through 3.3(2). Starting with release 3.3(3), the same counters are provided in the Cisco Media Streaming Application object. These counters provide the overall status of the MOH server itself on a per-CallManager basis because an MOH server is registered with only one CallManager at a time. Table 12-1 lists these counters and explains their use and interpretation.

Table 12-1 *Cisco Music on Hold Server/Cisco Media Streaming Application Counters*

Counter Name Through Release 3.3(2)/ Counter Name as of Release 3.3(3)	Information Provided
ConnectionState/MOHConnectionState	For each CallManager associated with an MOH server, this represents the current registration state to CallManager. • 0—No registration to any CallManager • 1—Registration to the primary CallManager • 2—Registration to the secondary CallManager This is important because a 2 indicates that the MOH server has failed over to its secondary CallManager. This should not change what audio source the user hears because all MOH servers should have the same audio source files.
NumberOfActiveAudioSources/ MOHAudioSourcesActive	The number of active (currently in use) audio sources for this MOH server. Some of these audio sources may not be actively streaming audio data if there are no devices listening. The exception is for multicast audio sources, which will always be streaming audio. Note: Current behavior for this counter is such that when an audio source is in use, even after the listener has disconnected, this counter will always have one input stream for each configured MOH codec. For unicast streams, the stream may be in a suspended state where no audio data is received until a device connects to listen to the stream. Is this the number you expect? If five audio sources are configured, you should see five active sources in this counter. If you don't see the expected number of audio sources, check for the following problems:

Table 12-1   *Cisco Music on Hold Server/Cisco Media Streaming Application Counters (Continued)*

Counter Name Through Release 3.3(2)/ Counter Name as of Release 3.3(3)	Information Provided
	• The process of adding the audio sources might have failed. Check the audio source configuration in CallManager Administration (**Service > Media Resource > Music on Hold Audio Source**) to be sure that all audio sources you have configured are accurately reflected in this counter. • If zero audio sources are shown in this counter and you know you have configured some, check to be sure the Cisco IP Voice Media Streaming Application is running. • If you don't see the number of audio sources you expect to see, there could be a problem with the actual audio source files—for example, the files have been moved, saved to the wrong location, or inadvertently deleted. You should check to be sure the audio sources are saved to the proper location on the TFTP server. To determine the proper location, check the location specified in the DefaultTFTPMOHFilePath field of the Cisco MOH Audio Translator service (**Service > Service Parameters >** *select a server* **> Cisco MOH Audio Translator**) and then look in that directory for the files.
NumberOfActiveStreams/MOHStreamsActive	The total number of active (currently in use) simplex (one direction) streams for all connections. There is one output stream for each device listening to a unicast audio source and one input stream for each active audio source, multiplied by the number of MOH codecs. Note: Current behavior for this counter is such that when an audio source has been used once, it will always have one input stream for each configured MOH codec. For unicast streams, the stream may be in a suspended state where no audio data is received until a device connects to listen to the stream.
NumberOfAvailableStreams/ MOHStreamsAvailable	The remaining number of streams allocated for the MOH device that are available for use. This counter starts as 408 plus the number of configured half-duplex unicast connections and is reduced by 1 for each active stream started. The counter is reduced by 2 for each multicast audio source, multiplied by the number of MOH codecs configured. The counter is reduced by 1 for each unicast audio source, multiplied by the number of MOH codecs configured.

continues

Table 12-1 *Cisco Music on Hold Server/Cisco Media Streaming Application Counters (Continued)*

Counter Name Through Release 3.3(2)/ Counter Name as of Release 3.3(3)	Information Provided
NumberOfLostConnections/ MOHConnectionsLost	The total number of times since the last restart of the Cisco IP Voice Media Streaming Application that a CallManager connection was lost.
	This counter should be used in combination with the ConnectionState/ MOHConnectionState counter.
	If this counter shows 1, and the ConnectionState/ MOHConnectionState counter shows 2, you know that a connection has been lost once and that the MOH server is currently registered to the secondary CallManager. If this counter is high, check the network for outages.
TotalNumberOfStreams/MOHStreamsTotal	The total number of simplex (one direction) streams that have connected to the MOH server since the Cisco IP Voice Media Streaming Application service started. This number increments with each endpoint placed on hold to receive music.

The counters described in Table 12-1 provide a high-level view of the server's status. The counters described in Table 12-2 provide a little more detail. The Cisco MOH Device object has individual counters for unicast and multicast streams.

Table 12-2 *Cisco MOH Device Counters*

Counter	Information Provided
MOHTotalUnicastResources	The total number of unicast MOH connections allowed by this MOH server. When the MOH server registers with CallManager, it advertises this number to CallManager.
MOHTotalMulticastResources	The total number of multicast MOH connections allowed to multicast addresses served by this MOH server.
MOHUnicastResourceActive	The number of active unicast MOH connections to this MOH server. Use this in combination with the MOHUnicastResourceAvailable counter.
MOHMulticastResourceActive	The number of currently active multicast connections to multicast addresses served by this MOH server.
	Only one multicast stream per audio source and per codec is coming from this server. Many different parties could currently be "listening." This counter tells you how many are.

Table 12-2   *Cisco MOH Device Counters (Continued)*

Counter	Information Provided
MOHUnicastResourceAvailable	The number of unicast MOH connections that are not active and are still available to be used at the current time for this MOH server. Use this in combination with the MOHUnicastResourceActive counter.
MOHMulticastResourceAvailable	The number of multicast MOH connections to multicast addresses served by this MOH server that are not active and are still available to be used at the current time for this MOH server.
MOHOutOfResources	The number of times the media resource manager (MRM) attempted to allocate an MOH resource from this MOH server and failed, for example because all available connections of the type requested were in use.
	If you see this counter going up, check the trace files. Either the MOH server is being oversubscribed or it lost registration to CallManager at some point. Also, check the NumberOfLostConnections or MOHConnectionsLost counter as described in Table 12-1. That counter tells you if the reason is lost connections.
MOHHighestActiveResources	This represents the largest number of simultaneously active MOH connections for this MOH server. This includes both multicast and unicast connections.
	This counter gives you an idea of the maximum load that has been placed on this server.

As you look at the status of your MOH resources, these counters can tell you much about their current state.

CCM Trace Files

CCM trace files can help provide additional insight into the operation of an MOH server.

First, you need to review the difference between unicast and multicast in regards to CallManager, MOH server, and endpoints.

With unicast, the MOH server is commanded to generate a stream to the IP address of the endpoint receiving the stream. The endpoint is told to listen to the stream, which includes various messages depending on the protocol and the type of endpoint. When the call is to be taken off hold, the MOH server is told to stop streaming, and the held party is connected to the appropriate endpoint.

With multicast, the MOH server is always streaming the multicast stream. As such, CallManager doesn't need to tell the MOH server to do anything. The endpoint is simply told to listen to the multicast stream.

That being said, you now know what you should expect to see.

Examples 12-1 through 12-3 show a CCM trace file of an IP Phone being told to listen to a multicast stream. The first part of the CCM trace, Example 12-1, shows a normal call setup to this IP Phone. Refer to Chapter 5, "IP Phones," for details on how to read traces like this.

Example 12-1 *Normal IP Phone Call Setup*

```
StationD:    56327c8 CallState callState=12(Proceed)
  lineInstance=1 callReference=16777242
StationD:    56327c8 CallInfo callingPartyName=''
  callingParty=2006 cgpnVoiceMailbox=2006
StationD:    56327c8 DialedNumber dialedNumber=2002
  lineInstance=1 callReference=16777242.
StationD:    56327c8 CallInfo callingPartyName=''
  callingParty=2006 cgpnVoiceMailbox=2006
StationD:    56327c8 StartTone tone=36(AlertingTone).
StationD:    56327c8 CallState callState=3(RingOut)
  lineInstance=1 callReference=16777242
StationD:    56327c8 SelectSoftKeys instance=1 reference=16777242
  softKeySetIndex=8 validKeyMask=-1.
StationD:    56327c8 DisplayPromptStatus timeOutValue=0
  promptStatus='Ring Out' lineInstance=1 callReference=16777242.
StationD:    56327c8 StopTone.
StationD:    56327c8 OpenReceiveChannel conferenceID=0
  passThruPartyID=385 millisecondPacketSize=20
  compressionType=4(Media_Payload_G711Ulaw64k)
  qualifierIn=?.  myIP: 414100a (10.16.20.4)
StationD:    56327c8 StopTone.
StationD:    56327c8 CallState callState=5(Connected)
  lineInstance=1 callReference=16777242
StationD:    56327c8 CallInfo callingPartyName=''
  callingParty=2006 cgpnVoiceMailbox=2006
StationD:    56327c8 SelectSoftKeys instance=1
  reference=16777242 softKeySetIndex=1 validKeyMask=-1.
StationD:    56327c8 DisplayPromptStatus timeOutValue=0
  promptStatus='Connected' lineInstance=1 callReference=16777242.
StationD:    56327c8 StartMediaTransmission conferenceID=0
  passThruPartyID=385 remoteIpAddress=514100a(10.16.20.5) remotePortNumber=24642
  milliSecondPacketSize=20 compressType=4(Media_Payload_G711Ulaw64k)
  qualifierOut=?.  myIP: 414100a (10.16.20.4)
StationInit: 56327c8 OpenReceiveChannelAck Status=0,
  IpAddr=0x414100a, Port=19878, PartyID=385
```

At this point, IP Phone A is in the middle of a call. The other party in this call, IP Phone B, presses **Hold**, and IP Phone A is told to listen to the multicast stream. Notice that IP Phone A is told to stop listening (**CloseReceiveChannel**) and to stop talking (**StopMediaTransmission**) to IP Phone B. (This assumes that the MOH server and specified

audio file are available.) Immediately after that, CallManager sends a
StartMulticastMediaReception command to IP Phone A. IP Phone A acknowledges this
with a **MulticastMediaReception** message. Finally, IP Phone A is commanded to change its
display. Example 12-2 demonstrates the media stream teardown between IP Phone A and IP
Phone B and the command to IP Phone A to start listening to the multicast stream. Remember,
the MOH server was already streaming this multicast stream, so CallManager doesn't need to
tell the MOH server to do anything. Notice the TCP handle 56327c8 indicating messages to
and from IP Phone A. Also, the IP address of IP Phone A is seen in the trace file as highlighted
in the example. Unfortunately the multicast address the CallManager is telling the IP Phone to
listen to is not printed in the CCM trace in some versions of CallManager, so the only way to
determine which multicast address is being used is to look at a sniffer trace. CallManager
3.3(2) and later displays the multicast IP address of the MOH stream as shown in Example 12-2.

Example 12-2 *IP Phone A Is Told to Stop "Listening" to IP Phone B and to Start "Listening" to the Multicast Stream*

```
StationD:     56327c8 CloseReceiveChannel conferenceID=0
  passThruPartyID=385.  myIP: 414100a (10.16.20.4)
StationD:     56327c8 StopMediaTransmission conferenceID=0
  passThruPartyID=385.  myIP: 414100a (10.16.20.4)
StationD:     56327c8 StartMulticastMediaReception
  multiCastStreamIP: 10101ef (239.1.1.1) multiCastPort: 16384
  myIP: 414100a (10.16.20.4)
StationInit: 56327c8 MulticastMediaReception
StationD:     56327c8 CallInfo callingPartyName=''
  callingParty=2006 cgpnVoiceMailbox=2006
```

In Example 12-3, the IP Phone B goes off hold, so CallManager sets up the stream between IP Phone A and IP Phone B again. Notice the TCP handle 56327c8 indicating
messages to and from IP Phone A as the IP Phone is told to stop listening
(**StopMulticastMediaReception**) to the multicast stream. Remember that since the MOH
server was already streaming this multicast stream, CallManager doesn't need to tell the
MOH server to stop streaming when phone-to-phone communication is reestablished.

Example 12-3 *IP Phone A Is Told to Stop "Listening" to the Multicast Stream, and the Call Is Reestablished with IP Phone B*

```
StationD:     56327c8 StopMulticastMediaReception
  myIP: 414100a (10.16.20.4)
StationD:     56327c8 StopTone.
StationD:     56327c8 OpenReceiveChannel conferenceID=0
  passThruPartyID=387 millisecondPacketSize=20
  compressionType=4(Media_Payload_G711Ulaw64k) qualifierIn=?.
  myIP: 414100a (10.16.20.4)
StationInit: 56327c8 OpenReceiveChannelAck Status=0,
  IpAddr=0x414100a, Port=20318, PartyID=387
StationD:     56327c8 CallInfo callingPartyName=''
  callingParty=2006 cgpnVoiceMailbox=2006
```

continues

Example 12-3 *IP Phone A Is Told to Stop "Listening" to the Multicast Stream, and the Call Is Reestablished with IP Phone B (Continued)*

```
StationD:    56327c8 StartMediaTransmission conferenceID=0
  passThruPartyID=387 remoteIpAddress=514100a(10.16.20.5)
  remotePortNumber=25082 milliSecondPacketSize=20
  compressType=4(Media_Payload_G711Ulaw64k)
  qualifierOut=?.   myIP: 414100a (10.16.20.4)
```

In Examples 12-4 through 12-8, we examine the same scenario but with a unicast stream. Because this is a different type of stream from multicast, the message setup is different. Example 12-4 shows a unicast stream. Remember that the receiving device is told to "listen," and the MOH server is told to generate a stream to the endpoint's IP address. Notice the TCP handle 5632b4c indicating messages to and from CallManager to the IP Phone. CallManager sets up a stream between Phone A and Phone B and then tears down the stream when the call is placed on hold to open a new stream to the MOH server.

Example 12-4 *IP Phone A Establishes a Call with IP Phone B, and the Stream Is Then Torn Down*

```
StationD:    5632b4c StartMediaTransmission conferenceID=0
  passThruPartyID=65 remoteIpAddress=714100a(10.16.20.7)
  remotePortNumber=20330 milliSecondPacketSize=20
  compressType=4(Media_Payload_G711Ulaw64k)
  qualifierOut=?.   myIP: 614100a (10.16.20.6)
StationInit: 5632b4c OpenReceiveChannelAck Status=0,
  IpAddr=0x614100a, Port=27110, PartyID=65
StationD:    5632b4c CloseReceiveChannel conferenceID=0
  passThruPartyID=65.   myIP: 614100a (10.16.20.6)
StationD:    5632b4c StopMediaTransmission conferenceID=0
  passThruPartyID=65.   myIP: 614100a (10.16.20.6)
```

The next trace, shown in Example 12-5, shows IP Phone A being told to start listening (**OpenReceiveChannel**) to the unicast stream from the MOH server. The IP Phone receiving the MOH stream is indicated by TCP handle 5632b4c. It is told to listen (**OpenReceiveChannel**) to the unicast stream.

Example 12-5 *IP Phone A Is Told to "Listen" to the Unicast MOH Stream*

```
StationD:    5632b4c OpenReceiveChannel conferenceID=0
  passThruPartyID=66 millisecondPacketSize=20
  compressionType=4(Media_Payload_G711Ulaw64k) qualifierIn=?.
  myIP: 614100a (10.16.20.6)
StationInit: 5632b4c OpenReceiveChannelAck Status=0,
  IpAddr=0x614100a, Port=27230, PartyID=66
```

The rest of the trace would look very much the same as the multicast stream. The key difference to focus on is the MOH setup. In the multicast trace, you saw the endpoint being told to listen to a multicast stream. In the unicast trace, the setup looks like any other voice stream setup. Example 12-6 displays the unicast setup messages.

Here, the IP Phone is told to **OpenReceiveChannel**, and it sends back an **OpenReceiveChannelAck** message.

Example 12-6 *Unicast Stream Setup and Teardown Messages*

```
StationD:     567459c OpenReceiveChannel conferenceID=0
  passThruPartyID=610
  millisecondPacketSize=20 compressionType=4(Media_Payload_G711Ulaw64k)
  qualifierIn=?.  myIP: 614100a (10.16.20.6)
StationInit: 567459c OpenReceiveChannelAck Status=0,
  IpAddr=0x614100a, Port=31268, PartyID=610
```

In Example 12-7, the MOH server is told to stream to the IP Phone with IP address 10.16.20.6.

Example 12-7 *MOH Server Sends a Unicast Stream to the IP Phone*

```
MohDControl - stationOutputStartMediaTransmission
  tcpHandle=56743a8 myIP: cf2590a (10.89.242.12)
MohDControl - RemoteIpAddr: 614100a (10.16.20.6)
  RemoteRtpPortNumber: 31268 msecPacketSize: 20 compressionType: 4
```

Finally, after the call is taken off hold, Example 12-8 shows that the IP Phone is told to **CloseReceiveChannel** and the MOH server is told to **StopMediaTransmission**.

Example 12-8 *MOH Server Stops Sending a Unicast Stream to the IP Phone*

```
StationD:     567459c CloseReceiveChannel conferenceID=0
  passThruPartyID=610. myIP: 614100a (10.16.20.6)
MohDControl - stationOutputStopMediaTransmission
  tcpHandle=56743a8 myIP: cf2590a (10.89.242.12)
```

Troubleshooting MOH

Someone places you on hold, and you don't hear any music. Use the following steps to pinpoint the problem:

Step 1   Check the MOH server registration status.

Step 2   Check the MRG and MRGL configuration.

Step 3   Verify router configuration for multicast (if multicast is used).

Step 4   Verify the multicast capability of the terminating voice gateway.

Step 5   Verify the codec used by all devices involved.

Step 6   Verify the location's configuration if you are using the centralized call processing model.

First, make sure that the MOH servers are registered. Then check the counters in PerfMon or the Real-Time Monitoring Tool in CallManager Serviceability to determine whether any available streams are present. It really doesn't matter which CallManager within the cluster the MOH server is registered to. It can be registered anywhere, as long as the endpoints in question have an MRGL that has access to that resource.

It is also important to see whether the MOH server has available streams. By default, the MOH server has 250 unicast streams and 30 multicast streams available. You can reduce these settings to minimize the load on a server. If someone expects to hear MOH and they don't, perhaps no available streams exist.

Check the **MOHOutOfResources** counter. It tells you how many times the MOH server has been out of resources.

Second, check the MRG/MRGL settings for the device expecting to hear MOH. Make sure its MRG/MRGL has an MOH server. It's possible that the holding party could have an audio source specified for user hold and network hold, but the held party might not have access to an MOH server. Figure 12-2 shows two IP Phones in a call. Party A is the holding party. As such, she presses the **Hold** button. Party B is the held party, but the only media resource included in its MRG/MRGL is a conference bridge.

The trace output in Examples 12-9 through 12-12 shows two IP Phones engaged in a call. IP Phone A puts IP Phone B on hold. CallManager tries to provide MOH but no resources are available. Instead, CallManager provides tone on hold to IP Phone B. Notice the TCP handle 783025c indicating messages to and from IP Phone A. The TCP handle of IP Phone B is 78301f8.

Figure 12-2 *IP Phone Without Access to an MOH Server*

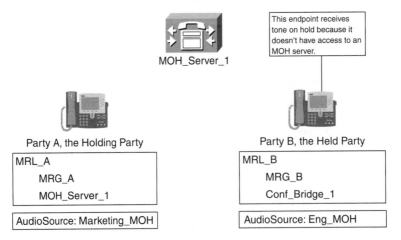

Example 12-9 shows the call setup between IP Phone A (TCP handle 783025c) and IP Phone B (TCP handle 78301f8). This trace begins from the point where IP Phone B answers the call.

Example 12-9 *IP Phone A Calls IP Phone B*

```
StationInit: 78301f8 OffHook.
StationD:    78301f8 ClearNotify.
StationD:    78301f8 SetRinger ringMode=1(RingOff).
StationD:    78301f8 SetLamp stimulus=9(Line) stimulusInstance=1
   lampMode=2(LampOn).
StationD:    78301f8 CallState callState=1(OffHook) lineInstance=1
   callReference=16777258
StationD:    78301f8 ActivateCallPlane lineInstance=1.
StationD:    783025c StopTone.
StationD:    783025c OpenReceiveChannel conferenceID=0 passThruPartyID=209
   millisecondPacketSize=20 compressionType=4(Media_Payload_G711Ulaw64k)
   qualifierIn=?.   myIP: 714100a (10.16.20.7)
StationD:    78301f8 StopTone.
StationD:    78301f8 OpenReceiveChannel conferenceID=0 passThruPartyID=225
   millisecondPacketSize=20 compressionType=4(Media_Payload_G711Ulaw64k)
   qualifierIn=?.   myIP: 614100a (10.16.20.6)
StationInit: 78301f8 OpenReceiveChannelAck Status=0, IpAddr=0x614100a, Port=25606,
   PartyID=225
StationD:    78301f8 StopTone.
StationD:    78301f8 CallState callState=5(Connected) lineInstance=1
   callReference=16777258
StationInit: 783025c OpenReceiveChannelAck Status=0, IpAddr=0x714100a, Port=18386,
   PartyID=209
StationD:    78301f8 SelectSoftKeys instance=1 reference=16777258
   softKeySetIndex=1 validKeyMask=-1.
StationD:    78301f8 DisplayPromptStatus timeOutValue=0 promptStatus='Connected'
   lineInstance=1 callReference=16777258.
StationD:    783025c StopTone.
StationD:    783025c CallState callState=5(Connected) lineInstance=1
   callReference=16777257
StationD:    783025c SelectSoftKeys instance=1 reference=16777257
   softKeySetIndex=1 validKeyMask=-1.
StationD:    783025c DisplayPromptStatus timeOutValue=0 promptStatus='Connected'
   lineInstance=1 callReference=16777257.
StationD:    783025c StartMediaTransmission conferenceID=0 passThruPartyID=209
   remoteIpAddress=614100a(10.16.20.6) remotePortNumber=25606
   milliSecondPacketSize=20 compressType=4(Media_Payload_G711Ulaw64k)
   qualifierOut=?.   myIP: 714100a (10.16.20.7)
StationD:    78301f8 StartMediaTransmission conferenceID=0 passThruPartyID=225
   remoteIpAddress=714100a(10.16.20.7) remotePortNumber=18386
   milliSecondPacketSize=20 compressType=4(Media_Payload_G711Ulaw64k)
   qualifierOut=?.   myIP: 614100a (10.16.20.6)
```

Example 12-10 shows IP Phone A pressing the **Hold** soft key to place IP Phone B on hold and the RTP streams are torn down.

Example 12-10 *IP Phone A Places IP Phone B on Hold*

```
StationInit: 783025c SoftKeyEvent softKeyEvent=3(Hold) lineInstance=1
  callReference=16777257.
StationD:     783025c CloseReceiveChannel conferenceID=0 passThruPartyID=209.
  myIP: 714100a (10.16.20.7)
StationD:     783025c StopMediaTransmission conferenceID=0 passThruPartyID=209.
  myIP: 714100a (10.16.20.7)
StationD:     78301f8 CloseReceiveChannel conferenceID=0 passThruPartyID=225.
  myIP: 614100a (10.16.20.6)
StationD:     78301f8 StopMediaTransmission conferenceID=0 passThruPartyID=225.
  myIP: 614100a (10.16.20.6)
```

Example 12-11 shows CallManager attempting MRG allocation. However, no MOH resources are available. Notice that first the **MrmAllocateMohResourceReq** indicates a request to the MRM for an MOH resource. You can see the MRM returns a list of three MOH servers: MOH_CLSTR1-A, MOH_CLSTR1-B, and MOH_CLSTR1-C. You then see CallManager go through the list and show a failure to allocate each resource with the message **device_lookup_DevicePidErr**. This message typically indicates the MOH server (the Cisco IP Voice Media Streaming Application service) is not running. Because there are no available resources, you finally see the message **MrmAllocateMohResourceErr - ERROR - no resources are available**.

Example 12-11 *CallManager Attempts to Allocate an MOH Resource for IP Phone B, but None Are Available*

```
MediaResourceManager::waiting_MrmAllocateMohResourceReq
MediaResourceManager::waiting_MrmAllocateMohResourceReq - MRGL SEARCH,
  TRY CREATING CHILD USING MRGL AND DEFAULT LIST
MRM::convertScmStringToRWCString MRG_CM_AB:MRG_CM_BA
MRM::getMohDeviceGivenMrgl
MRM::getMohDeviceGivenMrgl MOH_CLSTR1-A Group=0 Counter=0
MRM::getMohDeviceGivenMrgl MOH_CLSTR1-A Group=1 Counter=0
MRM::getMohDeviceGivenMrgl GETTING MOH FROM DEFAULT LIST
MRM::getMohDeviceGivenMrgl MOH_CLSTR1-B Group=2 Counter=0
MRM::getMohDeviceGivenMrgl MOH_CLSTR1-C Group=2 Counter=0
MediaResourceManager::waiting_MrmAllocateMohResourceReq -
  CREATED CHILD USING MRGL AND DEFAULT LIST
MediaResourceCdpc::sortDeviceGivenList
MediaResourceCdpc::sortDeviceGivenList Name=MOH_CLSTR1-A Group=0 Counter=0
MediaResourceCdpc::sortDeviceGivenList Name=MOH_CLSTR1-A Group=1 Counter=0
MediaResourceCdpc::sortDeviceGivenList Name=MOH_CLSTR1-B Group=2 Counter=0
MediaResourceCdpc::sortDeviceGivenList Name=MOH_CLSTR1-C Group=2 Counter=0
MediaResourceCdpc - Started
MediaResourceCdpc::waiting_MrmAllocateMohResourceReq
MediaResourceCdpc::findDeviceGivenList
MediaResourceCdpc::waiting_MrmAllocateMohResourceReq MtpDevice=MOH_CLSTR1-A
MediaResourceCdpc::device_lookup_DevicePidErr;
  Unable to locate DeviceName=MOH_CLSTR1-A
MediaResourceCdpc::waiting_MrmAllocateMohResourceReq
MediaResourceCdpc::findDeviceGivenList
```

Example 12-11 *CallManager Attempts to Allocate an MOH Resource for IP Phone B, but None Are Available (Continued)*

```
MediaResourceCdpc::waiting_MrmAllocateMohResourceReq MtpDevice=MOH_CLSTR1-A
MediaResourceCdpc::device_lookup_DevicePidErr;
  Unable to locate DeviceName=MOH_CLSTR1-A
MediaResourceCdpc::waiting_MrmAllocateMohResourceReq
MediaResourceCdpc::findDeviceGivenList
MediaResourceCdpc::waiting_MrmAllocateMohResourceReq MtpDevice=MOH_CLSTR1-B
MediaResourceCdpc::device_lookup_DevicePidErr;
  Unable to locate DeviceName=MOH_CLSTR1-B
MediaResourceCdpc::waiting_MrmAllocateMohResourceReq
MediaResourceCdpc::findDeviceGivenList
MediaResourceCdpc::waiting_MrmAllocateMohResourceReq MtpDevice=MOH_CLSTR1-C
MediaResourceCdpc::device_lookup_DevicePidErr;
  Unable to locate DeviceName=MOH_CLSTR1-C
MediaResourceCdpc::waiting_MrmAllocateMohResourceReq
MediaResourceCdpc::findDeviceGivenList
MediaResourceCdpc::mohErrorResponseToManager
MediaResourceManager::waiting_MrmAllocateMohResourceErr
MRM::waiting_MrmAllocateMohResourceErr - ERROR - no resources are available --
  ci = 16777259
```

Because there are no MOH resources available, Example 12-12 shows tone on hold being played to IP Phone B rather than MOH.

Example 12-12 *Tone on Hold Is Played to IP Phone B*

```
StationD:    78301f8 StartTone tone=53(HoldTone)
```

Resolving Problems Related to Multicast and Unicast

The next question to consider is whether the audio source in question is unicast or multicast. Now is a good time to ask that question because multicast creates a new area of investigation.

What is different between how an MOH stream is set up in unicast and how it is set up in multicast?

With unicast, the MOH server is told to stream to the endpoint that should receive the music stream. Because this is unicast, the MOH server must read the wave file in the necessary codec (or start encoding the fixed audio source) and then begin to stream. If 20 people are on hold, 20 separate streams are generated. When an endpoint goes off hold, CallManager tears down the stream.

With multicast, the MOH server is always playing the stream. When an endpoint is supposed to listen to that stream, the endpoint is simply told to listen to multicast address *x.x.x.x* on port *x*. When the endpoint goes off hold, it is told to stop listening to the multicast stream and is reconnected to the appropriate party. The routers between the MOH server and the endpoint must be configured to forward multicast packets. If one of these devices isn't, the endpoint doesn't hear any music.

NOTE	When troubleshooting multicast problems with Cisco IOS Software gateways, make sure the Cisco IOS Software load you are using can accept multicast MOH. Multicast MOH is supported for H.323 and MGCP endpoints in Cisco IOS Software version 12.2(11)T and later.

Remember that when the held party doesn't have an MRGL with an MOH source, it hears tone on hold instead of music because it doesn't have access to an MOH resource. When tone on hold is used, CallManager tells the IP Phone to simply play a tone. If someone does not hear music and expects to, it could be a configuration problem involving the MRGL. If the held party doesn't hear anything—including tone on hold—it might be an infrastructure issue.

If it is an infrastructure problem, it is most likely a configuration issue related to multicast. Look for the following line in your router configuration:

```
ip multicast-routing
```

Also, all interfaces where multicast packets will traverse need to have one of the following commands applied:

```
ip pim sparse-mode
```

```
ip pim dense-mode
```

Consult your router documentation for details about multicast routing.

The held party endpoint is told to listen to a multicast stream if multicast is enabled for that audio source. The endpoint doesn't know if that stream exists, so it simply obeys CallManager. The endpoint could be listening to an MOH server-generated multicast stream that never made it through all the infrastructure to the IP Phone's subnet. If that happens, it is time to check the router configuration. It might not be forwarding multicast packets, so the endpoint doesn't hear music.

Note that no errors show up in the CCM trace files or the MOH trace files if multicast packets are not being forwarded because the MOH server is successfully streaming a multicast stream. CallManager successfully commands the endpoint to listen to the multicast stream specified. The endpoint responds and "listens" to the stream. Neither device knows the stream isn't there, and both devices have done their respective part. It is like tuning a radio to a specific frequency and not hearing anything because the radio station is off the air.

Another common issue related to multicast occurs when the endpoint is a voice gateway. In this case, it is possible that the gateway that needs to hear the stream is incapable of hearing a multicast stream. Older voice gateway software might not be multicast-capable. Also, intercluster trunks do not support multicast, so that too would cause a problem.

Determining Why Tone on Hold Is Playing

There are several completely valid reasons for CallManager to play tone on hold to an endpoint that has been correctly configured for MOH. It is important that you understand why CallManager chooses tone on hold instead of MOH. With this information, you can determine if this instance of tone on hold was an intentional and preferred choice by CallManager or the result of a problem with MOH.

When two endpoints are to have a Real-Time Transport Protocol/User Datagram Protocol (RTP/UDP) stream set up by CallManager, the codec selection is part of the setup process. CallManager tells the devices which codec they must use. The codec to be used is based on two criteria:

- The codecs that the device can use
- The region imposed by CallManager

If two endpoints are capable of doing G.711 or G.729, CallManager can use either codec to set up the call. However, if a region has specified that those two endpoints must talk to each other with G.729, G.729 is the only codec used to set up the call. The same principle applies to MOH.

By default, the MOH server advertises only a capability of G.711 μ-law. If an endpoint is in another region enforcing the G.729 codec, CallManager chooses tone on hold because a stream cannot be played to that site (due to the mismatched codecs). You can change the codec advertisement in the service parameter configuration for the Cisco IP Media Voice Streaming Application. It can advertise G.711 μ-law, G.711 A-law, G.729, and wideband if you choose.

If you are going to use G.729 for MOH, be forewarned that you might have issues with the stream's quality. The G.729 codec does a great job of compressing the human voice, but it isn't always great with music. If you find that the music quality is poor, try a different audio source file.

If you have a centralized call processing model, you probably have remote sites using CallManager as the call processing engine. As such, you are also probably using the locations capability in CallManager to make sure that the WAN link isn't oversubscribed by voice traffic. If the connection is considered full based on the CallManager settings for that location, CallManager does not send an MOH stream across the link. Instead, it chooses tone on hold. Sending tone on hold to reduce resource constraints is preferable to oversubscribing the WAN.

Troubleshooting the Audio Translator

The MOH Audio Translator converts audio source files into various codecs so that the MOH server can use the files to provide MOH. The MOH Audio Translator service installs automatically during installation of the Cisco IP Voice Media Streaming Application. The installation program creates an input directory during installation in the following location: c:\Cisco\DropMOHAudioSourceFilesHere.

After the MOH Audio Translator service translates the audio files, it places the source audio file and the translated file in the output directory on the default MOH TFTP server. To change the output directory, modify the DefaultTFTPMOHFilePath parameter in CallManager Administration (**Service > Service Parameters** > *select a server* > **Cisco MOH Audio Translator**); however, make sure that the path points to the default MOH TFTP server.

The DefaultTFTPMOHFilePath parameter contains a universal naming convention (UNC) share name that displays in the format *computer name**directory name*.

CAUTION   The process of translating audio files is very processor-intensive. Do not drop audio files into this input directory on a CallManager server during operational hours! Ideally, run this service on a standalone MOH server or on the Publisher server to avoid degrading call processing performance.

When you map the audio source file to an audio source number, the default MOH TFTP server copies the files into one directory so that all the MOH servers can access them. The MOH server then downloads the files into the C:\Program Files\Cisco\MOH directory.

Valid input audio source files include most standard wave and MP3 files. Any sound file in a format that Windows DirectShow drivers understand natively will work. You place the audio source into the proper processing directory, at which point CallManager automatically detects and translates the file. The output files and source files move into the directory on the Default MOH TFTP server holding directory. This holding directory comprises the DefaultTFTPMOHFilePath with \MOH appended. Conversion of a 3 MB MP3 file or a 21 MB wave file takes approximately 30 seconds.

So what can go wrong?

First, the original audio file could be invalid. Make sure that you are using a valid wave or MP3 file. During the conversion, the files are copied to the TFTP/MOH path on the server. This path can be changed under the service parameter configuration for the Cisco IP Voice Media Streaming Application service, so make sure that the destination wasn't changed there. If those files were copied to the wrong place, the MOH server does not know where to go to read them.

Troubleshooting the Live Audio Source

In addition to the 50 wave file audio sources available by translating files through the Audio Translator service, CallManager can use a single fixed (live) audio source for MOH. The live audio stream can come from any device that can connect to the microphone or line input on a standard PC sound card. Currently CallManager only supports the SoundBlaster 16 PCI sound card and the built-in sound card on the 7815 platform. Check Cisco.com or the latest CallManager release notes for the current list of supported sound cards.

The two most common problems encountered when trying to use the live audio source are

- Incorrect configuration of the MOH fixed audio source device
- Improperly selected recording input

Configuring the Correct MOH Fixed Audio Source Device

One common problem that prohibits the live audio source from functioning is the misconfiguration of the MOH fixed audio source device. To verify the configuration, first check the device name for your sound card by opening the Recording Control applet (**Start > Settings > Control Panel > Sounds and Multimedia > Audio Tab > Sound Recording > Volume Button**).

At the bottom of the Recording Control applet you will see the name of the device. Figure 12-3 shows the Recording Control applet.

Figure 12-3 *Windows Recording Control Applet*

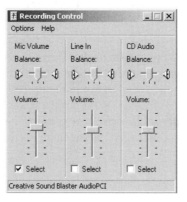

As you can see in Figure 12-3, the name of the sound device is Creative Sound Blaster AudioPCI. Once you have the device name, verify that the CallManager configuration matches.

To verify CallManager configuration, go to the Music on Hold (MOH) Audio Source Configuration page in CallManager Administration (**Service > Media Resource > Music**

on Hold Audio Source) and select audio source 51 from the list of MOH Audio Sources in the left-most column. Numbers 1 through 50 are for wave file audio sources and 51 is for the live audio source. In the MOH Fixed Audio Source Device field, enter the name of the audio device *exactly* as it appears at the bottom of the Recording Control applet. Include any spaces or special characters that appear in the name. In the case of Figure 12-3, you would enter **Creative Sound Blaster AudioPCI** in the MOH Fixed Audio Source Device field.

Sometimes different revisions of the Sound Blaster sound card have slightly different model names in the Recording Control applet. If you have multiple MOH servers in the cluster and the name of the audio device appears different on each server, you can override the global setting by configuring the device name on a per-server basis.

To override the device name on a particular server, go to the Music On Hold (MOH) Server Configuration page in CallManager Administration (**Service > Media Resource > Music on Hold Server**). Select the server you want to modify and enter the device name in the Fixed Audio Source Device field. If this field is blank, the name configured under audio source 51 is used.

You must reset the MOH server from CallManager Administration after making a configuration change. Note that this will interrupt the MOH stream to any calls currently on hold; however, the calls are not dropped.

Selecting the Proper Recording Input

For the MOH live audio source to work properly, you must select which sound card input the source is connected to. The two choices are typically either the microphone or line input.

To select the recording input, open the Recording Control applet again (**Start > Settings > Control Panel > Sounds and Multimedia > Audio Tab > Sound Recording > Volume Button**). This is the same applet shown in Figure 12-3. Click the **Select** checkbox below the correct input source. You can also adjust the volume level of the input source as well if the MOH is too loud or soft. If you select the wrong one, you will hear nothing when MOH is invoked because the MOH server is streaming blank audio packets.

Best Practices

Assume that a person who has been placed on hold doesn't hear music and expects to. The following list describes some of the steps to take to resolve the problem.

- Check to make sure the Cisco IP Voice Media Streaming Application service is running and that the MOH servers are registered.

- Check PerfMon or the Real-Time Monitoring Tool to see if streams are available.

- Check the MRG/MRGL configuration for the endpoint expecting to hear MOH. Make sure its MRG/MRGL has an MOH server.

- Verify that the multicast stream is making it to the network of the endpoint that needs to hear it. It could be that the infrastructure devices, such as routers and switches, are no longer forwarding this multicast stream. A sniffer trace is the easiest way to verify that the multicast stream has made it to the IP Phone's subnet. Also, if it is a gateway, make sure it is multicast-capable for voice.

- If the stream is unicast, make sure that the MOH server has connectivity to the held device.

Make sure that tone on hold isn't provided for a valid reason. Valid reasons for tone on hold include the following:

- **Codec mismatch**—By default, the MOH server advertises only a capability of G.711 μ-law. If an endpoint is in a region enforcing a codec other than G.711 μ-law, CallManager chooses tone on hold because a stream cannot be played to a site unless there is a matching codec. The codecs supported by the MOH server can be changed under the service parameter configuration for the Cisco IP Media Voice Streaming Application service. It can advertise G.711 μ-law, G.711 A-law, G.729, and wideband if you choose.

- **Locations enforcement**—If you have a centralized call processing model, you probably have remote sites using CallManager. As such, you are also likely to be using locations to make sure that the WAN link isn't oversubscribed. If the connection is considered full based on the CallManager settings for that location, CallManager does not send an MOH stream across that link. Instead, it sends tone on hold, which is preferable to oversubscribing the WAN.

- **No available streams**—The MOH server has a finite number of unicast streams it can generate. Suppose that you intentionally set the maximum number of streams to 40. If 40 endpoints are on hold, the 41st endpoint trying to receive an MOH stream receives tone on hold instead.

Summary

The Cisco IP Voice Media Streaming Application in CallManager provides MOH. MOH provides users with prerecorded or live audio while they wait on hold. The biggest challenge to troubleshooting MOH is simply knowing how it works. This chapter provided troubleshooting methodology for you to determine the root cause of an MOH problem and resolve it quickly.

## CHAPTER 13

Call Admission Control

The majority of Cisco IP Telephony installations depend on some form of *call admission control* (CAC). CAC is used in situations where there is a limited amount of bandwidth between telephony endpoints such as phones and gateways. CAC allows a call to be completed over the IP network if enough bandwidth is available; otherwise, the call is rejected or, in some situations, automatically routed over the Public Switched Telephone Network (PSTN) without the end user's knowledge.

If you have a single Cisco CallManager cluster located on a LAN, along with any other voice over IP (VoIP) devices, you probably don't need to read this chapter. CAC is used only when there is contention for limited bandwidth. This is an issue only when WAN connections are involved.

CAC is extremely important to ensure QoS when voice packets must travel over a WAN connection. As discussed in Chapter 7, "Voice Quality," a call using the G.729 codec uses a little over 24 kbps of bandwidth. If you have a WAN circuit with 64 kbps of bandwidth, you can put two calls (48 kbps) over that circuit without oversubscribing the WAN. If a third call is allowed to go over this WAN connection while the other two calls are still up, the result is that 72 kbps worth of traffic tries to travel down a 64 kbps pipe. Obviously, at least 8 kbps of that data is lost. The biggest problem is that the packet loss is distributed evenly over the three calls, so the voice quality of all three calls is affected, not just the third call that was made. If CAC is properly configured in this example, only two calls are allowed to exist over that WAN connection at any given time.

Two distinct CAC mechanisms are available in CallManager: locations-based CAC and gatekeeper CAC. *Locations-based CAC* limits the number of calls between devices registered to a single CallManager cluster. *Gatekeeper CAC* depends on an H.323 gatekeeper to control the number of calls between multiple CallManager clusters. Which CAC method you use depends largely on your deployment model. (See Chapter 2, "IP Telephony Architecture Overview," for more information on deployment models.) If you have a centralized CallManager cluster with one or more remote sites, you must use locations-based CAC. If you have distributed CallManager clusters connected via intercluster trunks, you must use gatekeeper CAC. You might have to use both locations-based CAC and gatekeeper CAC if you have a combination of the centralized and distributed models.

Always remember that CAC by itself does not guarantee voice quality. The WAN routers must be configured to ensure that voice packets get priority treatment over data traffic. This means that CAC and QoS are dependent on each other and that neither can work properly without the other. In other words, if your CAC policy admits 96 kbps of traffic on a WAN connection that prioritizes only 64 kbps of voice traffic, you will have voice quality problems. That being said, if you are having voice quality issues and you are using CAC, you should always keep in mind the concepts from Chapter 7 as well.

Locations-based CAC

The most commonly used CAC mechanism is locations based. Locations-based CAC is designed to operate in only a hub-and-spoke topology that has a central hub site with one or more remote sites that are directly connected to only the hub site. Locations-based CAC does not work properly in a partially- or fully-distributed environment where one or more of the remote sites have direct connections to each other. Nor does it work if you have spokes that do not connect directly to the hub. Locations-based CAC assumes that to get from one location to another, the packets must traverse the hub location.

The hub location is designated as the default location, named <none>. The hub location is also referred to as location 0 because CCM traces show devices in the hub as belonging to location 0. All other locations have a user-configurable name, along with a bandwidth amount in kbps. Figure 13-1 shows a typical hub-and-spoke topology with one central location and two remote sites.

The amount of bandwidth needed for a call depends on the codec being used for the particular call and the Layer 2 and Layer 3 data transport being used. CallManager allocates 80 kbps of bandwidth for a G.711 call, 24 kbps for a G.729 or G.723 call, and 272 kbps for a wideband call. These numbers do not necessarily correspond to the actual amount of bandwidth being used. Typically, G.729 is used over WAN connections to save bandwidth. When using 20 ms packets, G.729 consumes 8 kbps of bandwidth for the codec plus 16 kbps of bandwidth for the IP/UDP/RTP header overhead. Layer 2 headers increase this further. Refer to Chapter 7 for more information about how bandwidth required for a call depends on Layer 2 and Layer 3 headers and packetization size.

Many administrators assume they should set the location bandwidth in CallManager to be equal to the speed of the WAN connection. However, most installations require that you configure the bandwidth to a value that does not match the actual WAN bandwidth. If you are using RTP header compression, the IP/UDP/RTP headers are reduced to approximately 4 to 5 kbps. For a G.729 call, this equates to approximately 13 kbps of bandwidth required per call.

Because RTP header compression is done only between the WAN routers, neither CallManager nor the IP telephony endpoints (IP phones, gateways, and so on) are aware that RTP header compression is being used (with the exception of gateways that also function as WAN routers). However, even in this case the gateway functionality and WAN routing functionality are independent of each other. Because of this, you might have to tweak the numbers when you configure the location bandwidth in CallManager. For example, returning to the example of the 64 kbps WAN circuit, if RTP header compression is being used, you can easily fit four calls (4×13 kbps = 52 kbps), with bandwidth to spare. To compensate for this, you can trick CallManager into allowing four G.729 calls by configuring the bandwidth for this location to be 4×24 kbps = 96 kbps, even though the site really has only a 64 kbps connection.

Figure 13-1 *Locations-based CAC Hub-and-spoke Topology*

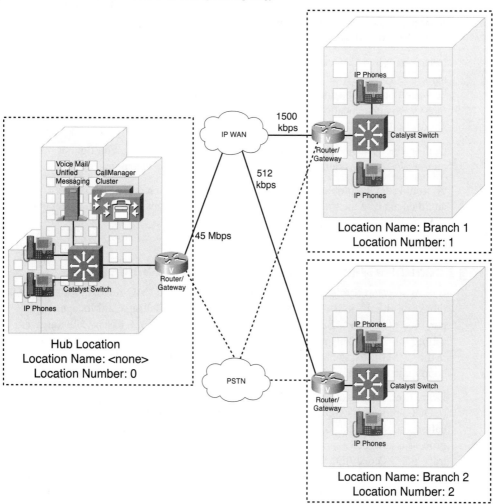

CallManager assumes that any devices that are in the same location have infinite bandwidth between them; therefore, a call between two devices in the same location is never restricted by locations-based CAC.

As of CallManager 3.3, CallManager supports the capability to perform automatic fallback to the PSTN if all WAN bandwidth is currently in use in a limited number of scenarios through a feature called *automated alternate routing* (AAR). If AAR is not configured, or if the call does not fall into the list of supported calls for AAR, or if you are using a version prior to CallManager 3.3, when not enough bandwidth is available to complete a call, the user sees a message on his phone that says "Not enough bandwidth," and he receives a reorder tone. You can configure this text via the CallManager service parameter **OutOfBandwidthText**.

Locations-based CAC requires very little configuration. You must configure each location name and associated bandwidth, where the associated bandwidth is the available bandwidth between this location and the hub location (location 0). Then you configure each device on the system into a location. That's all there is to it. Troubleshooting locations-based CAC is almost as easy.

Configuring AAR to allow for automatic PSTN fallback in case you run out of bandwidth on the WAN is considerably more complex. This topic is discussed later in this chapter.

To troubleshoot a problem with locations-based CAC, first enable the proper CCM traces, and then analyze the trace data to determine why locations-based CAC is not operating as expected.

Setting LocationsTraceDetailsFlag and CDCC Values

Before you start trying to troubleshoot a locations-based CAC-related problem, the first thing you should do is enable the **LocationsTraceDetailsFlag** CallManager service parameter (**Service > Service Parameters >** *select a server* **> Cisco CallManager**) by setting it to **True**. This parameter provides additional locations-related debug information in the CCM traces, such as the allocation and release of bandwidth, as well as a list of active bandwidth reservations and the amount of available bandwidth for each location.

Every time a call is attempted, CallManager creates a new Call Dependent Call Control (CDCC) process. A CDCC process is created inside CallManager for every instance of a call. As soon as a call is released, the CDCC process for that call terminates. Each CDCC process is assigned a unique process identifier (PID). The CDCC PID is shown in the CCM trace files as cdccPID. The cdccPID plays an important part in troubleshooting locations-based problems because it is shown in the trace files any time bandwidth is allocated or released. Using this information, you can determine exactly which call caused a particular bandwidth allocation and how much bandwidth was allocated from each location for that call.

The Role of Regions in CAC

Locations-based CAC depends on the region configuration. Remember that although locations-based CAC is solely responsible for CAC, regions are solely responsible for codec selection. The codec that is configured between two devices (via the regions configuration in CallManager Administration) determines how much bandwidth needs to be allocated for a call.

Locations-based CAC in Action

The best way to understand how to troubleshoot a locations-based CAC problem is to see what happens when a call using locations-based CAC is placed. Most of the information you need to troubleshoot a locations-based CAC problem can be found in the CCM traces on the CallManager servers.

Table 13-1 shows how the two IP phones are configured in this example.

Table 13-1   *IP Phone Configuration for This Example*

	Extension	Region	Location
Phone 1	13256	Branch 1	Branch 1
Phone 2	13257	Branch 3	Branch 3

The regions are configured so that G.729 is used for any call between Branch 1 and Branch 3. The Branch 1 location is configured for 1500 kbps of bandwidth, and the Branch 3 location is configured for 128 kbps of bandwidth.

When you configure a location by selecting **System > Location** in CallManager Administration, the location is assigned a unique number that identifies this location. These location identifiers are assigned at configuration time and are not user-selectable. To determine the location identifier that has been assigned to a particular location, you have to look in the SQL database. The easiest way to do this is to bring up Microsoft SQL Query Analyzer as follows:

Step 1   On the server running the Publisher database for CallManager, select **Start > Programs > Microsoft SQL Server 7.0 > Query Analyzer**.

Step 2   In the Connect to SQL Server dialog box, put a period (.) in the **SQL Server** box.

Step 3   Select **Use Windows NT Authentication**, and click **OK**.

Step 4   At the top of the query window, select the highest-numbered CCM database from the popup menu (for example, CCM0305).

As soon as the Query Analyzer is open, enter the following query:

```
SELECT id, name, kbits
FROM location
ORDER BY id
```

Press **F5** to execute the query. In the bottom pane, you should see something like the output shown in Example 13-1 (the output should match your configured locations).

Example 13-1 *SQL Query Results Listing Locations Identifiers*

```
id          name                                               kbits
----------  -------------------------------------------------  ----------

1           Branch 1                                           1500
2           Branch 2                                           512
3           Branch 3                                           128
4           Branch 4                                           96
5           Branch 5                                           48
6           Branch 6                                           256
7           Branch 7                                           512
8           Branch 8                                           1500

(8 row(s) affected)
```

As you can see in Example 13-1, the branch names and IDs match because the locations were entered into CallManager Administration in numerical order. On the other hand, if you entered Branch 3 before Branch 2, Branch 3 would have location ID 2, and Branch 2 would have location ID 3. The query also shows you the configured bandwidth for each location.

Now that you have this information, you can look at a trace to understand what is happening. The test call is a call from 13256 to 13257. Immediately after you place the call, the CCM trace shows the results in Example 13-2 as long as the **LocationsTraceDetailsFlag** is enabled. For more information about enabling CCM traces, refer to Chapter 3, "Understanding the Troubleshooting Tools."

Example 13-2 *CCM Trace Results for a Test Call from 13256 to 13257*

```
Locations: reserve: cdccPID=(2.13.132) adding entry.
Locations: reserve: cdccPID=(2.13.132) Orig=1 reserved bw=24 curr=1476 max=1500
Locations: reserve: cdccPID=(2.13.132) Dest=3 reserved bw=24 curr=104 max=128
Locations: broadcast local location table update to all active nodes:
  remote node=1
Locations: cdccPID(2.13.53) locA=0 (-1/-1) locB=2 (432/512) bw=80 userLoc=0
  (-1/-1) mediaLoc=0 (-1/-1) bwForMedia=-1
Locations: cdccPID(2.13.132) locA=1 (1476/1500) locB=3 (104/128) bw=24 userLoc=0
  (-1/-1) mediaLoc=0 (-1/-1) bwForMedia=-1
Locations: Displaying Locations List
Locations: location=1 curr=1476 max=1500
Locations: location=2 curr=432 max=512
Locations: location=3 curr=104 max=128
Locations: location=4 curr=96 max=96
Locations: location=5 curr=48 max=48
Locations: location=6 curr=256 max=256
Locations: location=7 curr=512 max=512
Locations: location=8 curr=1500 max=1500
```

The following text examines one piece of the trace at a time to help you better understand.

The first three lines tell you the ccdcPID for this call, along with the location ID for each device involved and the amount of bandwidth required for the call:

```
Locations: reserve: cdccPID=(2.13.132) adding entry.
Locations: reserve: cdccPID=(2.13.132) Orig=1 reserved bw=24 curr=1476 max=1500
Locations: reserve: cdccPID=(2.13.132) Dest=3 reserved bw=24 curr=104 max=128
```

As you can see, the cdccPID for this call is (2.13.132). The originating IP phone in the call is in location ID 1, which is Branch 1 if you look at the SQL query that generated the output in Example 13-1, and the destination phone is in location ID 3, which is Branch 3. You can also see that the bandwidth required for this call is 24 kbps, which is correct because CallManager is configured to use G.729 for this call. You can also see the location's current remaining bandwidth, along with the maximum bandwidth for that location. Note that the current bandwidth listed already takes into account the allocation for this call.

The next line indicates that the locations database is being propagated to the other nodes in the CallManager cluster. This feature is available in CallManager version 3.0(10) and later:

```
Locations: broadcast local location table update to all active nodes: remote node=1
```

What follows in the trace is a list of all currently active calls that have locations bandwidth allocated to them. If you have a large number of active calls across locations, this list can be quite long, so a recommended precaution is that you not enable the CallManager service parameter, **LocationsTraceDetailsFlag**, unless you are troubleshooting a locations-based CAC problem.

```
Locations: cdccPID(2.13.53) locA=0 (-1/-1) locB=2 (432/512) bw=80 userLoc=0
    (-1/-1) mediaLoc=0 (-1/-1) bwForMedia=-1
Locations: cdccPID(2.13.132) locA=1 (1476/1500) locB=3 (104/128) bw=24 userLoc=0
    (-1/-1) mediaLoc=0 (-1/-1) bwForMedia=-1
```

You can see that currently two active calls have locations bandwidth allocated. The first is a call from location ID 0 to location ID 2. As mentioned earlier, location ID 0 is the hub location that is configured as location <none> in CallManager Administration. You can also see that this call is using the G.711 codec because the bandwidth allocated to the call is 80 kbps. The section "Locations-based CAC Reservations for Music on Hold Resources" covers the userLoc, mediaLoc, and bwForMedia fields in greater detail.

The second call is the call just placed. You can see the information on this line matches the information that was presented in the first three lines of the trace.

The last part of the trace lists all the configured locations and the amount of bandwidth currently allocated to each location:

```
Locations: Displaying Locations List
Locations: location=1 curr=1476 max=1500
Locations: location=2 curr=432 max=512
Locations: location=3 curr=104 max=128
Locations: location=4 curr=96 max=96
Locations: location=5 curr=48 max=48
Locations: location=6 curr=256 max=256
Locations: location=7 curr=512 max=512
Locations: location=8 curr=1500 max=1500
```

The traces look similar when the call is torn down. Continuing with the same call used in the preceding example, the trace looks like Example 13-3 when the call is torn down.

Example 13-3 *CCM Trace Results After the Call from 13256 to 13257 Is Torn Down*

```
Locations: release: cdccPID=(2.13.132) Orig=1 released bw=24 curr=1500 max=1500
Locations: release: cdccPID=(2.13.132) Dest=3 released bw=24 curr=128 max=128
Locations: release: cdccPID=(2.13.132) removing entry.
Locations: broadcast local location table update to all active nodes: remote node=1.
Locations: cdccPID(2.13.53) locA=0 (-1/-1) locB=2 (432/512) bw=80 userLoc=0 (-1/-1)
  mediaLoc=0 (-1/-1) bwForMedia=-1
Locations: Displaying Locations List
Locations: location=1 curr=1500 max=1500
Locations: location=2 curr=432 max=512
Locations: location=3 curr=128 max=128
Locations: location=4 curr=96 max=96
Locations: location=5 curr=48 max=48
Locations: location=6 curr=256 max=256
Locations: location=7 curr=512 max=512
Locations: location=8 curr=1500 max=1500
```

As you can see, the first two lines show that the bandwidth for the call with cdccPID=(2.13.132) is being released. You can see the bandwidth to location ID 1 and location ID 3 being released. The rest of the trace is identical to the bandwidth reservation trace, showing all currently active calls with bandwidth reserved, along with the list of locations and their available bandwidth.

So far, you have seen what happens when things work, but how do you identify a call that was rejected because of insufficient bandwidth? In the following trace, we'll make the same call again, but this time we'll set the bandwidth for the Branch 1 location to 20 kbps and see what happens.

If 13256 (Branch 1) calls 13257 (Branch 2), you see the following in the trace:

```
Locations: reserve: cdccPID=(2.13.142) Orig=1 not enough bw. bw=24 curr=20 max=20
```

You can see that location ID 1 (Branch 1) has only 20 kbps available. You are trying to reserve 24 kbps. As a result, the following messages are sent to the IP phone:

```
StationD:    66b030c StartTone tone=37(ReorderTone).
StationD:    66b030c DisplayText text='Not Enough Bandwidth'.
StationD:    66b030c DisplayNotify timeOutValue=10 notify='Not Enough Bandwidth'.
```

These three lines tell the IP phone to play reorder tone and display the text "Not Enough Bandwidth" on the screen for 10 seconds. If you suspect you are having problems with calls not completing because of insufficient bandwidth, do a text search through the CCM trace directory (as discussed earlier) for the text "not enough bw" to track down any calls that were rejected because of insufficient bandwidth. You can also search for "Not Enough Bandwidth"; however, this text might change, depending on what you have configured in the **OutOfBandwidthText** CallManager service parameter. The text **not enough bw** will be there regardless of how the **OutOfBandwidthText** CallManager service parameter is configured.

Note that this message appears only on devices that can display a message initiated by CallManager. This means that a call coming in from the PSTN on a gateway that terminates on another device across a locations boundary receives reorder tone. The user receives no indication as to why the call failed if there is not enough bandwidth to allow the call and no rerouting is configured.

Locations Reservations for Media Resources

Calls between locations are not the only time CallManager needs to reserve bandwidth across the WAN. You might encounter several instances where a media resource might be located across the WAN, but all the IP phones or gateways using those resources are in the same location. Two examples of this are conference resources and Music on Hold (MOH) servers. As of CallManager 3.3, transcoders are not factored into calculating locations bandwidth, so be very careful when using transcoders and locations simultaneously.

Locations-based CAC Reservations for Music on Hold Resources

Table 13-2 shows how the two IP phones and the MOH server are configured in the examples.

Table 13-2   *IP Phone Configuration for the Examples*

	Extension	Region	Location
Phone 1	13256	Branch 1	Branch 1
Phone 2	13257	Branch 1	Branch 1
MOH Server	—	Default	<none>

Within Branch 1, the codec is configured for G.711, but between Branch 1 and the Default region, the codec is G.729. The Branch 1 location is configured for 48 kbps.

If you make a call from 13256 to 13257, the first locations-related message you see in the trace is this:

```
Locations: reserve: cdccPID=(2.13.169) Orig=Dest=1 no need to reserve bw.
```

Because both the origination and destination devices are in the same location (Branch 1), there is no need to reserve bandwidth. Later in the call, 13257 puts 13256 on hold, as shown in the following trace:

```
StationInit: 66b0370 SoftKeyEvent softKeyEvent=3(Hold) lineInstance=1
  callReference=33554825.
```

Next you see the MOH server being allocated based on the MRGL configured on extension 13256 and a bandwidth reservation:

```
MediaResourceCdpc::device_lookup_DevicePidRes MohResource=MOH_FTL-CM02
Locations: reserve for MediaResource: cdccPID=(2.13.169) Media Source=0 no need
   to reserve bw for MediaResource
Locations: reserve for MediaResource: cdccPID=(2.13.169) adding entry for
   MediaResource.
Locations: reserve for MediaResource: cdccPID=(2.13.169) Orig=1 bw added &
   deducted for MediaResource=24 curr=24 max=48
Locations: broadcast local location table update to all active nodes:
   remote node=1.
Locations: cdccPID(2.13.53) locA=0 (-1/-1) locB=2 (432/512) bw=80 userLoc=0
   (-1/-1) mediaLoc=0 (-1/-1) bwForMedia=-1
Locations: cdccPID(2.13.169) locA=0 (-1/-1) locB=0 (-1/-1) bw=0 userLoc=1
   (24/48) mediaLoc=0 (-1/-1) bwForMedia=24
```

Notice in the preceding trace that instead of using **locA** and **locB** to indicate the locations where CallManager needs to reserve bandwidth, the following fields are used instead:

- **userLoc**—Indicates the location of the device using the media resource. In this case, the IP phone is in Branch 1.

- **mediaLoc**—Indicates where the media resource resides. In this case, the MOH server is in the <none> location (location 0).

- **bwForMedia**—Indicates 24 because the regions configuration dictates that G.729 is used for calls between the Default region and the Branch 1 region.

If bandwidth availability is insufficient, tone on hold is played instead of MOH. The following trace shows what happens if not enough bandwidth is available for the MOH stream:

First, you see the hold soft key press:

```
StationInit: 66b030c SoftKeyEvent softKeyEvent=3(Hold) lineInstance=1
   callReference=33554849.
```

Next, the MOH resource is allocated, and an attempt to reserve bandwidth occurs; however, as you can see, there is not enough bandwidth:

```
MediaResourceCdpc::device_lookup_DevicePidRes MohResource=MOH_FTL-CM02
Locations: reserve for MediaResource: cdccPID=(2.13.172) Media SOurce=0 no need
   to reserve bw for MediaResource.
Locations: reserve for MediaResource: cdccPID=(2.13.172) UserParty=1 not enough
   bw for UserParty. curr=20 max=20 bw required for MediaResource=24
Locations: cdccPID(2.13.53) locA=0 (-1/-1) locB=2 (432/512) bw=80 userLoc=0
   (-1/-1) mediaLoc=0 (-1/-1) bwForMedia=-1
Locations: Displaying Locations List
Locations: location=1 curr=20 max=20
Locations: location=2 curr=432 max=512
Locations: location=3 curr=128 max=128
Locations: location=4 curr=96 max=96
Locations: location=5 curr=48 max=48
Locations: location=6 curr=256 max=256
Locations: location=7 curr=512 max=512
Locations: location=8 curr=1500 max=1500
MohDControl - ERROR AllocateMohResourceReq failed - not enough location bandwidth,
   AudioSourceID and MuticastFlag = 2, 0
MediaResourceCdpc::resource_rsvp_AllocateMohResourceErr Device=MOH_FTL-CM02
MediaResourceCdpc::waiting_MrmAllocateMohResourceReq
```

```
MediaResourceCdpc::findDeviceGivenList
MediaResourceCdpc::mohErrorResponseToManager
MediaResourceManager::waiting_MrmAllocateMohResourceErr
MRM::waiting_MrmAllocateMohResourceErr - ERROR - no resources are
   available -- ci = 33554851
```

A few lines further down, you finally see CallManager tell the held party phone to play hold tone because no MOH resources are available:

```
StationD:    66b0370 StartTone tone=53(HoldTone).
```

As you can see, the CCM traces are very readable. As long as you know what you're looking for, troubleshooting a locations-based CAC problem should be fairly straightforward.

Locations-based CAC Reservations for Ad Hoc or Meet-Me Conferences

Just to complicate things a bit, let's take a look at an Ad Hoc conference. Locations-based CAC for an Ad Hoc or Meet-Me conference is very similar to that of a call between two IP phones in different locations. As you saw in Chapter 11, "Conference Bridges, Transcoders, and Media Termination Points," when CallManager creates an Ad Hoc or Meet-Me conference, it sets up a call between the conference bridge and each device being added to the conference. So for a three-party conference, CallManager must place three individual "calls" from the conference participants to the conference bridge device. Each participant must be allocated its own bandwidth if it needs to traverse locations boundaries to get to the conference bridge device.

Table 13-3 shows how the regions and locations are configured for this example.

Table 13-3 *Region and Location Configuration for This Example*

	Extension	Region	Location
Phone 1	13256	Branch 1	Branch 1
Phone 2	13257	Branch 1	Branch 1
MOH server	—	Default	<none>
Conference bridge device	—	Default	<none>
PSTN gateway	—	Default	<none>

For example, assume that you have two IP phones in Branch 1, and Branch 1 has 48 kbps of bandwidth allocated to it. A hardware conference bridge resource is available at the hub location, as well as a gateway to the PSTN.

If you set up a call between the two IP phones in Branch 1, no locations bandwidth is required because the two devices are in the same location. However, if either of these two IP phones wants to conference in a third phone (regardless of what location this phone is in), the conference resource is across the WAN, so each phone needs enough bandwidth for a stream to this conference bridge device. For this example, analyze what happens when you make a call between the two IP phones in Branch 1 and then try to conference a participant from the PSTN.

Begin by placing a call from 13256 to 13257. Because both IP phones are in the same location, you see the following in the CCM trace:

```
Locations: reserve: cdccPID=(2.13.165) Orig=Dest=1 no need to reserve bw.
```

Next, phone 13256 presses the **Confrn** soft key. Notice the allocation of a conference bridge device named **b00210505003**:

```
StationInit: 66b030c SoftKeyEvent softKeyEvent=13(Confrn) lineInstance=1
MRM::waiting_MrmAllocateUcbResourceRes - return to CC bridge = b00210505003
```

When 13256 presses the **Confrn** soft key, 13257 is placed on hold while 13256 calls the third conference participant. Because the MOH resources are across the WAN, CallManager must reserve bandwidth to allow the MOH stream to come across:

```
Locations: reserve for MediaResource: cdccPID=(2.13.165) Media SOurce=0
  no need to reserve bw for MediaResource.
Locations: reserve for MediaResource: cdccPID=(2.13.165) adding entry for
  MediaResource.
Locations: reserve for MediaResource: cdccPID=(2.13.165) Orig=1 bw added &
  deducted for MediaResource=24 curr=24 max=48
```

While 13257 is on hold, 13256 dials 95551234, which is routed out the PSTN gateway at the hub location. Because this call must traverse the WAN, bandwidth must be allocated for this call. Notice that the cdccPID is new because this is a new call:

```
Digit analysis: match(fqcn="13256", cn="13256", pss="Internal:Local:Long Distance:
  International", dd="95551234")

Locations: reserve: cdccPID=(2.13.166) Dest=0 no need to reserve bw.
Locations: reserve: cdccPID=(2.13.166) adding entry.
Locations: reserve: cdccPID=(2.13.166) Orig=1 reserved bw=24 curr=0 max=48
```

Notice that at this point, all the bandwidth to Branch 1 is in use—24 kbps for the MOH stream to 13257 and 24 kbps for the call between 13256 and the PSTN. As soon as the PSTN answers, 13256 presses the **Confrn** soft key again:

```
StationInit: 66b030c SoftKeyEvent softKeyEvent=13(Confrn) lineInstance=1
  callReference=33554819.
```

Now CallManager must close the media stream between the PSTN and 13256 as well as the MOH stream to 13257. This also results in bandwidth being released. First, CallManager releases the bandwidth for the call between 13256 and the PSTN:

```
Locations: release: cdccPID=(2.13.166) Orig=1 released bw=24 curr=24 max=48
Locations: release: cdccPID=(2.13.166) Dest=0 no bw to release.
Locations: release: cdccPID=(2.13.166) removing entry.
```

Next, the bandwidth for the MOH stream is released:

```
Locations: release for MediaResource: cdccPID=(2.13.165) UserParty=1
  released bw for User party=24 curr=48 max=48
Locations: release for MediaResource: cdccPID=(2.13.165)  Media Source =0
  infinite bw available for MediaResource
```

At this point, no bandwidth is reserved for the Branch 1 location, as evidenced by **curr=48** in the preceding trace portion. This bandwidth is quickly reallocated when 13256 and 13257 are added to the conference that has just been created. First you see 13256 get added to the conference. (Remember, you saw that the conference ID that was allocated for this conference is **b00210505003**.)

```
Digit analysis: match(fqcn="13256", cn="13256", pss="Phone Line 1:Internal:
  Local:Long Distance:International", dd="b00210505003")
Locations: reserve: cdccPID=(2.13.165) Dest=0 no need to reserve bw.
Locations: reserve: cdccPID=(2.13.165) modifying entry.
Locations: reserve: cdccPID=(2.13.165) Orig=1 reserved bw=24 curr=24 max=48
```

Next, 13257 is added to the conference:

```
Digit analysis: match(fqcn="13257", cn="13257", pss="Phone Line 1:Internal:
  Local:Long Distance:International", dd="b00210505003")

Locations: reserve: cdccPID=(2.13.168) Dest=0 no need to reserve bw.
Locations: reserve: cdccPID=(2.13.168) adding entry.
Locations: reserve: cdccPID=(2.13.168) Orig=1 reserved bw=24 curr=0 max=48
```

Finally, the PSTN participant is added. Because the PSTN gateway and the conference bridge are in the same location, no bandwidth is allocated for the PSTN participant:

```
Digit analysis: match(fqcn="9.@", cn="95551234", pss="Internal",
  dd="b00210505003")

Locations: reserve: cdccPID=(2.13.167) Orig=Dest=0 no need to reserve bw.
```

Notice that each participant in the conference has a unique cdccPID. This is because each participant is now treated as a separate call into the conference bridge device. Because every participant now has a unique cdccPID, bandwidth can be released as each participant drops out of the conference. There's no need to discuss the release process for a conference bridge because it is identical to the process of releasing bandwidth for any other call between two devices as explained in the section "Locations-based CAC in Action."

One important thing to note is that if there is not enough bandwidth for one of the participants to join a conference call, that participant just hears reorder tone. All other participants who have enough bandwidth to get to the conference bridge are added to the conference bridge.

Finding Bandwidth Leaks

You might find yourself in a situation where you can't place as many calls as you want to or from a particular location. It is possible that one or more calls with active reservations exist that you think should not have a reservation active. CCM traces help you determine exactly where all your bandwidth is being used.

You might have noticed in the trace examples that the cdccPID values have been incrementing sequentially. This is not a coincidence; the last digit of the cdccPID increments by 1 for each call attempt. Because of this fact, it is usually obvious if there is a call that has been active for a very long time. For example, take a look at the CCM trace shown in Example 13-4.

Example 13-4   *CCM Trace Showing the cdccPID for Each Call*

```
Locations: reserve: cdccPID=(2.13.2182) adding entry.
Locations: reserve: cdccPID=(2.13.2182) Orig=1 reserved bw=24 curr=1476 max=1500
Locations: reserve: cdccPID=(2.13.2182) Dest=3 reserved bw=24 curr=104 max=128
Locations: broadcast local location table update to all active nodes: remote node=1
Locations: cdccPID(2.13.53) locA=0 (-1/-1) locB=2 (432/512) bw=80 userLoc=0
```

continues

Example 13-4 *CCM Trace Showing the cdccPID for Each Call (Continued)*

```
   (-1/-1) mediaLoc=0 (-1/-1) bwForMedia=-1
Locations: cdccPID(2.13.2182) locA=1 (1476/1500) locB=3 (104/128) bw=24 userLoc=0
   (-1/-1) mediaLoc=0 (-1/-1) bwForMedia=-1
Locations: Displaying Locations List
Locations: location=1 curr=1476 max=1500
Locations: location=2 curr=432 max=512
Locations: location=3 curr=104 max=128
Locations: location=4 curr=96 max=96
Locations: location=5 curr=48 max=48
Locations: location=6 curr=256 max=256
Locations: location=7 curr=512 max=512
Locations: location=8 curr=1500 max=1500
```

As you can see in this trace, the current call has a cdccPID of (2.13.2182). In the location table, you can also see that there is a call with cdccPID (2.13.53). This tells you that there have been more than 2000 call attempts between the time the call with cdccPID (2.13.53) was attempted and the time the call with cdccPID (2.13.2182) was attempted. Depending on the amount of traffic on your CallManager server, this might or might not be a significant number. To find out why the call with cdccPID (2.13.53) still has a bandwidth reservation, you must do a text search through the CCM trace file directory for the phrase "cdccPID(2.13.53)." Assuming that the trace files have not wrapped and overwritten the trace where the bandwidth was allocated for cdccPID (2.13.53), you will find out how that call got set up. You should then know exactly which devices were involved in setting up that call. You can either check the devices to see if they are still on the call or search though the traces for activity related to those devices.

Under no circumstance should locations bandwidth remain allocated after CallManager knows a call has been torn down. However, there is one case in the event of a CallManager failure in which you might end up with a temporary oversubscription of a WAN link while media streams are preserved, as discussed in the following section.

Locations and Call Preservation Interaction

As of CallManager release 3.1(1), most calls are preserved in the event of a CallManager server failure. For a detailed explanation of calls that are not preserved, refer to Chapter 10, "Call Preservation." Call preservation preserves the media streams only for active calls. Call preservation does not preserve any kind of signaling between most endpoints. This presents a minor problem for locations-based CAC.

The problem is that as soon as a failure occurs, the remaining CallManager servers in the cluster remove bandwidth reservations that were initiated by the CallManager server that failed. Because there is no way for the other CallManager servers in the cluster to know when the preserved calls end, they just clear the bandwidth allocation immediately. This means that CallManager can inadvertently allow more calls than the bandwidth allows for because it does not take into account the bandwidth being used by the preserved calls.

For example, assume that a location has only 24 kbps available and that an active call to that location is using that 24 kbps. Any other calls to that location result in a "Not Enough Bandwidth" message displayed on the IP phone. While this call is up, suppose that the CallManager server to which the phones involved in this call are registered goes down for some reason (crash, network failure, and so on). The call is preserved, and the IP phones continue their conversation; however, the backup CallManager in the cluster removes the locations reservation for this call because it no longer knows about the call. While this call is preserved, all the other IP phones that were registered to the CallManager server that went down fail over to their backup CallManager. At this point, the CallManager servers in the cluster think that 24 kbps of bandwidth is available and allow a call to this location to be completed. Depending on how your WAN link is configured, there is a chance that both the new call and the preserved call will experience voice quality issues because of WAN oversubscription. Luckily, this problem is self-correcting. Whenever the preserved call is disconnected, the locations database is once again correct.

CallManager failures are extremely rare. Even if there is a failure, the conditions must be such that the number of preserved calls plus active calls to a location exceeds the bandwidth available to that location. In most deployments, it is unlikely that this will cause a problem; however, you should keep this possibility in mind when troubleshooting locations-based CAC problems.

Troubleshooting Automated Alternate Routing

In CallManager 3.3 and later you can configure CallManager to automatically reroute calls when not enough WAN bandwidth is available. This feature is called automated alternate routing (AAR).

From a locations-based CAC perspective, there is not much to troubleshooting AAR. When a call fails because of insufficient WAN bandwidth, the CCM traces look exactly as they appear in the previous examples. The only difference is that instead of displaying **OutOfBandwidthText**, the phone shows "Network Congestion, Rerouting." CallManager then prefixes the appropriate digits as dictated by the AAR configuration in CallManager Administration (**System > AAR Group**) and places a brand new call, just as if the user had dialed the number directly from his or her phone. The only difference is that the calling search space used for the rerouted call is the AAR calling search space configured for the device. This allows you to configure a less-restrictive calling search space for the purposes of rerouting a call. For example, you might have an IP phone that is permitted to call only internal extensions, but you want to allow that phone to reroute through the PSTN when there is not enough WAN bandwidth. In this case, the AAR calling search space allows calls through a local gateway to the PSTN that would be otherwise inaccessible by the normal calling search space configured on the device.

If your calls are failing after the rerouting, troubleshoot the call like any other direct call out a gateway. Refer to Chapter 9, "Call Routing," and Chapter 6, "Voice Gateways," for more information on troubleshooting calls through a gateway.

As you have seen, locations-based CAC allows you to easily control the number of calls allowed across your WAN to ensure voice quality; however, locations-based CAC works only within a single cluster. To perform CAC between clusters, you must use an H.323 gatekeeper.

Gatekeeper Call Admission Control

CallManager clusters can be interconnected to each other using virtual trunks called *intercluster trunks*. An intercluster trunk uses the H.323 protocol to communicate between CallManager clusters. In a distributed CallManager deployment, each cluster is separated by WAN links. As a result, you need a mechanism to control the number of calls that can be placed between clusters. CallManager can use an H.323 gatekeeper to provide CAC on intercluster trunks.

The focus here is on Cisco's IOS Software gatekeeper functionality, although CallManager should interoperate with any standards-compliant H.323 gatekeeper. The gatekeeper functionality in Cisco IOS Software is called Multimedia Conference Manager (MCM). MCM functionality is an optional feature available on various platforms, including the Cisco 2500, Cisco 2600, Cisco 3600, Cisco 3700, and Cisco 7200 series routers.

Note that CallManager supports only direct endpoint call signaling mode. In this mode, the gatekeeper is used for CAC and dial plan resolution, but the call signaling (H.225 and H.245) occurs directly between the two endpoints, without the gatekeeper's involvement. This is opposed to gatekeeper-routed call signaling mode, in which call signaling is sent through the gatekeeper in addition to CAC and dial plan messaging. CallManager does not support gatekeeper-routed call signaling mode.

For additional information on H.323 gatekeepers, refer to the following URL:

www.cisco.com/warp/public/788/voip/understand-gatekeepers.html

The basic idea behind gatekeeper CAC is that each CallManager cluster registers with the gatekeeper and uses it to determine whether it is allowed to make a call to another CallManager cluster. The bandwidth for each cluster is configured on the gatekeeper, so CallManager is never aware of how much bandwidth is actually available to it. CallManager merely sends a message to the gatekeeper, asking whether CallManager is allowed to make a call to a particular number.

The ITU-T H.323 specification defines gatekeeper functionality. This subset of functionality is called Registration, Admission, and Status (RAS). Table 13-4 shows the RAS messages used between a CallManager and a gatekeeper.

Table 13-4   *H.323 RAS Messages*

Message Name	Description
Registration Request (RRQ) Gatekeeper ← CCM	Sent from CallManager to the gatekeeper when CallManager wants to register with the gatekeeper. Also sent from CallManager periodically as a KeepAlive while registered.
Registration Confirm (RCF) Gatekeeper → CCM	Sent from the gatekeeper to CallManager in response to an RRQ confirming the registration. Also sent as a KeepAlive acknowledgment in response to an RRQ message received while already registered.
Registration Reject (RRJ) Gatekeeper → CCM	Sent from the gatekeeper to CallManager in response to an RRQ rejecting the registration.
Unregistration Request (URQ) Gatekeeper ← CCM	Sent from CallManager to the gatekeeper, indicating that CallManager wants to unregister from the gatekeeper.
Unregistration Confirm (UCF) Gatekeeper → CCM	Sent from the gatekeeper to CallManager in response to a URQ allowing CallManager to unregister from the gatekeeper.
Unregistration Reject (URJ) Gatekeeper → CCM	Sent from the gatekeeper to CallManager in response to a URQ rejecting CallManager's request to unregister from the gatekeeper.
Admission Request (ARQ) Gatekeeper ← CCM	When CallManager is originating or accepting a call on a gatekeeper-controlled device, this message is sent from CallManager to the gatekeeper to ask the gatekeeper to admit a call.
Admission Confirm (ACF) Gatekeeper → CCM	Sent from the gatekeeper to CallManager in response to an ARQ to permit a call to proceed. The ACF also contains the IP address of the device to which CallManager should set up the call. In the context of CAC, an ACF means that there is enough bandwidth to allow the call.
Admission Reject (ARJ) Gatekeeper → CCM	Sent from the gatekeeper to CallManager in response to an ARQ to reject a call. In the context of CAC, an ARJ means that there is not enough bandwidth to allow the call.
Disengage Request (DRQ) Gatekeeper ← CCM	Sent from CallManager to the gatekeeper, asking the gatekeeper to disconnect an active call and return the bandwidth for that call to the pool of available bandwidth.
Disengage Confirm (DCF) Gatekeeper → CCM	Sent from the gatekeeper to CallManager in response to a DRQ allowing a call to be disconnected and confirming that the bandwidth allocated for that call is returned to the pool of available bandwidth.
Disengage Reject (DRJ) Gatekeeper → CCM	Sent from the gatekeeper to CallManager in response to a DRQ denying the request to disconnect an active call.

To troubleshoot a gatekeeper CAC problem, first check the CallManager and gatekeeper configuration, and then enable the proper traces to determine why gatekeeper CAC is failing.

Checking Gatekeeper Configuration

The first thing to do when troubleshooting a gatekeeper CAC-related problem is to ensure that the gatekeeper configuration is correct. Example 13-5 shows a sample configuration from a gatekeeper.

Example 13-5 *Sample Gatekeeper Configuration*

```
gatekeeper
 zone local ftl-cm02-03 cisco.com
 zone local ftl-cm4a cisco.com
 zone prefix ftl-cm02-03 1....
 zone prefix ftl-cm02-03 2....
 zone prefix ftl-cm02-03 3....
 zone prefix ftl-cm02-03 4....
 zone prefix ftl-cm02-03 5....
 zone prefix ftl-cm02-03 6....
 zone prefix ftl-cm4a 7....
 gw-type-prefix 1#* default-technology
 bandwidth total zone ftl-cm02-03 256
 bandwidth total zone ftl-cm4a 256
 no shutdown
```

First of all, every CallManager cluster should belong to one zone. Because the gatekeeper controls these zones, you need to define them as local zones. Give the zone a name that is descriptive and easy to identify. This zone name should match what is configured in CallManager Administration for each cluster. If you put multiple clusters in the same zone, you will have problems because the gatekeeper will not know which calls should go to which cluster.

Next, check to make sure the dial plan is correct. Example 13-5 uses a five-digit dial plan. Calls to numbers between 10000 and 69999 are routed to the cluster that registers with the **ftl-cm02-03** zone, and calls to numbers between 70000 and 79999 are routed to the cluster that registers with the **ftl-cm4a** zone.

If you are not prepending technology prefixes to the dialed digits when you route calls to the gatekeeper, you need to ensure you have a default technology prefix configured on the gatekeeper. Make sure the line **gw-type-prefix 1#* default-technology** is present in the configuration and that the prefix (minus the *) is configured on all CallManager clusters that are registering with this gatekeeper. Failure to do so results in calls failing to complete.

To get a better understanding of the importance of a technology prefix, you should understand how IOS gatekeepers make call routing decisions. The document

"Understanding Cisco IOS H.323 Gatekeeper Call Routing" on Cisco.com explains this in detail:

www.cisco.com/warp/public/788/voip/gk-call-routing.html

Finally, make sure the bandwidth from one zone to another is configured correctly. Gatekeeper CAC is similar to locations-based CAC in that CallManager requests different amounts of bandwidth depending on the codec being used for the call; however, the amount of bandwidth requested differs between locations-based CAC and gatekeeper CAC. With gatekeeper CAC, CallManager requests 128 kbps for a G.711 call and 20 kbps for a G.729 call. As observed earlier with locations-based CAC, these numbers probably do not accurately reflect the amount of bandwidth each call will really consume, so you have to tweak the numbers so that you allow a specific number of calls by configuring the bandwidth instead of just setting the bandwidth to the link speed. For example, if you are using RTP header compression and G.729 for your calls, each call consumes only 12 to 13 kbps as opposed to the 20 kbps that CallManager asks the gatekeeper for. For example, if you want to allow four calls to a particular zone (which would consume 48 to 52 kbps of bandwidth), you should configure the bandwidth for that zone to 80 kbps to compensate for the difference between the actual bandwidth being used and the bandwidth being requested.

NOTE	Example 13-5 uses the command **bandwidth total zone**. In earlier versions of Cisco IOS Software, the command to configure bandwidth for a zone was **zone bw**. Both commands do the same thing.

Verifying Gatekeeper Configuration on CallManager

After you have verified that everything is configured correctly on the gatekeeper, make sure the gatekeepers are configured correctly in CallManager (**Device > Gatekeeper**). Figure 13-2 shows the gatekeeper configuration on a CallManager 3.2 server.

The **Gatekeeper Name** should be the gatekeeper's IP address or DNS name. The **Registration Request Time To Live** indicates the interval at which CallManager sends RRQs to the gatekeeper as KeepAlives. The **Registration Retry Timeout** is the amount of time that CallManager waits after a failure to register with the gatekeeper before trying to reregister. You should always set Terminal type to **Gateway** when configuring the gatekeeper to communicate between CallManager clusters.

Figure 13-2 *Gatekeeper Configuration in CallManager Administration for Release 3.2*

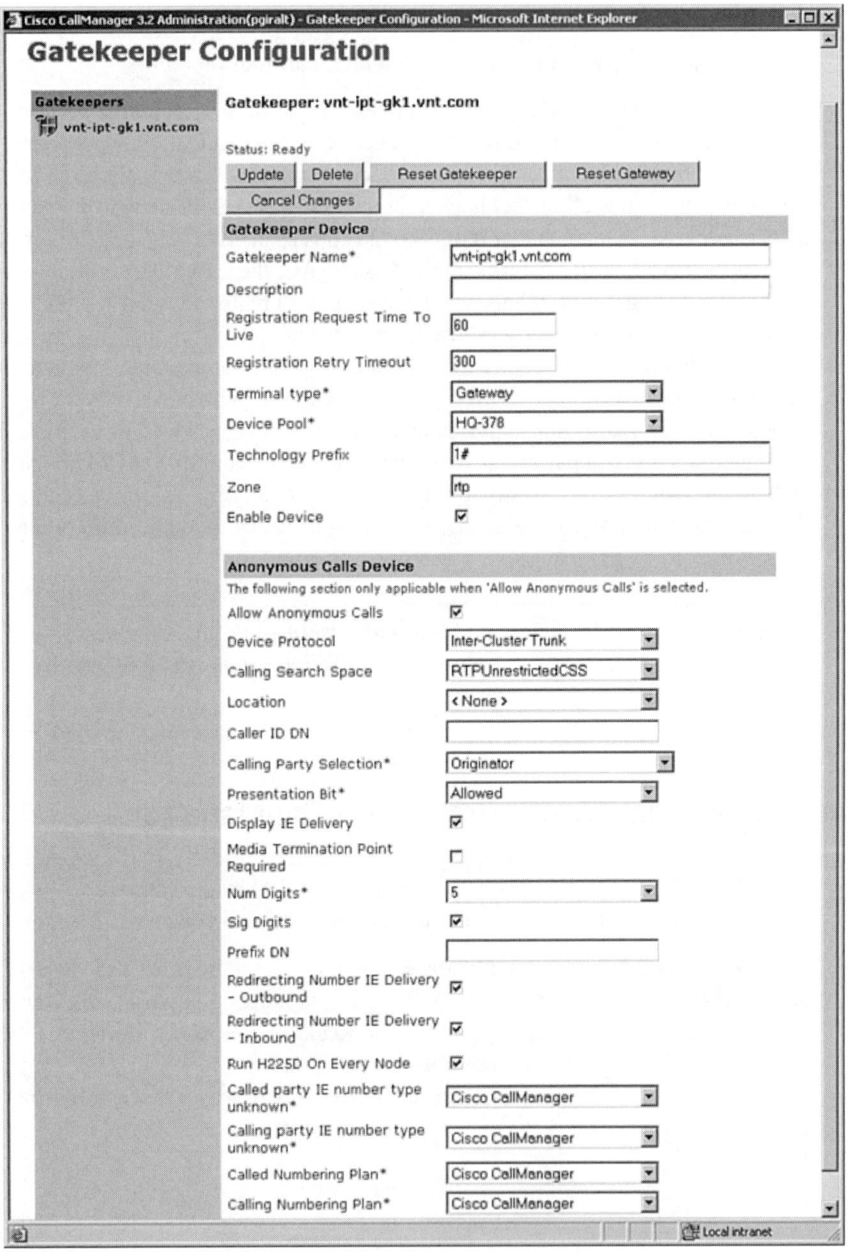

CallManager 3.1 and 3.2 have a device called AnonymousDevice that is created when you select **Allow Anonymous Calls** under the Anonymous Calls Device section of the gatekeeper configuration. AnonymousDevice allows you to route calls to a gatekeeper and let

the gatekeeper decide which IP address to send the call to. In contrast, you can use a gatekeeper just for CAC without allowing it to perform IP address selection. When you select **Allow Anonymous Calls**, the device named AnonymousDevice appears as an H.323 gateway, just like any other H.323 gateway device you have configured. It can be added to route groups, route lists, and route patterns like any other H.323 gateway. The difference is that instead of sending a setup directly to the H.323 gateway's IP address, it sends an admission request to the gatekeeper and uses the IP address returned in the admission confirm message.

The AnonymousDevice has a configuration option for **Device Protocol**. This option allows you to select what kind of devices are registered to the gatekeeper in addition to the CallManager cluster you are configuring. If there are any non-CallManager H.323 endpoints to which you want to be able to route calls, select **H.225**. CallManager 3.2 and later versions automatically detect when a gatekeeper-controlled call is between two CallManagers and switch to the intercluster trunk variant of H.323. Prior to CallManager 3.2, you could not combine CallManagers and non-CallManager devices.

The device pool that is configured on the Gatekeeper Configuration page is important. This device pool configures several parameters that you might not realize at first. First, the device pool contains a CallManager group. The CallManager group determines which CallManager in the cluster registers with the gatekeeper. Only one CallManager in a cluster should be registered with a gatekeeper at any given time. If the primary CallManager fails, the next available CallManager in the cluster should attempt to register with the gatekeeper. Additionally, the gatekeeper's device pool determines which codec is used for calls routed through the AnonymousDevice. This is important because the codec determines how much bandwidth CallManager requests.

The last two fields under the Gatekeeper Device configuration are the Technology Prefix and Zone. These must match the gatekeeper's configuration. The **Enable Device** checkbox must be selected for CallManager to register with the gatekeeper.

After you have properly configured the gatekeeper, you must click the **Reset Gatekeeper** and **Reset Gateway** buttons to start the CallManager processes that register with the gatekeeper. With everything properly configured, you can verify whether everything is working correctly.

In CallManager version 3.3 and later (**Device > Gatekeeper**), gatekeeper configuration is substantially different, as shown in Figure 13-3. As of CallManager version 3.3, a CallManager cluster can register with multiple gatekeepers.

Notice that the **Anonymous Calls Device** configuration section is missing. This is because CallManager 3.3 and later does away with the concept of AnonymousDevice and introduces the concept of a trunk device (select **Device > Trunk**). A trunk device can be one of the following:

- H.225 trunk (gatekeeper-controlled)
- Intercluster trunk (gatekeeper-controlled)
- Intercluster trunk (non-gatekeeper-controlled)

Figure 13-3 *Gatekeeper Configuration in CallManager Administration for Release 3.3*

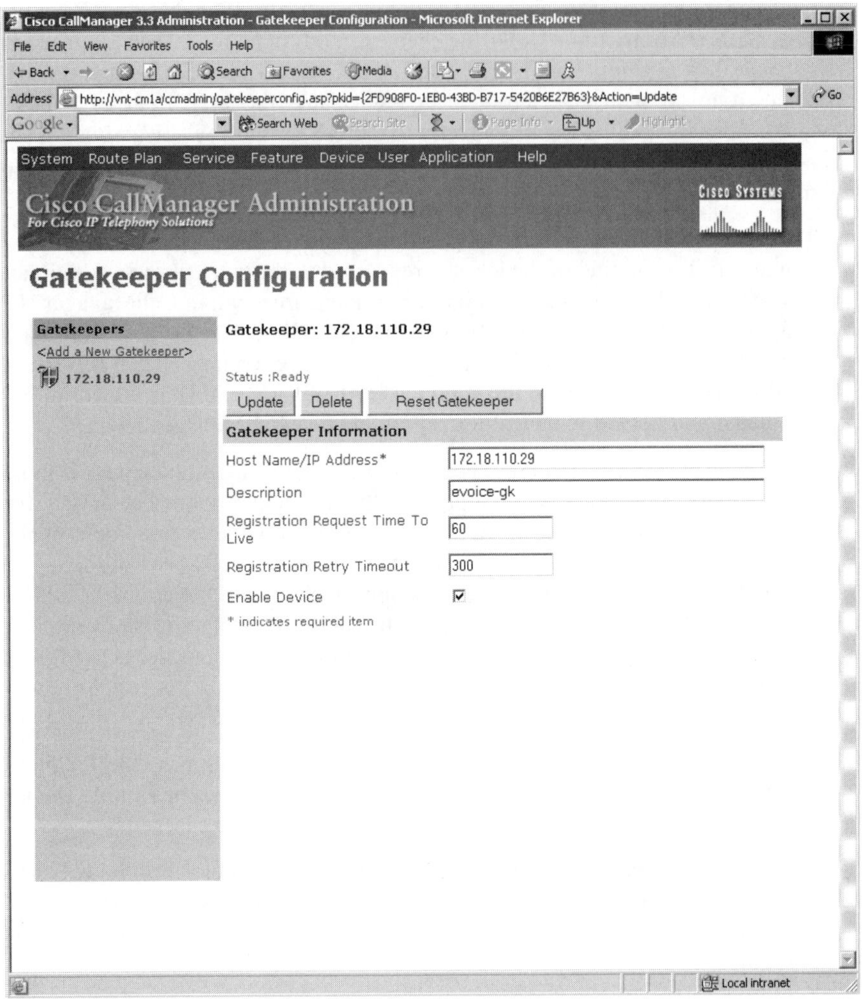

The functionality of AnonymousDevice can be emulated in CallManager 3.3 and later by creating a gatekeeper-controlled trunk device. The difference is that in CallManager 3.3 and later you can configure multiple devices that function like the AnonymousDevice, but you can route calls to different gatekeepers if you so choose. Also, calls can be received from multiple gatekeepers.

From a CAC point of view, the important things to note are the zone and technology prefix configured for a particular trunk device. This configuration dictates which zone on the gatekeeper is used to admit calls that are destined out a particular trunk device.

CallManager Registration with Gatekeeper

The first thing you should look for after checking the configuration is to make sure the CallManager clusters you are working with have registered correctly with the gatekeeper. The easiest way to do this is by looking on the gatekeeper. Issue the command **show gatekeeper endpoints**. The output should look similar to Example 13-6.

Example 13-6   **show gatekeeper endpoints** *Command Output*

```
Router#show gatekeeper endpoints
                GATEKEEPER ENDPOINT REGISTRATION
                ================================
CallSignalAddr  Port  RASSignalAddr  Port  Zone Name      Type    F
--------------- ----- -------------- ----- ---------      ----   --
172.18.116.69   1720  172.18.116.69  1710  ftl-cm4a       VOIP-GW
   H323-ID: 172.18.116.69
172.18.116.71   1720  172.18.116.71  1710  ftl-cm02-03    VOIP-GW
   H323-ID: 172.18.116.71
Total number of active registrations = 2
```

As you can see, two CallManagers are registered with this gatekeeper. One is registered with the zone **ftl-cm4a**, and the other is registered with the zone **ftl-cm02-03**. They are both registered as terminal type **VOIP-GW**, which is correct because it matches what you configured in CallManager Administration. In CallManager 3.2 and earlier the terminal type is configured in the Gatekeeper Configuration page (**Device > Gatekeeper**). In CallManager 3.3 and later the terminal type is configured on the Trunk Configuration page (**Device > Trunk**). In IOS, the type **VOIP-GW** is equivalent to **Gateway** in CallManager and type **VOIP-TERM** is equivalent to **Terminal**.

If your CallManager is not registering with the gatekeeper, or if it is registering with the wrong zone, the first thing you should do is recheck your configuration in CallManager Administration on the Gatekeeper Configuration page (**Device > Gatekeeper**). Next, make sure you have IP connectivity between the gatekeeper and CallManager. It is possible that something is configured that is causing the gatekeeper to reject the CallManager registration. To check whether CallManager is attempting to register, enter the command **debug ras**. If you are accessing the gatekeeper via a Telnet session, be sure to also enter **terminal monitor** so that the debug messages appear on your screen.

The easiest way to force CallManager to send a Registration Request (RRQ) is to click the **Reset Gatekeeper** button on the Gatekeeper Configuration page in CallManager

Administration. If CallManager was not previously registered, you should see something like the output shown in Example 13-7, with **debug ras** enabled in the gatekeeper.

Example 13-7 *Output for a Previously Unregistered CallManager, Forcing an RRQ*

```
Dec   3 00:37:49.592:  RecvUDP_IPSockData   successfully rcvd message of
  length 12 from 172.18.116.71:1710
Dec   3 00:37:49.592: URQ (seq# 2) rcvd
Dec   3 00:37:49.592:  IPSOCK_RAS_sendto:   msg length 4 from
  10.192.123.33:1719 to 172.18.116.71: 1710
Dec   3 00:37:49.592:          RASLib::RASSendURJ: URJ (seq# 2) sent to 172.18.116.71
Dec   3 00:37:49.736:  RecvUDP_IPSockData   successfully rcvd message of length 104
  from 172.18.116.71:1710
Dec   3 00:37:49.736: RRQ (seq# 2) rcvd
Dec   3 00:37:49.740:  IPSOCK_RAS_sendto:   msg length 104 from
  10.192.123.33:1719 to 172.18.116.71: 1710
Dec   3 00:37:49.740:          RASLib::RASSendRCF: RCF (seq# 2) sent to 172.18.116.71
```

The first thing you see in this trace is CallManager sending an Unregister Request (URQ) to make sure it is not registered with the gatekeeper before trying to register. In this case, the gatekeeper sends back an Unregister Reject (URJ) because CallManager was not registered, so the gatekeeper cannot unregister it.

Next, CallManager sends an RRQ and receives a Registration Confirm (RCF). If there had been a failure, the gatekeeper would have sent a Registration Reject (RRJ) instead. For example, take a look at the **debug** output in Example 13-8, with **debug ras** enabled on the gatekeeper.

Example 13-8 **debug ras** *on a Gatekeeper Showing a Registration Rejection*

```
Router#debug ras
Dec   3 00:46:08.223: RRQ (seq# 2) rcvd
Dec   3 00:46:08.223:  IPSOCK_RAS_sendto:    msg length 12 from 10.192.123.33:1719
  to 172.18.116.71: 1710
Dec   3 00:46:08.223:          RASLib::RASSendRRJ: RRJ (seq# 2) sent to 172.18.116.71
```

Unfortunately, **debug ras** does not give you any details as to why the registration was rejected. To see the actual RRJ message, enable **debug h225 asn1** on the gatekeeper. The RRJ looks similar to Example 13-9.

Example 13-9 *ASN.1 Output Indicating the Registration Rejection Reason*

```
Router#debug h225 asn1
value RasMessage ::= registrationReject :
    {
      requestSeqNum 2
      protocolIdentifier { 0 0 8 2250 0 2 }
      rejectReason discoveryRequired : NULL
    }
```

Unfortunately, the rejectReason is usually not very descriptive either. In this case, the reason of **discoveryRequired** is misleading. The generation of this error was forced by the configuration of **no zone subnet ftl-cm02-03 172.18.116.0/24 enable** on the gatekeeper. This command rejects any registrations from the 172.18.116.0/24 subnet. As soon as you remove that line from the configuration, CallManager can register successfully. The gatekeeper usually sends **rejectReason discoveryRequired** as the reason, regardless of what the real problem is, so don't be misled. Nearly all registration problems with Cisco IOS Software gatekeepers are the result of a misconfiguration, so if you are getting an RRJ, double-check that the configuration on the gatekeeper matches that on CallManager. Also remember that you must perform this configuration for each CallManager cluster registered to the gatekeeper.

TIP   Although the easiest way to see the ASN.1 messages is through the use of the **debug h225 asn1** command on the gatekeeper, you can see the same messages in the CCM trace if you set the SDL Trace Type Flags to **0x8000EB15**. This is useful if you are trying to troubleshoot a registration problem on a non-Cisco gatekeeper.

Call Setup with Gatekeeper

As soon as your CallManagers are registered with the gatekeeper, you can attempt a call using the gatekeeper for CAC. Assume that you have two clusters registered to a gatekeeper. You use the same configuration that was presented in the preceding section. An IP phone on the first cluster has a directory number of 13258 and wants to make a call to 71003, which resides on a second cluster. AnonymousDevice is configured on both CallManager clusters to allow for gatekeeper-routed calls. Although this example shows you the call flow for a call using AnonymousDevice, the same concepts apply for a call using a gatekeeper-controlled gateway device. The only difference is that the IP address for the call setup is decided by the gatekeeper when using AnonymousDevice as opposed to being selected by the IP address configured for the trunk device in CallManager. Figure 13-4 shows the call flow for a call from 13258 to 71003.

Figure 13-4 *Call Flow for a Gatekeeper CAC Intercluster Call*

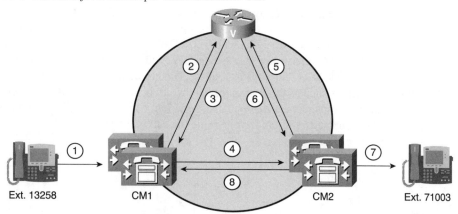

The call steps illustrated in Figure 13-4 are as follows:

Step 1   13258 dials the phone number 71003.

Step 2   CM1 sends GK1 an ARQ, asking permission to call 71003.

Step 3   GK1 does a lookup, finds CM2 registered for zone prefix 7, and returns an ACF with an IP address of CM2.

Step 4   CM1 sends an H.225 call setup to CM2 with the phone number 71003.

Step 5   CM2 sends GK1 an ARQ, asking permission to answer CM1's call.

Step 6   GK1 returns an ACF with an IP address of CM1.

Step 7   CM2 sets up a call to 71003.

Step 8   When 71003 answers, CM2 sends an H.225 connect to CM1.

Look at debugs for this call. When troubleshooting a gatekeeper CAC problem, the best place to start is by looking at the debugs on the gatekeeper. For the preceding call, first look at the **debug ras** shown in Example 13-10.

Example 13-10 **debug ras** *Output of a Successful Call*

```
Router#debug ras
Dec  3 01:59:45.603:  RecvUDP_IPSockData  successfully rcvd message of length 99
  from 172.18.116.71:1710
Dec  3 01:59:45.603: ARQ (seq# 71) rcvd
Dec  3 01:59:45.603:  IPSOCK_RAS_sendto:   msg length 23 from 10.192.123.33:1719
  to 172.18.116.71: 1710
Dec  3 01:59:45.603:       RASLib::RASSendACF: ACF (seq# 71) sent to 172.18.116.71
Dec  3 01:59:45.623:  RecvUDP_IPSockData  successfully rcvd message of length 101
  from 172.18.116.69:1710
Dec  3 01:59:45.623: ARQ (seq# 256) rcvd
Dec  3 01:59:45.627:  IPSOCK_RAS_sendto:   msg length 23 from 10.192.123.33:1719
  to 172.18.116.69: 1710
Dec  3 01:59:45.627:       RASLib::RASSendACF: ACF (seq# 256) sent to 172.18.116.69
```

As you can see, the gatekeeper first receives an ARQ from 172.18.116.71, which is a server in the CallManager cluster that 13258 is registered to. The gatekeeper then sends an ACF to allow the call. You then see 172.18.116.69, a CallManager server in the destination cluster, sending an ARQ to make sure its zone has enough bandwidth to accept the call. The gatekeeper also sends an ACF for this request. The problem with **debug ras** is that you do not see any details such as the amount of bandwidth being requested. Before looking at some of the additional debugs to see this information, you should familiarize yourself with some of the commands you can look at while the call is active.

The first command is **show gatekeeper calls**, shown in Example 13-11. It shows all active gatekeeper calls and how much bandwidth they have been allocated.

Example 13-11 show gatekeeper calls *Command Output*

```
Router#show gatekeeper calls
Total number of active calls = 1.
                        GATEKEEPER CALL INFO
                        ====================
LocalCallID                       Age(secs)   BW
43-201                               10          20(Kbps)
  Endpt(s): Alias        E.164Addr     CallSignalAddr  Port  RASSignalAddr   Port
    src EP: 172.18.116.7 13258         172.18.116.71   1720  172.18.116.71   1710
    dst EP: 172.18.116.6 71003         172.18.116.69   1720  172.18.116.69   1710
```

You can see that the call has been active for 10 seconds and has been allocated 20 kbps, which indicates that this call is using the G.729 codec. You can also see the calling and called party numbers in the E.164Addr column.

For additional information about the amount of bandwidth in use and the available bandwidth for each zone on the gatekeeper, use the command **show gatekeeper zone status**, as demonstrated in Example 13-12.

Example 13-12 show gatekeeper zone status *Command Output*

```
Router#show gatekeeper zone status
ftl-cm02-03  cisco.com     10.192.123.33    1719  LS
  BANDWIDTH INFORMATION (kbps) :
    Maximum total bandwidth    :    256
    Current total bandwidth    :    20
    Maximum interzone bandwidth :
    Current interzone bandwidth :    20
    Maximum session   bandwidth :
    Total number of concurrent calls : 1
  SUBNET ATTRIBUTES :
    All Other Subnets : (Enabled)
  PROXY USAGE CONFIGURATION :
    Inbound Calls from all other zones :
      to terminals in local zone ftl-cm02-03 : use proxy
      to gateways in local zone ftl-cm02-03  : do not use proxy
      to MCUs in local zone ftl-cm02-03   : do not use proxy
    Outbound Calls to all other zones :
      from terminals in local zone ftl-cm02-03 : use proxy
      from gateways in local zone ftl-cm02-03  : do not use proxy
      from MCUs in local zone ftl-cm02-03   : do not use proxy

ftl-cm4a     cisco.com     10.192.123.33    1719  LS
  BANDWIDTH INFORMATION (kbps) :
    Maximum total bandwidth    :    256
    Current total bandwidth    :    20
    Maximum interzone bandwidth :
    Current interzone bandwidth :    20
    Maximum session   bandwidth :
  SUBNET ATTRIBUTES :
```

continues

Example 13-12 **show gatekeeper zone status** *Command Output (Continued)*

```
    All Other Subnets : (Enabled)
  PROXY USAGE CONFIGURATION :
    Inbound Calls from all other zones :
      to terminals in local zone ftl-cm4a : use proxy
      to gateways in local zone ftl-cm4a  : do not use proxy
      to MCUs in local zone ftl-cm4a  : do not use proxy
    Outbound Calls to all other zones :
      from terminals in local zone ftl-cm4a : use proxy
      from gateways in local zone ftl-cm4a  : do not use proxy
      from MCUs in local zone ftl-cm4a  : do not use proxy
```

The important lines to look at are **Maximum total bandwidth** and **Current total bandwidth**. These lines show you how much bandwidth remains for each zone.

If the gatekeeper rejects a call, you might need to turn on additional debugs on the gatekeeper to see why the call is being rejected. Let's see what happens if you turn on **debug h225 asn1**.

First, you see the ARQ shown in Example 13-13.

Example 13-13 **debug h225 asn1** *Output Showing an Admission Request*

```
Router#debug h225 asn1
value RasMessage ::= admissionRequest :
    {
        requestSeqNum 282
        callType pointToPoint : NULL
        endpointIdentifier {"62BD484800000003"}
        destinationInfo
        {
          e164 : "71003"
        }
        srcInfo
        {
          e164 : "13258"
        }
        srcCallSignalAddress ipAddress :
        {
          ip 'AC127445'H
          port 1720
        }
        bandWidth 200
        callReferenceValue 10
        conferenceID '009269048A06711D0A0020C20A11B311'H
        activeMC FALSE
        answerCall TRUE
        canMapAlias FALSE
        callIdentifier
        {
          guid '009269048A06711D0A0020C20A11B311'H
        }
        willSupplyUUIEs FALSE
    }
```

Notice the line **bandWidth 200**. The bandwidth listed here is actually 10 times larger than the requested bandwidth. In this case, the bandwidth requested is 20 kbps. For a G.711 call, you would see **bandWidth 1280**, which represents 128 kbps. This does not mean you should configure the bandwidth to be 10 times the number. The configuration should still be 20 for G.729 or 128 for G.711.

TIP

The ITU-T H.225 specification defines the value for the **bandWidth** message as the number of 100 bits requested for the bidirectional call, so a 128 kbps call is 128,000 bps or 1280×100 bits per second.

Immediately after receiving the ARQ, the gatekeeper sends the message shown in Example 13-14.

Example 13-14 *ASN.1 Debug of a Registration Rejection from the Gatekeeper*

```
Router#debug h225 asn1
Dec  3 02:18:14.812: RAS OUTGOING PDU ::=

value RasMessage ::= admissionReject :
    {
       requestSeqNum 282
       rejectReason requestDenied : NULL
    }
```

Once again, the **rejectReason** that the gatekeeper gives is not very descriptive. In this case, the call failed because it did not have enough bandwidth available for that zone, but this is not clear from the debug. To verify this, you would have to issue the command **show gatekeeper zone status** to see if there is enough bandwidth to allow the call.

Other than not enough bandwidth, other likely reasons for the call to get rejected are

- No zone prefix is configured that matches the dialed digits.
- No CallManager is registered in the zone where the call is supposed to terminate.

Both of these conditions should have been detected when you verified the configuration and checked CallManager's registration with the gatekeeper.

Armed with the information in this chapter, you should be able to troubleshoot almost any gatekeeper CAC-related problem.

Call rerouting to the PSTN when there is insufficient bandwidth using gatekeeper CAC relies on the configuration of your route lists and route groups. Route lists and route groups are covered in Chapter 9. You should configure the gatekeeper-controlled device to be the first in a route list, followed by the secondary device, which routes the call to the PSTN. When there is insufficient bandwidth to route a call to a gatekeeper-controlled device, the call uses the next device configured in your route list. You can then perform any digit transformations on the route list to modify the called party number so that it is routed properly over the PSTN.

Best Practices

There are a few things you can do when configuring CAC to make troubleshooting easier. First, give your locations descriptive names that allow you to easily identify which devices are associated with a particular location. Similarly, be sure to give your gatekeeper zones descriptive names as well so you can easily identify which zones belong to each CallManager cluster. For example, use the name of the Publisher server as the name of the gatekeeper zone.

Also, try to avoid the possibility of more than one codec being used at any time over the WAN. Most administrators choose to use G.729 over the WAN because a G.729 call consumes far less bandwidth than a G.711 call, allowing you to get the most number of calls possible over a WAN connection. The important thing is that you make sure that every call over the WAN uses the same codec, such as G.729. This is important because, as mentioned earlier, the bandwidth configured for locations-based CAC and gatekeeper CAC does not actually match the bandwidth available on the WAN link. Mixing multiple codecs over the WAN complicates these calculations and in some cases makes it impossible to properly determine a number in the configuration that will maximize the number of calls that can be placed over the WAN without oversubscribing the WAN. As a general rule, stick to G.729 or G.711, but not both.

Note that all current CAC mechanisms rely on a device always remaining within the same location or zone. This presents a problem for mobile devices such as Cisco IP SoftPhone because they are hard-coded to a specific location. This is less of an issue with IP phones because they usually do not cross locations boundaries when being moved. However, be aware that if a device is moved from one location to another, failure to reconfigure the locations information might result in calls across the WAN that are not accounted for as part of the CAC mechanism being used.

Summary

This chapter explored the two CAC mechanisms available in CallManager. Locations-based CAC is used within a CallManager cluster, and gatekeeper CAC is used between two or more CallManager clusters. The best way to troubleshoot a CAC problem is to understand how the two CAC mechanisms are supposed to work so that you can identify where in the process the call is failing.

## CHAPTER 14

Voice Mail

Many IP telephony systems have some form of voice mail to take messages when users cannot answer their phones. Cisco CallManager is compatible with a variety of voice mail systems that integrate with CallManager through various methods. This chapter does not attempt to explain how to troubleshoot the actual voice mail systems that can integrate with CallManager. Instead, it focuses on troubleshooting the integration between CallManager and the voice mail systems.

This chapter focuses on the following types of voice mail systems:

- Cisco Unity
- Third-party voice mail integrated via Simple Message Desk Interface (SMDI)
- Octel voice mail integrated via a DPA 7610 or DPA 7630

Cisco Unity

Cisco Unity is Cisco's voice mail and unified messaging system. Unity integrates with CallManager via the Skinny Client Control Protocol (Skinny protocol). As just mentioned, this chapter does not cover how to troubleshoot the Unity product itself, because that would take a book of its own. You would also need to understand Microsoft Exchange and/or Lotus Domino, which are an integral part of Unity. Instead, this chapter covers how Unity integrates with CallManager and how to troubleshoot problems such as calls not forwarding to voice mail or to the correct mailbox.

CallManager Integration

Unity uses the telephony application programming interface (TAPI) protocol to communicate with a variety of private branch exchange (PBX) switches. Each switch has a TAPI service provider (TSP) that translates TAPI to the native language the PBX speaks. In the case of CallManager, the TSP translates from TAPI to Skinny protocol.

From CallManager's perspective, Unity is just a set of Skinny devices, similar to a set of Cisco 79xx series IP Phones. In fact, much of the troubleshooting for Unity is identical to troubleshooting an IP phone.

Verifying Version Compatibility

The biggest reason for problems with the integration between CallManager and Unity is an incompatible TSP. The release notes for each version of Unity include a compatibility matrix indicating which TSP is compatible with which version of Unity and CallManager. Ensure that the version of CallManager you are running is compatible with both the TSP and Unity and that the TSP is also compatible with Unity.

To determine the version number of the currently installed TSP, go to the C:\WINNT\System32 directory on the Unity server and find the file named AvSkinny.tsp. Right-click it and select **Properties**. Select the **Version** tab on the dialog box that appears, as shown in Figure 14-1. You should see a file version number at the top, such as 6.0.2.0, which corresponds to TSP version 6.0(2).

Figure 14-1   *AvSkinny.tsp File Properties Version Tab*

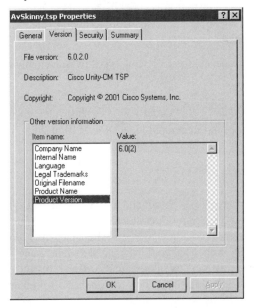

Verifying TSP Configuration

After you have verified that you are using a compatible TSP, check the TSP configuration to ensure it is correct. Go to the Phone and Modem Options control panel on the Unity server. On the Advanced tab you should see a provider named **Cisco Unity-CM TSP** (also named **Av-Cisco Service Provider** in older versions of the TSP). Select it and then click the **Configure** button. You should see your CallManager listed. Select the CallManager IP address, and then click **Settings**. You should see a window similar to Figure 14-2.

Figure 14-2 *Cisco Unity TSP Configuration*

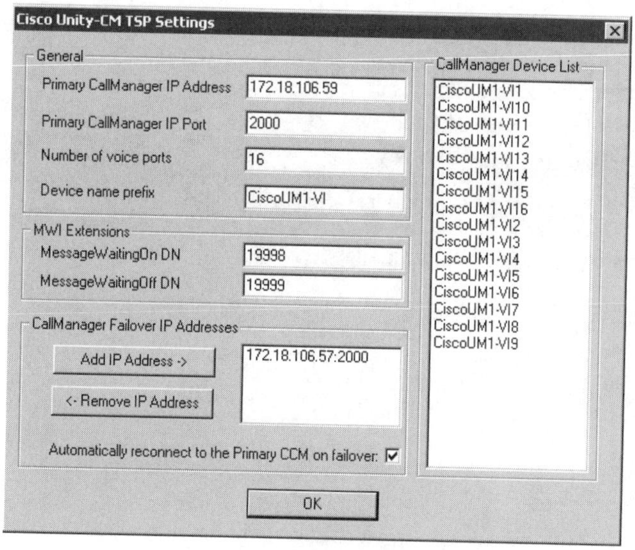

Check the configured settings to ensure they match what you have configured in CallManager. To see the equivalent configuration on the CallManager side, open the Cisco Voice Mail Port Configuration screen in Cisco CallManager Administration (**Feature > Voice Mail > Cisco Voice Mail Port**), as shown in Figure 14-3. Pay special attention to the names of the ports. Normally the ports are named something like CiscoUM-VI*x* where *x* is a number. Make sure the port names are identical to the port names in the CallManager Device List in the TSP configuration. If they aren't, Unity will not register properly.

In the TSP configuration, ensure that the other parameters are configured correctly as well. The **Primary CallManager IP Address** parameter should have the IP address of the CallManager to which you want Unity to be registered under normal operating conditions. This is not to be confused with the Publisher, which is generally not used for call processing under normal operating conditions. You can configure a list of backup CallManagers in the CallManager Failover IP Addresses section of the TSP configuration screen.

The TSP configuration also has a Test button you can use to ensure that TSP can successfully register its ports with CallManager. If the test passes, there is a good chance you have the TSP and CallManager configured to the point where Unity can register with CallManager.

Another important thing to check that might seem obvious but is often overlooked is to ensure that there is proper IP connectivity between CallManager and the Unity server. Obviously Unity cannot register with CallManager if it is unreachable. Just ping CallManager from the Unity server to ensure IP connectivity, assuming that no firewall device between CallManager and the Unity server is configured to pass Skinny messages but block Internet Control Message Protocol (ICMP) echoes (pings).

Figure 14-3 *Cisco Voice Mail Port Configuration in CallManager Administration*

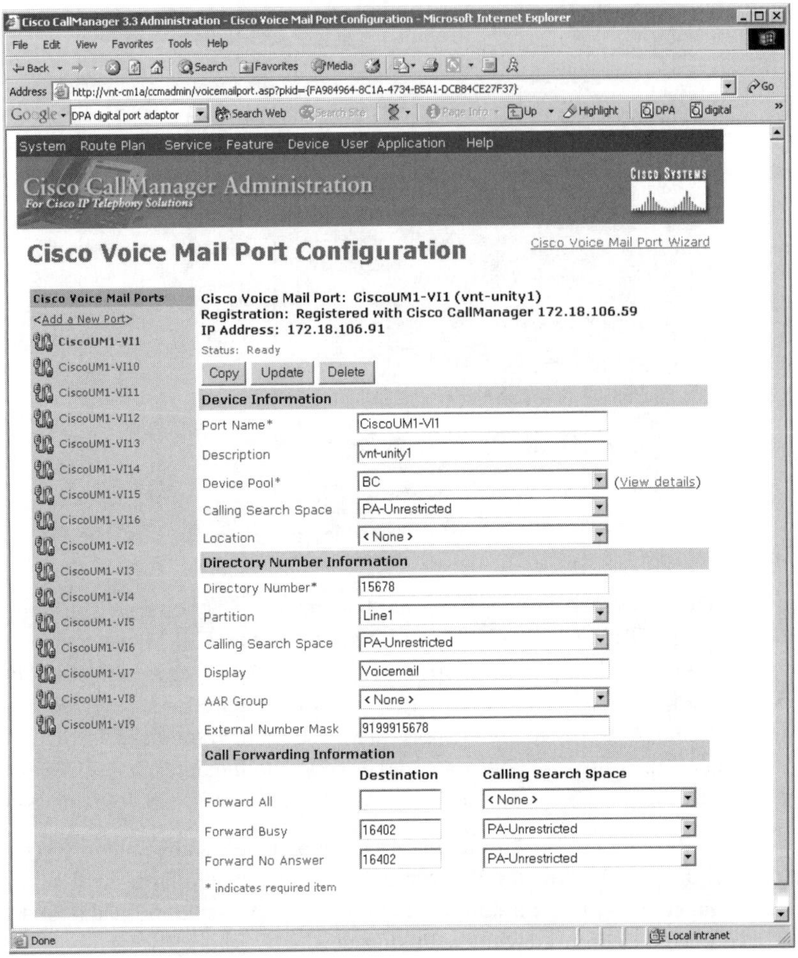

Verifying Cisco Unity Switch Configuration

One common configuration problem is selecting the wrong switch type in the Unity configuration. When Unity is first installed, you are prompted for the integration type. You can also modify this setting after Unity has been installed. You can access the switch configuration in Unity Administration by selecting **Switch > IP Switch**. To properly integrate with CallManager, configure the settings as follows:

Manufacturer: CISCO
Model: CALLMANAGER
Switch PBX Software Version: 3.0(1) OR LATER
Integration: TAPI

If these settings are wrong, change them to match the preceding specifications, and restart Unity. The message waiting indicator (MWI) on and off codes should be blank on this page because these are configured in the TSP configuration.

Failure to properly configure the switch settings can result in behavior such as long pauses between logins and prompts and even users being sent to the wrong mailboxes.

You should also verify that the switch settings are correct in the Registry on the Unity server.

CAUTION   Using Registry Editor incorrectly can cause serious problems that may require you to reinstall your operating system. Do not modify the Registry unless you feel comfortable doing so.

Check the following registry entries to ensure they are correct:

HKLM\SOFTWARE\Active Voice\MIU\1.0\Initialization\Switch 0\"
Switch Configuration File"="CISCO0002.INI"

HKLM\SOFTWARE\Active Voice\MIU\1.0\Initialization\Switch 1\"
Switch Configuration File"="CISCO0002.INI"

If you do not have a switch 1 key, this is not a problem unless you have a dual-switch integration (such as, integrating Unity with a CallManager and a traditional PBX at the same time). Just ensure that the switch 0 configuration is correct for CallManager integration to work.

Message Waiting Indicator (MWI)

Trouble turning MWIs on and off is a fairly common problem, especially in environments with complex dial plans that contain several partitions and calling search spaces. Most of these problems are the result of configuration errors.

Unity can turn an MWI on or off by dialing a user-defined MWI on or off number. Prior to CallManager release 3.2, there was a single MWI on number and a single MWI off number. In CallManager release 3.2 and later, you can define as many MWI on and off numbers as you like.

Unity notifies CallManager which extension to turn the MWI on or off for by setting the calling party number to the number of the station on which Unity wants to turn the lamp on or off. For example, if the MWI on number is 1999 and Unity wants to turn on the MWI for extension 3000, Unity goes off-hook on one of its ports and dials 1999; however, Unity sets the calling party number to 3000. CallManager looks at the calling party number and lights the lamp for extension 3000; however, partitions and calling search spaces add some additional complexity. Unity accomplishes this through the use of the

StationOffHookWithCgpn message. Note that Unity can light the MWI for only a phone registered to the same CallManager cluster as the Unity server. To light the MWI on multiple CallManager clusters, you must register some Unity ports to each CallManager cluster on which you want to be able to light the MWI.

As of CallManager 3.2, there is a Message Waiting Configuration page in CallManager Administration (**Feature > Voice Mail > Message Waiting**) similar to the one shown in Figure 14-4.

Figure 14-4 *CallManager Message Waiting Configuration*

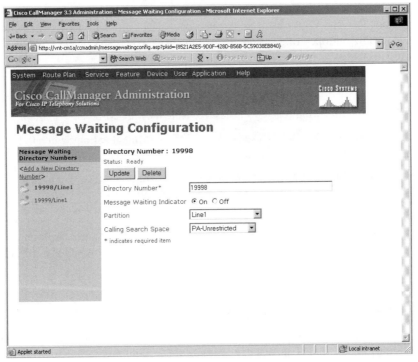

Notice that the Message Waiting Configuration page allows you to configure both a partition and a calling search space associated with the MWI on and off numbers. These play a crucial role in determining whether Unity can turn an MWI on or off.

A discussion of the partition is warranted at this point. The MWI on/off numbers are directory numbers (DNs) just like any other directory number in the system. Just as a line on a phone can appear in a partition, so can the MWI on and off numbers. This means that the Unity voice mail ports configured in CallManager Administration must have a calling search space that can dial the partition in which the MWI on/off number resides. If Unity cannot reach the partition in which the MWI on/off number resides, MWI will not work.

The next parameter that is important is the calling search space. Because CallManager supports overlapping dial plans through the use of partitions and calling search spaces, there needs to be a way to decide which phones the MWI on/off number has access to for the purpose of turning the MWI on or off. For example, you might have an IP phone with a DN of 2000 in partition Tenant_A_Lines and another IP phone with a DN of 2000 in partition Tenant_B_Lines. Because these are two separate partitions, a way to determine which of the two MWI lamps to turn on must be available. This is where the calling search space parameter comes into play. The calling search space determines which partitions the MWI on/off number searches when trying to turn on the MWI. For example, if the calling search space for the MWI on number includes the Tenant_A_Lines partition, the phone with the DN in the Tenant_A_Lines partition can have the MWI turned on or off. The opposite is true if the calling search space includes only the Tenant_B_Lines partition. If the calling search space includes both partitions, normal dialing rules apply. Because 2000 is an equivalent match for two IP phones, the order of the partitions in the calling search space breaks the tie, so the MWI turns on and off for whichever partition is listed first in the calling search space.

If you are using Cisco Personal Assistant, make sure the calling search space for the MWI on/off numbers does not include the partition in which your interceptor ports reside. Failure to do so results in a nonfunctional MWI since the call to the MWI number gets intercepted by Personal Assistant. If you do not have Cisco Personal Assistant and have no idea what's being discussed here, don't worry about it.

Also remember that any MWI changes that occur in Unity while Unity cannot talk to CallManager are not buffered until CallManager can be reached. This means that your MWI might get out of synch. Unity has an option to automatically resynch the MWI for all devices at a specified time every day to ensure that the system automatically corrects such an event.

Also note that if Unity makes MWI changes while the Publisher server is down, the MWI changes take effect; however, they are not written to the CallManager database. This means that if the IP phone is reset for any reason, the "old" MWI setting returns.

Dual-Tone Multifrequency (DTMF) Relay Problems

In general, DTMF relay is important for any voice mail system. As you've probably discovered by now, DTMF is carried out-of-band in an IP telephony network to ensure that the tones do not get corrupted while being transported as voice over IP packets due to codec compression or packet loss/jitter. Voice mail is highly reliant upon DTMF tones, because this is how the user interacts with the voice mail system.

When you deal with IP phones that dial directly into voice mail, DTMF is carried out-of-band the entire time because the phone sends a Skinny message indicating the digit to be played, and CallManager forwards that Skinny message to Unity, so in this case no actual tones are played. When a call to voice mail comes from the PSTN, however, there is usually a conversion from in-band DTMF to out-of-band DTMF relay at the gateway. For CallManager MGCP gateways, this is always on by default; however, on H.323 gateways, it needs to be explicitly configured. If you are having problems where users dial in from the PSTN, and it seems as though Unity is just ignoring the user's key presses, check to make sure DTMF relay is functioning properly. For more information about troubleshooting DTMF relay problems, refer to Chapter 6, "Voice Gateways."

Additional Unity Troubleshooting

Other than what has been mentioned so far, from a CallManager perspective, Unity ports are identical to any other Skinny endpoint registered to CallManager. This means that you can follow the same methodology for troubleshooting problems with Skinny client registration, forwarding, dialing, transfer, hold, and so on. As long as you remember that a Unity port is just like an IP phone, you should have no problems troubleshooting the integration. Note, however, that call preservation works differently in Unity than on an IP phone. Calls to Unity are not preserved in the case of a CallManager or Unity failure. The reason for this is that without CallManager performing the call signaling, there is no way to pass DTMF digits to Unity, and without that, there is not much you can do in Unity. Therefore, calls in Unity are dropped in the event of a failure.

More Troubleshooting Resources for Unity

Unity is a complex product. Therefore, troubleshooting the Unity product itself is complex and deserving of an entire book of its own. For additional Unity troubleshooting assistance, visit the Networking Professionals Connection Unity forum at

http://forums.cisco.com/eforum/servlet/NetProf?page=Voice_and_Video_discussion

Also be sure to visit the home page of one Unity's creators, Jeff Lindborg:

www.answermonkey.net/

SMDI Integration

One of the most prevalent ways to integrate a PBX with a legacy voice mail system is via the Bellcore-defined Simple Message Desk Interface (SMDI) integration. SMDI uses an RS-232 serial connection to pass information about the calling party number—Automatic Number Identification (ANI)—and the redirecting party number—Redirecting Dialed Number Identification Service (RDNIS). RDNIS is used to inform a voice mail system who the originally intended recipient for a call was. For example, if a call from extension 1000 to extension 2000 forwards to voice mail at extension 3000, the ANI is 1000, the DNIS is 3000, and the RDNIS is 2000. SMDI can also turn MWIs on and off. SMDI is defined in Bellcore specification TR-NWT-000283.

The serial connection is used to pass only the additional information that the voice mail system needs to route the call to the proper mailbox. All other call signaling is handled via either an analog or digital gateway.

There are two primary methods to integrate an SMDI-compliant voice mail system with CallManager:

- Use the Cisco Messaging Interface (CMI) service on one or more CallManagers in the cluster.

- Use an async port on a Cisco VG248 voice gateway to perform the SMDI messaging.

Although the two integrations are very different from a CallManager perspective, the messages sent to and from the voice mail system via the RS-232 connection are identical regardless of which device you are using for the integration.

Understanding SMDI Messages

To understand how to troubleshoot SMDI voice mail integration, it helps to understand the SMDI protocol. SMDI is a very simple protocol. You see only four kinds of messages between CallManager and the voice mail system:

- Call history information for calls to voice mail from CallManager

- Turn on and off MWI from voice mail to CallManager

- Error messages from CallManager to voice mail

These messages are all transmitted as strings of standard ASCII characters. As you'll see later, this makes troubleshooting much easier. Before you look at the format of each message, Table 14-1 defines the items in SMDI messages/commands.

Table 14-1   *Notations in SMDI Messages/Commands*

Symbol	Definition
<CR>	The ASCII carriage return character (0x0D).
<LF>	The ASCII line feed character (0x0A).
md-num	An arbitrary 3-digit zero-padded message desk number between 001 and 999. This value is typically 001.
md-port	The message desk port. This is the line number that the incoming call is being delivered on. It is a 4-digit number between 0000 and 9999. It should correspond to an agreed-upon system for numbering the trunks connecting CallManager to the voice mail system.

continues

Table 14-1   *Notations in SMDI Messages/Commands (Continued)*

Symbol	Definition
fwd-type	A single character indicating the forwarding type: • **D**—Direct call • **A**—Forward all calls • **B**—Forwarded on busy • **N**—Forwarded on no answer • **U**—Forwarded, reason unknown
fwd-sta	The original destination called party number or RDNIS for the call. This indicates which subscriber mailbox number the voice mail system should use to select the correct greeting. The specification says that this number can be 10 digits, 7 digits, or a variable number of digits. Most systems pad zeros to the phone number to make the number of digits equal to 10. For example, when forwarding to extension 15000, the *fwd-sta* field is sent as 0000015000. If the type of forwarding is D, indicating a direct call from a station, the *fwd-sta* field is eliminated from the message.
<SP>	The ASCII space character (0x20).
source-num	The number of the station that originated the call, or ANI. If the call's source is unavailable, the *source-num* field is eliminated from the message or is replaced with all zeros.
station-number	The number of the station that the voice mail system wants to turn on an MWI light for.
error-code	Used to indicate an error condition. The two choices for *error-code* are • **INV**—Indicates an invalid station number • **BLK**—Indicates a temporary block state
<^D>	The ASCII Ctrl-D character (0x04).
<^Y>	The ASCII Ctrl-Y character (0x19).

Let's look at the format of each message.

Call History Information for Calls to Voice Mail from CallManager

When a call is sent from CallManager to the voice mail system, CallManager must provide the voice mail system with several pieces of information for the voice mail system to properly answer the call with the correct greeting. The bearer path to most SMDI voice mail systems is one or more analog loop start circuits, although some SMDI voice mail systems integrate with T1/E1 channel-associated signaling (CAS) or Primary Rate Interface (PRI).

Analog and CAS connections do not have a mechanism to provide information about the ANI and/or the RDNIS. The purpose of the call history information message is to provide information about the ANI and RDNIS as well as the forwarding reason.

Refer to Table 14-1 for descriptions of the notations in SMDI messages/commands. The format of the call history information message is as follows:

<CR><LF>MD *md-num md-port fwd-type fwd-sta* <SP> *source-num* <SP><CR><LF><^Y>

In this message definition, items in angle brackets represent special characters. Space characters in the message are used only where specified by <SP>. For example, a call from extension 12345 to 56789 that forwarded to voice mail port 15 because 56789 was busy would look like this:

<CR><LF>MD0010015B0000056789<SP>0000012345<SP><CR><LF><^Y>

Message Waiting Indicator On/Off Messages

One of the primary purposes of SMDI is to let a voice mail system turn the MWIs on and off, depending on whether there are messages in a user's mailbox. The SMDI protocol provides one command to turn on an MWI for an IP phone and another command to turn the MWI off. OP is the command to turn on an MWI. In this case the command is actually the ASCII characters O and P. Refer to Table 14-1 for descriptions of the notations in SMDI messages/commands.

To turn on an MWI, the voice mail system sends the following command to CallManager:

OP:MWI<SP> *station-number* ! <^D>

RMV is the command to turn off an MWI. In this case the command is actually the ASCII characters R, M, and V. Refer to Table 14-1 for descriptions of the notations in SMDI messages/commands.

To turn off an MWI, the voice mail system sends the following command to CallManager:

RMV:MWI<SP> *station-number* ! <^D>

For both of these commands, *station-number* is defined as a 10-digit, 7-digit, or variable-length 1-to-10-digit station number. <^D> is the Ctrl-D ASCII character (0x04).

For example, to turn on the MWI for extension 12345, the voice mail system sends the following command:

OP:MWI<SP>0000012345!<^D>

To turn the MWI off, the voice mail system sends the following command:

RMV:MWI<SP>0000012345!<^D>

Error Messages

There are two situations in which CallManager sends an error/diagnostic message to the voice mail system:

- When an MWI command is sent for an invalid station
- When the system is busy and cannot respond to a command immediately

Refer to Table 14-1 for descriptions of the notations in SMDI messages/commands. Both messages have the following format:

<CR><LF> MWI *station-number* <SP> *error-code* <CR><LF><^Y>

The two choices for *error-code* are

- INV—Indicates an invalid station number
- BLK—Indicates a temporary block state

For example, assume that the voice mail system sends the following SMDI message to CallManager:

OP:MWI<SP>0000012345!<^D>

This command tells CallManager to turn on the MWI for extension 12345. CallManager looks for this number. If the extension is invalid, CallManager returns the following message:

<CR><LF>0000012345<SP>INV<CR><LF><^Y>

This message tells the voice mail system that it has attempted to turn on the MWI for an extension that does not exist.

Cisco Messaging Interface

The first way to interface to an SMDI voice mail system is by using the Cisco Messaging Interface (CMI). CMI is a service that can run on one or more CallManager nodes in the cluster. CMI uses one of the available COM ports on the server to connect to the voice mail system.

CMI is typically used to connect CallManager to a third-party voice mail system via analog ports on a WS-X6624 analog Foreign Exchange Station (FXS) gateway or MGCP-controlled FXS analog ports on a Cisco IOS Software voice gateway. One very important point to note is that there are restrictions on what kind of gateway can be used to connect to a voice mail system when you're using SMDI. CallManager must be able to know exactly which port to send a call to the voice mail system so that it can send the proper message desk port number. If CallManager can't control which port gets used, it cannot send the proper data to the voice mail system. For example, if CallManager is integrated with a Cisco IOS Software gateway using the H.323 protocol, CallManager sends a call setup message to the gateway, and the gateway decides which port to send the call out. In this case, CallManager does not know which port was chosen, so it cannot send the proper information via SMDI. As a general rule, you cannot perform SMDI integration via H.323 unless you will use the SMDI connection only for MWI on/off functionality.

The first step if you are having problems integrating to a voice mail system using CMI is to ensure that everything is properly configured.

CMI Configuration Parameters

The CMI service has only a few configuration parameters; however, failure to correctly configure one of them can keep voice mail integration from working properly. Table 14-2 defines the CMI service parameters. These parameters are defined in further detail following Table 14-2.

Table 14-2   *CMI Service Parameters*

Parameter	Description
BackupCallManagerName	Defines the names of the CallManager nodes that the CMI service registers with if the local CallManager service is unavailable. You can use either the name of a CallManager or its IP address. The default value is blank.
BaudRate	Defines the connection rate for the RS-232 connection that CallManager uses to connect to the voice mail system. The majority of voice mail systems use 9600 baud. The default value is 9600.
CallManagerName	Defines the name of the CallManager node that the CMI service registers with first. You can use either the name of a CallManager or its IP address. If this parameter is blank, the local machine is assumed. The default value is blank.
DataBits	Defines the number of data bits to use to send data on the RS-232 connection that CallManager uses to connect to the voice mail system. Valid values are 7 and 8. The majority of voice mail systems use 7 data bits. The default value is 7.
DialingPlan	This parameter is one of four that are used by CMI to register an intercept for the voice mail system with which CMI will work. This parameter is optional. Note that small systems without a complex dialing plan usually need only the **VoiceMailDn** parameter. The default value is blank.

continues

Table 14-2   *CMI Service Parameters (Continued)*

Parameter	Description
InputDnSignificantDigits	This parameter is designed to accommodate the differences between voice mailbox numbers and directory numbers. If a legacy voice mail system has mailbox numbers that are not longer than the directory numbers on the system, this parameter can be used to strip the most-significant digits. The numeric value of this parameter indicates how many digits should be used.
	For example, a value of 5 would cause CallManager to only examine the last five digits of an MWI message sent by the voice mail system.
	The default value is 10.
KeepAliveDn	This is a string parameter. For most voice mail systems, a blank value is acceptable; however, some Octel systems periodically send an invalid DN specifically for the purpose of verifying that the attached CallManager is functioning properly. In this case, you can turn off **ValidateDns** if you know the directory number that the Octel system uses as a KeepAlive. By programming that directory number into the **KeepAliveDn** parameter, you ensure that the invalid directory number message is returned to the voice mail system when needed.
	The default value is blank.
MessageDeskNumber	Specifies the message desk number configured on the voice mail system. This number is typically 1 because that is what is configured on the legacy voice mail system. The valid values are from 1 to 999.
	The default value is 1.
MwiSearchSpace	Indicates the ordered list of partitions that CallManager searches for the directory number that is specified for MWI on/off operation. To specify multiple partitions, use colons to separate partitions in a list.
	The default value is blank.
OutputDnFormat	This value is used to format the value of *fwd-sta* that is formatted in the SMDI message sent to the voice mail system (see Table 14-1 for more information).
	The original destination called party number or RDNIS is padded with leading zeros if it is shorter than what is listed in this parameter.
	The default value is %010s.

Table 14-2   *CMI Service Parameters (Continued)*

Parameter	Description
OutputExternalFormat	This value is used to format the value of *source-num* that is formatted in the SMDI message sent to the voice mail system (see Table 14-1 for more information).
	In case **OutputExternalFormat** is empty or the call is OnNet (the length of the caller phone number is less than 7), **OutputDnFormat** is used to format the value of *source-num*.
	The default value is %010s.
Parity	This parameter defines the RS-232 connection that CMI uses to connect to the voice mail system. The parity settings can be **None**, **Even**, **Odd**, **Mark**, or **Space**. Settings are usually **Even** or **None**; **Mark** and **Space** are rarely used. Using just the first character of the parity name also works, for example, **E** for **Even**.
	The default value is Even.
RouteFilter	This parameter is one of four that are used by CMI to register an intercept for the voice mail system with which CMI will work. This parameter is optional.
	The default value is blank.
SerialPort	This parameter defines the RS-232 connection that CMI uses to connect to the voice mail system. The **SerialPort** name should match the port number you have the serial cable connected to. For MCS servers this is either COM1 for the first serial port or COM2 for the second serial port.
	The default value is COM1.
SsapiKeepAliveInterval	You should not change this parameter from its default value unless you are directed to by the Cisco Technical Assistance Center (TAC).
	During normal operations, CMI is attached to a CallManager. When this is the case, CMI sends a KeepAlive message to CallManager at the rate (in seconds) specified by this parameter. This is a numeric parameter.
	The default value is 30 and should not be changed.
StopBits	This parameter defines the number of stop bits sent after each data byte on the RS-232 connection that CMI uses to connect to the voice mail system. This value can be either 1 or 2.
	The default value is 1.

continues

Table 14-2   *CMI Service Parameters (Continued)*

Parameter	Description
UseZerosForUnknownDn	When CMI receives call information about a call routed to an SMDI-compliant voice mail system, this parameter determines how CMI sends information for an unknown or nonnumeric calling party number. When this parameter is set to True, CMI sends a string of zeros for the calling party number. If set to False, CMI leaves the calling party number empty for an unknown or nonnumeric CallingParty number. The default for this parameter is True.
ValidateDns	When CMI receives incoming lamp commands from the voice mail system, it normally validates the associated DN against an existing DN known to CallManager. If the DN is not found, an invalid DN message is sent to the voice mailbox. On a system with a lot of traffic to and from the voice mail system, you may choose to skip this validation process by setting the **ValidateDns** parameter to **False**. The default value is True.
VoiceMailDn	This parameter is one of four that are used by CMI to register an intercept for the voice mail system with which CMI will work. This parameter represents the voice mail access number and is a mandatory parameter. The default value is blank.
VoiceMailPartition	This parameter is one of four that are used by CMI to register an intercept for the voice mail system with which CMI will work. It defines the partition in which the voice mail DN resides. This parameter is optional. The default value is blank.

The first parameters to ensure that you have set correctly are the ones that deal with the characteristics of the SMDI link:

- **BaudRate**
- **DataBits**
- **Parity**
- **StopBits**

Most SMDI voice mail systems are configured for 9600 baud, 7 data bits, even parity, and 1 stop bit by default. Check the configuration on the voice mail system and make sure both sides match.

The CMI service works by intercepting all calls to a particular phone number and using that as a trigger to send SMDI messages. For this to work, you must have your route patterns and route groups properly configured to ensure successful SMDI integration. For clarity, look at the following example of a correctly configured system. To properly configure SMDI integration with the CMI service, you must perform the following tasks:

Step 1   Configure the gateway ports.

Step 2   Add a route group that includes each of the gateway ports.

Step 3   Add a route list that includes the route group configured in Step 2.

Step 4   Create a route pattern for the voice mail pilot number.

Assume that you have an eight-port voice mail system that connects to CallManager via analog FXS ports. You have a WS-X6624 module, and the first eight ports are wired to the voice mail system. When you configure the WS-X6624 in CallManager, make sure you do not put directory numbers on the first eight ports. Figure 14-5 shows how the first eight ports should be configured.

Figure 14-5 *WS-X6624 Gateway Configuration*

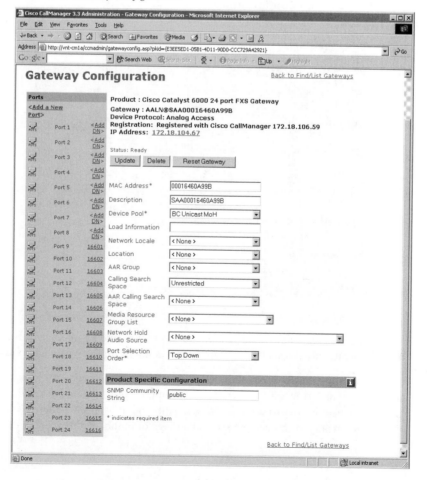

After configuring the gateway, you must configure a route group containing each of the ports for that gateway (**Route Plan > Route Group >** *find and select an existing route group or click the link to* **Add a New Route Group**). This is important because the order of the ports in the route group determines the port numbers that are sent to the voice mail system via SMDI. For example, Figure 14-6 shows the route group containing the eight voice mail ports that were just configured. Notice that each port has a distinct number in the Order column. This order is what determines the port number sent via SMDI.

Figure 14-6 *Route Group Configuration*

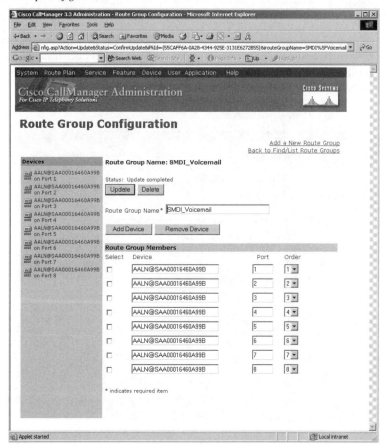

After you have created the route group, you must put it into a route list. This route list should contain only the single route group that contains all the voice mail ports.

Finally, you must create the pilot directory number used to access voice mail. This is the number users dial to access voice mail and the number you want the system to forward calls to when the user is busy or does not answer. Although most route patterns usually contain one or more wildcard characters to match a range of numbers, this route pattern should match only a single DN. Figure 14-7 (which you can navigate to by selecting **Route Plan > Route Pattern >** *find and select an existing route pattern or click the link to* **Add a New Route Pattern**) shows the route pattern 15705 configured in the Line1 partition. Notice that the route pattern routes the call to the SMDI_VM route list, which contains the SMDI_Voicemail route group shown in Figure 14-6.

Figure 14-7 *Route Pattern Configuration*

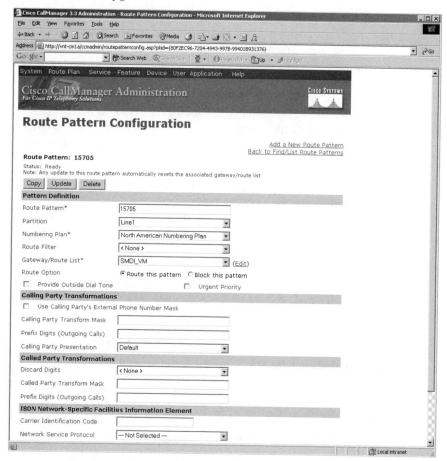

With all this configured, you should now be able to place a call and have the voice mail system answer. At this point, however, the SMDI link might not be functioning; therefore, the voice mail system might answer with the general auto attendant greeting (sometimes called *open trees*).

You can now look at the remainder of the SMDI configuration. Continuing with the example, the voice mail pilot number is 15705, and it is in the Line1 partition. This means that you configure the CMI service parameters for **VoiceMailDn** to 15705 and **VoiceMailPartition** to Line1. Be sure to enter these parameters correctly; don't include any additional spaces or change the capitalization from what has been configured in CallManager Administration. Failure to put the correct number and partition here keeps the CMI service from intercepting calls to voice mail.

Finally, make sure you have the **SerialPort** parameter configured to be the same port where you have the RS-232 serial cable connected to the voice mail system.

Note that you should configure the CMI service only on the node(s) in the cluster that have an RS-232 connection to the voice mail system. For each pilot number, only one CMI service in the cluster can intercept calls for that number. This means that if you configure CMI on more than one node in the cluster, only one of those nodes actively tries to send SMDI messages. If that node has no RS-232 cable, the message never gets to the voice mail system. The CMI service is typically configured on two nodes in the cluster, and a Y-adapter is used to connect both CallManager nodes to the voice mail system. This way, either of the two nodes can send SMDI messages to the voice mail system, depending on which node is active.

As soon as you have all this configured, you should be able to see CallManager sending SMDI messages for calls placed to the voice mail number. The first place to look to see what is being sent and received by CallManager on the SMDI connection is the CMI trace files.

Reading CMI Traces

Trace files for CMI are located in C:\Program Files\Cisco\Trace\CMI by default. Before looking at the trace files, make sure the trace levels are set appropriately. To enable CMI tracing, follow these steps:

Step 1   In CallManager Serviceability, select **Trace > Configuration**.

Step 2   From the list on the left, select the server you want to configure.

Step 3   In the Configured Services box, select **Cisco Messaging Interface**.

Step 4   Select the **Trace On** checkbox.

Step 5   Set the **Debug Trace Level** to **Detailed**.

Step 6   Select the **Cisco Messaging Interface Trace Fields** checkbox.

Step 7   Select the **Enable All Trace** checkbox.

Step 8   Select the **Enable File Trace Log** checkbox.

Step 9   Click **Update**.

Now stop and restart the CMI service on the node on which tracing is enabled. If you look at the newest trace file in the CMI directory, you should see something similar to the output

shown in Example 14-1 a few lines from the beginning of the trace file. You can search for
CMIProcessConfigItems.

First you see a list of all the configured parameters. These should match the service
parameters you have configured for CMI.

Example 14-1 *CMI Configuration Parameters Shown in the CMI Trace*

```
-->CMIProcessConfigItems::CMIProcessConfigItems()
   CMIProcessConfigItems::CMIProcessConfigItems() Serial port params =
      COM1:9600,Even,7,1
   CMIProcessConfigItems::CMIProcessConfigItems() VoiceMailDn = 15705
   CMIProcessConfigItems::CMIProcessConfigItems() VoiceMailPartition = Line1
   CMIProcessConfigItems::CMIProcessConfigItems() MwiSearchSpace = Line1
   CMIProcessConfigItems::CMIProcessConfigItems() CallManagerName =
   CMIProcessConfigItems::CMIProcessConfigItems() BackupCallManagerName =
   CMIProcessConfigItems::CMIProcessConfigItems() OutputDnFormat = %010s
   CMIProcessConfigItems::CMIProcessConfigItems() OutputExternalFormat = %010s
   CMIProcessConfigItems::CMIProcessConfigItems() InputDnSignificantDigits = 10
   CMIProcessConfigItems::CMIProcessConfigItems() DialingPlan =
   CMIProcessConfigItems::CMIProcessConfigItems() Routefilter =
   CMIProcessConfigItems::CMIProcessConfigItems() ValidateDns = TRUE
   CMIProcessConfigItems::CMIProcessConfigItems() KeepAliveDn =
   CMIProcessConfigItems::CMIProcessConfigItems() SsapiKeepAliveInterval = 30
   CMIProcessConfigItems::CMIProcessConfigItems() MessageDeskNumber = 1
   CMIProcessConfigItems::CMIProcessConfigItems() UseZerosForUnknownDn = TRUE
<--CMIProcessConfigItems::CMIProcessConfigItems()
```

Next the CMI service attempts to register with the primary CallManager (usually the node
on which the CMI service is running), as shown in Example 14-2.

Example 14-2 *CMI Trace Showing the CMI Service Registering with CallManager*

```
-->CMISsapiClient::AttemptConnect()
   CMISsapiClient::AttemptConnect() Attempting connection to primary CM:
   CMISsapiClient::AttemptConnect() Resolved name to IP address: 172.18.106.58
<--CMISsapiClient::AttemptConnect()
-->CMIControl::::PollConfigThread()
-->CMISsapiClient::RecvSsRegisterManagerResMsg()
   CMISsapiClient::RecvSsRegisterManagerResMsg() Received RegisterManagerResMsg
      userdata = 29597584
   CMISsapiClient::RecvSsRegisterManagerResMsg() Sending RegisterInterceptReqMsg
      userdata = 29597584, fSsKey = 7864, fDn = 15705, ServicePriority = 739404346
<--CMISsapiClient::RecvSsRegisterManagerResMsg()
-->CMISsapiClient::RecvSsRegisterInterceptResMsg()
   CMISsapiClient::RecvSsRegisterInterceptResMsg() Receive
      RecvSsRegisterInterceptResMsg userdata = 29597584, fSsKey = 7864,
      fSsType = 0, fSsNodeId = 1
```

Next the CMI service opens the serial port. The parameters for the serial port (Serial Port, Baud Rate, Start Bits, Stop Bits, and Parity) were previously listed in the CMI service parameters. Look at the trace in Example 14-3, and ensure that the serial port is opened.

Example 14-3 *CMI Trace Showing the Serial Port Being Opened*

```
-->CMISerialWorker::CMISerialWorker()
-->CMISerialWorker::OpenPort()
   CMISerialWorker::OpenPort() Opening the com port
   CMISerialWorker::OpenPort() CreateFile returned a handle of 776
   CMISerialWorker::OpenPort() Com port has been opened
<--CMISerialWorker::OpenPort()
<--CMISerialWorker::CMISerialWorker()
```

If for some reason the serial port is in use by another application (such as HyperTerminal), the trace looks like Example 14-4 instead.

Example 14-4 *CMI Trace Showing a Failure to Open the Configured Serial Port*

```
-->CMISerialWorker::CMISerialWorker()
-->CMISerialWorker::OpenPort()
   CMISerialWorker::OpenPort() Opening the com port
   CMISerialWorker::OpenPort() CreateFile returned a handle of -1
kSerialPortOpenningError - Error when CMI tries to open the Windows NT serial port.
   Serial Port Openning Error:Windows NT returned an error opening the
   serial port: ( 5 ) - Access is denied App ID:Cisco Messaging Interface
   Cluster ID:VNT-CM1A-Cluster Node ID:172.18.106.58<CT::Alarm>
<?xml version="1.0" encoding="ISO-8859-1"?><Tracelist>
<--CMISerialWorker::OpenPort()
<--CMISerialWorker::CMISerialWorker()
   CMISsapiClient::RecvSsRegisterInterceptResMsg() Caught exception in
      SSAPIClient, going non-functional: CMI throws the exception due to
      kSerialPortOpenningError{OpenningError}. CMI stops
<--CMISsapiClient::RecvSsRegisterInterceptResMsg()
```

CMI attempts to reopen the serial port every minute if it is unable to open the port for some reason.

As soon as the service has registered and the serial port is open, any calls to the pilot number should result in an SMDI message sent out by the CMI service. Remember that if multiple CMI services register for the same DN and partition, you see activity on only one of the actively registered nodes.

For example, if extension 15600 makes a direct call to the pilot number, 15705, the trace looks like Example 14-5.

Example 14-5 *CMI Trace Showing a Direct Call to Voice Mail*

```
-->CMISsapiClient::RecvSsDataIndMsg()
<--CMISsapiClient::RecvSsDataIndMsg()
-->CMISsapiClient::RecvSsInterceptIndMsg()
  CMISsapiClient::RecvSsInterceptIndMsg() Received RecvSsInterceptIndMsg
    userdata = 29597584, Key = 7864, fDn = 15705
  CMISsapiClient::RecvSsInterceptIndMsg() SendSsExtendCallReqMsg userdata =
    29597584, Key = 7864
<--CMISsapiClient::RecvSsInterceptIndMsg()
-->CMISsapiClient::RecvSsExtendCallResMsg()
  CMISsapiClient::RecvSsExtendCallResMsg() Received RecvSsExtendCallResMsg:
    userdata = 29597584, Key = 7864, NodeId = 2, Party = 33555187
  CMISsapiClient::RecvSsExtendCallResMsg() Send CallInfoReqMsg
<--CMISsapiClient::RecvSsExtendCallResMsg()
-->CMISsapiClient::RecvSsDataIndMsg()
  CMISsapiClient::RecvSsDataIndMsg() Received RecvSsDataIndMsg:
    userdata = 29597584, Key = 0, NodeId = 2, Party = 33555187
<--CMISsapiClient::RecvSsDataIndMsg()
-->CMISsapiClient::RecvSsCallInfoResMsg()
  CMISsapiClient::RecvSsCallInfoResMsg() Received Call Info:
    userdata = 29597584, fSsType = 0, fSsKey = 7864, fdls2 = 1
  CMISsapiClient::RecvSsCallInfoResMsg()
    CallingParty = 15600, CallingPattern = 15600, VoiceMailBox = ,
    OriginalCalledParty = 15705, OriginalPattern = 15705, VoiceMailBox = ,
    Forwarded Reason Code = 0
  CMISsapiClient::RecvSsCallInfoResMsg() CallingParty has no VoiceMailBox,
    using its Dn!
  CMISsapiClient::RecvSsCallInfoResMsg() Original CalledParty has no VoiceMailbox,
    using its Dn!
-->CMISsapiClient::SendCall()
  CMISsapiClient::SendCall() Direct Call: port - 1, callingparty - 0000015600
  CMISsapiClient::SendCall() Construct SMDI message:
    <CR><LF>MD0010001D<0x20>0000015600<0x20><CR><LF><^Y>
-->CMISerialWorker::SendBuffer()
  CMISerialWorker::SendBuffer() Send Buffer -
    <CR><LF>MD0010001D<0x20>0000015600<0x20><CR><LF><^Y>
<--CMISerialWorker::SendBuffer()
<--CMISsapiClient::SendCall()
<--CMISsapiClient::RecvSsCallInfoResMsg()
```

As you can see, the CMI service sends the following SMDI message to the voice mail system:

```
<CR><LF>MD0010001D<0x20>0000015600<0x20><CR><LF><^Y>
```

This message means that message desk 1, port 1 received a direct call to voice mail from DN 15600. The voice mail system should use this information to answer port 1. It typically prompts the user to enter her password to retrieve her messages.

The other type of call history message you see is when a call is forwarded to voice mail. Example 14-6 shows such a call.

Example 14-6 *CMI Trace Showing a Call Forwarded to Voice Mai*

```
-->CMISsapiClient::RecvSsDataIndMsg()
<--CMISsapiClient::RecvSsDataIndMsg()
-->CMISsapiClient::RecvSsInterceptIndMsg()
   CMISsapiClient::RecvSsInterceptIndMsg() Received RecvSsInterceptIndMsg userdata
      = 29597584, Key = 7864, fDn = 15705
   CMISsapiClient::RecvSsInterceptIndMsg() SendSsExtendCallReqMsg
      userdata = 29597584, Key = 7864
<--CMISsapiClient::RecvSsInterceptIndMsg()
-->CMISsapiClient::RecvSsExtendCallResMsg()
   CMISsapiClient::RecvSsExtendCallResMsg() Received RecvSsExtendCallResMsg:
      userdata = 29597584, Key = 7864, NodeId = 2, Party = 33555219
   CMISsapiClient::RecvSsExtendCallResMsg() Send CallInfoReqMsg
<--CMISsapiClient::RecvSsExtendCallResMsg()
-->CMISsapiClient::RecvSsDataIndMsg()
   CMISsapiClient::RecvSsDataIndMsg() Received RecvSsDataIndMsg:
      userdata = 29597584, Key = 0, NodeId = 2, Party = 33555219
<--CMISsapiClient::RecvSsDataIndMsg()
-->CMISsapiClient::RecvSsCallInfoResMsg()
   CMISsapiClient::RecvSsCallInfoResMsg() Received Call Info:
      userdata = 29597584, fSsType = 0, fSsKey = 7864, fdls2 = 1
   CMISsapiClient::RecvSsCallInfoResMsg()                      CallingParty =
      9195551234, CallingPattern = , VoiceMailBox = , OriginalCalledParty = 15600,
      OriginalPattern = 15600, VoiceMailBox = 15600, Forwarded Reason Code = 2
   CMISsapiClient::RecvSsCallInfoResMsg() CallingParty has no VoiceMailBox, using
its Dn!
   CMISsapiClient::RecvSsCallInfoResMsg() Original CalledParty has a VoiceMailbox,
using it
-->CMISsapiClient::SendCall()
   CMISsapiClient::SendCall() NO-ANSWER-Forwarded Call: port - 1,
      calledparty - 0000015600, callingparty - 9195551234
   CMISsapiClient::SendCall() Construct SMDI message:
      <CR><LF>MD0010001N0000015600<0x20>9195551234<0x20><CR><LF><^Y>
-->CMISerialWorker::SendBuffer()
   CMISerialWorker::SendBuffer() Send Buffer -
      <CR><LF>MD0010001N0000015600<0x20>9195551234<0x20><CR><LF><^Y>
<--CMISerialWorker::SendBuffer()
<--CMISsapiClient::SendCall()
<--CMISsapiClient::RecvSsCallInfoResMsg()
```

In this example, the SMDI message sent to the voice mail system is as follows:

```
<CR><LF>MD0010001N0000015600<0x20>9195551234<0x20><CR><LF><^Y>
```

This message indicates that message desk 1, port 1 received a call from 9195551234 that was forwarded from extension 15600 because that extension did not answer. This message should cause the voice mail system to play the greeting for the user at extension 15600.

So what do you do if you don't see these messages in the CMI trace files? The first thing to check is to make sure the CMI service is running. As long as the service is running and the trace levels are set correctly, you should see some kind of trace files being generated. Check for any failures, such as the serial port already being open. Also be absolutely sure the **VoiceMailDn** and **VoiceMailPartition** service parameters are set correctly. The majority of the time, this kind of problem is caused by an improperly configured **VoiceMailDn** or **VoiceMailPartition**. Also, be sure you have configured only one node in the cluster for CMI. If you are using redundant CMI processes, check both; only one of the two will be sending SMDI messages, and only one will be generating meaningful trace information.

If you are still having problems, you should make sure that calls are reaching the voice mail ports in the first place. The easiest way to accomplish this with an analog FXS integration is to disconnect the voice mail system from the first analog port and place a standard analog phone into that port. Now when a call is made to the voice mail pilot number, the analog phone should ring. If the calls are not getting through to the analog phone, troubleshoot this like any other gateway problem, as described in Chapter 6.

If you are seeing the SMDI messages in the trace file but the voice mail system is not receiving them or is giving you the open trees prompt instead of the individual user's greeting or mailbox, the next logical step is to verify that CallManager is indeed sending the SMDI messages out the serial port.

Using HyperTerminal to Diagnose SMDI Problems

Because SMDI is a simple ASCII text-based protocol, any terminal software can easily emulate the connection between a voice mail system and a CallManager. The easiest way to do this is by using HyperTerminal, which is included with all versions of Microsoft Windows since Windows 95 (including Windows 95, Windows 98, Windows NT, Windows 2000, and Windows XP). All you need is a male-to-male DB9 serial cable. Or, if you have two console kits that ship with any Cisco router or switch, you can make the correct cable. Just connect two of the DB9-to-RJ-45 connectors to each other using a flat rollover cable. A rollover cable is one in which the pins are reversed from one end to the other (meaning 1 <-> 8, 2 <-> 7, 3 <-> 6, 4 <-> 5). Connect one end of the cable to the serial port on the CallManager server that is running the CMI service. If your voice mail system is currently connected to that machine, temporarily unplug it. Either connect the other end of your cable to another Windows PC that has HyperTerminal installed, or connect it to the other serial port (for example, COM2) on CallManager. Now you should have your PC in the place of the voice mail system.

Open HyperTerminal. You are prompted to name your connection. Name it anything you want, such as SMDI Test. You should then see a box similar to Figure 14-8. Choose the COM port where you connected the serial cable to your PC, and then click **OK**. You should then be prompted for the COM port properties, as shown in Figure 14-9. Select the same settings you configured in the CMI service parameters (which should also be the same as what you have configured on your voice mail system).

Figure 14-8 *HyperTerminal Connect Port Selection*

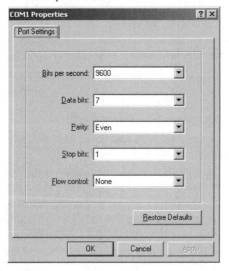

Figure 14-9 *HyperTerminal COM Port Properties*

You should now see a blank HyperTerminal window. Place a direct call to your voice mail system. You should see the associated SMDI message appear on your screen. For example, Figure 14-10 shows the output of four SMDI messages. The first two and the last one are all direct calls to voice mail from extension 15600. The third is a call from extension 2000 that forwarded to voice mail because extension 15600 did not answer.

If you do not see anything on your console, yet you are still seeing SMDI messages appear in the CMI traces, the most likely problem is a cabling issue. Ensure that you have a good cable, and, if possible, try replacing it. There is a small possibility that a problem exists with the serial port on CallManager. To ensure that this is not the problem, try switching to the second COM port on the machine. *Remember, you have to change the **SerialPort** CMI service parameter and restart the CMI service for this change to take effect immediately.*

Figure 14-10 *SMDI Messages Viewed Via HyperTerminal*

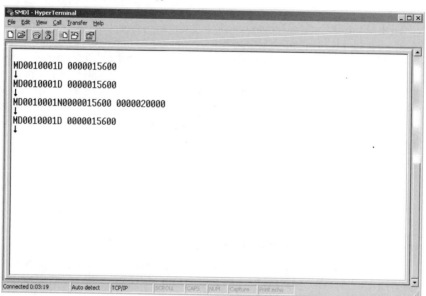

If you are seeing the messages in your HyperTerminal window and the voice mail system still does not answer with the correct voice mailbox, there are still a few things to check.

The first thing to check is if you can turn on any tracing on the voice mail system. Try to see if the voice mail system is also seeing the SMDI messages. If it is, there is likely a misconfiguration somewhere. Various configuration parameters have not been discussed. These all relate to the number of digits that are sent to and received from the voice mail system. In our examples so far, all you have seen are 10-digit numbers being sent between CallManager and the voice mail system, even though the phones have 5-digit extensions. If the voice mail system is expecting more or fewer digits than what CallManager is sending, the voice mail system might ignore the message and, as a result, not play the proper greeting. The three CMI service parameters that are significant in this respect are

- **OutputDnFormat**
- **OutputExternalFormat**
- **InputDnSignificantDigits**

Most voice mail systems expect CallManager to send it 10 digits for all numbers delivered to the voice mail system, even if the phone number is shorter. For example, if you are using 5-digit extensions, CallManager pads five zeros in front of the 5-digit extension when the phone number is sent to the voice mail system. You can change this behavior by using the **OutputDnFormat** and **OutputExternalFormat** parameters. **OutputDnFormat** specifies the number of digits sent for *fwd-sta*, the RDNIS information. Change this parameter if the voice mail system expects to see fewer than 10 digits for the RDNIS information.

The same holds true if the voice mail system needs to see a smaller number of digits for the calling party number (*source-num*). To modify the number of digits sent for *source-num*, use the **OutputExternalFormat** service parameter. Note that this service parameter takes effect only if the calling party number is seven digits in length or greater. Otherwise, whatever is listed for **OutputDnFormat** also is used to decide how many digits to send for the calling party number. This is useful when you want the calling party number to be the length of your internal extensions (for example, four or five digits) but want the calling party number to be 10 digits when a call is coming in from the PSTN. Check with your voice mail vendor to see how many digits the voice mail system is expecting, and adjust on CallManager accordingly.

So far the focus has been on ensuring that the voice mail system receives the information necessary to answer the call correctly; however, the second important function of SMDI is the capability for the voice mail system to turn MWIs on and off.

Message Waiting Indicator Problems

One of the most common problems encountered when integrating with an SMDI voice mail system with CallManager is the inability to turn MWI lamps on or off. If you are unable to get the voice mail system to answer with the correct greeting, go back and make sure you can get that part working, because that will ensure that the SMDI connection is functioning—at least from CallManager to the voice mail system.

MWI in SMDI is very straightforward. The voice mail system sends a simple command to turn the light either on or off (as discussed earlier). You should be aware, however, of several things that might cause problems if not configured properly.

The most important configuration parameter for MWI is the **MwiSearchSpace** service parameter. When the CMI service receives a message to turn an MWI on or off, it needs to send this message to CallManager. With partitions and calling search spaces, however, it is possible to have multiple phones with the same extension. For this reason, CMI must be configured to know which partitions to try when lighting the MWI lamp. Note that the name of the service parameter **MwiSearchSpace** is misleading, because you do not put the name of a calling search space in this parameter. Instead, you must enter an ordered list of partitions to search for lighting the MWI lamps.

For example, if all your IP phones have their first line in a partition called PhonesLine1, and you have several other partitions, such as Internal, LongDistance, International, and so on, the CMI service needs to be capable of accessing the lines in the PhonesLine1 partition to light the MWI on those phones. Therefore, you must configure the PhonesLine1 partition in the **MwiSearchSpace** service parameter. If you want the CMI service to search more than one partition, list each one, and separate each partition with a colon (:). For example, if you have partitions Branch_A_Phones and Branch_B_Phones, and you want to light the MWI on all the phones in both partitions, set the **MWISearchSpace** service parameter to Branch_A_Phones:Branch_B_Phones. Note that the character string you enter for **MWISearchSpace** can be up to 512 characters. Anything past 512 is ignored. If you need to use a search space that is more than 512 characters, you can create a translation pattern in a partition that you enter into the **MWISearchSpace** parameter. On the translation pattern, set the calling search space to one that includes all the partitions you want to be able to turn on the MWI and do not set any calling or called party transformations.

To troubleshoot an MWI problem, take it one step at a time. First look at the CMI trace, and then look at the SDL trace.

The first place to look is in the CMI trace files to see if the voice mail system is sending the CMI service an MWI message. Example 14-7 demonstrates an incoming MWI on message for extension 15600.

Example 14-7 *CMI Trace Showing an Inbound MWI for Extension 15600*

```
   CMISerialWorker::SerialThread() Saw EOT, inbound message:
     [OP:MWI<0x20>0000015600!<EOT>]
 -->CMISsapiClient::LampOnOff()
   CMISsapiClient::LampOnOff() Lamp on - 0000015600
   CMISsapiClient::LampOnOff() Processed number = 15600
   CMISsapiClient::LampOnOff()  Turn Lamp on - 15600
 <--CMISsapiClient::LampOnOff()
```

This trace is very simple. As far as the CMI service is concerned, it sent a message to CallManager to turn on the MWI light for this number. But in this case, the light did not go on. At least you know the message is getting to CallManager and the extension number is correct. The next place to look is the SDL trace to see if the message got to CallManager. Copy the timestamp where you see the "Turn Lamp on" message. In Example 14-7, the timestamps have been removed for ease of reading.

Next, open the SDL trace file that corresponds to the timeframe in which the "Lamp on" message was received, and search for that timestamp. You should see something similar to the trace output shown in Example 14-8.

Example 14-8 *SDL Trace Showing an MWI Message When Misconfigured*

```
SdlSig   | SsInfoReq                              | wait
  | SSAPIManager(1,100,86,1)        | SSAPIManager(1,100,86,1)
  | (1,100,86,1).4190-(*:*)
  | [NP - HP: 0, NP: 0, LP: 0, VLP: 0, LZP: 0]
 SsType=0 SsKey=0 SsNodeId=1 SsParty=0 DeviceId=(0,0,0)
 partitionSearchSpace= dn=15600 FeatureId=122 FeatureValue=2 WhichLamps=0
 LampPersistence=0 SsSignal=0 SsCause=0
SdlSig   | SsInfoReq                              | wait
  | Cc(1,100,13,1)                  | SSAPIManager(1,100,86,1)
  | (1,100,86,1).4190-(*:*)
  | [NP - HP: 0, NP: 0, LP: 0, VLP: 0, LZP: 0]
 SsType=16777243 SsKey=0 SsNodeId=1 SsParty=0 DeviceId=(0,0,0)
 partitionSearchSpace= dn=15600 FeatureId=122 FeatureValue=2 WhichLamps=0
 LampPersistence=0 SsSignal=0 SsCause=0
SdlSig   | DbVoiceMailUpdtReq                      | initialized
  | Db(1,100,20,1)                  | Cc(1,100,13,1)
  | (1,100,86,1).4190-(*:*)                |
```

continues

Example 14-8 *SDL Trace Showing an MWI Message When Misconfigured (Continued)*

```
    [NP - PQ: 0]
SdlSig-O | DbVoiceMailUpdtReq                    | NotApplicable_RemoteSignal
    | Db(3,100,20,1)                   | Db(1,100,20,1)
    | (1,100,86,1).4190-(*:*)
    | [NP - HP: 0, NP: 1, LP: 0, VLP: 0, LZP: 0]
SdlSig-O | DbVoiceMailUpdtReq                    | NotApplicable_RemoteSignal
    | Db(2,100,20,1)                   | Db(1,100,20,1)
    | (1,100,86,1).4190-(*:*)            |
    [NP - HP: 0, NP: 0, LP: 0, VLP: 0, LZP: 0]
```

Notice in Example 14-8 that the line labeled **partitionSearchSpace** is blank. This
corresponds to the **MwiSearchSpace** service parameter. If the DN whose MWI light you
are trying to turn on is in a partition, the lack of a search space explains why the light did
not turn on.

If the search space was configured correctly, the CMI trace would look identical because,
as mentioned earlier, from the CMI service's perspective, everything worked correctly. On
the CallManager side, the SDL trace looks slightly different when the search space is
correct, as demonstrated in Example 14-9.

Example 14-9 *SDL Trace Showing an MWI on Message When Configured Properly*

```
SdlSig    | SsInfoReq                         | wait
    | SSAPIManager(1,100,86,1)      | SSAPIManager(1,100,86,1)
    | (1,100,86,1).4254-(*:*)           |
    [NP - HP: 0, NP: 0, LP: 0, VLP: 0, LZP: 0]
    SsType=0 SsKey=0 SsNodeId=1 SsParty=0 DeviceId=(0,0,0)
    partitionSearchSpace=Line1 dn=15600 FeatureId=122 FeatureValue=2 WhichLamps=0
    LampPersistence=0 SsSignal=0 SsCause=0
SdlSig    | SsInfoReq                         | wait
    | Cc(1,100,13,1)                 | SSAPIManager(1,100,86,1)
    | (1,100,86,1).4254-(*:*)           |
    [NP - HP: 0, NP: 0, LP: 0, VLP: 0, LZP: 0]
    SsType=16777245 SsKey=0 SsNodeId=1 SsParty=0 DeviceId=(0,0,0)
    partitionSearchSpace=Line1 dn=15600 FeatureId=122 FeatureValue=2 WhichLamps=0
    LampPersistence=0 SsSignal=0 SsCause=0
SdlSig    | DbVoiceMailUpdtReq                 | initialized
    | Db(1,100,20,1)                 | Cc(1,100,13,1)
    | (1,100,86,1).4254-(*:*)            | [NP - PQ: 0]
SdlSig-O | CcInfoReq                          | NotApplicable_RemoteSignal
    | LineControl(2,100,34,92)       | Cc(1,100,13,1)
    | (1,100,86,1).4254-(*:*)           |
    [NP - HP: 0, NP: 0, LP: 0, VLP: 0, LZP: 0]
SdlSig-O | DbVoiceMailUpdtReq                 | NotApplicable_RemoteSignal
    | Db(3,100,20,1)                 | Db(1,100,20,1)
    | (1,100,86,1).4254-(*:*)           |
    [NP - HP: 0, NP: 1, LP: 0, VLP: 0, LZP: 0]
SdlSig-O | DbVoiceMailUpdtReq                 | NotApplicable_RemoteSignal
    | Db(2,100,20,1)                 | Db(1,100,20,1)
    | (1,100,86,1).4254-(*:*)           |
    [NP - HP: 0, NP: 0, LP: 0, VLP: 0, LZP: 0]
```

Notice that the SDL trace has an additional signal that was not present in the nonworking scenario. This is the **CcInfoReq** signal. Notice that it is destined to a **LineControl** process on node 2 of the cluster. If you look on node 2 of the cluster, you will see something similar to Example 14-10.

Example 14-10 *SDL Trace from Node 2 Showing an MWI On Message*

```
SdlSig-I  I CcInfoReq                              I idle
  I LineControl(2,100,34,92)        I Cc(1,100,13,1)
  I (1,100,86,1).4254-(*:*)                I
  [NP - HP: 0, NP: 0, LP: 0, VLP: 0, LZP: 0]
SdlSig    I CcInfoReq                              I restart0
  I StationD(2,100,89,280)          I LineControl(2,100,34,92)
  I (1,100,86,1).4254-(*:*)                I
  [NP - HP: 0, NP: 7, LP: 0, VLP: 0, LZP: 0]
SdlSig    I StationOutputSetLamp              I restart0
  I StationD(2,100,89,280)          I StationD(2,100,89,280)
  I (1,100,86,1).4254-(*:*)                I
  [NP - HP: 0, NP: 13, LP: 0, VLP: 0, LZP: 0]
  StimulusName=VoiceMail Mode=LampOn Instance=1
SdlSig    I StationOutputDisplayPromptStatus  I restart0
  I StationD(2,100,89,280)          I StationD(2,100,89,280)
  I (1,100,86,1).4254-(*:*)                I
  [NP - HP: 0, NP: 12, LP: 0, VLP: 0, LZP: 0]
  TimeOutValue=0   Status=_$   Line=0   CI=0
SdlSig-I  I DbVoiceMailUpdtReq                I initialized
  I Db(2,100,20,1)                  I Db(1,100,20,1)
  I (1,100,86,1).4254-(*:*)                I
  [NP - PQ: 0]
```

Notice that the LineControl instance is the same on both nodes, **LineControl(2,100,34,92)**. This represents the instance of LineControl for the DN on which the lamp is to be turned on. The next thing you see in the SDL trace is a **StationOutputSetLamp** signal telling the IP phone's StationD instance to turn on the lamp. If you look at the CCM trace at the same timestamp as the StationOutputSetLamp signal, you should see the trace output shown in Example 14-11.

Example 14-11 *CCM Trace Showing the SetLamp Message*

```
StationD: abcd214 SetLamp stimulus=15(VoiceMail) stimulusInstance=1
  lampMode=2(LampOn).
StationD: abcd214 SetLamp stimulus=15(VoiceMail) stimulusInstance=0
  lampMode=2(LampOn).
StationD: abcd214 DisplayPromptStatus timeOutValue=0 promptStatus='_$' content=
  'You have a voice mail' lineInstance=0 callReference=0 ver=80000004.
```

If the messages are getting all the way from the voice mail system to the CallManager SDL trace and the MWI is not lighting, there is a very good chance that the problem is the **MwiSearchSpace** parameter. Refer to the previous sections for instructions on properly configuring the MwiSearchSpace parameter.

Cisco VG248 SMDI Integration

The second platform available to integrate to a voice mail system using SMDI is the VG248 analog gateway. The VG248 has two async ports that allow it to connect directly to the voice mail system without requiring the use of the CMI service on a CallManager node. One of the async ports connects to the voice mail system, and the second port can be used to daisy-chain multiple VG248s for voice mail systems that have more than 48 voice mail ports. It can also be used to connect to a legacy PBX so that CallManager and the legacy PBX can both share a single SMDI port on the voice mail system.

The format of the SMDI messages and the concepts of how SMDI works are no different when you integrate CallManager to a voice mail system using a VG248. The biggest difference is that the VG248 takes care of creating the SMDI messages and interpreting any messages sent by the voice mail system, such as MWI on/off messages. The VG248 integrates with CallManager using the Skinny protocol. In fact, from CallManager's perspective, each VG248 port is no different from a 7960 IP Phone. For this reason, troubleshooting the ports on a VG248 is identical to troubleshooting an IP Phone, which was discussed in Chapter 4, "Skinny Client Registration," and Chapter 5, "IP Phones." Therefore, this chapter covers only how to troubleshoot the SMDI integration portion of the VG248.

Verifying Configuration Parameters

The VG248 has configuration parameters similar to those found in the CMI service parameters.

To view the SMDI configuration, select **Configure > SMDI**. You should see a menu similar to that shown in Example 14-12.

Example 14-12 *VG248 SMDI Configuration Menu*

```
----------------------------------------------------------------
       |              Cisco VG248 (vnt-vg248-1)                |
-------- ------------------------------------------------ ----
       | SMDI                                            |
       |-----------------------------------------------|
       | Pilot directory number           (4058)       |
       | Number of SMDI ports             (48)         |
       | First voice mail port number     (1)          |
       | SMDI number length               (10)         |
       | Truncate SMDI number if too long (no)         |
       | SMDI number format               ()           |
       | Message desk number              (1)          |
       | Forward MWIs to CallManager      (yes)        |
       | Forward MWIs to Async 2          (no)         |
       | Forward INV responses to Async 1 (no)         |
       | CallManager MWI on DN            (19998)      |
       | CallManager MWI off DN           (19999)      |
       | Keep alive SMDI number           (5551212)    |
       | Disconnect notification          (no)         |
       | Async port serial settings                    |
       ------------------------------------------
```

Table 14-3 describes the purpose of each of the configuration parameters.

Table 14-3   *VG248 SMDI Configuration Parameters*

Parameter	Description
Pilot directory number	Corresponds to the number users dial on their IP phones to access voice mail. This helps the VG248 distinguish between calls made to retrieve a user's voice mail and calls made to leave a voice mail for another user.
Number of SMDI ports	By default, none of the ports on the VG248 are configured to send SMDI information about calls made to them. To enable SMDI, you must assign the number of SMDI ports a value from 1 to 48. Using fewer than 48 ports for SMDI means that the remaining ports can be used to connect analog phones, modems, or fax machines.
	If you use fewer than 48 ports for SMDI, you must ensure that the SMDI ports are consecutive, beginning with port 1. For example, if this value is set to 10, VG248 ports 1 through 10 should be connected to the voice mail system, and ports 11 through 48 are available for other analog devices.
	If you fail to connect the ports in sequential order, users will receive the general greeting instead of a specific user greeting when a call is extended on the out-of-order ports because the VG248 and the voice mail system do not agree on the port numbering.
First voice mail port number	With a single VG248 connected to a voice mail system, port 1 on the VG248 should be connected to port 1 of the voice mail system, and similarly for the other VG248 ports.
	However, with multiple VG248 devices connected to a single voice mail system (such as in a daisy-chain configuration), this simple mapping is possible only on the first VG248. On the other VG248 devices, port 1 must connect to higher voice mail port numbers.
	Using this setting, you can identify the first port used on the voice mail system. This value should correspond to the port number on the voice mail system to which port 1 is connected. In all cases, connections from a single VG248 must use consecutive, successive ports of the voice mail system.
	For example, if two VG248 devices are connected to a 96-port voice mail system, one VG248 connects to ports 1 to 48, and the other connects to ports 49 to 96. On the first VG248 device, set the **First voice mail port number** to 1 (the default value), and on the second VG248, set the value to 49.
	As another example, if 80 voice mail ports are in use, and two VG248 devices each provide 40 ports, the **Number of SMDI ports** on each VG248 is set to 40, and the **First voice port number** is set to 1 on the first VG248 and to 41 on the second VG248.

continues

Table 14-3   *VG248 SMDI Configuration Parameters (Continued)*

Parameter	Description
SMDI number length	Traditional SMDI includes caller and called party information as 7-digit numbers, although most modern voice mail systems usually require 10 digits.
	If the number is shorter than 7 digits, extra digits (typically zeros) are added to the left. For example, the extension number 12345 becomes 0012345 when sent via SMDI. Because 7 digits are not enough for external caller ID, however, an extended SMDI format is available that uses 10-digit numbers.
	Most voice mail systems are flexible, supporting either SMDI format; however, some older systems insist on receiving exactly seven digits. Check the voice mail system's documentation to determine which setting is appropriate.
	You can set the VG248 to output either 7- or 10-digit numbers. It should match the value required by your voice mail system. You can also set the number length to **unpadded**, which indicates that the voice mailbox numbers are always passed unmodified between CallManager and the analog voice mail system.
Truncate SMDI number if too long	If SMDI extension numbers are longer than the traditional 7 or 10 digits, the VG248 can either output the entire number or truncate the extension number to the length you defined in the **SMDI number length**. If you have set the **SMDI number length** to **unpadded**, the **Truncate SMDI number if too long** setting has no effect.
	Most voice mail systems can accept longer numbers, but some systems insist on exactly 7 or 10 digits. Check which format your system supports before selecting this option.
SMDI number format	When the **SMDI number length** is configured to 7 or 10 digits, the VG248 adds digits to any SMDI extension numbers that are shorter. Normally, it does so by adding zeros to the left of the number, so that, for example, 1234 becomes 0001234 in the 7-digit case.
	However, the **SMDI number format** allows other digits to be used. For example, with an **SMDI number format** of 1234567, the extension number 8989 becomes 1238989. Zeros are used for any additional required digits. So, if **SMDI number length** is 10, the final extension number is 0001238989. If the **SMDI number length** is set to **unpadded**, this setting has no effect.
	You might need to use this parameter if the extension numbers on CallManager do not match those configured on the voice mail system and you need to add some digits to convert the CallManager extension number to a longer number required by the voice mail system.
Message desk number	Typically, a voice mail system is configured with a single message desk number (normally 1), and incoming SMDI messages are required to use this value for proper operation. You need to set the message desk number on the VG248 to match the value used by the voice mail system.

Table 14-3   *VG248 SMDI Configuration Parameters (Continued)*

Parameter	Description
Forward MWIs to CallManager	Specifies whether the VG248 sends MWI commands it receives from the voice mail system to CallManager. This is enabled by default and must be set to True for MWI to function when integrating with CallManager. If you enable this parameter, you must identify the directory number used to set MWI commands (see the parameter, **CallManager MWI on DN**).
Forward MWIs to Async 2	Specifies whether the VG248 forwards SMDI MWI commands received from the voice mail system to the next device in the SMDI chain. You should only enable this parameter if you have a PBX connected to the Async 2 port that needs to also receive MWI messages received by Async 1.
Forward INV responses to Async 1	Some PBX systems generate an INV (invalid) response to MWI commands from the voice mail system if an error occurs. The VG248 cannot distinguish which extension numbers are connected to the legacy PBX and which are connected to CallManager. Therefore, MWI commands are sent to both systems. If the VG248 is connected to a legacy PBX and CallManager (such as in the multiplexing configuration), the PBX is likely to generate these error responses to commands it receives from the VG248. Disabling this option prevents the voice mail system from seeing all the invalid messages sent by the PBX or another device on Async 2.
CallManager MWI on DN	If you have enabled the VG248 to forward MWI commands from the voice mail system to CallManager, you must identify the directory number used to set MWI commands. In CallManager version 3.1 and earlier, this is configured in the CallManager service parameter **MessageWaitingOnDN** (**System > System Parameters**). In CallManager version 3.2 and later, this is accomplished in the Message Waiting Configuration (**Feature > Voice Mail > Message Waiting**).
CallManager MWI off DN	If you have enabled the VG248 to forward MWI commands from the voice mail system to CallManager, you must identify the directory number used to clear MWI commands. In CallManager version 3.1 and earlier, this is configured in the CallManager service parameter **MessageWaitingOffDN** (**System > System Parameters**). In CallManager version 3.2 and later, this is accomplished in the Message Waiting Configuration (**Feature > Voice Mail > Message Waiting**).
Keep alive SMDI number	Some voice mail systems use a **Keep alive SMDI number** to determine whether the SMDI connection is active. The voice mail system sends out a test MWI operation for this voice mailbox number and expects to receive a negative response from the attached VG248. You must configure the VG248 with this KeepAlive number so that it distinguishes the MWI commands on this number from those on a real extension number. By default, this value is set to 5551212, which is a number commonly used by analog voice mail systems.

continues

Table 14-3 *VG248 SMDI Configuration Parameters (Continued)*

Parameter	Description
Disconnect notification	When a remote party hangs up, the voice mail system should detect this so that it can hang up also, freeing the port for use by another caller. If this parameter is set to **Yes**, the VG248 sends an additional SMDI message to the voice mail system when a call into it has finished. This message is not part of the SMDI standard. By default, this option is set to **No**.
Async port serial settings	Specifies the baud rate, data bits, stop bits, and parity for each of the async ports. The baud rate must match on both of the asynch ports; however, the other parameters can be different.

When integrating to an SMDI voice mail system through a VG248, CallManager does not know there is an SMDI connection. The VG248 handles the creation and reception of SMDI messages.

To see the SMDI messages being sent and received by the VG248, perform the following steps:

Step 1 Enable the SMDI trace by selecting **Diagnostics > Event Log > Set Logging Levels > SMDI**.

Step 2 Set this parameter to **Errors + warnings + info + trace**.

Step 3 On the **Event Log** menu, change the **Set logged ports** setting to the port you want to monitor to avoid having excessive debug information on the screen.

Step 4 After you have enabled tracing, select **Event Log > View Recent**.

Step 5 Place a call to the analog port you enabled tracing for. You should see a line appear on your screen showing the SMDI message. For example:

```
474 00:14:52   31s T SMDI     Tx 1:\r\nMD0010001D 0000015000 \r\n^Y
```

You can see that the SMDI message indicates a direct call to message desk 1, port 1 from phone number 15000. From an SMDI perspective, the same troubleshooting rules apply here as they do for the CMI service, as discussed previously. Be sure to turn off tracing when you are done troubleshooting.

Message Waiting Indicator Problems

Troubleshooting MWI problems with the VG248 is basically a combination of the troubleshooting methodology for CMI and the troubleshooting methodology for Unity. To troubleshoot an MWI problem on the VG248, do the following:

- Check VG248 SMDI trace for MWI messages
- Check VG248 Port 0 configuration and registration status
- Check Skinny traces on the VG248

The first piece is ensuring that the VG248 is receiving the SMDI messages and is configured to send them to CallManager. To check if the messages are being received, enable the SMDI trace as described in the preceding section. With tracing enabled, you should see MWI on and off commands similar to this:

```
476 00:35:04   46s T SMDI      Rx 1:OP:MWI 0000015000!^D
477 00:35:20   16s T SMDI      Rx 1:RMV:MWI 0000015000!^D
```

One common reason for MWI not functioning is forgetting to configure port 0 on the VG248. Port 0 is a virtual port used by the VG248 to send MWI on/off messages to CallManager. If this port is not assigned a DN and is not registered with CallManager, MWI will not function.

Also note that the same restrictions discussed regarding partitions and calling search spaces in the discussion about Unity (see the section, "Message Waiting Indicator (MWI)") apply here as well. Port 0 must have a calling search space that can call the MWI on/off numbers configured in the system.

You can verify that port 0 is registered properly by selecting **Display > Port Status** from the VG248. The first line should say **Device level CallManager connection: Up**. If you select this line and press **Enter**, you should see details about the virtual port similar to those shown in Example 14-13.

Example 14-13 *VG248 Port Status Screen*

```
  ------------------------------------------------------------------
  | Device level CallManager connection                            |
  |----------------------------------------------------------------|
  |                                                                |
  |   CallManager link : up                                        |
  |   TFTP server      : 172.18.106.58                             |
  |   Device name      : VGC0653d6b2eb00                           |
  |   Directory number : 15711  (external mask="15711")            |
  |   Forwarded to     : <not forwarded>                           |
  |   Call state       : idle                                      |
  |   Remote party     : <none>                                    |
  |   Remote address   : <none>                                    |
  |   Codec in use     : <none>                                    |
  |   MWI              : off                                        |
  |                                                                |
  |   CallManager name            IP address     State     Type    |
  |   ---------------             ----------     -----     ----     |
  |   172.18.106.59          172.18.106.59:2000  Active    Normal   |
  |   172.18.106.57          172.18.106.57:2000  Standby   Normal   |
  |                                                                |
  |                                                                |
  |                                                                |
  ---|                            <press space for statistics>  |---
  WA -------------------------------------------------------------
```

If the port is not registered, first make sure it is configured as a device in CallManager and that it has a DN assigned to it. If it still does not register, troubleshoot this like any other Skinny device registration problem, as discussed in Chapter 4.

After you have ensured that the port is registered, you can enable Skinny traces for the virtual port to see the VG248 sending the MWI on message. Select **Diagnostics > Event log > Set logging levels** and change the SCCP (Skinny) level to **Errors + warnings + info + trace**. Now go back and view the recent log entries. You should see something similar to Example 14-14 when an MWI message is received from the voice mail system via SMDI.

Example 14-14 *VG248 Event Log Showing SCCP Traces*

```
600 00:47:28   16s T SMDI      Rx 1:RMV:MWI 0000015000!^D
601 00:47:28    6 T SCCP     0 TX: SCCP_OFFHOOK_CALLING_PARTY_NUMBER 15000
602 00:47:28   12 T SCCP     0 RX: SCCP_SET_LAMP_MODE 9/1 = 2
603 00:47:28    5 T SCCP     0 RX: SCCP_CALL_STATE 1
604 00:47:28    4 T SCCP     0 TX: SCCP_KEY_PAD *
605 00:47:28    6 T SCCP     0 TX: SCCP_KEY_PAD *
606 00:47:28    4 T SCCP     0 TX: SCCP_KEY_PAD *
607 00:47:28    4 T SCCP     0 TX: SCCP_KEY_PAD *
608 00:47:28    5 T SCCP     0 TX: SCCP_KEY_PAD *
609 00:47:28   27 T SCCP     0 RX: SCCP_START_TONE 33
610 00:47:28    5 T SCCP     0 RX: SCCP_STOP_TONE
611 00:47:28    4 T SCCP     0 RX: SCCP_CALL_STATE 12
612 00:47:28    6 T SCCP     0 RX: SCCP_CALL_INFORMATION 15711 -> 19999
613 00:47:28   18 T SCCP     0 RX: SCCP_SET_SPEAKER_MODE 2
614 00:47:28    5 T SCCP     0 RX: SCCP_CALL_STATE 2
615 00:47:28    6 T SCCP     0 Set idle; flag=1, new_config=0
616 00:47:28    5 T SCCP     0 RX: SCCP_SET_LAMP_MODE 9/1 = 1
617 00:47:28    4 T SCCP     0 RX: SCCP_DEFINE_TIME_DATE
618 00:47:28    5 T SCCP     0 RX: SCCP_STOP_TONE
```

You can see that the VG248 received an SMDI message to clear the MWI on extension 15000. Immediately following that, you see port 0 on the VG248 place a call to 19999, which happens to be the MWI off number configured on this CallManager and VG248. The important thing to note is the message **OFFHOOK_CALLING_PARTY_NUMBER 15000**, which tells you which MWI the VG248 is attempting to turn off.

Make sure port 0 (extension 15711 in Example 14-14) has a calling search space that can dial the MWI on/off numbers (extension 19999 in this case). This is one of the most common reasons for MWI to not work properly.

Octel Voice Mail Digital Integration Via a DPA Voice Mail Gateway

A very popular voice mail system used in IP telephony networks is the Octel line of voice mail products, such as the Octel 200, 250, 300, and 350.

These Octel voice mail systems can integrate with CallManager using one of three different cards. The first uses an analog connection in conjunction with a serial SMDI connection. This integration is covered in the earlier section "SMDI Integration."

The other two integrations are called digital integration because Octel emulates the behavior of a digital phone set. The only difference between the two digital integrations is that one emulates an Avaya/Lucent digital set, and the other emulates a Nortel digital set. An Octel with digital integration is designed to connect directly to a digital line card on an Avaya/Lucent PBX or a Nortel PBX.

The Cisco DPA 7630 voice mail gateway allows CallManager to integrate with an Octel voice mail system designed to integrate with an Avaya/Lucent PBX. The Cisco DPA 7610 voice mail gateway allows CallManager to integrate with an Octel voice mail system designed to integrate with a Nortel PBX. Both the DPA 7630 and DPA 7610 can also operate in hybrid mode, where they allow an existing Avaya/Lucent or Nortel PBX to integrate with the Octel voice mail at the same time as CallManager, allowing for a seamless user transition from a traditional PBX to IP telephony.

The DPA voice mail gateways appear like 24 Skinny protocol-based IP phone devices in CallManager. In fact, the DPA has no special device configuration. Each port is configured as a 30VIP IP Phone device. The Skinny signaling is the same as what you see when troubleshooting Skinny messages to newer phones like a 7960. Each port on the DPA registers with CallManager just like any other IP phone, including downloading a .cnf file from the TFTP server and registering to the CallManager server specified in the list.

Verify Cabling

The most common problems encountered when integrating to an Octel using a Cisco DPA voice mail gateway involve cabling. A DPA cannot be connected to an Octel system using a straight-through 25-pair telco cable. Figure 14-11 shows the pinouts for the telco connectors on a DPA 7630. The DPA 7630 has three connectors with eight ports each.

Figure 14-11 *DPA 7630 Telco Connector Pinouts*

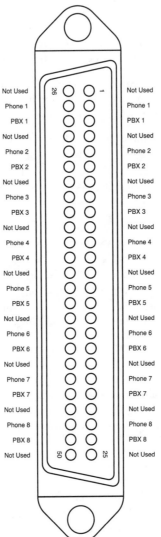

Figure 14-12 shows the wiring connections between the connector on the DPA and the connector on the Octel. Notice that the DPA ports skip a pair of pins between each port, but the Octel does not.

Figure 14-12 *DPA 7630 Wiring to the Octel System*

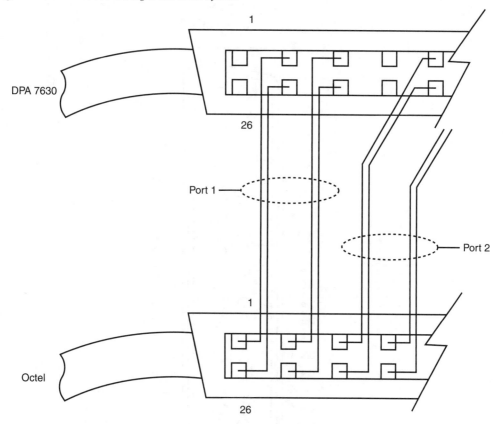

Figure 14-13 shows the pinouts for the telco connector on a DPA 7610. The DPA 7610 has a single connector for all 24 ports.

Figure 14-13 *DPA 7610 Telco Connector Pinouts*

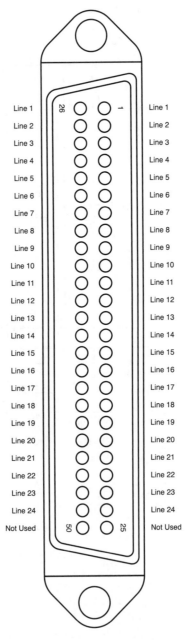

Figure 14-14 shows the wiring connections between the connector on the DPA and the connector on the Octel. Notice that the 24 ports from the DPA's single connector must be cross-connected to three separate connectors on the Octel, because each Octel card has only eight ports. Also notice that no pairs are skipped on the DPA between ports, but a single pair is skipped on the Octel side between ports.

Figure 14-14 *DPA 7610 Wiring to the Octel System*

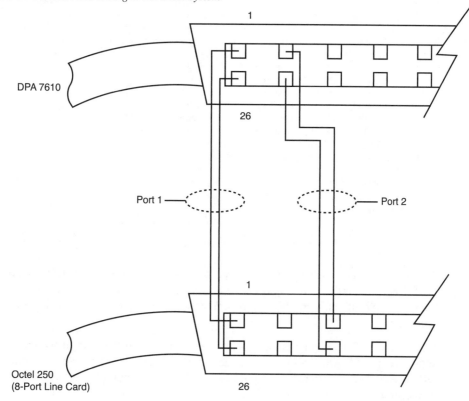

Check Port Status

After you have verified your cabling, you can check the status of the DPA ports from the DPA menu interface. The menu interface is accessible via either the console or a Telnet session.

From the main menu, access the Port Status page (**Display > Port status**). You should see a page similar to Example 14-15.

Example 14-15 *Checking the DPA Port Status*

```
    ------------------------------------------------------------
  |                    Cisco DPA 7630 (SEP036b9b9c99)             |
    ------------------------------------------------------------

  ------------------------------------------------------------------
| Port status                                                       |
|------------------------------------------------------------------|
|   # Type     Status              # Type     Status                |
|   -- ------  ------------------   -- ------  ------------------    |
|   1 Call     DN=29111 On Hook    13 Down                          |
|   2 Call     DN=19101 On Hook    14 Down                          |
|   3 Call     DN=19102 On Hook    15 Down                          |
|   4 Call     DN=19103 On Hook    16 Down                          |
|   5 Call     DN=19104 On Hook    17 Down                          |
|   6 Call     DN=19105 On Hook    18 Down                          |
|   7 Call     DN=19106 On Hook    19 Down                          |
|   8 Call     DN=19107 On Hook    20 Down                          |
|   9 Down                         21 Down                          |
|  10 Down                         22 Down                          |
|  11 Down                         23 Down                          |
|  12 Down                         24 Down                          |
|                                  25 Virtual DN=19100 Q=0          |
|                                                                   |
    ------------------------------------------------------------------
```

Twenty-five ports are listed. The first 24 ports correspond to the 24 physical ports on the DPA. The 25th port is a virtual port that the DPA uses to turn MWI on and off for phones connected to CallManager. This is very similar to how Unity does it by dialing the MWI on/off numbers.

Notice that the first eight ports are up and have a status of On Hook. Ports 9 through 24 all show a status of Down. This is because they are not physically connected to anything. The DPA does not attempt to register a port with CallManager until it has established a connection to the Octel on a given port.

You can select one of the ports and get detailed registration information for it. Example 14-16 shows the details for port 1.

Example 14-16 *Checking Detailed Registration Information for a Specific DPA Port*

```
                       ---------------------------------------------------
               |                   Cisco DPA 7630 (SEP036b9b9c99)                 |
                       ---------------------------------------------------

      - -------------------------------------------------------------------- -
    | | Port 1                                                             | |
    |-|-----------------------------------------------------------------|-|
    | |                                                                     | |
    | |    Codec in use            : none                                   | |
    | |                                                                     | |
    | |                                                                     | |
    | |    CallManager connection  : up                                     | |
    | |    CallManager device name : SEP036b9b9c9901                        | |
    | |                                                                     | |
    | |    CallManager name                    IP address     State         | |
    | |    ----------------                    ----------     -----         | |
    | |    -                                   14.84.221.10:2000   Active    | |
    | |    -                                   14.84.223.10:2000   Standby   | |
    | |    -                                   14.84.204.10:2000   Idle      | |
    | |                                                                     | |
    | |                                                                     | |
    | |                                                                     | |
      - -------------------------------------------------------------------- -
```

Notice that the port has a list of CallManager IP addresses, just as an IP phone would have a CallManager list for registration. You can also see the device name for this port that matches the device name in CallManager. If a port fails to register with CallManager, troubleshoot it just as you would any other Skinny device registration problem. Refer to Chapters 4 and 5 for more information about troubleshooting Skinny device registration problems.

The DPA ports can have one of five different statuses, as shown in Table 14-4.

Table 14-4 *DPA Voice Mail Gateway Port Types*

Port Type	Description
Call	This port is used for general call processing.
Oct MWI	This port is used to receive MWI commands from the Octel system.
PBX MWI	This port is used to set MWI commands on the Definity or Meridian 1 PBX systems.
Virtual	This "port" is an IP phone used for setting MWI commands on CallManager.
Down	The link to the Octel or PBX port is not connected. Unused ports display as **Down**.

Table 14-5 shows the various values for **Port status** and what they mean. Although the 7630 and 7610 are nearly identical, there are a few statuses that apply to only one gateway or the other.

Table 14-5   *DPA Voice Mail Gateway Port Statuses*

Port Status	Description	Which Port Type Uses It	DPA 7630/7610
Octel registering	Indicates an intermediate state when the DPA 7630/7610 starts up a port's connection to the Octel system.	• Call • Oct MWI	DPA 7630/7610
Octel link down	The port previously had a connection to the Octel system, but the connection is down.	• Call • Oct MWI	DPA 7630/7610
CM link registering	Indicates an intermediate state when the DPA 7630/7610 is registering an IP phone with CallManager.	• Call • Oct MWI • Virtual	DPA 7630/7610
CM link down	Indicates an intermediate state when the DPA 7630/7610 has successfully started the port connected to the Octel system but cannot establish a connection to CallManager.	• Call • Oct MWI • Virtual	DPA 7630/7610
DN=*xxxx substate*	The normal status of the ports. The Octel port has started, and the IP phone associated with the port has registered and has a directory number assigned to it. DN=*xxxx* indicates the directory number and *substate* indicates current port activity: • On hook • Off hook • Call in—The Octel-emulated phone is ringing.	• Call • Oct MWI	DPA 7630/7610

Table 14-5   *DPA Voice Mail Gateway Port Statuses (Continued)*

Port Status	Description	Which Port Type Uses It	DPA 7630/7610
DN=*xxxx substate* (*continued*)	• Call out—Octel has made an outgoing call. • *xxxx*—Octel has dialed out. • On call—The Octel port is on a call. • Transfer—The Octel system is transferring the caller. • Outcall—Octel is dialing out a number. • Hanging up—The DPA 7630/7610 is waiting for the Octel system to hang up.		
DN=*xxxx*, Q=*yyyy*	The IP phone is up with the assigned directory number, and MWI messages are queued for CallManager. DN=*xxxx* indicates the directory number and Q=*yyyy* indicates the number of messages in queue to be sent out that DPA port.	Virtual	DPA 7630/7610
Down	The PBX port is down, or the port has no physical link to the PBX.	PBX MWI	DPA 7630/7610
Registering	The PBX port is starting up.	PBX MWI	DPA 7630/7610
Q=*xxxx*	The PBX port is up, and MWI messages are queued. Q=*yyyy* indicates the number of messages in queue to be sent out that DPA port.	PBX MWI	DPA 7630

continues

Table 14-5   *DPA Voice Mail Gateway Port Statuses (Continued)*

Port Status	Description	Which Port Type Uses It	DPA 7630/7610
O=*xxxx*	The DPA is dialing out the MWI command *xxxx* to the PBX. For example, O=*4023976 means the DPA is dialing the digits *4023976 towards the PBX.	PBX MWI	DPA 7630/7610
Disabled	The port is connected but is either disabled or misconfigured.	PBX MWI	DPA 7610
Idle	The port is available to set MWIs but is currently inactive.	PBX MWI	DPA 7610
O=*number*	The port is setting an MWI on the given extension.	PBX MWI	DPA 7630/7610
Busy	The port is busy preparing to set an MWI.	PBX MWI	DPA 7610

Troubleshooting DPA MWI Problems

MWI problems are common in DPA integrations and are usually the result of misconfiguration.

For the DPA to turn MWI on or off on an IP phone, the DPA must be configured with the same MWI on/off numbers that are configured in CallManager. Prior to CallManager version 3.2, the MWI on/off numbers are configured as CallManager service parameters (**Service > Service Parameters**); however, in CallManager version 3.2, they are configured on the Message Waiting Configuration page (**Feature > Voice Mail > Message Waiting**). These numbers should match what is configured on the DPA under **Configure > CallManager**.

The DPA voice mail gateway uses the virtual phone port (port 25) for MWI on/off functions. For this to work, the phone device for port 25 must have a calling search space that allows it to dial the partition in which the MWI on/off numbers are configured in CallManager version 3.2 and later. Prior to CallManager version 3.2, the phone device for port 25 must have a calling search space that allows it to dial the partition in which the phone DNs reside, which you want to be able to turn the MWI on/off for.

When using a DPA 7630, the Octel uses feature codes to turn MWI on and off. These feature codes must match between the Octel and the DPA. Use the following steps to compare the feature codes:

Step 1 Verify the configuration on the DPA by selecting **Configure > Octel/ Definity integration**.

Step 2 Examine the values for the parameters Definity MWI ON pre-extension dial string and Definity MWI OFF pre-extension dial string.

Step 3 Now compare to the configuration on the Octel by going to menu 6.2 on the Octel.

Step 4 Examine the values for the parameters **Dialing Sequence to Activate Message Waiting** and **Dialing Sequence to Deactivate Message Waiting**. These should match the configuration on the DPA.

Note that the Octel parameter has the letter **N** after the dial string. For example, if the MWI on the pre-extension is configured as ***4** on the DPA, you will see ***4N** on the Octel. You might also see a **P** on the Octel. This tells the Octel to pause between the time it dials the prefix and the time it dials the number of the extension it wants to modify the MWI for. This is not necessary when you're integrating with a DPA, so you can safely remove it.

Using the DPA Event Log

The DPA voice mail gateways provide a variety of tracing facilities to help you troubleshoot problems on the DPA. You access the event log on the DPA by selecting **Diagnostics > Event log**. From the **Event log** menu, you can enable a variety of trace facilities. You should not normally have to use these. However, if you want to get detailed information about what is happening on a particular DPA port, go to **Set Logging levels** and set the level for the item you want to troubleshoot to **Errors + warnings + info + trace**. For example, if you want to see all the Skinny messages between the DPA and CallManager, enable the CSSP trace. Use the **Set Logged port** option to select which ports you want to view the event log for. You can specify a single port or a range of ports.

Best Practices

- Always make sure your Unity TSP is compatible with the versions of Unity and CallManager you are using. Check network connectivity between Unity and CallManager.

- Always remember that voice mail systems are usually nothing more than automated phones. Much of the troubleshooting methodology that applies to Skinny devices and gateways applies to voice mail systems.

- Be sure to check your MWIs to ensure that they are functioning properly after any voice mail-related configuration changes or upgrades. MWI problems are among the most common voice mail-related problems. It usually takes some time before users figure out they have been receiving voice mails but were not informed of their arrival. Proactively checking this can help you avoid such a service-affecting problem.

- For SMDI integrations, ensure the settings on the voice mail system match the settings on CallManager, whether you are using the CMI service or a VG248 to provide SMDI connectivity.

- Ensure your MWI on/off numbers are configured properly when using Unity, the VG248, or DPA integration.

- Ensure your Skinny voice mail ports (Unity, VG248, or DPA) have a calling search space that allows them to access the devices necessary to turn on the MWI lamps.

Summary

Voice mail is an essential feature in most IP telephony systems. There are three primary methods to integrate with a voice mail system:

- Cisco Unity
- Third-party voice mail integrated via SMDI
- Octel voice mail digital integration via a DPA voice mail gateway

This chapter covered how to troubleshoot the integration between CallManager and the various voice mail systems. You also learned where to look when the voice mail system is not receiving the information it needs to properly answer calls or turn on and off the MWI lamps.

## CHAPTER 15

Survivable Remote Site Telephony (SRST)

One of the most powerful advantages of IP Telephony is the ability to deploy a centralized Cisco CallManager cluster with one or more remote sites connected to the central site via a WAN connection. Unfortunately, this means that if your WAN goes down, you lose phone service at the remote site. To remedy this problem, Cisco developed Survivable Remote Site Telephony (SRST) services for a variety of routers running Cisco IOS Software.

Note that SRST is very different from another Cisco IOS Software feature called IOS Telephony Services (ITS), which allows a Cisco IOS Software router to perform call processing without a CallManager in the network with far fewer features than what are available in CallManager. This chapter discusses only SRST.

SRST Operation

SRST is a feature available in Cisco IOS Software that allows a router at a remote branch to assume basic call processing responsibilities in the event that IP Phones at a remote site are unable to contact the central CallManager. Figure 15-1 shows how a router running SRST fits into an IP Telephony network.

When the connection between the IP Phones at the remote site and CallManager fails, the SRST router assumes call processing responsibilities. For this transfer of responsibility to work, the IP Phones at the remote site must be SRST-capable, and SRST must be enabled for those devices.

A Cisco IP Phone treats the IP address of the SRST gateway almost the same way it treats any other CallManager on its CallManager list. This means that the phone always tries to register with the two highest CallManagers on the list. If the first two are not available, the IP Phone continues down the list always trying to maintain a connection to two available CallManagers. For example, if the IP Phone has a list of three CallManager servers, it normally has a connection to the first two; however, if the first CallManager fails, the IP Phone maintains a connection to the second and third CallManagers. When the first CallManager returns to service, the IP Phone reconnects to the first CallManager and disconnects from the third, still maintaining a connection with the second CallManager. When the IP Phone loses connectivity to all CallManager servers on its CallManager list, it tries the SRST router as a last resort.

Figure 15-1   *SRST Topology*

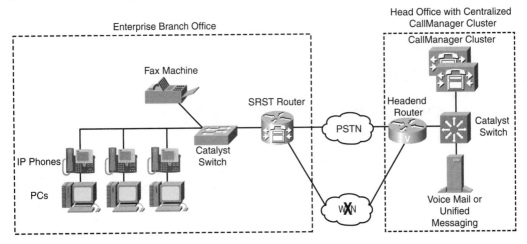

Before going into the operation and troubleshooting of SRST, it is important to understand some of the limitations of SRST. SRST provides only basic survivability for remote sites in the event of a WAN outage. When the IP Phone is in fallback mode, the prompt on the phone displays the message, "CM Fallback Service Operating" to inform users that fallback mode is active. You should set user expectations as to what this mode means and what functionality they lose while in fallback mode.

SRST is not designed to be a full-featured CallManager; be aware of the following restrictions:

- Some devices are not supported in SRST mode, including any CTI application (for example, Cisco IP SoftPhone). The ATA 186 and VG248 currently cannot register with an SRST gateway, although there are plans for these gateways to be supported.

- Extension mobility does not work in SRST mode.

- SRST does not have a concept of partitions or calling search spaces. You can use class of restriction (CoR) in SRST to create some restrictions. However, CoR is not nearly as flexible as partitions and calling search spaces, and the information is not automatically populated on the SRST router.

- Each IP Phone has only one line instance per physical line button. When registered to a CallManager, a phone can have up to two calls per line (future versions beyond CallManager 3.3 may allow for more than two). Transfers and conferencing are special cases in SRST that work on one line.

- All transfers are blind transfers. This can be confusing to users who are accustomed to performing consultation transfers.

- Message waiting indicators (MWIs) might be out of synch when recovering from SRST mode. Most voice mail systems have a method to automatically resynchronize MWI every night.

- All forwarding (busy, no answer, and forward all) is lost in SRST mode. Therefore, if line 1 on an IP Phone is busy, the next call doesn't automatically go to line 2, as it might when the phone is registered to CallManager. Only global call forwarding (the same number for everyone) can be configured for SRST mode.

- In SRST mode, all call routing decisions are made on the SRST gateway through dial peer configuration, so anything not explicitly configured on the SRST gateway will not work. An IP Phone registered to an SRST gateway can call any endpoint that is directly registered to the SRST gateway, any POTS port on the SRST gateway, or an IP endpoint via H.323.

- MGCP endpoints do not function in SRST mode; however, as of Cisco IOS Software Release 12.2(11)T, MGCP endpoints can be configured to become H.323 endpoints when SRST mode is operating due to a WAN failure.

SRST Configuration

If you are having problems with SRST, the first thing to check is the configuration to ensure that SRST is enabled on both the SRST router and the IP Phone.

TIP   Cisco IOS Software releases refer to IP Phones running under SRST as ephones.

For SRST to function on an SRST-capable router, you must ensure the following configuration:

```
call-manager-fallback
  ip source-address 14.84.41.1 port 2000
  max-ephones 24
  max-dn 48
```

The **ip source-address** parameter should match the IP address of the Ethernet/Fast Ethernet interface your IP Phones use as their default gateway or the IP address configured in CallManager as the SRST Reference. The **max-ephones** parameter specifies the maximum number of IP Phones that are allowed to register with the SRST router. **max-dn** specifies the total number of lines (directory numbers) that are allowed to register. These two parameters are limited, depending on the platform. They should be configured based on the number of SRST client licenses you purchased.

NOTE

The number of devices that can register with an SRST router depends on the platform and the Cisco IOS Software version you are using. Refer to Cisco.com for the latest platform and SRST Cisco IOS Software release information.

As of CallManager Release 3.1(3a), you can enable or disable SRST on a per-IP Phone basis. Between 3.1(1) and 3.1(3a), SRST was enabled for all phones. Prior to CallManager 3.1, SRST required special phone loads that were SRST-enabled.

In CallManager 3.3(1) and later, the SRST router does not have to be the default gateway of the IP Phone. Instead, you can configure an SRST Reference in CallManager Administration (**System > SRST**) and configure SRST on a per-device pool basis to be disabled, use the phone's default gateway, or use a specific SRST Reference. This gives you additional flexibility to have multiple IP subnets at a remote site and still use the same gateway for SRST operation.

To check to see if SRST is enabled or disabled on an IP Phone prior to CallManager 3.3(1), select **Device > Phone** in Cisco CallManager Administration, and search for the phone you want to check. Near the bottom of the Phone Configuration page, you should see something similar to Figure 15-2.

Figure 15-2 *SRST Phone Configuration in CallManager Administration Prior to Release 3.3(1)*

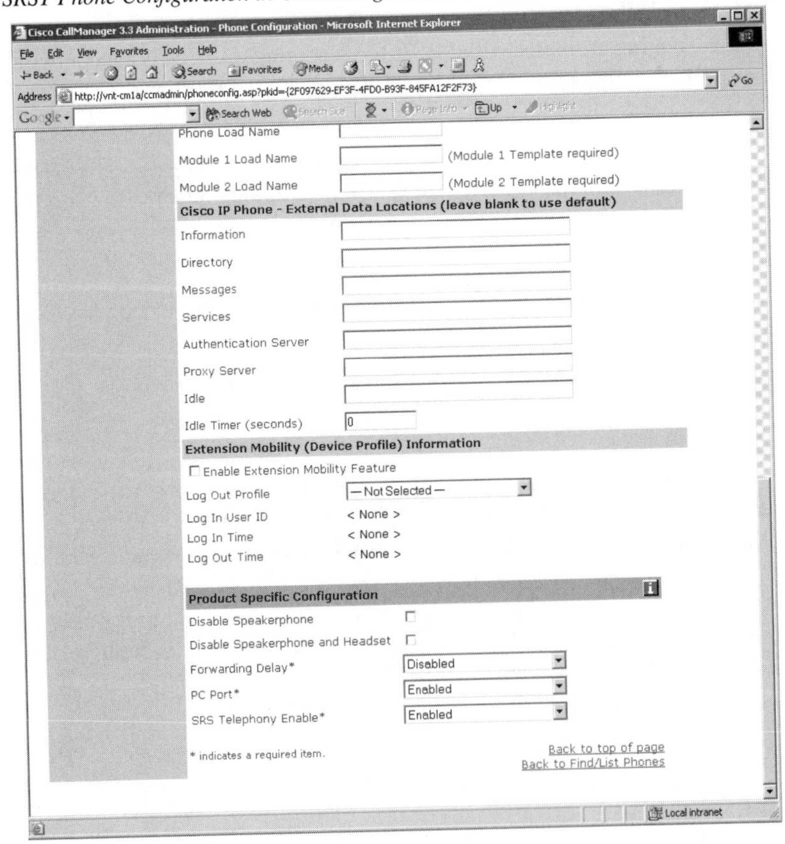

Ensure that the IP Phone configuration indicates that SRST is enabled. In CallManager 3.3(1) and later this configuration is on the device pool level and can be verified by selecting **System > Device Pool** in CallManager Administration. Figure 15-3 shows a device pool with the SRST Reference configured for **Use Default Gateway**.

Figure 15-3 *SRST Device Pool Configuration in CallManager Administration as of Release 3.3(1)*

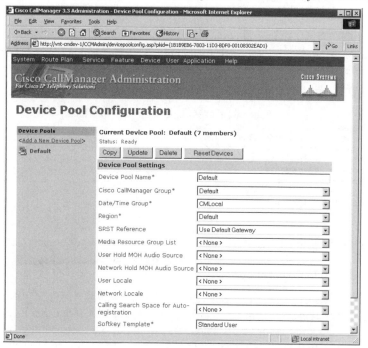

The setting to enable or disable SRST and the SRST reference are passed to the IP Phone via TFTP. You can check to see if the IP Phone's .cnf.xml file has the correct parameter listed. Look in the C:\Program Files\Cisco\TFTPPath directory on the TFTP server for a file named SEP*MACAddress*.cnf.xml, where *MACAddress* is the MAC address of the IP Phone you have enabled for SRST.

In CallManager 3.3(1) and later you must disable caching of configuration files for CallManager to write these files to disk. To disable caching of configuration files, go to the service parameters configuration for the TFTP service in CallManager Administration (**Service > Service Parameters >** *select a server* **> Cisco TFTP**), and then click the **Advanced** button. Set the parameter **Enable Caching of Configuration Files** to **False** and click **Update**. Within a few minutes, the TFTP server will generate the configuration files in the C:\Program Files\Cisco\TFTPPath directory on the TFTP server.

NOTE   You should disable file caching only for troubleshooting purposes. Always re-enable caching to improve TFTP server performance.

Once you open the configuration file, you should see a string similar to this in the file on a CallManager prior to CallManager 3.3(1):

```
<vendorConfig>
<disableSpeaker>false</disableSpeaker>
  <disableSpeakerAndHeadset>false</disableSpeakerAndHeadset>
  <forwardingDelay>1</forwardingDelay>
  <pcPort>0</pcPort><SRSTEnable>1</SRSTEnable></vendorConfig>
```

Notice that the setting for SRSTEnable is **1**. This means that SRST is enabled. If SRST is disabled, the SRSTEnable flag is set to 0.

If you are running CallManager 3.3(1) and later, the file will look similar to the following:

```
<srstInfo  uuid= "{C80CAFE0-AF65-43D6-A1F1-435AD998BD26}">
<name>Use Default Gateway</name>
<srstOption>Use Default Gateway</srstOption>
<userModifiable>false</userModifiable>
<ipAddr1></ipAddr1>
<port1>2000</port1>
<ipAddr2></ipAddr2>
<port2>2000</port2>
<ipAddr3></ipAddr3>
<port3>2000</port3>
</srstInfo>
```

Notice the setting for srstOption is **Use Default Gateway**. This setting reflects the configuration setting and the list of IP addresses if configured to use a specific SRST Reference as opposed to the default gateway.

If the Phone Configuration or Device Pool Configuration page in CallManager Administration shows one setting (for example, Enabled, Use Default Gateway, and so on) but the .cnf.xml file for that IP Phone shows that SRST is disabled, you might have a problem with database change notifications to the TFTP server. Stop and restart the Cisco TFTP service on the CallManager node acting as your TFTP server. This should rebuild all the TFTP files with the latest data.

IP Phone Registration

After you have verified your configuration, SRST should be functioning. In the event of a WAN outage, the IP Phones at the remote site lose IP connectivity to their CallManager(s). As a last resort, an SRST-enabled IP Phone attempts to register with its default gateway or SRST Reference. The phone assumes that its default gateway or SRST Reference is an SRST-capable router, not a CallManager. The signaling involved in registering to an SRST router is similar to when an IP Phone registers with CallManager; however, some additional messaging occurs that allows the SRST router to learn about the dial plan. The important thing to remember is that the IP Phone decides when to register with the SRST router and when to register with CallManager.

In CallManager Administration, you define IP Phones and assign lines and speed dials to the phone. SRST has no mechanism for you to configure lines or speed dials. SRST works by learning about the dial plan from the IP Phones as they register. Therefore, for SRST to work, an IP Phone must be registered with a CallManager before it attempts to register with the SRST gateway.

For example, assume you have configured an IP Phone in CallManager with two lines, 1000 and 2000, and a speed dial. When the IP Phone loses communication with the CallManager server(s), it attempts to register with the default gateway or SRST Reference. If the default gateway is an SRST router, the IP Phone registers and tells the SRST router that it has extension 1000 on line 1, extension 2000 on line 2, and a speed dial on button 3.

When the SRST router learns about the phone numbers, it adds them to the dial plan on the router. You can enable debugs to see the entire registration process. Enable the command **debug ephone register**. Example 15-1 shows the resulting output.

Example 15-1 **debug ephone register** *Output*

```
Router#debug ephone register
May 11 14:52:12.175:
Skinny StationAlarmMessage on socket [3] 14.84.41.15
May 11 14:52:12.175: severityInformational p1=2304 [0x900] p2=254366734 [0xF29540E]
May 11 14:52:12.175: Name=SEP0008A3FD3B09 Load=3.1(1.2) Last=CM-ICMP-Unreach
```

NOTE   Most **debug ephone** commands can be followed by the MAC address of the device you want to debug. This lets you debug a single IP Phone even under heavy call volume because the amount of debugging is restricted to the phone you specify. You can enter the **debug ephone** commands multiple times with different MAC addresses, and you see the debugs for all the MAC addresses. You can use **no debug ephone** to turn off debugging for a particular MAC address.

The first message in Example 15-1 shows you the **StationAlarmMessage** from the IP Phone, indicating to the router that there is a problem. You then see the name of the device sending the message, the load running on the IP Phone, and the reason for the message. In this case, the IP Phone is registering with the SRST gateway because it received an Internet Control Message Protocol (ICMP) unreachable message from somewhere in the network when attempting to contact CallManager. This is likely caused by a WAN link failure, leading to the router losing its route to CallManager.

Note that the message in Example 15-1 was received on **socket [3]**. You see [3] in front of most messages, indicating which socket the message refers to. This allows you to distinguish between different IP Phones if multiple phones are registering at the same time.

Example 15-2 shows the IP Phone register with the SRST router with the StationRegisterMessage.

Example 15-2 *Continuation of the* **debug ephone register** *Command*

```
May 11 14:52:12.175: ephone-(-1)[3] StationRegisterMessage (0/0/24) from
  14.84.41.15
May 11 14:52:12.175: ephone-(-1)[3] Register StationIdentifier DeviceName
  SEP0008A3FD3B09
May 11 14:52:12.175: ephone-(-1)[3] StationIdentifier Instance 1    deviceType 7
May 11 14:52:12.175: ephone-(-1) Allow any Skinny Server IP address 14.84.41.1
```

Next, the SRST router associates this IP Phone with an ephone identifier, as shown in Example 15-3. Notice that the beginning of the debug lines changes from **ephone-(-1)[3]**, as in Example 15-2, to **ephone-1[3]**, as in Example 15-3.

Example 15-3 *Continuation of the* **debug ephone register** *Command*

```
May 11 14:52:12.175: ephone-1[3]:new phone associate OK on socket [3]
May 11 14:52:12.175: Skinny Local IP address = 14.84.41.1 on port 2000

May 11 14:52:12.175: Skinny Phone IP address = 14.84.41.15 52845
May 11 14:52:12.175: ephone-1[3]:RegisterAck sent to ephone 3: keepalive period 30
```

Next, the IP Phone and SRST router exchange capabilities, as shown in Example 15-4.

Example 15-4 *Continuation of the* **debug ephone register** *Command*

```
May 11 14:52:12.175: ephone-1[3]:CapabilitiesReq sent
May 11 14:52:12.175: ephone-1[3]:Skinny IP port 28110 set for socket [3]
May 11 14:52:12.427: ephone-1[3]:CapabilitiesRes received
May 11 14:52:12.427: ephone-1[3]:Caps list
G711Ulaw64k
May 11 14:52:12.427: G711Alaw64k
May 11 14:52:12.427: G729
May 11 14:52:12.427: G729AnnexA
May 11 14:52:12.427: G729AnnexB
May 11 14:52:12.427: G729AnnexAwAnnexB
May 11 14:52:12.427: Unrecognized Media Type 25
May 11 14:52:12.427:
```

Now the SRST router needs to get information about the number of lines and speed dials on the IP Phone, as well as the directory numbers assigned to those lines. Notice in Example 15-5 that this IP Phone has two lines and two speed dials configured.

Example 15-5 *Continuation of the* **debug ephone register** *Command*

```
May 11 14:52:12.427: ephone-1[3]:ButtonTemplateReqMessage
May 11 14:52:12.427: ephone-1[3]:ButtonTemplateReq requesting fallback info
May 11 14:52:12.679: ephone-1[3]:Malloc OK for ServerResMessage
May 11 14:52:12.931: ephone-1[3]:Limiting number of line buttons on 7960 from 6 to 20
May 11 14:52:14.443: ephone-1[3]:ButtonTemplateReqMessage
May 11 14:52:14.443: ephone-1[3]:Setting 2 lines 2 speed-dials on phone (max_line 6)
May 11 14:52:14.443: ephone-1[3]:First Speed Dial Button location is 3 (0)
```

Example 15-5 *Continuation of the* **debug ephone register** *Command (Continued)*

```
May 11 14:52:14.443: ephone-1[3]:Configured 4 speed dial buttons
May 11 14:52:14.443: ephone-1[3]:ButtonTemplate lines=2 speed=2 buttons=6 offset=0
May 11 14:52:14.695: ephone-1[3]:StationSoftKeyTemplateReqMessage
May 11 14:52:14.695: ephone-1[3]:StationSoftKeyTemplateResMessage
May 11 14:52:14.947: ephone-1[3]:StationSoftKeySetReqMessage
May 11 14:52:14.947: ephone-1[3]:StationSoftKeySetResMessage
```

Example 15-6 shows the SRST router receiving the information about the two lines. Line 1 on the IP Phone has extension 10033, and line 2 has extension 10040.

Example 15-6 *Continuation of the* **debug ephone register** *Command*

```
May 11 14:52:15.199: ephone-1[3]:StationLineStatReqMessage from ephone line 2
May 11 14:52:15.199: ephone-1[3]:StationLineStatReqMessage ephone line 2 DN 2 =
  10040
May 11 14:52:15.199: ephone-1[3]:StationLineStatResMessage sent to ephone (1 of 2)
May 11 14:52:15.451: ephone-1[3]:StationLineStatReqMessage from ephone line 1
May 11 14:52:15.451: ephone-1[3]:StationLineStatReqMessage ephone line 1 DN 1 =
  10033
May 11 14:52:15.451: ephone-1[3]:StationLineStatResMessage sent to ephone (2 of 2)
May 11 14:52:15.451: ephone-1[3]:SkinnyCompleteRegistration
```

As Example 15-7 confirms, now the IP Phone informs the SRST router of the speed dials that are configured.

Example 15-7 *Continuation of the* **debug ephone register** *Command*

```
May 11 14:52:15.703: ephone-1[3]:StationSpeedDialStatReqMessage speed 4
May 11 14:52:15.703: ephone-1[3]:No speed-dial set 4
May 11 14:52:15.703: ephone-1[3]:StationSpeedDialStatMessage sent
May 11 14:52:15.955: ephone-1[3]:StationSpeedDialStatReqMessage speed 3
May 11 14:52:15.955: ephone-1[3]:No speed-dial set 3
May 11 14:52:15.955: ephone-1[3]:StationSpeedDialStatMessage sent
May 11 14:52:16.207: ephone-1[3]:StationSpeedDialStatReqMessage speed 2
May 11 14:52:16.207: ephone-1[3]:Speed Dial 2: 10030
May 11 14:52:16.207: ephone-1[3]:StationSpeedDialStatMessage sent
May 11 14:52:16.459: ephone-1[3]:StationSpeedDialStatReqMessage speed 1
May 11 14:52:16.459: ephone-1[3]:Speed Dial 1: 10032
May 11 14:52:16.459: ephone-1[3]:StationSpeedDialStatMessage sent
May 11 14:52:16.711: ephone-1[3]:StationServerReqMessage from ephone
May 11 14:52:16.711: ephone-1[3]:Free OK for ServerResMessage
May 11 14:52:16.711: Using Server List from phone
May 11 14:52:16.711: CM1 14.84.211.10
May 11 14:52:16.711: CM2 0.0.0.0
May 11 14:52:16.711: CM3 0.0.0.0
May 11 14:52:16.711: CM4 0.0.0.0
May 11 14:52:16.711: CM5 0.0.0.0
May 11 14:52:16.711: ephone-1[3]:StationServerResMessage sent to ephone
```

At this point, your IP Phone should be registered with the SRST router. To verify which IP Phones are currently registered and their current state, use the command **show ephone**. You should see something like the results shown in Example 15-8.

Example 15-8 show ephone *Output*

```
Router#show ephone
ephone-1 Mac:0008.A3FD.3B09 TCP socket:[3] activeLine:0 REGISTERED
mediaActive:0 offhook:0 ringing:0 reset:0 reset_sent:0 paging 0 debug:0
IP:14.84.41.15 53179 Telecaster 7960  keepalive 0 max_line 6
button 1: dn 3  number 10033  CM Fallback IDLE
button 2: dn 4  number 10040  CM Fallback IDLE
speed dial 1:10032 John Smith
speed dial 2:10030 Fred Flintstone


ephone-2 Mac:0008.E37F.970A TCP socket:[1] activeLine:0 REGISTERED
mediaActive:0 offhook:0 ringing:0 reset:0 reset_sent:0 paging 0 debug:0
IP:14.84.41.16 51261 Telecaster 7910  keepalive 1 max_line 2 dual-line
button 1: dn 1  number 10031  CM Fallback IDLE


ephone-3 Mac:0008.E31B.78EC TCP socket:[2] activeLine:0 REGISTERED
mediaActive:0 offhook:0 ringing:0 reset:0 reset_sent:0 paging 0 debug:0
IP:14.84.41.17 52291 Telecaster 7960  keepalive 0 max_line 6
button 1: dn 2  number 10034  CM Fallback IDLE
```

Notice that the output in Example 15-8 indicates the IP Phone's MAC address, the TCP socket number, the number of active lines, and whether the phone is registered. It also shows you the IP Phone's state, its model number, and a list of the buttons and the directory numbers assigned to them.

Also, each ephone is assigned a unique ephone ID, starting from 1 and going as high as the configured number of **max-ephone**. Example 15-8 shows information for ephone-1 through ephone-3.

A common reason for IP Phones not being able to register with the SRST router is that the router runs out of either ephones or ephone directory numbers (**ephone-dn**) to assign to a device. For example, if no more ephones are available, you see the results shown in Example 15-9.

Example 15-9 *Output of* **debug ephone register** *When No More ephones Are Available*

```
Router#debug ephone register
May 11 17:47:09.955:
Skinny StationAlarmMessage on socket [1] 14.84.41.16
May 11 17:47:09.955: severityInformational p1=2308 [0x904] p2=271143950
[0x1029540E]
May 11 17:47:09.955: Name=SEP0008E37F970A Load=3.1(1.2) Last=Initialized
May 11 17:47:09.955: ephone-(-1)[1] StationRegisterMessage (1/1/1) from 14.84.41.16
May 11 17:47:09.955: ephone-(-1)[1] Register StationIdentifier DeviceName
SEP0008E37F970A
```

Example 15-9 *Output of* **debug ephone register** *When No More ephones Are Available (Continued)*

```
May 11 17:47:09.955: ephone-(-1)[1] StationIdentifier Instance 1     deviceType 6
May 11 17:47:09.955: ephone-(-1) Allow any Skinny Server IP address 14.84.41.1
May 11 17:47:09.955: ephone Associate FAIL: max phone count 1 exceeded on socket [1]
May 11 17:47:09.955: Skinny register (phones=1/1/1) REJECT from IP 14.84.41.16
May 11 17:47:10.207: CLOSED Skinny socket 1 at hdr errno=0 (2 active)
error code 0
```

The debug in Example 15-9 tells you that the number of ephones has been exceeded, and the registration is being rejected. You will see this repeatedly because the IP Phone continues to retry.

The result is different if not enough ephone directory numbers (**ephone-dn**) are available. In this case, the IP Phone registers; however, it does not get all of the lines that were available when the phone was previously registered to a CallManager. In this case, you see the following in the output of **debug ephone register**:

```
.May 11 17:51:30.949: current dn 3 exceeds the max-dn 2
```

In this case, the router in question is configured for a maximum of two directory numbers, and this IP Phone is trying to add a third line. This can occur if you have several IP Phones with a large number of lines. To ensure that enough ephone directory numbers are available for all the IP Phones, you can limit the number of lines that a particular phone can register with the SRST router by using the configuration commands shown in Example 15-10.

Example 15-10 *Configuring SRST Directory Number Registration Limits*

```
call-manager-fallback
  limit-dn 7910 1
  limit-dn 7935 1
  limit-dn 7940 2
  limit-dn 7960 2
```

As you can see, the limits can be configured on a per-IP Phone–type basis, so you can allow 7960s to have up to four lines but 7940s only one line, for example.

If you encounter registration problems, you might need to get a sniffer trace of the registration process to see where it is failing. There might be an IP connectivity problem between the SRST router and the IP Phone trying to register. A simple test is to ensure that the SRST router can ping the IP address of the IP that won't register. For further information on troubleshooting device registration, refer to Chapter 4, "Skinny Client Registration."

SRST Dial Plan

When an ephone-dn is created, it gets assigned to a virtual voice port on the SRST router. Lines on an IP Phone in SRST mode are treated very similarly to Foreign Exchange Station (FXS) ports. A set of virtual dial peers is created for these ports to allow them to coexist with any other dial peers configured on the gateway.

To view the ephone-dn configuration and the virtual dial peers, use the command **show ephone-dn**. You can get a summarized version of the same information using the command **show ephone-dn summary**, as shown in Example 15-11.

Example 15-11 *Displaying the **ephone-dn** Configuration and the Virtual Dial Peers*

```
Router#show ephone-dn summary
PORT      DN STATE    MWI_STATE     CODEC     VAD VTSP STATE              VPM STATE
========  ==========  ============  ========  === ====================   =========
50/0/1    IDLE        NONE          -         - -                        EFXS_ONHOOK
50/0/2    IDLE        NONE          -         - -                        EFXS_ONHOOK
50/0/3    IDLE        NONE          -         - -                        EFXS_ONHOOK
50/0/4    IDLE        NONE          -         - -                        EFXS_ONHOOK
50/0/5    INVALID     NONE          -         - -                        EFXS_INIT
50/0/6    INVALID     NONE          -         - -                        EFXS_INIT
50/0/7    INVALID     NONE          -         - -                        EFXS_INIT
50/0/8    INVALID     NONE          -         - -                        EFXS_INIT
50/0/9    INVALID     NONE          -         - -                        EFXS_INIT
50/0/10   INVALID     NONE          -         - -                        EFXS_INIT
```

Currently, four voice ports, 50/0/1 through 50/0/4, are created and in the IDLE state. The remainder are unused. To look at the phone numbers associated with the ephone directory numbers (**ephone-dn**), use the command **show dial-peer voice summary**, as demonstrated in Example 15-12.

Example 15-12 *Displaying the **ephone-dn** Configuration and the Virtual Dial Peers*

```
Router#show dial-peer voice summary
dial-peer hunt 0
              AD                                      PRE PASS
TAG     TYPE  MIN  OPER PREFIX   DEST-PATTERN         FER THRU SESS-TARGET    PORT
20001   pots  up   up            10031                0                       50/0/1
20002   pots  up   up            10034                0                       50/0/2
20003   pots  up   up            10033                0                       50/0/3
20004   pots  up   up            10040                0                       50/0/4
20005   pots  up   down                               0                       50/0/5
20006   pots  up   down                               0                       50/0/6
20007   pots  up   down                               0                       50/0/7
20008   pots  up   down                               0                       50/0/8
20009   pots  up   down                               0                       50/0/9
20010   pots  up   down                               0                       50/0/10
```

These temporary dial peers are no different from any of the other dial peers discussed in Chapter 6, "Voice Gateways," other than the fact that they exist only while the IP Phone is registered with the SRST router. This means that all the dial peer matching rules discussed in Chapter 6 apply here.

Because these temporary dial peers coexist with other dial peers on the system, you must ensure that they do not conflict with each other. For example, in Example 15-12, one of the IP Phones has extension 10031. If another dial peer has a destination pattern of 10031 configured, it might interfere with the operation of the SRST IP Phone that has extension 10031.

Debugging Call Control in SRST Mode

When IP Phones are in fallback mode, registered to an SRST router, normal CCM traces are no longer available. However, Cisco IOS Software provides similar debugging facilities that allow you to track the operation of the IP Phones while in fallback mode.

As mentioned earlier, each IP Phone registered to an SRST router is assigned an ephone ID and a TCP socket number. Each of these represents unique identifiers that can be used to correlate a particular device to a line of debug output. Use the ephone identifier and/or TCP socket number the same way you would use a TCP handle when looking through a CCM trace.

The first command that gives you basic call setup information is **debug ephone state**. You can also enable the debug for just a particular IP Phone if you are interested in seeing debugs for a single IP Phone as opposed to all the IP Phones. To enable the debug for a particular IP Phone, use **debug ephone state mac-address** *mac address* where *mac address* is the MAC address in dotted hexadecimal notation. For example, to view the debug for the IP Phone with MAC address 00D001234567 you must enter **debug ephone state mac-address 00d0.0123.4567**. Examples 15-13 through 15-27 examine a call between two IP Phones registered to an SRST router.

Example 15-13 shows the output from **debug ephone state**, which indicates that ephone-3 goes off-hook on DN 2.

Example 15-13 *Output of* **debug ephone state**

```
Router#debug ephone state
.May 12 14:12:22.696: ephone-3[2]:OFFHOOK
.May 12 14:12:22.696: ephone-3[2]:SIEZE on activeline 0
.May 12 14:12:22.696: ephone-3[2]:SetCallState line 1 DN 2 ref 17 TsOffHook
.May 12 14:12:22.696: DN 2 Voice_Mode
```

If you look at the output from **show ephone** in Example 15-14, you can see ephone-3's characteristics.

Example 15-14 *Output of* **show ephone** *Displaying the Characteristics of ephone-3*

```
Router#show ephone
ephone-3 Mac:0008.E31B.78EC TCP socket:[2] activeLine:0 REGISTERED
mediaActive:0 offhook:0 ringing:0 reset:0 reset_sent:0 paging 0 debug:1
IP:14.84.41.17 52962 Telecaster 7960  keepalive 2439 max_line 6
button 1: dn 2  number 10034  CM Fallback IDLE
```

You can also see that DN 2 is extension 10034. Example 15-15 continues with the output of **debug ephone state** from Example 15-13. In the continued output, you see a call from DN 2 to DN 3. You can also see ringback applied to DN 2 and ringing applied to DN 3.

Example 15-15 *Continuation of the* **debug ephone state** *Output*

```
.May 12 14:12:30.760: ephone-3[2]:Skinny-to-Skinny call DN 2 to DN 3 instance 1
.May 12 14:12:30.760: ephone-3[2]:SetCallState line 1 DN 2 ref 17 TsRingOut
.May 12 14:12:30.760: ephone-3[2]:Call Info DN 2 line 1 ref 17 called 10033 calling
   10034
            origcalled  calltype 2
.May 12 14:12:30.760: ephone-3[2]: 10034 calling
.May 12 14:12:30.760: ephone-3[2]: 10033
.May 12 14:12:30.760: ephone-1[4]:SetCallState line 1 DN 3 ref 18 TsRingIn
.May 12 14:12:30.760: ephone-1[4]:Call Info DN 3 line 1 ref 18 called 10033 calling
   10034
            origcalled  calltype 1
.May 12 14:12:30.760: ephone-1[4]: 10034 calling
.May 12 14:12:30.760: ephone-1[4]: 10033
.May 12 14:12:30.760: ephone-1[4]:Ringer Inside Ring On
```

Notice that the called IP Phone is extension 10033, which corresponds to DN 3. Also notice that the called IP Phone has an ephone identifier of ephone-1. At this point, ephone-3 is hearing ringback, and ephone-1 is ringing.

Example 15-16 shows where ephone-3 answers the IP Phone.

Example 15-16 *Continuation of the* **debug ephone state** *Output*

```
.May 12 14:12:37.312: ephone-1[4]:OFFHOOK
.May 12 14:12:37.312: ephone-1[4]:Ringer Off
.May 12 14:12:37.312: ephone-1[4]:ANSWER call
.May 12 14:12:37.312: ephone-1[4]:Answer Incoming call from ephone-(3) DN 2
.May 12 14:12:37.312: ephone-1[4]:SetCallState line 1 DN 3 ref 18 TsConnected
.May 12 14:12:37.312: ephone-3[2]:SetCallState line 1 DN 2 ref 17 TsConnected
```

Next, the audio path is opened between the two IP Phones using G.711 μ-law as the codec. The IP Phones send back an open receive channel acknowledgment, and the SRST router tells each IP Phone to start media transmission to the other phone. Example 15-17 shows this series of transactions.

Example 15-17 *Continuation of the* **debug ephone state** *Output*

```
.May 12 14:12:37.312: ephone-3[2]:OpenReceive DN 2 codec 4:G711Ulaw64k
   duration 20 ms bytes 160
.May 12 14:12:37.312: ephone-1[4]:OpenReceive DN 3 codec 4:G711Ulaw64k
   duration 20 ms bytes 160
.May 12 14:12:37.312: DN 2 End Voice_Mode
.May 12 14:12:37.312: DN 2 Voice_Mode
.May 12 14:12:37.312: DN 3 Voice_Mode
.May 12 14:12:37.564: ephone-3[2]:OpenReceiveChannelAck:IP 14.84.41.17, port=23656,
                 dn_index=2, dn=2
.May 12 14:12:37.564: ephone-1[4]:StartMedia 14.84.41.17 port=23656
.May 12 14:12:37.564: DN 2 codec 4:G711Ulaw64k duration 20 ms bytes 160
.May 12 14:12:37.564: ephone-1[4]:OpenReceiveChannelAck:IP 14.84.41.15, port=23054,
                 dn_index=3, dn=3
.May 12 14:12:37.564: ephone-3[2]:StartMedia 14.84.41.15 port=23054
.May 12 14:12:37.564: DN 2 codec 4:G711Ulaw64k duration 20 ms bytes 160
```

Now both IP Phones are engaged in an active call. If you enter **show ephone** while the call is active, the output looks like Example 15-18.

Example 15-18 *Output of* **show ephone** *During an Active Call*

```
Router#show ephone
ephone-1 Mac:0008.A3FD.3B09 TCP socket:[4] activeLine:1 REGISTERED
mediaActive:1 offhook:1 ringing:0 reset:0 reset_sent:0 paging 0 debug:1
IP:14.84.41.15 52490 Telecaster 7960  keepalive 59 max_line 6
button 1: dn 3  number 10033  CM Fallback CONNECTED
button 2: dn 4  number 10040  CM Fallback IDLE
speed dial 1:10032 John Smith
speed dial 2:10030 Fred Flintstone
Active Call on DN 3:10033 14.84.41.15 23054 to 14.84.41.17 23656 via 14.84.41.15
G711Ulaw64k  160 bytes no vad
Tx Pkts 559 bytes 96148 Rx Pkts 748 bytes 128656 Lost 0
Jitter 0 Latency 0

ephone-3 Mac:0008.E31B.78EC TCP socket:[2] activeLine:1 REGISTERED
mediaActive:1 offhook:1 ringing:0 reset:0 reset_sent:0 paging 0 debug:1
IP:14.84.41.17 52962 Telecaster 7960  keepalive 2461 max_line 6
button 1: dn 2  number 10034  CM Fallback CONNECTED
Active Call on DN 2:10034 14.84.41.17 23656 to 14.84.41.15 23054 via 14.84.41.17
G711Ulaw64k  160 bytes no vad
Tx Pkts 748 bytes 128656 Rx Pkts 559 bytes 96148 Lost 0
Jitter 0 Latency 0
```

You might be wondering how the SRST router knows information about transmit and receive packets if the RTP stream is going directly between the two IP Phones and is not traversing the SRST router. This works because the SRST router polls each IP Phone every

5 seconds for its statistics. If you enable **debug ephone statistics**, you can see the polling and results every 5 seconds, as demonstrated in Example 15-19.

Example 15-19 *Output of* **debug ephone statistics**

```
Router#debug ephone statistics
.May 12 14:12:56.547: ephone-1[4]:GetCallStats line 1 ref 18 DN 3: 10033
.May 12 14:12:56.547: ephone-3[2]:GetCallStats line 1 ref 17 DN 2: 10034
.May 12 14:12:56.799: ephone-3[2]:Call Stats for line 1 DN 2 10034 ref 17
.May 12 14:12:56.799: ephone-3[2]:TX Pkts 20001 bytes 3440172
  RX Pkts 19812 bytes 3407664
.May 12 14:12:56.799: ephone-3[2]:Pkts lost 0 jitter 0 latency 0
.May 12 14:12:56.799: ephone-3[2]:Src 14.84.41.17 23656
  Dst 14.84.41.15 23054 bytes 160 vad 0 G711Ulaw64k
.May 12 14:12:56.799: ephone-1[4]:Call Stats for line 1 DN 3 10033 ref 18
.May 12 14:12:56.799: ephone-1[4]:TX Pkts 19812 bytes 3407664
  RX Pkts 20001 bytes 3440172
.May 12 14:12:56.799: ephone-1[4]:Pkts lost 0 jitter 0 latency 0
.May 12 14:12:56.799: ephone-1[4]:Src 14.84.41.15 23054
  Dst 14.84.41.17 23656 bytes 160 vad 0 G711Ulaw64k
```

Example 15-20 shows ephone-1 going on-hook, which tears down the call.

Example 15-20 *Continuation of the* **debug ephone state** *Output*

```
.May 12 14:13:01.513: ephone-1[4]:ONHOOK
.May 12 14:13:01.513: ephone-3[2]:CloseReceive
.May 12 14:13:01.513: ephone-3[2]:StopMedia
.May 12 14:13:01.513: ephone-1[4]:call clean up this DN 3 was called by other DN 2
.May 12 14:13:01.513: this ephone-1 other ephone-(3) other DN state CONNECTED
.May 12 14:13:01.513: ephone-1[4]:CloseReceive
.May 12 14:13:01.513: ephone-1[4]:StopMedia
.May 12 14:13:01.513: DN 3 End Voice_Mode
.May 12 14:13:01.513: ephone-1[4]:SetCallState line 1 DN 3 ref 18 TsOnHook
.May 12 14:13:01.513: ephone-1[4]:SpeakerPhoneOnHook
.May 12 14:13:01.513: DN 2 End Voice_Mode
.May 12 14:13:01.513: ephone-3[2]:SetCallState line 1 DN 2 ref 17 TsOnHook
.May 12 14:13:01.513: ephone-3[2]:SpeakerPhoneOnHook
.May 12 14:13:01.513: ephone-1[4]:SpeakerPhoneOnHook
.May 12 14:13:01.613: DN 3 Voice_Mode
.May 12 14:13:01.613: DN 3 End Voice_Mode
.May 12 14:13:01.625: SkinnyReportDnState DN 2 ONHOOK
```

The output from **debug ephone state** is usually detailed enough for most troubleshooting; however, the output is not as detailed as the output of a CCM trace where you see every Skinny message back and forth between the IP Phone and CallManager. For this level of detail, enable **debug ephone detail** on the SRST router.

Example 15-21 shows output of the same call as before, but with **debug ephone detail** enabled. First you see ephone-3 press the **NewCall** soft key, which causes DN 2 to go off-hook. For readability purposes, some of the redundant messages have been removed from the trace; however, you might see some additional SkinnyGetCallState messages when you run this on a router.

Example 15-21 *Output of* **debug ephone detail**

```
Router#debug ephone detail
.May 12 14:46:27.063: ephone-3[2]:SoftKeyEventMessage event 2 line 0 callref 0
.May 12 14:46:27.063: ephone-3[2]:SK NEWCALL line 0 ref 0
.May 12 14:46:27.063: SkinnyGetCallState for DN 2 IDLE
.May 12 14:46:27.063: called DN -1, calling DN -1 phone -1 s2s:0
.May 12 14:46:27.063: ephone-3[2]:OFFHOOK
.May 12 14:46:27.063: ephone-3[2]:SIEZE on activeline 0
.May 12 14:46:27.063: ephone-3[2]:Sieze auto select line 1
.May 12 14:46:27.063: ephone-3[2]:UpdateCallState DN 2 state 2 calleddn -1
.May 12 14:46:27.063: ephone-3[2]:Binding ephone-3 to DN 2 s2s:0
.May 12 14:46:27.063: Assign Call Ref 21 to DN 2
.May 12 14:46:27.063: Skinny Call State change for DN 2 SIEZE
.May 12 14:46:27.063: ephone-(3) DN 2 calledDn -1 callingDn -1 0.0.0.0 port=0
.May 12 14:46:27.063: SkinnyUpdateCstate DN 2 state 1
.May 12 14:46:27.063: ephone-3[2]:SetCallState line 1 DN 2 ref 21 TsOffHook
.May 12 14:46:27.063: ephone-3[2]:ClearCallPrompt line 1 ref 21
.May 12 14:46:27.063: ephone-3[2]:SelectPhoneSoftKeys set 4 for line 1 ref 21
.May 12 14:46:27.063: SkinnyGetCallState for DN 2 SIEZE
.May 12 14:46:27.063: called DN -1, calling DN -1 phone 3 s2s:0
.May 12 14:46:27.063: ephone-3[2]:SetLineLamp 1 to ON
.May 12 14:46:27.063: ephone-3[2]:SpeakerPhoneOffHook mute 0
.May 12 14:46:27.067: SetDnCodec DN 2 codec 4:G711Ulaw64k  vad 250 size 160
.May 12 14:46:27.067: DN 2 Voice_Mode
.May 12 14:46:27.067: dn_tone_control DN=2 tonetype=0:DtSilence onoff=0 pid=115
.May 12 14:46:27.067: ephone-3[2]:Tone Off ignored - already sent
.May 12 14:46:27.067: dn_tone_control DN=2 tonetype=33:DtInsideDialTone onoff=1
   pid=115
.May 12 14:46:27.067: Skinny StartTone 33 sent on  ephone socket [2]
   DtInsideDialTone
```

Now that ephone-3 is playing a dial tone, the user at ephone-3 begins dialing, as demonstrated in Example 15-22.

Example 15-22 *Continuation of the* **debug ephone detail** *Output*

```
.May 12 14:46:34.119: ephone-3[2]:KeypadButtonMessage 1
.May 12 14:46:34.119: ephone-3[2]:Store ReDial digit: 1
.May 12 14:46:34.119: ephone-3[2]:SkinnyTryCall to 1 instance 1 start at 0
.May 12 14:46:34.119: dn_tone_control DN=2 tonetype=0:DtSilence onoff=0 pid=115
.May 12 14:46:34.119: ephone-3[2]:StopTone sent to ephone
.May 12 14:46:34.875: ephone-3[2]:KeypadButtonMessage 0
.May 12 14:46:34.875: ephone-3[2]:Store ReDial digit: 10
.May 12 14:46:34.875: ephone-3[2]:SkinnyTryCall to 10 instance 1 start at 0
.May 12 14:46:34.875: dn_tone_control DN=2 tonetype=0:DtSilence onoff=0 pid=115
.May 12 14:46:34.875: ephone-3[2]:Tone Off ignored - already sent
.May 12 14:46:35.883: ephone-3[2]:KeypadButtonMessage 0
.May 12 14:46:35.883: ephone-3[2]:Store ReDial digit: 100
.May 12 14:46:35.883: ephone-3[2]:SkinnyTryCall to 100 instance 1 start at 0
```

continues

Example 15-22 *Continuation of the* **debug ephone detail** *Output (Continued)*

```
.May 12 14:46:35.883: dn_tone_control DN=2 tonetype=0:DtSilence onoff=0 pid=115
.May 12 14:46:35.883: ephone-3[2]:Tone Off ignored - already sent
.May 12 14:46:38.151: ephone-3[2]:KeypadButtonMessage 3
.May 12 14:46:38.151: ephone-3[2]:Store ReDial digit: 1003
.May 12 14:46:38.151: ephone-3[2]:SkinnyTryCall to 1003 instance 1 start at 0
.May 12 14:46:38.151: dn_tone_control DN=2 tonetype=0:DtSilence onoff=0 pid=115
.May 12 14:46:38.151: ephone-3[2]:Tone Off ignored - already sent
.May 12 14:46:40.167: ephone-3[2]:KeypadButtonMessage 3
.May 12 14:46:40.167: ephone-3[2]:Store ReDial digit: 10033
```

Example 15-23 shows the message SkinnyTryCall make a match for DN 3. This causes the SRST router to tell ephone-3 to play a ringback tone.

Example 15-23 *Continuation of the* **debug ephone detail** *Output*

```
.May 12 14:46:40.167: ephone-3[2]:SkinnyTryCall to 10033 instance 1 start at 0
.May 12 14:46:40.167: ephone-3[2]:SkinnyTryCall to 10033 instance 1 match DN 3
.May 12 14:46:40.167: SkinnyGetCallState for DN 3 IDLE
.May 12 14:46:40.167: called DN -1, calling DN -1 phone -1 s2s:0
.May 12 14:46:40.167: ephone-3[2]:Skinny-to-Skinny call DN 2 to DN 3 instance 1
.May 12 14:46:40.167: ephone-3[2]:UpdateCallState DN 2 state 1 calleddn 3
.May 12 14:46:40.167: ephone-3[2]:Binding ephone-3 to DN 2 s2s:0
.May 12 14:46:40.167: Binding calledDn 3 to DN 2
.May 12 14:46:40.167: Skinny Call State change for DN 2 ALERTING
.May 12 14:46:40.167: ephone-(3) DN 2 calledDn 3 callingDn -1 0.0.0.0 port=0
.May 12 14:46:40.167: SkinnyUpdateCstate DN 2 state 3
.May 12 14:46:40.167: ephone-3[2]:SetCallState line 1 DN 2 ref 21 TsRingOut
.May 12 14:46:40.167: ephone-3[2]:CallPrompt line 1 ref 21: Ring Out
.May 12 14:46:40.167: ephone-3[2]:SelectPhoneSoftKeys set 8 for line 1 ref 21
.May 12 14:46:40.167: SkinnyGetCallState for DN 2 ALERTING
.May 12 14:46:40.167: called DN 3, calling DN -1 phone 3 s2s:0
.May 12 14:46:40.167: ephone-3[2]:SetLineLamp 1 to ON
.May 12 14:46:40.167: SetCallInfo calling dn 2 dn 2
calling [10034] called [10033]
.May 12 14:46:40.167: SetCallInfo DN 2 is not skinny-to-skinny
.May 12 14:46:40.167: ephone-3[2]:Call Info DN 2 line 1 ref 21 called 10033
   calling 10034
              origcalled  calltype 2
.May 12 14:46:40.167: ephone-3[2]: 10034 calling
.May 12 14:46:40.167: ephone-3[2]: 10033
.May 12 14:46:40.167: dn_tone_control DN=2 tonetype=0:DtSilence onoff=0 pid=115
.May 12 14:46:40.167: ephone-3[2]:Tone Off ignored - already sent
.May 12 14:46:40.171: SkinnyUpdateDnState by EFXS_PROCEEDING
   for DN 2 to state ALERTING
.May 12 14:46:40.171: ephone-3[2]:UpdateCallState DN 2 state 1 calleddn 3
.May 12 14:46:40.171: ephone-3[2]:Binding ephone-3 to DN 2 s2s:0
.May 12 14:46:40.171: Binding calledDn 3 to DN 2
.May 12 14:46:40.171: Skinny Call State change for DN 2 ALERTING
.May 12 14:46:40.171: ephone-(3) DN 2 calledDn 3 callingDn -1 0.0.0.0 port=0
.May 12 14:46:40.171: ephone-3[2]:SetLineLamp 1 to ON
.May 12 14:46:40.171: SetCallInfo calling dn 2 dn 3
```

Example 15-23 *Continuation of the* **debug ephone detail** *Output (Continued)*

```
calling [10034] called [10033] calling name 10034
.May 12 14:46:40.171: SetCallInfo DN 3 is not skinny-to-skinny
.May 12 14:46:40.171: Binding callingDn 2 to DN 3 at SetCallInfo
.May 12 14:46:40.171: Skinny-to-Skinny Call DN 2 to DN 3
.May 12 14:46:40.171: SkinnyUpdateDnState by EFXS_RING_GENERATE
  for DN 3 to state RINGING
.May 12 14:46:40.171: UpdateCallState DN 3 state 7 phone-ref -1 calleddn -1
.May 12 14:46:40.171: Assign Call Ref 22 to DN 3
```

Because this call is routed to ephone-1, the SRST router tells ephone-1 to ring and display the call information about the inbound call, as demonstrated in Example 15-24.

Example 15-24 *Continuation of the* **debug ephone detail** *Output*

```
.May 12 14:46:40.171: Skinny Call State change for DN 3 RINGING
.May 12 14:46:40.171: ephone-(-1) DN 3 calledDn -1 callingDn 2 0.0.0.0 port=0
incoming
.May 12 14:46:40.171: SkinnyUpdateCstate DN 3 state 4
.May 12 14:46:40.171: DN 3 ephone-1 state set to 4
.May 12 14:46:40.171: ephone-1[4]:SetCallState line 1 DN 3 ref 22 TsRingIn
.May 12 14:46:40.171: ephone-1[4]:CallPrompt line 1 ref 22: Ring In
.May 12 14:46:40.171: ephone-1[4]:SelectPhoneSoftKeys set 3 for line 1 ref 22
.May 12 14:46:40.171: ephone-1[4]:Set Defer Ring Timestamp 40175005 for line 2 DN 4
.May 12 14:46:40.171: SkinnyGetCallState for DN 3 RINGING
.May 12 14:46:40.171: called DN -1, calling DN 2 phone -1 incoming s2s:1
.May 12 14:46:40.171: ephone-1[4]:DisplayCallInfo incoming call
.May 12 14:46:40.171: ephone-1[4]:Call Info DN 3 line 1 ref 22 called 10033
  calling 10034
             origcalled  calltype 1
.May 12 14:46:40.171: ephone-1[4]: 10034 calling
.May 12 14:46:40.171: ephone-1[4]: 10033
.May 12 14:46:40.171: ephone-1[4]:Internal RINGING
.May 12 14:46:40.171: ephone-1[4]:Ringer Inside Ring On
.May 12 14:46:40.175: ephone-1[4]:SetLineLamp ignored for telecaster phones with 2
lines
.May 12 14:46:40.175: Check AUTO phone -1
.May 12 14:46:40.175: SetDnCodec DN 2 codec 4:G711Ulaw64k  vad 250 size 160
.May 12 14:46:40.175: dn_tone_control DN=2 tonetype=36:DtAlertingTone onoff=1
  pid=115
.May 12 14:46:40.175: Skinny StartTone 36 sent on  ephone socket [2]
  DtAlertingTone
```

At this point, ephone-1 is ringing, and ephone-3 is hearing ringback. Example 15-25 shows where ephone-1 goes off-hook to answer the call. This causes the ringer to be disabled.

Example 15-25 *Continuation of the* **debug ephone detail** *Output*

```
.May 12 14:46:52.264: ephone-1[4]:OFFHOOK
.May 12 14:46:52.264: ephone-1[4]:Disable Ringer line 1
.May 12 14:46:52.264: ephone-1[4]:STOP RINGING
.May 12 14:46:52.264: ephone-1[4]:Ringer Off
```

continues

Example 15-25 *Continuation of the* **debug ephone detail** *Output (Continued)*

```
.May 12 14:46:52.264: SkinnyGetCallState for DN 3 RINGING
.May 12 14:46:52.264: called DN -1, calling DN 2 phone -1 incoming s2s:1
.May 12 14:46:52.264: ephone-1[4]:Auto select answer line 1 dn -1
.May 12 14:46:52.264: ephone-1[4]:ANSWER call
.May 12 14:46:52.264: Calling DN 2 from Called DN 3 explicit
.May 12 14:46:52.264: ephone-3[2]:Calling ephone-3 is bound to Calling DN 2
.May 12 14:46:52.264: ephone-1[4]:Answer Incoming call from ephone-(3) DN 2
.May 12 14:46:52.264: ephone-1[4]:UpdateCallState DN 3 state 4 calleddn -1
.May 12 14:46:52.264: ephone-1[4]:Binding ephone-1 to DN 3 s2s:1
.May 12 14:46:52.264: Skinny Call State change for DN 3 CONNECTED
.May 12 14:46:52.264: ephone-(1) DN 3 calledDn -1 callingDn 2 0.0.0.0 port=0
   incoming
.May 12 14:46:52.264: SkinnyUpdateCstate DN 3 state 5
.May 12 14:46:52.264: ephone-1[4]:SetCallState line 1 DN 3 ref 22 TsConnected
.May 12 14:46:52.264: ephone-1[4]:CallPrompt line 1 ref 22: Connected
.May 12 14:46:52.264: ephone-1[4]:SelectPhoneSoftKeys set 1 for line 1 ref 22
.May 12 14:46:52.264: ephone-1[4]:SetLineLamp ignored for telecaster phones
   with 2 lines
.May 12 14:46:52.264: ephone-3[2]:UpdateCallState DN 2 state 4 calleddn 3
.May 12 14:46:52.264: ephone-3[2]:Binding ephone-3 to DN 2 s2s:1
.May 12 14:46:52.264: Binding calledDn 3 to DN 2
.May 12 14:46:52.264: Skinny Call State change for DN 2 CONNECTED
.May 12 14:46:52.264: ephone-(3) DN 2 calledDn 3 callingDn -1 0.0.0.0 port=0
.May 12 14:46:52.264: SkinnyUpdateCstate DN 2 state 5
.May 12 14:46:52.264: ephone-3[2]:SetCallState line 1 DN 2 ref 21 TsConnected
.May 12 14:46:52.264: ephone-3[2]:CallPrompt line 1 ref 21: Connected
.May 12 14:46:52.264: ephone-3[2]:SelectPhoneSoftKeys set 1 for line 1 ref 21
.May 12 14:46:52.264: ephone-3[2]:SetLineLamp 1 to ON
.May 12 14:46:52.268: ephone-3[2]:StopTone sent to ephone
```

Next the media streams are set up between the two IP Phones using G.711 μ-law as the codec, as demonstrated in Example 15-26.

Example 15-26 *Continuation of the* **debug ephone detail** *Output*

```
.May 12 14:46:52.268: ephone-3[2]:OpenReceive DN 2 codec 4:G711Ulaw64k
   duration 20 ms bytes 160
.May 12 14:46:52.268: ephone-1[4]:OpenReceive DN 3 codec 4:G711Ulaw64k
   duration 20 ms bytes 160
.May 12 14:46:52.268: dn_tone_control DN=3 tonetype=0:DtSilence onoff=0 pid=115
.May 12 14:46:52.268: ephone-1[4]:Tone Off ignored - already sent
.May 12 14:46:52.268: dn_support_g729 true DN 2 ephone-3
.May 12 14:46:52.268: dn_support_g723 false DN 2 ephone-3
.May 12 14:46:52.268: dn_support_g729 true DN 3 ephone-1
.May 12 14:46:52.268: dn_support_g723 false DN 3 ephone-1
.May 12 14:46:52.268: DN 2 End Voice_Mode
.May 12 14:46:52.268: SetDnCodec DN 2 codec 4:G711Ulaw64k  vad 0 size 160
.May 12 14:46:52.268: DN 2 Voice_Mode
.May 12 14:46:52.268: SetDnCodec DN 3 codec 4:G711Ulaw64k  vad 0 size 160
.May 12 14:46:52.268: DN 3 Voice_Mode
.May 12 14:46:52.268: SkinnyUpdateDnState by MSG_RX_VOICE_MODE
```

Example 15-26 *Continuation of the* **debug ephone detail** *Output (Continued)*

```
   for DN 3 to state CALL_START
.May 12 14:46:52.268: ephone-1[4]:UpdateCallState DN 3 state 12 calleddn -1
.May 12 14:46:52.268: ephone-1[4]:Binding ephone-1 to DN 3 s2s:1
.May 12 14:46:52.268: ephone-1[4]:Call Start ignored - mediaActive set
.May 12 14:46:52.272: SkinnyUpdateDnState by EFXS_OPEN_VOICE_PATH
   for DN 2 to state CALL_START
.May 12 14:46:52.272: ephone-3[2]:UpdateCallState DN 2 state 12 calleddn 3
.May 12 14:46:52.272: ephone-3[2]:Binding ephone-3 to DN 2 s2s:1
.May 12 14:46:52.272: Binding calledDn 3 to DN 2
.May 12 14:46:52.272: ephone-3[2]:Call Start ignored - mediaActive set
.May 12 14:46:52.272: dn_tone_control DN=2 tonetype=0:DtSilence onoff=0 pid=115
.May 12 14:46:52.272: ephone-3[2]:Tone Off ignored - already sent
.May 12 14:46:52.520: ephone-3[2]:Update Stats Total for DN 2
.May 12 14:46:52.520: ephone-1[4]:Update Stats Total for DN 3
.May 12 14:46:52.520: ephone-3[2]:OpenReceiveChannelAck:IP 14.84.41.17,
   port=20080, dn_index=2, dn=2
.May 12 14:46:52.520: ephone-3[2]:Outgoing calling DN 2 Far-ephone-1 called DN 3
.May 12 14:46:52.520: ephone-3[2]:s2s=1 DN:2
.May 12 14:46:52.520: ephone-1[4]:StartMedia 14.84.41.17 port=20080
.May 12 14:46:52.520: DN 2 codec 4:G711Ulaw64k duration 20 ms bytes 160
.May 12 14:46:52.520: ephone-1[4]:OpenReceiveChannelAck:IP 14.84.41.15,
   port=19476, dn_index=3, dn=3
.May 12 14:46:52.520: Calling DN 2 from Called DN 3 explicit
.May 12 14:46:52.520: ephone-3[2]:Calling ephone-3 is bound to Calling DN 2
.May 12 14:46:52.520: ephone-1[4]:Incoming called DN 3 Far-ephone-3 calling DN 2
.May 12 14:46:52.520: ephone-1[4]:s2s=1 DN:3
.May 12 14:46:52.520: ephone-3[2]:StartMedia 14.84.41.15 port=19476
.May 12 14:46:52.520: DN 2 codec 4:G711Ulaw64k duration 20 ms bytes 160
```

At this point, the two IP Phones are connected, and the RTP streams are open. Next, ephone-1 goes on-hook, and the call is cleared, as demonstrated in Example 15-27.

Example 15-27 *Continuation of the* **debug ephone detail** *Output*

```
.May 12 14:47:22.760: ephone-1[4]:ONHOOK
.May 12 14:47:22.760: Calling DN 2 from Called DN 3 explicit
.May 12 14:47:22.760: ephone-3[2]:Calling ephone-3 is bound to Calling DN 2
.May 12 14:47:22.760: ephone-3[2]:CloseReceive
.May 12 14:47:22.760: ephone-3[2]:StopMedia
.May 12 14:47:22.760: ephone-1[4]:call clean up this DN 3 was called by other DN 2
.May 12 14:47:22.760: this ephone-1 other ephone-(3) other DN state CONNECTED
.May 12 14:47:22.760: ephone-1[4]:CloseReceive
.May 12 14:47:22.760: ephone-1[4]:StopMedia
.May 12 14:47:22.760: UpdateCallState DN 3 state 0 phone-ref -1 calleddn -1
.May 12 14:47:22.760: DN 3 End Voice_Mode
.May 12 14:47:22.760: SetCallInfo calling dn -1 dn 3
calling [] called []
.May 12 14:47:22.760: SetCallInfo DN 3 is not skinny-to-skinny
.May 12 14:47:22.760: Skinny Call State change for DN 3 IDLE
.May 12 14:47:22.760: ephone-(-1) DN 3 calledDn -1 callingDn -1 0.0.0.0 port=0
.May 12 14:47:22.760: SkinnyUpdateCstate DN 3 state 2
```

continues

Example 15-27 *Continuation of the* **debug ephone detail** *Output (Continued)*

```
.May 12 14:47:22.760: ephone-1[4]:SetCallState line 1 DN 3 ref 22 TsOnHook
.May 12 14:47:22.760: ephone-1[4]:ClearCallPrompt line 1 ref 22
.May 12 14:47:22.760: ephone-1[4]:SelectPhoneSoftKeys set 0 for line 1 ref 22
.May 12 14:47:22.760: ephone-1[4]:Clean Up Speakerphone state
.May 12 14:47:22.760: ephone-1[4]:SpeakerPhoneOnHook
.May 12 14:47:22.760: ephone-1[4]:Clean up activeline 1
.May 12 14:47:22.760: ephone-1[4]:Tone Off ignored - already sent
.May 12 14:47:22.760: ephone-1[4]:SetLineLamp ignored for telecaster phones
  with 2 lines
.May 12 14:47:22.760: UnBinding ephone-1 from DN 3
.May 12 14:47:22.760: UnBinding calling DN 2 from DN 3
.May 12 14:47:22.760: UpdateCallState DN 2 state 0 phone-ref -1 calleddn -1
.May 12 14:47:22.760: DN 2 End Voice_Mode
.May 12 14:47:22.760: SetCallInfo calling dn -1 dn 2
calling [] called []
.May 12 14:47:22.760: SetCallInfo DN 2 is not skinny-to-skinny
.May 12 14:47:22.760: Skinny Call State change for DN 2 IDLE
.May 12 14:47:22.764: ephone-(-1) DN 2 calledDn -1 callingDn -1 0.0.0.0 port=0
.May 12 14:47:22.764: SkinnyUpdateCstate DN 2 state 2
.May 12 14:47:22.764: ephone-3[2]:SetCallState line 1 DN 2 ref 21 TsOnHook
.May 12 14:47:22.764: ephone-3[2]:ClearCallPrompt line 1 ref 21
.May 12 14:47:22.764: ephone-3[2]:SelectPhoneSoftKeys set 0 for line 1 ref 21
.May 12 14:47:22.764: ephone-3[2]:Clean Up Speakerphone state
.May 12 14:47:22.764: ephone-3[2]:SpeakerPhoneOnHook
.May 12 14:47:22.764: ephone-3[2]:Clean up activeline 1
.May 12 14:47:22.764: ephone-3[2]:Tone Off ignored - already sent
.May 12 14:47:22.764: ephone-3[2]:Clean Up phone offhook state
.May 12 14:47:22.764: ephone-3[2]:SetLineLamp 1 to OFF
.May 12 14:47:22.764: UnBinding ephone-3 from DN 2
.May 12 14:47:22.764: UnBinding called DN 3 from DN 2
.May 12 14:47:22.764: ephone-1[4]:Far-end cleanup skiping ephone-3 DN 2
  non-active line 0
.May 12 14:47:22.764: ephone-1[4]:SpeakerPhoneOnHook
.May 12 14:47:22.764: ephone-1[4]:ClearCallPrompt line 0 ref 0
.May 12 14:47:22.764: ephone-1[4]:SelectPhoneSoftKeys set 0 for line 0 ref 0
.May 12 14:47:22.764: ephone-1[4]:CallPrompt line 0 ref 0:
  CM Fallback Service Operating
.May 12 14:47:22.864: SetDnCodec DN 3 codec 4:G711Ulaw64k  vad 0 size 160
.May 12 14:47:22.864: DN 3 Voice_Mode
.May 12 14:47:22.864: DN 3 End Voice_Mode
.May 12 14:47:22.864: dn_tone_control DN=3 tonetype=0:DtSilence onoff=0 pid=115
.May 12 14:47:22.864: No active phone for DN 3 instance 1
.May 12 14:47:22.876: SkinnyReportDnState DN 2 ONHOOK
.May 12 14:47:22.876: dn_tone_control DN=2 tonetype=0:DtSilence onoff=0 pid=115
.May 12 14:47:22.876: No active phone for DN 2 instance 1
```

As you can see, **debug ephone detail** is far more detailed than **debug ephone state** and therefore is not needed for most troubleshooting. However, it provides additional information that you might need when troubleshooting a problem that **debug ephone state** does not give you.

Problems with Transferring Calls in SRST Mode

Prior to Cisco IOS Software Release 12.2(8)T, call transfer while in SRST mode was supported only between registered IP Phones and POTS ports. This means that the transfer destination for a call was not allowed to be a VoIP destination. This is problematic in situations where a remote site has an SRST router and one or more additional voice gateways. As long as all SRST routers and voice gateways are running Cisco IOS Software Release 12.2(8)T or later, transfers to VoIP destinations are supported; however, they are not enabled by default.

For example, assume that an SRST router has the configuration shown in Example 15-28.

Example 15-28 *SRST Router Configuration*

```
dial-peer voice 10000 voip
 destination-pattern 10...
 session target ipv4:14.84.0.130
 dtmf-relay h245-alphanumeric
 codec g711ulaw
 ip qos dscp cs5 media
 no vad
!
!
call-manager-fallback
ip source-address 14.84.41.1 port 2000
 max-ephones 24
 max-dn 48
!
```

In this case, an IP Phone registered with the SRST router can place a call to any extension from 10000 to 10999 by going through the gateway under dial peer 10000. However, with this configuration, transfers fail to any extension that needs to match dial peer 10000. Example 15-29 shows the output if you enable **debug ephone detail**.

Example 15-29 *Output of* **debug ephone detail**

```
Router#debug ephone detail
May 12 17:06:31.942: ephone-1[4]:KeypadButtonMessage 1
May 12 17:06:31.942: ephone-1[4]:StopTone sent to ephone
May 12 17:06:31.942: ephone-1[4]:SkinnyTryCall to 1 instance 1 start at 0
May 12 17:06:31.942: ephone-1[4]:No Transfer-Pattern match for 1
May 12 17:06:32.446: ephone-1[4]:KeypadButtonMessage 0
May 12 17:06:32.446: ephone-1[4]:SkinnyTryCall to 10 instance 1 start at 0
May 12 17:06:32.446: ephone-1[4]:No Transfer-Pattern match for 10
May 12 17:06:32.698: ephone-1[4]:KeypadButtonMessage 0
May 12 17:06:32.698: ephone-1[4]:SkinnyTryCall to 100 instance 1 start at 0
May 12 17:06:32.698: ephone-1[4]:No Transfer-Pattern match for 100
May 12 17:06:33.202: ephone-1[4]:KeypadButtonMessage 1
May 12 17:06:33.202: ephone-1[4]:SkinnyTryCall to 1001 instance 1 start at 0
May 12 17:06:33.202: ephone-1[4]:No Transfer DN match for 1001
May 12 17:06:33.202: ephone-1[4]:No Transfer-Pattern match for 1001
May 12 17:06:33.202: Skinny StartTone 37 sent on  ephone socket [4] DtReorderTone
```

Notice that after dialing 1001, the SRST router instructs the IP Phone to play a reorder tone. This is because it does not have a local pattern that matches 1001, and it doesn't have a transfer pattern that matches that number either. To allow transfers to a dial peer, you must configure a transfer pattern to allow the transfer, as demonstrated in Example 15-30.

Example 15-30 *Configuring a Transfer Pattern for the SRST Router*

```
call-manager-fallback
ip source-address 14.84.41.1 port 2000
 max-ephones 24
 max-dn 48
 transfer-pattern 10...
```

Remember that a transfer can also fail if you have a problem with the H.323 or POTS leg of the call. If you have problems transferring to a number, try dialing the number directly (as opposed to transferring a call to that number), and make sure that the number can be successfully called. If you have problems dialing the number, transfers obviously will not work either. If you have problems with VoIP or POTS calls, refer to Chapter 6 for additional gateway troubleshooting techniques.

IP Phones Stuck in SRST Mode

If you end up with IP Phones that are registered with the SRST router after the WAN connectivity has been restored, you can take some steps to determine why this is occurring. An IP Phone that is registered to the SRST router should periodically attempt to reconnect to all the CallManager nodes in its CallManager list until it can reregister with any of the CallManagers on the list. This is no different from the behavior when an IP Phone fails over to a backup CallManager because the primary has failed. Power-cycling the IP Phone should force it to reregister with the primary CallManager.

If the IP Phone is not reregistering with the primary CallManager, the best thing to look at is a sniffer trace. First, look to see if the IP Phone is trying to establish a TCP connection on port 2000 to the primary CallManager. If you see the IP Phone attempting the connection, but you don't see a response from CallManager, follow the steps outlined in Chapter 4 to determine why the phone is unable to register. The problem might be that although the WAN is restored, network connectivity is not fully restored or is degraded between the IP Phone and CallManager.

If you do not see the IP Phone attempting to connect to the primary CallManager in the sniffer trace, there is a problem with the phone. Search Cisco Bug Toolkit (discussed in Chapter 3) for any known issues in the phone load you are running, or open a case with the Cisco Technical Assistance Center and attach the sniffer trace showing the IP Phone not attempting to reregister with the primary CallManager.

Voice Mail and Forwarding Features in SRST Mode

When an IP Phone is registered with CallManager, CallManager stores the phone's voice mail pilot number. In SRST mode, the SRST router needs to be configured to act when the user presses the **messages** button. Because the WAN is down, the voice mail system is probably inaccessible by any means other than the PSTN. You should configure the SRST router to route calls to the voice mail system via the PSTN when the **messages** button is pressed. This is configured as follows:

```
call-manager-fallback
  voicemail 914445551212
```

The **messages** button then is treated like a speed dial to the configured pilot number. Note that when you place a call through the PSTN, the calling party number information presented to the voice mail system might be different than when the call is made OnNet. This might result in the voice mail system not recognizing the subscriber and playing a generic greeting.

Forwarding in SRST mode is very different than when the IP Phone is registered to CallManager. In SRST mode, there is a single global destination where calls are forwarded when busy or when there is no answer. You can configure the busy and no answer forwarding destination for all IP Phones registered to the SRST router as follows:

```
call-manager-fallback
  call-forward busy 914445551212
  call-forward noan 914445551212 timeout 20
```

Note that any configured forwarding behavior on CallManager does not apply in SRST mode. Unless the PSTN is providing redirected dial number ID service (RDNIS) to the location where the voice mail system resides, the voice mail system likely will answer with a generic greeting, as opposed to the personal greeting for the user who got forwarded to voice mail. Also, when in SRST mode, the voice mail system has no way to turn MWIs on or off. Be sure to set user expectations when operating in SRST mode to ensure that they know what to expect in the event of a WAN failure.

DHCP Considerations When Using SRST

Most IP Telephony administrators choose to use DHCP to assign IP addresses to their IP Phones for ease of administration. One important thing to consider is when your remote sites do not have a local DHCP server.

An IP Phone has two timers that determine the way it renews its DHCP lease: T1 and T2. T1 is the time that the IP Phone begins trying to renew its address by sending a unicast DHCP request message to the DHCP server that gave it the address. T1 defaults to 50 percent of the lease duration and is user-configurable using DHCP option 58. T2 is the time that the IP Phone begins trying to rebind by sending a broadcast DHCP request to any server. T2 defaults to 87.5 percent of the lease duration and is user-configurable through DHCP option 59. The actual lease duration is sent using DHCP option 51.

For example, if the lease is set to expire in eight days, the IP Phone attempts to renew with the DHCP server that gave it the address it has in four days. If the IP Phone is unable to renew its lease after seven days, it starts sending broadcast DHCP requests in an attempt to obtain a new IP address. If the IP Phone is unable to renew its lease after it has expired, the phone resets and becomes inoperable until it can obtain a new DHCP lease.

This is an important consideration when SRST is involved. If a remote site does not have a local DHCP server, the worst-case scenario is that an IP Phone could be halfway through the lease when the WAN goes down (because presumably if the lease were more than halfway elapsed, the phone would have renewed it already). This means that, assuming that your lease is eight days, if the WAN fails and you are running in SRST mode, the IP Phones will stop working as early as four days after the WAN failure if the WAN is not restored. In this case, four days is probably plenty of time. However, if you set a short lease time, such as one hour, IP Phones might start resetting if the WAN is down for more than half an hour. After an hour of WAN outage, *all* the IP Phones will be down.

To ensure that this does not cause you any problems, either make the lease times fairly long (several days), or use a local DHCP server. All versions of code that support SRST also support DHCP server functionality, so you can use the SRST router to provide IP addresses via DHCP for the site. The only drawback to this is that you must configure the DHCP scopes individually on each SRST router instead of on one centralized DHCP server. Because this is a one-time configuration, this is usually not a major drawback.

Best Practices

SRST is a fairly simple feature to configure. Therefore, there is little you must do to ensure successful operation. Keep the following best practices in mind:

- If possible, have inbound calls for a remote site come in on a gateway local to that site, such as the SRST router. This lets you maintain both inbound and outbound calling in the event of a WAN failure.

- Set your DHCP lease times to several days, or use a local DHCP server to ensure that IP Phones do not reset themselves when their lease expires during a WAN outage.

- Ensure that the dial peers configured on the gateway do not conflict with any of the temporary dial peers that are created when the IP Phones register to the SRST router.

- Use transfer patterns to allow transfers to non-IP Phone destinations. Also ensure that all voice gateways are running a version of Cisco IOS Software that permits transferring calls from an SRST router.

Summary

SRST lets you deploy a centralized CallManager cluster with many remote sites while ensuring that the IP Phones continue to work in the event of a WAN outage. Trouble-shooting SRST is fairly simple because SRST is far less complex than CallManager. As soon as an IP Phone is registered with an SRST router, troubleshooting inbound and outbound calling problems is identical to any other call through a Cisco IOS Software gateway (as described in Chapter 6).

## CHAPTER 16

Applications

Cisco AVVID IP Telephony allows for the creation of many different applications to interoperate within the converged network. Several Cisco applications provide various services within AVVID. These applications include services such as the following:

- Customer Response Applications (CRA), including IP Interactive Voice Response (IP IVR) and IP Auto Attendant (IP AA)
- Extension mobility for release 3.1, 3.2, and 3.3
- Cisco CallManager Attendant Console (formerly known as Cisco WebAttendant)
- Personal Assistant
- Cisco IP SoftPhone
- Cisco IP Phone services
- Cisco IP Videoconferencing
- Cisco Conference Connection
- Cisco Emergency Responder

Cisco AVVID provides so many solutions that addressing every application that works with Cisco CallManager would require a book unto itself. Many of these applications have troubleshooting documentation on Cisco.com, or you can navigate to the applications by starting at the following URL:

www.cisco.com/univercd/cc/td/doc/product/voice/

In this chapter, we discuss some of the troubleshooting topics and encourage you to consult the troubleshooting documentation on Cisco.com for additional information.

Chapter 14, "Voice Mail," covered many voice mail-related issues, so for Unity, please refer to that chapter. Also, many white papers are available for Unity on Cisco.com or at the following URL:

www.cisco.com/univercd/cc/td/doc/product/voice/c_unity/index.htm

There are also troubleshooting guides for each release of Unity. From the preceding link, click the version of Unity you are using and then click the link to "Troubleshooting Guide."

Customer Response Applications (CRA)

CallManager offers various protocols to interface with external applications. Telephony Application Programming Interface (TAPI) and Java Telephony Application Programming Interface (JTAPI) are two such protocols that are generically referred to as Computer Telephony Interface (CTI) protocols. Applications that use TAPI or JTAPI are generally referred to as CTI applications.

CTI applications require that you install a piece of CallManager software on the server running the CTI application. For a TAPI application, this is called the TAPI Service Provider (TSP). For JTAPI it is called the JTAPI Plugin.

A CTI application only communicates via TAPI or JTAPI to the TSP or JTAPI Plugin respectively. CallManager uses a protocol named Computer Telephony Interface Quick Buffer Encoding (CTIQBE) to communicate between the TSP or JTAPI Plugin and CallManager.

The TSP and JTAPI Plugin do not communicate directly with CallManager. Instead, CTI applications communicate with the CTI Manager service running on one or more servers in the cluster. The CTI Manager service in turn communicates with the CallManager services running on the various nodes in the cluster. CTI Manager provides redundancy by allowing a TSP or JTAPI Plugin to communicate with more than one CTI Manager service and also provides a layer of abstraction that allows a CTI application to monitor or control a device registered to any server in the cluster. Prior to CallManager 3.1 there was no CTI Manager. This required a CTI application to be registered to the same CallManager server as the device it wanted to control.

Checking TSP or JTAPI Plugin Versions

For any TAPI or JTAPI application, one of the first things you should do when trouble-shooting a problem is to ensure the TAPI or JTAPI versions are consistent between CallManager and the application server. The easiest way to determine this is to run the TSP or JTAPI plugin installer on the application server. You can access the TSP or JTAPI plugin that matches your version of CallManager from the Install Plugins page in CallManager Administration (**Application > Install Plugins**).

When you run the TSP or JTAPI plugin installer on a server that already has the TSP or JTAPI plugin installed, the installer either states it is going to upgrade from one version to another (and lists the versions) or asks if you want to reinstall the same version of the TSP or JTAPI plugin. If it asks you to reinstall the same version, you are running the correct version. If the version numbers are different, upgrade to match the version running on the CallManager server and reboot your application server when prompted at the end of the installation.

IP IVR and IP AA

The primary application platform addressed here is CRA release 3.0. CRA uses JTAPI to communicate with CallManager and primarily provides IVR, AA, and ICD capabilities to CallManager.

TIP

You can find many troubleshooting scenarios with resolutions for CRA version 2.2 at the following URL:

www.cisco.com/univercd/cc/td/doc/product/voice/sw_ap_to/apps_22/trbl22/index.htm

In the future, similar troubleshooting information may be posted for later versions as well. Check the following URL for any troubleshooting links for the release of CRA that you are using:

www.cisco.com/univercd/cc/td/doc/product/voice/sw_ap_to/

Auto Attendant (AA) is just an example of an Integrated Voice Response (IVR) script. As such, the discussions of IVR and AA are grouped. Both entities are powered by CRA, and both have the same basic requirements in order to work. Before any troubleshooting begins, you must verify two important items:

- Check to make sure your version of CRA is compatible with the version of CallManager used. The CallManager Release Notes always specify application compatibility, so check the Release Notes to verify version compatibility between CallManager and your applications. As directory schemas and JTAPI implementations change, the interoperability changes. Make sure the CallManager version and CRA version match.

  You can review the CallManager compatibility matrix at the following URL:

  www.cisco.com/univercd/cc/td/doc/product/voice/c_callmg/ccmcomp.htm

- Any time you upgrade your CallManager version, install the corresponding JTAPI plugin on the CRA server to match the CallManager JTAPI version as mentioned in the section "Checking TSP or JTAPI Plugin Versions."

- Check to make sure there is network connectivity between the CRA server and the CallManager servers. If DNS is used, make sure name resolution works properly. The CRA server needs to find CallManager to register, so network connectivity and name resolution must be working.

Figure 16-1 depicts the signaling relationship between the CRA application server and CallManager.

Figure 16-1   *CallManager, Applications Server, and IP Phone Interaction*

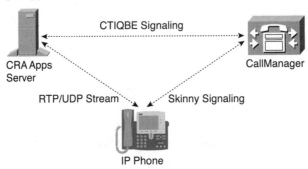

Notice that the RTP/UDP stream occurs between the endpoint, such as an IP phone, and the application server. The Skinny protocol signaling is between the IP phone and CallManager. The JTAPI signaling is between the application server and the JTAPI Plugin, which in turn communicates with CallManager using the CTIQBE protocol. If the signaling between the application server and CallManager is interrupted or never established, none of the applications will work.

The CRA application server is given the IP address or name of two servers running the CTI Manager service. If a CallManager fails, the CTI Manager ensures that the application registers with the next available CallManager.

Figure 16-2 shows the relationship between the application server, CTI Manager, and CallManager.

The CTI Manager keeps a record of every available CallManager so that applications can register to whichever CallManager the CTI Manager specifies. If a CallManager fails, the CTI Manager can get the application registered to the next available CallManager. Because the application can specify two CTI Managers, two CTI Managers are always available to proxy the registration to the available CallManager.

CRA Administration Problems

When you first bring up the CRA Administration (http://*server IP address*/appadmin), it should take you to the Directory Configuration initialization page allowing you to configure the Directory settings mentioned in the next section.

If the CRA Administration page does not come up, it is possible that there is a problem with accessing the required java classes that allow the web pages to function. The most likely suspect is the Classpath entries.

Figure 16-2 *Applications Server, CTI Manager, and CallManager Relationship*

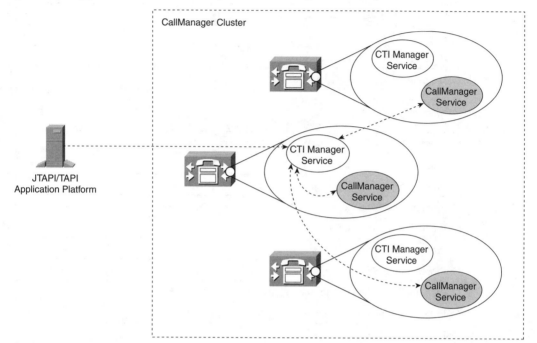

The .jar (java resource) files listed in Table 16-1 (for CRA 2.x) or Table 16-2 (for CRA 3.0) should be in the Classpath in the system variables of a CRA server that has IP IVR/IP AA/ IP ICD and the Agent Desktop and Reporting Clients installed. These .jar files contain the java software used to control the CRA Administration web pages as well as the CRA Engine that runs the applications. Add these entries and restart the server, or reinstall CRA to make sure these entries are created.

You can add the Classpath entries on the CRA server by right-clicking **My Computer > Properties > Advanced** tab **> Environment Variable**. The Classpath is located in the System Variables area. Select the **Classpath** variable and click **Edit**. In the **Variable Value** field, add the Classpath entries in Tables 16-1 or 16-2, depending on the version of CRA you have installed, using a semicolon as a separator between the entries (no spaces).

Table 16-1 *CRA 2.x Classpath Entries*

CRA 2.x System Classpath Entries
C:\Program Files\wfavvid\CiscoUtil.jar
C:\Program Files\wfavvid\dlconcurrent.jar
C:\Program Files\wfavvid\collections.jar
C:\Program Files\wfavvid\wfrepos.jar
C:\Program Files\wfavvid\CiscoSysService.jar
C:\Program Files\wfavvid\CiscoWFAPI1.0.jar
C:\Program Files\wfavvid\CiscoWFFBase.jar
C:\Program Files\wfavvid\rmi.zip
C:\Program Files\wfavvid\providerutil.jar
C:\Program Files\wfavvid\jndi.jar
C:\Program Files\wfavvid\lda.jar
C:\Program Files\wfavvid\stepsIVR.jar
C:\Program Files\wfavvid\wfccndomain.jar
C:\Program Files\wfavvid\xalan.jar
C:\Program Files\wfavvid\xerces.jar
C:\Program Files\wfavvid\SubsystemRmCm.jar
C:\inetpub\wwwroot\AppAdmin\reporting\lib\rmiswing.jar
C:\WINNT\java\lib\jtracing.jar
C:\Program Files\wfavvid\Reporting\Lib\rmiswing.jar
C:\Program Files\wfavvid\ldap.jar
C:\Program Files\wfavvid\License.jar
C:\WINNT\java\lib\jtapi.jar

Table 16-2 *CRA 3.0 Classpath Entries*

CRA 3.x System Classpath Entries
C:\WINNT\Java\Lib\jtapi.jar
C:\WINNT\Java\Lib\DirUser.jar
C:\WINNT\Java\Lib\Xerces.jar
C:\WINNT\Java\Lib\DirUserNotification.jar
C:\Program Files\wfavvid\collections.jar

Table 16-2   *CRA 3.0 Classpath Entries (Continued)*

C:\Program Files\wfavvid\rmi.zip
C:\Program Files\wfavvid\providerutil.jar
C:\Program Files\wfavvid\jndi.jar
C:\Program Files\wfavvid\ldap.jar
C:\Program Files\wfavvid\xalan.jar
C:\Program Files\wfavvid\xerces.jar
C:\Program Files\wfavvid\CiscoBulkJar.jar
C:\Program Files\wfavvid\alarm.jar
C:\inetpub\wwwroot\AppAdmin\reporting\lib\rmiswing.jar

Once you have verified that the Classpath is correct, the directory configuration can be verified.

Directory Configuration

Where CallManager uses Microsoft SQL server to store its configuration data, CRA uses an LDAP directory. This LDAP directory is the same directory used to store user information (not configuration data) for CallManager.

When you first install CRA or if you select the Directory Setup page in CRA Administration (**System > Configuration and Repository**), you must configure the location of the LDAP directory where you want CRA to store its configuration information. The directory initialization sets up the directory with the appropriate configuration. You can use either the embedded directory (DC Directory), Active Directory, or Netscape iPlanet to store the CRA configuration information. You should use whichever directory you are currently using for your CallManager user information. The directory configuration must be correct, or the CRA server will not work correctly.

Table 16-3 lists the default entries for a standard DC Directory installation. If you are using DC Directory, the information in Table 16-3 should match your configuration. If the port, distinguished name (DN), password, or base context is wrong, directory initialization will not succeed. You can see the Directory values in the Directory Setup page (**System > Configuration and Repository**) in CRA Administration.

Table 16-3 *Default Entries for a Standard DC Directory Installation*

Entry	Default Value
Directory port number	8404
Directory user (DN)	cn=Directory Manager, o=cisco.com
Directory password	This is a password you define when you install CallManager. If you forgot your password, refer to Chapter 18, "LDAP Integration and Replication," in the section "Troubleshooting the CallManager Embedded Directory" to recover your password.
User Base	ou=Users, o=cisco.com
Base context	o=cisco.com

Table 16-4 lists the typical entries if you're using Active Directory.

Table 16-4 *Typical Entries for an Active Directory Installation*

Entry	Default Value
Directory port number	389
Directory user (DN)	cn=Administrator, cn=Users, dc=cisco, dc=com
Directory password	This is a password you define in your Active Directory for the user specified as the Directory User above.
User Base	cn=Users, dc=cisco, dc=com
Base context	dc=cisco, dc=com

There are two basic branches in the directory for the CRA server:

- One branch for configuration
- One branch for the workflow repository

The main reason that profiles are used is to accommodate multiple IP IVR installations with a single CallManager. If you have two IP IVRs and one CallManager, the configuration for each IP IVR needs to be stored in separate branches in the directory so that they can be managed separately. However, if the workflows (scripts) are to be shared, both IP IVRs can load their workflows from the same directory branch. This means that you can set up the directory configuration in both IP IVRs to point to the same repository profile and maintain one set of scripts.

To examine what has been configured in the DC Directory, access DC Directory Administrator (**Start > Programs > DC Directory Administrator**). A standard CRA installation has a branch called cisco.com. Under that branch is a CCN Apps branch. In this branch are branches for Configuration and Workflows. Each of these branches has a branch for all the profiles that have been initialized. Figure 16-3 shows the DC Directory Admin window with the profiles expanded.

Figure 16-3 *DC Directory Admin Window Showing Profiles*

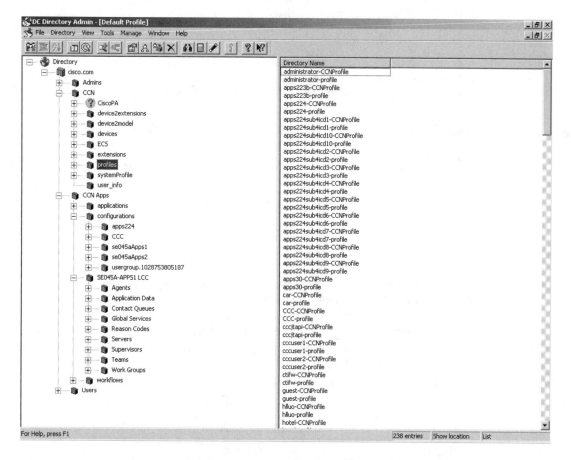

For Active Directory installations, the process involves running the Active Directory plugin on CallManager. This allows CallManager to reference the Active Directory. For information about integrating your CallManager with Active Directory, refer to Chapter 18.

Following the configuration of the directory in CRA Administration, the system updates the **ccndir.ini** file, which resides in the C:\WINNT\system32\ccn directory. Various processes use this .ini file to determine how to locate the LDAP directory.

Example 16-1 provides a sample Active Directory ccndir.ini file.

Example 16-1 *Sample Active Directory ccndir.ini File*

```
# Directory Administrator's Password
MGRPW    "1c0c1f1c371a1a0700"

# Directory Server URL
```

continues

Example 16-1   *Sample Active Directory ccndir.ini File (Continued)*

```
LDAPURL    "ldap://172.20.229.99:389"

# Base    DN for Users
USERBASE    "cn=Users, dc=unity, dc=cisco, dc=com"

# Base    DN for CCN APPS
CCNAPPSBASE    "ou=CCN Apps, dc=unity, dc=cisco, dc=com"

# Directory Administrator's DN
MGRDN    "cn=Administrator, cn=Users, dc=unity, dc=cisco, dc=com"

# CCN APPS    Profile    name
CCNAPPSPROFILE    "AD-IVR1"

# PROFILEBASE for profiles
PROFILEBASE    "ou=profiles, ou=CCN, dc=unity, dc=cisco, dc=com"

Directory Server Type
DS    "ADS"
```

Table 16-5 lists and describes other files that are created during configuration of the directory in CRA Administration. If your attempt to initialize with Active Directory fails, check whether these files have actually been created. For the .ini file, check C:\WINNT\system32\ccn; for the .properties files, check C:\Program Files\wfavvid. Then make sure you are supplying the correct port, username, and password information, as well as the appropriate base context.

Table 16-5   *Other Files Created with an Active Directory Installation*

File	Contents of the File
ccndir.ini	LDAP and profile information
system.properties	System information
wfengine.properties	Engine configuration properties
SubsystemJtapi.properties	JTAPI subsystem properties
SubsystemGED125.properties	Intelligent Contact Management (ICM) subsystem properties
domains.properties	Domain-specific information

Verifying Configuration

For an application to function properly, the configuration on CRA must match what is configured for that application in CallManager. For any application to work, a call must arrive for the application through a CTI route point. The CRA server then presents this call to an IVR script. When the script accepts the call, the call is redirected to a CTI port for media termination.

Table 16-6 provides the high-level checklist to begin the troubleshooting process.

Table 16-6   *CRA/CallManager Configuration Checklist*

CRA AA/IVR Tasks	CallManager Tasks
Specify the CTI route point (it must match the CTI route point on CallManager).	Create the CTI route point and assign a directory number (DN).
Specify the CTI port group (it must match the CTI ports on CallManager).	Create the CTI ports. Ensure the DNs configured on the CTI ports are consecutive.
Specify the user/password for CTI port groups.	Create a user in the CallManager user directory (**User > Add a New User**). Assign a password to the user and the associate all CTI route points and CTI ports controlled by the CRA server with this user. Also ensure that the **Enable CTI Application Use** checkbox is selected for the user.

This is just the beginning but often a small discrepancy here is the cause of the problem. You should verify the following configuration items:

- The CTI route points *must* match.

- The CTI ports *must* match, and they must be a consecutive range of numbers.

- The CTI route points and CTI ports *must* be associated with the designated user.

- The CRA server *must* use the correct username and password.

If you do not verify these configuration items, you could waste a lot of time troubleshooting the system when the problem lies in a simple configuration error. The following sections address CRA Administration problems that affect IP IVR, IP AA, and pre-3.3 versions of extension mobility.

Engine Status

If the applications server is properly configured, the application engine (**System > Engine**) shows that it is running with the JTAPI subsystem, shown as **IN_SERVICE**. If the JTAPI subsystem status shows that it is unavailable, make sure the application engine host name or IP address (**System > Engine > Engine Configuration**) is valid. It is best to use an IP address to eliminate any DNS issues. Figure 16-4 shows the Engine status screen in CRA Administration.

Figure 16-4 *Engine Status in CRA Administration*

If the JTAPI subsystem shows **OUT_OF_SERVICE**, none of the CTI route points/CTI ports were correctly initialized or registered to CallManager. Make sure CallManager is up and that the application server has connectivity to CallManager.

If connectivity appears to be good, check the JTAPI Configuration page in CRA Administration (**Subsystems > JTAPI**). The JTAPI Configuration page should have the IP address of one or more CallManagers running the CTI Manager service. Confirm that the servers in the CallManager cluster whose IP address(es) appear in the **JTAPI Provider(s)** field have the CTI Manager service active.

The **User ID** and **Password** fields listed on the JTAPI Configuration page are extremely important. The CRA Engine uses this username and password to log into the CTI Manager service. CallManager only allows the CTI application (in this case CRA) access to devices that you have associated with this user. This means that any CTI route points and CTI ports that CRA needs control of must be associated with this user in CallManager Administration (**User > Global Directory**).

To verify your JTAPI configuration (**Subsystems > JTAPI**), the following must be configured correctly on the CRA server:

- On the JTAPI Configuration page in CRA Administration, the **JTAPI Provider(s)** must point to a functioning CTI Manager service in the CallManager cluster.

- On the JTAPI Configuration page in CRA Administration, the **User ID** and **Password** fields must match with a user configured in CallManager's LDAP directory. We call this user the *JTAPI user*.

- The JTAPI user must have the **Enable CTI Application Use** checkbox selected in CallManager Administration (**User > Global Directory**). Failure to select this checkbox causes CallManager to deny any CTI application login attempts for this username.

- You must have all the CTI route points and CTI ports you want to use with the CRA server associated with the JTAPI user in CallManager Administration. In CRA 3.0 and later, CRA Administration does not let you configure a particular CTI route point or CTI port until the CRA server has successfully authenticated with CallManager and retrieved a list of controlled devices.

If the JTAPI subsystem shows **PARTIAL_SERVICE**, there is a good chance you have something partially misconfigured. It could be that the CTI port range configured in CRA Administration does not match the CTI ports configured in CallManager. It could also be that a particular CTI route point or CTI port is not associated with the JTAPI user.

Check the log files (**System > Engine > Trace Files**) to determine what CTI port or CTI route point is not being registered. To configure the information returned in the log files, you need to specify trace configuration settings (**System > Engine > Trace Configuration**), as described in Table 16-7 later in this chapter; however, this information should be in the trace using the default trace settings.

Open the most recent Multimedia Interactive Voice Response (MIVR) trace file from CRA Administration (**System > Engine > Trace Files**) and search for the word "exception." Most error conditions have the word "exception" as part of the trace line. For example, the following trace line shows an error registering a CTI port:

```
%MIVR-SS_TEL-3-UNABLE_REGISTER_CTIPORT:Unable to register CTI Port:
  CTI Port=16003,Exception=com.cisco.jtapi.InvalidArgumentExceptionImpl:
  Address 16003 is not in provider's domain.
```

The statement "Address 16003 is not in the provider's domain" nearly always means that the device the CRA server is trying to use is not associated with the JTAPI user. You can see that the particular CTI port in this case has DN 16003 configured.

A similar condition is encountered if a CTI route point is not properly associated as shown in the following:

```
%MIVR-SS_TEL-2-UNABLE_REGISTER_CALLBACK:Unable to register
   Callback for CTI Route point: Route Address=14001,
   Exception=com.cisco.jtapi.InvalidArgumentExceptionImpl:
   Address 14001 is not in provider's domain.
```

Notice the CTI route point with DN 14001 is not able to register because it is not associated with the JTAPI user.

If you see errors such as these in the trace files, check the device association for the JTAPI user and ensure **Enable CTI Application User** is selected. Once you have corrected any problems with the device association or configuration, stop and restart the CRA Engine from CRA Administration (**System > Engine**).

If the CRA server is not generating trace files or you need more detailed tracing information, you must enable additional trace flags.

Collecting Traces

It is important to have a good strategy in place when analyzing traces for IP IVR and IP AA types of calls. CallManager is involved in the call, but so is the CRA engine. Traces can be collected on both entities. Generally, you'll start with the application engine debugging and then move to CCM traces.

As you gain experience, you will know which logs need to be collected for a particular type of problem. If you aren't sure, it is best to collect more, not less. For application-related problems, you should collect CCM and SDL traces on CallManager.

For the CCM trace configuration (**CallManager Serviceability > Trace > Configuration > *select a server* > Cisco CallManager**), set the **Debug Trace Level** to **Detailed**.

Also ensure the following service parameters (**CallManager Administration> Service > Service Parameters > *select a server* > Cisco CallManager**) are set for the SDL traces:

- SdlTraceTypeFlags = 0x8000CB15
- SdlTraceDataFlags = 0x00000110
- SdlTraceDataFlags = True

On the application server, you should collect several trace files. Table 16-7 lists the trace levels for this server. Trace files on the CRA server are usually referred to as Multimedia Interactive Voice Response (MIVR) traces. Enable only the traces for the application you are troubleshooting. You usually want to have at least **SS_TEL** enabled and then add any of the others if you need them. For example, if you are troubleshooting ICD, you should enable SS_CM, SS_RM, and SS_RMCM in addition to SS_TEL.

Table 16-7   *Application Server Trace Settings*

Component	Subfacility	Trace Level	Purpose	Configuration Location
MIVR	SS_TEL	DEBUG/All	Telephony call events	In CRA Administration, click **System > Engine > Trace Configuration**
MIVR	SS_CM	DEBUG/All	ICD Contact Manager events	In CRA Administration, click **System > Engine > Trace Configuration**
MIVR	SS_RM	DEBUG/All	ICD Resource Manager events	In CRA Administration, click **System > Engine > Trace Configuration**
MIVR	SS_RMCM	DEBUG/All	ICD events	In CRA Administration, click **System > Engine > Trace Configuration**
JTAPI	All	DEBUG/All	Telephony call events	**Start > Programs > Cisco JTAPI > JTAPI Preferences**

Active trace level changes take effect immediately (no restart required); inactive trace level changes take effect the next time the subsystem is used.

Now that you have trace configured, you need to understand the different call states. Understanding what the call states means helps you understand what point in the call you are in when reading an MIVR trace file. Table 16-8 lists the different call states.

Table 16-8   *CRA Call States*

State	Description
Received	The call was received at a specified CTI route point.
Accepted	The call was routed to a CTI port.
Rejected	The call failed to be routed to a CTI port. It could also be that no ports were available.
Attributed	A task was invoked to handle the processing for this call.
Answered	The associated application answered the call.
Abandoned	The caller disconnected the call before the application terminated normally.
Disconnected	The application terminated the call.
Transferred	The application successfully transferred the call.
Aborted	The call was terminated prematurely due to an error or because the application ended without disconnecting or transferring the call.

The following examples show some actual MIVR traces.

The trace shown in Example 16-2 is of a call to an IP IVR script that performs basic auto attendant functionality. The basic order of events is as follows:

1   Extension 101380 calls CTI route point 5000.

2   CTI port 3041 is assigned, and the application (AA) answers.

3   The caller listens to the prompt and enters 1.

4   The caller listens to the prompt and enters 1586#.

5   AA redirects the caller to extension 1586.

Example 16-2 shows the first event in the MIVR trace—a received call from 101380 to CTI route point 5000.

Example 16-2   *Trace Output: A Received Call from Extension 101380 to CTI Route Point 5000*

```
86: Aug 21 09:07:47.984 PDT %MIVR-SS_TEL-7-UNK:Call.received() Call[id: 7,
   media: 116/1, state = RECEIVED, dn = 5000, ani = 101380, lrd = null,
   type = DIRECT_CALL, route = null, port = null, task = -1, app = null,
   aborting = false, transferring = false, disconnecting = false]
```

The application now starts handling the call. An application task ID is assigned. In this case, it is **3000000007**. The task ID is assigned for the duration of the call, so you can track this task ID through the trace file if you have multiple calls occurring simultaneously in a trace file. Example 16-3 shows the continued trace output.

Example 16-3   *Trace Output: An Application Task Is Assigned to Handle the Call*

```
87: Aug 21 09:07:47.984 PDT %MIVR-SS_TEL-7-UNK:Number of active ports: 0
90: Aug 21 09:07:48.000 PDT %MIVR-SS_TEL-7-UNK:Call.associated()
   Call[id: 7, media: 116/1, state = RECEIVED, dn = 5000, ani = 101380, lrd = null,
   type = DIRECT_CALL, route = TPG[type = Workflow, id = 48]-TR[num = 5000],
   port = TPG[type = Workflow, id = 48]-TP[num = 3041], task = -1, app = null,
   aborting = false, transferring = false, disconnecting = false]
IVR Associated call to CTI Port 3041
95: Aug 21 09:07:48.609 PDT %MIVR-SS_TEL-7-UNK:Call.accepted()
   Call[id: 7, media: 116/1, state = ACCEPTED, dn = 5000, ani = 101380, lrd = null,
   type = DIRECT_CALL, route = TPG[type = Workflow, id = 48]-TR[num = 5000],
   port = TPG[type = Workflow, id = 48]-TP[num = 3041], task = -1, app = null,
   aborting = false, transferring = false, disconnecting = false]
   Call was routed to the available CTI Port 3041
97: Aug 21 09:07:48.625 PDT %MIVR-SS_TEL-7-UNK:Call.attributed() Call[id: 7,
   media: 116/1, state = ATTRIBUTED, dn = 5000, ani = 101380, lrd = null,
   type = DIRECT_CALL, route = TPG[type = Workflow, id = 48]-TR[num = 5000],
   port = TPG[type = Workflow, id = 48]-TP[num = 3041], task = 3000000007,
   app = WFApp[id = -1, name = Auto Attendant, enabled = true, wf = aarv.aef,
   max = 39], aborting = false, transferring = false, disconnecting = false]
```

Notice in Example 16-3 that the workflow handling this call is called aarv.aef.

In Example 16-4, you see the call answered by the auto attendant.

Example 16-4   *Trace Output: The Call Is Answered*

```
103: Aug 21 09:07:48.656 PDT %MIVR-SS_TEL-7-UNK:Call.answered()
   Call[id: 7, media: 116/1, state = ANSWERED, dn = 5000, ani = 101380, lrd = null,
   type = DIRECT_CALL, route = TPG[type = Workflow, id = 48]-TR[num = 5000],
   port = TPG[type = Workflow, id = 48]-TP[num = 3041], task = 3000000007,
   app = WFApp[id = -1, name = Auto Attendant, enabled = true, wf = aarv.aef,
   max = 39], aborting = false, transferring = false, disconnecting = false]
```

The application now performs its programmed steps. Because this is an auto attendant, it plays a Welcome wave file and then a Menu wave file, as shown in Example 16-5.

Example 16-5   *Trace Output: The Application Performs Programmed Steps*

```
105: Aug 21 09:07:49.078 PDT %MIVR-SS_TEL-7-UNK:CallID:7 MediaId:116/1
   Task:3000000007MediaManager playing C:\Program Files\wfavvid\Prompts\user\
   en_US\AAWelcome.wav
107: Aug 21 09:07:51.171 PDT %MIVR-SS_TEL-7-UNK:CallID:7 MediaId:116/1
   Task:3000000007MediaManager playing C:\Program Files\wfavvid\Prompts\user\
   en_US\AArvMainMenu.wav
```

Example 16-6 shows the caller pressing 1.

Example 16-6   *Trace Output: The User Presses 1*

```
108: Aug 21 09:07:54.406 PDT %MIVR-SS_TEL-7-UNK:CallID:7 MediaId:116/1
   Task:3000000007 Digit received: 1
109: Aug 21 09:07:54.406 PDT %MIVR-SS_TEL-7-UNK:PLAYMsgHandler case dtmf
110: Aug 21 09:07:54.921 PDT %MIVR-SS_TEL-7-UNK:CallID:7 MediaId:116/1
   Task:3000000007 Digit entered during output:1
```

This message indicates that the digit 1 that was received, which interrupted the wave file being played. The IVR script then prompts the user to dial the extension number they want to reach. The user dials the first digit in the extension number, 1, which interrupts the prompt asking the user to enter the extension number. Then the caller dials the remaining digits (5, 8, 6, and #), as shown in Example 16-7.

Example 16-7   *Trace Output: The Wave File Is Interrupted; the Remaining Digits Are Dialed*

```
111: Aug 21 09:07:54.921 PDT %MIVR-SS_TEL-7-UNK:CallID:7 MediaId:116/1
   Task:3000000007MediaManager playing C:\Program Files\wfavvid\Prompts\user\
   en_US\AAEnterExtn.wav
Played AAEnterExtn.wav
```

continues

Example 16-7 *Trace Output: The Wave File Is Interrupted; the Remaining Digits Are Dialed (Continued)*

```
112: Aug 21 09:07:56.718 PDT %MIVR-SS_TEL-7-UNK:CallID:7 MediaId:116/1
   Task:3000000007 Digit received: 1
113: Aug 21 09:07:56.718 PDT %MIVR-SS_TEL-7-UNK:PLAYMsgHandler case dtmf
114: Aug 21 09:07:57.343 PDT %MIVR-SS_TEL-7-UNK:CallID:7 MediaId:116/1
   Task:3000000007 Digit received: 5
115: Aug 21 09:07:57.359 PDT %MIVR-SS_TEL-7-UNK:CallID:7 MediaId:116/1
   Task:3000000007 Digit received: 8
116: Aug 21 09:07:57.390 PDT %MIVR-SS_TEL-7-UNK:CallID:7 MediaId:116/1
   Task:3000000007 Digit entered during output:1
117: Aug 21 09:07:57.609 PDT %MIVR-SS_TEL-7-UNK:CallID:7 MediaId:116/1
   Task:3000000007 Digit received: 6
118: Aug 21 09:07:58.171 PDT %MIVR-SS_TEL-7-UNK:CallID:7 MediaId:116/1
   Task:3000000007 Digit received: #
```

With the digits received, Example 16-8 shows the JTAPI redirect beginning. In this case the JTAPI redirect is similar to a blind transfer where the application does not wait for the called party to answer before completing the transfer.

Example 16-8 *Trace Output: The Digits Are Received; the JTAPI Redirect Begins*

```
119: Aug 21 09:07:58.171 PDT %MIVR-SS_TEL-7-UNK:CallID:7 MediaId:116/1
   Task:3000000007, Redirecting call to: 1586
```

With the transfer complete, the CTI port drops out of the call. The **Call.abandoned** message highlighted in Example 16-9 is normal given this call-flow scenario.

Example 16-9 *Trace Output: The Transfer Is Complete; the CTI Port Drops Out of the Call*

```
123: Aug 21 09:07:58.500 PDT %MIVR-SS_TEL-7-UNK:CallID:7 MediaId:116/1
   Task:3000000007, TerminalConnection to Terminal: CTIP3041 is DROPPED
124: Aug 21 09:07:58.500 PDT %MIVR-SS_TEL-7-UNK:Call.abandoned()
   Call[id: 7, media: 116/1, state = ABANDONED, dn = 5000, ani = 101380, lrd = null,
   type = DIRECT_CALL, route = TPG[type = Workflow, id = 48]-TR[num = 5000],
   port = TPG[type = Workflow, id = 48]-TP[num = 3041], task = 3000000007,
   app = WFApp[id = -1, name = Auto Attendant, enabled = true, wf = aarv.aef,
   max = 39], aborting = false, transferring = false, disconnecting = false]
```

Table 16-9 details some additional CTI error codes that can be found in the traces.

Table 16-9 *CTI Error Codes*

CTI Error Code	Error Name	Description
0x8CCC0001	Timeout	Indicates a timeout occurred on the JTAPI request to CTI. This can be configured in the JTAPI Preferences (**Start > Programs > Cisco JTAPI > JTAPI Preferences > Advanced tab**). The default is 30 seconds.

Table 16-9   *CTI Error Codes (Continued)*

CTI Error Code	Error Name	Description
0x8CCC0004	Illegal Handle	This is a generic failure caused by an invalid call handle, line handle, or device handle sent in the requests from JTAPI to CTI or from CTI to CallManager.
0x8CCC0005	Undefined Line	Indicates JTAPI/TSP tried to open an invalid line (DN). This can also happen when you're trying to set the message waiting indicator on a device's non-existing line.
0x8CCC0006	Illegal Calling Party Number	Indicates CTI received a request to make a call from a DN that was not on the device.
0x8CCC0007	Call Already Exists	Indicates the application was trying to make a call (or retrieve a call from hold) from a DN that already had an active call.
0x8CCC0008	Line Control Failure	Indicates an internal failure occurred when trying to make a call.
0x8CCC0009	Illegal Call State	Indicates the request was given in the wrong call state, such as trying to answer a connected call.
0x8CCC000A	Call Handle Not an Incoming Call	Indicates the application was trying to answer or accept an outgoing call.
0x8CCC000B	Transfer Failed— Destination Unallocated	Indicates the application was trying to transfer to an invalid destination.
0x8CCC000D	Transfer Failed— Destination Busy	Indicates the destination was busy.
0x8CCC000E	Transfer Failed	Indicates the transfer failed for unknown reasons.
0x8CCC000F	Hold Failed	Indicates the hold failed because another hold was in progress.
0x8CCC0011	Retrieve Failed	Indicates the retrieve failed because another retrieve was in progress.
0x8CCC0014	Database Error— Illegal Device Type	Indicates the device type was incorrect.
0x8CCC0015	Database Error	Indicates an internal DB error occurred.
0x8CCC0016	Cannot Terminate Media on Phone	Indicates the application was trying to register an IP phone. (It can register only CTI ports.)

continues

Table 16-9   *CTI Error Codes (Continued)*

CTI Error Code	Error Name	Description
0x8CCC0019	Unknown Global Call Handle	Indicates the application might have used a stale call. A stale call is one that no longer exists, yet the application believes the call is still active.
0x8CCC001A	Device Not Open	Indicates the application was trying to do something on a device that was not yet opened.
0x8CCC001B	Associated Line Not Open	Indicates the application was trying to answer or accept a call before opening the line.
0x8CCC001C	SSAPI Not Registered	Indicates an internal CTI error occurred. SSAPI registration was needed for the redirect.
0x8CCC001D	Redirect Call Does Not Exist	Indicates that the application was trying to redirect a call that does not exist in CallManager.
0x8CCC0031	Redirect Error	Indicates a generic error resulted in redirecting a call.
0x8CCC0032	Redirect Call—Call Table Full	Indicates a temporary failure because too many calls were active in CallManager.
0x8CCC0033	Redirect Call— Protocol Error	Indicates that a protocol error in CTI and CallManager communication occurred. This can be caused by a JTAPI version mismatch between the CRA server and CallManager.
0x8CCC0034	Redirect Call— Unknown Destination	Indicates the application was trying to redirect the call to an unknown destination.
0x8CCC0035	Redirect Call— Digit Analysis Timeout	Indicates an internal CallManager error occurred.
0x8CCC0036	Redirect Call— Media Connection Failed	Indicates the redirect failed due to a media error such as a codec mismatch. Remember CRA only supports the G.711 codec for media termination. Other codecs require that you have transcoding resources available on the network.
0x8CCC0037	Redirect Call— Party Table Full	Indicates an internal CallManager error occurred.
0x8CCC0038	Redirect Call— Originator Abandoned	Indicates the call originator dropped the call before the redirect was complete.
0x8CCC003B	Redirect Call— Pending Redirect Transaction	Indicates the redirect failed because a redirect was already in progress.

Table 16-9 *CTI Error Codes (Continued)*

CTI Error Code	Error Name	Description
0x8CCC0041	Cannot Open Device	Indicates a device-open failure occurred when the device was shut down.
0x8CCC0042	Transfer Failed— Outstanding Transfer	Indicates the transfer failed due to an outstanding transfer request.
0x8CCC0043	Transfer Failed— Call Control Timeout	Indicates an internal CallManager failure occurred in the transfer operation.
0x8CCC0044	Call Handle Unknown to Line Control	Indicates an internal CallManager failure occurred in the transfer operation.
0x8CCC0045	Operation Not Available in Current State	Indicates the conference bridge was not configured or the Cisco IP Voice Media Streaming Application service was not running.
0x8CCC0046	Conference Full	Indicates the maximum number of conference connections was reached.
0x8CCC0047	Maximum Number of CTI Connections Reached	Indicates the provider open failed because the maximum number of application connections to CTI was exceeded.
0x8CCC0050	Incompatible Protocol Version	Indicates JTAPI Plugin/TSP version was not compatible with the CallManager CTI version.
0x8CCC0051	Unrecognized PDU	Indicates the message received was not recognized.
0x8CCC0052	Illegal Message Format	Indicates the message format was invalid.
0x8CCC005E	Directory Temporarily Unavailable	Indicates a temporary failure in the directory occurred.
0x8CCC005F	Directory Login Not Allowed	Indicates the user was not authorized to use the CTI application. Ensure the **Enable CTI Application Use** checkbox is enabled in CallManager Administration for the JTAPI user.
0x8CCC0060	Directory Login Failed	Indicates a login ID/password error with the JTAPI user occurred. Verify the username and password on both the CRA server and on the User Configuration page in CallManager Administration.
0x8CCC0061	Provider Not Open	Indicates CTI failed to open the JTAPI provider due to database/directory issues.

continues

Table 16-9   *CTI Error Codes (Continued)*

CTI Error Code	Error Name	Description
0x8CCC0063	Not Initialized	Indicates CTI was in the process of coming up but had not yet completed its initialization.
0x8CCC0064	Cluster Link Failure	Indicates the CTI Manager service lost the TCP link with CallManager nodes in the cluster.
0x8CCC0066	Digit Generation Already In Progress	Indicates the DTMF digits dialing failed due an existing DTMF digit dial.
0x8CCC0067	Digit Generation on Wrong Call Handle	Indicates the call handle does not exist.
0x8CCC0068	Digit Generation on Wrong Call State	Indicates the call was not in an active state when digit generation is requested.
0x8CCC0069	Digit Generation on Call State Changed	Indicates DTMF failed due to a change in the call state.
0xDEADBEEF	Provider Closed	Indicates CTI closed the provider.
0x8CCC0071	Invalid Line Handle	Indicates the line handle was invalid.
0x8CCC0077	Device Out Of Service	Indicates the device was unregistered due to rehoming, CallManager failure, and so on.
0x8CCC0078	Message Waiting Destination Invalid	Indicates the destination was invalid when you tried to set or reset the message waiting indicator.
0x8CCC007D	Conference Inactive	Indicates the conference complete was attempted without setting up the consult call.
0x8CCC007E	Transfer Inactive	Indicates the transfer complete was attempted without setting up the consult call.

Extension Mobility for CallManager 3.1 and 3.2

Extension mobility is a feature that appeared in CallManager 3.1. It allows users to log in to any extension mobility-enabled 7960/7940 IP Phone. After a user logs in, the IP Phone downloads all the information related to the device profile, in effect becoming your personal office phone (the same as if you were sitting at your desk). This includes line number, calling search spaces, speed dials, and services.

Before CallManager 3.3, the CRA Engine facilitated the extension mobility feature. If you are troubleshooting extension mobility on CallManager 3.1 or 3.2, follow the instructions presented in this section. In CallManager 3.3, one service that runs on the CallManager server performs the login and logout functionality so CRA is no longer needed. For more information about extension mobility in CallManager release 3.3, see the section "Extension Mobility for CallManager 3.3."

To better understand how to troubleshoot extension mobility, you should become familiar with several terms:

- **Device Profile**—Information that defines the configuration of a particular device without being assigned to a device. This information includes line appearances, speed dials, and services. A device profile can be viewed as a template for a physical phone.

- **Default Device Profile**—The profile that is assigned to a phone device when a user has logged out. This can be either an Auto-generated Device Profile or a User Device Profile.

- **User Device Profile**—A device profile that is used to configure line appearances, speed dials, and services for a user.

- **Auto-Generated Device Profile (ADP)**—A device profile that is a snapshot of the phone device prior to enabling extension mobility. This can be used as the default device profile.

- **Application User ID**—The user ID that is created in CallManager to perform login and logout functions. This user ID is the one specified when creating the application on the CRA server. The Application User ID is never associated with a device/profile.

- **User ID**—The username that an individual user uses to log into a device.

A device profile allows you to configure almost everything about a phone, but the configuration is not associated with a physical device. Device profiles contain information such as phone button templates, including any Cisco 7914 expansion modules, services, speed dials, and line appearances. Note that a device profile is configured as a Cisco IP Phone 7960 device. There is no way to select a Cisco IP Phone 7940 phone button template, even though extension mobility has limited support on the 7940 phone. A 7940 can have one of two phone templates: 1-line or 2-line. You can configure which of the two is used on a system-wide basis by using the extension mobility service parameter **7940 Phone Template For EM Login** (**Service > Service Parameters** > *select a server* > **Cisco Extension Mobility**). For the 2-line template, the first two lines configured on the device profile are used. For the 1-line template, the first line and first speed dial configured on the device profile are used.

There are two types of device profiles used in extension mobility: a user device profile and an ADP.

The user device profile is the profile that an individual user has configured for them by the system administrator. The user device profile can be treated like any other phone device. The user can access this profile via the Cisco CallManager User Options web page (http://*Publisher IP Address*/CCMUser) and add services and speed dials the same way they would on a physical phone. The user device profile is the template that gets applied to a phone when the user logs in. A user device profile can be used for both user login and the default (logged out) configuration for an IP phone.

When an IP phone is configured for extension mobility, you must choose to **Use Current Device Settings** or **Select a User Device Profile** for the logout profile (**Device > Phone**). The ADP is a special device profile that gets generated when an IP phone is configured for extension mobility and is not configured to use a user device profile as the default device profile. If **Use Current Device Settings** is chosen, the system creates a device profile with the name ADP*XXXXXXXXXXXX* where *XXXXXXXXXXXX* is the MAC address of the device configured for extension mobility.

When an IP phone registers with CallManager, the phone requests the SEP*XXXXXXXXXXXX*.cnf.xml file from the TFTP server. Extension mobility works by swapping the contents of the SEP*XXXXXXXXXXXX*.cnf.xml file with either the user device profile or the ADP, depending on the login or logout status of the IP phone.

When a user is logged in, CallManager also swaps the configuration of the physical IP phone in the CallManager database with the user device profile for the user that logged in. This means that if you look at the physical IP phone in CallManager Administration while a user is logged in, the lines and configuration of the physical phone shows up with the information from the device profile.

To properly configure extension mobility, you must make configuration changes in both CRA Administration and CallManager Administration. First, look at the configuration required on CallManager. Then we'll examine the configuration on CRA.

CallManager Extension Mobility Configuration

For extension mobility to work properly, you must configure the following on CallManager:

Step 1 Enable extension mobility service-wide.

Step 2 Add two IP Phone services (Login and Logout).

Step 3 Create device and user profiles so that users can use the login service on an extension mobility-enabled IP Phone.

First, you must enable extension mobility system-wide. This is done in the service parameters area of Cisco CallManager Administration (**Service > Service Parameters > *select a server* > click the Cisco Extension Mobility** *service*). You can also define the maximum login time and the multiple login behavior. The Cisco Extension Mobility service only needs to be configured and run on the Publisher node.

Second, you need to add two services to the Cisco IP Phone Services page (**Feature > Cisco IP Phone Services**). One can be named Login, and the other can be named Logout. In the **Service URL** field, enter **http://*CRAServerName*:8080/Login**, where *CRAServerName* is the DNS host name or IP address of the application engine, and where **/Login** matches the HTTP trigger you will create on the CRA server. Perform the same steps for the **/Logout** trigger and service.

NOTE	The login and logout you just configured are services like any other. If they do not show up on the IP Phone, review Chapter 5 to see how to resolve problems with Cisco IP Phone services.

Third, you must create the extension mobility user and grant authentication proxy rights. This user is created so that the extension mobility application on the CRA server can access the directory. It is essential that the username and password of this user account match the username and password you define on the login and logout Generic Applications page.

For example, create a user named **EMUser** with a password of **Cisco** in CallManager Administration (**User > Add a New User**). After inserting the user into the CallManager user directory, configure the extension mobility profile for the user (select **Extension Mobility** from the **User Configuration** page) and make sure **Enable Authentication Proxy Rights** is selected for this user. Make a note of the username and password because you must use the same values to configure the **ExtensionMobilityUserID** and **ExtensionMobilityPassword** parameters on the CRA server.

Finally, you must individually enable IP Phones for extension mobility, create user device profiles, and then associate these profiles with the users in the LDAP directory.

To enable a phone for extension mobility, select the **Enable Extension Mobility Feature** checkbox on the Phone Configuration page for the device in CallManager Administration (**Device > Phone**).

User device profiles are created in CallManager Administration on the **User Device Profile Configuration** page (**Device > Device Profile > Add a New User Device Profile**).

User device profiles are associated with a user on the User Information page in CallManager Administration (**User > Global Directory >** *search for a user*) by selecting the extension mobility application profile configuration on the left.

Once you have configured extension mobility on CallManager, you can proceed to extension mobility configuration for the CRA server.

CRA Extension Mobility Configuration

You must complete three basic configuration steps on the CRA server:

Step 1 Configure the LDAP directory services.

Step 2 Configure the login and logout scripts.

Step 3 Configure the HTTP triggers for the login and logout scripts.

Configuring the LDAP directory services is the starting point for all CRA activities (including AA and IVR configuration). This step is particularly important for extension mobility. Directory configuration was already covered in the section "Directory Configuration" earlier in this chapter. Before you continue, ensure the directory is properly configured.

Extension mobility is designated as a generic application in CRA. You must add two applications under the Generic Applications section for extension mobility to work:

- hotel.aef
- hotelout.aef

The application ID assigned to each really doesn't matter because that ID is used by only CRA.

What is important to check is the application's status: whether the application is enabled or disabled. If extension mobility isn't working, make sure the application itself (both hotel.aef and hotelout.aef) is enabled. Also, **ExtensionMobilityUserID** and **ExtensionMobilityPassword** must be added so that they match the user ID and password created on CallManager. This user ID is very important because you must tell CallManager that this user has proxy rights to log in and log out any user, not just devices and device profiles associated with this user.

You can determine if the application is enabled by viewing the Cisco Script Application page in CRA Administration (**Applications > Configure Applications >** *choose Login or Logout application*).

Finally, the HTTP triggers are added to CRA. You must add a login and logout trigger. Enter a name for the trigger, such as **/Login**. You must use a forward slash (not a backslash) in front of the name.

NOTE   The trigger name must match the Service URL you specify in the Cisco IP Phone Services Configuration page in CallManager Administration (**Feature > Cisco IP Phone Services**). A forward slash must be in front of the name because CallManager points to http://*appservername*:8080/*trigger_name*. See Figures 16-5 and 16-6 for comparison of the crucial fields.

Figure 16-5 */login Trigger in CRA*

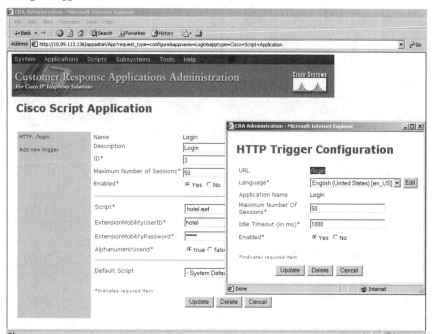

This HTTP trigger/CallManager Service URL disagreement is a frequent cause of problems with extension mobility. The trigger can have any name as long as it matches, but typically **/Login** and **/Logout** are the two triggers added. These are associated with the hotel.aef and hotelout.aef applications, respectively.

Figures 16-5 and 16-6 show the crucial fields highlighted. Figure 16-5 shows the HTTP Trigger Configuration window in CRA while Figure 16-6 shows the Service URL field in CallManager Administration. Notice that the "/login" is the same in both places. If it is not, the service does not work.

Finally, be aware that these HTTP triggers are reached via a Tomcat servlet running on the CRA server. This servlet listens on port 8080, not port 80. CRA administration is accomplished via IIS on port 80, but the HTTP triggers are accessed via port 8080. The Login/Logout IP Phone services configured on CallManager must specify port 8080.

Figure 16-6 */login Service in CallManager Administration*

Configuration Summary

Review your configuration for extension mobility. First, make sure there are no network connectivity issues or DNS name resolution issues between the application server and CallManager. Next, check the CRA configuration.

You must ensure the correct configuration of four areas on the CRA side.

For LDAP directory configuration, do the following:

- Make sure the directory type is correct.

- Make sure the TCP port is correct. The DC Directory uses port 8404. The standard LDAP port for Active Directory and Netscape iPlanet is 389, but those ports can be changed. This field must match how they are configured.

- Make sure the Directory user and password are correct.

- Make sure the User Base is correct.

For the login and logout scripts, do the following:

- Make sure both scripts are enabled.

- If in doubt about the state of the scripts, click **Reload**, thereby refreshing the application.

- Make sure the extension mobility user ID and password for this application are correct.

For the HTTP triggers, do the following:

- Make sure they match the names specified in CallManager Administration.

- Make sure the Tomcat servlet is running. Do this by simply browsing to http://*CRAServerName*:8080. This verifies that Tomcat is running. If it is not running, restart the CRA engine.

For the CallManager portion, do the following:

- Make sure that extension mobility is enabled service-wide.

- Make sure the two IP Phone services (Login and Logout) are configured correctly with the right IP address or DNS host name with port 8080 specified.

- Make sure the extension mobility user exists, the username and password match the settings on the CRA engine, and the user has the **Enable Proxy Authentication Rights** checkbox selected.

Understanding the Login and Logout process

To best understand how to troubleshoot an extension mobility problem you should understand exactly how the login process works:

Step 1   The user presses the **services** button on their IP Phone and the phone sends an HTTP request to retrieve the list of available services for the phone. If the user or administrator has added the login service for this IP Phone, the user should have the login service available.

Step 2   Selecting the login service sends an HTTP request to the CRA server for the /login trigger.

Step 3   If the device name is not presented during the /login request, the login script discovers the device name by querying the URL **http://**phone's IP address**/DeviceInformationX** on the IP Phone that sent the request for the login page and extracts the value in the **Hostname** field.

Step 4   The script sends XML output to the IP Phone requesting the user's ID and password. The phone displays "Please sign on" and the script ends.

Step 5 Once the user ID and password have been entered, the information is sent back to the application in the form of a new /login trigger that contains the user ID and password entered by the user.

Step 6 When the application receives the user ID and password, it authenticates the user by looking in the DC Directory LDAP directory for the user ID and password.

Step 7 The login script running on the CRA server sends an HTTP request to the Publisher server login service to perform the appropriate database operations. The URL for the login service is specified in DC Directory and should be **http://***Publisher IP address***/LoginService/login.asp**. The following information is passed to the login service:

— Application user ID and password

— Device identifier (MAC address)

— Extension mobility user ID and password

Step 8 The CallManager login service uses the application user ID and password to perform a user login on behalf of the end user. The user ID sent for the application user ID must have **Authentication Proxy Rights** enabled for the login to work.

Step 9 The login service adds the user ID and login time to the device record in the SQL database and copies the device profile for the user who logged in to the physical device.

Step 10 The login service sends a database change notification to restart the affected device so it can reregister with CallManager to obtain the new profile.

Step 11 Finally, the login service registers the login with the extension mobility logout service to start the countdown timer for automatic logout. For automatic logout to work, you must set the **Enforce Maximum Login Time** to True and then specify the **Maximum Login Time** on the Service Parameters Configuration page for extension mobility in CallManager Administration (**Service > Service Parameters >** *select a server >* **Cisco Extension Mobility**).

The logout process is very similar to the login process.

Step 1 The user presses the **services** button on the IP Phone and the phone sends an HTTP request to retrieve the list of available services for the phone. If the user or administrator has added the logout service on the device profile that is logged in, the user should have the logout service available. Remember that any services that were available on the IP Phone prior to logging in are overwritten by those specified on the device profile, so make sure you configure the logout service on any device profile you create. If not, the user won't be able to logout on demand. The IP Phone will still logout, but only after the **Maximum Login Time** timer has expired if the **Enforce Maximum Login Time** service parameter is enabled. An administrator can also log out the phone manually in the Phone Configuration page (**Device > Phone**).

Step 2   Selecting the logout service sends an HTTP request to the /logout trigger on the CRA server.

Step 3   If the device name is not presented during the /logout request, the logout script discovers the device name by querying the URL **http://***phone's IP address***/DeviceInformationX** on the phone that sent the request for the logout page and extracting the value specified in the **Hostname** field.

Step 4   The logout script running on the CRA server sends an HTTP request to the Publisher server login service to perform the appropriate database operations. Note that although the service on the Publisher is called the login service, it actually performs both logins and logouts. The URL for the login service is specified in DC Directory and should be **http://***Publisher IP address***/LoginService/login.asp**. The following information is passed to the login service:

— Application user ID and password

— Device identifier (MAC address)

Step 5   The CallManager logout service uses the application user ID and password to perform a user logout on behalf of the end user. The user ID sent for the application user ID must have **Authentication Proxy Rights** enabled for the login to work.

Step 6   The login service removes the user ID and login time from the SQL database and removes the logout request from the logout service for the device that the user had logged into.

Step 7   The login service sends a database change notification to restart the affected device so it can reregister with CallManager to obtain its original profile.

Troubleshooting Extension Mobility on CallManager 3.1 and 3.2

Although the process is fairly straightforward, there are several services involved in extension mobility and a malfunction in any one of them can cause extension mobility to stop working.

Table 16-10 contains a list of common problems and steps you can take to resolve the problem:

Table 16-10 *Extension Mobility Troubleshooting Tips*

Symptom or Error Message	Resolution
Pressing the **services** button on an IP Phone returns "invalid host" or nothing.	Check the **Services URL** entry in Enterprise Parameters (**System > Enterprise Parameters**). http://*IP address*/CCMCIP/getservicesmenu.asp
Pressing the **services** button on an IP Phone returns "No services Configured..."	Check that the services for the IP Phone or user device profile have the login or logout service properly configured.
After selecting the login or logout service, the IP phone displays "Requesting."	Check to make sure the Application Engine is running on the CRA server (**System > Engine**). Check the URL specified for the service in CallManager Administration. Make sure it's pointing to the right IP address (CRA server) and port 8080. Also check to see if port 8080 is blocked from the CRA sever to the IP Phone.
After selecting the login or logout service, nothing happens.	Check the trigger in CRA. The trigger name and URL in CallManager Administration must match exactly (note that the field is case sensitive).
IP phone displays "Login Unsuccessful" when trying to log in.	The username entered was not found in the LDAP directory. Check the username and password. Make sure you can log into the Cisco CallManager User Options web page on the server at http://*Publisher IP address*/CCMUser.
After entering a username and password, the IP phone returns to the login screen.	This can occur if Internet Explorer on either the CallManager server or the CRA server is configured to use a proxy server. To resolve this, from an Internet Explorer window, go to **Tools > Internet Options > Connection > LAN Settings**. Make sure the **Use a proxy server** checkbox is *not* selected. If you are running CRA 2.2(3a) or earlier, upgrade to 2.2(4). There is a defect in earlier versions that might exhibit symptoms such as this.
After login or logout, the IP phone resets (goes back to configuring IP) instead of restarting.	The IP phone is using DNS to resolve the CallManager name. Change the server name to an IP address in CallManager Administration (**System > Server**). Reset the IP phone and try the login/logout procedure again.
After entering the user ID and password, the IP phone displays "Authentication error."	Check the user ID and password you are using to log into the IP phone to be sure the values entered match the values configured in CallManager Administration.

Table 16-10 *Extension Mobility Troubleshooting Tips (Continued)*

Symptom or Error Message	Resolution
After entering the user ID and password, the IP phone displays "App authentication error."	Check the Application user ID and password on the CRA server. Also, verify the machine name is valid (no underscore characters). If the server has an invalid character in the machine name (for example, an underscore (_) character), then the login service cannot resolve the server name and does not work. Unfortunately, because of SQL server limitations, the only way to change the name of a CallManager server is to reinstall the CallManager service.
After entering username and password, the IP phone displays "Proxy Not Allowed."	Ensure that the application user ID being used by the CRA server is configured in CallManager with **Enable Authentication Proxy Rights** selected.
After entering username and password, the IP phone displays "LoginServer conn. Error."	This error indicates the CRA login script is unable to contact the login service on the Publisher. There are several possible reasons for this problem to occur. The IP address of the Publisher changed after the original installation, or the DNS name of the CallManager server cannot be resolved. To resolve this use the following steps: **Step 1** Open DC Directory Administrator on the Publisher (**Start > Programs > DC Directory Administrator**). **Step 2** Log in using the Directory Manager password you configured when you installed CallManager. **Step 3** Navigate to **cisco.com > CCN > systemProfiles**. Select the **Hoteling Profile**. **Step 4** Verify the IP address in the **URL** field. This should be the IP address of the Publisher server. If the **URL** field contains the name of the Publisher, verify that DNS name lookup is working properly from the server on which extension mobility is installed or change the URL to use the IP address of the Publisher.

continues

Table 16-10 *Extension Mobility Troubleshooting Tips (Continued)*

Symptom or Error Message	Resolution
After entering username and password, the IP phone displays "LoginServer conn. Error." (*Continued*)	This error can also happen when integrating with Microsoft Active Directory and the base context for the CRA engine is incorrect. To correct this problem, on the CRA server, set the base context to include a **cisco ou** (not just a **cisco dc**). So for the fictional company mycompany.com, the base context would be ou=cisco,dc=cisco,dc=mycompany,dc=com (change the mycompany entry to your company name).
	Note: When the base context is changed, the application settings must be reconfigured to find the directory information in the new context.
	If problems persist, use the sample login application at the following URL: http://*Publisher IP address*/ LoginService/Tools/sampleloginapp.asp.
	If you get an error indicating the page was not found, ensure the World Wide Web Publishing service is up and running on the Publisher. If it is running, try restarting the World Wide Web Publishing service. You may see the following error: "Error Parser Class Not Found org.apache.xerces.parsers.SAXParser null." If you see this error or a page not found even after restarting the World Wide Web Publishing service, the virtual directory was not created for the login service and the Classpath was not inserted during installation. To correct this, do the following:
	Step 1 Open the Computer Management applet (**Start > Programs > Administrative Tools > Computer Management**).
	Step 2 Navigate to the Internet Information Services Default Web Site (**Computer Management (local) > Services and Applications > Internet Information Services > Default Web Site**).
	Step 3 Right-click on Default Web Site and select **New > Virtual Directory**.
	Step 4 Click **Next**.

Table 16-10 *Extension Mobility Troubleshooting Tips (Continued)*

Symptom or Error Message	Resolution	
After entering username and password, the IP phone displays "LoginServer conn. Error." (*Continued*)	**Step 5**	Enter **LoginService** as the alias and click **Next**.
	Step 6	Enter **C:\CiscoWebs\LoginService** for the directory and click **Next**.
	Step 7	Click **Next**. You should now see **LoginService** under the Default Web Site.
	Step 8	Right-click on **LoginService** and select **Properties**.
	Step 9	Change the application protection to **High (Isolated)**.
	Step 10	Click the **Directory Security** tab.
	Step 11	Under Anonymous access and authentication control, click **Edit**.
	Step 12	Make sure that **Anonymous access** is selected.
	Step 13	Click **Edit** for the account used for anonymous access.
	Step 14	Change the username to **administrator** or any user that has administrative access on the server.
	Step 15	Verify that **Allow IIS to control password** is selected.
	Step 16	Click **OK**.
	Step 17	Click **OK**.
	Step 18	Next, add the system variables for the Classpath. Right-click on My Computer and select **Properties**.
	Step 19	Click the **Advanced** tab.
	Step 20	Click the **Environment Variables** button.
	Step 21	If the Classpath variable does not exist, click **New**. If it is on the list, select it and click **Edit**.
	Step 22	Ensure the **Variable Name** says **Classpath**.

continues

Table 16-10 *Extension Mobility Troubleshooting Tips (Continued)*

Symptom or Error Message	Resolution	
After entering username and password, the IP phone displays "LoginServer conn. Error." (*Continued*)	**Step 23**	The value for Classpath should include the following path. If there are existing values, add a semicolon at the end and append the following: C:\WINNT\Java\Lib\DirUser.jar; C:\WINNT\Java\Lib\Xerces.jar; C:\WINNT\Java\Lib\ DirUser-Notification.jar
	Step 24	Click **OK** three times to save the new environment variable.
	Step 25	Stop and restart the **IIS Admin** service (**Start > Programs > Administrative Tools > Services**).
	Another reason for this problem is if the administrator account on the CallManager server has been renamed or removed. The IIS LoginService virtual web uses the administrator account for access to this web page. If the user ID "administrator" is no longer present in the system, then the LoginService is not available for logging in users. To remedy this situation, do the following:	
	Step 1	Open the Computer Management applet (**Start > Programs > Administrative Tools > Computer Management**).
	Step 2	Navigate to the Internet Information Services Default Web Site (**Computer Management (local) > Services and Applications > Internet Information Services > Default Web Site**).
	Step 3	Right-click on **LoginService** and select **Properties**.
	Step 4	Click the **Directory Security** tab.
	Step 5	Under Anonymous access and authentication control, click **Edit**.
	Step 6	Make sure that **Anonymous access** is selected.
	Step 7	Click **Edit** for the account used for anonymous access.

Table 16-10 *Extension Mobility Troubleshooting Tips (Continued)*

Symptom or Error Message	Resolution
After entering username and password, the IP phone displays "LoginServer conn. Error." (*Continued*)	**Step 8** Change the username to any local user that has administrative access on the server.
	Step 9 Verify that **Allow IIS to control password** is selected.
	Step 10 Click **OK**.
	Step 11 Click **OK**.
	Step 12 Stop and restart the **IIS Admin** service (**Start > Programs > Administrative Tools > Services**).
	If you are using an IBM 340 series server, it might not have anonymous access correctly configured for login. To resolve this problem, enable IIS to control the password for anonymous devices by performing the following steps:
	Step 1 On the Cisco CallManager server, choose **Start > Programs > Administrative Tools > Internet Services Manager**.
	Step 2 Expand the tree on the left side of the page by selecting the machine name.
	Step 3 Choose **Default Web Site > LoginService**.
	Step 4 Right-click **LoginService** in the left pane and select **Properties**.
	Step 5 Click the **Directory Security** tab.
	Step 6 Under Anonymous access and authentication control, click **Edit**.
	Step 7 Make sure that **Anonymous access** is selected.
	Step 8 Click **Edit** for the account used for anonymous access.
	Step 9 Verify that **Allow IIS to control password** is selected.
	Step 10 Click **OK**.
	Step 11 Click **OK**.
	Step 12 Close the Internet Services Manager.

continues

Table 16-10 *Extension Mobility Troubleshooting Tips (Continued)*

Symptom or Error Message	Resolution
When reverting back to the default profile after logging out from an IP phone, services are no longer available.	After adding the services to an IP phone from the Phone Configuration page in CallManager Administration (**Device > Phone**), the **Update** button must be pressed so the auto-generated default profile gets updated.
After logging in, the user does not have any services available.	The user profile did not have any services associated with it when loaded on the IP phone. Solution: First, change the user profile to include the Login/Logout services. Second, change the phone the user is logged in on to include the login/logout services. Once updated, the user will get the logout service.

Whenever there is a problem with authentication of any user (either an extension mobility user or the application user), use the URL http://*Publisher IP address*/CCMUser and attempt to login. If login fails, extension mobility will not work as expected. Double-check the username and password before proceeding.

To verify that the login service is functioning properly, access a test login service available as part of CallManager. The URL is

http://*Publisher IP address*/LoginService/Tools/sampleloginapp.asp

Figure 16-7 shows the sample login application used to test the extension mobility login service.

In the **App ID** field, enter the user ID for the user with proxy authentication rights. In the **Password** field, enter the password for that user. Enter the device name of a device configured for extension mobility, the user ID for the user you want to log into the IP phone, and the device profile you want to use to log into that phone. When you click the **Login** button, the IP phone should restart with the new profile. If not, you will see an error message indicating what the problem is. This sample application can be used to narrow down the problem to either a CallManager login service problem or a CRA problem.

Figure 16-7 *Extension Mobility Sample Login Application*

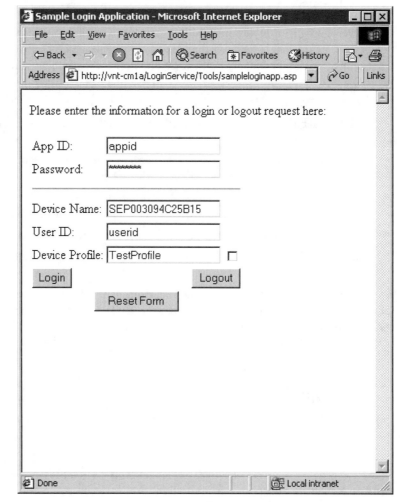

Extension Mobility for CallManager 3.3

Prior to release 3.3, the CRA Engine is required for the extension mobility feature to work. If you are troubleshooting extension mobility on CallManager 3.1 or 3.2, follow the instructions presented in the preceding section, "Extension Mobility for CallManager 3.1 and 3.2."

In CallManager 3.3 and later, the CRA Engine is no longer used for extension mobility. The extension mobility service that runs on CallManager is completely responsible for login and logout including the end user authentication. The following are changes in CallManager 3.3:

- **Easier configuration and installation**—The CRA engine is no longer required and because it is no longer required, there is also no need to configure generic applications or triggers. All functionality is already built into the extension mobility service.

- **Better tracing facilities**—Traces are available in the C:\Program Files\Cisco\Trace\emapp directory.

- **Flexible user ID**—Allows you to specify either alphanumeric or numeric user ID to be used for login.

- **A single IP Phone service for both login and logout**—The IP Phone service for login and logout toggles depending on whether the phone is already logged in or not.

- **Device profile selection**—A user who logs in can choose from a list of device profiles to log in with if there is more than one device profile associated with the user.

- **Localization support**—Supports all the locales supported by CallManager.

- **Alarms and PerfMon support**—Supports monitoring for errors and real-time information.

The process of logging in and logging out in CallManager 3.3 is virtually identical to CallManager 3.1 and 3.2. The biggest difference is the lack of the CRA engine. To configure extension mobility in CallManager 3.3, the configuration of user device profiles and the association of the device profiles with users is identical to previous versions.

From a configuration standpoint, the biggest change is the URL you use to access the extension mobility service. Instead of pointing the service to the IP address of the CRA server on port 8080, you must use the following as the Extension Mobility Service URL:

> http://*Publisher IP address*/emapp/EMAppServlet?device=#DEVICENAME#

NOTE   The URL listed above is case-sensitive. Ensure "**emapp**" is in all lowercase and "**EMAppServlet**" has the proper capitalization.

In CallManager 3.3, the **#DEVICENAME#** portion of the URL has a special meaning. When an IP phone sees this as part of the URL, it replaces that portion of the URL with its device name when it sends the HTTP request to the web server. This makes the login less complex because the extension mobility service does not have to query the IP phone for its device name because it is already part of the URL.

If you are converting from CallManager 3.1 or 3.2 to 3.3, you must change the URL to the Extension Mobility Service URL shown above. In CallManager 3.1 and 3.2 there were two separate services: one for login and another for logout. You can eliminate one and just keep one service or just put the same URL for both login and logout.

The HTTP portion of the extension mobility service runs as part of the Cisco Tomcat service. One of the first troubleshooting steps if you are having problems accessing the login service is to ensure the Cisco Tomcat service is running.

Understanding the Login and Logout Process

To best understand how to troubleshoot an extension mobility problem you should understand exactly how the login process works:

Step 1 The user presses the **services** button on their IP Phone and the phone sends an HTTP request to retrieve the list of available services for the phone. If the user or administrator has added the login service for this IP Phone, the user should have the login service available.

Step 2 Selecting the login service sends an HTTP request to the EMApp virtual web on the CallManager web server. The IP Phone replaces #DEVICENAME# in the URL with the phone's device name. This virtual web is controlled by the Cisco Tomcat service.

Step 3 The script sends XML output to the phone requesting the user's ID and password. The phone displays "Please sign on" and the script ends.

Step 4 Once the user ID and password have been entered, the information is sent back to the EMApp.

Step 5 When the user ID and password are received by the application, it authenticates the user by looking in the DC Directory LDAP directory for the user ID and password.

Step 6 The EMApp virtual web sends an HTTP request to the Publisher server login service to perform the appropriate database operations. The URL for the login service is specified in DC Directory and should be http://*Publisher IP address*/LoginService/login.asp. The following information is passed to the login service:

— Application user ID and password

— Device identifier (MAC address)

— Extension mobility user ID and password

Step 7 The CallManager login service uses the application user ID and password to perform a user login on behalf of the end user. The user ID sent for the application user ID must have **Authentication Proxy Rights** (**User > Add a New User >** *select* **Extension Mobility**) enabled for the login to work. In CallManager 3.3, this user is automatically configured with the username EMApp and should not have to be configured. The

EMApp user does not show up in the global directory; however, you can see it if you look directly in the DC Directory using DC Directory Administrator.

Step 8 The login service adds the user ID and login time to the device record in the SQL database and copies the device profile for the user who logged in to the physical device.

Step 9 The login service sends a database change notification to restart the affected device so it can reregister with CallManager to obtain the new profile.

Step 10 Finally, the login service registers the login with the extension mobility logout service to start the countdown timer for automatic logout. For automatic logout to work, you must set the **Enforce Maximum Login Time** to True and then specify the **Maximum Login Time** on the Service Parameters Configuration page for extension mobility in CallManager Administration (**Service > Service Parameters >** *select a server* **> Cisco Extension Mobility**).

The logout process is very similar to the login process.

Step 1 The user presses the **services** button on the IP Phone and the phone sends an HTTP request to retrieve the list of available services for the phone. If the user or administrator has added the logout service on the device profile that is logged in, the user should have the logout service available. Remember that any services that were available on the IP Phone prior to logging in are overwritten by those configured on the device profile, so make sure you configure the logout service on any device profile you create. If not, the user won't be able to logout on demand. The IP Phone will still logout, but only after the **Maximum Login Time** timer has expired if the **Enforce Maximum Login Time** service parameter is enabled. An administrator can also log out the phone manually in the Phone Configuration page (**Device > Phone**).

Step 2 Selecting the logout service sends an HTTP request to the EMApp virtual web on the CallManager web server. The IP Phone replaces #DEVICENAME# in the URL with the phone's device name. This virtual web is controlled by the Cisco Tomcat service.

Step 3 The EMApp vitual web sends an HTTP request to the Publisher server login service to perform the appropriate database operations. Note that although the service on the Publisher is called the login service, it actually performs both login and logout. The URL for the login service is specified in DC Directory and should be http://*Publisher IP address*/ LoginService/login.asp. The following information is passed to the login service:

— Application user ID and password

— Device identifier (MAC address)

Step 4   The CallManager login service uses the application user ID and password to perform a user logout on behalf of the end user. The user ID sent for the application user ID must have **Authentication Proxy Rights** enabled for the login to work.

Step 5   The login service removes the user ID and login time from the SQL database and removes the logout request from the logout service for the device that the user had logged into.

Step 6   The login service sends a database change notification to restart the affected device so it can reregister with CallManager to obtain its original profile.

Troubleshooting Extension Mobility on CallManager 3.3

Troubleshooting extension mobility on CallManager 3.3 is very similar to troubleshooting extension mobility on CallManager 3.1 or CallManager 3.2. Many of the common troubleshooting techniques presented in Table 16-10 apply to CallManager 3.3 as well, so be sure to use Table 16-10 as a reference for all extension mobility problems. There are some additional error messages you might encounter when using extension mobility in CallManager 3.3. Table 16-11 lists some common error messages and error codes and how to resolve the problem.

Table 16-11   *Extension Mobility in CallManager 3.3 Error Messages*

Error Message or Error Code	Resolution
Error: [0]	Check if the CallManager services are running.
Error: [2] or Error: [3]	Check whether the EMApp user ID and password are configured in the Windows registry at the following key: HKEY_LOCAL_MACHINE\SOFTWARE\Cisco Systems, Inc.\Directory Configuration\AppUsers\EMApp If not, then the directory installation failed. Try re-running the CallManager installer.
Device does not allow logon	Make sure **Enable Extension Mobility Feature** is enabled and a logout profile is selected on the Phone Configuration page in CallManager Administration (**Device > Phone**).

continues

Table 16-11 *Extension Mobility in CallManager 3.3 Error Messages (Continued)*

Error Message or Error Code	Resolution
Error: [6] or Error: [12]	There is no device profile associated with the user attempting to log in. To correct this error, make sure an existing device profile is associated in the directory with the user. If there is no device profile created for the user, add a device profile for the user and associate it in the directory with the user.
Error: [9]	There is a problem communicating with the LDAP directory. Ensure the DC Directory service is running. If you are having problems with your LDAP directory, refer to Chapter 18.
Error: [10]	The EMApp user does not have **Enable Authentication Proxy Rights** selected. In CallManager 3.3, this user does not appear in the Global Directory in CallManager Administration. To check the status of the **Enable Authentication Proxy Rights** configuration, you must directly access the directory through the DC Directory Administrator.
	Step 1 Open the DC Directory Administrator (**Start > Programs > DC Directory Administrator**).
	Step 2 Log in using the Directory Manager password you configured when you installed CallManager. If you have lost your Directory Manager password, refer to Chapter 18 for instructions on how to recover the password.
	Step 3 Navigate to **Directory > cisco.com > CCN > profiles** and locate the profile named **EMApp-CCNProfile**.
	Step 4 Double-click on **EMApp-CCNProfile**.
	Step 5 The field labeled **Authentication Proxy Rights** should say **true**.
	Step 6 If it says **false** or is blank, click **Modify**.
	Step 7 Enter **true** in the **Authentication Proxy Rights** field.
	Step 8 Click **OK**.
	Step 9 Close the DC Directory Administrator.
Another user logged in	You cannot log in a user when another user is already logged in. Logout the other user and try logging in again.
System not enabled for login	The extension mobility service is not enabled on the server. In CallManager Serviceability, go to **Tools > Service Activation >** *select a server* and ensure the Cisco Extension Mobility service is activated.

Table 16-11 *Extension Mobility in CallManager 3.3 Error Messages (Continued)*

Error Message or Error Code	Resolution
User logged in elsewhere	The system is configured to not allow multiple logins. You can enable multiple logins by making a selection in the Multiple Logins Allowed service parameter in CallManager Administration (**Service > Service Parameters >** *select a server* **> Cisco Extension Mobility**). You can also logout the user from the other phone they are logged into and then retry the login attempt.
Error: [100]	The URL is probably incorrect. Check the URL of the service configured in CallManager Administration (**Feature > Cisco IP Phone Services**). It should end with **?device=#DEVICENAME#**
Error: [101]	Either the IIS on the extension mobility server is down or the URL of the Login service is not configured in LDAP. To check configuration in LDAP, open DC Directory Administrator on the Publisher (**Start > Programs > DC Directory Administrator**), login using the Directory Manager password you configured when you installed CallManager, and navigate to **cisco.com > CCN > systemProfiles**. Select the **Hoteling Profile** and verify the IP address in the URL field. This should be the IP address of the Publisher server.

For additional troubleshooting information, you can enable tracing for the extension mobility service. On the Extension Mobility Service Parameters page (**Service > Service Parameters >** *select a server* **> Cisco Extension Mobility**), change the **Debug traces on** parameter to **True** and restart the Cisco Tomcat service.

NOTE   Restarting the Tomcat service will disrupt other services running on Cisco Tomcat such as CAR and Cisco IP Manager Assistant. The restart should be done at a non-critical time.

Once the debug flag is enabled, the debug traces are available in the following directory: C:\Program Files\Cisco\Trace\emapp.

Cisco CallManager Attendant Console

Cisco Attendant Console (formerly known as Cisco WebAttendant) is a client/server application that provides manual attendant console functionality. The Attendant Console client is associated with an IP Phone and allows an attendant to place, receive, and dispatch calls to all users within the CallManager cluster. The interface allows the attendant to control all the lines on the associated IP Phone. It also monitors the line status for all lines within the cluster and allows the attendant to quickly view the state of any line.

Attendant Console is the replacement for Cisco WebAttendant. Cisco WebAttendant ships with all versions of CallManager up to CallManager 3.2. However, Cisco highly recommends that users of CallManager 3.1 and later replace the WebAttendant application with Attendant Console for increased functionality and stability. For this reason, we only discuss Attendant Console here.

This section covers some common problems associated with Attendant Console. It is important to recognize the different components involved with Attendant Console:

- The server component is called Cisco Telephony Call Dispatcher (TCD) and resides on the CallManager server.
- The client component runs on a PC running Windows 98, Windows NT, Windows 2000, or Windows XP.

The following sections examine the different pieces you need to check when troubleshooting problems with Attendant Console.

Understanding the Server Components

The server component of Attendant Console runs as the Telephony Call Dispatcher (TCD) service on one or more CallManager servers in the CallManager cluster.

One function of the TCD service is to keep track of line states for all the IP phones in the cluster. The TCD service on a single CallManager server is only able to obtain line state information about IP phones registered to the CallManager service on the same server on which the TCD service is running. The TCD service on each node in the cluster shares information with the other TCD services so that all the TCD services have a snapshot of the line states anywhere in the cluster.

Note that in CallManager 3.1 and earlier, the TCD service has no mechanism to update line states until there is a line state change. In CallManager 3.2 and later, the TCD service is able to get an immediate snapshot of the line states for all lines in the cluster.

The TCD service is also responsible for accepting calls on pilot points and dispatching the calls to agents that are online using the Attendant Console. A *pilot point* is a virtual DN that alerts TCD to receive and direct calls to hunt group members. A *hunt group* comprises a list of destinations that determine the call redirection order. In CallManager 3.1 and CallManager 3.2, the configuration of pilot points and hunt groups is accessed from the **Service > Cisco WebAttendant** menu in CallManager Administration. In CallManager 3.3 and later, however, the menu item is renamed **Cisco CM Attendant Console**.

Both the TCD service and the Attendant Console client rely on the CTI Manager service for call control to CallManager. Ensure that both the CTI Manager service and the TCD service are running on your CallManager servers.

Because the TCD service uses CTI to log into the CTI Manager service, it must have a username and password to log in to the CTI Manager. By default the TCD service uses the username **ac** and the password **12345**. For Attendant Console to work properly, you must create a user in the CallManager Global Directory that matches the user the TCD service is using to log in. You can either create a user called **ac** with password **12345**, or you can change the defaults and use any username and password you like.

To change the username or password, first create the user in the CallManager Global Directory (**User > Global Directory**). Ensure the user has **Enable CTI Application Use** selected on the User Configuration page in CallManager Administration. In CallManager 3.3 and later, also make sure **Call Park Retrieval Allowed** is enabled if you want the Attendant Console users to be able to monitor and retrieve parked calls.

Once you have created the user, follow these steps to change the username and password used by the TCD service to log into the CTI Manager service:

Step 1 Open a command window by executing **Start > Run > cmd.exe**.

Step 2 Enter **cd C:\Program Files\Cisco\CallManagerAttendant**.

Step 3 Enter **bin\acenc.exe** *new password*, where *new password* is the new password you would like to use. Write down the new password or copy it to the clipboard.

Step 4 Enter **notepad etc\ACServer.properties**.

Step 5 Locate the **JTAPI_USERNAME=** line and enter the username you want to use after the **JTAPI_USERNAME=**—for example, JTAPI_USERNAME=ac.

Step 6 Locate the **JTAPI_PASSWORD=** line and enter the password you obtained in Step 3 after **JTAPI_PASSWORD=**—for example, JTAPI_PASSWORD=5e51405d76.

Step 7 Save the file and exit Notepad.

Step 8 Restart **Cisco Telephony Call Dispatcher** service (**CallManager Serviceability > Tools > Control Center**).

Step 9 Repeat Steps 1 through 8 on all CallManager nodes in the cluster.

The **ac** user must be associated with all the IP Phones on which you want to use Attendant Console. Failure to associate an IP Phone with the **ac** user results in the inability to initialize call control on the Attendant Console client.

Understanding the Attendant Console Client

The Attendant Console client is a java application that allows an attendant to control an IP Phone and monitor line state information across a CallManager cluster. Remember that the Attendant Console TCD service is not compatible with the legacy Cisco WebAttendant. Any time you upgrade your CallManager version, reinstall the Attendant Console client to match the updated version.

There are a few client login problems to look at. The first and most obvious problem is related to an incorrect username and password, which can prevent Attendant Console from coming online. The Attendant Console user is created on the Cisco CM Attendant Console User Configuration page in CallManager Administration (select **Service > Cisco CM Attendant Console >** *click the link in the upper-right corner to* **Cisco CallManager Attendant Console User Configuration**). If necessary, reset the password to ensure that the client matches the username and password.

The associated IP Phone must be registered for call control to function on the Attendant Console client. If the IP Phone is not registered, begin troubleshooting the registration problem. Until this issue is addressed, the client login will not work correctly. For registration troubleshooting, see Chapter 4, "Skinny Client Registration."

Troubleshooting Attendant Console

The majority of Attendant Console problems are due to a simple misconfiguration. Table 16-12 lists a variety of common problems encountered with Attendant Console and suggestions on how to resolve them.

Table 16-12 *Common Problems and Resolutions for Cisco CallManager Attendant Console*

Problem	Resolutions
When a call is made to a pilot point, you get fast busy. Or The lines on a controlled IP Phone are disabled in the Attendant Console client.	• Make sure the TCD service is running on all the CallManager servers. • Make sure the CTI Manager service is running on all the CallManager servers. • The pilot point or the controlled IP Phones are not in the controlled device list of the **ac** user. You must create a user with the ID **ac** in CallManager Administration (**User > Global Directory**), and associate all pilot points and attendant IP Phones with this user. Make sure that this user has **Enable CTI Application Use** selected. Follow the instructions in the previous section for changing the username and password. If integrating with Active Directory, you must create the **ac** user in the Active Directory. • The user(s) specified in the user/line pair(s) in the hunt group associated with the pilot point is not online. From the Attendant Console client, log in and go online.

Table 16-12 *Common Problems and Resolutions for Cisco CallManager Attendant Console (Continued)*

Problem	Resolutions
Line state is not updated in the Speed Dial and Directory windows on the Attendant Console client.	Line state updates from the server to the client are sent using User Datagram Protocol (UDP) packets. If a Network Address Translation (NAT) device or a firewall separates the client and server, the client most likely cannot receive line state updates from the server. Ensure that both client and server are on the same side of the NAT device or the firewall and ensure there are no access lists blocking UDP packets between the CallManager servers and the Attendant Console clients.
	Remember, UDP does not provide any mechanisms for retransmission, so any packet loss might cause the line state for a specific line to get out of sync.
I just added a user in CallManager Administration, but I don't see that user in the directory window on the Attendant Console client.	By default the directory is synchronized every three hours based on the **DirectorySyncPeriod** service parameter for the TCD service.
	The server extracts the user list from the LDAP directory when one of the following conditions is met:
	• TCD service is started and the **DirectorySyncPeriod** is not zero
	• **DirectorySyncPeriod** expires
	• **DirectorySyncPeriod** changed in CallManager Administration (**Service > Cisco CM Attendant Console >** *click the link to* **Cisco CallManager Attendant Console Server Configuration >** *select a server*)
	Also, the client loads the user list only at login. For the client to see an updated user list from the server, the attendant needs to logout and login again after any one of the preceding conditions has been met.
	Also, users without telephone numbers do not appear on the client. Make sure that all relevant users have DNs configured for them in the directory. .
Initial line state shows Unknown status for all DNs; however, the state is updated when the line state changes.	You are running CallManager version 3.1. Initial line state is not available until CallManager 3.2.
Line states of some DNs show Unknown state.	Make sure the TCD service is running on all CallManager servers that have IP phones registered to them, including any backup CallManager servers that might have phones registered in the event of a failover.
	If you are running CallManager 3.1 or 3.2, make sure you installed the new Attendant Console on all the servers in the cluster.

continues

Table 16-12 *Common Problems and Resolutions for Cisco CallManager Attendant Console (Continued)*

Problem	Resolutions
In CallManager 3.1, the longest idle algorithm is not working properly. Even though there are a number of hunt group lines available, the server is sending the calls only to a few lines.	This is because CallManager 3.1(x) does not allow the TCD service to retrieve the initial line state information, so TCD assumes the lines are not available until a state transition occurs on each line. Call all the hunt group lines once so that the server gets the initial line state of the hunt group line, or upgrade to CallManager 3.2 or later so that the initial line state is available.
When a call is not answered by the attendant and forwarded to voice mail, the voice mail system plays the attendant greeting instead of the pilot point greeting.	The TCD service parameter **ResetOriginalCalled** controls whether the original called party number is reset when a call is presented to an attendant. When set to **true**, a call that forwards to an attendant and then forwards to voice mail receives the mailbox for the attendant. When set to **false**, the caller receives the mailbox for the pilot point DN because it is the original called party number. If you are using Cisco Unity, ensure that you are using TSP version 6.0(2) or later.
Login failed when a user attempts to log in at the Attendant Console client.	Remember that users for Attendant Console are created in the Cisco CallManager Attendant Console User Configuration page (**Service > Cisco CM Attendant Console > Cisco CallManager Attendant Console User Configuration**), not the User Configuration page (**User > Global Directory**). Ensure the username and password configured in CallManager Administration match the username and password being used at the client.
You receive the message "connect to the same operator terminal" on the Attendant Console client.	Attendant Console does not support placing a call to another line that is controlled by the same Attendant Console client.
The directory on the Attendant Console client does not show the expected directory list.	By default the Attendant Console client application shows the user list data in the following order of precedence: 1 User list filename explicitly defined in the **Settings > Advanced** tab in the Attendant Console client. 2 **userlist\CorporateDirectory.txt** if it exists on the server. 3 **userlist\AutoGenerated.txt** if it exists on the server. By default the AutoGenerated.txt file is used because the user list filename is blank by default and the CorporateDirectory.txt file does not exist by default.

Cisco Personal Assistant

Cisco Personal Assistant provides users with customized call routing based on a variety of routing rules based on called party number, calling party number, time of day, and Microsoft Exchange schedule status. Personal Assistant also offers speech recognition capabilities that allow you to dial numbers, create conference calls, and browse voice mail with only the sound of your voice.

Personal Assistant is a complex application and requires a book of its own for troubleshooting it. There are several things to check from a CallManager perspective if you encounter problems with Personal Assistant.

TIP   You can find troubleshooting tips for Cisco Personal Assistant on Cisco.com at the following URL:

www.cisco.com/univercd/cc/td/doc/product/voice/assist/assist3/eng/admgd/patrbl.htm

---

Call Routing Problems and Personal Assistant

Most problems with Personal Assistant are due to call routing problems. Be sure to read through all of Chapter 9, "Call Routing" and become extremely familiar with how partitions and calling search spaces work.

Personal Assistant works by intercepting calls that are destined to IP phones managed by Personal Assistant. It accomplishes this through a CTI route point that matches the DNs for all the phones controlled by Personal Assistant. For example, if your extension range is 20000 through 29999, you use a CTI route point with a DN of 2XXXX to intercept all the calls.

As mentioned in Chapter 9, CallManager performs closest-match routing when attempting to route a call. This means that if you have a CTI route point with a DN of 2XXXX and an IP phone configured with DN 20001, CallManager routes the call to the phone directly. To force CallManager to route calls to the Personal Assistant CTI route point and not to the IP phone directly, you must place the IP phone DNs in a partition that is not in the calling search space of other devices in the system. When Personal Assistant intercepts the call, it has a calling search space that allows it to redirect the call to the IP phone when necessary.

If Personal Assistant is not intercepting calls (which means it cannot apply call routing rules), make sure you have created the required interceptor ports and configured the Personal Assistant servers correctly for those ports. The following web page on Cisco.com explains how to configure your partitions, calling search spaces, and CTI route points correctly:

www.cisco.com/univercd/cc/td/doc/product/voice/assist/assist3/eng/admgd/pacm.htm

If Personal Assistant never intercepts calls, potential problems might be

- The CTI route points and translation patterns are not configured with the correct partition or calling search space.
- The calling phone's calling search space might not include the PA partition as the first partition.
- The Personal Assistant server is not configured to intercept calls for the called phone.
- The CTI route points used as interceptor ports are not assigned to the Personal Assistant JTAPI user.

If you are sure you have followed those directions, you can get more details by checking the CCM trace files. Chapter 9 details how to read trace files when troubleshooting calling search space and partition problems.

Personal Assistant and Message Waiting Indicator Issues

See Chapter 14 for a troubleshooting tip involving PA and MWI in the section "Message Waiting Indicator (MWI)" under "Cisco Unity."

Cisco IP SoftPhone

Cisco IP SoftPhone is a java application that can run on most Windows 98, Windows NT, Windows 2000, and Windows XP computers. This section discusses a few of the common errors that could occur with Cisco IP SoftPhone.

TIP   You can find troubleshooting tips (in up to five languages, depending on the version) for Cisco IP SoftPhone on Cisco.com or at the following URL:

www.cisco.com/univercd/cc/td/doc/product/voice/c_ipphon/ip_7960/softphon/index.htm

Click the link to the version of SoftPhone you are using, for example, "Cisco IP SoftPhone Version 1.3," choose your language, click the link to **Cisco IP SoftPhone Administrator Guide (1.3)**, and then click the link to **Troubleshooting**.

Line Number Displays, But No Dial Tone

If the Cisco IP SoftPhone shows up with the line number but does not go off-hook, it is because an administrator created a CTI route point and associated it with the user instead of a CTI port. Delete the CTI route point and create a CTI port on the Phone Configuration page in CallManager Administration (**Device > Phone**).

Echo Problems with Cisco IP SoftPhone

See Chapter 7, "Voice Quality," and refer to the section called "Eliminating Echo Problems on Cisco IP SoftPhone" for help with this problem.

One-way Audio and Using Cisco IP SoftPhone over VPN

When using a virtual private network (VPN) connection on a PC, that PC is assigned a VPN adapter IP address. The PC also has an interface IP address that corresponds to the local IP subnet for that PC. While the VPN tunnel is active, all traffic on the corporate network appears to originate from the VPN adapter IP address. By default, Cisco IP SoftPhone uses the interface IP address when CallManager asks SoftPhone for its IP address. CallManager then tells the remote end of the call to send packets to the SoftPhone's interface IP address. The interface IP address is usually not reachable from the corporate network. The result is a one-way audio stream. SoftPhone should be sending the VPN adaptor IP address instead.

To ensure two-way audio when using NAT or utilizing VPN client software, make sure that you have configured the VPN IP address, instead of the interface IP address, under the Network Audio Settings on Cisco IP SoftPhone. To get there, do the following:

Step 1 Open Cisco IP SoftPhone and click the **Settings** icon.

Step 2 Click the **Audio settings** tab.

Step 3 Click **Network Audio Settings**.

Step 4 There are three ways to get the correct IP address advertised. The three methods are

- **Automatic Selection**—This setting requires the file getIP.asp to be present on the web server where you installed the SoftPhone web installer. SoftPhone uses this URL to obtain its IP address from the web server. The URL depends on what virtual web you selected when you installed the SoftPhone web installer. For example, if you selected "softphone" as the name of your web installer directory and you are using the English version of SoftPhone, the URL is http://*Server IP Address*/softphone/en/../getIP.asp. Enter the URL you see on your SoftPhone into a standard web browser. You should see a line of text that begins with your IP address.

- **Select Address**—There is a pull-down menu of addresses on the local machine. Select the one that is most appropriate.

- **Specify Address**—The address to be advertised can be manually entered if needed.

Step 5 Click **OK** when finished.

Cisco IP SoftPhone must be restarted for the changes to take effect.

Cisco IP SoftPhone Has No Lines

There are a few common reasons why a line may not show up on SoftPhone. Some of the most common reasons are

- The user has not been assigned a line in CallManager Administration. Check the Device Association page in CallManager Administration (**User > Global Directory >** *search for and select a user* **> Device Association**) to ensure that there are lines assigned to this user.

- There is a username or password mismatch. Verify username and password settings. You might have to reboot the SoftPhone client PC after changing the username or password.

- The Microsoft Network settings are not properly configured on the SoftPhone client PC. If the SoftPhone client is installed on a Windows 98 or Windows 95 system, make sure that **File and Printer sharing for Microsoft Networks** is enabled (**Programs > Settings > Control Panel > Network > Access Control tab > File and Print Sharing**). Also make sure you are running the **Client for Microsoft Networks** (**Programs > Settings > Control Panel > Network > Configuration** tab) and you have **User-level access control** enabled (**Programs > Settings > Control Panel > Network > Access Control** tab).

Cisco IP Phone Services

Applications (known as phone services) deliver interactive content to Cisco IP Phones. Applications are created to provide various services to phone users and can be as simple or complex as the service developer chooses to make them. Cisco provides a few basic phone services in the Cisco IP Phone Services Software Developer's Kit, accessible at the following link (which requires CCO login) or by searching for "Cisco IP Phone SDK" on Cisco.com:

> www.cisco.com/pcgi-bin/dev_support/access_level/
> products.cgi?product=IP_PHONE_SERV

Phone services are configured in CallManager Administration (**Feature > Cisco IP Phone Services**), subscribed to by users through the Cisco CallManager User Options web page, and accessed through the **services** button on the IP Phone.

Phone services are usually developed within a company based on the company's needs. For detailed information about creating, coding, validating, and deploying Cisco IP Phone services, consult the Cisco Press book *Developing Cisco IP Phone Services* (ISBN: 1-58705-060-9) available at ciscopress.com and other local or online booksellers.

Services are very simple to write; the most common problem with a service is usually a disagreement between the service code and the Cisco IP Phone schema. The CD-ROM included with *Developing Cisco IP Phone Services* provides a tool called the XML Validator, which takes the service code you or someone in your company writes and validates it against the Cisco IP Phone schema.

For more information about troubleshooting IP phones, refer to Chapter 5 in this book.

Cisco IP Videoconferencing (IP/VC)

The Cisco videoconferencing solution is the Cisco IP/VC product family, which comprises several products. The IP/VC 3500 Series consists of the IP/VC 3510 Multipoint Control Unit, the IP/VC 3520 and 3525 Gateways, and the IP/VC 3530 Video Terminal Adapter. In addition, the Cisco Multimedia Conference Manager is an H.323 gatekeeper/proxy. The Cisco IP/VC product family is designed to work with H.323 standards-based video-conference client devices from a variety of vendors.

The Multimedia Conference Manager (MCM) software is part of Cisco IOS Software. It functions as a high-performance H.323 gatekeeper and proxy, enabling network managers to control bandwidth and priority settings for H.323 videoconferencing services based on individual network configurations and capacities. The MCM is available across a wide range of Cisco router platforms, including the Cisco 2500, 2600, 3600, and the MC3810 multiservice access concentrator.

These products, and the solutions they enable, are developed for enterprises and service providers who want a reliable, easy-to-manage, cost-effective network infrastructure for videoconferencing applications deployment. The Cisco IP/VC product family enables videoconferencing over IP networks and at the same time integrates legacy H.320 systems and networks protecting original investments that enterprises make in videoconferencing.

The IP Videoconferencing design guide provides a great deal of useful information:

www.cisco.com/warp/public/779/largeent/netpro/avvid/srnd.html

You can learn more about IP/VC at the following links:

www.cisco.com/warp/public/cc/pd/mxsv/ipvc3500/index.shtml
www.cisco.com/univercd/cc/td/doc/product/ipvc/

Cisco Conference Connection

Cisco Conference Connection (CCC) is a Meet-Me audio conference server that integrates with CallManager. A Conference Connection server has two distinct components:

- An IP IVR front-end that accepts calls and parses user input to determine the conference ID and directs the party to the appropriate conference.

- An H.323 multipoint conference unit (MCU) that performs mixing of audio streams.

Future versions of Conference Connection might allow the use of external hardware digital signal processor (DSP) resources for audio stream mixing; however, versions 1.1 and 1.2 only support software conferencing that runs on the Conference Connection server.

The IP IVR portion of a Conference Connection server is nothing more than a CRA server that can only run the Conference Connection IP IVR scripts. If you are having problems dialing into the Conference Connection CTI route point, follow the troubleshooting methodology outlined in the earlier "Customer Response Applications (CRA)" section.

If the JTAPI subsystem is out of service in CRA, Conference Connection will not work. If the subsystem is down, perform the following tasks:

- Check to make sure that the CallManager server is up and running.

- Make sure that the CallManager service and the CTI Manager service are running. If they are not running, go to Windows Services and start each service.

- On the Conference Connection server (**Application Administration > JTAPI**), ensure that the IP address matches the IP address(es) of one or more CallManager servers running the CTI Manager service.

- Open the Configure page on the Conference Connection server (**Application Administration > Engine > Configure**). The Application Engine Hostname (IP address) must match the IP address configured on the Conference Connection server. If it does not, enter the correct IP address and click **Update**.

TIP	You can find troubleshooting tips for Cisco Conference Connection release 1.1(1) on Cisco.com or at the following URL: www.cisco.com/univercd/cc/td/doc/product/voice/cccdocs/admingd/rdzc5.htm

Ensure the Necessary Services Are Started

Several services must all be running in order for Conference Connection to work. The following services should be configured with a Startup Type of **Automatic**:

- Cisco Application Engine
- Conferencing Gateway
- Cisco AVVID Alarm Service

Also, these services should be running and configured with a Startup Type of **Automatic**:

- IIS Admin Service
- World Wide Web Publishing Service
- Event Log

Additionally, CallManager itself must be running for Conference Connection to successfully interoperate with CallManager.

Using Event Viewer with Conference Connection

You can use the Windows Event Viewer to look at the application events log when trying to troubleshoot Conference Connection. Open the Event Viewer from the Windows 2000 desktop by selecting **Start > Programs > Administrative Tools > Event Viewer**.

Cisco Emergency Responder (ER)

Cisco Emergency Responder (ER) enables emergency agencies to identify the location of 911 callers and eliminates the need for any administration when IP phones move from one location to another. Enhancing the existing E9-1-1 functionality of CallManager, Cisco ER's real-time location-tracking database and improved routing capabilities direct emergency calls to the appropriate Public Safety Answering Point (PSAP) based on the caller's location.

TIP   You can find troubleshooting tips for Cisco Emergency Responder release 1.1(1) on Cisco.com or at the following URL:

www.cisco.com/univercd/cc/td/doc/product/voice/respond/res_1_1/admin/ e911trbl.htm

---

Summary

This chapter covered a diverse set of applications that might require troubleshooting from time to time. The majority of the problems with applications are caused by configuration errors, largely because the configuration for CallManager and several applications servers can be complex.

Whatever the reason, you must thoroughly check the configuration on both sides. Make a checklist, and see if all pieces have been correctly configured. If everything appears to be correct, you can begin an in-depth analysis using trace files. Consult the application documentation and Cisco.com for additional troubleshooting tips for each application.

## CHAPTER 17

SQL Database Replication

At the heart of Cisco CallManager is a Structured Query Language (SQL) relational database based on Microsoft SQL Server 7.0 in CallManager releases 3.0 through 3.2 and Microsoft SQL Server 2000 in CallManager release 3.3. This database stores the majority of the configuration information for CallManager. Almost anything you configure in CallManager Administration adds to, deletes from, or modifies information in the SQL database.

The exception is user information (for example, username, password, PIN, device association, and so on), which is stored in an LDAP directory—either DC Directory, Microsoft Active Directory, or iPlanet Directory Server. Directory replication is covered in Chapter 18, "LDAP Integration and Replication."

This chapter covers the following:

- The Publisher-Subscriber model for database replication
- The role of name resolution and passwords in replication
- Using Enterprise Manager to troubleshoot replication problems
- Tracking down errors in Replication Monitor
- Re-establishing a broken subscription
- Troubleshooting CDR database replication

Understanding the Publisher-Subscriber Model

CallManager uses a single Publisher with multiple Subscribers model. The first CallManager server in a cluster is designated as the Publisher, and subsequent CallManager servers are Subscribers. The Publisher database is read-write, and the Subscribers are read-only. Any configuration changes to the database must be done on the Publisher and then replicated to the Subscribers. Figure 17-1 illustrates the relationship between the Publisher and Subscribers. Notice that the replication is one-way.

Figure 17-1 *CallManager Publisher-Subscriber Relationship*

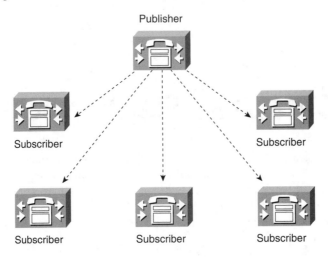

The Subscriber databases use transactional replication to keep their local database synchronized with the master database on the Publisher. *Transactional replication* means that an initial snapshot of the database is taken when the Subscriber first needs to replicate the database data, but from that point on, only database changes are replicated. This keeps the amount of bandwidth needed for database replication low because the only time a database changes is when a configuration change is made.

CallManager creates up to three separate databases on the Publisher server in the cluster:

- A database that stores CallManager configuration information

- A database that stores the call detail record (CDR) information

- If the CDR Analysis and Reporting (CAR) tool (formerly called the Administrative Reporting Tool) is installed, a database is created on the Publisher by the CAR tool.

The CallManager configuration database is named CCM03*xx*, where *xx* is a two-digit number. When a Publisher is first installed, the database is named CCM0300. Each CallManager in the cluster has a copy of this database. Most CallManager version upgrades increment this number by one. CallManager keeps the current version and one previous version. For example, if your database is named CCM0301 and the previous database is named CCM0300, when you upgrade to the next version of CallManager, the database is named CCM0302 and the CCM0300 database is removed, leaving you with CCM0301 and CCM0302. Currently, the older of the two databases is not used for anything other than troubleshooting database migration problems. There is no way to revert to the older database.

Some Cisco platforms that incorporate CallManager, such as the Cisco ICS 7750, might include additional databases for other purposes.

CAUTION   Never add new databases to the SQL Server on CallManager. The CallManager installer assumes that only certain databases exist on the CallManager server. It might get confused if it finds unknown databases on the server.

Subscriber servers in the cluster only have a copy of the CallManager configuration database. Prior to CallManager 3.2, all Subscribers also had a database to store CDRs. However, in CallManager 3.2 and later, all CDR information is passed to the Publisher in flat text files before being written to a database.

The Publisher server in the cluster also has a database named CDR that stores the CDR information. Prior to CallManager 3.2, all Subscribers also had a copy of this database that behaved slightly differently from the configuration database in that the Subscriber's CDR databases were read/write. Prior to CallManager 3.2, all CDRs were written locally to the CDR database, and the Cisco Database Layer Monitor service was responsible for copying these records back to the Publisher. When the Publisher server is offline for whatever reason (power outage, network outage, or hardware failure), the Subscriber servers can continue to process calls. During this time, the Subscribers write the CDRs to their local CDR database until the Publisher comes back online. When the Publisher comes back online, the records are moved from the Subscribers to the Publisher CDR database. As soon as the records have been pushed to the Publisher, the CDRs are deleted from the Subscriber.

In CallManager 3.2 and later, Subscribers perform a similar task of writing CDRs locally and then replicating them to the Publisher, except that CDRs are stored in a flat text file on the Subscribers instead of being written to a SQL database. The Database Layer Monitor service is still responsible for moving the CDRs from the Subscribers to the Publisher. A new service named the CDR Insert Service exists on servers running CallManager 3.2 and later. This service runs only on the Publisher in the cluster. The purpose of the CDR Insert Service is to take the flat files that have been moved to the Publisher and insert those records into the CDR database.

The Publisher also has a database named **art** that stores data for the CAR tool. The database is named art because CAR used to be called the Administrative Reporting Tool (ART). CAR is bundled with CallManager 3.2 and later (**Application > Install Plugins**) and is available as a separate download for CallManager 3.0 and 3.1.

CAR takes data from the CDR database and converts it into a format that makes it easier for CAR to generate reports and analyze the CDR data. CAR periodically looks through the CDR database for changes and copies the data to its own database. This copy operation is typically performed daily, but the frequency can be configured in CAR. The data in this database is not replicated to any other members of the cluster, which means that you cannot use CAR if the Publisher is down. Because the Subscribers automatically keep CDRs while the Publisher is down and CAR obtains its data from the central CDR database on the

Publisher, CAR is protected from losing data in the event of a network outage or other failure of the Publisher server as long as the Publisher returns to service in the same state it was in prior to the failure.

Troubleshooting the Publisher-Subscriber Relationship

When should you suspect a replication problem? You probably won't notice you're having a replication problem until it's too late. When everything is up and running, Subscribers do not rely on their local databases. Instead, they always read the configuration data they need directly from the Publisher database. This ensures that you're always using data that is correct up to the second. Any configuration changes can take up to 60 seconds to replicate to the Subscribers. The only time the locally replicated database on a Subscriber is used is when the Publisher is unavailable. The Database Layer Monitor service is responsible for monitoring the availability of the Publisher and switching between the Publisher database and the Subscriber database in the event of a failure.

If database replication is not functioning correctly, some devices might not operate as expected because they are using old configuration data. If devices have been added recently, they might not have been replicated to the Subscriber and might not be able to register at all.

The best thing you can do is perform some testing when you are first bringing up your CallManager cluster. As soon as you have everything configured and working as expected, unplug the Ethernet cable from the Publisher, effectively removing it from the network. Next, restart the CallManager service on your Subscribers. If all devices can successfully register as expected, there's a good chance your database replication is working correctly. Later in this chapter you will see how to use Enterprise Manager to verify that database replication is working correctly.

The Role of Name Resolution and Passwords in Replication

One of the most common causes of replication problems is lack of proper name resolution. Microsoft SQL Server relies on NetBIOS names to contact other SQL Servers. The best way to ensure that your NetBIOS name resolution is always correct and consistent is to use LMHOSTS files on all the CallManager servers in your cluster. The LMHOSTS file is found in the C:\WINNT\System32\drivers\etc directory. By default there is a file named lmhosts.sam, which is a sample file showing the file structure of an LMHOSTS file. Copy lmhosts.sam to a file in the same directory, and call it LMHOSTS with no extension. To ensure that you're looking at files with their full extensions, open My Computer in Windows Explorer and select **Tools > Folder Options**. Click the **View** tab. Make sure the box that says **Hide file extensions for known file types** is unchecked. To copy the file, do the following:

Step 1   Right-click the file named lmhosts.sam and select **Copy**.

Step 2   Right-click in the same window and select **Paste**. You get a file named **Copy of lmhosts.sam**.

Step 3   Right-click this file, select **Rename**, and enter the new name of the file, **LMHOSTS** (do not add an extension).

If you want to use LMHOSTS for NetBIOS name resolution, the LMHOSTS file should contain an entry for each CallManager in the cluster, and each CallManager in the cluster should have a copy of the LMHOSTS file. Example 17-1 shows a typical LMHOSTS file.

Example 17-1 *Typical LMHOSTS File*

```
10.1.1.1          CALLMANAGERPUB      #PRE
10.1.1.2          CALLMANAGERSUB1     #PRE
10.2.1.1          CALLMANAGERSUB2     #PRE
10.2.1.2          CALLMANAGERSUB3     #PRE
```

If you add the **#PRE** keyword, as shown in Example 17-1, the entries are added to the name resolution table when the server boots up instead of being added when needed.

To check what is currently in the NetBIOS name cache, open a command prompt on a CallManager server and enter the command **nbtstat -c**, as demonstrated in Example 17-2.

Example 17-2 *Checking NetBIOS Name Cache Contents*

```
C:\>nbtstat -c
Local Area Connection:
Node IpAddress: [172.18.106.58] Scope Id: []

                NetBIOS Remote Cache Name Table

        Name            Type      Host Address    Life [sec]
    ---------------------------------------------------------
        VNT-CM1B    <20> UNIQUE      172.18.106.59      570
        VNT-CM1B    <00> UNIQUE      172.18.106.59      570
        VNT-CER1A   <20> UNIQUE      172.18.106.62      322
```

Make sure the names in the list are correct. Only names that are in the cache are shown. If you are not using LMHOSTS, you should have a WINS server on your network to handle NetBIOS name resolution. If all CallManager servers are on the same subnet, they should be able to resolve NetBIOS names using subnet broadcasts because servers running Windows 2000 advertise their names to all other servers on the same subnet. However, you shouldn't rely on this method because it makes it fairly easy for a rogue PC on the network to corrupt the name cache on other machines if a duplicate name is added to the network. Use LMHOSTS to ensure that nothing is left to chance.

If one of the servers does not appear in the list, issue the command **nbtstat -a** *server_name,* as demonstrated in Example 17-3.

Example 17-3 *Checking NetBIOS Name Cache Contents*

```
C:\>nbtstat -a vnt-cm1b
Local Area Connection:
Node IpAddress: [172.18.106.58] Scope Id: []

        NetBIOS Remote Machine Name Table

    Name              Type        Status
    ---------------------------------------------
    VNT-CM1B     <00>  UNIQUE    Registered
    VNT-CM1B     <03>  UNIQUE    Registered
    VNT-CM1B     <20>  UNIQUE    Registered
    INet~Services <1C> GROUP     Registered
    IS~VNT-CM1B....<00> UNIQUE   Registered
    ADMINISTRATOR <03>  UNIQUE   Registered
```

You can then issue **nbtstat -c** again to see the server's IP address.

It's likely that a large percentage of replication problems are the result of improperly configured name resolution, so be sure to get this right when you first install the cluster. Also, be aware that an LMHOSTS file might be present when you are changing a CallManager's IP address because you need to change the LMHOSTS files on all the other nodes in the cluster that have the old IP address in their LMHOSTS files.

In addition to NetBIOS name resolution, CallManager also relies on proper DNS name resolution. DNS name resolution can be statically configured similar to the way NetBIOS names are configured in the LMHOSTS files. Static DNS entries are stored in the C:\WINNT\System32\drivers\etc directory in a file named **hosts**. The format of the hosts file is identical to the LMHOSTS file with the exception that the #PRE keyword is not allowed. You can verify DNS name resolution by using the **nslookup** command from a command prompt as shown in Example 17-4. Notice the IP address matches the IP address in Example 17-2.

Example 17-4 *Using* **nslookup** *to Verify DNS Name Resolution*

```
C:\>nslookup vnt-cm1b.cisco.com
Server:  dns-server.cisco.com
Address:  10.1.1.1

Name:     vnt-cm1b.cisco.com
Address:  172.18.106.59
```

Improperly configured passwords are also a common reason for database replication problems. For database replication to function properly, several passwords must be configured identically on all nodes of the cluster:

- Windows Administrator user
- Windows SQLSvc user
- SQL Server sa user

The Administrator and SQLSvc users are Windows accounts that have *superuser* access to the CallManager server. An account with superuser access is one that has full control over the operating system and is allowed access to all system resources. The Administrator account on each machine in the cluster must have the same password. The same holds true for the SQLSvc password. When CallManager is installed, the password for the SQLSvc user is auto-generated by the CallManager installer. This password is unique for each CallManager cluster. You can change the SQLSvc password provided that this is done properly and that it is done on every node of the cluster.

In CallManager release 3.3(2) and later, you must *not* manually set the password for the SQLSvc account (or any other service accounts such as CCMService). Instead, you must use the Cisco-provided password change utility available on Cisco.com and bundled with CallManager release 3.3(3) and later. If you change the password manually, you will not be able to upgrade your CallManager to the next release until you use the password utility to reset the passwords. You will also have problems adding additional servers to the cluster. The password change utility performs all the operations necessary to change the password for the SQLSvc user and all services that log in using the SQLSvc account. You can access the password change utility on the Software Download page for CallManager 3.3 (requires CCO login):

www.cisco.com/cgi-bin/tablebuild.pl/callmgr-33

To properly change the password in CallManager release 3.0, 3.1, or 3.2, you must first enter the new password for the user then change all the services that log on using the SQLSvc account to use the new password. The following procedure explains how to change the SQLSvc password on each node of the cluster:

CAUTION   This procedure applies only to CallManager release 3.0, 3.1, and 3.2. If you perform this procedure on release 3.3 and later, you will encounter problems when attempting to upgrade CallManager.

Step 1   Select **Start > Programs > Administrative Tools > Computer Management**.

Step 2   Click **+** (the plus sign) beside **Local Users and Groups** in the left column.

Step 3   Click **Users**.

Step 4   Right-click **SQLSvc** in the right column and select **Set Password**.

Step 5   Enter the new password and confirm it.

Step 6   Click **OK** to confirm and close the Change Password dialog box.

Step 7   Click + beside **Services and Applications** in the left column.

Step 8   Click **Services**.

Step 9   In the right column, click and highlight **MSSQLServer**.

Step 10 Right-click **MSSQLServer** and select **Properties**.

Step 11 Select the **Log On** tab.

Step 12 Change the password and confirm that it matches the SQLSvc user password you set in Step 5.

Step 13 Click **OK** to return to the Services list.

Step 14 Click and highlight **SQLServerAgent**.

Step 15 Right-click **SQLServerAgent** and select **Properties**.

Step 16 Click the **Log On** tab.

Step 17 Change the password to match the SQLSvc user password you set in Step 5.

Step 18 Click **OK** to return to the Services list.

Step 19 Click and highlight **Cisco Database Layer Monitor**.

Step 20 Right-click **Cisco Database Layer Monitor** and select **Properties**.

Step 21 Click the **Log On** tab.

Step 22 Change the password to match the SQLSvc user password you set in Step 5.

Step 23 Click **OK** to return to the Services list.

Step 24 Close the Computer Management window.

Step 25 Select **Start > Programs > Administrative Tools > Component Services**.

Step 26 Click + beside **Component Services**.

Step 27 Click + beside **Computers**.

Step 28 Click + beside **My Computer**.

Step 29 Click + beside **COM+ Applications**.

Step 30 Right-click **DBL** and select **Properties**.

Step 31 Click the **Identity** tab.

Step 32 Change the password and confirm that it matches the SQLSvc user password you set in Step 5.

Step 33 Click **OK** to go back to the Component Services window.

Step 34 Right-click **DBL** and click **Shut Down**.

Step 35 Right-click **DBL** and click **Start**.

Step 36 Close the Component Manager window.

Be sure to perform this procedure on all the nodes in the cluster.

You must follow a similar procedure to change the password for the local administrator. This procedure can be safely performed on all releases of CallManager, including CallManager 3.3. The following procedure explains how to change the administrator password on each node of the cluster:

Step 1 Select **Start > Programs > Administrative Tools > Computer Management**.

Step 2 Click + (the plus sign) beside **Local Users and Groups** in the left column.

Step 3 Click **Users**.

Step 4 Right-click **Administrator** in the right column and select **Set Password**.

Step 5 Enter the new password and confirm it.

Step 6 Click **OK** to confirm and close the Change Password dialog box.

Step 7 Click + beside **Services and Applications** in the left column.

Step 8 Click **Services**.

Step 9 In the right column, click and highlight **stiBack for Cisco IP Telephony Applications**. (The service name might be slightly different on older versions of CallManager.)

Step 10 Right-click **stiBack for Cisco IP Telephony Applications** and select **Properties**.

Step 11 Select the **Log On** tab.

Step 12 Change the password and confirm that it matches the Administrator user password you set in Step 5.

Step 13 Click **OK** to return to the Services list.

Step 14 If you do not have the Tool for Auto-Registered Phone Support (TAPS) installed, skip to Step 19. Click and highlight **Cisco TAPS**.

Step 15 Right-click **Cisco TAPS** and select **Properties**.

Step 16 Click the **Log On** tab.

Step 17 Change the password to match the Administrator user password you set
in Step 5.

Step 18 Click **OK** to return to the Services list.

Step 19 Close the Computer Management window.

Again, be sure to make this change on all nodes in the cluster. The best way to ensure that
the password change took effect is to reboot all the servers in the cluster and ensure that all
the services where you changed the password still start.

The system administrator (sa) user account is an account within Microsoft SQL Server that
has superuser access to all the databases in the SQL Server. The easiest way to properly
change this password and ensure that all services using the password are changed
accordingly is to rerun the CallManager installer on the Publisher. This does not affect any
of your data, but at the end of the installation, you are prompted for the SQL Administrator
password. This is the password for the sa account. After doing this on the Publisher, do the
same for all the Subscribers.

Microsoft SQL Server Enterprise Manager

To diagnose and correct database replication problems, you need to become familiar with
Microsoft SQL Server Enterprise Manager. This tool is installed as part of SQL Server 7.0
and SQL Server 2000 on the CallManager servers. For SQL 7.0, you access it by selecting
Start > Programs > Microsoft SQL Server 7.0 > Enterprise Manager. For SQL 2000,
you access it by selecting **Start > Programs > Microsoft SQL Server 2000 > Enterprise
Manager**. Figure 17-2 shows the Enterprise Manager.

After you open Enterprise Manager, expand the tree on the left until you get to the
databases. Under **Databases** you should see one or more databases that begin with CCM03
(for example, in Figure 17-2, you see CCM0314). Normally the highest-numbered database
is the current CallManager database. You can check which database is currently in use by
looking in the Windows Registry.

CAUTION You can cause serious damage to the Windows operating system if you are not careful when
using the Windows Registry Editor. Do not make any changes to any of the fields in the
Registry unless told to do so by a TAC support engineer.

Figure 17-2 *Microsoft SQL Server Enterprise Manager*

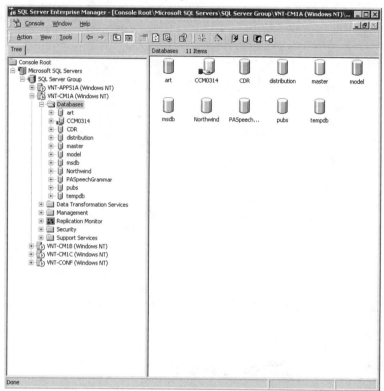

To open Registry Editor, select **Start > Run** and enter **regedit**. After it is open, expand the tree on the left to HKEY_LOCAL_MACHINE\SOFTWARE\Cisco Systems, Inc.\DBL. You should see something similar to Figure 17-3.

On the right side, you see one or more keys that begin with the word DBConnection. The key labeled DBConnection0 should always be the Publisher CallManager. In Figure 17-3, you can see that CCM0301 is the current CallManager database. Note that this is not from the same CallManager server shown in Figure 17-2 because you would expect to see CCM0314 as the database in the registry for the CallManager shown in Figure 17-2.

Go back to Enterprise Manager in Figure 17-2. In the left pane, you can navigate through the database hierarchy. In Figure 17-2, you can see one CallManager database. Notice a small hand under the CCM0314 database. The hand indicates that this database is being published. You also can see that a Publications folder under each database is being published. If you click the database under the Publications folder, on the right side you see a list of all the subscriptions and their status. All the subscriptions should be Active. If you see a subscription that has failed, you need to use Replication Monitor to investigate why the error has occurred. The following section covers how to work with Replication Monitor.

Figure 17-3 *CallManager Database Configuration in the Windows Registry*

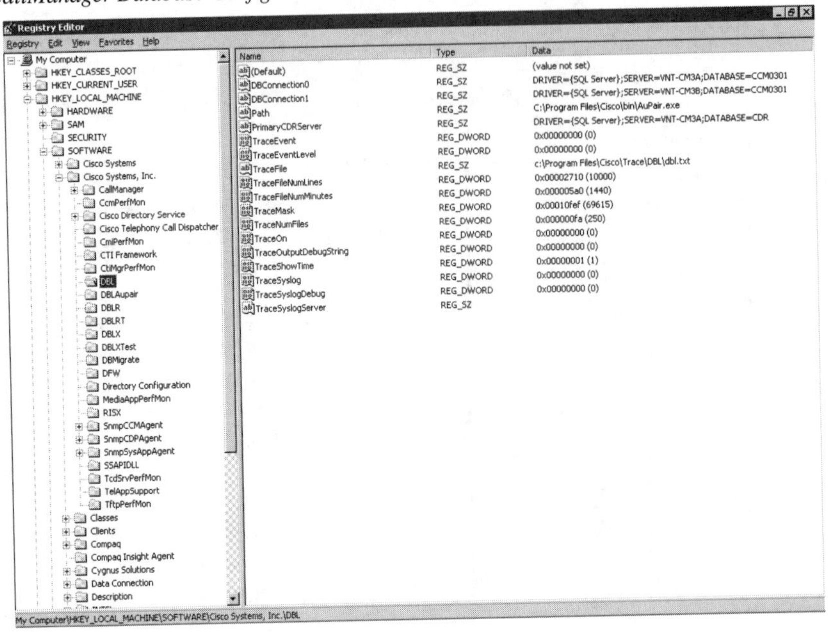

Correcting Replication Errors

Enterprise Manager contains a utility called Replication Monitor that lets you ensure that replication is working correctly. This utility is available only on the Publisher server.

Microsoft SQL Server accomplishes database replication through a variety of *replication agents,* a process that performs a specific task. The three replication agents you should be familiar with are the snapshot agent, the log reader agent, and the distribution agent.

As mentioned earlier, CallManager uses transactional replication to replicate data from the Publisher to the Subscribers. To start a transactional replication, the Subscriber needs to retrieve an initial snapshot of the entire database. The *snapshot agent* is responsible for collecting the information for database snapshots. All Subscribers are configured to run the snapshot agent nightly at 11:30. The snapshot agent takes a snapshot only if a subscription needs a snapshot because it got out of sync with the Publisher for some reason. If no subscriptions require a snapshot, the snapshot agent does nothing when it is run at 11:30 p.m. every day.

The *log reader agent* is responsible for moving any changes to the Publisher database, called transactions, to the distribution database. The distribution database is then used to replicate the changes to the Subscribers.

The *distribution agent* is responsible for taking the information from the distribution database and moving it to the Subscribers.

For more details about how Microsoft SQL Server performs database replication, refer to Microsoft's page titled "How Replication Works," available at msdn.microsoft.com/library/default.asp?url=/library/en-us/replsql/replintro_5ir2.asp.

To open Replication Monitor, navigate to **Microsoft SQL Servers > SQL Server Group > *Server Name* > Replication Monitor**. The first time you open Replication Monitor, a box appears that says "Replication Monitor can automatically refresh the status of the replication agents by periodically polling the Distributor for reports of recent replication activity." Click **Yes** to this box.

Then a Refresh Rate and Settings box appears. Keep the defaults by clicking **OK**.

If there are any replication errors, the icon next to Replication Monitor has a red circle with a white X in it, indicating an error. If you expand the folders below Replication Monitor, they also have a red mark, indicating where the error is originating. Figure 17-4 shows the error icons that result from a problem with the distribution agent.

Figure 17-4 *Replication Monitor Errors*

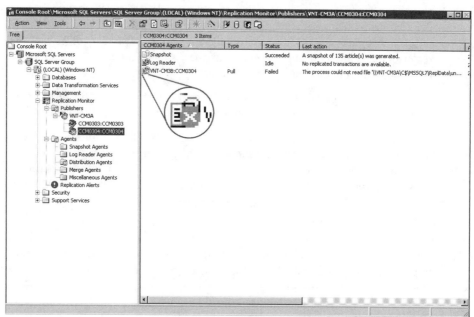

As you can see in Figure 17-4, the error is on the distribution agent for the subscription to VNT-CM3B for database CCM0304. You can also see that the status is Failed and an error message is listed. If you right-click the line marked Failed and choose **Error Details**, you see a box similar to Figure 17-5.

Figure 17-5   *Distribution Agent Error Details*

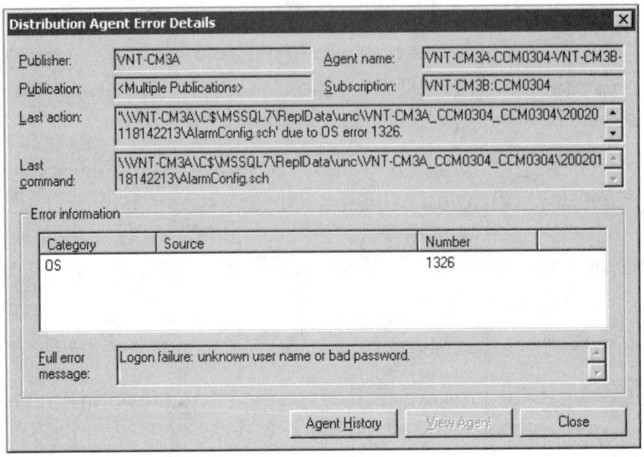

If you look at the bottom of Figure 17-5, you see the **Full error message:** section. The message is "Logon failure: unknown user name or bad password." This error indicates any number of things. Obviously it can indicate that a password is set incorrectly; however, in this case the problem is that the Subscriber is being rebooted. Because the Subscriber was offline, the login attempts to that server failed. After the Subscriber comes back online, the red error marks in Replication Monitor disappear. You might have to press the **F5** key to refresh the status of the Replication Monitor.

This is only an example. You might see a variety of error messages for several agents. The errors are generally plain text descriptions as opposed to cryptic error codes.

If you see an error on any of the agents, click that folder. The various agents are listed on the left side. The pane on the right shows which agents are in an error condition. If you right-click the agent and select **Agent History**, you see a log of past transactions. It is possible that you might have a stale entry for an agent that corresponds to an old database that no longer exists. You can safely delete entries like this.

CAUTION   Be careful not to delete an agent for the CallManager database currently in use. Doing so might require a fresh installation of CallManager to restore everything to the correct state.

You can also right-click any of the agents and select **Agent Properties**. The owner of all the agents should be the user named **sa**. **sa** is a SQL user account created by the CallManager installer that has superuser privileges in Microsoft SQL Server. If the owner is not **sa**, the agent might not run, and you will end up with errors. You can change the owner in the Agent Properties screen.

Re-establishing a Broken SQL Replication Subscription

In some cases where a SQL replication subscription has been broken, you might just need to rebuild the subscription. One example is if your Publisher fails and you need to restore the machine from a backup. In this case, you rebuild the machine from scratch and restore the database with the MCS Backup/Restore utility bundled with CallManager. After restoring the data to the Publisher, you must rebuild the database subscriptions to the Subscribers.

After you have verified proper name resolution, follow the instructions given here to re-create the subscription using Enterprise Manager. Follow this procedure for each Subscriber whose subscription is broken.

First, you must delete the Subscriber's subscription on the Publisher. Then you re-create the subscription on the Subscriber server.

To re-create a subscription, perform the following steps, as described in detail in the following sections:

Step 1   Delete the subscription from the Publisher.

Step 2   Add the subscription to the Subscriber SQL Server.

Step 3   Start the snapshot agent.

Deleting the Subscription from the Publisher

To delete the subscription from the Publisher, follow these steps:

Step 1   Under the Enterprise Manager on the Publisher, navigate the SQL Server tree and locate the Publication for the CCM03*xx* database (**Microsoft SQL Servers > SQL Server Group** > *Machine_name* > **Databases > CCM03***xx* **> Publications**).

Step 2   Select the CallManager subscription that is failing, and delete the entry. Be sure to select the subscription on the right that corresponds with the Subscriber you are trying to re-create the subscription to. If the subscription is not listed, proceed to the next section to re-create it.

Step 3   When prompted to delete the entry on the Subscriber system, click **Yes**.

Step 4   A warning appears, indicating that the subscription has been removed at the Publisher but not the Subscriber. You are asked if you want to connect to the Subscriber and delete the subscription. Click **Yes**.

Step 5   The next message indicates that the subscription has been deleted but the data has not. Click **OK**.

Step 6   Perform the steps in the following section to add the subscription to the Subscriber SQL Server.

Adding the Subscription to the Subscriber SQL Server

Next, you must add the subscription back into the Subscriber SQL Server. Open Enterprise Manager on the Subscriber server. To re-create the subscription, go to the current CallManager database (you can find this using Registry Editor, as mentioned earlier).

Step 1   Navigate to the Pull Subscriptions folder for the most current database (**Microsoft SQL Servers > SQL Server Group >** *Machine_name* **> Databases > CCM03***xx* **> Pull Subscriptions**).

Step 2   Right-click the Pull Subscriptions folder and select **New Pull Subscription**.

Step 3   The next page is the Pull Subscription Wizard. Click **Next**.

Step 4   Click the **Register Server** button.

Step 5   For the server name, type the name of the Publisher.

Step 6   Select **Use SQL Server authentication** and use a login name of **sa** and the sa password you entered when you installed the Publisher server.

Step 7   Click **OK**.

Step 8   On the Choose Publication screen, expand the Publisher, select the **CCM03***xx* database, and click **Next**.

Step 9   On the Specify Synchronization Agent Login screen, select **Using SQL Server Authentication of this account**. The login name is **sa**, and the password is the SQL SA password you specified on the Publisher during installation.

Step 10 On the **Specify Immediate-Updating Subscription(s)** popup, select **Yes, make this an immediate-updating subscription(s)**, and click **Next**.

Step 11 On the Initialize Subscription screen, select **Yes, initialize the schema and data at the Subscriber**, and click **Next**.

Step 12 On the Set Distribution Agent Schedule popup, select **Continuously** and click **Next**.

Step 13 The next step verifies that both the SQL Server agent and the Microsoft Distributed Transaction Coordinator (DTC) services are running. Click **Next**.

Step 14 On the Completing the Pull Subscription Wizard screen, click **Finish**. The Wizard sets up the subscription and displays a success message when it is done.

Step 15 Follow the instructions in the following section to start the snapshot agent.

Starting the Snapshot Agent

Now that the subscription has been created, you must run the snapshot agent to get the data to the distributor so that the Subscriber can pull it for synchronization. By default, the snapshot agent runs every night at 11:30; however, you can force it to start just to get the new subscription updated.

On the Publisher SQL Server, navigate to **Replication Monitor > Publishers >** *Machine_name* **> CCM03***xx***:CCM03***xx*. Right-click the **Snapshot** entry on the right and choose **Start**. The snapshot agent runs at this point. It takes about 3 to 5 minutes to complete the task. You can press **F5** to refresh the status. As soon as the snapshot agent completes, the pull agent starts applying the snapshot to the Subscriber. This takes another 3 to 5 minutes for a typical database of 500 to 1000 users. It might take longer for larger databases.

As soon as the pull subscription has completed, go back to the Subscriber and open the Pull Subscriptions folder again for the CCM03*xx* database. The subscription should be in a running state and waiting for updates. If the last action still reads "Waiting for snapshot agent to become available," press **F5** to refresh the screen.

The Subscriber is now resynchronized with the Publisher, and updates are being recorded in the local Subscriber SQL database.

Reinitializing a Subscription

There might be other times when one of the error messages you see in Replication Monitor indicates that you must reinitialize the subscription. To do this, you can once again use Enterprise Manager.

On the Publisher, open the Publications folder for the database you want to reinitialize (select **Microsoft SQL Servers > SQL Server Group >** *Machine_name* **> Databases > CCM03***xx* **> Publications > CCM03***xx*).

In the left pane, right-click the subscription you want to reinitialize, and click the **Reinitialize** option.

A message appears, indicating that the reinitialization will occur the next time the snapshot agent is run. You can force the snapshot agent to run by following the instructions outlined in the preceding section, "Starting the Snapshot Agent."

CDR Replication Issues

As mentioned previously, all CDRs are written locally to either the Subscriber's CDR database or a flat text file on the Subscriber. They are then pushed to the Publisher by the Database Layer Monitor service. As described in the following sections, you might not see CDRs from a particular Subscriber coming into the Publisher for a couple of reasons.

Subscriber Is Not Configured to Generate CDRs

The first thing you should check is whether the Subscriber is configured to generate CDRs. The CallManager service parameter **CDREnabled** (**Service > Service Parameters > select a server > Cisco CallManager**) dictates whether CDRs are written for calls that are processed on CallManager. Each server has its own CDREnabled service parameter, so be sure to enable it for each node in the cluster running the CallManager service.

If the **CDREnabled** flag is set to **True** and you are still not getting CDRs in the Publisher, you can check to see if they are being generated on the Subscriber.

To do this in CallManager 3.0 and 3.1, open Enterprise Manager and navigate to the Tables folder under the CDR database (**Microsoft SQL Servers > SQL Server Group > Machine_name > Databases > CDR > Tables**). Right-click the table named CallDetailRecord and select **Open Table > Return all rows**. You should see entries in this table. If there are entries here but they are not on the Publisher, you probably have a problem with the Database Layer Monitor service. If this is the case, follow the instructions in the next section, "Database Layer Monitor Is Not Running Properly."

In CallManager 3.2 and later, the process of replicating CDRs is slightly more complex. The additional complexity is designed to improve the performance of writing CDRs to the Publisher database. To better understand how to troubleshoot CDR problems in CallManager 3.2 and beyond, you should become familiar with how the process works.

Figure 17-6 provides a high-level overview of how CDRs are copied from the Subscribers to the Publisher.

The CallManager service running on each server is responsible for creating a flat file containing a comma-separated value (CSV) line for each CDR. The location of this file is determined by the enterprise parameter **Local CDR Path**. The default value for **Local CDR Path** is C:\Program Files\Cisco\CallDetail. That directory contains two subdirectories—CDR and CMR. The CDRs and call management records (CMRs, also known as diagnostic CDRs) are stored in their corresponding directories.

As soon as the enterprise parameter named **CDR File Time Interval** expires, the CallManager service closes the current flat file and opens a new one. It also notifies the Database Layer Monitor service that there is a new file to move to the Publisher. The CallManager service opens the flat files with exclusive rights. This means that you cannot copy, open, or move the file until the CallManager service has closed it.

The Database Layer Monitor service then takes the completed file and copies it to the Publisher by following the enterprise parameter named **CDR UNC Path**. By default, **CDR UNC Path** is set to a Windows share named CDR on the Publisher that corresponds to the C:\Program Files\Cisco\CallDetail directory. This means that by default the Database Layer Monitor service moves the flat text files from the C:\Program Files\Cisco\CallDetail directory on the Subscribers to the same directory on the Publisher.

Figure 17-6 *CDR Data Storage Process*

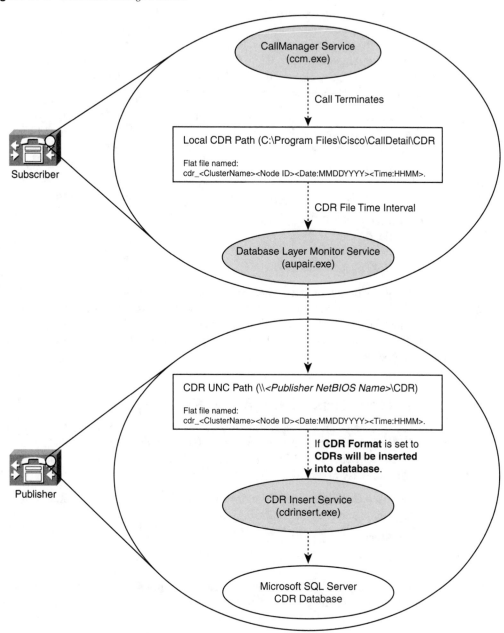

As soon as the flat files arrive on the Publisher, if the **CDR Format** enterprise parameter is set to **CDRs will be inserted into database**, the Cisco CDR Insert service reads these flat files and moves the CDR data into the CDR SQL Database. As soon as the data is in the SQL database, the flat files are deleted. If the **CDR Format** enterprise parameter is set to **CDRs will be kept in flat files**, the Cisco CDR Insert service does nothing. Be careful when using this option. The flat files are never deleted from the Publisher, so you might run out of hard drive space if you do not manually delete them.

To verify that CDRs are being generated on a system running CallManager 3.2 or later, open Windows Explorer to C:\Program Files\Cisco\CallDetail\CDR. You should see a file in the following format:

cdr_*<ClusterName><Node ID><Date:MMDDYYYY><Time:HHMM>*

For example, the file cdr_VNT-CM1A-Cluster02070420021940 translates to

Cluster name: VNT-CM1A-Cluster
Node ID: 02
Date: July 4, 2002
Time: 7:40 p.m.

If everything is working properly, there should be exactly one file in this directory. If multiple files exist in a Subscriber's directory, the CallManager service is successfully creating the CDR record flat files, but the Database Layer Monitor service is not copying them to the Publisher. You should check to see if the Database Layer Monitor service is running properly.

Database Layer Monitor Is Not Running Properly

To determine if the Database Layer Monitor service is running, open the Services control panel (**Start > Programs > Administrative Tools > Services**). There should be a service named Cisco Database Layer Monitor. If there is no such service, you have found the problem. This is easy to remedy.

To add the Cisco Database Layer Monitor service to a machine where it is missing, open a command prompt and enter the following command:

```
C:\>aupair -service
```

CAUTION   Be absolutely certain that the Cisco Database Layer Monitor service is not on the list before issuing the **aupair -service** command. Running this command while the service is installed removes the service.

Refresh the Services control panel by pressing **F5**. You should see the Cisco Database Layer Monitor service running.

If the Cisco Database Layer Monitor service was already installed and you are still having the problem, try restarting the service. Restarting the Cisco Database Layer Monitor service does not affect call processing on CallManager. However, it might briefly affect the ability of users on that server to set their phones to Call Forward All by using the **CFwdAll** soft key. Therefore, you might want to wait until a scheduled outage window to perform this just to be on the safe side.

Additional Problems with Writing CDRs

In CallManager 3.2 and later, there are several other reasons for CDRs not being written properly. The Database Layer Monitor service on the Subscriber relies on having access to a Windows share on the Publisher, as defined in the **CDR UNC Path** enterprise parameter. To verify that this is working, log into the Subscriber and select **Start > Run**. Enter the UNC path as specified in the **CDR UNC Path** enterprise parameter, such as \\CALLMANAGERPUB\CDR. You should see an Explorer window appear with the CDR folder on the Publisher. If you get an error such as invalid login or nonexistent path, verify that your passwords are synchronized (as discussed in the section "The Role of Name Resolution and Passwords in Replication" earlier in this chapter). Also check to see if the C:\Program Files\Cisco\CallDetail directory is still shared on the Publisher.

If the files are arriving at the Publisher but are not making it into the CDR database, you need to check a few things:

- Ensure that the **CDR Format** enterprise parameter is set to **CDRs will be inserted into database**.

- Ensure that the Cisco CDR Insert service is running on the Publisher.

- Ensure that the **Off Cluster CDR DSN** enterprise parameter is blank. If this parameter is not blank, the CDR Insert service attempts to move the CDRs from the flat files on the Publisher to the database listed in the **Off Cluster CDR DSN** enterprise parameter (**System > Enterprise Parameters**). When the parameter is blank, the service assumes the local machine.

If you are still experiencing problems with CDRs, narrow down which piece of the process is broken. Remember that the CallManager service is responsible for generating the flat files, so check CCM traces and CallManager service parameters to ensure that the CDR configuration is correct.

If the problem lies in the Database Layer Monitor's moving of CDRs from the Subscriber to the Publisher, enable Detailed tracing for the Database Layer Monitor service and look through the aupair trace files found in the C:\Program Files\Cisco\Trace\DBL directory.

When the service is working properly, you should see something like the trace output shown in Example 17-5.

Example 17-5 *Trace to Ensure That the Database Layer Monitor Service Is Working Properly*

```
CMoveCDRFilesWorker::AreWeThePrimary() Compare IP    [172.18.106.59] [VNT-CM1A]
CMoveCDRFilesWorker::AreWeThePrimary() Not the primary
<--CMoveCDRFilesWorker::AreWeThePrimary()
    CMoveCDRFilesWorker::DoWork()
      Src [c:\Program Files\Cisco\CallDetail\] Dst [\\VNT-CM1A\CDR\]
-->CMoveCDRFilesWorker::MoveFile()
    CMoveCDRFilesWorker::MoveFile()
      Filename [cdr_VNT-CM1A-Cluster02070420021718]
-->CMoveCDRFilesWorker::IsFileReady()
    CMoveCDRFilesWorker::IsFileReady() [c:\Program Files\Cisco\CallDetail\CDR\
      cdr_VNT-CM1A-Cluster02070420021718]
<--CMoveCDRFilesWorker::IsFileReady()
-->CMoveCDRFilesWorker::MoveFile()
    CMoveCDRFilesWorker::MoveFile() Moving [c:\Program Files\Cisco\CallDetail\CDR\
      cdr_VNT-CM1A-Cluster02070420021718]->[\\VNT-CM1A\CDR\CDR\
      cdr_VNT-CM1A-Cluster02070420021718]
<--CMoveCDRFilesWorker::MoveFile()
<--CMoveCDRFilesWorker::MoveFile()
-->CMoveCDRFilesWorker::MoveFile()
    CMoveCDRFilesWorker::MoveFile() Filename [cdr_VNT-CM1A-Cluster02070420021719]
-->CMoveCDRFilesWorker::IsFileReady()
    CMoveCDRFilesWorker::IsFileReady() [c:\Program Files\Cisco\CallDetail\CDR\
      cdr_VNT-CM1A-Cluster02070420021719]
<--CMoveCDRFilesWorker::IsFileReady()
<--CMoveCDRFilesWorker::MoveFile()
-->CMoveCDRFilesWorker::MoveFile()
    CMoveCDRFilesWorker::MoveFile() Filename [cmr_VNT-CM1A-Cluster02070420021718]
-->CMoveCDRFilesWorker::IsFileReady()
    CMoveCDRFilesWorker::IsFileReady() [c:\Program Files\Cisco\CallDetail\CMR\
      cmr_VNT-CM1A-Cluster02070420021718]
<--CMoveCDRFilesWorker::IsFileReady()
-->CMoveCDRFilesWorker::MoveFile()
    CMoveCDRFilesWorker::MoveFile() Moving [c:\Program Files\Cisco\CallDetail\CMR\
      cmr_VNT-CM1A-Cluster02070420021718]->[\\VNT-CM1A\CDR\CMR\
      cmr_VNT-CM1A-Cluster02070420021718]
<--CMoveCDRFilesWorker::MoveFile()
<--CMoveCDRFilesWorker::MoveFile()
-->CMoveCDRFilesWorker::MoveFile()
    CMoveCDRFilesWorker::MoveFile() Filename [cmr_VNT-CM1A-Cluster02070420021719]
-->CMoveCDRFilesWorker::IsFileReady()
    CMoveCDRFilesWorker::IsFileReady() [c:\Program Files\Cisco\CallDetail\CMR\
      cmr_VNT-CM1A-Cluster02070420021719]
<--CMoveCDRFilesWorker::IsFileReady()
<--CMoveCDRFilesWorker::MoveFile()
<--CMoveCDRFilesWorker::DoWork()
```

Look for errors in the aupair trace that might indicate where the problem is.

If the CDRs are making it to the Publisher but are not being written to the CDR database, check the InsertCDR log files on the Publisher. Make sure you set the trace level for the Insert CDR service to Detailed.

When functioning properly, the trace should look similar to Example 17-6.

Example 17-6 *Trace to Ensure That the Insert CDR Service Is Working Properly*

```
-->CMonitor::ProcessDirectoryChange ()
-->CMonitor::AreWeThePrimary()
-->::GetMyLocalHostName
   ::GetMyLocalHostName Local Host Name  Resolved [VNT-CM1A]
<--::GetMyLocalHostName
   CMonitor::AreWeThePrimary() Compare Local [VNT-CM1A] [VNT-CM1A]
<--CMonitor::AreWeThePrimary()
   CMonitor::ProcessDirectoryChange () Get connection
   CMonitor::ProcessDirectoryChange () Is database ready
-->CMonitor::IsDatabaseReady
<--CMonitor::IsDatabaseReady
   CMonitor::ProcessDirectoryChange () Look for CDRs
-->CMonitor::ConvertFile
   CMonitor::ConvertFile Processing file
      [\\VNT-CM1A\CDR\CDR\cdr_VNT-CM1A-Cluster02070420021718]
-->CMonitor::SetupColumnNames
<--CMonitor::SetupColumnNames
-->CMonitor::SetupColumnTypes
<--CMonitor::SetupColumnTypes
   CMonitor::ConvertFile 2 records in 141 ms
   CMonitor::ConvertFile Remove file
<--CMonitor::ConvertFile
   CMonitor::ProcessDirectoryChange () Look for CMRs
-->CMonitor::ConvertFile
   CMonitor::ConvertFile Processing file
      [\\VNT-CM1A\CDR\CMR\cmr_VNT-CM1A-Cluster02070420021718]
-->CMonitor::SetupColumnNames
<--CMonitor::SetupColumnNames
-->CMonitor::SetupColumnTypes
<--CMonitor::SetupColumnTypes
   CMonitor::ConvertFile 2 records in 93 ms
   CMonitor::ConvertFile Remove file
<--CMonitor::ConvertFile
   CMonitor::ProcessDirectoryChange () Remove connection
<--CMonitor::ProcessDirectoryChange ()
```

Best Practices

Ideally, database replication is configured automatically and should never be a concern for day-to-day operations; however, there are a few things you can do to make sure replication problems do not arise:

- Make sure that name resolution is working correctly. Use both hosts and LMHOSTS files on all CallManager servers in the cluster to make sure that there is no reliance on external DNS or WINS servers. Name resolution is essential for proper database replication. Remember that just because you can ping a machine by name does not mean that name resolution is fully functional. Use **nslookup** and **nbtstat** to verify DNS and NetBIOS name resolution, as described earlier in this chapter.

- When bringing up a new system, be sure to test replication before going live. Unplug the Publisher from the network and make sure that all the Subscribers can continue to function without the Publisher. While in this state, force all the phones to reregister. Either reset them or reset the Subscribers to make sure that phones can register successfully while the Publisher is down. It's better to find out you have a problem before going live than to have a Publisher failure occur in production with the Subscribers unable to take over. Remember that while the Publisher is down, you can't make any configuration changes. Also, services such as the Call Forward All button on users' IP Phones and extension mobility do not work without the Publisher online, because they need to be able to write data to the configuration database.

- Use Enterprise Manager to periodically check the Replication Monitor for any errors, especially after a CallManager version upgrade, just to be sure your replication is functioning correctly. Also check replication after any kind of network outage that may have caused the Publisher and Subscriber to lose IP connectivity, including events where the Publisher or Subscribers are rebooted.

- Always keep regular backups of your CallManager database using the Cisco IP Telephony Applications Backup utility included with CallManager. This utility keeps a backup of all relevant information needed to rebuild a server in the event of a hardware or software failure. For more information on backing up your CallManager cluster, check the CallManager documentation or search Cisco.com for "Backing Up and Restoring Cisco CallManager."

Summary

SQL database replication is essential for proper CallManager operation and failover. This chapter explored the following topics:

- The Publisher-Subscriber model for database replication
- The role of name resolution in replication
- Using Enterprise Manager to troubleshoot replication problems
- Tracking down errors in Replication Monitor
- Re-establishing a broken subscription
- Troubleshooting CDR database replication

For the most part, database replication just works, and you don't have to worry about it. But an issue might come up that requires you to open Enterprise Manager and take a look. It cannot be stressed enough how important name resolution is to having replication work correctly.

When encountering database replication problems, use the Enterprise Manager tool as outlined in this chapter to diagnose the problem and correct it.

## CHAPTER 18

LDAP Integration and Replication

In Cisco CallManager, all the device and configuration-related information is stored in the SQL database. User information, however, is stored in a Lightweight Directory Access Protocol (LDAP) database. This is either the integrated DC Directory database or a third-party LDAP server such as Active Directory or Netscape iPlanet.

LDAP provides an optimized way for applications to access user-related information. This method allows for a high number of reads, writes, searches, and changes. Companies can centralize their user information in an LDAP directory and have a single repository for applications to access.

LDAP directories are also very flexible. They have a directory schema, which refers to the type of stored information and the rules it defines. You can extend this schema by adding attributes to accommodate specific applications.

Besides CallManager, many other Cisco applications are directory-enabled:

- Cisco IP Interactive Voice Response (IVR) and Cisco IP Auto Attendant (AA)—Starting with release 2.1(2), IP IVR and IP AA supports integration with both Microsoft Active Directory and iPlanet Netscape Directory Server, and it integrates with other Cisco applications.

- Cisco IP Integrated Call Distributor (ICD)—Starting with release 2.1(3), IP ICD supports integration with both Microsoft Active Directory and iPlanet Netscape Directory Server, and it integrates with other Cisco applications.

- Cisco Personal Assistant (PA)—Starting with release 1.2, which requires CallManager 3.1, PA supports integration with both Microsoft Active Directory and iPlanet Netscape Directory Server, and it integrates with other Cisco applications.

- Cisco Unity 2.46 uses Microsoft Exchange 5.5 as the LDAP directory. It cannot integrate with other Cisco applications, and it cannot use Microsoft Active Directory or iPlanet Netscape Directory Server.

- Cisco Unity 3.x uses either Microsoft Exchange 5.5 as the LDAP directory or Microsoft Active Directory when integrated with Microsoft Exchange 2000.

- Cisco Unity 4.x uses either Microsoft Active Directory or Lotus Domino as the LDAP directory.

As you can see, LDAP is a big part of the entire Cisco Architecture for Voice, Video, and Integrated Data (AVVID) solution. It is vital, therefore, to understand what part it plays and how to troubleshoot problems with it.

This chapter covers the following topics:

- Directory integration versus directory access
- Using the CallManager embedded directory
- Integrating with Active Directory
- Integrating with Netscape iPlanet

Directory Integration Versus Directory Access

Before discussing the various directory integration scenarios, it is important to make a distinction between directory integration and directory access. If an endpoint simply needs to perform a user search, directory access is all that is needed.

A user of a 79*xx* IP Phone can press the **directories** button and invoke an XML "form" on which she can enter a first or last name to search for. After the request is executed, a number of matching entries are returned. The user can then choose the desired match and press the **Dial** soft key to complete the call. Figure 18-1 shows the steps involved in a direct user search request sent to the LDAP server via CallManager.

Figure 18-1 *Directory Access for a Cisco IP Phone*

Directory integration is a whole different matter. With directory integration, several applications store their user-related information in this directory instead of or in addition to their own database. By default, CallManager stores all its user-related information in an embedded directory. (All the dial plan and configuration information is stored in the SQL database.)

CallManager can also integrate with a third-party corporate directory. Currently, CallManager integrates with only Microsoft Active Directory and Netscape iPlanet. This is a great advantage because all user information, such as e-mail address, phone number, postal address, and so on, is stored in a central location, and there is only this single directory infrastructure to support. If you have multiple clusters, they can all point to this one centralized directory. Figure 18-2 depicts the centralized directory infrastructure.

Figure 18-2 *Multiple CallManager Clusters with a Centralized Directory*

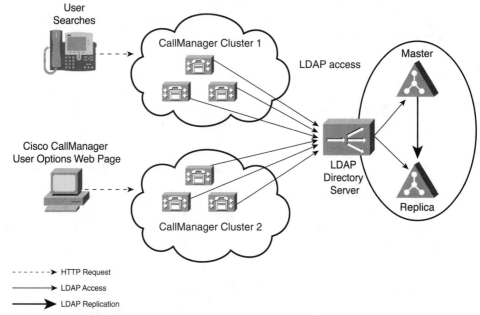

If the only need is for the username lookup capability that directory access provides, directory integration is not needed. You simply need to resolve an LDAP query, rendering the integration process unnecessary.

If, however, you want the benefit of having one user directory database that multiple CallManager clusters integrate with, the integration process is an appropriate option to pursue.

Providing Endpoints with Corporate Directory Access

Remember that endpoint directory access does not need any integration. All that the endpoint does is send an XML query to a web server that then sends an LDAP query to the LDAP server for resolution. To the end user, the result of the query is the same.

IP Phones are the most common endpoints to request LDAP information. The 7940 and 7960 IP Phones search the directory when the user presses the **directories** button. When the user executes a search using the **directories** button, the IP Phone sends an HTTP request to a web server to get the requested information. The web server responds with an Extensible Markup Language (XML) message that the IP Phone can interpret and display.

The HTTP server operates as a proxy in this instance. It receives the HTTP message from the IP Phone and translates it into an LDAP request that is sent to the directory server. The response it receives from the directory server is interpreted and is sent back to the IP Phone in an encapsulated XML object.

Figure 18-3 demonstrates the steps involved when CallManager is *not* integrated with the corporate directory. Notice that CallManager is not involved in the message exchange.

Figure 18-3 *Cisco IP Phone Directory Access*

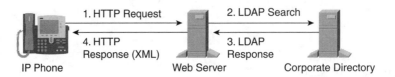

You can configure the proxy function provided by the web server using the Cisco IP Phone Services Software Developer Kit (SDK), which includes the Cisco LDAP search server. When you install the Cisco IP Phone Services SDK, the Cisco LDAP search server gets installed automatically.

TIP	You can download the Cisco IP Phone Services SDK from the Enterprise area on the Developer Support Central website (www.cisco.com/warp/public/570/). You can also learn more about building custom directories in the Cisco Press book *Developing Cisco IP Phone Services* (ISBN: 1-58705-060-9).

The Cisco IP Phone Services SDK allows you to make the necessary customizations for any LDAP server. Example 18-1 shows an example of how Microsoft Active Server Pages (ASP) code can be modified to point to the corporate directory server's name or IP address. In this example, ldap.cisco.com is the server, and the subtree is ou=people,o=cisco.com. Also, if anonymous searches are not permitted on the corporate directory, some authentication credentials can be entered as well.

Example 18-1 *Cisco IP Phone Directory Access*

```
[...]
// Server setup
s.Server = "ldap.cisco.com";
s.Port = 389;

//Authenticate and set scope
//s.AuthName = "cn=Directory Manager, o=cisco.com";
//s.AuthPasswd = "password";
s.SearchBase = "ou=people,o=cisco.com";
[...]
```

After this customization is complete, a configuration change is needed in CallManager. In the Enterprise Parameters Configuration page in Cisco CallManager Administration (**System > Enterprise Parameters**), the **URL Directories** field must be set to point to the appropriate web server that has the **ldapdirectory.asp** file customized.

For more information, refer to the book, *Developing Cisco IP Phone Services*.

Troubleshooting Corporate Directory Access

Corporate directories are LDAP servers such as Microsoft Active Directory or Netscape iPlanet. When you find a problem with this type of directory access, you should investigate the following:

- **Network issues**—As always, the endpoint's request could fail because of any number of network-related problems. These include network outages, host name resolution problems, and so on. Remember also that the web server must have network access to the directory it is requesting information from.

- **Incorrect LDAP ASP file**—If you have created an ASP file to facilitate an LDAP request on the IP Phone's behalf, make sure it has the correct information in it. For instance, if the ASP file attempts to connect to the directory with a wrong IP address, the query fails.

- **Web server**—Make sure the web server is running. If the IP Phone sends its HTTP request to a web server that isn't running, the request fails.

Troubleshooting directory access is fairly straightforward. Because the focus here is a device sending an HTTP request to a web server and that web server sending an LDAP request to the directory, the possible areas of failure are few. After all, this is only a directory lookup—not a full directory integration.

The part that makes troubleshooting directory access difficult is that there are no log files to easily view what is happening. Sniffer traces are an ideal way to troubleshoot this problem because Sniffer can show you the packet flow between the phone and the web server as well as the LDAP connection between the web server and the LDAP server. Sniffer decodes the HTTP packets and the LDAP packets into human-readable format. You can then see any error messages reported by the web server or LDAP server to isolate the problem.

Using the CallManager Embedded Directory

One of the directory options is the embedded directory that is already a part of CallManager. The embedded directory is a popular choice because it is integrated with CallManager by default upon installation. The embedded directory, named DC Directory, is an LDAP-v3-compliant directory provided by Data Connection, Ltd.

The embedded LDAP directory is recommended when

- A corporate directory does not exist, and there is no interest in deploying one.

- There is only one CallManager cluster, or there are multiple clusters but there is no requirement to share user information across them.

- It is deemed unacceptable to extend the corporate directory schema and add the Cisco Directory Information Tree (DIT) to the directory tree. This tree adds device and other related information that is used in conjunction with the users listed in the corporate directory.

The embedded directory resides on all members of a CallManager cluster. In fact, the directory replication in many ways mirrors the SQL replication that occurs between the members of a cluster. The directory master resides on the Publisher server, and all the replicas reside on each Subscriber server.

If you make a change to a Subscriber, it doesn't go into the Subscriber's database directly. Rather, that change is sent to the Publisher's DC Directory where it is inserted into the database and then replicated out to all of the Subscribers. Consequently, if the Publisher is down, no changes can be made to the DC Directory on any server.

Figure 18-4 shows the directory master/replica relationship.

Troubleshooting the CallManager Embedded Directory

So what types of problems can you encounter with the embedded directory? Typically the realization that something is wrong comes from attempting to add a user or search for users via CallManager Administration and receiving the "Cannot create user object" or the "Sorry your session object has timed out. Click here to Begin a New search" error. Other problems can include the following:

- You can add a user to one server, but not to another server

- Added users show up on some servers, but not all

The directory is normally very stable. However, certain events can cause a problem. For example, a CallManager upgrade also upgrades the embedded directory. If problems occur during the upgrade, you might encounter a problem with the embedded directory.

Whatever the case might be, you should investigate any irregularities by checking the directory's integrity. Begin by checking the directory configuration.

Figure 18-4 *Directory Master/Replica Relationship in a Cluster*

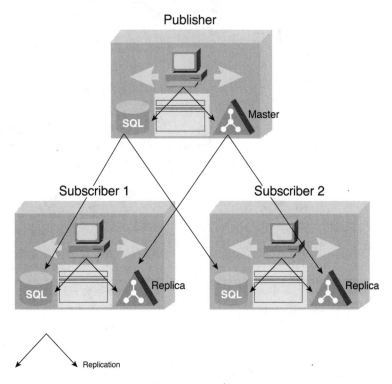

The first item to check when you suspect a problem is the state of the service. Make sure the DC Directory service is running (**Start > Programs > Administrative Tools > Service Control Manager**). If it isn't running, check the system Event Viewer log (**Start > Programs > Administrative Tools > Event Viewer**) for events that relate to the DC Directory.

Second, it is important to note that the DC Directory might sometimes pause itself as a preventive measure. When the system runs low on resources, such as disk space, it pauses itself to prevent data corruption. The Event Viewer has an entry indicating the paused service and the reason for the paused state. You can restart the service, but do not do so until you have resolved the resource shortage.

Sometimes—especially after a CallManager version upgrade—the DC Directory may stay paused for several minutes while it reindexes the database. This is normal and event log messages indicate DC Directory is reindexing. If you restart the service in this case, you just restart the reindexing process, so be sure to look in the event log before restarting the DC Directory service, as you may just prolong the problem.

If the DC Directory Service is running, you need to verify the configuration. Make sure you are logged in under the local administrator account before proceeding with the following steps.

Step 1   Launch the DC Directory Administrator by clicking **Start > Programs > DC Directory Administrator**.

Step 2   When the DC Directory Administrator Login window appears, click **Next**.

Step 3   Enter the username **Directory Manager** and the Directory Manager password you selected when you installed CallManager, and then click **Finish**. Figure 18-5 shows the screen that appears if the DC Directory is correctly configured.

Figure 18-5 *DC Directory Screen*

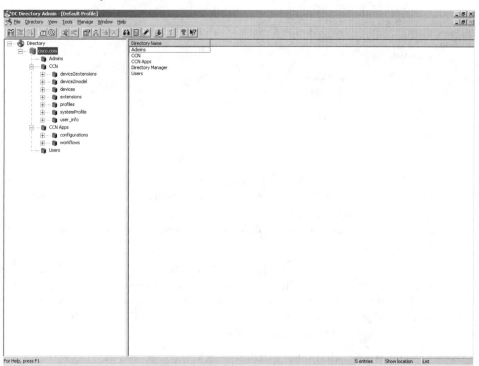

If this logon fails, it could simply be because the password you used is incorrect. You can check to see if your password is correct by using the passwordutils.exe utility.

The password is stored in an encrypted value in the registry, so you first need to determine the encrypted value of the password. Do this by using the passwordutils.exe program, which is located in the C:\dcdsrvr\bin directory.

Step 1 Open a command line and go to **C:\dcdsrvr\bin**.

Step 2 Type **passwordutils** followed by the DC Directory administrator password and press **Enter**. For example, if your password is **cisco** enter: **passwordutils cisco**.

Step 3 The passwordutils program returns the encrypted version of your password. For example,

```
C:\dcdsrvr\bin>passwordutils cisco
Encrypted Password: 0c0a000a2c
Original  Password: cisco
Decrypted Password: cisco
```

Step 4 Write down or copy the Encrypted Password value. You will need this information for the registry.

Step 5 Select **Start > Run**.

Step 6 In the Open field, type **regedit**. The Registry Editor window appears.

Step 7 In the Registry Editor window, navigate to the Directory Configuration folder (**HKEY_LOCAL_MACHINE > SOFTWARE > Cisco Systems, Inc. > Directory Configuration**).

Step 8 Double-click the **MGRPW** entry. The Edit String window appears.

Step 9 Compare the value in the **Value Data** field with the decrypted value shown in the passwordutils.exe results.

If the value in the registry does not match the output of the passwordutils utility, you are using the wrong password to access DC Directory. If you forgot the original password, you can replace the registry entry with the output from passwordutils to change the DC Directory password and then restart the World Wide Web Publishing service. You must do this on all the nodes in the cluster.

If, after changing the password, you still get a screen indicating a logon failure, try logging in by selecting Auth Level **none**. If you get a message asking if you want to configure the directory, cancel the setup and exit. The directory is not configured correctly, and you need to fix it manually on both the Publisher and the Subscriber, as described in the following sections.

Reconfiguring DC Directory on the Publisher

The reconfiguration steps for the DC Directory are different for CallManager 3.3 than for earlier versions of CallManager. In CallManager 3.3, the reconfiguration scripts have been rewritten and are greatly simplified.

However, if you have an earlier version of CallManager, you should check with TAC or search the Cisco website to see if any new scripts have been released for your version of CallManager. If not, proceed with the instructions presented in the later section "CallManager 3.0–3.2 Reconfiguration Steps."

CallManager 3.3 Reconfiguration Steps

Let's take a look at the new scripts and how they are to be used. Before running these scripts, make sure that there is network connectivity between all servers involved. Table 18-1 shows the scripts discussed in this section and their uses.

Table 18-1   *Scripts for CallManager 3.3*

Script	Description
reconfig_cluster	Reconfigures the replication agreements between all of the DC Directory databases in the cluster. It does not delete or modify existing directory data and only needs to be run on the Publisher server.
clean_publisher	Removes the replication agreements to all non-existent Subscribers from the Publisher DC Directory. It does not delete or modify existing directory data and only needs to be run on the Publisher after removing a Subscriber server.
avvid_srepl	Reconfigures the replication agreement between the Subscriber and Publisher DC Directory.
avvid_migrate_save	Saves the data in the C:\dcdsrvr\run\dcx500\config\ Migration-Backup directory.
avvid_migrate_restore	Restores data from the C:\dcdsrvr\run\dcx500\config\ Migration-Backup directory.

The key script is called **reconfig_cluster**. To execute this script, perform the following steps:

Step 1   On the Publisher server, select **Start > Run** and type **cmd**. A command window opens.

Step 2   In the command window, type **cd c:\dcdsrvr\bin**. The specified directory appears.

Step 3   Type **reconfig_cluster** *Directory Manager Password* where *Directory Manager Password* is the password for the Directory Manager, and press **Enter**.

Another script is called **clean_publisher**. This is only used if you are going to remove a server from a CallManager cluster. After removing the server, this script can be run on the Publisher. To execute the **clean_publisher** script, perform the following steps:

Step 1   On the Publisher server, select **Start > Run** and type **cmd**. A command window opens.

Step 2   In the command window, type **cd c:\dcdsrvr\bin**. The specified directory appears.

Step 3   Type **clean_publisher** and press **Enter**.

If you had only one Subscriber with replication problems, you should use the **avvid_srepl** script. The script has to be run on the Subscriber, and it reconfigures the replication agreement between the Subscriber and Publisher DC Directory instead of reconfiguring the whole cluster.

If all servers need to be reconfigured, use the **reconfig_cluster** script, as described earlier in this section. If only one Subscriber needs repair, use **avvid_srepl**. To execute the **avvid_srepl** script, perform the following steps on the Subscriber with replication problems:

Step 1   On the Subscriber server, select **Start > Run** and type **cmd**. A command window opens.

Step 2   In the command window, type **cd c:\dcdsrvr\bin**. The specified directory appears.

Step 3   Type **avvid_srepl** *Publisher Name Directory Manager Password* where *Publisher Name* is the name of the Publisher server and *Directory Manager Password* is the password for the Directory Manager, and press **Enter**.

Finally, two scripts are available to save and restore the actual data. If you need to save the data in the directory, use the **avvid_migrate_save** script. To restore this data, use **avvid_migrate_restore**. To execute either one of these scripts, perform the following steps on the Publisher:

Step 1   On the Publisher server, select **Start > Run** and type **cmd**. A command window opens.

Step 2   In the command window, type **cd c:\dcdsrvr\bin**. The specified directory appears.

Step 3   Type **avvid_migrate_save** to save the data, or if you are restoring the saved data, type **avvid_migrate_restore** and press **Enter**.

CallManager 3.0–3.2 Reconfiguration Steps

If an updated script is not available for your version of CallManager, you will need to follow the traditional steps for reconfiguration. You must perform the following directions precisely to manually fix the configuration. You must use the correct password for this to work, or you will simply be running reconfiguration scripts that fail because of a wrong password.

To verify that you have the right password, follow the steps outlined in the earlier section "Using the CallManager Embedded Directory."

WARNING   Failure to follow these instructions exactly could result in the loss of all your directory data.

These steps must be completed on all servers in the cluster. When working on the Subscribers, make sure you can ping both the Publisher and the Subscriber by name before beginning the process. First, you must save the existing DC Directory data. If you have no data in the directory that you need to save, you can skip to Step 7.

Step 1   On the Publisher server, select **Start > Run** and type **cmd**. A command window opens.

Step 2   In the command window, type **cd c:\dcdsrvr\bin**. The specified directory appears.

Step 3   Type **avvid_save**. This command saves all the data in the directory to a file. Example 18-2 shows sample output for this step.

NOTE   This procedure cannot be run via Terminal Services. You need to be on the server itself or connected via Telnet for these steps to be successful.

Example 18-2   *Verifying the Correct Configuration for the DC Directory Service*

```
C:\dcdsrvr\bin>avvid_save

*****************************************
*                                       *
* -- CISCO User Preferences Support -- *
*                                       *
*****************************************

C:\>REM patch for Spirian install- initialize the DCD environment vars

C:\>set DCX500RUN=C:\dcdsrvr
```

Example 18-2   *Verifying the Correct Configuration for the DC Directory Service (Continued)*

```
C:\>set DCDCONFIG=C:\dcdsrvr\run\dcx500\config

C:\>set PATH=C:\WINNT\system32;C:\WINNT;C:\WINNT\System32\Wbem;c:\sti;c:\cpqutil
;c:\utils;C:\MSSQL7\BINN;C:\WINNT\bin;C:\Program Files\Cisco\bin;C:\dcdsrvr\bin;
C:\dcdsrvr\lib;C:\dcdsrvr\bin;C:\dcdsrvr\lib;

C:\>set DCX500_SCHEMA_PORT=8404

C:\>mkdir C:\dcdsrvr\run\dcx500\config\Backup
A subdirectory or file C:\dcdsrvr\run\dcx500\config\Backup already exists.

Saving User Information...

C:\>call C:\dcdsrvr\bin\dcdexprt EXPORT C:\dcdsrvr\run\dcx500\config\Backup\avvi
dusers.txt /o=cisco.com/ou=users
Info MLK0096:
3 entries exported to file C:\dcdsrvr\run\dcx500\config\Backup\avvidusers.txt.

Saving Profile Information...
Info MLK0096:
5 entries exported to file C:\dcdsrvr\run\dcx500\config\Backup\avvidprofiles.txt
.

Saving Apps20 Information...
Info MLK0096:
1 entries exported to file C:\dcdsrvr\run\dcx500\config\Backup\avvidapps20.txt.

Saving Admin Information...
Info MLK0096:
1 entries exported to file C:\dcdsrvr\run\dcx500\config\Backup\avvidadmins.txt.

Saving PA node Information...
Error MLK0039:
Export of tree failed: DumpTree of /o=cisco.com/ou=ccn/cn=CiscoPA failed..

Error MLK0045:
Failed to export tree.

Info MLK0096:
1 entries exported to file C:\dcdsrvr\run\dcx500\config\Backup\avvidpauser.txt.

Saving E911 node Information...
Error MLK0039:
Export of tree failed: DumpTree of /o=cisco.com/ou=ccn/ou=ECS failed..

Error MLK0045:
Failed to export tree.
Press any key to continue . . .
```

Step 4 You must now check two directories for any error logs. Go to C:\dcdsrvr\run\dcx500\config and C:\dcdsrvr\run\dcx500\config\backup. Check to see if there is an **avvidprofiles.txt.err** or **avvidusers.txt.err** file in either folder. If you see either error in either directory, *do not proceed*. Verify that the DC Directory service is running. If the DC Directory service is stopped, restart the service and go back to Step 1.

Step 5 Next, check to see if any of these errors are related to certain applications being installed. For instance, you could see errors related to Personal Assistant when Personal Assistant isn't being used in the cluster. In this case, you can safely ignore the error because it is only a notification, not a problem.

Step 6 Examine the following two files to make sure they are populated with the exported directory users and profiles:

C:\dcdsrvr\run\dcx500\config\Backup\avvidusers.txt

C:\dcdsrvr\run\dcx500\config\Backup\avvidprofiles.txt

Additional files might appear if other applications are installed.

Step 7 Stop the directory service. You can do this using the Service Manager (**Start > Programs > Administrative Tools > Services >** *stop the service named* **DC Directory Server**).

Step 8 At the command prompt, type **cleandsa**. This erases the existing directory. Example 18-3 shows the resulting output from this command.

Example 18-3 **cleandsa** *Command Output*

```
C:\dcdsrvr\bin>cleandsa
------------------------------------------------------------------
A secured DC Directory Information Base exists.
If you choose to continue, this DIB will be deleted and replaced
with a clean DIB. Any existing directory entries will be lost!
------------------------------------------------------------------
Hit a key now to discard current DIB or Ctrl-C to abort
Copying configuration files...
Initialising DC Directory Information Base...
Setting up attribute categories...
DC Directory Information Base initialised successfully
```

Step 9 Using Windows Explorer, navigate to C:\dcdsrvr\bin.

Step 10 Right-click on the file named **avvid_cfg** and select **Edit**. The file should open in Notepad.

Step 11 Search for a line in the file similar to the following:

```
call %DCX500RUN%\bin\dcdbtapp /n:0x0400000083 Person
"Directory Manager" <password> >>%LOG%\avvid_cfg.log
2>>%LOG%\avvid_cfg_err.log
```

Step 12 Make sure the password listed after **"Directory Manager"** matches the password you verified in the MGRPW entry in the registry. (Refer to the section "Troubleshooting the CallManager Embedded Directory" earlier in this chapter for instructions on verifying the MGRPW entry.) If this password is wrong, the directory configuration will fail.

Step 13 Return to the command prompt and type **avvid_cfg**. This command re-configures the database. Example 18-4 shows sample output for this step.

Example 18-4   **avvid_cfg** *Command Output*

```
C:\dcdsrvr\bin>avvid_cfg
*****************************************
*                                       *
* -- CISCO User Preferences Support -- *
*                                       *
*****************************************

A subdirectory or file C:\dcdsrvr\suspense already exists.
A subdirectory or file C:\dcdsrvr\log already exists.

Stopping DC Directory...

Updating Directory Schema

Starting DC Directory...

Waiting for DC Directory to initialize...

Configuring DC Directory...

Setting up AVVID ACLs...

Indexing AVVID attributes...

Load password encription policy

Allow authenticated user to modify the ciscoCCNatAssociatedPC attribute

Remove anonymous browse...

Creating OUs to store AVVID configuration information

Creating a default entity reference in the RootDSE

Changing DCDirectory Log On account to LocalSystem
```

Step 14 After Step 13 is complete, return to the command prompt and type **avvid_restore**. This command imports the data saved in the first step back into the directory.

Step 15 The Publisher repair is complete. Example 18-5 shows sample output for this step.

Example 18-5 **avvid_restore** *Command Output*

```
C:\dcdsrvr\bin>avvid_restore
******************************************
*                                        *
* -- CISCO User Preferences Support -- *
*                                        *
******************************************

C:\>REM patch for Spirian install- initialize the DCD environment vars

C:\>set DCX500RUN=C:\dcdsrvr

C:\>set DCDCONFIG=C:\dcdsrvr\run\dcx500\config

C:\>set PATH=C:\WINNT\system32;C:\WINNT;C:\WINNT\System32\Wbem;c:\sti;c:\cpqutil
;c:\utils;C:\MSSQL7\BINN;C:\WINNT\bin;C:\Program Files\Cisco\bin;C:\dcdsrvr\bin;
C:\dcdsrvr\lib;C:\dcdsrvr\bin;C:\dcdsrvr\lib;;C:\dcdsrvr\bin;C:\dcdsrvr\lib;;C:\
dcdsrvr\bin;C:\dcdsrvr\lib;

C:\>set DCX500_SCHEMA_PORT=8404

Restoring Profile Information...

C:\>call C:\dcdsrvr\bin\dcdimprt APPLY C:\dcdsrvr\run\dcx500\config\Backup\avvid
profiles.txt
Error MLK0005:
Failure adding directory entry - entry skipped.
  Name of entry: /o=cisco.com/ou=CCN/ou=profiles

Error MLK0005:
Failure adding directory entry - entry skipped.
  Name of entry: /o=cisco.com/ou=CCN/ou=profiles/cn=ctifw-CCNProfile

Error MLK0005:
Failure adding directory entry - entry skipped.
  Name of entry: /o=cisco.com/ou=CCN/ou=profiles/cn=ctifw-profile

Info MLK0400:
Entry added to directory.
  Name of entry: /o=cisco.com/ou=CCN/ou=profiles/cn=test-CCNProfile

Info MLK0400:
Entry added to directory.
  Name of entry: /o=cisco.com/ou=CCN/ou=profiles/cn=test-profile

Restoring User Information...

Error MLK0005:
Failure adding directory entry - entry skipped.
  Name of entry: /o=cisco.com/ou=users
```

Example 18-5   **avvid_restore** *Command Output (Continued)*

```
Error MLK0005:
Failure adding directory entry - entry skipped.
  Name of entry: /o=cisco.com/ou=users/cn="CTI Framework"

Info MLK0400:
Entry added to directory.
  Name of entry: /o=cisco.com/ou=users/cn=test

Restoring Apps20 Information...

Error MLK0005:
Failure adding directory entry - entry skipped.
  Name of entry: /o=cisco.com/ou="CCN Apps"

Restoring Admins Information...

Error MLK0005:
Failure adding directory entry - entry skipped.
  Name of entry: /o=cisco.com/ou=Admins



Restoring PA node Information...

Error GEI0002:
Failure to open file 'C:\dcdsrvr\run\dcx500\config\Backup\avvidpaserver.txt'

Error MLK0005:
Failure adding directory entry - entry skipped.
  Name of entry: /o=cisco.com/ou=ccn/ou=user_info

Restoring E911 node Information...

Error GEI0002:
Failure to open file 'C:\dcdsrvr\run\dcx500\config\Backup\avvide911.txt'

Press any key to continue . . .
```

After completing the Publisher repair, you must perform very similar steps on every Subscriber. There are some differences when working with Subscribers, so carefully follow the steps described in the following section.

Reconfiguring DC Directory on Subscribers

You must perform the following directions precisely to manually fix the DC Directory configuration on Subscribers.

WARNING   Failure to follow these instructions exactly could result in the loss of all your directory data.

These steps must be completed on all members of the cluster. When working on the Subscriber servers, make sure you can ping both the Publisher and the Subscriber by name before beginning the process.

Step 1   Make sure you have performed the steps detailed in the earlier section "Reconfiguring DC Directory on the Publisher." You can verify that the steps for reconfiguring the DC Directory on the Publisher were completed successfully by going to the Global Directory pages on the Publisher. Search for existing users, and add a test user. If you succeed at both tasks, you can move to the Subscribers.

Step 2   Select **Start > Run** and type **cmd**. A command window opens.

Step 3   Type **cd c:\dcdsrver\bin**. The specified directory appears.

Step 4   Stop the directory service. You can do this using the Service Manager (**Start > Programs > Administrative Tools > Services**). Stop the service named **DC Directory Server**.

Step 5   At the command prompt, type **cleandsa**. This erases the existing directory on the Subscriber. Example 18-6 shows sample output for this step.

Example 18-6   **cleandsa** *Command Output*

```
C:\dcdsrvr\bin>cleandsa
------------------------------------------------------------------
A secured DC Directory Information Base exists.
If you choose to continue, this DIB will be deleted and replaced
with a clean DIB. Any existing directory entries will be lost!
------------------------------------------------------------------
Hit a key now to discard current DIB or Ctrl-C to abort
Copying configuration files...
Initialising DC Directory Information Base...
Setting up attribute categories...
DC Directory Information Base initialised successfully
```

Step 6   Type **avvid_scfg** *PublisherHostname SubscriberHostname*. You must resolve this host name to the correct IP address. You can test this by typing **ping** *PublisherHostname,* where *PublisherHostname* is the actual host name of your CallManager Publisher (not the IP address or DNS name). You should get a response. If not, the **avvid_scfg** command runs and appears to work, but replication is not fixed.

Assume that you have two CallManagers. One is called CM_Pub, and the other is CM_Sub. You type in **avvid_scfg CM_Pub CM_Sub**. This step re-establishes the Publisher/replica relationship. It is very important that you run **avvid_scfg** on the Subscribers, not **avvid_cfg**.

Step 7 Repeat Step 6 on all Subscriber servers.

The directory has now been reconfigured and the replication re-established.

TIP   It's a good idea to verify functionality after performing these steps on each Subscriber. Go into the Global Directory in CallManager Administration on each Subscriber and check to make sure users can be searched for and added.

Understanding and Troubleshooting Active Directory Integration

If an enterprise already has a corporate directory, it is probably best to integrate the IP Telephony applications with the corporate directory. This centralizes user information and allows the information to be shared among different applications. Integration also reduces administration because there is only one place to add users instead of having to enter user information into multiple locations. CallManager does not need to be a part of the same domain to integrate with Active Directory.

When Active Directory integration occurs, basically the corporate schema is extended by the addition of a DIT for information specific to Cisco applications. This means that the existing schema remains intact, with a separate tree added that doesn't interfere with the existing data. This separate directory tree is called an LDAP auxiliary class. Figure 18-6 shows a typical directory information tree.

With existing integration, this tree remains intact. An additional tree is added for Cisco applications. Figure 18-7 shows the added organizational unit containing Cisco-related information.

The CallManager Directory Service makes use of an LDAP auxiliary class to associate user properties (such as the mapping between the username and a telephone extension) with the existing user object in the corporate directory schema.

Figure 18-6 *Typical Directory Information Tree*

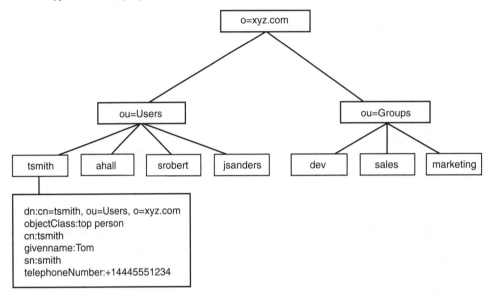

Figure 18-7 *Added Cisco Directory Information Tree*

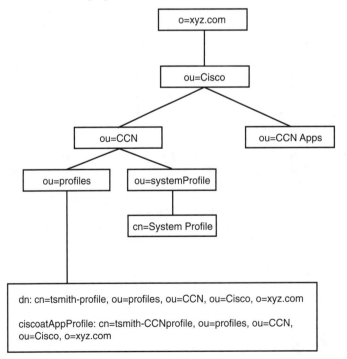

It is very important to note that multiple clusters can use the same corporate directory, but each cluster has its own DIT. If you have two clusters, the added DITs would look like Figure 18-8.

Figure 18-8 *Two CallManager Clusters with Two DITs*

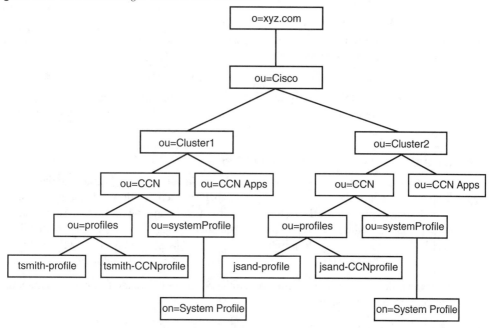

Of course, this is only a brief overview of what happens during directory integration. With that in mind, it is time to turn your attention to common problems you might encounter with Active Directory integration.

Troubleshooting Common Problems with Installing the Customer Directory Configuration Plugin

One of the CallManager plugins is the Cisco Customer Directory Configuration Plugin (**Application > Install Plugins**). This program creates the Cisco DIT in Active Directory and configures CallManager to read and write to that directory. Be sure to run this program during off-peak times because CPU usage is very high when it is installing.

The Cisco Customer Directory Configuration Plugin can successfully install and establish integration only with proper network connectivity and proper administrative rights to the Active Directory controller(s). An LDAP administrator distinguished name and a password are needed to install this plugin on the server. A distinguished name uniquely identifies a user or a group so that it can be found in the directory. A distinguished name usually has three main attributes:

- A user's name or user ID
- An organization name
- A country designation

However, more designations can be added such as the state or group the user belongs to. An example of a distinguished name is

```
cn=Addis Hallmark, ou=IP Telephony, o=Cisco, st=CA, c=US
```

For the plugin to install correctly, an administrator distinguished name must be used with read/write/modify privileges for the part of the directory where the DIT will be added.

Preparing Active Directory to Allow Schema Modifications

Active Directory doesn't simply allow schema modifications at any time. The directory is a critical part of an organization, and it would not be prudent to allow the schema to casually be modified. To prepare for the Active Directory integration, you must make some changes to the domain controller so that a DIT can be added. This step is sometimes missed, but it is critical that you do this before running the plugin. The plugin installation can fail if you do not take the proper steps. The plugin stops before completing and indicates a problem.

To set the domain controller to allow schema modifications, do the following on a domain controller for your active directory:

Step 1 Log in as domain administrator with schema admin rights.

Step 2 Register the DLL for schema modifications (this must be done on the domain controller). Browse to the C:\winnt\system32 directory and double-click the file called **schmmgmt.dll**. When prompted for the program you want to use to open this file, select **other** and choose the **regsvr32.exe** program in the C:\winnt\system32 directory.

The DLL is now registered.

Step 3 Next, change schema modification permissions. To do this, select **Start > Run** and in the command window, type **mmc /all**.

Step 4 Select **Console > Add/Remove Snap in**.

Step 5 Click **Add**.

Step 6 Select **Active Directory Schema**. Click **Add** and then **Close**.

Step 7 Click **OK**.

Step 8 Select Active Directory Schema. Right-click and select **Operation Master**. Figure 18-9 shows the Change Schema Master window.

Figure 18-9 *Change Schema Master Window*

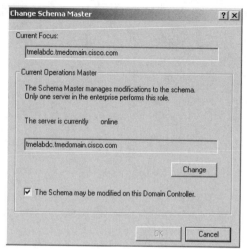

Step 9   Check the box that says **The Schema may be modified on this Domain Controller** as shown in Figure 18-9.

Step 10 Click **OK**. Schema modifications are now allowed.

The previous steps are very important to make sure that the permissions are set correctly to allow for schema modifications. With these changes made, you can verify the accuracy of the domain name so the Cisco Customer Directory Configuration Plugin can run successfully.

Ensuring Domain Name Accuracy for Active Directory

Another common installation problem is not getting the Active Directory domain name right. During the Cisco Customer Directory Configuration Plugin installation process, you are prompted for the name of the Active Directory domain name. It is important that you provide the exact Active Directory domain name.

Here is how to find the right Active Directory domain name: On the domain controller, go to **Start > Programs > Administrative Tools > Active Directory Users and Computers**. Figure 18-10 shows the Change Schema Master dialog. The selected attribute is the domain name. In this case, it is tmedomain.cisco.com.

The tmedomain.cisco.com name should be used when prompted by the Cisco Customer Directory Configuration Plugin.

Figure 18-10   *Active Directory Domain*

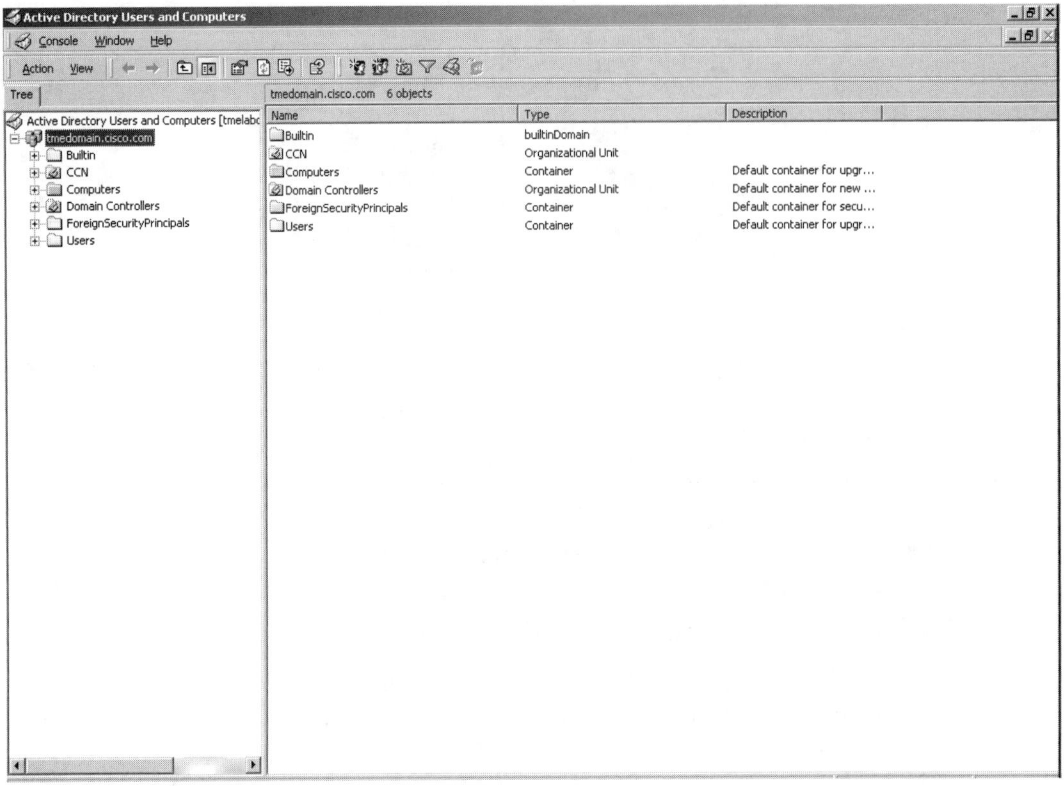

Verifying Distinguished Name Administrative Rights After Cisco Customer Directory Configuration Plugin Failure

If the plugin installation seems to fail, a very likely cause is that the distinguished name that was used does not have the proper administrative rights to modify the schema. Double-check the username and password, and check with the domain's administrator to make sure the appropriate settings are being used. The plugin displays an error that says "Setup failed to connect. Please enter your Host name, Port Number, Directory Administrator DN, and password again."

Checking Log Files for Errors

You can also check the log files under C:\dcdsrvr\log. There might be files named **ad_***. They might contain error information, but that does not always mean the installation failed. For example, if the schema already exists and the user chooses to install it again, doing so will result in errors in this file.

Log files are usually most helpful to TAC or CallManager engineering for very difficult problems. They are not always helpful and descriptive to the administrator. Nevertheless, in nearly every case, the reasons for failure are related to the various issues that have been addressed in previous sections.

Miscellaneous Troubleshooting Items

If the Cisco Customer Directory Configuration Plugin installation completed successfully, the directory integration should be complete. You might, however, run into a few oddities that you need to know how to deal with.

First, it is best to create new users in CallManager Administration (**User > Add a New User**). If you create users in Active Directory, they might not show up in CallManager Administration. The reason is that the E-mail field in Active Directory is not mandatory. From CallManager's perspective, however, it *is* mandatory for the user to be seen in CallManager Administration. Even though the E-mail field does not appear on the User Information page in CallManager Administration, the information in that field is used to indicate a valid entry in the directory.

You can easily fix this problem by double-clicking the user in question in the Active Directory Users and Computers console. Complete the E-mail field with the correct user-name, as shown in Figure 18-11. Also be sure to populate the First name and Last name fields.

Figure 18-11 *Active Directory User Properties*

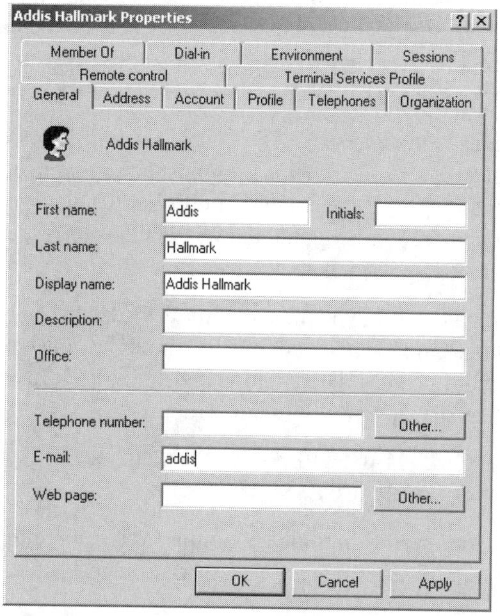

Another possible issue is the inability to add or delete users in CallManager Administration that are in the corporate directory. The reason for this is that you cannot add or delete user entries from your corporate directory by using CallManager Administration by default.

The error normally seen with this problem is "Error: The phone administrator is currently not allowed to add or delete users."

If you want to have this ability, you can enable this capability by performing the following:

Step 1   Select **Start > Run** and type **regedit**.

Step 2   Go to the following key:

HKEY_LOCAL_MACHINE > SOFTWARE > Cisco Systems, Inc. > Directory Configuration

Step 3   You should see a key named **DIRACCESS**. By default, the value of this key is set to False. Change the value of this key to **True**.

Step 4   Restart the IIS Admin Service.

Understanding and Troubleshooting Netscape iPlanet Integration

Netscape iPlanet integration is simpler to understand and troubleshoot than the other directory options we have discussed. The configuration steps for the Cisco Customer Directory Configuration Plugin in CallManager Administration (**Application > Install Plugins**) are nearly identical when used for Netscape. No changes are needed to enable schema modifications. As always, the Cisco Customer Directory Configuration Plugin must be run on all servers in the CallManager cluster.

One big difference is that Netscape Directory Server does not allow remote schema modifications. Because of this, the schema files must be copied manually to the directory server when you run the Plugin on the database Publisher. Running the Plugin on the database Subscribers does not require copying the schema files or restarting Netscape Directory Server. When this step is complete, the Netscape directory server must be restarted.

For this integration to work, you must modify the Registry on every CallManager server in the cluster. Users cannot be added or deleted through CallManager Administration by default. Only CallManager-related fields can be modified. To enable full read/write access, the following Registry key must be set to True:

HKEY_LOCAL_MACHINE > SOFTWARE > Cisco Systems, Inc. > Directory Configuration > DIRACCESS

There are many similarities in troubleshooting Active Directory integration and Netscape iPlanet integration. As such, it is not necessary to repeat the same steps in detail in this section. In particular, the "Troubleshooting Common Problems with Installing the Customer Directory Configuration Plugin" and "Miscellaneous Troubleshooting Items" apply to both integration processes.

The key factors to successfully integrating with iPlanet are

1 Make sure there is network connectivity between CallManager and the iPlanet directory.

2 Ensure that DNS name resolution is working.

3 Copy schema files manually to the directory server when you run the Plugin on the database Publisher.

4 Provide the proper administrator name during the plugin installation.

5 Set the Registry key properly on CallManager.

Best Practices

Network issues can affect directory problems like any other network device. Various network problems like DNS name resolution, incorrect IP addressing, or network outages can affect the directory. When troubleshooting, check these issues first. They are easily overlooked, but they can be the simple answer to problem at hand. If you do not do this, you may go through a lot of work to reconfigure the database only to find out it was a network connectivity issue.

Remember that endpoint directory access does not require directory integration, so choose the best option for your deployment.

When troubleshooting directory access, remember that the IP Phone sends an HTTP request to a web server, which in turn sends an LDAP request to the directory. As such, both parts of this communication must be investigated for any errors.

For CallManager 3.3 and later, use the new scripts that are provided (as discussed in the section, "CallManager 3.3 Reconfiguration Steps"). These scripts greatly simplify the process of reconfiguration. If you have an older version, check on Cisco.com or with TAC to see if a new script has been provided for your version. If not, carefully follow the reconfiguration steps provided in this chapter. When integrating with Active Directory, make sure to follow the instructions carefully. Small omissions can present big problems. The registry must be modified. The domain administrator account must have schema admin rights. The domain administrator name and password must be properly supplied when using the plugin. These small but important details are essential to having a successful integration.

Summary

IP Telephony brings communication capabilities to a new level by integrating with applications. LDAP directories facilitate this by allowing applications to interface with the directory. This combination provides a rich framework for applications to be written. This also allows existing enterprises to continue expanding on the benefits that a central directory provides.

LDAP is a big part of the Cisco AVVID IP Telephony solution, and troubleshooting effectively is important to the success of every entity that depends on the directory.

Cisco IP Telephony Protocol and Codec Information and References

This appendix lists and describes protocols and codecs in a Cisco IP Telephony network.

Protocols

Table A-1 provides the protocol name, a brief description, and the standards body corresponding to the protocol or the Request for Comments (RFC) number. RFCs are a series of notes about the Internet dating from 1969. Anyone can submit an Internet document to the Internet Engineering Task Force (IETF), the main standards organization for the Internet, but the IETF decides whether the document becomes an RFC. An RFC number designates each RFC. After it is published, an RFC never changes. Modifications to an original RFC are assigned a new RFC number. You can find all RFCs online at www.ietf.org/rfc/rfc*xxxx*.txt, where *xxxx* is the RFC number.

Other protocols, such as those published by the International Telecommunications Union (ITU), the Institute of Electrical and Electronics Engineers (IEEE), Telcordia (formerly Bellcore), the Telecommunications Industry Association (TIA), and the American National Standards Institute (ANSI), must be purchased from the respective standards body. More information is available on each organization's web page:

> **ITU**—www.itu.int
> **IEEE**—standards.ieee.org
> **ANSI**—www.ansi.org
> **EIA/TIA**—www.tiaonline.org
> **Telcordia**—www.telcordia.com

Additionally, the European Telecommunications Standards Institute (ETSI) offers its publications free of charge if you register on its web site, www.etsi.org.

Table A-1 *Protocol Information*

Protocol	Description	Standards Body and Specification
802.1Q	The Ethernet trunking protocol used to separate a physical link into different logical networks using VLAN tagging.	IEEE 802.1q
Analog Ground Start	Can be used by Foreign Exchange Office (FXO) interfaces. Provides analog telephony over a two-wire circuit. Differs from Loop Start signaling in the way on-hook and off-hook transitions are performed.	Telcordia (Bellcore) GR-506-CORE
Analog Loop Start	Used by Foreign Exchange Station (FXS) and FXO interfaces. Provides analog telephony over a two-wire circuit. Nearly all residential phone service customers have analog Loop Start service.	Telcordia (Bellcore) GR-506-CORE
DHCP	Dynamic Host Configuration Protocol. A network service whose primary purpose is to automatically assign IP addresses to new devices that connect or existing devices that reconnect to the network.	RFC 2131
E&M Delayed Start	A form of T1 Channel Associated Signaling (CAS). Used to connect an IP Telephony network to the PSTN or a PBX.	EIA/TIA-464B/C and ANSI T1.403
E&M Immediate Start	A form of T1 CAS. Used to connect an IP Telephony network to the PSTN or a PBX.	EIA/TIA-464B/C and ANSI T1.403
E&M Wink Start	A form of T1 CAS. Used to connect an IP Telephony network to the PSTN or a PBX.	EIA/TIA-464B/C and ANSI T1.403
EIGRP	Enhanced Interior Gateway Routing Protocol. A Cisco-proprietary routing protocol widely deployed in many networks. A white paper describing the protocol and its operation is available at www.cisco.com/warp/public/103/eigrp-toc.html.	Cisco Systems
H.225	See H.323. H.225 is used for call control functions. H.225 is very similar to ISDN Q.931. In fact, many parts of the H.225 specification refer to the Q.931 specification. H.225 uses messages such as setup, call proceeding, connect, and release complete to establish and tear down a call. The specification is available for purchase from the ITU at www.itu.int/rec/ recommendation.asp?type=items&lang=e&parent= T-REC-H.225.0-200011-I.	ITU-T H.225.0

Table A-1   *Protocol Information (Continued)*

Protocol	Description	Standards Body and Specification
H.245	See H.323. Terminal capabilities exchange is one of the most important functions of the H.245 protocol. This is how Cisco CallManager and the gateway let each other know what capabilities they support for a particular call. The specification is available for purchase from the ITU at www.itu.int/rec/ recommendation.asp?type=items&lang=e&parent=T-REC-H.245-200107-I.	ITU-T H.245
H.323	H.323 is an umbrella recommendation from the ITU that sets standards for multimedia communications over packet-based networks. It is considered an umbrella recommendation because most of the signaling protocols used by H.323 devices are actually defined in various other ITU speci-fications. H.323 uses other specifications to control call setup (H.225) and to exchange endpoints' capabilities (H.245). Multiple versions of H.323 exist, the most current being H.323 version 4. CallManager supports H.323 version 2 in CallManager releases 3.0 through 3.3. Cisco supports H.323 version 2 as of Cisco IOS Software Release 12.0(5)T in all H.323-enabled devices, including all versions of Cisco IOS Software Release 12.1 and 12.2. This is a peer-to-peer protocol. In H.323, each gateway con-trols its own interfaces and communicates with other gate-ways using ISDN-like signaling. The specification is available for purchase from the ITU at www.itu.int/rec/ recommendation.asp?type=items&lang=e&parent=T-REC-H.323-200011-I.	ITU-T H.323
IP	Internet Protocol. A Layer 3 network protocol by which one computer can communicate packets of information to another computer on a network.	RFC 791
ISDN BRI and T1/E1 PRI	Not a protocol of its own. Several protocols are used for ISDN BRI and T1 and E1 PRI signaling, including Q.921 and Q.931. In addition to these protocols, various vendors have developed extensions to Q.931, resulting in several ISDN protocol variants.	ITU-T Q.921 ITU-T Q.931

continues

Table A-1 *Protocol Information (Continued)*

Protocol	Description	Standards Body and Specification
JTAPI	Java Telephony Application Programming Interface. JTAPI is a portable, object-oriented API for Java-based computer telephony applications. JTAPI serves a broad audience, from call center application developers to web page designers. JTAPI supports both first- and third-party telephony application domains. The API is designed to make programming simple applications easy while providing features that are necessary for advanced telephony applications. For additional information, visit http://java.sun.com/products/jtapi/jtapi-1.2/Overview.html.	Sun Microsystems
LDAP	Lightweight Directory Access Protocol. LDAP provides an optimized way for applications to access user-related information. This method allows for a high number of reads, writes, searches, and changes. Companies can centralize their user information in an LDAP directory and have a single repository for applications to access.	RFC 1777
MGCP	Media Gateway Control Protocol. A UDP-based, plain-text, master/slave protocol whereby a call agent—in this case, CallManager—controls the function of a particular gateway. Messages are sent as ASCII-encoded text.	RFC 2705
NTP	Network Time Protocol. An Internet standard protocol (built on top of TCP/IP) that ensures accurate synchronization to the millisecond of computer clock times in a network of computers.	RFC 1305
OSPF	Open Shortest Path First. The OSPF protocol is based on link-state technology. This is a departure from the Bellman-Ford vector-based algorithms used in traditional Internet routing protocols such as Routing Information Protocol (RIP). OSPF has introduced new concepts such as authentication of routing updates, Variable-Length Subnet Masks (VLSM), and route summarization. In addition to RFC 2328, the OSPF Design Guide contains an excellent overview. You can find it at www.cisco.com/warp/public/104/1.html.	RFC 2328
Q.850	Defines cause codes for the cause information element used in both Q.931 and H.225 signaling. These cause codes are most commonly used to indicate why a call is disconnected.	ITU-T Q.850

Table A-1   *Protocol Information (Continued)*

Protocol	Description	Standards Body and Specification
Q.921	The ISDN protocol is documented in the ITU-T ISDN Q.931 specifications. Q.921 documents the link layer protocol. It is basically used to ensure reliable delivery of ISDN messages and to establish the D-channel.	ITU-T Q.921
Q.931	The Integrated Services Digital Network (ISDN) protocol is documented in the ITU-T ISDN Q.931 specifications. Q.931 documents Layer 3 signaling.	ITU-T Q.931
Q.Sig	A unified international corporate network signaling standard. As of CallManager release 3.3, Q.Sig is supported for basic call routing functionality.	www.qsig.ie/qsig/ad.htm
RAS	Registration, Admission, and Status. Defined as part of the ITU-T H.225.0 specification.	ITU-T H.225.0
RIP	Routing Information Protocol. A distance vector routing protocol used in some networks. RIP is a fairly simple protocol based on hop count. It has some limitations in comparison to more sophisticated protocols such as EIGRP and OSPF.	RFC 2453
RSVP	Resource Reservation Protocol. A new Internet protocol developed to support specified qualities of service.	RFC 2205
RTP	Real-Time Transport Protocol. An Internet-standard protocol for the transport of real-time data, including audio and video.	RFC 1889
RUDP	Reliable User Datagram Protocol. A Cisco-proprietary protocol that provides reliable transport over UDP. It is used on some MGCP gateway and call agent platforms to perform PRI backhaul; however, this protocol is not used on CallManager or its associated gateways. TCP is used to backhaul PRI signaling instead.	Cisco Systems
SCCP or Skinny client or Skinny protocol	Skinny Client Control Protocol. A Cisco-proprietary protocol that provides a lightweight yet feature-rich way to facilitate a master/slave relationship between CallManager and an IP phone. You can learn more about the Skinny protocol at the Cisco AVVID Partner Program: www.cisco.com/warp/public/779/largeent/partner/esap/.	Cisco Systems
SGCP or Skinny gateway	Skinny Gateway Control Protocol. Used for signaling to various gateways in CallManager versions prior to CallManager 3.1. Most now use MGCP, with the exception of the Cisco Access Analog Trunk and Analog Station series gateways.	Cisco Systems

continues

Table A-1 *Protocol Information (Continued)*

Protocol	Description	Standards Body and Specification
SMDI	Simple Message Desk Interface. SMDI utilizes an RS-232 serial connection to pass information about the calling party number (ANI) and redirecting party number (RDNIS). It also can turn message waiting indicators (MWI) on and off.	Telcordia (Bellcore) specification TR-NWT-000283
T.30	Fax Group 3 is a standards-based technology that is made up primarily of the T.4 and T.30 ITU recommendations. T.30 details the fax negotiations and communication protocol.	ITU-T T.30
T.38 fax relay	Standards-based T.38 fax for voice over IP (VoIP). T.38 uses UDP to transport fax data. Unfortunately, CallManager does not support T.38 fax, so T.38 should not be used in an IP Telephony environment (as opposed to a toll-bypass environment).	ITU-T T.38
T.4	Fax Group 3 is a standards-based technology that is made up primarily of the T.4 and T.30 ITU recommendations. T.4 pertains to how the fax image is encoded by a fax device.	ITU-T T.4
TAPI	Telephony Application Programming Interface. A standard developed by Microsoft to let Microsoft Windows applications interface with telephony applications. TAPI is one of the various CTI protocols supported by CallManager. For more information, visit www.microsoft.com/.	Microsoft Corporation
TCP	Transmission Control Protocol. A connection-oriented Layer 4 network protocol that provides for the reliable end-to-end, ordered delivery of IP packets.	RFC 793
TFTP	Trivial File Transfer Protocol. A UDP-based protocol that permits the transmission of files between network devices.	RFC 1350
UDP	User Datagram Protocol. A connectionless Layer 4 network protocol that runs on top of IP networks and offers a direct way to send and receive datagrams (also known as packets) over an IP network.	RFC 768
V.21 HDLC	V.21 modulated High-level Data Link Control. V.21 HDLC data frames are passed in fax transmission at a speed of 300 bps. These data frames are sent in a standard sequence between the originating and terminating fax devices. During this period, each fax device exchanges its capabilities, and both fax devices agree on the fax session characteristics before the page transmission takes place.	ITU-T V.21

Codecs

Table A-2 provides the codec name, a brief description, and the compression rate. Compression rates are shown without headers because this value depends on the transport medium (for example, Ethernet, Frame Relay, ATM, and so on) and the packetization size of each packet. For more information on packetization, refer to Chapter 7, "Voice Quality."

NOTE   Using the values in Table A-2 for each codec, you can factor the compression rate with headers by adding 12 kbps for IP, UDP, and RTP headers. If you are using RTP header compression, add 4–5 kbps for the IP, UDP, and RTP headers to the values provided in Table A-2.

Table A-2   *Codec Information*

Codec	Description	Compression Rate Without Headers	Standard
G.711	An uncompressed voice codec using 8-bit samples at 8000 samples per second. Samples are encoded using either A-law or μ-law companding.	64 kbps	ITU-T G.711
G.729	Coding of speech using conjugate structure algebraic code excited linear prediction (CS-ACELP).	8 kbps	ITU-T G.729
G.729a	A reduced-complexity version of the G.729 CS-ACELP speech codec.	8 kbps	ITU-T G.729, Annex A
G.729b	A silence-compression scheme for G.729.	8 kbps	ITU-T G.729, Annex B
G.729ab	A reduced-complexity version of the G.729b codec.	8 kbps	ITU-T G.729, Annex B
G.726	Adaptive Differential Pulse Code Modulation (ADPCM) codec.	40, 32, 24, or 16 kbps	ITU-T G.726
G.723	A dual-rate speech coder for multimedia communications.	5.3 kbps/6.3 kbps	ITU-T G.723.1
Wideband	An uncompressed voice codec using 16-bit samples at 16,000 samples per second. Provides better than toll-quality voice.	256 kbps	Cisco proprietary
GSM	Global System for Mobile Communications. The codec used to compress voice samples on GSM cellular phones. The specification for GSM is available at the following site: http://pda.etsi.org/pdahome.asp?wki_id=1580	13 kbps	ETSI GSM 06.10 v3.2.0

NANP Call Routing Information

The information contained in this appendix is actual information that comes from the North American Numbering Plan (NANP) file located in the C:\Program Files\Cisco\Dial Plan directory. This file shows how each part of an NANP number corresponds to a specific placeholder.

This information is particularly useful when you're applying route filters. Each component of every possible NANP number is broken down in this file. With a route filter, you can take the whole NANP and filter it down by forcing certain placeholders to exist, not exist, or match a particular pattern. For CallManager 3.3 and previous releases, this is the only numbering plan included for use with the @ wildcard. Other numbering plans must be created manually by adding a number of individual route patterns based on your local numbering plan.

Using this file, you can find the pattern you want to filter, and then choose the appropriate settings on the Route Filter Configuration page in Cisco CallManager Administration (**Route Plan > Route Filter >** *find and select a route filter*).

This appendix is included for a couple of reasons. First, it demonstrates just how many patterns are contained in the @ wildcard. This is difficult for some to grasp until you actually see all that is contained in the NANP. Second, it displays the placeholder of each part of the NANP. This information enables you to understand and apply route filters. By reviewing the details of the NANP below, you can correlate that with the route filter you want to build and proceed accordingly.

```
# P:        Digit pattern -- PATTERN TAG
# T: Type of Number -- I(nternational) or N(ational)
# W:   Network Specific Facilities -- OP or OP/P or OPXXX or OPXXXX
#
# U: Urgent pattern? (Call extended immediately on match)

# 0
P:  0                   LOCAL-OPERATOR
T:  N
W:  OP

# 00
P:  00                  LONG-DISTANCE-OPERATOR
T:  N
W:  OP/P
```

```
# 0+[2-9][02-9]XXXXX
P:  0                   LOCAL-OPERATOR
P:  [2-9][02-9]X        OFFICE-CODE
P:  XXXX                SUBSCRIBER
T:  N
W:  OP

# 0+[2-9]X[02-9]XXXX
P:  0                   LOCAL-OPERATOR
P:  [2-9]X[02-9]        OFFICE-CODE
P:  XXXX                SUBSCRIBER
T:  N
W:  OP

# 0+[2-9][02-9]X[2-9]XXXXXX
P:  0                   LONG-DISTANCE-OPERATOR
P:  [2-9][02-9]X        AREA-CODE
P:  [2-9]XX             OFFICE-CODE
P:  XXXX                SUBSCRIBER
T:  N
W:  OP

# 0+[2-9]X[02-9][2-9]XXXXXX
P:  0                   LONG-DISTANCE-OPERATOR
P:  [2-9]X[02-9]        AREA-CODE
P:  [2-9]XX             OFFICE-CODE
P:  XXXX                SUBSCRIBER
T:  N
W:  OP

# 1+01XXXX+0+[2-9][02-9]XXXXX
P:  101                 TRANSIT-NETWORK-ESCAPE
P:  XXXX                TRANSIT-NETWORK
P:  0                   LONG-DISTANCE-OPERATOR
P:  [2-9][02-9]X        OFFICE-CODE
P:  XXXX                SUBSCRIBER
T:  N
W:  OPXXXX

# 1+01XXXX+0+[2-9]X[02-9]XXXX
P:  101                 TRANSIT-NETWORK-ESCAPE
P:  XXXX                TRANSIT-NETWORK
P:  0                   LONG-DISTANCE-OPERATOR
P:  [2-9]X[02-9]        OFFICE-CODE
P:  XXXX                SUBSCRIBER
T:  N
W:  OPXXXX

# 1+01XXXX+0+[2-9][02-9]X[2-9]XXXXXX
P:  101                 TRANSIT-NETWORK-ESCAPE
P:  XXXX                TRANSIT-NETWORK
P:  0                   LONG-DISTANCE-OPERATOR
P:  [2-9][02-9]X        AREA-CODE
P:  [2-9]XX             OFFICE-CODE
P:  XXXX                SUBSCRIBER
T:  N
W:  OPXXXX

# 1+01XXXX+0+[2-9]X[02-9][2-9]XXXXXX
P:  101                 TRANSIT-NETWORK-ESCAPE
P:  XXXX                TRANSIT-NETWORK
P:  0                   LONG-DISTANCE-OPERATOR
P:  [2-9]X[02-9]        AREA-CODE
P:  [2-9]XX             OFFICE-CODE
```

```
P:  XXXX            SUBSCRIBER
T:  N
W:  OPXXXX

# 1+01XXXX+1+[2-9][02-9]XXXXX
P:  101             TRANSIT-NETWORK-ESCAPE
P:  XXXX            TRANSIT-NETWORK
P:  1               LOCAL-DIRECT-DIAL
P:  [2-9][02-9]X    OFFICE-CODE
P:  XXXX            SUBSCRIBER
T:  N

# 1+01XXXX+1+[2-9]X[02-9]XXXX
P:  101             TRANSIT-NETWORK-ESCAPE
P:  XXXX            TRANSIT-NETWORK
P:  1               LOCAL-DIRECT-DIAL
P:  [2-9]X[02-9]    OFFICE-CODE
P:  XXXX            SUBSCRIBER
T:  N

# 1+01XXXX+1+[2-9][02-9]X[2-9]XXXXXX
P:  101             TRANSIT-NETWORK-ESCAPE
P:  XXXX            TRANSIT-NETWORK
P:  1               LONG-DISTANCE-DIRECT-DIAL
P:  [2-9][02-9]X    AREA-CODE
P:  [2-9]XX         OFFICE-CODE
P:  XXXX            SUBSCRIBER
T:  N

# 1+01XXXX+1+[2-9]X[02-9][2-9]XXXXXX
P:  101             TRANSIT-NETWORK-ESCAPE
P:  XXXX            TRANSIT-NETWORK
P:  1               LONG-DISTANCE-DIRECT-DIAL
P:  [2-9]X[02-9]    AREA-CODE
P:  [2-9]XX         OFFICE-CODE
P:  XXXX            SUBSCRIBER
T:  N

# 1+01XXXX+[2-9]11
P:  101             TRANSIT-NETWORK-ESCAPE
P:  XXXX            TRANSIT-NETWORK
P:  [2-9]11         SERVICE
T:  N
W:  OPXXXX
U:  Y

# 1+01XXXX+[2-9][02-9]XXXXX
P:  101             TRANSIT-NETWORK-ESCAPE
P:  XXXX            TRANSIT-NETWORK
P:  [2-9][02-9]X    OFFICE-CODE
P:  XXXX            SUBSCRIBER
T:  N

# 1+01XXXX+[2-9]X[02-9]XXXX
P:  101             TRANSIT-NETWORK-ESCAPE
P:  XXXX            TRANSIT-NETWORK
P:  [2-9]X[02-9]    OFFICE-CODE
P:  XXXX            SUBSCRIBER
T:  N

# Interdigit timing between 7D and 10D metro numbers
# are added to the dialing tree by specifying patterns
# containing specific local area codes using route filters
# 1+01XXXX+[2-9][02-9]X[2-9]XXXXXX
```

```
P:  101                TRANSIT-NETWORK-ESCAPE
P:  XXXX               TRANSIT-NETWORK
P:  [2-9][02-9]X       LOCAL-AREA-CODE
P:  [2-9]XX            OFFICE-CODE
P:  XXXX               SUBSCRIBER
T:  N

# 1+01XXXX+[2-9]X[02-9][2-9]XXXXXX
P:  101                TRANSIT-NETWORK-ESCAPE
P:  XXXX               TRANSIT-NETWORK
P:  [2-9]X[02-9]       LOCAL-AREA-CODE
P:  [2-9]XX            OFFICE-CODE
P:  XXXX               SUBSCRIBER
T:  N

# 1+[2-9]11
P:  1                  LOCAL-DIRECT-DIAL
P:  [2-9]11            SERVICE
T:  N
U:  Y

# 1+[2-9][02-9]XXXXX
P:  1                  LOCAL-DIRECT-DIAL
P:  [2-9][02-9]X       OFFICE-CODE
P:  XXXX               SUBSCRIBER
T:  N

# 1+[2-9]X[02-9]XXXX
P:  1                  LOCAL-DIRECT-DIAL
P:  [2-9]X[02-9]       OFFICE-CODE
P:  XXXX               SUBSCRIBER
T:  N

# 1+[2-9][02-9]X[2-9]XXXXXX
P:  1                  LONG-DISTANCE-DIRECT-DIAL
P:  [2-9][02-9]X       AREA-CODE
P:  [2-9]XX            OFFICE-CODE
P:  XXXX               SUBSCRIBER
T:  N

# 1+[2-9]X[02-9][2-9]XXXXXX
P:  1                  LONG-DISTANCE-DIRECT-DIAL
P:  [2-9]X[02-9]       AREA-CODE
P:  [2-9]XX            OFFICE-CODE
P:  XXXX               SUBSCRIBER
T:  N

# [2-9]11
P:  [2-9]11            SERVICE
T:  N
U:  Y

# [2-9][02-9]XXXXX
P:  [2-9][02-9]X       OFFICE-CODE
P:  XXXX               SUBSCRIBER
T:  N

# [2-9]X[02-9]XXXX
P:  [2-9]X[02-9]       OFFICE-CODE
P:  XXXX               SUBSCRIBER
T:  N

# Interdigit timing between 7D and 10D metro numbers
# are added to the dialing tree by specifying patterns
```

```
# containing specific local area codes using route filters
# [2-9][02-9]X[2-9]XXXXXX
P:  [2-9][02-9]X       LOCAL-AREA-CODE
P:  [2-9]XX            OFFICE-CODE
P:  XXXX               SUBSCRIBER
T:  N

# [2-9]X[02-9][2-9]XXXXXX
P:  [2-9]X[02-9]       LOCAL-AREA-CODE
P:  [2-9]XX            OFFICE-CODE
P:  XXXX               SUBSCRIBER
T:  N

# 010
P:  01                 INTERNATIONAL-ACCESS
P:  0                  INTERNATIONAL-OPERATOR
T:  I
W:  OP

#### Satellite services need special handling

# 01+881+X+NN
P:  01                 INTERNATIONAL-ACCESS
P:  881                COUNTRY-CODE
P:  X                  SATELLITE-SERVICE
P:  !                  NATIONAL-NUMBER
T:  I
W:  OP

# 01+881+X+NN+#
P:  01                 INTERNATIONAL-ACCESS
P:  881                COUNTRY-CODE
P:  X                  SATELLITE-SERVICE
P:  !                  NATIONAL-NUMBER
P:  #                  END-OF-DIALING
T:  I
W:  OP

# 011+881+X+NN
P:  01                 INTERNATIONAL-ACCESS
P:  1                  INTERNATIONAL-DIRECT-DIAL
P:  881                COUNTRY-CODE
P:  X                  SATELLITE-SERVICE
P:  !                  NATIONAL-NUMBER
T:  I

# 011+881+X+NN+#
P:  01                 INTERNATIONAL-ACCESS
P:  1                  INTERNATIONAL-DIRECT-DIAL
P:  881                COUNTRY-CODE
P:  X                  SATELLITE-SERVICE
P:  !                  NATIONAL-NUMBER
P:  #                  END-OF-DIALING
T:  I

# 1+01XXXX+01+881+X+NN
P:  101                TRANSIT-NETWORK-ESCAPE
P:  XXXX               TRANSIT-NETWORK
P:  01                 INTERNATIONAL-ACCESS
P:  881                COUNTRY-CODE
P:  X                  SATELLITE-SERVICE
P:  !                  NATIONAL-NUMBER
T:  I
W:  OPXXXX
```

```
# 1+01XXXX+01+881+X+NN+#
P:  101            TRANSIT-NETWORK-ESCAPE
P:  XXXX           TRANSIT-NETWORK
P:  01             INTERNATIONAL-ACCESS
P:  881            COUNTRY-CODE
P:  X              SATELLITE-SERVICE
P:  !              NATIONAL-NUMBER
P:  #              END-OF-DIALING
T:  I
W:  OPXXXX

# 1+01XXXX+011+881+X+NN
P:  101            TRANSIT-NETWORK-ESCAPE
P:  XXXX           TRANSIT-NETWORK
P:  01             INTERNATIONAL-ACCESS
P:  1              INTERNATIONAL-DIRECT-DIAL
P:  881            COUNTRY-CODE
P:  X              SATELLITE-SERVICE
P:  !              NATIONAL-NUMBER
T:  I

# 1+01XXXX+011+881+X+NN+#
P:  101            TRANSIT-NETWORK-ESCAPE
P:  XXXX           TRANSIT-NETWORK
P:  01             INTERNATIONAL-ACCESS
P:  1              INTERNATIONAL-DIRECT-DIAL
P:  881            COUNTRY-CODE
P:  X              SATELLITE-SERVICE
P:  !              NATIONAL-NUMBER
P:  #              END-OF-DIALING
T:  I

#### From this point down, the table is generated
#### by a python script that takes country codes and
#### generates ndp entries.
####
#### The national.c file is then generated by
#### type ndp internationalndp | perl -s ...

# 01+2[07]+NN
P: 01              INTERNATIONAL-ACCESS
P: 2[07]           COUNTRY-CODE
P: !               NATIONAL-NUMBER
T: I
W: OP

# 01+2[07]+NN+#
P: 01              INTERNATIONAL-ACCESS
P: 2[07]           COUNTRY-CODE
P: !               NATIONAL-NUMBER
P: #               END-OF-DIALING
T: I
W: OP

# 011+2[07]+NN
P: 01              INTERNATIONAL-ACCESS
P: 1               INTERNATIONAL-DIRECT-DIAL
P: 2[07]           COUNTRY-CODE
P: !               NATIONAL-NUMBER
T: I

# 011+2[07]+NN+#
P: 01              INTERNATIONAL-ACCESS
```

```
P: 1                    INTERNATIONAL-DIRECT-DIAL
P: 2[07]                COUNTRY-CODE
P: !                    NATIONAL-NUMBER
P: #                    END-OF-DIALING
T: I

# 101XXXX+01+2[07]+NN
P: 101                  TRANSIT-NETWORK-ESCAPE
P: XXXX                 TRANSIT-NETWORK
P: 01                   INTERNATIONAL-ACCESS
P: 2[07]                COUNTRY-CODE
P: !                    NATIONAL-NUMBER
T: I
W: OPXXXX

# 101XXXX+01+2[07]+NN+#
P: 101                  TRANSIT-NETWORK-ESCAPE
P: XXXX                 TRANSIT-NETWORK
P: 01                   INTERNATIONAL-ACCESS
P: 2[07]                COUNTRY-CODE
P: !                    NATIONAL-NUMBER
P: #                    END-OF-DIALING
T: I
W: OPXXXX

# 101XXXX+011+2[07]+NN
P: 101                  TRANSIT-NETWORK-ESCAPE
P: XXXX                 TRANSIT-NETWORK
P: 01                   INTERNATIONAL-ACCESS
P: 1                    INTERNATIONAL-DIRECT-DIAL
P: 2[07]                COUNTRY-CODE
P: !                    NATIONAL-NUMBER
T: I
W: OPXXXX

# 101XXXX+011+2[07]+NN+#
P: 101                  TRANSIT-NETWORK-ESCAPE
P: XXXX                 TRANSIT-NETWORK
P: 01                   INTERNATIONAL-ACCESS
P: 1                    INTERNATIONAL-DIRECT-DIAL
P: 2[07]                COUNTRY-CODE
P: !                    NATIONAL-NUMBER
P: #                    END-OF-DIALING
T: I

# 01+2[1-689]X+NN
P: 01                   INTERNATIONAL-ACCESS
P: 2[1-689]X            COUNTRY-CODE
P: !                    NATIONAL-NUMBER
T: I
W: OP

# 01+2[1-689]X+NN+#
P: 01                   INTERNATIONAL-ACCESS
P: 2[1-689]X            COUNTRY-CODE
P: !                    NATIONAL-NUMBER
P: #                    END-OF-DIALING
T: I
W: OP

# 011+2[1-689]X+NN
P: 01                   INTERNATIONAL-ACCESS
P: 1                    INTERNATIONAL-DIRECT-DIAL
P: 2[1-689]X            COUNTRY-CODE
```

```
P: !                      NATIONAL-NUMBER
T: I


# 011+2[1-689]X+NN+#
P: 01                     INTERNATIONAL-ACCESS
P: 1                      INTERNATIONAL-DIRECT-DIAL
P: 2[1-689]X              COUNTRY-CODE
P: !                      NATIONAL-NUMBER
P: #                      END-OF-DIALING
T: I


# 101XXXX+01+2[1-689]X+NN
P: 101                    TRANSIT-NETWORK-ESCAPE
P: XXXX                   TRANSIT-NETWORK
P: 01                     INTERNATIONAL-ACCESS
P: 2[1-689]X              COUNTRY-CODE
P: !                      NATIONAL-NUMBER
T: I
W: OPXXXX


# 101XXXX+01+2[1-689]X+NN+#
P: 101                    TRANSIT-NETWORK-ESCAPE
P: XXXX                   TRANSIT-NETWORK
P: 01                     INTERNATIONAL-ACCESS
P: 2[1-689]X              COUNTRY-CODE
P: !                      NATIONAL-NUMBER
P: #                      END-OF-DIALING
T: I
W: OPXXXX


# 101XXXX+011+2[1-689]X+NN
P: 101                    TRANSIT-NETWORK-ESCAPE
P: XXXX                   TRANSIT-NETWORK
P: 01                     INTERNATIONAL-ACCESS
P: 1                      INTERNATIONAL-DIRECT-DIAL
P: 2[1-689]X              COUNTRY-CODE
P: !                      NATIONAL-NUMBER
T: I
W: OPXXXX


# 101XXXX+011+2[1-689]X+NN+#
P: 101                    TRANSIT-NETWORK-ESCAPE
P: XXXX                   TRANSIT-NETWORK
P: 01                     INTERNATIONAL-ACCESS
P: 1                      INTERNATIONAL-DIRECT-DIAL
P: 2[1-689]X              COUNTRY-CODE
P: !                      NATIONAL-NUMBER
P: #                      END-OF-DIALING
T: I


# 01+3[0-469]+NN
P: 01                     INTERNATIONAL-ACCESS
P: 3[0-469]               COUNTRY-CODE
P: !                      NATIONAL-NUMBER
T: I
W: OP


# 01+3[0-469]+NN+#
P: 01                     INTERNATIONAL-ACCESS
P: 3[0-469]               COUNTRY-CODE
P: !                      NATIONAL-NUMBER
P: #                      END-OF-DIALING
T: I
W: OP
```

```
# 011+3[0-469]+NN
P: 01                 INTERNATIONAL-ACCESS
P: 1                  INTERNATIONAL-DIRECT-DIAL
P: 3[0-469]           COUNTRY-CODE
P: !                  NATIONAL-NUMBER
T: I

# 011+3[0-469]+NN+#
P: 01                 INTERNATIONAL-ACCESS
P: 1                  INTERNATIONAL-DIRECT-DIAL
P: 3[0-469]           COUNTRY-CODE
P: !                  NATIONAL-NUMBER
P: #                  END-OF-DIALING
T: I

# 101XXXX+01+3[0-469]+NN
P: 101                TRANSIT-NETWORK-ESCAPE
P: XXXX               TRANSIT-NETWORK
P: 01                 INTERNATIONAL-ACCESS
P: 3[0-469]           COUNTRY-CODE
P: !                  NATIONAL-NUMBER
T: I
W: OPXXXX

# 101XXXX+01+3[0-469]+NN+#
P: 101                TRANSIT-NETWORK-ESCAPE
P: XXXX               TRANSIT-NETWORK
P: 01                 INTERNATIONAL-ACCESS
P: 3[0-469]           COUNTRY-CODE
P: !                  NATIONAL-NUMBER
P: #                  END-OF-DIALING
T: I
W: OPXXXX

# 101XXXX+011+3[0-469]+NN
P: 101                TRANSIT-NETWORK-ESCAPE
P: XXXX               TRANSIT-NETWORK
P: 01                 INTERNATIONAL-ACCESS
P: 1                  INTERNATIONAL-DIRECT-DIAL
P: 3[0-469]           COUNTRY-CODE
P: !                  NATIONAL-NUMBER
T: I
W: OPXXXX

# 101XXXX+011+3[0-469]+NN+#
P: 101                TRANSIT-NETWORK-ESCAPE
P: XXXX               TRANSIT-NETWORK
P: 01                 INTERNATIONAL-ACCESS
P: 1                  INTERNATIONAL-DIRECT-DIAL
P: 3[0-469]           COUNTRY-CODE
P: !                  NATIONAL-NUMBER
P: #                  END-OF-DIALING
T: I

# 01+3[578]X+NN
P: 01                 INTERNATIONAL-ACCESS
P: 3[578]X            COUNTRY-CODE
P: !                  NATIONAL-NUMBER
T: I
W: OP

# 01+3[578]X+NN+#
P: 01                 INTERNATIONAL-ACCESS
```

```
P: 3[578]X           COUNTRY-CODE
P: !                 NATIONAL-NUMBER
P: #                 END-OF-DIALING
T: I
W: OP

# 011+3[578]X+NN
P: 01                INTERNATIONAL-ACCESS
P: 1                 INTERNATIONAL-DIRECT-DIAL
P: 3[578]X           COUNTRY-CODE
P: !                 NATIONAL-NUMBER
T: I

# 011+3[578]X+NN+#
P: 01                INTERNATIONAL-ACCESS
P: 1                 INTERNATIONAL-DIRECT-DIAL
P: 3[578]X           COUNTRY-CODE
P: !                 NATIONAL-NUMBER
P: #                 END-OF-DIALING
T: I

# 101XXXX+01+3[578]X+NN
P: 101               TRANSIT-NETWORK-ESCAPE
P: XXXX              TRANSIT-NETWORK
P: 01                INTERNATIONAL-ACCESS
P: 3[578]X           COUNTRY-CODE
P: !                 NATIONAL-NUMBER
T: I
W: OPXXXX

# 101XXXX+01+3[578]X+NN+#
P: 101               TRANSIT-NETWORK-ESCAPE
P: XXXX              TRANSIT-NETWORK
P: 01                INTERNATIONAL-ACCESS
P: 3[578]X           COUNTRY-CODE
P: !                 NATIONAL-NUMBER
P: #                 END-OF-DIALING
T: I
W: OPXXXX

# 101XXXX+011+3[578]X+NN
P: 101               TRANSIT-NETWORK-ESCAPE
P: XXXX              TRANSIT-NETWORK
P: 01                INTERNATIONAL-ACCESS
P: 1                 INTERNATIONAL-DIRECT-DIAL
P: 3[578]X           COUNTRY-CODE
P: !                 NATIONAL-NUMBER
T: I
W: OPXXXX

# 101XXXX+011+3[578]X+NN+#
P: 101               TRANSIT-NETWORK-ESCAPE
P: XXXX              TRANSIT-NETWORK
P: 01                INTERNATIONAL-ACCESS
P: 1                 INTERNATIONAL-DIRECT-DIAL
P: 3[578]X           COUNTRY-CODE
P: !                 NATIONAL-NUMBER
P: #                 END-OF-DIALING
T: I

# 01+4[013-9]+NN
P: 01                INTERNATIONAL-ACCESS
P: 4[013-9]          COUNTRY-CODE
P: !                 NATIONAL-NUMBER
```

```
T: I
W: OP

# 01+4[013-9]+NN+#
P: 01                    INTERNATIONAL-ACCESS
P: 4[013-9]              COUNTRY-CODE
P: !                     NATIONAL-NUMBER
P: #                     END-OF-DIALING
T: I
W: OP

# 011+4[013-9]+NN
P: 01                    INTERNATIONAL-ACCESS
P: 1                     INTERNATIONAL-DIRECT-DIAL
P: 4[013-9]              COUNTRY-CODE
P: !                     NATIONAL-NUMBER
T: I

# 011+4[013-9]+NN+#
P: 01                    INTERNATIONAL-ACCESS
P: 1                     INTERNATIONAL-DIRECT-DIAL
P: 4[013-9]              COUNTRY-CODE
P: !                     NATIONAL-NUMBER
P: #                     END-OF-DIALING
T: I

# 101XXXX+01+4[013-9]+NN
P: 101                   TRANSIT-NETWORK-ESCAPE
P: XXXX                  TRANSIT-NETWORK
P: 01                    INTERNATIONAL-ACCESS
P: 4[013-9]              COUNTRY-CODE
P: !                     NATIONAL-NUMBER
T: I
W: OPXXXX

# 101XXXX+01+4[013-9]+NN+#
P: 101                   TRANSIT-NETWORK-ESCAPE
P: XXXX                  TRANSIT-NETWORK
P: 01                    INTERNATIONAL-ACCESS
P: 4[013-9]              COUNTRY-CODE
P: !                     NATIONAL-NUMBER
P: #                     END-OF-DIALING
T: I
W: OPXXXX

# 101XXXX+011+4[013-9]+NN
P: 101                   TRANSIT-NETWORK-ESCAPE
P: XXXX                  TRANSIT-NETWORK
P: 01                    INTERNATIONAL-ACCESS
P: 1                     INTERNATIONAL-DIRECT-DIAL
P: 4[013-9]              COUNTRY-CODE
P: !                     NATIONAL-NUMBER
T: I
W: OPXXXX

# 101XXXX+011+4[013-9]+NN+#
P: 101                   TRANSIT-NETWORK-ESCAPE
P: XXXX                  TRANSIT-NETWORK
P: 01                    INTERNATIONAL-ACCESS
P: 1                     INTERNATIONAL-DIRECT-DIAL
P: 4[013-9]              COUNTRY-CODE
P: !                     NATIONAL-NUMBER
P: #                     END-OF-DIALING
T: I
```

```
# 01+42X+NN
P: 01                    INTERNATIONAL-ACCESS
P: 42X                   COUNTRY-CODE
P: !                     NATIONAL-NUMBER
T: I
W: OP

# 01+42X+NN+#
P: 01                    INTERNATIONAL-ACCESS
P: 42X                   COUNTRY-CODE
P: !                     NATIONAL-NUMBER
P: #                     END-OF-DIALING
T: I
W: OP

# 011+42X+NN
P: 01                    INTERNATIONAL-ACCESS
P: 1                     INTERNATIONAL-DIRECT-DIAL
P: 42X                   COUNTRY-CODE
P: !                     NATIONAL-NUMBER
T: I

# 011+42X+NN+#
P: 01                    INTERNATIONAL-ACCESS
P: 1                     INTERNATIONAL-DIRECT-DIAL
P: 42X                   COUNTRY-CODE
P: !                     NATIONAL-NUMBER
P: #                     END-OF-DIALING
T: I

# 101XXXX+01+42X+NN
P: 101                   TRANSIT-NETWORK-ESCAPE
P: XXXX                  TRANSIT-NETWORK
P: 01                    INTERNATIONAL-ACCESS
P: 42X                   COUNTRY-CODE
P: !                     NATIONAL-NUMBER
T: I
W: OPXXXX

# 101XXXX+01+42X+NN+#
P: 101                   TRANSIT-NETWORK-ESCAPE
P: XXXX                  TRANSIT-NETWORK
P: 01                    INTERNATIONAL-ACCESS
P: 42X                   COUNTRY-CODE
P: !                     NATIONAL-NUMBER
P: #                     END-OF-DIALING
T: I
W: OPXXXX

# 101XXXX+011+42X+NN
P: 101                   TRANSIT-NETWORK-ESCAPE
P: XXXX                  TRANSIT-NETWORK
P: 01                    INTERNATIONAL-ACCESS
P: 1                     INTERNATIONAL-DIRECT-DIAL
P: 42X                   COUNTRY-CODE
P: !                     NATIONAL-NUMBER
T: I
W: OPXXXX

# 101XXXX+011+42X+NN+#
P: 101                   TRANSIT-NETWORK-ESCAPE
P: XXXX                  TRANSIT-NETWORK
P: 01                    INTERNATIONAL-ACCESS
```

```
P: 1                        INTERNATIONAL-DIRECT-DIAL
P: 42X                      COUNTRY-CODE
P: !                        NATIONAL-NUMBER
P: #                        END-OF-DIALING
T: I

# 01+5[1-8]+NN
P: 01                       INTERNATIONAL-ACCESS
P: 5[1-8]                   COUNTRY-CODE
P: !                        NATIONAL-NUMBER
T: I
W: OP

# 01+5[1-8]+NN+#
P: 01                       INTERNATIONAL-ACCESS
P: 5[1-8]                   COUNTRY-CODE
P: !                        NATIONAL-NUMBER
P: #                        END-OF-DIALING
T: I
W: OP

# 011+5[1-8]+NN
P: 01                       INTERNATIONAL-ACCESS
P: 1                        INTERNATIONAL-DIRECT-DIAL
P: 5[1-8]                   COUNTRY-CODE
P: !                        NATIONAL-NUMBER
T: I

# 011+5[1-8]+NN+#
P: 01                       INTERNATIONAL-ACCESS
P: 1                        INTERNATIONAL-DIRECT-DIAL
P: 5[1-8]                   COUNTRY-CODE
P: !                        NATIONAL-NUMBER
P: #                        END-OF-DIALING
T: I

# 101XXXX+01+5[1-8]+NN
P: 101                      TRANSIT-NETWORK-ESCAPE
P: XXXX                     TRANSIT-NETWORK
P: 01                       INTERNATIONAL-ACCESS
P: 5[1-8]                   COUNTRY-CODE
P: !                        NATIONAL-NUMBER
T: I
W: OPXXXX

# 101XXXX+01+5[1-8]+NN+#
P: 101                      TRANSIT-NETWORK-ESCAPE
P: XXXX                     TRANSIT-NETWORK
P: 01                       INTERNATIONAL-ACCESS
P: 5[1-8]                   COUNTRY-CODE
P: !                        NATIONAL-NUMBER
P: #                        END-OF-DIALING
T: I
W: OPXXXX

# 101XXXX+011+5[1-8]+NN
P: 101                      TRANSIT-NETWORK-ESCAPE
P: XXXX                     TRANSIT-NETWORK
P: 01                       INTERNATIONAL-ACCESS
P: 1                        INTERNATIONAL-DIRECT-DIAL
P: 5[1-8]                   COUNTRY-CODE
P: !                        NATIONAL-NUMBER
T: I
W: OPXXXX
```

```
# 101XXXX+011+5[1-8]+NN+#
P: 101                    TRANSIT-NETWORK-ESCAPE
P: XXXX                   TRANSIT-NETWORK
P: 01                     INTERNATIONAL-ACCESS
P: 1                      INTERNATIONAL-DIRECT-DIAL
P: 5[1-8]                 COUNTRY-CODE
P: !                      NATIONAL-NUMBER
P: #                      END-OF-DIALING
T: I

# 01+5[09]X+NN
P: 01                     INTERNATIONAL-ACCESS
P: 5[09]X                 COUNTRY-CODE
P: !                      NATIONAL-NUMBER
T: I
W: OP

# 01+5[09]X+NN+#
P: 01                     INTERNATIONAL-ACCESS
P: 5[09]X                 COUNTRY-CODE
P: !                      NATIONAL-NUMBER
P: #                      END-OF-DIALING
T: I
W: OP

# 011+5[09]X+NN
P: 01                     INTERNATIONAL-ACCESS
P: 1                      INTERNATIONAL-DIRECT-DIAL
P: 5[09]X                 COUNTRY-CODE
P: !                      NATIONAL-NUMBER
T: I

# 011+5[09]X+NN+#
P: 01                     INTERNATIONAL-ACCESS
P: 1                      INTERNATIONAL-DIRECT-DIAL
P: 5[09]X                 COUNTRY-CODE
P: !                      NATIONAL-NUMBER
P: #                      END-OF-DIALING
T: I

# 101XXXX+01+5[09]X+NN
P: 101                    TRANSIT-NETWORK-ESCAPE
P: XXXX                   TRANSIT-NETWORK
P: 01                     INTERNATIONAL-ACCESS
P: 5[09]X                 COUNTRY-CODE
P: !                      NATIONAL-NUMBER
T: I
W: OPXXXX

# 101XXXX+01+5[09]X+NN+#
P: 101                    TRANSIT-NETWORK-ESCAPE
P: XXXX                   TRANSIT-NETWORK
P: 01                     INTERNATIONAL-ACCESS
P: 5[09]X                 COUNTRY-CODE
P: !                      NATIONAL-NUMBER
P: #                      END-OF-DIALING
T: I
W: OPXXXX

# 101XXXX+011+5[09]X+NN
P: 101                    TRANSIT-NETWORK-ESCAPE
P: XXXX                   TRANSIT-NETWORK
P: 01                     INTERNATIONAL-ACCESS
```

```
P: 1                        INTERNATIONAL-DIRECT-DIAL
P: 5[09]X                   COUNTRY-CODE
P: !                        NATIONAL-NUMBER
T: I
W: OPXXXX

# 101XXXX+011+5[09]X+NN+#
P: 101                      TRANSIT-NETWORK-ESCAPE
P: XXXX                     TRANSIT-NETWORK
P: 01                       INTERNATIONAL-ACCESS
P: 1                        INTERNATIONAL-DIRECT-DIAL
P: 5[09]X                   COUNTRY-CODE
P: !                        NATIONAL-NUMBER
P: #                        END-OF-DIALING
T: I

# 01+6[0-6]+NN
P: 01                       INTERNATIONAL-ACCESS
P: 6[0-6]                   COUNTRY-CODE
P: !                        NATIONAL-NUMBER
T: I
W: OP

# 01+6[0-6]+NN+#
P: 01                       INTERNATIONAL-ACCESS
P: 6[0-6]                   COUNTRY-CODE
P: !                        NATIONAL-NUMBER
P: #                        END-OF-DIALING
T: I
W: OP

# 011+6[0-6]+NN
P: 01                       INTERNATIONAL-ACCESS
P: 1                        INTERNATIONAL-DIRECT-DIAL
P: 6[0-6]                   COUNTRY-CODE
P: !                        NATIONAL-NUMBER
T: I

# 011+6[0-6]+NN+#
P: 01                       INTERNATIONAL-ACCESS
P: 1                        INTERNATIONAL-DIRECT-DIAL
P: 6[0-6]                   COUNTRY-CODE
P: !                        NATIONAL-NUMBER
P: #                        END-OF-DIALING
T: I

# 101XXXX+01+6[0-6]+NN
P: 101                      TRANSIT-NETWORK-ESCAPE
P: XXXX                     TRANSIT-NETWORK
P: 01                       INTERNATIONAL-ACCESS
P: 6[0-6]                   COUNTRY-CODE
P: !                        NATIONAL-NUMBER
T: I
W: OPXXXX

# 101XXXX+01+6[0-6]+NN+#
P: 101                      TRANSIT-NETWORK-ESCAPE
P: XXXX                     TRANSIT-NETWORK
P: 01                       INTERNATIONAL-ACCESS
P: 6[0-6]                   COUNTRY-CODE
P: !                        NATIONAL-NUMBER
P: #                        END-OF-DIALING
T: I
W: OPXXXX
```

```
# 101XXXX+011+6[0-6]+NN
P: 101                    TRANSIT-NETWORK-ESCAPE
P: XXXX                   TRANSIT-NETWORK
P: 01                     INTERNATIONAL-ACCESS
P: 1                      INTERNATIONAL-DIRECT-DIAL
P: 6[0-6]                 COUNTRY-CODE
P: !                      NATIONAL-NUMBER
T: I
W: OPXXXX

# 101XXXX+011+6[0-6]+NN+#
P: 101                    TRANSIT-NETWORK-ESCAPE
P: XXXX                   TRANSIT-NETWORK
P: 01                     INTERNATIONAL-ACCESS
P: 1                      INTERNATIONAL-DIRECT-DIAL
P: 6[0-6]                 COUNTRY-CODE
P: !                      NATIONAL-NUMBER
P: #                      END-OF-DIALING
T: I

# 01+6[7-9]X+NN
P: 01                     INTERNATIONAL-ACCESS
P: 6[7-9]X                COUNTRY-CODE
P: !                      NATIONAL-NUMBER
T: I
W: OP

# 01+6[7-9]X+NN+#
P: 01                     INTERNATIONAL-ACCESS
P: 6[7-9]X                COUNTRY-CODE
P: !                      NATIONAL-NUMBER
P: #                      END-OF-DIALING
T: I
W: OP

# 011+6[7-9]X+NN
P: 01                     INTERNATIONAL-ACCESS
P: 1                      INTERNATIONAL-DIRECT-DIAL
P: 6[7-9]X                COUNTRY-CODE
P: !                      NATIONAL-NUMBER
T: I

# 011+6[7-9]X+NN+#
P: 01                     INTERNATIONAL-ACCESS
P: 1                      INTERNATIONAL-DIRECT-DIAL
P: 6[7-9]X                COUNTRY-CODE
P: !                      NATIONAL-NUMBER
P: #                      END-OF-DIALING
T: I

# 101XXXX+01+6[7-9]X+NN
P: 101                    TRANSIT-NETWORK-ESCAPE
P: XXXX                   TRANSIT-NETWORK
P: 01                     INTERNATIONAL-ACCESS
P: 6[7-9]X                COUNTRY-CODE
P: !                      NATIONAL-NUMBER
T: I
W: OPXXXX

# 101XXXX+01+6[7-9]X+NN+#
P: 101                    TRANSIT-NETWORK-ESCAPE
P: XXXX                   TRANSIT-NETWORK
P: 01                     INTERNATIONAL-ACCESS
```

```
P: 6[7-9]X              COUNTRY-CODE
P: !                    NATIONAL-NUMBER
P: #                    END-OF-DIALING
T: I
W: OPXXXX


# 101XXXX+011+6[7-9]X+NN
P: 101                  TRANSIT-NETWORK-ESCAPE
P: XXXX                 TRANSIT-NETWORK
P: 01                   INTERNATIONAL-ACCESS
P: 1                    INTERNATIONAL-DIRECT-DIAL
P: 6[7-9]X              COUNTRY-CODE
P: !                    NATIONAL-NUMBER
T: I
W: OPXXXX


# 101XXXX+011+6[7-9]X+NN+#
P: 101                  TRANSIT-NETWORK-ESCAPE
P: XXXX                 TRANSIT-NETWORK
P: 01                   INTERNATIONAL-ACCESS
P: 1                    INTERNATIONAL-DIRECT-DIAL
P: 6[7-9]X              COUNTRY-CODE
P: !                    NATIONAL-NUMBER
P: #                    END-OF-DIALING
T: I


# 01+7+NN
P: 01                   INTERNATIONAL-ACCESS
P: 7                    COUNTRY-CODE
P: !                    NATIONAL-NUMBER
T: I
W: OP


# 01+7+NN+#
P: 01                   INTERNATIONAL-ACCESS
P: 7                    COUNTRY-CODE
P: !                    NATIONAL-NUMBER
P: #                    END-OF-DIALING
T: I
W: OP


# 011+7+NN
P: 01                   INTERNATIONAL-ACCESS
P: 1                    INTERNATIONAL-DIRECT-DIAL
P: 7                    COUNTRY-CODE
P: !                    NATIONAL-NUMBER
T: I


# 011+7+NN+#
P: 01                   INTERNATIONAL-ACCESS
P: 1                    INTERNATIONAL-DIRECT-DIAL
P: 7                    COUNTRY-CODE
P: !                    NATIONAL-NUMBER
P: #                    END-OF-DIALING
T: I


# 101XXXX+01+7+NN
P: 101                  TRANSIT-NETWORK-ESCAPE
P: XXXX                 TRANSIT-NETWORK
P: 01                   INTERNATIONAL-ACCESS
P: 7                    COUNTRY-CODE
P: !                    NATIONAL-NUMBER
T: I
W: OPXXXX
```

```
# 101XXXX+01+7+NN+#
P: 101                  TRANSIT-NETWORK-ESCAPE
P: XXXX                 TRANSIT-NETWORK
P: 01                   INTERNATIONAL-ACCESS
P: 7                    COUNTRY-CODE
P: !                    NATIONAL-NUMBER
P: #                    END-OF-DIALING
T: I
W: OPXXXX

# 101XXXX+011+7+NN
P: 101                  TRANSIT-NETWORK-ESCAPE
P: XXXX                 TRANSIT-NETWORK
P: 01                   INTERNATIONAL-ACCESS
P: 1                    INTERNATIONAL-DIRECT-DIAL
P: 7                    COUNTRY-CODE
P: !                    NATIONAL-NUMBER
T: I
W: OPXXXX

# 101XXXX+011+7+NN+#
P: 101                  TRANSIT-NETWORK-ESCAPE
P: XXXX                 TRANSIT-NETWORK
P: 01                   INTERNATIONAL-ACCESS
P: 1                    INTERNATIONAL-DIRECT-DIAL
P: 7                    COUNTRY-CODE
P: !                    NATIONAL-NUMBER
P: #                    END-OF-DIALING
T: I

# 01+8[1246]+NN
P: 01                   INTERNATIONAL-ACCESS
P: 8[1246]              COUNTRY-CODE
P: !                    NATIONAL-NUMBER
T: I
W: OP

# 01+8[1246]+NN+#
P: 01                   INTERNATIONAL-ACCESS
P: 8[1246]              COUNTRY-CODE
P: !                    NATIONAL-NUMBER
P: #                    END-OF-DIALING
T: I
W: OP

# 011+8[1246]+NN
P: 01                   INTERNATIONAL-ACCESS
P: 1                    INTERNATIONAL-DIRECT-DIAL
P: 8[1246]              COUNTRY-CODE
P: !                    NATIONAL-NUMBER
T: I

# 011+8[1246]+NN+#
P: 01                   INTERNATIONAL-ACCESS
P: 1                    INTERNATIONAL-DIRECT-DIAL
P: 8[1246]              COUNTRY-CODE
P: !                    NATIONAL-NUMBER
P: #                    END-OF-DIALING
T: I

# 101XXXX+01+8[1246]+NN
P: 101                  TRANSIT-NETWORK-ESCAPE
P: XXXX                 TRANSIT-NETWORK
```

```
P: 01                   INTERNATIONAL-ACCESS
P: 8[1246]              COUNTRY-CODE
P: !                    NATIONAL-NUMBER
T: I
W: OPXXXX

# 101XXXX+01+8[1246]+NN+#
P: 101                  TRANSIT-NETWORK-ESCAPE
P: XXXX                 TRANSIT-NETWORK
P: 01                   INTERNATIONAL-ACCESS
P: 8[1246]              COUNTRY-CODE
P: !                    NATIONAL-NUMBER
P: #                    END-OF-DIALING
T: I
W: OPXXXX

# 101XXXX+011+8[1246]+NN
P: 101                  TRANSIT-NETWORK-ESCAPE
P: XXXX                 TRANSIT-NETWORK
P: 01                   INTERNATIONAL-ACCESS
P: 1                    INTERNATIONAL-DIRECT-DIAL
P: 8[1246]              COUNTRY-CODE
P: !                    NATIONAL-NUMBER
T: I
W: OPXXXX

# 101XXXX+011+8[1246]+NN+#
P: 101                  TRANSIT-NETWORK-ESCAPE
P: XXXX                 TRANSIT-NETWORK
P: 01                   INTERNATIONAL-ACCESS
P: 1                    INTERNATIONAL-DIRECT-DIAL
P: 8[1246]              COUNTRY-CODE
P: !                    NATIONAL-NUMBER
P: #                    END-OF-DIALING
T: I

# 01+8[03579]X+NN
P: 01                   INTERNATIONAL-ACCESS
P: 8[03579]X            COUNTRY-CODE
P: !                    NATIONAL-NUMBER
T: I
W: OP

# 01+8[03579]X+NN+#
P: 01                   INTERNATIONAL-ACCESS
P: 8[03579]X            COUNTRY-CODE
P: !                    NATIONAL-NUMBER
P: #                    END-OF-DIALING
T: I
W: OP

# 011+8[03579]X+NN
P: 01                   INTERNATIONAL-ACCESS
P: 1                    INTERNATIONAL-DIRECT-DIAL
P: 8[03579]X            COUNTRY-CODE
P: !                    NATIONAL-NUMBER
T: I

# 011+8[03579]X+NN+#
P: 01                   INTERNATIONAL-ACCESS
P: 1                    INTERNATIONAL-DIRECT-DIAL
P: 8[03579]X            COUNTRY-CODE
P: !                    NATIONAL-NUMBER
P: #                    END-OF-DIALING
```

```
T: I

# 101XXXX+01+8[03579]X+NN
P: 101                    TRANSIT-NETWORK-ESCAPE
P: XXXX                   TRANSIT-NETWORK
P: 01                     INTERNATIONAL-ACCESS
P: 8[03579]X              COUNTRY-CODE
P: !                      NATIONAL-NUMBER
T: I
W: OPXXXX

# 101XXXX+01+8[03579]X+NN+#
P: 101                    TRANSIT-NETWORK-ESCAPE
P: XXXX                   TRANSIT-NETWORK
P: 01                     INTERNATIONAL-ACCESS
P: 8[03579]X              COUNTRY-CODE
P: !                      NATIONAL-NUMBER
P: #                      END-OF-DIALING
T: I
W: OPXXXX

# 101XXXX+011+8[03579]X+NN
P: 101                    TRANSIT-NETWORK-ESCAPE
P: XXXX                   TRANSIT-NETWORK
P: 01                     INTERNATIONAL-ACCESS
P: 1                      INTERNATIONAL-DIRECT-DIAL
P: 8[03579]X              COUNTRY-CODE
P: !                      NATIONAL-NUMBER
T: I
W: OPXXXX

# 101XXXX+011+8[03579]X+NN+#
P: 101                    TRANSIT-NETWORK-ESCAPE
P: XXXX                   TRANSIT-NETWORK
P: 01                     INTERNATIONAL-ACCESS
P: 1                      INTERNATIONAL-DIRECT-DIAL
P: 8[03579]X              COUNTRY-CODE
P: !                      NATIONAL-NUMBER
P: #                      END-OF-DIALING
T: I

# 01+88[02-9]+NN
P: 01                     INTERNATIONAL-ACCESS
P: 88[02-9]               COUNTRY-CODE
P: !                      NATIONAL-NUMBER
T: I
W: OP

# 01+88[02-9]+NN+#
P: 01                     INTERNATIONAL-ACCESS
P: 88[02-9]               COUNTRY-CODE
P: !                      NATIONAL-NUMBER
P: #                      END-OF-DIALING
T: I
W: OP

# 011+88[02-9]+NN
P: 01                     INTERNATIONAL-ACCESS
P: 1                      INTERNATIONAL-DIRECT-DIAL
P: 88[02-9]               COUNTRY-CODE
P: !                      NATIONAL-NUMBER
T: I

# 011+88[02-9]+NN+#
```

```
P: 01                          INTERNATIONAL-ACCESS
P: 1                           INTERNATIONAL-DIRECT-DIAL
P: 88[02-9]                    COUNTRY-CODE
P: !                           NATIONAL-NUMBER
P: #                           END-OF-DIALING
T: I


# 101XXXX+01+88[02-9]+NN
P: 101                         TRANSIT-NETWORK-ESCAPE
P: XXXX                        TRANSIT-NETWORK
P: 01                          INTERNATIONAL-ACCESS
P: 88[02-9]                    COUNTRY-CODE
P: !                           NATIONAL-NUMBER
T: I
W: OPXXXX


# 101XXXX+01+88[02-9]+NN+#
P: 101                         TRANSIT-NETWORK-ESCAPE
P: XXXX                        TRANSIT-NETWORK
P: 01                          INTERNATIONAL-ACCESS
P: 88[02-9]                    COUNTRY-CODE
P: !                           NATIONAL-NUMBER
P: #                           END-OF-DIALING
T: I
W: OPXXXX


# 101XXXX+011+88[02-9]+NN
P: 101                         TRANSIT-NETWORK-ESCAPE
P: XXXX                        TRANSIT-NETWORK
P: 01                          INTERNATIONAL-ACCESS
P: 1                           INTERNATIONAL-DIRECT-DIAL
P: 88[02-9]                    COUNTRY-CODE
P: !                           NATIONAL-NUMBER
T: I
W: OPXXXX


# 101XXXX+011+88[02-9]+NN+#
P: 101                         TRANSIT-NETWORK-ESCAPE
P: XXXX                        TRANSIT-NETWORK
P: 01                          INTERNATIONAL-ACCESS
P: 1                           INTERNATIONAL-DIRECT-DIAL
P: 88[02-9]                    COUNTRY-CODE
P: !                           NATIONAL-NUMBER
P: #                           END-OF-DIALING
T: I


# 01+9[0-58]+NN
P: 01                          INTERNATIONAL-ACCESS
P: 9[0-58]                     COUNTRY-CODE
P: !                           NATIONAL-NUMBER
T: I
W: OP


# 01+9[0-58]+NN+#
P: 01                          INTERNATIONAL-ACCESS
P: 9[0-58]                     COUNTRY-CODE
P: !                           NATIONAL-NUMBER
P: #                           END-OF-DIALING
T: I
W: OP


# 011+9[0-58]+NN
P: 01                          INTERNATIONAL-ACCESS
P: 1                           INTERNATIONAL-DIRECT-DIAL
```

```
P: 9[0-58]              COUNTRY-CODE
P: !                    NATIONAL-NUMBER
T: I

# 011+9[0-58]+NN+#
P: 01                   INTERNATIONAL-ACCESS
P: 1                    INTERNATIONAL-DIRECT-DIAL
P: 9[0-58]              COUNTRY-CODE
P: !                    NATIONAL-NUMBER
P: #                    END-OF-DIALING
T: I

# 101XXXX+01+9[0-58]+NN
P: 101                  TRANSIT-NETWORK-ESCAPE
P: XXXX                 TRANSIT-NETWORK
P: 01                   INTERNATIONAL-ACCESS
P: 9[0-58]              COUNTRY-CODE
P: !                    NATIONAL-NUMBER
T: I
W: OPXXXX

# 101XXXX+01+9[0-58]+NN+#
P: 101                  TRANSIT-NETWORK-ESCAPE
P: XXXX                 TRANSIT-NETWORK
P: 01                   INTERNATIONAL-ACCESS
P: 9[0-58]              COUNTRY-CODE
P: !                    NATIONAL-NUMBER
P: #                    END-OF-DIALING
T: I
W: OPXXXX

# 101XXXX+011+9[0-58]+NN
P: 101                  TRANSIT-NETWORK-ESCAPE
P: XXXX                 TRANSIT-NETWORK
P: 01                   INTERNATIONAL-ACCESS
P: 1                    INTERNATIONAL-DIRECT-DIAL
P: 9[0-58]              COUNTRY-CODE
P: !                    NATIONAL-NUMBER
T: I
W: OPXXXX

# 101XXXX+011+9[0-58]+NN+#
P: 101                  TRANSIT-NETWORK-ESCAPE
P: XXXX                 TRANSIT-NETWORK
P: 01                   INTERNATIONAL-ACCESS
P: 1                    INTERNATIONAL-DIRECT-DIAL
P: 9[0-58]              COUNTRY-CODE
P: !                    NATIONAL-NUMBER
P: #                    END-OF-DIALING
T: I

# 01+9[679]X+NN
P: 01                   INTERNATIONAL-ACCESS
P: 9[679]X              COUNTRY-CODE
P: !                    NATIONAL-NUMBER
T: I
W: OP

# 01+9[679]X+NN+#
P: 01                   INTERNATIONAL-ACCESS
P: 9[679]X              COUNTRY-CODE
P: !                    NATIONAL-NUMBER
P: #                    END-OF-DIALING
T: I
```

```
W: OP

# 011+9[679]X+NN
P: 01                       INTERNATIONAL-ACCESS
P: 1                        INTERNATIONAL-DIRECT-DIAL
P: 9[679]X                  COUNTRY-CODE
P: !                        NATIONAL-NUMBER
T: I

# 011+9[679]X+NN+#
P: 01                       INTERNATIONAL-ACCESS
P: 1                        INTERNATIONAL-DIRECT-DIAL
P: 9[679]X                  COUNTRY-CODE
P: !                        NATIONAL-NUMBER
P: #                        END-OF-DIALING
T: I

# 101XXXX+01+9[679]X+NN
P: 101                      TRANSIT-NETWORK-ESCAPE
P: XXXX                     TRANSIT-NETWORK
P: 01                       INTERNATIONAL-ACCESS
P: 9[679]X                  COUNTRY-CODE
P: !                        NATIONAL-NUMBER
T: I
W: OPXXXX

# 101XXXX+01+9[679]X+NN+#
P: 101                      TRANSIT-NETWORK-ESCAPE
P: XXXX                     TRANSIT-NETWORK
P: 01                       INTERNATIONAL-ACCESS
P: 9[679]X                  COUNTRY-CODE
P: !                        NATIONAL-NUMBER
P: #                        END-OF-DIALING
T: I
W: OPXXXX

# 101XXXX+011+9[679]X+NN
P: 101                      TRANSIT-NETWORK-ESCAPE
P: XXXX                     TRANSIT-NETWORK
P: 01                       INTERNATIONAL-ACCESS
P: 1                        INTERNATIONAL-DIRECT-DIAL
P: 9[679]X                  COUNTRY-CODE
P: !                        NATIONAL-NUMBER
T: I
W: OPXXXX

# 101XXXX+011+9[679]X+NN+#
P: 101                      TRANSIT-NETWORK-ESCAPE
P: XXXX                     TRANSIT-NETWORK
P: 01                       INTERNATIONAL-ACCESS
P: 1                        INTERNATIONAL-DIRECT-DIAL
P: 9[679]X                  COUNTRY-CODE
P: !                        NATIONAL-NUMBER
P: #                        END-OF-DIALING
T: I
```

Decimal to Hexadecimal and Binary Conversion Table

Decimal Value	Hexadecimal Value	Binary Value
0	00	0000 0000
1	01	0000 0001
2	02	0000 0010
3	03	0000 0011
4	04	0000 0100
5	05	0000 0101
6	06	0000 0110
7	07	0000 0111
8	08	0000 1000
9	09	0000 1001
10	0A	0000 1010
11	0B	0000 1011
12	0C	0000 1100
13	0D	0000 1101
14	0E	0000 1110
15	0F	0000 1111
16	10	0001 0000
17	11	0001 0001
18	12	0001 0010
19	13	0001 0011
20	14	0001 0100
21	15	0001 0101
22	16	0001 0110

continues

Decimal Value	Hexadecimal Value	Binary Value
23	17	0001 0111
24	18	0001 1000
25	19	0001 1001
26	1A	0001 1010
27	1B	0001 1011
28	1C	0001 1100
29	1D	0001 1101
30	1E	0001 1110
31	1F	0001 1111
32	20	0010 0000
33	21	0010 0001
34	22	0010 0010
35	23	0010 0011
36	24	0010 0100
37	25	0010 0101
38	26	0010 0110
39	27	0010 0111
40	28	0010 1000
41	29	0010 1001
42	2A	0010 1010
43	2B	0010 1011
44	2C	0010 1100
45	2D	0010 1101
46	2E	0010 1110
47	2F	0010 1111
48	30	0011 0000
49	31	0011 0001
50	32	0011 0010
51	33	0011 0011
52	34	0011 0100

Decimal Value	Hexadecimal Value	Binary Value
53	35	0011 0101
54	36	0011 0110
55	37	0011 0111
56	38	0011 1000
57	39	0011 1001
58	3A	0011 1010
59	3B	0011 1011
60	3C	0011 1100
61	3D	0011 1101
62	3E	0011 1110
63	3F	0011 1111
64	40	0100 0000
65	41	0100 0001
66	42	0100 0010
67	43	0100 0011
68	44	0100 0100
69	45	0100 0101
70	46	0100 0110
71	47	0100 0111
72	48	0100 1000
73	49	0100 1001
74	4A	0100 1010
75	4B	0100 1011
76	4C	0100 1100
77	4D	0100 1101
78	4E	0100 1110
79	4F	0100 1111
80	50	0101 0000
81	51	0101 0001
82	52	0101 0010

continues

Decimal Value	Hexadecimal Value	Binary Value
83	53	0101 0011
84	54	0101 0100
85	55	0101 0101
86	56	0101 0110
87	57	0101 0111
88	58	0101 1000
89	59	0101 1001
90	5A	0101 1010
91	5B	0101 1011
92	5C	0101 1100
93	5D	0101 1101
94	5E	0101 1110
95	5F	0101 1111
96	60	0110 0000
97	61	0110 0001
98	62	0110 0010
99	63	0110 0011
100	64	0110 0100
101	65	0110 0101
102	66	0110 0110
103	67	0110 0111
104	68	0110 1000
105	69	0110 1001
106	6A	0110 1010
107	6B	0110 1011
108	6C	0110 1100
109	6D	0110 1101
110	6E	0110 1110
111	6F	0110 1111
112	70	0111 0000

Decimal Value	Hexadecimal Value	Binary Value
113	71	0111 0001
114	72	0111 0010
115	73	0111 0011
116	74	0111 0100
117	75	0111 0101
118	76	0111 0110
119	77	0111 0111
120	78	0111 1000
121	79	0111 1001
122	7A	0111 1010
123	7B	0111 1011
124	7C	0111 1100
125	7D	0111 1101
126	7E	0111 1110
127	7F	0111 1111
128	80	1000 0000
129	81	1000 0001
130	82	1000 0010
131	83	1000 0011
132	84	1000 0100
133	85	1000 0101
134	86	1000 0110
135	87	1000 0111
136	88	1000 1000
137	89	1000 1001
138	8A	1000 1010
139	8B	1000 1011
140	8C	1000 1100
141	8D	1000 1101
142	8E	1000 1110

continues

Decimal Value	Hexadecimal Value	Binary Value
143	8F	1000 1111
144	90	1001 0000
145	91	1001 0001
146	92	1001 0010
147	93	1001 0011
148	94	1001 0100
149	95	1001 0101
150	96	1001 0110
151	97	1001 0111
152	98	1001 1000
153	99	1001 1001
154	9A	1001 1010
155	9B	1001 1011
156	9C	1001 1100
157	9D	1001 1101
158	9E	1001 1110
159	9F	1001 1111
160	A0	1010 0000
161	A1	1010 0001
162	A2	1010 0010
163	A3	1010 0011
164	A4	1010 0100
165	A5	1010 0101
166	A6	1010 0110
167	A7	1010 0111
168	A8	1010 1000
169	A9	1010 1001
170	AA	1010 1010
171	AB	1010 1011
172	AC	1010 1100

Decimal Value	Hexadecimal Value	Binary Value
173	AD	1010 1101
174	AE	1010 1110
175	AF	1010 1111
176	B0	1011 0000
177	B1	1011 0001
178	B2	1011 0010
179	B3	1011 0011
180	B4	1011 0100
181	B5	1011 0101
182	B6	1011 0110
183	B7	1011 0111
184	B8	1011 1000
185	B9	1011 1001
186	BA	1011 1010
187	BB	1011 1011
188	BC	1011 1100
189	BD	1011 1101
190	BE	1011 1110
191	BF	1011 1111
192	C0	1100 0000
193	C1	1100 0001
194	C2	1100 0010
195	C3	1100 0011
196	C4	1100 0100
197	C5	1100 0101
198	C6	1100 0110
199	C7	1100 0111
200	C8	1100 1000
201	C9	1100 1001
202	CA	1100 1010

continues

Decimal Value	Hexadecimal Value	Binary Value
203	CB	1100 1011
204	CC	1100 1100
205	CD	1100 1101
206	CE	1100 1110
207	CF	1100 1111
208	D0	1101 0000
209	D1	1101 0001
210	D2	1101 0010
211	D3	1101 0011
212	D4	1101 0100
213	D5	1101 0101
214	D6	1101 0110
215	D7	1101 0111
216	D8	1101 1000
217	D9	1101 1001
218	DA	1101 1010
219	DB	1101 1011
220	DC	1101 1100
221	DD	1101 1101
222	DE	1101 1110
223	DF	1101 1111
224	E0	1110 0000
225	E1	1110 0001
226	E2	1110 0010
227	E3	1110 0011
228	E4	1110 0100
229	E5	1110 0101
230	E6	1110 0110

Decimal Value	Hexadecimal Value	Binary Value
231	E7	1110 0111
232	E8	1110 1000
233	E9	1110 1001
234	EA	1110 1010
235	EB	1110 1011
236	EC	1110 1100
237	ED	1110 1101
238	EE	1110 1110
239	EF	1110 1111
240	F0	1111 0000
241	F1	1111 0001
242	F2	1111 0010
243	F3	1111 0011
244	F4	1111 0100
245	F5	1111 0101
246	F6	1111 0110
247	F7	1111 0111
248	F8	1111 1000
249	F9	1111 1001
250	FA	1111 1010
251	FB	1111 1011
252	FC	1111 1100
253	FD	1111 1101
254	FE	1111 1110
255	FF	1111 1111

Performance Objects and Counters

This appendix lists and describes the performance objects and counters in a Cisco IP Telephony network. Some pertinent Windows 2000 counters are also described.

Cisco Performance Objects and Counters

The following sections list the available CallManager-related objects and briefly describe the statistics they provide. Some objects and counters changed between versions 3.3(1) and 3.3(3), as noted in the following sections.

- Cisco Analog Access
- Cisco CallManager
- Cisco CallManager Attendant Console
- Cisco CallManager System Performance
- Cisco CTI Manager
- Cisco Gatekeeper
- Cisco H.323
- Cisco HW Conference Bridge Device
- Cisco Lines
- Cisco Locations
- Cisco Media Streaming Application
- Cisco Media Termination Point
- Cisco Messaging Interface
- Cisco MGCP FXO Device
- Cisco MGCP FXS Device
- Cisco MGCP Gateways
- Cisco MGCP PRI Device
- Cisco MGCP T1 CAS Device
- Cisco MOH Device

- Cisco MTP Device
- Cisco Music on Hold Server
- Cisco Phones
- Cisco SW Conference Bridge Device
- Cisco TFTP
- Cisco Transcode Device
- Cisco Unicast Hardware Conference Bridge Device
- Cisco Unicast Software Conference Bridge Device
- Cisco WebAttendant

NOTE   The information in the following tables is provided for your reference. New features and bug fixes cause the counters and objects to be routinely updated. Only counters of installed components are available. Check the Real-Time Monitoring Tool or Microsoft Performance (PerfMon) for the latest objects and counters. Also, when you add a counter from the Add window in PerfMon, you can click the **Explain** button to get a short description of the counter.

Cisco Analog Access Object

The counters described in this section provide port and call information about Skinny protocol-based Analog Access gateways. In CallManager 3.1 and later, the only Skinny-based Analog Access gateways are the legacy AS-*X* and AT-*X* gateways. Prior to CallManager 3.1, the WS-X6624 and WS-X6608 were Skinny-based gateways, but they are now MGCP-based gateways.

Table D-1 lists all the counters in the Cisco Analog Access object and describes what each counter represents.

Table D-1   *Cisco Analog Access Counters*

Counter	Description
OutboundBusyAttempts	The total number of times that a call through the Analog Access gateway was attempted when all ports were busy.
PortsActive	The number of ports that are currently in use (active). A port is active when a call is in progress on that port.
PortsOutOfService	The number of ports that are currently out of service. This counter only applies to Loop Start and Ground Start trunks.

Cisco CallManager Object

The counters discussed in this section allow you to monitor the activity of the CallManager service. The CallManager service is responsible for the majority of call processing and device registration.

Table D-2 lists all the counters in the Cisco CallManager object and describes what each counter represents.

Table D-2   *Cisco CallManager Counters*

Counter Name as of Release 3.3(3)/ Counter Name Through Release 3.3(2)	Description
CallManagerHeartBeat	The heartbeat of CallManager. This is an incremental count that indicates that CallManager is alive and running. If the count does not increment, then CallManager is down (dead).
	The heartbeat increments once every 2 seconds, so you can use this value to determine how long the CallManager service has been running since the last restart.
	Note that the heartbeat does not begin incrementing until after CallManager has completed initializing, which may take several minutes on a large database.
CallsActive	The number of streaming connections that are currently in use (active). In other words, the number of calls that actually have a voice path connected on this CallManager.
CallsAttempted	The total number of attempted calls. Any time a phone goes off-hook and back on-hook, it is considered an attempted call, regardless of whether any digits were dialed or if it connected to a destination. Some call attempts are made by the system during feature operations (such as transfer and conference) and are considered attempted calls.

continues

Table D-2 *Cisco CallManager Counters (Continued)*

Counter Name as of Release 3.3(3)/ Counter Name Through Release 3.3(2)	Description
CallsCompleted	The number of calls that were actually connected (a voice path was established) through this CallManager and that have already ended. This number increments when the call is terminated.
CallsInProgress	The number of calls currently in progress on this CallManager, including all active calls. This includes calls that do not have a voice path established (such as when a caller hears ringback before a voice path is established). As soon as all calls that are in progress have connected, the number of CallsInProgress and the number of CallsActive are the same.
FXOPortsActive	The number of Foreign Exchange Office (FXO) ports that are in an active call on this CallManager. This includes both MGCP and Skinny-based ports.
FXOPortsInService	The number of FXO ports that are available for use or that are in use in the system. This includes both MGCP and Skinny-based ports.
FXSPortsActive	The number of Foreign Exchange Station (FXS) ports that are in an active call on this CallManager. This includes both MGCP and Skinny-based ports.
FXSPortsInService	The number of FXS ports that are available for use or that are in use in the system. This includes both MGCP and Skinny-based ports.
MTPOutOfResources/ MediaTermPointsOutOfResources	The number of times CallManager attempted to allocate an MTP resource from one of the MTP devices that is registered with this CallManager when none were available. This also means that no transcoders were available to act as MTPs.
MTPResourceActive/ MediaTermPointsResourceActive	The total number of MTPs that are currently in use (active) on all MTP devices that are registered with this CallManager. An MTP in use is one MTP resource that has been allocated for use in a call.

Table D-2   *Cisco CallManager Counters (Continued)*

Counter Name as of Release 3.3(3)/ Counter Name Through Release 3.3(2)	Description
MTPResourceAvailable/ MediaTermPointsResourceAvailable	The total number of MTPs that are not in use and are available to be allocated on all MTP devices that are registered with this CallManager.
MOHMulticastResourceActive	The total number of multicast MOH connections that are currently in use (active) on all MOH servers that are registered with this CallManager.
MOHMulticastResourceAvailable	The total number of multicast MOH connections that are not being used on all MOH servers that are registered with this CallManager.
MOHOutOfResources	The number of times that the Media Resource Manager (MRM) attempted to allocate an MOH resource when all available resources on all MOH servers registered with this CallManager were already active.
MOHTotalMulticastResources	The total number of multicast MOH resources or connections provided by all MOH servers that are currently registered with this CallManager.
MOHTotalUnicastResources	The total number of unicast MOH resources or streams provided by all MOH servers that are currently registered with this CallManager.
MOHUnicastResourceActive	The total number of unicast MOH connections that are currently in use (active) on all MOH servers that are registered with this CallManager.
MOHUnicastResourceAvailable	The total number of unicast MOH connections that are currently available (not being used) on all MOH servers that are registered with this CallManager.
PRIChannelsActive	The number of MGCP-controlled PRI voice channels that are in an active call on this CallManager.
PRISpansInService	The number of MGCP-controlled PRI spans that are currently available for use.

continues

Table D-2   *Cisco CallManager Counters (Continued)*

Counter Name as of Release 3.3(3)/ Counter Name Through Release 3.3(2)	Description
RegisteredAnalogAccess	The number of Cisco Access Analog gateways that are registered with this system. This does not include the number of Cisco Analog Access ports.
RegisteredHardwarePhones	The number of Cisco hardware IP phones (for example, models 7960, 7940, 7910, and so on) that are currently registered in the system.
RegisteredMGCPGateway	The number of MGCP gateways currently registered in the system.
RegisteredOtherStationDevices	The number of station devices other than Cisco hardware IP phones that are currently registered in the system (for example, Cisco IP SoftPhone, CTI port, CTI route point, and Cisco voice mail port).
T1ChannelsActive	The number of MGCP-controlled T1 CAS voice channels that are in an active call on this CallManager.
T1SpansInService	The number of MGCP-controlled T1 CAS spans that are currently available for use.
TranscoderOutOfResources	The total number of times CallManager attempted to allocate a transcoder resource from one of the transcoder devices that is registered to this CallManager when none were available.
TranscoderResourceActive	The total number of transcoders that are in use on all transcoder devices registered with this CallManager. A transcoder in use is one transcoder resource that has been allocated for use in a call.
TranscoderResourceAvailable	The total number of transcoders that are not in use and are available to be allocated, on all transcoder devices that are registered with this CallManager.

Table D-2   *Cisco CallManager Counters (Continued)*

Counter Name as of Release 3.3(3)/ Counter Name Through Release 3.3(2)	Description
HWConferenceActivePaticipants/ UnicastHardwareConferenceActiveParticipants	The number of participants that are in all active conferences that are using a hardware-based (Cisco Catalyst 6000, Cisco Catalyst 4000, and Cisco VG200) conference bridge allocated from this CallManager.
HWConferenceCompleted/ UnicastHardwareConferenceCompleted	The total number of conferences that used a hardware conference bridge (hardware-based conference devices such as Cisco Catalyst 6000, Cisco Catalyst 4000, and Cisco VG200) allocated from this CallManager and that have been completed, which means that the conference bridge has been allocated and released. A conference is activated when the first call is connected to the bridge. The conference is completed when the last call disconnects from the bridge.
HWConferenceOutOfResources/ UnicastHardwareConferenceOutOfResources	The total number of times CallManager attempted to allocate a hardware conference resource from those that are registered to this CallManager when none were available.
HWConferenceResourceActive/ UnicastHardwareConfResourceActive	The total number of conference resources that are in use on all hardware conference devices (Cisco Catalyst 6000, Cisco Catalyst 4000, and Cisco VG200) that are registered with this CallManager. A conference is considered active when one or more calls are connected to a bridge.
HWConferenceResourceAvailable/ UnicastHardwareConfResourceAvailable	The number of hardware conference resources that are not in use and are available to be allocated on all hardware-based conference devices (such as Cisco Catalyst 6000, Cisco Catalyst 4000, and Cisco VG200) that are registered with this CallManager. Each conference resource represents the availability of three full-duplex streams on this CallManager.

continues

Table D-2   *Cisco CallManager Counters (Continued)*

Counter Name as of Release 3.3(3)/ Counter Name Through Release 3.3(2)	Description
SWConferenceActiveParticipants/ UnicastSoftwareConferenceActiveParticipants	The number of participants that are in all active conferences that are using a software conference bridge allocated from this CallManager.
SWConferenceCompleted/ UnicastSoftwareConferenceCompleted	The total number of conferences that used a software conference bridge allocated from this CallManager and have been completed, which means that the conference bridge has been allocated and released. A conference is activated when the first call is connected to the bridge. The conference is completed when the last call disconnects from the bridge.
SWConferenceOutOfResources/ UnicastSoftwareConferenceOutOfResources	The total number of times CallManager attempted to allocate a software conference resource from those that are registered to this CallManager when none were available. This counter includes failed attempts to add a new participant to an existing conference.
SWConferenceResourceActive/ UnicastSoftwareConfResourceActive	The total number of conference resources that are in use on all software conference devices that are registered with this CallManager. A conference is considered active when one or more calls are connected to a bridge.
SWConferenceResourceAvailable/ UnicastSoftwareConfResourceAvailable	The number of new software-based conferences that can be started at this point in time for this CallManager. A minimum of three streams must be available for each new conference.

Cisco CallManager Attendant Console Object—Release 3.3(2)

The counters discussed in this section describe the types of data collected by the Telephony Call Dispatcher service (TcdSrv). The TCD service is the server-side component for all the Cisco CallManager Attendant Console/Cisco WebAttendant client applications. TCD provides call control and line state service to Attendant Console and WebAttendant clients. It also provides hunt group functionality.

Prior to CallManager release 3.3(2), this object was named Cisco WebAttendant.

Table D-3 lists all the counters under the Cisco CallManager Attendant Console object and describes what each counter represents.

Table D-3 *Cisco CallManager Attendant Console Counters*

Counter Name as of Release 3.3(2)/Counter Name Through Release 3.3(1)	Description
CallsActive/TotalActiveCalls	This counter should not be used. Information in this counter may not accurately reflect the total number of active calls.
CallsRedirected/TotalRedirectedCalls	The total number of redirected calls for this TCD service. This number increments each time a pilot point receives a call and redirects the call to a member of its hunt group.
CallsTotal/TotalCalls	The total number of all calls that have been made since the TCD service started.
CcmLineLinkState	The line state. Values are 0, 1, 10, or 11: • **0**—The TCD service has not registered or has not received line link state information from CallManager • **1**—The TCD service has registered and is receiving line link state information from CallManager • **10**—The TCD service has logged into CTI but has not registered or has not received line link state information from CallManager • **11**—The TCD service has logged into CTI and has registered and is receiving line link state information
ClientsOnline/TotalOnlineClients	The total number of Cisco CallManager Attendant Console clients that are currently online. Attendant Console clients include all users configured in the Attendant Console User Configuration screen in CallManager Administration that are currently online. This number increments by one for each client that goes online, and decrements by one for each client that goes offline.
ClientsRegistered/ TotalRegisteredClients	The total number of registered clients for this TCD service. This number increments by one for each new registration of a Cisco CallManager Attendant Console client when the client application logs in.

continues

Table D-3 *Cisco CallManager Attendant Console Counters (Continued)*

Counter Name as of Release 3.3(2)/Counter Name Through Release 3.3(1)	Description
ClientsTotal/TotalClients	The total number of Cisco CallManager Attendant Console clients that are currently registered with the TCD service. Attendant Console clients are all users configured in the Attendant Console User Configuration screen in CallManager Administration.
HeartBeat	The heartbeat of the Telephony Call Dispatcher (TCD) service. This is an incremental count that indicates that TCD service is alive and running. If the count does not increment, then the TCD service is down (dead).
LinesActive/TotalActiveLines	This counter should not be used. Information in this counter may not accurately reflect the total number of active lines.
LinesIdle/TotalIdleLines	This counter should not be used. Information in this counter may not accurately reflect the total number of idle lines.
LinesTotal/TotalLines	This counter should not be used. Information in this counter may not accurately reflect the total number of lines.
PilotPointsTotal/TotalPilotPoints	The total number of pilot points that have been configured in CallManager Administration.
StartTime	The time that the TCD service started, expressed as the number of milliseconds elapsed since midnight, January 1, 1970 (Epoch time). The tool, CDR Time Converter, described in Chapter 3, "Understanding the Troubleshooting Tools," provides a quick and easy way to convert this number to a standard date and time format.
Version	The version of the TCD service.

Cisco CallManager System Performance Object

The counters discussed in this section provide system performance information to help you decipher CPU utilization spikes on CallManager. These counters detail which queue level the usage is attributed to, so even when the CPU spikes to 100 percent utilization, you can understand where the spike is occurring and determine whether it will result in degraded CallManager performance.

Table D-4 lists all the counters under the Cisco CallManager System Performance object and describes what each counter represents.

Table D-4   *Cisco CallManager System Performance Counters*

Counter	Description
EngineeringCounter1	This counter is not used unless directed by a Cisco Engineering Special build. Information in this counter will be used by Cisco for diagnostic purposes.
EngineeringCounter2	
EngineeringCounter3	
EngineeringCounter4	
EngineeringCounter5	
EngineeringCounter6	
EngineeringCounter7	
EngineeringCounter8	
QueueSignalsPresent 1-High	Indicates the number of high-priority signals in the CallManager queue. High priority signals include timeout events, internal CallManager KeepAlives, certain gatekeeper events, and internal process creation, among other events. A large number of high priority events in this queue will cause degraded performance on CallManager, resulting in slow call connection or loss of dial tone. Use this counter in conjunction with the QueueSignalsProcessed 1-High counter to determine the processing delay on CallManager.
QueueSignalsPresent 2-Normal	Indicates the number of normal-priority signals in the CallManager queue. Normal priority signals include call processing functions, key presses, on-hook and off-hook notifications, among other events. A large number of normal priority events in this queue will cause degraded performance on CallManager, sometimes resulting in delayed dial tone, slow call connection, or loss of dial tone. Use this counter in conjunction with the QueueSignalsProcessed 2-Normal counter to determine the call processing delay on CallManager. Remember that high priority signals must complete before normal priority signals begin to process, so check the high priority counters as well to get an accurate picture of the potential delay.
QueueSignalsPresent 3-Low	Indicates the number of low-priority signals in the CallManager queue. Low priority signals include station device registration (except the initial station registration request message) among other events. A large number of signals in this queue could result in delayed device registration, among other events.

continues

Table D-4 *Cisco CallManager System Performance Counters (Continued)*

Counter	Description
QueueSignalsPresent 4-Lowest	Indicates the number of lowest-priority signals in the CallManager queue. Lowest priority signals include the initial station registration request message during device registration, among other events. A large number of signals in this queue could result in delayed device registration, among other events.
QueueSignalsProcessed 1-High	Indicates the number of high-priority signals processed by CallManager for the last one-second interval. Use this counter in conjunction with the QueueSignalsPresent 1-High counter to determine the processing delay on this queue.
QueueSignalsProcessed 2-Normal	Indicates the number of normal-priority signals processed by CallManager for the last one-second interval. Use this counter in conjunction with the QueueSignalsPresent 2-Normal counter to determine the processing delay on this queue. Remember that high priority signals are processed before normal priority signals.
QueueSignalsProcessed 3-Low	Indicates the number of low-priority signals processed by CallManager for the last one-second interval. Use this counter in conjunction with the QueueSignalsPresent 3-Low counter to determine the processing delay on this queue. The number of signals processed gives an indication of how much device registration activity is being processed in this time interval.
QueueSignalsProcessed 4-Lowest	Indicates the number of lowest-priority signals processed by CallManager for the last one-second interval. Use this counter in conjunction with the QueueSignalsPresent 4-Lowest counter to determine the processing delay on this queue. The number of signals processed gives an indication of how many devices began the CallManager registration process in this time interval.
QueueSignalsProcessed Total	Provides a sum total of all queue signals processed by CallManager for each one-second period for all queue levels: high, normal, low, and lowest.

Cisco CTI Manager Object

The counters discussed in this section supply information including the number of Computer Telephony Integration (CTI)-controlled devices, lines, and connections that have been established with this CallManager. CTI connections include Applications servers, Cisco CallManager Attendant Console, Cisco IP SoftPhone, and any other third-party TAPI- or JTAPI-controlled device.

Table D-5 lists all the counters in the Cisco CTI Manager object and describes what each counter represents.

Table D-5   *Cisco CTI Manager Counters*

Counter Name as of Release 3.3(3)/ Counter Name Through Release 3.3(2)	Description
CcmLinkActive/NumOfActiveCmLink	The total number of active CallManager links. CTI Manager maintains links to all active CallManagers in the cluster.
CTIConnectionActive/NumOfCtiConnection	The total number of CTI clients currently connected to the CTI Manager. This counter increments by one when new connection is established, and decrements by one when a connection is released. The maximum number of active connections is determined by the CTI Manager service parameter MaxCTIConnections.
DevicesOpen/NumOfOpenDevices	The total number of devices configured in CallManager that are controlled or monitored by CTI applications. Devices include hardware IP phones, CTI ports, CTI route points, and so on.
LinesOpen/NumOfOpenLines	The total number of lines configured in CallManager that are controlled or monitored by CTI applications.
QbeVersion	The version number of the Quick Buffer Encoding (QBE) interface used by the CTI Manager.

Cisco Gatekeeper Object

The counters discussed in this section provide information about registered Cisco gatekeeper devices.

Table D-6 lists all the counters under the Cisco Gatekeeper object and describes what each counter represents.

Table D-6 *Cisco Gatekeeper Counters*

Counter	Description
ACFsReceived	This counter represents the total number of RAS Admission Confirm messages received from the configured gatekeeper and its alternate gatekeepers.
ARQsAttempted	This counter represents the total number of RAS Admission Request messages attempted via the configured gatekeeper and its alternate gatekeepers.
RasRetries	This counter represents the number of retries due to loss or delay of all RAS acknowledgement messages on the configured gate-keeper and its alternate gatekeepers.

Cisco H.323 Object

The counters discussed in this section provide information about H.323 devices. H.323 devices include station devices such as NetMeeting and H.323-compliant gateways such as Cisco 2600, 3600, and 5300. Each H.323 device is listed by name. The name is obtained from CallManager Administration.

Table D-7 lists all the counters in the Cisco H.323 object and describes what each counter represents.

Table D-7 *Cisco H.323 Counters*

Counter	Description
CallsAttempted	The total number of calls that have been attempted on this device, including both successful and unsuccessful call attempts.
CallsCompleted	The total number of successful calls made from the device.
CallsInProgress	The number of calls currently in progress on this device.

Cisco HW Conference Bridge Device—Release 3.3(2)

The counters discussed in this section provide information about registered Cisco hardware conference bridge devices. Prior to CallManager release 3.3(2), this object was named Cisco Unicast Hardware Conference; there are no changes to the counter names.

Table D-8 lists all the counters under the Cisco HW Conference Bridge Device object and describes what each counter represents.

Table D-8   *Cisco HW Conference Bridge Device Counters*

Counter	Description
HWConferenceActiveParticipants	The number of participants currently active in all the conferences for this HW Conference device.
HWConferenceCompleted	The total number of conferences that have been allocated and released on this HW Conference device. A conference is started when the first call is connected to the bridge. The conference is completed when the last call disconnects from the bridge.
OutOfResources	The total number of times an attempt was made to allocate a conference resource from this HW Conference device and failed—for example, because all resources were already in use.
ResourceActive	The number of resources that are currently in use (active) for this HW Conference device.
ResourceAvailable	The total number of resources that are not active and are still available to be used at the current time for this HW Conference device.

Cisco Lines Object

The counter discussed in this section provides information about the number of Cisco lines (directory numbers) that can be dialed and connected to a device. Lines represent all directory numbers that terminate on an endpoint. The directory number that is assigned to it identifies the line. The Lines object does not include directory numbers that include wildcards such as a pattern for a Digital or Analog Access gateway.

Table D-9 describes the counter in the Cisco Lines object.

Table D-9   *Cisco Lines Counter*

Counter	Description
Active	The state of the line, either active or not active. A zero indicates the line is not in use. Of the number is greater than zero, the line is active and the number represents the number of calls currently in progress on that line. If more than one call is active, this indicates the call is on hold either because of being placed on hold specifically (user hold), or because of a network hold operation (for example, a transfer is in progress and it is on transfer hold). This applies to all directory numbers assigned to any device.

Cisco Locations Object

The counters discussed in this section provide information about all locations defined in Cisco CallManager.

Table D-10 lists all the counters under the Cisco Locations object and describes what each counter represents.

Table D-10 *Cisco Locations Counters*

Counter Name as of Release 3.3(3)/ Counter Name Through Release 3.3(2)	Description
BandwidthAvailable/ CurrentAvailableBandwidth	The current bandwidth available in a given location. A value of zero indicates that no bandwidth is available.
BandwidthMaximum/MaxAvailableBandwidth	The maximum bandwidth available in a given location. A value of zero indicates that infinite bandwidth is available.

Cisco Media Streaming App Object

The counters discussed in this section provide information about software media termination point, software conference bridge, and music on hold. The Cisco IP Voice Media Streaming Application generates these counters.

Table D-11 lists all the counters in the Cisco Media Streaming App object through CallManager release 3.3(2) and describes what each counter represents.

Table D-12 lists all the counters in the Cisco Media Streaming App object starting in CallManager release 3.3(3) and describes what each counter represents. Note that in release 3.3(3), the counters defined in Table D-11 are removed and the counters described in Tables D-13, D-22, and D-24 move to this object—with name changes.

Table D-11 *Cisco Media Streaming App Counters Through Release 3.3(2)*

Counter	Description
HeartBeat	The heartbeat of the process. This is an incremental count that indicates that the Cisco IP Voice Media Streaming Application is alive and running. If the count does not increment, the Cisco IP Voice Media Streaming Application is down (dead).
IOCTL Errors	The number of input/output control (IOCTL) errors. The count increments when an application has trouble communicating with the Media Streaming Application kernel mode driver.
Missing Device Driver Errors	The number of missing device driver errors.

Table D-11   *Cisco Media Streaming App Counters Through Release 3.3(2) (Continued)*

Counter	Description
Out of Streams	The number of times a stream was requested but was unavailable.
StartTime	The time that the Cisco IP Voice Media Streaming Application service started, expressed as the number of milliseconds elapsed since midnight, January 1, 1970 (Epoch time). The tool, CDR Time Converter, described in Chapter 3 provides a quick and easy way to convert this number to a standard date and time format.

Table D-12   *Cisco Media Streaming App Counters Starting in Release 3.3(3)*

Counter	Description
CFBConferencesActive	The number of active (currently in use) conferences.
CFBConferencesTotal	The total number of conferences that have been started since the Cisco IP Voice Media Streaming Application service started.
CFBConnectionsLost	The total number of times since the last restart of the Cisco IP Voice Media Streaming Application that a CallManager connection to the conference bridge was lost.
CFBConnectionState	For each CallManager associated with a software conference bridge, this represents the current registration state to CallManager. • **0**—No registration to any CallManager • **1**—Registration to the primary CallManager • **2**—Registration to the secondary CallManager
CFBStreamsActive	Total number of currently active simplex (one direction) streams for all conferences. Each stream direction counts as one stream. In a three-party conference, the number of active streams would be 6.
CFBStreamsAvailable	The remaining number of streams allocated for the conference bridge that are available for use. This counter starts as 2 multiplied by the number of configured connections (defined in the Cisco IP Voice Media Streaming App service parameter for Conference Bridge, Call Count) and is reduced by one for each active stream started.
CFBStreamsTotal	The total number of simplex (one direction) streams that have been connected to the conference bridge since the Cisco IP Voice Media Streaming Application service started.

continues

Table D-12 *Cisco Media Streaming App Counters Starting in Release 3.3(3) (Continued)*

Counter	Description
MOHAudioSourcesActive	The number of active (currently in use) audio sources for this MOH server. Some of these audio sources may not be actively streaming audio data if there are no devices listening. The exception is for multicast audio sources, which will always be streaming audio. NOTE: Behavior for this counter as of release 3.3(3) is such that when an audio source is in use, even after the listener has disconnected, this counter will always have one input stream for each configured MOH codec. For unicast streams, the stream may be in a suspended state where no audio data is received until a device connects to listen to the stream.
MOHConnectionsLost	The total number of times since the last restart of the Cisco IP Voice Media Streaming Application that a CallManager connection to the MOH server was lost.
MOHConnectionState	For each CallManager associated with an MOH, this represents the current registration state to CallManager. • **0**—No registration to any CallManager • **1**—Registration to the primary CallManager • **2**—Registration to the secondary CallManager
MOHStreamsActive	The total number of active (currently in use) simplex (one direction) streams for all connections. There is one output stream for each device listening to a unicast audio source and one input stream for each active audio source, multiplied by the number of MOH codecs. NOTE: Behavior for this counter as of release 3.3(3) is such that when an audio source has been used once, it will always have one input stream for each configured MOH codec. For unicast streams, the stream may be in a suspended state where no audio data is received until a device connects to listen to the stream.
MOHStreamsAvailable	The remaining number of streams allocated for the MOH device that are available for use. This counter starts as 408 plus the number of configured half-duplex unicast connections, and is reduced by 1 for each active stream started. The counter is reduced by 2 for each multicast audio source, multiplied by the number of MOH codecs configured. The counter is reduced by 1 for each unicast audio source, multiplied by the number of MOH codecs configured.
MOHStreamsTotal	The total number of simplex (one direction) streams that have connected to the MOH server since the Cisco IP Voice Media Streaming Application service started.

Table D-12   *Cisco Media Streaming App Counters Starting in Release 3.3(3) (Continued)*

Counter	Description
MTPConnectionsLost	The total number of times since the last restart of the Cisco IP Voice Media Streaming Application that a CallManager connection to the MTP device was lost.
MTPConnectionsTotal	The total number of MTP instances that have been started since the Cisco IP Voice Media Streaming Application service started.
MTPConnectionState	For each CallManager associated with an MTP, this represents the current registration state to CallManager. • **0**—No registration to any CallManager • **1**—Registration to the primary CallManager • **2**—Registration to the secondary CallManager
MTPInstancesActive	The number of active (currently in use) instances of MTP.
MTPStreamsActive	The total number of currently active simplex (one direction) streams for all MTP connections. Each stream direction counts as one stream.
MTPStreamsAvailable	The remaining number of streams allocated for the MTP device that are available for use. This counter starts as 2 multiplied by the number of configured connections (defined in the Cisco IP Voice Media Streaming App service parameter for MTP, Call Count) and is reduced by one for each active stream started.
MTPStreamsTotal	The total number of simplex (one direction) streams that have been connected to the MTP device since the Cisco IP Voice Media Streaming Application service started.

Cisco Media Termination Point Object—Through Release 3.3(2)

For software media termination points, the counters discussed in this section provide information about the availability of streams and the connection state.

NOTE   Starting in CallManager release 3.3(3), this object is removed and the counters in this object move to the Cisco Media Streaming App Object.

Table D-13 lists all the counters in the Cisco Media Termination Point object and describes what each counter represents.

Table D-13 *Cisco Media Termination Point Counters*

Counter	Description
ConnectionState	For each CallManager associated with an MTP, this represents the current registration state to CallManager. • **0**—No registration to any CallManager • **1**—Registration to the primary CallManager • **2**—Registration to the secondary CallManager
NumberOfActiveConnections	The number of active (currently in use) instances of MTP.
NumberOfActiveStreams	The total number of currently active simplex (one direction) streams for all connections. Each stream direction counts as one stream.
NumberOfAvailableStreams	The remaining number of streams allocated for the MTP device that are available for use. This counter starts as 2 multiplied by the number of configured connections (defined in the Cisco IP Voice Media Streaming App service parameter for MTP, Call Count) and is reduced by one for each active stream started.
NumberOfLostConnections	The total number of times since the last restart of the Cisco IP Voice Media Streaming Application that a CallManager connection was lost.
TotalNumberOfConnections	The total number of MTP instances that have been started since the Cisco IP Voice Media Streaming Application service started.
TotalNumberOfStreams	The total number of simplex (one direction) streams that have been connected to the MTP device since the Cisco IP Voice Media Streaming Application service started.

Cisco Messaging Interface Object

The counters discussed in this section provide communication information between CallManager and Cisco Messaging Interface (CMI) for voice mail systems using SMDI.

Table D-14 lists all the counters in the Cisco Messaging Interface object and describes what each counter represents.

Table D-14 *Cisco Messaging Interface Counters*

Counter Name as of Release 3.3(3)/Counter Name Through Release 3.3(2)	Description
HeartBeat	The heartbeat of the CMI service. This is an incremental count that indicates that the CMI service is alive and running. If the count does not increment, then the CMI service is down (dead).
SMDIMessageCountInbound/Inbound SMDI Message Count	The running count of inbound SMDI messages since the last restart of the CMI service.
SMDIMessageCountInbound24Hour/24-hour Inbound SMDI Message Count	The rolling count of inbound SMDI messages in the last 24 hours.
SMDIMessageCountOutbound/Outbound SMDI Message Count	The running count of outbound SMDI messages since the last restart of the CMI service.
SMDIMessageCountOutbound24Hour/24 hour Outbound SMDI Message Count	The rolling count of outbound SMDI messages in the last 24 hours.
StartTime	The time that the CMI service started, expressed as the number of milliseconds elapsed since midnight, January 1, 1970 (Epoch time). The tool, CDR Time Converter, described in Chapter 3 provides a quick and easy way to convert this number to a standard date and time format.

Cisco MGCP FXO Device Object

The counters discussed in this section provide status information for MGCP-based analog FXO trunks.

Table D-15 lists all the counters under the Cisco MGCP FXO Device object and describes what each counter represents.

Table D-15 *Cisco MGCP FXO Device Counters*

Counter	Description
CallsCompleted	The total number of successful calls made from the port on this MGCP FXO device.
OutboundBusyAttempts	The total number of times that a call through the port on this MGCP FXO device was attempted when there were no voice channels available.
PortStatus	The status of the FXO port associated with this MGCP FXO device.

Cisco MGCP FXS Device Object

The counters discussed in this section provide status information for registered MGCP-based analog FXS devices. One instance of this object is created for each port on a Cisco Catalyst 6000 24 port FXS Analog Interface Module gateway. For example, for a fully configured Catalyst 6000 Analog Interface Module, there would be 24 separate instances of this object.

Table D-16 lists all the counters under the Cisco MGCP FXS Device object and describes what each counter represents.

Table D-16   *Cisco MGCP FXS Device Counters*

Counter	Description
CallsCompleted	The total number of successful calls made from this port on the MGCP FXS device.
OutboundBusyAttempts	The total number of times that a call through this port on the MGCP FXS device was attempted when there were no voice channels available.
PortStatus	The status of the FXS port associated with this MGCP FXS device.

Cisco MGCP Gateways Object

The counters discussed in this section provide information about the ports, spans, and channels in registered MGCP gateways.

Table D-17 lists all the counters under the Cisco MGCP Gateways object and describes what each counter represents.

Table D-17   *Cisco MGCP Gateways Counters*

Counter	Description
FXOPortsActive	The number of FXO ports that are currently active in a call in the gateway.
FXOPortsInService	The number of FXO ports that are currently available for use in the gateway.
FXSPortsActive	The number of FXS ports that are currently active in a call in the gateway.
FXSPortsInService	The number of FXS ports that are currently available for use in the gateway.
PRIChannelsActive	The number of PRI voice channels that are currently active in a call in the gateway.
PRISpansInService	The number of PRI spans that are currently available for use in the gateway.
T1ChannelsActive	The number of T1 channel associated signaling (CAS) voice channels that are currently active in a call on the gateway.
T1SpansInService	The number of T1 CAS spans that are currently available for use in the gateway.

Cisco MGCP PRI Device Object

The counters discussed in this section provide call and channel status information for MGCP PRI gateways.

Table D-18 lists all the counters under the Cisco MGCP PRI Device object and describes what each counter represents.

Table D-18   *Cisco MGCP PRI Device Counters*

Counter	Description
CallsCompleted	The total number of successful calls made from this MGCP PRI device.
Channel 1 Status Channel 2 Status Channel 3 Status Channel 4 Status Channel 5 Status Channel 6 Status Channel 7 Status Channel 8 Status Channel 9 Status Channel 10 Status Channel 11 Status Channel 12 Status Channel 13 Status Channel 14 Status Channel 15 Status Channel 16 Status Channel 17 Status Channel 18 Status Channel 19 Status Channel 20 Status Channel 21 Status Channel 22 Status Channel 23 Status Channel 24 Status Channel 25 Status	The status of the indicated B-Channel associated with this MGCP PRI device. Possible values: • **0**—Unknown; indicates the status of the channel could not be determined. • **1**—Out of service; indicates that this channel is not available for use. • **2**—Idle; indicates that this channel has no active call and is ready for use. • **3**—Busy; indicates an active call on this channel. • **4**—Reserved; indicates that this channel has been reserved for use as a D-channel or for use as a Synch-Channel for E-1.

continues

Table D-18 *Cisco MGCP PRI Device Counters (Continued)*

Counter	Description
Channel 26 Status	
Channel 27 Status	
Channel 28 Status	
Channel 29 Status	
Channel 30 Status	
Channel 31 Status	
DataLinkInService	The state of the Data Link (D-Channel) on the corresponding Digital Access gateway. This value will be set to 1 (one) if the Data Link is up (in service) or 0 (zero) if the Data Link is down (out of service).
OutboundBusyAttempts	The total number of times a call through this MGCP PRI device was attempted when there were no voice channels available.

Cisco MGCP T1 CAS Device Object

The counters discussed in this section provide call and channel status information for MGCP T1 CAS gateways.

Table D-19 lists of all the counters under the Cisco MGCP T1CAS Device object and describes what each counter represents.

Table D-19 *Cisco MGCP T1CAS Device Counters*

Counter	Description
CallsCompleted	The total number of successful calls made from this MGCP T1 CAS device.
Channel 1 Status	The status of the indicated B-Channel associated with this MGCP T1 CAS device. Possible values:
Channel 2 Status	
Channel 3 Status	• **0**—Unknown; indicates the status of the channel could not be determined.
Channel 4 Status	
Channel 5 Status	• **1**—Out of service; indicates that this channel is not available for use.
Channel 6 Status	• **2**—Idle; indicates that this channel has no active call and is ready for use.
Channel 7 Status	
Channel 8 Status	• **3**—Busy; indicates an active call on this channel.
Channel 9 Status	• **4**—Reserved; indicates that this channel has been reserved for use as a D-channel or for use as a Synch-Channel for E-1.
Channel 10 Status	
Channel 11 Status	
Channel 12 Status	

Table D-19   *Cisco MGCP T1CAS Device Counters (Continued)*

Counter	Description
Channel 13 Status	
Channel 14 Status	
Channel 15 Status	
Channel 16 Status	
Channel 17 Status	
Channel 18 Status	
Channel 19 Status	
Channel 20 Status	
Channel 21 Status	
Channel 22 Status	
Channel 23 Status	
Channel 24 Status	
OutboundBusyAttempts	The total number of times that a call through the MGCP T1 CAS device was attempted when there were no voice channels available.

Cisco MOH Device Object

The counters discussed in this section provide information about MOH resource availability. MOH is a component of the Cisco IP Voice Media Streaming Application.

Table D-20 lists all the counters under the Cisco MOH Device object and describes what each counter represents.

Table D-20   *Cisco MOH Device Counters*

Counter	Description
MOHHighestActiveResources	The largest number of simultaneously active MOH connections on this MOH server. This includes both multicast and unicast connections.
MOHMulticastResourceActive	The number of currently active multicast connections to multicast addresses served by this MOH server.
MOHMulticastResourceAvailable	The number of MOH multicast connections to multicast addresses served by this MOH server that are not active and are still available to be used at the current time for this MOH server.

continues

Table D-20 *Cisco MOH Device Counters (Continued)*

Counter	Description
MOHOutOfResources	The number of times the Media Resource Manager (MRM) attempted to allocate an MOH resource when all available resources on all MOH servers registered with this CallManager were already active.
MOHTotalMulticastResources	The total number of multicast MOH connections allowed to multicast addresses served by this MOH server.
MOHTotalUnicastResources	The number of unicast MOH connections allowed by this MOH server.
MOHUnicastResourceActive	The number of active unicast MOH connections to this MOH server.
MOHUnicastResourceAvailable	The number of unicast MOH connections that are not active and are still available to be used at the current time for this MOH server.

Cisco MTP Device Object

The counters discussed in this section provide information about registered MTP resource availability. MTP is a component of the Cisco IP Voice Media Streaming Application.

Table D-21 lists all the counters under the Cisco MTP Device object and describes what each counter represents.

Table D-21 *Cisco MTP Device Counters*

Counter	Description
OutOfResources	The total number of times an attempt was made to allocate an MTP resource from this MTP device and failed—for example, because all resources were already in use.
ResourceActive	The number of MTP resources that are currently in use (active) for this MTP device.
ResourceAvailable	The total number of MTP resources that are not active and are still available to be used at the current time for the MTP device.

Cisco Music on Hold Server Object—Through Release 3.3(2)

The counters discussed in this section provide stream information on a per-CallManager basis. These counters apply to this MOH server only.

NOTE   Starting in CallManager release 3.3(3), this object is removed and the counters in this object move to the Cisco Media Streaming App Object.

Table D-22 lists all the counters under the Cisco Music on Hold Server object and describes what each counter represents.

Table D-22   *Cisco Music on Hold Server Counters*

Counter	Description
ConnectionState	For each CallManager associated with an MOH, this represents the current registration state to CallManager. • **0**—No registration to any CallManager • **1**—Registration to the primary CallManager • **2**—Registration to the secondary CallManager
NumberOfActiveAudioSources	The number of active (currently in use) audio sources for this MOH server. Some of these audio sources may not be actively streaming audio data if there are no devices listening. The exception is for multicast audio sources, which will always be streaming audio. NOTE: Behavior for this counter as of release 3.3(2) is such that when an audio source is in use, even after the listener has disconnected, this counter will always have one input stream for each configured MOH codec. For unicast streams, the stream may be in a suspended state where no audio data is received until a device connects to listen to the stream.
NumberOfActiveStreams	The total number of active (currently in use) simplex (one direction) streams for all connections. There is one output stream for each device listening to a unicast audio source and one input stream for each active audio source, multiplied by the number of MOH codecs. NOTE: Behavior for this counter as of release 3.3(2) is such that when an audio source has been used once, it will always have one input stream for each configured MOH codec. For unicast streams, the stream may be in a suspended state where no audio data is received until a device connects to listen to the stream.
NumberOfAvailableStreams	The remaining number of streams allocated for the MOH device that are available for use. This counter starts as 408 plus the number of configured half-duplex unicast connections, and is reduced by 1 for each active stream started. The counter is reduced by 2 for each multicast audio source, multiplied by the number of MOH codecs configured. The counter is reduced by 1 for each unicast audio source, multiplied by the number of MOH codecs configured.

continues

Table D-22 *Cisco Music on Hold Server Counters (Continued)*

Counter	Description
NumberOfLostConnections	The total number of times since the last restart of the Cisco IP Voice Media Streaming Application that a CallManager connection was lost.
TotalNumberOfStreams	The total number of simplex (one direction) streams that have connected to the MOH server since the Cisco IP Voice Media Streaming Application service started.

Cisco Phones Object

The counter described in this section can be used to determine the total number of calls that have been made per device (not per line) since the system started. This represents the number of registered IP phones, including both hardware-based and other station devices.

Table D-23 describes the counter under the Cisco Phones objects.

Table D-23 *Cisco Phones Counter*

Counter	Description
CallsAttempted	The number of calls that have been attempted from this phone. Each time the phone goes off-hook and then on-hook, it is considered an attempted call. This number is incremented for each call attempt on a per-device basis. It includes all call attempts, whether or not they were successful.

Cisco SW Conference Bridge Object—Through Release 3.3(2)

The counters discussed in this section provide stream information on a per-CallManager basis for software-based conferences.

NOTE Starting in CallManager release 3.3(3), this object is removed and the counters in this object move to the Cisco Media Streaming App Object.

Table D-24 lists all the counters in the Cisco SW Conference Bridge object and describes what each counter represents.

Table D-24   *Cisco SW Conference Bridge Counters*

Counter	Description
ConnectionState	For each CallManager associated with a software conference bridge, this represents the current registration state to CallManager. • **0**—No registration to any CallManager • **1**—Registration to the primary CallManager • **2**—Registration to the secondary CallManager
NumberOfActiveConferences	The number of active (currently in use) conferences.
NumberOfActiveStreams	The number of currently active simplex (one direction) streams for all conferences. Each stream direction counts as one stream. In a three-party conference, the number of active streams would be 6.
NumberOfAvailableStreams	The remaining number of streams allocated for the conference bridge that are available for use. This counter starts as 2 multiplied by the number of configured connections (defined in the Cisco IP Voice Media Streaming App service parameter for Conference Bridge, Call Count) and is reduced by one for each active stream started.
NumberOfLostConnections	The total number of times since the last restart of the Cisco IP Voice Media Streaming Application that a CallManager connection was lost.
TotalNumberOfConferences	The total number of conferences that have been started since the Cisco IP Voice Media Streaming Application service started.
TotalNumberOfStreams	The total number of simplex (one direction) streams that have been connected to the conference bridge since the Cisco IP Voice Media Streaming Application service started.

Cisco SW Conference Bridge Device Object—Release 3.3(2)

The counters discussed in this section provide information about software conference resource availability. Prior to CallManager release 3.3(2), this object was called Cisco Unicast Software Conference Bridge Device.

Table D-25 lists all the counters under the Cisco SW Conference Bridge Device object and describes what each counter represents.

Table D-25 *Cisco SW Conference Bridge Device Counters*

Counter	Description
OutOfResources	The total number of times an attempt was made to allocate a conference resource from this SW conference device and failed—for example, because all resources were already in use.
ResourceActive	The number of resources that are currently in use (active) for this SW conference device.
ResourceAvailable	This represents the total number of resources that are not active and are still available to be used at the current time for this SW conference device.
SWConferenceActiveParticipants	The number of participants currently active in all the conferences for this SW conference device.
SWConferenceCompleted	The total number of conferences that have been allocated and released on this SW conference device. A conference is started when the first call is connected to the bridge. The conference is completed when the last call disconnects from the bridge.

Cisco TFTP Object

The counters discussed in this section show database changes processed by the Cisco TFTP server. Information in these counters applies to this Cisco TFTP server only.

Table D-26 lists all the counters in the Cisco TFTP object and describes what each counter represents.

Table D-26 *Cisco TFTP Counters*

Counter Name as of Release 3.3(3)/ Counter Name Through Release 3.3(2)	Description
BuildAllChangeNotifications — This counter is added in CallManager release 3.3(3).	The number of times the TFTP server, since the TFTP service started, has built all the configuration files in response to a database change notification that affects all devices. This counter increments by one every time the TFTP server performs a new build of all configuration files (not when the notification request is received).
BuildDuration — This counter is added in CallManager release 3.3(3).	The length of time in seconds that the last build of file(s) took.

Table D-26 *Cisco TFTP Counters (Continued)*

Counter Name as of Release 3.3(3)/ Counter Name through Release 3.3(2)	Description
BuildGatewayChangeNotifications — This counter is added in CallManager release 3.3(3).	The number of times the TFTP server has built the configuration files in response to a database change notification for gateway-related files. This counter increments by one every time the TFTP server performs a new build of the configuration files (not when the notification request is received).
BuildOneChangeNotifications — This counter is added in CallManager release 3.3(3).	The number of times the TFTP server built a configuration file for one device, for example a particular phone. This counter increments by one every time the TFTP server builds a configuration file for a device (not when the notification request is received).
BuildStartTime — This counter is added in CallManager release 3.3(3).	The time that the last build of file(s) started, expressed as the number of milliseconds elapsed since midnight, January 1, 1970 (Epoch time). The tool, CDR Time Converter, described in Chapter 3 provides a quick and easy way to convert this number to a standard date and time format.
HeartBeat	This represents the heartbeat of the TFTP server. This is an incremental count that indicates that the TFTP server is alive and running. If the count does not increment, then the TFTP server is down (dead).
ChangeNotifications/ TotalChangeNotifications	The total number of CallManager database change notifications handled by the TFTP server. Each time a device configuration is updated in CallManager Administration, the TFTP server is sent a database change notification to rebuild the XML file for the updated device.
RequestsInProgress — This counter is added in CallManager release 3.3(3).	The number of file requests currently being processed by the TFTP server. This counter increments for each new file request and decrements for each file request successfully sent. This counter gives you an indication of the current load of the TFTP server.

continues

Table D-26 *Cisco TFTP Counters (Continued)*

Counter Name as of Release 3.3(3)/ Counter Name Through Release 3.3(2)	Description
SegmentsAcknowledged/ TotalSegmentsAcknowledged	The total number of data segments acknowledged by the client devices. Files are sent to the requesting device in data segments of 512 bytes and for each 512-byte segment, the device sends the TFTP server an acknowledgment message. Each additional data segment is sent upon receipt of the acknowledgment message until the complete file has been successfully transmitted to the requesting device.
SegmentsSent/TotalSegmentsSent	The total number of data segments sent by the TFTP server. Files are sent to the requesting device in data segments of 512 bytes.
StartTime — In CallManager release 3.3(3), this counter will be removed. See the counter, BuildStartTime instead.	The time that the TFTP server started, expressed as the number of milliseconds elapsed since midnight, January 1, 1970 (Epoch time). The tool, CDR Time Converter, described in Chapter 3 provides a quick and easy way to convert this number to a standard date and time format.
TFTPRequests/TotalTftpRequests	The total number of file requests (such as requests for XML configuration files, phone firmware files, audio files, and so on) handled by the TFTP server. This counter represents the sum total of the following counters since the TFTP service started: TFTPRequestsProcessed, TFTPRequestsNotFound, TFTPRequestsOverflow, TFTPRequestsAborted.
TFTPRequestsAborted/ TotalTftpRequestsAborted	The total number of TFTP requests that were canceled (aborted) unexpectedly by the TFTP server. Requests could be aborted if the requesting device cannot be reached (for instance, the device lost power) or if the file transfer was interrupted due to network connectivity problems.
TFTPRequestsNotFound/ TotalTftpRequestsNotFound	The total number of TFTP requests where the requested file was not found. When the TFTP server does not find the requested file, an error message is sent to the requesting device.

Table D-26 *Cisco TFTP Counters (Continued)*

Counter Name as of Release 3.3(3)/ Counter Name Through Release 3.3(2)	Description
TFTPRequestsOverflow/ TotalTftpRequestsOverFlow	The total number of TFTP requests that were rejected because the maximum number of allowable client connections was exceeded, or because of some other resource limitation. The maximum number of allowable connections is set in the Cisco TFTP advanced service parameter, Maximum Serving Count. This counter increments if the TFTP service is currently building configuration files because the TFTP service denies all requests while rebuilding files.
TFTPRequestsProcessed/ TotalTftpRequestsLocal	The total number of TFTP requests successfully processed by the TFTP server.

Cisco Transcode Device Object

The counters discussed in this section provide information about registered transcoder resource availability.

Table D-27 lists all the counters under the Cisco Transcode Device object and describes what each counter represents.

Table D-27 *Cisco Transcode Device Counters*

Counter	Description
OutOfResources	The total number of times an attempt was made to allocate a transcoder resource from this transcoder device and failed—for example, because all resources were already in use.
ResourceActive	The number of transcoder resources that are currently in use (active) for this transcoder device.
ResourceAvailable	The total number of transcoder resources that are not active and are still available to be used at the current time for this transcoder device.

Cisco Unicast Hardware Conference Object

The name of this object changed in CallManager release 3.3(2). For counter descriptions applicable through CallManager release 3.3(2), see the section, "Cisco HW Conference Bridge Device—Release 3.3(2)."

Cisco Unicast Software Conference Bridge Device Object—Through Release 3.3(1)

The counters discussed in this section provide information about unicast software conference resource availability. Starting in CallManager release 3.3(2), this object name changes to Cisco SW Conference Bridge Device. See the section, "Cisco SW Conference Bridge Device Object—Release 3.3(2)" for counter descriptions. The counters themselves remain the same across the releases, just the object name changes.

Cisco WebAttendant Object—Through Release 3.3(1)

Starting in CallManager release 3.3(2), this object is called Cisco CallManager Attendant Console. See the section, "Cisco CallManager Attendant Console Object" for counter descriptions.

Windows 2000 Objects

In addition to the objects included with CallManager, several objects are included as part of Windows 2000 Server. Some of these objects and their counters prove useful when you're troubleshooting high CPU utilization problems and/or memory utilization problems.

Although covering each object and counter that comes standard with Windows 2000 is beyond the scope of this chapter, Table D-28 lists some of the more useful counters. You can find complete information about Windows counters in the Windows 2000 Performance Counter Reference (Counters.chm) on the Windows 2000 Resource Kit companion disc.

Table D-28   *Subset of Windows 2000 Counters*

Object	Counter	Description
Memory	Available Mbytes	The amount of physical memory, in megabytes, available to processes running on the computer. This counter displays the last observed value only; it is not an average. Note that this does not include virtual memory in use.
Process	% Processor Time	Similar to the Processor object and % Processor Time counter, except that you can set this counter to indicate the processor utilization by a single process by selecting a process instance.
Process	Private Bytes	The total amount of physical memory in bytes that cannot be shared with other processes used by the selected process instance.
Process	Virtual Bytes	The total amount of both physical and virtual memory used by the selected process instance.
Processor	Processor Time	The percentage of processor time spent executing nonidle threads, or simply the system's total CPU utilization.

This glossary lists terms and acronyms that are applicable to this book. You can find additional information at the following location:

www.cisco.com/univercd/cc/td/doc/product/voice/evbugl4.htm

GLOSSARY

SYMBOL

μs. microseconds.

μ-law. A North American standard for converting analog data into digital form using pulse code modulation.

A

AAR. Automatic Alternate Routing. A CallManager feature that allows you to automatically reroute calls when not enough WAN bandwidth is available. Works in conjunction with locations-based call admission control.

ACELP. Algebraic Code Excited Linear Prediction. An algorithm used to compress human voice before it is transmitted over a packet network.

ACOM. Combined loss. The total echo return loss seen across an echo canceller's terminals. It is the sum of ERL and ERLE.

acoustic echo. A form of echo that occurs when the acoustic energy from a device such as a handset, headset, or speakerphone enters the microphone of the same device.

AD. Active Directory. A Windows 2000 LDAP directory service.

ad hoc. Improvised or impromptu.

Ad Hoc conference. A type of conference in the CallManager system that requires a user (called the conference controller) to include conference attendees by calling them individually. See also *Meet-Me conference*.

AIM. Advanced Integration Module. A variety of modules available for Cisco IOS routers and voice gateways that provide additional functionality such as voice DSP resources.

A-law. A European standard for converting analog data into digital form using pulse code modulation.

algorithmic delay. The look-ahead delay that occurs when a coder (such as G.729) tries to compress a block of audio. The coder looks at the subsequent audio block to make the calculation for the current sample. This means that the current sample must be delayed by the amount of the look-ahead time before being compressed. G.729 has an algorithmic delay of 5 ms, and G.723.1 has an algorithmic delay of 7.5 ms.

ANI. Automatic number identification (also known as calling party number). A service that provides the phone number of an incoming call.

ANSI. American National Standards Institute.

API. Application programming interface. Usually a set of libraries with accompanying header files that application programmers can use in their programs to interact with a third-party application.

ARP. Address resolution protocol. Allows a device on an IP network to obtain the Layer 2 address (MAC address) of a device on its local subnet using that device's IP address.

ASCII. American Standard Code for Information Interchange. A code for representing English characters as numbers, with each letter assigned a number from 0 to 127. Directory numbers in CCM trace files are represented in ASCII.

ASIC. Application-specific integrated circuit. A chip designed for a particular application.

ASN.1. Abstract Syntax Notation. Used to encode messages in various protocols, including H.225 and H.245.

ASP. Active server page. A web page that uses ActiveX scripting to dynamically control the Web page's content. Cisco CallManager Administration relies on active server pages.

B

B-channel. Bearer channel. A fundamental component of ISDN interfaces. It carries 64 kbps in both directions, is circuit-switched, and can carry either voice or data.

bandwidth. A measurement of the amount of data per unit of time that a communications interface can send or receive.

BAT. Bulk Administration Tool. A web-based tool bundled with CallManager that allows you to add, update, or delete large numbers of users and devices in the CallManager database.

BDPU. Bridge protocol data unit. Used by LAN switches participating in the Spanning Tree Protocol to discover the network topology to ensure a loop-free bridged network.

bit mask. A string of bits that each represent a particular trace setting. Commonly used in SDL tracing.

blind transfer. A form of transfer whereby the user redirects a call to another extension without speaking to the party where the call is being redirected. See also *consultation transfer.*

BootP. Bootstrap protocol.

BRI. Basic Rate Interface. The basic ISDN configuration consisting of two B-channels that can each carry voice or data at a rate of 64 kbps and one D-channel that carries call control information.

C

call admission control (CAC). Ensures that voice QoS is maintained across constricted WAN links and automatically diverts calls to alternative PSTN routes when WAN bandwidth is unavailable. There are two types of CAC: locations-based CAC and gatekeeper CAC. CAC is used in situations where there is a limited amount of bandwidth between telephony endpoints such as phones and gateways.

call leg ID. Call leg identifier. A value appearing in CCM traces and CDRs, unique among all CallManager nodes in a cluster, that identifies each participant in a call.

calling search space. An ordered list of partitions used by CallManager digit analysis to decide which endpoint to extend a call to.

CallManager. A Cisco AVVID IP Telephony service whose primary function is the control and routing of calls to and from voice-enabled IP devices.

CAM table. Content Addressable Memory table. A table maintained by Layer 2 network switches that maps a MAC address to the port where the MAC address was learned.

CAR. CDR Analysis and Reporting tool. A web-based tool bundled with CallManager Serviceability that helps you analyze the raw data that comprises the CDR database and create reports based on your search criteria.

CAS. Channel-associated signaling. See *robbed-bit signaling*.

CatOS. Cisco Catalyst operating system. The operating system that runs on Catalyst 4000, 5000, and 6000 series LAN switches.

CBL. Color block logic. The ability of a LAN switch with VLAN support to block all packets on a particular VLAN from entering or exiting a particular port while allowing traffic for other VLANs to pass. Cisco IP Phones do *not* have CBL.

CBR. Constant bit rate.

CCAPI. Call control application programming interface. The call routing engine in Cisco IOS voice gateways.

CCC. Cisco Conference Connection. A Meet-Me audio conference server that integrates with CallManager.

CCM. An abbreviation of Cisco CallManager.

CCMAdmin. A shortened term for Cisco CallManager Administration.

CCO. Cisco Connection Online. Cisco's web site for product information, customer support, and distribution of software: Cisco.com.

CDCC. Call-Dependent Call Control. A CDCC process is created inside CallManager for every instance of a call.

CDP. Cisco Discovery Protocol.

CDR. Call detail record. A record that CallManager logs after a call completes to permit billing or auditing of system use.

CDR Analysis and Reporting Tool. See CAR.

CDR data. The grouping of CDRs and CMRs.

central office. A telecommunications office centralized in a specific locality to handle the telephone service for that locality.

CFA. Call Forward All.

CFB. Call Forward Busy.

CFF. Call Forward on Failure.

CFNA. Call Forward No Answer.

CGI. Common gateway interface. A standard method of interacting with a web server for requests and responses.

CID. callID.

CIP. Cisco IP Phone.

CIPT. Cisco IP Telephony.

CIR. Committed information rate. The amount of bandwidth a service provider guarantees over a Frame Relay network without dropping packets.

Cisco AVVID IP Telephony. The IP Telephony feature of the Cisco Architecture for Voice, Video, and Integrated Data.

Cisco CallManager Administration. The web-based interface to CallManager. CallManager Administration allows you to add, update, or delete users, devices, and the system configuration for CallManager.

Cisco CallManager node. See *Cisco CallManager server*.

Cisco CallManager server. A Cisco-certified Windows 2000 server that is running CallManager software.

Cisco CallManager User Options. A website that users can access to make changes to their IP phone's configuration, including setting or canceling Call Forward All designations, managing speed dials, and managing IP phone service subscriptions.

CLI. Command-line interface.

closest-match routing. A call routing feature whereby CallManager matches the dialed number that has the most explicit route pattern match. The most explicit match is selected based on the number of possible matches that could occur for a given pattern.

CM. An abbreviation of CallManager.

CMI. Cisco Messaging Interface. Allows a CallManager cluster to integrate with third-party voice mail systems using the SMDI protocol.

CMM. Communications Media Module.

CMR. Call management record (also known as a diagnostic record). A record that CallManager logs that provides information about the media session on which a device participated.

CNAME. Canonical name. A record created on a DNS server that serves as an alias for another DNS address. For example, a CNAME entry can be created for Cisco.com that points to the DNS record www.cisco.com.

CO. See *central office*.

codec. Coder-decoder. A media-encoding scheme by which an end device encodes speech or visual information into a digital representation for transmission across a media connection and decodes the digital representation into speech or visual information for playback by the recipient.

coder delay. The time taken by the DSP to compress a block of PCM samples. Because different coders work in different ways, this delay varies with processor speed and the voice codec used. Also known as processing delay. A form of fixed delay.

comfort noise. A small amount of quiet noise during a phone conversation, usually characterized as a slight hiss on the line. Comfort noise makes users feel like there is still someone on the other end of the line, even when no one is speaking.

conference controller. The user who calls the first conference attendee (in the case of Ad Hoc conferencing) or who establishes the Meet-Me conference number.

consultation transfer. A form of transfer whereby the user discusses the redirected call with the intended recipient before completing the transfer operation.

CoR. Class of restriction. A Cisco IOS Software feature that provides the ability to deny certain call attempts based on who originates the call.

CoS. Class of service. Any form of Layer 2 quality of service marking. For Ethernet, this is typically 802.1p priority bits.

CPU. Central processing unit. The chip or chips inside a computer that execute the instructions that permit applications to function.

CRA. Cisco Customer Response Applications. A suite of CTI-based applications including IP AA, IP IVR, and IP ICD.

crosstalk. When the electrical energy in an analog circuit where the receive and transmit pairs are separate "leaks" from one side to the other because of inductance between the two pairs of wires.

cRTP. Compressed RTP.

CS-ACELP. Conjugate Structure Algebraic Code Excited Linear Prediction. An algorithm used to compress human voice before it is transmitted over a packet network.

CSV. Comma-separated value. A type of file in which commas are used to separate individual fields of a complex data record and new lines indicate the end of an individual record.

CTI. Computer telephony integration. A set of protocols that allow a call processing engine such as Cisco CallManager to integrate with third-party applications. TAPI and JTAPI are examples of CTI protocols.

CUG. Closed User Group. A restricted group of users on an ISDN network. Members of a specific CUG can communicate among themselves but not with users outside the group.

D

D-channel. Data channel. In an ISDN interface, the D-channel is used to carry control signals and customer call data in a packet-switched mode. In a BRI, the D-channel runs at 16 kbps. In a PRI, the D-channel runs at 64 kbps.

dB. decibel.

DBL. Database layer. A set of software components that provide a programming interface to the SQL database containing all the CallManager configuration information.

DDI. Digit discard instruction. A form of called-number transformation that, with one exception, works only when used with the @ wildcard (the exception is the PreDot DDI).

dejitter buffer. A feature on any VoIP end-point that transforms variable delay into a fixed delay by holding the first sample received for a period of time before playing it.

delay. A voice quality issue. The amount of time it takes the sound from a talker's mouth to reach the far-end listener's ear.

DHCP. Dynamic Host Configuration Protocol. A network service whose primary purpose is to automatically assign IP addresses to new devices that connect to the network or existing devices that reconnect to the network.

Dick Tracy. A tool used to troubleshoot problems on various gateways based on MGCP or the Skinny protocol.

DID. Direct inward dial. A type of central office trunk that provides additional routing information on incoming calls. DID allows trunk calls to be routed directly to a specific directory number instead of being routed to a common attendant.

DN. Directory number. The numerical address assigned to an endpoint such as a phone, gateway port, or route point within an enterprise.

DNIS. Digital Number Identification Service (also known as the called party number). The digits for the phone number being dialed.

DNS. Domain Name System. A network service whose primary function is to convert fully qualified domain names (textual) into numerical IP addresses and vice versa.

DOD. Direct outward dialing. A service that permits a device in the enterprise to place calls directly to the public network.

doubletalk. Occurs when both parties on a call talk at the same time.

DRAM. Dynamic RAM.

DSCP. Differentiated Services Code Point, or DiffServ CodePoint. A marker in the header of each IP packet that prompts network routers and switches to apply differentiated grades of service to various packet streams.

DSP. Digital signal processor. A specialized type of CPU used for computationally in-tensive tasks. CallManager uses DSP resources to process voice streams. For example, DSPs are used to transcode voice and join multiple streams into a conference.

DSP farm. An IP endpoint with a large number of DSP resources for providing services such as conferencing and transcoding.

DTMF. Dual-Tone Multifrequency. A common tone-signaling method used by touchtone phones in which two pure frequencies are superimposed.

E

E1. A digital trunk specification that permits the transfer of 2.048 Mbps of information.

E.164 address. A fully qualified numerical address for a device attached to a national network. The ITU-T specification E.164 defines the framework in which nations manage their national numbering plans.

E&M. Ear and Mouth. A trunking arrangement generally used for two-way switch-to-switch or switch-to-network connections.

echo canceller. A device or system that reduces or eliminates echoes in voice transmission systems.

echo canceller coverage. The maximum length of the tail circuit the echo canceller converges on.

EIA/TIA. Electronics Industries Alliance (www.eia.org)/Telecommunications Industry Association (www.tiaonline.org).

EIGRP. Enhanced Interior Gateway Routing Protocol.

enbloc sending. A method of sending a call setup where the complete called party number is sent as part of the setup message.

endpoint. A device or software application that provides real-time, two-way com-munication for users.

ER. Cisco Emergency Responder. An application that lets emergency agencies identify the location of 911 callers and eliminates the need for any administration when IP phones move from one location to another.

ERL. Echo return loss. The echo level loss provided by the tail circuit.

ERLE. Echo return loss enhancement. A measure of returning echo attenuation through the echo canceller.

ESF. Extended Superframe. See also *robbed-bit signaling*.

Ethernet. A LAN architecture that uses a bus or star topology and supports data transfer rates of 10 Mbps. CallManager uses a newer version of Ethernet called 100BASE-T or Fast Ethernet, which supports data transfer rates of 100 Mbps. See also *Fast Ethernet* and *Gigabit Ethernet*.

ETSI. European Telecommunications Standards Institute.

extension mobility. A CallManager feature that allows a user to log in to any extension mobility-enabled 7960/7940 IP Phone. After a user logs in, the IP Phone downloads all the information related to the device profile, in effect becoming the user's personalized phone, including line number, calling search spaces, speed dials, and services.

F

failback. The process whereby devices in a Cisco IP Telephony network register themselves to their primary CallManager node when it becomes available after a failover to a backup CallManager node.

failover. The process whereby devices in a Cisco IP Telephony network register themselves to the backup CallManager nodes if they lose their connection to their primary CallManager. Phones open a connection to the backup CallManager at the same time they register to the primary CallManager so that they can failover faster.

fallback. The process of offering a call to a less-desirable route after all desirable routes have been exhausted.

fast busy. See *reorder tone*.

Fast Ethernet. A LAN architecture that supports data transfer rates of 100 Mbps. See also *Ethernet* and *Gigabit Ethernet*.

FAQ. Frequently asked question.

Fax Group 3. A standards-based technology that is made up primarily of the T.4 and T.30 ITU recommendations. T.4 pertains to how the fax image is encoded by a fax device, and T.30 details the fax negotiations and communication protocol. Group 3 fax devices are designed for use over the PSTN.

fax passthrough. A method of sending faxes through a voice codec. In a Cisco IP Telephony network, G.711 is currently the only codec that supports fax passthrough.

fax relay. A protocol used by fax devices that terminates the modulated fax signal, extracts the digital information, and then relays the digital information through the data network using data packets.

firewall. A computer system placed at the junction between a private computer network and other computer networks. It is designed to protect systems of a private network from users in the other networks.

fixed delay. Delays in a call that are constant for every call regardless of varying network conditions. See also *coder delay, packetization delay, propagation delay,* and *serialization delay*.

FLP. Fast Link Pulse.

forwarding loop. A condition caused when calls are routed back and forth between two endpoints in an endless loop.

fractional PRI. A T1 or E1 PRI where only a fraction of the B-channels are provisioned to carry voice or data traffic. The remaining B-channels are unused. As of release 3.3, CallManager does not support fractional PRIs.

FXO. Foreign Exchange Office. A VoIP gateway providing analog access to the central office's line termination.

FXS. Foreign Exchange Station. A VoIP gateway providing analog access to a POTS station.

G

G.711. A simple codec used to encode voice communications that requires 64 kbps bandwidth.

G.723. A codec used to encode voice communications that requires either 5.3 or 6.3 kbps bandwidth.

G.729. A codec used to encode voice communications that requires 8 kbps bandwidth.

gatekeeper CAC. Uses an H.323 gatekeeper to control the number of calls between multiple CallManager clusters. See also *call admission control (CAC)*.

Gb. Gigabit.

Gigabit Ethernet. A LAN architecture that supports data transfer rates of 1 Gbps (1000 Mbps). See also *Ethernet* and *Fast Ethernet*.

glare. A condition that occurs when two devices attempt to seize the same trunk at the same time. Glare is common when both sides are configured to use Bottom-Up or Top-Down because both sides are trying to use the channels in the same order.

GSM. Global system for mobile communications. The codec used to compress voice samples on GSM cellular phones.

H

H.323. A recommendation from ITU-T that contains a complex set of protocols designed to facilitate media communication sessions over an IP network.

hair pinning. See *tromboning*.

HDSM. High-Density Service Module.

HDV. High-Density Voice Module.

held party. The party who is placed on hold.

hexadecimal (hex). Refers to the base-16 number system, which consists of 16 unique symbols: the numbers 0 to 9 and the letters A to F. IP addresses in CCM trace files are sometimes represented in hex.

holding party. The party who initiates a hold action.

HTTP. Hypertext Transfer Protocol. A simple, stateless request/response protocol that is used at the application level.

hub. An Ethernet device that repeats Ethernet packets accepted on one port and transmits them on all other ports of the hub.

hybrid. A telephony device that converts two-wire analog circuits to four-wire analog circuits.

I

ICCP. Intracluster Control Protocol. A signaling protocol used by CallManager servers to communicate runtime data.

ICMP. Internet Control Message Protocol. A protocol that supports packets containing error, control, and informational messages.

IE. Information element. Carries a specific piece of information within a Q.931 or H.225 message.

IE. See *Internet Explorer*.

IEEE. Institute of Electrical and Electronics Engineers.

IETF. Internet Engineering Task Force. The main standards organization for the Internet.

IIS. Internet Information Server. A Microsoft service designed to permit users to create and manage Internet services such as web servers.

in-band. The exchange of call control information on the same channel as the telephone call or data transmission.

initial playout delay. The process of holding the first voice sample received for a period of time before playing it. Used for the dejitter buffer.

inside dial tone. The initial dial tone provided when a user goes off-hook on an IP phone.

intercluster trunk. A virtual trunk connecting CallManager clusters. An intercluster trunk uses the H.323 protocol to communicate between CallManager clusters.

interdigit timeout. The number of seconds CallManager delays routing a call if an immediate pattern match is not made when a user dials a phone number.

Internet Explorer. Microsoft's version of a web browser.

IP. Internet protocol. A Layer 3 protocol used by one computer to communicate packets of information to another computer on a network.

IP AA. IP Auto Attendant. An application designed to distribute calls by automated means. Part of CRA.

IP ICD. IP Integrated Contact Distribution. A voice application that provides call center functionality by queuing and delivering calls to agents. Part of CRA.

IP IVR. IP Interactive Voice Response. A voice application that provides a telephone user interface and that can retrieve data and redirect calls. Part of CRA.

IP Telephony. The implementation of telephony over a data network using the IP Layer 3 protocol.

IP/VC. Cisco IP videoconferencing. Enables videoconferencing over IP networks.

ISDN. Integrated Services Digital Network. An international communications standard for sending voice, video, and data over digital telephone lines or normal telephone wires.

ITU. International Telecommunications Union.

ITU-T. ITU Telecommunications Standardization Sector.

IXC. Interexchange carrier, or long distance company. A company whose chief responsibility is the interconnection of local exchange carriers.

J–K

jitter. The difference in time between a packet's expected arrival time and the time the packet actually arrives. Also called variable delay.

JTAPI. Java Telephony Application Programming Interface. A CTI protocol that allows applications to use CallManager's call control functionality.

kbps. Kilobits per second.

L

LAN. Local-area network. A high-speed, low-error data network covering a relatively small geographic area (up to a few thousand meters). LANs connect workstations, peripherals, terminals, and other devices in a single building or other geographically limited area. LAN standards specify cabling and signaling at the OSI model's physical and data link layers. Ethernet, Fast Ethernet, and Gigabit Ethernet are widely used LAN technologies.

LCD. Liquid crystal display.

LDAP. Lightweight Directory Access Protocol. A protocol that defines a programming interface that can be used to access computer-based directories. LDAP directories are a specialized format of database that is often used to hold user information in large organizations. CallManager uses an LDAP directory to store user information.

legacy. Using established, possibly outdated, methods.

LFI. Link fragmentation and interleaving.

line appearance. A logical entity on a phone or gateway that can terminate calls, often associated with a particular button on a phone. Line appearances have addresses called DNs.

listener echo. A form of echo in which one party in the call hears the other person's words repeated.

LLQ. Low Latency Queuing.

loading coil. A device used when the local loop is longer than 18,000 feet to compensate for the capacitance of such a long cable run.

locations-based CAC. A feature in CallManager that limits the number of calls between devices registered to a single CallManager cluster. See *call admission control (CAC)*.

logical channel. A network pathway that carries a streaming data connection between two endpoints.

M

MAC address. Media Access Control address. A hardware address that uniquely identifies a device.

MAN. Metropolitan-area network. A network that spans a metropolitan area. Generally, a MAN spans a larger geographic area than a LAN but a smaller geographic area than a WAN.

mask. A CallManager call routing feature that provides specific number presentation and digit manipulation. Masks format a calling or called party number in a specific way.

MCS. Media Convergence Server. A Cisco-certified server that comes preinstalled with the components that comprise Cisco AVVID IP Telephony.

media resource. A network device that terminates a media stream to provide some service to IP telephony endpoints such as IP phones and voice gateways.

Meet-Me conference. A type of conference that allows attendees to dial into the conference after a user (called the conference controller) has created the conference. See also *Ad Hoc conference*.

MFT. Multi-Flex Trunk. Interface cards for Cisco IOS voice gateways and routers used to terminate a T1 or E1 connection.

MGCP. Media Gateway Control Protocol. A UDP-based, plain-text, master/slave protocol whereby a call agent—in this case, CallManager—controls the function of a particular gateway. Messages are sent as ASCII-encoded text.

MGCP package. A grouping of the events and signals supported by a particular type of MGCP endpoint.

MH. Modified Huffman. A compression and encoding method for fax images. MH usually compresses at a 20:1 ratio.

MIVR. Multimedia Interactive Voice Response. A type of trace file for CRA.

MLP. Multilink Point-to-Point Protocol. A method of splitting, recombining, and sequencing datagrams across multiple logical data links. MLP allows packets to be fragmented and the fragments to be sent at the same time over multiple point-to-point links to the same remote address.

most-significant bit. The first bit of a binary number.

MR. Modified Read. A compression and encoding method for fax images. MR encoding typically provides a 20 percent compression improvement over MH but is slightly less resilient to errors.

ms. Milliseconds.

msec. Milliseconds.

MTP. Media termination point. A device that terminates a media stream for the purpose of allowing the stream to be redirected.

MWI. Message waiting indicator. An audible or visual alert that signals a user to the presence of a new voice mail message.

N

NANP. North American Numbering Plan. The default numbering plan that ships with CallManager. It applies to the United States and Canada.

NAT. Network Address Translation. An Internet standard that lets a LAN use one set of IP addresses for internal traffic and a second set of addresses for external traffic.

network hold. A type of hold operation whereby the user invokes a feature operation such as transfer, conference, or call park that requires CallManager to place the call on hold while performing the feature operation. See also *user hold*.

NLP. Nonlinear processor.

NM. Network module.

no-way audio. A voice quality problem in which no audio is heard on both sides of a conversation, even though the participants are speaking.

NTP. Network Time Protocol. An Internet standard protocol (built on top of TCP/IP) that ensures accurate synchronization to the millisecond of computer clock times in a network of computers.

O

off-hook. Literally, the action of removing the handset from the hookswitch. In modern telephony, this term indicates that the phone is no longer in the idle state. On Cisco IP Phones, off-hook can be accomplished in many ways, not limited to the following: lifting the handset, pressing the **Speaker** button, and pressing the **Answer** or **NewCall** soft keys.

OffNet. A term applied to calls between the enterprise and another telephone network (generally the PSTN).

one-way audio. A voice-quality problem in which one side of the conversation cannot hear the other.

on-hook. Literally, the action of returning the handset to the hookswitch. In modern telephony, this term indicates that the phone has returned to the idle state. On Cisco IP Phones, on-hook can be accomplished in many ways, not limited to the following: returning the handset to the cradle, pressing the **Speaker** button, and pressing the **EndCall** soft key.

OnNet. A term applied to calls that are placed and received within the same enterprise.

open trees. A general auto attendant greeting on a voice mail system.

OS. Operating system. Software running on a hardware platform that gives other applications access to the resources (such as processor, memory, and network interfaces) that the hardware platform provides.

OSI. Open System Interconnection. An ISO standard for worldwide communications that defines a networking framework for implementing protocols in seven layers.

OSPF. Open Shortest Path First.

out-of-band. The exchange of call control information on a different channel than the telephone call or data transmission.

outside dial tone. For OffNet calls, the dial tone (sometimes called the secondary dial tone) provided when a user goes off-hook and dials an access code on an IP phone.

overlap receiving. Allows the PSTN to send a setup message with only part of the called party number.

overlap sending. Allows CallManager to send a setup message to the PSTN with only part of the called party number.

P–Q

PA. Personal Assistant. An application that works with CallManager. It is designed to permit a user to customize call forwarding behavior based on who is calling and to locate a user given multiple possible destinations.

packet loss concealment. A Cisco IOS Software feature in which lost scan lines in fax images are repeated to spoof the receiving fax machine into believing that it is receiving all the data.

packetization delay. The time taken to fill a packet payload with encoded/compressed speech and add the various IP/UDP/RTP headers. A form of fixed delay.

page transmission. Occurs when the training part of the fax negotiation phase is complete. The page information is coded into scan lines with a standard resolution of 203H × 98V dots per inch. Fax images are typically compressed and encoded using either Modified Huffman (MH) or Modified Read (MR) encoding.

parser. A program that breaks an input stream into syntactic elements. Cisco IP Phones have an XML parser that breaks out individual element values for the phone's firmware.

partition. A group of directory numbers and route patterns used to divide a route plan into subsets.

PAT. Port Address Translation. A feature that lets you address hosts on a LAN with inside local addresses and filter them through one globally routable IP address.

PBX. Private branch exchange. A small phone system located at a customer site. The PBX is used to supplement or replace functionality that might normally be provided by a central office.

PC. Personal computer.

PCM. Pulse code modulation. A sampling technique for digitizing analog signals, especially audio signals.

PerfMon. Microsoft Performance. An administrative tool provided by the Windows 2000 operating system used to monitor a variety of performance objects.

performance object. A set of counters reported by a process or application running on the system that can be monitored using PerfMon or the RTMT.

PIM. Power interface module.

PLAR. Private line automatic ringdown. A call routing feature whereby a phone immediately places a call to a specified destination when taken off-hook.

playout delay. Also known as jitter buffer size. The amount of time packets are stored in the jitter buffer before being played out to the listener.

POTS. Plain old telephone service. Generally used to refer to the PSTN.

POTS dial peer. Defines the characteristics of a traditional telephony network connection on a Cisco IOS voice gateway. The POTS dial peer maps a dial string to a specific voice port on the local gateway. Normally, the voice port connects the gateway to the local PSTN, a PBX, or an analog telephone.

power cycle. To reset a device by interrupting and restoring power to it.

PPP. Point-to-Point Protocol.

pps. Packets per second.

PRI. Primary Rate Interface. A type of ISDN service designed for large organizations. Includes B-channels (bearer channels) for voice or data and one D-channel (data channel) for signaling. PRI comprises 23 B-channels in North America and 30 B-channels in Europe.

propagation delay. The amount of time it takes for a single bit of data to get from one side of a digital connection to the other. A form of fixed delay.

PSAP. Public Safety Answering Point. A physical location where 911 emergency telephone calls are received and then are routed to the proper emergency services. Used in CIPT in conjunction with Cisco ER.

PSTN. Public Switched Telephone Network. The international phone system.

Publisher. The master database in a CallManager cluster.

PVC. Permanent virtual circuit. A virtual circuit that is permanently available. Usually refers to a virtual connection through a service provider's Frame Relay or ATM network.

PVDM. Packet Voice/Data Module.

Q.931. An ITU-T specification that defines the Layer 3 messages used on an ISDN circuit's D-channel.

QoS. Quality of service. A distributed multimedia system's traffic-management mechanisms that permit it to guarantee the transmission of coherent information. Such mechanisms include traffic classification, traffic prioritization, bandwidth management, and admissions control.

Q.Sig. A unified international corporate network signaling standard. As of CallManager release 3.3, Q.Sig is supported for basic call routing functionality. You can learn about the Q.Sig standards at the following link: www.qsig.ie/qsig/ad.htm.

R

RAS. Registration, Admission, and Status. A portion of the H.323 specification that defines a gatekeeper's operation.

RDNIS. Redirected dial number ID service (also called the redirecting party number or the original called party number). Typically used to convey information about the original called party to a voice mail system.

red alarm. On a digital interface such as T1, a remote alarm that informs the other side that it is not receiving any framing. See also *yellow alarm*.

reorder tone. A fast, cyclical tone that CallManager uses to indicate some sort of problem during call establishment. Commonly called fast busy.

reset. A command that causes a device to completely power-cycle and begin the registration process again as if it had just been plugged in.

restart. A command that tells a device to unregister and then reregister with CallManager.

RFC. Request for Comments. A series of notes about the Internet dating from 1969.

ringback. The tone heard at the calling party's end when the called party's phone rings.

robbed-bit signaling. Also known as channel-associated signaling (CAS), this is called robbed-bit signaling because some bits from each T1 speech bearer channel are "robbed" and used for signaling. On a T1 with

Superframe (SF) framing, these are called the A and B bits, whereas a T1 with Extended Superframe (ESF) framing has A, B, C, and D bits. A gateway uses these bits to indicate on-hook, off-hook, and ringing.

route filter. A call routing feature used with numbering plans when using the @ wildcard.

route pattern. Represents one or more strings of dialed digits used to route a call to a particular destination.

rsh. Remote shell. A protocol used to establish a remote terminal session to a Cisco IOS device.

RSVP. Resource Reservation Protocol. An Internet protocol that supports the reservation of resources across an IP network.

RTCP. Real time control protocol; the control protocol that works in conjunction with RTP. RTCP control packets are periodically transmitted by each participant in an RTP session to all other participants. Feedback of information to the application can be used to control performance and for diagnostic purposes.

RTMT. Real-Time Monitoring Tool. A web-based application bundled with CallManager Serviceability that provides up-to-the-second information about the state of a CallManager cluster.

RTP. Real-Time Transport Protocol. An Internet-standard protocol for the transport of real-time data, including audio and video.

RU. Rack unit.

S

SABME. Set Asynchronous Balanced Mode Extended.

SCCP. See *Skinny protocol*.

SDI. System Diagnostic Interface.

SDK. Software Development Kit. A set of programming interfaces and documentation provided to programmers seeking to interface with a given operating system, application, or other product.

SDP. Session Description Protocol. Defined in RFC 2327.

secondary line. Any line appearance on a station other than the primary.

serialization delay. The delay required to clock an IP packet out a network interface. It is directly related to the clock rate on the interface. A form of fixed delay.

service parameters. Settings on CallManager that take effect on a service-wide basis.

SF. Superframe. See also *robbed-bit signaling*.

SGCP. See *Skinny gateway protocol*.

SID. Silence Information Description.

sidetone. Occurs in almost every telephone device when some of the transmit signal is fed back into the earpiece so that the user can hear himself or herself speaking.

silence suppression. See *VAD*.

SIP. Session Initiation Protocol. A signaling protocol that initiates call setup, routing, authentication, and other feature messages to endpoints within an IP domain. SIP is used in some phones and gateways and might be added as a CallManager protocol in future releases.

Skinny client. A client using the Skinny protocol, such as a Cisco IP Phone.

Skinny gateway protocol. Skinny Gateway Control Protocol. A now-obsolete protocol used by gateway devices to communicate with CallManager.

Skinny protocol. Skinny Client Control Protocol. A protocol used by devices to communicate with CallManager. Commonly referred to as Skinny.

sniffer trace. A packet-capture tool that lets you see exactly what is happening on the network at any given time.

SOAP. Simple Object Access Protocol. A way for applications to communicate with each other over the Internet, independent of platform.

soft key. A context-sensitive digital display button on the bottom row of the display on Cisco IP Phones 7940 and 7960.

SQL. Structured Query Language. A standard language defined to permit reading from and writing to databases.

SRST. Survivable Remote Site Telephony. A software feature available in Cisco IOS that lets a router at a remote branch assume basic call processing responsibilities in the event that phones at a remote site are unable to contact the central CallManager.

SSAPI. Supplementary Services API. A messaging interface provided by CallManager to allow the CMI service to light message waiting indicators and to allow the Cisco Database Layer Monitor service to issue change notification commands.

ssh. Secure shell. A protocol that can be used to create a remote session to a Cisco IOS device. Uses encryption to secure the connection.

station. Any device that provides a user with a direct interface to a voice network.

StationD. A Skinny message sent from CallManager to an IP phone.

StationInit. A Skinny message sent from an IP phone to CallManager.

STP. Spanning Tree Protocol. A link-management protocol that is part of the IEEE 802.1 standard for media access control bridges used to prevent Layer 2 bridge loops.

stream. A one-way, active media session connected through a simplex (one-direction) logical channel from one device to another.

subnet. A portion of a network that shares a common address component. On TCP/IP networks, subnets are defined as all devices whose IP addresses have the same prefix. For example, all devices with IP addresses that start with 100.100.100. would be part of the same subnet.

Subscriber. One or more duplicate databases serving the CallManager system. Subscriber databases are updated with information from the Publisher database.

subscriber. A user of a (usually public) telephone network.

superuser. An account with superuser access has full control over the operating system and is allowed to access all system resources.

switchback. The process whereby devices unregister with one CallManager node and reregister with a higher-priority CallManager node. See *failback*.

switchover. A process whereby a secondary call agent assumes control of the call signaling and media control for a call that earlier was controlled by a different call agent. See *failover*.

T

T1 CAS. T1 channel-associated signaling. A dedicated phone connection supporting data rates of 1.544 Mbps using channel-associated signaling.

T1 PRI. T1 primary rate interface. A dedicated phone connection supporting data rates of 1.544 Mbps using an ISDN primary rate interface.

tail circuit. The part of the telephony network facing out from an echo canceller. In an
IP Telephony environment, the tail circuit encompasses everything from the voice gateway's connection to the PSTN all the way to the terminating phone.

tail circuit delay. The time between the point where the original audio signal exits the echo canceller and the time it returns as echo.

talker echo. A form of echo in which one party in the call hears himself or herself echoed.

TAPI. Telephony Application Programming Interface. An API for providing telephone services to applications running on the Microsoft Windows operating system.

TCD. Telephony Call Dispatcher. The server component of Cisco CallManager Attendant Console. TCD keeps track of line states for all the IP phones in the cluster and is responsible for accepting calls on pilot points and dispatching the calls to agents that are online using the Attendant Console.

TCP. Transmission Control Protocol. A connection-oriented protocol that provides for the reliable end-to-end, ordered delivery of IP packets.

TCP handle. A unique value in a CCM trace file that identifies a specific Skinny client registered to a specific CallManager server.

TDM. Time Division Multiplexing. A method of transporting information for multiple endpoints across a single interface that relies on assigning each endpoint a specific window of time when it has exclusive access to the interface.

TEI. Terminal Endpoint Identifier.

TELR. Talker Echo Loudness Rating.

TFTP. Trivial File Transfer Protocol. A User Datagram Protocol (UDP)-based protocol that permits the transmission of files between network devices.

TIA. Telecommunications Industry Association.

timestamp. The date and time listed at the beginning of a line in a debug or trace file that tells you the exact time when the event listed in the debug or trace occurred.

TLV. Type, Length, and Value.

token reject. A Skinny message sent by CallManager to an IP phone in response to a token request when it is too busy to accept a registration.

token request. A Skinny message sent by an IP phone to its primary CallManager before a failback to ensure that the primary CallManager can service the registration request.

training. A phase in fax machine negotiation that determines the speed at which a fax machine sends its information.

transactional replication. A form of database replication. An initial snapshot of the database is taken when the Subscriber first needs to replicate the database data, but from that point on, only database changes are replicated.

transcoder. A hardware device that allows devices with incompatible codecs to communicate with each other.

transformation. See *mask*.

translation pattern. A CallManager call routing feature that allows you to take an originally dialed number and change all or part of the calling and called number into another number. A translation pattern transforms the calling and called party numbers through the use of calling and called party transformations that are configured as part of the translation pattern.

tromboning. Also called *hair pinning*. A call comes in a gateway and is forwarded back out another channel on that (or a different) gateway, with the end result being that two channels are tied up. So named because the result is like a trombone's U shape.

TSV. Tab-separated value. A file format in which a record's individual data fields are separated by a tab character and records are separated by new lines.

U

UAf. Unnumbered Acknowledge frame.

UDP. User Datagram Protocol. A connectionless protocol that, like TCP, runs on top of IP networks.

UNC. Universal naming convention.

URL. Uniform resource locator.

user hold. A type of hold operation whereby the user presses the **Hold** soft key to put a call on hold. See also *network hold*.

User-User IE. An IE that carries H.323-specific information such as signaling IP addresses. The User-User IE is coded in a format called *ASN.1*.

UTP. Unshielded twisted pair.

UUIE. See *User-User IE*.

V

VAD. Voice activity detection (also called silence suppression). A CallManager feature that detects when there is silence in a conversation. With VAD enabled, the endpoint stops sending voice packets filled with silence and indicates to the far end that there is a silent period. Substantial bandwidth savings can be achieved by enabling VAD, although some voice-quality issues might arise.

variable delay. See *jitter*.

VIC. Voice interface card.

VLAN. Virtual local-area network.

VNC. Virtual Network Computing. A remote display system that allows you to view a remote desktop environment.

VoATM. Voice over Asynchronous Transfer Mode. Not supported by CallManager.

VoFR. Voice over Frame Relay. Not supported by CallManager.

VoIP. Voice over IP. The process of routing voice communications over a network running Internet Protocol.

VoIP dial peer. Defines the attributes of a packet voice network connection on a Cisco IOS voice gateway. A VoIP dial peer maps a dial string to a remote network device and also sets the network connection's attributes, such as the codec to use, the capability to do VAD, and DTMF relay configuration.

VoX. Voice over *X,* where *X* represents any one of the following protocols: IP, ATM, or Frame Relay.

vty. Virtual terminal. A terminal session created with a Cisco IOS device over the network as opposed to via the console port. Protocols such as Telnet, rsh, and ssh can be used to establish a vty session.

VWIC. Voice/WAN Interface Card.

W–X–Y–Z

WAN. Wide-area network. A data communications network that serves users across a broad geographic area and often uses transmission devices provided by common carriers.

web server. A server machine that provides dynamic or static content using HTTP.

wink. When the terminating side of a gateway using CAS is ready to receive the digits, it goes off-hook for approximately 200 ms and then goes back on-hook.

XML. Extensible markup language. The universal format for structured documents and data on the web.

yellow alarm. On a digital interface such as T1, an alarm that indicates that the side in yellow alarm is receiving frames that indicate that the far end is in red alarm. See also *red alarm.*

Symbols

! wildcard, 460
. wildcard, 461
@ wildcard, 461
    DDIs, 487–494
    route filters, 506–507
        multiple clauses, 512
        NANP tags, 508–510

Numerics

3-port switch operation, Cisco 79xx series IP phones, 161–164
7-digit local calls, delayed routing, 466–469
10-10-Dialing DDI, 487
10-10-Dialing Trailing-# DDI, 487
11/10D->7D DDI, 487
11/10D->7D Trailing-# DDI, 487
11D->10D DDI, 488
11D->10D Trailing-# DDI, 488
802.1Q protocol, 850
911 routing, Cisco ER, 478
6608 T1/E1 module
    configuring, 325–337
    D-channel establishment, 337, 340–343
        advanced troubleshooting, 344–359
    T1 CAS, 359–367
6624 Port FXS Analog Interface Module
    configuring, 367–379
7960/7940 IP Phones
    extension mobility, 756–758
        configuring, 758–763
        login/logout process, 763–765
        resolving common problems, 765–768, 772
79xx IP Phones
    3-port switch operation, 161–164
    network settings, 123–126

A

AA (Auto Attendant), 737
    traces, collecting, 748–752
AAR (automatic alternate routing), 478
acknowledgments, 238
ACOM (combined loss), 417
acoustic echo, isolating, 412
acquiring
    Dick Tracy tool, 105
    Q.931 Translator, 100
active connections, 155
AD (Active Directory)
    Customer Directory Configuration plugin, troubleshooting, 839–844
    LDAP integration, 837–839
Ad Hoc conferences, 565
    error messages, 597–598
    locations-based CAC bandwidth reservations, 633–635
adjusting
    fax relay data rate, 451–452
    interdigit timeout, 467
Administrative Reporting Tool (ART), 795
alarms
    configuring on CallManager Serviceability, 82
    StationAlarmMessage field definitions, 158–160
alerts
    configuring on CCEmail, 81
    enabling on PerfMon, 75
algorithmic delay, 386
"Already In Conference" error messages, troubleshooting, 597
analog gateways, VG248 SMDI integration, 686–692
Analog Ground Start, 850
Analog Loop Start, 850
analyzing collected data
    case study, 18–19
    CCM traces, 42, 50–57
        through MGCP T1 PRI gateways, 58–60
    CMI traces, 674–679
    deductive reasoning, 11–12
    ISDN traces, 258–262

calling name display, 270

cause codes, 262–269

numbering type/plan mismatches, 269–270

timer information, 271–276

locations-based CAC trace information, 628–631

SDL traces, 60–63

verifying IP network integrity, 12–13

Anlagenanschluss, 213

ANS (answer tone), 439

ANSI (American National Standards Institute) web site, 849

appearances, held calls, 524

applications

CallManager Serviceability, 82

alarms, 82

Control Center, 85

RTMT, 85–88

Service Activation, 84

traces, configuring, 83

CAR, 90

CCC, 790–791

CCEmail

alerting methods, 81

configuring, 76–80

Cisco Attendant Console, 779–780

client, 781–782

resolving common problems, 782–784

server components, 780–781

Cisco AVVID IP Telephony, 34

Cisco ER, 791

Cisco IP SoftPhone, 786–788

Cisco Personal Attendant, resolving call routing problems, 785–786

CRA, 736

CTI, 736

Dick Tracy, 101–104

CLI/embedded Tracy, 105

directory-enabled, 819–820

Enhanced Q.931 Translator, 98–100

Event Viewer, 91

alarm definitions, 92–93

PerfMon

alerts, 75

counter logging, 71–75

versus RTMT, 68–69

viewing real-time statistics, 69–71

Q.931 Translator, 95–97

VNC, 108

Windows Terminal Services, 107

applying transformations

cumulative effect, 497–499

order of application, importance of, 496–497

area codes

blocking, 548–549

versus local area code, 510

ART (Administrative Reporting Tool), 795

assigning calling search spaces to devices, 471–473

audio sources (MOH), 601–603

Audio Translator, troubleshooting, 618

live

selecting recording input, 620

troubleshooting, 619–620

mulitcast

troubleshooting, 616

versus unicast, 615

Audio Translator, troubleshooting, 618

automatic alternate routing (AAR), 478

automatic time synchronization, configuring on CallManager servers, 39

auto-registration, controlling with PLAR, 545–546

B

backhauling, 553

on MGCP PRI gateways, 256–258

backup CallManager, 154

BackupCallManagerName parameter (CMI), 667

bandwidth requirements, locations-based CAC, 624–626

BaudRate parameter (CMI), 667

best practices, troubleshooting Cisco IP Phones, 165–166

binary values, converting to decimal and hexadecimal values, 881–889

bit masks, 63

configuring for SDL traces, 63–67

blind transfers, 529–531

blocked calls, 473

blocking area codes, 548–549

buffering delay. *See* queueing delay

Bug Toolkit, 106–107
busy calls, forwarding, 480

C

CAC (call admission control), 24, 623
    gatekeeper CAC, 638
        call setup, 647–651
        CallManager registration, 645–647
        RAS messages, 639
        verifying configuration, 640–645
    locations-based, 623–624
        bandwidth requirements, 624–626
        call preservation, 636–637
        CCM traces, enabling, 626
        conference bandwidth reservations,
           633–635
        configuring, 630
        detecting bandwidth leaks, 635–636
        location identifiers, 628
        MOH bandwidth reservations, 631–633
        regions, 627–629
        trace information, analyzing, 628–631
call admission control. *See* CAC
call control, CCAPI debug commands, 196–205
call forwarding, 479
    CFA, 480–485
        restricting, 546–547
    CFB, 480
    CFF, 485–486
    CFNA, 479–480
    to voice mail, reading CMI traces, 678
call history information messages (SMDI), 665
call hold feature (CallManager), 522–529
call legs, 175. *See also* dial peers
call park feature (CallManager), 531
    troubleshooting, 532–533
call pickup feature (CallManager), troubleshooting,
    533–538
call preservation
    locations-based CAC, 636–637
    SRST, 562
    troubleshooting, 561

call routing
    called party transformations, effect on, 513–514
    Cisco Personal Attendant, 785–786
    closest-match routing, 461–464
        unexpected outside dial tone,
           troubleshooting, 465–466
    dial peers
        call legs, 175
        destination-pattern parameter, 176–179
        incoming called number command,
           181–184
        matching, 175
        optional parameters, 179–181
    NANP, 857–879
    pattern matching
        blocked calls, 473
        multiple partitions within calling search
           space, 474–475
    problem resolution methodology, 515–516
        reading CCM traces, 516–521
    route patterns
        urgent priority, 502
        wildcards, 460–461
    toll fraud, preventing, 544–549
    translation patterns, 501–506
call setup, gatekeeper CAC, 647–651
call statistics menu (Cisco IP Phones), 165
call transfer feature (CallManager), 529–531
called party transformations
    effect on call routing, 513–514
    masks, 495–496
        cumulative effect of changes, 497–499
        order of application, 496–497
    overriding, 499
CallerID service parameter transformation, 500
calling party transformations, 513–514
    masks, 495–496
        cumulative effect of changes, 497–499
        order of application, 496–497
    overwriting, 499
calling search spaces, 469–473
    AAR, 637
    applying to voice mail systems, 547
    call forwarding, 479
        CFA, 480–485, 546–547
        CFB, 480

CFF, 485–486
CFNA, 479–480
device-level, 476–477
event-specific, 478
line-level, 476–477
multiple partitions, pattern-matching rules, 474–475
CallManager. *See also* CallManager Serviceability
audio sources
mulitcast versus unicast, 615
selecting recording input, 620
troubleshooting live sources, 619–620
call hold feature, 522–529
call park feature, 531–533
call pickup feature, 533–538
call processing messages, 140, 144–147
call transfer feature, 529–531
calling IP phone interaction, 150
Cisco AVVID IP Telephony call processing, 24
centralized deployment model, 26
distributed deployment model, 27
multiple-site deployment model, 25
single-site deployment model, 24
closest-match routing, 461–464
unexpected outside dial tone, troubleshooting, 465–466
Database Layer Monitor
CDR replication, troubleshooting, 813–815
verifying operation, 812–813
delayed routing, 466–469
digit analysis behavior, 463–464
embedded LDAP directory, 823–825
logon failures, troubleshooting, 827
reconfiguring on Publisher server, 828–835
reconfiguring on Subscriber server, 835–837
endpoints, 551
MOH, troubleshooting, 611–615
nonsurvivable endpoints, 557
CTI/TAPI endpoints, 559
H.323 gateways, 558–559
Skinny gateways, 557

object counters, 893–898
Cisco CallManager Attendant Console object counters, 898–900
Cisco CallManager System Performance object counters, 900–902
Cisco CIT Manager object counters, 903
partitions, 470
service parameters, transformations, 500–501
survivable endpoints, 552
IP Phones, 552–553
MGCP gateways, 553–557
TOH, 602
investigating instances of, 617
trace files
analyzing SCCP messages, 148–154
call state field values, 525
configuring in CallManager Serviceability, 42–50
digit analysis results, 149
fields, 44–46
for MGCP T1 PRI gateways, 58–60
MOH, troubleshooting, 608–611
reading, 42, 50–57
reviewing for call routing problems, 516–521
unregistered IP Phones, troubleshooting
checking inline power, 114–117
verifying network connectivity, 117–127
CallManager Serviceability, 82
alarms, 82
configuring CCM traces, 42–50
Control Center, 85
RTMT, 85
CTI Apps tab, 88
Devices tab, 86
Performance tab, 86
Service Activation, 84
traces, configuring, 83
CallManagerName parameter (CMI), 667
capability bits, 200
DTMF relay, 202
fax, 201
capturing IP IVR/AA traces, 748–752
CAR (CDR analysis and reporting), 90
case studies
data analysis, 18–19
data collection, 14–18

Catalyst 4000 series switches
AGM, hardware conferencing, 587
Catalyst 4224 switch, voice gateway
functionality, 173–174
Catalyst 6000 series
6608 T1/E1 modules
configuring, 325–337
D-channel establishment, 337, 340–359
T1 CAS, troubleshooting, 359–367
6608/6624 voice gateway modules
DHCP, troubleshooting, 314–320
powering up, 313–314
registration, troubleshooting, 324–325
TFTP, troubleshooting, 320–324
6624 FXS Analog Interface Module,
configuring, 367–379
CMM switch, voice gateway functionality, 174
CatOS switches, time synchronization, 41
CCAPI (call control application programming
interface) debugs, 196–205
CCC (Cisco Conference Connection), 790–791
CCEmail
alerting methods, 81
configuring, 76–80
CCMAdmin
reset command, 156
restart command, 156
CDCC (Call Dependent Call Control) processes,
tracing locations-based CAC, 626
CDR Time Converter, 90–91
CDRs (call detail records), 89
CAR, 90
configuring Subscriber replication, 810–812
replication, troubleshooting, 813–815
storing in Publisher server, 795
timestamps, 90–91
centralized CallManager architecture, locations-
based CAC, 26, 623–624
AAR, troubleshooting, 637
analyzing, 628–631
bandwidth requirements, 624–626
call preservation, 636–637
CCM traces
analyzing, 628–631
enabling, 626

conference bandwidth reservations, 633–635
configuring, 627–631
detecting bandwidth leaks, 635–636
MOH bandwidth reservations, 631–633
regions, 627
CFA (call forward all), 480–485
restricting, 546–547
CFB (call forwardbusy), 480
CFF (call forward on failure), 485–486
CFNA (call forward no answer), 479–480
CgpnScreeningIndicator service parameter
transformation, 500
choppy voice quality, sources of
packet drops, 397–400
queuing delay, 401
VAD, 402–404
Cisco 7910 IP Phone, 32
Cisco 7914 IP Phone Expansion Module, 32
Cisco 7935 IP Conference Station, 32
Cisco 7960/7940 IP Phones, 31
Cisco Attendant Console, 779–780
client, 781–782
resolving common problems, 782–784
server components, 780–781
Cisco AVVID IP Telephony
applicaitons, 34
call processing
centralized deployment model, 26
distributed deployment model, 27
multiple-site deployment model, 25
single-site deployment model, 24
clients, 29–31
Cisco 7910 IP Phone, 32
Cisco 7914 IP Phone Expansion
Module, 32
Cisco 7935 IP Conference Station, 32
Cisco 7960/7940 IP Phones, 31
IP Telephony infrastructure, 23–24
network infrastructure, 23
voice gateways, 32
Cisco CallManager Administration, viewing Route
Plan Report, 466
Cisco CallManager Attendant Console object
counters, 898–900
Cisco CallManager System Performance object
counters, 900–902

Cisco CIT Manager object counters, 903
Cisco Customer Directory Configuration plugin,
  troubleshooting installation, 839–843
Cisco DPA 7630 voice mail gateway, 702
  Octel voice mail system integration with
    CallManager, 693, 697–703
      MWI problems, troubleshooting, 702
      port statuses, 700–702
      verifying cabling, 693
Cisco ER (Emergency Responder), 478, 791
Cisco Gatekeeper object counters, 904
Cisco H.323 object counters, 904
Cisco HW Conference Bridge Device object
  counters, 905
Cisco IOS Software
  debugs, enabling, 185–187
  dial peers
    call legs, 175
    destination-pattern parameter legs,
      176–179
    incoming called number command,
      181–184
    matching, 175
    optional parameters, 179–181
Cisco IOS voice gateways, 169
  2600 series routers, 171–172
  3600 series routers, 172
  3700 series routers, 173
  digital interfaces
    ISDN PRI signaling, 210–214
    T1 CAS, 214–218
    timestamps, configuring, 185
    verifying physical layer connectivity,
      208–210
  eliminating sources of echo, 421–424
  H.323, 281
    H.225 call flow, 288–294
    H.225 signaling, 283–284
    H.245 call signaling, 295–307
    IEs, 284–287
  MGCP
    cause codes (traces), 262–269
    commands, 219–221
    DTMF packages, 231–232
    DTMF trunk packages, 236–237
    endpoint identifiers, 218–219
    FXO/FXS signaling, 249–256

generic media packages, 231
handset emulation packages, 235–236
line packages, 234–235
MF packages, 232–238
packages, 229–230
parameter lines, 221–229
PRI backhaul, 256–258
numbering type/plan mismatches,
  269–270
reading ISDN traces, 258–262
response codes, 239–240
response headers, 238
RTP packages, 236
T1 CAS, 276–281
timers, 271–276
trunk packages, 233
verifying registration status, 240–249
resolving one-way/no-way audio problems,
  407–410
TDM interfaces, troubleshooting, 187
  with debug commands, 192–205
  with show commands, 187–192
VG200, 170
Cisco IP Phone Services SDK, 822
Cisco IP Phones
  79xx series
    3-port switch operation, 161–164
    call processing messages, 140, 144–148
    network settings, 123–126
    SCCP, troubleshooting, 139–140
  active connections, 155
  best practices for troubleshooting, 165–166
  directory problems, troubleshooting, 160–161
  dropped calls, troubleshooting, 157
  failback, 156
  failover, 155
    troubleshooting, 158–160
  resetting, 156
  restarting, 156
  service problems, troubleshooting,
    160–161, 789
  Skinny client registration process
    messages, 127–132
      verifying with status messages, 133–135
  soft keys, 147
  TCP handle, deriving from CCM traces, 148
  Temporary Failure messages, 561–562

Cisco IP SoftPhone, 786–788
    eliminating sources of echo, 428–429
Cisco IP/VC products, 789
Cisco Lines object counters, 905
Cisco Locations object counters, 906
Cisco Media Streaming App object counters, 906–909
Cisco Media Termination Point object counters, 909–910
Cisco Messaging Interface object counters, 910–911
Cisco MGCO FXI Device object counters, 911
Cisco MGCO FXS Device object counters, 912
Cisco MGCP Gateways object counters, 912
Cisco MGCP PRI Device object counters, 913–914
Cisco MGCP T1 CAS Device object counters, 914–915
Cisco MOH Device object counters, 915–918
Cisco MTP Device object counters, 916
Cisco Personal Attendant, resolving call routing problems, 785–786
Cisco Phones object counters, 918
Cisco SW Conference Bridge Device object counters, 918–920
Cisco TFTP object counters, 920–923
Cisco Transcoder Device object counters, 923
Cisco Unity, 655
    DTMF, 661–662
    MWI, 659–661
    switch configuration, verifying, 658–659
    troubleshooting resouces, 662
    TSP
        compatibility, verifying, 655–656
        configuring, 656–657
Cisco WebAttendant. *See* Cisco Attendant Console
Cisco WS-X6608 gateway, eliminating sources of echo, 424–427
CLI Tracy, 105
clients
    Cisco 7910 IP Phone, 32
    Cisco 7914 IP Phone Expansion Module, 32
    Cisco 7935 IP Conference Station, 32
closest-match routing, 461–464
    unexpected outside dial tone, troubleshooting, 465–466

clusters
    database replication, Publisher-Subscriber model, 793–796
    intercluster trunks, 311
        codec mismatches, 312
    master/replica relationship, 823
    passwords, configuring on nodes, 798– 802
"CM Down, Features Disabled" message (Cisco IP Phones), 158
CMI (Cisco Messaging Interface), 666–667
    service parameters, 667–671, 674
    traces, reading, 674–679
    troubleshooting with HyperTerminal, 679–682
CMRs (Call Management Records), 89
codec complexity, 171
codecs
    CallManager selection process, 568
    capability bits, 200
    configuring between regions, 569
    GSM, 855
    transcoding, 565
    wideband, 855
coder delay, isolating, 386
collecting data, 4
    analyzing, 11
        CCM traces, 42, 50–57
        CMI traces, 674–679
        ISDN traces, 258–262
        locations-based CAC traces, 628–631
        SDL traces, 60–63
    case study, 14–18
    IP IVR/AA traces, 748–752
    isolating root cause of problems, 6
        deductive reasoning, 11–12
        earliest occurence of problem, referencing device-based time, 10–11
        with topology information, 7–9
    user information, 10
    verifying IP network integrity, 12–13
comfort noise, 402
commands
    debug ephone, 713
    debug ephone detail, 723–728
    debug ephone register, 714–717
    debug ephone state, 719–722
    debug vstp tone, 192–196

fax interface-type, 454
fax nsf, 453
fax rate, 451
fax-relay ecm disable, 452
frame-clock-select, 210
incoming called number, 182–184
show call active voice, 191, 404
show call active voice brief, 449
show ephone, 720
show gatekeeper calls, 649
show gatekeeper endpoints, 645
show gatekeeper zone status, 649
show voice port summary, 188–189
conferencing
    Ad Hoc, error messages, 597–598
    failures, troubleshooting, 592–597
configuration parameters, VG248, 686–690
configuring
    6608 T1/E1 digital gateway, 325–337
        D-channel establishment, 337, 340–359
        T1 CAS, troubleshooting, 359–367
    6624 FXS Analog Gateway, 367–379
    CallManager Serviceability
        alarms, 82
        CCM traces, 42–50
        Service Activation, 84
        traces, 83
    CCEmail, 76–80
    CMI, service parameters, 667–671, 674
    codecs between regions, 569
    CRA, LDAP directories, 741–745
    dial peers, 176–177
        incoming called number command, 181–184
        optional parameters, 179–181
        variable-length matching, 178–179
    extension mobility, 758–763
    fax/modem passthrough on WS-X6608 port, 441
    locations-based CAC, 627–631
    MWI, parameters, 682–685
    passwords on cluster nodes, 798–802
    regions, 571
    SDL traces, 63–67

SRST, 709–712
    DHCP support, 732
    transfer patterns, 730
Subscriber CDR replication, 810–812
connectivity
    troubleshooting unregistered Skinny clients, 117–127
        configuration files, 121–127
        IP addressing, 118–121
        VLAN configuration, 118
    verifying, 12–13
Control Center (CallManager Serviceability), 85
converting decimal values
    to binary, 881–889
    to hex, 881–889
CoR (class of restriction), 708
corporate directories
    Cisco IP phone directory integration, 820
    LDAP integration
        with Active Directory, 837–839
        with Netscape iPlanet, 844
    providing endpoint access, 821–823
    troubleshooting, 823
counters
    Cisco analog access, 892
    Cisco CallManager Attendant Console object, 898–900
    Cisco CallManager object, 893–898
    Cisco CallManager System Performance object, 900–902
    Cisco CTI Manager object, 903
    Cisco Gatekeeper object, 904
    Cisco H.323 object, 904
    Cisco HW Conference Bridge Device object, 905
    Cisco Lines object, 905
    Cisco Locations object, 906
    Cisco Media Streaming App object, 906–909
    Cisco Media Termination Point object, 909–910
    Cisco Messaging Interface object, 910–911
    Cisco MGCP FXO Device object, 911
    Cisco MGCP FXS Device object, 912
    Cisco MGCP Gateways object, 912
    Cisco MGCP PRI Device object, 913–914
    Cisco MGCP T1 CAS Device object, 914–915
    Cisco MOH Device object, 915–918

Cisco MTP Device object, 916
Cisco Phones object, 918
Cisco SW Conference Bridge Device object,
918–920
Cisco TFTP object, 920–923
Cisco Transcoder Device object, 923
enabling logging on PerfMon, 71–75
Windows 2000 objects, 924–925
CRA (customer response application), 736
AA, 737
compatibility with CCM, verifying, 737
extension mobility
configuring, 759–763
login/logout process, 763–765
resolving common problems,
765–768, 772
LDAP directory, configuring, 741–745
CRA Administration, 738–741
engine status, verifying, 745–748
CTI (Computer Telephony Interface)
applications, 736
CRA
AA, 737
extenion mobility, 759–769, 772
IVR, 737
LDAP directory, configuring, 741–745
CRA Administration, troubleshooting, 738–741
CTI Manager, 738
nonsurvivable CTI/TAPI endpoints, 559
verifying TSP version, 736
CTI Apps tab (RTMT), 88
CTI Manager, 738
CTIQBE (Computer Telephony Interface Quick
Buffer Encoding), 736
cumulative transformations, 497–499
Customer Directory Configuration plugin,
troubleshooting installation, 839–843

D

data analysis, 4–5
case study, 14–19
CCM traces, 42, 50–57
through MGCP T1 PRI gateways, 58–60
CMI traces, 674–679
deductive reasoning, 11–12

ISDN traces, 258–262
calling name display, 270
cause codes, 262–269
numbering type/plan mismatches,
269–270
timer information, 271–276
isolating root cause, 6
with topology information, 7–9
locations-based CAC trace information,
628–631
SDL traces, 60–63
user information, 10
verifying IP network integrity, 12–13
Database Layer Monitor
troubleshooting CDR replication, 813–815
verifying operation, 812–813
database replication
name resolution, 796–797
passwords, changing, 798–802
Publisher-Subscriber model, 793–796
troubleshooting with Microsoft SQL Server
Enterprise Manager, 802–803
DataBits parameter (CMI), 667
DC Directory, 823–825
logon failures, troubleshooting, 827
reconfiguring
on Publisher server, 828–835
on Subscriber server, 835–837
DC Directory Administrator, launching, 826
DDIs (digit discard instructions), 486–494
alternate expansion of DDI acronym, 486
debug ephone command, 713
debug ephone detail command, 723–728
debug ephone register command, 714–717
debug ephone state command, 719–722
debug vtsp tone command, 192–196
debugs
enabling on Cisco IOS Software, 185–187
SRST call control, 719–720
decimal values, converting to hexadecimal and
binary values, 881–889
deductive reasoning, 11–12
default MRGL, 568
dejitter delay, isolating source of, 393–395

delay, 384. *See also* echo
    effect on signaling, 395–396
    isolating sources of
        dejitter delay, 393–395
        fixed delay, 385–389
        variable delay, 390–395
delayed routing, troubleshooting, 466–469
Delayed Start (E&M), 850
deriving TCP handles of Cisco IP Phones from
    CCM traces, 148
destination-pattern parameter (dial peers), 176–179
developing phone services, 789
DEVICE_RESET message (SCCP), 157
DEVICE_RESTART message (SCCP), 157
device-level calling search spaces, 476–477
devices
    Cisco IOS Software gateways
        eliminating sources of echo, 421–424
        resolving one-way/no-way audio
            problems, 407–410
    Cisco IP SoftPhones, eliminating sources of
        echo, 428–429
    codecs
        CallManager selection process, 568
        capability bits, 200
        configuring between regions, 569
        G.711, 855
        G.723, 855
        G.726, 855
        G.729, 855
        G.729a, 855
        G.729ab, 855
        G.729b, 855
        transcoding, 565
    echo cancellers, 384
        operation of, 416–418
    fax machines, 433
        encoding schemes, 434
        fax/modem passthrough, 437–439
        isolating problems, 449–450
        jitter, 446
        negotiation, 434
        NSF field, modifying, 453
        packet loss, 446
        page transmission, 434
        passthrough, 440

        physical layer errors, troubleshooting,
            447–449
        switching fax protocol, 454
        T.30 transmissions, 435–437
    media resources, 565
    modems
        passthrough, 439
        physical layer errors, troubleshooting,
            447–449
    MOH fixed audio sources, verifying
        configuration, 619–620
    time synchronization
        CatOS, 41
        Cisco IOS, 40–41
    transcoders, 571–577
        out-of-resource conditions, 578–580
        with conference bridge resources,
            581–585
        with MOH servers, 585
Devices tab (RTMT), 86
DHCP (Dynamic Host Configuration Protocol), 850
    troubleshooting on 6608/6624 modules,
        314–320
dial peers
    answer-address command, 182
    call legs, 175
        callID assignment, 199–200
        capabilities, 200–203
        inbound, disconnects, 204
        tear down, 204–205
    destination-pattern parameter, 176–179
    inbound peer matching, 181–182
        based on port configuration, 183
    incoming called-number command, 181–184
    interdigit timeout, 177–178
    longest-match routing, 177
    optional parameters, 179–181
    outbound peer matching, 182–183
    peer ID 0, characteristics, 183–184
    POTS, 175
        as destination, 179
        optional parameters, 180–181
    priority, assigning, 177
    session-target ipv4 command, 179
    temporary dial peers, viewing, 719
    variable-length destination patterns, 178

viewing configuration with CCAPI debugs, 197–200

VoIP, 175

Dial Plan Path service parameter transformation, 501

dialing forest traces, 538–542
    verbose mode, 543

dialing transformations. *See* transformations

DialingPlan parameter (CMI), 667

Dick Tracy, 101–104
    acquiring, 105
    CLI/embedded Tracy, 105

digit analysis, 461–464
    CCM trace results, 149
    dialing forest traces, 538–542
        verbose mode, 543
    identifying potential route pattern matches within partitions, 517–521

digital integration, Octel voice mail systems and CallManager, 693, 698–700

digital interfaces
    ISDN PRI signaling, 210–212
        configuring, 213–214
    physical layer, verifying connectivity, 208–210
    T1 CAS, 214–218

directories, LDAP
    access, 820
    integration, 820
    schema, 819

Directories button (Cisco IP Phones), request failures, 160–161

directory-enabled Cisco applications, 819

disabling ECM on fax relay, 452–453

disconnected FXO interfaces, troubleshooting, 205

displaying
    e-phone-dn configuration, 718
    SRST polling statistics, 722

distributed CallManager architecture, gatekeeper CAC, 623, 638
    call setup, 647–651
    CallManger registration, 645–647
    RAS messages, 639
    verifying configuration, 640–645

distributed deployment model, CallManager, 27

distribution agent, 804

DNS name resolution in database replication, 798

DPA voicemail gateway
    event logging, 703
    Octel/CallManager integration, 693, 697–703
        MWI problems, troubleshooting, 702
        port statuses, 700–702
        verifying cabling, 693

dropped calls, 551–552
    media processing resources, 560
    troubleshooting, 157, 561

DSPs (digital signal processors), codec complexity, 171

DT-24+/DE-30+ gateways, eliminating sources of echo, 424–427

DTMF (Dual-Tone MultiFrequency) tones, importance to voice mail systems, 661–662

DTMF packages (MGCP), 231–232
    trunk packages, 236–237

DTMF relay (H.245), 303–307

Dynamic Host Configuration Protocol. *See* DHCP

E

E&M Delayed Start, 850

echo
    eliminating sources of, 418–429
    perception of as problem, 414–416
    sources of, isolating, 411
        acoustic echo, 412
        electrical echo, 411–412

echo cancellers, 384
    operation, 416–418

ECM (error control mode), disabling on fax relay, 452–453

EIA/TIA web site, 849

EIGRP (Enhanced Interior Gateway Routing Protocol), 850

electrical echo, isolating, 411–412

eliminating
    possible causes using deductive reasoning, 11–12
    sources of echo, 418–429

embedded LDAP directory, 823–825
    logon failures, troubleshooting, 827
    reconfiguring
        on Publisher server, 828–835
        on Subscriber server, 835–837

embedded Tracy tool, 105

empty capabilities set, 565

enabling

    debugs on Cisco IOS Software, 185–187

    fax relay debugs, 455–456

    H.323 Fast Connect, 396

encoding schemes, fax machines, 434

endpoint directory access, 821–823

endpoint identifiers (MGCP), 219

endpoints

    nonsurvivable, 557

        CTI/TAPI endpoints, 559

        H.323 gateways, 558–559

        Skinny gateways, 557

    survivable, 552

        IP Phones, 552–553

        MGCP gateways, 553–557

end-to-end delay, ITU-T specifications, 384

Enhanced Interior Gateway Routing Protocol
(EIGRP), 850

Enhanced Q.931 Translator, 98–100

Enterprise Manager, troubleshooting database
replication errors, 802–804

ephone-dn configuration, viewing, 718

Epoch time, 90–91

ER (Emergency Responder), 478

ERL (echo return loss), 417

ERLE (echo return loss enhancement), 417

error codes, Extension Mobility (CallManager 3.3),
777–779

error messages, SMDI, 666

event-specific calling search spaces, 478

"exceeds maximum parties" error messages, 597

extension mobility, 756–758

    CallManager 3.1/3.2, 756–772

        login/logout process, 763–765

    CallManager 3.3, 772–773

        error codes, 777–779

        login/logout process, 774–777

    configuring, 758–763

    resolving common problems, 765–772

F

failback behavior in Cisco IP Phones, 156

failed conferences, troubleshooting, 592–597

failover

    behavior in Cisco IP Phones, 155

    troubleshooting, 158–160

Fast Connect, enabling, 396

Fax Group 3, 433

fax interface-type command, 454

fax machines, 433

    encoding schemes, 434

    isolating problems, 449–450

    jitter, 446

    negotiation, 434

    NSF field, modifying, 453

    packet loss, 446

    page transmission speed, 434

    physical layer errors on digital interfaces,
447–449

    switching fax protocol, 454

    T.30 transmissions, 435–437

fax nsf command, 453

fax preamble, 440

fax rate command, 451

fax relay, 444–445

    adjusting data rate, 451–452

    debugs, enabling, 455–456

    ECM, disabling, 452–453

    switching to fax passthrough, 450

    T.38, 445–446

    troubleshooting, 450

fax/modem passthrough, 437, 440

    NSE, 439

    NTE, 438

    troubleshooting, 450

    verifying configuration, 441–444

fax-relay ecm disable command, 452

features of CallManager

    call hold, 522–529

    call park, 531–533

    call pickup, 533–538

    call transfer, 529–531

fields of CCM traces, 44–46

filtering CCM trace results, 49–50

firewalls, resolving one-way/no-way audio
problems, 410

firmware, Cisco IP Phones, 165
fixed delay, 384
 coder delay, isolating, 386
 effect on signaling, 395–396
 packetization delay, isolating, 386–387
 propagation delay, isolating, 389
 serialization delay, isolating, 387–389
 sources of, isolating, 385
formatting
 called/calling party numbers with
  transformations, 501–506
 called/calling party tranformations with masks,
  495–496
  cumulative effect of changes, 497–499
  order of application, 496–497
forwarding in SRST mode, 731
frame-clock-select command, 210
FXO interface
 disconnects, 205
 supervisory disconnect tone, 207
FXO/FXS signaling on MGCP gateways, 249–256
FXS (Foreign Exchange Station) gateways, applying
 restrictive calling search spaces, 547–548

G

G.711 codecs, 855
 fax passthrough, 437
G.723 codecs, 855
G.726 codecs, 855
G.729 codecs, 855
G.729a codecs, 855
G.729ab codecs, 855
G.729b codecs, 855
garbled audio, sources of
 packet drops, 397–400
 queuing delay, 401
 VAD, 402–404
gatekeeper CAC, 638
 call setup, 647–651
 CallManager registration, 645–647
 RAS messages, 639
 verifying configuration, 640–645

gateways, Cisco IOS MGCP
 FXO/FXS signaling, 249–256
 PRI backhaul, 256–258
 reading ISDN traces, 258–276
 T1 CAS, 276–281
 verifying registration status, 240–249
gathering data, 4
 analyzing collected data
  case study, 18–19
  CCM traces, 42, 50–60
  CMI traces, 674–679
  deductive reasoning, 11–12
  ISDN traces, 258–262
 case study, 14–18
 earliest occurence of problem, referencing
  device-based time, 10–11
 isolating root cause, 6–9
 user information, 10
 verifying IP network integrity, 12–13
generic media packages (MGCP), 231
Group 3 fax devices, 433
group pickup, 533–538
GSM (Global System for Mobile Communications)
 codecs, 855

H

H.225 signaling, 283, 850
 call flow, 288–294
 call setup messages, 283–284
H.245, 851
 call signaling, 295
  DTMF relay, 303–307
  logical channel signaling, 300–303
  maser/slave determination, 296
  terminal capabilities exchange, 297–300
H.323, 281, 851
 gatekeepers, 638
 H..225 signaling
  call flow, 288–294
 H..245 signaling, 295
  DTMF relay, 303–307
  logical channel signaling, 300–303
  master/slave determination, 296
  terminal capabilities exchange, 297–300

H.225 signaling, 283
    call setup messages, 283–284
IEs, 284–287
nonsurvivable endpoints, 558–559
null capabilities set, 565
versus MG CP, 281
H.323 Fast Connect, enabling, 396
handset emulation packages (MGCP), 235–236
hardware conferencing
    "No Conference Bridge Available"messages,
    587–591
    Catalyst 4000 AGM, 587
held calls, 522–525
held party, 602
hexadecimal conversion table, 881–889
high complexity calls, 171
high-compression codecs, 437
    fax relay, 444–445
    T.38, 445–446
holding party, 602
hub-and-spoke topology, locations-based CAC, 624
    AAR, troubleshooting, 637
    analyzing trace information, 628–631
    bandwidth requirements, 624–626
    call preservation, 636–637
    CCM traces, enabling, 626
    conference bandwidth reservations, 633–635
    configuring, 627–631
    detecting bandwidth leaks, 635–636
    location identifier assignments, 628
    MOH bandwidth reservations, 631–633
    regions, 627
HyperTerminal, troubleshooting CMI problems,
    679–682

I

i button (Cisco IP Phones), logging call
   statistics, 165
identifying root cause of problems, 6–9
IEEE (Institute of Electrical and Electronic
   Engineers) web site, 849
IEs (information elements), 284–287
Immediate Start (E&M), 850

inbound call legs, 175
incoming called-number command, dial peer
   configuration, 182–184
initiating transactional replication, 804
inline power problems (Cisco IP Phones),
   troubleshooting unregistered Skinny clients,
   114–117
InputDnSignificantDigits parameter (CMI), 668
inside dial tone, 465
installation of Cisco Customer Directory
   Configuration plugin, troubleshooting,
   839–843
intercluster trunks, 311
    codec mismatches, 312
interdigit timeout, adjusting, 466–467
international numbers, preventing unauthorized
   access, 545
Intl TollBypass DDI, 488
Intl TollBypass Trailing-# DDI, 488
investigating sources of delay, 385
    fixed delay, 385
        coder delay, 386
        packetization delay, 386–387
        propagation delay, 389
        serialization delay, 387–389
    variable delay
        dejitter delay, 393–395
        low-speed links, 391–393
        queuing delay, 390–391
IP addressing
    SRST, DHCP support, 732
    resolving one-way/no-way audio problems,
    405–406
    verifying IP Phone configuration, 118–121
IP IVR traces, collecting, 748–752
IP Phones
    auto-registration, controlling, 545–546
    call forward fields, 479
        CFA, 480–485
        CFB, 480
        CFF, 485–486
        CFNA, 479–480
    directory access, 820

extension mobility, 756–758
   configuring, 758–763
   login/logout process, 763–765
   resolving common problems,
      765–768, 772
Skinny client registration
   troubleshooting inline power, 114–117
   troubleshooting network connectivity,
      117–127
   verifying, 133
IP Telephony infrastructure, call processing, 24
   centralized deployment model, 26
   distributed deployment model, 27
   multiple-site deployment model, 25
   single-site deployment model, 24
IP/VC products, 789
iPlanet (Netscape), LDAP integration, 844
IPV MSApp (Cisco IP Voice Media Streaming
   Application), software conferencing, 586
ISDN (Integrated Services Digital Network)
   Anlagenanschluss, 213
   PRI signaling, 210–212
      configuring on Cisco IOS voice gateways,
         213–214
   traces, reading from MGCP gateways, 258–276
isolating
   fax problems, 449–450
   root cause of problems, 6
      case study, 16
      with topology information, 7–9
   sources of echo, 411
      acoustic echo, 412
      electrical echo, 411–412
   sources of fixed delay, 385
      coder delay, 386
      packetization delay, 386–387
      propagation delay, 389
      serialization delay, 387–389
   sources of variable delay
      dejitter delay, 393–395
      low-speed links, 391–393
      queuing delay, 390–391
   voice quality problems
      packet drops, 397–400
      queuing delay, 401
      VAD, 402–404

ITS (IOS Telephony Services), 707
ITU-T
   H.225 specification, 651
   Recommendation G.114, delay
      specifications, 384
   web site, 849
IVR (Integrated Voice Response) scripts, 737

J

jitter
   effect on fax machines and modems, 446
   isolating source of, 391–392
JTAPI (Java Telephony Application Programming
   Interface), 852
   verifying CRA engine status, 745–748

K-L

KeepAliveDn parameter (CMI), 668

LDAP (Lightweight Directory Access Protocol), 852
   Active Directory integration, 837–839
   corporate directory access, 821–823
   Customer Directory Configuration plugin,
      troubleshooting, 839–844
   directories, 819
      configuring, 741–743
      verifying configuration, 745
   directory integration versus directory
      access, 820
   embedded directories, 823–825
      logon failures, troubleshooting, 827
      reconfiguring on Publisher server,
         828– 835
      reconfiguring on Subscriber server,
         835–837
   iPlanet integration, 844
LFI (link fragmentation and interleaving), 391
line packages (MGCP), 234–235
line-level calling search spaces, 476–477
listener echo, isolating sources of, 412–413
live audio sources, troubleshooting, 619–620
LMHOSTS file, name resolution, 796–797
local area code versus area code, 510

local calls, delayed routing, 466–469

locating alarm definitions, 93–94

locations-based CAC, 623–624

    bandwidth requirements, 624–626

    call preservation, 636–637

    CCM traces, enabling, 626

    conference bandwidth reservations, 633–635

    configuring, 627–631

    detecting bandwidth leaks, 635–636

    location identifier assignments, 628

    MOH bandwidth reservations, 631–633

    regions, 627

    trace information, analyzing, 628–631

log reader agent, 804

logging call statistics on Cisco IP Phones, 166

logical channel signaling (H.245), 300–303

login/logout process

    Extension Manager (CallManager 3.3), 774–777

    extension mobility, 763–765

low-speed links, isolating delay source, 391–393

M

manual time synchronization, configuring on CallManager servers, 40

masks, 495–496

master/replica relationship in clusters, 823

master/slave determination in H.245 call signaling, 296

MatchingCgpnWithAttendantFlag service parameter transformation, 500

MCM (Multimedia Conference Manager), 638

media processing resources, 560

media resource group lists (MRGLs), 566, 602

media resource groups (MRGs), 566, 602

media resources, 565

    selecting, 567

medium complexity calls, 171

Meet-Me conferences, 565

    locations-based CAC bandwidth reservations, 633–635

Message Waiting Indicator On/Off Messages (SMDI), 665

MessageDeskNumber parameter (CMI), 668

messages

    "CM Down, Features Disabled," troubleshooting, 158

    in H.225 call setup, 283–284

    IP Phone status, verifying registration, 133–135

    SCCP, 140, 144–147

        in CCM traces, 148–154

    Skinny client registration process, 127–132

    SMDI, 664–666

    T.30, 435–437

    "Temporary Failure," troubleshooting dropped calls, 561–562

messaging. *See* voice mail systems

methodology for resolving call routing problems, 515–516

    reading CCM traces, 516–521

MF packages (MGCP), 232–233

MF trunk packages (MGCP), 237–238

MGCP (Media Gateway Control Protocol), 852

    commands, 219–221

    endpoint identifiers, 218–219

    packages, 229–230

        DTFM package, 231–232

        DTMF trunk package, 236–237

        generic media package, 231

        handset emulation package, 235–236

        line package, 234–235

        MF package, 232–233

        MF trunk package, 237–238

        RTP package, 236

        trunk package, 233

    parameter lines, 221–229

    response codes, 239–240

    response headers, 238

    See also Cisco IOS MGCP gateways

MGCP gateways, survivable endpoints, 553–557

MGCP T1 PRI gateways, tracing calls, 58–60

Microsoft AD (Active Directory)

    Customer Directory Configuration plugin, troubleshooting, 839–844

    LDAP integration, 837–839

Microsoft Event Viewer, 91

    alarm definitions, 92–93

Microsoft PerfMon, 68
   alerts, 75
   counter logging, 71–75
   versus RTMT, 68–69
   viewing real-time statistics, 69–71
Microsoft SQL Server Enterprise Manager, 802–803
   Replication Monitor
      correcting replication errors, 804–806
      reestablishing broken replication
      subscription, 807–809
      reinitializing subscriptions, 809
misconfigured 6608 T1/E1 modules,
   troubleshooting, 326–337
MIVR traces, capturing, 748–752
models of Cisco 2600 series routers, 171–172
modems
   jitter, 446
   packet loss, 446
   passthrough, 437
      ANS, 439
      NSE, 439
      NTE, 438
      verifying configuration, 441–444
   physical layer errors, troubleshooting, 447–449
modules
   6608 T1/E1
      advanced troubleshooting, 344–359
      configuring, 325–337
      D-channel establishment, 337, 340–343
      T1 CAS, troubleshooting, 359–367
   6608/6624 voice gateways
      DHCP, troubleshooting, 314–320
      powering up, 313–314
      registration, troubleshooting, 324–325
      TFTP, troubleshooting, 320–324
   6624 Port FXS Analog Interface Module,
      configuring, 367–379
MOH (Music On Hold). *See also* TOH
   audio sources, 601–603
      multicast versus unicast, 615–616
      selecting recording input, 620
   Audio Translator, troubleshooting, 618
   CAC bandwidth reservations, 631–633
   performance counters, 915–918
   troubleshooting, 611–615
      CCM trace files, 608–611
      performance counters, 605–607
MOHAudioSourcesActive counter
   (CallManager 3.3), 604
MOHConnectionsLost counter
   (CallManager 3.3), 606
MOHConnectionState counter
   (CallManager 3.3), 604
MOHHighestActiveResources counter
   (CallManager 3.3), 607
MOHMulticastResourceActive counter
   (CallManager 3.3), 606
MOHMulticastResourceAvailable counter
   (CallManager 3.3), 607
MOHOutOfResources counter
   (CallManager 3.3), 607
MOHStreamsActive counter (CallManager 3.3), 605
MOHStreamsAvailable counter
   (CallManager 3.3), 605
MOHStreamsTotal counter (CallManager 3.3), 606
MOHTotalMulticastResources counter
   (CallManager 3.3), 606
MOHTotalUnicastResources counter
   (CallManager 3.3), 606
MOHUnicastResourceActive counter
   (CallManager 3.3), 606
MOHUnicastResourceAvailable counter
   (CallManager 3.3), 607
MRGLs (media resource group lists), 566, 602
MRGs (media resource groups), 566, 602
MTPs (media termination points), null capabilities
   set, 565
multicast audio sources (MOH), troubleshooting,
   615–616
multiple-site deployment model (CallManager), 25
MWIs (Message Waiting Indicators), 709
   configuration parameters, 682–685
   toggling on/off, 659, 661
   VG248 platform, troubleshooting, 690–692
MwiSearchSpace parameter (CMI), 668

N

name resolution
    LMHOSTS file, 796–797
    NetBIOS in database replication, 796–798
NANP (North American Numbering Plan)
    call routing information, 857–879
    route filters, 506–510
        multiple clauses, 512
    tags, 507
NAT (Network Address Translation), resolving one-way/no-way audio problems, 410
negotiation process, fax machines, 434
NetBIOS name resolution in database replication, 796–798
Netscape iPlanet, LDAP integration, 844
network diagrams, required information, 7–9
network hold MOH audio source, 601
network integrity, verifying, 12–13
network settings, Cisco 79xx IP Phones, 123–126
Network Time Protocol. *See* NTP
"No Conference Bridge Available," troubleshooting, 587–591
NoDigits DDI, 488
nonproduction hours, troubleshooting methodologies, 5–6
nonsurvivable endpoints, 557
    CTI/TAPI endpoints, 559
    H.323 gateways, 558–559
    Skinny gateways, 557
no-way audio, isolating sources of
    Cisco IOS Software gateways, 408–410
    firewalls, 410
    IP connectivity, 405–406
    NAT, 410
    PAT, 410
NSE (Named Service Event), 439
NSF (Nonstandard Facilities) field, modifying, 453
NTE (Named Telephony Event), 438
NTP (Network Time Protocol), 852
    time synchronization, 39
        on CatOS devices, 41
        on Cisco IOS devices, 40–41
null capabilities set, 565

numbering plans
    NANP, call routing information, 857–879
    route filters, 506–507
        multiple clauses, 512
        NANP tags, 508–510

O

object counters
    Cisco analog access, 892
    Cisco CallManager, 893–898
    Cisco CallManager Attendant Console, 898–900
    Cisco CallManager System Performance, 900–902
    Cisco CIT Manager, 903
    Cisco Gatekeeper, 904
    Cisco H.323, 904
    Cisco HW Conference Bridge Device, 905
    Cisco Lines, 905
    Cisco Locations, 906
    Cisco Media Streaming App, 906–909
    Cisco Media Termination Point, 909–910
    Cisco Messaging Interface, 910–911
    Cisco MGCP FXO Device, 911
    Cisco MGCP FXS Device, 912
    Cisco MGCP Gateways, 912
    Cisco MGCP PRI Device, 913–914
    Cisco MGCP T1 CAS Device, 914–915
    Cisco MOH Device, 915–918
    Cisco MTP Device, 916
    Cisco Phones, 918
    Cisco SW Conference Bridge Device, 918–920
    Cisco TFTP, 920–923
    Cisco Transcoder Device, 923
    logging on PerfMon, 71–75
    Windows 2000, 924–925
obtaining
    Dick Tracy tool, 105
    Enhanced Q.931 Translator, 100
Octel voice mail systems, CallManager integration, 693, 698–700
OffHookMessage message, SCCP call processing, 144

one-way audio, isolating sources of
  Cisco IOS Software gateways, 408–410
  firewalls, 410
  IP connectivity, 405–406
  NAT, 410
  PAT, 410
open trees, 673
operating systems, Windows 2000
  CCEmail, 76–81
  performance counters, 924–925
operation of echo cancellers, 416–418
optional dial peer parameters, 179–181
OSI reference model, verifying connectivity at every
  layer, 12–13
OSPF (Open Shortest Path First), 852
outbound call legs, 175
out-of-resource conditions, 578–580
OutputDnFor parameter (CMI), 668
OutputExternalFormat parameter (CMI), 669
OverlapReceivingForPriFlag service parameter
  transformation, 501
overwriting transformations, 499

P

packages (MGCP), 229–230
  DTMF, 231–232
  DTMF trunkRTP, 236–237
  generic media, 231
  handset emulation, 235–236
  line, 234–235
  MF, 232–233
  MF trunkRTP, 237–238
  RTP, 236
  trunk, 233
packet drops
  as source of voice quality degradation, 397–400
  effect on fax machines and modems, 446
packet-capture software, 106
packetization delay, isolating, 386–387
page transmission speed, 434
parameter lines (MGCP), 221–229
Parity parameter (CMI), 669
parked calls, 531
  troubleshooting, 532–533

partitions, 469–470. *See also* calling search spaces
  calling search spaces, AAR, 637
  identifying potential route pattern matches,
    517–519
  pattern-matching rules, 474–475
passwords, configuring on cluster nodes, 798–802
PAT, resolving one-way/no-way audio
  problems, 410
pattern matching. *See also* calling search spaces
  blocked calls, 473
  closest-match routing, 461–464
  delayed routing, troubleshooting, 466–469
  multiple partitions within a calling search space,
    474–475
  variable-length, 178–179
  wildcards, 460–461
PBXs (private branch exchanges), troubleshooting
  calling name display problems, , 270
perception of echo as problematic, 414–416
PerfMon, 68. *See also* CCEmail
  alerts, 75
  counter logging, 71–75
  versus RTMT, 68–69
  viewing real-time statistics, 69–71
performance counters
  Cisco analog access, 892
  Cisco CallManager, 893–898
  Cisco CallManager Attendant Console,
    898–900
  Cisco CallManager System Performance,
    900–902
  Cisco CIT Manager, 903
  Cisco Gatekeeper, 904
  Cisco H.323, 904
  Cisco HW Conference Bridge Device, 905
  Cisco Lines, 905
  Cisco Locations, 906
  Cisco Media Streaming App, 906–909
  Cisco Media Termination Point, 909–910
  Cisco Messaging Interface, 910–911
  Cisco MGCP FXO Device, 911
  Cisco MGCP FXS Device, 912
  Cisco MGCP Gateways, 912
  Cisco MGCP PRI Device, 913–914
  Cisco MGCP T1 CAS Device, 914–915
  Cisco MOH Device, 915–918
  Cisco MTP Device, 916

Cisco Phones, 918
Cisco SW Conference Bridge Device, 918–920
Cisco TFTP, 920–923
Cisco Transcoder Device, 923
logging on PerfMon, 71–75
MOH, monitoring, 605–607
Windows 2000, 924–925
Performance tab (RTMT), 86
phone registration, SRST, 712–717
phone services, 789
physical layer
connectivity, verifying on digital interfaces,
208–210
troubleshooting fax/modem errors, 447–449
pinpointing earliest occurence of problems, 10
referencing device-based time, 11
plain-text protocols, 218
PLAR (Private Line Automatic Ringdown),
controlling IP phone auto-registration, 545–546
plugins, Cisco Customer Directory Configuration,
troubleshooting installation, 839–843
polling statistics (SRST), viewing, 722
POTS dial peers, 175
variable-length pattern matching, 179
power denial, 206
powering 6608/6624 voice gateway modules,
313–314
PreAt 10-10-Dialing DDI, 489
PreAt 10-10-Dialing Trailing-# DDI, 489
PreAt 11/10D->7D DDI, 490
PreAt 11/10D->7D Trailing-# DDI, 490
PreAt 11D->10D DDI, 491
PreAt 11D->10D Trailing-# DDI, 491
PreAt DDI, 489
PreAt Intl TollBypass DDI, 492
PreAt Intl TollBypass Trailing-# DDI, 492
PreAt Trailing-# DDI, 489
PreDot 10-10-Dialing DDI, 493
PreDot 10-10-Dialing Trailing-# DDI, 493
PreDot 11/10D->7D DDI, 493
PreDot 11/10D->7D Trailing-# DDI, 493
PreDot 11D->10D DDI, 494
PreDot 11D->10D Trailing-# DDI, 494
PreDot DDI, 487, 492
PreDot Intl TollBypass DDI, 494

PreDot Intl TollBypass Trailing-# DDI, 495
PreDot IntlAccess IntlDirectDial DDI, 494
PreDot Trailing-# DDI, 493
preventing
service-affecting problems, 5–6
toll fraud, 544–549
PRI backhaul on MGCP gateways, 256–258
primary CallManager, 154
processing delay, isolating, 386
production hours, troubleshooting
methodologies, 5–6
progress tones, 307
propagation delay, isolating, 389
Publisher server
DC, reconfiguring, 828–835
Replication Monitor
correcting replication errors, 804–806
reestablishing broken replication
subscription, 807–809
reinitializing subscriptions, 809
Publisher-Subscriber model
database replication, 793–796
name resolution
LMHOSTS file, 796–797
NetBIOS, 796–798
Subscriber server, configuring CDR
replication, 810–812

Q

Q.850, 852
Q.921, 853
Q.931 Translator, 95–97. *See also* Enhanced Q.931
Translator
queuing delay
as source of voice quality degradation, 401
isolating source of, 390–391

R

RAS (Registration, Admission, and Status) messages, 639, 853

reading traces

CCM traces, 42, 50–57

through MGCP T1 PRI gateways, 58–60

CMI traces, 674–679

ISDN traces from MGCP gateways, 258–262

calling name display, 270

cause codes, 262–269

numbering type/plan mismatches, 269–270

timer information, 271–276

SDL traces, 60–63

Real-Time Monitoring Tool, monitoring MOH performance counters, 605–607

real-time statistics, viewing with PerfMon, 69–71

reconfiguring DC

on Publisher server, 828–835

on Subscriber server, 835–837

recording input of live audio sources, selecting, 620

redirecting calls, group pickup, 533–538

reestablishing broken replication subscription, 807–809

regions, 571

codec configuration, 568–569

codec matrix, 571–577

configuring for locations-based CAC, 627

registration (Skinny clients)

608/6624 modules, 324–325

checking phone status display, 133

inline power, troubleshooting, 114–117

messages, 127–132

network connectivity, 117, 120–127

configuration files, 121–127

IP addressing, 118–121

VLAN configuration, 118

verifying with IP Phone status messages, 133–135

reinitializing subscriptions, 809

remote access tools

VNC, 108

Windows Terminal Services, 107

replication

correcting with replication agents, 804–806

name resolution, 796–797

of CDRs

configuring, 810–812

troubleshooting, 813–815

passwords, configuring on cluster nodes, 798–802

Publisher-Subscriber model, 793–796

reestablishing broken subscription, 807–809

troubleshooting with Microsoft SQL Server Enterprise Manager, 802–803

Replication Monitor

reestablishing broken replication subscription, 807–809

reinitializing subscriptions, 809

troubleshooting replication errors, 804–806

resetting

Cisco IP Phones, 156

NSF field, 453

resolving call routing problems, 515–516

reading CCM traces, 516–521

response codes, 239–240

response headers, 238

restarting Cisco IP Phones, 156

restrictions of SRST, 708

ringback, troubleshooting absence of, 307

during call transfer, 309

on IP phones calling PSTN, 308

on PSTN phones calling IP phones, 309

RIP (Routing Information Protocol), 853

robbed-bit signaling, 214

rollover cables, 679

route filters, 506–507

multiple clauses, 512

NANP tags, 508–510

route patterns. *See also* translation patterns

closest-match routing, 461–464

pattern-matching, delayed routing, 466–469

urgent priority, 502

wildcards, 460–461

Route Plan Report, viewing in Cisco CallManager Administration, 466

RouteFilter parameter (CMI), 669

routers, voice gateway functionality
Cisco 2600 series, 171–172
Cisco 3600 series, 172
Cisco 3700 series, 173
routing calls to voice mail (SRST), 731
RSVP (Resource Reservation Protocol), 853
RTMT (Real-Time Monitoring Tool), 85
CTI Apps tab, 88
Devices tab, 86
Performance tab, 86
verifying Skinny client registration, 135–137
RTP (Real-Time Protocol), 853
dropped calls, 551–552
packages (MGCP), 236
RUDP (Reliable User Datagram Protocol), 853

S

sa (system administrator) user account, changing
password, 802
sample CCM trace, 51
SCCP (Skinny Client Control Protocol), 139
messages
analyzing in CCM traces, 148–154
call processing, 140, 144–148
DEVICE_RESET, 157
DEVICE_RESTART, 157
Skinny client registration, 127–135
608/6624 modules, 324–325
checking phone status display, 133
configuration files, 121–127
inline power, troubleshooting, 114–117
IP addressing, 118–121
messages, 127–132
network connectivity, troubleshooting,
117, 120–127
verifying with RTMT, 135–137
verifying with status messages, 133–135
scheduled outages, preventing service-affecting
problems, 5–6
SDI traces, reading, 42, 50–57
SDKs, Cisco IP Phone Services, 822
SDL traces
configuring, 63–67
reading, 60–63
troubleshooting held calls, 527–529

secondary CallManager, 154
selecting
appropriate troubleshooting tools, 13
MRGLs, 567
recording input for live audio sources, 620
serialization delay, isolating, 387–389
SerialPort parameter (CMI), 669
Service Activation, configuring on CallManager
Serviceability, 84
service parameters
CMI, 667–671, 674
transformations, 500–501
VG248, 686–690
service-affecting problems, preventing, 5–6
services button (Cisco IP Phones), request failures,
160–161
SGCP (Skinny Gateway Control Protocol), 853
shared lines, calling search spaces, 477
show call active voice brief command, 449
show call active voice command, 191, 404
show ephone command, 720
show gatekeeper calls command, 649
show gatekeeper endpoints command, 645
show gatekeeper zone status command, 649
show voice port summary command, 188–189
signaling
H.225, 283–284
problem isolation, 18
silence suppression. *See* VAD
single-site deployment model (CallManager), 24
Skinny Client Control Protocol. *See* SCCP
Skinny clients, registration
608/6624 modules, 324–325
checking phone status display, 133
configuration files, 121–127
inline power, troubleshooting, 114–117
IP addressing, 118–121
messages, 127–132
network conenctivity, troubleshooting,
117, 120–127
verifying with RTMT, 135–137
verifying with status messages, 133–135
Skinny gateways, nonsurvivable endpoints, 557

SMDI (Simple Message Desk Interface), 854
    CallManager integration, 662–666
    messages, 664–666
    MWI, configuration parameters, 682–685
    VG248 SMDI integration, 686
        configuration parameters, 686–690
        MWI problems, troubleshooting, 690–692
snapshot agent, 804
sniffer traces, 106
soft keys, 147
    events, 522–523
software conferencing
    "No Conference Bridge Available" messages,
        troubleshooting, 587–591
    IPV MSApp, 586
sources of delay, investigating
    fixed delay, 385
        coder delay, 386
        packetization delay, 386–387
        propagation delay, 389
        serialization delay, 387–389
    variable delay
        dejitter delay, 393–395
        low-speed links, 391–393
        queuing delay, 390–391
sources of echo
    eliminating, 418–429
    isolating, 411
        acoustic echo, 412
        electrical echo, 411–412
SQL servers
    database replication
        changing passwords, 798–802
        name resolution, 796–798
    Microsoft SQL Server Enterprise Manager,
        802–803
    Publisher-Subscriber model, 793–796
SRST (Survivable Remote Site Telephony), 562
    call control, debugging, 719–720
    call tranfer, debugging, 729–730
    configuring, 709–712
    CoR, 708
    DHCP support, 732
    ephone-dn configuration, viewing, 718
    forwarding calls, 731
    phone registration, 712–717
    polling, 722

    restrictions, 708
    routing calls to voice mail system, 731
    transfer patterns, configuring, 730
SsapiKeepAliveInterval parameter (CMI), 669
standards
    ITU-T H.225 specification, 651
standby CallManager, 154
StationActivateCallPlane message, SCCP call
    processing, 144
StationAlarmMessage, 129
    field definitions, 158–160
StationCallInfo message, SCCP call processing, 145
StationCallState message, SCCP call
    processing, 145
StationClearNotify message, SCCP call
    processing, 146
StationClearPromptStatus message, SCCP call
    processing, 146
StationCloseReceiveChannel message, SCCP call
    processing, 146
StationConnectionStatisticsRequest message, SCCP
    call processing, 146
StationConnectionStatisticsResponse message,
    SCCP call processing, 147
StationDisplayNotify message, SCCP call
    processing, 145
StationDisplayPromptStatus message, SCCP call
    processing, 144
StationKeepAliveAck messages, 129
StationKeepAliveMsg, 129
StationKeypadButtonMessage message, SCCP call
    processing, 144
StationOpenReceiveChannel message, SCCP call
    processing, 146
StationOpenReceiveChannelAck message, SCCP
    call processing, 146
StationOutputDisplayText message, SCCP call
    processing, 144
StationRegisterAck messages, 129
StationRegisterMessage, 129
StationRegisterReject messages, 129
StationSelectSoftKeys message, SCCP call
    processing, 144
StationSetLamp message, SCCP call
    processing, 144
StationSetRinger message, SCCP call
    processing, 145

StationSetSpeakerMode message, SCCP call processing, 146

StationSoftKeyEventMessage message, SCCP call processing, 147

StationStartMediaTransmission message, SCCP call processing, 146

StationStartTone message, SCCP call processing, 144

StationStopMediaTransmission message, SCCP call processing, 146

StationStopTone message, SCCP call processing, 146

status messages (IP Phones), verifying Skinny client registration, 133–135

StopBits parameter (CMI), 669

StripPoundCalledPartyFlag service parameter transformation, 501

Subscriber server, 794
    CDR replication, configuring, 810–812
    DC, reconfiguring, 835–837

subscriptions, reinitializing, 809

substrings, 507
    tags, 507–510

supervisory disconnect tone, 207–208

survivable endpoints, 552
    dropped calls, troubleshooting, 561–562
    IP Phones, 552–553
    MGCP gateways, 553–557

switching. fax protocol, 454

T

T.30 fax transmissions, 435–437, 854

T.38 fax relay, 445–446, 854

T1 CAS (Channel Associated Signaling), troubleshooting
    on 6608 module, 359–367
    on Cisco IOS voice gateways, 214–218
    on MGCP-enabled ports, 276–281

tags, 507–510

tail circuits, 416

talker echo, isolating sources of, 412–413

TAPI (Telephony Application Programming Interface), 854

TCP (Transmission Control Protocol), 854
    backhauling, 554
    failback, 156
    failover, 155

TCP handle, 52

TDM interfaces
    ISDN PRI, 210–212
        configuring on Cisco IOS voice gateways, 213–214
    on Cisco IOS voice gateways, 187
        debug commands, 192–205
        show commands, 187–192

Telcordia web site, 849

temporary dial peers, viewing, 719

Temporary Failure messages (IP Phones), 561–562

terminal capabilities exchange in H.245 call signaling, 297–300

terminal emulation, troubleshooting HyperTerminal CMI problems, 679–682

Terminal Services, 107

TFTP (Trivial File Transfer Protocol), 854
    configuration files, 154
    troubleshooting on 6608/6624 modules, 320–324

third-party voice mail systems, applying restrictive calling search spaces, 547–548

time synchronization, 38
    on CallManager servers, 39–40
    on CatOS devices, 41
    on Cisco IOS devices, 40–41

timestamps
    configuring, 185
    on CDRs, 90–91

toggling MWI on/off, 659, 661

TOH (tone on hold), 602
    investigating instances of, 617

toll fraud, preventing, 544–549

topologies, required documentation, 9

traces. *See also* CDRs
    CCM
        analyzing SCCP messages, 148–154
        call state field values, 525
        configuring for CallManager serviceability, 42–50
        digit analysis results, 149
        fields, 44–46
        reading, 42, 50–57

reviewing for call routing problems,
516–521
through MGCP T1 PRI gateways, 58–60
CMI, reading, 674–679
configuring
for locations-based CAC, 626
for CallManager Serviceability, 83
dialing forests, 538–542
verbose mode, 543
IP IVR/AA, capturing, 748–752
ISDN, analyzing, 258–276
MOH, troubleshooting, 608–611
SDL
configuring, 63–67
reading, 60–63
troubleshooting held calls, 527–529
sniffer traces, 106
Trailing-# DDI, 495
training, 434
transactional replication, 794
initiating, 804
transcoders, 565, 571–577
out-of-resource conditions, 578–580
with conference bridge resources, 581–585
with MOH servers, 585
transfer patterns, configuring, 730
transferred calls, 529–531
transformations, 513–514
DDIs, 486–494
overriding, 499
rules
cumulative effect of changes, 497–499
order of application, 496–497
service parameter-related, 500–501
translation patterns, 501–506
translation patterns, 501–506
transmission rates
fax devices, 434
fax relay, adjusting, 451–452
transmitting faxes through voice codecs, 437
troubleshooting methodologies
data analysis, case study, 18–19
data collection, 4–5
analyzing collected data, 11
case study, 14–18
earliest occurence of problem, 10–11
identifying root cause of problem, 6

isolating root cause of problem, 7–9
user information, 10
production versus nonproduction outages, 5–6
trunk packages (MGCP), 233
trunks, intercluster, 311
codec mismatches, 312
TSP (TAPI service provider)
verifying compatibility with Cisco Unity,
655–656
verifying configuration, 656–657

U

UDP (User Datagram Protocol), 854
umbrella recommendations, H.323, 281
unanswered calls, forwarding, 479–480
unauthorized access to international numbers,
preventing, 545
unexpected outside dial tone, troubleshooting,
465–466
unicast audio sources (MOH), troubleshooting,
615–617
Unity voice mail systems
applying restrictive calling search spaces, 547
DTMF, 661–662
MWI, 659–661
troubleshooting resources, 662
verifying switch configuration, 658–659
verifying TSP compatibility, 655–656
verifying TSP configuration, 656–657
UnknownCallerId service parameter
transformation, 501
UnknownCallerIdFlag service parameter
transformation, 501
UnknownCallerIdText service parameter
transformation, 501
unregistered IP Phones, tracing, 131–132
unregistered Skinny clients
troubleshooting inline power problems,
114–117
troubleshooting network connectivity, 117,
120–127
configuration files, 121–127
IP addressing, 118–121
VLAN configuration, 118
urgent priority route patterns, 502

user hold audio source (MOH), 601
user information, collecting, 10
user search requests, directory access, 820
UseZerosForUnknownDn parameter (CMI), 670
utilities, CDR Time Converter, 91.
    See also applications

V

V.21 HDLC, 854
VAD (voice activity detection)
    as source of voice quality degradation, 402–404
    comfort noise, 402
ValidateDns parameter (CMI), 670
variable delay, 384
    dejitter delay, isolating, 393–395
    effect on signaling, 395–396
    low-speed links, isolating, 391–393
    queuing delay, isolating, 390–391
variable-length matching (dial peers), 178–179
VAT (Voice Anomaly Tracking), 166
verbose dialing forest traces, 543
verifying
    CAC configuration, 640–645
    Cisco IOS MGCP registration status, 240–249
    Cisco IP Phone firmware, 165
    Cisco Unity switch configuration, 658–659
    CRA engine status, 745–748
    Database Layer Monitor operation, 812–813
    fax/modem passthrough configuration,
      441–444
    IP network integrity, 13
    LDAP directory configuration, 745
    MOH fixed audio source device configuration,
      619–620
    physical layer connectivity on digital interfaces,
      208–210
    Skinny client registration with RTMT, 135–137
    SRST configuration, 709–712
    TSP compatibility with Cisco Unity, 655–656
    TSP configuration, 656–657
    TSP version on CTI applications, 736
VG200 voice gateway, 170

VG248 voice gateway, 521
    SMDI integration, 686
      configuration parameters, 686–690
      MWI problems, troubleshooting, 690–692
viewing
    ephone-dn configuration, 718
    real-time statistics with PerfMon, 69–71
    Route Plan Report in Cisco CallManager
      Administration, 466
    SRST polling statistics, 722
virtual dial peers, viewing, 719
VNC (Virtual Computer Networking), 108
Voice Codec Bandwidth Calculator, 106
voice codecs, fax/modem passthrough, 437
voice gateways
    Catalyst
      Catalyst 4224, 173–174
      Catalyst 6000 CMM, 174
      configuring 6624 Analog Interface
        Module, 367–379
    Cisco AVVID IP Telephony, 32
    Cisco IOS, 169
      2600 series routers, 171–172
      3600 series routers, 172
      3700 series routers, 173
      H.323, 281–307
      MGCP, 218–240
      T1 CAS, troubleshooting, 214–218
      timestamps, configuring, 185
      troubleshooting TDM interfaces, 187–205
      VG200, 170
    Dick Tracy tool, 101–104
      CLI/embedded Tracy, 105
    FXO interface, troubleshooting
      disconnects, 205
voice mail systems
    applying restrictive calling search spaces, 547
    Cisco Unity, 655
      DTMF, 661–662
      MWI, 659–661
      troubleshooting resources, 662
      verifying switch configuration, 658–659
      verifying TSP compatibility, 655–656
      verifying TSP configuration, 656–657

CMI, 666–667
    service parameters, 667–671, 674
    traces, reading, 674–679
    troubleshooting with HyperTerminal, 679–682
Octel, CallManager integration, 693, 698–700
SMDI
    CallManager integration, 662–666
    messages, 664–666
    MWI, 682–685
    VG248 integration, 686–692
voice quality
    choppy audio, isolating sources of, 397–404
    echo
        acoustic echo, 412
        electrical echo, 411–412
        eliminating sources of, 418–429
        isolating sources of, 411
        perception of as problem, 414–416
    one-way/no-way audio, isolating sources of, 405–410
voice streaming
    dropped calls
        media processing resources, 560
        RTP/UDP, 551–552
    nonsurvivable endpoints, 557
        CTI/TAPI endpoints, 559
        H.323 gateways, 558–559
        Skinny gateways, 557
    survivable endpoints, 552
        IP Phones, 552–553
        MGCP gateways, 553–557
VoiceMailDn parameter (CMI), 670
VoiceMailPartition parameter (CMI), 670
VoIP dial peers, 175
    variable-length pattern matching, 179
VSTP (Voice Telephony Service Provider) states, 190–191
    debug commands, 193–196

W-X-Y-Z

WANs, fax relay, 444–445
wideband codecs, 855
wildcards, 460
    ! wildcard, 460
    . wildcard, 461
    @ wildcard, 461
        DDIs, 487–494
        route filters, 506–512
        multiple clauses, 512
    X wildcard, 460
NANP tags, 508–510
Windows 2000
    CCEmail
        alerting methods, 81
        configuring, 76–80
    object counters, 924–925
Windows Terminal Services, 107
Wink Start (E&M), 850
winks, 214
WS-X6608 module, 587

X wildcard, 460

Developing Cisco IP Phone Services

Darrick Deel, Mark Nelson, and Anne Smith

1-58705-060-9 • **Available Now**

Developing Cisco IP Phone Services uses detailed code samples to explain the tools and processes used to develop custom phone services. You'll learn about XML, CallManager, Cisco IP Phones, and the history behind why Cisco chose XML to deploy phone services. You'll find detailed information to help you learn how to build a service, how to build a directory, and how to integrate your service with Cisco CallManager. This book complements and expands on the information provided in the Cisco IP Phone Services Software Developer's Kit (SDK). With the information in this book, you can maximize your productivity using the tools provided in the SDK and the custom tools provided on the companion CD-ROM. Beginner and advanced service developers alike benefit from the information in this book. *Developing Cisco IP Phone Services* represents the most comprehensive resource available for developing services for Cisco IP Phones.

Cisco CallManager Fundamentals

Anne Smith, John Alexander, Chris Pearce, Delon Whetten

1-58705-008-0 • **Available Now**

Cisco CallManager Fundamentals provides examples and reference information about CallManager, the call processing component of the Cisco AVVID (Architecture for Voice, Video, and Integrated Data) IP Telephony solution. *Cisco CallManager Fundamentals* uses examples and architectural descriptions to explain how CallManager processes calls. This book details the inner workings of CallManager so that those responsible for designing and maintaining a Voice over IP (VoIP) solution from Cisco Systems® can understand the role each component plays and how they interrelate. You will learn detailed information about hardware and software components, call routing, media processing, system management and monitoring, and call detail records. The authors, all members of the CallManager group at Cisco Systems, also provide a list of features and Cisco solutions that integrate with CallManager.

Cisco IP Telephony

David Lovell

1-58705-050-1 • **Available Now**

Master the fundamentals of implementing a Cisco IP Telephony (CIPT) solution that can be run over a data network. *Cisco IP Telephony* focuses on using Cisco CallManager and other IP telephony components connected in LANs and WANs. Learn how to install, configure, support, and maintain a CIPT network while preparing for the CIPT #9E0-402 exam with this Self-Study Guide.